P9-CQN-673

POLITICAL PARTIES
OF
THE WORLD

4th edition

SHELTON STATE LIBRARY

Compiled and edited by

Alan J. Day, Richard German, and John Campbell

Contributing editor: Ciarán Ó Maoláin

Cartermill
Publishing

Political Parties of the World 4th edition

Published by Cartermill International Ltd,
Maple House, 149 Tottenham Court Road,
London W1P 9LL, United Kingdom.
Telephone: (0171) 896 2424
Facsimile: (0171) 896 2449

First three editions published by Longman Group UK Limited
First edition published 1980
Second edition published 1984
Third edition published 1988

This edition first published in 1996 by Cartermill International Limited

ISBN 1-86067-029-6

© Cartermill International Ltd 1996

Co-published in the United States and Canada by Stockton Press,
345 Park Avenue South, 10th floor, New York, NY 10010-1707, USA
Tel: 212-689-9200
Fax: 212-689-9711

ISBN: 1-56159-144-0

All rights reserved. No part of this publication may be reproduced,
stored on a retrieval system, or transmitted in any form or by any means,
electronic, mechanical, photocopying, recording or otherwise, without
either the prior written permission of the Publishers or a licence
permitting restricted copying issued by the Copyright Licensing
Agency Ltd., 90 Tottenham Court Road, London W1P 9HE.

A catalogue record for this book is available from the British Library.

Typeset in 9/10pt Times New Roman
Printed and bound in Great Britain by Bookcraft (Bath) Ltd.

Contents

Introduction..vii
About the Authors...ix

Afghanistan	1	Comoros	149
Albania	4	Congo	152
Algeria	8	Costa Rica	158
Andorra	14	Côte d'Ivoire	161
Angola	16	Croatia	164
Antigua and Barbuda	22	Cuba	170
Argentina	23	Cyprus	171
Armenia	29	Turkish Republic of Northern	
Australia	32	Cyprus	175
Austria	40	Czech Republic	177
Azerbaijan	44		
		Denmark	185
Bahamas	48	Danish Dependencies	192
Bahrain	48	Faroe Islands	192
Bangladesh	49	Greenland	195
Barbados	55	Djibouti	196
Belarus	56	Dominica	198
Belgium	61	Dominican Republic	199
Belize	68		
Benin	70	Ecuador	202
Bhutan	74	Egypt	208
Bolivia	75	El Salvador	210
Bosnia and Hercegovina	81	Equatorial Guinea	216
Botswana	85	Eritrea	218
Brazil	86	Estonia	219
Brunei	91	Ethiopia	223
Bulgaria	91		
Burkina Faso	100	Fiji	226
Burundi	104	Finland	228
		France	234
Cambodia	108	French Overseas Departments	253
Cameroon	113	French Guiana	254
Canada	117	Guadelope	255
Cape Verde	120	Martinique	256
Central African Republic	122	Réunion	257
Chad	126	French Overseas Territories	258
Chile	131	French Polynesia	258
China	136	Mayotte	259
Colombia	143	New Caledonia	260

St Pierre and Miquelon...................261
Wallis and Futuna Islands.............262

Gabon.......................................263
Gambia.....................................264
Georgia....................................266
Germany...................................270
Ghana......................................280
Greece.....................................282
Grenada....................................287
Guatemala.................................289
Guinea.....................................296
Guinea-Bissau............................297
Guyana....................................299

Haiti..302
Honduras..................................304
Hungary...................................307

Iceland....................................312
India.......................................315
Indonesia.................................321
Iran..322
Iraq..324
Ireland....................................325
Israel......................................330
Italy.......................................334

Jamaica...................................345
Japan......................................346
Jordan.....................................349

Kazakhstan...............................352
Kenya.....................................354
Kiribati...................................357
Korea, North.............................357
Korea, South.............................358
Kuwait....................................360
Kyrgyzstan...............................361

Laos.......................................363
Latvia.....................................364
Lebanon...................................367
Lesotho...................................370
Liberia....................................372
Libya......................................373
Liechtenstein.............................373
Lithuania.................................375
Luxembourg..............................377

Macedonia................................380
Madagascar...............................383
Malawi....................................385
Malaysia..................................387
Maldives..................................391
Mali.......................................391
Malta......................................394
Marshall Islands.........................395
Mauritania................................396
Mauritius.................................398
Mexico....................................400
Micronesia, Federated States of............405
Moldova..................................405
Monaco...................................408
Mongolia.................................408
Morocco..................................410
Mozambique.............................412
Myanmar (Burma).......................415

Namibia...................................417
Nauru.....................................418
Nepal......................................419
Netherlands...............................421
Netherlands Dependencies...................426
    Aruba.................................426
    Netherlands Antilles...................427
New Zealand..............................428
New Zealand Associated Territories......431
Nicaragua.................................432
Niger......................................438
Nigeria....................................441
Norway....................................442

Oman......................................445

Pakistan...................................446
Palau......................................449
Palestinian Entity........................449
Panama....................................451
Papua New Guinea.......................456
Paraguay..................................458
Peru.......................................462
Philippines...............................468
Poland.....................................471
Portugal...................................478
    Macao.................................482

Qatar......................................483

Romania 483
Russia 490
Rwanda..500

St Christopher and Nevis.....................503
St Lucia...504
St Vincent and the Grenadines.............505
San Marino...506
São Tomé and Príncipe 508
Saudi Arabia 509
Senegal...509
Seychelles...512
Sierra Leone.......................................513
Singapore 515
Slovakia 516
Slovenia 521
Solomon Islands 524
Somalia...525
   Somaliland 526
South Africa 527
Spain..531
Sri Lanka 546
Sudan...549
Suriname...550
Swaziland...553
Sweden...554
Switzerland 559
Syria...565

Taiwan 567
Tajikistan 568
Tanzania 571
Thailand 573
Togo...575
Tonga...577
Trinidad and Tobago...........................577
Tunisia 579
Turkey..581
Turkmenistan......................................586
Tuvalu..588
Uganda 589
Ukraine...590

United Arab Emirates...........................599
United Kingdom..................................599
  Northern Ireland 609
UK Crown Dependencies 616
  Channel Islands.............................617
  Isle of Man...................................617
UK Dependent Territories 618
  Anguilla..618
  Bermuda.......................................619
  British Virgin Islands 620
  Cayman Islands 621
  Falkland Islands............................621
  Gibraltar 622
  Hong Kong....................................623
  Montserrat 624
  Pitcairn Islands.............................625
  St Helena and Dependencies 626
  Turks and Caicos Islands................626
United States of America.......................627
US Dependent Territories 630
  American Samoa 630
  Guam 630
  Northern Mariana Islands..............631
  Puerto Rico 631
  US Virgin Islands 632
Uruguay..633
Uzbekistan..638

Vanuatu 640
Venezuela 642
Vietnam 647

Western Sahara 649
Western Samoa 650

Yemen 651
Yugoslavia...652

Zaïre 656
Zambia 658
Zimbabwe 659

Index of Principal Organisations..663

Introduction

Since the publication of the third edition of *Political Parties of the World* (PPW) in 1988, the world has undergone a seismic political transformation, stemming in particular from the collapse of communism in Eastern Europe in 1989 and the demise of the Soviet Union two years later. The latter development accounts for 14 of the 25 independent countries which exist today but did not in 1988 (i.e. not counting Russia, as being the successor of the Soviet Union in many respects). The break-up of post-communist Czechoslovakia and Yugoslavia have produced another six, the remainder being mainly former dependencies in the Pacific which have achieved full independence. More importantly for this fourth edition of PPW, the ending of the Cold War and the redrawing of the political map of the world have generated a tremendous surge of multi-party democracy, not only in the former communist states but also in most African and some other countries previously governed under one-party systems. In 1988 over a third of the world's countries were one-party states of one sort or another. Very few are left in 1996, with the result that there has been exponential growth in the sheer number of active political parties around the globe, and particularly in Eastern Europe and Africa.

The aim of PPW is to make available within a single volume concise, current and objective information (including address, telephone and fax number, leadership data, orientation, electoral performance and political history) on significant parties in all countries and dependent territories of the world, placed within the context of the prevailing constitutional, electoral and parliamentary situation. For the reasons cited above, the present volume incorporates major revision and updating as compared with its predecessor, although the basic country-by-country arrangement is the same. Parties are again presented in alphabetical order of the English translation of their title, with those currently represented in the national legislature being covered in main entries and "other parties" listed at the end of each section. As with the previous three editions, the aspiration of the editors has been to contribute to a greater knowledge and awareness of the phenomenon of political parties as well as to facilitate inter-country comparison of what is now a key facet of political life almost everywhere in the world.

Important features of the worldwide party scene which emerge from the present volume include:

(i) the growing number and influence of Islamic fundamentalist formations in the Muslim world, most of them seized by hostility to what they perceive to be decadent Western social mores and culture;

(ii) the continuing importance of racial and/or religious identity as a determinant of party political affiliation;

(iii) the often related rise of regional political movements demanding greater autonomy from central government, and in some cases outright separation;

(iv) the dominance in the 1990s of the philosophy of the free-market economy right across the traditional political spectrum (at least in the developed world), with once anti-market left-wing parties having to find other reasons for their existence; and

(v) a parallel and somewhat contradictory recent tendency on the part of voters in Eastern Europe, disenchanted by their early experience of the market economy, to opt for parties that are "successors" to the former ruling Communist parties, albeit now espousing democratic socialism rather than Marxism-Leninism.

As regards the thorny question of defining what constitutes a political party (as opposed to a pressure group or protest movement), the compilers have again accepted self-definition

vii

as a political party as the basic criterion for inclusion, finding in practice that this almost always means that the organization is seeking to obtain or retain direct political power over the process of government at some level, usually through the ballot box. As in previous editions, illegal, guerrilla and terrorist movements have not usually been included, with the partial exception that such movements have been covered in a few countries where the political situation is fluid and where they may become legal political parties in the accepted sense.

Information sources for the present volume have included data provided by the parties themselves (although the editors are entirely responsible for the way that such material has been used) and by the four major international party organizations, namely the Christian Democrat International, the International Democrat Union, the Liberal International and the Socialist International. Also important has been input from national bodies responsible for registering political parties (usually the electoral commission), from the secretariats of national parliaments in many countries, from London embassies and high commissions, and from British embassies and high commissions abroad. On the complexities of the new multi-party systems of Eastern Europe and the former Soviet republics, much valuable guidance has been provided by the well-informed writers and researchers of the Open Media Research Institute (OMRI) in Prague, who have unfailingly responded promptly to requests for information and whose daily *News Digest* of political developments in ex-communist Europe has been a key source for the present volume.[1] Particular acknowledgement should also be made to *Keesing's Record of World Events* [2], for its monthly coverage of political, electoral and constitutional developments worldwide, and to the *Political Handbook of the World* [3], the estimable American annual reference work, which has been an invaluable source of current party data for Third World countries in particular.

Appreciation is also recorded for particular assistance of various kinds from the following individuals; Dr James Jupp of the Australian National University, Canberra; Frank Nugent, in the Office of the President of the Senate, Canberra; Paul Fox at the UK embassy in Baku, Azerbaijan; Shaikat Rushdee Haque at the British high commission in Dhaka for his/her patient unravelling of the party scene in Bangladesh; Loreta Bertosa of the Croatian embassy in London; Soteris Georgiallis of the Cyprus high commission in London; Jeremy Astill-Brown of the British embassy in Addis Ababa, Ethiopia; Bharti Tiwari and N.K. Sapra, of the secretariats of, respectively, the upper and lower houses of the Indian parliament; Dr Stephen Gundle of the Royal Holloway University of London, for help on recent Italian party developments; Elise Manganaro of the Lebanese Center for Policy Studies, New Jersey, USA; Berend Jan van den Boomen of the Alfred Mozer Foundation in the Netherlands; Angela A. Andal of the British embassy in Manila, Philippines; Dr Vladimir Kolossov of the Russian Academy of Sciences, Moscow; and Dr Hans Hirter of Bern University, Switzerland.

Any errors or omissions in the present volume are the responsibility of the Authors, who would welcome communications on any such shortcomings via Cartermill Publishing.

London, October 1996

Notes

1. For background to the re-emergence of parties in ex-communist Europe extensive use has been made of *Political Parties of Eastern Europe, Russia* and *the Successor States*, edited by Bogdan Szajkowski (Cartermill, 1994); also available on CD-ROM.
2. Published by Keesing's Worldwide, 7979 Old Georgetown Road, Suite 900, Bethesda, Maryland 20814, USA.
3. Published by CSA Publications, Binghamton University, N.Y. 13902-6000, USA; available outside North America from Macmillan Publishers, 25 Eccleston Place, London, SW1W 9NF.

About the Authors

John Campbell is a former researcher at the University of Bristol and is currently a research consultant in the area of international relations and the international economy. He has published widely in the field of international affairs and was co-editor of the sixth edition of *Treaties and Alliances of the World* (Cartermill, 1995).

Alan J. Day has edited or contributed to a number of reference titles, including the first three editions of *Political Parties of the World, Border and Territorial Disputes* (3rd ed., Cartermill, 1991) and *Think Tanks: An International Directory* (Cartermill, 1993). He is currently editor of *The Annual Register.*

Richard German, a former chief indexer for *Keesing's Record of World Events*, has worked as a writer at the Central Office of Information (COI) specializing in current affairs reference publications and information material. Since the beginning of 1995 he has been a freelance writer, continuing to contribute to joint COI-HMSO publications as well as undertaking other commissions.

Ciarán Ó Maoláin, a former associate editor of *Keesing's Record of World Events*, is director of Caradoc current affairs research and publishing company. He was a contributing editor of the third edition of *Political Parties of the World* and has compiled other major reference works, including *Latin American Political Movements* (1985), *The Radical Right: A World Directory* (1987) and *European Directory of Migrant and Ethnic Minority Organizations* (1995).

Afghanistan

Capital: Kabul

Population: 21,500,000 (1995E)

The Islamic State of Afghanistan was proclaimed in April 1992 as successor to the Soviet-backed regime of President Mohammed Najibullah, which had been overthrown by opposition *mujaheddin* ("holy warriors") following the end of the 1979–89 Soviet military intervention. Under arrangements agreed by nine major *mujaheddin* movements in mid-1993, there is a President who is head of the Leadership Council and chair of the Defence Commission and who appoints a Vice-President. Primary responsibility for the conduct of policy rests with a Prime Minister and Council of Ministers, appointed on a multi-party basis. A Council of Resolution and Settlement (*Shura-i-Ahl-i-Hal wa Aqd*), nominally composed of 1,336 elected and appointed representatives, met in Kabul in December 1992, being described as a "constituent assembly" and subsequently designating 250 of its own members to serve as an interim legislature.

The last general elections (only the third in the country's history) were held in April 1988 under the Najibullah regime and resulted in the then ruling People's Democratic Party of Afghanistan (PDPA), renamed the Homeland Party in June 1990, winning a majority of seats in both houses of the then National Assembly.

Afghan Islamic Association

Jamaat-i-Islami Afghanistan

Address. c/o President's Office, Kabul

Leadership. Ustad Burhanuddin Rabbani (chair)

Fundamentalist in orientation, this grouping founded in 1970 has its main support in the Sunni Moslem Tajik tribes of northern Afghanistan. During the 1979-89 Soviet intervention it was one of the *mujaheddin* groups based in Peshawar, Pakistan (although it also maintained an office in the Iranian capital) and gained kudos from the successes of Ahmed Shah Masoud (the movement's military commander) against Soviet forces in the Panjsher Valley. In January 1980 it took part in the formation at Islamabad, Pakistan, of the Islamic Alliance for the Liberation of Afghanistan, also known as the National Alliance, while in May 1985 two factions of the grouping joined the more fundamentalist Islamic Union of Afghan Holy Warriors, founded at Peshawar. Following the Soviet withdrawal in 1989, Masoud was instrumental in forging the Tajik–Pushtun alliance which finally toppled the Najibullah regime in April 1992, becoming Defence Minister for three months. In June 1992 Rabbani took over as head of the Leadership Council (and thus as head of state) and in December 1992 was formally elected President by a constituent assembly. In June 1993 he succeeded in bringing certain dissident move-

ments into the government, notably the Hekmatyar faction of the Islamic Party amd the Shia Islamic Unity Party of Afghanistan. However, from January 1994 the Rabbani administration faced an insurgency by ultra-fundamentalist elements of the Islamic Party (including forces declaring their loyalty to Hekmatyar) allied with the Uzbek militia leader, Gen. Abdul Rashid Dostam. By mid-1994 the latter forces had been driven out of Kabul, but towards the end of the year Rabbani faced a new challenge from the fundamentalist *talibaan* movement, consisting mainly of fundamentalist Pushtun student fighters opposed to all existing *mujaheddin* groups and said to be backed by Pakistan. By mid-1995, however, pro-Rabbani forces appeared to have gained the upper hand against the *talibaan* and other opposition groups.

Afghan National Liberation Front (ANLF)

Jabh-i-Nijat-i-Milli Afghanistan

Leadership. Imam Sibghatullah Mujaddedi

The ANLF was launched in March 1979 with a call for a *jihad* (holy war) against the then Kabul regime and embraced the Khalis faction of the Islamic Party. A relatively moderate Sunni *mujaheddin* group, it joined the Islamic Alliance for the Liberation of Afghanistan set up at Islamabad in January 1990 as well as the more fundamentalist Islamic Union of Afghan Holy Warriors created

1

at Peshawar in May 1985. Head of the Naqsh-bandiyah Sufi order in Afghanistan, Imam Mujad-dedi became president of the interim Afghan government set up by moderate Peshawar-based groups in February 1989 in the wake of the Soviet military withdrawal. In November 1990 he and the leader of the National Islamic Front reportedly had talks with President Najibullah at Geneva, in an abortive effort to form a coalition government. On Najibullah's fall in April 1992 Imam Mujad-dedi became head of state of the new Islamic republic proclaimed in Kabul by the victorious *mujaheddin* groups, but gave way to the leader of the Afghan Islamic Association in June 1992.

Islamic Party
Hizb-i-Islam

Leadership. Gulbuddin Hekmatyar (leader of Hekmatyar faction), Mawlawi Mohammed Yunis Khalis (leader of Khalis faction)

Based in the Pushtun tribes of south-east Afghanistan, the Islamic Party emerged as the largest and most radical of the fundamentalist *mujaheddin* movements opposed to the pro-Soviet Najibullah regime, being committed to the restoration of the monarchy. It was split in 1979 on personality differences between Hekmatyar and Khalis, both factions continuing to advocate the creation of a strictly Islamic state. The Khalis faction, with a large following among Afghan refugees in Pakistan, was reportedly the favoured conduit for US aid via the CIA, while Hekmatyar was linked to the March 1990 coup attempt by Lieut.-Gen. Shahnawaz Tanay, the hardline communist Defence Minister. Both factions joined the Islamic Alliance for the Liberation of Afghanistan, formed at Islamabad in January 1980, the Khalis faction through its membership of the Afghan National Liberation Front; both also joined the Islamic Union of Afghan Holy Warriors formed at Peshawar in May 1985. Both factions were original members of the Afghan interim government set up in Peshawar in February 1989, but the Hekmatyar faction quickly withdrew following armed clashes with the Afghan Islamic Association, to be followed by the Khalis faction in May 1991. Neither faction was included in the post-Najibullah government established in April 1992, the result being violent clashes between government and non-government *mujaheddin* forces. Under an Islamabad peace accord of March 1993 the Hekmatyar faction joined a broad-based government in June 1993, with Hekmatyar becoming Prime Minister, while the Khalis faction remained outside. In January 1994, however, Hekmatyar effectively broke with the government, his forces launching a new insurgency, in alliance with the Uzbek militia leader, Gen. Abdul Rashid Dostam, who objected to Tajik dominance in

Kabul. In May 1994 Hekmatyar rejected a proposal by President Rabbani that both leaders should resign and that new elections should be held. The following month Hekmatyar's and Dostam's forces were driven out of Kabul and in November Hekmatyar was officially replaced as Prime Minister. In February 1995 Hekmatyar and his followers were defeated by the newly-emerged *talibaan* student fundamentalist fighters and forced to abandon their bases around Kabul and to flee northwards; however, in the face of subsequent government military successes, the Hekmatyar faction became effectively allied with the *talibaan* from mid-1995.

Islamic Revolutionary Movement
Harakat-i-Inqilab-i-Islami

Leadership. Mawlawi Mohammed Nabi Mohammedi

Led by a traditional Islamic scholar with pronounced anti-Shia views, this relatively moderate formation joined both the Islamic Alliance for the Liberation of Afghanistan, founded at Islamabad in January 1980, and the more fundamentalist Islamic Union of Afghan Holy Warriors, created at Peshawar in May 1985. It was allied with the Afghan National Liberation Front and the National Islamic Front, as Pakistan-based *mujaheddin* groups in receipt of CIA funding, but was weakened in 1981 by the defection of at least two fundamentalist factions. In April 1992 it became a component of the post-Najibullah regime in Kabul.

Islamic Unity
Ittehad-i-Islami

Leadership. Abdul Rasul Sayaf, Ahmad Shah Ahmadzay

This militant Sunni fundamentalist grouping has received financial and military backing from Saudi Arabia, representing as it does the puritanical current of Saudi-inspired Wahhabi Islam. During the 1980s it opposed acceptance of US/Western support by the *mujaheddin* opposition, preferring the concept of an Islamic holy war against a Soviet-backed regime. Abdul Rasul Sayaf became leader of the Islamic Union of Afghan Holy Warriors on its formation in May 1985 and was subsequently appointed prime minister in the interim Afghan government proclaimed in Peshawar in February 1989. Islamic Unity participated in the post-Najibullah government set up in Kabul in April 1992 and became involved in pitched battles with dissident Shia forces of the pro-Iranian Islamic Unity Party of Afghanistan. It was also a member of the broader-based government installed in June 1993.

Islamic Unity Party of Afghanistan (IUPA)
Hizb-i-Wahdat-i-Islami-i-Afghanistan

Leadership. Abdul Karim Khalili (provisional leader), Rehmat Ullah Mutazawi (secretary-general)

Formerly called the Islamic Coalition Council of Afghanistan (founded in June 1987), the IUPA itself was launched in June 1990 as an alliance of Shia *mujaheddin* movements mostly based in Tehran, namely the Afghani Nasr Organization (*Sazmane Nasr*) led by Khalili, the largest of the Iran-based Shia opposition groups; the Afghanistan Party of God (*Hizbollah-i-Afghanistan*) led by Alhaj Shaikh Ali Wosoqus-alam Wosoqi and previously allowed to operate by the Kabul regime; the Dawa Party of Islamic Unity of Afghanistan (*Dawa-i-Ittehad-i-Islami Afghanistan*), with support in Ghazni province; the Guardians of the Islamic Jihad of Afghanistan (*Pasdaran-i-Jihad-i-Afghanistan*); the Islamic Force of Afghanistan (*Nehzat-i-Afghanistan*), based in the Jogore area; the Islamic Struggle for Afghanistan (*Narave Islami Afghanistan*) led by Zaidi Mohazzizi; the Party of God (*Hizbollah*) led by Qari Ahmed (or Yakdasta); the United Islamic Front of Afghanistan (*Jabhe Muttahid-i-Afghanistan*), with strong support among ethnic Hazara; and the Unity Council (*Shura-i-Ittefaq*), the largest Shia opposition movement with support concentrated in the Hazarajat area. Also declared as an IUPA component was the Peshawar-based Islamic Movement of Afghanistan (*Harakat-i-Islami Afghanistan*) led by Ayatollah Aseh Mohseni, although the latter's anti-Iranian stance raised a question-mark over his movement's relationship with the IUPA.

Following the fall of the Najibullah regime in April 1992, IUPA forces joined with those of the Islamic Party in contesting the Kabul dominance of non-Shia factions. Under the March 1993 Islamabad accord, the main IUPA groups (and the Hekmatyar faction of the Islamic Party) joined the Kabul government in June. When Hekmatyar's forces and the Uzbek militia of Gen. Abdul Rashid Dostam launched a new insurgency in January 1994, the IUPA gave qualified backing to the Rabbani regime in power. In March 1995, however, government forces moved against IUPA positions in Kabul, forcing the IUPA into a precarious alliance with the anti-government *talibaan* fighters then encircling the capital. As government forces got the upper hand, the alliance broke down and the IUPA leader, Abdul Ali Mazari, was killed on March 13 while in the custody of the *talibaan*, being provisionally replaced as IUPA leader by Khalili.

National Islamic Front (NIF)
Mahaz-i-Milli-i-Islami

Leadership. Pir Sayed Ahmed Gailani

Originally called the Afghan Islamic and National Revolutionary Council, the Pushtun-based NIF was the most liberal of the Pakistan-based anti-Najibullah movements (the Western media also reporting that its leaders were the best-dressed *mujaheddin*). Pro-monarchist in orientation, it joined both the Islamic Alliance for the Liberation of Afghanistan, set up at Islama-bad in January 1980, and the more fundamental-ist Islamic Union of Afghan Holy Warriors, proclaimed at Peshawar in May 1985. The latter alliance represented an expansion of a grouping of the same name which the NIF had formed in June 1981 with the Afghan National Liberation Front and the Islamic Revolutionary Movement. Favouring the restoration of Mohammed Zahir Shah (deposed as king of Afghanistan in 1973), Pir Gailani rejected President Najibullah's offer of power-sharing in July 1987; he was also reported to have had talks with Najibullah at Geneva in November but to have turned down a proposal, engineered by the US and Soviet governments, that he head a coalition government. Following Najibullah's fall in April 1992, the NIF became a component of the new Islamic regime.

Union of the Companions of the Prophet
Ittehad-i-Ansarollah

Leadership. Haji Zafar Mohammed Khadem

This moderate Islamic formation was set up in 1988 with the approval of the Najibullah regime. On the fall of the latter in April 1992 it found itself largely superseded by the victorious *mujaheddin* movements which took power in Kabul.

Albania

Capital: Tirana

Population: 3,500,000 (1995E)

The Republic of Albania was proclaimed under a new interim constitution adopted on April 29, 1991, replacing the Socialist People's Republic of Albania in existence since 1946. In December 1990 the government had bowed to popular pressure by authorizing the formation of parties to compete with the communist-era ruling party, which in June 1991 changed its name from Party of Labour of Albania to Socialist Party of Albania. Supreme political authority is vested in the unicameral People's Assembly (*Kuvënd Popullore*), whose 140 members are elected for a four-year term by universal suffrage of those aged at least 18 years. Of the total, 100 deputies are elected in single-member constituencies in two rounds of voting; the other 40 seats are filled from national party lists according to the proportional first-round share of parties with at least 4% of the total vote. Electoral legislation enacted in February 1991 banned "extremist" parties and those based exclusively in ethnic minorities. The Albanian President is elected by the Assembly for a four-year term (and may not hold party office); the Assembly also elects the Council of Ministers. Having been proclaimed an atheist state in 1967, Albania opted for freedom of religion in April 1991. Some 70% of the population espouse the Islamic faith.

General elections on March 22 and 29, 1992, resulted as follows: Democratic Party of Albania 92 seats (62.8% of the first-round vote); Socialist Party of Albania 38 (25.7%); Social Democratic Party of Albania 7 (4.4%); Human Rights Union Party (the list of the Democratic Union of the Greek Minority/Omonia) 2 (2.9%); Albanian Republican Party 1 (3.1%). The official results of the next elections, held on May 26 and June 16, 1996, gave the Democratic Party 122 seats, the Socialists 10, the Republicans 3, the Human Rights Union Party 3 and the Democratic Party of the Right 2. However, most international observers endorsed Albanian opposition claims that the poll had not been fairly conducted.

Albanian Republican Party
Partia Republikana Shqipërisë (PRS)
Address. Bulevardi Deshmoret e Kombit, Tirana
Telephone. (#355–42) 32511
Fax. (#355–42) 28361
Leadership. Sabri Godo (chair), Fatmir Mediu (vice-chair), Çerçiz Mingomataj (secretary-general)

Founded in January 1991 with support from the Italian Republican Party, the conservative, pro-market PRS has its main power base in southern Albania and enjoys considerable rural support for its policy of exempting peasants from taxation for several years in the interests of rebuilding agriculture. It failed to win a seat in the March-April 1991 Assembly elections but was nevertheless included in the "non-partisan" coalition government appointed in June. In the March 1992 elections the party took one seat, opting to join a coalition headed by the Democratic Party of Albania and being allocated the transport and communications portfolio and two posts of deputy minister. The first PRS congress in June 1992 was marred by a major split in the party, resulting in the creation of distinct right-wing and centrist groups, including the Republican Alliance Party, the Republican Alternative Party (led by Shemshedin Memia) and the Right-wing Republican Party (led by Hysen Cobani). The party withdrew from the ruling coalition at the time of a major ministerial reshuffle in December 1994, issuing a critique of the government's "shortcomings" but nevertheless promising to take a "constructive" approach. The party boycotted the second round of the May-June 1996 general elections, the disputed official results of which gave it three seats.

Democratic Alliance of Albania
Aleanca Demokratike ë Shqipërisë (ADS)
Address.. c/o Kuvënd Popullore, Tirana
Leadership. Neritan Çeka (chair), Arben Imami

4

The centre-right ADS was founded in October 1992 by dissident elements of the ruling Democratic Party of Albania opposed to the "autocratic rule" of President Berisha, who accused it of having pro-Serbian tendencies. For the May 1996 legislative elections it entered the "Pole of the Centre" alliance with the Social Democratic Party of Albania; but the banning of several ADS candidates under the 1995 Genocide Act, because of their communist-era role, created difficulties for the party. The ADS joined an opposition boycott of the second round of the May-June 1996 general elections.

Democratic Party of Albania
Partia Demokratika ë Shqipërisë (PDS)
   Address. Rruga Konferenca e Perez 120, Tirana
   Telephone. (#355–42) 23525
   Fax. (#355–42) 28463
   Leadership. Sali Berisha (chair of national council), Tritan Shehu (president)

The PDS was launched in December 1990 as Albania's first authorized opposition party since World War II, on a platform of human rights' observance, a free enterprise economy, better relations with neighbouring states and eventual membership of the European Union. It was derived from a movement of dissident intellectuals led by the writer Ismail Kadare, who had used the institutions of the then ruling Party of Labour of Albania (PLA) to undermine the communist system from within. An interview with Kadare published by the PLA youth organ in March 1990, in which he called for the deposition of the PLA regime, marked the real beginning of the revolt of the intellectuals. In his first published interview (in May 1990), cardiologist Sali Berisha, another early member, urged intellectuals to act as an embryonic opposition movement in a country destroyed by communist totalitarianism. Although Kadare himself moved to Paris in October 1990, teachers and students at Tirana University continued the movement and founded the PDS immediately after the PLA central committee had endorsed the legalization of opposition parties. The PDS won 75 of 250 Assembly seats in the first post-communist elections in March-April 1991, after which it opted in June to join a "non-partisan" coalition government with the Socialist Party of Albania (PSS, formerly the PLA), until withdrawing in December 1991 in protest against the slow pace of reform.

Drawing substantial membership and support from the lower ranks of the PSS and the state bureaucracy, the PDS won a landslide victory in the March 1992 Assembly elections. By now PDS chair, Berisha was the following month elected President of Albania by 96 Assembly votes to 35, following which the PDS became the dominant formation in a coalition with the Social Democratic Party of Albania (PSDS) and the Albanian Republican Party (PRS), under the premiership of Aleksander Meksi. The party chairmanship passed to Eduard Selami. Serious post-election tensions in the PDS were highlighted by the departure of six moderate leftists in July 1992 to form the Democratic Alliance Party of Albania. The PDS-led government was accused of increasing authoritarianism in 1993–94, although the party took steps to expel several declared right-wing extremists, who later formed the Democratic Party of the Right. Concerned with the status of ethnic Albanians in the Federal Yugoslav province of Kosovo, the PDS maintained close ties with the Democratic Alliance of Kosovo and sought to use its governmental influence to induce the Belgrade authorities to moderate their security regime in the province.

The PDS polled strongly in partial local elections in June 1994, winning 47% of the vote. But the rejection of a new government-proposed constitution in a referendum on Nov. 6, 1994, represented a major setback for the party, which was accused by other formations of seeking to increase presidential powers at the expense of the People's Assembly. President Berisha responded by carrying out a major government reshuffle in December, retaining Meksi as Prime Minister but losing the PRS and the PSDS as formal coalition partners. At a special PDS conference in March 1995, Selami was dismissed as party chair, having opposed the President's plan to hold another referendum on the new draft constitution. He was replaced in March 1996 by Tritan Shehu, as the PDS launched its election campaign on a platform of lower taxes and more privatization. The following month Selami and seven others were ousted from the PDS national council.

Amid opposition charges of electoral fraud and intimidation, the PDS was officially stated to have won 122 of the 140 seats in the May-June 1996 parliamentary elections.

The PDS is affiliated to the European Democrat Union and in 1994 claimed a membership of 80,000.

Democratic Party of the Right
Partia Demokratike e Djathte (PDD)
   Address. c/o Kuvënd Popullore, Tirana
   Leadership. Petrit Kalakula (chair)

The PDD was founded in March 1994 by the right-wing *Balli Kombëter* faction of the ruling Democratic Party of Albania, its original joint leaders having been Abdi Baleta and Kalakula (a former Agriculture Minister). The party advocates a "greater Albania" and support for Kosovo's Albanians as well as the complete restoration of property nationalized under communism. Weakened by Baleta's formation of the breakaway Party of National Restoration early in 1996, the PDD was credited with winning two seats in the May-June elections, in which it participated in an opp-position boycott of the second round.

Democratic Union of the Greek Minority/Concord

Bashkimia Demokratik i Minoritet Grek/Omonia
   Leadership. Sotiris Kyriazatis (president), Theodhori Bezhani (chair)

Representing Albania's ethnic Greek minority, this party originated in a clandestine opposition movement of the communist era and was officially founded in December 1990. It contested the March-April 1991 Assembly elections as Omonia, winning five of the 250 seats, but subsequently found itself covered by a ban, enacted in January 1992, on parties of an ethnic minority character. It therefore contested the March 1992 Assembly elections on the list of the Human Rights Union Party, which won two out of 140 seats. Omonia has come under violent challenge from Albanian nationalists who depict it as supporting the transfer to Greece of southern Epirus (home of many ethnic Greeks but nevertheless containing an ethnic Albanian majority). Claiming a membership of 60,000, Omonia has declared that any territorial change can come only by negotiation and has concentrated its efforts on securing improved rights and conditions for ethnic Greeks in Albania. Its agitation nevertheless helped to promote the largescale flight of ethnic Greeks into Greece in the early 1990s, this movement giving rise to a series of border incidents.

Amid a deterioration in Albanian-Greek relations, six prominent Omonia members were among many ethnic Greeks detained in May 1994 in a government crackdown on suspected subversion. In September five of the six were convicted by a Tirana court on treason and other charges, including "carrying out the orders of a foreign secret service", conspiracy and illegal possession of weapons, and were sentenced to prison terms of between six and eight years. The court found that the accused had received some $130,000 from the Athens government for the purchase of arms intended to be used for secessionist purposes. The five sentenced included the Omonia chair, Theodhori Bezhani. In December 1994, however, one of the five received a presidential pardon, while the other four were released in February 1995 after the Court of Appeal had ruled that there had been "procedural violations" in their trial.

Human Rights Union Party

Partia Bashkimi i te Drejtava te Njeriut (PBDN)
   Address. c/o Kuvënd Popullore, Tirana
   Telephone. (#355–42) 27170
   Fax. (#355–42) 28361
   Leadership. Vasil Melo (president)

The PBDN was formally launched in February 1992, following the enactment of legislation banning parties based on "ethnic principles". The new law was directed in particular at the Democratic Union of the Greek Minority (Omonia), which had won five Assembly seats in the March 1991 elections. In the further Assembly elections of March 1992 the PBDN (including Omonia representatives) won two of the 140 seats with 2.9% of the first-round vote. Its manifesto called for the "full democratization of the social order in Albania", economic reform in the direction of a market economy and peasant ownership of the land. In the disputed 1996 elections the PBDN was awarded three seats.

Social Democratic Party of Albania

Partia Social Demokratike ë Shqipërisë (PSDS)
   Address. Rr. Asim Vokshi 26, Tirana
   Telephone. (#355–42) 27485
   Fax. (#355–42) 23338
   Leadership. Skënder Gjinushi (chair), Paskal Milo (deputy chair), Gaqo Apostoli (general secretary)

Tracing its descent from pre-communist workers' parties, the PSDS was founded in March 1991 on a democratic socialist platform and won seven Assembly seats in the March 1992 elections, subsequently joining the coalition government headed by the Democratic Party of Albania. In late 1994, however, the PSDS opted to withdraw from the coalition amid differences over a new government-proposed constitution, this decision leading to the formation of the breakaway Social Democratic Union. For the 1996 legislative elections the PSDS formed the "Pole of the Centre" alliance with the Democratic Alliance of Albania, both formations joining in the opposition boycott of the June run-off voting on the grounds that the first round in May had been unfairly conducted.

Claiming a membership of 20,000, the PSDS is a consultative member of the Socialist International.

Social Democratic Union of Albania

Unioni Socialdemokrate ë Shqipërisë (USdS)
   Address. c/o Kuvënd Popullore, Tirana
   Leaders. Teodor Laco, Vullnet Ademi

The USdS was launched in January 1995 by two ministers hitherto associated with the Social Democratic Party of Albania (PSDS), who had opposed the PSDS's decision to withdraw from the coalition government dominated by the Democratic Party of Albania.

Socialist Party of Albania
Partia Socialiste Shqipërisë (PSS)

Address. Bulevardi Deshmoret e Kombit, Tirana
Telephone. (#355–42) 23408
Fax. (#355–42) 27417
Leadership. Fatos Nano (chair, imprisoned), Servet Pellumbi (acting chair), Namik Dokle and Illr Meta (vice-chairs), Gramoz Ruci (general secretary)

The PSS is descended from the former ruling Party of Labour of Albania (PLA), itself the successor to the Albanian Communist Party founded in November 1941. The latter had led resistance to the Italian occupation during World War II, the Communist-dominated Democratic Front under Enver Hoxha declaring Albania's liberation in November 1944 and forming a provisional government. The party became the sole authorized formation in 1946 following the Front's overwhelming victory in the December 1945 elections and was renamed the PLA in November 1948 to signify its supposedly broad popular base. Opposed to Yugoslav "revisionism" and the Soviet party's alleged abandonment of Marxism-Leninism under Khrushchev, the PLA aligned itself with the Communist Party of China from 1961 until the late 1970s, after which it became equally hostile to both the USSR and China. Changes in the PLA politburo in November 1981 were followed in December by the "liquidation" (as confirmed some years later) of Prime Minister Mehmet Shehu, whose supporters were then executed or imprisoned.

Hoxha died in April 1985 and was succeeded as party leader by President Ramiz Alia, who moved to end Albania's isolation but who initially took a hardline stance against the post-1989 political changes in Eastern Europe. In November 1990, however, a PLA congress bowed to the new realities by endorsing limited pluralism and deciding that the posts of head of state and party leader were incompatible. Popular demonstrations in December 1990 yielded the actual legalization of several opposition parties, but the PLA's strong rural base enabled it to win a two-thirds majority in multi-party elections in March-April 1991.

In May 1991 President Alia surrendered the PLA leadership, while the following month a party congress, featuring unprecedented criticism of past actions, adopted the new PSS name to signify an abandonment of Marxist precepts and elected a new leadership, former Prime Minister Fatos Nano becoming party chair. Concurrent popular demonstrations forced Alia to appoint a "non-partisan" government under Ylli Bufi of the PSS and including representatives of former opposition parties. But continuing unrest obliged the PSS to surrender the premiership in December 1991, when Albania's first non-party Prime Minister since World War II was appointed. In further Assembly elections in March 1992 the PSS was heavily defeated by the Democratic Party of Albania (PDS) and went into opposition, while Alia resigned as President in April. The party's largely intact organization enabled it to stage a partial recovery in municipal elections in July-August 1992 (when it took 41% of the vote); but in 1993 the PSS was weakened by the prosecution of Alia, Nano and other leaders for alleged corruption and abuse of power under the previous regime. Nano was convicted on various charges in April 1994 and sentenced to 12 years' imprisonment (later reduced), while in July Alia was also found guilty, although his nine-year sentence was later reduced prior to his release in July 1995, when he vowed to resume active politics. Despite his conviction, Nano remained PSS chair, with deputy chair Servet Pellumbi becoming acting chair. Pressure on the PSS was maintained with the conviction in June 1995 of Ilir Hoxha (son of Enver) for "inciting national hatred" by denouncing the PDS government and praising the former communist regime. In September 1995 the Supreme Court rejected Nano's appeal against his conviction.

In November 1995 the PSS deputies were among those who unsuccessfully opposed legislation requiring senior public officials to be screened for their activities in the communist era. Under this so-called Genocide Act, a number of proposed PSS candidates were barred from contesting the 1996 legislative elections, the actual conduct of the first round of which in May was widely regarded as riddled with fraud and intimidation. The PSS accordingly led an opposition boycott of the second round and was credited with only 10 seats when the official results were published.

Other Parties

Albanian Agrarian Party (*Partia Agrar Shqiptare*, PAS), a pro-market formation advocating land privatization, founded in February 1991, led by Prof. Lufter Xhuveli, unsuccessful in recent Assembly elections. *Address*. Rr. Budi 6, Tirana

Albanian Communist Party (*Partia Komuniste Shqiptare*, PKS), formed in June 1991 by a faction of the Party of Labour of Albania opposed to its conversion into the Socialist Party of Albania, legalized in November but banned in mid-1992 as an extremist organization.

Albanian Green Party (*Partia e Blerte Shqiptare*, PBS), founded in March 1991 as the Albanian Ecology Party, led by Nasi Bozhegu, Nevroz Paluka and Namik Huti.

Albanian Liberal Party (*Partia Liberale Shqiptare*, PLS), legalized in October 1991, led by Valter File, backed Democratic Party of Albania in March 1992 elections.

Albanian National Democratic Party (*Partia Nacional Demokratike Shqipërisë*, PNDS), founded in 1991, led by Fatmir Çekani.

Cameria Political and Patriotic Association (*Shoqata Politike-Patriotike Çamëria*, SPPÇ), founded in 1991 to represent the interests of the Çam people, led by Abaz Dojaka.

Democratic Prosperity Party (*Partia e Prosperitetit Demokratike*, PPD), led by Yzeir Fetahu.

Democratic Unity Party (*Partia e Bashkimit Demokratike*, PBD), led by Xhevdet Libohova.

Independent Centre Party (*Partia Indipendente Centriste*, PIC), founded in August 1991, led by Edmond Gjokrushi, backed Democratic Party of Albania in March 1992 elections. *Address.* Rr. Qemal Stafa 120, Tirana

Islamic Democratic Union (*Unioni Democratike Islami*, UDI), founded by Muslims of the Durres region, refused official recognition in May 1993 and March 1996 because of its religious basis.

Movement of Legality Party (*Partia Lëvizja e Legalitetit*, PLL), founded in February 1991, led by Agustin Shashaj and Nderim Kupi, political wing of the small Albanian monarchist movement, whose 50th anniversary celebrations in November 1993 were briefly attended by Leka, son of the late King Zog (who had fled the country in 1939). *Address.* Rr. P. Shkurti pall. 5/1, Tirana

National Front Party (*Partia e Bashkimi Kombëtare*, PBK), led by Abaz Ermenji, who returned to Albania in October 1995 after 49 years in exile.

Party of National Progress (*Partia e Progresit Kombëtare*, PPK), founded in September 1991, led by Myrto Xhaferri, of right-wing orientation. *Address.* Rr. 8 Nentori 1282, Vlora

Party of National Restoration (*Partia per Rimekembjen Kombëtare*, PRK), extreme nationalist formation founded in early 1996 by Abdi Baleta (hitherto a leader of the Democratic Party of the Right), advocates the unification of all Albanian-populated lands in the Balkans, by force if necessary.

Party of National Unity (*Partia e Unitetit Kombëtare*, PUK or UNIKOMB), an ultra-nationalist formation launched in June 1991, led by Idajet Beqiri, with links with Kosovo Albanians, declined to participate in March 1992 Assembly elections because of "anti-democratic" electoral law; Beqiri received a six-month prison sentence in July 1993 for asserting that President Berisha wanted to install a fascist dictatorship; he was in further trouble in January 1996, when he was arrested on charges of having committed crimes against humanity as a communist-era prosecutor. *Address.* Rr. Alqi Kondi, Tirana

People's Party (*Partia Popullore*, PP), an anti-communist formation founded in August 1991 as the Albanian People's Party League, renamed in September 1992, led by Bashkim Driza and Xhemal Borova, unsuccessful in recent Assembly elections.

People's Unity Party (*Partia Bashkimi Popullor*, PBP), led by Gjergj Ndoja.

Social Labour Party of Albania (*Partia Social Punëtore ë Shqipërisë*, PSPS), founded in March 1992, led by Ramadan Ndreka.

Algeria

Capital: Algiers

Population: 28,500,000 (1995E)

The Democratic and Popular Republic of Algeria, under an amendment to its 1976 constitution adopted in 1989, moved from the status of one-party state in which the National Liberation Front (FLN) was the "vanguard, leadership and organization of the people with the aim of building socialism" to being a qualified multi-party democracy. The constitution provides for an executive President, who is directly elected by universal suffrage of those aged at least

18 for a renewable five-year term and who appoints and presides over a Council of Ministers. The constitution also provides for a 430–seat unicameral National People's Assembly (*Majlis Ech Chaabi al-Watani*), elected for five-year term from single-member constituencies in two rounds of voting on the French model. Under the 1989 constitutional amendment, "associations of a political nature" are permitted to exist, provided they do not "threaten the basic interest of the state" and are not exclusively based on "religion, language, region, sex, race or profession".

Contested by 49 separate parties, the first round of Assembly elections on December 26, 1991, resulted in 231 of the 430 seats being filled outright, as follows: Islamic Salvation Front (FIS) 188 (47.5% of the vote); Socialist Forces Front 25 (15%); FLN 15 (23.5%); independents 3. In light of the likely FIS victory and following the resignation of President Chadli Bendjedid (FLN) on Jan. 11, 1992, the second round of voting was cancelled by elements of the FLN regime and a state of emergency declared. Presidential powers were assumed by an army-dominated five-member High State Committee, but this body was disbanded in January 1994 upon the appointment on Brig.-Gen. Liamine Zéroual as President, on the nomination of the High Security Council (HSC). In May 1994 President Zéroual inaugurated a non-elected National Transition Council (NTC) of 200 members to replace the HSC as interim legislature. In the first round of presidential elections held on Nov. 16, 1995, but boycotted by the FIS and most other opposition parties, Brig.-Gen. Zéroual was elected outright, being credited with 61.3% of the vote.

Challenge

Ettahaddi

Address. 61 blvd Krim Belkacem, Telemly, Algiers

Telephone. (#213-2) 718991

Fax. (#213-2) 718993

Leadership. Cherif al-Hashemi (secretary-general)

This party was established in January 1993 as successor to the Socialist Vanguard Party (*Parti de l'Avant-Garde Socialiste*, PAGS), itself descended from the Algerian Communist Party (CPA) founded in the 1930s. Originally supported mainly by Europeans, the CPA had participated in the anti-colonialist struggle but had been banned after independence in 1962 and dissolved in 1964, many members joining the ruling National Liberation Front (FLN). It was relaunched in 1966 by FLN left-wingers as the PAGS and legalized in 1989 on a democratic socialist platform. The party boycotted the December 1991 Assembly elections and became committed, under its new name, to "the revolutionary transition of Algeria to modernity and progress". In April 1993 al-Hashemi was wounded in a presumed fundamentalist attack.

Islamic Renaissance Movement

Harakat al-Nahda al-Islamiyya (En-Nahda)
Mouvement de la Renaissance Islamique (MRI)

Address. 4 ave des Ecoles, Place des Martyrs, Algiers

Telephone. (#213-2) 667666

Fax. (#213-2) 667666

Leadership. Sheikh Abdallah Djaballah

This moderate Islamist party sprang from a Constantine University movement of the 1970s. It was unsuccessful in December 1991 Assembly elections and subsequently declared itself in favour of dialogue with the government to bring about a national consensus. Its leader participated in a conference of Algerian opposition parties held in Rome in January 1995 and endorsed a resultant draft peace agreement, but this text did not impress the regime in Algiers. The MRI joined other opposition parties in boycotting the November 1995 presidential elections.

Islamic Salvation Front

Front Islamique du Salut (FIS)

Leadership. Abassi Madani (president), Ali Belhadj (vice-president), Abdelkader Hashani (leader in 1991 elections), Rabeh Kebir, Anouar Haddam (spokesmen in exile)

Formed from student and other Islamist groups dating from the early 1970s, the FIS obtained official recognition in February 1989 amid a rising tide of opposition to the government of the National Liberation Front (FLN). In municipal elections in June 1990 FIS candidates took 55% of the popular vote, winning control of 853 municipalities and 32 out of 48 provinces. Serious clashes between FIS supporters and the security forces resulted, in June 1991, in the postponement of Assembly elections and the arrest of hundreds of FIS activists, including Madani and Belhadj. Divisions between moderates and extremists in the remaining leadership resulted in the former prevailing in their view that the FIS should contest the elections, set for December 1991, and call off street demonstrations. A party programme published for the elections envisaged the renovation of social, economic and political life according to Islamic precepts and the historical experience of the Algerian people. Specific pledges included segregation of the sexes at school and at work, compulsory wearing of the veil by women and a ban on alcohol consumption. Led in the elections by Hashani and presenting candidates for all 430 seats, the FIS took a commanding lead in the first-round voting, winning 188 seats outright (and 47.5% of the vote). With the FIS poised to secure a substantial overall majority in the second round, Hashani made it clear that an FIS government would seek an early presidential election and, "should that be the people's demand", embark upon constitutional reform; he gave no specific commitment to the multi-party system, but stressed that Islamicization would be pursued by legal means.

Hashani and Kebir were among several FIS leaders arrested in January 1992 following the cancellation of the second electoral round and the military's effective assumption of power. Upon petition by the High State Council, the FIS was banned by a court ruling in March 1992 (upheld by the Supreme Court in April) on the grounds that it had violated the 1989 law prohibiting a religious basis for parties. In a major clamp-down on FIS activists, many thousands were arrested and detained in desert concentration camps. FIS moderates, committed to non-violence, sought political accomodation with the regime (and the FIS leadership denied any involvement in the assassination of head of state Mohammed Boudiaf in June 1992); but the initiative passed inreasingly to radical splinter-groups favouring armed struggle, notably to the Armed Islamic Group (GIA). In July 1992 both Madani and Belhadj were sentenced to 12 years' imprisonment after being convicted on insurgency charges. The following month Kebir escaped from detention and was later granted political asylum in Germany, together with Ossama Madani, son of Abbasi. In September 1993 the German authorities refused an Algerian extradition request for these two, who had both been sentenced to death *in absentia* for their alleged part in a bomb attack at Algiers airport in August 1992.

In 1993–94 attacks on security personnel and foreign nationals mounted, as did arrests and executions of FIS militants, bringing the country to a state of virtual civil war. In February 1994 the new Zéroual government released two senior FIS figures in an effort to promote political talks; but a subsequent unofficial dialogue involving FIS representatives produced no agreement. In September Madani and Belhadj were transferred from prison to house arrest in a regime move to promote further dialogue; when this did not occur, both were reimprisoned in November. The release of the two FIS leaders was the main demand of the hijackers of a French airliner at Algiers in December; presumed to be members of the GIA, all four were killed by French security forces at Marseilles. The episode generated much press speculation on whether the GIA and the official armed wing of the FIS (called the Islamic Salvation Army) had merged, as some unconfirmed reports had suggested. French sources, citing official Algerian figures, put the death toll in Algeria's internal conflict in 1994 at some 40,000, the majority of them civilians.

In January 1995 the FIS was represented at a conference of Algerian opposition parties held in Rome, but a draft peace plan drawn up on that occasion found little favour with the Algerian government. The following month several prominent FIS members were among many killed when the Algerian security forces put down a revolt by Islamist prisoners at the Serkadji prison in Algiers. Talks between FIS leaders and the government were initiated in April, initially in secret, but broke down in July, with the government claiming that the FIS had entered new conditions at a late stage and had refused to give a commitment to pluralist democracy. Having again been released to house arrest during the talks, Madani and Belhadj were again returned to prison when the talks failed. The FIS boycotted the November 1995 presidential elections, claiming after the result was declared that the turnout had been only about 30% rather the 75% cited by the Algerian authorities. Growing divisions in the Islamist opposition were highlighted in December 1995 by the execution by a GIA firing squad of two aides of the FIS leader who had criticized the GIA's campaign of violence.

Movement for Democracy in Algeria
Mouvement pour la Démocratie en Algérie (MDA)

    Address. 41 rue Didouche Mourad, Algiers

    Telephone. (#213-2) 610878

    Fax. (#213-2) 610878

    Leadership. Ahmed Ben Bella, Hocine Guermouche

The MDA was originally founded in May 1984 by ex-President Ben Bella, who had been deposed in 1965 and had languished in prison or under house arrest until 1979, when he went into exile in France, where the first MDA congress was held at a secret location, and then to Switzerland. Seeking to initiate "Algeria's apprenticeship in democracy" and espousing a moderate Islamism, the party formed an opposition alliance with the secular Socialist Forces Front (FFS) in December 1985. With the advent of pluralism in 1989, it proclaimed itself "a party for all Algerians" and secured legalization in early 1990; but it boycotted the June 1990 local polls on the grounds that Assembly elections should be held first. Ben Bella returned from exile in September 1990 but led the MDA to a poor performance in the December 1991 Assembly elections, in the first round of which it failed to win a seat despite fielding 339 candidates. Opposing the military-led regime installed in January 1992, Ben Bella in June 1992 initiated the formation of an alliance of opposition parties which called for a government of national unity and a return to multi-party democracy, also urging an end to repression of Islamist elements. Having rejected involvement in the regime-sponsored National Patriotic Rally, the MDA boycotted the "national consensus conference" convened in January 1994. However, following Zéroual's accession to the presidency, it joined other mainstream parties in participating in a new dialogue process aimed at finding a political accomodation. In January 1995 Ben Bella attended the Rome conference of Algerian opposition parties at which a draft peace plan was formulated. The government's rejection of the plan impelled the MDA and other opposition parties to boycott the November 1995 presidential elections.

Movement of the Islamic Society

Harakat al-Mujtamaa al-Islami (Hamas)
   Address. 63 ave Ali Adade, El Mouradia, Algiers
   Telephone. (#213-2) 660945
   Fax. (#213-2) 660899
   Leadership. Sheikh Mahfoud Nahnah
   This moderate Islamist party was formed in 1990, declaring its opposition to the radicalism of the Islamic Salvation Front. It failed to win a seat in the first round of the December 1991 Assembly elections and was subsequently supportive of the regime's anti-fundamentalist campaign, being the only significant party to participate in the "national consensus conference" convened by the government in January 1994. Sheikh Mahfoud Nahnah was a candidate in the November 1995 presidential elections, coming in second place with 25.4% of the vote. After the result was declared, Sheikh Nahnah asserted that 4 million names added to the electoral register since 1991 could not be justified by population growth; he also claimed that his supporters and monitors had been intimidated by the authorities. Nevertheless, in January 1996 Hamas accepted two portfolios in a government reshuffle announced by President Zéroual.

National Liberation Front

Front de Libération Nationale (FLN)
   Address. 7 rue du Stade Hydra, Algiers
   Telephone. (#213-2) 592149
   Fax. (#213-2) 591732
   Leadership. Abdelhamid Mehri (secretary-general)
   The FLN was founded at Cairo in November 1954 under the leadership of Ahmed Ben Bella and other nationalists as an anti-colonialist, socialist, non-aligned, pan-Arabist and pro-Islam movement dedicated to ending French rule. After achieving independence and coming to power in 1962, it experienced internal strife in which Ben Bella was initially victorious but which eventually resulted in his replacement in July 1965 by Col. Houari Boumedienne, who held the government and party leadership until his death in December 1978. The FLN was then reorganized and given a new statute at its fourth congress in January 1979, at which Bendjedid Chadli was elected party leader and designated as sole candidate for the presidency in elections the following month. Re-elected unopposed in January 1984, Bendjedid embarked upon a programme of economic reform, emphasizing "pragmatic" socialism and the virtues of the private enterprise, to the chagrin of the FLN's socialist old guard. He also, following anti-FLN riots in late 1978, sought to democratize political structures, to which end the posts of head of state and party leader were made incompatible by decision of an FLN congress in November. Bendjedid was succeeded as FLN secretary-general by his brother-in-law, Abdelhamid Mehri, and himself took the new post of party president.

The move to multi-party democracy in 1989 revealed the extent of popular discontent with the FLN, which suffered a serious rebuff in local elections in June 1990 marking the emergence of the fundamentalist Islamic Salvation Front (FIS) as a major force. Subsequent anti-government demonstrations resulted in the formation in June 1991 of the first post-independence government not dominated by the FLN, Bendjedid resigning as party president the same month. In Assembly elections in December 1991 the FLN trailed a poor third in the first-round voting despite putting up 429 candidates, after which the military intervened to prevent a likely FIS victory in the second and Bendjedid resigned as President. Although the new regime included many figures associated with the years of FLN rule, the party itself effectively went into opposition, joining other parties in calling for a transitional government of national unity and condemning the use of military courts to enforce emergency regulations banning fundamentalist political activity. It also declined to join a regime-sponsored National Patriotic

Rally, announced in June 1992 as a new "foundation" for political co-operation; for its pains the FLN was dispossessed of its state-owned properties, including its party headquarters in Algiers. In March 1994 the FLN joined other parties in opening a dialogue with the new Zéroual government, while in January 1995 Mehri attended the Rome conference of Algerian opposition parties at which a peace plan was drawn up, although without substantive effect. A member of the FLN central committee, Ahmed Kasmi, was found beheaded in February 1995, apparently the victim of Islamic militants. The FLN joined the opposition parties' boycott of the November 1995 presidential elections, after which Mehri made a conciliatory statement calling on the government to enter into real dialogue with the FIS.

Rally for Culture and Democracy

Rassemblement pour la Culture et la Démocratie (RCD)
  Address. 87A rue Didouche Mourad, Algiers
  Telephone. (#213-2) 736201
  Fax. (#213-2) 736220
  Leadership. Saïd Saadi (secretary-general)

Based in the Berber community, the secular RCD was formed in February 1989 on a platform of "economic centralism" and official recognition of the Berber language. It took third place in the June 1990 local elections (which were boycotted by the rival Berber-based Socialist Forces Front), winning 5.7% of the vote and majorities in 87 municipalities and the province of Tizi Ouzou. In the December 1991 Assembly elections, however, none of its 300 candidates were elected in the first round. The RCD joined other mainstream parties in opposing the military-led regime installed in January 1992, until Zéroual's accession to the presidency in January 1994 heralded a more conciliatory government stance, enabling political dialogue to commence in March. Saïd Saadi was a candidate in the November 1995 presidential elections, winning 9.3% of the vote.

Socialist Forces Front

Front des Forces Socialistes (FFS)
  Address. 56 ave Souidani Boudjemaa, 16000 Algiers
  Telephone. (#213–2) 593313
  Fax. (#213–2) 591145
  Leadership. Hocine Aït-Ahmed (president)

Originally founded in 1963 and revived and legalized in November 1989, the FFS espoused democratic socialist principles as contrasted with the state centralism of the then ruling National Liberation Front (FLN). Its leader is one of the surviving *neuf historiques* who launched the Algerian war of independence against France in November 1954. Following independence in 1962, he instigated an unsuccessful Berber revolt against the Ben Bella government in 1963. Arrested in October 1964, Aït-Ahmed was sentenced to death in April 1964 (the sentence being commuted to life imprisonment) but escaped abroad in May 1966. After Aït-Ahmed had returned to Algeria from Switzerland in December 1989, the FFS urged its supporters to boycott the June 1990 local elections (arguing that Assembly balloting should be held first), achieving large support for this line in the Berber (*Amazghiya*) heartland of Kabylie region east of Algiers. After an abortive attempt in 1991 to create a broad coalition to oppose the Islamic Salvation Front (FIS), the FFS emerged as the leading non-Islamist party in the first round of Assembly elections in December 1991. It put up 317 candidates and won 25 seats outright with 15% of the vote, on a platform advocating a mixed economy, regional autonomy and recognition of the Berber language. Having ruled out a second-round alliance with either the FLN or the FIS, Aït-Ahmed strongly criticized the subsequent military intervention and returned to exile in Switzerland.

Calling for a government of national unity and and an end to anti-FIS repression, the FFS rejected affiliation with the National Patriotic Rally launched by the government in June 1992 and also boycotted the "national consensus conference" convened in January 1994. Nevertheless, having urged moderate army elements to join with the democratic opposition, the FFS responded to the conciliatory overtures of the new Zéroual government in March 1994, while insisting that political dialogue must result in a resumption of multi-party democracy. In January 1995 Aït-Ahmed attended the Rome conference of Algerian opposition parties at which a putative peace plan was formulated. Following its rejection by the government, the FFS was one of several opposition parties that boycotted the November 1995 presidential elections. Aït-Ahmed returned to Algeria in March 1996 to attend the second FFS congress, which appealed for national dialogue to achieve civil peace.

The FFS claims a membership of 30,000 and is a consultative member of the Socialist International.

Other Parties

Algerian Movement for Justice and Development (*Mouvement Algérien pour la Justice et le Développement*, MAJD), founded in 1990 by Kasdi Merbah, a former Prime Minister following his resignation from the National Liberation Front (FLN), claiming to represent the dominant socialist current of the pre-Chadli era, unsuccessful in the December 1991 Assembly elections.

Algerian National Party (*Parti National Algérien*, PNA), a moderate Islamist formation founded in 1989, advocating economic liberalization and the restoration of publicly-owned land to its previous owners.

Algerian People's Party (*Parti du Peuple Algérien*, PPA), led by Mohammed Memchaoui, an Islamist formation.

Algerian Renewal Party (*Parti pour le Renouveau de l'Algérie*, PRA), led by Noureddine Boukrouh, a moderate Islamist and pro-market formation which emerged in 1988, won no seats in the December 1991 Assembly elections, subsequently aligned with progressive FLN elements; Boukrouh contested the November 1995 presidential elections, winning 3.8% of the vote, and in January 1996 a PRA member was appointed to the government.

Arab-Islamic Rally (*Rassemblement Arabe-Islamique*, RAI), led by Laid Grine and Ali Zeghdad, an Islamist and pan-Arab formation.

Community (*El Oumma*), headed by veteran pre-independence leader Benyoussef Ben Khedda, advocating the application of Islam as being superior to both capitalism and socialism.

Democratic Progressive Party (*Parti Démocratique Progressif*, PDP), led by Saci Mabrouk, a centrist formation.

National Party for Development and Solidarity (*Parti National pour le Développement et la Solidarité*, PNDS), led until early 1994 by Rabah Bencherif, a centre-right party which took two municipalities in the June 1990 local elections with 1.6% of the popular vote.

National Renewal Front (*Front National de Renouvellement*, FNR), led by Zineddine Cherifi, a centrist formation.

National Republican Alliance (*Alliance Républicaine Nationale*, ARN), founded in mid-1995 by Redha Malek (a former Prime Minister), opposed to any concessions to Islamic fundamentalism.

Party of God (*Hizbollah*), led by Jamal al-Din Bardi, an Islamist formation denied legalization in 1990, reported to be active in the fundamentalist struggle from 1992 onwards.

Party of Islamic and Democratic Arab Unity (*Parti de l'Unité Arabe Islamique et Démocratique*, PUAID), led by Belhadj Khalil Harfi, legalized in 1990, Islamist formation advocating the creation of a united Islamic community stretching from the Gulf to the Atlantic.

People's Association for Unity and Action (*Association du Peuple pour l'Unité et l'Action*, APUA), founded in 1990, led by Mehdi Abbes Allalou, centrist in orientation.

Progressive Republican Party (*Parti Républicain Progressif*, PRP), founded in 1990, led by Khadir Driss.

Social Authenticity Movement (*Mouvement Social de l'Authenticité*, MSA), led by Babouche Mohammed Ameziane, based in the Berber community, represented at the Rome peace conference of opposition parties in January 1995.

Social Democratic Party (*Parti Social-Démocrate*, PSD), led by Abderrahmane Abjerid and Abdelkader Bouzar, founded in 1989 on a centrist, pro-market platform, won two municipalities in the June 1990 local elections but failed to make an impact in the December 1991 Assembly balloting.

Social Liberal Party (*Parti Social-Libéral*, PSL), led by Ahmed Khelil, a centrist formation.

Socialist Workers' Party (*Parti Socialiste des Travailleurs*, PST), legalized in early 1990, a left-wing secular party seeking to promote Trotskyist ideas in Algeria.

Union for Democracy and Liberty (*Union pour la Démocratie et la Liberté*, UDL), led by Moulay Boukhalafa and Turki Zaghloul, a centrist formation.

Union of Democratic Forces (*Union des Forces Démocratiques*, UFD), founded in 1989 under the leadership of Ahmed Mhasas, who had served as Agriculture Minister in the post-independence period.

Workers' Party (*Parti des Travailleurs*, PT), led by Louisa Hannoun, who attended the Rome conference of opposition parties in January 1995.

Andorra

Capital: Andorra la Vella　　　　　　　　　　　　　　　**Population:** 65,000 (1995E)

Andorra effectively gained independence on May 4, 1993, with the entry into force of its first written constitution, adopted by referendum on March 14. The sovereignty hitherto vested in the President of the French Republic and the Bishop of Urgel (in Spain) as Co-Princes was transferred to Andorra itself as a "parliamentary co-principality". The Co-Princes were retained with the status of a single constitutional monarch, with much-reduced powers, and were still represented by their respective appointees as Permanent Delegates, and locally by the *Veguer de França* and the *Veguer Episcopal*. The unicameral legislature, the 28–member General Council of the Valleys (*Consell General de las Valls d'Andorra*), is elected for a four-year term by universal franchise of Andorran citizens aged 18 and over, 14 members being chosen on a national list system and 14 elected locally to represent the seven constituent parishes. Most residents are ineligible to vote, being French or Spanish nationals. The General Council, under the new dispensation, selects the Head of Government (*Cap del Govern*) who presides over a 10–member Executive Council or Cabinet (*Govern d'Andorra*); neither the Head of Government nor the ministers may be members of the General Council.

Political parties were legalized by the 1993 constitution, which also formalized trade union and civil rights and the separation of the judiciary from the executive and legislative branches. Various ad hoc groupings had contested earlier elections, and the General Council elections on Dec. 12, 1993, marked the development of these groups into political parties. The largest share of the vote, 26.4%, went to the National Democratic Grouping (AND), giving it 8 seats; the Liberal Party (PL) took 5 seats (22%); New Democracy (ND) 5 (19.1%); the National Andorran Coalition (CNA) 2 (17.2%); and the National Democratic Initiative (IDN) 2 (15.3%). The remaining six seats went to independents, four of whom formed the Canillo-Massana Group, two joining the CNA.

Formal political parties, as opposed to loosely-organized groupings drawing on allegiance to personalities, clan or locality, are as yet a novelty in the co-principality, having had no legal existence until 1993. No fewer than 18 associations of various kinds presented or endorsed candidates in the 1993 elections, but few could properly be regarded as parties. A limiting factor in the development of a fully-fledged party system is the small size of the electorate (under 10,000 adult Andorran citizens). Realignments of party interests in the General Council before the next election, due in 1997, were expected to clarify the basic cleavage between outward-looking, modernizing viewpoints and the more parochial conservative forces.

Liberal Party
Partit Lliberal (PL)

Address. carrer Mossen Tremosa 6–1er, Andorra la Vella

Telephone. (#376) 820031, 829345

Fax. (#376) 823724

Leadership. Marc Forné Molné (leader), Francesc Cerqueda Pascuet (leader of parliamentary group), Joan Tomás Roca (president), Gerard Sasplugas Mateu (secretary general), Joan Samarra (director)

In the December 1993 election this centre-right party secured five seats on the General Council with 1,591 votes (22 per cent), and voted against the nomination of Oscar Ribas Reig of the National Democratic Grouping as head of government in January 1994. When his coalition partners in New Democracy withdrew their backing for budget proposals, Forné garnered sufficient votes from other parties (including two from Ribas's party) to form a new administration with six other Liberal ministers and three non-party ministers.

The party, also known as the Liberal Union

14

(*Unió Lliberal*, UL), was admitted to observer membership of the Liberal International in 1994.

National Andorran Coalition
Coalició Nacional Andorrana (CNA)
Address. a/c MI Simó Duró Coma, Consell General, Casa de la Vall, Andorra la Vella
Telephone. (#376) 821234
Leadership. Antoni Cerqueda Gispert (president of parliamentary group)

Following the 1993 elections, the two members of the General Council elected as CNA candidates abstained in the vote to form the first Executive Council under the new constitution. The CNA's support is spread around the country rather than being concentrated in particular parishes, its two seats coming from the national list voting rather than from the parish constituencies. However, two independent councillors subsequently joined the CNA bloc.

National Democratic Grouping
Agrupament Nacional Democratic (AND)
Address. a/c MI Jordi Torres Alís, Consell General, Casa de la Vall, Andorra la Vella
Telephone. (#376) 821234
Leadership. Oscar Ribas Reig (leader), Ladislau Baró Solà (president of parliamentary group)

The AND is a centre-right liberal nationalist formation formed by Ribas, who presided over the executive council in 1982–84 and 1990– 94, including a ten-month period as the first Head of Government under the new constitution. The AND emerged as the largest party in the December 1993 elections, following which Ribas was re-elected Head of Government on Jan. 19, 1994, and subsequently formed a coalition government consisting of the AND, the National Democratic Initiative and New Democracy (ND); but he resigned on Nov. 25, 1994, after losing a confidence vote by 20 votes to eight when the five ND councillors refused to endorse his 1995 budget. The resignation of Ribas in November 1994 was the third such event in his career: he had quit office in 1984 over a tax policy dispute and had again briefly resigned in 1992 to face down conservative critics of constitutional change. Reforms introduced under Ribas reflected a modernizing liberal agenda: they included the introduction of a penal code abolishing capital punishment, implementation of the new constitution (which secured 74.2% approval), customs union with the European Union and admission to the United Nations in July 1993. More controversially, he proposed to widen indirect taxation beyond sales to cover banking, insurance and other sectors to finance infrastructural development, and it was on this issue that his government fell. However, two AND members voted in the successor government only on condition that it agreed to implement a budget on broadly similar lines.

New Democracy
Nova Democracia (ND)
Address. a/c MI Jordi Cinca Mateos, Consell General, Casa de la Vall, Andorra la Vella
Telephone. (#376) 821234
Leadership. Jaume Bartumeu Cassany (president of parliamentary group)

The centre-left ND secured five General Council seats in December 1993, with the third-largest share of the popular vote. It supported the government led by the National Democratic Coalition installed in early 1994. Its withdrawal from the alliance in November, in a dispute over fiscal policy, precipitated the formation of a new executive.

Other Parties

Canillo-Massana Group (*Agrupament Canillo-Massana*, ACM), a bloc of four General Council members elected as independents, with Josep Garrallà Rossell as president. *Address*. a/c MI Josep Areny Fité, Consell General, Casa de la Vall, Andorra la Vella

National Democratic Initiative (*Iniciativa Democratica Nacional*, IDN), led by Vicenç Mateu Zamora and described as left-leaning; the IDN's two General Council seats won in 1993 were insufficient to secure formal recognition as a parliamentary group. *Address*. a/c MI Vicenç Alay Ferrer, Consell General, Casa de la Vall, Andorra la Vella.

Angola

Capital: Luanda

Population: 11,500,000 (1995E)

Angola achieved independence from Portugal in November 1975 as the People's Republic of Angola, with what became the Popular Movement for the Liberation of Angola-Party of Labour (MPLA-PT) becoming the sole ruling party in Luanda. By early 1976 the MPLA government, assisted by Cuban military forces, had established control over most of Angola, although the competing Union for the Total Independence of Angola (UNITA), backed by South Africa and the USA, remained active in the south. Following the signature in December 1988 of the Brazzaville Agreement, providing for the withdrawal of Cuban and South African troops, the MPLA-PT in December 1990 abandoned Marxism-Leninism and embraced "democratic socialism". The Lisbon Accord of May 1991 provided for an end to the civil war with UNITA and for reform of the political structure, including the introduction of a multi-party system. Under constitutional amendments adopted in August 1992, the country was renamed the Republic of Angola and provision made for a "semi-presidential" system headed by an executive President, directly elected for a five-year term in two rounds of voting, who appoints a Prime Minister. Legislative authority is vested in a National Assembly (*Assembléia Nacional*) elected for a four-year term by universal adult suffrage and proportional representation, with 130 members being returned nationally, 90 from provincial constituencies and possibly three by Angolans living abroad.

A law enacted in May 1991 specifies that political parties "must be national in character and scope". Specifically prohibited are parties that "are local and regional in character; foster tribalism, racism, regionalism or other forms of discrimination against citizens or affect national unity and territorial integrity; use or propose the use of violence to pursue their aims. . .; adopt a uniform for their members or possess clandestine parallel structures; use military, para-military or militarized organization; [or] are subordinate to the policy of foreign governments, bodies or parties". The 1991 law also makes provision for registered parties to receive state financial assistance on the basis of their support in the most recent general election and the number of candidates presented.

Multi-party elections to the new People's Assembly on Sept. 29–30, 1992, produced the following results: MPLA-PT 129 seats (53.7% of the national vote); UNITA 70 (34.1%); Social Renewal Party 6 (2.3%); National Front for the Liberation of Angola 5 (2.4%); Liberal Democratic Party 3 (2.4%); Democratic Renewal Party 1 (0.9%); Democratic Alliance of Angola 1 (0.9%); Social Democratic Party 1 (0.8%); Angola Youth, Worker and Peasant Alliance Party 1 (0.4%); Angolan Democratic Forum 1 (0.3%); Democratic Party for Progress-Angolan National Alliance 1 (0.3); Angolan National Democratic Party 1 (0.3%). By agreement of the parties, the three seats for Angolans abroad were not filled. In concurrent presidential elections, incumbent José Eduardo dos Santos (MPLA-PT) won 49.6% of the first-round vote, just short of the 50% needed to make a second round unnecessary, although this was not held. A newly-appointed transitional government headed by the MPLA-PT included representatives of four smaller parties, while six posts were allocated to UNITA. The latter nevertheless disputed the official election results and resumed military activities. Direct negotiations between the two sides opened in Lusaka in November 1993 after UNITA had declared its acceptance of the September 1992 election outcome. This process yielded the signature of a ceasefire and power-sharing agreement in the Zambian capital on Nov. 20, 1994.

16

Angolan Democratic Forum

Forum Democrático Angolano (FDA)
Address. c/o Assembléia Nacional, Luanda
Leadership. Jorge Rebelo Pinto Chikoto (president), Manuel Adão Domingos (secretary-general)

Registered in February 1992, the FDA was led by former members of the National Union for the Total Independence of Angola (UNITA) who claimed that UNITA had been guilty of human rights abuses. In the September 1992 National Assembly elections, the FDA won one of the 220 seats at issue with 0.3% of the popular vote. Generally supportive of the government of the Popular Movement for the Liberation of Angola-Party of Labour (MPLA-PT), the FDA was allocated one cabinet post in the "unity" government announced in December 1992.

Angolan Democratic Liberal Party

Partido Democrático Liberal Angolano (PDLA)
Address. c/o Assembléia Nacional, Luanda
Leadership. Honorato Lando (president)

Founded after the move to multi-party democracy in May 1991, the centrist PDLA was unsuccessful in the September 1992 Assembly elections, although its president was placed fifth of the 11 first-round presidential candidates, with 1.9% of the popular vote.

Angolan Democratic Party

Partido Democrático Angolana (PDA)
Address. c/o Assembléia Nacional, Luanda
Leadership. António Alberto Neto (president)

The FDA was founded in 1992, its leader expressing criticism of both the government of the Popular Movement for the Liberation of Angola-Party of Labour (MPLA-PT) and the main opposition National Union for the Total Independence of Angola (UNITA). In the September 1992 presidential election, Neto was third-placed of the 11 first-round candidates, although with only 2.2% of the popular vote, while the party failed to secure representation in the simultaneous Assembly elections.

Angolan National Democratic Party

Partido Nacional Democrático de Angola (PNDA)
Address. c/o Assembléia Nacional, Luanda
Leadership. Paulino Pinto João (president)

The PNDA was founded following the transition to multi-party democracy in May 1991 (at first called the Angolan National Democratic Convention) and joined the pro-democracy National Opposition Council in October 1991. The PNDA leader had previously been a senior member of the ruling Popular Movement for the Liberation of Angola-Party of Labour (MPLA-PT). In the September 1992 presidential election the PNDA endorsed the candidacy of Daniel Chipenda, also a former senior member of the MPLA-PT who had opposed the nomination of incumbent President dos Santos for the presidency. Chipenda was placed eighth among the 11 first-round candidates, with 0.5% of the vote, while in the simultaneous Assembly balloting the PNDA won one of the 220 seats at issue, with 0.3% of the vote.

Democratic Alliance of Angola

Aliança Democrática de Angola (ADA)
Address. c/o Assembléia Nacional, Luanda
Leadership. Simba da Costa (president)

The ADA was created by a number of opposition parties prior to the September 1992 multi-party elections. It took only 0.9% of the popular vote in the Assembly balloting, winning one of the 220 seats at issue.

Democratic Party for Progress-Angolan National Alliance

Partido Democrático para Progresso-Aliança Nacional Angolano (PDP-ANA)
Address. c/o Assembléia Nacional, Luanda
Leadership. Nfulumpinga Lando Victor (president)

The right-wing FDP-ANA came into being following the move to multi-partyism in May 1991, led by a former member of the National Front for the Liberation of Angola. Advocating capitalism and humanism, it joined the pro-democracy National Opposition Council in October 1991. In the September 1992 Assembly elections it won one of the 220 seats with 0.3% of the popular vote.

Democratic Renewal Party

Partido Renovador Democrático (PRD)
Address. c/o Assembléia Nacional, Luanda
Leadership. Luis da Silva dos Passos (president), Vicente Junior (secretary-general)

The PRD was founded by surviving dissidents of the Popular Movement for the Liberation of Angola-Party of Labour (MPLA-PT) who had staged an abortive coup in 1977. At first regarded as one of the best-organized of the new Angolan parties which emerged following the move to multi-partyism in May 1991, the PRD joined the pro-democracy National Opposition Council formed in October 1991 and declared its intention to form a post-election coalition government with the National Union for the Total Independence of Angola (UNITA). However, it was weakened by a split in April 1992, when honorary president Joaquim Pinto de Andrade and other leaders resigned in protest against alleged vote-rigging in PRD executive elections. Forecasts by dos Passos

17

that the party would win 20% of the vote in the September 1992 elections, taking support from the MPLA-PT, proved wide of the mark: he was placed sixth out of 11 first-round candidates in the presidential contest, with 1.5% of the vote, and the PRD won only one Assembly seat out of 220, with 0.9% of the vote. Nevertheless, the party obtained representation at junior level in the "unity" government announced in December 1992.

Front for the Liberation of the Enclave of Cabinda
Frente para a Libertação do Enclave de Cabinda (FLEC)
Address. c/o Assembléia Nacional, Luanda
Leadership. Henrique Tiaho Nzita, Luis de Ganzaga Ranque Franque, Francisco Xavier Lubota

FLEC was founded in 1963 as a nationalist movement seeking separate independence for Cabinda, an oil-rich coastal enclave which is not contiguous with Angola proper, being bordered by Congo and Zaïre. Encouraged by the Portuguese colonial authorities as an ally of sorts against the Popular Movement for the Liberation of Angola (MPLA), FLEC refused to co-operate with other nationalist movements and rejected the claim of the MPLA government installed in Luanda at independence in November 1975 that Cabinda was part of Angola. Forced on the defensive by Cuban-supported government troops, FLEC was also weakened in the late 1970s by internal divisions which resulted in the creation of several factions. Two of these declared "independent" governments in Cabinda and one claimed in 1979 to control 30% of Cabindan territory. But guerrilla action by the FLEC factions was sporadic in the 1980s, being usually directed at state oil installations and similar targets. The withdrawal of Cuban troops in 1990–91 prompted a revival of FLEC, which condemned the May 1991 Lisbon Accord between the government and the National Union for the Total Independence of Angola (UNITA) for its failure to contemplate Cabindan independence. In 1992 the various FLEC factions came together to mount actions designed to disrupt the September Assembly elections, subsequently claiming that the participation rate of under 20% in Cabinda demonstrated a desire for independence. In May 1993 FLEC declared that the US recognition of the government in Luanda did not extend to Cabinda and warned foreign nationals to leave the territory if their companies supported "the extermination of the Cabindan people". The Angolan government claimed that FLEC was being armed by "Congolese politicians" and was reported to be seeking an alliance with a FLEC splinter group to offset the perceived possibility of a FLEC-UNITA joint front.

Liberal Democratic Party
Partido Liberal Democrático (PLD)
Address. c/o Assembléia Nacional, Luanda
Leadership. Amália de Vitoria Pereira (chair)

The PLD was formed following the move to multi-partyism in May 1991 and joined the pro-democracy National Opposition Council established in October that year. In the September 1992 elections the PLD leader came tenth out of 11 candidates in the first round of the presidential contest, with only 0.3% of the vote, but in the simultaneous Assembly balloting the party won three out of 220 seats, with 2.4% of the vote.

National Front for the Liberation of Angola
Frente Nacional de Libertação de Angola (FNLA)
Address. c/o Assembléia Nacional, Luanda
Leadership. Holden Roberto (president)

The FNLA was founded in March 1962 as a merger of the *União das Populações de Angola* (UPA) led by Roberto and the *Partido Democrático Angolano* (PDA), two northern nationalist movements which had launched an anti-Portuguese peasants' revolt the previous year. Based in Zaïre and backed by President Mobutu, the FNLA the following month formed the "revolutionary Angolan government-in-exile" (GRAE), with Roberto as prime minister. Although vigorously anti-communist, the FNLA secured the backing of China, which switched its support from the pro-Soviet Popular Movement for the Liberation of Angola (MPLA) in December 1962; it was also at various times aided by South Africa and the USA. In 1966 it was weakened by the formation of the breakaway National Union for the Total Independence of Angola (UNITA), but it subsequently allied itself with UNITA in a pre-independence struggle for supremacy with the MPLA, interspersed with the signature of abortive "unity" pacts.

Following the left-wing military coup in Lisbon in April 1974, Portugal signed ceasefire agreements with the FNLA and UNITA, but a powerful pro-Soviet faction of the new Portuguese regime favoured the MPLA. In January 1975 all three Angolan movements received OAU recognition and formed a transitional government, but hostilities between them resumed almost immediately, with the FNLA-UNITA alliance receiving active military support from South Africa. On the MPLA's declaration of an independent People's Republic of Angola in November 1975, the FNLA and UNITA declared a rival Democratic Republic. However, following the withdrawal of South African forces in early 1976, Cuban-backed MPLA troops established control of most of Angola, driving FNLA forces into Zaïre and winning a decisive victory over them at Kifangondo in November 1977. The FNLA then ceased to be a significant force and President Mobutu (Roberto's brother-in-law) transferred Zaïrean support to UNITA, which continued to resist the MPLA-PT (as it now was) in the south. Expelled from Zaïre in 1979 (and subsequently from Senegal and Gabon), Roberto was eventually granted asylum in France.

Following the signature of the May 1991 Lisbon Accord between the MPLA-PT government and UNITA, Roberto returned to Angola at the end of August and announced his candidacy for the presidency in the planned multi-party elections. After some dispute over whether it had a military wing (possession of which was supposed to disqualify parties), the FNLA was registered as a political party and in October 1991 joined the pro-democracy National Opposition Council. In the September 1992 elections Roberto came fourth in the first-round presidential balloting, with 2.1% of the vote, while the FNLA won five of the 220 seats in the new National Assembly. It was then included in the "unity" government announced in December 1992.

National Union for the Total Independence of Angola

União Nacional para a Independência Total de Angola (UNITA)

Address. c/o Assembléia Nacional, Luanda

Leadership. Jonas Malheiro Savimbi (president), Gen. Paulo Lukamba Gato (secretary-general)

UNITA was founded in March 1966 by a breakaway faction of the National Front for the Liberation of Angola (FNLA) consisting mainly of elements of the former *União das Populaçoes de Angola* (UPA) led by Savimbi, who had resigned as foreign minister in the FNLA-sponsored "revolutionary Angolan government-in-exile" (GRAE) in July 1964. Based in Ovimbundu and Chokwe tribes of central and southern Angola, UNITA had Maoist ideological roots but moved to an anti-leftist stance as it adopted a policy of co-operation with the Portuguese authorities against the dominant Soviet-backed Movement for the Liberation of Angola (MPLA). After the left-wing military coup in Lisbon in April 1974, UNITA signed a separate ceasefire agreement with Portugal in June. In 1975, following the collapse of an OAU-sponsored transitional government of all three liberation movements, UNITA forces, allied with the FNLA, came increasingly into conflict with the MPLA, receiving substantial military support from South Africa. According to later South African accounts, the 2,000 South

African troops sent into Angola could have captured the whole country by late 1975 had not Savimbi insisted that he wanted control only of areas of UNITA support in the interests of reaching a settlement with the MPLA.

Following the declaration of the independent People's Republic of Angola by the MPLA in November 1975, Cuban-supported government troops launched an offensive against the FNLA and UNITA, whose capacity to resist was seriously weakened by the withdrawal of South African forces across the Namibian border early in 1976. By late February UNITA had been forced to vacate all its positions and to resort to guerrilla warfare in the bush. A UNITA congress at Cuanza (central Angola) in May 1976 called for intensified armed struggle "against the regime imposed by the Cubans and Russians" and approved a reorganization of UNITA structures, including the creation of an armed people's militia. Subsequent clashes between UNITA and forces of the MPLA-PT (as it became in 1977) led to widespread losses and chaotic conditions, especially in the south. From 1982 onwards UNITA attacks were increasingly directed at economic targets, including the Benguela railway from the coast to Zaïre; abduction of foreign specialists and their families also become a regular UNITA practice. In September 1985 the South African government admitted that it had provided military and humanitarian aid to UNITA for a number of years with the aim of halting "Marxist infiltration and expansionism". In mid-1985 the US Congress voted to repeal the 1976 Clarke Amendment which had prohibited US financial or military aid for UNITA. Savimbi paid an official visit to Washington in January 1976, reportedly securing a pledge of covert US aid from President Reagan.

After military setbacks for UNITA and South African forces in early 1988, UNITA came under further pressure later that year when it was agreed that South African and Cuban forces would be withdrawn from Angola as part of the Namibian peace settlement. The MPLA-PT government showed its willingness to negotiate by releasing 700 UNITA detainees in June 1988 and by conceding UNITA's demand for multi-partyism (as endorsed by an MPLA-PT congress in December 1990). Talks in Lisbon resulted in the signature in May 1991 of the Estoril Accord providing for a ceasefire, demobilization of forces and democratic elections. Savimbi returned to Luanda in September 1991 and in December UNITA published an election manifesto identifying the economic uplift-ment of the people as a central aim. In early 1992 UNITA was damaged by the defection of two senior members, amid charge and counter-charge cataloguing nefarious activities on both sides.

Tending to sour UNITA-US relations, the episode deprived UNITA of support in Cabinda (where the defectors came from) and narrowed its ethnic base to the Ovimbundu in the south.

In the September 1992 Assembly elections UNITA came a poor second to the MPLA-PT, winning only 70 of the 220 seats; but Savimbi did better in the simultaneous presidential poll, taking 40.1% of the first-round vote. Despite the verdict of international observers that the polling had been fair in the main, UNITA alleged widespread fraud in both contests and ordered its troops, most of whom had evaded demobilization, to resume armed struggle. The naming of a "unity" government in December with one cabinet and five other posts reserved for UNITA did not resolve the crisis. Conflict of unprecedented ferocity ensued, with UNITA making major advances not only in the south but also in central and northern Angola. It continued unabated after the opening of peace talks in Lusaka in November 1993 on the basis that UNITA would accept the 1992 elections results. Factors impelling UNITA to negotiate included the USA's decision to recognize the MPLA-PT government in May 1993 (implying the end of US backing for UNITA) and the imposition of a mandatory UN oil and arms embargo against UNITA in September. Factors impelling it to continue fighting included the temporary weakness of Angolan government forces, many of which had been demobilized under the 1991 accord.

Amid continued fighting between UNITA and government forces, the Lusaka talks on power-sharing appeared to make some headway in mid-1994 but then encountered familiar deadlock, following which UNITA suffered serious military reverses. In September Savimbi announced the creation in Huambo of a new UNITA political and administrative body, designated a ministry and headed by Gen. Paulo Lukamba Gato; but on Nov. 10 government troops captured Huambo, forcing Savimbi and other UNITA leaders to flee. A ceasefire and power-sharing agreement was at last signed in Lusaka on Nov. 20, 1994, but Savimbi signalled his displeasure with continued advances by government forces by leaving the signature to the then UNITA secretary-general, Gen. Eugenio Manuvakola. Amid efforts by UN mediators to consolidate the Lusaka agreement, a UNITA congress at Bailundo (in Huambo province) in February 1995 was marked by serious divisions between those favouring the accord and hardliners. On Savimbi's proposal, delegates voted to accept the agreement; but a senior UNITA defector, Col. Isaac Zabarra, claimed subsequently that Savimbi in reality rejected the Lusaka accord and had instructed his military leaders to use the ceasefire to reorganize UNITA forces. According to Col. Zabarra, several UNITA leaders identified with the peace process were under detention, including Gen. Manuvakola. At the Bailundo congress, the latter was replaced as UNITA secretary-general by Gen. Gato.

Savimbi had talks with President dos Santos in Lusaka in June 1995 and again in Gabon in August, reportedly agreeing in principal to accept a vice-presidency in the government and to implement the other power-sharing clauses of the November 1994 accord. However, the MPLA-PT regime's insistence on the prior disarming of UNITA guerrillas and their confinement to barracks pending the creation of a national army remained a major obstacle to implementation of the accord.

Party of the Alliance of Youth, Workers and Peasants of Angola
Partido da Aliança da Juventude, Operários e Camponeses de Angola (PAJOCA)
Address. c/o Assembléia Nacional, Luanda
Leadership. Miguel João Sebastião (president)
PAJOCA was founded following the move to multi-party democracy in May 1991 and aligned itself with the government of the Popular Movement for the Liberation of Angola-Party of Labour in opposing calls for a national conference to decide a new political structure. In the September 1992 elections it won one of the 220 Assembly seats at issue, with 0.4% of the vote, and was included in the new "unity" government announced in December 1992.

Popular Movement for the Liberation of Angola-Party of Labour
Movimento Popular de Libertação de Angola-Partido de Trabalho (MPLA-PT)
Address. c/o Assembléia Nacional, Luanda
Leadership. José Eduardo dos Santos (chair), Lopo do Nascimento (secretary-general)
The MPLA was founded in 1956 as a merger of two nationalist movements, the *Partido da Luta Unida dos Africanos de Angola* and the (Communist) *Movimento para a Independencia de Angola*, initially under the leadership of Mário de Andrade and, from 1962, that of Agostinho Neto. Backed by the USSR, it played a leading part in the struggle against Portuguese rule, sometimes in collaboration but usually in conflict with the two other nationalist movements, the National Front for the Liberation of Angola (FNLA) and the National Union for the Total Independence of Angola (UNITA). On Portugal's transference of sovereignty to "the Angolan people" in November 1975, the MPLA proclaimed the People's Republic of Angola in Luanda, with Neto as President and

do Nascimento as Prime Minister, and secured recognition from many states (although not the USA). By February 1976 the MPLA government, assisted by Cuban forces, was in control of the greater part of the country, although UNITA continued to conduct military operations in the south.

Pre-independence dissension within the MPLA resurfaced in 1976, when Andrade and other leaders of his *Revolte Activa* faction were arrested; the following year another dissident faction attempted a coup in Luanda (the survivors of which later formed the Democratic Renewal Party). At its first congress in December 1977 the MPLA restructured itself as a Marxist-Leninist "vanguard of the proletariat" and added the suffix Party of Labour to its title to signify its claim to unite the working and intellectual classes. Further internal divisions in 1978 resulted in the abolition of the post of Prime Minister in December 1978 and the dismissal of do Nascimento and other ministers. Neto died in Moscow in September 1979 and was succeeded as President and party leader by dos Santos, whose preference for a negotiated settlement with UNITA and rapprochement with the West was resisted by the hardline pro-Soviet faction. At the second party congress in December 1985 the MPLA-PT central committee was enlarged to give the President's supporters a majority, three veteran hardliners being dropped from the resultant political bureau.

The third MPLA-PT congress in December 1990 ratified a central committee recommendation that Angola should "evolve towards a multi-party system", dos Santos acknowledging that the collapse of communism in Eastern Europe indicated a need for democratic reform and that collectivist policies had failed. The congress approved the jettisoning of Marxist-Leninist ideology, which was to be replaced by a commitment to "democratic socialism", including a free enterprise economy and protection of private property and foreign investment. Under the May 1991 Lisbon Accord with the UNITA, the MPLA-PT government made provision for the legalization of competing parties and for multi-party elections. These changes were approved by a special MPLA-PT congress in May 1992, when reformers secured the enlargement of the central committee from 180 to 193 members and the election to it of representatives of the business community, intellectuals and some former dissidents.

Elections in September 1992 resulted in the MPLA-PT winning a decisive majority in the new National Assembly, while dos Santos narrowly failed to win an outright majority in the first round of simultaneous presidential balloting. UNITA's rejection of the results and resumption of armed struggle meant that the second presidential round could not be held. A new "unity" government appointed in December 1992 was dominated by the MPLA-PT but included nominees of four small parties as well as, notionally, UNITA representatives. In 1993 MPLA-PT hardliners regained influence with criticism of the leadership for precipitate army demobilization under the Lisbon Accord, to the advantage of UNITA in the renewed civil war.

In May 1993 the USA at last recognized the MPLA-PT government, signalling an end to its support for UNITA, which in November indicated its acceptance of the September 1992 election results. Peace talks then resumed in Lusaka between the MPLA-PT-led government and UNITA on an agenda which included power-sharing at national and provincial level. After intensified conflict from mid-1994, a ceasefire and power-sharing agreement was signed in the Zambian capital on Nov. 20, 1994, as government forces made important advances against UNITA. A year later, however, the agreement remained unimplemented, despite two face-to-face meetings between dos Santos and UNITA leader Jonas Savimbi in June and August 1995, principally because of the difficulty of arranging for the disarming of guerrilla forces.

Social Democratic Party
Partido Social Democrático (PSD)
    Address. c/o Assembléia Nacional, Luanda
    Leadership. José Manuel Miguel (president)
The PSD was created following the move to multi-party democracy in May 1991. It joined the pro-democracy National Opposition Council established in October 1991, when Miguel criticized the National Union for the Total Independence of Angola for failing to implement the terms of the May 1991 Lisbon Accord with the government. In the September 1992 elections the PSD presidential candidate, Bengue Pedro João, was placed seventh among 11 first-round candidates, with just under 1% of the vote, while in the Assembly balloting the party won one seat and 0.8% of the vote.

Social Renewal Party
Partido Renovador Social (PRS)
    Address. c/o Assembléia Nacional, Luanda
    Leadership. António João Machicungo (co-ordinator)
The centrist PRS was formed following the move to multi-partyism in May 1991 and subsequently joined other opposition parties in calling for a national conference to agree a new political system. In the September 1992 elections it took third place in the Assembly balloting, winning six of the 220 seats at issue.

Other Parties

Angolan Democratic Liberal Party (*Partido Democrático Liberal Angolano*, PDLA), a centrist formation led by Honorato Lando, who was placed fifth of 11 presidential candidates, with 1.9% of the vote, in the September 1992 elections.

Angolan Liberal Party (*Partido Angolano Liberal*, PAL), founded in 1991, unsuccessful in the September 1992 elections.

Angolan Social Democratic Party (*Partido Social Democrático de Angola*, PSDA), founded in 1990 in Zaïre by Angolan exiles, led by André Milton Kilandamoko, who in 1991 held separate talks with the National Union for the Total Independence of Angola (UNITA) and the National Front for the Liberation of Angola (FNLA).

National Union for the Liberation of Cabinda (*União Nacional de Libertação de Cabinda*, UNLC), led by Lumindo Dimbi, Cabindan separatist movement, allied from May 1992 with the Front for the Liberation of the Enclave of Cabinda.

Antigua and Barbuda

Capital: St John's

Population: 67,500 (1995E)

Antigua and Barbuda became internally self-governing in 1967 and independent from the United Kingdom in 1981. The head of state is the British sovereign, represented by a Governor-General who is appointed on the advice of the Antiguan Prime Minister. Legislative power is vested in a bicameral parliament, the lower chamber (House of Representatives) of which is directly elected for up to five years. The Prime Minister and Cabinet are responsible to parliament and are appointed to office by the Governor-General acting upon its advice. Barbuda, the smaller of the country's two inhabited constituent islands, maintains a considerable degree of control over its local affairs. In power since 1976, the Antiguan Labour Party won 11 seats in the House elections of March 8, 1994, the United Progressive Party 5 and the Barbuda People's Movement 1.

Antigua Labour Party (ALP)
Address. St Mary's Street, St John's
Telephone. (#1–809) 462-1059
Leadership. Lester Bird (leader)
Long affiliated with the Antigua Trades and Labour Union (of which Vere Bird, Prime Minister and ALP leader until 1994, was a founder member), the party was continuously in power in the colony from 1946 to 1971. Returned to office in 1976, the domestically-conservative ALP has since remained the ruling party, most recently securing a fifth successive term with 11 of the 17 seats in the House of Representatives in the March 1994 general election (after which Vere Bird was succeeded as Prime Minister by his son, Lester).

Barbuda People's Movement (BPM)
Address. c/o House of Representatives, St John's
Leadership. Thomas Hilbourne Frank (leader)
The BPM campaigns for separate status for Barbuda. It controls the local Barbuda Council, and won the single Barbudan seat in the House of Representatives in the 1994 elections.

United Progressive Party (UPP)
Address. c/o House of Representatives, St John's
Leadership. Baldwin Spencer (leader)
The UPP was formed in early 1992 by the merger of the Antigua Caribbean Liberation Movement (founded in 1977 as a "new left" organization), the Progressive Labour Movement (established in 1970, and the ruling party from 1971 to 1976), and the United National Democratic Party (a formation identified with business and professional interests, which arose from the merger of the small United People's Movement and National Democratic Party in 1986). In the 1994 elections the UPP was runner-up with five lower house seats, gaining nearly 44 per cent of the vote.

Other Parties

Barbuda Independence Movement (BIM), advocating island self-government and led by Arthur Shabazz-Nibbs.

Barbuda National Party (BNP), headed by Eric Burton.

Workers Amalgamated Congressional Symbolization (WACS), launched in 1994.

Argentina

Capital: Buenos Aires

Population: 34,981,000 (1995E)

Upon returning to civilian rule in 1983 following seven years of military rule by successive juntas, most of the constitutional structure of 1853 was reintroduced. The republic comprises a Federal District, 23 Provinces (the National Territory of Tierra del Fuego having been upgraded in 1991). Each province has its own elected governor and legislature, concerned with all matters not delegated to the Federal Government. The federal legislature consists of a Chamber of Deputies of 254 members elected for four years terms with half of the seats renewable every two years, and a Senate. Two members are nominated to the Senate by the legislature of the each of the 23 provinces for nine year terms (with one third of the seats renewable every three years).

A new constitution entered into effect on Aug. 24, 1994, under which each province elects a third senator to represent minorities, and the President, hitherto appointed by an electoral college, is directly elected for a four year term (reduced from the six years allowed under the 1853 constitution) with re-election allowed for only one consecutive term. Run-off elections for presidential and vice presidential election also take place unless a candidate obtains 45% of the vote (or 40% with a 10% advantage over the second placed candidate). The new constitution also allows for an autonomous government for the capital Buenos Aires, with a directly elected mayor. As previously, in the absence of the President, the president of the Senate assumes the presidency. The cabinet is appointed by the President who exercises executive power and is head of state.

At Constituent Assembly balloting on April 10, 1994, both of the leading formations experienced setbacks. The *Peronistas* (Justicialist Party, PJ) were held to a plurality of 136 seats on a 37.7% share of the vote, while the Radical Civic Union (UCR) won 75 seats on 19.9% vote share. The most striking gain was registered by the left-of-centre Broad Front (FG) coalition, which captured 31 seats as contrasted with only three Chamber seats in 1993. At the general election of May 14, 1995, Menem surpassed poll projections by easily winning direct election to a new four-year mandate on a 49.8% vote share—20.6% more than that of his nearest competitor, José Octavio Bordon, who headed a recently formed leftist coalition that included the FG. By contrast, the UCR candidate, Horatio Massacesi, came in third with 17.1% of the vote. (Results: Carlos Raúl Menem, PJ, 49.8%; José Octavio Bordon, Front for a Country in Solidarity, 29.2%; Horatio Massacesi, UCR, 17.1; others, 3.9%). The PJ also won control of a majority of lower house seats and nine of 14 contested regional governorships.

Broad Front
Frente Grande (FG)
Leadership. Carlos "Chacho" Alvarez (1995 presidential candidate)

A left wing grouping, the FG is also one of the newest parties in Argentine politics. The party was launched in October 1993 to coincide with the forthcoming congressional elections. In the final results the party obtained three seats. However at Constituent Assembly balloting in May 1994, the party hugely increased its share of the vote, taking third position largely on its policy of constitutional reform.

23

Christian Democratic Party
Partido Demócrata Christiano (PDC)
Address. Combate de los Pozos 1055, Buenos Aires 1222
Telephone. (#54–1) 263269
Fax. (#54–1) 263324
Leadership. Esio Ariel Silveira (president); Augusto Conte (congressional bloc president)

A well-established centrist party and an official affiliate of the Christian Democrat International, the PDC is a traditional grouping of Christian Democrats, remaining one of the smaller parties in the electoral system.

The PDC was one of the five small parties in the *Multipartidaria* democratic movement. The party's presidential candidate won 0.3% of the national vote in the 1983 October, elections and obtained a seat in the Chamber of Deputies. A rapprochement with the Peronists (PJ) in 1984 led to a conflict in the party which caused a majority of the centre-left Humanism and Liberation faction to split away and join the Intransigent Party (PI). In the congressional elections of September 1987, the party received only 0.2% of the national vote despite greater unity within the party. To improve their electoral chances the PDC joined the FREJUPO electoral alliance supporting the Peronists' presidential candidate Carlos Saúl Menem, who won the election on May 14, 1989. The Christian Democrats' support was rewarded with the appointment of Antonio Ermán González as Social Security Minister who, on Dec. 15, 1989, was transferred to the important Economy Ministry. The PDC withdrew from the FREJUPO alliance backing the government in October 1990 in protest against González' economic measures.

The party was a founding member of the Front for a Country in Solidarity (FREPASO) alliance in 1994.

Communist Party of Argentina
Partido Comunista de la Argentina (PCA)
Address. Av. Entre Ríos 1039, 1080 Buenos Aires
Leadership. Patricio Echegaray, Luis Heller, Ernestol Salgado, Athos Fava (general secretary)

A centrist party in Argentine politics, the PCA was formed in 1918 as the International Socialist Party by expelled members of the Socialist Party. The party took on its present name in 1920. By the 1940s the rise of Peronism meant a falling off of the party's support among the nation's workers. The party was banned following Péron's overthrow by the military, and alternated between legality and underground work between 1959 and 1971, and wavering policies during the subsequent return of Péron and then a second phase of military rule.

Following the collapse of communism in the Eastern bloc countries, the party has gone through a process of self-examination. In June 1987 the PCA joined with the Humanist Party (*Partido Humanista, PH*) and ten other small groups to form the Broad Front of Liberation (*Frente Amplio de Liberación, FRAL*) as an electoral challenge to the UCR and PJ. In the build-up to the 1989 elections FRAL joined with a number of other left-of-centre alliances to form the United Left (*Izquierda Unida, IU*) led by Néstor Vicente. The IU was hoping to become the country's fourth electoral force with policies such as non-payment of foreign debt and the nationalization of all banks. However, the alliance was only able to secure 2.4% of the vote in 1989 and failed to obtain a seat in Congress.

Front for a Country in Solidarity
Frente Pais Solidario (FREPASO)
Leadership. José Octavio Bordon (1995 presidential candidate)

One of the newest and one of the most important parties in Argentina, FREPASO was launched in late 1994 as a moderate left coalition designed to incorporate the Broad Front (FG), the Christian Democractic Party (PDC), Open Politics for Social Integrity (PAIS) and Socialist Unity (US). It includes a number of independent communists and socialists. The Front's presidential candidate, José Octavio Bordon, secured second place behind Carlos Menem on May 14, 1995, polling 29.2% of the vote. FREPASO as a whole secured 26 seats in the legislative poll leaving the Front third overall. On May 17, 1995, FREPASO passed into being as a permanent structure.

Intransigent Party
Partido Intransigente (PI)
Address. Riobamba 482, 1025 Buenos Aires
Leadership. Oscar Allende (congressional bloc president)

The PI is a left-of-centre split from the UCR, leaving its former partners in 1956. The UCRI changed its name to Intransigent Party in 1972 after the rival People's UCR won the exclusive right to be called Radical Civic Union (UCR). For the presidential elections of 1973 the party joined forces with the Communist Party (PCA) and two other small parties and fielded Oscar Alende as their candidate, who, however, polled only 7.4% of the vote. Following the coup of 1976 the PI was banned and many activists were imprisoned and tortured.

In the first presidential election since Argentina's return to democracy in October 1983 Oscar Alende, with Lisandro Viale as his running mate, came third but won only 2.3% of the valid vote. With its support waning, the PI joined the

FREJUPO alliance backing the Peronist candidate Carlos Saúl Menem for the May, 1989 elections. Menem won the presidency with a majority in the electoral college (48.5% of the national vote). The PI left FREJUPO in October 1990 over the government's economic policies.

It won one chamber seat in 1993 and none in 1995.

Justicialist Party
Partido Justicialista (PJ-Peronist)
   Address. Callao 1134 P.1, 1023 Buenos Aires
   Leadership. Carlos Saúl Menem (chair)
   Founded in 1945, the PJ is a Peronist party, populist in outlook and encompassing groups from the far right to the far left. Formerly the Justicialist Nationalist Movement (*Movimiento Nacionalista Justicialista*, MNJ) the PJ grew out of the extreme nationalist *peronista* movement led by Lt.-Gen. Juan Domingo Péron Sosa during his 1946-55 presidency. As President, Péron pursued corporatist nationalist policies inspired by Italian fascism and through his wife Evita Duarte de Péron advocated social improvement. Péron's populism and strong personal image attracted support from the trade unions, Roman Catholics, dissidents from the Radical Civic Union (UCR) and some conservatives alike. However, amid rising popular discontent in 1955 he was overthrown by the military and exiled to Spain. Military government continued almost unbroken in Argentina until the triumphant return of Péron from Spain in 1973 to once again become President following a victory for the Peronist left wing under Héctor J Cámpora. However, Péron's death the following year and the succession of his third wife María Estela (Isabelita) Martínez de Péron to the position of president spelt the end of this second brief period of MNJ Peronist rule. The military staged a successful coup in March 1976 and remained in power until 1983 following the débâcle of the Falklands War.

From 1983 the PJ went through a major period of redefinition following the death of Péron.

Seven years of brutal military repression, however, could not erase the memory of the Peronist government of 1973-76. In the October 1983 elections following the Falklands/Malvinas war and the collapse of the military regime, the Peronists lost to the Radical Civic Union (UCR) in both the presidential and congressional elections but beat the UCR in the provincial governorship elections. The party, with Isabelita Perón restored as its figurehead, obtained 40.5% of the vote which translated into 111 seats in Congress, and its presidential candidate Italo Lúder came second with 40.2% of the vote (compared to Raúl Alfonsín of the UCR's 51.8%). This defeat resulted in a long period of internal turmoil which

split the Peronist movement into two main rival factions with parallel leaderships: the right-wing *oficialistas* (official wing) and the *renovadores* (renewalist wing). The party congress in July 1985, intended to reunite the party, resulted in an *oficialista* takeover of the party machinery. All *oficialista* candidates were confirmed for the forthcoming congressional elections because of a boycott by the left wing who subsequently put forward their own alternative candidates under the name of the *Frente Renovador* (Renewalist Front), led by Antonio Cafiero. Neither the official PJ, which fought the election as the leading party in the FREJULI alliance, nor the Renovation Front did very well and the overall PJ representation in the congress was reduced by 10 seats.

Despite further splits within the two factions in 1986 which led to four distinct PJ blocs in Congress, the Peronists began to gain in popularity. Benefiting from widespread discontent with the UCR government's austerity measures and its lenient treatment of the army, the PJ won the highest number of votes (41.5%) in the partial congressional elections of Sept. 6, 1987, and narrowed the gap between the PJ and UCR representation in Congress. As well as increasing their congressional seats to 105, the PJ won 16 provincial governorships, including that of the crucial province of Buenos Aires. With the general election of 1989 in view the PJ regrouped. Isabelita Perón was finally replaced as the party's president and a party leadership comprising *oficialistas, renovadores* and the "Federalism and Liberation" faction, linked to Carlos Saúl Menem, was elected. Small left-wing and right-wing factions were ignored and Herminio Iglesias' right-wing group, which had contested the elections separately under the name of the October 17 Party, was expelled the following December.

The modern party has itself been re-defined from 1989 when Carlos Saúl Menem gained the leadership of the party and the nation. The dominant pro-government *menemista* faction, promoting a free market economy and wholesale privatisation, has taken the party far to the right. Menem took office in July 1989 and since then has struggled with a fundamentally destabilized economy with policies as diverse as rationing, an expansion of the state privatization programme, and large reductions in the workforce of the state iron and steel plants. Although Menem largely continued Alfonsín's policy of leniency towards the military, measures such as an amnesty for crimes perpetrated during the so-called "dirty war" of 1976-83 could not prevent increasingly vocal discontent over army low pay and lack of status.

The PJ's electoral performance since 1989 has

been a strong one and Menem himself has overcome a long period of unpopularity in his party for his perceived abandonment of Peronism. In congressional and gubernatorial elections held in August, September, October and December 1991, the Justicialist Party (PJ-"Peronists") increased their seats in the Chamber of Deputies from 112 to 119, and won the governorships of 14 provinces. The Peronists won the Chamber of Deputies elections (for 127 seats) on Oct. 3, 1993, increasing their total number of seats to 125; this total was further raised, to 137 seats, in the elections (for 130 seats) on May 14, 1995. They took nine of the 14 provincial governorships at stake. The Peronists had won 136 seats in the elections held on April 10, 1994, to the new 305-member Constituent Assembly, which was responsible for the amendment of the 1853 constitution. Carlos Saúl Menem of the Peronists was re-elected President on May 14, 1995, with 49.8% of the vote and was sworn into office on July 8 along with the majority of the previous cabinet. The Oct. 8, 1995, Senate election for the federal district of Buenos Aires was won by the centre-left Frepaso coalition with 45.7% of the vote defeating the Radical Party (UCR) with 24.3% and the Peronists with 22.6%. The Peronists held power in 14 of the 23 provinces following provincial elections staged between July and October 1995.

Internally the party is divided into three main factions: "Renewalists", left-wing, led by Antonio Cafiero (former governor of Buenos Aires province and former president of the party); "Menemists", supporters of Carlos Menem; and "Officialists", orthodox Peronists. Despite these divisions Menem is generally supported and recent election results are generally interpreted as an acknowledgement by the electorate that Menem's bitter economic pill is working. The Peronists held power in 14 of the 23 provinces following provincial elections staged between July and October 1995.

Movement for Dignity and Independence

Movimiento por la Dignidad y la Independecia (MDI or MODIN)

Leadership. Lt.-Col. Aldo Rico (1995 presidential candidate)

MODIN was formed in 1990 and led by the cashiered Lt.-Col. Aldo Rico, who led military uprisings at Easter 1987 and in January 1988. In the 1991 provincial elections the grouping proved to be the third political force in Buenos Aires province (Argentina's largest electoral district) where it won three seats in the Federal Chamber of Deputies and obtained 10% of the vote.

In September 1991 Aldo Rico announced that he was considering standing as a candidate in the 1995 presidential elections.

The party was formally registered as a nation-wide group in mid-1993. It came in fourth in the Constituency Assembly ballots in 1994 on a 9.1% share of the vote. It won seven Chamber seats in 1993 but was unable to hold on to any of them in 1995.

Movement of Integration and Development

Movimiento de Integración y Desarrollo (MID)

Address. Ayacucho 49, P.1, 1025 Buenos Aires

Leadership. Aldo Rico (1995 presidential candidate)

Describing itself as "developmentalist", the party was formed by Arturo Frondizi, who was overthrown as President of Argentina by the military in 1962. He and his supporters split away from the Intransigent Party (PI) and formed the MID in 1963. In 1973 the MID joined the Peronist-led FREJULI alliance which backed the successful campaigns of Héctor Cámpora in the May elections and Péron in the September elections. In 1988 the party became a founder member of the FREJUPO electoral alliance formed to bring the Peronists back to power and assisted with the successful campaign of Carlos Menem elected in May 1989. The MID continued with its membership of the FREJUPO alliance despite heavy criticism of the Menem government.

The MID won one lower house seat in 1993 and two in 1995 on a joint ticket with the UCR.

Open Politics for Social Integrity

Política Abierto para la Integridad Social (PAIS)

Leadership. José Octavio Bordon

PAIS was launched in September 1994 by the anti-Menem PJ senator, José Octavio Bordon. It soon became one of the backbones of the left-wing Front for a Country in Solidarity (FREPASO).

Progressive Democratic Party

Partido Demócrata Progresista (PDP)

Address. Chile 1934, 1227 Buenos Aires

Leadership. Rafael Martinez Raymonda (leader)

The PDP participated in the 1980 talks with the military regime negotiating the normalization of political activities and in August of the same year it joined the Union of the Democratic Centre (UCeDé). In the presidential elections of 1983, however, the party's leader, Martínez, stood as candidate for the Democratic Socialist Alliance against the UCeDé's candidate Álvaro Alsogaray and obtained 0.3% of the vote. The PDP contested the partial congressional elections of 1985 as a separate party and gained one seat in the Chamber of Deputies. In the elections of September 1987 the party's share of the national vote was 1.3% and it increased its representation in the Chamber to two seats.

The PDP thereafter joined forces again with the UCeDé and in the presidential elections of May 14, 1989, Alberto Natale of the PDP was running-mate to the UCeDé presidential candidate Álvaro Alsogaray who came third with 6.4% of the vote. The party won three lower house seats in 1995, two on a joint ticket with the Corrientes Liberal Party (*Partido Liberal de Corrientes*, PLC).

Radical Civic Union

Unión Cívica Radical (UCR)

Address. Alsina 1786, 1088 Buenos Aires

Leadership. Rodolfo Terragno (president)

As Argentina's premier centrist/moderate left party, the UCR has been the dominant mainstream opposition to the PJ until recent times. Classed as one of the main so-called "traditional" parties, the UCR has recently suffered from an increasing trend of voter wariness of the traditional parties.

The UCR was set up after the radical faction split away from the mainstream Civic Union and led an unsuccessful revolt against the Conservative government. One of the party's main demands was the enfranchisement of all adult male Argentinians and it did not participate in any elections until 1912 when that demand was met. In 1916, the UCR formed its first government and remained in power until 1930, when President Hipólito Yrigoyen was ousted by a military coup. After losing the elections to the UCR's direct rivals, the Peronists, in both 1945 and 1951, the UCR suffered internal problems which culminated in a dramatic split in 1956, caused by the nomination as the UCR's presidential candidate of Arturo Frondizi of the Intransigent faction who was favourable to some co-operation with the Peronists. Frondizi became the candidate of the newly formed UCR *Intrasigente* (Intransigent UCR, see Movement of Integration and Development and Intransigent Party) and with assistance from the Peronists won the presidency in 1958.

The conservative wing of the party, led by the former UCR presidential candidate Ricardo Balbín, formed the UCR *del Pueblo* (People's UCR—UCRP) in 1956 which was to become the official UCR in 1972, when a court ruling awarded it the sole right to the name. The UCRP supported the military coup against Frondizi in 1962 and in the subsequent elections of 1963 the UCRP's candidate Arturo Umberto Illía was elected President. He was himself overthrown three years later in 1966 in a coup led by Gen. Ogania which was supported by the UCRI. Ricardo Balbín stood again in the 1973 presidential elections for the now renamed UCR and was heavily defeated by Peronists in both the April and September polls.

In 1981 the UCR helped to form a five-party democratic alliance opposed to the military junta which called for the restoration of democracy.

When the junta was deposed a year later, the UCR's candidate Raúl Alfonsín Foulkes celebrated a landslide victory in the general election of Oct. 20, 1983. He won 317 of the 600 seats in the electoral college which gave him 51.8% of the electoral college vote. The UCR also won a majority of Chamber of Deputies seats (129 out of 256) but only 16 of the 48 Senate seats and seven of the 24 provincial governorships, including Buenos Aires.

Alfonsín, inaugurated on Dec. 23, 1983, proceeded to make good his election promises of reorganizing the armed forces and putting an end to the cycle of political instability and military intervention. Over half the military high command was forced into retirement and members of the military juntas since 1976 were prosecuted for murder, torture and abduction and were sentenced in December 1985 and May 1986. However, after uprisings in a number of army garrisons in April 1987 and persistent rumours of an impending coup, Alfonsín introduced the law of "Due Obedience", dropping all prosecutions against lower-ranking army and police officers indicted for human rights violations. Further military uprisings by officers demanding greater army spending and an extension of the military amnesty to higher-ranking officers nevertheless followed in January and December 1988, followed in January 1989 by an incident, thought to have been provoked by the armed forces, in which a left-wing group attacked La Tablada barracks in order to suppress a rumoured military coup.

Spiralling inflation and a highly unstable economy forced Raúl Alfonsín to relinquish power to Carlos Menem in July 1989, five months before he was due to retire as President on Dec. 10. The UCR remained the main opposition party and the unsuccessful UCR presidential candidate, Angeloz, was invited by President Menem to join his Cabinet in February 1990. He refused the post and instead called for all political parties to sign a pact under which a plan for effective government would be drawn up to preserve and consolidate democracy in an extreme social and economic crisis.

Such proposals and the UCR's criticism of government policies, however, did not improve the party's electoral chances. In the 1991 mid-term elections the UCR lost five seats thus reducing its congressional strength to 85 delegates, and in the gubernatorial elections the UCR managed to retain only three governorships. One of the victims of this poor electoral showing was Alfonsín himself, who, following strong criticism from within the UCR, resigned the party leadership in mid-November. He then became head of the "Movement for the Defence of the Principles of Social Democracy" faction within the UCR.

Upon his resignation, Alfonsín announced the formation of an internal faction within the UCR, the Movement for Social Democracy (*Movimiento por la Democracia Social*, MDS) which would campaign for the defence of traditional UCR democratic principles. He was then re-elected party leader by an overwhelming majority in November 1993. In the subsequent 1995 presidential elections, the party's chosen nominee, Horatio Massacesi could only poll a disappointing third with 17.1% of the vote. However, in legislative balloting the UCR retained the second highest representation with 69 seats (down 14).

Republican Force
Fuerza Republicana (FR)
Address. Pte. Péron 318, P.1 Of.5, 1008 Buenos Aires
Leadership. Gen. (retd.) Antonio Domingo Bussi (leader)
A right-wing party, controlling the northwestern Tucumán district, the FR had loose links with the previous military regime and increased its seats in the Chamber of Deputies from two to four in the October 1991 mid-term elections. The party went on to win three lower house seats in October 1993, adding another in 1995.

Socialist Unity
Unidad Socialista (US)
Address. Avda Entre Rios 1018, 1080 Buenos Aires
Telephone. (#54–1) 306 7293
Fax. (#54–1) 305 7428
Leadership. Enrique Inda (PSA); Amerigo Ghioldi (PSD); Rubén Giustiniani (PSP)
As well as being part of the FREPASO coalition, the US is itself a union of the three remaining portions of the 1958 Argentine Socialist Party: the Authentic Socialist Party (*Partido Socialista Auténtico, PSA*); the Democratic Socialist Party (*Partido Socialista Democático, PSD*); and the Popular Socialist Party (*Partido Socialista Popular, PSP*), the latter being recognised as the Argentine affiliate of the Socialist International.

Union of the Democratic Centre
Union del Centro Democrático (UCeDé)
Address. Av. R S Peña 628, P.1 Of.2, 1008 Buenos Aires
Leadership. Frederico Clerici (president)
More right-wing than centrist, the UCeDé is a conservative party standing for a free market economy and a reduced public sector.
Originally a coalition of eight small centre-right parties, the UCeDé was formed and led by Álvaro Alsogaray, who could count an important

position in the 1976 military government among his previous government posts. The party in the October 1983 general elections won only two seats in the Chamber of Deputies, Alsogaray receiving only 0.3% of the presidential vote. In order to improve its chances in the Federal Capital of Buenos Aires in the November 1985 elections, the UCeDé formed the "Popular Centrist Alliance" coalition with the Capital Democratic Party (PDC) and Federalist Centre Party (PFC), both of which are not defunct. The vote for the alliance increased to 3.5% of the national vote.

Although Alsogaray was elected as presidential candidate in June 1988, the party leadership at the same time decided to support the Peronist campaign, hoping thereby to raise the UCeDé's profile. This strategy led to the party polling 9.5% of the national vote, giving the UCeDé nine seats out of the 127 up for election in the May 14, 1989, election. Alsogaray came third with 6.4% of the presidential vote. In June 1989 the party leadership was transferred to Federico Clerici.

In May 1989 with Alsogaray as its candidate the party polled 6.4% of the presidential vote, placing them a disappointing third overall. The party's legislative vote was only 2.6%, increasing only marginally to 3.0% in 1995.

Other Parties

Argentine Socialist Confederation (*Confederación Socialista Argentina*, CSA), led by Oscar Palmeiro.

Blue and White (*Azul y Blanco*); named after the national colours the party was formed in September 1994 by a group of MODIN dissidents dissatisfied with their party's support for the PJ in the 1995 elections; led by Luis Polo.

Democratic Integration (*Partido de Integración Democratica*, PID), led by Ricardo Hilleman.

Federal Party (*Partido Federal*, PF), *Address.* Av. De Mayo 962, P.1, 1084 Buenos Aires.

Marxist-Leninist Communist Workers Party (*Partido Obrero Comunista Marxista-Leninista*, POCML), led by Elías Seman and Roberto Cristina.

Movement to Socialism (*Movimiento al Socialism*, MAS), led by Marcello Parrilli and Luis Zamora.

National Centre Party (*Partido Nacional de Centro*, PNC), led by Raúl Rivanera Carles and founded in 1980.

Nationalist Workers' Party (*Partido Nacionalista de los Trabajadores*, PNT), led by Alejandro Biondini, an anti-Zionist party launched in 1990. Biondini was a former PJ member and was leader of the extreme right-wing group *Alerta Nacional*. The swastika is the party's official symbol.

Popular Christian Party (*Partido Popular Cristiano*, PPC), led by José Antonio Allende.

Popular Conservative Party (*Partido Conservador Popular*, PCP), a right-wing party founded by Vicente Solano Lima. The party, led by J. Amoedo since Solano's death in 1984, has a very small following. *Address*. Alberti 950, 1121 Buenos Aires.

Popular Left Front (*Frente de Izquierda Popular*, FIP), led by Jorge Abelardo Ramos.

Social Democracy (*Democracia Social*, DS), organized in 1981 by former junta member Adm. Emilio Massera.

Socialist Workers' Party (*Partido de los Trabajadores por el Socialismo*, PTS), led by Emilio Albamonte and Hugo Manes.

Union for the New Majority (*Unión para la Nueva Mayoría*, UNM), formed in 1986 by José Antonio Romero Feris.

Workers' Party (*Partido Obrero*, PO), led by Jorge Altamira and Juan Carlos Capurro; a Trotskyite party formed in 1982. *Address*: Ayacucho 444, 1026 Buenos Aires. .

Workers' Socialist Party (*Partido Socialista de los Trabajadores*, PST), led by Nora Ciapponi.

Armenia

Capital: Yerevan

Population: 3,900,000 (1995E)

The former Soviet republic of Armenia declared independence as the Republic of Armenia in August 1990 and became a sovereign member of the Commonwealth of Independent States (CIS) on the latter's creation in December 1991. Independent Armenia retained its Soviet-era constitution, with some adjustments to cater for multi-partyism, until the approval by referendum on July 5, 1995, of a new text establishing a democratic "presidential" system. Directly elected for a five-year term, the executive President appoints the Prime Minister and other ministers and may dissolve the National Assembly and call new elections. Legislative authority is vested in the unicameral Assembly (*Geraguin Khorhurt*), elected for a four-year term by universal adult suffrage.

In a presidential election on Oct. 16, 1991, the incumbent candidate of the Pan-Armenian National Movement (PANM), Levon Ter-Petrosyan, was returned to power with 83% of the votes cast. Legislative elections held on July 5, 1995 (with some later re-runs being necessary), for an Assembly of 190 members (150 by majority voting and 40 by proportional representation) resulted in the Republic Bloc alliance (headed by the PANM and also including the Armenian Christian Democratic Union, the Democratic Liberal Party of Armenia, the Intellectual Armenian Union, the Republican Party of Armenia and the Social Democratic Hnchakian Party) winning 119 seats, the Shamiram Women's Party 8, the Armenian Communist Party 7, the National Democratic Union of Armenia 5, the National Self-Determination Union 3, the Armenian Revolutionary Federation (*Dashnak*) 1, the Ramkavar-Azatakan Party 1 and independents 45. (There was one vacancy at the final declaration of results.) The 1995 constitution provided that the Assembly would be reduced to 131 members at the next election.

Armenian Christian Democratic Union (ACDU)
Address. 8 Abovian Street, Yerevan
Telephone. (#374–2) 561067
Fax. (#374–2) 561963

Leadership. Azat Arshakian (chair), Aram Mkrtchian (co-ordinator)
The ACDU was founded at Armenian independence, its leader having been elected a deputy in

1990. The party was supportive of the government of the Pan-Armenian National Movement (PANM) elected in 1990, issuing a joint political declaration with the PANM, the Democratic Liberal Party of Albania and three small parties in September 1994. It formed part of the victorious Republic Bloc in the 1995 legislative elections. Advocating Christian democracy on the West European model but adapted to Armenian conditions, the ACDU is affiliated to the Christian Democrat International.

Armenian Communist Party (ACP)

Address. c/o Geraguin Khorhurt, Yerevan
Leadership. Sergey Badalyan (first secretary)

Armenia's sole ruling party in the Soviet era, the ACP could manage only second place in multiparty legislative elections in 1990 and was suspended in September 1991. Many of its members in the state bureaucracy joined the new ruling Pan-Armenian National Movement; others opted for the Democratic Party of Armenia. Re-legalized in 1994, the ACP took a poor third place in the 1995 Assembly elections, winning 12% of the proportional vote and only seven seats.

Armenian Revolutionary Federation

Hai Heghapokhakan Dashnaktsutyun (HHD/Dashnak)

Address. c/o Geraguin Khorhurt, Yerevan
Leadership. Rouben Hakobian (chair), Seiran Baghdasarian (spokesman)

Dating from 1891, the *Dashnak* movement was the ruling party in pre-Soviet independent Armenia and retained a large following in the Armenian diaspora after it had been outlawed by the Bolsheviks in 1920. Re-established in 1991 as a nationalist opposition party with socialist overtones, *Dashnak*) put up the actor Sos Sargsyan in the October 1991 presidential election but received only 4% of the vote. The party became a fierce critic of the conduct of the war in Nagorno-Karabakh by the government of the Pan-Armenian National Movement, which claimed that HHD leaders in exile had co-operated with the Soviet security authorities. The then HHD parliamentary leader, Gagik Ovanessian, was expelled from the party in June 1994 for publicly criticizing its "Bolshevik" methods. In late December 1994 the HHD was suspended by presidential decree, on the grounds that it had engaged in terrorism, political assassination and drug-trafficking. It therefore did not participate as a party in the July 1995 legislative elections, although it secured representation by other means.

Democratic Liberal Party of Armenia (DLPA/Ramkavar)

Address. c/o Geraguin Khorhurt, Yerevan
Leadership. Rouben Mirzakhanyan (chair)

Descended from the historic *Ramkavar* movement influential among Soviet-era Armenians overseas, the DLPA was registered in Armenia in June 1991. Right-of-centre in orientation, it drew support from the professional classes and supported the government of the Pan-Armenian National Movement (PANM) elected in 1990. In September 1994 it issued a declaration jointly with the PANM and four small parties praising the government's achievements since independence while listing its shortcomings and itemizing desired improvements. The DLPA formed part of the victorious Republic Bloc in the 1995 Assembly elections, although it was weakened by a split which yielded the separate .

Democratic Party of Armenia (DPA)

Address. c/o Geraguin Khorhurt, Yerevan
Leadership. Aram Sarkisian (chair)

The DPA was established in late 1991 as the would-be successor to the former ruling Armenian Communist Party (ACP), which was suspended in September 1991 after having secured the second-largest number of seats in the 1990 legislative elections. Many senior Communists switched allegiance to the ruling Pan-Armenian National Movement rather than to the DPA, which was also weakened by the revival of the ACP in 1994. In the 1995 legislative elections the DPA took only 1.8% of the vote and failed to win representation.

Intellectual Armenian Union (IAU)

Address. c/o Geraguin Khorhurt, Yerevan
Leadership. H. Tokmajian (chair)

The IAU was registered in June 1994, subsequently becoming a signatory of the joint political declaration issued in September at the instigation of the ruling Pan-Armenian National Movement (PANM). It formed part of the victorious Republic Bloc in the 1995 Assembly elections.

National Democratic Union of Armenia (NDUA)

Address. c/o Geraguin Khorhurt, Yerevan
Leadership. Vasken Manukian (chair)

The NDUA was formed by Vasken Manukian following his resignation as Prime Minister in September 1991, when he also left the ruling Pan-Armenian National Movement. In mid-1994 the NDUA organized largescale demonstrations against the government in Yerevan. It won 7.5% of the vote and five Assembly seats in the 1995 Assembly elections.

National Self-Determination Union (NSDU)

Address. c/o Geraguin Khorhurt, Yerevan
Leadership. Parouyr Hayrikian (chair)

The right-wing NSDU contested the 1995 Assembly elections as an opposition party, winning 5.6% of the national vote and three seats.

Pan-Armenian National Movement (PANM)

Address. c/o President's Office, Yerevan
Leadership. Levon Ter-Petrosyan (leader), Fr Husik Lazarian (president)

Established in November 1989, the PANM originally grouped pro-independence elements of the then ruling Armenian Communist Party (ACP). Its early leaders included Ter-Petrosyan, who in the Soviet era had been a prominent member of the unofficial Karabakh Committee advocating the transfer of the Armenian-populated enclave of Nagorno-Karabakh from Azerbaijan to Armenia. In his youth Ter-Petrosyan had been arrested in 1965 at a demonstration in Yerevan marking the 50th anniversary of the Turkish massacre of Armenians during World War I. Calling for Armenia's negotiated withdrawal from the Soviet Union, the PANM swept the May 1990 legislative elections and subsequently led Armenia to full independence. Following the dissolution of the ACP, Ter-Petrosyan secured a popular mandate in October 1991 when he was directly elected President with 83% support from those voting. The PANM's dominance was not seriously affected by the formation of the breakaway National Democratic Union of Armenia in 1991, nor by the revival of the ACP in 1994. In the 1995 legislative elections it headed the Republic Bloc, which won an absolute majority of Assembly seats. As the governing party, the PANM strongly advocates that the conflict with Azerbaijan should be pursued to a successful conclusion, by which it means the transfer of Nagorno-Karabakh, with territorial adjustments to make it contiguous with Armenia proper.

Republic Bloc

Hanrapetoutioun
Address. c/o Geraguin Khorhurt, Yerevan
Leadership. Levon Ter-Petrosyan

This alliance was formed for the 1995 Assembly elections on the initiative of the ruling Pan-Armenian National Movement and also included the Armenian Christian Democratic Union, the Democratic Liberal Party of Armenia, the Intellectual Armenian Union, the Republican Party of Armenia and the Social Democratic Hnchakian Party. The alliance won an aggregate vote share of 42.6% in the proportional balloting and a total of 119 of the 190 seats. Its overall parliamentary majority was subsequently enhanced by the adhesion of several deputies elected as independents.

Republican Party of Armenia (RPA)

Address. c/o Geraguin Khorhurt, Yerevan
Leadership. Ashot Navasardyan (chair)

The RPA was founded in May 1991 by a breakaway faction of the National Self-Determination Union. It formed part of the victorious Republic Bloc in the 1995 Assembly elections.

Shamiram Women's Party (SWP)

Address. c/o Geraguin Khorhurt, Yerevan
Leadership. Nadezhda Sarkisian (chair)

The SWP took as its title the Armenian version of the name of the legendary Queen Semiramis of Assyria, who survived her husband and built the Hanging Gardens of Babylon. Led by a popular singer, the party advocates women's rights and permits only women to be members. It took an impressive 17% of the vote in the 1995 Assembly elections, winning eight seats to become the largest single opposition party and the best-represented specifically women's formation in Europe (and probably in the world).

Social Democratic Hnchakian Party (SDHP)

Address. c/o Geraguin Khorhurt, Yerevan
Leadership. Yeghia Najaryan (chair)

The SDHP was registered in October 1991 and was a signatory of the September 1994 joint declaration issued on the initiative of the ruling Pan-Armenian National Movement (PANM). It formed part of the victorious Republic Bloc in the 1995 Assembly elections.

Other Parties

Agrarian Democratic Party of Armenia, led by Telman Dilanyan, registered in September 1992.

Armenian Labour Union, led by Hamlet Karayan, registered in March 1993.

Armenian Monarchists' Party, led by Aghasi Yesayan, registered in October 1992.

Armenian National Congress, led by Miasnik Hakobyan, registered in January 1992.

Armenian Royalist Party, led by Tigran Petrosyants, registered in April 1992.

Constitutional Rights Union, led by Hrand Khachatryan, registered in August 1991.

Democratic Forces of Dilijan Union, led by Zhora Madatyan, registered in March 1993.

Democratic Party of Armenia, led by Aram Sargsyan, registered in October 1991.

Green Union of Armenia, led by Hakob Sanasar-ian.

International Armenian Assembly, led by Serzh Dzhilavian.

Labour Party of Albania, led by L. Yesayan, registered in May 1994.

National Conservative Party of Armenia, registered in June 1991.

National Renaissance Party, led by Hovik Vas-ilyan, registered in December 1991.

National Salvation Party, led by Anton Vardan-yan, registered in May 1992.

National Social Democratic Union of Abovyan, led by Valeri Sargsyan, registered in August 1991.

National Unity Party, led by Tigran Nikoghosyan, registered in April 1993.

Nzhtehyan Chauvinist Party, led by Gevorg Hov-sepyan, registered in July 1991.

Party of Democratic Freedom, led by Rouben Mirzakhanian.

Racist Party of Armenia, led by Shant Harouty-ounyan, registered in July 1991.

Radicals' Party of Armenia, led by Valery Vardan-yan, registered in December 1991.

Ramkavar-Azatakan Party, a breakaway faction of the Democratic Liberal Party of Armenia, won one seat in the 1995 Assembly elections.

Traditionalist Democratic Armwomall Party, led by Armenouhi Ghazaryan, registered in February 1994, the political arm of the Armenian Women's Alliance.

Universal Prosperity Party, led by Armen Kirako-syan, registered in April 1992.

Australia

Capital: Canberra, ACT

Population: 18,000,000 (1995E)

The Commonwealth of Australia is a parliamentary democracy with the British monarch as non-executive head of state, represented by a locally nominated Governor-General. Australia comprises six states, each with its own directly-elected assembly with extensive powers, and two territories. There is a bicameral federal Parliament. The membership of the Senate is currently fixed at 76: 12 members from each state, directly elected for a six-year term (with half the seats renewed at three-year intervals), and two members each from the Northern Territory and the Australian Capital Territory (ACT), directly elected for three-year terms. The members of the House of Representatives–currently totalling 148–serve a three-year term. Either the House or both chambers may be dissolved early by the Governor-General, whose powers are by convention exercised in accordance with the advice of the Australian government. Elections to the House, and to most state lower chambers, use the alternative vote system in single-member constituencies; those to the Senate, and the Tasmanian lower house, use proportional representation in multi-seat constituencies. Federal and state elections are on the basis of universal and (with some exceptions) compulsory suffrage. The Governor-General appoints the Prime Minister, who is normally the majority leader in the federal House of Representatives, and who exercises executive power along with a cabinet drawn from and answerable to Parliament; broadly similar arrangements apply at state level, each state having its own constitution and a government led by a state premier.

The activities of political parties are regulated principally by the Commonwealth Electoral Act and the Australian Electoral Commission. On the recommendation of an all-party parliamentary committee in 1994, the Act was amended to increase public funding of parties, along with stricter requirements to disclose donations to party funds. Federal funds are allocated on the basis of votes cast in the most recent general election, among those parties which were registered on the day before the election was called: each party is entitled to A$1.50 per vote won in polling to the House of Representatives and to the Senate, so that the total available for 1995 was of the order of A$30 million (twice the 1993 figure).

After winning five general elections in a row, the Australian Labor Party (ALP) lost power on March 2, 1996, the seat distribution in the House of Representatives becoming Liberal Party of Australia (LPA) 76, ALP 49, National Party of Australia (NPA) 18, independents 5. As a result of simultaneous elections for half the Senate seats, the composition of the upper house became ALP 30, LPA 29, Australian Democrats 7, NPA 6, Western Australia Greens 2, independents 2.

Five states have bicameral legislatures; Queensland and the Northern Territory have single-chamber Legislative Assemblies, while the ACT's unicameral House of Assembly has a non-legislative role.

New South Wales. Australia's most populous state has a 99–member Legislative Assembly and an upper house, the Legislative Council, with 60 members. Assembly elections are held at maximum intervals of four years, and a quarter of Council seats are renewed at each election. A Liberal-National alliance ended 12 years of ALP rule in 1988, and retained power in 1991, but elections in March 1995 returned Labor to office (with 48 seats in the Assembly, to 47 for the coalition).

Queensland. The Legislative Assembly's 89 members represent single-seat constituencies and are elected for three-year terms. In 1989 the ALP ousted the National Party, which had ruled the state for 30 years. Labor retained office in the September 1992 election and again in July 1995, although on the latter occasion it was reduced to 45 seats against 43 for the National and Liberal parties and one independent right-winger, its narrow majority being rendered uncertain by a successful legal challenge to one of the results.

South Australia. The House of Assembly has 47 members, serving a three-year term, and the Legislative Council has 22 seats. The ALP, having been in power since 1982, held only 10 seats in December 1993, when the Liberals won 37.

Tasmania. The island state comprises five constituencies, each returning seven members for a four-year term in the House of Assembly. The 19–member Legislative Council is directly elected, each member serving for six years; three seats are renewed each year and four every sixth year. In elections on Feb. 25, 1996, the ruling Liberals won 16 Assembly seats, the ALP 14, the Greens 4 and an independent 1.

Victoria. The 88 members of the Legislative Assembly are elected every three years, along with half of the 44 Legislative Council members, who serve a six-year term. After 10 years in office, the ALP suffered a comprehensive defeat in the election of October 1992, the resultant Liberal/National coalition being re-elected on March 30, 1996, with 58 lower house seats against 29 for the ALP and one independent.

Western Australia. The House of Assembly, with 57 members, is subject to election every three years. Half of the Legislative Council's 34 members are also elected at three-year intervals, serving for six years. After 10 years in government and implicated in various corruption scandals, the ALP lost control of the House in February 1993, retaining only 24 seats against 32 for the Liberal-National alliance and 1 independent.

Australian Capital Territory. The directly-elected House of Assembly in Canberra, with 18 members, exists to advise the federal government on ACT affairs. After a long period of Labor dominance, power passed narrowly to the Liberals in the February 1995 election.

Northern Territory. The sparsely-populated territory's unicameral Legislative Assembly has 25 members directly elected under a two-party preferred vote system. Elections in June 1994 gave a seventh consecutive victory to the Country Liberal Party (CLP), with 56% of the vote and 17 seats. The ALP took seven seats and one independent was returned.

Australian Democrats

Address. 10–12 Brisbane Avenue, Barton, ACT 2600; PO Box 5089, Kingston, ACT 2604

Telephone. (#61–6) 273-1059

Fax. (#61-6) 273-1251

Leadership. Heather Southcott (national president), Cheryl Kernot (deputy president, parliamentary leader)

Founded in May 1977 by former Liberal Party cabinet minister Donald L. (Don) Chipp, by a merger of the Australia Party and the New Liberal Movement, the Democrats (as the party is informally known) pursued a centre-left, issue-driven agenda which distinguished them from the main traditional parties. They emphasized their independence from both organized labour and business interests. The party supports participatory democracy, open government, nuclear disarmament, protection of the environment, civil liberties and social justice including freedom from discrimination on grounds of race or gender. It is opposed to privatization and deregulation and advocates a role for the state in defence of the disadvantaged, favouring higher public investment in education, welfare and poverty reduction.

Winning 9.4% of the vote and two Senate seats in December 1977, it gained three more in October 1980 and from mid-1981 held the balance of power in the upper house. It retained five seats in 1983, growing to seven in 1984 and 1987, and held eight after the March 1993 election. Chipp retired in 1986, making way for Senator Janine Haines to become the first woman leader of a parliamentary party in Australia. Democrats were also elected to the Legislative Councils of South Australia and New South Wales and the Houses of Assembly for Tasmania and the ACT. In the 1996 national elections, the Democrats again failed to win representation in House of Representatives (despite doubling their vote share to 6.8%) but retained an effective balance of power in the Senate, with seven seats.

Australian Labor Party (ALP)

Address. National Secretariat, 19 National Circuit, Barton, ACT 2600; PO Box E1, Queen Victoria Terrace, ACT 2600

Telephone. (#61-6) 273-3133

Fax. (#61-6) 273-2031

Leadership. Kim Beazley (leader), Gareth Evans (deputy leader), Barry Jones (national president), Bill Ludwig (senior vice-president), Gary Gray (national secretary)

Founded in 1901 from state labour parties, the first of which arose in 1891, the ALP is Australia's oldest national political party, and since 1922 the only one to have held power other than in coalition. It seeks "the democratic socialization of industry, production, distribution and exchange to the extent necessary to eliminate exploitation and other anti-social features". It defends social justice and economic security; freedom of speech, education, assembly, organization and religion; personal liberties and minority rights; free elections, democracy and the rule of law. In recent years, its policies have also emphasized sex and race equality, recognition of Aboriginal rights, the pursuit of an independent foreign policy focusing on free trade and Australia's role in the Asian-Pacific region, and progress towards the adoption of a republican form of constitution.

The party was created as the political arm of the trade union movement (with which it retains close links) and gained representation in the first Commonwealth elections in 1901, with 16 seats in the House and eight in the Senate. The first ALP government was formed in 1904, lasting for three months under John Watson. A minority Labor government held office from October 1907 to June 1909, and the party returned to office with a majority in both House and Senate from April 1910 to May 1913. Elections in September 1914 returned it to government but during World War I it was damaged by divisions on the issue of conscription, and lost office. It was October 1929 before the ALP regained power, under J.H. Scullin's leadership, only to lose it in November 1931 following a parliamentary defeat. Factional disputes helped to keep the party in opposition until the elections of October 1941, following which it remained in power until December 1949 under Prime Minister John Curtin (who died in July 1945) and his successor J.B. (Ben) Chifley. Chifley was followed in 1951 by H.V. Evatt, who led the ALP to three consecutive defeats. The Cold War years saw the ALP embattled by anti-communist factions, leading to a series of splits and the formation of the breakaway Democratic Labor Party.

Under the leadership of Gough Whitlam, the party's fortunes recovered in the late 1960s. Regaining a narrow majority in both chambers in 1972, the party formed a new government with Whitlam as Prime Minister. This administration abolished compulsory military service, pulled Australian forces out of the Vietnam war, established diplomatic ties with China and lowered the voting age to 18. But its failure to secure a Senate majority in May 1974 brought on a constitutional crisis, culminating in Governor-General John Kerr's controversial intervention to dismiss the Whitlam cabinet in November 1975. The ALP lost the following month's election, recovering some ground in the October 1980 elections under the leadership of William (Bill) Hayden, a former president of the Australian Council of Trade Unions (who became Governor-General of Australia in 1989). His successor in the union

34

post, Robert (Bob) Hawke, was chosen to lead the party into the March 1983 elections, from which it emerged in triumph with 75 of the 125 House seats. When the House was enlarged to 148 seats, Labor returned 82 representatives in December 1984, rising to 86 in July 1987. Elections in March 1990 reduced it to 78 seats, its majority slipping from 24 seats to eight.

Under Hawke the ALP discarded many of its traditional policy commitments and pursued an anti-inflation economic policy. Disputes between the party's socialist left, traditionally based in the trade union movement, and its more pragmatic parliamentary caucus came to a head. In April 1989, a left-wing tendency broke off to form the Socialist Party of Australia, leaving the pragmatists in control. During 1991 Hawke's leadership was twice challenged by the federal Treasurer, Paul Keating. Succeeding at the second attempt in December, Keating took over as Prime Minister at a time of considerable economic difficulties. The ALP suffered setbacks in state elections but recovered its standing nationally in time for the March 1993 federal election, in which it obtained a fifth consecutive term, winning 80 seats for a lower house majority of 13. In the following year the government successfully tabled a Native Title Bill providing for recognition of Aboriginal land claims and pledged to abolish the monarchy by the turn of the century. Four ALP cabinet ministers resigned between December 1993 and March 1994 in controversial circumstances.

In June 1995 Prime Minister Keating (of Catholic Irish descent) published plans for a referendum to complete the transition to republican status in 2001, envisaging that the place of the monarch would be taken by a non-political, popularly-elected President. However, such aims did not enthuse voters sufficiently for Labor to win a sixth term in the March 1996 elections, when it retained only 49 seats (on a 38.8% first-preference vote share) and went into opposition. Keating resigned as ALP leader immediately after the contest and was succeeded by Kim Beazley, the former Deputy Prime Minister.

The ALP is officially committed to having at least 35% women parliamentarians at federal and state levels by 2002. There is an autonomous Young Labor Association. The ALP is affiliated to the Socialist International and the Asia-Pacific Socialist Organization.

Country Liberal Party (CLP)

Address. PO Box 4194, Darwin, NT 5794
Telephone. (#61–89) 818986
Leadership. Marshall Perron

Conservative in outlook and closely aligned to the federal Liberal Party of Australia, the CLP (formally registered as the Northern Territory Country Liberal Party) has governed the Northern Territory since the first territorial legislative election in 1974. Led by the NT chief minister, it scored a seventh consecutive election victory in June 1994, with 56% of the vote. In the 1996 federal elections its one seat was regarded as part of the Liberal Party tally.

The Greens

Address. PO Box 1220, Sydney, NSW 2001
Telephone. (#61–2) 216-4454, 249-0220
Leadership. Bob Brown, Norm Sanders (leaders), Doug Hine (secretary), Hazen Waller (convenor), Gosta Lynga (international secretary)

Declining to describe themselves as a party, the Australian Greens act as the federal co-ordinating body for numerous state, territorial and local ecologist parties, including the Greens Western Australia as well as parties in NSW, Queensland, South Australia, Tasmania, Victoria and the ACT. The movement drew many adherents from the Nuclear Disarmament Party launched by Australian Labor Party (ALP) dissidents in 1984. Although never yet represented in the federal lower house, the formation has been influential in securing the inclusion of environmental commitments in the programmes of other parties.

The Greens Western Australia (GWA)

Address. PO Box 8087, Stirling Street, Perth, WA 6849
Telephone. (#61–9) 221-4550
Fax. (#61–9) 221-4515
Leadership. Senators Christabel Chamarette and Dee Margetts (leaders), Stewart Jackson (secretary)

An ecologist party broadly aligned with, but independent of, the federal Greens, the Greens Western Australia have representation in the state parliament as well as two federal senators (as confirmed in the March 1996 general elections).

Liberal Party of Australia

Address. Blackall Street, corner Macquarie Street, Barton, ACT 2600; PO Box E13, Queen Victoria Terrace, ACT 2600
Telephone. (#61–6) 273-2564
Fax. (#61–6) 273-1534
Leadership. John W. Howard (leader), Peter Costello (deputy leader), Tony Staley (federal president), Andrew Robb (secretary-general)

The Liberal Party (as it is invariably called) has been, since its foundation by Sir Robert Gordon Menzies in October 1944, the main anti-socialist party in Australia, representing views ranging from the centre to the conservative right. Its core values are support for free enterprise and individual initiative, for the family and for "a common set of

Australian values" in a multi-cultural society. It opposes state ownership of other than essential public services and advocates conservative economic policies, including rewarding enterprise through low levels of personal taxation. Internationally, it supports peace and co-operation, notably with the United States and the Commonwealth.

The party originated in succession to the United Australia Party, which merged with other forces opposed to the Australian Labor Party. The Liberals won power in Western Australia, South Australia and Victoria in 1947, and went into coalition with the (then) Country Party to form a federal government in 1949. Menzies was federal Prime Minister up to his retirement in 1966, when he was succeeded by Harold Holt. Holt supported the US intervention in Vietnam; domestically his main achievement was the abandonment of the White Australia immigration policy. His death in a swimming accident in 1967 precipitated a battle for the leadership which weakened the party, but the coalition remained in office until 1972. After losing its House majority, the Liberal-Country alliance retained a lead in the Senate which it used effectively against the ALP government.

Invited by the Governor-General to form a minority government in November 1975, Liberal leader Malcolm Fraser secured a majority for the alliance in elections in December, and retained office in 1977 and 1980. Returned to opposition by the March 1983 elections, the Liberals subsequently underwent an intricate series of leadership changes. Andrew Peacock, who took over as leader after the 1983 defeat, was replaced by John Howard in September 1985. The alliance with the National Party (the former Country Party) temporarily collapsed in 1987. Following the July 1987 federal election, in which the Liberals lost two seats in the House to hold 45, Peacock was appointed Howard's deputy, eventually ousting him and being reappointed leader in May 1989. But when the 1990 election saw the opposition fail to overturn Labor's majority, Peacock again resigned, to be succeeded by Dr John R. Hewson. (Peacock was to announce his retirement from political life in September 1994.) Unpopular budget measures proposed by Hewson, including a 15% goods and services tax and cutbacks in the welfare state, were seen as contributing to the opposition's failure to oust an embattled Labor government in 1993, and Howard made another, unsuccessful bid for the Liberal leadership. Hewson stepped down in May 1994, to be succeeded by the Alexander Downer. However, after eight months in the post, during which he secured the abandonment of the consumption tax plan but got into political difficulties on other issues, Downer

gave up the Liberal leadership on Jan. 26, 1995. Howard was elected unopposed to the post on Jan. 30, completing his comeback at a time of auspicious opinion poll ratings for the opposition.

The Liberals expressed reservations about the ALP's proposal to abolish the Australian monarchy, though neither Hewson nor Howard adopted explicitly anti-republican positions. The issue had caused some friction with the firmly monarchist Nationals, the outcome being a Liberal pledge to convene a 'people's convention' to consider the constitutional options before any form decision was taken. Howard declared, on resuming the leadership, that the Liberals were opposed to tax increases and favoured reductions in public expenditure, this platform taking the party to a sweeping victory in the March 1996 general elections (on a 38.7% vote share), after which Howard formed a coalition government with the National Party.

The Liberal Party is structured in seven autonomous state and territory divisions (everywhere but the Northern Territory where it is associated with the Country Liberal Party). An autonomous Young Liberal Movement groups members aged 16–30 and there are women's councils at state and federal levels. The party is affiliated to the International Democrat Union and the Pacific Democrat Union.

National Party of Australia

Address. John McEwen House, National Circuit, Barton, ACT 2600; PO Box E265, Queen Victoria Terrace, ACT 2600

Telephone. (#61–6) 273 3822

Leadership. Timothy (Tim) Fischer (leader), John Anderson (deputy leader), John Paterson (federal president), Cecile Ferguson (national director)

A conservative force, traditionally identified with rural interests, the National Party emerged from Western Australia's state parliament in 1914 and developed a federal platform within two years under its original title of the Country Party. Its electoral appeal has been based on defending free enterprise, family values, national security and development while emphasising the concerns of people outside the relatively populous southeastern coastal areas. The Country Party entered a federal coalition pact with the Liberal Party of Australia in 1949 and, as the junior partner, shared power with it until 1972. After changing its name to the National Country Party in 1974, it returned to federal office, again in partnership with the Liberals, from 1975 to 1983. By the time it reverted to opposition, it had assumed its present title. The two conservative parties have remained allies on the opposition benches, but have differences in emphasis, in geographical spread and occasionally on policy matters and electoral strategy. The Nationals have shown a strong ideological commitment to the preservation of the monarchy, on which the Liberals have been divided, and the parties have disagreed on whether they should refrain from contesting each other's safe seats.

The National Party's strongest base has been in Queensland, where the state government was led for two decades by the controversial right-winger Sir Johannes Bjelke-Petersen; he resigned in December 1987 after failing in a bid to take over the party's federal leadership (and was later criticized by a commission inquiring into allegations of gerrymandering). At national level, the party lost two seats in the June 1987 election, leaving it with 19 members in the House, but picked up a sixth Senate seat. Leader Ian Sinclair was replaced by Charles Blunt, who lost his seat in the party's election disaster of 1990 and was succeeded by Tim Fischer. Left with only 14 seats in the House, the party was severely dented by the findings of an official inquiry into corruption in the Queensland state administration. Over 200 officials and businessmen, Bjelke-Petersen included, were eventually to face criminal charges in the former National Party stronghold. The Australian Labor Party victory in 1993 heightened the National Party's differences with the Liberals, leading to demands for an increased share of shadow cabinet portfolios for the smaller party. These problems were overcome

The party's membership is put at 130,000. The Young National Party is an autonomous organization. Internationally, the National Party is affiliated to the Pacific Democrat Union.

Minor Parties

Abolish Self-Government Coalition, contested the 1993 federal election, without success

Aboriginal Provisional Government, a political movement advocating self-rule for indigenous peoples. *Address.* 198 Elizabeth Street, Hobart, Tasmania

ACT Referendum First Group, confined to the Capital Territory around Canberra, and campaigning for more participatory democracy in the Territory (the present Assembly having a purely advisory remit).

Advance Australia Party, a minor right-wing formation, registered in the late 1980s with the Australian Electoral Commission.

Australia First, a right-wing party active in the early 1990s.

Australian Family Movement (AFM), right-wing group nationally registered in the late 1980s.

Australian League of Rights, an unregistered extreme right-wing antisemitic movement led by Eric Butler, does not contest elections. *Address.* McHarg Road, Happy Valley, Adelaide

Australian National Action (ANA), a fascist grouping led by Jim Saleam (in prison at the time of writing) and Michael Brander; does not contest elections.

Australian Republican Movement, an anti-monarchist pressure group founded 1991, with branches across Australia; leadership includes the prominent lawyer Malcolm Turnbull (chair) and Michael Ward (executive director). *Address.* 1 Chifley Square, GPO Box 5150, Sydney, NSW 2001

Australian Shooters' Party (ASP), a firearm owners' pressure group which presented candidates in the 1993 federal elections and secured the election of leader John Tingle to the New South Wales upper house in March 1995. *Address.* Carver Crescent, Baulkham Hills, Sydney, NSW

Australian Workers' Party (AWP), won 0.5% of the vote in the 1996 Senate elections.

Australians Against Further Immigration Party (AAFI), a populist movement opposed in particular to non-European immigration, led by Rodney Spencer; having achieved up to 13% of the vote at previous by-elections, it won only 0.7% at the 1996 general elections. *Address.* West Ryde, Sydney, NSW

Australians for Constitutional Monarchy, an anti-republican pressure group, whose director, Tony Abbott, entered the House of Representatives as a Liberal Party of Australia candidate in a 1994 by-election. *Address.* GPO Box 9841, Canberra, ACT 2601

Australia's Indigenous Peoples Party (AIPP), campaigning in the 1993 elections on a platform of enhanced rights for Aboriginals and Torres Strait Islanders.

Call to Australia (CTA), a right-wing party also known after its leader, a Protestant fundamentalist minister, as the Fred Nile Group; registered in New South Wales (where it has legislative representation), Tasmania and Victoria; took 0.4% in the 1996 federal elections. *Address.* PO Box 154, Forest Hill, Melbourne, Victoria

Citizens' Electoral Councils of Australia Group, a registered party (which generally does not contest elections) promoting the esoteric conspiracy theories of the US-based movement led by Lyndon LaRouche.

Communist League, a small Marxist formation not registered with the Electoral Commission. *Address.* 19 Terry Street, Surry Hills, NSW 2010

Communist Party of Australia (Marxist-Leninist) (CPA-ML), a Maoist grouping formed by the late Ted Hill in 1964 after the Sino-Soviet split, drawing in some former members of the (then) Communist Party of Australia; published the weekly *Vanguard* and the monthly *Australian Communist*. *Address.* 168 Day St, Sydney, NSW 2000

Confederate Action Party of Australia, contested the 1993 elections in Queensland and New South Wales constituencies, without success. *Address.* 5 Tonkin Street, Cronulla, Sydney, NSW

Conservative Party of Australia (CPA), a small party, registered nationally in the late 1980s.

Daylight Saving Extension Party, a pressure group campaigning for legislation to extend daylight saving time mainly in the interests of road safety. *Address.* 7 Cammeray Road, Cammeray, Sydney, NSW

Deadly Serious Party of Australia, a party registered with the federal Electoral Commission in the mid-1980s, seeking protest votes against the compulsory voting requirement; perhaps unsurprisingly, it did not receive many votes.

Defence and Ex-Services Party of Australia, a nationally-registered right-wing party active in the late 1980s.

Democratic Labor Party (DLP), formerly the Australian Labor Party (Anti-Communist); founded in 1955 by right-wing, chiefly Roman Catholic, dissidents from the Australian Labor Party, it held between two and five Senate seats in the period 1956 to 1974 and generally supported the foreign policy line of Liberal-National coalition governments; despite winning about 10% of the vote in December 1977, it has never won a seat in the federal House of Representatives and scored a negligible vote share in 1980 and subsequent elections; its leadership includes John Mulholland (secretary). *Address.* PO Box 855, Mulgrave, Victoria 3170

Democratic Socialist Party (DSP), a radical leftist/ecologist group founded in 1972 as the

Socialist Workers' Party (SWP), an affiliate of the Trotskyist Fourth International United Secretariat; the SWP fielded 38 candidates in the 1983 election to win 0.5% of the vote; in June 1985, at the first national congress of the Nuclear Disarmament Party, 30% of delegates walked out, alleging an attempted SWP takeover; enjoying some student following, the DSP has branches in all states and the ACT; leadership includes James Percy and Claudine Holt. *Address.* 23 Abercrombie Street, Chippendale, NSW 2008

EFF Political Party, also known as **Independent EFF**, a grouping whose three unsuccessful candidates in the 1993 elections included its leader, Joe Bryant. *Address.* 418 Roper Road, St Mary's, Sydney, NSW

Family Law Reform Party, an unregistered party. *Address.* 19 Bourke Street, Ringwood, Melbourne, Victoria

Federal Party of Australia (FPA), contested the 1993 elections, without success.

Grey Power, a pensioners' pressure group which took 8% of the poll in Western Australia's state election in February 1989, and developed a national presence; the party came under the influence of far-right factions and, although it contested the 1993 elections, it was virtually inactive by the mid-1990s. *Address.* 58 Sorrell Street, North Parramatta, Sydney, NSW

International Socialists (IS), a Trotskyist group active in Brisbane, Sydney and elsewhere. *Address.* 109 Edward Street, Brisbane, Queensland

Janet Powell Independents Network, registered as a party for the 1993 federal elections.

National Front, a neo-fascist movement, not registered with the electoral authorities.

Natural Law Party, which contests elections in order to promote the transcendental meditation practices of the international Maharishi Mahesh Yogi new religious movement; took 0.4% in the 1996 House elections. *Address.* 200 Smith Street, Thornbury, Melbourne, Victoria

New Left Party (NLP), formed in 1989 when the Communist Party of Australia (CPA) dissolved itself and many of its members joined with the Association of Communist Unity (ACU), a revisionist splinter group of the Socialist Party of Australia, to launch the NLP; having distanced itself from both Chinese and Soviet trends in the international communist movement, adopting an independent position akin to Eurocommunism, the CPA sought alliances with a range of social and political movements.

Nuclear Disarmament Party (NDP), formed in June 1984 by elements of the Australian Labor Party to campaign for the prohibition of nuclear weapons, nuclear power and the mining of uranium (of which Australia has a large proportion of the world's reserves); in the 1984 Senate election it won a single seat, but its senator quit the NDP the following year to form the Vallentine Peace Group; another NDP senator was elected in June 1987, but the party was subsequently riven by allegations of Trotskyist infiltration, and is no longer registered; its leader Pete Garrett (a rock musician) and many of its members subsequently became active in Green politics.

One Australia Movement (OAM), a minor party, registered with the Australian Electoral Commission in the late 1980s.

Pensioner- and Citizen-Initiated Referendum Alliance, contested the 1993 elections.

Rainbow Alliance, a Victorian radical ecologist coalition. *Address.* 124 Napier Street, Fitzroy, Melbourne, Victoria

Republican Party of Australia (RPA), formed to advance the campaign for the removal of the British monarchy from the Australian constitution; it contested the 1993 elections, although its principal objective had by then been adopted as Australian Labor Party policy; in March 1995 the party named the Prince of Wales as "Republican of the Year" for his supposed contribution to anti-monarchical sentiment; led by Peter Considine (executive director). *Address.* Castle Hill, Sydney, NSW

ReWorking Australia, and unregistered group. *Address.* 122 Little Eveleigh, Redfern, Sydney, NSW

Rex Connor (Snr) Labor Party, a splinter group of the ALP which contested the 1993 elections, without success.

Rural Australia Party, formerly known as the Farm and Town Party; no significant following.

Social Credit Movement of Australia, a small group advocating the redistributionist theories of the late (British) monetary reformer C.H. Douglas; through the Social Credit League, these ideas achieved significant electoral support in Australia in the 1930s, but association with the extreme right had marginalized the movement by the 1970s. *Address.* 76 Sunbury Street, Geebung, Brisbane, Queensland

Socialist Forum, a left-wing group in Victoria. *Address.* 317 Barkly Street, Brunswick, Melbourne, Victoria

Socialist Labor League, a Trotskyist group aligned with the faction of the (UK) Workers' Revolutionary Party led by the late Gerry Healy, and subsequently with his Marxist Party.

Socialist Party, formed by left-wing dissidents who quit the Australian Labor Party in April 1989, disagreeing with the ALP government's foreign policies in particular.

Socialist Party of Australia (SPA), led by Peter Dudley Symon (general secretary) and Dr H. Middleton; an orthodox communist party, seeking a socialist republic with an independent foreign policy, the SPA was formed in December 1971 by a group which left the Communist Party of Australia in protest at the latter's criticisms of Soviet policies; the SPA's membership in the late 1980s was estimated at less than 1,000, some of whom left to form the Association of Communist Unity and later the New Left Party; the party, which contested the 1993 elections without success, publishes a fortnightly organ, *The Socialist*, and is in contact with similarly orthodox communist parties abroad; won 1.1% of the vote in the 1996 Senate elections. *Address.* 65 Campbell Street, Surry Hills, NSW 2010

Southern Cross Republican Action Party, a radical anti-monarchist group. *Address.* 25 Leslie Street, Brunswick, Melbourne, Victoria

Spartacist League of Australia and New Zealand (SLANZ), an unregistered party representing a current of Trotskyism. *Address.* 329 Lt Collins Street, Melbourne, Victoria; 800 George Street, Sydney, NSW

Tasmanian Independent Group, the personal vehicle of state Senator Brian Harradine.

Torres United Party (TUP), seeking to represent the 5,000 indigenous inhabitants of the Torres Strait Islands, and the 20,000 Islanders resident in mainland Queensland.

Unite Australia Party (UAP), also known as **United**; registered with the federal Electoral Commission in the late 1980s. *Address.* United Sydney Team, 168 Flood Street, Leichhardt, Sydney, NSW

Vallentine Peace Group, led by Jo Vallentine; founded as the Nuclear-Free Australia Party in December 1985, as the result of a split within the Nuclear Disarmament Party, the Group advocated world peace, nuclear disarmament and the maintenance of Australia as a nuclear-free zone; Vallentine, the NDP's first member of the federal Senate, led the breakaway in protest at alleged Trotskyist infiltration of that party by the, and retained her position in the July 1987 election; the new formation became known as the Vallentine Peace Group but was also referred to as the Western Australia Anti-Nuclear Party. *Address.* PO Box 137, West Perth, WA 6005

Weekend Trading Party, which was registered nationally but has been active mainly in Victoria; this small group campaigns against legal restrictions on Sunday shopping.

World Socialist Party of Australia (WSPA), a small, independent Marxist party, with limited grassroots influence in the trade union movement, publishing *Socialist Comment*; the group is an offshoot of the Socialist Party of Great Britain and is affiliated to the World Socialist Movement. *Address.* PO Box 1440, Melbourne, Victoria; GPO Box 2291, Sydney, NSW; PO Box 1357, Brisbane, Queensland.

Austria

Capital: Vienna

Population: 7,950,000 (1995E)

First founded in 1919, the Republic of Austria was re-established after World War II and obtained international recognition as a "sovereign, independent and democratic state" under the Austrian State Treaty signed on 15 May 1955 by Austria, France, the UK, the USA and the USSR. The Austrian constitution provides for a parliamentary system of government based on elections by secret ballot and by "free, equal and universal suffrage"; as amended in 1945, it proscribes any attempt to revive the pre-war Nazi Party. There is a bicameral parliament consisting of a 183–member lower house called the National Council (*Nationalrat*) and a 63–member upper house called the Federal Council (*Bundesrat*), both together forming the Federal Assembly (*Bundesversammlung*). The *Nationalrat* is elected for a four-year term under an exact proportional representation system (subject to a minimum requirement of 4% of the national vote) by all citizens over 19 years of age. Members of the *Bundesrat* are elected for from four to six years by the legislatures of the nine Austrian provinces (*Länder*), each of which has an elected assembly (*Landtag*). The President of the Republic (*Bundespräsident*) is elected for a six-year term (to a maximum of two terms) by universal suffrage, the functions of the post being mainly ceremonial but including the appointment of the Federal Chancellor (*Bundeskanzler*) as head of government, who recommends ministeral appointments for confirmation by the President. Each member of the government must enjoy the confidence of a majority of members of the *Nationalrat*.

Under the Parties Financing Act of 1975, parties represented in the *Nationalrat* are granted federal budget support (for publicity and campaigning) in the form of a basic sum and additional amounts in proportion to the number of votes received in the previous election, subject to at least 1% of the valid votes being obtained. The total amount of such financial support available in 1993 was 203.5 million schillings (about $17 million), including a basic sum of 3 million schillings for each party represented. Separate state assistance is available to research foundations run by parties, totalling 119.3 million schillings ($10 million) in 1993.

Elections to the *Nationalrat* on Dec. 17, 1995, resulted as follows: Social Democratic Party of Austria 71 seats (with 38.1% of the vote); Austrian People's Party 53 (28.3%); Freedom Movement 40 (21.9%); Liberal Forum 10 (5.5%) Green Alternative 9 (4.8%).

Austrian People's Party
Österreichische Volkspartei (ÖVP)

Address. Lichtenfelsgasse 7, A-1010 Vienna
Telephone. (#43–1) 401260
Fax. (#43-1) 4012-6429
Leadership. Wolfgang Schüssel (chair), Aloïs Mock (honorary chair), Ingrid Korosec (secretary-general)

Founded in 1945 from pre-war Christian Democratic groups, the ÖVP was the leading government party in 1945–66, in coalition with what later became the Social Democratic Party of Austria (SPÖ). In sole power from 1966, the ÖVP was narrowly defeated by the SPÖ in the 1970 election, after which it was in opposition for 16 years. Although it lost ground in the 1986 election, simultaneous SPÖ losses dictated the formation of a "grand coalition" of the two major parties, which survived through the 1990 election and beyond, with the ÖVP as junior partner. Meanwhile, the party had become enmeshed in public controversy over the wartime record of Kurt Waldheim, whose election as President in 1986 with ÖVP backing was accompanied by claims that as a Germany Arm officer he had participated in Nazi atrocities in the Balkans during World War II.

Waldheim's successor as President, Thomas Klestil, was elected in 1992 as the ÖVP nominee. But provincial elections in the early 1990s showed falling support for the ÖVP, mainly to the benefit of the right-wing Freedom Party of Austria (which became the Freedom Movement in 1995). This trend was confirmed in the October 1994 federal election, in which the ÖVP's representation fell from 60 to 52 seats and its share of the vote to a low of 27.7%. The party nevertheless continued its coalition with the SPÖ, this being the only viable option if the FPÖ was to be excluded from the government. But Vice-Chancellor Erhard Busek later paid the price of the ÖVP's election setback, being replaced as party chair in April 1995 by the Economics Minister, Wolfgang Schüssel, who therefore also became Vice-Chancellor.

The ÖVP/SPÖ coalition unexpectedly collapsed in October 1995 over budget policy differences, precipitating a new federal election on Dec. 17. To general surprise, the ÖVP emerged with slightly higher representation of 53 seats, on a vote share of 28.3%. In March 1996 the ÖVP entered a further coalition headed by the SPÖ.

Claiming a membership of c.350,000, the ÖVP is affiliated to the International Democrat Union and the Christian Democrat International; its representatives in the European Parliament sit in the European People's Party group.

Freedom Movement
Die Freiheitlichen (DF)

Address. Kärntner Strasse 28/0, A-1010 Vienna
Telephone. (#43–1) 512-3535
Fax. (#43–1) 512-3277
Leadership. Jörg Haider (chair), Edith Haller (deputy chair), Walter Meischberger and Herbert Scheibner (secretaries-general)

This party took its present name in January 1995, when the Freedom Party of Austria (FPÖ) decided that, such was the public antipathy to traditional party politics, the descriptor "party" should be dropped. The FPÖ was formed in 1956 as a merger of three right-wing formations, notably the League of Independents, which had won 14 lower house seats in 1953. FPÖ representation languished in the 1960s and 1970s, although some of its policies, including exact proportional representation, were enacted. In 1983 it won 12 seats and joined a coalition government with what later became the Social Democratic Party of Austria (SPÖ). Subsequently, the moderate federal leadership of Norbert Steiger came into increasing ideological conflict with the right-wing Carinthian FPÖ, which contested the 1984 provincial election on a platform of opposition to the provision of bilingual education for the Slovene minority. This argument culminated in Steiger being replaced by right-winger Jörg Haider in September 1986.

The SPÖ responded by terminating the ruling coalition, but in the resultant federal elections in November 1986 the FPÖ almost doubled its vote share to 9.7%, on a populist platform which included opposition to foreign immigration. Developing such policies in the 1990 election, the opposition FPÖ increased its vote to 16.6%, thereafter also making a series of major gains in provincial elections. The party failed in 1993 to bring about a national referendum on the immigration issue, and Haider's opposition to the government's aim of European Union membership failed to prevent the Austrian electorate voting decisively in favour in June 1994. But after registering a further advance in the Vorarlberg provincial election in September 1994, in the following month's federal elections the FPÖ's share of the vote rose to 22.6% (and 42 seats), although the party remained in opposition.

Following the collapse of the coalition of the SPÖ and the Austrian People's Party (ÖVP) in October 1995, general elections in December resulted in an unexpected failure to progress by what was now the Freedom Movement, which slipped to 40 seats and 21.9%.

Claiming 50,000 members, the FPÖ was an affiliate of the Liberal International until being replaced in that organization by the breakaway

Liberal Forum. The movement's representatives in the European Parliament are part of the "unattached" contingent.

Green Alternative

Grüne Alternativen (GA)

Address. Lindengasse 40, A-1070 Vienna

Telephone. (#43–1) 521–250

Fax. (#43–1) 526–9110

Leadership. Peter Pilz (chair), Madeleine Petrovic (parliamentary leader)

The GA was formed in 1987 as a union of three alternative groupings which had won a total of eight seats in the 1986 federal election, although the conservative United Greens of Austria subsequently opted to retain organizational independence. The GA increased its representation to 10 seats in the 1990 election and thereafter opposed the government's successful policy of European Union membership. In the October 1994 federal elections the formation advanced to 7% of the national vote, giving it 13 seats as against 10 previously. It fell back to 4.8% and nine seats in the December 1995 elections.

The GA's single representative in the European Parliament is a member of the Green Group.

Liberal Forum

Liberales Forum (LF)

Address. Reichsratstrasse 7/2, A-1010 Vienna

Telephone. (#43–1) 402-7873

Fax. (#43–1) 406–7889

Leadership. Heide Schmidt (leader), Gerhard Kratky (secretary-general)

The LF was launched in February 1993 by five lower house deputies of the Austrian Freedom Party (FPÖ), which later became the Freedom Movement. The dissidents disagreed with the strident right-wing and anti-foreigner stance of the FPÖ's post-1986 leadership headed by Jörg Haider. The chief defector, Heide Schmidt, had been the FPÖ presidential candidate in 1992, winning 16.4% of the first-round vote. The Forum backed the successful government line in favour of EU membership in the June 1994 referendum. In the October 1994 federal elections it prevented an even bigger advance for its parent party by itself winning 11 seats on the strength of 5.7% of the popular vote. In the December 1995 contest, however, it fell back to 10 seats and 5.5%.

In 1993 the LF was designated to replace the FPÖ as the Austrian affiliate of the Liberal International. Its single representative in the European Parliament is a member of the European Liberal, Democratic and Reformist Group.

Social Democratic Party of Austria

Sozialdemokratische Partei Österreichs (SPÖ)

Address. Löwelstrasse 18, A-1014 Vienna

Telephone. (#43–1) 534–27280

Fax. (#43–1) 535–9683

Leadership. Franz Vranitzky (chair), Heinz Fischer (parliamentary leader), Josef Cap and Brigitte Ederer (general secretaries)

The SPÖ is descended from the Social Democratic Workers' Party dating from 1874, which advocated social revolution and the transformation of the Austro-Hungarian Empire into a federal state of coexisting nations. It had no direct political influence before World War I, although it became the largest parliamentary party on the strength of universal male franchise. On the establishment of the Austrian Republic in 1919 it was briefly in government under Karl Renner, but went into opposition in 1920, remaining committed to "Austro-Marxism" and prepared to resort to armed struggle if the bourgeoisie sought to resist social revolution. The party came under increasing pressure in the early 1930s, as the pro-fascist Dollfus government adopted authoritarian methods, dissolving the *Nationalrat* in March 1933 and introducing rule by decree. The party's paramilitary Republican Defence League, itself already banned, responded by mounting an uprising in Vienna in February 1934 but was quickly defeated. Following the proclamation of a quasi-fascist constitution three months later, the party went underground and participated with other democratic forces in anti-fascist resistance until German forces occupied Austria in 1938.

On the re-establishment of the Republic in 1945, the SPÖ adopted a pro-Western stance and participated in a broad-based coalition government including the Communist Party of Austria. From November 1947, however, it became the junior partner in a two-party coalition with the Austrian People's Party (ÖVP) that endured until 1966, when the SPÖ went into opposition. In 1970 it returned to power as the sole governing party under the leadership of Bruno Kreisky, forming a minority government until 1971, when it gained an absolute majority in the lower house which it retained in the 1975 and 1979 elections. A party congress in 1978 renounced public ownership as a necessary requirement of democratic socialism.

Losing its overall majority in the 1983 election, the SPÖ formed a coalition with the Freedom Party of Austria (FPÖ)—later the Freedom Movement—and Kreisky handed over the government and party leadership to Fred Sinowatz. The latter resigned in June 1986 as a result of the controversial election of Kurt Waldheim as President and was replaced as Chancellor by Franz

Vranitzky. In September 1986, because of the FPÖ's swing to the right, the SPÖ terminated the coalition but lost ground sharply in November elections. It therefore formed a "grand coalition" with the ÖVP in January 1987, under Vranitzky's chancellorship, thereby provoking the resignation of Kreisky as SPÖ honorary chair. Later that year an SPÖ congress gave qualified support to the government's privatization programme.

The SPÖ/ÖVP coalition was maintained after the October 1990 elections, in which the SPÖ remained substantially the largest party. In 1991 the party renamed itself "Social Democratic" rather than "Socialist", retaining the SPÖ abbreviation. The government's key external policy of EC/EU membership was endorsed by the electorate in June 1994 by a 2:1 majority. In the October 1994 federal elections, however, the SPÖ vote slipped to a new post-war low of 35.2% and the party opted to continue its coalition with the ÖVP. In October 1995, however, the coalition collapsed over budget policy differences, with the result that new lower house elections were held in December. Against most predictions, Vranitzky led the SPÖ to a significant electoral recovery, yielding 71 seats and 38.1% of the vote. In March 1996 he was appointed to a fifth term as Chancellor, heading a further coalition between the SPÖ and the ÖVP.

The SPÖ has an official membership of 700,000 and is a founding member of the Socialist International. Its representatives in the European Parliament are members of the Party of European Socialists.

Other Parties

Austrian Family Party (*Österreichische Familienpartei*, ÖFP), founded in 1982 by Leopold Kendöl, president of the Austrian Catholic Family Association.

Austrian Natural Law Party (*Österreichische Naturgesetz Partei*, ÖNP), won 0.05% of the vote in 1994.

Best Party (*Die Beste Partei*, DBP), won 0.01% of the national vote in 1994.

Christian Electors' Union (*Christliche Wähler Gemeinschaft*, CWG), won 0.2% of the national vote in 1994.

Civic Greens of Austria (*Bürgerliche Grüne Österreichs*, BGÖ), won 0.05% of the national vote in 1994.

Communist Party of Austria (*Kommunistische Partei Österreiches*, KPÖ), led by Otto Bruchner, founded by pro-Soviet Social Democrats in 1919, in government in 1945–47 and represented in the lower house until 1959, reputedly the richest Austrian party on the strength of industrial holdings acquired under the post-war Soviet occupation, took only 0.3% of the vote in 1994. *Address.* Höchstädtplatz 1, A-1206 Vienna.

Economy Party (*Wirschaftspartei*, WP), founded in 1992 by Vienna businessman Martin Zumtobel as an anti-establishment, pro-market formation.

League of Democratic Socialists (*Bund Demokratischer Sozialisten*, BDS), a Marxist grouping with links with the Socialist Party of Great Britain. *Address.* Gussriegelstrasse 50, A-1000 Vienna.

No (*Nein*), being the chosen 1994 electoral designation of the Citizens' Initiative against the Abandonment of Austria (*Bürgerinitiave gegen den Ausverkauf Österreichs*), which won 0.9% of the popular vote in that year's contest.

People's True Extra-Parliamentary Opposition (*Volkstreue Ausserparlamentarische Opposition*, VAPO), extreme right-wing group, founded by Gottfried Küssel, identified with attacks on immigrants in the early 1990s; arrested in January 1992, Küssel was sentenced to 11 years' imprisonment in October 1994 for founding VAPO.

Revolutionary Marxist Group (*Gruppe Revolutionärer Marxisten*, GRM), a small Trotskyist formation founded in 1972, led by Hermann Dworczak, affiliated to the Fourth International, United Secretariat.

United Greens of Austria (*Vereinte Grüne Österreichs*, VGÖ), led by Adi Pinter, founded in 1982 by conservative ecologists and briefly part of the coalition which became the Green Alternative, winner of one lower house seat in 1986 but none in 1990 or 1994 (taking only 0.1% of the vote on the latter occasion).

Azerbaijan

Capital: Baku

Population: 7,600,000 (1995E)

The Azerbaijan Republic declared independence from the USSR in August 1991, becoming a sovereign member of the Commonwealth of Independent States (CIS) created on the dissolution of the USSR in December 1991. Interim constitutional arrangements based on the 1978 Soviet-era text applied until the adoption of a new constitution in November 1995, providing for an executive President, who is directly elected by universal adult suffrage for a five-year term and who appoints the Prime Minister and other ministers. Legislative authority is vested in a 125-seat National Assembly (*Milli Majlis*), also elected for a five-year term, with 100 members being returned from single-member constituencies and 25 proportionally from party lists which obtain at least 8% of the national vote.

Since independence Azerbaijan has moved to a limited multi-party system, qualified by the exigencies of an ongoing war with Armenia, internal political conflict and the continuing preponderance of former Communists in the state bureaucracy. Stringent registration requirements for Assembly elections held on Nov. 12 and 26, 1995, resulted in only eight parties being deemed eligible to stand (and about a dozen being deemed ineligible), with the consequence that a UN/OSCE monitoring mission subsequently concluded that the elections had not been conducted fairly. The official results showed that, of the 109 seats filled, the ruling New Azerbaijan Party (YAP) and its allies (including pro-government independents) had won 103, with the Azerbaijan Popular Front (AKC) and the Azerbaijan National Independence Party being credited with three each. Further polling in February 1996 for 15 of the 16 unfilled seats resulted in the YAP and its allies increasing their representation to 115 seats, while the AKC took an additional seat and the Muslim Democratic Party won one. In a presidential election held on June 7, 1992, Abulfaz Elchibey (AKC) had been victorious with 59.4% of the vote. Following Elchibey's deposition a year later, a further presidential contest on Oct. 3, 1993, was won by Geidar Aliyev (YAP) with 98.8% of the vote.

Azerbaijan Independence Party
Müstaqil Azerbaycan Partiyasi (MAP)
> Address. 11/28 Keçid, 370073 Baku
> Telephone. (#994-12) 394602
> Leadership. Nizami Suleymanov (chair)

The MAP leader contested the June 1992 presidential election, being at that time head of the Democratic Union of Azerbaijan's Intelligentsia. The MAP is closely allied with the New Azerbaijan Party headed by President Geidar Aliyev.

Azerbaijan National Independence Party
Azerbaycan Milli Istiqlal Partiyasi (AMIP)
> Address. 179 Azadlig Street, 370087 Baku
> Telephone. (#994-12) 627576
> Leadership. Etibar Mamedov (chair)

The AMIP was founded in July 1992 by Mamedov, who had been a prominent leader of the then ruling Azerbaijan Popular Front (AKC) but had defected in light of resistance to his hardline nationalist approach to the Nagorno-Karabakh conflict with Armenia. Mamedov had been an initial candidate for the June 1992 presidential election but had withdrawn claiming that the arrangements favoured the AKC candidate. He found no more acceptance of his line from Geidar Aliyev of the New Azerbaijan Party when the latter came to power in June 1993 and refused a post in the Aliyev government. Thereafter Mamedov and the AMIP vigorously opposed the government's preference for the deployment of Russian troops in Azerbaijan to help guarantee a Nagorno-Karabakh settlement. The AMIP was officially stated to have won three seats in the November 1995 Assembly elections on the basis of a national vote share of 9%.

44

Azerbaijan Popular Front
Azerbaycan Khalq Cabhasi (AKC)
Address. 1 Injasanat Street, 370000 Baku
Telephone. (#994-12) 921483
Fax. (#994-12) 989004
Leadership. Abulfaz Elchibey (president), Ibrahim Ibrahimli (chair), Ali Kerimov (deputy chair)

The AKC was founded in 1989 under the leadership of Elchibey (then a teacher of oriental philosophy) as a broad-based opposition movement calling for reform of the then Communist-run political system. The movement took a broadly pan-Turkic line, supporting nationalist calls for the acquisition of Azeri-populated areas of northern Iran. In January 1990 AKC members were among 150 people killed by the security forces in Baku and elsewhere in disturbances arising from AKC-led anti-Armenian demonstrations. Allowed to contest the Supreme Soviet elections of September-October 1990, the AKC-led opposition won only 45 of the 360 seats (with a vote share of 12.5%). Together with other opposition parties, the AKC boycotted the direct presidential election held in September 1991 but subsequently brought about the resignation President Mutalibov in March 1992. In a further presidential election in June 1992, Elchibey was returned with 59.4% of the vote against four other candidates.

In government, the AKC blocked ratification of Azerbaijan's CIS membership but came under increasing pressure from opposition groups, notably the New Azerbaijan Party led by Geidar Aliyev and the forces of Col. Surat Guseinov. Replaced as head of state by Aliyev in June 1993, Elchibey fled to Nakhichevan and disputed the official results of an August referendum (boycotted by the AKC) in which only 2% of voters were said to have expressed confidence in Elchibey. Aliyev secured popular endorsement as President in September 1993, in direct elections that were also boycotted by the AKC. The authorities subsequently launched a crackdown against the AKC, raiding its headquarters in Baku in February 1994 and arresting 100 AKC supporters for "resisting the police". AKC leaders claimed that weapons said to have been found at the building had been planted by the police. Nevertheless, the AKC was able in 1994-95 to command substantial popular support for its opposition to the Aliyev government's policy of seeking a Nagorno-Karabakh settlement via close relations with Russia.

In May 1995 Elchibey repeated the AKC's call for the creation of a "greater Azerbaijan", to include the estimated 15 million ethnic Azeris inhabiting northern Iran (twice as many as the entire population of Azerbaijan proper). The Iranian authorities responded by cutting off electricity supplies to Elchibey's stronghold of Nakhichevan. In the same month Shahmerdan Jafarov, an AKC deputy, was stripped of his parliamentary immunity and accused of setting up illegal armed groups in Nakhichevan, where Elchibey's residence was reportedly surrounded by government troops. On June 17 Jafarov was shot in a clash in the enclave, subsequently dying of his injuries, while in October 1995 former Foreign Minister Tofik Gasymov of the AKC was arrested and charged with involvement in a coup attempt earlier in the year. In the November 1995 Assembly elections the AKC was officially credited with winning three proportional seats on the basis of a national vote share of 10%. It increased its tally to four in balloting for unfilled seats in February 1996.

Azerbaijan Revolutionary Revival Party
Azerbaycan Inqilabi Dirçeliš Partiyasi (AIDP)
Address. 14 Yeni Guneshli, massif A-B/apt. 61-62, Baku
Telephone. (#994-12) 625842
Leadership. Sayad Sayadov (chair)

The AIDP was created by former members of the Azerbaijan Communist Party (AKP) following the latter's suspension in 1992. It continued activities despite the relegalization of the AKP in November 1993 under the name Azerbaijan United Communist Party.

Azerbaijan United Communist Party
Azerbaycan Vahid Kommunist Partiyasi (AVKP)
Address. 29 Hussein Javid Prospekti, Room 637te, Baku
Telephone. (#994-12) 380151
Leadership. Ramiz Ahmedov (chair)

The Azerbaijan Communist Party (AKP) was relaunched in November 1993 as the AVKP. The AKP had governed the republic during the Soviet era, latterly under the hardline rule of Ayaz Mutalibov. In elections to the 360-member Azerbaijan Supreme Soviet in September-October 1990, the AKP had won 280 of the 340 seats contested (with 78% of the vote) and Mutalibov had been re-elected President unopposed in September 1991 in direct elections boycotted by the opposition parties. Following military setbacks in Nagorno-Karabakh, Mutalibov had been forced to resign in March 1992 and had fled to Russia after a shortlived return to power in May (for which alleged coup attempt criminal charges were later preferred against him). The AKP had been effectively suspended under the subsequent government of the Azerbaijan Popular Front (AKC), which had replaced the Supreme Soviet with an interim 50-member National Assembly dominated by AKC members. Nevertheless, party members, some of whom set up the Azerbaijan Revolutionary Revival Party (AIDP), had remained preponderant in the state bureaucracy and former AKP deputies had continued to regard the 1990 Supreme Soviet as the legitimate legislative body. The relaunching of the party in November 1993 under the AVKP rubric was aimed at rallying these elements in opposition to the government of Geidar Aliyev of the New Azerbaijan Party, although the AIDP remained in existence. On Sept. 1, 1995, the Supreme Court banned the AVKP in light of Justice Ministry allegations that the party had engaged in anti-state activities by advocating union with other ex-Soviet republics. On Sept. 19, however, the Court reversed its decision, which it described as "groundless and illegal", thus enabling the party to contest legislative elections in November.

Muslim Democratic Party
Yeni Musavat Partiyasi (YMP)
  Address. 37 Azerbaijan Prospekt, 370001 Baku
  Telephone. (#994-12) 981870
  Fax. (#994-12) 983165
  Leadership. Isa Gambarov (chair), Niyazi Ibrahimov (general secretary)
  The YMP (usually referred to as *Musavat*) was founded in June 1992, indirectly descended from the pre-Soviet *Musavat* nationalists, of moderate Islamic, pan-Turkic orientation. It was closely allied with the Azerbaijan Popular Front under the 1992–93 government, when Gambarov was chair of the interim National Assembly. The party came into sharp conflict with succeeding government of Geidar Aliyev of the New Azerbaijan Party and won only one seat in the legislative elections held in November 1995 and February 1996.

New Azerbaijan Party
Yeni Azerbaycan Partiyasi (YAP)
  Address. 6 Landau Street, 370073 Baku
  Telephone. (#994-12) 393875
  Leadership. Geidar Aliyev (chair), Ali Nagiyev (deputy chair)
  The YAP was founded by Aliyev in September 1992 as an alternative to the then ruling Azerbaijan Popular Front (AKC) following his exclusion from the June 1992 presidential election because he was over a newly-decreed age limit of 65. At the time he held the presidency of the Azerbaijani enclave of Nakhichevan and had previously been a politburo member of the Soviet Communist Party and first secretary of the party in Azerbaijan (from 1969); he had also served as a Soviet deputy premier until being dismissed by Mikhail Gorbachev in 1987 for alleged corruption. Returning to Nakhichevan, he had become chair of its Supreme Soviet in September 1991 and had

conducted an independent foreign policy for the enclave, signing a ceasefire with Armenia and developing relations with Russia, Turkey and Iran. The new party pledged itself to the defence of the rights of all individuals, regardless of nationality, and the creation of a law-based state.

Aliyev used the YAP to rally opposition to the AKC government of Abulfaz Elchibey, who was deposed in June 1993 with assistance from Col. Surat Guseinov, a former wool merchant who had recently been dismissed as commander of Azerbaijani forces in Nagorno-Karabakh. Elected interim head of state, Aliyev appointed Col. Guseinov as Prime Minister and received popular endorsement of sorts in a presidential election in October 1993 (for which the 65–year age limit was rescinded), being credited with 98.8% of the vote against two other candidates, neither of whom represented major opposition parties. Meanwhile, at Aliyev's urging in September, parliamentary approval had at last been given to Azerbaijan's membership of the CIS. The new government launched a crackdown against the AKC, while Aliyev moved to improve Azerbaijan's regional relations and sought a settlement of the conflict with Armenia involving the deployment of Turkish troops in Nagorno-Karabakh and the return of a limited Russian military presence in Azerbaijan proper.

In a further power struggle in October 1994, Col. Guseinov was dismissed as Prime Minister and replaced by Fuad Kuliyev. The YAP regime accused Col. Guseinov of treasonable activities, reportedly in connivance with opposition groups and the Russian authorities. The episode therefore marked a distinct cooling between the YAP government and Moscow. In the November 1995 legislative elections the YAP formed a front with the Azerbaijan Independent Democratic Party, the Motherland Party and United Azerbaijan, being credited with 62% of the national vote in its own right and winning an overwhelming majority of Assembly seats when pro-government independents were included in the tally.

Social Democratic Party
Sosial-Demoktarik Partiyasi (SDP)
  Address. 3/28 May Street, Apr. 11, 370014 Baku
  Telephone. (#994-12) 933378
  Fax. (#994-12) 987555
  Leadership. Araz Alizade (chair)
  The SDP was founded in 1989 by Alizade, who withdrew as a candidate for the September 1991 presidential elections in protest against the government's conduct of the poll. The party seeks to be a moderate left-wing formation on the West European social democratic model.

Other Parties

Azerbaijan Democratic Party (*Azerbaycan Democrat Partiyasi*, ADP), led by Sardar Jalal, founded in 1994.

Azerbaijan Independent Democratic Party (*Azerbaycan Müstaqil Demokrat Partiyasi*, AMDP), led by Leyla Yunusova, allied with the ruling New Azerbaijan Party in the 1995 Assembly elections.

Azerbaijan National Democratic Party, led by Rafik Abdullayev, who was an unsuccessful candidate in the June 1992 presidential elections.

Azerbaijan Peasant Party (*Azerbaycan Kendli Partiyasi*, AKP), led by Firuz Mustafayev.

Azerbaijan Renaissance and Progress Party (*Azerbaycan Dirçeliš ve Teraqqi Partiyasi*, ADTP), led by Azad Nabiyev.

Green Party of Azerbaijan, a small grouping which has found little space for the advocacy of environmentalism in present conditions.

Islamic Party of the Republic of Azerbaijan, founded in December 1992, seeking a revival of Islamic culture in an independent Azerbaijan.

Labour Party (*Isçi Partiyasi*, IP), led by Sabutai Hajiyev, who was arrested in October 1995 and charged with illegal possession of arms.

Motherland Party (*Anavatan Partiyasi*, AP), modelled on the Turkish party of the same name, allied with the ruling New Azerbaijan Party in the 1995 Assembly elections.

National Statehood Party, contested the 1995 Assembly elections as an opposition party, without success.

Party of Entrepreneurs (*Azad Sahibkarlar Partiyasi*, ASP), led by Eldar Azizov, a centrist formation that was unsuccessful in the 1995 Assembly elections.

Party of Equality of the Peoples of Azerbaijan, led by Fahraddin Aydayev.

People's Freedom Party, led by Panah Shahsevenli.

True Path Party (*Dogru Yol Partiyasi*, DYP), founded in April 1992 and modelled on the Turkish party of the same name, led by Tamerlan Kareyev (hitherto a leader of the Azerbaijan Popular Front), who was an unsuccessful candidate in the June 1992 presidential elections.

United Azerbaijan (*Azerbaycan Vahid*, AV), led by Kerrar Abilov, who contested the October 1993 presidential elections as an apparent token candidate, receiving only 0.3% of the vote, allied with the ruling New Azerbaijan Party in the 1995 Assembly elections.

Bahamas

Capital: Nassau   **Population:** 275,000 (1995E)

The Bahamas gained independence from the United Kingdom in 1973. The head of state is the British sovereign, represented by a Governor-General, but effective executive authority is exercised by the Prime Minister and other ministers. Legislative power is vested in a bicameral parliament consisting of a popularly-elected 49–member House of Assembly and an appointed 16–member Senate. The victory of the Free National Movement (FNM). In the general election of Aug. 19, 1992, the Free National Movement came to power with a final tally of 34 Assembly seats, against 15 for the Progressive Liberal Party.

Free National Movement (FNM)
Address. POB N-10713, Nassau
Telephone. (#1–809) 393–7863
Leadership. Hubert Ingraham (leader)
The conservative FNM was founded in the early 1970s by the merger of the United Bahamian Party and an anti-independence dissident faction of the Progressive Liberal Party (PLP). Reconstituted in 1979 as the Free National Democratic Movement, the organization absorbed defectors from the Bahamian Democratic Party and the Social Democratic Party, and was recognized as the official opposition in 1981 (subsequently reverting to the name FNM). In the 1992 elections it won 33 seats in the House of Assembly, forming a new government under the premiership of the party leader (and later being awarded an additional seat).

Progressive Liberal Party (PLP)
Address. c/o House of Assembly, Nassau
Telephone. (#1–809) 325–2900

Leadership. Sir Lynden Pindling (leader)
The populist PLP was founded in 1953 as a mainly Black-supported party. A leading proponent of Bahamian independence, it came to power in 1967 and won a further four successive general elections on a platform of economic self-reliance and greater government involvement in a mixed economy. The party lost power in the 1992 elections when it secured only 16 of the 49 House of Assembly seats. In January 1993 the electoral court awarded one seat previously given to the PLP to the Free National Movement.

Other Parties

People's Democratic Force (PDF), launched in 1989 and led by Fred Mitchell.

Vanguard Nationalist and Socialist Party (VNSP), a left-wing group founded in 1971 and led by John McCartney.

Bahrain

Capital: Manama   **Population:** 520,000 (1995E)

The State of Bahrain, independent since 1971, is an absolute monarchy whose Emir governs through an appointed Cabinet. The 1973 constitution provides for a National Assembly consisting of the Cabinet and 30 other members to be elected by popular vote. However, the last National Assembly was dissolved in August 1975 for having conducted debates "dominated by ideas alien to the society and values of Bahrain". Under a limited political reform announced in December 1992, the Emir in January 1993 appointed a 30–member Consultative Council charged with offering "advice and opinion" on government legislation and also able to make legislative proposals of its own in certain areas. In the absence of legal political parties, there are a number of clandestine groups, mainly based in the majority Shia Muslim community and opposed to the government of the Sunni Muslim Emir. An outbreak of overt Shia opposition in December 1994 was firmly repressed by the authorities, but unrest continued in 1995-96.

Bangladesh

Capital: Dhaka   **Population:** 120,000,000 (1995E)

The People's Republic of Bangladesh achieved sovereignty in 1971, having previously formed the eastern part of Pakistan (which had become independent from Britain in 1947). After a brief period of parliamentary democracy until August 1975, the country was then ruled by a series of military dictatorships, albeit with increasing scope for party activity, until Lt.-Gen. (retd.) Hussain Mohammed Ershad was finally forced to resign in December 1990. Under amendments to the 1972 constitution approved by referendum in September 1991, full legislative authority was restored to the unicameral National Parliament (*Jatiya Sangsad*) of 330 members elected for a five-year term. Of these, 300 are returned from individual constituencies by universal suffrage of those aged 18 and over, and can be of either sex, and the other 30 are women elected by the directly-elected members. The country's President is elected by the *Jatiya Sangsad*, also for a five-year term, and has largely ceremonial powers. Executive power is vested in the Prime Minister and Council of Ministers, formally appointed by the President but responsible to the *Jatiya Sangsad*.

General elections to the *Jatiya Sangsad* on Feb. 27, 1991, together with immediate repolling for three seats and by-elections in 11 constituencies on Sept. 11, produced the following distribution of the 300 elective seats: Bangladesh Nationalist Party (BNP) 142; Awami League 91; National Party 35; Bangladesh Islamic Assembly 18; Communist Party of Bangladesh 5; National Socialist Party (Siraj) 1; Workers' Party of Bangladesh 1; National Awami League (Muzaffar) 1; independents 3; others 3. Of the 30 seats reserved for women, the BNP obtained 28 and the Bangladesh Islamic Assembly 2. After a long political crisis, general elections on Feb. 15, 1996, were boycotted by the main opposition parties and resulted in the ruling BNP winning an overwheling majority. Amid continuing deadlock, a new BNP government resigned at the end of March 1996, a neutral caretaker Prime Minister being appointed pending new elections on June 12. They resulted in the Awami League winning 146 of the 300 elective seats, the BNP 116, the National Party 32, the Bangladesh Islamic Assembly 3, the National Socialist Party–Rab 1, the Democratic Unity Alliance 1, an independent 1 and other parties 38. Of the 30 women's seats, the Awami League obtained 27 and the National Party 3.

Awami League (AL)

Address. 23 Bangabandha Avenue, Dhaka

Leadership. Sheikh Hasina Wazed (president), Zillur Rahman (general secretary)

The AL was founded in 1949 as the Awami (i.e. People's) Muslim League by left-wing Bengali nationalists opposed to the right-wing orientation of the Muslim League after the 1947 partition. It headed coalition governments in East Pakistan in 1956–58 and was concurrently represented in the central government, although it was weakened by secession of pro-Soviet elements in 1957 to form the National Awami Party. In elections held in 1970 the AL won 151 of the 153 East Pakistan seats in the central parliament on a pro-independence and secular platform. Led by Sheikh Mujibur Rahman, it then brought about the secession of what was renamed Bangladesh, assisted by the Indian Army, and became the ruling party on the establishment of the new state in

1971. In 1972 the AL underwent a split when young advocates of "scientific socialism" broke away to form the National Socialist Party. In January 1975 Sheikh Mujib introduced a presidential form of government and moved to a one-party system by creating the Bangladesh Peasants' and Workers' Awami League, within which all existing parties were required to operate. However, Sheikh Mujib was overthrown and killed by the military in August 1975, the AL being temporarily banned.

Resuming activity under the leadership of Sheikh Hasina (Mujib's daughter), the AL headed the Democratic United Front coalition which backed the candidacy of Gen. Mohammed Ataul Ghani Osmani in the June 1978 presidential election, won by Gen. Ziaur (Zia) Rahman of what became the Bangladesh Nationalist Party (BNP). In the 1979 parliamentary elections the AL won 40 of the 300 elective seats, while in the November 1981 presidential contest the AL candidate, Kamal Hossain, was officially credited with 25.4% of the vote in a disputed result. Following Lt.-Gen. Ershad's seizure of power in March 1982, the AL was prominent in demanding a return to democracy, forming a 15–party left-wing alliance, which in September 1983 joined the BNP and its allies in creating the Movement for the Restoration of Democracy (MRD). Leftist elements of the AL broke away in July 1983 to form the Peasants' and Workers' Awami League (which was reintegrated with the parent party in 1991).

MRD pressure produced a partial resumption of legal party activity from January 1986 and the calling of parliamentary elections for May 1986. But the MRD parties were divided on whether adequate concessions had been made, with the result that the BNP and its allies boycotted the poll whereas the AL and seven associated parties opted to participate, being credited with 76 of the 300 elective seats in disputed results. AL and other opposition members boycotted the opening of parliament in July in protest at the slow progress of democratization, setting up a "people's parliament", of which Sheikh Hasina was elected leader. Both the AL and the BNP boycotted the October 1986 presidential contest, after which efforts by the Ershad government to entice the AL to attend parliament were eventually rebuffed.

The AL was then a leading organizer of a series of mass demonstrations and strikes demanding Ershad's resignation, culminating in the "siege of Dhaka" of November 1987, when over two million opposition supporters sought to immobilize government activity in the capital, Sheikh Hasina being briefly held under house arrest as a result. Both main MRD parties declined to paticipate in the March 1988 parliamentary elections. Renewed opposition demonstrations from October 1990 yielded the departure of Ershad in December and the holding of parliamentary elections in February 1991, when the AL came a poor second to the BNP in terms of seats although with a similar percentage share of the popular vote. As the main opposition party, the AL came into renewed conflict with the BNP, accusing it of corruption and abuse of government power, but was weakened by the formation in August 1993 of the breakaway People's Forum. Local elections in January 1994 brought advances for the AL in Dhaka and elsewhere, while a BNP victory in a parliamentary by-election in March was hotly disputed by the AL on the grounds of alleged vote-rigging.

In September 1994 the AL took the lead in a new opposition campaign intended to force the government's resignation, the appointment of a neutral interim administration and the calling of new elections; to these ends it began a boycott of parliament in December 1994. Although this action was declared unconstitutional by the High Court, in January 1995 Sheikh Hasina declared the boycott "irrevocable" and the AL thereafter stepped up its campaign of strikes and other actions aimed at forcing new elections under a caretaker government. Elections eventually held in February 1996 were boycotted by the AL and the other main opposition parties, with the result that new elections were held in June. These produced a relative majority for the AL, enabling Sheikh Hasina to form a coalition government that included the National Party.

Bangladesh Islamic Assembly
Jamaat-i-Islami Bangladesh (JIB)
   Address. 505 Elephant Road, Bara Maghbazar, Dhaka 1217
   Leadership. Gholam Azam (president), Maulana Matiur Rahman Nizami (parliamentary leader)
   The JIB was originally founded in 1941 under the British Raj and opposed the creation of a separate Muslim state as being contrary to the principles of Islam. It combined this line with pronounced anti-Hindu and anti-Indian attitudes. After the 1947 partition its main strength was in West Pakistan, but Gholam Azam built up a considerable following in East Pakistan. Opposed to the secular socialism and Bengali nationalism of the Awami League (AL), the JIB campaigned against the Bangladesh independence movement in 1970–71. On the creation of the new state, the party was banned and Azam was deprived of his citizenship for alleged collaboration with Pakistan.

Following the overthrow of the AL government by the military in 1975, the JIB regained legal status in 1977 within the Islamic Democratic League, but was weakened in 1978 when its dominant liberal wing joined the new Bangladesh

50

Nationalist Party. The party's fundamentalist wing responded by relaunching the JIB in May 1979 under the leadership of Abbas Ali Khan as proxy for Azam, who had returned from exile. After the March 1982 military coup, the JIB maintained its distance from the main opposition alliances, although it made similar demands that the Ershad regime should restore democracy. In the May 1986 parliamentary elections JIB candidates were returned in 10 of the 300 elective seats.

The resignation of Ershad in December 1990 served to sharpen the JIB's Islamist profile, which in the 1991 parliamentary elections yielded 18 elective seats and, by dint of post-election co-operation with the BNP, two of the 30 seats reserved for women. In December 1991 Azam was elected to resume the party leadership, even though his lack of Bangladeshi citizenship made this technically illegal. Popular pressure then mounted, led by the AL, for Azam to be brought to trial for crimes allegedly committed during the 1970–71 independence struggle. Such demands were resisted by the BNP government, which accepted a High Court ruling in April 1993 that Azam should be granted citizenship (this being upheld by the Supreme Court in June 1994).

In 1994 the JIB was prominent in the fundamentalist campaign against the Bangladeshi writer Taslima Nasreen for alleged defamation of Islam in a novel. In 1995 the party participated in AL-led strikes and civil disobedience aimed at forcing the government's resignation and the calling of new elections. Elections eventually held in February 1996 were boycotted by the JIB and the other main opposition parties.

Bangladesh Nationalist Party (BNP)
Bangladesh Jatiyatabadi Dal
    Address. Sattar House, 19/A Road No. 16, Dhanmondi R/A, Dhaka 9
    Leadership. Begum Khaleda Zia (chair), Prof. A.Q.M. Badruddoza Chaudhury (vice-chair), Abdus Salam Talukder (general secretary)

The centre-right BNP was launched in September 1978 by the then President, Gen. Ziaur (Zia) Rahman, on the basis of the Nationalist Front which had successfully campaigned for his election in June 1978. In the parliamentary elections of February 1979 the BNP obtained 49% of the vote and two-thirds of the seats on a platform of inscribing Islam into the constitution and pursuing social justice rather than socialism. Martial law and the state of emergency were lifted in the course of 1979, and the BNP attracted various defectors from other parties. President Zia was assassinated in May 1981 in an apparent coup attempt and was succeeded by Vice-President Abdus Sattar, senior BNP vice-chair, who secured

a popular mandate in presidential elections in November 1981. On Lt.-Gen. Ershad's seizure of power in March 1982 the BNP went into opposition, joining with the Awami League (AL) and other parties in creating the Movement for the Restoration of Democracy (MRD) in September 1983. In January 1984 Begum Khaleda, the late President's widow, succeeded Sattar as leader of the main BNP (the party having in 1983 suffered defections by elements opposed to confrontation with the Ershad regime).

MRD pressure produced a partial resumption of legal party activity from January 1986 and the calling of parliamentary elections for May 1986. But the MRD parties were divided on whether adequate concessions had been made, with the result that the BNP and its allies boycotted the poll whereas the AL and its major allies opted to participate. MRD co-operation resumed after the legislative elections and both the BNP and the AL boycotted the October 1986 presidential contest. The BNP was then in the forefront of a series of mass demonstrations and strikes demanding Ershad's resignation, culminating in the "siege of Dhaka" of November 1987 when over two million MRD supporters sought to immobilize government activity in the capital, Begum Khaleda being briefly held under house arrest as a result. Both main MRD parties declined to paticipate in the March 1988 parliamentary elections, after which the BNP was again distracted by internal factionalism.

Renewed opposition demonstrations from October 1990 yielded the departure of Ershad in December. In parliamentary elections in February 1991 the BNP ended up with a comfortable majority of seats (although it took only some 35% of the popular vote) and Begum Khaleda was sworn in as the country's first woman Prime Minister. In October 1991 the BNP nominee, Abdur Rahman Biswas, was elected President by the new *Jatiya Sangsad*). In government, the BNP dropped its previous aim of restoring presidential government but found itself in renewed conflict with the AL, now the main opposition party. It was also, in 1993, accused of corruption and abuse of power, while facing increasing hostility from Islamic groups. Local elections in January 1994 brought setbacks for the BNP in Dhaka and elsewhere at the hands of the AL. A BNP victory in a parliamentary by-election in March was hotly disputed by the AL, which alleged official vote-rigging.

From May 1994 the BNP government faced an opposition boycott of parliament and other protest action aimed at forcing early general elections. Amid mounting pressure, Begum Khaleda in September 1995 offered to hold talks with the opposition parties, while rejecting their demand for a caretaker government. As civil disturbances continued, President Biswas in November 1995 announced the dissolution of parliament, preparatory to general elections that were eventually held in February 1996. With the main opposition parties boycotting the poll, the BNP won almost all the elective seats and formed a new government under Begum Khaleda. However, amid undiminished civil disobedience by the opposition, the BNP leader resigned at the end of March, giving way to a neutral caretaker Prime Minister until new elections in June, in which the BNP was decisively defeated.

Communist Party of Bangladesh (CPB)

Address. 21/1 Purana Paltan, Dhaka 2

Leadership. Mujahidul Islam Selim (general secretary)

The CPB was founded in 1948 as the East Pakistan section of the Communist Party of Pakistan (CPP), itself an offshoot of the Communist Party of India. The party was illegal for most of its early pro-Soviet history, although it had several members elected to the East Pakistan Assembly in 1954 as candidates of a four-party Unity Front. Driven underground by the promulgation of martial law in October 1958, the CPP virtually ceased to exist as an organized party in West Pakistan and was further weakened by the secession of its pro-Chinese wing in the mid-1960s. In East Pakistan the pro-Soviet wing in 1968 formed an independent party, which was renamed the CPB on the creation of Bangladesh in 1971 and became a legal party supportive of the Awami League (AL) government. Following the overthrow of the latter in 1975, the CPB was again banned in 1977, before achieving a degree of legality in 1978. In April 1980 the party's then general secretary and 52 other leading members were arrested on sedition charges.

In the wake of the March 1982 military coup, the CPB joined the 15–party alliance of left-wing opposition parties headed by the AL and participated actively in the campaign for a return to democracy. It was one of the eight parties of this alliance, including the AL, which contested the May 1986 elections, its tally of six seats being the party's first-ever representation in its own name. Thereafter the CPB remained closely allied with the AL, joining the general opposition boycott of the March 1988 parliamentary elections. Following the exit of President Ershad in December 1990 and the restoration of parliamentary democracy, the CPB won five of the 300 elective seats in the 1991 parliamentary elections. Meanwhile, the collapse of communism in Europe had inspired new thinking in the party leadership, with then leader Saifuddin Ahmed

Manik advocating the abandonment of Marxism-Leninism but being opposed by a majority of the CPB central committee. Eventually, in June 1993, the Manik faction broke away, later joining the new People's Forum, while in April 1994 the rump CPB became a component of the Left Democratic Front.

Democratic Unity Alliance

Ganotantrik Oikya Jote (GOJ)

Leadership. Rotating

This assemblage of nine mainly centre-right parties was launched in October 1994, none of them having parliamentary representation. It was headed by the National People's Party (*Jatiya Janata Dal*, JJD), which had been founded in 1976 by the Bangladeshi military commander in the 1971 war of independence, Gen. (retd.) Mohammed Ataul Ghani Osmani, who won over four million votes in the 1978 presidential election and 300,000 in 1981. Following his death in 1985, the JJD had entered a fissiparous phase, splitting into at least four factions. The other major GOJ component was the National Awami Party (Bhashani) (NAP-B), descended from the original NAP founded in 1957 by Awami League dissidents led by Maulana Abdul Hamid Khan Bhashani and more especially from a pro-Chinese minority faction which in 1967 broke away from what became the National Awami Party (Muzaffar). Following the death of Maulana Bhashani in 1976, the NAP-B had itself split into numerous factions laying claim to his name. The new GOJ won a single seat in the June 1996 elections.

Left Democratic Front (LDF)

Bam Ganotantrik Front

Address. c/o Jatiya Sangsad, Dhaka

Leadership. Rotates monthly between constituent party leaders

The LDF was launched in April 1994 as an alliance of eight left-orientated parties, namely: the faction of the National Socialist Party (JSD) led by Hasanul Huq Inu; the Communist Party of Bangladesh led by Mujahidul Islam Selim; the Bangladesh Socialist Party (Khaleque) led by Khalequzzaman Bhuiyan; the Bangladesh Socialist Party (Mahbub) led by A.F.M. Mahbubul Huq; the Workers' Party of Bangladesh (WPB) led by Rashed Khan Menon; the Workers' and Peasants' Socialist Party (*Krishak Sramik Samajbadi Dal*, KSSD) led by Nirmal Sen; the Equalitarian Party (*Samyabadi Dal*) led by Dilip Barua; and the Unifying Process (*Oikya Prokria*, OP) led by Nayeem Jahangir.

Of these constituent formations, the JSD (Inu) had opposed participation in the 1986 elections, whereas they were contested by the Siraj and Rab factions of the JSD. The Bangladesh Socialist Party (*Bangladesh Samajtantrik Dal*, BSD) had been formed as the result of a 1980 split in the JSD and had itself later split into two groups, both of which had refused to follow the Awami League (AL), to which they were then allied, in contesting the 1986 elections. The KSSD, dating from 1969, had also been allied with the AL after the 1982 Ershad coup but had also declined to contest the 1986 elections. The OP leader had previously been convenor of the Independence Party (*Swadhinata Dal*).

The LDF participated in the opposition campaign to bring about the resignation of the Zia government, calling a strike in April 1995 that paralysed Dhaka and other major cities.

National Awami Party (Muzaffar) (NAP-M)

Address. 20 Dhanmondi Hawkers Market, Dhaka 5

Leadership. Muzaffar Ahmed (president), Pankaj Bhattacharya (general secretary)

The NAP was originally founded in 1957 by a leftist, anti-Western faction of the Awami League (AL) led by Maulana Abdul Hamid Khan Bhashani. In 1967 the NAP split into a pro-Soviet majority led by Muzaffar and a pro-Chinese minority led by Maulana Bhashani. The NAP-M took an active part in the 1971 independence struggle and adopted a policy of "constructive opposition" to the post-independence AL government. Having won one parliamentary seat in the 1979 elections, the NAP-M joined the AL-led alliance which opposed the post-1982 Ershad military regime and was one of eight opposition parties to contest the 1986 elections, winning two seats. Following the restoration of parliamentary democracy in 1990, the NAP-M won one seat in the 1991 elections.

National Democratic Alliance (NDA)

Address. 68 Jigatola Road, Dhaka 9

Leadership. Khandaker Moshtaque Ahmed (leader), Lt.-Col. (retd.) Khandaker Abdur Rashid (chair)

The NDA was created in February 1993 as an alliance of 10 Islamic parties of conservative and moderate Islamist orientation, headed by Moshtaque Ahmed's own Democratic (*Ganotantrik*) League and the Freedom Party of Abdur Rashid. It also embraced the Progressive Democratic Force (*Progotishil Ganotantrik Shakti*, PROGOSH) led by Lt.-Col. (retd.) Shariar Rashid Khan; two factions of the National Democratic Party (*Jatiya Ganotantrik* Party), one led by Shafiul Alam Prodhan and designated JAGPA, the other led by Salahuddin Qader Chaudhury and designated NDP; the Progressive Nationalist

Party (*Progotishil Jatiyatabadi Dal*, PJD) led by Shawkat Hossain Nilu; the Peasant Subjects' (*Krishak Proja*) Party led by A.S.M. Solaiman; a faction of the Muslim League; the Bangladesh Caliphate Movement (*Khelafat Andolan*) led by Maulana Mohammed Ullah Hafezji Huzur; and the Islamic Constitutional Movement (*Islami Shashontontro Andolan*, ISA) led the Pir of Charmonai.

Moshtaque Ahmed was briefly President of Bangladesh following the overthrow of Sheikh Mujubur Rahman's Awami League (AL) government in August 1975 and founded the Democratic League the following year. He spent 1977–80 in prison following a conviction for corruption and abuse of power, the League being banned in 1977–78. Following the Ershad military coup of March 1982, Moshtaque Ahmed became leader of the National Unity Front (NUF) of right-wing opposition parties, which mostly boycotted the May 1986 elections. In the 1980s the Democratic League was weakened by two splits, one breakaway group objecting to the leader's alleged co-operative attitude towards the Ershad regime and the other allying itself with the Bangladesh Nationalist Party (BNP). Nevertheless, Moshtaque Ahmed relaunched the NUF in 1991 as a precursor to what became the NDA.

Abdur Rashid was one of the three principal leaders (the so-called "majors") of the 1975 coup, in which Sheikh Mujib and members of his family were killed; on their own overthrow in November 1975 the "majors" were allowed to seek exile in Libya. Following his return to Bangladesh in, Abdur Rashid backed the unsuccessful presidential bid of fellow "major" Sayed Faruq Rahman (now a lieutenant-general) in October 1986, although his million-plus votes encouraged the two to launch the Freedom Party in August 1987. Its supporters clashed frequently with those of the AL, whose leader, Sheikh Hasina Wajed, consistently demanded that the "majors" should be brought to trial for her father's murder. The PROGOSH leader, Rashid Khan, was also one of the "majors" of 1975, while the National Democratic Party had been founded in 1980 by former AL student elements that gravitated to the right in the Zia era.

The PJD had been founded by BNP dissidents who wished to contest the 1986 elections (in which they were unsuccessful). The leader of the *Krishak Proja* Party had previously headed a faction of the Peasants' and Workers' Party (*Krishak Sramik Dal*, KSD), descended from Bengal's first peasant party founded in 1914. The NDA's Muslim League component consisted of some of the elements of the historic party which had rejected incorporation into the National Party prior to the 1986

53

elections. The Caliphate Movement had been founded by Maulana Hafezji Huzur in 1981 to his support presidential candidacy that year, which yielded some 387,000 votes and inspired him to stand again in October 1986, when he came second with some 1,500,000 votes. Meanwhile, the Movement had fielded 43 candidates in the May 1986 parliamentary elections, none being elected amid a split which produced a breakaway group led by Azizul Huq.

National Party
Jatiya Dal

Address. 104 Road No. 3, Dhanmondi R/A, Dhaka 9

Leadership. Lt.-Gen. (retd.) Mohammad Ershad (leader), Mizanur Rahman Chowdhury (acting chair), Raushan Ershad (presidium member), Anwar Hossain Manju (general secretary)

The *Jatiya Dal* was launched in January 1986 as a political base for Lt.-Gen. Ershad, who had seized power in March 1982, and succeeded an earlier National Front of pro-Ershad formations headed by the People's Party (*Jana Dal*), itself launched in November 1983, and including the United People's Party, the Democratic Party and breakaway factions of the Bangladesh Nationalist Party (BNP) and the Muslim League. The new formation, which was joined by all the then government ministers, advocated national unity on the basis of independence and sovereignty, faith in Islam, nationalism, democracy and social progress. In the May 1986 parliamentary elections the *Jatiya Dal* won 180 of the 300 elective seats and all 30 of those reserved for women. In September 1986 Ershad was elected as party chair (having resigned as Army Chief of Staff) and the following month was returned as President with 83.6% of the vote in a presidential election boycotted by the main opposition parties.

Having gained an even bigger majority (251 elective seats) in the March 1988 parliamentary elections, which were also boycotted by the opposition, the *Jatiya Dal* government was gradually paralysed by renewed popular agitation. Shunned by opposition leaders and in the end deserted by the military establishment, Ershad resigned in December 1990 and was later arrested, put on trial, sentenced and convicted, together with several close associates. The *Jatiya Dal* continued in business under new management, which in January 1991 "begged forgiveness" from the people for the Ershad years. In the February 1991 parliamentary elections, the party won 35 of the 300 elective seats, with some 10% of the popular vote, and became part of the opposition to the new BNP government. In September 1993 a pro-Ershad faction of the party formed the National Party (Nationalist), which quickly established control of the party as such.

In 1994-95 the *Jatiya Dal* participated in the opposition campaign to force the resignation of the Zia government and the calling of new elections. In April 1995 it called a strike on its own account following the killing of one of its leaders in Khulna. Having joined the opposition boycott of the February 1996 elections, the *Jatiya Dal* won 32 elective seats in the June contest (and a further three women's seats). It then opted to join a coalition government headed by the Awami League, reportedly in return for a promise that Ershad would be released on parole, which he was soon afterwards. Taken by Ershad, the decision to accept office generated some internal internal dissent and provoked the resignation from the party of its former parliamentary leader, Moudad Ahmed.

National Socialist Party (Rab)
Jatiya Samajtantric Dal (Rab) (JSD-Rab)

Address. c/o Jatiya Sangsad, Dhaka

Leadership. A.S.M. Abdul Rab

The JSD-Rab is derived from one of the several factions of the original JSD, which had been founded in 1972 by young Awami League dissidents, including Abdul Rab and Shajahan Siraj, who espoused notions of scientific socialism. They contended that the capitalist class was maintaining "monopolistic" economic and political power through "controlled democracy" in alliance with "imperialism", in the struggle against which the armed forces had a legitimate role to play. The JSD gained an urban following for its militant opposition to the AL government and was banned in 1975 after its armed wing, called the Revolutionary People's Army, had allegedly attempted to seize power. It welcomed the military coup of August 1975 and played a prominent role in elevating Gen. Ziaur (Zia) Rahman to power later that year. Nevertheless, Gen. Zia disowned the JSD, whose leaders were arrested and brought to trial in 1976 on sedition charges, one being executed. Reactivated from November 1978, the JSD won nine of the 300 elective seats in the February 1979 elections, but its presidential candidate in November 1981 forfeited his deposit.

JSD factional strife intensified following the Ershad military takeover of March 1982, with the result that in January 1984 Abdul Rab formed the breakaway JSD (Rab), the rump party becoming known as the JSD (Siraj). Both factions joined the Movement for the Restoration of Democracy and were among the eight AL-led opposition parties which contested the May 1986 elections, the JSD (Rab) obtaining four seats and the JSD (Siraj) three. Thereafter, both factions adhered to the general opposition boycott of the electoral process under the Ershad regime, although they ceased to be formally allied with the AL. Following the restoration of democracy, the JSD (Siraj) won one seat in the 1991 parliamentary elections but the JSD (Rab) failed to register. In August 1993 the JSD (Siraj) became part of the People's Forum and another faction led by Hasanul Huq Inu joined the new Left Democratic Front in April 1994. In contrast, the JSD (Rab) remained a separate formation, won one seat in the June 1996 elections and was included in the new coalition headed by the AL (Abdul Rab becoming Minister of Special Affairs).

People's Forum (PF)
Gano Forum
Address. 23 DIT Road, Malibagh, Dhaka
Leadership. Kamal Hossain (chair)

The PF was founded in August 1993 by a dissident faction of the Awami League (AL) led by Kamal Hossain, who had been the first Law Minister of independent Bangladesh, the framer of its constitution and later Foreign Minister in the 1971–75 AL government. Advocating "violence-free politics, economic progress at the grass-roots and basic amenities for all", the new party backed the demand of the main opposition parties that the next general elections should be held under a caretaker government (i.e. one not controlled by the Bangladesh Nationalist Party). Influential PF recruits included Saifuddin Ahmed

Manik, who had vacated the leadership of the Communist Party of Bangladesh after failing to persuade it to renounce Marxism-Leninism. The PF also included the faction of the National Socialist Party led by Shajahan Siraj, which had won one seat in the 1991 elections.

Workers' Party of Bangladesh (WPB)
Address. 31/E-F Topkhana Road, Dhaka
Leadership. Rashed Khan Menon (general secretary)

Originally Marxist-Leninist in orientation, the WPB won one seat in the 1979 parliamentary elections and joined the left-wing alliance headed by the Awami League (AL) which opposed the post-1982 Ershad military regime. It broke with the AL by refusing to contest the May 1986 elections and later joined a five-party alliance of left-wing parties opposed to electoral politics while Ershad remained in power. Meanwhile, a WPB faction favouring electoral participation had broken away under the leadership of Nazrul Islam and had won three seats in the 1986 poll. The WPB secured only one seat in the 1991 elections, won by Menon himself, and in April 1994 became a member of the eight-party Left Democratic Front opposed to the government of the Bangladesh Nationalist Party.

Barbados

Capital: Bridgetown   **Population:** 260,000 (1995E)

Barbados gained independence from the United Kingdom in 1966. The head of state is the British sovereign, represented by a Governor-General, with effective executive power residing in the Prime Minister and the government. Legislative power is vested in a bicameral parliament, consisting of a 28–member House of Assembly elected every five years by universal adult suffrage, and a 21–member Senate. Senators are appointed to office by the Governor-General (12 on the advice of the Prime Minister, two on that of the Leader of the Opposition, and seven at the discretion of the Governor-General to represent social, religious and economic interests).

In a premature general election held on Sept. 6, 1994, the main opposition Barbados Labour Party returned to power with 19 of the Assembly seats, against the Democratic Labour Party's 8 and the National Democratic Party's 1.

Barbados Labour Party (BLP)
Address. Grantley Adams House, 111 Roebuck Street, Bridgetown
Telephone. (#1–809) 429-1990
Fax. (#1-809) 437-8792

Leadership. Owen Arthur (leader), Louis R. Tull (chair), Pat Thorington (general secretary)

Founded in 1938, the moderate, social democratic BLP held office in the pre-independence period from 1951 to 1961 under the leadership of

Sir Grantley Adams. It then went into opposition until the 1976 elections when, led by J.M.G. (Tom) Adams (Sir Grantley's son), it was returned to power. The party was affected by factional splits after Tom Adams's death in 1985 and was defeated heavily in the polls the following year, thereafter remaining in opposition until the general election in September 1994. The party, under Owen Arthur's leadership (from July 1993), then won 19 of the 28 House of Assembly seats with just over 48% of the votes cast, thus returning to power after eight years in opposition.

The BLP is a full member party of the Socialist International.

Democratic Labour Party (DLP)

Address. George Street, Belleville, St Michael
Telephone. (#1–809) 429-3104
Leadership. David Thompson (leader)

With a democratic socialist orientation, the DLP was formed in 1955 principally by dissident members of the Barbados Labour Party disenchanted with the leadership. Between 1961 and 1976 it was the governing party (during which time it led Barbados to independence), but then spent the following ten years in opposition before returning to power in the 1986 elections on an essentially right-of-centre programme. The then party leader and Prime Minister, Errol Barrow,

died in 1987 and was succeeded by Erskine Sandiford. The party won the 1991 elections, but suffered a resounding defeat in the September 1994 polls (called early by Sandiford in response to an internal DLP revolt). Leadership of the party, whose parliamentary strength fell to eight seats, was assumed by David Thompson.

National Democratic Party (NDP)

Address. 3 Sixth Avenue, Belleville
Telephone. (#1–809) 429 6882
Leadership. Richard (Richie) Haynes (leader)

The NDP was formed in February 1989 following the resignation of Dr. Haynes (a former finance minister) and three other parliamentary deputies from the then ruling Democratic Labour Party. The party lost its four seats in the 1991 elections, but regained one (with nearly 13% of the votes cast) in the 1994 polls.

Other Parties

People's Pressure Movement (PPM), a small grouping established in 1979.

Workers Party of Barbados (WPB), a socialist party formed in 1985 by George Belle.

Belarus

Capital: Minsk

Population: 10,500,000 (1995E)

The Soviet Socialist Republic of Byelorussia declared independence in August 1991, adopted the name Republic of Belarus the following month and became a sovereign member of the Commonwealth of Independent States (CIS) on the demise of the USSR in December 1991. The ruling republican Communist Party was suspended at independence and, on its revival in 1993, appeared to have lost the allegiance of most of the Soviet-era personnel who remained in control of government and state structures. A new constitution approved in March 1994 defines Belarus as "a unitary, democratic, socially-oriented, law-governed state". It provides for an executive President, who is directly elected by universal adult suffrage for a five-year term (once renewable) and appoints the Prime Minister and Council of Ministers. Under legislation and amendments enacted in February and May 1995, the President may be impeached and removed from office in certain circumstances, but has the right to dissolve the legislature "in the event of systematic or gross violation of the constitution". The legislature is the unicameral Supreme Council of 260 members, also directly elected for a five-year term in two rounds of voting, with successful candidates requiring an overall majority in a turnout of more than 50% of eligible voters.

In presidential elections in June-July 1994, an independent candidate, Alyaksandr Lukashenka, was elected in the second round with 80.1% of the vote against 14.1% for another independent candidate. In November 1994 the Belarusan Patriotic Movement (BPR) was launched with the aim of providing political support for President Lukashenka. In legislative elections on May 14 and 28, 1995, well under half of the 260 seats were filled, whereas a complement of two-thirds was required for the new body to be quorate. Further elections on Nov. 29 and Dec. 10, 1995, increased the number of seats properly filled to 198 (i.e. above the quorum threshold), the results showing that pro-government parties, including the Communist Party of Belarus (42 seats) and the Agrarian Party of Belarus (33 seats), held an overall majority.

Agrarian Party of Belarus

Agrarnaya Partiya Belarusi (APB)

Address. c/o Supreme Council, Minsk

Leadership. Syamyon Sharetski (chair)

Established in 1994, the APB provides a national political framework for agrarian interests associated with the communist-era agricultural system, being opposed in particular to the restoration of individual peasant ownership of the land. It emerged as the most powerful agrarian party in the 1995 legislative elections, winning 33 seats. In January 1996 APB leader Sharetski was elected to the chairmanship of the new Supreme Council.

All-Belarusan Party of People's Unity and Accord

Usebelaruskaya Partiya Narodnaya Adzinstva i Zgody (UPNAZ)

Address. c/o Supreme Council, Minsk

Leadership. Dzmitry Bulakhau (chair)

Founded in 1994, the centrist UPNAZ contested the first rounds of the 1995 parliamentary elections as part of the alliance which later became the United Civic Party of Belarus. After the third round it was credited with winning two seats in its own right.

Belarusan Patriotic Movement

Belaruski Patryatychny Rukh (BPR)

Address. c/o Supreme Council, Minsk

Leadership. Mikhail Chyrhir (chair)

The BPR was launched in November 1994 as a new party dedicated to supporting President Lukashenka, who had been elected earlier in the year as an independent. Having come to prominence as an anti-corruption parliamentarian, Lukashenka had appointed Mikhail Chyrhir, a pro-market reformer, as Prime Minister and had promised early parliamentary elections; but his espousal of more traditional theses was apparent in his declared preference for "a state-regulated economy", his strong advocacy of full economic union with Russia and his support for the retention of the Russian military presence in Belarus. The BPR aspired in particular to attract those in the state bureaucracy and elsewhere who had been disinclined to declare specific political allegiance following the demise of the Communist-run Soviet system. The party gave strong backing to the signature in Minsk in February 1995 of a Belarusan-Russian friendship treaty, together with treaties on joint border protection and the creation of a single administration to run the two states' customs union created in April 1994. Shortly after the signature, President Lukashenka cited the aspiration of neighbouring Poland and Lithuania to join NATO as reason for closer security co-operation between Belarus and Russia. As regards the President's political leanings, Western press reports claimed that he was ideologically close to the radical Russian nationalist Vladimir Zhirinovsky, leader of the Liberal Democratic Party of Russia.

In four referendums held on May 14, 1995, popular endorsement was given to BPR plans for closer links with Russia and also to an extension of presidential powers. In the protracted legislative elections of 1995, pro-Lukashenka forces won an overall majority in the new chamber, the BPR itself being credited with only one seat, although many of the 95 deputies elected without party attribution belonged to the presidential tendency.

Belarusan Peasants' Party

Belaruskaya Syalanskaya Partiya (BSP)

Address. Gaya 38, PO Box 333, 220108 Minsk

Telephone. (#7–0172) 771905

Fax. (#7-0172) 779651

Leadership. Yaugen Lugin (chair), Mikhail Antanenka (deputy chair)

The BSP was founded in 1990 as a reincarnation of the pre-Soviet agrarian movement, pledged to securing the restoration of peasant land ownership. It associated itself with the opposition Belarusan Popular Front—Revival in the pressure for political and economic reform. In the 1994 presidential elections, however, it presented its own candidate, Alyaksandr Dubko (chair of the Agrarian Union of Belarus), who won 6% of the first-round vote in June. In the 1995 legislative elections, the BSP was heavily outpolled by the pro-collectivism Agrarian Party of Belarus, winning only one seat.

Belarusan Popular Front–Revival

Narodni Front Belarusi–Adradzhennie (NFB-A)

Address. PO Box 208, 220040 Minsk

Telephone. (#7–0172) 314893

Fax. (#7–0172) 395869

Leadership. Zyanon Paznyak (president), Vintsuk Viachorka (secretary)

The NFB-A was launched in June 1989 (as the NFB) at a conference held in Vilnius (Lithuania) of representatives of groups and organizations united by the belief that Belarus should be governed by its own independent authorities rather than by Moscow. The then Communist Party regime had refused to allow the conference to be held in the republic and had denounced its organizers as "extremists". Elected party leader at the Vilnius session was Zyanon Paznyak, an archaeologist who in 1988 had published evidence of mass graves found at Kurapaty, near Minsk, on the site of a detention/execution camp established on Stalin's orders in 1937. Founding or subsequent NFB-A participating parties included the Belarusan Christian Democratic Union, the Belarusan Peasants' Party, the Belarusan Social Democratic Party, the Movement for Democratic Reforms, the National Democratic Party and the United Democratic Party of Belarus. Other participating organizations included the Belarusan Association of Servicemen and the Writers' Union of Belarus.

As European communism began to crumble from late 1989, the new movement had some impact in Belarus, where Belarusan replaced Russian as the official language in January 1990 and where opposition candidates were allowed to run in the April 1990 Supreme Soviet elections. However, the entrenched position of the Communist Party enabled it to win a large majority, the NFB-A being confined to 34 seats in the 360–member legislature. Thereafter, the NFB-A sought to accelerate the government's hesitant moves to assert sovereignty and was strongly critical of its initial support for the attempted coup by hardliners in Moscow in August 1991. It therefore welcomed the resultant downfall of the Minsk conservatives and the advent of the Shushkevich government, supporting the latter's declaration of independence in late August. But the simultaneous suspension of the Communist Party deprived the opposition of a valuable target: although effectively a continuation of the previous regime, the new government could depict itself as independent.

Remaining in opposition, the NFB-A concentrated on attacking the sluggish pace of political and economic reform. In 1992 and 1993 it twice collected the requisite 350,000 signatures for the holding of a referendum on early multi-party elections, but neither petition was accepted by a legislature dominated by conservative elements under the umbrella of the Popular Movement of Belarus. The NFB-A opposed the new presidential constitution introduced in March 1994, on the grounds that a democratic parliament had not yet been elected. It also opposed the treaty on monetary union with Russia signed by the government in April and Belarusan participation in the CIS security pact. In the direct presidential elections of June-July 1994, Paznyak stood as the NFB-A candidate but received only 13.8% of the first-round vote and was eliminated. In the second round, NFB-A support swung overwhelmingly behind Alyaksandr Lukashenka as being the more reformist of the two candidates on offer.

Opposed to the government's policy of close integration with Russia, the NFB-A won no seats in the 1995 parliamentary elections. Following the signature of a treaty of union by Belarus and Russia in April 1996, NFB-A leaders came under pressure from the authorities for organizing anti-government protests.

As a pluralist organization that includes a strong Christian democratic current, the NFB-A is affiliated to the Christian Democrat International.

Belarusan Social Democratic Party
Satsiyal-Demokratychnaya Partiya Belarusi (SDPB/Hramada)
  Address. Partizansky 83/53, 220026 Minsk
  Telephone. (#7–0172) 464691
  Fax. (#7-0172) 457852
  Leadership. Mykola Statkevich (chair)

The SDPB was founded in 1991 as a latter-day revival of the Revolutionary *Hramada* (Assembly) Party (founded in 1903), which spearheaded the early movement for the creation of a Belarusan state but was outlawed following the declaration of the Soviet Socialist Republic in January 1919. The revived party, also known as the *Hramada*, participated in the opposition Belarusan Popular Front, supporting the latter's unsuccessful candidate in the first round of the June-July 1994 presidential elections. In the 1995 legislative elections it won two seats and later increased its parliamentary group to 15 members.

Communist Party of Belarus
Kommunisticheskaya Partiya Belarusi (KPB)
  Address. Lunacharskaga 5, 220071 Minsk
  Telephone. (#7-0172) 337757
  Fax. (#7-0172) 323123
  Leadership. Syarhei Kalyakin (parliamentary chair), Vasil Novikau (1994 presidential candidate)

The Soviet-era Communist Party had originated as a regional committee of the Russian Social Democratic Labour Party (formed in 1904) covering both Belarus and Lithuania. Established as the ruling Communist Party of the Soviet Socialist Republic of Byelorussia in 1920, the party suffered heavily during Stalin's terror of the 1930s, when almost all of its leaders were liquidated and party membership fell by more than half. Enlarged by Soviet territorial acquisitions from Poland in World War II, the Byelorussian SSR was given UN membership in 1945 but its ruling party and government remained wholly subservient to Moscow. From mid-1989 the republican leadership came under official Soviet criticism for lacking "tolerance. . .and readiness to make compromises". It therefore allowed candidates of the opposition Belarusan Popular Front—Revival (NFB-A) to contest the April 1990 Supreme Soviet elections, correctly calculating that its control of the levers of power would ensure a decisive Communist victory. But the conservative Minsk leadership miscalculated when it backed the abortive coup by hardliners in Moscow in August 1991. In the immediate aftermath, the hardline Chairman of the Supreme Soviet (head of state), Nikalai Dzementsei, was replaced by the reformist Stanislau Shushkevich; independence from the USSR was declared; the first secretary of the republican Communist Party, Anatol Malofeev, resigned from the Soviet politburo; and the party itself was suspended and its property nationalized.

The party remained under suspension for 18 months, although the government structure and the legislature continued to be under the control of people appointed or elected as Communists. At government level, Shushkevich came into increasingly bitter dispute with the hardline Prime Minister, Vyacheslau Kebich, who commanded majority support from the so-called Belarus Group of conservative deputies for his resistance to political and economic reform. The re-legalization of the Communist Party in February 1993 did little to clarify true allegiance, in part because government members preferred to retain the "independent" label. There were, moreover, competing versions of the party owing to a leadership dispute: in addition to the party led by Novikau as chair and Malofeev as (again) first secretary, another faction emerged under the leadership of Viktor Chykin, who in October 1993 founded the Movement for Democracy, Social Progress and Justice as a merger of seven hardline communist groups. However, the various factions came under the umbrella of the loose alliance of conservative parties called the Popular Movement of Belarus (NDB), which backed the ousting of Shushkevich in January 1994 and his replacement by hardliner Mechyslau Hryb. According to Shushkevich, this change marked "the restoration of *nomenklatura* power".

Having embraced the concept of multipartyism, the Novikau-Malofeev KPB contested the June-July 1994 presidential elections in its own right, with Novikau as candidate. Its problem was that voters had other "establishment" candidates to choose from, including Kebich and Shushkevich, both standing as independents. The result of the first round was last place out of six candidates for Novikau, who managed only 4.6% of the vote. But forecasts that *"nomenklatura* power" would ensure victory for Kebich proved wide of the mark: relegated to a poor second place in the first round, he was heavily defeated in the second by another independent, Alyaksandr Lukashenka, a moderate conservative who in his parliamentary role as anti-corruption supremo had played a key role in the ousting of Shushkevich. Lukashenka subsequently received the support of the new "presidential" Belarusan Patriotic Movement, but the KPB's stronger organization enabled it to become the largest formal party in the 1995 legislative elections, in which it won 42 seats.

Liberal Democratic Party of Belarus
Liberalna-Demokratychnaya Partiya Belarusi (LDPB)
Address. 2 Pyaschanaya 9, 220091 Minsk
Telephone. (#7-0172) 695909
Fax. (#7-0172) 477257
Leadership. Vasil Kryvenkiy (chair)
The right-wing pan-Slavic LDPD is the Belarus fraternal party of the Liberal Democratic Party of Russia and therefore advocates close links with Russia. It is a component of the conservative Popular Movement for Belarus.

National Democratic Party of Belarus
Natsyianal-Demokratychnaya Partiya Belarusi (NDPB)
Address. Timashenka 24, 220116 Minsk
Telephone. (#7-0172) 570823
Fax. (#7-0172) 369972
Leadership. Anatoly Astapenka, Viktar Naumenko, Uladzimir Astapenka, Mikola Mikhnouski
The NDPB was founded in 1990 as a pro-market, nationalist formation seeking the political and cultural renaissance of Belarus. It became a member of the Belarusan Popular Front—Revival.

Party of People's Accord
Partiya Narodnaya Zgody (PNZ)
Address. c/o Supreme Council, Minsk
Leadership. Lanid Sechka (chair)
The PNZ is a technocratic party emphasizing the need for economic reform, independent of the pro-democracy and conservative alliances, although it backed the Belarusan Popular Front—Revival candidate in the 1994 presidential elections after its then leader, Henadz Karpenka, had failed to meet the nomination requirements. The party won eight of the declared seats in the 1995 legislative elections.

Popular Movement of Belarus
Narodni Dirzhenie Belarusi (NDB)
Address. c/o Supreme Council, Minsk
Leadership. Syarhey Haydukkevich (chair)

The NDB was created in 1992 as an alliance of pro-government conservative groupings favouring a cautious approach to political and economic reform. Aiming to counter the influence of the pro-democracy Belarusan Popular Front—Revival (NFB-A), the NDB embraced both the hardline left and the pan-Slavic right on a joint platform advocating the maintenance of close relations with Russia and resistance to Western capitalist encroachment. Its leaders had mostly prospered under the Soviet-era rule of the republican Communist Party, the suspension of which in August 1991 had not affected the predominance of supposedly former Communists in the government and in the Supreme Soviet elected in 1990. Although the head of state elected in September 1991, Stanislau Shushkevich, had come to prominence in the late 1980s campaigning on the Chernobyl nuclear disaster, Prime Minister Vyacheslau Kebich was a hardline career politician backed by the conservative Belarus Group controlling the legislature. Such elements formed the core of the NDB, which naturally embraced the Communist Party of Belarus following its return to legality in 1993 as well as the right-wing ethno-nationalist Liberal Democratic Party and Slavic Assembly of Belarus. By early 1994 the NDB claimed to have over 500,000 members throughout the country.

The fall of Shushkevich in January 1994 (over dubious corruption charges) and the election of Mechyslau Hryb as head of state strengthened the position of the NDB hardliners. This was apparent in the introduction of a new presidential constitution in March 1994, the signature the following month of a monetary union treaty with Russia and moves to participate in CIS collective security arrangements. In the June-July 1994 presidential elections, however, the hardliners were unexpectedly outmanoeuvred by the NDB's more moderate wing. Standing as an independent, Kebich secured only 17.3% of the first-round vote, ahead of the NFB-A candidate and Shushkevich (also standing as an independent) but well behind a third independent, Alyaksandr Lukashenka, who took 44.8%. In the second round, Lukashenka registered a massive 80.1% of the vote, while Kebich could manage only 14.1%, despite being backed by most sitting deputies.

Socialist Party of Belarus
Satsiyalicheskaya Partiya Belarusi (SPB)
Address. c/o Supreme Council, Minsk
Telephone. (#7-0172) 293738
Leadership. Vyacheslau Kuznyatsow (chair)

The SPB was founded at a Minsk congress in July 1994 as one of a number of attempts, in the wake of the mid-1994 presidential elections, to provide a new political home for those favouring the retention or restoration of elements of the pre-independence system. The deputy chair of the Belarus legislature was elected to lead the SPB, which called for the political union of the members of the Commonwealth of Independent States. The new party appeared to differ little in its policy prescriptions from the Belarusan Patriotic Movement, founded later in 1994 to provide a political base for President Lukashenka.

United Civic Party of Belarus
Abyadnanaya Grazhdanskaya Partiya Belarusi (AGPB)
Address. Sudmalisa 10, PO Box 299, 220094 Minsk
Telephone. (#7-0172) 457322
Fax. (#7-0172) 729505
Leadership. Stanislau Bahdankevich (president)

The pro-market AGPB was founded in October 1995 as a merger of the United Democratic Party of Belarus (ADPB) led by Alyaksandr Dabravolsky and the Civic Party. The leader of the new party had been dismissed as president of the National Bank the previous month after disagreeing with President Lukashenka's pro-Russian policies. The ADPB had been founded in November 1990 as a merger of three recently-formed pro-democracy groupings, including Communists for Perestroika and the Democratic Party. Drawing its main support from the technical and scientific professional strata, it had become a member of the opposition Belarusan Popular Front—Revival, supporting the latter's unsuccessful candidate in the 1994 presidential elections. In the 1995 legislative elections the AGPB was credited with winning nine seats, later becoming the core of the Civic Action parliamentary group which by April 1996 had 18 members.

In February 1996 the AGPB was joined by the Belarusan Christian Democratic Union (BKDZ), led by Pyatro Silko and an affiliate of the Christian Democrat International. This party had been founded in 1991 as the successor to the pre-Soviet Christian Democratic Association and had become a member of the opposition Belarusan Popular Front—Revival, supporting the latter's unsuccessful candidate in the first round of the 1994 presidential elections.

Other Parties

Belarusan Ecological Party, founded in 1993, led by Alyaksandr Mikulich, won one seat in the 1995 legislative elections.

Belarusan Humanitarian Party, founded in 1994, led by Yaugen Novikau.

Belarusan National Party, registered with the Justice Ministry in September 1994.

Belarusan Party of Labour (*Belaruskaya Partiya Pratsy*, BPP), founded in 1993, led by Alyaksandr Bukhvostau.

Belarusan Party of Labour and Justice, founded in 1993, led by Anatol Nitylkin, won one seat in the 1995 legislative elections.

Belarusan Republican Party, founded in 1994, led by Valery Artysheuski.

Belarusan Social Sporting Party, won one seat in the 1995 legislative elections.

Green Party of Belarus, founded in 1992, led by Mikalay Kartash, won one seat in the 1995 legislative elections.

Movement for Democratic Reforms, led by Olha Abramova and Leonid Zlatnikau, also known as Democratic Belarus, a member of the Belarusan Popular Front—Revival.

Polish Democratic Union (*Polskaye Demokratchnaye Zhurtavannye*, PDZ), founded in 1993, led by Eduard Akhrem.

Republican Party, led by Uladzimir Balazar, registered in February 1994, concentrates on economic reform requirements, independent of the pro-democracy and conservative alliances.

Slavic Assembly of Belarus, a non-communist pan-Slavic formation aligned with the Popular Movement of Belarus, advocating the union of Belarus, Russia and Ukraine, led by Andrey Tsegalka.

Belgium

Capital: Brussels   **Population:** 10,060,000 (1995E)

The Kingdom of Belgium is a constitutional monarchy with a parliamentary democracy in which most political parties are based in the country's linguistic communities, principally the majority Flemish-speaking population in the north and the French-speaking Walloon community in the south. The constitutional monarch, as head of state, has limited powers, with central executive authority residing in the Prime Minister and the Council of Ministers responsible to a federal bicameral legislature. The lower house is the 150–member Chamber of Representatives (*Chambre des Représentants/Kamer van Volksvertegenwoordigers*), reduced from 212 to 150 members from 1995 and elected for a maximum four-year term by universal (and compulsory) suffrage of those aged 18 and over according to a system of proportional representation. The Chamber has virtually equal powers with the upper house, which is the 71-member Senate (*Sénat/Senaat*), 40 of whose members are elected directly and the remainder indirectly, also for a four-year term. A lengthy process of constitutional reform, inaugurated in 1970 and involving the phased devolution of substantial powers to the linguistic regions, culminated with the final parliamentary approval on July 14, 1993, of legislation transforming Belgium into a federal state. Under the changes, the country is divided into three regions (Flanders, Wallonia and bilingual Brussels), each with a government and directly-elected legislature endowed with broad economic and social powers, and into three linguistic communities (Flemish, French and German) for cultural purposes.

There is no public funding of political parties in Belgium, although the electoral code and other laws give them certain facilities during election campaigns that amount to indirect state subsidy.

General elections to the Chamber of Representatives on May 21, 1995, resulted as follows: Christian People's Party (Flemish) 29 seats (with 17.2% of the vote); Flemish Liberals and Democrats 21 (13.1%); Socialist Party (Walloon) 21 (11.9%); Socialist Party (Flemish) 20

(12.6%); Liberal Reform Party (Walloon) and Democratic Front of French-Speakers 18 (10.3%); Christian Social Party (Walloon) 12 (7.7%); Flemish Bloc 11 (7.8%); People's Union (Flemish) 5 (4.7%); Ecologist Party (Walloon) 6 (4.0%); Live Differently (Flemish Ecologists) 5 (4.4%); National Front 2 (2.3%).

Christian People's Party

Christelijke Volkspartij (CVP)
 Address. Tweekerkenstraat 41, B-1040 Brussels
 Telephone. (#32–2) 238–3811
 Fax. (#32–2) 238–3871
 Leadership. Johan van Hecke (president), Yves Leterme (secretary-general)

Historically descended from the *Katholieke Vlaamse Volkspartij*, which was the Flemish wing of the pre-war Belgian Catholic Party, the CVP was created in 1945 as the Flemish counterpart of the French-speaking Christian Social Party (PSC), initially within a single party structure. From 1947 the CVP/PSC participated in successive coalition governments, except for the period 1954–58. By the mid-1960s the CVP and the PSC had effectively become separate parties, the former considerably larger than the latter in terms of electoral support. Consistently the strongest single parliamentary party, the CVP has provided the Prime Minister in recent coalitions, with the Socialists and the Democratic Front of French-Speakers of Brussels in 1979–80; with the Socialists and Liberals briefly in 1980; with the Socialists in 1980–81; with the Liberals in 1981–88; with the Socialists and the People's Union in 1988–91; and with the Socialists since 1992.

After 13 years of almost continuous incumbency as CVP Prime Minister, Wilfried Martens gave way to Jean-Luc Dehaene in the government formed in March 1992. In the November 1991 Chamber elections the CVP's representation fell from 43 to 39 seats out of 212 and its share of the vote from 19.5% to 16.7%. In the June 1994 European Parliament elections the party took 17% of the vote (compared with 21.1% in 1989) and four of the 25 Belgian seats. In further Chamber elections in May 1995 the CVP unexpectedly increased its vote share to 17.2%, winning 29 out of 150 seats, so that Dehaene remained head of a federal coalition with the Socialists. In simultaneous elections for the 118-member Flemish regional council the CVP won a plurality of 35 seats (with 26.8% of the vote), providing the minister-president of Flanders in the person of Luc van den Brande, who headed a coalition with the Flemish Socialists.

The CVP is a member of the Christian Democrat International, the European Union of Christian Democrats and the European People's Party.

Christian Social Party

Parti Social Chrétien (PSC)
 Address. Rue des Deux Églises 41/45, B-1040 Brussels
 Telephone. (#32–2) 238–0111
 Fax. (#32–2) 238–0129
 Leadership. Gérard Deprez (president), Pierre Scharff (secretary-general)

The PSC has its historical origins in the Catholic Union, one of several such organizations set up in Belgium in the 19th century. It is directly descended from the Belgian Catholic Party (PCB) created in 1936 and more specifically from the *Parti Catholique Social* (PCS), the PCB's French-speaking section. As the country's strongest party, the PCB took part in coalition governments before and during World War II, the PCS providing Belgium's wartime Prime Minister. At Christmas 1945 the PCB was reconstituted, the PCS becoming the PSC and the Flemish wing becoming the Christian People's Party (CVP), at that stage within one overall party structure. Having confirmed its dominant position in the 1946 elections, the joint party entered a coalition with the Socialists in 1947. Since then the PSC/CVP tandem has participated continuously in the central government except for the period 1954–58.

From the mid-1960s the PSC and CVP were effectively two separate parties, the former becoming substantially the smaller of the two. The PSC has therefore been a junior partner in recent coalitions headed by the CVP, with the Socialists and the Democratic Front of French-Speakers of Brussels in 1979–80; with the Socialists and Liberals briefly in 1980; with the Socialists in 1980–81; with the Liberals in 1981–88; with the Socialists and the People's Union in 1988–91; and with the Socialists since 1992. In the November 1991 Chamber elections PSC representation slipped from 19 to 18 seats out of 212 and its vote share from 8% to 7.8%. In the June 1994 European Parliament elections the PSC retained two of the 25 Belgian seats but its vote share fell to 6.9% from 8.1% in 1989. This setback coincided with disclosures of financial corruption in the Brussels section of the party. Nevertheless, in the May 1995 Chamber elections the PSC retained a 7.7% vote share, winning 12 of the 150 seats, and took third place in the simultaneous elections to the Walloon regional council, with 16 of the 75 seats and 21.6% of the vote. Thereafter, in addition to remaining in the federal coalition, the PSC also maintained its coalition with the Walloon Socialists in the regional government of Wallonia.

The PSC is a member of the Christian Democrat International, the European Union of Christian Democrats and the European People's Party.

Democratic Front of French-Speakers
Front Démocratique des Francophones (FDF)

Address. Chaussée de Charleroi 127, B-1060 Brussels

Telephone. (#32-2) 538-8320

Fax. (#32-2) 539-3650

Leadership. Olivier Maingain (president), Serge de Patoul (secretary-general)

Founded in May 1964 with the aim of preserving the French character of the Belgian capital, the FDF incorporated various militant francophone groupings of Brussels. Its three Chamber seats in the 1965 elections were increased to 10 by 1977, after which it joined a coalition government with the Christian Socials and Socialists and assisted with the enactment of the 1978 Egmont Pact on regional devolution. Under the plan, Brussels was to become a separate (bilingual) region, i.e. not included in surrounding Flanders as some Flemish nationalists had demanded. Having risen to 11 seats in 1978, the FDF went into opposition again from 1980 and slipped to six seats in 1981. Two of these deputies defected to the Walloon Socialist Party in March 1985 and the FDF was reduced to three seats in the October 1985 elections, retaining them in 1987 and 1991.

The FDF retained representation in the May 1995 Chamber elections by virtue of an alliance with the Liberal Reform Party (PRL). In simultaneous elections, the PRL/FDF alliance became the largest bloc in the Brussels regional council, winning 28 of the 75 seats (with 35% of the vote), and the second largest in the Walloon regional council, with 19 of the 75 seats and a 23.7% vote share. The FDF was allocated one portfolio in the six-party Brussels regional government.

Ecologist Party
Ecologistes Confédérés pour l'Organisation de Luttes Originales (ECOLO)

Address. Rue Charles VI 12, B-1030 Brussels

Telephone. (#32-2) 218-3035

Fax. (#32-2) 217-5290

Leadership. Isabelle Durant, Dany Josse, Jacky Morael (secretaries)

Originally founded in 1978 by Walloon environmentalists, ECOLO was reorganized for the 1981 elections, in which it co-operated with the Flemish Live Differently (AGALEV) grouping and won two Chamber seats. Having established a significant local government presence, ECOLO increased its Chamber tally to five seats in 1985 (standing independently), but slipped back to three seats in 1987. The November 1991 elections brought a major advance, to 10 seats out of 212, with 5.1% of the vote, double the party's 1987 share. In the June 1994 European Parliament elections ECOLO won 4.8% of the national vote and one seat, compared with 6.3% and two seats in 1989. Its share in the May 1995 Chamber elections fell back to 4.0%, giving it six of the 150 seats, while in simultaneous regional polling it won eight and seven seats respectively on the 75-member Walloon and Brussels regional councils (with 10.4% and 9.0% respectively).

ECOLO has links in the international Green movement, its single representative in the European Parliament being a member of the Green Group.

Flemish Bloc
Vlaams Blok (VB)

Address. Madouplein 8, Bus 9, B-1030 Brussels

Telephone. (#32–2) 219-6009

Fax. (#32-2) 217-5275

Leadership. Karel Dillen (chair), Roeland Raes (secretary)

The ultra-nationalist Flemish Bloc first came into being for the December 1978 elections as an alliance between the Flemish People's Party, established in 1977 by Lode Claes following a split in the People's Union (VU), and the Flemish National Party, led by Dillen and also founded in 1977. Having won one seat in that contest, the two parties formally merged in May 1979 on a platform of opposition to the 1978 Egmont Pact on devolution on the grounds that it demanded too many concessions of Flemings. Having increased its Chamber tally to two seats in 1987, the Bloc experienced a surge of support in the 1990s on a platform which now emphasized opposition to immigration. In the November 1991 elections the Bloc's representation in the Chamber increased to 12 seats and its vote share to 6.6%, ahead of the VU, for long the main vehicle of Flemish nationalism. During the campaign brown-shirted VB militants were involved in numerous violent incidents involving foreigners.

In the June 1994 European Parliament elections the Bloc won two seats and increased its vote to 7.8% (from 4.1% in 1989) on a platform which combined anti-immigration policies with opposition to the Maastricht process of European union. It made further advances in local elections in October 1994, winning representation in 82 of the 308 municipal councils and a total of 202 seats nationally. The Bloc headed the poll in Antwerp, winning 29% of the vote and 18 of the 55 seats, but its leader in the city, Filip Dewinter, was excluded from the mayorship by a combination of the other parties represented. The VB again registered 7.8% of the national vote in the May 1995 Chamber elections, giving it 11 out of 150 seats, while in simultaneous polling for the 118-member Flemish regional council it won 15 seats with a 12.3% vote share.

The VB's single representative in the European Parliament is among the "unattached" contingent.

Flemish Liberals and Democrats
Vlaamse Liberalen en Demokraten (VLD)
   Address. Melsensstraat 34, B-1000 Brussels
   Telephone. (#32–2) 512–7870
   Fax. (#32–2) 512–6025
   Leadership. Herman de Croo (president), Clair Ysebaert (secretary-general)

The VLD is descended from the historic Belgian Liberal Party, which was founded in 1846 as the country's earliest political formation. It was in power in 1857–70 and 1878–84 but was then overtaken on the left by the new Belgian Labour Party, becoming the country's third political force behind the Catholics and Socialists. Having participated in a succession of coalitions after World War II, notably the 1954–58 Socialist-Liberal government, the Liberal Party was reconstituted in 1961 as the Party of Liberty and Progress (PLP). In 1970 the Flemish wing (*Partij voor Vrijheid en Vooruitgang*, PVV) became an autonomous formation, leaving the PLP as a Walloon party. Having participated in various coalitions in the 1970s, both the PVV and its Walloon counterpart, by now called the Liberal Reform Party (PRL), were in government with the Christian People's and Christian Social parties in 1981–88, being regarded as the right-wing component of the coalition. In the November 1991 general elections the opposition PVV increased its Chamber representation from 25 to 26 seats out of 212 and its vote share from 11.5% to 11.9%.

In November 1992, in a move to broaden its support base, the PVV switched to its current VLD designation, also using the sub-title Party of Citizens (*Partij van de Burger*). In the June 1994 European Parliament elections the VLD took 11.4% of the vote and three of the 25 Belgian seats, against 10.6% and two seats for the PVV in 1989. In municipal and provincial elections in October 1994 the VLD replaced the Flemish Socialists as the second-largest party in Flanders. It made a further advance in the May 1995 Chamber elections, winning 21 of the 150 seats with 13.1% of the vote, but not enough to oust the incumbent coalition. In simultaneous regional polling the VLD consolidated its position as second party in Flanders, winning 26 of the 118 seats in the Flemish regional council. In light of the party's relatively disappointing performance, Guy Verhof-stadt resigned as leader and was succeeded in September 1995 by Herman de Croo.

Claiming a membership of 73,300, the VLD is a member party of the Liberal International and also of the Liberal, Democratic and Reformist Group of the European Parliament.

Liberal Reform Party
Parti Réformateur Libéral (PRL)
   Address. Rue de Naples 41, B-1050 Brussels
   Telephone. (#32–2) 500–3511
   Fax. (#32–2) 500–3500
   Leadership. Louis Michel (president), Jacques Simonet (secretary-general), Lucien Vandermeulen (director)

Descended from the historic Belgian Liberal Party and its successors (see previous entry), the French-speaking PRL came into being in June 1979 as a merger of the Party of Reforms and Liberty of Wallonia (PRLW) and the Brussels Liberal Party. Of these, the PRLW had been formed in November 1976 as successor to the Party of Libery and Progress (*Parti de la Liberté et du Progrès*, PLP), which had continued as the main Walloon Liberal party after the Flemish wing had become a separate formation in 1970. The Brussels Liberals had adopted the party's historic name in June 1974 as successor to the distinct Liberal Democrat and Pluralist Party (PLDP) founded in January 1973. The PLP and the successor PRL (with the Flemish Liberals, who were consistently the stronger) participated in various coalitions, most recently with the Christian People's Party and the Christian Social Party in 1981–88, being regarded as the coalition's right-wing component.

In the November 1991 general elections, the opposition PRL's representation in the Chamber fell from 23 to 20 seats out of 212 and its vote share from 9.4% to 8.2%. In the June 1994 European Parliament elections the PRL won 9.0% of the vote and three seats compared with 8.7% and two seats in 1989. For the May 1995 Chamber elections the PRL presented a joint list with the Democratic Front of French-Speakers (FDF) of Brussels, winning 18 out of 150 seats on a 10.3% vote share. In simultaneous elections, the PRL/FDF alliance became the largest bloc in the Brussels regional council, winning 28 of the 75 seats (with 35% of the vote), and the second largest in the Walloon regional council, with 19 of the 75 seats and a 23.7% vote share. The PRL was allocated two portfolios in the six-party Brussels regional government.

Claiming a membership of 35,000, the PRL is a member party of the Liberal International and also of the Liberal, Democratic and Reformist Group of the European Parliament.

Live Differently

Anders Gaan Leven (AGALEV)

Address. Tweekerkenstraat 78, B-1040 Brussels

Telephone. (#32-2) 230-6666

Fax. (#32-2) 230-4786

Leadership. Johan Malcorps (secretary of collective leadership)

This Flemish environmentalist formation won two Chamber seats in the 1981 elections standing jointly with the Walloon Ecologist Party. Established as an independent party in 1982, AGALEV increased its representation to four seats in 1985, six in 1987 and seven in November 1991, when its share of the poll was 4.9%. In the June 1994 European Parliament elections, it retained one seat with 6.7% of the vote (as against 7.6% in 1989), while in the May 1995 Chamber elections it slipped to 4.4% of the national vote, winning five out of 150 seats. In simultaneous regional balloting, AGALEV took 7.1% of the vote in Flanders, winning seven of the 118 regional council seats.

AGALEV has contacts with the international Green movement; its single member of the European Parliament sits in the Green Group.

National Front

Front National (FN)

Address. Clos du Parnasse 12, B-1040 Brussels

Telephone. (#32-2) 511-7577; 512-0575

Leadership. Daniel Feret (president)

The extreme right-wing FN, modelled on the National Front of France, was founded in 1983 on a platform of opposition to non-white immigration. Based in the French-speaking community, it achieved a breakthrough in the November 1991 elections, winning one Chamber seat with 1.1% of the vote. A further advance came in the June 1994 European Parliament elections, when it took 2.9% of the vote and one of the 25 Belgian seats. In October 1994 the FN leadership announced the expulsion of a member who had been shown on television desecrating a Jewish grave. In local elections the same month the party doubled its share of the vote in Wallonia compared with the previous contest in 1988. In the May 1995 Chamber elections the NF advanced to 2.3% of the national vote, winning two seats, while in simultaneous regional balloting it won 5.2% of the vote in Wallonia and two of the 75 seats on the Walloon regional council.

The FN's single representative in the European Parliament is one of the "unattached" contingent.

People's Union

Volksunie (VU)

Address. Barrikadenplein 12, B-1000 Brussels

Telephone. (#32-2) 219-4930

Fax. (#32-2) 217-3510

Leadership. Bert Anciaux (president), Chris Vandenbroeke (secretary)

The VU was founded in December 1954 as a nationalist party seeking autonomy for Flanders on a "socially progressive, tolerant, modern and forward-looking" platform. It made a breakthrough in the 1965 Chamber elections, winning 12 seats, which it increased to 20 in 1969 and to 22 in 1974. It fell back to 20 seats in 1977, in which year it entered government for the first time, in coalition with the Christian Socials, Socialists and Democratic Front of French-Speakers (FDF) of Brussels, with the task of enacting regional devolution plans. Enshrined in the 1978 Egmont Pact, these were opposed by many VU militants as being inimical to Flemish interests, the result being the secession of a VU faction which later became part of the Flemish Bloc (VB). The VU retained only 14 seats in the December 1978 elections and reverted to opposition status. Rebuilding its strength, it won 20 seats in 1981 but slipped again in 1985 to 16. Having again won 16 seats in the December 1987 elections, it accepted participation in a coalition with the Christian Socials and Socialists formed in March 1988 but withdrew in September 1991 over an arms export controversy.

In the November 1991 elections the VU retained only 10 seats (and 5.9% of the vote), being overtaken by the VB. In the June 1994 European Parliament elections it slipped to 4.4% of the vote, from 5.4% in 1989, while retaining one seat. The May 1995 Chamber elections yielded a further setback for the VU, which fell to 4.7% of the national vote and five seats (out of 150). In simultaneous regional elections it won 9% of the vote in Flanders and nine of the 118 regional council seats, while in Brussels it won one seat and was allocated one portfolio in the six-party Brussels regional government.

The VU's single member of the European Parliament sits in the European Radical Alliance group.

Radical Reformist Fighters in the Struggle for an Honest Society

Radikale Omvormers Strijders en Strubbelaars voor een Eerlijke Maatschappij (ROSSEM)

Address. Petunialaan 2, B-8301 Knokke-Heist

Telephone. (#32-50) 515590

Leadership. Jean-Pierre van Rossem (leader)

Formed prior to the 1991 Chamber elections, this populist/alternative formation compiled its full title so that its acronym would be the same as the last name of its founder and leader, a wealthy anarchist. Despite the arrest of the latter on fraud charges shortly before polling, the so-called ROSSEM List took three Chamber seats, with 3.2% of the vote. A five-year prison sentence passed on van Rossem in February 1995 could not be carried out because he was covered by parliamentary immunity. Nevertheless, the party did not contest the May 1995 Chamber elections.

Socialist Party
Parti Socialiste (PS)

Address. Blvd de l'Empereur 13, B-1000 Brussels

Telephone. (#32–2) 548–3211
Fax. (#32–2) 548-3380
Leadership. Philippe Busquin (chair), Roger Gaillez (national secretary)

Dating as a separate French-speaking party from October 1978, the PS is descended from the Belgian Labour Party (POB) founded in April 1885 with its base in industrial Wallonia and its support in organized labour. After obtaining universal male suffrage through a general strike, the POB was well-represented in the Chamber from 1894 and was admitted to the government-in-exile formed at Le Havre (France) in 1915 during World War I. In 1938 Paul-Henri Spaak became Belgium's first POB Prime Minister, but the German occupation of Belgium in 1940 forced the party underground under the leadership of Achille van Acker. Reconstituted in 1944 as the Belgian Socialist Party, with direct membership rather than group affiliation, it took part in postwar coalition governments until 1949 and again (with the Liberals) in 1954–58. Thereafter it was in coalition with the Christian Socials in 1961–66 and 1968–72; with the Christian Socials and Liberals in 1973–74; and with the Christian Socials, the Democratic Front of French-Speakers (FDF) and the People's Union (VU) in 1977–78. In October 1978 the Socialists emulated the other main Belgian political formations by formalizing the separation of their Flemish and French-speaking wings into autonomous parties, respectively the PS and the SP (see next entry).

Both the PS and the SP participated in coalitions with the Christian Socials and the FDF in 1979–80; with the Christian Socials and Liberals briefly in 1980; and with the Christian Socials in 1980–81. Both parties were then in opposition until, having become the largest lower house force in the December 1987 elections (for the first time since 1936), they joined a coalition with the Christian Socials and the VU in March 1988. Following the VU's withdrawal in September 1991, both Socialist parties lost ground in Chamber elections the following month (the PS falling from 40 to 35 seats out of 212 on a vote share of 15.6%) and joined a new coalition with the two Christian Social parties in March 1992. Concurrently, the PS also headed the regional governments of Wallonia and Brussels, championing the channelling of

redevelopment resources to French-speaking areas and the maintenance of a large nationalized sector.

The murder in Liège in July 1991 of André Cools (a former PS Deputy Prime Minister) led eventually to the uncovering of the Agusta scandal, involving allegations of financial corruption in the party leadership in connection with a 1988 government contract for military helicopters awarded to an Italian firm. In January 1994 the disclosures resulted in the resignations of Guy Coëme (as federal Deputy Prime Minister), Guy Spitaels (as minister-president of Wallonia) and Guy Mathot (as interior minister of Wallonia), although all three denied any impropriety. In European Parliament elections in June 1994, the PS vote share slipped to 11.3% (from 14.5% in 1989 and 13.6% in the 1991 national balloting), so that it won only three of the 25 Belgian seats.

The May 1995 elections demonstrated the party's resilience, the PS winning 21 out of 150 seats on an 11.9% vote share and remaining a member of the federal centre-left coalition. In simultaneous regional elections the PS remained by far the strongest party in Wallonia, taking 30 of the 75 regional council seats with a 35.2% vote share, so that Robert Collignon (PS) remained minister-president of Wallonia. In the Brussels region the PS won 21.4% and 17 seats out of 75, enabling Charles Picqué of the PS to remain head of government in charge of a six-party administration.

The PS is a full member party of the Socialist International and also participates in the Party of European Socialists.

Socialist Party
Socialistische Partij (SP)

Address. Keizerslaan 13, B-1000 Brussels
Telephone. (#32–2) 548–3211
Fax. (#32–2) 548–3590
Leadership. Louis Tobback (chair), Linda Blomme (national secretary)

As the Flemish section of the post-war Belgian Socialist Party, the SP had its origins in the *Belgische Werklieden Partij* founded in October 1885 as the Flemish wing of the Belgian Labour Party; it became an autonomous party on the formal separation of the two Socialist wings in October 1978. Before and subsequently it participated in all the central coalition governments of which the Walloon PS was a member (see previous entry). Having formally renounced Marxism and class struggle in 1980, the SP became more "social democratic" in orientation than its Walloon counterpart, distancing itself in particular from the pro-nationalization line of the latter. For long the weaker of the two parties electorally, the SP maintained its Chamber representation at 32 seats out of 212 in December 1987 but fell back to 28 seats in November 1991. In the June 1994 European Parliament elections the SP retained three Belgian seats but its vote share slipped to 10.8%, from 12.4% in the 1989 Euro-elections and 12.0% in the 1991 national poll.

Following the appointment of Willy Claes (then SP Deputy Premier and Foreign Minister) to the post of NATO secretary-general in October 1994, Frank Vandenbroucke replaced him in the government and was succeeded as SP chair by Louis Tobback, hitherto Interior Minister. In March 1995 Vandenbroucke became the most senior casualty to date of the Agusta bribery scandal, resigning from the government after admitting that in 1991 he knew that the party held a large sum of undeclared money in a bank safe deposit. Also implicated was Claes, who as Economic Affairs Minister in 1988 had been closely involved in the helicopter contract at the centre of the bribery allegations. Despite these difficulties, the SP advanced to 12.6% in the May 1995 general elections (ahead of the Walloon Socialists), winning 20 of the 150 Chamber seats. In the simultaneous regional polling, it took 25 of the 118 Flemish council seats (with a 19.4% vote share) and continued to participate in the Flanders government. In October 1995 Claes was obliged to resign his NATO post when the Belgian parliament voted in favour of his being brought to trial.

The SP is a full member party of the Socialist International and also participates in the Party of European Socialists.

Walloon Party
Parti Wallon (PW)

Address. 14 rue du Faubourg, B-1430 Quenast
Leadership. Jean-Claude Piccin (president)

The PW is a left-wing nationalist party advocating a socialist Wallonia, founded in 1985 as a merger of the *Rassemblement Wallon* (RW) and other radical Walloon groups. Founded in 1968, the RW had participated in a coalition government with the Christian Socials and Liberals in 1974–77, helping to secure the passage of the Egmont Pact on devolution; but it had been weakened by defections of moderates to what became the Liberal Reform Party. Whereas the RW won two Chamber seats in the 1981 elections on a joint list with the Democratic Front of French-Speakers, in 1985 the PW failed to gain representation and was no more successful in the 1987, 1991 and 1995 contests.

Other Parties

Christian Social Party (*Christlich-Soziale Partei*, CSP), the Christian Social party of Belgium's

small German-speaking minority, secured one seat in the June 1994 European Parliament elections (with only 0.2% of the overall vote), effectively on the ticket of the (Flemish) Christian People's Party.

Communist Union of Belgium (*Union des Communistes de Belgique/Unie van Kommunisten van België*, UCB/UKB), led by Pierre Beauvois, descended from the historic Belgian Communist Party (PCB/KPB) founded in 1921, powerful after World War II on a pro-Soviet tack but in decline since the mid-1950s, unrepresented in the Chamber since 1985, has renounced Marxism-Leninism in favour of socialist democracy, renamed the UCB/UKB in 1990. *Address.* Ave de Stalingrad 18–20, B-1000 Brussels

Democratic Union for the Respect of Labour (*Respect voor Arbeid en Democratie/Union Démocratique pour le Respect du Travail*, RAD/UDRT), Poujadist formation founded in 1978, led by Robert Hendrick, won one Chamber seat in 1978, three in 1981, one in 1985 and none since then. *Address.* Chaussée de Boondael 548, B-1050 Brussels

Humanist Feminist Party (*Humanistische Feministische Partij/Parti Féministe Humaniste*, HFP/PFH), originally founded in 1972, adopted its present name in 1990, seeking to promote women's rights and female representation in elected bodies. *Address.* Ave des Phalènes 35, B-1050 Ixelles

Marxist-Leninist Communist Party of Belgium (*Parti Communiste Marxiste-Léniniste de Belgique*, PCMLB), led by Fernand Lefebvre, one of Europe's oldest Maoist formations, founded in 1963 by dissidents of the main Communist Party, adopted present name in 1970.

Movement for the Liberty of the Citizen (*Mouvement pour la Liberté du Citoyen*, MPLC), led by Luc Rykerman and Paul Moors. *Address.* Ave de Scheuf 46, B-1070 Brussels

Party of Belgian German-Speakers (*Partei der Deutschsprachigen Belgier*, PDB), led by Rudolf Pankert and Martin Schröder, founded in 1971 to campaign for equal rights for the German-speaking minority. *Address.* Kaperberg 6, B-4700 Eupen

Party of Labour (*Partij van de Arbeid/Parti du Travail de Belgique*, PvdA/PTB), led by Ludo Martens, founded in 1979 in opposition to the reformism of the Belgian Communist Party, part of the All Power to the Workers (*Alle Macht Aan de Arbeiders*, AMADA) movement in the 1979

Euro-elections, unsuccessful then and subsequently in securing representation. *Address.* Lemonnier-laan 171/2, B-1000 Brussels

Return to Liège (*Retour à Liège*), led by José Happart, the electoral movement of the French-speaking majority of the Voeren/Les Fourons commune situated in Flemish Limburg, linked with the Walloon Socialist Party (PS); elected mayor in October 1994, Happart refused to use Flemish as required by law, eventually standing down in favour of a bilingual colleague.

Belize

Capital: Belmopan

Population: 200,000 (1995E)

Belize became independent within the British Commonwealth on Sept. 21, 1981. A Legislative Assembly has been in existence since 1935 and was given responsibility for internal self-government under the old constitution of 1954. Since independence the country has since been governed by the People's United Party, with the exception of the period 1984-89.

Under the 1981 constitution the Belizan head of state is the British monarch, represented by a Governor-General. He or she acts on the advice of a Cabinet headed by a Prime Minister. The Governor-General appoints the Prime Minister, who is the leader of the party with a parliamentary majority. The Prime Minister is assisted by a Deputy Prime Minister and other ministers appointed by the Governor-General on the advice of the Prime Minister. The Governor-General is also advised by an appointed Belize Advisory Council. Legislative authority is vested in the bicameral National Assembly, comprising an appointed eight-member Senate and a House of Representatives with 28 elected members. Legislation may be introduced in either house, except financial legislation, which must be introduced in the lower house.

Belize uses the first-past-the-post electoral system, with successful candidates requiring a simple majority in one of the 28 single-member constituencies. The eight members of the Senate are officially appointed by the Governor-General: five on the advice of the Prime Minister, two on that of the Leader of the Opposition and one after consulting the Belize Advisory Council. The National Assembly sits for a five-year term subject to dissolution. The 1954 constitution granted universal adult suffrage. All citizens over the age of 18 are entitled to vote.

The Peoples' United Party (PUP) was unexpectedly defeated in the election of June 30, 1993. The contest, called 15 months before it was constitutionally due, resulted in the United Democratic Party (UDP) winning 16 seats and the PUP 13.

National Alliance for Belizean Rights (NABR)
Address. c/o House of Representatives, Belmopan.
Leadership. Philip S. W. Goldson (national co-ordinator)

The newest party in Belizean politics, the NABR was organized in February 1992 by former UDP members disaffected by the maritime concessions given to Guatemala (resulting in a non-aggression pact between the two countries on April 16, 1993).

Despite being a party founded in disagreement with the United Democratic Party, the NABR campaigned alongside it in the 1993 elections and was subsequently included in the Esquivel government.

Peoples' United Party (PUP)
Address. c/o House of Representatives, Belmopan.
Leadership. Said Musa (chair)

Founded in 1950, the centrist PUP has traditionally drawn more of its support from Catholics, Indians and Spanish-speakers than from the black population. The party was founded as a left-wing reformist party motivated by co-operatist ideas and supported by the General Workers' Union, of which Price was president, and the Roman Catholic Church. In 1951-54 the PUP was thought to have had close relations with the like-minded reformist Arbenz government in Guatemala (deposed by the USA) and campaigned for independence from Britain, a position which helped it win a comprehensive victory in the 1954 general election. Price became PUP leader in 1956 when a faction in the party opposed to independence broke away to form the National Independence Party (NIP). In 1957 the party won all nine assembly seats, and in the elections in 1961 to an enlarged legislature took all 18 seats. Price became the First Minister in 1961 and Premier in 1965. The party then had an unbroken run in office until 1984, during which time the country gained its independence, in September 1981, and Price became Prime Minister.

In the first post-independence election in 1984 the PUP suffered a dramatic defeat, receiving only seven seats in the enlarged 28-member House. As part of the post-electoral shock, former PUP ministers Louise Sylvestre and Fred Hunter left to form the (now defunct) Belize Popular Party (BPP) in July 1985 in protest at a perceived move to the left within the party. To counter-balance this tendency and restore the predominance of the party's centrist faction, the Christian Democratic Party (CDP), led by former United Democratic Party (UDP) leader Theodore Aranda, joined the PUP in 1988. The party returned to power in 1989 when it won 15 seats, narrowly defeating the UDP which gained 13 seats in the general election. Price, once again appointed Prime Minister, named a Cabinet balancing the different wings of the party. He promised a mixed economy with a measure of state planning to counteract what he characterized as the UDP government's "savage economic liberalism". The PUP's parliamentary majority was increased when an expelled UDP representative switched political allegiances immediately after the election. The party then consolidated its position by winning all nine seats in the local elections to the Belize city council held on Dec. 7, 1989.

Significantly, during Price's post-1989 term of office the country identified itself more closely with the region, being accepted as a member of the Organization of American States (OAS) in January 1991 and being offered observer status at the inauguration of the Central American Parliament (Parlacén) in October. This process of integration was reinforced in September 1991 by the establishment of diplomatic relations with neighbouring Guatemala, which had long claimed sovereignty over the country.

Since 1993, a number of party members have undergone investigations for bribery and charges were in fact brought. However, as of mid-1996 decisions were still pending.

United Democratic Party (UDP)

Address. c/o House of Representatives, Belmopan.

Leadership. Manuel A Esquivel (leader); Alfredo Martinez (chair)

Founded in September 1973, the conservative and free market UDP has a predominantly black (Creole) ethnic base but it also claims to have support from the Mayan and Mestizo sectors.

The UDP emerged from the fusion of the National Independence Party, the Liberal Party and the People's Development Movement as a right-wing opposition to the People's United Party (PUP). In the 1979 general election, it won 46.8% of the vote and five seats on the basis of a campaign alleging that the government was influenced by communism. Opposed to hasty independence from Britain until Guatemala's claims over the country had been neutralized diplomatically, the party unsuccessfully sought a referendum on independence in 1981, subsequently boycotted a parliamentary committee mandated to study the question and refused to participate in the official celebrations, held in September, once independence had been achieved. In July of the same year, radical UDP members had formed the Belize Action Movement (BAM) which co-ordinated sometimes violent anti-government demonstrations.

Esquivel became leader of the party in 1982, deposing Theodore Aranda, who resigned to form the (now defunct) Christian Democrat Party. Esquivel led the party to power in 1984 on a free-market pro-Western platform which also emphasized the country's sovereignty rights and non-alignment. It won a comprehensive victory over the PUP with 21 seats to seven. The party was the unexpected loser of the general election of September 1989, by 15 seats to 13, despite Esquivel's prediction that his free-market economic policies and the promise of increased US investment would receive strong endorsement from the electorate.

Esquivel participated in a bipartisan team which toured the country in October 1991 explaining the implications of the September establishment of diplomatic relations with Guatemala and the significance of a Maritime Areas Bill, establishing conditions for Guatemalan access to the Caribbean Sea.

However, not all sectors of the party approved of the normaliztion of relations with Guatemala. Minority member Philip Goldson resigned from his position as deputy secretary-general, left the party, and helped launch the National Alliance for Belizean Rights (NABR).

At local elections held on March 8, 1994, the UDP won all seven of the country's town boards, an increase of five from the previous poll.

Benin

Capital: Porto Novo

Population: 5,500,000 (1995E)

Benin achieved independence from France in 1960 as Dahomey, was renamed the People's Republic of Benin in 1972 and became the Republic of Benin in 1990. The People's Republic was proclaimed following a military coup led by Mathieu Kérékou, who installed a Marxist-Leninist regime with the People's Revolutionary Party of Benin (PRPB) as the sole ruling party. The Republic of Benin was proclaimed under new constitutional arrangements approved by referendum on Dec. 2, 1990, and providing for multi-party democracy (the PRPB having dissolved itself in April). Under the new system, the executive President, who appoints the Council of Ministers, is directly elected for a five-year term by universal suffrage of those aged at least 18. Legislative authority is vested in a unicameral National Assembly (*Assemblée Nationale*) of 83 members, which is elected for a four-year term by universal adult suffrage according to a department-based system of proportional representation and which may not be dissolved by the President.

Presidential elections held in two rounds on March 10 and 24, 1991, were won by Nicéphore Soglo (backed by a coalition of parties), who defeated Gen. Kérékou (standing without party attribution) in the run-off ballot by 68% to 32%, after no candidate had obtained the required absolute majority in the first round. The following year President Soglo became identified with the new Benin Renaissance Party (PRB). Contested by over 30 distinct parties, elections to the National Assembly held on March 28, 1995, followed by re-runs in 13 constituencies on May 28 resulted in the PRB becoming the largest party, with 21 seats, while seven other pro-Soglo parties won one seat each. The other 55 seats went to nine anti-Soglo parties, among which the Party of Democratic Renewal took 18, the Action Front for Renewal and Development 14, the Social Democratic Party 8, the Rally of Liberal Democrats for National Reconstruction 4, Our Common Cause 4, the Alliance for Democracy and Progress 3 and the Impulse for Progress and Democracy 2.

In further presidential elections on March 3 and 17, 1996, President Soglo was defeated in the second round by Kérékou, who received 52.5% of the vote against 47.5% for the incumbent.

Action Front for Renewal and Development
Front d'Action pour le Renouveau et le Développement (FARD)
Address. c/o Assemblée Nationale, Porto Novo
Leadership. Salif Aka (secretary-general)

Proclaiming itself to be a party of national unity on its foundation in 1994 by five opposition deputies, the FARD formed part of the anti-Soglo group of parties in the 1995 Assembly elections, in which it increased its representation to 14 seats.

African Rally for Progress and Solidarity
Rassemblement Africain pour le Progrès et la Solidarité (RAPS)
Address. c/o Assemblée Nationale, Porto Novo
Leadership. Florentin Mito-Baba, Lazare Kpa-toukpa, Rigobert Ladikpo

The RAPS was launched in late October 1993 as an alliance of 11 parties and associations supportive of the government of President Soglo. The leaders listed above were cabinet ministers at the time of the creation of the alliance, which came shortly after the President's narrow majority in the Assembly had been threatened by defections. Perplexingly for the distant observer, the President's own Benin Renaissance Party (PRB) did not join the RAPS, which was reduced to one Assembly seat in the 1995 elections. Matters became clearer in July 1995 when a majority of the RAPS leadership opted to join the PRB.

Alliance for Democracy and Progress
Alliance pour la Démocratie et le Progrès (ADP)
Address. c/o Assemblée Nationale, Porto Novo
Leadership. Adekpedjou Akindes

The ADP contested the February 1991 Assembly

elections in alliance with the Democratic Union for Social Renewal, jointly winning two of the 64 seats. It formed part of the anti-Soglo front in the 1995 Assembly elections, winning three seats.

Alliance for Social Democracy
Alliance pour la Social-Démocratie (ASD)
   Address. c/o Assemblée Nationale, Porto Novo
   Leadership. Robert Dossou

The ASD contested the February 1991 Assembly elections in an alliance with the Bloc for Social Democracy which jointly won three of the 64 seats. The ASD leader, Robert Dossou, had been Minister of Planning under the Kérékou regime and had chaired the organizing committee of the February 1990 National Conference which had opted for multi-party democracy. He became Minister of Foreign Affairs and Co-operation in the post-election Soglo administration, retaining the post after the 1995 Assembly elections, in which the ASD won one seat.

Benin Renaissance Party
Parti de la Renaissance du Bénin (PRB)
   Address. c/o Assemblée Nationale, Porto Novo
   Leadership. Nicéphore Soglo (president), Rosine Soglo

The formation of the PRB was announced in March 1992 by President Soglo's wife, Rosine Soglo, and was intended as a new political base for the President, who had been elected in March 1991 with the backing of the Union for the Triumph of Democratic Renewal (*Union pour la Triomphe du Renouveau Démocratique*, UTRD). A former World Bank official, Soglo had been named Prime Minister in February 1990 by a National Conference charged with establishing a new political structure for Benin. After heading the first-round balloting in the subsequent presidential contest, Soglo had secured a decisive 68% advantage over President Kérékou in the second, thus becoming the first successful challenger to an incumbent head of state in black continental Africa.

The three component parties of the UTRD were the Democratic Union of Progressive Forces (UDFP) led by Timothée Adanlin, the Movement for Democracy and Social Progress (MDPS) led by Joseph Marcelin Degbe and the Union for Freedom and Development (ULD) led by Marius Francisco. In the February 1991 Assembly elections the UTRD had become the largest grouping with 12 of the then 64 seats, the UTRD contingent forming the nucleus of the broader Renewal (*Renouveau*) Group which by mid-1992 numbered 34 deputies and thus gave the government a working majority. In July 1993 President Soglo effectively assumed the leadership of the PRB, saying that he would "come down into the political arena" and promote the new party as a "catalyst" for the country's emerging democracy. His decision contributed to strains within the presidential coalition in the Assembly, where 15 members of the Renewal Group defected in October 1993, claiming that they had been "marginalized" by the President. Later the same month, however, 11 pro-Soglo parties and associations, including the UTRD rump (but not the PRB), formed the African Rally for Progress and Solidarity (RAPS), thus restoring the government's Assembly majority.

Further strains were apparent in September 1994, when President Soglo declared his intention to introduce the latest budget by decree, thus ignoring parliamentary opposition to the measure. In October 1994 the PRB absorbed the small Pan-African Union for Democracy and Solidarity (*Union Panafricaine pour la Démocratie et la Solidarité*, UPDS). But presidential efforts to elevate the PRB into the dominant party were confounded by voters in the 1995 Assembly elections, in which the PRB won only 21 of the 83 seats (and its allies a further seven), while anti-Soglo parties aggregated 55 seats. In July 1995 the PRB was formally joined by a majority of the RAPS leadership.

In that he also held French citizenship, Soglo's quest for a second term in the 1996 presidential elections appeared at first to be ruled out by the passage in September 1995 of a law barring anyone with dual nationality from standing. In the event, he entered the contest in March 1996 and was unexpectedly defeated in the second round by the resurrected Gen. Kérékou, who had retained powerful support in the state bureaucracy. Having at first complained of electoral fraud, Soglo accepted the voters' verdict on April 2.

Communist Party of Benin
Parti Communiste de Benin (PCB)
   Address. c/o Assemblée Nationale, Porto Novo
   Leadership. Pascal Fatondji (first secretary)

The PCB was granted legal registration in October 1993, being the successor to the Dahomey Communist Party (PCD) founded in 1977 in opposition to the brand of Marxism-Leninism propagated by Kérékou regime. Once labelled "pro-Albanian" in ideological orientation, the banned PCD had come to notice in 1985 when some 100 alleged members had been detained in a government crackdown. Operating mainly from exile in Paris, the PCD had maintained an underground network in Benin, which had displayed its influence in the trade union movement during protest demonstrations in late 1989. The PCD had boycotted the 1990 negotiations on transition to multi-partyism, most of its leaders remaining in exile at that stage. By 1993, however, many had returned to Benin and, undeterred by the demise of communism elsewhere in the world, had reconstituted the party under the PCB rubric. The party won one seat in the 1995 Assembly elections on a platform of opposition to President Soglo, although it was quickly induced to join the presidential tendency in the new legislature.

National Movement for Democracy and Development

Mouvement National pour la Démocratie et le Développement (MNDD)

    Address. c/o Assemblée Nationale, Porto Novo

    Leadership. Bertyin Borna

The MNDD contested the February 1991 Assembly elections in a three-party alliance with the Movement for Solidarity, Union and Progress and the Union for Democracy and National Reconstruction. The joint tally of the alliance was six of the 64 seats. Forming part of the presidential tendency in the 1995 elections, the MNDD won one seat.

National Rally for Democracy

Rassemblement Nationale pour la Démocratie (RND)

    Leadership. Théophile Paoleti Behanzin

The RND was founded in May 1990 as a merger of the National Front for Democracy (FND) and the Democratic Republican Movement (MDR). These parties had been part of a broader opposition Rally of Democratic Forces, founded in January 1990 and bringing together prominent opposition leaders for the following month's National Conference which agreed a new political system. The RND presented candidates in the November 1990 local elections and won seven seats in the Assembly elections of February 1991. The then RND leader, Joseph Keke, was an initial candidate for the March 1991 presidential election, but withdrew before polling in favour of Nicéphore Soglo, candidate of the Union for the Triumph for Democracy and the eventual victor. Keke also failed to be elected to the Assembly presidency in July 1991, despite being President Soglo's preferred candidate. In August 1991 the RND was weakened by the defection of former President Justin Tometin Ahomadegbe, who had been leader of the FND constituent of the RND. The RND failed to win representation in the 1995 Assembly elections; nevertheless, in the post-election government RND member Pierre Nevi retained the justice portfolio to which he had been appointed in May 1994,

National Union for Democracy and Progress

Union Nationale pour la Démocratie et le Progrès (UNDP)

    Address. c/o Assemblée Nationale, Porto Novo

    Leadership. Emile Zinsou

The UNDP was launched on the advent of multi-partyism in 1990 and became a component of the loose Rally of Democratic Forces. Its leader had been President from mid-1968 until being deposed by the military in late 1969 and was one of four former heads of state who pressed for democratic reform at the February 1990 National Conference. The UNDP presented candidates in the November 1990 local elections and the following month campaigned for a "no" vote in the constitutional referendum, in part because of provisions debarring presidential candidates over the age of 70 (which meant that Zinsou could not stand). In the February 1991 Assembly elections, the UNDP won only one of the 64 seats. It retained its one seat in the 1995 elections, in which it was one of the "presidential tendency" parties.

Our Common Cause

Notre Cause Commune (NCC)

    Address. c/o Assemblée Nationale, Porto Novo

    Leadership. Albert Tevoedjire

The NCC was founded as a vehicle for the presidential ambitions of Tevoedjire, a former deputy director of the International Labour Organization, who in March 1990 became the first opposition figure to declare his candidacy. To this end, the NCC was an early constituent of the National Rally for Democracy, but Tevoedjire was expelled from the latter in September 1990. The NCC then registered as a political party in its own right and won six of the 64 seats in the Assembly elections of February 1991. In the presidential contest the following month, Tevoedjire came in third place, with 14% of vote, and declined to give his endorsement to either of the candidates who went forward to the second round. Increasingly critical of the post-1991 Soglo administration, the NCC leader in October 1994 categorically rejected government claims of opposition involvement in recent bombing attacks. As one of the group of anti-Soglo parties, the NCC won four seats in the 1995 Assembly elections. In November 1995 the party selected former President Mathieu Kérékou as its presidential candidate for 1996, apparently without consulting him.

Party of Democratic Renewal

Parti du Renouveau Démocratique (PRD)

    Address. c/o Assemblée Nationale, Porto Novo

    Leadership. Adrien Houngbedji

The PRD contested the February 1991 Assembly elections in an alliance with the National Party for

Democracy and Development which came in second place, although together they won only nine of the 64 seats. Houngbedji was subsequently elected president of the National Assembly, despite not having the backing of President Soglo. In the 1995 Assembly elections the PRD headed the victorious group of anti-Soglo parties, winning 18 of the 83 seats in its own right. In that he also held French citizenship, Houngbedji's expected candidacy for the 1996 presidential election appeared to be blocked by the passage of a law in September 1995 banning anyone with dual nationality from standing for the presidency.

Rally of Liberal Democrats for National Reconstruction
Rassemblement des Démocrates Libéraux pour la Réconstruction Nationale (RDL-Vivoten)
    Address. c/o Assemblée Nationale, Porto Novo
    Leadership. Sévérin Adjovi
    Led by a businessman based in Paris, this party contested the February 1991 Assembly elections in its own right, winning four of the 64 seats. As part of the opposition, it again won four seats (out of 83) in the 1995 Assembly elections.

Social Democratic Party
Parti Social-Démocrate (PSD)
    Address. c/o Assemblée Nationale, Porto Novo
    Leadership. Bruno Amoussou
    The PSD was formed on the introduction of multi-partyism in 1990 and presented candidates in the November 1990 local elections. It contested the February 1991 Assembly elections in alliance with the National Union for Solidarity and Progress, registering a joint tally of eight of the 64 seats. It retained eight seats in the 1995 elections (out of 83), forming part of the victorious group of anti-Soglo parties.

Union for National Democracy and Solidarity
Union pour la Démocratie et la Solidarité Nationale (UDSN)
    Address. c/o Assemblée Nationale, Porto Novo
    Leadership. Adamou N'Diaye
    The UDSN was one of the "presidential tendency" parties in the 1995 Assembly elections, in which it won one seat.

Other Parties

Action and Progress Generation (*Action Génération Progrès*, AGP), led by Yves Edgar Monou, founded in 1994, unsuccessful in the 1995 Assembly elections.

Benin Workers' Party (*Parti des Ouvriers Béninois*, POB), founded in 1994, unsuccessful in the 1995 Assembly elections.

Bloc for Social Democracy (*Bloc pour la Social-Démocratie*, BSD), led by Michel Magnide, contested the 1991 Assembly elections in alliance with the Alliance for Social Democracy, together winning three of the 64 seats; failed to win representation in 1995.

Chameleon Alliance (*Alliance Caméléon*, AC), a new formation seeking to embrace disparate political currents, won one Assembly seat in 1995 as an anti-Soglo party.

Democratic Union for Social Renewal (*Union Démocratique pour le Renouveau Social*, UDRS), led by Deni Amoussou-Yeye, contested the 1991 Assembly elections in alliance with the Alliance for Democracy and Progress, jointly winning two of the 64 seats, but failed to gain representation in 1995.

Impulse for Progress and Democracy (*Impulsion pour le Progrès et la Démocratie*, IPD), a new formation that won two Assembly seats in 1995 as part of the anti-Soglo opposition.

Movement for Solidarity, Union and Progress (*Mouvement pour la Solidarité, l'Union et le Progrès*, MSUP), led by Adebo Adeniyi Djamiou, contested the 1991 Assembly elections in a three-party alliance with the National Movement for Democracy and Development and the Union for Democracy and National Reconstruction, the joint tally being six of the 64 seats; failed to gain representation in 1995.

National Party for Democracy and Development (*Parti National pour la Démocratie et le Développement*, PNDD), led by Joseph Copiery, contested the 1991 Assembly elections in an alliance with the Party of Democratic Renewal which came in second place, although together they won only nine of the 64 seats; failed to gain representation in 1995.

National Party of Labour (*Parti National du Travail*, PNT), led by Inoussa Bello, contested the February 1991 Assembly elections in an alliance with the Republican People's Union which yielded only one of the 64 seats; failed to gain representation in 1995.

National Union for Solidarity and Progress (*Union Nationale pour la Solidarité et le Progrès*, UNDP), led by Eustache Sarre, contested the 1991 Assembly elections in alliance with the Social Democratic Party, jointly winning eight of the 64 seats; failed to gain representation in 1995.

New Generation (*Nouvelle Génération*, NG), a recently-formed pro-Soglo party that took one seat in the 1995 Assembly elections.

Rally for Democracy and Pan-Africanism (*Rassemblement pour la Démocratie et le Pan-Africainisme*, RDPA), led by Dominique Hoyminou, founded in mid-1994 by a faction of the Pan-African Union of Democracy and Solidarity that opposed the latter's merger with the Benin Renaissance Party.

Rally for Democracy and Progress (*Rassemblement pour la Démocratie et le Progrès*, RDP), won one seat in the 1995 Assembly elections as part of the anti-Soglo opposition.

Republican People's Union (*Union Républicaine du Peuple*, URP), led by Michel Toko, contested the 1991 Assembly elections in alliance with the National Party of Labour, this joint endeavour yielding one of the 64 seats; failed gain representation in the 1995 Assembly elections.

Union for Democracy and National Reconstruction (*Union pour la Démocratie et la Réconstruction Nationale*, UDRN), led by Azaria Fakorede, contested the 1991 Assembly elections in a three-party alliance with the National Movement for Democracy and Development and the Movement for Solidarity, Union and Progress, their joint tally being six of the 64 seats; failed to gain representation in 1995.

Union for Democracy and Solidarity (*Union pour la Démocratie et la Réconstruction Nationale*, UDRN), led by Adamou Mama, contested the 1991 Assembly elections in its own right, winning five of the 64 seats; failed to gain representation in 1995.

Union of Progressive Forces (*Union des Forces du Progrès*, UFP), led by Machoudi Dissoudi, established in May 1990 as successor to the former ruling People's Revolutionary Party of Benin (which had voted to dissolve itself the previous month) but marginalized in the rapidly-changing political situation created by the advent of multi-partyism.

Bhutan

Capital: Thimphu

Population: 1,750,000 (1995E)

The Kingdom of Bhutan is an hereditary monarchy in which power is shared between the King (assisted by a Royal Advisory Council), the Council of Ministers, the National Assembly (*Tsongdu*) and the monastic head of Bhutan's Buddhist priesthood. The Council of Ministers is appointed by the King and may be dismissed by him with the consent of the National Assembly, which was established in 1953 as the principal legislative body. The unicameral National Assembly has 151 members, of whom 106 are directly elected for three-year terms by univeral adult suffrage; 10 are elected indirectly by religious bodies; one is elected by the Chamber of Commerce and Industry; 18 are the leaders of district governments; and 16 are government nominees (usually ministers or royal advisers). There are no legal political parties, such activity being largely confined to dissident ethnic Nepali groups based in Nepal or India.

Bolivia

Capital: La Paz (Sucre is the judicial capital) **Population:** 7,400,000 (1995E)

Bolivia claimed independence from Spain in 1925 and its first constitution was enforced in November 1826. Since then Bolivia has suffered 189 military coups and had several new constitutions. Bolivian politics since the World War II, despite the continued persistence of military intervention, have been dominated by the Nationalist Revolutionary Movement (MNR)—later the Historic Nationalist Revolutionary Movement (MNRH)—under its veteran leader Victor Paz Estenssoro, who came to power in the popular revolution of 1952. Bolivia was subsequently under the rule of military juntas almost continuously between 1964 and 1982, when it was returned to civilian rule under President Hernan Siles Zuazo.

The present constitution dates from 1947 and was resurrected after a coup in 1964. Executive power is vested in the President who appoints the Cabinet, as well as the nine departmental prefects, the country's diplomatic representatives, archbishops and bishops. He is assisted by a Vice-President and a bicameral Congress which is made up of a 27-seat Senate and a 130-seat Chamber of Deputies. The President is elected by direct suffrage for a four-year term and is not eligible to serve two consecutive terms. If no candidate emerges from the election with an absolute majority the newly-elected Congress appoints a President. Senators (three for each of the nine provinces) and deputies are elected by proportional representation, also for a four-year term.

There has been universal suffrage in Bolivia since the 1952 popular uprising, when the vote was also given to women and illiterates over the age of 21 and the age of suffrage for married people was reduced to 18. Voting is compulsory, and non-participation in the ballot can result in loss of certain legal rights for up to three months, such as the use of banks.

Gonzalo Sanchez de Lozada of the MNR was the winner of the June 6, 1993, presidential election. In concurrent congressional elections, the MNR won 52 seats in the Chamber of Deputies and 17 in the Senate, short of an overall majority. This resulted in a pact with centre parties, the Civic Solidarity Union (UCS) and the Free Bolivia Movement (MBL), in return for cabinet posts. The government took office on August 6, 1993. The UCS, which left the government in September 1994 after months of disagreement, rejoined on June 15, 1995.

Bolivian Communist Party
Partido Comunista de Bolivia (PCB)

Leadership. Humberto Ramirez (secretary-general)

Founded in 1950, the PCB was orthodox communist before the collapse of the Soviet Union and the Eastern Bloc, since when internal factions have plagued the party.

Formed by dissident members of the Party of the Revolutionary Left (PIR) youth section, the PCB attained legal status after the 1952 revolution. The party at first supported the revolutionary MNR government but soon became critical of its one-party rule and stood against it in the general election of 1956, in alliance with the PIR. It won only 1.5% of the vote and in 1960, when

the PCB contested an election by itself for the only time in its history, it found support among only 1% of the voters. In 1965 the party split into a pro-Soviet and a pro-Chinese faction and both were banned in 1967 even though their involvement with the guerrillas of Che Guevara's National Liberation Army, then attempting to ignite a domestic revolution, was limited to some pro-Soviet PCB youth section members who were subsequently expelled. Although the ban was later lifted, the PCB was again driven underground during the Bánzer military regime of 1971 to 1978.

The PCB, under new leadership, fought the 1985 general election in the United People's Front alliance with the Revolutionary Party of the National Left (PRIN) and two dissident factions of the

MIR, which won four Congressional seats. In July of that year, it expelled a minority faction which included a large part of the PCB youth wing. In an attempt to improve its appeal to young voters the party joined the left-wing Patriotic Alliance for the 1987 municipal elections and in September 1988 it became a founder member of the United Left (IU). In the general election of May 7, 1989, the IU candidate Antonio Araníbar Quiroga (see Free Bolivia Movement) won a negligible percentage of the valid vote but the alliance gained 10 seats in the Chamber of Deputies.

Christian Democratic Party
Partido Demócrata Cristiano (PDC)
    Address. Casilla M. 10044, La Paz
    Telephone. (#591-2) 321918
    Leadership. Dr Jorge Agreda Valderrama (president)
The PDC is a centre-left Roman Catholic grouping that was founded in 1954 as the Social Christian Party by Remo di Natale.

In the 1962 partial elections its leader Benjamín Miguel obtained the party's first congressional seat, and at its November 1964 congress, the party took its present name. Although it boycotted the general election of 1966, called by the military junta, the PDC accepted the Labour portfolio in 1967 in a military government from which it resigned when the President, Gen. Barrientos, sent in the army to fight protesting miners. Thereafter the PDC opposed all subsequent military regimes, which eventually led to the exile of both Miguel and the party's organizing secretary, Félix Vargas, from 1974 until after President Bánzer was overthrown in 1978. In the general election of July 1979 the PDC, in an alliance with the Nationalist Revolutionary Movement-Historic (MNRH) and three minor parties, won nine seats in the Chamber of Deputies and three in the Senate. It was given a cabinet post after democracy was restored in October 1982. In the general election of 1985 the PDC's presidential candidate, Luis Ossio Sanjinés, won a mere 1.4% of the vote while the party's representation in Congress dwindled to three seats. In the run-up to the May 1989 elections, the PDC negotiated an alliance with the left-wing MIR, but when the talks broke down in January 1989, the PDC agreed to join forced with the right-wing Nationalist Democratic Action (ADN). Ossio Sanjinés became Bánzer's running mate in the presidential elections on May 7, 1989. On Aug. 6 he was appointed vice-president of the new Patriotic Accord coalition government as a result of the pact with the ADN. In a major cabinet re-shuffle in August 1991, Ossio Sanjinés retained his post but was unsuccessful in demanding an enlarged "quota of power" for the PDC in government.

The party campaigned as a member of the Patriotic Agreement (*Acuerdo Patriótico*, AP) in 1993. The PDC is an affiliate of the Christian Democrat International.

Civic Solidarity Union
Unión Cívica Solidaridad (UCS)
    Address. c/o Camara de Diputadoc, La Paz
    Leadership. Max Fernández Rojas
An off-shoot of the National Civic Union (*Unión Cívica Nacional*, UCN), the UCS was founded in 1988 as a vehicle for the presidential campaign of Max Fernández Rojas. Rojas won a surprising third place in the May 1989 election with 22.8% of the vote. However, his candidacy was subsequently nullified by the Electoral Court after he was found to have forged 40,000 of the 60,000 votes he received. He nevertheless announced his candidature for the 1993 presidential elections where he polled a 13.1% vote share.

Following this election in which Sánchez de Lozada won the presidency, the UCS was invited to be one of three parties in a new government coalition with the Free Bolivia Movement (MBL) and the Nationalist Revolutionary Movement (MNR).

Conscience of the Fatherland
Conciencia de Patria (Condepa)
    Address. c/o Camara de Diputados, La Paz
    Leadership. Julio Mantilla Cuéllar
In July 1991, Condepa joined the MNRH and the MBL in breaking off talks with the AP, claiming that it had violated the impartiality of the new electoral law, approved by Congress in June, by appointing its own preferred choices to the new Electoral Court. In the municipal elections of December 1991, however, Condepa candidate Julio Mantilla Cuéllar was elected mayor of La Paz, with 26.35% of the vote, and the party also won the major neighbouring city of El Alto with 34% of the vote, both results representing the party's most significant achievement to date. Mantilla pledged to use his office to bring justice to the poorest sectors of the population.

In a general election on May 7, 1989, Condepa won nine seats in the Chamber of Deputies and two in the Senate. During the presidential run-off in the Congress in August, the party threw its support behind Paz Zamora, candidate of the Movement of the Revolutionary Left (MIR), but the party remained in opposition to the subsequent Patriotic Accord (AP) government. The party was later placed fourth in the 1993 legislative balloting, winning 14 seats overall.

Free Bolivia Movement

Movimiento Bolivia Libre (MBL)

Address. Calle Batallón, Victoria esq Armentia 807, Casilla 10382, La Paz

Telephone. (#591-2) 340257

Fax. (#591-2) 392242

Leadership. Antonio Araníbar Quiroga (1993 presidential candidate)

This nominally left-wing party was founded in 1985. The party was formed by the then general secretary of the main Movement of the Revolutionary Left (MIR), Antonio Araníbar Quiroga, after he and a left-wing section of the MIR split away in protest against participation in the Siles Zuazo government. Araníbar fought the 1985 election as the presidential candidate of the left-wing People's United Front alliance and won 2.2% of the vote, while the alliance obtained four seats in Congress.

The municipal elections of 1987 showed an increase in MBL's support—the party won in Bolivia's legal capital Sucre and came second in Cochabamba. In 1988 its electoral success brought the MBL to the leadership of the newly formed United Left (IU). Araníbar fought for the Presidency as candidate for the IU in the May 1989 elections but won a negligible percentage of the vote. In February 1990 the MBL left the alliance.

In 1990 and 1991, the party was prominent in protracted opposition dialogue with the Patriotic Accord (AP) government over such issues as the independence of the Supreme Court and the establishment of a new electoral system presided over by a impartial electoral court.

Leftist Nationalist Revolutionary Movement

Movimiento Nacionalista Revolucionario de Izquierda (MNRI)

Leadership. Dr Hernán Siles Zuazo

The MNRI was founded after the left wing of the Nationalist Revolutionary Movement (MNR) split away in the early 1970s. It was led by the MNR founding member and former President (1956-60) Hernán Siles Zuazo. The party was the leading force of the Popular Democratic Unity (UDP) alliance during the 1978 general election. Siles Zuazo won both the 1979 and 1980 presidential elections with 36 and 38.7% of the vote, but each time was prevented from taking power by a military coup. In October 1982 he was finally allowed to return from his Peruvian exile and take office.

His UDP government, which was increasingly dominated by the MNRI, rapidly lost support from the left, the unions and the peasantry as it tried to placate multilateral lending agencies in the search for international loans, to the neglect of initiating urgent social reforms.

The elections of June 1985 resulted in the massive defeat of the MNRI presidential candidate, Roberto Jordán Pando, who received a mere 4.8%

of the vote, the party obtaining only eight seats in the Congress. It proved to be a setback from which the party never recovered.

After this defeat, the party proceeded to split into a number of factions including the centre-right Nationalist Revolutionary Movement—April 9th Revolutionary Vanguard (*Movimiento Nacionalista Revolucionario–Vanguardia Revolucionaria 9 de Abril*, MNR-V) and the Leftist Nationalist Revolutionist Movement—One (*Movimiento Nacionalista Revolucionario Izquierdo–Uno*, MNRI-1) each of which subsequently campaigned separately.

Movement of the Revolutionary Left

Movimiento de la Izquierda Revolucionaria (MIR)

Address. Avenida América 119, 20 Piso, La Paz

Telephone. (#591-2) 392939

Fax. (#591-2) 710380

Leadership. Jaime Paz Zamora

Founded in 1971, the MIR has much left-wing rhetoric but in power has proved to be conservative. Gaining its main power base from the liberal urban middle class, the MIR arose out of a merger of small left-wing groups and young Christian Democrats and was formed in opposition to the 1971 military coup. It drew considerable support from the radical student movement and was linked to the National Liberation Army (ELN) in the early years of the Bánzer military dictatorship (1971-78).

It gradually moved away from its Marxist roots but nevertheless remained in strong opposition to the regime which continued to persecute and imprison members of the MIR, among them Bánzer's future political ally, Jaime Paz Zamora (see Patriotic Accord).

The party contested the elections of 1978, 1979 and 1980 as part of an alliance led by the Leftist Nationalist Revolutionary Movement (MNRI) with Jaime Paz Zamora as running-mate to the victorious but ill-fated MNRI leader, Hernán Siles Zuazo, in 1979 and 1980.

Zamora came third with 8.8% of the vote in the July 1985 presidential contest and in the simultaneous congressional elections the depleted MIR won 16 seats. When Congress had to vote in the second round of the presidential elections, the MIR joined with other centre-left parties in electing the presidential runner-up Victor Paz Estenssoro of the Nationalist Revolutionary Movement-Historic (MNRH) in preference to ex-dictator Bánzer.

In late 1988 the MIR approached the Christian Democratic Party with a view to forming an alliance but when by January 1989 they had not come any closer to an agreement, the MIR decided to contest the May 1989 general election alone, winning 41 congressional seats, Zamora being placed a close third with 19.64% of the vote in the presidential race. However, with no conclusive winner in the presidential election, the runner-up, Gen. Hugo Bánzer, of the right-wing Nationalist Democratic Action (ADN), withdrew and switched 46 ADN congressional members to Jaime Paz Zamora who, on Aug. 6, was duly elected by Congress to be President.

The price exacted for this support was the necessity for the MIR to share power with the ADN in a "Patriotic Accord" (AP). In an August 1991 major cabinet reshuffle, three MIR ministerial posts were allocated to members of the MIR-New Majority (MIR-NM) faction, who, due to the domination of the ADN, had previously been circumspect in their support for the party's involvement in the AP coalition. However in March 1992, the MIR-NM confirmed its support for Bánzer as AP candidate in the 1993 presidential elections.

Paz Zamora entered into "permanent" retirement in March 1994, but returned less than eight months later following the arrest on drugs charges of the party's secretary-general, Oscar Eid Franco.

The MIR is the Bolivian affiliate of the Socialist International.

Nationalist Democratic Action
Acción Democrática Nacionalista (ADN)

Leadership. Gen. (retd.) Hugo Bánzer Suárez (leader), Jorge Ouiroga (general secretary).

The ADN was formed as a vehicle for former dictator Gen. (retd.) Hugo Bánzer Suárez (1971-78) for the July 1979 general election in which he came third with 14.9% of the vote. In the 1980 general election his share of the vote increased slightly to 16.9% and the ADN won 30 congressional seats which were finally taken up when Congress was recalled in September 1982. The ADN initially supported the July 1980 coup led by Gen. Luis García Meza but in April 1981 this backing was withdrawn. A month later Bánzer was arrested on a charge of plotting a counter-coup.

The general election of July 1985 resulted in Bánzer winning the largest volume of votes, 28.6%, and the ADN gained 51 seats in Congress. However, because no presidential candidate had obtained a clear majority, a centre-left alliance in Congress elected Víctor Paz Estenssoro of the Nationalist Revolutionary Movement-Historic (MNRH) as President.

For the general election of May 7, 1989, the ADN entered into an alliance with the Christian Democratic Party (PDC). Bánzer, the alliance's joint candidate, won 22.7% of the vote in the presidential election and was narrowly beaten by the MNRH candidate, Gonzalo Sánchez de Losada. Personal dislike between the two candidates, however, prevented the ADN-MNRH pact from being renewed and ensured that neither was elected President. On August 5, a day before the scheduled second round of voting in Congress,

Bánzer withdrew from the race and switched the votes of the 46 ADN congressional members to the Movement of the Revolutionary Left (MIR), enabling its candidate, Jaime Paz Zamora, to be elected to the presidency.

The subsequent ADN-MIR-led Patriotic Accord (AP) coalition government assumed power on Aug. 8, 1989. In return for the presidency, Paz Zamora awarded the ADN 10 out of 18 ministerial posts, including the most important portfolios of finance, defence and foreign affairs. Bánzer personally took the chair of the *Consejo del Gobierno de Unidad y Convergencia* (Political Council of Convergence and National Unity), a post which gave him effective control over government policy, appointments to top public positions and changes in the hierarchy of the armed forces.

The ADN's dominance in the AP coalition was underlined in ministerial changes in August 1991 and March 1992, when it retained the most influential portfolios. Some prominent ADN ministers were replaced in government to enable them to join Bánzer's campaign staff for the forthcoming 1993 presidential elections. In the same month, MIR leaders had ratified Bánzer as the AP's presidential candidate.

However, once again Bánzer Suárez could only manage second place in the presidential elections, being well beaten by Gonzalo Sánchez de Lozada. The AP was consequently dissolved in August 1993, with Bánzer Suárez resigning as ADN leader in November. In February 1995, however, Bánzer Suárez changed his mind, announcing a return to public life and to leadership of the ADN.

Nationalist Revolutionary Movement
Movimiento Nacionalista Revolucionario (MNR)

Address. Jenaro Sanjines 541, Pasaje Kuljis, La Paz

Leadership. Gonzalo Sánchez de Lozada

This right-wing party was founded in June 1941 as the Nationalist Revolutionary Movement (MNR), although in later years it became known as the Historic Nationalist Revolutionary Movement (MNHR). The party is now again usually referred to as the MNR following the demise of previous factions. Although a right-wing grouping, the party has consistently stood for the development of neo-liberal economic policies.

Founded by among others Victor Paz Estenssoro, the left-wing Hernán Siles Zuazo and the fascist sympathiser Carlos Montenegro, the party's policies reflected its leader's attempt to combine the nationalist developmentalist ideas of the Peruvian American Popular Revolutionary Alliance Party (APRA) with those of European fascism, especially as extolled by the Italian dictator Benito Mussolini. The MNR first participated in government in 1943-33 under President Villaroel.

When the military overthrew Villaroel in 1946, numerous MNR leaders were killed or exiled. Paz Estenssoro fought the elections of May 1951 from exile as the MNR's presidential candidate and won the highest vote (although not an outright majority). The incumbent President, however, handed over power to a military junta which, less than a year later, was toppled by an MNR-led popular uprising, known thereafter as the 1952 Revolution, assisted by the police and tin miners. Paz Estenssoro was finally allowed to return from Argentina and was appointed President in April 1952.

Paz Estenssoro's coalition government with the Labour Party introduced a number of progressive reforms, including the nationalization of the mines, agrarian reform and the enfranchisement of illiterates. The MNR remained in power for two more terms, with Siles Zurazo taking over the presidency in 1956 and Paz Estenssoro being elected President again in 1960.

In November 1964, following widespread strikes and disorder, Estenssoro was overthrown and forced into exile by his Vice-President, Gen. René Barrientos Ortuño, who took power with the assistance of the army. The MNR was thrown into disarray and only re-emerged on the political scene in 1971 as supporters of the military coup of Gen. Hugo Bánzer (see Nationalist Democratic Action).

The MNR participated in Bánzer's government until 1974 when it was expelled for protesting that the promised process of democratization had not begun. By then, the left wing of the party, led by Siles Zuazo, had already broken away and formed the Nationalist Revolutionary Movement of the Left (MNRI), to which Paz Estenssoro's faction, MNRH, came second in the 1979 and 1980 presidential elections; Paz Estenssoro was beaten by Siles in both elections, winning only 35.9% and 20.1% of the vote respectively. The MNRH, however, won 44 seats in the Congress.

Following another period of military government (1980-82) and three years of opposition to the MNRI government, Paz Estenssoro once again made a bid for the presidency. In the general election of June 1985 he obtained 26.4% of the vote, 2.2% less than the ADN's candidate, Bánzer.

However, in a run-off congressional vote in August 1985, the centre-left parties added their votes to those of the 59 MNRH Congressmen and brought Paz to power. His third term in office set a future precedent for the party and the country. He quickly introduced a strict austerity programme to reduce rampant inflation, a policy persisted with despite the collapse of the international tin market in late 1985.

Faced with general labour unrest, repressed under a 90-day state of siege, Paz Estenssoro found greater common ground with the right-wing ADN than with his erstwhile supporters of the centre left. A "Pact for Democracy" between the MNRH and the ADN was duly signed in October 1985. In the municipal elections of December 1987 the MNRH polled poorly, amid widespread discontent with the government. This was further fuelled by the USA-assisted anti-drug programme which threatened the livelihood of many peasant coca growers, whose numbers had been swollen by unemployed miners. Nevertheless, in the general election of May 7, 1989, the MNRH presidential candidate Gonzalo Sánchez de Lozada, the former Minister of Planning, headed the poll with 23.07% of the vote, not sufficient to give him the presidency. A run-off election in the newly elected Congress, in which the MNRH had 49 seats, did not produce a renewal of the "Pact of Democracy" with the ADN. Personal animosity between de Lozada and ADN leader Bánzer resulted in the ADN switching its support to Jaime Paz Zamora of the Movement of the Revolutionary Left (MIR), who was elected President.

Three months after the election of Zamora as President, the 84-year old Paz Estenssoro announced his desire to resign the party leadership. At the next party congress in mid-1990 the decision was formalized and Gonzalo Sánchez de Lozada was elected as his successor. On Oct. 27, 1992, Sánchez de Lozada resigned as party president and as 1993 MNR presidential candidate following a death threat from an MNR congressional deputy. However, he resumed both activities on Nov. 20, 1992. At the nationwide poll of June 6, 1993, Sánchez de Lozada again defeated Bánzer Suárez to take the presidency. In the later legislative balloting the MNR raised its representation to 69 out of 157 seats, thus confirming its status as the dominant ruling party.

Patriotic Alliance
Alianza Patriótico (AP)
    Leadership. Walter Delgadillo Terceros
    Founded in 1985, the party was formed by Walter Delgadillo, the leader of the radical MIR faction MIR-Masses, the former leader of the Bolivian Workers' Centre (COB) trade union confederation. In September 1988 the AP became the founder member of the United Left (IU) for which Delgadillo fought the 1989 elections as the running-mate of Antonio Aranibar Quiroga of the Free Bolivia Movement.

Socialist Party—One
Partido Socialista—Uno (PS-1)
    Leadership. Ramiro Velasco; Roger Cortez
    Founded in 1988, the PSI was formed by the merger of three minor parties which had sup-

ported the former President, Gen. Alfredo Ovando Candía. In the mid-1970s the party suffered a split: the right wing led by Guillermo Aponte backed the MRNI and the left renamed itself the Socialist Party-One. In the elections of 1978, 1979 (in which the PS1 won five congressional seats) and 1980 (winning 11 congressional seats), the PS1 fielded Marcelo Quiroga Santa Cruz as its presidential candidate. He was assassinated by troops during the 1980 military coup and thereafter the party's popularity declined.

The party contested the 1985 elections with little success, coming sixth with 2.2% of the vote and winning five seats in the Congress. The PS1, which strongly opposed the Paz Estenssoro government's economic and social policies (see Nationalist Revolutionary Movement-Historic), joined the United Left (IU) at its inception in 1988. When the date for the municipal elections for 1991 was announced, the PS1 argued that they should be postponed so that more people would have the chance to register on the electoral roll.

As in 1985, Ramiro Velasco was the party's 1993 Presidential Candidate.

Tupaj Katari Revolutionary Movement— Liberation

Movimiento Revolucionario Tupaj Katari—Liberación (MRTK-L)

Address. 939 Avenida Baptista, Casilla 9133, La Paz

Telephone. (#591-2) 354784

Leadership. Víctor Hugo Cárdenas Conde (president); Norberto Perez Hidalgo (secretary-general)

A splinter group of its smaller parent, the Tupaj Katari Revolutionary Movement (*Movimiento Revolucionario Tupaj Katari*—MRTK), the MRTK-L out-polled its weak parent party in 1985, winning two Congressional seats, both of which were subsequently lost in 1989. In late 1992 the MNR sought to widen the popularity of its electoral ticket by offering the MRTK-L's leader, Victor Cárdenas, as Gonzalos Sánchez de Lozada's running mate.

United Left

Izquierda Unida (IU)

Leadership. Germán Guttierez

In 1989 the United Left coalition was formed to campaign in the 1989 elections following the demise of the previous leftist coalition, the United People's Front (*Frente del Pueblo Unido*, FPU). The IU was the product of an alliance of eight parties formed to contest the May 1989 general election. Led by the Free Bolivia Movement (MBL), the IU fielded MBL leader Antonio Araníbar Quiroga as its presidential candidate with Walter Delgadillo of the Patriotic Alliance (AP) as his running mate. The IU won 12 congressional

seats, a poor result compared with that achieved by its component parties in the 1985 elections, as Araníbar won a negligible percentage of the total vote. However, in the municipal elections of December 1989 the IU retained the MBL's hold on power in the (official) capital, Sucre. Two months later, however, the MBL left the alliance, leaving it in a state of disarray. In the municipal elections in December, it won 4% of the total vote.

The IU put forward Ramiro Velasco of the Socialist Party–One as its presidential candidate in the 1993 election, at which it lost all ten of its legislative seats. The alliance includes the Bolivian Communist Party, the Patriotic Alliance and the Socialist Party–One.

Other Parties

Left Revolutionary Front

Frente Revolucionario de Izquierda (FRI)

Leadership. Oscar Zamora Medinacelli

Headed by Oscar Zamora Medinacelli, the FRI has been quite successful as a vehicle for the political ambitions of its leader if not in a strictly electoral sense. Zamora Medinacelli was also a founder member of the MIR (see above) founded in 1971. For the elections of 1985, Zamora Medinacelli formed an alliance with the MNR and gained from it the Senate Presidency. He achieved similar success in 1989 by backing the MIR-ADN coalition which yielded him the job of labour minister in the government of his nephew, Paz Zamora. In August 1991, the FRI joined the Patriotic Accord government and he re-obtained the Labour portfolio in an August 1991 reshuffle.

This post he resigned in 1992 to accept the vice-presidential position on the presidential campaign ticket of the ADN's Hugo Bánzer, a former military dictator of Bolivia.

National Leftist Revolutionary Party

Partido Revolucionario de Izquierda Nacionalista (PRIN)

Leadership. Juan Lechín Oquendo

PRIN was founded in 1964 as a splinter from the MNR embodying various national labour principles under its charismatic leader, Juan Lechín Oquendo. It represented in national politics the opinions of the Miners' Federation (*Federación Sindical de Trabajadores Mineros Bolivianos*—FSTMB) and the Bolivian Workers' Federation (*Central Obrera Boliviano*—COB), both of which had Oquendo as president until 1986.

Revolutionary Workers' Party

Partido Obrero Revolucionario (POR)

Leadership. Guillermo Lora Escobar

A Trotskyite party with limited support and three prominent internal factions.

Bosnia and Hercegovina

Capital: Sarajevo   **Population:** 3,000,000 (1995E)

The Republic of Bosnia and Hercegovina declared independence from the Socialist Federal Republic of Yugoslavia (SFRY) in March 1992 and was admitted to the UN in May 1992. Its pre-independence ethnic composition by main group was 44% Muslim, 31% Serb and 17% Croat, a mixture which precipitated a bloody civil war in which the neighbouring states of Croatia and rump Yugoslavia (Serbia and Montenegro) became involved. In December 1992 the Serbian Republic of Bosnia and Hercegovina was proclaimed in the Serb-controlled areas, while the Croat-controlled area declared the Croatian Republic of Herceg-Bosna in August 1993. A US-brokered agreement signed in Washington in March 1994 by Bosnian Muslim and Bosnian Croat representatives provided for a power-sharing (Muslim-Croat) Federation of Bosnia and Hercegovina to exist in parallel with the Republic. US mediation was also instrumental in achieving a definitive peace agreement between the warring parties, initialled in Dayton, Ohio, on Nov. 21, 1995, and formally signed in Paris on Dec. 14. The accord specified that the Republic of Bosnia and Hercegovina would remain a single sovereignty but would consist of two "entities", namely the Federation of Bosnia and Hercegovina (covering 51% of the country's territory) and the Serbian Republic of Bosnia and Hercegovina (49%). Its responsibilities including foreign relations, trade and customs, monetary policy and communications, the central government was to be headed by a three-person presidency (one "Bosniac", one Croat and one Serb) and a Council of Ministers. It was also to have a bicameral legislature, consisting of a 15-member House of Peoples indirectly elected by the legislatures of the "entities" (10 from the Federation and five from the Serbian Republic) and a 42-member House of Representatives directly elected from each "entity" (28 from the Federation and 14 from the Serbian Republic).

Of the two "entities", the Federation of Bosnia and Hercegovina is headed by a President and Vice-President, each elected by the legislature and drawn alternately from the Muslim and Croat communities. The President, with the agreement of the Vice-President, nominates the Prime Minister and Council of Ministers for endorsement by the bicameral legislature, consisting of an indirectly-elected upper House of Peoples (containing equal Muslim and Croat representation) and a directly-elected House of Representatives. The Serbian Republic of Bosnia and Hercegovina is headed by a President, who is elected by the unicameral and directly-elected People's Assembly, which also elects the Prime Minister and Council of Ministers on the nomination of the President.

Pre-independence elections to the two houses of the former republican Assembly in November-December 1990 produced the following results for the Chamber of Citizens/ Chamber of Communes: Party of Democratic Action 43/43 seats; Serbian Democratic Party 34/38; Croatian Democratic Union 21/23; Party of Democratic Changes 15/4; Alliance of Reform Forces 12/0; Muslim Bosniac Organization 2/0; Democratic Party of Socialists 1/1; Democratic League of Greens 1/0; Liberal Party 1/0; Serbian Renaissance Movement 0/1. (In subsequent changes in the party structure, the Alliance of Reform Forces became the Union of Bosnian Social Democrats; the Muslim Bosniac Organization and the Liberal Party merged to form the Liberal Bosniac Organization; and the Party of Democratic Changes merged with the Democratic Party of Socialists to form the Socialist Democratic Party.)

Muslim Parties

Democratic People's Community
Demokratska Narodna Zajednica (DNZ)
Leadership. Fikret Abdić (president)

The DNZ was founded in April 1996 by Abdić as the successor to his Muslim Democratic Party (MDS), which itself had originated in the declaration in September 1993 of the "autonomous province of Western Bosnia" by the Muslim-populated enclave of Bihać in north-western Bosnia-Hercegovina, by then a UN-designated "safe area". The breakaway was led by Abdić, who had been elected to the collegial presidency in 1990 as a candidate of the Party of Democratic Action (SDA) but had later fallen out with the SDA leader, President Izetbegović. The immediate cause of the split was anger at the reluctance of the Izetbegović government to sign a peace agreement with the Serbs and Croats. A wealthy chicken farmer and entrepreneur, Abdić had, in the last years of the communist era, been heavily implicated in the Agrokomerc financial scandal. He quickly signed local "treaties of lasting peace" with the Croat and Serbian leaders, his MDS forces subsequently acting as a deterrent to encroachment by the surrounding Serbs. In August 1994, however, they succumbed to Bosnian government forces, Abdić being forced to flee from his stronghold in the town of Velika Kladusa and to take refuge in the Krajina (then Serb-controlled Croatian territory).

In September 1994 the MDS initiated the creation of the broader Muslim Democratic Alliance (*Muslimanski Demokratski Savez*) of Bihać Muslim groups. In late December Velika Kladusa was recaptured by Abdić's forces making common cause with the Serbs. But Bihać itself remained under Bosnian government control, which was strengthened by the fall of western Krajina to Croat government forces in August 1995. Thereafter Abdić was reported to have made an accomodation with the Croats.

Party of Democratic Action
Stranka Demokratske Akcije (SDA)
Address. c/o Skupština, Sarajevo
Leadership. Alija Izetbegović (president), Irfan Ajanović (secretary)

The SDA was founded in May 1990 as a nationalist organization representing Muslims and became the largest Assembly party in elections in November-December 1990, winning a total of 86 seats with 36% of the popular vote. In simultaneous elections to the seven-member collegial presidency, the two guaranteed Muslim seats were won by SDA candidates (Izetbegović and Fikret Abdić) and the seventh "open" seat also went to the SDA. Under Izetbegović's presidency, Bosnia-Hercegovina moved somewhat reluctantly to full independence in March 1992. The new state's government was supposed to be a coalition of the SDA, the Serbian Democratic Party and the Croatian Democratic Union (HDZ), but deepening hostilities between the communities resulted in the effective breakdown of inter-party co-operation by late 1992. In December 1992 Izetbegović stood down as SDA president to placate Serb and Croat objections to the head of state being leader of an ethnically-based party. In late 1993 the SDA was weakened by the the formation of the breakaway Muslim Democratic Party by Muslims in Bihać led by Abdić. The creation of the (Muslim-Croat) Federation of Bosnia-Hercegovina in March 1994 yielded a theoretical resumption of the SDA-HDZ governmental alliance at the new federal level. At the same time, Izetbegović resumed the formal SDA leadership. In April 1996, as campaigning started for post-Dayton legislative elections, the SDA was weakened by the formation of the breakaway Party for Bosnia and Hercegovina.

Serb Parties

Serbian Democratic Party
Srpska Demokratska Stranka (SDS)
Address. c/o Assembly Building, Pale
Leadership. Radovan Karadzić (president)

The SDS was launched in July 1990 as the political vehicle of Bosnian Serb nationalism and secured most of the ethnic Serb vote in the November-December 1990 elections, winning 72 of the 240 Assembly seats and securing the two guaranteed Serb seats on the collegial presidency with about 25% of the popular vote. It joined a post-election coalition with the (Muslim) Party of Democratic Action and the Croatian Democratic Union, arguing that Bosnia-Hercegovina should remain within a federal Yugoslavia. When the government opted for independence, the SDS withdrew from the Assembly in Sarajevo and in March 1992 led the proclamation of the Serbian Republic of Bosnia-Hercegovina in Serb-controlled territory, with its own assembly at Pale. Thereafter the SDS was closely identified with the Bosnian Serbs' military struggle and was technically banned by the central government in June 1992.

Under the leadership of Karadzić, the SDS secured the Bosnian Serbs' rejection of successive international peace plans, on the grounds that they involved the surrender of too much Serb-controlled territory and did not guarantee sovereignty for a Bosnian Serb entity. For this reason the party came into apparent conflict with the political leadership of rump federal Yugoslavia (Serbia and Montenegro), which opted in favour a settlement with a view to securing the lifting of

UN sanctions. The SDS also condemned the US-inspired creation of the (Muslim-Croat) Federation of Bosnia-Hercegovina in March 1994. Military exigencies subsequently dominated political affairs among the Bosnian Serbs, whose SDS leadership came under increasing Yugoslav and international pressure in 1995 to accept a settlement that would preserve the nominal sovereignty of Bosnia-Hercegovina and reduce the Bosnian Serbs' effective control to around half of the state's territory. In consequence, serious divisions became apparent in the SDS. In April 1995 Radovan Karadzić was named as a suspected war criminal by the UN War Crimes Tribunal at The Hague. Under the US-brokered peace agreement concluded at Dayton, Ohio, in November 1995, indicted war criminals were specifically excluded from standing for office in post-settlement political structures.

Serbian Renaissance Movement
Srpski Pokret Obnove (SPO)
    Address. c/o Assembly Building, Pale
    Leadership. Vuk Drasković, Milan Trivunčić
    The SPO is the counterpart in Bosnia-Hercegovina of the ultra-nationalist Serbian Renaissance Movement of rump Yugoslavia (Serbia and Montenegro). It won only one Assembly seat in the November-December 1990 elections and in 1992 supported the dominant Serbian Democratic Party in the proclamation of the Serbian Republic of Bosnia and Hercegovina. In the post-Dayton era the SPO sought to rally support from ethnic Serbs who remained in the Muslim-Croat area.

Socialist Party of the Serbian Republic
Socijalisticka Partija i Republika Srpska (SPRS)
    Address. c/o Assembly Building, Pale
    Leadership. Dragutin Ilić (president)
    The SPRS is closely aligned with the Socialist Party of Serbia in Federal Yugoslavia, becoming in the post-Dayton era a vigorous opponent of the dominant Serbian Democratic Party led by Radovan Karadžić, in line with Belgrade's increasing disenchantment with the latter.

Croat Parties

Croatian Democratic Union
Hrvatska Demokratska Zajednica (HDZ)
    Address. c/o Assembly Building, Grude
    Leadership. Ivo Lozancić (president), Pero Marković (general secretary)
    The HDZ was launched in Bosnia-Hercegovina in August 1990 on the reported initiative of the ruling Croatian Democratic Union of Croatia. In the pre-independence Assembly elections of

November-December 1990 it took most of the ethnic Croat vote, winning a total of 44 seats, and also returned the two guaranteed members of the collegial presidency (Stjepan Kljuić and Franjo Boras) with some 20% of the popular vote. The HDZ joined a post-election coalition government with the main Muslim and Serb parties but strains developed over the Bosnian Croats' ambilavence on whether there should be an independent state of Bosnia-Hercegovina. The party effectively withdrew from the central government in 1992 and in August 1993 spearheaded the proclamation of the Croatian Republic of Herceg-Bosna in the Croat-populated western region, with its own assembly at Grude. A change of policy in Zagreb, however, resulted in HDZ participation in the March 1994 agreement to set up a (Muslim-Croat) Federation of Bosnia-Hercegovina in the territory not under Bosnian Serb control. In July 1994 the Herceg-Bosna leader, Mate Boban, was succeeded as HDZ president by Dario Kordić, who was later replaced by Ivo Lozancić.

Croatian Peasant Party
Hrvatska Seljaćka Stranka (HSS)
    Address. c/o Assembly Building, Grude
    Leadership. Ivo Komšić (president)
    The HSS is the counterpart in Bosnia-Hercegovina of the Croatian Peasant Party of Croatia, its leader having been a vice-president of the former ruling League of Communists of Yugoslavia. It was initially overshadowed by the Croatian Democratic Union (HDZ) as the vehicle for Bosnian Croat aspirations. However, it attracted increasing support in 1994 for its opposition to the degree of accomodation with the Bosnian Muslims officially favoured by the HDZ leadership.

Multi-Ethnic Parties

Democratic League of Greens
Demokratski Savez Zelena (DSZ)
    Address. c/o Skupština, Sarajevo
    Leadership. Dražen Petrović
    This formation emerged before the 1990 Assembly elections in Bosnia-Hercegovina, in which Petrović won the party's only seat. Its scope for action on ecological concerns was subsequently severely curtailed by the onset of civil war.

Liberal Bosniac Organization
Liberalna Bosniak Organizacija (LBO)
    Address. c/o Skupština, Sarajevo
    Leadership. Rasim Kadić (president), Muhamed Filipović (vice-president)
    The LBO was created in 1992 as a merger of the Liberal Party (*Liberalna Stranka*, LS) and the Muslim Bosniac Organization (*Muslimanska Boš-*

njačka Organizacija, MBO). These two moderate parties had emerged in 1990, the LS as an offshoot of the Liberal Democratic Party of Slovenia and the MBO as a breakaway from the Party of Democratic Action led by Adil Zulfikarpašič, a wealthy foreign-based businessman, and Muhamed Filipović, a philosopher. In the November-December 1990 Assembly elections the LS had won one seat and the MBO two, finding its support in the Sarajevo middle class. Zulfikarpašič and Filipović subsequently diverged on strategy, the former opposing the formation of the LBO and resigning from the party (to become Bosnian ambassador to Switzerland). Seeking to articulate a distinctly Bosnian national identity embracing "the three great cultural-religious traditions", the LBO advocates a market economy, the privatization of socially-owned property, the rule of law and the autonomy of educational and legal institutions vis-à-vis the state.

Party for Bosnia and Hercegovina
Stranka za Bosne i Hercegovina (SBiH)
    Leadership. Haris Silajdžić (president)
    The SBiH was founded in April 1996 by Silajdžić, who had resigned as prime minister of the Bosnian government in January after coming into dispute with alleged Islamic fundamentalist tendencies in the dominant Party of Democratic Action (SDA). For the post-Dayton legislative elections the new party sought to rally moderate non-sectarian support. In June 1996 Silajdžic was beaten up by SDA supporters during an election meeting in Bihać.

Republican Party
Republicanska Stranka (RS)
    Address. c/o Skupština, Sarajevo
    Leadership. Stjepan Kljuić (president)
    This party was formed in 1993 by Kljuić, who had been elected to the collegial presidency of Bosnia-Hercegovina in 1990 as a candidate of the Croatian Democratic Union (HDZ) but had later become unhappy with the HDZ's identification with ethnic Croat aims. The new party declared a firm commitment to a multi-ethnic state.

Socialist Democratic Party
Socijalistička Demokratska Partija (SDP)
    Address. c/o Skupština, Sarajevo
    Leadership. Nijaz Duraković (president), Krsto Stjepanović (secretary-general)
    The SDP was formed in 1992 as a combination of two parties deriving from the Bosnian sections of the political formations of the communist era, namely: the Party of Democratic Changes (*Stranka*

Demokratskih Promjena), founded in March 1990 as successor to the former ruling League of Communists of Yugoslavia (LCY); and the Democratic Party of Socialists (*Demokratska Stranka Socijalista*, DSS), founded as the Democratic Socialist League in June 1990 as successor to the Socialist League of the Working People of Yugoslavia (the LCY's front organization). In the November-December 1990 Assembly elections, the Party of Democratic Changes had won 19 of the 240 seats and the DSS two, deriving much benefit from their inheritance of the party apparatus of the communist era. The two parties had thus become jointly the largest opposition grouping in the new Assembly, although the onset of civil war had the effect of marginalizing them politically. The merged SDP describes itself as a "modern party of left orientation" in favour of a regulated market economy; it disavows any specific ethnic/national identification.

Union of Bosnian Social Democrats
Zajednica Socijalistička Demokratska Bosna (ZSDB)
    Address. c/o Skupština, Sarajevo
    Leadership. Selim Beslagić (president), Milodrag Janković (deputy president), Sejfudin Tokić (mayor of Tuzla)
    This party was founded in September 1990 as the Alliance of Reform Forces (*Savez Reformskih Snaga*, SRS), which was created as an electoral vehicle by the then federal Yugoslav Prime Minister, Ante Marković, in the hope of preserving the federation. Aiming to transcend divisive ethnic loyalties, Marković chose to launch the SRS in Bosnia-Hercegovina, as being the most ethnically diverse of the then Yugoslav republics. In the November-December 1990 Assembly elections in Bosnia-Hercegovina, the Tuzla-based SRS won 12 seats and an SRS candidate for the collegial presidency (Nenad Kecmanović, then SRS leader in the republic, and a Serb) took 21% of the vote but was not elected to one of the two posts guaranteed to Serbs because candidates of the Serbian Democratic Party polled rather better. Of the SRS parties subsequently formed in the Yugoslav republics, only the one in Bosnia-Hercegovina made an appreciable impact, but even there was damaged by the previous regime's record of mismanagement and corruption. Its subsequent change of name and leadership was intended to repair this negative image. The reorganized party committed itself to full parliamentary democracy, modernization of state institutions and economic reconstruction on the basis of a regulated market economy.

Botswana

Capital: Gaborone

Population: 1,450,000 (1995E)

The Republic of Botswana, which became independent from Britain in 1966, is a unitary multi-party democracy. Under its 1966 constitution, executive power is vested in the President as head of state, elected for a renewable five-year term by an absolute majority of the elected members of the National Assembly, which has legislative authority. A constitutional amendment tabled in late 1995 specified that one person could not serve more than two presidential terms, although the change was not retrospectively applicable to the current incumbent. The President appoints a Vice-President from among the members of the Assembly as well the members of the Cabinet, over which he presides. The National Assembly, also having a term of five years, consists of 40 members directly elected from single- member constituencies by universal suffrage of those aged 21 and over, as well as four members elected by the elected Assembly members (from a list of eight submitted by the President) and three ex-officio members (the Speaker, the non-voting Attorney-General and the President). There is also a 15–member House of Chiefs, composed of representatives of the principal ethnic groupings, which considers draft legislation on constitutional or chieftaincy matters (but has no veto) and may make representations to the President on tribal matters.

In elections for the elective seats in the National Assembly on Oct. 15, 1994, the Botswana Democratic Party won 26 (with 53.1% of the vote) and the Botswana National Front 13 (37.7%), with polling being postponed in one constituency.

Botswana Democratic Party (BDP)

Address. POB 28, Gaborone

Telephone. (#267) 352564

Fax. (#267) 313911

Leadership. Sir Ketumile Masire (president), Pontashego Kedikilwe (chair), Daniel Kwelagobe (secretary-general)

The BDP was founded in 1962 as the Bechuanaland Democratic Party, adopting its present name in 1965, when it won a decisive majority in pre-independence elections. Favoured by the British colonial authorities and white residents for its relative moderation, the party led Botswana to independence in September 1966, its then leader, Sir Seretse Khama, becoming President. Pursuing conservative domestic policies and adopting a pragmatic line externally (notably in regard to South Africa), the BDP was returned to power with further large majorities in the 1969, 1974 and 1979 elections. On Khama's death in 1980, he was succeeded as President and party leader by Vice-President Quett (now Ketumile) Masire. The BDP won further landslide victories in the 1984 and 1989 elections but faced increasing popular unrest in the early 1990s as well as opposition charges of graft and corruption. In March 1992 the report of a commission of inquiry into land allocations resulted in the resignations of Peter S. Mmusi as Vice-President and of Daniel Kwelagobe as Agriculture Minister, both men also losing their senior party posts. However, at a BDP congress in June 1993 Mmusi and Kwelagobe were elected party chair and secretary-general respectively, while some senior cabinet ministers failed to secure election to the BDP central committee. Thereafter, tensions increased between the Mmusi/Kwelagobe faction and the traditional leadership of southern cattle-raisers typified by Lt.-Gen. Mompati Merafhe. Also apparent was a struggle for the succession to the ailing Masire.

The BDP retained an overall majority in the October 1994 Assembly elections, but its support slipped sharply to 53.1% (from 64.8% in 1989) and several cabinet ministers lost their seats. Mmusi died during the election campaign. The new Assembly re-elected Masire as President, while the post-election government included Kwelagobe as Minister of Works, Transport and Communications. In July 1995 the Presidential Affairs and Public Administration Minister, Pontashego Kedikilwe, was elected as BDP chair.

Botswana National Front (BNF)

Address. Bag BO45, Gaborone

Telephone. (#267) 309180

Leadership. Kenneth Koma (chair), James Pilane (secretary-general)

The BNF was established shortly before independence in 1966 by opposition elements desirous of providing an alternative to the dominant Botswana Democratic Party (BDP). It won three Assembly seats in 1969, two in 1974 and 1979 and four in 1984, this last tally increasing to seven by late 1985 as a result of a by-election victory and two BDP defections. In 1989 the BNF fell back to three elective seats, although its share of the vote increased from 20.4% in 1984 to 26.9%. Based in the urban working class, the BNF had a Marxist orientation in the 1980s (and was portrayed as subversive by the BDP government) but moved to a social democratic stance after the 1989 elections. In August 1990 it set up a joint action committee with two other opposition parties, namely the Botswana People's Party and the Botswana Progressive Union. In October 1991 this was converted into the more formal Botswana People's Progressive Front (BPPF), which called for the creation of an all-party commission to supervise the next elections, claiming that the previous contest had been rigged.

Revelations of corruption in ruling circles in 1992 generated increasing support for the BPPF alliance, which staged a series of mass protest demonstrations calling on the government to resign. In 1993, however, dissension developed within the BPPF over whether the alliance should boycott the next elections if its demands for electoral reform were not met. In the event, the BNF contested the October 1994 elections in its own right, substantially increasing its vote share (to 37.7%) and winning 13 elective seats, including all four in Gaborone.

Other Parties

Botswana Freedom Party (BFP), founded in September 1989 by dissidents of the Botswana National Front, led by Leach Tlhomelang, unsuccessful in recent elections.

Botswana Independence Party (BIP), led by Motsamai Mpho, founded in 1962 by dissidents of the Botswana People's Party, unrepresented in the National Assembly since 1979, originally leftist in orientation, in 1991 declined to participate in an opposition alliance headed by the Botswana National Front because of its alleged militancy.

Botswana Labour Party (BLP), moderate left-wing party led by Lenyeletse Koma, founded in 1989 by dissidents of the Botswana National Front, did not contest the 1989 elections, unsuccessful in those of 1994.

Botswana Liberal Party (BLP), founded in 1983, led by Martin Chakalisa, unsuccessful in recent elections.

Botswana People's Party (BPP), founded in 1960, led by Knight Maripe, formed the official opposition at independence in 1966, but thereafter lost support, ceasing to be represented in the Assembly in 1989 and again failing to win a seat in 1994 (with a vote share of 4.6%).

Botswana Progressive Union (BPU), launched by radical elements in 1982, led by G.G. Bagwasi, made no impact in the 1984 and 1989 elections, in 1991 joined an opposition alliance headed by the Botswana National Front, but contested the 1994 elections in its own right, again failing to win a seat.

Independent Freedom Party (IFP), part of the opposition to the ruling Botswana Democratic Party, took 2.9% of the vote in the 1994 Assembly elections but failed to win a seat.

Brazil

Capital: Brasilia

Population: 156, 296, 000 (1995E)

The Federative State of Brazil became independent from Portugal in 1822 and a federal republic in 1889. It comprises 23 states, three territories and a federal district (Brasilia). National legislative authority rests with the bicameral National Congress, comprising a Chamber of Deputies which is directly elected every four years by a system of proportional representation, and an 81-member Federal Senate elected for eight-year terms by elections at four-year intervals for, alternately, one third and two thirds of the members. Congressional elections are by universal and compulsory adult suffrage with one third of the Senators elected indirectly. Executive power is exercised by the President who appoints and leads the Cabinet. A new constitution entered into effect on Oct. 6, 1988, which confirmed a five-year presidential term, and removed many of the restrictions imposed under military rule between 1964 and 1985. On May 25, 1994, congressional deputies voted by 323 to 29 to amend the constitution reducing the presidential term from five to four years.

Each state has its own government, with a structure that mirrors the federal level, enjoying all the powers (defined in its own constitution) which are not specifically reserved for the federal government or assigned to the municipal councils. The head of the state executive is the Governor, elected by direct popular vote under the federal constitution. The one-chamber state legislature is a State Assembly. The state judiciary follows the federal pattern and has its jurisdiction defined so as to avoid any conflict or superimposition with the federal courts.

Presidential elections on Oct. 3, 1994, were won by Fernando Henrique Cardoso, candidate of the centre-left Brazilian Social Democratic Party (PSDB) with a resounding 54.3% absolute majority. The PSDB, the Brazilian Democratic Movement Party (PMDB) and the Liberal Front Party (PFL) were victorious in simultaneous legislative elections. Cardoso was sworn in as President, with Marco Maciel as Vice-President, on Jan. 1, 1995, when a new coalition Cabinet of 21 ministers took office, featuring a high proportion of independent technocrats. The new Cabinet was formally installed on Feb. 1, 1995. The PSDB won sufficient congressional pluralities to give the new President broad support for a constitutional reform programme.

As of mid-1996, the government coalition members were the PSDB, the PFL, the Brazilian Labour Party (PTB) and the Liberal Party (PL).

Brazilian Labour Party
Partido Trabalhista Brasileiro (PTB)
　Address. Praça dos Três Poderes, Ala Nilo Coelho, Senado Federal, 70. 168-970 Brasilia—DF
　Telephone. (#55-61) 311 4059
　Fax. (#55-61) 321 0146
　Leadership. Rodrigues Palma; Celso Pecanha
　Founded in 1980, the centrist PTB is another direct successor of the pre-1965 Brazilian Workers' Party founded in the 1940s by former president Vargas. A small party, it gained 19 deputies in the 1986 elections and joined the opposition against President Sarney. The party went to win two governorships in the early 1990s.

Brazilian Social Democratic Party
Partido da Social Democracia Brasileira (PSDB)
　Address. Praça dos Três Poderes, 2 Andar, Senado Federal, 70. 168-970 Brasilia—DF
　Telephone. (#55-61) 322 0045; 311 3566
　Fax. (#55-61) 226 9447
　Leadership. Fernando Henrique Cardoso (president)
　The centre-left PSDB was founded in June 1988 using a manifesto based upon social justice, economic development, land reform and environmental protection. It also called for the establishment of a true parliamentary system within four years.
　The PSDB was formed by members of the *históricos* faction of the Party of the Brazilian Democratic Movement (PMDB) opposed to President Sarney's retention of the presidential system and his determination not to shorten his term of office. The catalyst, however, was the unsuccessful challenge by Mario Covas, PMDB leader in the Constituent Assembly, for the PMDB leadership. The new party also attracted defectors from the Liberal Front Party (PFL), the Brazilian Socialist Party (PSB), the Brazilian Labour Party (PTB) and the Social Democratic Party (PDS), and soon after its formation the PSDB became the third largest party in Congress, with eight senators and 60 deputies. The first electoral test for the party came on Nov. 15, 1989 when Covas stood as presidential candidate. He came fourth with 11.52% of the valid vote.
　In 1994 the party joined the Liberal Front Party (PFL), the Brazilian Labour Party (PTB) and the Liberal Party (PL) in supporting the successful presidential campaign of Fernando Henrique Cardoso.

Brazilian Socialist Party
Partido Socialista Brasileiro (PSB)
　Address. Praça dos Três Poderes, Anexo IV, Gabinete 846, Câmara dos Deputados, 70. 169-970 Brasilia—DF
　Telephone. (#55–61) 425 2222
　Fax. (#55-61) 318 2846
　Leadership. Miguel Arraes de Alencar (president)
　Founded in 1985, the PSB managed to send only one deputy and two senators to Congress following the elections of November 1986. However, by October 1990 the party had established itself as a left-wing opposition party and increased its

representation in the Chamber of Deputies to 12 seats. The PSB formed part of the left-wing bloc openly hostile to the Collor government.

The PSB withdrew from the Franco government coalition in August 1993. It then went on to win two state governorships in 1994.

Communist Party of Brazil
Partido Comunista do Brasil (PCdoB)
Leadership. Haroldo Lima, João Amazonas
The PCdoB originated in a Maoist faction within the Brazilian Communist Party (PCB, now renamed the Popular Socialist Party, PSP). It split away from the PCB and set up as a separate party under the PCB's original name after the Communist Party had abandoned internationalism. Banned as soon as it was founded, the PCdoB worked within the Brazilian Democratic Movement (MDB—see Party of the Brazilian Democratic Movement), the official opposition party. After the death of Mao and the arrest of the "gang of four" in 1976, the PCdoB turned away from China and became pro-Albanian.

In the same year a raid by security forces on a secret meeting in São Paulo resulted in the murder of three central committee members, including the party founder Pedro de Aranjo Pomar, and the arrest of six other members. The 1979 amnesty allowed the party to operate more openly, although it remained officially illegal until June 1985.

Following the defeat of the PT's presidential candidate, Lula da Silva, the PCdoB campaigned again by itself in the 1990 congressional elections and won five seats in the Chamber. As part of a large left-of-centre opposition bloc, the PCdoB strongly opposed the policies of President Collor.

It won five Chamber seats in 1990, and 10 in 1994.

Democratic Labour Party
Partido Democrático Trabalhista (PDT)
Address. Rua 7 de Septembro 141—3 Andar, CEP 20050 Centro, Rio de Janeiro RJ
Telephone. (#55–21) 221 0093
Fax. (#55–21) 521 3849
Leadership. Leonel de Moura Brizola
History. Founded by Leonel Brízola, Doutel de Andrade (party vice-president until his death in January 1991) and other exiled members of the old Brazilian Labour Party (PTB) after their return to Brazil under the 1979 amnesty, the party had to adopt its current name after a dissident group won a court case over the old party name in 1980 (see PTB). The PDT had the support of 10 deputies from the start and in the general election of 1982 it increased its representation to 24 deputies and one senator thus forming the largest labour bloc in Congress.

Although the party had thrown its weight behind Tancredo Neves, the victorious Democratic Alliance candidate in the 1985 presidential elections, it was one of the few parties to take an early stand against the economic policies of his running-mate and replacement, President Sarney. This unpopular stand, however, was vindicated in 1988, when, following social and industrial tensions, the PDT made major gains in the November municipal elections at the expense of the ruling Party of the Brazilian Democratic Movement (PMDB). However, by the time of the elections in November 1989, the majority of voters had turned away from the centre-left and placed their hopes in a newcomer in politics, the conservative Fernando Collor de Mello.

The PDT recovered in the October 1990 congressional and gubernatorial elections, increasing its representation in the Chamber of Deputies from 24 to 46 seats, and thus becoming the third largest party.

Brizola went on to stand as the PDT presidential candidate in 1994 coming in fifth with 2.59% of the vote.

The party is a full member of the Socialist International.

Liberal Front Party
Partido da Frente Liberal (PFL)
Address. Praça dos Três Poderes, 26 Andar, Senado Federal, 70. 168-970 Brasilia—DF
Telephone. (#55-61) 311 4305; 311 4306
Fax. (#55-61) 311 1390
Leadership. Jorge Bornhausen
This centre-right party was founded in 1984 and was formed by the liberal faction of the right-wing Social Democratic Party (PDS) following disagreements over the appointment of Paulo Salim Maluf as the party's candidate for the 1985 presidential elections. The PFL, with José Sarney (president of the military's official party ARENA, 1970-79, and president of the PDS, 1979-84) and the Brazilian Vice-President António Aureliano Chaves de Mendonca among its leaders, and 72 deputies and 12 senators having sworn allegiance to the party, became Brazil's third largest party in parliament almost overnight. Although the PFL was not officially a legal political party until June 1985, it nevertheless formed a Democratic Alliance with the Party of the Brazilian Democratic Movement (PMDB) in order to contest the indirect presidential elections of Jan. 15, 1985, which José Sarney won.

In September 1987 the PFL officially withdrew from the Democratic Alliance, claiming that it was too dominated by the PMDB, although some PFL members retained their cabinet and other government posts.

Sarney finally acquiesced to the popular demands for early elections, called in November 1989. The

PFL's candidate for the presidency was Sarney's Mines and Energy Minister, António Aureliano Chaves de Mendonca, who obtained only a small percentage of the valid votes. In the elections of the following year, however, his party won the highest number of state governors' posts and again proved to be the second most popular party, having gained 92 seats in the Chamber of Deputies.

In 1992 the PFL was the largest pro-government formation in the Chamber of Deputies, thus becoming the largest grouping in the Cardoso coalition government. However, despite its position in the coalition it could hold on to only two of the state governorships won in 1989.

The party is an observer member of the Liberal International.

Liberal Party
Partido Liberal (PL)

Address. Praça dos Três Poderes, Anexo I, salas 5 e 6, Câmara dos Deputados, 70. 169-970 Brasilia—DF

Telephone. (#55-61) 318 5899
Fax. (#55-61) 223 9444
Leadership. Álvaro Valle

Founded in 1985, the centre-right PL secured seven seats in the Chamber of Deputies and one Senate seat in the 1989 elections, bringing this number up to 15 in the 1990 elections. As a small party the PL stands for the country's tradesmen and supports free enterprise and fair wages for all.

National Reconstruction Party
Partido da Reconstrução Nacional (PRN)

Address. Rua Visconde de Inhaúma, sala 112, Rio de Janeiro—RJ, 20.091-000

Telephone. (#51–21) 236 1463
Fax. (#55–21) 253 0756
Leadership. Fernando Collor de Mello

Founded in 1989, the PRN was formed as an electoral vehicle for the presidential ambitions of Fernando Collor de Mello, who previous to his candidature was governor of the small north-eastern state of Alagoas. His election promises included social spending, the rooting-out of government corruption and privilege and the streamlining of the civil service and privatizations, policies which appealed to the business community as well as the poor. A lavish campaign on TV Globo, owned by Collor's parents, and other media, together with widespread discontent with the Sarney government, helped Collor win 30.48% of the vote, the highest amount of the valid poll.

Collor was inaugurated in March 1990, and with only 24 PRN representatives in the Congress called for national unity. After offering the defeated PT a share in government, which was refused, he appointed a Cabinet mainly composed of independents. Collor de Mello governed by executive persuasion, criticized by many as an "autocratic" style of government.

In an effort to restore his political standing, Collor submitted to Congress two bills to fight official corruption and took visible steps to disband his unofficial inner cabinet of friends and advisors—popularly known as the "Republic of Alagoas" after his home state—who were accused of influence-peddling. Collor's wife had been forced to resign as head of a government welfare agency in August 1992 accused of the misappropriation of funds.

In late 1992, President Collor de Mello was, like his wife, forced to resign following several high-profile charges of corruption. Although he was acquitted in December 1994 of all charges, he has been banned from running for elective office until the year 2000 because of a Senate conviction for "lack of decorum".

Party of the Brazilian Democratic Movement
Partido do Movimento Democrático Brasiliero (PMDB)

Address. Praça dos Três Poderes, 2 Andar, Senado Federal, 70. 168-970 Brasilia—DF

Telephone. (#55-61) 224 0569; 318 5120; 318 5121
Fax. (#55-61) 223 5405
Leadership. Paes de Andrade (president)

The PMDB is the main centrist, Christian Democrat party in Brazil and was founded in 1980. Formed by the moderate elements of the Brazilian Democratic Movement (MDB), disbanded in 1979 and the sole opposition party tolerated under the 14-year military dictatorship, the PMDB inherited a large majority of the old party's branches and 120 members of Congress. Its campaign for democratization attracted support from a wide section of society, ranging from left-wing forces, such as the illegal Communist Party (now the Popular Socialist Party) and trade unions to moderate conservatives. In November 1986, the PMDB became the most powerful party in Brazil, with 22 governorships, 260 out of 487 seats in the Chamber of Deputies and 46 out of 72 seats in the Senate, and thus also dominated the Constituent Assembly which President Sarney established in February 1987 to draft the 1988 constitution. However, by September 1987, with the economy in turmoil, an agrarian reform plan held in disrepute and a raging controversy regarding the length of his presidential mandate, the Democratic Alliance was dissolved. Sarney agreed to hand over power in March 1990 and in September 1988 endorsed Ulysses Guimarães' bid to become his successor.

In March 1991 the 20-year party leadership of Guimarães finally ended, when he was defeated in a party election by Orestes Quércia. In October the following year, Guimarães was killed in a helicopter crash. Then, in 1994, Quércia himself was forced to resign amid allegations of corruption. The largest portion of the Franco coalition in 1994, the PMDB won nine of the of 26 gubernatorial elections and secured a plurality of seats in both houses of Congress.

Popular Socialist Party
Partido Popular Socialista (PPS)
Address. Praça dos Três Poderes, Anexo II, Câmara dos Deputados, 70. 169-970 Brasilia—DF
Telephone. (#55-61) 311 2164
Fax. (#55-61) 323 6389
Leadership. Roberto Freire

Originally founded in 1922 as the Communist Party of Brazil, the party was renamed under Roberto Freire as the PPS in January 1992. The party is independent communist on the "eurocommunist" model and supported the liberation of the former autocratic Soviet Union, describing Marxism-Leninism as "corruption by Stalin of the thoughts of Marx, Engels and Lenin". In 1992 the party voted to allow the pursuit of socialism through democratic means. The PSP mainly campaigns for job creation, the abolition of "unproductive landholdings" and the autonomy of Amazonia.

Progressive Renewal Party
Partido Progressista Reformador (PPR)
Leadership. Paulo Salim Maluf

A centre-right party based in Brazil's south and south-east, the PPR was formed in 1993 as a merger of the Social Democratic Party (PDS) and the Christian Democratic Party (PDC).

Workers' Party
Partido dos Trabalhadores (PT)
Address. Rua Conselheiro Nébias, 1052—Campos Elízios, 01.203-002 São Paulo—SP
Telephone. (#55–11) 223 7999
Fax. (#55–11) 222 9665
Leadership. José Dirceu

The PT was the country's first independent labour party and has long endorsed a "pure form of socialism" that rejected orthodox Marxism. Recently it has been proved to be the second force in Brazilian politics.

The party was founded by the leader of the powerful United Confederation of Workers (CUT), Luís Inácio da Silva (known universally as 'Lula'), Jaco Bítar and Airton Soares and emerged from the growing São Paulo *autêntico* independent trade union movement in the late 1970s. Many of the PT's leaders and members had been supporters of the former Brazilian Labour Party (PTB) which had backed the former Presidents Vargas and Kubitschek in the 1950s. Although chiefly supported by urban industrial workers, the party was also active in rural areas. In 1981 Lula da Silva and nine other PT members received sentences from two to three and a half years for incitement to murder, having made speeches at a peasant leader's funeral which was later followed by revenge murders. They were finally acquitted in 1984.

In the first congressional elections the party participated in, it received only six seats in the Chamber of Deputies. The more open elections of 1986 gave the PT 19 seats in the Chamber. However, opposition to President Sarney's austerity measures and support for the strikes and demonstrations called by the CUT greatly broadened the PT's electoral appeal. This became evident in the municipal elections of 1988 when the PT won control of 36 important towns and Luiza Erundina da Souza became mayor of the city of São Paulo, the first woman mayor in Brazil. In the Presidential election of Nov. 15, 1989, the PT formed a Popular Front together with the Brazilian Socialist Party (PSB), the Communist Party of Brazil (PCdoB) and other left-wing parties.

In late 1991 the party underwent a fundamental change of identity voting to abandon a former commitment to "democratic socialism" in favour of coexistence and indeed co-operation with other groups, be they socialist or not. Standing in the subsequent presidential election, Da Silva came in second to President Collor in 1989, achieving the same placing in 1994 behind Fernando Henrique Cardoso.

Other Parties

Christian Socialist Party (*Partido Socialista Cristão,* PSC), centrist party led by Victor Jorge Abdala Nossels.

Democratic Socialist Party (*Partido Socialista Democrático,* PSD), currently without a leader.

Nationalist Party (*Partido Nacionalista,* PN), led by Livia Maria.

Progressive Party (*Partido Progressista,* PP), led by Alvaro Dias.

Progressive Reform Party (*Partido Progressista Reforma,* PPR), led by 1994 presidential candidate Esperidão Amin.

Renovating Labour Party (*Partido Trabalhista Renovador,* PTR), formerly known as the Revolutionary Labour Party (*Partido Trabalhista Revolucionario,* PTR).

Socialist Workers' Party (*Partido Socialista de Trabalhadores,* PST).

Brunei

Capital: Bandar Seri Bagwan   **Population:** 290,000 (1995E)

The Sultanate of Brunei, having been a British protectorate since 1888, gained internal self-government in 1971 and became fully independent in 1984. Under the 1959 constitution, supreme executive authority is vested in the Sultan, who presides over and is assisted by a Council of Cabinet Ministers, a Privy Council and a Religious Council. There is also a non-elective Legislative Council (*Majlis Meshuarat Negeri*) of 21 members. The Sultan has ruled by decree since December 1962, when a revolt by forces associated with the left-wing People's Party of Brunei (*Partai Rakyat Brunei*, PRB), which had won all the elective seats in legislative elections in August 1962, was put down by the authorities and the party banned. In 1966 a semi-official People's Independence Front was formed as an amalgamation of all existing political formations, but this entity became inactive with the achievement of independence and was de-registered in early 1985. Two new parties then achieved legal status, namely the Brunei National Democratic Party (BNDP) in 1985 and the Brunei National United Party (BNUP) in 1986, the former a moderate Islamist opposition formation and the latter a pro-government offshoot of the BNDP. However, the BNUP quickly became inactive and was de-registered, while in March 1988 the government announced that it had dissolved the BNDP (and arrested its leaders) and that "no other political parties" existed in Brunei. In February 1991 an Islamist "Society of Companions" was banned by royal decree for allegedly spreading teachings contrary to Islam (Brunei's official religion).

Bulgaria

Capital: Sofia   **Population:** 9,000,000 (1995E)

The Republic of Bulgaria was proclaimed as a multi-party parliamentary democracy in November 1990, replacing the People's Republic which had existed since the Bulgarian Communist Party (BCP) came to power after World War II. Under a new constitution formally effective since July 1991 and declaring Bulgaria to be a "democratic, constitutional and welfare state", the President is directly elected (with a Vice-President) for a five-year term and nominates the Prime Minister and Council of Ministers for parliamentary endorsement. Legislative authority is vested in a unicameral National Assembly (*Narodno Sobraniye*), whose 240 members are elected for a four-year term by universal suffrage of those aged 18 and over. Elections are held under a system of proportional representation, the threshold for representation being 4% of the national vote. The 1991 constitution guarantees freedom of political activity with the exception of parties with separatist aims or likely to promote ethnic or religious divisions.

Elections to the National Assembly on Dec. 18, 1994, resulted as follows: Bulgarian Socialist Party (successor to the BCP), allied with the Ecoglasnost Political Club and the Bulgarian Agrarian National Union–Aleksandur Stamboliyski, 125 seats (43.5% of the vote); Union of Democratic Forces (SDS) 69 (24.2%); People's Union (of the Bulgarian Agrarian National Movement and the Democratic Party) 18 (6.5%); Movement for Rights and Freedoms 15

(5.4%); Bulgarian Business Bloc 13 (4.7%). In presidential elections on Jan. 12 and 19, 1992, Zhelyu Zhelev (SDS) had been the victor in the second round with 53% of the votes cast, having won 45% in the first round.

Bulgarian Agrarian National Union-Aleksandur Stamboliyski

Bulgarski Zemedelski Naroden Sayuz-Aleksandur Stamboliyski (BZNS-AS)

Address. c/o, Narodno Sobraniye, 1000 Sofia

Leadership. Svetoslav Shivarov, Vasil Chichibaba

The BZNS-AS is descended from one of the world's oldest peasant parties, founded in 1899 to represent what then constituted 80% of the Bulgarian population. After World War I a BZNS government was in power from 1920 under Aleksandur Stamboliyski until being overthrown by a right-wing coup in 1923 in which Stamboliyski was killed. During World War II left-wing BZNS elements participated in the Fatherland Front led by the Bulgarian Communist Party (BCP), which came to power in 1944 following the ejection of German forces by the Red Army. The anti-Communist wing of the party, led by Nikola Petkov, refused to participate in the obligatory Front list for the October 1946 elections, the Front's victory in which entrenched the BZNS pro-Communists. Petkov was hanged for alleged treason in September 1947. Under the subsequent People's Republic, the BZNS was always represented in the Assembly (with about a quarter of the seats) as well as in successive governments (usually holding the agriculture portfolio). The party had no record of ever contesting BCP decisions, and its vetted membership was limited to 120,000.

As East European communism began to crumble in late 1989, the BZNS asserted its independence of the BCP by replacing its long-time leader (and Deputy Premier), Petur Tanchev, and by refusing to participate in the government formed in February 1990. Meanwhile, the party's traditionalist faction led by Milan Drenchev had formed the separate Bulgarian Agrarian National Union-Nikola Petkov, which became a component of the opposition Union of Democratic Forces (SDS). In the June 1990 Assembly elections the rump BZNS won 16 of the 400 seats and in December 1990 joined a national unity coalition with the Bulgarian Socialist Party (the former BCP) and elements of the SDS. However, the party failed to secure representation in the further elections of October 1991, despite having attracted a faction of the BZNS-Nikola Petkov back into its ranks and standing as the BZNS-United (E); it won only 3.9% of the national vote, just below the 4% minimum required for representation.

Thereafter, the manoeuvrings of the assorted factions claiming descent from the historic party became increasingly hard to follow, as various unity schemes proved abortive and other splits occurred. The BZNS-AS designation was eventually adopted by those favouring alliance with the BSP, this ticket (which included the Ecoglasnost Political Club) winning a decisive victory in the December 1994 Assembly elections. Two BZNS-AS ministers were included in the BSP-led government formed in January 1995.

Bulgarian Agrarian National Union–Nikola Petkov

Bulgarski Zemedelski Naroden Sayuz–Nikola Petkov (BZNS-NP)

Address. 4/A Slaveikov Square, 1000 Sofia

Telephone. (#359-2) 393325

Fax. (#359-2) 885549

Leadership. Georgi Petrov (chair)

The BZNS-NP was formed in November 1989 by traditionalist elements of the Bulgarian Agrarian National Union (BZNS) led by Milan Drenchev and was named after the Agrarian leader executed by the Communists in September 1947 (see previous entry). Rejecting the pro-Communist line of the main BZNS, the BZNS-NP joined the Union of Democratic Forces (SDS) and figured in the SDS list of candidates for the June 1990 Assembly elections. It advocated full political democracy and a market economy based on private agriculture. After the rump BZNS had joined a coalition government in December 1990, a faction of the BZNS-NP reunited with the parent party to form BZNS-United (E) for the October 1991 elections, while the bulk of the remaining BZNS-NP opted to stand independently of the SDS. Neither list secured representation. In February 1992 Drenchev was replaced as BZNS-NP leader by Anastasia Dimitrova-Moser, who advocated co-operation with the SDS minority government by now in office. The following month the BZNS-NP faction which had remained in the SDS opted to set up its own organization within the SDS, so that there were now at least three separate Agrarian parties deriving from the historic BZNS and little prospect that stated intents of reunification would bear fruit.

Prior to the December 1994 Assembly elections, Dimitrova-Moser's faction of the BZNS formed the People's Union alliance with the Democratic Party, while the remainder of the BZNS-NP participated in the defeated SDS electoral front.

The BZNS-NP is listed as an affiliate of the Christian Democrat International.

Bulgarian Business Bloc
Bulgarski Biznes Blok (BBB)

Address. c/o Narodno Sobraniye, 1000 Sofia

Leadership. Georgi Ganchev (president)

The BBB was founded in November 1990 by leading businessman Valentin Mollov as a right-wing, pro-market formation advocating the conversion of Bulgaria into a tariff- and tax-free zone so that it could act as a conduit for commerce between the former Soviet republics and the West. It won 1.3% of the vote (and no seats) in the 1991 elections but attracted growing support under the new leadership of the charismatic Georgi Ganchev, a former fencing champion whose accounts of a colourful past attracted much media publicity. In the December 1994 Assembly elections the BBB broke through to representation, winning 4.7% of the vote and 13 of the 240 Assembly seats. The party improved slightly to 5% in municipal elections in October 1995.

Bulgarian Social Democratic Party
Bulgarska Sotsialdemokraticheska Partiya (BSDP)

Address. 37 Ekzarch Yossif Street, 1504 Sofia

Telephone. (#359–2) 390112; 831962

Fax. (#359–2) 390086

Leadership. Petar Dertliev (chair), Stefan Radoslavov (general secretary)

The BSDP traces its descent from the historic BSDP founded in 1891 and more especially from the non-revolutionary "broad" party resulting from the secession in 1903 of the "narrow" revolutionary wing which in 1919 became the Bulgarian Communist Party. The BSDP opposed right-wing regimes of the inter-war period. During World War II left-wing Social Democrats joined the Communist-dominated Fatherland Front, which came to power in 1944 on Bulgaria's liberation by the Red Army. The party's anti-Communist wing, calling themselves Independent Socialists, was powerless to resist the post-war consolidation of Communist power. Following the declaration of a People's Republic in December 1947, the BSDP was merged with the Communist Party in 1948 (although it was never formally banned). Over the next four decades exiles kept the party alive as the Socialist Party, which was re-established in Bulgaria in 1989 under the leadership of Dertliev, a veteran of the pre-1948 party and a former political prisoner.

In March 1990 the party reverted to the historic BSDP title in view of the imminent decision of the Communist Party to rename itself the Bulgarian Socialist Party (BSP). As a component of the opposition Union of Democratic Forces (SDS), the BSDP took 29 of the 144 seats won by the SDS in the June 1990 Assembly elections. The following month Dertliev was the initial SDS candidate for the presidency but withdrew to allow SDS chair Zhelyu Zhelev to be elected unopposed in the sixth round of Assembly voting. The BSDP supported the decision of some SDS elements to enter a BSP-dominated coalition government in December 1990 but thereafter came into increasing conflict with the SDS pro-market wing. Whereas the latter advocated fullscale economic liberalization, the BSDP favoured a welfare market economy (including private, co-operative and state sectors) and argued that privatized industries should become co-operatives where possible. In the October 1991 Assembly elections it headed a separate SDS-Centre list, which failed to surmount the 4% representation threshold.

The BSDP backed Zhelev's successful candidacy in the January 1992 direct presidential elections and thereafter sided with the President in his developing conflict with the SDS minority government. Following the appointment of a non-party "government of experts" in December 1992, the BSDP warned that it marked a reassertion of Communist influence. In March 1993, seeking to establish a credible third force between the BSP and an SDS seen as moving to the right, the BSDP launched the Bulgarian Social Democratic Union, which the following month was enlarged into a Council of Co-operation of centre-left parties, two of them with Assembly representation. Further alliance-building by the BSDP resulted in the formation of the Democratic Alternative for the Republic (which included the Green Party) for the December 1994 Assembly elections, but its vote share of 3.8% was below the 4% minimum required for representation. An extraordinary BSDP congress in April 1995 endorsed the established line of seeking an alliance of all social democratic forces, rejecting a minority argument that the party should federate with the ruling BSP.

The BSDP is a full member party of the Socialist International.

Bulgarian Socialist Party
Bulgarska Sotsialisticheska Partiya (BSP)

Address. 20 Positano Street, PO Box 382, Sofia

Telephone. (#359–2) 85141

Fax. (#359–2) 871292

Leadership. Zhan Videnov (chair), Rumen Serbezov (secretary)

The BSP dates from April 1990, when the then ruling Bulgarian Communist Party (BCP) changed its name, abandoned Marxism-Leninism (although not Marxist theory) and embraced democratic socialism. The BCP traced its descent from the Bulgarian Social Democratic Party (BSDP), founded in 1891, which in 1903 split into left-wing "narrow" and non-revolutionary "broad" parties. The BCP as such dated from 1919, when the pro-Bolshevik "narrow" party became a founder member of the Third International (Comintern), later organizing armed opposition to right-wing regimes of the inter-war period and renaming itself the Workers' Party in 1927. Finally banned in 1934, the party was for a decade based in Moscow, where many of its exiled leaders were executed in Stalin's purges.

During World War II (in which Bulgaria was allied to Germany until mid-1944) the party played a leading role in the anti-Nazi resistance, its activities being directed by Georgi Dimitrov, Bulgarian secretary-general of the Comintern. In September 1944 the Communist-dominated Fatherland Front (FF), including left-wing Agrarians and Social Democrats, took power in Sofia, assisted by the conquering Red Army. In the post-war period the Communists consolidated their position, Dimitrov becoming Prime Minister after the October 1946 elections and a People's Republic being declared in December 1947. In 1948 the rump of the BSDP was merged with the Workers' Party, the resultant formation readopting the BCP rubric. It thus effectively became the sole ruling party, although the Bulgarian Agrarian National Union (BZNS) remained a component of the Front (the smaller members of which were dissolved in 1949).

On Dimitrov's death in 1949 the BCP leadership passed to Vulko Chervenkov, but he was replaced in 1954 by Todor Zhivkov after being accused of fostering a personality cult. Under Zhivkov's long rule Bulgaria remained closely aligned with the USSR and participated in the 1968 Soviet-led intervention in Czechoslovakia. At one stage he even proposed that Bulgaria should become a constituent republic of the USSR. In 1971 Zhivkov added the post of head of state to his BCP leadership and subsequently appeared to be grooming his daughter Lyudmila for the succession, until her sudden death in 1981. At the 13th BCP congress in April 1986 he announced a reform programme reflecting the Gorbachev *glasnost* and *perestroika* initiatives in the USSR; but reform proved difficult to accomplish because of party in-fighting. Amidst the rapid collapse of European communism in late 1989, Zhivkov was replaced as BCP leader and head of state by Petur Mladenov, whose palace coup was supported by those concerned at Zhivkov's repression of ethnic Turks and apparent grooming of his playboy son Vladimir for the succession. A purge of Zhivkov and his supporters followed, accompanied by denunciations of 35 years of "feudal, repressive, corrupt and incompetent" government.

The BCP's "leading role" in society and the state was terminated under constitutional amendments enacted in January 1990, following which an extraordinary party congress on Jan. 30-Feb.2 renounced "democratic centralism", replaced the BCP central committee with a supreme council and its politburo and secretariat with a presidium, and opted for a "socially-oriented market economy". In keeping with a pledge to separate state and party functions, the party leadership passed to Aleksandur Lilov (a prominent BCP reformer of the Zhivkov era), with Mladenov remaining head of state. Later in February 1990, paradoxically, the BCP was obliged to form the first openly all-Communist government in Bulgaria's history when the BZNS, now asserting its independence, opted to go into opposition and the new Union of Democratic Forces (SDS) refused to join a national unity coalition. Dissatisfaction with the pace of change led in February to the emergence of a reformist BCP faction called the Alternative Socialist Association; in the same period the Communist Youth League and the official trade union federation reconstituted themselves as bodies independent of the BCP, while the FF became the Fatherland Union. In April 1990, following a ballot of party members, the BCP officially renamed itself the BSP, which in multi-party elections in June resisted the East European trend by being returned to power with 211 of the 400 seats. Although the SDS did well in Sofia and other cities, the ruling party's organizational strength in rural areas made the difference.

In July 1990 Mladenov resigned as head of state, after disclosures about his role in the suppression of anti-government demonstrations in December 1989. He was succeeded by SDS leader Zhelyu Zhelev in August, in which month the BSP's headquarters building in Sofia was burnt down during an SDS-led demonstration. In December 1990 the BSP also vacated the premiership, although it remained the largest component in a coalition with the SDS and the BZNS. The adoption of a new democratic constitution in July 1991 was followed by political dissension over the BSP's attitude to the August coup attempt by hardliners in Moscow, seen by many as initially supportive. In further elections in October 1991 the BSP was allied with eight small parties and organizations on a platform of preserving the "Bulgarian spirit and culture", including the moderate Bulgarian Liberal Party, the Christian Republican Party and the nationalist Fatherland Party of Labour, but was narrowly defeated by the SDS. It therefore went into opposition for first time since 1944 and in November 1991 the BSP Assembly group adopted the name Union for Social Democracy.

At a party congress in December 1991, described as the 40th (i.e. since 1891), Lilov was replaced as leader by Zhan Videnov, who advocated a "modern left socialist party" and easily defeated the candidate of the reformist social democrats, Georgi Pirinski. The BSP also suffered a narrow defeat in the direct presidential election held in January 1992, although its preferred candidate secured 46.5% of the second-round vote.

In September 1992 the decision of the (ethnic Turkish) Movement for Rights and Freedoms (DPS) to withdraw support from the SDS minority government enabled the BSP to reassert its influence. A "government of experts" headed by Lyuben Berov (non-party), appointed in December, was backed by most BSP deputies (although a faction led by former leader Lilov voted against) in effective alliance with the DPS. Thereafter, as the government achieved a degree of stability by not hurrying privatization and deregulation of the economy, the BSP was content to avoid direct governmental responsibility during a period of transition, while relying on the Communist-era establishment network and the party's strength in the Assembly to influence government decision-making. By mid-1993 the BSP was again the largest Assembly party, due to the steady erosion of SDS affiliation. Dissent rumbled on in the party, however, as indicated by the launching in June 1993 of the centre-left Civic Alliance for the Republic, which included some BSP dissidents. In May 1994 a proposal by Berov to appoint a BSP member as Economy Minister was successfully opposed by the DPS on the grounds that it would signify BSP control of the government.

On the resignation of the Berov government in September 1994, the BSP declined the opportunity to try to form a new administration, preferring early elections. These were held in December, the BSP being allied principally with the Bulgarian Agrarian National Union–Aleksandur Stamboliyski and the Ecoglasnost Political Club. The outcome was an overall Assembly majority for the BSP-led list and the formation of a coalition government in January 1995 under the premiership of Videnov which committed itself to a socially-oriented market economy and integration into European institutions. In local elections in October-November 1995 the BSP consolidated its position as the strongest party, winning 41% of the first-round vote in its own right.

Democratic Party
Demokratiecka Partiya (DP)

Address. 8 blvd Dondoukov, 1000 Sofia
Telephone. (#359-2) 802046
Fax. (#359-2) 803411
Leadership. Stefan Savov (president), Peter Stankov (general secretary)

Descended from the conservative Christian party of the same name founded in 1896, the DP was revived in 1989 and joined the opposition Union of Democratic Forces (SDS). Following the SDS victory in the October 1991 elections, Stefan Savov was elected president of the National Assembly. However, shortly before the fall of the minority SDS government, he resigned as Assembly president on Sept. 24, 1992, after being named in a censure motion tabled by the opposition Bulgarian Socialist Party and supported by some SDS dissidents. For the December 1994 Assembly elections the DP broke with the SDS, forming the People's Union with a faction of the Bulgarian Agrarian National Union. The alliance took third electoral place, with 18 of the 240 seats.

The DP is affiliated to both the Christian Democrat International and the International Democrat Union.

Ecoglasnost Movement
Dvizhenie Ekoglasnost

Address. 28 Marin Drinov Street, 1504 Sofia
Leadership. Petur Slabakov (chair), Georgi Avramov (secretary)

The Ecoglasnost dissident movement was formed by anti-Communist environmentalists in April 1989 under the leadership of the zoologist Petur Beron and the actor Petur Slabakov. Ecoglasnost was the principal organizer of the popular demonstrations which surrounded the downfall of Todor Zhivkov in November 1989 and became a leading component of the opposition Union of Democratic Forces (SDS). On the election of Zhelyu Zhelev as President in July 1990, Beron succeeded him as SDS chair but was forced to resign in December by disclosures about his past role as a government informer. His successor, Filip Dimitrov, was also from the Ecoglasnost Movement and led the SDS to a narrow victory in the October 1991 Assembly elections, becoming Prime Minister of an SDS minority government. In those elections, a radical Ecoglasnost faction, taking the name Green Party, presented a separate SDS-Liberal list with other left-of-centre groups but failed to secure representation. Following the fall of the Dimitrov government in October 1992, the Ecoglasnost Movement became concerned at the rightward drift of the SDS. Some elements moved to centre-left alliances initiated by the Bulgarian Social Democratic Party, while the Ecoglasnost Political Club opted for alignment with the (ex-Communist) Bulgarian Socialist Party for the December 1994 elections and therefore found itself on the winning side, unlike the parent formation.

Ecoglasnost Political Club

Politicheski Klub Ekoglasnost (PKE)

Address. 37 Exarch Yossif Street, 8th floor, 1000 Sofia

Leadership. Boris Kolev (chair), Georgi Georgiev

The PKE is one of several factions that emerged from the original pro-democracy Ecoglasnost Movement, which dominated the first post-Communist governments and formed part of the Union of Democratic Forces (SDS). It participated in the SDS-Centre alliance in the 1991 elections but opposed the SDS government's shift to the right in 1992. Further policy tensions developed after the SDS went into opposition in December 1992, with the result that the PKE opted to join an alliance headed by the (ex-Communist) Bulgarian Socialist Party (BSP) for the December 1994 Assembly elections. It was allocated the environment portfolio in the resultant BSP-led government.

Movement for Rights and Freedoms

Dvizhenie za Prava i Svobodi (DPS)

Address. 50/B/55 Petar Topalov Shmid, Ivan Vazov Street, 1408 Sofia

Telephone. (#359-2) 519822

Leadership. Ahmed Dogan (president), Osman Oktay (secretary)

The DPS was founded in January 1990 based mainly (but not entirely) in the Muslim ethnic Turkish community, forming some 10% of Bulgaria's population. The policies of compulsory assimilation practised in the 1980s by the Zhivkov regime, resulting in the flight of many ethnic Turks to Turkey and elsewhere, formed the background to the DPS's aims, which included full political, cultural and religious rights but excluded any fundamentalist or separatist objectives. In the June 1990 Assembly elections the DPS won 23 of the 400 seats at issue with 6% of the national vote. From December 1990 it participated in a national unity coalition under a non-party Prime Minister, together with the dominant Bulgarian Socialist Party (BSP) and the Union of Democratic Forces (SDS). In further elections in October 1991 it improved its posititition, winning 24 of 240 seats with 7.6% of the vote.

From November 1991 the DPS gave crucial parliamentary backing to a minority SDS administration, being rewarded with the lifting of a ban on optional Turkish-language instruction in secondary schools. But the SDS government's subsequent pro-market policies were described as "blue fascism" by the DPS, which withdrew its support in September 1992, thereby precipitating the government's fall in October. After the BSP had failed to fill the political vacuum, the DPS successfully nominated a non-party Prime Minister

(Lyuben Berov) to head a "government of experts" which included semi-official DPS representation. In the Assembly vote to endorse the new government in December 1992, the DPS was supported by most BSP deputies and by some SDS dissidents. In 1993 the DPS backed the Berov government but was weakened by internal dissension and by continuing emigration of ethnic Turks. In March 1994, after Berov had suffered a heart attack, the DPS Deputy Premier, Evgeni Matinchev (an ethnic Bulgarian), became acting Prime Minister. In May 1994 the DPS successfully opposed the ailing Berov's proposal to appoint a BSP member as Economy Minister. Weakened by the launching of at least two breakaway parties in 1994, the DPS slipped to 5.4% of the vote and 15 seats out of 240 in the December elections, therefore reverting to opposition status. It won 8.2% of the vote in municipal elections in October 1995, following which the party mounted a protest campaign against the decision of the authorities to annul its victory in the south-eastern town of Kurdzhali on the grounds of voting irregularities.

People's Union

Narodni Sayuz (NS)

Address. c/o Narodno Sobraniye, 1000 Sofia

Leadership. Stefan Savov (DP), Anastasia Dimitrova-Moser (BZNS)

The People's Union was formed before the December 1994 Assembly elections by the Democratic Party (DP) and a faction of the Bulgarian Agrarian National Union (BZNS) led by Dimitrova-Moser, daughter of G.M. Dimitrov, a pre-war Agrarian leader who had emigrated to the USA after World War II. She had been a key participant in earlier struggles for supremacy among the many factions claiming descent from the historic BZNS, becoming leader of the BZNS–Nikola Petkov in February 1992. At that stage this group and the DP participated in the broad Union of Democratic Forces (SDS), but the latter became increasingly divided after it lost power in December 1992 and various groups broke away in 1993–94. The People's Union was the most successful of these in the 1994 elections, winning 6.5% of the vote and 18 of the 240 seats. In municipal elections in October 1995 the NS share of the vote improved to 12.3%.

Union of Democratic Forces

Sayuz na Demokratichni Sili (SDS)

Address. 134 Rakovski Street, 1000 Sofia

Telephone. (#359-2) 882501

Leadership. Ivan Kostov (chair of co-ordinating council), Mihan Drenchev and Hristafor Sbev (deputy chairs)

The SDS was established in December 1989 by

10 fledgling pro-democracy movements, notably the Support (*Podkrepa*) independent trade union federation (formed in February 1989 by Konstantin Trenchev), the Ecoglasnost environmentalist movement and Citizens' Initiative (GI). The other founder members were the Bulgarian Agrarian National Union-Nikola Petkov (BZNS-NP); the Bulgarian Social Democratic Party (BSDP); the Independent Association for the Defence of Human Rights in Bulgaria, led by Ilya Minev; the Club of Persons Illegally Repressed After 1945, led by Dimitur Bakalov; the Committee for Religious Rights, Freedom of Conscience and Spiritual Values, led by Hristofor Subev (a priest); the Federation of Clubs for Democracy, led by Petko Simeonov (later founder of the Liberal Party); and the Federation of Independent Student Societies. In the period up to the June 1990 elections the SDS was also joined by the Radical Democratic Party (RDP); what became the United Christian Democratic Centre (OHZ); the Democratic Party (DP); the Christian Democratic Union (HDS); and the Alternative Social-Liberal Party (ASP). The Bulgarian Democratic Forum (BDF) and the Republican Party (RP) became observer members of the SDS.

Chaired by Zhelyu Zhelev (a dissident philosophy professor of the Zhivkov era), the SDS entered into talks with the ruling Bulgarian Communist Party (BCP) in January 1990, first on ethnic Turkish rights (which the SDS supported) and then on the country's political future. The SDS was permitted to launch its own newspaper (*Demokratsija*) and negotiated detailed arrangements for multi-party elections, but it refused to join a coalition government with the BCP at that stage. The SDS campaign for the Assembly elections held in June 1990 was seen as negative and flawed by over-gearing to international opinion, the result being a decisive victory for the Bulgarian Socialist Party (BSP), the new name of the BCP. Nevertheless, following the resignation of the BSP incumbent, the new Assembly elected Zhelev as President of Bulgaria in August 1990, after the original SDS candidate, Petur Dertliev of the BSDP, had been withdrawn. SDS deputies and their supporters in the country kept up vigorous opposition to the BSP government, which resigned in November 1990 and was replaced in December by a coalition, headed by a non-party Prime Minister, consisting of the BSP, elements of the SDS and the rump Bulgarian Agrarian National Union. Also in December 1990, SDS chair Petur Beron (who had succeeded Zhelev on his elevation to the presidency) was obliged to resign following disclosures about his past activities as a government informer. He was succeeded by Filip Dimitrov, also of the SDS environmentalist wing.

Despite being in government, the SDS maintained an opposition mode and in August 1991 made much political capital out of the BSP's ambiguous response to the abortive coup by hardliners in Moscow. However, dissension between moderate and radical elements resulted in the presentation of three distinct SDS lists in the new Assembly elections of October 1991 as well as a separate BZNS-NP list. The party components of the SDS proper, also designated the SDS-Movement and still embracing various civil movements, included the ASP, the BDF, two dissident factions of the BSDP, the GI, the main DP, part of the Ecoglasnost movement, the RDP, the RP and the UDC. An SDS-Centre alliance was headed by the main BSDP and included the Alternative Socialist Association and factions of the DP and Ecoglasnost. An SDS-Liberal list included the Green Party, the OHZ, a faction of the DP and the Federation of Clubs for Democracy. The outcome was a narrow plurality for the main SDS, which won 110 of the 240 seats and 34.4% of the vote, just ahead of the BSP. Neither the SDS-Centre (3.2%) nor the SDS-Liberals (2.8%) secured representation. The main SDS proceeded to form Bulgaria's first wholly non-Communist government since World War II, headed by Dimitrov, with the parliamentary support of the (ethnic Turkish) Movement for Rights and Freedoms (DPS). In direct presidential elections in January 1992, Zhelev secured a popular mandate as the SDS candidate, winning 53% of the second-round vote (following an inconclusive 45% in the first).

The minority SDS government quickly fell out with the trade unions (including the *Podkrepa* federation), which opposed aspects of its pro-market economic programme. Serious strains also developed between President Zhelev and the Dimitrov government, while the SDS Assembly group, harbouring over 20 distinct party groupings, became riven with dissension. Having been told by Zhelev in August 1992 to end its "war against everyone", the Dimitrov government fell in October after the DPS had withdrawn its support and made common cause with the BSP in a no-confidence vote. The successor DPS-proposed "government of experts" under Lyuben Berov was approved by the Assembly in December 1992 with the support of most BSP and some 20 SDS deputies. The latter included the ASP deputies (who later joined the Bulgarian Social Democratic Union headed by the BSDP) and those of what became the New Union for Democracy. Seen as increasingly conservative in orientation, the anti-Berov SDS in mid-1993 mounted demonstrations against President Zhelev for his alleged connivance with "re-communization". In June 1993 the

Vice-President elected with Zhelev in January 1992, the poet Blaga Dimitrova, resigned and was not replaced.

By early 1994 SDS numbers in the Assembly had fallen to some 90 deputies, less than the BSP's committed parliamentary strength, while the Berov team was widely credited with having restored political stability. In April 1994 Zhelev sought to re-establish his SDS credentials by withdrawing political support from the government, charging it with having delayed privatization and with failure to attract foreign investment. The Berov government survived no-confidence votes in May but the validity of the results was disputed by the SDS, which in June launched a boycott of proceedings in the Assembly. Following the resignation of the Berov government in September 1994, the SDS declared a preference for new elections but was further weakened by the formation of the separate People's Union by former SDS formations.

Held in December 1994, the elections resulted in defeat for the SDS, which won only 24.2% of the vote and 69 of the 240 seats. Soon afterwards Dimitrov was replaced as SDS leader by Ivan Kostov (a former Finance Minister), who headed a party which, as the principal opposition formation, was now more cohesive by virtue of previous defections into electorally unsuccessful entities. Having failed to secure the passage of a motion of no confidence in the government in September 1995 (although it attracted 102 votes), the SDS won 24.7% of the first-round vote in municipal elections the following month.

Other Parties and Alliances

Alternative Social-Liberal Party (*Alternativna Sotsialliberlna Partiya*, ASP), led by Nikolay Vasilev, founded in 1990 by reform Communists, joined the Union of Democratic Forces, but was expelled in December 1992 because its deputies had backed the installation of the Berov government; in April 1993 it joined the Council of Co-operation with a dozen other centre-left parties supportive of President Zhelev and in the December 1994 elections was part of the Democratic Alternative for the Republic headed by the Bulgarian Social Democratic Party. *Address.* 10A blvd V. Levski, 1000 Sofia

Alternative Socialist Association (*Alternativo Sotsialistichesko Obedinienie*, ASO), led by Manol Manolov, founded in 1990 by a reformist Communist Party faction, joined the Union of Democratic Forces (SDS) in 1991, was part of the unsuccessful SDS-Centre coalition in the October 1991 elections, in 1993 joined the Bulgarian Social Democratic Union headed by the Bulgarian Social Democratic Party. *Address.* 12 blvd Vitosha, 1000 Sofia

Bulgarian Communist Party (*Bulgarska Komunisticheska Partiya*, PKP), led by Ivan Spasov, founded in 1990 as the self-proclaimed successor to the then ruling party on the latter's transformation into the Bulgarian Socialist Party (BSP), formed part of BSP-led alliance in the 1991 elections; not to be confused with the **Bulgarian Communist Party (Marxist)** led by Boris Petkov or the **Bulgarian Communist Party (Revolutionary)** led by Angel Tsonev, both also claiming the legitimate Marxist-Leninist succession. *Address.* 5B blvd Mladezhki Prohod, 1404 Sofia

Bulgarian Democratic-Constitutional Party (*Bulgarska Demokrat-Konstitucionna Partiya*, BDKP), led by Ivan Ambarev.

Bulgarian Democratic Forum (*Bulgarski Demokraticheski Forum*, BDF), led by Vasil Zlatarov, of conservative orientation, successor to the pre-communist Union of Bulgarian National Legions, became observer member of Union of Democratic Forces. *Address.* 82 G.S. Rakovski Street, 1505 Sofia

Bulgarian Labour Social Democratic Party (*Bulgarska Rabotnicheska Sotsialdemokraticheska Partiya*, BRSP), led by Mahol Dimitrov, in 1993 joined the Bulgarian Social Democratic Union headed by the Bulgarian Social Democratic Party. *Address.* 2/32/5 Suhodolska Street, 1373 Sofia

Bulgarian Liberal Party (*Bulgarska Liberalna Partiya*, BLP), led by Vikan Vergev and Ekaterina Zahareva, in 1991 elections was part of the coalition headed by the Bulgarian Socialist Party. *Address.* 4 Haidushka Gora Street, 1000 Sofia

Bulgarian National Democratic Party (*Bulgarska Natsionalna Demokraticheska Partiya*, BNDP), led by Lchezar Stoyanov, won 0.3% of the vote in the 1991 elections. *Address.* 25 blvd Vitosha, 1000 Sofia

Bulgarian National Democratic Union (*Bulgarski Natsionalen Demokraticheski Sayuz*, BNDS), led by Nikolay Genchev.

Bulgarian National Party (*Bulgarska Narodna Partiya*, BNP), led by Dimitur Brankov.

Bulgarian National Radical Party (*Bulgarska Natsionalna Radikalna Partiya*, BNRP), led by Ivan Georgiev, won 1.1% of the vote in the 1991 elections. *Address.* 6 Alen Street, 1000 Sofia

Christian Democratic Union (*Hristiyan Demokrat-icheska Sayuz*, HDS), led by Julius Pavlov, affiliate of the Christian Democrat International, participant in the Union of Democratic Forces. *Address*. 134 Rakowski Street, 1000 Sofia

Christian Republican Party (*Hristiyan-Republikanska Partiya*, HRP), led by Konstantin Adzharov, a conservative grouping which in the 1991 elections participated in the coalition headed by the Bulgarian Socialist Party. *Address*. PO Box 113, 1066 Sofia

Citizens' Initiative (*Grazhdanska Initsiativa*, GI), led by Todor Gagalov and Lyubomir Sobadjiev, founded in 1988-89 from earlier human rights organizations, was founder member of Union of Democratic Forces (SDS) in December 1989, later also known as the Civic Initiative Movement. *Address*. 39 blvd Dondoukov, 1000 Sofia

Conservative Party (*Konservativna Partiya*, KP), led by Ivan Edisonov.

Constitutional Alliance (*Konstitucionen Sayuz*, KS), led by Manol Zhurnalov, a pro-monarchist formation founded in January 1991.

Democratic Party 1896 (*Demokratiecka Partiya 1896*), led by Stefan Raychevski, founded in 1994 by a faction of the Democratic Party which opposed the creation of the People's Union and preferred to stay in the Union of Democratic Forces.

Democratic Party of Justice in the Republic of Bulgaria (*Demokraticheska Partiya na Spravedlivostta v Republika Bulgariya*, DPSRP), founded in 1994 as a breakaway of the ethnic Turkish Movement for Rights and Freedoms, led initially by Nedim Gendzhev, who was succeeded by Ali Ibrahimov on being reinstated as Chief Mufti.

Democratic Women's Union (*Demokratichen Sayuz Zhenite*, DSZ), led by Nora Ananieva and Emilia Maclarova.

Fatherland Party of Labour (*Otechestvena Partiya na Truda*, OPT), nationalist formation led by Rumen Popov, advocating "Bulgaria for the Bulgarians" and therefore opposed to special rights for ethnic Turks, won one Assembly seat in the June 1990 elections, formed alliance with the Bulgarian Socialist Party for the October 1991 elections but lost its representation. *Address*. 3 Slavyanska Street, 1000 Sofia

Green Party (*Zelena Partiya*, ZP), led by Aleksandur Karakachanov, derives from the Ecoglasnost Movement of anti-communist environmentalists which played a key role in bringing an end to one-party Bulgarian communism in 1989-90 as part of the Union of Democratic Forces (SDS); one radical group formed the ZP for the 1991 elections and was part of the SDS-Liberal coalition, whose vote share of 2.8% was insufficient to give it representation; in the December 1994 elections the ZP was part of the Democratic Alternative for the Republic, headed by the Bulgarian Social Democratic Party, but its vote share of 3.8% was also below the required minimum. *Address*. 3 Alabin Street, 1000 Sofia

Kingdom Bulgaria (*Tsarstvo Bulgariya*), an alliance formed for the October 1991 elections (in which it won 1.8% of the vote) to advocate the restoration of King Simeon II, including the Committee for the Restoration of Parliamentary Monarchy, the Constitutional Union of Plovdiv, the Crown Movement of Gabrovo, the Kingdom of Bulgaria Union of Rousse, the Prosvetlenie Association of Sofia, the St John of Rila Club of Sofia, the Third Bulgarian Kingdom Committee of Sofia, the Nadezhda Union of Dobrich and the Union of Simeon the Great of Lovich. *Address*. Vassil Kolarov 45, 7000 Ruse

Liberal Congress Party (*Partiya Liberalen Kongres*, PLK), led by Yanko Yankov, founded in 1989 as the Socialist Party, renamed the Social Democratic Party (Non-Marxist) in 1990, renamed as the PLK in 1991. *Address*. 39 blvd Donkoukov, 1000 Sofia

Liberal Democratic Party (*Liberalno-Demokraticheska Partiya*, LDP), led by Hristo Santulov, founded in November 1989.

Liberal Party (*Liberalna Partiya*, LP), led by Petko Simeonov, former leader of the Federation of Clubs for Democracy, a component of the Union of Democratic Forces (SDS), contested October 1991 elections on the SDS-Liberals list (with the Green Party), launched as an autonomous party in November 1991.

New Social Democratic Party (*Nova Sotsial-demokraticheska Partiya*, NSDP), led by Vasil Mihailov, founded in 1994 by a faction of the Bulgarian Social Democratic Party which opted to remain under the umbrella of the Union of Democratic Forces.

New Union for Democracy, also known as **New Choice** and **Centre New Policy** (an affiliate of the

Liberal International), was launched in 1993 by Dimitur Ludzhev (a former Defence Minister) and included deputies of the Union of Democratic Forces (SDS) who had voted to approve the Berov "government of experts" in December 1992, against the official SDS line; on the resignation of the Berov government in September 1994, the new party's nomination of Ludzhev for the premiership was rejected by the National Assembly; in the December 1994 elections it failed to surmount the 4% barrier. *Address*. 129 Vitosha Street, 1408 Sofia

Party of Democratic Change (*Partiya na Demokratichnite Promeni*, PDP), led by Mukkades Nalbant and Mekhmed Hodzha, a splinter group of the ethnic Turkish Movement for Rights and Freedoms founded in 1994.

Party of Free Democrats (*Partiya ne Svobodnite Demokrati*, PSD), led by Kiril Dukov.

Party of Free Democrats–Centre (*Partiya ne Svobodnite Demokrati–Centar*, PSD-C), led by Khristo Santulov.

Radical Democratic Party (*Radikalna Demokraticheska Partiya*, RDP), led by Elka Konstantinova and Aleksandur Yordanov, descended from a pre-war party, revived in 1989 and a participant in the Union of Democratic Forces in recent elections, member of the Liberal International. *Address*. 34 blvd Dondukova, 1000 Sofia

Republican Party (*Republicanska Partiya*, RP), led by Lenko Roussanov and Ivan Sotirov, founded

in 1990, supportive of a mixed economy and the depoliticization of government and state bodies, became observer member of the Union of Democratic Forces. *Address* 46 blvd Gen. Ckobelev, 1606 Sofia

Svoboda Coalition for the Turnovo Constitution, alliance formed for the October 1991 elections (in which it won 0.7% of the vote), consisting of the Bulgarian Democratic Party for European Federation, the Bulgarian People's Party, the Conservative Party, the Liberal Democratic Party, the Party of Freedom and Progress and the United Agrarian Party.

Turkish Democratic Party (*Turska Demokraticheska Partiya*, TDP), led by Adem Kenan, ethnic Turkish fundamentalist formation founded in 1991 by a dissident faction of the Movement for Rights and Freedoms; was refused registration in mid-1994 on the grounds of its ethnic base.

Union of Democratic Muslims (*Sayuz na Demokratichni Myusyulmani*, SDM), led by Dimitur Chaushev and Yuli Mladenov Bakardzhiev.

United Christian Democratic Centre (*Obedinen Hristijandemokratitcheski Zentar*, OHZ), led by Stefan Sofianski, affiliated to the Christian Democrat International and the International Democrat Union, participant in the Union of Democratic Forces (SDS), originally as the United Democratic Centre, part of the SDS-Liberal coalition for the 1991 elections. *Address*. 134 Rakwski Street, 1000 Sofia.

Burkina Faso

Capital: Ouagadougou

Population: 10,000,000 (1995E)

Burkina Faso achieved independence from France in August 1960 and was called Upper Volta until August 1984. After 20 years of alternating parliamentary and military rule, a military coup in 1980 led to the installation of a radical left-wing regime by Capt. Thomas Sankara, who was overthrown (and killed) in a further coup in 1987 led by Capt. Blaise Compaoré at the head of an army faction called the Popular Front. Following the African trend, the government brought military rule to an end in June 1991 on the approval by referendum (and immediate promulgation) of a new constitution providing for multi-party democracy. Under its terms, an executive President is directly elected for a seven-year term by universal adult suffrage in two rounds of voting if no candidate secures an absolute majority in the first. The President appoints the Prime Minister and Council of Ministers subject to parliamentary approval. Legislative authority resides in the Assembly of People's Deputies (*Assemblée des Députés Populaires*), which is popularly elected for a five-year term on a constituency basis and currently has 107 members.

Presidential elections on Dec. 1, 1991, were boycotted by the opposition parties, with the result that Compaoré was elected unopposed in a turnout of only 28%. Assembly elections on May 24, 1992, resulted as follows: *Popular Front parties* – Organization for Popular Democracy–Labour Movement 78 seats; African Independence Party 2; Burkinabe Socialist Party 1; Movement of Progressive Democrats 1; Movement for Social Democracy 1; Union of Social Democrats 1; *other parties* – National Convention of Progressive Patriots–Social Democratic Party 12; African Democratic Assembly 6; Alliance for Democracy and Federation 4; Union of Independent Social Democrats 1.

African Democratic Rally

Rassemblement Démocratique Africain (RDA)
  Address. BP 347, Ouagadougou
  Leadership. Gérard Kango Ouedraogo (secretary-general)

The RDA is descended from the nationalist movement of the same name founded in 1946 to promote independence in French West Africa, its local branch, the Voltaic Democratic Union (UDV), becoming the dominant party in the two decades after independence in 1960. Revived in 1991, the RDA selected Gérard Kango Ouedraogo (a former Prime Minister) as its presidential candidate, but in the event the party joined the general opposition boycott of the December 1991 election. It participated in the May 1992 Assembly elections, achieving third place with six seats, and subsequently secured one portfolio in the broad coalition government appointed in June.

African Party for Independence

Parti Africain pour l'Indépendence (PAI)
  Address. 01 BP 1035, Ouagadougou 01
  Leadership. Philippe Ouedraogo (secretary-general)

The PAI was active as a pro-Soviet Marxist party in the 1970s but was banned following the 1983 Sankara coup. Following the 1987 Compaoré coup, it became a component of the ruling umbrella Popular Front (FP). It backed Compaoré's candidacy in the December 1991 presidential poll and won two seats in the May 1992 Assembly elections.

Alliance for Democracy and Federation

Alliance pour la Démocratie et la Fédération (ADF)
  Address. PB 1943, Ouagadougou
  Leadership. Herman Yaméogo

The ADF was launched in December 1990, its leader (son of a President deposed in 1966) having in 1978 founded the opposition National Union for the Defence of Democracy (UNDD). He later became leader of the Movement of Progressive Democrats (MDP) but broke away to form the ADF after the MDP had been expelled from the ruling umbrella Popular Front in June 1990 because of his alleged "irresponsible" behaviour. In February 1991 the ADF issued a joint statement with the Alliance for Democracy and Social Development calling for a transitional government and the exclusion of the ruling Popular Front parties from elections. Yaméogo was appointed Agriculture Minister in June 1991 but he and two other ADF ministers resigned in August in protest against the slow pace of democratization. The ADF boycotted the December 1991 presidential election but Yaméogo again accepted a cabinet post in February 1992. The party won four seats in the May 1992 Assembly elections, its leader remaining a minister of state in the coalition government appointed in June.

Burkinabe Socialist Party

Parti Socialiste Burkinabe (PSB)
  Address. 01 PO 1417, Ouagadougou 01
  Leadership. Ouindelasida François Ouedraogo

Launched on the restoration of multi-party democracy in 1991, the PSB became one of the smaller components of the ruling umbrella Popular Front headed by the Organization for Popular Democracy–Labour Movement and backed the candidacy of Compaoré in the December 1991 presidential elections. In won one seat in the May 1992 Assembly elections and was allocated one post in the broad coalition appointed in June.

Congress for Democracy and Progress

Congrès pour la Démocratie et le Progrès (CDP)
  Address. c/o Assemblée des Députés Populaires, Ouagadougou
  Leadership. Blaise Compaoré (president), Christian Roch Kaboré (first vice-president), Kanidoua Naboho (secretary-general)

The CDP was created early in 1996 as a merger of President Compaoré's Organization for Popular Democracy–Labour Movement (ODP-MT) and some 10 other pro-regime parties. The ODP-MT had been created in April 1989 by a merger of the Burkinabe Union of Communists (UCB) and a faction of the Union of Communist Struggles (ULC), from which the UCB had previously split. It was intended originally to provide a single-party base for the Compaoré regime by unifying "all political tendencies in the country" and became the leading component of the pro-Compaoré Popular Front (*Front Populaire*, FP), first created in October 1987 and reorganized in 1991. Meanwhile, the first ODP-MT secretary-general, Clément Ouedraogo (former UCB leader), had been dismissed in April 1990 for "serious failures of principle and party policy". At a congress in March 1991, the ODP-MT formally renounced Marxism-Leninism and embraced a free enterprise, pro-Western philosophy, while remaining unenthusiastic about multi-party politics.

Asserting its autonomy and dominance within the FP, the ODP-MT backed Compaoré's (uncontested) presidential candidacy in December 1991 and in May 1992 unexpectedly won a large majority in Assembly elections (which were condemned as fraudulent by the opposition parties). The ODP-MT was the leading party in the post-election coalition government headed by Youssouf Ouedraogo, which included six other parties, several of them outside the FP. In March 1994 Ouedraogo was replaced by Christian Roch Kaboré after failing to reach a wage agreement with the trade unions in the wake of the devaluation of the CFA franc. In January 1995 the leader of the ODP-MT youth wing, Moumouni Ouedraogo, was killed in disturbances preceding local elections the following month. On the creation of the CDP in February 1996, Kaboré was replaced as Prime Minister by Kadre Desiré Ouedraogo and became first vice-president of the new party as well as special adviser to the presidency.

Movement for Social Democracy

Mouvement pour la Démocratie Sociale (MDS)

Address. c/o Assemblée des Députés Populaires, Ouagadougou

Leadership. Jean-Marc Palm (secretary-general)

The MDS is derived from the Burkinabe Communist Group (GCB), founded in 1984 by a breakaway faction of the Voltaic Revolutionary Communist Party (PCRV). Palm was appointed Minister of External Relations after the 1987 Compaoré coup but was dismissed in April 1989 when he opposed the merging of the GCB into the new Organization for Popular Democracy–Labour Movement (ODP-MT). Relaunched as the MDS in 1991 and now propounding democratic socialism rather than Marxism-Leninism, the party won one seat in the May 1992 Assembly elections and was included in the broad coalition government appointed in June.

Movement of Progressive Democrats

Mouvement des Démocrates Progressistes (MDP)

Address. c/o Assemblée des Députés Populaires, Ouagadougou

Leadership. Lassane Ouangraoua (secretary-general)

The MDP was established by Herman Yaméogo following the 1987 Compaoré coup and became a non-socialist component of the ruling umbrella Popular Front (PF). In mid-1990 the expulsion of the MDP from the PF, on the grounds of Yaméogo's "irresponsible" behaviour (including alleged embezzlement of party funds), provoked the creation of the MDP (Orthodox) led by Yaméogo and the MDP (Reformist). Of these factions, the former later became the Alliance for Democracy and Federation and the latter rejoined the PF under its original rubric. The MDP won one seat in the May 1992 Assembly elections.

National Convention of Progressive Patriots–Social Democratic Party

Convention Nationale des Patriotes Progressistes–Parti Social-Démocrate (CNPP-PSD)

Address. 01 BP 2143, Ouagadougou 01

Leadership. Mamadou Simpore (president)

The CNPP-PSD was expelled from the ruling umbrella Popular Front in March 1991, after criticizing the reluctance of the dominant Organization for Popular Democracy–Labour Movement (ODP-MT) to proceed to a full national conference on political change. It was one of the "group of 13" opposition parties which walked out of the alternative consultative assembly convened in June 1991; later the same month it joined a transitional government but withdrew within a fortnight. In September 1991 it was a founding member of the Confederation of Democratic Forces (*Confédération des Forces Démocratiques*, CFD), which became the main umbrella organization of the pro-democracy opposition. Having originally nominated Pierre-Claver Damiba as its candidate, the CNPP-PSD joined the general opposition boycott of the December 1991 presidential election. However, it participated in the May 1992 Assembly elections, becoming the largest opposition party with 12 seats (and lodging vigorous allegations of electoral fraud). It obtained three portfolios in the post-election broad coalition headed by the ODP-MT. In May 1993 the retirement from political life of the CNPP-PSD leader, Pierre Tapsoba, precipitated a power struggle for the succession, leading to the formation of the breakaway Party for Democracy and Progress and to a reduction in the rump CNPP-PSD's parliamentary strength to four seats.

Party for Democracy and Progress
Parti pour la Démocratie et le Progrès (CDP)
    Address. BP 606, Ouagadougou
    Telephone. (#226) 362190
    Fax. (#226) 362902
    Leadership. Joseph Ki-Kerbo (general secretary)
The CDP came into being as a result of a power struggle in the National Convention of Progressive Patriots–Social Democratic Party (CNPP-PSD) in 1993. Prof. Ki-Zerbo had been placed fourth in presidential elections in 1978 as candidate of what became the socialist-oriented Voltaic Progressive Front (*Front Progressiste Voltaïque*, FPV), which was banned after the 1980 Sankara coup. The FPV was later accepted into membership of the Socialist International under Ki-Zerbo's leadership in exile. On the restoration of multi-partyism in 1991, Ki-Kerbo returned to Burkina Faso and became associated with the CNPP-PSD, heading the allied Union of Independent Social Democrats (*Union des Sociaux-Démocrates Indépendants*, USDI) in the May 1992 Assembly elections, in which it won one seat. Ki-Zerbo broke with the CNPP-PSD following the retirement of its leader in May 1993, complaining of the "suspicion, internal quarrels and absence of motivation" generated by the resultant succession struggle. His new CDP was formally constituted at a congress in April 1994, when it claimed to have the support of nine of the 13 CNPP-PSD/USDI deputies and thus to be the second strongest party in the Assembly.

Union of Social Democrats
Union des Sociaux-Démocrates (USD)
    Address. c/o Assemblée des Députés Populaires, Ouagadougou
    Leadership. Alain Yoda (secretary-general)
The USD was founded in November 1990 as a "progressive and anti-imperialist" grouping and joined the ruling umbrella Popular Front supportive of President Compaoré. It won one seat in the May 1992 Assembly elections.

Other Parties

Alliance for Democracy and Social Development (*Alliance pour la Démocratie et le Développement Social*, ADDS), led by Etienne Traoré, is closely aligned with the Alliance for Democracy and Federation.

Burkinabe Labour Party (*Parti du Travail du Burkina*, PTB), founded in 1990 by Clément Oumarou Ouedraogo, who became prominent in the opposition Confederation of Democratic Forces (CFD) but who was assassinated in December 1991.

Burkinabe Socialist Bloc (*Bloc Socialiste Burkinabe*, BSB), led by Ernest Nongoma Ouedraogo, formed in November 1991 to pursue the leftist policies of the 1983–87 Sankara regime, derived from the Sankarist Movement (MS) formed in 1988, opposed to the Compaoré regime but not part of main pro-democracy opposition, boycotted May 1992 Assembly elections although the constituent United Forces (*Forces Unis*, FU) led by Victor Yaméogo broke ranks to contest the poll (without success).

Ecologist Party for Progress (*Parti Ecologiste pour le Progrès*, PEP), led by Salvi Charles Somé, founded in April 1991.

Group of Revolutionary Democrats (*Groupement des Démocrates Révolutionnaires*, GDR), led by Ludovic Tou, a member of the pro-Compaoré Popular Front until its expulsion in early 1991, susbequently a component of the opposition Confederation of Democratic Forces (CFD).

Movement for Progress and Tolerance (*Mouvement pour le Progrès et la Tolérance*, MPT), led by Emmanuel Nayabtigungu Congo Kabore (a former government Secretary-General), founded as an "anti-imperialist and nationalist/progressive" party, more prepared for co-operation with Compaoré regime than other opposition parties.

Party for Democracy and Assembly (*Parti pour la Démocratie et le Rassemblement*, PDR), launched in mid-1993.

Party of the Convergence of Liberties and Integration (*Parti de la Convergence pour les Libertés et l' Intégration*, PCLI), launched in mid-1993.

Patriotic League for Development (*Ligue Patriotique pour le Développement*, LIPAD), led by Hamidou Coulibaly, founded in 1973 as a splinter of the African Party for Independence and initially influential under the 1983–87 Sankara regime, part of the opposition to the post-1987 Compaoré regime.

Social Progress Party (*Parti du Progrès Social*, PPS), led by Alain Zougba, descended from the Union of Communist Struggles (ULC) founded in 1980 by Maoist and Trotskyist students and represented in the post-1983 Sankara government but marginalized under post-1987 Compaoré regime (Zougba being dismissed from ministerial office in 1989 for refusing to take the ULC into the Organization for Popular Democracy–Labour Movement), relaunched as the PPS in 1991 and thereafter part of the anti-Compaoré opposition.

Union for Democracy and Social Progress (*Union pour la Démocratie et le Progrès Social*, UDPS), led by Jean-Claude Kambire, founded in early 1991 as a pro-democracy party.

Union of Burkinabe Democrats and Patriots (*Union des Démocrates et Patriotes Burkinabe*, UDPB), led by Joseph Ouedraogo, member of the pro-Compaoré Popular Front.

Union of Greens for the Development of Burkina (*Union des Verts pour le Développement du Burkina*, UVDB), led by Ram Ouedraogo, founded in 1991, its leader was the first declared candidate for the December 1991 presidential election, but he later withdrew along with all other opposition nominees.

Workers' Revolutionary Party of Burkina (*Parti Révolutionnaire des Travaillistes du Burkina*, PRTB), an anti-Compaoré grouping dating from the late 1980s.

Burundi

Capital: Bujumbura

Population: 6,000,000 (1995E)

Burundi was granted independence as a monarchy in 1962, having previously been administered by Belgium since the termination of German rule during World War I, first under a League of Nations mandate and from 1946 as a UN trusteeship. The overthrow of the monarchy in 1966 and the declaration of the Republic of Burundi was followed, from 1976, by a series of military regimes and one-party government, latterly under Maj. Pierre Buyoya. Following the African trend, Buyoya published a National Unity Charter in May 1990, under which Burundi moved to civilian rule and "controlled" multi-partyism; but the transition served to unleash conflict between the majority Hutu ethnic group and the minority Tutsis who had traditionally exercised dominance. A new constitution approved in March 1992 provides for an executive President, who is directly elected by universal adult suffrage for a five-year term (renewable once) and who appoints the Prime Minister. Legislative authority is vested in a unicameral National Assembly (*Assemblée Nationale*), currently of 81 members, which is directly elected for a five-year term by proportional representation from party lists, subject to a minimum requirement for representation of 5% of the overall vote. Political parties must, to obtain registration, subscribe to the 1990 National Unity Charter, eschew racial, religious and royalist identification and have founder members from each of Burundi's 15 provinces. A "convention of government" concluded by the main parties in September 1994 (and incorporated into the constitution) provided for formalized power-sharing in government structures between representatives of the Hutu and Tutsi ethnic groups.

The first round of presidential elections on June 1, 1993, resulted in an outright victory for Melchior Ndadaye of the Burundi Front for Democracy (FRODEBU), who secured 64.8% of the vote, against 32.4% for incumbent Buyoya (candidate of the Union for National Progress, UPRONA) and 1.4% for a candidate of the People's Reconciliation Party (PRP). In Assembly elections on June 29, 1993, FRODEBU won 65 seats and UPRONA the other 16. Ndadaye was killed in an attempted coup in October 1993 and was succeeded in January 1994 by Cyprien Ntaryamira (FRODEBU), who under emergengy constitutional revisions was elected by the National Assembly rather than by popular vote. Three months later, on April 6, 1994, Ntaryamira himself died in an air crash and was succeeded by Sylvestre Ntibantunganya (FRODEBU).

Burundi Front for Democracy
Front pour la Démocratie au Burundi
(FRODEBU)
    Address. c/o Assemblée Nationale, Bujumbura
    Leadership. Jean Minani (president)

FRODEBU began as an informal alliance of opposition groups which campaigned for a "no" vote in the March 1992 constitutional referendum on the grounds that the Buyoya regime had refused to convene a full national conference to agree the transition to multi-partyism. Following the promulgation of the new constitution, FRODEBU registered as a political party, containing both Hutus and Tutsis. The first round of presidential elections on June 1, 1993, resulted in an outright victory for Melchior Ndadaye, the FRODEBU leader, who secured 64.8% of the vote, against 32.4% for incumbent Buyoya, of the Union for National Progress (UPRONA). In Assembly elections on June 29, 1993, FRODEBU won 65 of the 81 seats with 71.4% of the vote. The accession to power of Ndadaye, a member of the majority Hutu ethnic group, marked an interruption of centuries of rule by the Tutsi minority, although UPRONA members were allocated the premiership and six portfolios in the post-election coalition government. Ndadaye was killed in an attempted coup by militant Hutu dissidents in October 1993 and was succeeded in January 1994 by Cyprien Ntaryamira (FRODEBU), also a Hutu, who likewise appointed a Tutsi (and UPRONA member) as Prime Minister of a broad coalition government charged with promoting inter-ethnic peace. Nevertheless, some FRODEBU leaders were implicated in Hutu revenge attacks on Tutsis.

On April 6, 1994, Ntaryamira himself died in an unexplained air crash near Kigali (together with the President of Rwanda) and was succeeded by Sylvestre Ntibantunganya (FRODEBU), a Hutu, who was formally endorsed by the National Assembly on Sept. 30, 1994. Immediately prior to his endorsement, FRODEBU signed the "convention of government" providing for power-sharing with other parties. Following Ntibantunganya's inauguration on Oct. 1, a new government included representatives of FRODEBU (the dominant party), UPRONA (which continued to hold the premiership) and five other parties. Subsequent strains between the main coalition partners were partially resolved in January 1995 by the election of Léonce Ngendakumana of FRODEBU as Assembly speaker with UPRONA support, while the controversial original nominee for the post, Jean Minani, became FRODEBU president in place of President Ntibantunganya.

FRODEBU continued to participate in the re-formed power-sharing government installed in March 1995, holding 10 portfolios. In May President Ntibantunganya rejected suggestions that the territories of Burundi and Rwanda should be reorganized into ethnically pure Hutu and Tutsi states. The following month he was rebuffed by his own FRODEBU Assembly deputies when he sought approval to rule by decree, amid a serious deterioration in the internal security situation. In September 1995 FRODEBU and other "presidential bloc" ministers, calling themselves

the Force for Democratic Change (*Force pour le Changement Démocratique*, FCD), issued a statement criticizing the UPRONA Interior Minister for having rejected an assertion by the US ambassador to Burundi that the security situation caused him "deep concern". The same statement accused the Interior Minister of refusing to apply the political parties law and of failing to take action to curb the continuing violence.

Guarantor of the Freedom of Speech in Burundi
Inkinzo y'Igambo Ry'abarundi
Address. c/o Ministry of Culture, Bujumbura
Leadership. Alphonse Rugumbarara (president)
Although not represented in the Assembly elected in June 1993, *Inkinzo* was included in the broad coalition government appointed in February 1994, its president becoming Minister of Culture, Youth and Sports. It signed the September 1994 "convention of government" and was also included in the successive multi-party cabinets installed in October and March 1995, holding one portfolio.

People's Reconciliation Party
Parti de la Réconciliation du Peuple (PRP)
Leadership. François Mbesherubusa (president)
The PRP was founded in September 1991 by elements favouring a restoration of the (Tutsi) monarchy and power-sharing between ethnic groups in a parliamentary system. It secured official registration in July 1992, notwithstanding a provision in the new parties law enacted in April debarring parties with royalist aspirations (among other categories). Its presidential candidate, Pierre-Claver Sendegeya, trailed a poor third in the June 1993 voting, winning 1.4% of the vote; later the same month the PRP failed to win a seat in Assembly elections. The party was nevertheless included in the broad coalition government appointed in February 1994 and signed the September 1994 "convention of government" on power-sharing between the main parties.

Rally for Democracy and Economic and Social Development
Rassemblement pour la Démocratie et le Développement Economique et Social (RADDES)
Address. c/o Ministry of Trade and Industry, Bujumbura
Leadership. Joseph Nzeyimana (president), Astère Nzisibira
RADDES was founded on the move to multi-partyism in 1992 but failed to make any impact in the June 1993 Assembly elections. It was nevertheless included in the broad coalition government formed in February 1994, Nzeyimana becoming

Minister of Trade and Industry after having protested vigorously about an initial allocation of portfolios. RADDES signed the September 1994 "convention of government" on power-sharing between the main parties and was also included in the coalition government appointed in October. It retained the Trade and Industry portfolio in the new government appointed in March 1995, although it passed to Astère Nzisibira.

Rally of the People of Burundi
Rassemblement du Peuple du Burundi (RPB)
    Address. c/o Ministry of Energy and Mines, Bujumbura
    Leadership. Emmanuel Sindayigaya
    Founded in 1992, the mainly Hutu RPB was third-placed party in the June 1993 Assembly elections, although without surmounting the 5% barrier to representation. It was nevertheless included in the coalition government appointed in October 1994, having backed the power-sharing "convention of government" concluded the previous month. In March 1995 the RPB leader, Ernest Kabushemeye, was killed in renewed inter-ethnic fighting and replaced as Minister of Energy and Mines by Emmanuel Sindayigaya.

Union for National Progress
Union pour le Progrès National (UPRONA)
    Address. BP 1810, Bujumbura
    Leadership. Maj. Pierre Buyoya (chairman), Charles Mukasi (president)
    Founded in 1959 by Prince Louis Rwagasore, UPRONA has over the years undergone various adjustments in its French title, although all have retained the UPRONA acronym. It was in the forefront of the struggle against Belgian rule, winning an overwhelming majority in Assembly elections in 1961 (after which Prince Rwagasore was assassinated) and leading Burundi to full independence as a monarchy the following year. Having retained its majority in the 1965 Assembly elections (and lost two more Prime Ministers by assassination), UPRONA was proclaimed the sole ruling party on the overthrow of the (Tutsi) monarchy by the Tutsi-dominated army in 1966, whereupon Michel Micombero was installed as President. He was ousted in 1976 by Col. Jean-Baptiste Bagaza (a Tutsi), who declared the Second Republic and reorganized UPRONA as the ruling party. At its first congress in December 1979 UPRONA adopted a new charter and statutes, defining the party as a democratic centralist organization dedicated to the struggle against exploitation and imperialism and in favour of self-reliance, the preservation of national culture, and co-operation in community development.

A new constitution for Burundi, drafted by the UPRONA central committee and providing for a return to civilian rule, secured referendum approval in November 1981. In August 1984 Bagaza was re-elected President as the UPRONA (and only) candidate, but in September 1987 he was overthrown (while out of the country) by a military coup led by Maj. Pierre Buyoya, another Tutsi and a then little-known UPRONA central committee member. Although Buyoya dismissed the incumbent UPRONA central committee, he was backed by the party's national secretariat, which was instructed to establish a new structure for UPRONA. Full party activity was resumed in 1989 (after a spate of Tutsi-Hutu conflict), with Nicolas Mayugi (a Buyoya nominee and a Hutu) as UPRONA secretary-general. Under a National Unity Charter published by Buyoya in May 1990, the UPRONA central committee in December 1990 took over the functions of the Military Committee for National Salvation. Having at that stage shown a preference for "democracy within the single party", Buyoya in May 1991 declared his support for a measure of pluralism, which was enshrined in the new constitution adopted in March 1992. At an extraordinary congress the same month UPRONA delegates elected a new 90–member central committee and also endorsed Mayugi as party president in succession to Buyoya (who stood down in accordance with the new constitution). That Mayugi and a majority of the new central committee were Hutus (despite UPRONA's membership being 90% Tutsi) reflected the regime's sensitivity to charges that it was dominated by the minority Tutsis.

The stratagem did not help Buyoya in the presidential elections of June 1993, when he was defeated outright in the first round by the Hutu candidate of the Burundi Front for Democracy (FRODEBU). UPRONA was also decisively defeated in Assembly elections later the same month, winning only 16 of the 81 seats, after which the party complained of "ethnic manipulation" by FRODEBU. Nevertheless, UPRONA accepted representation in the post-election government, the premiership going to Sylvie Kinigi, a Tutsi and former UPRONA member, who became Burundi's first woman Prime Minister. Following the murder of President Ndadaya in October 1993, UPRONA again charged FRODEBU leaders of fomenting anti-Tutsi violence but accepted participation in a broad coalition government formed in February 1994 and headed by UPRONA member Anatole Kanyenkiko, a Tutsi.

The death of President Ntaryamira in April 1994 gave rise to fears of a tribal bloodbath on the Rwandan scale, to avert which UPRONA eventually co-operated in the elevation to the presidency of the FRODEBU Speaker of the National Assembly, a Hutu, and continued to participate in the coalition government. The intitial UPRONA candidate for the presidency had been Charles Mukasi, who replaced Mayugi as party president. UPRONA was a signatory of the September 1994 "convention of government" providing for power-sharing between the main parties. Following the parliamentary confirmation of the FRODEBU President in September 1994, UPRONA was the second-strongest party in new broad coalition appointed in October, with Kanyenkiko continuing as Prime Minister. However, the latter was expelled from UPRONA in January 1995 (for having dismissed two UPRONA ministers at the President's behest) and was eventually replaced by Antoine Nduwayo after UPRONA had mounted anti-Kanyenkiko demonstrations.

In June 1995 most UPRONA Assembly deputies supported the President's unsuccessful request to be allowed to rule by decree. The following month UPRONA unsuccessfully demanded the dissolution of the Assembly and new elections, claiming that many FRODEBU deputies had fled the country. In September Nduwayo and the UPRONA Interior Minister, Gabriel Sinarinzi, came under attack from FRODEBU and other members of the government for downplaying the extent of violence in Burundi and for allegedly resisting multi-party democracy. He was dismissed from the government in October 1995.

Other Parties

Independent Workers' Party (*Parti Indépendant des Travailleurs*, PIT), led by Nicéphore Ndimurukundo, included in the coalition governments appointed from October 1994.

National Alliance for Rights and Development (*Alliance Nationale pour les Droits et le Développement*, ANADDE), founded in 1992.

Party for the Liberation of the Hutu People (*Parti pour la Libération du Peuple Hutu*, PALIPE-HUTU), led by Rémy Gahutu, militant Hutu organization founded among exiles in Rwanda, active in inter-ethnic slaughter in Burundi in the 1990s.

People's Party (*Parti Populaire*, PP), led by Shadrack Niyonkuru, registered in July 1992, unsuccessful in the June 1993 Assembly elections, but included in the coalition government appointed in October 1994.

Social Democratic Party (*Parti Social-Démocrate*, PSD), founded in 1993.

Social Development Union (*Union du Développement Social*, UDS).

Cambodia

Capital: Phnom Penh   **Population:** 9,800,000 (1995E)

The Kingdom of Cambodia achieved independence in 1953 after 90 years of French rule, with King Norodom Sihanouk becoming head of state but vacating the throne in 1955 in order to preserve his political authority. Prince Sihanouk (as he then became) steered a neutral and non-aligned course for 15 years but fell victim to the escalating Vietnam conflict in 1970, being deposed and replaced by a pro-US regime headed by Lon Nol. This provoked a massive insurrection by the Chinese-backed communist Khmers Rouges (KR), who seized power in 1975, proclaimed Democratic Kampuchea (DK) in 1976 and engaged in a three-year reign of terror under Pol Pot. In 1979 the DK regime was overthrown by Vietnamese-backed communist rebels, who established the People's Republic of Kampuchea (PRK) in 1981 under the leadership of the pro-Soviet Kampuchean People's Revolutionary Party (KPRP). But the DK government-in-exile, headed by Prince Sihanouk and dominated by the KR, retained UN recognition and pursued a guerrilla war against the PRK government. The PRK was renamed the State of Cambodia (SOC) in 1989, as Vietnamese forces began to withdraw, facilitating the signature of a UN-brokered peace agreement in Paris in October 1991. This instrument provided for the country to be administered by a UN Transitional Authority in Cambodia (UNTAC) pending democratic elections and the formation of a new government. A Supreme National Council (SNC), originally formed in September 1990 under the chairmanship of Prince Sihanouk, supposedly embraced all the contending factions. However, amid continuing hostilities, the KR (now calling themselves the Cambodian National Unity Party) boycotted UN-supervised elections in May 1993, allowing the Sihanoukist United National Front for an Independent, Neutral, Peaceful and Co-operative Cambodia (FUNCINPEC) to win a narrow majority over the ex-KPRP, now called the Cambodian People's Party (CPP). A coalition government of FUNCINPEC, the CPP and two smaller parties was formed and on Sept. 21, 1993, a new constitution was promulgated re-establishing the monarchy in the context of a pluralistic, liberal and democratic political system. Three days later a seven-member Throne Council elected Sihanouk to resume the throne he had vacated 38 years earlier.

The elections to the 120–member Constituent (later National) Assembly, held on May 23, 1993, resulted as follows: FUNCINPEC 58 seats (with 45.5% of the vote); CPP 51 (38.2%); Buddhist Liberal Democratic Party 10; National Liberation Movement of Cambodia 1.

Buddhist Liberal Democratic Party (BLDP)
Kanakpak Preacheathippatai Serei Preah Puthasasna

Address. 197 Keo Mony Blvd, Phnom Penh

Telephone. (#855-23) 26175

Leadership. Ieng Mouli (president), Pen Thol (deputy chair), Son Soubert (secretary-general)

The BLDP was founded in 1992 as the successor to the Khmer People's National Liberation Front (KPNLF), itself the political heir of the 1970–75 pro-US regime of Lon Nol. The KPNLF was launched in 1979 by Son Sann (a Prime Minister under the pre-1970 Sihanouk regime), first in France and then in Cambodia, as a democratic, non-communist movement opposed to the pro-Vietnam regime installed in Phnom Penh that year. Initially also opposed to the *Khmers Rouges* (KR), the KPNLF was the political wing of the Free Khmers (*Khmers Serei*) guerrilla army, which raised a considerable anti-communist following on the strength of US and ASEAN aid. In June 1982, however, the KPNLF joined the Coalition Government of Democratic Kampuchea (CGDK) in alliance with Sihanoukist forces and the KR, Son Sann becoming the CGDK Prime Minister. Military reverses for the KPNLF in the 1980s were compounded by internal divisions, so that the Front had little influence in shaping the Paris peace agreement of October 1991, although it had two seats on the 12–member Supreme National Council (SNC) established by the contending factions the previous year.

Authorized to establish a presence in Phnom Penh, the KPNLF transformed itself into a political party in May 1992, the chosen BLDP rubric being intended to demonstrate its non-communist, traditionalist but pro-market orientation. In the Assembly elections of May 1993, the BLDP won only 10 of the 120 seats but was subsequently included in the new coalition government headed by the Sihanoukist United National Front for an Independent, Neutral, Peaceful and Co-operative Cambodia (FUNCINPEC) and the pro-Vietnamese Cambodian People's Party (CPP). In July 1995 Son Sann was replaced as BLDP leader by Ieng Mouli, who had the public backing of FUNCINPEC and the CPP.

Cambodian National Unity Party (CNUP)
Kanakpak Samakki Cheat Kampuchea
   Address. c/o National Assembly, Phnom Penh
   Telephone. (#855-23) 26499
   Leadership. Khieu Samphan (president), Son Sen (vice-president)

The CNUP was launched in 1992 as the latest political arm of the *Khmers Rouges* (KR), succeeding the Party of Democratic Kampuchea (PDK). The KR had been set up in 1967 as the armed wing of the Communist Party of Kampuchea (CPK), the name which the then dominant pro-Chinese faction had given to the Kampuchean People's Revolutionary Party (KPRP), which was itself descended from the original Indo-Chinese Communist Party founded in 1930 (and is now called the Cambodian People's Party). Pro-Chinese as opposed to pro-Soviet ascendancy in the Cambodian communist movement dated from a secret congress in 1960 (later alternatively described as the KPRP's second and the CPK's first) which opted for armed struggle against the Sihanouk government and elected younger, Paris-educated intellectuals to the leadership, including Tou Samouth as general secretary and Pol Pot (then called Saloth Sar), Ieng Sary and Son Sen to other leading posts. The party also opted to change its name, although not until 1966 was the CPK title generally established. Meanwhile, the pro-Vietnamese (i.e. pro-Soviet) Tou Samouth had been assassinated in 1962, possibly on the orders of Pol Pot, who was elected party general secretary in early 1963 and then went underground together with other radical leaders.

The KR launched a major peasant revolt in north-western Cambodia in 1967–68 and attracted the support of some communists who had previously operated within the Sihanouk regime,

notably Khieu Samphan. It was also prepared in those days to use Vietnamese *Viet Cong* irregulars to advance its military cause. The advent of the pro-US Lon Nol regime in 1970 produced an uneasy reconciliation between the KR and the CPK's pro-Vietnamese wing, with the party as a whole joining the Beijing-based government-in-exile headed by Prince Sihanouk. Although on the military front the KR made up only a small proportion of the Sihanoukist forces which opposed the Lon Nol regime, politically the KR became dominant. From 1973 Pol Pot began purging pro-Vietnamese elements from the CPK, with the result that, following the fall of the Lon Nol regime in 1975, the KR-dominated faction of the CPK came to power in Phnom Penh. The first head of state of the new regime, Prince Sihanouk, was replaced by Khieu Samphan in April 1976, and in September 1977 it was officially confirmed that the ruling party in what was now called Democratic Kampuchea was the CPK led by Pol Pot. This regime launched one of the most brutal social transformation programmes in history, involving the forcible transfer of the urban population to the countryside and mass executions of huge numbers of alleged reactionaries.

The response of the pro-Vietnamese faction of the CPK was an armed insurgency, supported by Vietnamese forces, which yielded the overthrow of the KR regime in January 1979 and the eventual establishment of the People's Republic of Kampuchea (PRK) led by what reverted to being called the KPRP. Having resumed armed struggle on the ground, the KR leadership in December 1981 announced the dissolution of the CPK, which was later replaced by the PDK. The KR also renewed its alliance with the Sihanoukists, joining the Coalition Government of Democratic Kampuchea (CGDK) formed in June 1982 under the titular leadership of Prince Sihanouk and also including the Khmer People's National Liberation Front (which later became the Buddhist Liberal Democratic Party). Despite much international condemnation of the brutality of the Pol Pot regime, combined Chinese and US influence ensured that the CGDK retained UN recognition, despite increasing KR dominance therein. To appease world opinion, Pol Pot and other infamous KR figures were removed from public leadership posts in the 1980s. However, although Son Sen took over the KR military command and Khieu Samphan became vice-chairman of the CGDK, Pol Pot was thought to have retained crucial influence as general secretary of the clandestine PDK structure. Also suspect was the PDK's declaration in mid-1985 that it had embraced a "new ideology of democratic socialism".

From bases on the Thai border, the KR-led

forces of the CGDK stepped up their military operations when Vietnamese troops began to withdraw in 1989. Nevertheless, UN-brokered negotiations entered a positive phase, producing agreement in September 1990 on the creation of a Supreme National Council (SNC) representing both the CGDK and the KPRP government of the former PRK, now called the State of Cambodia (SOC). The KR representatives on the SNC, which was chaired by Prince Sihanouk, were Khieu Samphan and Son Sen. This led on to the signature in October 1991 of the UN-brokered Paris agreement providing for military demobilization and multi-party elections, pending which the CGDK parties were authorized to return to Phnom Penh. After initial obstruction from anti-KR demonstrators, Khieu Samphan and Son Sen established a KR compound in the Cambodian capital in December 1991 and declared the party's intention to contest elections. To this end, in November 1992 the KR announced that the CNUP had been created to replace the PDK, with Khieu Samphan and Son Sen becoming chair and vice-chair respectively. It had previously been announced that Pol Pot had retired from the KR leadership, although reports to the contrary persisted. The CNUP programme pledged the party "to respect and abide by a parliamentary regime" and to implement "a liberal economic system".

In the event, amid continuing hostility between the SNC components, the KR/CNUP decided to boycott the Assembly elections held in May 1993, on the grounds that the UN had failed to verify the complete withdrawal of Vietnamese troops. The boycott turned out to be a serious tactical error, in that the Sihanoukist United National Front for an Independent, Neutral, Peaceful and Co-operative Cambodia (FUNCINPEC) and the new Cambodian People's Party (CPP), successor to the KPRP, emerged as joint victors and thereafter consolidated their anti-KR alliance. In political and military opposition to the new ruling coalition led by FUNCINPEC and the CPP, the KR/CNUP no longer had the overt backing of China, which endorsed the post-election restoration of old friend Sihanouk to the Cambodian throne. Less overtly, China continued to regard the KR as an ally against the ambitions of the pro-Vietnamese CPP to become dominant in Phnom Penh.

After a series of military reverses, the KR/CNUP entered into talks with the government in May 1994, but these broke down in June when the KR/CNUP refused to declare a ceasefire in advance of a power-sharing agreement. On the initiative of the CPP, the KR/CNUP headquarters in Phnom Penh was speedily closed and its officials expelled from the country. The following month the Cambodian National Assembly enacted legislation banning the KR, membership of which became punishable by up to 30 years' imprisonment. The KR reacted by announcing in July 1994 a "provisional government of national union and national salvation", headed by Khieu Samphan and located in the northern province of Prey Vihear. Kidnappings and murders of Western travellers followed later in the year. A government amnesty for KR activists was said to have yielded some 7,000 surrenders by January 1995; but up to 10,000 hard-core KR fighters were thought to remain in the field. The most senior KR defector was Sar Kim Lemouth, who in February 1995 was reported to have told government officials that Pol Pot remained a key leader of the movement.

Cambodian People's Party (CPP)
Kanakpak Pracheachon Prachor
   Address. Chamcarmon, Blvd Norodom, Phnom Penh
   Telephone. (#855-23) 25403
   Leadership. Chea Sim (president), Hun Sen (vice-president), Heng Samrin (honorary chair)

The CPP was launched in October 1991 as a non-communist successor to the communist Kampuchean People's Revolutionary Party (KPRP), then the ruling party in Phnom Penh. The KPRP was itself descended from the Indo-Chinese Communist Party founded in 1930, which had divided into separate sections for Cambodia, Laos and Vietnam in 1951. Following the end of French rule in 1953, the KPRP in Cambodia for some years conducted peaceful opposition to the Sihanouk government, operating within the Masses Party and also seeking to infiltrate the ruling Popular Socialist Community Party. In 1960 the party was radicalized at a secret congress which opted for armed struggle and elected younger, Paris-trained intellectuals to the leadership, including Tou Samouth as general secretary and Pol Pot (then called Saloth Sar), Ieng Sary and Son Sen to other leading posts. The party also opted to change its name, although not until 1966 was the new title Communist Party of Kampuchea (CPK) generally accepted. Meanwhile, Tou Samouth had been assassinated in 1962, possibly on the orders of Pol Pot, who was elected general secretary in early 1963 and then went underground together with other radical leaders.

Pro-Chinese and Maoist in orientation, the Pol Pot faction became known as the *Khmers Rouges* (KR) and launched a major peasant revolt in north-western Cambodia in 1967. The advent of the pro-US Lon Nol regime in 1970 produced an uneasy reconciliation between the KR and the CPK's pro-Vietnamese (and pro-Soviet) wing, the party as a whole joining the Beijing-backed government-in-exile headed by Prince Sihanouk.

From 1973, however, Pol Pot began purging pro-Vietnamese elements from the CPK, with the result that, following the fall of the Lon Nol regime in 1975, the KR-dominated faction of the CPK was able to take power in Phnom Penh in 1976. In September 1977 it was officially confirmed that the ruling party in Democratic Kampuchea was the CPK led by Pol Pot. The response of the pro-Vietnamese faction was an armed revolt and the formation in "liberated" areas of the Kampuchean National United Front for National Salvation (KNUFNS). With assistance from Vietnamese forces, the KNUFNS overthrew the Pol Pot regime in January 1979, in which month a "reorganization" congress in Phnom Penh decided that the CPK should revert to the KPRP rubric and elected a new leadership with Pen Sovan as general secretary. Under the 1981 constitution inaugurating the People's Republic of Kampuchea (PRK), the KPRP was confirmed as the sole legal party and the leading force of the Kampuchean United Front for National Construction and Defence (KUFNCD) as successor to the KNUFNS. Following an apparent internal power struggle, Pen Sovan was replaced as KPRP general secretary by Heng Samrin in December 1981.

The departure of Vietnamese forces from 1989, the renaming of the PRK as the State of Cambodia (SOC) and the conversion of the KUFNCD into the United Front for the Construction and Defence of the Cambodian Fatherland (UFCDCF) led to the signature of the Paris peace agreement in October 1991 and impelled the KPRP to undertake another transformation. An extraordinary congress in October 1991 not only changed the party's name to its present form but also renounced Marxism-Leninism and embraced multi-party democracy and a free enterprise economy. Other decisions included the removal of the hammer and sickle from the party's emblem and the merging of the former politburo and secretariat into a single standing committee of the central committee. In leadership changes, the relatively hardline president of the National Assembly, Chea Sim, became party leader and the moderate faction leader, Prime Minister Hun Sen, became deputy leader, while Heng Samrin was allocated the cosmetic post of honorary chair. In the UN-supervised Assembly elections of May 1993, the CPP benefitted from a boycott followed by the KR, now called the Cambodian National Unity Party (CNUP), to win 51 of the 120 seats, in close second place behind the Sihanoukist United National Front for an Independent, Neutral, Peaceful and Co-operative Cambodia (FUNCINPEC).

The CPP then experienced divisions between those who favoured acceptance of the results and alliance with the Sihanoukists, including Chea Sim and Hun Sen, and the CPP hardliners, notably Gen. Sin Song (SOC National Security Minister), who apparently aspired to a coup. After the collapse of the "secession" of seven eastern provinces (declared by Gen. Sin Song and other CPP dissidents in mid-June 1993), early in July the CPP entered a coalition with FUNCINPEC and two smaller parties. A feature of the new government was the appointment of the CPP's powerful organization chief, Sar Kheng, to the influential post of Deputy Prime Minister and Interior Minister, in which he was seen as a rival to Hun Sen, the CPP Second Prime Minister. In September 1993 the CPP supported the new monarchical constitution and the restoration of Prince Sihanouk to the throne, and the following month Chea Min was again elected as president of the National Assembly. In subsequent negotiations between the government and the KR/CNUP, the latter's power-sharing demands were strongly resisted by the CPP, which was seen by some in FUNCINPEC as aiming to use its position as the best-organized Cambodian party to achieve dominance. On the collapse of the talks in June 1994, the CPP was the driving force in a decision to expel the remaining KR/CNUP representatives from Phnom Penh and to enact a legal ban on KR membership. The following month the government claimed to have foiled another coup attempt by Gen. Sin Song, Prince Norodom Chakkrapong (a son of King Sihanouk) and other CPP members. Factional conflict in the CPP intensified in September 1994 when Hun Sen released a list of 43 persons suspected of involvement in the plot, including Sar Kheng. However, the latter was reported to have the support of Chea Sim (his brother-in-law) and of senior army and police officers.

Khmer Nation Party (KNP)

Address. c/o National Assembly, Phnom Penh
Leadership. Sam Rangsi

The KNP was launched in November 1995 by Sam Rangsi, who had achieved national popularity as an anti-corruption Finance Minister until his dismissal in October 1994 and had subsequently become a critic of the government dominated by the United National Front for an Independent, Neutral, Peaceful and Co-operative Cambodia (FUNCIPEC). In May 1995 he had been expelled from FUNCINPEC for his opposition activities, and the following month was deprived of his National Assembly seat. The formation of the KNP elicited threats of violence against Ram Rangsi from his political opponents and an assertion by the government that the new party did not conform to current legislation.

National Liberation Movement of Kampuchea

Mouvement de la Libération Nationale de Kampuchea (MOULINAKA)

Address. c/o National Assembly, Phnom Penh

Leadership. Chea Chhut (president)

MOULINAKA was one a number of pro-Sihanouk movements which came together in the United National Front for an Independent, Neutral, Peaceful and Co-operative Cambodia (FUNCINPEC) formed in 1982. Following the signature of the October 1991 peace agreement it resumed a separate identity and became closely aligned with the Buddhist Liberal Democratic Party. In the May 1993 Assembly elections MOULINAKA won only one of the 120 seats and was included in the subsequent coalition government headed by FUNCINPEC.

United National Front for an Independent, Neutral, Peaceful and Co-operative Cambodia

Front Uni National pour une Cambodge Indépendente, Neutre, Pacifique et Coopérative (FUNCINPEC)

Address. 61 Street 214, Phnom Penh

Telephone. (#855-23) 26053

Fax. (#855-23) 26144

Leadership. Prince Norodom Ranariddh (president), Princess Monique and Nhiek Tioulong (vice-presidents)

FUNCINPEC was launched in March 1982 by King (as he later again became) Sihanouk as the political wing of the Sihanoukist National Army (ANS), then in conflict with the pro-Vietnamese regime of the Kampuchean People's Revolutionary Party (KPRP) in power in Phnom Penh. FUNCINPEC was seen as the successor of Sihanouk's Confederation of Khmer Nationalists and included several earlier pro-Sihanouk movements which had opposed the 1970–75 Lon Nol government and 1976–79 regime of the *Khmers Rouges* (KR) headed by Pol Pot. Despite this recent history, in June 1982 FUNCINPEC renewed its earlier alliance with the KR by forming the Coalition Government of Democratic Kampuchea (CGDK), which also included the Khmer People's National Liberation Front (KPNLF), later renamed the Buddhist Liberal Democratic Party (BLDP). Under the titular leadership of Prince Sihanouk, the CGDK came to be dominated by the KR, as armed struggle against the Phnom Penh regime was interspersed with bouts of conflict between the CGDK components. Despite much international condemnation of the excesses of the Pol Pot regime, combined Chinese and US influence ensured that the CGDK retained UN recognition. US and other Western aid was channelled to FUNCINPEC and the KPNLF (rather than to the Chinese-backed KR), but the non-communist components of the CGDK forces remained ill-disciplined and poorly motivated compared with the KR.

Following the announcement of Vietnam's military withdrawal in 1989, UN-brokered negotiations produced agreement in September 1990 on the creation of a Supreme National Council (SNC) representing both the CGDK and the government of what was by now called the State of Cambodia (SOC). Having become chairman of the SNC, Prince Sihanouk resigned as FUNCINPEC and ANS leader and was succeeded by his son, Prince Norodom Ranariddh. However, notwithstanding assertions of his political neutrality by Prince Sihanouk, FUNCINPEC remained loyal to its founder. On the strength of the Paris peace agreement of October 1991, FUNCINPEC and the other CGDK parties were authorized to return to Phnom Penh, where the KPRP meanwhile changed its name to Cambodian People's Party (CPP) and abandoned Marxism-Leninism. This transformation facilitated the development of a tactical FUNCINPEC-CPP alliance against the KR and the latter's new political wing, the Cambodian National Unity Party (CNUP). The CNUP's decision to boycott the May 1993 Assembly elections left the way open for FUNCINPEC to become the largest party, with 58 of the 120 seats, followed by the CPP with 51. Prince Ranariddh became First Prime Minister in the subsequent coalition government of FUNCINPEC, the CPP, the BLDP and the National Liberation Movement of Kampuchea (MOULINAKA), while Prince Sihanouk himself was restored to the Cambodian throne in September 1993.

Assisted by KR/CNUP intransigence, FUNCINPEC's alliance with the CPP mainstream held during 1994, despite various attempts by CPP radicals to overturn the post-election arrangements. Within FUNCINPEC, however, there remained considerable suspicion of the CPP's real intentions, given the latter's powerful organizational base and its continued alignment with Vietnam. Accordingly, some FUNCINPEC elements advocated the formation of an anti-CPP alliance with the KR, pointing out that such a rapprochement would be likely to have the backing of China. Other strains within the party were evident in October 1994 in the dismissal of the popular anti-corruption Finance Minister, Sam Rangsi, in the interests of what Prince Ranariddh termed the need for "unity and cohesion", and the resignation of Prince Sereivut as Foreign Minister out of solidarity with Sam Rangsi, who later announced the creation of the Khmer Nation Party. A half-brother of King Sihanouk, Prince Sereivut was in November 1995 charged with the attempted murder of Second Prime Minister Hun Sen of the CPP, but the following went into exile in France under a deal brokered by King Sihanouk.

Cameroon

Capital: Yaoundé   **Population:** 14,000,000 (1995E)

French-administered (East) Cameroon achieved independence in 1960 and the following year was united with the southern part of British-administered (West) Cameroon, both areas having been under German colonial rule until World War I. A one-party state established in 1966 under the National Cameroon Union, renamed the Cameroon People's Democratic Movement (CPDM) in 1985, gave way to a multi-party system in 1990. Under its 1972 constitution as amended, the Republic of Cameroon has an executive President who is elected for a seven-year term (once renewable) by universal suffrage of those aged 20 and over, requiring only a relative majority in a single voting round. The President is head of state and government, appointing the Prime Minister and other members of the government. Legislative authority is vested in a bicameral parliament consisting of a National Assembly (*Assemblée Nationale*) of 180 members directly elected by proportional representation for a five-year term and of a Senate (*Sénat*). Under laws enacted in 1990–91, political parties may not be based on regional or tribal support and may not form coalitions for electoral purposes. Registered parties are eligible for financial support from state funds for their electoral campaigns.

Assembly elections held on March 1, 1992, resulted as follows: CPDM 88 seats; National Union for Democracy and Progress (UNDP) 68; Union of the Peoples of Cameroom 18; Movement for the Defence of the Republic 6. A presidential election on Oct. 11, 1992, was won by incumbent Paul Biya of the CPDM, with 39.98% of the popular vote against 35.97% for the candidate of the Social Democratic Front, 19.22% for the UNDP nominee and 4.83% for three other candidates.

Cameroon People's Democratic Movement (CPDM)

Rassemblement Démocratique du Peuple Camerounais (RDPC)

Address. BP 867, Yaoundé

Leadership. Paul Biya (president), Joseph Charles Doumba (secretary-general), Grégoire Owona (deputy secretary-general)

The CPDM is the successor, created in March 1985, to the Cameroon National Union (UNC), which was established as the sole ruling party in 1966 as a merger of the francophone Cameroon Union (UC) and five other parties, including three of anglophone identity. The UC had taken Cameroon to independence in 1960 under the leadership of Ahmadou Ahidjo (a Muslim), whose post-1966 one-party UNC government claimed credit for economic advances. When Ahidjo unexpectedly resigned in November 1982, he was succeeded as President and party leader by Paul Biya (a Christian), who had held the premiership since 1975. After surviving coups attempts in 1983 and 1984, Biya was confirmed in office in an April 1988 one-party presidential election (officially with 100% of the vote). Meanwhile, the UNC had renamed itself the CPDM, against strong internal opposition from the party's anglophone wing.

From mid-1990 the CPDM government accepted opposition demands for a transition to multi-party democracy, although Biya refused to convene a sovereign national conference on political change. In Assembly elections in March 1992 the CPDM maintained its dominance, although its 88–seat tally was short of an overall majority. The CPDM benefited from a boycott by some opposition parties and from its following in the francophone Christian south, but gained little support in the anglophone west or the Muslim north. In the October 1992 presidential election, Biya as CPDM candidate won a narrow victory over the nominee of the Social Democratic Front, which made vigorous allegations of electoral fraud. In November 1992 the post-April coalition government of the CPDM and the small Movement for the Defence of the Republic was expanded to include the other two parties represented in the Assembly. In 1993–94 the government came under persistent pressure from the political opposition and also faced growing secessionist tendencies in anglophone areas. It was reported in September 1994 that an assassination plot against President Biya had been foiled the previous May.

Democratic Union of Cameroon
Union Démocratique du Cameroun (UDC)
　　Address. BP 1638, Yaoundé
　　Leadership. Adamou Ndam Njoya (president)
　　The UDC achieved legal status in April 1991, its president having been a senior minister under the pre-1982 Ahidjo regime. Together with the Social Democratic Front (SDF), it headed the boycott of the March 1992 Assembly elections by some opposition parties on the grounds that the electoral arrangements gave an unfair advantage to the ruling Cameroon People's Democratic Movement. It changed tack for the October 1992 presidential poll, in which Njoya came in fourth place with 3.6% of the votes cast. Thereafter strains developed betweem the UDC and the SDF: in January 1993 the UDC vice-president, Benjamin Menga, was fatally injured in an attack in which the SDF was implicated.

Front of Allies for Change
Front des Alliés pour le Changement (FAC)
　　Address. c/o Assemblée Nationale, Yaoundé
　　Leadership. Samuel Eboua
　　The FAC was launched in October 1994 as an alliance of 16 opposition parties opposed to President Biya, headed by the Social Democratic Front (SDF). In December that year it declined to participate a "constitutional consultative committee" proposed by the President to promote political reconciliation. In February 1995 the FAC rotating leadership passed from SDF leader John Fru Ndi to Samuel Eboua, former leader of the National Union for Democracy and Progress.

Movement for the Defence of the Republic
Mouvement pour la Défense de la République (MDR)
　　Address. BP 895, Yaoundé
　　Leadership. Dakole Daissala (president)
　　The MDR was founded on the eve of the March 1992 Assembly elections, in a move to divide Muslim allegiance in northern Cameroon at the expense of the opposition National Union for Democracy and Progress (UNDP). Previously a prominent dissident, the MDR leader had spent seven years in detention in connexion with a coup attempt in 1984. Based particularly in the Kirdi ethnic group, the MDR won six of the 180 Assembly seats, enough to give it the immediate balance of power between the ruling Cameroon People's Democratic Movement (CPDM) and the

opposition parties. Daissala and four other MDR nominees were appointed to the CPDM-led government which was installed in April 1992 and expanded in November to include the other two parties represented in the Assembly.

National Union for Democracy and Progress
Union Nationale pour la Démocratie et le Progrès (UNDP)
　　Address. BP 656, Douala
　　Leadership. Maigari Bello Bouba
　　The UNDP was founded in 1991 mainly by supporters of ex-President Ahidjo and was based in the Muslim community (forming 22% of the population). In early 1992 its first leader, Samuel Eboua, was displaced by Bello Bouba, who had been Prime Minister in 1982–83 following Ahidjo's resignation but had later been implicated in an alleged plot to restore Ahidjo. Having initially decided to boycott the March 1992 Assembly elections, the UNDP changed its mind and proceeded to win 68 of the 180 seats at issue, only 20 seats behind the ruling Cameroon People's Democratic Movement (CPDM). In the October 1992 presidential election the UNDP leader came in third place with 19.2% of the vote and afterwards joined the leader of the Social Democratic Front in challenging the validity of the official results. Nevertheless, in November 1992 the UNDP accepted participation in a coalition government of all four Assembly parties under the leadership of the CPDM.
　　The basic impasse persisted in subsequent years. In November 1994 UNDP deputies launched a boycott of the Assembly in protest against the arrest of some 30 party activists four months earlier. The party called off the boycott the following month (without securing the release of its members), but a presidential initiative to achieve reconciliation quickly collapsed when the UNDP and other parties refused to participate in a "constitutional consultative committee".

Social Democratic Front (SDF)
　　Address. PO Box 89, Bamenda
　　Leadership. John Fru Ndi (president)
　　Founded in early 1990, the SDF gained legal recognition in March 1991 after a year in which its anti-government rallies had frequently been subject to official repression. Based in the English-speaking north and west, the SDF opted to boycott the May 1992 Assembly elections but changed its line for the October 1992 presidential contest. Standing as the SDF candidate, John Fru Ndi attracted support from anglophone and francophone voters, winning 36% of the popular vote and thus coming a close second to incumbent Paul Biya of the Cameroon People's Democratic

Movement (CPDM). Supported by many foreign observers, the SDF claimed that the presidential poll had been fraudulent, but its petition was rejected by the Supreme Court. In November 1992 the SDF refused to join a new CPDM-led coalition government, calling instead for the convening of an all-party national conference on the country's political future. It then initiated the formation of a 10–party opposition alliance called the Union for Change (*Union pour le Change*), with Fru Ndi as its leader, which launched a campaign of popular protests against the Biya government. The latter responded in March 1993 by banning demonstrations involving "a risk of violence" and by arresting over 100 opposition activists.

In June 1993 Fru Ndi refused to participate in a government-proposed "grand national debate" on constitutional reform, the idea of which generated some dissension within the SDF between moderates and radicals. An SDF congress in August 1993 endorsed the moderates' call for acceptance of the 1992 election results and participation in constitutional talks; but renewed harassment of Fru Ndi (who briefly took refuge in the Netherlands embassy in November 1993) reopened the government-opposition divide. In May 1994 Assanga Assiga was suspended as SDF secretary-general for making unauthorized contact with the government on possible SDF participation in a national unity coalition. In July 1994 the SDF reacted to a major cabinet reshuffle by repeating its call for a sovereign national conference and for an interim government involving "all the nation's active political forces". In October 1994 the SDF spearheaded the creation of a new 16-party opposition alliance called the Front of Allies for Change.

Union of the Peoples of Cameroon
Union des Populations du Cameroun (UPC)
   Address. BP 8647, Douala
   Leadership. Ndeh Ntumazah (chairman), Augustin Frederic Kodock (secretary-general)
The UPC was founded in the late 1940s as a Marxist-Leninist party opposed to French rule, under which it was banned in 1955. Relegalized at independence in 1960, it won 22 seats in the 1961 Assembly elections but became split into pro-Soviet and Maoist factions, both of which went underground in armed opposition to the one-party regime created in 1966. By 1970 the UPC insurgency had been largely suppressed, party leader Ernest Ouandié being executed in January 1971 after being convicted of "attempted revolution". Led by Ngouo Woungly-Massaga, the UPC survived in exile (based in Paris) and regained legal status in February 1991 as a social democratic formation. Meanwhile, Woungly-Massaga had left the UPC to form the People's Solidarity Party,

after failing to persuade his colleagues to join an anti-Biya united front and being accused by them of abuse of office. The leadership passed to Ndeh Ntumazah, a UPC founder, who led half the party into a boycott of the March 1992 Assembly elections, while the other half followed Augustin Frederic Kodock (UPC secretary-general) in putting up candidates, 18 of whom were elected. The split in the party deepened when Kodock alienated many of his colleagues by accepting a ministerial post in the coalition government formed in November 1992.

Other Parties

Alliance for Democracy and Development (*Alliance pour la Démocratie et le Développement*, ADD), led by Garga Haman Adji.

Alliance for Democracy and Progress of Cameroon (*Alliance pour la Démocratie et le Progrès du Cameroun*, ADPC), led by Aboukar Koko, legalized in June 1991. *Address.* BP 231, Garoua

Authentic Democrats of Cameroon (*Démocrates Authentiques du Cameroun*, DAC), led by Jean-Baptiste Ayissi-Ntsama, legalized in July 1991. *Address.* BP 4452, Yaoundé

Autonomous Socialist Party (*Parti Socialiste Autonome*, PSA), led by David Diffoum, legalized in October 1991. *Address.* BP 1445, Douala

Cameroon Alliance for Progress and Emancipation of the Dispossessed (*Alliance Camerounaise pour le Progrès et l'Emancipation des Dépossédés*, ACPED), led by Augustin Bohin Bohin. *Address.* BP 6527, Yaoundé

Cameroon Ideological Party (CIP), led by Oben Isaac Enow, legalized in July 1991. *Address.* BP 37, Muyuka

Cameroon Liberal Congress (CLC), led by Ngunjoh Tafoh, legalized in August 1991. *Address.* BP 4022, Bamenda

Cameroon National Party (*Parti National du Cameroun*, PNC), a pro-Biya formation whose leader, Tita Fomukong, was killed during an election riot in October 1992. *Address.* BP 230, Bamenda

Cameroon Party of Democrats (*Parti des Démocrates Camerounais*, PDC), led by Louis-Tobie Mbida and Gaston Bikele Ekami, founder of the National Convention of the Cameroonian Opposition (CNOC) in October 1992, affiliated to the Christian Democrat International. *Address.* BP 6909, Douala

Cameroon Patriotic Movement (*Mouvement Patriotique Camerounais*, MPC), led by Arab Alli Alam, legalized in October 1991. *Address.* BP 6017, Douala

Cameroon Progressive Party (*Parti Progressiste Camerounais*, PPC), led by Jean Pahai, legalized in June 1991. *Address.* BP 755, Yaoundé

Cameroon Rally for the Republic (*Rassemblement Camerounais pour la République*, RCR), led by Samuel Wouafo, legalized in October 1991. *Address.* BP 116, Bandjoun

Cameroon Social Union (*Union Social du Cameroun*, USC), led by Nicole Okala.

Cameroon Socialist Party (*Parti Socialiste Camerounais*, PSC), led by Appolinaire Guillaume Nseth-Nseth, legalized in May 1991. *Address.* BP 12501, Douala

Defence of the Cameroon Environment (*Défense de l'Environnement Camerounais*, DEC), led by Ndih Nkeh, legalized in November 1991. *Address.* BP 6361, Yaoundé

Democratic Socialist Party (*Parti Socialiste Démocratique*, PSD), led by Joseph Nsame Mbongo, legalized in March 1991. *Address.* BP 141, Douala

Green Party for Democracy in Cameroon (*Parti Vert pour la Démocratie au Cameroun*, PVDC), led by Justin-Aimé Fogoum, legalized in July 1991. *Address.* BP 2104, Douala

Integral Democracy of Cameroon (*Démocratie Intégrale du Cameroun*, DIC), led by Blazius Isaka, legalized in February 1991. *Address.* BP 8647, Douala

Liberal Alliance Party (*Parti de l'Alliance Libérale*, PAL), led by Célestin Bedzigui, legalized in June 1991. *Address.* BP 13233, Douala

Liberal Convention (*Convention Libérale*, CL), led by Pierre- Flambeau Ngayap, legalized in June 1991. *Address.* BP 2363, Douala

Liberal Democratic Alliance (LDA), anglophone grouping led by Henri Fossung, launched in 1993 to campaign for speedier constitutional reform.

Liberal Democratic Party (*Parti Libéral Démocrate*, PLD), led by Njoh Litumbe, legalized in March 1991. *Address.* BP 68, Buea

Movement for Justice and Liberties (*Mouvement pour la Justice et les Libertés*, MJL), led by François-Xavier Tsoungui, legalized in August 1991. *Address.* BP 642, Yaoundé

National Democratic Party (NDP), led by Henry Fossung, legalized in March 1991. *Address.* BP 116, Buea

National Progress Party (*Parti National pour le Progrès*, PNP), led by Antar Gassagay, legalized in July 1991. *Address.* BP 1011, Douala

National Union of the Cameroon People (*Union National du Peuple Camerounais*, UNPC), led by Mahaman Nagambo, legalized in August 1991. *Address.* BP 2748, Douala

Pan-African Congress of Cameroon (*Congrès Panafricain du Cameroun*, CPC), led by Noucti Tchokwago, legalized in March 1991. *Address.* BP 1248, Yaoundé

Party of Ants (*Parti des Fourmis*, PDF), led by David Dieudonné Boo, legalized in July 1991. *Address.* BP 7373, Yaoundé

Peasants' Movement of Cameroon (*Mouvement des Paysans du Cameroun*, MPC), led by Henri Matip Libam.

People's Action Party (*Parti de l'Action du Peuple*, PAP), led by Victor Mukwele Ngoe, legalized in April 1991. *Address.* BP 79, Kumba

People's Solidarity Party (*Parti de la Solidarité du Peuple*, PSP), founded by Ngouo Woungly-Massaga in 1991 following his break with the Union of the Peoples of Cameroon, presented 25 candidates in March 1992 elections, without success.

Progressive Movement (*Mouvement Progressif*, MP), led by Jean- Jacques Ekindi, legalized in August 1991, in January 1994 joined opposition front with Social Democratic Party of Cameroon, Social Movement for New Democracy and other groups. *Address.* BP 2500, Douala

Rally for National Unity (*Rassemblement pour l'Unité Nationale*, RUN), led by François Seunkam, legalized in March 1991. *Address.* BP 100, Yaoundé

Regrouping of Nationalist Forces (*Regroupement des Forces Nationalistes*, RFN), led by Richard Polog, legalized in August 1991. *Address.* BP 1722, Douala

Regrouping of Patriotic Forces (*Regroupement des Forces Patriotiques*, RFP), led by Ema Otou, legalized in August 1991. *Address.* BP 6110, Yaoundé

Renewal Movement of the African People (*Mouvement Rénovateur du Peuple Africain*, MORDA), led by Joseph Leboux Tegue, legalized in December 1991.

Republican Party of the Cameroon People (*Parti Républicain du Peuple Camerounais*, PRPC), led by André Ateba Ngoua, legalized in March 1991. *Address.* BP 6654, Yaoundé

Social Democratic Action of Cameroon (*Action Sociale Démocratique du Cameroun*, ASDC), led by Said Sindan el Hadj Sadjo, legalized in March 1991.

Social Democratic Party of Cameroon (*Parti Social-Démocrate du Cameroun*, PSDC), led by Jean-Michel Tekam, legalized in December 1991, in January 1994 joined opposition front with Progressive Movement, Social Movement for New Democracy and other groups.

Social Democratic Union (*Union Social Démocrate*, USD), led by Jean-Pierre Mbele, legalized in June 1991. *Address.* BP 7125, Yaoundé

Social Movement for New Democracy (*Mouvement Social pour la Nouvelle Démocratie*, MSND), founded in 1991 by Yondo Mandengue Black (former Bar Association president), who was active in the early pro-democracy movement and served a prison term in 1990, in January 1994 joined opposition front with Progressive Movement, Social Democratic Party of Cameroon and other groups. *Address.* BP 1641, Douala

Social Programme for Liberty and Democracy (*Programme Sociale pour la Liberté et la Démocratie*, PSLD), an opposition party whose leader, Massok Mboua, was arrested in February 1995.

Unified Socialist Movement (*Parti Socialiste Unifié*, PSU), led by Daniel Sohfone, legalized in April 1991. *Address.* BP 12106, Douala

Unified Workers' Party of Cameroon (*Parti Ouvrier Unifiés du Cameroun*, POUC), led by Dieudonné Bizole.

Union of Cameroon Republicans (*Union des Républicains du Cameroun*, URC), led by Ernest Koumbin Bilitik, legalized in March 1991. *Address.* BP 4435, Douala

Union of Democratic Forces of Cameroon (*Union des Forces Démocratiques du Cameroun*, UFDC), led by Victorin Hameni Bialeu, legalized in March 1991, boycotted March 1992 Assembly elections in protest against electoral law banning party alliances; Bialeu was detained in November 1992 for alleged anti-government activities. *Address.* BP 7190, Yaoundé

Union of Initiatives for National Entente (*Union des Initiatives pour l'Entente Nationale*, UIEN), led by Blaise Echemo Djamen, legalized in July 1991. *Address.* BP 10081, Douala

United Front of Cameroon (*Front Uni du Cameroun*, FUC), led by Jean Njeunga, legalized in October 1991. *Address.* BP 4372, Douala

Canada

Capital: Ottawa   **Population:** 29,000,000 (1995E)

The Dominion of Canada is a member of the Commonwealth with the British sovereign as head of state represented by a Governor-General. The federal legislature comprises a Senate of 104 members appointed by the Governor-General, and a House of Commons of 295 members. The latter is elected for a maximum of five years by universal adult suffrage under a simple majority system in single-member constituencies. The Governor-General appoints the Prime Minister and, on the latter's recommendation, the members of the Cabinet.

Parties winning at least 12 seats in a federal election are eligible for state financial support in proportion to the number of seats obtained.

In the federal general election of Oct. 25, 1993, the then ruling Progressive Conservative Party (PCP) experienced a crushing defeat, retaining only 2 seats in the Commons (although with 16.1% of the vote), while the Liberal Party of Canada (LCP) won 177 (41.6%), the Quebec Bloc (BQ) 54 (13.9%), the Reform Party of Canada (RPC) 52 (18.1%), the New Democratic Party (NDP) 9 (6.6%), and an independent conservative 1.

Canada consists of 10 provinces and two territories. Each province has a Lieutenant-Governor representing the British sovereign, an elected legislature, and an executive council led by a Premier. There is considerable decentralization of authority to the provincial governments. In October 1995 the people of Quebec voted narrowly against leaving the Canadian federation by a margin of less than 1% in a referendum in which more than 93% of the electorate participated. Seats in the provincial legislatures were distributed as follows as a result of the most recent elections (the months of which are shown in parentheses): *Alberta* (June 1993)—PCP 51, LCP 32; *British Columbia* (May 1996)—NDP 39, LPC 33, RPC 3; *Manitoba* (April 1995)—PCP 31, NDP 23, LPC 3; *New Brunswick* (September 1995)—LPC 48, PCP 6, NDP 1; *Newfoundland and Labrador* (February 1996)—LPC 37, PCP 9, NDP 1, independent 1; *Nova Scotia* (May 1993)—LPC 40, PCP 9, NDP 3; *Ontario* (June 1995)—PCP 82, LPC 30, NDP 17, independent 1; *Prince Edward Island* (March 1993)—LPC 31, PCP 1; *Quebec* (September 1994)—Quebec Party 77, LPC 47, Democratic Action of Quebec 1; *Saskatchewan* (June 1995)—NDP 42, LPC 11, PCP 5.

The two territories, in which the chief executive officer is the federally-appointed Commissioner, have a lesser degree of government responsibility. In elections to the 24-member legislature of the *Northwest Territories* in October 1995, all successful candidates were independents. Elections to the *Yukon* legislature in October 1992 resulted in the Yukon Party winning 7 seats, the NDP 6, the LPC 1 and independents 3.

Liberal Party of Canada (LPC)

Address. 200 Laurier Ave West, Suite 200, Ottawa, Ontario, K1P 6M8

Telephone. (#1–613) 237-0740

Fax. (#1–613) 235-7208

Leadership. Jean Chrétien (leader), Daniel Hays (president), George Young (national director)

Founded in 1867, the Liberal Party has been the ruling party in Canada for the larger part of the 20th century. In recent decades, advocating centrist policies under the leadership of Pierre Trudeau, it was returned to office at federal general elections in 1968, 1972, 1974, and again in 1980, following a brief minority Progressive Conservative Party (PCP) administration. However, in 1984, in the face of increasing unpopularity, Trudeau resigned and the party was decisively beaten at the polls by the Progressive Conservatives, who then retained power until 1993. In the federal elections in October of that year, the Liberals were returned with 177 of the 295 House of Commons seats. A Liberal government was sworn in under the premiership of Jean Chrétien, who led the subsequent campaign by pro-federalists against Quebec separatism in the October 1995 referendum.

As of June 1996 the Liberal Party controlled the provincial governments in Prince Edward Island, Nova Scotia, New Brunswick, and Newfoundland and Labrador, and was the principal opposition party in Alberta, British Columbia and Quebec. The party is affiliated to the Liberal International.

New Democratic Party (NDP)

Address. 900–81 Metcalfe Street, Ottawa, Ontario, K1P 6K7

Telephone. (#1–613) 236-3613

Fax. (#1–613) 230-9950

Leadership. Alexa McDonough (leader), Iain Angus (president), David Woodbury (federal secretary)

Established in 1961, the social democratic NDP was the third main party at federal level behind the Liberal Party of Canada (LPC) and the Progressive Conservative Party (PCP) until the 1993 general election, when it slipped to fifth in terms of vote share (6.6%) and retained only nine of the 43 seats in the House of Commons which it had won in the 1988 polling. At the provincial level, the NDP in June 1995 retained power in its traditional stronghold of Saskatchewan, but lost power to the PCP in Ontario, Canada's most populous province, which had governed since 1990. In May 1996 the party narrowly retained office in British Columbia. In Yukon the NDP took six of the 17 seats in the territorial legislature in the elections in October 1992, but was ousted as the governing party by the Yukon Party.

The NDP is a member party of the Socialist International.

Progressive Conservative Party (PCP)

Address. 275 Slater Street, Suite 600, Ottawa, Ontario, K1P 5H9

Telephone. (#1–613) 238-6111

Fax. (#1–613) 563-7892

Leadership. Jean Charest (leader), Gerry St.-Germain (president), Jean-Carol Pelletier (national director)

The PCP, with a history dating back to 1854, stands for the preservation of the monarchy and parliamentary democracy, the multicultural composition of Canada and its bilingual nature, private enterprise, individual liberties and social welfare. The period from 1963 to 1984 was spent almost entirely in opposition to Liberal Party of Canada administrations, although a minority PCP government was briefly in power under Joe Clark from May 1979 until its collapse nine months later. Under the subsequent leadership of Brian Mulroney, the party won the 1984 federal election by a substantial majority. Having retained power in the 1988 elections, PCP popularity diminished to an unprecedented level and the party was decimated in the October 1993 federal polls, retaining only two seats. Kim Campbell, who had replaced Mulroney in June 1993, resigned the following December and was replaced by Jean Charest.

At the provincial level the PCP controlled, as at mid-1996, the governments in Ontario (which it had regained convincingly from the NDP in elections in June 1995), Manitoba and Alberta. The party is affiliated to the International Democrat Union.

Quebec Bloc

Bloc Québécois (BQ)

Address. Room 488, West Block, House of Commons, 111 Wellington Street, Ottawa, Ontario

Telephone. (#1–613) 996-5535

Fax. (#1–613) 954-2121

Leadership. Michel Gauthier (parliamentary leader), François Landry (director-general)

The BQ was formed by Lucien Bouchard in May 1990 as the federal voice of Quebec separatism, committed to the achievement of sovereignty for the predominantly French-speaking province. Although fielding candidates only in Quebec, it won 54 of the 295 seats in the House of Commons in the federal elections in October 1993, becoming the second largest party and the official opposition. In support of the provincial Quebec

Party, Bouchard and the BQ campaigned intensively in the run-up to the October 1995 referendum on independence, which was lost only by the narrowest of margins. In the wake of the referendum, Bouchard was inaugurated as Premier of Quebec in January 1996, having been elected unopposed as leader of the provincial Quebec Party. In the same month Michel Gauthier replaced Bouchard as parliamentary leader of the BQ.

Quebec Party

Parti Québécois (PQ)

Address. 7370 rue St-Hubert, Montreal, Quebec, H2R 2N3

Telephone. (#1–514) 270 5400

Fax. (#1–514) 270 2865

Leadership. Lucien Bouchard (leader)

Founded in 1968 by René Lévesque, the social democratic and separatist PQ was the governing party in the province of Quebec from 1976 to 1985. However, it failed in a referendum in 1980 to obtain a mandate to negotiate "sovereignty-association" with the federal government, and was subsequently weakened by divisions between moderate and hardline party factions over the separatist issue. In December 1985 the party was ousted by the Liberal Party of Canada, which retained office until the provincial elections in September 1994 in which the PQ, under the leadership of Jacques Parizeau, won a comfortable majority of seats (although only by a margin of 44.7% to 44.3% of the vote). A new referendum on independence for Quebec took place in October 1995, resulting in a very close victory for the opponents of separation. Parizeau subsequently resigned and was replaced in January 1996 as PQ leader and Quebec Premier by Lucien Bouchard, whose federal Quebec Bloc had supported the secessionist campaign in the October referendum. Bouchard vowed to continue the PQ's campaign for separation.

Reform Party of Canada (RPC)

Address. 833 4th Ave, SW, Suite 600, Calgary, Alberta, T2P 0K5

Telephone. (#1–403) 269-1990

Fax. (#1–403) 269-4077

Leadership. Preston Manning (leader), Glen McMurray (executive director)

Launched in 1987 as a populist movement, the neo-conservative Reform Party opposes bilingualism and multiculturalism, advocates fiscal reform, a reduction in immigration, and increased powers for federal government. Having attracted just 2% of the vote in the 1988 polling and won one seat in a subsequent by-election, the party's vote share rose dramatically in the 1993 federal election to

18% (predominantly in western Canada), giving it 52 seats in the House of Commons. It thus became the main voice of the right, eclipsing the Progressive Conservative Party (PCP). Thereafter the RPC acquired an image of intolerance and extremism, which critics blamed for a decline in its electoral support and its failure to attract any significant support in eastern Canada.

Other Parties

Canadian Greens, an environmental group active at federal level but without parliamentary representation, led by Deborah Roberts.

Communist Party of Canada (CPC), led by William Kashtan and George Hewison, founded in 1921.

Confederation of Regions Party of New Brunswick, formed in 1989 to represent the interests of the anglophone population of the province of New Brunswick, won eight seats in the provincial legislature in 1991, led by Greg Hargrove.

Democratic Action of Quebec (*Action Démocratique de Québec*, ADQ), launched in 1994 by former members of the Liberal Party of Canada, originally supported Quebec's continued inclusion within the Canadian confederation with greater autonomy, but backed the unsuccessful separatist cause in the 1995 referendum; won 6.5% of the vote in the September 1994 provincial elections and its leader, Marc Dumont, won a seat in the legislature.

Equality Party (EP), formed to represent the English-speaking minority in Quebec, led by Keith Henderson.

National Union (*Union Nationale*, UN), standing for Quebec's autonomy within the Canadian confederation, based on the concept of a French-Canadian nation, and for strong links with France; led by Jean-Marie Beliveau.

Social Credit Party (SOCRED), currently led by Donna Barnett, the governing party in Alberta from 1935 to 1971 and in British Columbia from 1952 to 1972 and from 1975 to 1991, not represented at federal level since 1980, riven by scandal and dissension in 1990s.

Western Canada Concept, led by Douglas Christie.

Yukon Party (YP), won seven of the 17 seats in the Yukon territory legislature in elections in October 1992 and formed a minority administration headed by John Ostashek, replacing a government of the New Democratic Party.

Cape Verde

Capital: Praia   **Population:** 400,000 (1995E)

The Republic of Cape Verde achieved independence from Portugal in 1975 and had a one-party system under what became the African Party for the Independence of Cape Verde (PAICV) until moving to multi-partyism under legislation enacted in September 1990. The 1980 constitution as amended in 1990 provides for an executive President who appoints the government and who is directly elected for a five-year term by universal suffrage of those aged 18 and over. Legislative authority is vested in a unicameral National People's Assembly (*Assembléia Nacional Popular*) of 72 members, who are directly elected for a five-year term from 21 multi-member constituencies.

In Assembly elections held on Dec. 17, 1995, the ruling Movement for Democracy (MPD) won 50 seats and 61.3% of the vote; the PAICV 21 and 29.7%; and the Democratic Convergence Party 1 and 6.7%. In a presidential election on Feb. 18, 1996, the MPD candidate, António Mascarenhas Monteiro, was re-elected unopposed, having in 1991 defeated the then incumbent PAICV nominee by 73.5% to 26.5%.

African Party for the Independence of Cape Verde

Partido Africano da Independência de Cabo Verde (PAICV)

Address. CP 22, Praia, São Tiago

Telephone. (#238) 612136

Fax. (#238) 615239

Leadership. Gen. Pedro Verona Rodrigues Pires (president), Aristides Lima (general secretary)

The PAICV originated as the islands' branch of the African Party for the Independence of Guinea and Cape Verde (PAIGC), which had been founded by Amilcar Cabral in 1956 to oppose Portuguese colonial rule. The PAIGC led both Guinea-Bissau and Cape Verde to independence in 1974–75, becoming the sole ruling party in each. Following the November 1980 coup in Guinea-Bissau, the Cape Verde party reconstituted itself as the PAICV in January 1981, under the leadership of President Arístides Maria Pereira. Under the 1980 constitution the PAICV was defined as the leading force in society and nominated all candidates in legislative elections. However, an extraordinary PAICV congress in February 1990 endorsed constitutional changes providing for the introduction of a multi-party system, to herald which Pereira resigned as party general secretary in July and was replaced the following month by Gen. Pires, the Prime Minister since 1975. In multi-party elections in January 1991 the PAICV was heavily defeated by the opposition Movement for Democracy (MPD), winning only a third of the popular vote and only 23 of the 79 seats. The following month Pereira, standing effectively as the PAICV candidate, went down to an even heavier defeat in presidential balloting, managing only just over a quarter of the vote.

In opposition for the first time, the PAICV underwent some internal strains and suffered a further rebuff in local elections in December 1991. In August 1993 a party congress elected Pires to the newly-created post of president, while Aristides Lima, the PAICV leader in the Assembly, took the vacated job of general secretary.

The PAICV is a consultative member of the Socialist International.

Cape Verdean Independent Democratic Union

União Caboverdeana Independente e Democrática (UCID)

Address. CP 348, TV Šao Tiago 7, PRC Nova, São Vicente

Telephone. (#238) 312168

Leadership. Celso Celestino (president)

The conservative UCID was founded in 1974 by emigré opponents of the then one-party government, notably the US-based John Wahnon. In mid-1982 16 alleged UCID members received prison sentences for conspiracy to overthrow the regime. Re-emerging in the transition to multi-party democracy in 1990, the UCID entered into a co-operation agreement with the Movement for Democracy (MPD). It failed to win any seats in the January 1991 Assembly elections but in the December 1991 local elections it was successful on São Vicente island. The UCID is an affiliate of the Christian Democrat International.

Democratic Convergence Party

Partido da Convergência Democrática (PCD)

Address. c/o Assembléia Nacional Popular, Praia

Leadership. Enrico Monteiro (chair)

Founded in 1994, the centrist PCD won only one seat in the December 1995 legislative elections, with 6.7% of the popular vote.

Movement for Democracy

Movimento para Democracia (MPD)

Address. c/o Assembléia Nacional Popular, Praia

Leadership. Carlos Alberto Wahnon de Carvalho Veiga (chair)

The MPD was founded by Lisbon-based exiles who in April 1990 issued a manifesto demanding the introduction of multi-party democracy and a free enterprise economy. The concurrent move of the ruling African Party for the Independence of Cape Verde (PAICV) in that direction enabled the MPD leaders to return to Praia and to negotiate on a timetable for elections with the government. In mid-1990 the MPD signed a co-operation agreement with the conservative Cape Verde Independent Democratic Union to extend its influence throughout the islands. In the Assembly contest in January 1991 the MPD registered a landslide victory, winning 56 of the 79 seats and nearly two-thirds of the popular vote. In presidential balloting the following month, moreover, the MPD candidate and then leader, António Mascarenhas Monteiro (a former PAICV member), overwhelmingly defeated the PAICV incumbent, winning nearly three-quarters of the vote. The resultant MPD government under the premiership of Carlos Veiga quickly experienced tensions between radical and more cautious reformers. The dismissal of Jorge Carlos Fonseca as Foreign Minister in March 1993 intensified internal divisions, which erupted in February 1994 when the reappointment of Veiga as MPD chair provoked the resignations of several leading party members. Nevertheless, the MPD won a further convincing victory in legislative elections in December 1995, while President Monteiro was re-elected unopposed in Febrary 1996.

Other Parties

Democratic Socialist Party (*Partido Socialista Democrático*, PSD), led by João Alem, founded in 1992.

People's Union for the Independence of Cape Verde–Revived (*União do Povo para Independência de Cabo Verde– Ressusitacão*, UPICV-R), led by José Leitão da Grãça, founded in 1990 as a revival of a pre-independence movement.

Central African Republic

Capital: Bangui

Population: 3,300,000 (1995E)

The Central African Republic (CAR) became independent from France in 1960 and a one-party state from 1962. Military rule was imposed in 1966 by Col. Jean-Bedel Bokassa, who created the Central African Empire in 1977 but was deposed in 1979 by ex-President David Dacko, who revived the CAR. Military rule under Gen. André Kolingba from 1981 gave way in 1986 to a semi-civilian one-party regime under Kolingba's Central African Democratic Rally (RDC), which in turn gave way to multi-party democracy in 1991. Under a new constitution introduced in January 1995, the previous "semi-presidential" arrangements gave way to a fully presidential system in which the President, directly elected for a six-year term (renewable once), was to "embody and symbolize national unity" and was empowered to give policy direction to the Prime Minister. The latter is responsible to an 85–member National Assembly (*Assemblée Nationale*), directly elected for a five-year term by universal adult suffrage in two rounds of voting. The 1995 constitution also provided for the establishment of directly-elected regional assemblies.

Assembly elections held on Aug. 22, Sept. 19 and Oct. 3, 1993, resulted as follows: Central African People's Liberation Party (MLPC) 34 seats; RDC 13; Patriotic Front for Progress 7; Liberal Democratic Party 7; Alliance for Democracy and Progress 6; David Dacko supporters 6; National Convention 3; Social Democratic Party 3; Movement for Social Evolution in Black Africa 1; Civic Forum 1; Central African Republican Party 1; Democratic Movement for the Renaissance and Evolution of Central Africa 1; independents 2. Presidential elections held on Aug. 22 and Sept. 19, 1993, resulted in the election of the MLPC candidate, Ange-Félix Patassé, with 52.5% of the second-round vote.

Alliance for Democracy and Progress
Alliance pour la Démocratie et le Progrès (ADP)
Address. c/o Assemblée Nationale, Bangui
Leadership. François Pehoua, Didier Mangue

The ADP was launched in 1991 and became a founder member of the opposition Consultative Group of Democratic Forces (CFD) headed by the Patriotic Front for Progress. The ADP suffered a setback in October 1992 when its first leader, Jean-Claude Conjugo, was killed by security forces during a trade union demonstration. In March 1993 the party expelled its first general secretary, Tehakpa Mbrede, when he accepted a ministerial post under the Kolingba regime. In the 1993 presidential elections the ADP supported the unsuccessful CFD candidate, while the simultaneous legislative elections gave the ADP six of the 85 seats. In October 1993 the ADP broke with the

CFD by accepting representation in a coalition government headed by the Central African People's Liberation Movement.

Central African Democratic Rally
Rassemblement Démocratique Centrafricain (RDC)
Address. c/o Assemblée Nationale, Bangui
Leadership. André Dieudonné Kolingba (leader), Laurent Gomina- Pampali (general secretary)

Founded in May 1986 as the sole ruling party of the regime of Gen. Kolingba, who had come to power in a bloodless military coup in 1981, the RDC held its inaugural congress in February 1987. Launched as the country moved to semi-civilian rule, the RDC was intended to represent all political and social tendencies except those seeking "to impose a totalitarian doctrine". The RDC provided the only authorized candidates in elections held in July 1987. The RDC at first resisted the post-1989 world trend against one-party regimes, but in April 1991 President Kolingba announced his conversion to multi-partyism and his party followed suit. At an extraordinary party congress in August 1991, he resigned as RDC leader with the aim of "putting himself above all political parties". Thereafter Kolingba and the RDC resisted opposition demands for a sovereign national conference and instead promoted the idea of a "grand national debate", which was boycotted by most other parties when it was held in mid-1992. The first attempt to hold democratic elections, in October 1992, was aborted by the authorities, reportedly with the opposition well ahead of the RDC.

In the first round of rescheduled presidential elections in August 1993, Kolingba trailed in a poor fourth place as the RDC candidate, winning only 12.1% of the vote and therefore being eliminated. Attempts by him to suppress the results were successfully resisted by the opposition, so that the RDC was obliged to hand over power to the Central African People's Liberation Movement (MLPC) after the second round in September. In simultaneous Assembly elections the RDC also polled weakly, winning only 13 of the 85 seats, although this tally made it the second strongest party after the MLPC. Having resumed effective leadership of the RDC, Kolingba was stripped of his military rank in March 1994, under a 1985 law (which he had signed as President) banning army officers from participating in elections or holding public office. This move, and the concurrent arrest of two senior RDC members on charges of "creating pockets of social tension", caused Kolingba to declare that democracy had been dangerously derailed.

Central African People's Liberation Movement
Mouvement pour la Libération du Peuple Centrafricain (MLPC)
    Address. c/o Assemblée Nationale, Bangui
    Leadership. Ange-Félix Patassé (president), Francis Albert Oukanga (secretary-general)
The MLPC was founded in Paris in mid-1979 by exiles led by Patassé, who as Bokassa's Prime Minister from September 1976 had overseen the creation of the Central African Empire in December 1976. Dismissed in July 1978 and forced to flee the country, he had then disclosed details of the barbarism and corruption of the Bokassa regime. The MLPC opposed the succeeding Dacko government established in September 1979 and Patassé, who returned to Bangui, spent a year in prison for "fomenting unrest", emerging to take second place in the March 1981 presidential elec-

tion. Again forced into exile in April 1982 (this time in Togo), Patassé was ousted as MLPC leader in September 1993 by a majority which favoured a leftist orientation and alliance with what became the Patriotic Front for Progress (FPP). The new leadership involved the MLPC in attempts to overthrow the Kolingba regime, but Patassé regained control by the time of the transition to multi-partyism, securing legalization for the MLPC in September 1991.

As MLPC presidential candidate, Patassé was well-placed in the first round of October 1992 elections, which were aborted by the authorities. In February 1993 Patassé accepted membership of a government-appointed transitional legislature but in April the MLPC refused to join a coalition administration. Concurrently, the MLPC leader dismissed as "slander" public allegations by the FPP leader that Patassé had links with international diamond merchants and right-wing mercenary groups. In resumed elections in August-September 1993, Patassé headed the field in the first ballot (with 37.3% of the vote) and won the run-off (with 52.5%) against the FPP leader. In simultaneous Assembly elections the MLPC became substantially the strongest party, although its 34 seats out of 85 left it without an overall majority. It therefore formed a coalition government, under the premiership of Jean-Luc Mandaba (MLPC vice-president), with the Liberal Democratic Party, the Alliance for Democracy and Progress and the six Assembly supporters of ex-President Dacko (later organized as the Movement for Democracy and Development).

President Patassé's powers were significantly enhanced under the new constitution introduced in January 1995 following approval in a referendum the previous month. In April 1995 Mandaba was forced to resign as Prime Minister after more than half the Assembly deputies had signed a no-confidence motion tabled by his own MLPC and citing government corruption, maladministration and lack of consultation. He was succeeded by Gabriel Koyambounou, a technocrat close to the President, at the head of a new government coalition of the "presidential majority" parties.

Central African Republican Party
Parti Républicain Centrafricain (PRC)
    Address. c/o Assemblée Nationale, Bangui
    Leadership. Ruth Rolland (president)
The PRC was launched in 1991 under the country's first female party leader, a former president of the CAR Red Cross. She had previously spent five years in prison following the advent of the Kolingba regime, which she had accused of tribalism and corruption. The PRC was a founder member of the opposition Consultative

Group of Democratic Forces (CFD) in late 1991, but its membership was suspended in December 1992 when Rolland accepted a ministerial post in the government of Timothée Malendoma of the Civic Forum. In August 1993 she became the first-ever woman candidate to contest an African presidential election but was placed last in the first round with only 1% of the vote. In the concurrent Assembly elections the PRC won one of the 85 seats.

Civic Forum
Forum Civique (FC)
Address. c/o Assemblée Nationale, Bangui
Leadership. Gen. (retd.) Timothée Malendoma (president)

The FC was one of many newly-founded parties which in late 1991 joined the opposition Consultative Group of Democratic Forces (CFD) headed by the Patriotic Front for Progress. Its CFD membership was suspended in August 1992, however, when it opted to participate in the "grand national debate" convened by the then Kolingba government. Its relations with the CFD worsened in December 1992 when Malendoma was appointed Prime Minister, although they recovered somewhat in February 1993 when the FC leader was dismissed by Kolingba for "blocking the democratic process". Malendoma won only 2% of the vote in the presidential election first round in August 1993, while the FC secured only one of the 85 Assembly seats in concurrent legislative elections.

Democratic Movement for the Renaissance and Evolution of Central Africa
Mouvement Démocratique pour la Renaissance et l'Évolution en Centrafrique (MDREC)
Address. c/o Assemblée Nationale, Bangui
Leadership. Joseph Bendouga (president)

Launched in mid-1991, the MDREC joined the opposition Consultative Group of Democratic Forces (CFD), headed by the Patriotic Front for Progress (FPP), which pressed for a sovereign national conference on political reform. In 1992 the MDREC leader spent six months in prison after being convicted of insulting President Kolingba. The party supported the unsuccessful CFD/FPP candidate in the August-September 1993 presidential election. In the simultaneous Assembly elections it won only one of the 85 seats.

Liberal Democratic Party
Parti Libéral-Démocrate (PLD)
Address. c/o Assemblée Nationale, Bangui
Leadership. Nestor Kombo-Naguemon (president)

The PLD was launched amid the transition to multi-partyism in 1991–92. Advocating a deregulated market economy, the party won seven of the 85 Assembly seats in the 1993 legislative elections and accepted representation in the coalition government formed in October 1993 under the leadership of the Central African People's Liberation Movement.

Movement for Democracy and Development
Mouvement pour la Démocratie et le Développement (MDD)
Address. c/o Assemblée Nationale, Bangui
Leadership. David Dacko (president)

The MDD was launched in January 1994 by ex-President Dacko, who had led the CAR to independence in 1960 and had established one-party rule in 1962 through the Movement for the Social Evolution of Black Africa (MESAN). He was overthrown in 1966 by his cousin, Col. Jean-Bedel Bokassa, who appropriated MESAN as his political vehicle and placed it under new management. In 1976 Dacko accepted appointment as a special adviser to Bokassa, shortly before the latter's controversial self-elevation to the status of Emperor, but in 1979, with the assistance of French paratroopers, led the ousting of Bokassa and the re-establishment of the republic. Installed as President again, Dacko in March 1980 founded the Central African Democratic Union (UDC) as the sole ruling party, but later accepted multi-party competition under a new constitution promulgated in February 1981.

Declared the victor in disputed presidential elections in March 1981, Dacko was overthrown six months later by Gen. André Kolingba and thereafter was a key figure in the exiled anti-Kolingba opposition. Returning to the CAR on the introduction of multi-partyism, Dacko held aloof from party identification, standing as an independent in the August 1993 first round of presidential elections, in which he was placed third with 20.1% of the vote. In the concurrent Assembly elections, nominally independent candidates identified with Dacko won six of the 85 seats and in October 1993 became part of a coalition headed by the Central African People's Liberation Movement. The subsequent creation of the MDD was intended to provide a party framework for the pro-Dacko element of the new government.

Movement for the Social Evolution of Black Africa
Mouvement de l'Évolution Sociale de l'Afrique Noir (MESAN)
Address. c/o Assemblée Nationale, Bangui
Leadership. Prosper Lavodrama, Joseph Ngbangadibo (faction leaders)

Descended from the party of the same name founded in 1949 by Abbé Barthélémy Boganda (who was killed in an air crash in 1959), MESAN took the country to independence in 1960 under the leadership of David Dacko. It became the sole ruling party in 1962 and retained that status following the overthrow of Dacko in 1966 by Col. Jean-Bedel Bokassa, who introduced new ruling party management. Outlawed under the post-1981 Kolingba regime and now no longer connected with Dacko, MESAN regained only limited influence after its revival in 1991, in part because it became riven by factional division. In the 1993 Assembly elections MESAN won only one of the 85 seats.

National Convention

Convention National (CN)
    Address. c/o Assemblée Nationale, Bangui
    Leadership. David Galiambo
    The CD was founded in October 1991, immediately becoming a founder member of the opposition Consultative Group of Democratic Forces (CFD) headed by the Patriotic Front for Progress (FPP). It backed the unsuccessful CFD/FPP candidate in the August-September 1993 presidential election, while winning three of the 85 seats in simultaneous Assembly elections.

Patriotic Front for Progress

Front Patriotique pour le Progrès (FPP)
    Address. BP 259, Bangui
    Telephone. (#236–61) 5223
    Leadership. Abel Goumba (president), Patrice Endjimoungou (secretary-general)
    The FPP was launched in 1981 as the (Congo-based) Ubangi Patriotic Front–Labour Party after veteran anti-Bokassa campaigner Goumba had broken with the post-Bokassa Dacko government. During the late 1980s the party co-operated closely with the Central African People's Liberation Movement (MLPC) when the latter was under left-wing leadership. It also forged links with the European democratic left, becoming an affiliate of the Socialist International. The party obtained legal recognition as the FPP in August 1991, but not before Goumba had spent six months in prison for participating in an unauthorized opposition attempt to initiate a national conference on political reform. In late 1991 the FPP took the lead in the formation of the Consultative Group of Democratic Forces (CFD), with 13 other parties and six trade unions, which refused to participate in a "grand national debate" proposed by President Kolingba.
    Standing as the CFD candidate in the October 1992 presidential elections, Goumba was reported to be leading the first-round count when the elections were aborted. In February 1993 Goumba accepted membership of a government-appointed

transitional legislature, but the CFD formations refused to join a coalition administration. When the electoral process was resumed in August 1993, Goumba took second place in the first round of presidential balloting, winning 21.7% of the vote. He therefore went forward to second round in September but was defeated by the MLPC candidate by 52.5% to 45.6%. In simultaneous legislative elections, the FPP won seven of the 85 seats in its own right. After the elections the CFD was weakened by the decision of the Alliance for Democracy and Progress to join an MLPC-led coalition government. Nevertheless, the FPP became an active focus of opposition to the new Patassé administration, opposing the move to a presidential constitution in January 1995.

Popular Assembly for the Reconstruction of Central Africa

Rassemblement Populaire pour la Reconstruction de la Centrafrique (RPRC)
    Leadership. Gen. François Bozize (president)
    The RPRC was launched in the wake of the advent of multi-partyism in 1991 and was at first closely associated with the Central African Republican Party. Gen. Bozize had previously been a leader of the pro-Libyan Central African Movement for National Liberation (MCLN), which had been founded in 1980 in opposition to the then Dacko government and had later mounted active opposition to the post-1981 Kolingba regime. In 1989 he had been detained after being extradited to the CAR from Benin (reportedly for a "fee" of $3 million) but had been acquitted in October 1991 on charges of involvement in a 1982 coup attempt. Standing as an independent in the 1993 presidential election, Gen. Bozize won only 1.5% of the first-round vote.

Social Democratic Party

Parti Social-Démocrate (PSD)
    Address. c/o Assemblée Nationale, Bangui
    Leadership. Enoch Dérant Lakoué (president)
    Founded in 1991, the PSD distanced itself from the main anti- Kolingba opposition, favouring instead an accomodation with the then ruling Central African Democratic Rally (RDC). The PSD leader was a candidate in the aborted October 1992 presidential election and in February 1993 accepted President Kolingba's invitation to become Prime Minister. However, he failed in his quest to bring other major opposition parties into the government, his role in which precipitated wholesale defections from the PSD. Standing again for the presidency, Lakoué obtained only 2.4% of the vote in the August 1993 first round, while in Assembly elections the PSD took three of the 85 seats. Thereafter it formed part of the opposition to the new Patassé administration.

Other Parties

Central African Socialist Movement (*Mouvement Socialiste Centrafricain*, MSC).

Movement for the Liberation of the Central African Republic (*Mouvement pour la Libération de la République Centrafricaine*, MLRC), led by Hughes Dobozendi.

National Union for the Defence of Democracy (*Union National pour la Défense de la Démocratie*, UNDD), led by Sylvestre Bangui.

People's Union for Economic and Social Development (*Union du Peuple pour le Développement Économique et Social*, UPDES), led by Hubert Katoussi Simani.

Chad

Capital: N'Djaména

Population: 6,500,000 (1995E)

The Republic of Chad achieved independence from France in 1960 and became a one-party state in 1962 under N'Garta Tombalbaye's Chadian Progressive Party. Tombalbaye's overthrow in 1975 ushered in a lengthy north-south civil war and a series of shortlived regimes, leading in late 1990 to the seizure of power by the Patriotic Salvation Movement led by Col. Idriss Déby. In October 1991 the new regime published legislation allowing the operation of political parties provided they renounced "intolerance, tribalism, regionalism, religious discrimination. . .and recourse to violence". In April 1993 a sovereign national conference agreed detailed arrangements for a transition to multi-party democracy. Under a charter agreed by the conference, Déby remained head of state but the conference itself elected a transitional Prime Minister and a 57–member Higher Transitional Council (*Conseil Supérieur de Transition*) to serve as an interim legislature pending general elections. The transitional period, involving popular approval of a new constitution and the holding of elections, was provisionally set at 12 months but was later extended for further 12-month periods in April 1994 and May 1995. In light of continuing rebel activity, the government in May 1994 established a National Reconciliation Committee to serve as a framework for the achievement of peace. In November 1995 a timetable was published scheduling a constitutional referendum for March 1996, presidential elections for June 1996 and legislative elections for December 1996. Under the so-called Franceville Accord, signed by the government and 13 opposition parties on March 9, 1996, a referendum on March 31 resulted in 63.5% approval of a new constitution modelled on that of France.

Action for Unity and Socialism
Action pour l'Unité et le Socialisme (ACTUS)
   Leadership. Fidèle Moungar (president)
   ACTUS originated as a faction of the Transitional Government of National Unity (GUNT), which had been created in 1979 to unite the forces of Hissène Habré and Goukhouni Oueddei but had disintegrated into opposing factions when the latter had driven the former from N'Djaména in 1980. When the former turned the tables in 1982, the GUNT became an anti-Habré, Libyan-backed grouping dominated by Oueddei's faction of the Chad National Liberation Front (FROLINAT), but was still very prone to divisions. In early 1990 the ACTUS faction announced that it was regrouping with another GUNT fac-

tion, the Revolutionary Movement of the Chadian People (*Mouvement Révolutionnaire du Peuple Tchadien*, MRPT) led by Bire Titinan, to form the Rally for Democratic Action and Progress (*Rassemblement pour l'Action Démocratique et le Progrès*, RADP). This alliance backed the successful offensive against the Habré regime by the Patriotic Salvation Movement (MPS) led by Idriss Déby, whose assumption of power in December 1990 was followed by the re-emergence of ACTUS as a distinct formation under the leadership of Fidèle Moungar, a prominent surgeon.
   In May 1992 Moungar was appointed Education Minister in an MPS-dominated coalition government and in April 1993 was elected Prime Minister by the sovereign national conference

which had been convened in January to agree transitional arrangements leading to multi-party elections. Expressing confidence that he could work with President Déby, Moungar identified the protection of human rights and security issues as his main priorities. In October 1993, however, he was forced to resign after the transitional legislature had passed a no-confidence motion apparently inspired by Déby in light of serious strains between the two. Moungar claimed that his ejection violated the procedures and principles agreed by the national conference.

Chad National Liberation Front
Front de Libération National Tchadien (FROLINAT)

Leadership. Goukhouni Oueddei (chair)

FROLINAT was originally founded in 1966 by Libyan-backed northerners opposed to the southern-based Tombalbaye government (1960–75) and subsequently underwent repeated splits and fragmentation. FROLINAT factions were key elements of the governments of both Goukhouni Oueddei (1980–82) and Hissène Habré (1982–90), although the latter's faction was merged into the ruling National Union for Independence and Revolution (UNIR) in 1984. Usually backed by Libya, Oueddei's faction dominated various anti-Habré alliances in the 1980s but Oueddei himself, based in Algeria, appeared to become marginalized, especially by the formation of the Patriotic Salvation Movement (MSP) by Idriss Déby. Following the MSP's assumption of power in December 1990, Oueddei made a highly-publicized return to N'Djaména in May 1991 for talks with President Déby on a transition to multi-party democracy. He later returned to Algiers and in mid-1992 affirmed that FROLINAT (his faction of which was also designated the Provisional Council of the Revolution) preferred political dialogue to armed struggle. In early 1993 Oueddei attended the sovereign national conference on political reform convened by the Déby government in N'Djaména, some two-thirds of the delegates at which had once belonged to one or other of the FROLINAT factions. By then, however, the initiative appeared to have passed to the MSP and to other parties and movements. In August 1995 Oueddei was reported to have joined forces with southern-based rebels which were continuing operations against the government despite the declaration of a national ceasefire the previous month.

Movement for Democracy and Development
Mouvement pour la Démocratie et le Développement (MDD)

Leadership. Goukhouni Guët, Aboubarkaye Haroun, Brahim Malla

The MDD was founded Nigeria in 1991 by exiled supporters of ex-President Hissène Habré, who had been overthrown in December 1990 by the Patriotic Salvation Movement (MSP) led by Idriss Déby. It was therefore in part a successor to the National Union for Independence and Revolution (UNIR), which had been created by Habré in 1984 as the ruling party of his regime. (Other ex-UNIR elements came to terms with the Déby government and in 1992 formed the National Democratic and Social Convention.) The MDD's military wing, called the Western Armed Forces (*Forces Armées Occidentales*, FAO), launched an offensive from the western border in late 1991 but an attempt to seize power in N'Djaména was defeated by government forces in January 1992. Soon afterwards several MDD leaders were reportedly kidnapped from Nigeria, among them Goukhouni Guët, whom the Déby government later named as being in its custody. In early 1993 the MDD/FAO reportedly split into a militant pro-Habré faction called the National Armed Forces of Chad (*Forces Armées Nationales du Tchad*, FANT) and a faction loyal to Guët. The latter was invited to the national conference on political reform held in N'Djaména in January-April 1993, while the former, led by Brahim Malla, continued the armed struggle and in January 1994 announced an alliance with the National Union for Democracy and Socialism (*Union Nationale pour la Démocratie et le Socialisme*, UNDS) led by Youssou Sougoudi. The government's announcement of a nationwide ceasefire in July 1995 was greeted with scepticism by the MDD. In November 1995, however, the MDD and the government signed a ceasefire agreement providing for an exchange of prisoners, the integration of selected MDD guerrillas into the national army and the return of the rest into civilian life.

Movement for Democracy and Socialism in Chad
Mouvement pour la Démocratie et le Socialisme en Tchad (MDST)

Leadership. Salomon (Ngarbaye) Tombalbaye (president), Abderahman Hamdane (executive secretary)

The MDST was founded in Nigeria in 1988 by anti-Habré exiles, including Salomon (Ngarbaye) Tombalbaye, son of independent Chad's first President (who was assassinated in 1975). Allied with the Patriotic Salvation Movement (MPS) in its successful offensive against the Habré regime in late 1990, the MDST elected Tombalbaye as its president in April 1992 and was legalized in June. Almost alone among the crop of new parties in Chad, the MDST advocated a socialist programme, while stressing the importance of full multi-party democracy. In May 1994 President Déby announced the appointment of Tombalbaye as

Health Minister, but the MDST leader declined the post on the grounds that he had not been consulted about it.

National Alliance for Democracy and Development
Alliance Nationale pour la Démocratie et le Développement (ANDD)
    Leadership. Salibou Garba (president)
    The ANDD was one of a number of parties formed in early 1992 on the fringes of the ruling Patriotic Salvation Movement (MPS). The Prime Minister appointed in May 1992, Joseph Yodemane, was at first described as being "close" to the ANDD, while one of his ministers, Nabia Ndali, was an actual party member. However, Ndali resigned in July 1992 as a result of a dispute between ANDD leaders and Yodemane, who was formally disowned by the party and later formed the National Alliance for Democracy and Renewal.

National Alliance for Democracy and Renewal
Alliance Nationale pour la Démocratie et le Renouveau (ANDR)
    Leadership. Joseph Yodemane (president)
    The ANDR was created by Yodemane after he had broken with the National Alliance for Democracy and Development in July 1992. He had been appointed Prime Minister of a coalition government two months previously and held this post until April 1993.

National Front of Chad
Front National du Tchad (FNT)
    Leadership. Alarit Bachar
    Based in central-eastern Chad, the rebel FNT entered into a peace agreement with the Déby government in October 1992 providing for its political and military integration into national structures. However, most FNT elements continued military activities, stepping them up in 1994. A further ceasefire agreement signed with the government by an FNT faction in October 1994 was disowned by Bachar as leader of the main FNT.

National Rally for Democracy and Progress
Rassemblement National pour la Démocratie et le Progrès (RNDP)
    Leadership. Delwa Kassiré Koumakoyé (president)
    The RNDP was founded in early 1992, its leader becoming spokesman of the National Co-ordination of the Opposition (CNO) created in May 1992 but later gravitating towards the ruling Patriotic Salvation Front (MPS), whose (unsuccessful) candidate he was for the chairmanship of the sovereign national conference convened in January 1993. In June 1993 Koumakoyé accepted the post of Justice Minister in a transitional coalition government and in November was elevated to the premiership. On the latter occasion he gave as his main aims the further demobilization of armed forces, a social pact with the trade unions, the preparation of elections and reconciliation with unreconciled rebel movements. In April 1995, however, he was dismissed by decision of the legislative Higher National Council, apparently at the instigation of President Déby, and in June participated in protest demonstrations against what he termed the government's "drift towards totalitarianism and dictatorship".

National Salvation Council for Peace and Democracy
Conseil de Salut National pour la Paix et la Démocratie (CSNPD)
    Leadership. Col. Moise Nodji Tchiete (president)
    The southern-based CSNPD was founded in mid-1992 by deserters from the northern-dominated national army and came into bloody conflict with the government in 1993. Talks between government and CSNPD representatives were subsequently initiated in Bangui under Central African Republic, UN and French auspices, these producing a ceasefire agreement in August 1994 under which government forces were to withdraw from the south, the CSNPD was to abandon armed struggle and its fighters were to be integrated into the national army. On being appointed a Chad army officer in November, CSNPD leader Tchiete, hitherto a lieutenant, was promoted to the rank of colonel. In April 1995 he was appointed Minister of Environment and Tourism in the new government headed by the Patriotic Salvation Movement.

Patriotic Salvation Movement
Mouvement Patriotique du Salut (MPS)
    Leadership. Idriss Déby (president), Nadjita Beassoumal (executive secretary)
    The MPS was founded in March 1990 by Libyan-based opponents of the French-backed regime of Hissène Habré, who had held power in Chad since 1982. The MPS leader had been a top adviser to Habré until participating in a coup attempt in April 1989, being the only one of the three principals to escape. The MPS at foundation included Déby's April 1 Action (*Action du 1 April*) based in the Zaghwa and Hadjerai tribes of central Chad; the southern-based Movement for Chadian National Salvation (*Mouvement pour le Salut National du Tchad*, MOSANAT); and remnants of the Chadian Armed Forces (*Forces Armées Tcha-*

diennes, FAT). Adopting a pro-democracy stance and advocating "neither capitalism nor socialism", the MPS launched a major offensive against the Habré government which brought it to power in N'Djaména, and Déby to the presidency, in December 1990. It then attracted the allegiance of other groups, including the Chadian People's Revolution (*Révolution du Peuple Tchadienne*, RPT) led by Adoum Togoi and a faction of the Chad National Liberation Front (FROLINAT), as it emphasized political reconciliation and moved towards multi-party democracy. Internal strains were highlighted by the arrest in October 1991 of MPS vice-president Maldom Baba Abbas for an alleged coup attempt, but he was rehabilitated in February 1992.

From May 1992 President Déby expanded the political basis of the government to include several new parties, notably Action for Unity and Socialism (ACTUS), the National Alliance for Democracy and Development, the National Rally for Democracy and Progress, the Rally of the Chadian People, the Union for Democracy and Progress, the Union for Democracy and the Republic (UDR), the Union for Renewal and Democracy and the Union of Democratic Forces. He also acceded to the convening in January 1993 of a sovereign national conference on the country's political future, making sure that some 75% of the delegates (representing 66 parties and organizations) were MPS supporters. The outcome in April 1993 was the adoption of a transitional charter which left Déby as head of state and commander-in-chief but provided for the election by the conference of the Prime Minister (the post going to Fidèle Moungar of ACTUS) and of an interim legislature pending the holding of multi-party general elections.

President Déby quickly fell out with Moungar, who was replaced in November 1993 by Delwa Kassiré Koumakoyé of the National Rally for Development and Progress, whose government, like its predecessor, was dominated by the MPS. Déby's good relations with Libya were highlighted at the end of May 1994 by the formal return to Chad of the disputed Aouzou Strip (held by Libya since 1973) in accordance with an International Court of Justice ruling of February 1994 in favour of Chad's claim. In October 1994 an MPS nominee, Mahamat Bachar Ghadaia, became chairman of the legislative Higher Transitional Council in place of Lol Mahamat Choua of the opposition Rally for Democracy and Progress. Criticized for the slow progress of political transition, Moungar became yet another ex-Prime Minister in April 1995, being replaced by Keibla Djimasta of the UDR.

Rally for Democracy and Progress
Rassemblement pour la Démocratie et le Progrès (RDP)

Leadership. Lol Mahamat Choua (president)

The RDP was launched in December 1991 under the leadership of Lol Mahamat Choua (mayor of N'Djaména), who in 1979 had briefly been President of an aborted national unity government and had later held ministerial office under the post-1982 Habré regime. Strong in the Kanem tribe around Lake Chad, the RDP came under heavy pressure from the security forces for its alleged involvement in the Kanem-backed coup attempt of January 1992. The party was nevertheless one of the first to be legalized in March 1992 and in May joined the National Co-ordination of the Opposition (CNO). It participated in the sovereign national conference of January-April 1993, its leader being elected chairman of the resultant Higher Transitional Council (CST), which was to serve as an interim legislature pending general elections. When the initial transitional period of 12 months was extended by a further year in April 1994, Choua complained publicly the Déby government had failed to make adequate preparations for democratic elections. His reward was to be ousted from the CST chairmanship in October 1994, whereupon he claimed at a press conference that the government had recently ordered the assassination of two RDP journalists and had arrested a dozen other RDP members.

Rally of the Chadian People
Rassemblement du Peuple Tchadien (RPT)

Leadership. Dangbe Laobele Damaye (president)

The RPT obtained legalization in April 1992 and the following month a party member, Jeremie Beade Toiria, was appointed Minister of Trade and Industry in a new coalition government. He resigned at his party's request in October 1993 after the government had placed a temporary ban on trade union activities.

Union for Democracy and the Republic
Union pour la Démocratie et la République (UDR)

Leadership. Keibla Djimasta, Jean Alingué Bawoyeu

The UDR was still awaiting official recognition when, in March 1992, it elected Jean Alingué Bawoyeu as its president on his appointment as Prime Minister by President Déby of the Patriotic Salvation Movement. The UDR leader ceased to be Prime Minister in May 1992, but the party continued to be represented in the government. In April 1995 the UDR regained the premiership in the person of Keibla Djimasta.

Union for Renewal and Democracy

Union pour le Renouveau et la Démocratie (URD)

Leadership. Wadal Abdelkader Kamougue (president)

Founded in March 1992 and legalized two months later, the URD consisted of supporters of Lt.-Gen. Kamougue, who had commanded anti-Habré forces in southern Chad in the 1980s and had been a vice-president of the Libyan-backed Transitional Government of National Unity (GUNT). Following the sovereign national conference held in early 1993, the URD leader was in April 1993 appointed Minister of Civil Service and Labour but was dismissed in May 1994 in the wake of a strike by civil servants.

Other Parties and Movements

Action for the Renewal of Chad (*Action pour le Rénouvellement du Tchad*, ART), led by Oumar Bouchar.

Action Forces Front for the Republic (*Front des Forces d'Action pour la République*, FFAR), led by Yorongar Lemohiban, a militant anti-Déby group.

African Party for Progress and Social Justice (*Parti Africain pour le Progrès et la Justice Sociale*, PAPJS), led by Neatobei Didier Valentin.

Alliance for Chadian Democracy (*Alliance pour la Démocratie du Tchad*, ADET), led by Tidjani Thiam (an oil trader), founded in April 1992, in coalition since late 1993 with the Democratic National Union (*Union National Démocratique*, UND) led by Facho Balaam and the Democratic Revolutionary Council–Rejection Front (*Conseil Démocratique Révolutionnaire–Front du Rejet*, CDR-FR) led by Gaileth Bourkou Mandah.

Chadian Democratic Union (*Union Démocratique Tchadienne*, UDT), led by Abderhamane Koulamallah, a businessman.

Chadian Social Democratic Party (*Parti Social-Démocrate du Tchad*, PSDT), a southern-based movement led by Niabe Romain, a businessman.

Chadian Union for Democracy and Progress (*Union Tchadienne pour la Démocratie et le Progrès*, UTDP), led by Elie Romba, legalized in March 1992.

Convention of Chadian Social Democrats (*Convention des Social-Démocrates Tchadiens*, CSDT), led by Younous Idedou, founded in April 1992 by

(among others) several former ministers of the Habré regime, dedicated to creating a "new Chad" and ending decades of civil war.

Democratic Revolutionary Council (*Conseil Démocratique Révolutionnaire*, CDR), led by Aboubakar Adzalo Barraka, allied to the Oueddei faction of the Chad National Liberation Front.

Democratic Union for Chadian Progress (*Union Démocratique pour le Progrès Tchadien*, UDPT), led by Elie Romba.

Movement for Unity and Democracy in Chad (*Mouvement pour l'Unité et la Démocratie au Tchad*, MUDT), led by Julien Marabaye.

National Council for the Recovery of Chad (*Conseil National de Redressement du Tchad*, CNRT), a southern-based movement led by Idriss Agar Bichara, formed in mid-1992 by Col. Abbas Koty (an ex-member of the Déby government who had fled after being accused of plotting a coup), deprived of its first leader when Koty was killed by security forces in August 1993 shortly after negotiating a reconciliation and integration pact with the Déby government, thereafter continued armed struggle.

National Movement of Chadian Renovators (*Mouvement National des Rénovateurs Tchadiens*, MNRT), led by Ali Muhammad Diallo, allied with the Oueddei faction of the Chad National Liberation Front.

National Union (*Union National*, UN), led by Abdoulaye Lamane (a former ambassador) and Mahamat Djerba (a former deputy leader of the Oueddei faction of the Chad National Liberation Front), founded in March 1992.

National Union for Democracy and Progress (*Union National pour la Démocratie et le Progrès*, UNDP), led by Abdelkader Yassine Bakit.

National Union for Democracy and Renewal (*Union National pour la Démocratie et le Rénouvellement*, UNDR), led by Saleh Kebzabo, who in September 1995 was arrested and charged with making illegal contacts with rebel groups.

Party for Freedom and Development (*Parti pour la Liberté et le Développement*, PLD), founded in late 1993 by Ibn Oumar Mahamat Saleh and Paul Saradori, following the former's dismissal in May as Minister of Planning and Co-operation, advocating the "rehabilitation" of Chad.

Rally for Development and Progress (*Rassemblement pour le Développement et le Progrès*, RDP), led by Mamadou Bisso, founded in December 1991, the target of government reprisal attacks following the January 1992 attempted takeover by the Movement for Democracy and Development.

Revolutionary Council of the Chadian People (*Conseil Révolutionnaire du Peuple Tchadien*, CRPT), led by Hamed Jacob.

Socialist Movement for Democracy in Chad (*Mouvement Socialiste pour la Démocratie en Tchad*, MSDT), led by Albert Mbainaido Djomia.

Union of Democratic Forces (*Union des Forces Démocratiques*, UFD), led by Ngawara Nahor, legalized in early 1992, one of the smaller parties included in the coalition government appointed in May 1992 under the leadership of the Patriotic Salvation Movement.

Union of Democratic Forces–Republican Party (*Union des Forces Démocratiques–Parti Républicain*, UFD-PR), led by Gali Gatta Ngothe.

Union of the Chadian People for National Reconstruction (*Union du Peuple Tchadien pour la Reconstruction Nationale*, UPTRN), led by Happa Karouma.

Chile

Capital: Santiago   **Population:** 14,300,000 (1995E)

The Republic of Chile won its independence in 1818. Prior to a right-wing military coup led by Gen. Augusto Pinochet Ugarte in September 1973 Chile had been a parliamentary democracy with an executive President and a National Congress elected by universal adult suffrage. After the coup, absolute power rested with the military junta, and increasingly with Pinochet, who in June 1974 was designated Supreme Chief of State, and in December, President of the Republic (although he did not formally assume that title until March 1981). The junta proclaimed various "constitutional acts" in 1976 purporting to establish an "authoritarian democracy", with executive and legislative authority vested in the President and the junta, assisted by a Cabinet.

In accordance with the March 1981 constitution, as amended and approved by referendum in July 1989, Chile is a democratic republic; executive power lies with the President, who is directly elected for a six-year term. Legislative power is held by a bicameral National Congress, comprising a 47-member Senate serving an eight-year term (of whom 38 are elected and nine are currently appointed directly by the outgoing government and the Supreme Court) and a 120-member Chamber of Deputies elected for a four-year term. The National Security Council, a direct legacy of military rule in a period of transition to full democracy, consists of the President, the presidents of the Supreme Court and the Senate, and heads of the armed forces and police.

The electoral law also provides for army-approved candidates for the Senate who do not necessarily need to win a majority in their constituency to be elected. Non-approved candidates need to obtain twice as many votes to win an election. According to a new constitutional reform approved by Congress on Nov. 9, 1991, municipal councils and mayors are elected by direct suffrage and hold their posts for a four-year period.

In a plebiscite held on Oct. 5, 1988, a majority of nearly 55% voted against Pinochet remaining in office for a further eight years upon the expiry of his term in 1990. In the resulting presidential elections held on Dec. 14, 1989, Patricio Aylwin Azócar of the Christian Democratic Party (PDC), who was also the representative of the 17-party Coalition of Parties for Democracy (CPD), was the clear winner. He took office on March 11, 1990. In the next presidential elections, held on Dec. 11, 1993, the CPD candidate, Eduardo Frei Ruíz-Tagle, also of the PDC, won with 58% of the vote. In simultaneous congressional elections, the CPD failed to secure a two thirds majority in either house. Frei took office on March 11, 1994. Included in his new Cabinet were members of the Socialist Party (PS), Party for Democracy (PPD), Social Democratic Party (PSD) and independents.

Central-Central Union

Unión de Centro-Centro (UCC)

Leadership. Francisco Javier Errazuriz

The UCC is a populist party and founding member of the UPP. The party is led by Francisco Javier Errazuriz, a well-known Chilean business-man and popularly known as "Fra Fra".

Centre Alliance Party

Partido Alianza de Centro (PAC)

Address. c/o Adolfo Balaf, Manizalef 1966, Santiago

Telephone. (#56-2) 219 1947

Fax. (#56-2) 251 8964

Leadership. Hernán Felipe Errazuriz Correa (president)

A centrist party with moderate conservative leanings, the PAC is the Chilean observer member of the Liberal International which it joined in 1991. Although a part of the successful CDP alliance which brought President Aylwin to power, it was not awarded with any government posts under the new government of President Frei in March 1994.

Christian Democratic Party

Partido Demócrata Cristiana (PDC)

Address. Alameda B. O'Higgins 1460, 1° piso interior, Santiago.

Telephone. (#56-2) 695 1025

Fax. (#56-2) 695 5396

Leadership. Alejandro Foxley Rioseco (president), Genaro Arriagada (secretary-general)

Founded in July 1957, the PDC is a Christian Democratic party and is an affiliate of the Christian Democrat Organisation of America (ODCA) and the Christian Democrat International.

The PDC was formed as a merger of the National Falange (founded 1934) and the majority faction of the Social Christian Conservative Party. The party's leader, Eduardo Frei Montalva, came third in the presidential elections of 1958. The party built up its support in rural areas, especially through illegal rural unions. In 1961 the PDC became the largest party in Congress (and remained so until the 1973 coup).

The Christian Democrats, with the help from the USA and funding from the US Central Intelligence Agency (CIA), formed an effective and hostile opposition to the Allende government (1970-73), increasing the pressure on Allende to grant concessions to them and the military.

The Pinochet coup was welcomed by a large majority of the party, including the then party president Patricio Aylwin Azócar. However, its allegiance to the junta diminished as Pinochet developed his own political agenda. In 1977, the PDC was banned, along with all other parties. In August 1983 the party founded the Democratic Alliance (AD), a centre-left alliance which superseded the *Multipartidaria* alliance formed only months earlier. In 1986 the party announced its acceptance of the military's 1980 Constitution but at the same time became the main force in the AD's campaign for free elections and was a signatory to the National Democratic Accord, an opposition document outlining the agenda for a transition to democracy.

Aylwin became the spokesman for the "Command for the No Vote" a 13-party opposition alliance which successfully campaigned against the extension of Pinochet's term as President, an issue submitted to a plebiscite on Oct. 5, 1988. The popular support, energy and enthusiasm generated by the "no" was harnessed to establish the Coalition for Democracy (CPD), a 17-member electoral alliance led by the Christian Democrats. In July 1989 the CPD parties agreed to support Aylwin as the main opposition presidential candidate. His campaign programme included pledges to investigate human rights abuses, improve education and health care and increase the minimum wage within the context of a sound economic programme designed to boost exports and control inflation. In the Dec. 14, 1989, elections, Aylwin was elected President with 55.2% of the valid votes. The PDC, with 38 seats in the Chamber of deputies and 13 seats in the Senate, became the largest party in the Congress.

Currently Chile's strongest party, the PDC is divided into right, centre and left-wing factions and took a third of the available votes in the 1992 municipal election as well as providing the successful presidential candidate in the December 1993 presidential elections, Eduado Frei Ruíz-Tagle.

Coalition of Parties for Democracy

Concertación de los Partidos por la Democracia (CPD)

Leadership. Eduado Frei Ruíz-Tagle

This centrist alliance was founded in its present form in November 1988, as a vehicle for Patricio Aylwin Azócar. In the December 1989 presidential campaign, Aylwin campaigned on a platform of social welfare and education reforms, an increase in the minimum wage, an end to human rights abuses, and increased exports with low inflation. This, originally, seven-party coalition (now six) has proved a successful force in Chilean politics.

The CPD arose out of the Democratic Alliance led by the Christian Democratic Party (PDC) and the "Command for the No Vote" opposition alliance which successfully campaigned to prevent Pinochet extending his presidential term of office beyond 1990, a view subsequently endorsed in a plebiscite held in October 1988. The CPD formed a united front against the right in the December 1989 general election and presented an all-encompassing proposal for constitutional reform in January 1990. Pinochet, under pressure from his own Cabinet and the right-wing National Renewal (PR) party, agreed to discuss the proposals the following March and in May Interior Minister Caceres put forward a 43-point proposal for constitutional amendments. These were cautiously welcomed by the CPD as a step towards an orderly transition to democracy.

In order not to fragment the pro-democracy vote in the Dec. 14, 1989, presidential election, the CPD's 17 member parties officially decided in July 1989 to back Patricio Aylwin, the CPD leader and already the presidential candidate for the PDC (the coalition's largest party).

After his inauguration in March 1990, Aylwin formed a CPD coalition government with Cabinet posts allocated to the main alliance parties proportionate to their representation in Congress. Aylwin had the difficult task of implementing the coalition's election promises while adopting a conciliatory approach towards the military and the two main right-wing parties. Thus Aylwin allowed Pinochet to remain Commander-in-Chief of the Armed Forces.

In November 1991 the CPD government also passed a new constitutional reform allowing local elections by direct suffrage and in March 1992 further proposed constitutional amendments were announced, which marked an attempt to distance the government further from the military. Chief among the proposed reforms would be the right of a future President to remove heads of the armed forces, forbidden under the then current 1980 military constitution.

In December, 1993, the alliance proved just as successful as their chosen candidate, Eduado Frei Ruíz-Tagle was elected President of the Republic and took office on March 11, 1994.

The current members of the ruling CPD coalition are the Christian Democratic Party, the Socialist Party of Chile, the Party for Democracy, the Radical Social Democratic Party, the Social Democratic Party and the Centre Alliance Party (see separate entries).

Communist Party of Chile
Partido Comunista de Chile (PCCh)
   Address. San Pablo 2271, Santiago
   Telephone. (#56-2) 724164
   Leadership. Gladys Marin (president)
   The PCCh is now a centre-left party having rejected Marxism-Leninism in 1991 in the wake of the collapse of the former Soviet Union and the Eastern bloc.
   Formed by Luis Emilio Recabarren as the

Socialist Workers' Party, the party adopted its present name in 1922, the year it joined the Third International.

The party contested the 1949 general election, obtaining six seats in the Chamber of Deputies under the name of National Democratic Front, which it retained until the PCCh was legalized in 1958. Joining forces with the Socialist Party (PSCh) in 1952, it supported the unsuccessful presidential campaign of Salvador Allende and continued to do so in the elections of 1958, 1964 and 1970. The party's representation in the lower house rose from 15 seats in 1961 to 18 in 1965 and to 22 seats in 1969. By the time it was invited into the Allende government in 1970, the PCCh was one of the largest Communist Parties outside the Eastern bloc.

The Communist Party was banned following the September 1973 military coup and many of its leaders and activists were imprisoned. Some leaders, including the party's long standing secretary-general Luís Corvalán Lepe, were allowed to go into exile in 1976.

Like other Marxist parties, the PCCh was not permitted to register in 1987 and for the December 1989 elections the party relied on the support of Christian Democrat-led Coalition for Democracy (CPD) and on PCCh-sponsored lists in exchange for the communist support elsewhere.

A month before the December 1989 general elections, the PCCh, joined the Broad Party of the Socialist Left (PAIS) which, however, collapsed shortly before the polling day. PCCh candidates won a total of 300,000 votes but due to an electoral law which required non-army candidates to win twice the number of votes to be elected, the party gained no seats in Congress. The party was legalized in October 1990.

Also, in January 1990 the party finally renounced its policy of violent struggle by declaring that it had severed all links with the Manuel Rodríguez Patriotic Front (*Frente Patriótica Manuel Rodríguez*, FPMR), an active left-wing guerrilla group in Chile. This enabled the party to enter the democratic process in October of that year.

Other small parties in the MIDA coalition are the Left Broad Force Party, the Socialist People's Movement Party and the Socialist Recuperation Movement.

Independent Democratic Union
Unión Demócrata Independiente (UDI)
   Address. Suecia 286, Providencia, Santiago
   Telephone. (#56-2) 233-0037
   Fax. (#56-2) 233-6189
   Leadership. Jovino Novoa Vásquez (president)
   The right-wing UDI was founded in the early 1980s under the leadership of Julio Dittborn Cordúa.

The UDI was formed as a right-wing pressure group whose original platform was for the military to authorize the creation of a nominal parliament in order to counteract growing popular demands for a transition to democracy. The UDI merged with two other groups to form the National Renewal (PR) party in 1987 but was expelled in April 1988. It supported Gen. Pinochet's attempt to extend his presidency, voted down in the October 1988 plebiscite. After Pinochet's defeat, the UDI decided against fielding their own presidential candidate. In an attempt to distance itself from the military regime, the party backed the presidential candidacy of Hernán Buechi, the Finance Minister and an independent right-wing technocrat who came second in the December 1989 elections.

The party was dealt a serious blow in April 1991 when its president, Jaime Guzmán, was assassinated. Although two left-wing guerrilla groups claimed responsibility, it was widely believed that he was shot by right-wing *agents provocateurs* in order to destabilize the government and prompt the intervention of the army.

Movement of the Allendist Democratic Left

Movimiento Izquierda Democrática Allendista (MIDA)

Leadership.; Eugenio Pizzaro (1993 presidential candidate)

This third major alliance in Chilean politics was launched in December 1991 with the PCCh (see below) as its principle component. Its leader, Andrés Pascal Allende, a nephew of the former president, was the former leader of the now defunct MIR. MIDA had a 6.6% share of the vote in the municipal elections of 1992 but only a 4.7% share in the 1993 presidential elections.

The member parties of the MIDA alliance are dominated by the Communist Party of Chile, other components being the Left Broad Force Party, the Socialist People's Movement and the Socialist Recuperation Movement.

National Advance Guard

Avanzada Nacional (AN)

Leadership. Col. (retd.) Alvaro Corbalán Castillo

Led and founded by Alvaro Corbalán, the AN is a far-right group that maintains strong links with the military and remains a strong supporter of former dictator General Pinochet.

It has campaigned with both the radical Party of the South (*Partido del Sur*, PSu) and the Radical Democracy Party (*Partido Democracia Radical*, PDR) (see below under the PNDC). The party maintains links with the Chilean state intelligence community under Pinochet.

National Party of Centrist Democracy

Partido Nacional de Democracia Centrista (PNDC)

Address. Compañia 1263, Santiago

Leadership. Julio Duran (president)

The PNDC is a right-of-centre party launched in 1990 by a merging of the following parties: the National Party (*Partido Nacional*, PN), the Radical Democracy Party (*Partido Democracia Radical*, PDR), National Vanguard (*Vanguardia Nacional*, VN) and the Free Democratic Centre (*Centro Democrática Libre*, CDL).

National Renewal

Renovación Nacional (RN)

Address. Antonio Varas 454, Providencia, Santiago

Telephone. (#56-2) 235-1337

Fax. (#56-2) 235-1338

Leadership. Andrés Allemand Zavala (president)

Founded in 1987, the right-wing RN campaigned in the 1989 election campaign as the party that would protect the 1980 Constitution installed by the Pinochet regime and prevent it from being dismantled wholesale.

The party was created by a merger of the National Union, the National Labour Front and the Independent Democratic Union (UDI, which was expelled a year later). Although pro-Pinochet, the RN distanced itself from his regime, and following the October 1988 plebiscite rejection of an extension of Pinochet's presidency the party tried to project a moderate image by declaring itself willing to negotiate with the pro-democracy movement. In early 1989 the RN put pressure on Pinochet to consider the constitutional reform proposals put forward by the Coalition for Democracy (CPD).

In May 1989 the RN announced the candidacy of Sergio Onofre Jarpa, a former Interior Minister, for the December 1989 presidential elections, but when he withdrew, the party backed the independent right-wing candidate Hernán Buechi, Pinochet's former Finance Minister.

The RN was not so much interested in becoming the dominant party in Congress as in beating its rival, the UDI, in the elections and thus establishing itself as the major right-wing party. Aided by the bias of the current electoral law towards military-approved right-wing candidates, the RN won the second largest representation in the legislature with 29 seats in the Chamber of Deputies and 11 in the Senate.

In 1992 the party's long-standing support for the military was ended following a scandal in which two of the party's leaders were forced to withdraw as presidential candidates after the discovery of a wire-tapping operation involving the army's communications battalion. One of the leaders, Sebastián Piñera, subsequently ran in the 1993 elections as an independent.

Party for Democracy

Partido por la Democracia (PPD)

Address. Padre Luis Valdivia 327, Santiago

Leadership. Jorge Schaulsohn Brodsky (president)

This party was founded in December 1987 by Ricardo Lagos as a political vehicle of the illegal Socialist Party (PS), of which all PPD members and leaders retained their leadership.

The party was founded by Ricardo Lagos as a political vehicle for the illegal Socialist Party (PS), of which all PPD members and leaders retained their membership. The PPD supported the "no" campaign leading up to the October 1988 plebiscite and was a member of the Coalition for Democracy (CPD) from its inception in November 1988. After the CPD victory in the December 1989 general election, the PPD became the third largest party in Congress with 17 seats in the Chamber and four seats in the Senate despite the anti-left bias in the electoral law.

The PPD and the PSCh formed a sub-pact for the June 1992 municipal poll and both supported Lagos Escobar for the presidency in 1993.

Radical Social Democratic Party

Partido Radical Social Democrata (PRSD)

Address. Miraflores 495, Santiago

Telephone. (#56-2) 639 1053

Fax. (#56-2) 639 1053

Leadership. Anselmo Sule Candia (president)

Chile's affiliate to the Socialist International, the PRSD, originally founded in 1863 as the Radical Party (PR), is the country's oldest extant party.

The PR was formed by a group which split away from the Liberal Party (PL). It was Chile's main progressive party in the decades around the turn of the century and was in government from 1938 to 1952.

The party lost power following bitter factional fights which led to the breakaway of two groups. The party held some ministerial posts in the National Party government of Jorge Alessandri (1958-64) but in 1969, after the defection of its right-wing faction to Alessandri's camp, it joined the broad Popular Unit (PU) alliance backing the presidential candidacy of Salvador Allende of the Socialist Party.

In the 1980s the Radical Party became an influential force in the CPD. Following the party's appalling showing in the 1993 elections it adopted its present name in 1994, changing from the Radical Party, (*Partido Radical*, PR).

Social Democratic Party

Partido Social Demócrata (PSD)

Address. 815 París, Casilla 50/220, Santiago

Telephone. (#56-2) 399064

Leadership. Arturro Venegas Gutiérrez (president)

A founding member of the Democratic Alliance in 1983 (the forerunner of the CPD), the party however supported an opposing alliance, the National Democratic Accord, and went on to defy the CPD by supporting General Pinochet in the October 1988 plebiscite. In April 1994 it was announced that the PR and the PSD would merge under a group title that had not yet been decided (although most likely the PRSD above).

Socialist Party of Chile

Partido Socialista de Chile (PS or PSCh)

Address. Concha y Toro 36, Santiago

Telephone. (#56-2) 338490

Fax. (#56-2) 382449

Leadership. Camilio Escalona (president), Gonzalo Martner (general-secretary)

Founded in 1933, the centre-left PS has the distinction of being one of Chile's oldest political parties.

The Socialist Party was formed by a merger of six parties which had supported the Socialist Republic proclaimed by Col. Marmaduke Grove which lasted 13 days. It had a strong trade union base and committed itself to Marxism-Leninism. Its ranks swelled by the merger with the Trotskyist Communist Left party, the PS won 19 seats in the Chamber of Deputies in the 1937 elections as part of a left-wing Popular Front alliance. After several conflicts with the Communist Party of Chile (PCCh) the Socialist Party suffered a major split in 1948, dividing into the Socialist Party of Chile (PSCh), which supported three deputies expelled from the PS for voting for the banning of the Communist Party (PCCh), and the Popular Socialist Party (PSP) which was led by Salvador Allende. The reunited Socialist Party (PS) joined the Popular Unity alliance (UP) in 1969 and with Allende as its candidate won the 1970 presidential elections, the PS receiving 22.8% of the overall UP vote.

Allende's reforms included the full nationalization of the copper industry, a price freeze and an increase in wages. The Socialists, who held four ministerial posts in the Allende coalition governments, proved to be the most radical force, initially supporting land and factory seizures but then increasingly calling for moderation and refusing to arm the working class when a coup seemed imminent. The Allende government, dogged by spiralling inflation, a US embargo, economic sabotage by the business sector and pressure from the army, made increasing concessions to the right and in late 1972 included members of the military in the cabinet.

After the 1973 coup, in which Allende lost his life, many of the PS leaders were either killed, imprisoned, tortured or exiled. The party fragmented as a result of disagreements over Allende's failure, and continued to split throughout the 1970s and 1980s.

In 1989, both the PS "Historic" and "Almeyda" factions participated with the Communist party (PCCh) in the short-lived Broad Party of the Socialist Left (PAIS). The PS-Almeyda and left-wing Radicals subsequently made a pact with the Coalition for Democracy (CPD) supporting the victorious presidential campaign of Patricio Aylwin in December 1989.

The party's current president and general secretary were named in 1992, and as of the start of 1996 the PS had secured three cabinet posts in the coalition government of President Frei Ruíz-Tagle, including José Miguel Insulza as the Minister for Foreign Affairs.

Union for the Progress of Chile
Unión por el Progreso de Chile (UPP)
Leadership. Arturo Alessandri Besa (1993 presidential candidate); Andres Allemand Zavala (RN)

The UPP alliance was organized prior to the presidential elections of 1993 which saw the elec-

tion of the CPD candidate Eduado Frei Ruíz-Tagle. As a strong alliance of the country's leading right-wing groups, the UPP is the effective opposition in Chile.

The UPP constituent parties are the Central–Central Union, the Independent Democratic Union and National Renewal.

Other Parties

Christian Social Movement (*Movimiento Social Cristiano*, MSC), led by Juan de Dios Carmona.

Left Broad Force Party (*Partido Fuerza Amplia de Izquierda*, PFAI) led by Eugenio Pizarro.

Republican Party (*Partido Republicano*, PR), led by Gabrielle Léon Echaiz.

Socialist People's Movement Party (*Partido Movimiento Pueblo Socialista*, PMPS), led by Eduardo Gutierrez.

Socialist Recuperation Movement (*Movimiento de Recuperación Socialista*, MRS), led by Mario Palestro.

Unitary Pinochetist Action (*Accíon Pinochetista Unitaria*, APU), led by Gonzalo Townsend Pinochet.

China

Capital: Beijing

Population: 1,200,000,000 (1995E)

The People's Republic of China (PRC) was proclaimed in 1949 on the victory of Mao Zedong's Communist Party of China (CPC) in a long civil war with Chiang Kai-shek's Nationalists. The first three PRC constitutions were promulgated in 1954, 1975 and 1978, the second and third specifically enshrining the leading role of the CPC. The 1982 constitution, the PRC's fourth and currently in force, describes China as "a socialist state under the people's democratic dictatorship led by the working class". It makes no reference to the role of the CPC in its main articles, although its preamble asserts that the Chinese people are "under the leadership of the CPC and the guidance of Marxism-Leninism and Mao Zedong Thought". The preamble also makes reference to "a broad patriotic united front" headed by the CPC and "composed of democratic parties and organizations", eight such parties being in nominal existence within this front, which is manifest in the China People's Political Consultative Conference (CPPCC). Legislative authority is vested in the unicameral National People's Congress (*Qanguo Renmin Daibiao Dahui*), whose members are indirectly elected for a five-year term by the people's congresses of China's 22 provinces, five autonomous regions and three municipalities (themselves elected by all citizens aged 18 and over) and by the People's Liberation Army (PLA). All candidates are approved by the CPC but are not necessarily party members. The National People's Congress (NPC) meets annually, legislative authority being exercised in the interim by a 155–member Standing Committee elected by the NPC. Executive authority is vested in a State Council (government) elected by the NPC, which also elects the President and Vice-President of the PRC for a concurrent five-year term. All effective power, however, resides in the leadership bodies of the CPC. Elections to the eighth NPC were held in early 1993 and resulted in the return of 2,977 deputies approved by the CPC.

Communist Party of China (CPC)

Zhongguo Gongchan Dang

Address. CPC Central Committee, Beijing

Leadership. Jiang Zemin (general secretary), Hu Jintao, Li Peng, Li Ruihuan, Gen. Liu Huaqing, Qiao Shi, Zhu Rongji (other members of politburo standing committee)

According to its authorized history, the CPC was founded in 1921 at a congress in Shanghai attended by a dozen delegates (among them Mao Zedong) from Marxist groups with a total membership of 57. Independent accounts say that the inaugural congress took place a year earlier but was expunged from later official histories because one of the founders (Zhang Shenfu) was rapidly expelled from the party. The accounts agree that soon after the Shanghai congress Chinese students in France (among them Zhou Enlai) formed a communist party and that, in China, Chen Duxiu became general secretary of the new party. The CPC's first programme advocated "science and democracy", the nurturing of Chinese culture and the abolition of feudalism. Party membership rose to 1,000 by 1925 and to 58,000 by 1927. Among its sources of support was the patriotic May 4 Movement, which had originated in Chinese outrage at the 1919 transfer of the leased port of Qingdao from Germany to Japan. Inspired by the 1919 Bolshevik Revolution, the CPC followed Soviet instructions to co-operate with the Nationalist government (headed by Chiang Kai-chek from 1925) and to infiltrate the ruling *Kuomintang* (KMT) party organization. Elected a politburo member in 1924, Mao took charge of the CPC peasant department in 1926 and advanced the then controversial thesis that the key revolutionary force in China was the poor peasantry not the (then small) industrial proletariat.

In 1927 Chiang broke with his increasingly numerous CPC allies, thousands of whom were massacred in Shanghai by Nationalist forces. A period of confusion followed, in which Chen Duxiu was replaced as CPC general secretary by Qu Qiubai and then by Li Lisan. Mao was sent to Hunan to organize a peasant revolt, but the "autumn peasant uprising" was a failure and Mao lost his seat on the politburo. He and about 1,000 followers nevertheless set up headquarters in

mountains on the Hunan-Jiangxi border, where he was joined in 1928 by Zhu De, who had lately headed an uprising in Nanchang and was to become the outstanding Communist military leader of the revolutionary period. From this base the Communists took control of most of Jiangxi and of large parts of Hunan and Fujian, where a Chinese Soviet Republic (CSR) was established in 1931 under the leadership of Mao and Zhu De. Meanwhile, Li Lisan had been removed from the CPC leadership in 1930 and Mao's belief in the revolutionary potential of the peasantry had begun to gain acceptance. The CPC central committee, which had been operating underground in Shanghai, joined Mao in Jiangxi in 1931, after which the CSR declared war on Japan in light of its invasion of Manchuria. Policy differences resulted in Mao's removal from his military and political posts in 1932–34, as KMT forces mounted a series of offensives against the Communists. The fifth such onslaught, involving some 900,000 troops, compelled the Communists to evacuate Jiangxi in October 1934 and to start out on their Long March to the remote north-west. During the march a conference at Zunyi (Guizhou province) in January 1935 elected Mao as chairman of the CPC military affairs committee (and thus effective party leader) and Zhang Wentian as general secretary. After a 6,000–mile trek, only 4,000 of the 86,000 people who had set out on the Long March reached Shaanxi and established new headquarters at Yanan.

In 1937 a revolt among his own followers impelled Chiang to enter into an alliance with the Communists to resist Japanese aggression. This broke down in the early 1940s, when KMT troops began attacking CPC units. From then on Chiang combined passive resistance to the Japanese with military operations against the Communists, who by 1944 were holding down two-thirds of the Japanese occupation forces. By 1945 the Communists controlled a large area of rural northern China and had some 900,000 regulars and over 2 million militia under arms, facing 4 million KMT troops holding all the main towns. The seventh CPC congress, held at Yenan in 1945, elected Mao as central committee chairman, adopted a new constitution embracing Mao Zedong Thought and noted that party membership had risen to 1,210,000. Under Moscow's instruction to come to terms with the KMT, Mao solicited US support for the formation of a post-war coalition government, but Chiang had Washington's ear. Renewed civil war broke out in 1946. Numerical superiority gave the KMT the advantage at first, but the tide turned in 1948 and Communist forces gained control of most of China in 1949. The People's Republic of China (PRC) was proclaimed by the CPC in Beijing on Oct. 1, 1949, with Mao as Chairman (President) and Zhou Enlai as Prime Minister of a nominal coalition government including some small non-communist parties (see below).

The new regime was confronted by an economy ruined by years of war, its problems soon being exacerbated by China's involvement in the Korean War of 1950–53. Communist China was therefore dependent for some years on Soviet economic and military aid, its first five-year plan (1953–57) being concentrated on the development of heavy industry. From 1955, however, Mao set out to develop a distinctively Chinese form of socialism, pushing through the collectivization of agriculture in 1955 and the transfer of private enterprises to joint state-private ownership in 1956. Following Khrushchev's denunciation of Stalin at the 20th Soviet party congress in 1956, the eighth CPC congress the same year approved the deletion of references to Mao Zedong Thought from the party constitution. It also revived the post of general secretary (vacant since 1937), to which Deng Xiaoping was elected, and created a new five-member standing committee of the CPC politburo (the first members being Mao, Deng, Zhu, Liu Shaoqi and Chen Yun). Party membership was reported to the congress as 10,734,385. Mao had by then enunciated the slogan "Let 100 flowers bloom, let 100 schools of thought contend", which he developed in 1957 by launching a "rectification campaign" in which the people were encouraged to criticize government and party officials. The response was so great that the campaign was changed into one against "rightists" (defined as critics of the regime). The non-communist ministers were dropped from the government.

In 1958 the CPC launched China on the Great Leap Forward, a grandiose attempt to develop Chinese socialism at high speed. Industrial and agricultural targets were repeatedly raised, agricultural co-operatives were grouped into large communes that also undertook small-scale manufacturing, and over 2 million "backyard furnaces" were set up for the local production of iron and steel. This policy quickly led to economic and political crisis. A CPC central committee meeting in December 1958 adopted a critical

resolution and Mao was forced to yield the PRC chairmanship to Liu Shaoqi in April 1959. A concurrent deterioration in relations with the USSR, mainly over ideological questions but also involving territorial issues, resulted in the termination of Soviet aid in 1960 and the onset of the Sino-Soviet dispute. This became official when the CPC broke off relations with the Soviet Communist Party in 1966, after which the only ruling Communist party to back China was that of Albania. Meanwhile, a series of disastrous harvests in the early 1960s had caused mass starvation and had impelled Deng and Liu not only to allow peasants to cultivate private plots but also to introduce bonuses and incentives in the industrial sector.

Regarding such policies as leading to a restoration of capitalism, or at least to Soviet-style revisionism, Mao in 1962 enunciated the slogan "Don't forget the class struggle". He was supported by Marshal Lin Biao, the Defence Minister, who promoted the study of Mao Zedong Thought in the army and in 1964 published a compendium of the leader's ideas in the famous *Little Red Book*. Opposition in the CPC leadership remained strong, however, and in October 1965 Mao moved from Beijing to Shanghai, which became his base for the campaign which became known as the Cultural Revolution. With army backing, he forced the CPC politburo, meeting in Shanghai on May 16, 1966, to issue a circular calling for a purge of "those representatives of the bourgeoisie who have sneaked into the party, the government, the army and various spheres of culture". Demonstrations against such elements began at Beijing University the same month, followed by the formation of Red Guard units of students and schoolchildren, who terrorized anyone suspected of bourgeois tendencies. Returning to Beijing, Mao presided over a CPC central committee meeting on Aug. 1–12, 1966, which issued instructions for the conduct of the Cultural Revolution. On Aug. 18 Mao and Marshal Lin (by now second in the party hierarchy) reviewed a parade over more than a million Red Guards in the capital. They received support from Zhou, who nevertheless endeavoured to moderate the excesses into which the Cultural Revolution quickly descended.

Having generated much public uneasiness, in 1967 the Red Guards were replaced as the main agents of the Cultural Revolution by the Revolutionary Rebels, consisting of adult workers. Pitched battles between rival factions followed in many parts of China, producing a state of virtual anarchy and obliging Mao to fall back on the support of the army. The party and government disintegrated, as almost all the leading members came under attack and were replaced.

The most virulent campaign was directed against Liu Shaoqi (the "number one capitalist roader"), who was removed from the chairmanship of the PRC in 1968 (the post being left vacant), expelled from the party and put in prison, where he died in 1969. Also purged was Deng Xiaoping ("number two capitalist roader"), whose post of general secretary was abolished by the 9th CPC congress in 1969. At that congress Marshal Lin became Mao's designated successor, Mao Zedong Thought was reinstated in the party constitution and a new politburo was elected dominated by Lin's military associates and recently-promoted politicians. But the new leadership was soon split on foreign policy questions. In light of the deepening Sino-Soviet rift, Mao and Zhou favoured détente with the USA; but this policy was opposed by Lin, whose supporters began to plan a coup. After the announcement in July 1971 that President Nixon would visit China in 1972, Mao again withdrew to Shanghai to rally support. When he returned to Beijing, Lin fled the country in September 1971 and was killed when his plane crashed or was shot down in Mongolia, whereupon his supporters on the CPC politburo were arrested.

Mao's failing health in his last years obliged him to live in seclusion. He presided over the 10th CPC congress in 1973 but apparently took no part in its deliberations, which ushered in a new power struggle between the moderates led by Zhou and the extremist "gang of four" politburo members headed by Mao's fourth wife, former actress Jiang Qing, who had the advantage of being able to claim that Mao supported them. Zhou secured the rehabilitation of many of those disgraced during the Cultural Revolution, including Deng, who became a Deputy Premier in 1973 and was readmitted to the CPC politburo in 1974. Zhou died in January 1976, however, and was succeeded as Prime Minister by Hua Guofeng, who took an anti-moderate line, assisted by serious disturbances in Beijing on April 5, 1976, that were labelled "counter-revolutionary". Later that month Deng was again removed from all his offices, accused of being an "unrepentant capitalist roader". Meanwhile, the CPC had begun propagating a new view of international relations called the Three Worlds Theory, rejecting the division of states into first (capitalist), second (socialist) and third (developing) worlds. Instead, the CPC advanced the notion that the two superpowers jointly formed one world (and were the main threat to peace), the other industrialized countries (both capitalist and socialist) a second world trying to free themselves from US or Soviet domination, and the developing countries of Asia, Africa and Latin America (including China) a third world which should seek alliance with the second against the first. This theory found little favour among pro-Chinese Communist parties, however, and was specifically rejected by the Albanian party.

Following Mao's death in September 1976 (at the age of 82), Hua Guofeng took over as CPC chairman (and chairman of the central military commission) and turned against the radicals. The "gang of four" and their supporters were arrested in October 1976 on charges of plotting to seize power and in July 1977 Deng was again rehabilitated to his former party and government posts. A massive campaign was launched against the alleged misdeeds of the "gang of four", of whom Jiang Qing and one other were, in 1981, sentenced to death and the other two to long prison sentences, as were six former associates of Lin Biao. (The executions were not carried out, and Jiang committed suicide in 1991.) Under Deng's influence, the theories and practices of the Great Leap Forward and the Cultural Revolution were gradually abandoned and earlier critiques of revisionism were admitted to be incorrect. The communes were dismantled and land was allocated to households on a contract basis. Central economic planning was relaxed and wages were related more closely to output. The formation of small private enterprises was encouraged and former capitalists' confiscated property was restored to them. Loans were accepted from external sources and foreign investment in joint enterprises was permitted. However, Deng defined the limits to change in his Four Principles of early 1979, requiring the China to keep to the socialist road, uphold the people's democratic dictatorship, maintain the CPC's leading role and stay true to Marxism-Leninism and Mao Zedong Thought. Thus Deng broke with the radical pro-democracy April 5 Movement (named after the 1976 clashes in Beijing), the better to deal with opposition to his reforms from the politburo conservatives headed by Hua.

The power struggle between Hua and Deng culminated in the former's replacement as Prime Minister in September 1980 and as CPC chairman in June 1981, respectively by Zhao Ziyang and Hu Yaobang, both Deng associates who had been disgraced during the Cultural Revolution. Deng himself became chairman of the powerful CPC central military commission (as well as a member of the politburo's standing committee). In this phase some 100,000 people disgraced after 1957 were rehabilitated, many of them posthumously (including Liu Shaoqi), and a 1981 central committee resolution condemned most of Mao's post-1957 policies, while conceding that his contribution to the revolution had outweighed his mistakes. The 12th CPC congress in September 1982 abolished the post of party chairman, Hu being elected to the strengthened post of general secretary (which had been revived in 1980), while Hua was excluded from the new politburo. A revised CPC constitution retained the reference to Mao Zedong Thought but defined it as representing the distilled wisdom of the party rather than a programme of action. The ascendancy of the reformers was indicated by the adoption of a report by Hu defining the party's "great tasks" as including "an all-round upsurge of the socialist economy". Under the new PRC constitution adopted in December 1982, Li Xiannian (a former close associate of Zhou) was elected to the restored post of President of China in June 1983.

There followed an extensive reorganization and relative rejuvenation of party and government bodies, with many "old guard" figures being replaced by supporters of Deng's pragmatic policies. The economy embarked on a phase of rapid expansion (growing at nearly 10% a year through the 1980s) and its integration into the world system gathered pace. This process was boosted by the signature in September 1984 of an agreement with Britain under which Hong Kong would revert to Chinese sovereignty in 1997 but retain its existing capitalist system for at least 50 years thereafter. Nevertheless, greater reliance on market forces led to increased corruption among party cadres, which in turn aroused popular discontent over the slow pace of political liberalization. Pro-democracy student demonstrations in several cities began in late 1986 and were stamped out only after some delay. Hu Yaobang was forced to resign as CPC general secretary in January 1987, being accused by Deng and others of excessive leniency to the demonstrators, and was replaced by Zhao Ziyang, who embarked on a campaign against "bourgeois liberalization". Zhao was formally confirmed in office at the 13th CPC congress in October-November 1987, when Deng stood down from the politburo's standing committee while retaining the chairmanship of the central military commission. Endeavouring to attune his policies to Deng's thinking, Zhao pushed ahead with economic reform, proposing in mid-1988 that state price controls should be abolished within five years. Although this reform was quickly postponed (so that Zhao was left isolated), popular pressure for political reform, led by intellectuals and focusing on official corruption and rapidly rising prices, gathered impetus in late 1988 and early 1989.

The sudden death in April 1989 of Hu Yaobeng, shortly after he had delivered an impassioned critique of government policy to the CPC politburo, gave renewed impetus to the pro-democracy movement. Demonstrations in Beijing's Tiananmen Square sparked similar protest rallies in other cities, gathering strength in mid-May during an historic visit to Beijing by Mikhail Gorbachev to mark the normalization of Sino-Soviet relations. For the demonstrators, mostly students but also including workers and intellectuals, Gorbachev's reformist policies in the USSR merited emulation in China. The Chinese leadership was at first split on how to deal with the crisis. Zhao favoured a conciliatory approach but lost the argument to the hardliners led by Prime Minister Li Peng. On June 3–4 army units were sent in to clear the square, this being accomplished in bloody fighting which left up to 1,000 demonstrators dead and many thousands injured. Similar crackdowns followed in other parts of China, although on a less violent scale. In the inevitable conservative backlash, Zhao and his supporters were ejected from their politburo and other party posts, the position of CPC general secretary going to Jiang Zemin, hitherto party secretary in Shanghai. He joined a politburo standing committee enlarged to six members, whose dominant figure at that time was Li Peng. Also in the conservative camp was Yang Shangkun, a politburo member who had been elected President of the PRC in April 1988 in succession to Li Xiannian.

At a CPC central committee meeting in October-November 1989 Deng Xiaoping finally vacated the chairmanship of the central military commission, his only remaining post, and was replaced by Jiang Zemin. But he remained the effective leader of the regime as China's "elder statesman", issuing instructions that economic reform should be suspended and an austerity drive launched to curb inflation. In an attempt to revive the political discipline of an earlier age, strident official warnings were issued against "bourgeois liberalization" and students at Beijing University were forced to undergo intensified ideological indoctrination and, in some cases, preliminary military training. In mid-1990 fears of an economic downturn led to a resumption of economic reform, while in 1991 some Zhao supporters were rehabilitated. Nevertheless, on the third anniversary of the Tiananmen Square massacre in June 1992, new regulations were published which placed even tighter restrictions on demonstrations. A 1992 codification of Deng's speeches asserted that the response to the "turmoil" of June 1989 had been correct. Differences persisted, however, as highlighted by the contrast in May-June 1992 between Li Peng's further warning against "bourgeois liberalization" and Jiang Zemin's criticism of "leftists" (i.e. conservatives) for using revolutionary slogans to "confuse the people".

The 14th CPC congress, held in October 1992,

was told that party membership stood at 52 million and elected a central committee (of 189 full and 130 alternate members) on which nearly half the members were new. Jiang was re-elected CPC general secretary (and chairman of the central military commission) and three of the other six members of the standing committee were also re-elected, although a majority of the other politburo members were also new, most of them Dengists. Features of the changes included the party demotion of both President Yang and his half-brother, Yang Baibing, who had been prominent Dengists but were now reportedly seen as an alternative power centre, and the inclusion of only one army representative (Gen. Liu Huaqing) on the new politburo.

Following the indirect election of nearly 3,000 CPC-approved deputies to the eighth National People's Congress (NPC) in early 1993, its first session in March elected Jiang as President of the PRC in succesion to Yang Shangkun. It also re-elected Li Peng as Prime Minister, although his receipt of an unprecedented 330 negative votes indicated strong underlying disapproval of his role in the 1989 events. Jiang thus became the first Chinese leader since Hua Guofeng (in the immediate post-Mao period) to hold the three top posts of party leader, chairmanship of the central military commission and head of state or government. But his designation as "core leader" was not necessarily indicative of dominant influence, the holder of which was not thought likely to emerge until after the death of Deng, in whom ultimate authority still resided. Meanwhile, the broad Dengist line of economic liberalization combined with political conservatism continued to deliver the goods in terms of economic expansion: according to IMF figures issued in March 1993, China had by 1992 become the world's third-largest economy after the USA and Japan. Nevertheless, concern about inflation and other negative phenomena continued to generate strains within the leadership, highlighted by regular switches of economic policy priorities in 1993-94.

A CPC central committee session in November 1993 adopted a new blueprint for what was termed a "socialist market economic system" and appeared to mark a crucial victory for those favouring rapid economic change. On the other hand, supporters of a centralized economy were boosted by the reappearance in February 1994 of veteran traditionalist Chen Yun (now 88), who called for the strengthening of central party authority. In March 1994 Prime Minister Li Peng told the NPC that a retrenchment plan involving the suspension of price liberalization (first tabled the previous year but quickly shelved) had been revived in the interests of maintaining social stability. A number of draft laws on further progress to a market economy were not put to the vote at the NPC session. In April 1994, moreover, there was a renewed crackdown on prominent dissidents in the run-up to the anniversary of the 1989 events. A session of the CPC central committee in September 1994 resolved that the "extensive and profound social change currently taking place in China" required the party "to do better in upholding and improving democratic centralism". It also approved appointments to the politburo and secretariat which appeared to strengthen the so-called "Shanghai clique" headed by Jiang Zemin and Deputy Premier Zhu Rongji. At the same time, the *People's Daily* (organ of the CPC) began citing the teachings of Confucius—once denounced by the Communists as the creator of Chinese feudalism—on the need for social and political harmony.

Amid ever more explicit reports of the declining health of Deng Xiaoping through 1995, a significant minority of NPC deputies opposed two nominations for vice-premiership posts submitted in March by Jiang Zemin in what was seen as a move to bolster his claim to the succession to Deng as paramount leader. The death of venerated former CPC politburo member Chen Yun in April reduced the ranks of Communist China's "eight immortals" to five, all now in their 80s or 90s. According to Prime Minister Li, the effective political leadership "has already been transferred from Deng Xiaoping, the second-generation leader, to President Jiang Zemin, who represents the third generation of Chinese leadership". In May Jiang launched a campaign against high-level corruption, requiring all state and party officials (and their children in some cases) to declare their incomes from all sources. The following month the authorities instituted a major clampdown on dissidents to coincide with the sixth anniversary of the Tiananmen Square massacre.

A further session of the CPC central committee in September 1995 approved China's ninth five-year plan, envisaging annual growth of 8-9% in 1996-2000 (compared with 11.7% in the eighth plan period), as well a longer-term target of a doubling of GNP between 2000 and 2010. Reports of the meeting indicated that concern about inflation had persuaded the party leadership to modify the previous emphasis on unrestrained growth. Appointments and promotions on the central military commission appeared to strengthen President Jiang's position. although followers of Deng in the People's Liberation Army remained prominent. The session also approved the removal from the CPC politburo of Chen Xitong, who had resigned from the party secretariat in April after being accused of corruption.

Other Parties

Eight other "democratic" parties are permitted to exist in China on the basis of participation in a "united front" with the CPC. Officially they are recognized as having co-operated with the CPC in the "war of resistance" against Japan (1937–45) and in the "war of liberation" against the *Kuomintang* (KMT), and as having played a role, as members of the China People's Political Consultative Conference (CPPCC), in the formulation of the first PRC constitution. Not allowed to operate during the Cultural Revolution, these essentially powerless parties re-emerged in the late 1970s. They are customarily allocated about 7% of the seats in the National People's Congress.

China Association for Promoting Democracy (*Zhongguo Minzhu Cujin Hui*), led by Lei Jieqiong and Chen Yiqun, founded in 1945 to represent literary, cultural and educational personnel, held sixth congress in November 1988, emphasizes importance of education in building a socialist society. *Address.* 98 Xinanli Guloufangzhuangchang, 100009 Beijing

China Democratic League (*Zhongguo Munzhu Tongmeng*), led by Fei Xiaotong and Wu Xiuping, founded in 1941 as the League of Democratic Parties and Organizations of China to unite intellectuals against the KMT, membership drawn from scientific, educational and cultural intellectuals, held sixth congress in October 1988. *Address.* 1 Beixing Dongchang Hutong, 100006 Beijing

China National Democratic Construction Association (*Zhongguo Minzhu Jianguo Hui*), led by Sun Qimeng and Feng Kexu, founded in 1945, membership drawn from industrialists and businessmen, promotes use of advanced technology and strengthened contact with overseas Chinese, held fifth congress in June 1988. *Address.* 93 Beiheyan Dajie, 100006 Beijing

China Party for Public Interests (*Zhongguo Zhi Gong Dang*), led by Dong Yinchu and Wang Songda, founded in San Francisco in 1925, descended from 19th-century secret society for overseas Chinese, advocates "reform and construction under the banner of socialism and patriotism", held ninth congress in December 1988.

Chinese Peasants' and Workers' Democratic Party (*Zhongguo Nonggong Minzhudang*), led by Lu Jiaxi and Zhang Shiming, descended from pre-war movement of anti-Chiang Kai-shek Nationalists who abandoned the objective of a bourgeois republic in 1935 and joined forces with the Communist Party of China, adopted present name in 1947, despite which it is based in the medical and scientific professions, gives priority to health and educational issues.

Revolutionary Committee of the Kuomintang (*Zhongguo Guomindang Geming Weiyuanhui*), led by Zhu Xuefan and Peng Qingyuan, founded in 1948 in Hong Kong by notional KMT members opposed to Chiang Kai-shek, seeks the "peaceful reunification of the motherland", membership drawn from health, finance, culture and education sectors, held seventh congress in November 1988, when it described itself as a "carrying forward Dr Sun Yat-sen's patriotic and revolutionary spirit".

September 3 Society (*Jiu San Xuehui*), founded in 1946 in Sichuan as the Democracy and Science Forum, renamed to commemorate the date of the Japanese surrender in 1945, membership drawn from scientists and technologists, held fifth congress in December 1988–January 1989.

Taiwan Democratic Self-Government League (*Taiwan Minzhu Zizhi Tongmeng*), led by Cai Zimin and Pan Yuanjing, founded in 1947 by pro-PRC Chinese from Taiwan, promotes contacts with Taiwan to further the goal of reunification.

Colombia

Capital: Bogota   **Population:** 35,100,000 (1995E)

The Republic of Colombia gained independence from Spain in 1819 after liberation by the forces of Simón Bolivar and, after several boundary changes, became a Republic in 1886. Until recently Colombian parliamentary politics was dominated by the Liberal Party (CPL) and the Conservative Party (now Social Conservative, PSC), which were both founded in the 1840s. Colombia's only military government this century was overthrown in 1958, when the two rival parties joined forces and formed a National Front coalition government which lasted from 1958 until 1974. The PL and PSC continued to dominate the political system until the general election of May 27, 1990, when other parties came to the fore.

Approved by 90% of the votes cast (26% of registered voters) in a referendum which took place simultaneously with the general election of May 27, 1990, a National Constitutional Assembly was established to revise the constitution of 1886. In December 1990, 70 members were directly elected and three seats were allocated by the government to former guerrilla groups. The Assembly opened on Feb. 5, 1991, and the new constitution came into force at midnight on July 5, 1991.

Executive authority is vested in the President. Under the new constitution new posts of Vice-President, Fiscal General, and Defender of the People were created to assist the President in policy-making. The President is also assisted by a 14-member Cabinet which he appoints. Legislative power is vested in a bicameral Congress, which was reduced to 102 seats in the Senate and 161 in the House of Representatives. Members of Congress cannot hold any other public post. The President was given temporary special legislative powers until a new Congress was installed on Dec. 1, 1991. The indigenous population was given judicial autonomy in minor internal disputes within certain recognized territories.

The President is elected directly for a four-year term by direct universal suffrage and may not serve a second consecutive term. A system of proportional representation operates for the election of members of both houses, who are also elected for a four-year period. The Senate has 99 nationally elected members; indigenous people in specific regions have two appointed senators selected in special elections and one elected senator. Each of the 23 departments, four intendencies and five commissaries (32 states) elects two members of the House of Representatives and further seats are allotted to each state on the basis of population. Governors, under the new constitution, are elected directly in the 27 departments and intendencies.

All Colombian citizens aged 18 or over are eligible to vote, except members of the armed forces on active service, the national police and people who have been deprived of their political rights. Women obtained the vote in 1957.

In legislative elections held on March 13, 1994, the Liberal Party (PL) retained its congressional majority, winning 89 seats in the House of Representatives and 52 in the Senate. The Social Conservative Party (PSC) won 56 seats in the House and 21 in the Senate. In the presidential elections held on May 30, the PL's Ernesto Samper Pizano gained 45.25% of the vote and the PSC's Andres Pastrana Arango gained 44.25%. In a second round of voting on June 19, Samper won with 50.37% of the vote against 48.64% for Pastrana and took office on Aug. 7. Included in his Cabinet were PSC ministers and one from the Alliance for Colombia (AC). The Cabinet was reshuffled in July 1995; all the members of the Cabinet resigned on Dec. 18, 1995 but most were reappointed.

Since the middle of the 19th century the Liberal and Conservative parties have been the leading groupings in Colombian politics. Towards the end of the 1930s the Communist Party began to take shape but failed to gain much support in national elections.

143

Christian Democratic Party

Partido Demócrata Cristiano (PDC)

Address. Avenida 42, No. 18-08, Bogotá

Telephone. (#57-1) 285 6639

Fax. (#57-1) 256 7118

Leadership. Luis Jaime Pabon Mahecha

It was founded in 1964 and was, until 1965, a member of the "United Front", led by the radical priest Fr Camilo Torres, before Torres chose to join the guerrilla struggle. Although electorally the party has been insignificant, the DC has been ideologically influential in Colombian politics.

The DC backed Belisario Betancur Cuartas of the then Conservative Party (see Social Conservative Party) in the presidential elections of 1970, 1978 and 1982 and its own presidential candidate in the 1974 elections came fifth. The party helped to found the Democratic Alliance April 19 Movement (see ADM19) in April 1990 having been banned from participation in the 1986 elections because of fraudulent electoral registration.

The party is the Colombia affiliate of the Christian Democrat International.

Democratic Alliance—April 19 Movement

Alianza Democrática—Movimiento 19 de Abril (AD-M19)

Address. Carrera 7 No. 33-49, Office 1501, Bogotá

Telephone. (#57-1) 342 4251

Fax. (#57-1) 245 4921

Leadership. Antonio Navarro Wolff (1994 presidential candidate); Carlos Alonso Lucio (leader of dissident faction)

Founded in 1973, this left-wing party and former guerrilla group has made a significant mark in Colombian politics with its stand for national independence and social justice and democracy. The M-19 was formed by National Popular Alliance (ANAPO) supporters as the party's armed wing in reaction to the disputed April 19, 1970, election results. The group's ideology was originally an amalgam of Marxism-Leninism and the radical liberal ideas of Jorge Eliécer Graitán (assassinated 1948), which attracted dissident members of the FARC guerrilla group to M-19. As its first public act, M-19 seized Simón Bolívar's sword and spurs in January 1974. ANAPO, which had shifted to the right, disassociated itself from M-19 soon after.

M-19 started its guerrilla activity, involving mainly kidnappings and sabotage of multinational companies, in 1976, with the abduction and killing of a trade union leader whom M-19 suspected of having links with the CIA. In early 1982 the guerrillas suffered heavy losses in counterinsurgency operations and clashes with the new right-wing paramilitary group Death to Kidnappers (MAS). In August 1984, M-19, by now Colombia's most prominent guerrilla group, announced its intention to become a political party.

In May 1988 M-19, in an attempt to force the government to hold peace talks, kidnapped the former PSC presidential candidate Alvaro Gómez Hurtado. The Barco government put forward a peace plan the following September as a result. The M-19 called a unilateral ceasefire, and negotiations began in January 1989. An agreement with the government on reintegration of the M-19 into civilian life was signed on March 17, 1989. The CNGSB subsequently announced that the M-19, having disregarded the agreed guidelines on negotiations, was no longer a member. In October 1989 the M-19 was constituted as a political party and on March 9, 1990, the guerrillas signed a final peace treaty with the government and surrendered their arms. In exchange the government guaranteed the M-19 a general amnesty, full political participation in elections and the holding of a referendum on the question of a new constitution.

In April 1990 the M-19 leader and popular presidential candidate for the newly-formed Democratic Alliance M-19 (ADM19) Carlos Pizarro Leongómez was gunned down, it was thought, at the instigation of the Medellín drugs cartel. He was replaced as candidate in the May presidential elections by Antonio Navarro Wolff who came third with 12.6% of the vote.

The M-19 won the majority of the 19 ADM-19 seats and as leaders of the Constitutional Assembly's largest opposition block made an important contribution to the drawing-up of the Constitution which came into effect in July 1991.

In the municipal elections of March 1992 the party suffered big losses, especially in the capital, Bogotà.

In the first round of presidential balloting on May 30, 1994, Navarro Wolff was again well beaten with a meagre 3.8% of the vote. Recently, a dissident faction, led by Carlos Alonso Lucio, a former guerrilla commando, has split away from the main party through deep dissatisfaction with the party's abandonment of its former "revolutionary principles".

Liberal Party

Partido Liberal (PL)

Address. Avenida Caracas No. 36-07, Bogotá

Telephone. (#57-1) 287 9740

Fax. (#57-1) 287 9740

Leadership. Emilio Lébolo (president), José Fernando Bautista (secretary-general)

Founded in the 1840s, the Colombian Liberal Party has been a mainstay of the country's political history. Traditionally centrist, the PL stand for free enterprise and privatisation, a raising of the standard of living and the fighting of drug trafficking.

The Liberal Party emerged from the rise of the American-born Spanish middle-classes influenced by European republican and radical utopian ideas. Although its major founding forces were the political discussion clubs which opposed Simón Bolivar, the PL's classic liberal reforms, such as the abolition of slavery, reduction of church power, decentralization of government, an end to state monopolies and the introduction of freedom of the press, were inspired by the earlier independence movement.

The Liberals and Conservatives agreed on a power-sharing arrangement whereby the presidency would be held by each party in rotation and the Cabinet posts would be divided equally between the two parties. This National Front agreement was approved by a referendum on December 1957 and in the subsequent general election the Liberal candidate, former President Lleras Camargo, became the first National Front President. Even though the parity agreement between the PL and PC officially expired in 1974, the Liberals, who won the elections of 1974 and 1978, continued to award half the Cabinet portfolios to Conservatives.

Liberal governments proved largely ineffective against the illegal drugs trade and the escalating violence which in 1988 alone saw an estimated 18,000 political and drug-cartel-related killings. In the political turmoil of 1989 leading PL members were among victims of the growing spate of assassinations of politicians: on March 3, 1989, the PL leader Ernesto Samper Pizano was seriously injured in an attack by right-wing paramilitaries, in which the Patriotic Union (UP) leader Antequera was killed, and in mid-August the popular leader of the PL's New Liberalism faction, Luis Carlos Galán Sarmiento, who was favoured as the PL's next presidential candidate, was murdered by killers hired by the Medellín or Cali drug barons.

The PL's relatively poor performance in the March 1988 municipal elections, caused by divisions in the party and the government's impotence against drug traffickers and the mounting violence, boded ill for the 1990 congressional elections. Nevertheless, on March 11, 1990, the PL increased their seats in the Senate to 72 and in the House of Representatives to 120. The PL also regained the important mayorships of Medellín and Bogotá which it had lost in 1988. The Liberal victory was crowned in the presidential election of May 17, 1990, when the PL candidate César Gaviria Trujillo won 47% of the vote.

His inauguration pledge to continue his predecessor's campaign against "narco-terrorism" but not his policy of extraditing drug traffickers came to fruition on Oct. 8, when Gaviria issued a decree offering drug barons, who called themselves the *"Extraditables"*, a guarantee that they would not be extradited to the USA if they surrendered to the authorities. Although this was generally seen as a concession to the Medellín cartel, the deal was followed by the surrender of several major drug traffickers and an end to all-out war between the government and the drug cartels. This in turn had the desired effect of stabilizing the country for economic growth. At the end of 1991 Gaviria announced a major investment in infrastructure to assist this trend. The Liberal government also continued the peace initiatives with the country's remaining guerrilla groups and by the time of the opening of the Constitutional Assembly in February 1991, peace agreements with the National Liberation Army (EPL), the Quintín Lame group and the Workers' Revolutionary Party (PRT) had been signed.

In April 1992, Lopez Michelsen resigned as party leader, ushering in a period of internal strife within the party that forced four successive factional leadership changes in a four month period. The PL's successful presidential election candidate, Ernesto Samper came from the party's left-wing faction the *Nuevo Liberaliso*, whereas his running-mate came from the right of the party. He won a marginal victory in the 1994 elections.

The PL is a consultative member of the Socialist International.

National Salvation Movement
Movimiento de Salvación Nacional (MSN)
Leadership. Dr Alvaro Gomez Hurtado (1990 presidential candidate)

The MSN was founded by Álvaro Gómez Hurtado and a splinter group from the Social Conservative Party (PSC) just before the presidential elections of May 27, 1990. Hurtado had been a PSC presidential candidate in 1974 and 1986 and was abducted by the M-19 guerrillas on May 29, 1988, and held for nearly two months as a bargaining tool to bring about peace talks. His split from the PSC to form the MSN seriously weakened his former party, as the presidential election results made clear. Gómez came second with 23.8% of the valid vote, almost twice the vote for the PSC candidate.

In the December 1990 Constitutional Assembly elections the MSN won 11 seats (two more than the PSC) out of the 70 allocated by direct vote. As the third largest party in the Constitutional Assembly, the MSN joined forces with the Democratic Alliance M-19 (ADM-19) against the ruling Liberal Party (PL). In its first legislative election on Oct. 27, 1991, the party again proved to be a major political force, winning five seats in the Senate, 12 in the House of Representative and one governorship. The MSN subsequently obtained the mines and energy portfolio in President Gaviria's Cabinet.

Patriotic Union
Unión Patriótica (UP)
Address. Calle 23 No. 17-51, Bogotá
Telephone. (#57-1) 342 4251
Fax. (#57-1) 281 9287
Leadership. Aida Abella (president)

The UP was formed by extreme left-wing groups including the Communist Party. For a long time it was known as the political arm of the Colombian Revolutionary Armed Forces (FARC), a guerrilla group that has been active in Colombia for over 30 years. The party campaigns for political and trade union liberties as well as agrarian reform.

The Patriotic Union was established by the Communist Party of Colombia (PCC) and other left-wing groups and trade unions in order to integrate the Revolutionary Armed Forces of Colombia (FARC) guerrilla group into Colombia's political system following President Betancur's peace initiative.

On Oct. 11, 1987, the former presidential candidate Pardo Leal was gunned down by right-wing paramilitaries and in early 1989 the UP leader José Antequera became the 928th member to be assassinated since the UP's foundation. The following February Bernardo Jaramillo Ossa, leader of the *Aperturista* faction (which wanted to distance itself from the FARC's armed struggle), was forced to travel to Europe for his personal safety. He returned for the legislative elections on March 11, 1990, in which he won the only UP seat in senate. He was murdered 11 days later at Bogotá airport by a hired gunman suspected to have been in the pay of the Medellín cartel, although the cartel denied involvement.

Jarmillo had brought together the PCC and *Aperturista* faction but soon after his death the *Aperturistas* clashed with the PCC and broke away from the UP to join the Democratic Alliance M-19 (ADM-19). No UP candidate stood in the May 1990 presidential election and in the December elections no UP candidate was elected to the Constitutional Assembly. The party played little part in the discussions leading up to the disbanding of Congress in July 1991 and in the October 1991 congressional elections it won only one seat in the Senate and two in the House of Representatives.

In 1994, with deaths of its members having rising to 2,300 people, the party declined to put forward a presidential candidate because of the potential risks for the candidate. Another leader,

Manuel Cepeda Vargas, who represented both the UP and the Communists in the Senate, was assassinated in August 1994.

Social Conservative Party
Partido Social Conservador (PSC)
Address. Avenida 22 No. 37-09, Bogotá
Telephone. (#57-1) 268 0006
Fax. (#57-1) 269 5354
Leadership. Jaime Arias Ramírez (president)

The conservative orientation of the PSC dates back to its founding in 1849 as the *Partido Conservador*, and has dictated its policies to date. The party stands for law and order and traditional religious values, its doctrine being based upon the encyclicals of the Roman Catholic Church.

The PSC was founded as the Conservative Party (PC) by Mariano Ospina Rodríguez, a leading member of the conservative Popular Societies, and supporters of President José Ignacio Márquez (1837-42). The party drew its members and leaders chiefly from the landed classes and monopoly capitalists. The party originally stood for protectionism and centralised state controlled by the traditional élite, their power being legitimized by the Roman Catholic Church which was given an important role in society.

President Betancur was inaugurated in August 1982 and his administration, hampered by a Liberal-dominated Congress, still managed to pass a variety of social and economic reforms. In November 1982, in an attempt to bring about peace, Betancur announced an amnesty for the country's guerrilla groups and in mid-1984 secured agreement for a year-long ceasefire with three groups, the Revolutionary Armed Forces of Colombia, the National Liberation Army and the April 19 Movement (M-19).

However this first step towards reconciliation with the country's guerrilla groups was quickly overshadowed by an escalating war with the powerful drug cartels. After the murder of Justice Minister Rodrigo Lara Bonilla in May 1984, Betancur imposed a state of siege and in November of the following year, with the internal situation rapidly deteriorating, he declared a state of economic and social emergency. In the subsequent congressional elections of March 9, 1986, and the presidential elections on May 25, the PC was defeated by its old rival, the PL, its seats in the Senate reduced to 45 and in the House of Representatives to 82.

In 1987 the PC changed its name to the current Social Conservative Party. The new PSC won 415 municipalities, only 12 fewer than the PL, in the March 1988 municipal elections, and defeated the PL in the important cities of Bogotá and Medellín. In late May 1988 the former presidential candidate Alvaro Gómez Hurtado, was abducted by the M-19 group for two months, which caused widespread protests against the government and demands for his release.

Gómez subsequently broke with the PSC in 1990 to form the National Salvation Movement (MSN), a move which greatly damaged the party. In the general election of March 11, 1990, the PSC came second with 41 seats in the Senate, and in the presidential elections of May 27 Rodrigo Lloreda Caicedo, the party's presidential candidate, came only fourth with 12.2% of the vote. In August 1990 President Gaviria appointed three PSC members to his new "national unity" Cabinet.

In 1994, the PSC's presidential candidate Andrés Pastrana Arango lost to Ernesto Samper of the PL by less than one percentage point in the second round of voting.

Other Parties

There are other legally active movements which fail however to gain any great support from the electorate. Although under the Colombian constitution these groups are free to act politically, very often they have not met minimum electoral requirements such as obtaining a certain number of votes in a previous election (more than 50,000). Thus in many cases they do not receive recognition from the National Electoral Council as political parties or movements.

Communist Party of Colombia

Partido Comunista de Colombia (PCC)

Address. Carrera 34, 9-28 Apartado Aéreo, 8886 Bogotá

Telephone. (#57-1) 334-1947

Fax. (#57-1) 281-8259

Leadership. Alvaro Vasquez del Real (general secretary)

Founded in 1930, the PCC is really communist in name only being a predominantly reformist party which campaigns for free social services, agrarian reform and nationalisation of the oil and gas industries.

The party originates in the Communist Group, later called the Socialist Revolutionary Party, which disbanded in 1930. The PCC became very active in peasants' land seizures and in dockers' and plantation workers' unions, and PCC candidates held seats in Congress under the Liberal (PL) governments of 1934-38 and 1942-45.

In 1985 the PCC became the main force behind the formation of the Patriotic Union (UP) which was set up in response to President Betancur's peace proposals to Colombia's guerrilla groups. The PCC has since operated with the UP as one, and following the UP's electoral successes, PCC members suffered increased repression. By 1987 the PCC claimed that some 500 of its members had been killed. Two central committee members (and UP leaders) were assassinated in early 1989: Téofilio Forero on Jan. 27 and José Antequera on March 3. The latter killing was claimed by the right-wing Death to Kidnappers (MAS) group and was suspected to be a retaliation for the killing a few days earlier of drug trafficker and "emerald king" Gilberto Molina.

In August 1992, the PCC was one of ten parties stripped of legal standing because of a failure to obtain more than 50,000 votes at the October 1991 election.

Hope, Peace and Liberty

Esperanza, Paz y Libertad (EPL)

Leadership. Bernardo Gutierrez Zuluaga (president)

Re-founded in March, 1991.

The EPL was formerly the guerrilla Popular Liberation Army (also EPL), founded in 1969 by the Communist Party of Colombia—Marxist-Leninist to conduct a "people's war". In August 1984, the EPL was one of the guerrilla groups to sign an initial one-year ceasefire agreement with the government, although some factions continued to clash with the army. The EPL did not join other guerrilla groups in the formation of the Simón Bolívar National Guerrilla Co-ordinating Board (CNGSB) after the peace plan broke down in 1985, but officially maintained the truce until November 1985, when a right-wing paramilitary group killed the EPL leader Oscar William Calvo.

In March 1989 the EPL, following the example of the M-19, agreed to hold peace talks with the government, and in the months of exploratory talks which followed, the guerrillas kept a unilateral ceasefire.

The truce came to an end in mid-November after an army raid on the EPL's main camp in which EPL commander Arnulfo Jiménez and 30 other guerrillas were killed. In February 1990, with elections due in March and May, the EPL announced a unilateral ceasefire. As a first step in demobilization the EPL congregated in the "neutral zone" of the northern coastal locality of Necoclí in mid-June. The group finally disbanded and reformed as a political party in March 1991 after signing a peace pact with the government in late January.

Humberto Javier Callegas Rúa, the second ranked dissident leader, was captured by police in on Jan. 2, 1993. The party's leader, Zuluaga, had a brief flirtation with the AD-M19 in late 1991 but returned to the EPL after a dispute with Navarro Wolff in September, 1993.

Metapolitical Unitarian Movement
Movimiento Unitario Metapolítico (MUP)
   Address. 60d-40 Calle 13, Santa Fe de Bogotá, DC
   Telephone. (#57-1) 292-1330
   Fax. (#57-1) 292-5502
   Leadership. Regina Betancourt de Liska (president)
   The MUP was founded in 1985 and its philosophy is what can best be described as a 'populist occult party. It won one seat in the October 1991 congressional elections, taken up by its leader, Regina Betancourt de Liska. In 1992, she proceeded to speak an incantation over the finance minister to prevent the progress of an unpopular finance bill.

National Restoration Movement
Movimiento de Restauración Nacional (MORENA)
   Leadership. Iván Roberto Duque (president)
   An extreme right-wing group founded in July 1989 with the assistance of the Association of Peasants and Ranchers (ACDEGAM) of the Middle Magdalena valley drug region which had been promoting paramilitary attacks on left-wing politicians, trade unionists and peasant organizers since 1983. MORENA is said also to have links with the Medellín cartel.

Socialist Workers' Party
Partido Socialista de los Trabajadores (PST)
   Leadership. María Socorro Ramirez (1978 presidential candidate)
   The party was founded in 1977 by members of the former *Bloque Socialista*. It has a very small national following and lost its mandate following a poor showing in the 1991 elections. At these elections the PST campaigned against the high cost of getting onto the electoral list.

Minor Parties

Christian National Party (*Partido Nacional Cristiano*, PNC), won one seat in the Senate in the October, 1991, congressional elections.

Movement for Workers' Self-Defence (*Movimiento de Autodefensa Obrera*, MAO), led by Adelaida Abadia Rey, this radical, and sometimes violent, Trotskyite party was founded in 1978.

National Conservative Movement (*Movimiento Nacional Conservador*, MNC), also won one seat in the Senate in the October, 1991, congressional elections.

National Progressive Movement (*Movimiento Nacional Progresista*, MNP) won one seat in the 1991 Senate elections.

United Movement for Colombia (*Movimiento Unidos por Colombia*, MUPC), achieved only one seat in the 1991 Senate elections.

Illegal Organizations

Simón Bolívar National Guerrilla Co-ordinating Board
Coordinadora Nacional Guerrillera Simón Bolívar (CNGSB)
   Leadership. Manuel Pérez (ELN); Manuel Marulanda Vélez (FARN)
   Founded in 1985, the CNGSB is a left-wing alliance of guerrilla groups whose demands include the dismantling of right-wing paramilitary groups, the democratization of economic policy, more regard for human rights and freedom of movement for all CNGSB members.
   The guerrilla alliance was formed by the M-19, Quintín Lame, and the Ricardo Franco Commando (which was expelled soon after) as the Guerrilla Co-ordinating Board (CNG). The aim behind the formation of the CNG was not only to co-ordinate Colombia's left-wing guerrilla groups, but also to co-operate in a united front with other Latin American guerrillas. In 1986 the CNG formed links with groups from Panama and Venezuela and participated in operations with the Ecuadorian "Alfaro Vive, Carajo!" and the Tupac Amaru Revolutionary Movement (MRTA) under the name Battalón América (American Battalion).
   To coincide with the opening of the Constitutional Assembly in early February 1991, the CNGSB launched a major country-side offensive with attacks on infrastructure and direct clashes with the army. By Feb. 20 the government had agreed to exploratory peace talks with the CNGSB, with a view to encouraging the guerrillas to give up arms and enter civilian life without losing face. There were still no conclusive results to these talks as of mid-1996.
   The main members of the CNGSB alliance are as follows:

Colombia Revolutionary Armed Forces
Fuerzas Armadas Revolucionarias de Colombia (FARC)
   Leadership. Manuel Marulanda Vélez; Alfonso Cano (second-in-command)
   Originally founded in 1949, the left-wing FARC is the oldest Latin America guerrilla group.
   It was founded by the peasant leader and member of the Communist Party of Colombia (PCC) central committee Fermin Charry Rincón, as the defence force of the Republic of Gaitania (an occupied area of approximately 2,000 square miles in the high Andes south of Bogotá).
   After the invasion of the territory by the Colombian army in 1964, the independent

republic's armed forces re-formed as a guerrilla force. The group, led by the PCC central committee member Manuel Marulanda, alias *Tirofijo* ("Sharpshooter"), since Charry's death in 1960, was officially recognized and given its present name by the PCC at its 1966 party congress.

A political party, the Patriotic Union (UP), was founded in 1985 by the PCC and other groups as a vehicle for the FARC's integration into the mainstream politics. The peace effort, however, was undermined by continuing army operations against the FARC and escalating assassinations of UP leaders by right-wing death squads which in October 1987 led to the FARC's joining the Simón Bolívar Guerrilla Co-ordinating Board (CNGSB).

In December 1988 the FARC declared a unilateral ceasefire (which they were accused of using to rearm) and in March 1989, together with other CNGSB groups, announced its willingness to hold peace talks.

In January, 1995, the group claimed that more talks with the government were on the way but nothing has as yet been forthcoming.

National Liberation Army

Ejército de Liberación Nacional (ELN)

Leadership. Manuel Pérez (alias "Poliarco"); Gerardo Bermudez (alias Francisco Gálan; in prison)

Founded in 1964, the ELN was once one of the major militant groups in the country. It was formed by Fabio Vásquez Castaño and was officially named the Unión Camilista-ELN after the radical priest, Camilo Torres who was killed in action a month after joining the ELN in 1966.

Since the integration of the former guerrilla groups, the M-19, Quintín Lame and the PRT, into mainstream politics, the ELN has mainly worked in conjunction with the FARC in both CNGSB operations and peace negotiations. In September 1991 a group split away from the ELN to form the Socialist Renewal Movement, in an attempt to negotiate a return to civilian life.

A breakaway from the group, the **Socialist Renovation Current**, eventually agreed a peace agreement with the government in early 1994 following a spate of military attacks on the ELN resulting in the deaths of some 200 of its members.

Comoros

Capital: Moroni   **Population:** 600,000 (1995E)

The Federal Islamic Republic of the Comoros (where the population is mostly Sunni Muslim) achieved independence from France in 1975. It later became a one-party state under the Comoran Union for Progress (UCP or UDZIMA) but moved to a multi-party system in 1989–92. Following an all-party national conference, a new constitution was approved by referendum in June 1992. It provides for an executive President, who is directly elected for a six-year term by universal suffrage of those aged 18 and over and who appoints the Prime Minister and government. Legislative authority is vested in a bicameral parliament consisting of a 42–member Federal Assembly (*Assemblée Fédérale*) as the lower house, which is directly elected for a four-year term in two rounds of voting, and a 15–member Senate (*Sénat*) as the upper house, chosen by an electoral college for a six-year term.

A presidential election on March 4 and 11, 1990, resulted in Saïd Mohamed Djohar (as candidate of the UCP/UDZIMA) being re-elected in the second round with 55.1% of the vote. The bulk of the UCP/UDZIMA became the Rally for Democracy and Renewal (RDR) prior to Federal Assembly elections on Dec. 12 and 20, 1993 (and repeat polling in eight constituencies on Dec. 26), which resulted as follows: RDR 24 seats; National Union for Democracy and Progress (UNDP) and allies 18. The UNDP parties subsequently formed the Forum for National Recovery (FRN).

An attempted coup in September 1995 raised question-marks over the position of President Djohar, who based himself in the French island of Réunion until, in January 1996, it was agreed that he would return to Moroni, assume a "symbolic" role as head of state and be effectively excluded from seeking a further presidential term by dint of an agreement that candidates should be aged between 40 and 70. In a presidential election on March 9 and 16, 1996, Mohamed Taki Abdoulkarim of the National Union for Democracy in the Comoros (UNDC) was elected with nearly two-thirds of the second-round vote.

Forum for National Recovery

Forum pour le Redressement National (FRN)
    Address. c/o Assemblée Fédérale, Moroni
    Leadership. Abbas Djoussouf (spokesman),
Saïd Hassan Saïd Hachim (parliamentary leader)

The FRN was created as an opposition alliance
in January 1994, a month after Assembly elections
in which the presidential Rally for Democracy and
Renewal (RDR) had won a substantial majority.
Five of the FRN parties had hitherto comprised
the National Union for Democracy and Progress
(*Union Nationale pour la Démocratie et le Progrès*,
UNDP), namely: the oppositon rump of the
Comoran Union for Progress (*Union Comorienne
pour le Progrès*, UCP or UDZIMA) led by Omar
Tamou; the Movement for Renovation and
Democratic Action (*Mouvement pour la Rénova-
tion et l'Action Démocratique*, MOURAD) led by
Abdou Issa; the National Union for Democracy
in the Comoros (UNDC) led by Mohamed Taki
Abdoulkarim (who later broke away from the
FRN); the Rally for Change and Democracy
(*Rassemblement pour le Changement et la Démocra-
tie*, RACHADE) led by Saïd Ali Youssouf; and
the Socialist Party of the Comoros (*Parti Socialiste des Comores*, PASOCO) led by Ali Idarousse.

Other participants in the FRN included the
Comoran Party for Democracy and Progress
(*Parti Comorien pour la Démocratie et le Progrès*,
PCDP) led by Ali Mroudjae and Abdou Soefou;
the Comoran Popular Front (*Front Populaire
Comorien*, FPC), also known as the Mohéli
Popular Front (*Front Populaire Mohélien*, FPM),
led by Mohamed Hassanali and Abdou Mous-
takim; the Democratic Front of the Comoros
(*Front Démocratique des Comores*, FDC) led by
Moustapha Saïd Cheikh; the Movement for
Democracy and Progress (*Mouvement pour la
Démocratie et le Progrès*, MDP), also known as
the Popular Democratic Movement (*Mouvement
Démocratique Populaire*, MDP), led by Abbas
Djoussouf; the National Salvation Party (*Parti du
Salut National*, PSN); and a splinter group of
RACHADE, called RACHADE R, led by Saïd
Hassan Saïd Hachim, who became Assembly
leader of the FRN.

The UCP/UDZIMA had been founded as the
sole government party in 1982 under President
Ahmed Abdullah Abderrahman and had been
inherited in 1989 by his successor, Saïd Mohamed
Djohar. Having backed the latter's successful
re-election campaign in 1990, the party became
increasingly estranged from Djohar and went into
opposition in 1991 in protest against the formation of a coalition government as a prelude to the
move to multi-partyism. The UCP/UDZIMA
participated in the national conference of early
1992 but opposed the resultant constitution and

did not contest the October 1992 Assembly elections, in part because its leaders had been
implicated in a coup attempt the previous month.

Of the other FRN participants, RACHADE
was founded in December 1990 by UDC/
UDZIMA dissidents, joined the coalition government formed in 1992 and approved the new
constitution, although it later called for President
Djohar's resignation. The PCDP also derived from
the UDC/UDZIMA, Ali Mroudjae having held
high government office under both Abdullah and
Djohar; standing for his new party in the March
1990 presidential elections, Mroudjae came fourth
and in 1991 took the PCDP into the opposition
camp. The FPC leader had also contested the 1990
presidential elections, subsequently joining the
transitional government of 1992 and backing the
new constitution, as did the FDC, whose leader
had previously been imprisoned for alleged
involvement in a 1985 coup attempt and had also
stood for the presidency in 1990. The MDP also
backed the 1992 constitution and joined the
interim government, its leader having been another
unsuccessful presidential contender in 1990; it
polled strongly in the November 1992 Assembly
elections and was the largest single party at the
dissolution in June 1993. The Islamist PSN won
one seat in the 1992 elections and became alienated from Djohar by the growing influence of the
President's son-in-law, Mohamed Saïd Abdullah
M'Changama.

The UNDC-led alliance won 18 of the 42
Assembly seats in the December 1993 Assembly
elections, the official outcome of which was
described as a "masquerade" by the opposition.
Contesting the results and the resultant appointment of an RDR Prime Minister, the opposition
parties nevertheless acknowledged that their divisions had assisted what they described as Djohar's
"political coup" and the "brutal interruption of
the transition to democracy". They therefore
agreed in January 1994 to form the FRN as a focus
of joint opposition.

Following an abortive coup by rebel soldiers and
mercenaries in September 1995, the FRN accepted
representation in a new "unity" government
announced in early November. However, in
presidential elections in March 1996 Abbas
Djoussouf, as FRN candidate, was easily defeated
by Taki Abdoulkarim of the UNDC.

Islands' Fraternity and Unity Party

*Chama cha Upvamodja na Mugnagna wa
Massiwa (CHUMA)*
    Leadership. Prince Saïd Ali Kemal (president),
Sy Mohamed Nacer-Eddine (secretary-general)

CHUMA was founded in the late 1980s as an
anti-Abdullah "patriotic alliance" of exiled groups
under the leadership of Kemal, grandson of the

last Sultan of the Comoros. He took third place in the first round of the March 1990 presidential elections (with 13.7% of the vote) and backed Djohar in the second, being rewarded with a cabinet post. CHUMA was also a member of the interim government formed in 1992 and endorsed the new constitution.

National Union for Democracy in the Comoros
Union Nationale pour la Démocratie aux Comores (UNDC)

Address. c/o President's Office, Moroni

Leadership. Mohamed Taki Abdoulkarim (chair), Mouni Madi (secretary-general)

The UNDC was founded in exile by Taki Abdoulkarim, who had been runner-up to Djohar in the March 1990 presidential elections with 44.9% of the second-round vote but had then returned to exile after being implicated in a coup attempt. In 1992 he was successively appointed "co-ordinator" and then Prime Minister of an interim coalition government, until being dismissed in July and going into hiding during the November 1992 Assembly elections, which the UNDC boycotted. It formed part of the opposition National Union for Democracy and Progress in the December 1993 Assembly elections and then of the opposition Forum for National Recovery (FRN). Following the September 1995 coup attempt, however, Taki Abdoulkarim opted to stand as UNDC candidate in the March 1996 presidential election, on a traditionalist Islamic and nationalist platform. Successfully depicting his principal FRN opponent as the candidate of France, he was elected with nearly two-thirds of the second-round vote and appointed a government which included representatives of the UCP/UDZIMA component of the FRN. Once elected, President Taki made it clear that the existing defence agreement with France would not only be maintained but possibly enhanced to allow for a permanent French military presence in the Comoros. He also promised to submit a new constitution for popular endorsement and to call new parliamentary elections in 1996.

Rally for Democracy and Renewal
Rassemblement pour la Démocratie et le Renouveau (RDR)

Address. c/o Federal Assembly, Moroni

Leadership. Mohamed Abdou Madi (secretary-general)

The RDR was created immediately prior to the December 1993 elections as a political vehicle for President Djohar. The latter had come to power in 1989 following the assassination of President Ahmed Abdullah Abderrahman and had inherited the latter's one-party regime of the Comoran

Union for Progress (UCP or UDZIMA). He had nevertheless permitted opposition candidates to contest the March 1990 presidential elections, in which he was the comfortable second-round victor with the official backing of the UCP/UDZIMA. On the formal move to multi-partyism in 1991–92, the UCP/UDZIMA ceased to be the government party. In Assembly elections in November 1992 Djohar backed the Union for Democracy and Development but there was no clear overall majority. After a period of political instability, the President dissolved the Assembly in June 1993 and new elections were eventually held in December. For these the RDR was created as a merger of the *Mwangaza* party (headed by the President's controversial son-in-law, Mohamed Saïd Abdullah M'Changama) and dissident groups of other parties. The outcome was an RDR victory, which was hotly contested by what became the opposition Forum for National Recovery (FRN), and the appointment of the RDR secretary-general as Prime Minister in January 1994. In major government changes in October 1994, however, Abdou Madi was replaced as Prime Minister by Halifa Houmadi, amid dissension within the RDR over privatization plans supported by the former but opposed by M'Changama.

Houmadi lasted until April 1995, when he was replaced by Caabi el-Yachroutou Mohamed, a former Finance Minister. In late September 1995 the Comoros experienced its 17th coup attempt since independence, when a group of rebel soldiers backed by foreign mercenaries seized power in Moroni and held it until being overcome early in October by forces sent in by France. Restored to office, President Djohar proceeded to form a "unity" government headed by the RDR but including representatives of the FRN, this lasting until a presidential election in March was won by the candidate of the National Union for Democracy in the Comoros.

Other Parties

Comoran Party for Progress (*Parti Comorien pour le Progrès*, PCP), known locally as *Marandrazi*, led by Choudjay Abdullah.

Comoran Party of Labour and Progress (*Parti Comorien du Travail et du Progrès*, PCTP), known locally as *Mayesha Bora*, led by Ahmed Saïd Islam, participated in the interim government formed in 1992.

National Federation for Progress (*Fédération Nationale pour le Progrès*, FNP), led by Ali Mirghane.

National Front for Justice (*Front National pour la Justice*, FNJ), led by Soidiki M'Bapandza, an Islamist formation.

National Solidarity for Democracy in the Comoros (*Solidarité Nationale pour la Démocratie aux Comores*, SNDC), led by Bacar M'Madi.

Party for Democracy and Progress in the Comoros (*Parti pour la Démocratie et le Progrès aux Comores*, PDPC), led by Mogne Attoumane.

Realizing Freedom's Promise (*Uhuru Wendza Zorenda*, UWEZO), led by Mouazoir Abdullah, founded in exile in the mid-1980s as the Union for a Democratic Comoran Republic (*Union pour une République Démocratique aux Comores*, URDC), adopted the UWEZO rubric in 1990, when it was a "presidential" party, although it subsequently opposed the 1992 constitution.

Congo

Capital: Brazzaville

Population: 2,600,000 (1995E)

The Republic of Congo achieved independence from France in 1960, became a one-party state in 1963, was renamed the People's Republic of Congo in 1970 but reverted to its orginal name in 1991 on moving to a multi-party system. Drawn up by a national conference convened in February 1991, a new constitution approved by referendum in March 1992 provides for an executive President, who is directly elected for a five-year term (once renewable) by universal suffrage of those aged 18 and over and who appoints the Prime Minister and other ministers. Legislative authority is vested in a bicameral parliament consisting of a 125–member National Assembly (*Assemblée Nationale*) as the lower house, elected for a five-year term in two rounds of voting, and a 60–seat Senate (*Sénat*), whose members are indirectly elected for a six-year term.

Legislative elections held in May-June 1993 and re-runs in 11 constituencies in October 1993 resulted as follows: Presidential Tendency 65 seats, of which the Pan-African Union for Social Democracy (UPADS) won 47, the Rally for Democracy and Development 6, the Union of Democratic Forces 3, the Congolese Renewal Party 2, the Union for Congolese Democracy 1, the Union for Development and Social Progress 1 and others 5; Opposition Coalition 56, of which the Congolese Movement for Democracy and Integral Development (MCDDI) won 28, the Congolese Labour Party 15, the Rally for Democracy and Social Progress 10, the Union for Democratic Renewal 2 and an independent 1; the Union for Democracy and the Republic 2; the Patriotic Union for National Renewal 1; and an independent 1. Presidential elections held on Aug. 2 and 16, 1992, had resulted in a second-round victory for Pascal Lissouba (UPADS) over the MCDDI candidate.

Congolese Labour Party
Parti Congolais du Travail (PCT)
   Address. c/o Assemblée Nationale, Brazzaville
   Leadership. Gen. Denis Sassou-Nguesso (president), Ambroise Noumazalaye (secretary-general)
   The PCT was launched in 1969 as the sole ruling party of the military regime of Capt. Marien Ngouabi, replacing the National Movement of the Revolution. Forming Africa's first Marxist-Leninist government, the party was riven by factional struggle in the 1970s: among several purges, one in 1972 ousted Ambroise Noumazalaye as first secretary and resulted in him being condemned to death, although he was later amnestied. The PCT establishment took a back seat to the military regime of 1977–79, but was then instrumental in the replacement of Gen. Jacques-Joachim Yhombi-Opango by Col. (as he then was) Sassou-Nguesso, who was elected party chairman and thus head of state at an extraordinary congress in March 1979. Victims of a purge of "leftists" in 1984 included Jean-Pierre Thystère-Tchikaya, who was subsequently condemned for involvement in bomb attacks but amnestied in 1988. Yhombi-Opango was later to found the Rally for Democracy and Development (RDD) and Thystère-Tchikaya the Rally for Democracy and Social Progress (RDPS).
   In mid-1990 the PCT opened the way for

President Sassou-Nguesso's decision of October that year to accede to pressure for a transition to multi-partyism. In December 1990 a PCT congress opted to abandon Marxism-Leninism and to embrace democratic socialism; it also reinstated Noumazalaye, who was elected to the new post of secretary-general. In early 1991 the party participated in the national conference which drafted a new constitution, although a hardline PCT faction bitterly criticized the surrender of authority to the conference and the resultant transitional government. From mid-1991 the latter took steps to remove PCT cadres from their entrenched position in the state bureaucracy, some prominent members being convicted of corruption. Paradoxically, the PCT's surrender of power meant that popular discontent now focused as much on the transitional government as on President Sassou-Nguesso and the former ruling party. Nevertheless, in the mid-1992 elections the PCT came in third place, with 19 Assembly and three Senate seats, while Gen. Sassou-Nguesso also took third place in the first round of the August 1992 presidential elections (with 16.9% of the vote) and was therefore eliminated. Accepting his defeat "with serenity", Sassou-Nguesso endorsed the successful candidacy of Pascal Lissouba of the Pan-African Union for Social Democracy (UPADS) in the second round and the PCT accepted membership of a post-election coalition government dominated by the UPADS.

Reports that a formal PCT/UPADS alliance had been agreed proved to be exaggerated, however. In late October 1992 the PCT deputies combined with those of the Union for Democratic Renewal (URD) to defeat the government on a no-confidence motion, as a result of which President Lissouba dissolved the Assembly and called new elections. In December 1992 both the PCT and the URD were included in an interim national unity government, which kept the peace until the elections began in May 1993. But opposition charges of electoral fraud in the first round of voting, and a joint PCT/URD boycott of the second round in June, were accompanied by escalating violence. Rejecting the official results giving the UPADS and its allies a comfortable overall Assembly majority, the PCT/URD axis refused to recognize the new UPADS-dominated cabinet headed by Yhombi-Opango (RDD) and named a parallel government headed by Thystère-Tchikaya (RDPS). Growing civil unrest, featuring bloody clashes between government and opposition militias in Brazzaville and elsewhere, was stemmed by a Gabonese-brokered accord concluded in August 1993 under which the disputed elections were re-run in 11 constituencies in October. Seven of these contests were won by the opposition (so that the PCT's final tally was 15 seats and one pro-PCT independent), but the UPADS and its allies still had an overall Assembly majority.

Further fighting ensued, especially around the PCT/URD stronghold of Bacongo in south Brazzaville, until the signature of a precarious ceasefire at the end of January 1994. The following month an international panel ruled that a further nine 1993 election results were invalid, but the government took no immediate steps to hold re-run contests. Nor was there was much progress in disarming the contending party militias, among which Sassou-Nguesso's so-called "Cobras" (including many former presidential guards) achieved particular notoriety. Amid continuing violence, the PCT in September 1994 announced the formation of a new opposition alliance called the United Democratic Forces.

Congolese Movement for Democracy and Integral Development

Mouvement Congolais pour la Démocratie et le Développement Intégral (MCDDI)

    Address. c/o Assemblée Nationale, Brazzaville

    Leadership. Bernard Kolelas (president)

    Founded in 1990, the centre-right MCDDI was a member of the broad Forces of Change coalition which spearheaded the transition to multi-partyism in 1991, Bernard Kolelas becoming an adviser to the Prime Minister of the resultant transitional government. In the mid-1992 legislative elections, the MCDDI became the second-strongest party, with 29 Assembly and 13 Senate seats. In the August 1992 presidential contest, Kolelas likewise took second place in the first voting round (with 22.9% of the vote), thus going on to the run-off, in which he was defeated by Pascal Lissouba of the Pan-African Union for Social Democracy (UPADS) by 61.3% to 38.7%. The MCDDI had meanwhile formed the seven-party Union for Democratic Renewal (URD), which opted to oppose the new UPADS-dominated government and procured an alliance with the former ruling Congolese Labour Party (PCT) for this purpose. Having brought down the government in October 1992, both the MCDDI-led URD and the PCT joined an interim national unity government formed in December 1992 pending new Assembly elections. These began in May 1993, but Kolelas claimed that "monstrous irregularities" had been perpetrated by the government in the first voting round and led an opposition boycott of the second in June. After Kolelas had urged the army to intervene to restore law and order (without result), the MCDDI/URD boycotted the new Assembly and participated in the formation of an alternative government to oppose the new UPADS-dominated coalition.

The immediate crisis was partially resolved by an electoral re-run in 11 constituencies in October 1993, as a result of which the final MCDDI tally in the 125–member Assembly was 28 seats (out of 56 held by the opposition parties).

Clashes between government forces and militiamen of the URD/PCT axis intensified in late 1993 and early 1994, until the signature of a ceasefire agreement in late January 1994 by UPADS and MCDDI representatives brought some respite. In July 1994 popular anti-government feeling in Brazzaville was demonstrated by the election of Kolelas as the capital's mayor. But the incipient accomodation between the MCDDI/URD and the UPADS-led government was consolidated in January 1995 when the URD accepted representation in a new coalition, thus apparently breaking with the PCT. The MCDDI's strong support in the capital was demonstrated in by-elections in May 1995; but the party was weakened the same month by a split that yielded the creation of the Party for Unity, Work and Progress.

Congolese Renewal Party
Parti Congolaise du Renouvellement (PCR)
    Address. c/o Assemblée Nationale, Brazzaville
    Leadership. Grégoire Lefouaba (president)
    The PCR was founded in late 1992 by Grégoire Lefouaba, who had previously been a member of the Congolese Labour Party. Forming part of the Presidential Tendency alliance in the mid-1993 Assembly elections, the party won two seats in its own right.

Pan-African Union for Social Democracy
Union Panafricaine pour la Démocratie Sociale (UPADS)
    Address. c/o Assemblée Nationale, Brazzaville
    Leadership. Pascal Lissouba (president), Christophe Moukoueke (secretary-general)
    The left-of-centre UPADS emerged from the opposition National Alliance for Democracy, formed in July 1991, and contested the 1992 elections in its own right, having attracted defectors from other parties. Its leader, Pascal Lissouba, had served as Prime Minister in 1963–66 and had narrowly failed to be elected head of the transitional government formed in mid-1991 as a result of the national conference. The UPADS became the largest party in the legislative elections of June-July 1992, winning 39 Assembly and 23 Senate seats. Lissouba then won the presidential elections of August 1992, heading the first-round vote with 35.9% and taking 61.3% of the second-round vote, thanks in part to being endorsed by the outgoing President, Denis Sassou-Nguesso of the Congolese Labour Party. (PCT). The UPADS/PCT axis did not last long, as the PCT formed an opposition alliance with the Union for Democratic Renewal (URD). The post-election UPADS-dominated coalition government lost a vote confidence at the end of October 1992, whereupon President Lissouba dissolved the Assembly the following month and called new elections.

A national unity government appointed in December 1992, including both the PCT and the URD, kept the peace until the elections began in May 1993. But opposition charges of electoral fraud in the first round of voting, and a joint PCT/URD boycott of the second round in June, were accompanied by escalating violence. On the strength of official results giving the UPADS and its allies a comfortable overall Assembly majority, Lissouba appointed a UPADS-dominated government headed by the leader of the Rally for Democracy and Development (RDD). It faced a parallel government named by the PCT/URD and growing disorder, as government forces and opposition militias fought regular battles in Brazzaville and elsewhere. Under a Gabonese-brokered accord concluded in August 1993, re-run elections were held in 11 constituencies in October, seven being won by the opposition. This outcome still left the UPADS and its allies with an overall Assembly majority of 65 seats. Further bloody clashes ensued, until the signature of a precarious ceasefire at the end of January 1994. The following month an international panel ruled that a further nine 1993 constituency results were invalid, but the government took no immediate steps to hold new contests.

The UPADS remained the dominant formation in a new coalition formed in January 1995 (again under the premiership of the RDD leader) and succeeded in persuading the URD to break with the PCT (by now heading the United Democratic Forces) by accepting ministerial representation. Immediately after the new government formation, however, 12 UPADS Assembly deputies resigned from the party, complaining that they had been marginalized, and subsequently formed the Union for the Republic.

Party for Unity, Work and Progress
Parti pour l'Unité, le Travail et le Progrès (PUTP)
    Address. c/o Assemblée Nationale, Brazzaville
    Leadership. Didier Sengha
    The PUTP was launched in May 1995 by a dissident faction of the Congolese Movement for Democracy and Integral Development (MCDDI), the breakaway party's leader, Didier Sengha, claiming that the MCDDI had ceased to care about "democracy, freedom, equity, legality and fraternity". The MCDDI leader, Bernard Kolelas, responded by accusing Sengha of financial misappropriation and embezzlement.

Patriotic Union for National Reconstruction

Union Patriotique pour la Réconstruction Nationale (UPRN)

Address. c/o Assemblée Nationale, Brazzaville

Leadership. Mathias Dzon

The UPRN was formed prior to the 1993 Assembly elections as a party at that stage independent of both the government and the opposition alliances. It won one seat in that contest and in September 1994 joined the opposition United Democratic Forces alliance headed by the Congolese Labour Party.

Rally for Democracy and Development

Rassemblement pour la Démocratie et le Développement (RDD)

Address. c/o Assemblée Nationale, Brazzaville

Leadership. Gen. Jacques-Joachim Yhombi-Opango (president)

The RDD was founded in 1990 as a political vehicle for Gen. Yhombi-Opango, who had become President of a military government in 1977 but had been ousted in 1979 and expelled from the then ruling Congolese Labour Party. The RDD was at first an influential element in the broad Forces of Change alliance which dominated the transitional government formed after the 1991 national conference. But by April 1992 the party was openly criticizing the Prime Minister for alleged misuse of public funds for electoral purposes. In the mid-1992 Assembly elections the RDD won five seats and thereafter aligned itself with the opposition to the newly-dominant Pan-African Union for Social Democracy (UPADS). However, in further Assembly elections in mid-1993 the RDD formed part of the UPADS-led Presidential Tendency alliance, winning six seats in its own right, whereupon Gen. Yhombi-Opango accepted appointment as Prime Minister in a new coalition government. In January 1995 he was reappointed as head of a broader coalition, still dominated by the UPADS but also including the Union for Democratic Renewal.

Rally for Democracy and Social Progress

Rassemblement pour la Démocratie et le Progrès Social (RDPS)

Address. c/o Assemblée Nationale, Brazzaville

Leadership. Jean-Pierre Thystère-Tchicaya

The RDPS was founded in 1990 by Thystère-Tchicaya, once an ideologist of the former ruling Congolese Labour Party (PCT), before being purged as a "leftist" in 1984. It won nine Assembly and five Senate seats in the mid-1992 elections, although Thystère-Tchikaya came a poor fifth in the first round of presidential elections in August, winning only 5.9% of the vote. The party was thereafter a member of the opposition Union for

Democratic Renewal (URD) led by the Congolese Movement for Democracy and Integral Development, whose post-election axis with the PCT resulted in the fall in late October of the coalition government dominated by the Pan-African Union for Social Democracy (UPADS). The RDPS participated in the opposition boycott of the second round of new Assembly elections in June 1993, when Thystère-Tchicaya was named as head of a parallel government set up by the URD and the PCT. Following electoral re-runs in 11 constituencies in October 1993, the RDPS tally in the Assembly was 10 seats. The party thereafter continued to form part of the opposition to the UPADS-dominated Lissouba administration.

Union for Congolese Democracy

Union pour la Démocratie Congolaise (UDC)

Address. c/o Assemblée Nationale, Brazzaville

Leadership. Sylvain Bemba, Félix Makosso

The formation of the UDC was announced in November 1989 in neighbouring Côte d'Ivoire, where Bemba, a former government official and associate of President Fulbert Youlou (1960–63), had been in exile for some 25 years. It was one of the first groups to challenge the one-party rule of the Congolese Labour Party and joined the National Alliance for Democracy, becoming closely aligned with the Pan-African Union for Social Democracy (UPADS). As part of the UPADS-led Presidential Tendency alliance in the mid-1993 Assembly elections, the UDC won one seat in its own right.

Union for Democracy and the Republic

Union pour la Démocratie et la République (UDR)

Address. c/o Assemblée Nationale, Brazzaville

Leadership. André Milongo

The UDR was founded in 1992 by Milongo (a former World Bank official), who in June 1991 had been elected transitional Prime Minister by the national conference convened to determine the country's constitutional future. He had then represented the broad coalition of pro-democracy parties called the Forces of Change (FDC), which designation was used by him in the 1992 legislative and presidential elections, although by then many of its original components were in open opposition to his government. In the legislative elections of June-July 1991, the FDC failed to win a seat in the Assembly and won only one in the Senate. In the August 1992 presidential elections, Milongo came in fourth place in the first round, with 10.2% of the vote. Launched after his electoral failure, the UDR gave broad support to President Lissouba and the new government dominated by his Pan-African Union for Social

Democracy (UPADS), without becoming a member of the Presidential Tendency coalition. In the 1993 Assembly elections, the UDR was at first credited with six seats on the strength of the disputed balloting of May-June, but its tally fell to two seats as a result of the re-runs in 11 constituencies in October. By the latter date, however, Milongo had been elected president of the Assembly.

Union for Democratic Renewal
Union pour la Renouveau Démocratique (URD)
   Address. c/o Assemblée Nationale, Brazzaville
   Leadership. Bernard Kolelas (MCDDI), Jean-Pierre Thystère- Tchicaya (RDPS)

The centre-right URD was created at the time of the mid-1992 elections as an alliance of seven parties, notably the Congolese Movement for Democracy and Integral Development (MCDDI) and the Rally for Democracy and Social Progress (RDPS), both with their main strength in central and southern Congo. Joining a post-election opposition axis with the former ruling Congolese Labour Party (PCT), the URD helped to bring about the fall in late October 1992 of the coalition government dominated by the Pan-African Union for Social Democracy (UPADS). It became a member of the interim national unity government formed in December 1992 but again came into conflict with the UPADS-dominated administration of President Lissouba when new elections were held. Claiming that the first round of voting in May 1993 had featured massive electoral fraud by the authorities, the URD and the PCT boycotted the second round in June and set up their own parallel government under the premiership of Thystère-Tchicaya, amid a descent into bloody civil conflict.

The impasse was partially resolved by repeat elections in 11 constituencies in October 1993, seven of them won by the opposition. As a result, however, the UPADS and its allies still had an overall majority in the 125–member Assembly and the opposition parties 56 seats, of which the URD parties held 40 (including two won by candidates standing under the URD rubric rather than for constituent parties). Further serious violence between government forces and the URD/PCT axis in late 1993 and early 1994 was temporarily stemmed by a ceasefire agreement of late January. The URD also welcomed the finding of an international panel in February 1994 that the 1993 election results were invalid in a further nine seats, although its demand for re-runs met with no immediate response from the UPADS-dominated government. However, little progress was subsequently made in disarming the opposing militias, that of the URD being concentrated in

the south Brazzaville stronghold of Kolelas, who was elected mayor of the capital in July 1994.

The URD at first aligned itself with the opposition United Democratic Forces (FDU) launched in September 1994 under the leadership of the PCT; but in January 1995 it broke with the FDU by accepting representation in a new coalition government headed by the UPADS.

Union for Development and Social Progress
Union pour le Développement et le Progrès Social (UDPS)
   Address. c/o Assemblée Nationale, Brazzaville
   Leadership. Jean-Michel Boukamba-Yangouma (president)

The UDPS was formed prior to the mid-1993 Assembly elections by a dissident group, headed by trade union leader Boukamba-Yangouma, of the Union for Social Progress and Democracy. As part of the Presidential Tendency alliance in those elections, it won one seat in its own right.

Union of Democratic Forces
Union des Forces Démocratiques (UFD)
   Address. c/o Assemblée Nationale, Brazzaville
   Leadership. David Charles Ganao (president)

The UFD formed part of the Presidential Tendency alliance in the mid-1993 Assembly elections, in which it won three seats in its own right. The UFD leader was an unsuccessful contender for the Assembly presidency, despite receiving opposition backing because of his reputed political objectivity.

Union for the Republic
Union pour la République (UR)
   Address. c/o Assemblée Nationale, Brazzaville
   Leadership. Benjamin Bounkoulou

This party was launched in March 1995 by 12 Assembly deputies who had resigned from the dominant Pan-African Union for Social Democracy in January on the grounds that they had become marginalized by the formation of a broad coalition government that month. Led by the outgoing Foreign Minister, the new party declared its qualified support for the Lissouba administration.

United Democratic Forces
Forces Démocratiques Unies (FDU)
   Address. c/o Assemblée Nationale, Brazzaville
   Leadership. Gen. Denis Sassou-Nguesso (PCT), Alfred Opimba (CAD), Nicéphore Fyla (PLR), Pierre N'Ze (UNDP), Mathias Dzon (UPRN), Gabriel Bokilo (URN)

The FDU was launched in September 1994 as an opposition alliance of six parties headed by the Congolese Labour Party (PCT) and including the

Convention for the Democratic Alternative (CAD), the Liberal Republican Party (PLR), the National Union for Democracy and Progress (UNDP), the Patriotic Union for National Reconstruction (UPRN) and the Union for National Recovery (URN). The FDU's leaders came mainly from northern Congo, in contrast to the central and southern provenance of the Union for Democratic Renewal (URD), then the FDU's ally in opposition to the government headed by President Lissouba's Pan-African Union for Social Democracy (UPADS). In January 1995 the FDU parties refused to participate in a new UPADS-led coalition, whereas the URD accepted representation. Clashes between government forces and the FDU-led opposition intensified in Brazzaville in September 1995.

Other Parties and Alliances

Convention for the Democratic Alternative (*Convention pour l'Alternatif Démocratique*, CAD), led by Alfred Opimba, joined the opposition United Democratic Forces in 1994.

Democratic Centre (*Centre Démocratique*, CD), founded in January 1993 as an alliance of six centrist parties, namely the Congolese Democratic Rally (*Rassemblement Démocratique Congolais*, RDC), the Movement for Freedom and Democracy (*Mouvement pour la Liberté et la Démocratie*, MLD), the National Rally for Development and Progress (*Rassemblement National pour la Développement et le Progrès*, RNDP), the Patriotic Movement of the Congo (*Mouvement Patriotique du Congo*, MPC), the Rally for Alternative Democracy (*Rassemblement pour l'Alternatif Démocratique*, RAD) and the Union for the Republic and Democracy (*Union pour la République et la Démocratie*, URD).

Liberal Republican Party (*Parti Libéral et Républicain*, PLR), led by Nicéphore Fyla, joined the opposition United Democratic Forces in September 1994.

National Union for Democracy and Progress (*Union Nationale pour la Démocratie et le Progrès*, UNDP), led by Pierre N'Ze, founded in 1990, was prominent in the early pro-democracy movement, but lost support to the Pan-African Union for Social Democracy, joined the opposition United Democratic Forces in 1994.

Party for Reconstruction and Development of the Congo (*Parti pour la Reconstruction et le Développement du Congo*, PRDC), led by Stéphane Bongho-Nouarra (a minister in the 1960s), founded in 1991, became a leading member of the National Alliance for Democracy (AND), which opposed the 1991–92 transitional government, became aligned with the post-AND Pan-African Union for Social Democracy, unsuccessful in the 1992 and 1993 Assembly elections, although Bongho-Nouarra was briefly Prime Minister (September-October 1992) after the first contest.

Rally of Congolese Democrats (*Rassemblement des Démocrates Congolais*, RDC), led by Gilbert Pongault, a Catholic party, with links with the Christian Democrat International.

Union for National Recovery (*Union pour le Recouvrement National*, URN), led by Gabriel Bokilo, joined the opposition United Democratic Forces in September 1994.

Union for Social Progress and Democracy (*Union pour le Progrès Social et la Démocratie*, UPSD), led by Ange-Édouard Poungui (Prime Minister in 1985–89), founded in 1991 by former prominent members of the Congolese Labour Party, joined the opposition National Alliance for Democracy, won two Assembly seats in the 1992 elections, thereafter gravitating to the anti-Lissouba opposition, weakened by the formation of the splinter Union for Development and Social Progress, failed to win representation in the 1993 elections.

Union of Social Democrats (*Union des Démocrates Sociaux*, UDS), led by Clément Mierassa, won three Assembly seats in 1992 but none in 1993.

Costa Rica

Capital: San José

Population: 3,400,000 (1995E)

Costa Rica gained independence from Spain in 1821 and was a member of the United Provinces of Central America until 1838. Following a bloody civil war in 1948 a new constitution was promulgated disbanding the army, an important factor behind the country's claim to be the longest lasting democracy in Latin America. The social democratic political tradition, represented by the National Liberation Party (PLN), barring brief periods, dominated national politics until 1990. The more conservative tradition, represented in a coalition in 1978, finally triumphed in February 1990 when the Social Christian Unity Party (PUSC) assumed power.

Under the 1949 constitution, a unicameral Legislative Assembly is made up of 57 members. Executive power rests with the President who appoints a Cabinet. A presidential candidate may not be a member of the clergy, related to an incumbent President or have served as either a cabinet minister, as a director of an autonomous state agency, or as a member of the Electoral Tribunal or the Supreme Court in the period immediately preceding the electoral campaign. The President may not stand for re-election for a period of eight years after the completion of one term of office.

The President is elected directly by universal adult suffrage for a four-year term. Members of the Legislative Assembly are elected by proportional representation for the same period to coincide with the presidential term. Voting is compulsory for all men and women over 18 and under 70 years of age.

José María Figueres of the National Liberation Party (PLN) won the presidential elections held on Feb. 7, 1994, taking office on May 8. In the simultaneous elections to the Legislative Assembly, the PLN won 28 seats, while the Social Christian Unity Party (PUSC) won 25 and independents 4.

National Liberation Party

Partido de Liberación Nacional (PLN)
  Address. P.O. Box 10051-1000, San José
  Telephone. (#506) 232 5133
  Fax. (#506) 231 4097
  Leadership. Rolando Araya Monge (president); Rolando González Ulloa (general secretary)

Founded in October 1951, the PLN is nominally social democratic but the party itself tends to pursue conservative policies when in office. The successor to the Social Democratic Party (PSD) (founded in 1948), the PLN was formed by supporters around José "Pepe" Figueres Ferrer who promised social and economical reforms, the restructuring of the government and the better management of the state-run sector. The party lost the presidential elections in 1958 but regained the presidency in 1962 and held it for the periods 1970-74, 1974-78, 1982-1986 and 1986-1990. The PLN also had near continuous control of the National Assembly during the same period except for the period 1978-1982 when it lost control to

an opposition Unity (*Unidad*) coalition (see Social Christian Unity Party, PUSC). The nomination of Oscar Arias Sánchez as presidential candidate in 1986 marked a rupture with the old guard in the party who had a conservative pro-USA foreign policy and were hostile to the Sandinistas in Nicaragua. Arias gained international status for his peace plan for Central America and as a consequence received the Nobel Prize for Peace in 1987. However, domestically, the effects of the foreign debt burden, and pressure from the conservative wing of the party for economic restructuring, including the privatization of the state sector and banking reform, led to the defeat of the more moderate social democratic wing. Drug-related scandals involving prominent party figures, including Daniel Odúber Quirós, party president from 1974-79, damaged the party's image and the shift in policy failed to restore it. The party's conservative candidate for the 1990 presidential elections, Carlos Manuel Castillo, was subsequently defeated. Then, on June 8, 1990, long-time party leader Figueres Ferrer died bringing on a new younger internal atmosphere.

At the presidential elections of Feb. 6, 1994, Figueres Ferrer's son, José María Figueres Olsen, defeated Miguel Angel Rodriguez of the PUSC by 49.6 to 47.5% of the vote.

The PLN is a full member party of the Socialist International. A 70-delegate national assembly is the party's supreme body and this elects a three-member national executive committee and a seven-member national political committee. In addition, there are seven provincial, 80 cantonal and 410 municipal committees, appointed by assemblies at the respective levels.

Social Christian Unity Party

Partido Unidad Social Cristiana (PUSC)

Address. Apartada 725-1007, Centro Colón, San José

Telephone. (#506) 534811

Fax. (#506) 240033

Leadership. Mario Quintana (president), Rafael Angel Calderon Fournier, Rodriego Carazo Odio, Miguel Angel Rodriguez (1994 presidential candidate)

The PUSC alliance was originally formed in 1978 and is a right-wing Christian Democrat grouping. The PUSC was the product of four parties—the Christian Democratic Party (PDC), founded in 1962), the Calderónist Republican Party (PRC, founded 1970), the Popular Union Party (PUP, founded 1974), and the Democratic Renewal Party (PRD, founded 1971)—which in 1978 formed a Unity (*Unidad*) coalition whose candidate Rodrigo Carazo Odio won the 1978 presidential elections and which took 28 seats in the National Assembly, one short of a majority. The coalition combined the right-wing republican tradition of ex-president Rafael Angel Calerón Guarda (1942-44) and the conservatism of the coffee barons with the guiding principles of Christian democracy. Carazo's government clashed with the trade unions and cooled relations with Cuba and with the Sandinistas in Nicaragua. The Unity candidate Rafael Angel Calderón Fournier lost the 1982 presidential elections and the party's strength in the assembly was reduced to 18 seats.

The first electoral test for the new PUSC was in 1986 when Calderón standing on a platform that advocated opposition to agrarian reform, cuts in public spending and the privatization of state assets came second in the presidential race to the PLN candidate but the party increased its number of seats in the assembly. In opposition, it pressed for the breaking of diplomatic relations with Nicaragua, tax reforms and increased law and order. Calderón finally gained the presidency in February 1990, and the party a majority in the Assembly, promising more moderate economic measures and new social packages for the majority of the population. Instead the government implemented drastic IMF-approved economic shock measures in June 1990 which provoked widespread opposition, particularly from public sector trade unions. Government attempts to form a social pact with the trade unions and business sector failed as did its attempt to gain public acceptance for a plan it proposed to deal with poverty.

As Calderón's popularity plummeted, many PUSC officials and delegates in the Assembly publicly characterized the government's emphasis on economic re-adjustment as "excessive" and argued that more pressing social problems were being neglected. However the conditions for a third phase of the government's economic structural re-adjustment policies were finalized with the IMF in January and February 1992.

The alliance lost a close election race in 1994 with their candidate Miguel Angel Rodriguez losing to the PLN's José María Figueres Olsen by 47.5 to 49.6% of the vote.

The party is a member of the Christian Democrat International.

Other Parties

Calderonist Republican Party

Partido Republicano Calderónista (PRC)

Leadership. Alvaro Cubillo Aguilar (president)

The party was formed in 1976 by a breakaway group from the National Union Party (PUN) and was named after former president Rafael Angel Calderón Guardia.

Cartago Agricultural Action

Unión Agrícola Cartaginesa (UAC)

Address. Frente Iglesias Cervantes, Alvarado Cartago

Leadership. Juan Guillermo Brenes Castilles (president)

The party, formerly known as the *Unión Agrícola Cartaginesa*, has always operated as a lobbyist at national level for the interests of Cartago, the country's fourth largest state. In the 1978 elections it won one seat in the Legislative Assembly which it lost in 1982, regained in 1986 and held on to in the presidential and legislative elections of February 1990.

Christian Democratic Party

Partido Demócrata Cristiano (PDC)

Leadership. Rafael Alberto Grillo Rivera (president)

A traditional Christian democrat party founded in 1962.

Costa Rican Peoples' Party
Partido del Pueblo Costarricense (PPC)

Leadership. Daniel Camacho (1990 presidential candidate); Lenín Chacon Vargas (secretary general)

Yet another splinter group, the PPC was formed in the early eighties by Manuel Mora Valverde, the founder of the Communist Party (PC) and a leader of the 1948 Civil War. Its pro-Cuba and pro-Castro stance put it at odds with the mainstream PVP (from which it had split) and in 1984 it joined with the New Republican Movement (MNR) to form the short-lived Patriotic Alliance.

The PPC won one seat in 1990 but none thereafter.

National Movement
Movimiento Nacional (MN)

Leadership. Mario Echandi Jiménez; Rodrigo Sancho Robles (secretary)

The MN began life as an offshoot from the former National Unification Party (PUN)—not to be confused with the National Union Party—see below. The MN is a conservative group whose leader obtained 3.7% of the 1982 presidential ballot vote. The party has made little showing since that time.

National Union Party
Partido Unión Nacional (PUN)

Leadership. Olga Marta Ulate Rojas (president)

A small party that was formed in April 1985 by the leader of the former Democratic Renovation Party (PRD), Oscar Aguilar Bulgarelli.

Popular Union Party
Partido Unión Popular (PUP)

Leadership. Cristián Tattenbach Yglesias (president); Juan Rafael Rodriguez Calvo (general secretary)

The Popular Union Party is a coalition of small right-wing interest groups.

Popular Vanguard Party
Partido Vanguardia Popular (PVP)

Leadership. Arnoldo Ferreto Segura (president); Humberto Elías Vargas Carbonell (secretary general)

The PVP was founded in 1931 as the Communist Party (PC) but constitutionally banned until 1975, and joined forces with the Costa Rican People's Party (PPC) (most of whose members were expelled from the "pro-Soviet" PVP in 1984 for being "Castroists") to support the PU candidate in the February 1990 presidential elections.

Then, running as a single party, the PVP managed to secure one seat in the 1990 ballots. At the party's 17th congress in September 1990 the majority of members voted not to restore the party's old "revolutionary character".

Minor Parties

There are over 30 minor parties which do not currently have full political status because they have failed to receive at least 1.5% of the national vote. A number of the parties below belong in this category.

Costa Rican Ecology Party (*Partido Ecológia Costarricense*, PEC), led by Alexander Bonilla.

Costa Rican Socialist Party (*Partido Socialista Costarricense*, PSC), a pro-Cuban Marxist party led by Alvaro Montero Mejía.

General Union Party (*Partido Unión Generaleña*, PUG) is a regional party which won one legislative seat in the 1990 election. It is led by Otto Guevara.

National Christian Alliance Party (*Alianza Nacional Cristiana*, ANC), led by Victor Hogo Gonzalez Montero.

New Republican Movement (*Movimiento Nueva Republica*, MNR), a moderate splinter from the radical Maoist Revolutionary Peoples' Movement (MRP), and is led by Sergio Erick Ardon.

Radical Democratic Party (*Partido Radical Demócrata*, PRD), a left-of-centre party led by Juan José Echeverria Brealey.

Workers' Party (*Partido de los Trabajadores*, PT) is the political wing of the Revolutionary Peoples' Movement (MRP), the Maoist and often violent revolutionary group. It is led by José Francisco Araya.

Côte d'Ivoire

Capital: Abidjan

Population: 14,600,000 (1995E)

The Republic of Côte d'Ivoire achieved independence from France in 1960 and was a de facto one-party state until 1990, when a multi-party system was introduced. Executive power is vested in the President, who is directly elected for a renewable five-year term by universal adult suffrage of those aged 21 and over and who appoints the Prime Minister and Council of Ministers. A new code enacted in December 1994 required all future presidential candidates to be Ivorian by birth and born of Ivorian parents, never to have renounced Ivorian citizenship and to have resided in the country for at least five years up to the election. Legislative authority is vested in a unicameral National Assembly (*Assemblée Nationale*) of 175 members, who are elected on a constituency basis, also for a five-year term.

The official results of presidential elections held on Oct. 22, 1995 (but boycotted by most opposition parties), showed a turnout of less than 50% and a victory for incumbent Henri Konan-Bédié of the Democratic Party of Côte d'Ivoire (PDCI), who was credited with 95.3% of the vote. Assembly elections on Nov. 26, 1995, resulted in 172 of the 175 seats being filled as follows: PDCI 148 (including four that were uncontested); Rally of Republicans 13; Ivorian Popular Front 11.

Democratic Party of Côte d'Ivoire
Parti Démocratique de la Côte d'Ivoire (PDCI)
   Address. BP 36, Abidjan 05
   Leadership. Henri Konan-Bédié (chair), Laurent Dona-Fologo (general secretary)

The PDCI was founded in 1946 as the local section of the pro-independence movement of French West Africa called the African Democratic Rally (*Rassemblement Démocratique Africain*, RDA), which designation is still a suffix of the PCDI's full official title. The party's Ivorian founder, Félix Houphouët-Boigny, sat in the French National Assembly from 1946 to 1959 (also holding ministerial office during this period), before returning home to lead Côte d'Ivoire to independence in 1960. For the next 30 years the PDCI was the only authorized party, although a one-party system was never formalized by law. Every five years a PDCI congress would draw up a list of Assembly candidates for endorsement by the electorate and would also renominate Houphouët-Boigny as the sole presidential candidate. By 1990 he had served six consecutive terms and was Africa's longest-serving head of state, running an administration committed to a free enterprise system, open access for Western capitalists and close relations with France (which remained Côte d'Ivoire's financial and military guarantor).

Bowing to a new wind of change in black Africa, Houphouët-Boigny in May 1990 publicly endorsed a transition to multi-partyism. The change was approved by a PDCI congress in October 1990, when changes in the party's structure were also agreed, including the revival of the post of general secretary (abolished in 1980) and the creation of an 80–member central committee with executive responsibilities. The congress also again endorsed Houphouët-Boigny as the PDCI candidate in the presidential election due later that month, resisting internal pressure from the party's "new guard" for the nomination of Henri Konan-Bédié, who as Assembly president was next in line to the President under a 1985 constitutional amendment. Houphouët-Boigny was duly re-elected with nearly 82% of the popular vote (according to official figures), defeating a candidate of the Ivorian Popular Front (FPI), who claimed that the elections had been fraudulent. In multi-party Assembly elections in November 1990, the PDCI swept to a landslide victory, winning 163 of the 175 seats, although again the results were disputed by the FPI. The PDCI therefore remained in power, despite a sharp deterioration in economic and social conditions since the late 1980s.

The move to multi-partyism served to reveal long-suppressed tribal divisions within the PDCI, reflecting broader tensions between Côte d'Ivoire's predominantly Muslim north and the Christian south of Houphouët-Boigny. The election of Laurent Dona-Fologo as party general secretary in April 1991 was in line with the President's ruling that the post should be held by someone not from his own ethnic background. Nevertheless, tension increased between heir apparent Konan-Bédié (a southerner) and then Prime Minister Alassane Ouattara (a northern Muslim), being sharpened by the death of Houphouët-Boigny in December 1993. An attempt by Ouattara to assume supreme power (with army backing) was successfully resisted by Konan-Bédié (with French backing), who proceeded to appoint a new Prime Minister and was succeeded as Assembly president by Charles Donwahi of the PDCI. Thereafter, the PDCI government resisted calls from some opposition parties for a national conference to determine the country's future political structure.

In April 1994 President Konan-Bédié was unanimously elected PDCI chair, thus ensuring his candidacy for the ruling party in the 1995 presidential elections. The following month Ouattara resigned from the PDCI and subsequently became identified with the breakaway Rally of Republicans. Assisted by the enactment in December 1994 of new presidential qualifications that effectively barred Ouattara from being able to stand, Konan-Bédié won 95.3% of the vote in the presidential elections of October 1995, his only opponent being a candidate of the Ivorian Workers' Party. The following month the PDCI retained its overwhelming majority in the Assembly.

Group for Solidarity
Groupement pour la Solidarité (GPS)
 Address. c/o Assemblée Nationale, Abidjan
 Leadership. Achi Kouman (ASD)
The GPS was created in April 1994 as an alliance of 19 centre-left opposition parties under the leadership of the chair of the Alliance for Social Democracy; it included the Ivorian Workers' Party (PIT), which had one seat in the National Assembly, and most of the formations listed below under "Other Parties". The GPS was a broader successor to the Union of Democratic Forces (*Union des Forces Démocratiques*, UFD) created in December 1992 as an alliance of 15 opposition parties headed by the PIT. The main opposition Ivorian Popular Front did not join either alliance because it disagreed with the other opposition parties' demand for a sovereign national conference to draw up a new political structure for Côte d'Ivoire.

Ivorian Popular Front
Front Populaire Ivorien (FPI)
 Address. BP 302, Abidjan 22
 Telephone. (#225) 243677
 Fax. (#225) 221918

 Leadership. Laurent Gbagbo (general secretary)
The FPI was founded in France in 1982 by the then exiled Laurent Gbagbo (a history professor), who was granted an amnesty on his return in September 1988 but was harassed by the authorities in his moves to establish the party in Côte d'Ivoire. At its founding (illegal) congress in November 1989, the FPI committed itself to a mixed economy with a private sector emphasis, thus placing itself to the left of the ruling Democratic Party of Côte d'Ivoire (PDCI). Legalized in May 1990, the FPI became the acknowledged leader of an opposition coalition which included the Ivorian Workers' Party, the Ivorian Socialist Party and the Union of Social Democrats. This coalition endorsed Gbagbo's candidature for the October 1990 presidential elections, as agreed the previous month by the first legal FPI congress. But sparse finance and organization compared with the resources of the PDCI contributed to Gbagbo's heavy defeat, the official results showing support of less than 18% for the FPI candidate. This outcome was hotly disputed by the FPI, which also denounced alleged government fraud in Assembly elections the following month, when the FPI was awarded only nine of the 175 seats. Its support in that contest came mainly from the north-east of the country and from the more affluent districts of Abidjan.

Amid growing popular unrest in 1991, the FPI declined to endorse a call by other opposition parties for a national conference to determine the future political structure; instead, it demanded the outright resignation of Houphouët-Boigny and announced a campaign of civil disobedience. Arrested in February 1992 amid anti-government demonstrations in Abidjan, Gbagbo and his chief lieutenant, Mollé Mollé, were sentenced the following month to two years' imprisonment, but were amnestied in July 1992 on the recommendation of the President. In October 1992 the FPI launched a new attack on the government for its failure to deal with the deteriorating economic and social situation; but it remained outside an opposition front of 15 other parties formed in December 1992 under the name. In the prelude to the death of Houphouët-Boigny in December 1993, the FPI publicly backed the Assembly president, Henri Konan-Bédié (PDCI), for the succession as provided for under constitutional law. However, when newly-installed President Konan-Bédié failed to offer Gbagbo the premiership, the FPI rejected his proposal that it should join a coalition with the PDCI and returned to opposition mode, although it did not join the Group for Solidarity formed by 19 opposition parties in April 1994.

In December 1994 Gbagbo was endorsed as the

FPI candidate in the 1995 presidential elections, but the party subsequently decided to boycott the contest. The FPI assailed the new presidential qualifications code as being "xenophobic and dangerous", joining with the Rally of Republicans in mounting anti-government demonstrations. In June 1995 an FPI leader, Abou Dramane Sangare, was beaten by police while in the office of the Security Minister; the same month the pro-FPI weekly *La Patrie* was suspended for three months and two of its journalists were sent to prison after being convicted of conspiring to give offence to the President. Having not contested the October 1995 presidential contest, the FPI won 11 seats in the following month's Assembly elections, although Gbagbo's constituency of Gagnoa was one of three in which voting was postponed because of inter-tribal violence.

Strongly based in the trade union movement, the FPI is a consultative member of the Socialist International.

Ivorian Workers' Party
Parti Ivoirien des Travailleurs (PIT)
   Address. BP 302, Abidjan 22
   Leadership. Francis Wodié (general secretary)
The left-of-centre PIT achieved legalization in May 1990 and joined a pro-democracy opposition alliance headed by the Ivorian Popular Front (FPI), backing the latter's unsuccessful candidate in the October 1992 presidential elections. In Assembly elections the following month the PIT was the only opposition party apart from the FPI to gain representation, Wodié winning a seat in the affluent Cocody suburb of Abidjan. Three PIT leaders were among those sentenced to prison terms in March 1992 for their participation in anti-government demonstrations the previous month, although all the detainees were amnestied four months later. Thereafter the PIT and the FPI drifted apart, with the latter declining to endorse the former's demand for a fullscale national conference to decide the country's future political system. In December 1992 the PIT joined with 14 other opposition parties (excluding the FPI) in an alliance called the Union of Democratic Forces. Shortly before President Houphouët-Boigny's death in December 1993, the PIT and five other parties called for the creation of a transitional all-party government. Wodié was the only opposition candidate in the October 1995 presidential election, being credited with 3.8% of the vote.

Rally of Republicans
Rassemblement des Républicains (RDR)
   Address. c/o Assemblée Nationale, Abidjan
   Leadership. Djény Kobina (secretary-general)
The RDR was formally launched in October 1994 by a dissident faction of the ruling Democratic Party of Côte d'Ivoire (PDCI) consisting mainly of "old guard" elements. Claiming to have the support of 31 Assembly deputies, the new party was joined by several former PDCI ministers. Its posters featured pictures of Alassane Ouattara, the former (northern Muslim) Prime Minister who had resigned from the PDCI in May 1994 six months after losing the power struggle for the succession to President Houphouët-Boigny. Ouattara had then taken up a post with the IMF in Washington and was thought likely to be the RDR candidate in the 1995 presidential elections. However, he was effectively barred from standing because his previous citizenship of Burkina Faso and overseas residence ran foul of a new qualifications code enacted in December 1994 by the PDCI Assembly majority. In the run-up to the elections, the RDR took a prominent role in anti-government demonstrations calling in particular for the electoral code to be rescinded. Having not contested the October 1995 presidential elections, the RDR won 13 seats out of 175 in the following month's balloting for the Assembly. However, the RDR leader, Djény Kobina, was prevented from standing by a Constitutional Court ruling that his parents had been Ghanaian.

Union of Political Parties for the Presidential Group of Côte d'Ivoire
Union des Parties Politiques pour le Groupe Présidentiel de la Côte d'Ivoire (UPPGPCI)
   Address. c/o Assemblée Nationale, Abidjan
   Leadership. Siriki Aboubacar Camara (chair)
Also known as the Presidential Group, the UPPGPCI was launched in March 1995 as a merger of five pro-government parties, including the African Federal Party and the Rally for the Forces of the Republic. The grouping backed victorious incumbent Henri Konan-Bédié of the Democratic Party of Côte d'Ivoire in the October 1995 presidential elections.

Other Parties

African Party for Ivorian Renaissance (*Parti Africain pour la Renaissance Ivoirienne*, PARI), founded in 1992.

Alliance for Social Democracy (*Alliance pour la Social-Démocratie*, ASD), led by Achi Kouman, founded in 1990, its leader was named as leader of the opposition Group for Solidarity formed in April 1994.

Democratic and Social Movement (*Mouvement Démocratique et Social*, MDS), founded in 1992.

Ivorian Communist Party (*Parti Communiste Ivoirien*, PCI), registered in 1990.

Ivorian Socialist Party (*Parti Socialiste Ivoirien*, PSI), led by Mandaouadjoa Koukakou (a former vice-president of the National Assembly), registered in 1990.

Liberal Party of Côte d'Ivoire (*Parti Libéral de la Côte d'Ivoire*, PLCI), led by Soumah Yadi, registered in 1990, right-wing opposition party.

Party for Social Progress (*Parti pour le Progrès Social*, PPS), led by Bamba Morifère (a wealthy businessman), registered in 1990, based in the Djoula ethnic group.

National Union for Democracy (*Union National pour la Démocratie*, UND), founded in 1990.

Republican Party of Côte d'Ivoire (*Parti Républicain de la Côte d'Ivoire*, PRCI), led by Robert Gbai-Tagro, founded in France in 1987 and registered in 1990, a right-wing liberal reformist party.

Social Democratic Party (*Parti Social-Démocrate*, PSD), led by Vincent Akadje, founded in 1990, left-of-centre formation.

Union of Social Democrats (*Union des Sociaux-Démocrates*, USD), led by Bernard Zadi-Zaourou, founded and registered in 1990, left-of-centre party opposed to state ownership.

Croatia

Capital: Zagreb

Population: 4,800,000 (1995E)

The Republic of Croatia declared independence from the Socialist Federal Republic of Yugoslavia in June 1991 and was admitted to UN membership in May 1992. Meanwhile, hostilities between Croatian forces and the Serb-dominated Yugoslav Federal Army had resulted in the declaration of what became the Republic of Serbian Krajina in Serb-populated areas of Croatia. The pre-independence ethnic composition of the republic was Croats 74.6% and Serbs 11.3%, with Muslims, Slovenes, Hungarians, Italians and Czechs forming small locally-significant other minorities. Under its 1990 constitution, Croatia is a unitary, democratic and social state, in which the "supreme head of the executive power" is the President, who is directly elected for a five-year term by universal adult suffrage and who appoints the Prime Minister and other ministers. Legislative authority is vested in the bicameral Assembly (*Sabor*), consisting of the upper House of Districts (*Županije Dom*) and the lower House of Representatives (*Predstavničke Dom*), both elected for a four-year term. The upper house has 63 elective members (three from each of the 21 districts of Croatia) plus up to five members nominated by the President. Under an electoral law enacted in September 1995, 92 of the lower house seats (including 12 assigned to Croatian citizens living abroad) are filled by proportional representation from party lists winning at least 5% of the vote, while 28 are filled by constituency-based majority voting and up to a further eight seats are reserved for ethnic minorities (including three for ethnic Serbs).

State financial support is available to parties which have representation in the *Sabor* in proportion to their number of members, a total sum of 18.6 million kunas (c.US$3 million) being allocated for this purpose in the 1994 budget.

Elections to the House of Representatives on Oct. 29, 1995, resulted in 127 seats being filled as follows: Croatian Democratic Union (HDZ) 75 (with 45.2% of the vote); Joint List Bloc 18 (18.3%); Croatian Social Liberal Party 12 (11.6%); Social Democratic Party of Croatia–Party of Democratic Reform 10 (8.9%); Croatian Party of Rights 4 (5.0%); Croatian Independent Democrats 1 (3.1%); ethnic minorities 7. In presidential elections on Aug. 2, 1992, Franjo Tudjman (HDZ) was re-elected with 56.7% of the votes cast.

Croatian Christian Democratic Union

Hrvatska Kršćanska Demokratska Unija (HKDU)

Address. Tkalčićeva 4, 41000 Zagreb

Telephone. (#385–41) 422062

Fax. (#385–41) 421969

Leadership. Marko Veselica (president), Ivan Cesar (vice-president)

The right-wing HKDU was formed in December 1992 as a merger of the Croatian Christian Democratic Party (HKDS) led by Cesar and a faction of the Croatian Democratic Party (HDS) led by Veselica. Founded in October 1989, the HKDS had won two seats in the 1990 pre-independence elections and had participated in the subsequent coalition headed by the Croatian Democratic Union (HDZ); it had failed to win a seat in the lower house elections of August 1992, when Cesar had come seventh out of eight candidates in the presidential balloting with 1.6% of the vote. The HDS had been founded in November 1989 by HDZ dissidents opposed to the parent party's reluctance to reject socialism; it had won nine seats in the 1990 elections but had failed to secure representation in 1992, when Veselica had come sixth in the presidential balloting with 1.7% of the vote. The merged party failed to win any seats in the February 1993 upper house elections. In the October 1995 lower house elections the HKDU formed part of the centre-right Joint List Bloc, winning one seat.

The HKDU inherited the HKDS's affiliation to the Christian Democrat International.

Croatian Democratic Union

Hrvatska Demokratska Zajednica (HDZ)

Address. Trg Hrvatskih Velikana 4, 41000 Zagreb

Telephone. (#385–41) 450338

Fax. (#385–41) 435314

Leadership. Franjo Tudjman (president), Gojko Sušak (vice- president), Ivić Pašalić (executive council chair), Zlatko Canjuga (general secretary)

Formally launched in February 1989 in opposition to the then Communist regime, the HDZ spearheaded the drive both to multi-party democracy and to independence from the Yugoslav federation. A nationalist party, it was joined by many of the elite of the Yugoslav regime, although Franjo Tudjman himself, a history professor with a military background, had been a prominent dissident in the 1970s and 1980s. Contesting the 1990 multi-party elections on a pro-autonomy platform, the HDZ won a landslide parliamentary majority, by virtue of which Tudjman was elected President in May 1990 by vote of the deputies. The HDZ government secured a 94% pro-independence verdict in a referendum in May 1991 and declared Croatia's independence the following month. In further elections in August 1992, the HDZ retained an overall parliamentary majority and Tudjman was directly re-elected President with 56.7% of the popular vote. Thereafter, the HDZ government was riven by dissension about how to deal with the civil war in neighbouring Bosnia-Hercegovina; also controversial was its maintenance of much of the communist-era panoply of central economic control, despite the party's claim to be of the centre-right. Nevertheless, the HDZ in February 1993 won 37 of the 63 elective seats in the upper house, thereafter accepting the small Croatian Peasant Party into the government.

In October 1993 a special HDZ congress approved a new party programme espousing Christian democracy, describing the HDZ as the guarantor of Croatian independence and defining the liberation of Serb-held Croatian territory as the government's most important task. In addition to re-electing Tudjman as party president, the congress elected the hardline nationalist Defence Minister, Gojko Sušak, as vice-president but also, on Tudjman's urging, replaced some other hardliners with moderates on the HDZ presidium. But the impact of this move was diminished by Tudjman's proposal that Jasenovać in southern (Serb-held) Croatia, site of the camp where the wartime pro- Nazi *Utsaša* regime had exterminated Serbs, Jews and Gypsies, should also commemorate "all the victims of communism" (including *Ustaša* officials executed after the war) as well as the Croatian dead in the 1991 war with Serbia. In February 1994 President Tudjman publicly apologized for having, in an earlier book, doubted the veracity of received accounts of the Nazi extermination of Jews during World War II; the following month he also apologized for the role of the *Ustaša* regime in such extermination.

In April 1994 the HDZ was weakened by the formation of the breakaway Croatian Independent Democrats by liberal elements which favoured alliance with the Muslims of Bosnia-Hercegovina against the Serbs and also objected to Tudjman's dictatorial tendencies. Further internal conflict was evident in the resignations of two prominent HDZ hardliners in September 1994, Vladimir Seks (as Deputy Prime Minister) and Branimir Glavas (as party chair in Osijek), in what appeared to be the start of a purge of the party's radical right wing. Nevertheless, Seks's popularity among HDZ deputies was demonstrated the following month when he was elected HDZ leader in the lower house. Buoyed by Croat military successes against the Serbs, the HDZ retained an overall majority in lower house elections in October 1995, although short of the two-thirds majority required for constitutional amendments and with a vote share of 45.2%.

The HDZ is affiliated to the Christian Democrat International.

Croatian Independent Democrats

Hrvatski Nezavisni Demokrati (HND)
Address. Kačićeva 16, 41000 Zagreb
Leadership. Stipe Mesić (president), Josip Manolić (vice- president)

The HND was founded at the end of April 1994 by a dissident group of the ruling Croation Democratic Union (HDZ) led by Mesić and Manolić and including some 16 parliamentary deputies. The former was then president of the lower house of the Croatian Assembly and the latter president of the upper house (both being replaced by HDZ nominees in May). The breakaway party consisted of moderate elements of the HDZ who accused President Tudjman of displaying authoritarian tendencies and bigotry. The origins of the split lay in the government's decision of early 1993 to abandon Croatia's military alliance with the Muslim-dominated government of Bosnia-Hercegovina and instead to support the separatist aims of the Bosnian Croats. Mesić, Manolić and other HDZ liberals had criticized this policy switch and had described the war in Bosnia as unnecessary and brutal. That the HDZ government, under US pressure, had in March 1994 again reversed its line by supporting the Washington agreement providing for a Muslim-Croat federation in Bosnia had not healed the party rift, which had become personalized by what Mesić described as the "crude Bolshevism" of the HDZ leadership's decision to strip Manolić of his party posts. In the October 1995 lower house elections the HND failed to achieve the minimum 5% of the vote required for proportional representation but elected one candidate in the constituency section.

Croatian National Party

Hrvatska Narodna Stranka (HNS)
Address. Gajeva 12/II, 41000 Zagreb
Telephone. (#385–41) 427749
Fax. (#385–41) 425332
Leadership. Savka Dabčević-Kučar (president), Krešimir Džaba (vice-president)

The HNS was founded in October 1990, although its core leadership had formed a coherent dissident group since the attempt in 1970–71 to liberalize the then ruling League of Communists of Croatia. It advocates "modernity" in political and economic structures, private enterprise, regionalism and the creation of a "civil society", drawing considerable support from ethnic Serbs. On its creation, it attracted the backing of five Assembly deputies elected under other labels in 1990 and in the August 1992 elections it won six lower house seats, while its president came third in the concurrent presidential contest with 6% of the national vote. In the February 1993 upper house elections the HNS won one of the elective seats. For the October 1995 lower house elections it was part of the centre-right Joint List Bloc, winning two seats.

Croatian Party of Rights

Hrvatska Stranka Prava (HSP)
Address. c/o Sabor, Trg Sv. Marka 7, 41000 Zagreb
Telephone. (#385–41) 444000, ext. 3314
Leadership. Boris Kandare (president), Anto Dapić (vice- president), Vlado Jukić (secretary)

Descended indirectly from a pre-war nationalist party of the same name, the far-right HSP was founded in February 1990 by Dobroslav Paraga and had considerable support among Croats outside Croatia. It advocates "national-state sovereignty throughout the whole of [Croatia's] historical and ethnic space", which has been taken to imply a territorial claim not just to the Croat-populated areas of Bosnia-Hercegovina but to the whole of that state. To these ends, the party formed a military wing called the Croatian Defence Association (*Hrvatska Obrambeni Savez*, HOS), which became heavily involved on the Croat side in inter-ethnic conflict in Bosnia (and was seen by many as the modern counterpart of the wartime pro-fascist *Ustaša* movement). The party won five lower house seats in the August 1992 elections and Paraga came fourth in the concurrent presidential contest, winning 5.4% of the national vote. It failed to win a seat in the February 1993 upper house elections, after which Paraga and three other HSP leaders were charged with terrorism and inciting forcible changes to the constitutional order. The government also applied to the Constitutional Court for a ban on the HSP.

In July 1993 Zagreb police evicted the party from its headquarters in the capital, on the grounds that its occupation of the state-owned building since 1991 was illegal. Steps were also taken by the authorities to curtail the independence of the HOS by integrating its forces into units controlled by the Defence Ministry. Meanwhile, Paraga had come under criticism for his leadership, this resulting in his being replaced by Kandare at an extraordinary congress in September 1993, when a new main committee was elected as the party's governing body. Having been acquitted of the charges against him in November 1993, Paraga proceeded to form the new Croatian Party of Rights 1861. In the October 1995 lower house elections the HSP just surmounted the 5% representation threshold.

Croatian Party of Slavonia and Baranja

Slavonsko-Baranjska Hrvatska Stranka (SBHS)
    Address. c/o Predstavničke Dom, Zagreb
    Leadership. Damir Jurić (president)

The SBHS represents ethnic Croats of territories occupied by Serbian forces in 1991 (but mostly recovered in 1995). It contested the October 1995 lower house elections as part of the opposition Joint List Bloc, winning one seat.

Croatian Peasant Party

Hrvatska Seljačka Stranka (HSS)
    Address. Trnskoga 8, 41000 Zagreb
    Telephone. (#385–41) 212325
    Fax. (#385–41) 217411
    Leadership. Zlatko Tomčić (president), Valentin Puževski (parliamentary chair)

The HSS is descended from the co-operative party founded by the Radić brothers in 1904, which became a standard-bearer of Croat nationalism in inter-war Yugoslavia but was suppressed by the wartime pro-Nazi *Ustaša* regime in Croatia. Revived in November 1989 and committed to pacifism, local democracy, privatization and rural co-operatives, the HSS won three seats in the August 1992 lower house elections and five in the February 1993 upper house balloting. It then effectively entered a coalition with the ruling Croatian Democratic Union. On succeeding Drago Stipać as HSS president in December 1994, however, Zlatko Tomčić vacated his post as Minister of Urban Planning, Housing and Construction. In the October 1995 lower house elections the HSS won 10 seats as part of the opposition Joint List Bloc.

Croatian Social Liberal Party

Hrvatska Socijalno-Liberalna Stranka (HSLS)
    Address. Galovićeva 8, 41000 Zagreb
    Telephone. (#385–41) 215704
    Fax. (#385–41) 214444
    Leadership. Dražen Budiša (president), Mate Meštrović (parliamentary chair), Božo Kovačević (secretary-general)

The HSLS was founded in May 1989 as a liberal party on the classic European model, emphasizing the "democratic and European tradition and orientation of Croatia". Having made little impact in the 1990 pre-independence elections, it became the second-strongest party in the lower house elections of August 1992, winning 14 seats, while its president took second place in the simultaneous presidential contest with 21.9% of the national vote. In the February 1993 upper house elections, the party won 16 of the 63 elective seats. Opposed to the government of the Croatian Democratic Union, the HSLS participated in an opposition boycott of parliament from May to September

1994 in protest against irregularities in the election of new presidents of the two houses in the wake of the formation of the Croatian Independent Democrats. In the October 1995 lower house elections the party took 11.6% of the vote and 12 seats, confirming its status as the strongest single opposition party.

The HSLS is an observer member of the Liberal International.

Dalmatian Action

Dalmatinska Akcija (DA)
    Address. Kružićeva 2/II, 58000 Split
    Telephone. (#385–58) 362060
    Fax. (#385–58) 517036
    Leadership. Mira Ljubić-Lorger (president)

Founded in December 1990, the DA seeks to represent the people of Dalmatia (many of them non-Croats), for which it seeks greater autonomy, and has drawn attention to the increased isolation of the region caused by the conflict between Croatia and Serbia and within Bosnia-Hercegovina. In the August 1992 lower house elections it participated in a regionalist alliance with the Istrian Democratic Assembly and the Rijeka Democratic League, winning one of the six seats accruing to that alliance. In October 1993 the Zagreb authorities launched a crackdown on DA activists, several of whom were arrested and charged with terrorist offences and illegal possession of arms.

Istrian Democratic Assembly

Istarski Demokratski Sabor (IDS)
    Sieta Democratica Istriana (SDI)
    Address. Flanatička 29/1, 52000 Pula
    Telephone. (#385–52) 43702
    Fax. (#385–52) 43707
    Leadership. Ivan Jakovčić (president)

The centre-right IDS confines its activities to the Istrian region, where it represents the aspirations of ethnic Italians and other minorities, advocating the creation of a "trans-border" Istria encompassing Croatian, Slovenian and Italian areas. It has been especially exercised by Croatian-Slovenian border definition issues and by the Croatian-Italian dispute over compensation for Italians who left Yugoslavia in the wake of the Istrian territorial gains by the latter after World War II. In the August 1992 lower house elections, the IDS was allied with Dalmatian Action and the Rijeka Democratic League in a regionalist front, winning four of the six seats taken by the alliance. In the February 1993 upper house elections the IDS won one elective seat and was allocated two more under the President's prerogative. In the same month it won 72% of the Istrian vote in local elections. In the October 1995 lower house elections it formed part of the centre-right Joint List Bloc, winning four seats within this alliance.

Joint List Bloc
Zajednica Lista (ZL)
    Address. c/o Predstavničke Dom, Zagreb
    Leadership. Zlatko Tomčić (HSS)

The centre-right ZL was formed as an opposition alliance for the October 1995 lower house elections, consisting of the Croatian Peasant Party (HSS), the Croatian Christian Democratic Union, the Croatian National Party, the Croatian Party of Slavonia and Baranja and the Istrian Democratic Assembly. The alliance won an aggregate vote share of 18.3% and 18 seats, making its the largest opposition force in the new house. It subsequently aligned with other opposition parties, notably the Croatian Social Liberal Party, to resist what was perceived to be the authoritarian tendencies of the ruling Croatian Democratic Union.

Rijeka Democratic League
Riječki Demokratski Savez (RDS)
    Address. Ciottina 19, 51000 Rijeka
    Telephone. (#385–41) 34743
    Leadership. Nikola Ivaniš (president), Franjo Butorac (secretary)

The left-of-centre RDS is based in the ethnic Italian minority of Rijeka, being concerned with issues of cultural expression, minority rights and education. It contested the August 1992 lower house elections in a regionalist alliance with Dalmatian Action and the Istrian Democratic Assembly, winning one of the six seats accruing to that alliance.

Serbian Democratic Party
Srpska Demokratska Stranka (SDS)
    Address. Jove Miodragovića 22, 59300 Knin
    Leadership. Jovan Rašković

The nationalist SDS was founded in February 1990 to represent ethnic Serbs in Croatia, while claiming to promote the rights of all ethnic minorities. It supported the creation of the breakaway Republic of Serbian Krajina (RSK), thus coming under official scrutiny in 1992 for its alleged threat to the constitutional order. The SDS candidate, Milan Martić, was elected RSK president in January 1994, but in 1995 was party was thrown into crisis by the recapture of most of the Krajina by Croatian government forces and by the resultant massive exodus of ethnic Serbs.

Serbian National Party
Srpska Narodna Stranka (SNS)
    Address. Trg Mažuranića 3, 41000 Zagreb
    Telephone. (#385–41) 451090
    Fax. (#385–41) 451090

    Leadership. Milan Dukić (president), Veselin Pejnović (vice-president)

Founded in May 1991, the SNS represents ethnic Serbs who regard Croatia as their homeland and therefore rejects the separatist solution represented by the self-proclaimed Republic of Serbian Krajina, as espoused by the Serbian Democratic Party. Although Croatia's Serb-populated areas were by then largely outside the control of the Zagreb government, the SNS won three seats in the August 1992 lower house elections. In mid-1995 the party's support base was sharply reduced by the flight of most ethnic Serbs from the Krajina on its recapture by Croatian government forces, while the reduction of guaranteed Serb seats in the Croation lower house from 13 to three narrowed its representative scope. In October 1995 SNS leader Milan Dukić asserted that at least 50% of the Krajina's former ethnic Serb population of 250,000 wished to return and condemned the government's rejection of a mass return to the area. In the October 1995 Croatian elections the SNS took two seats.

Social Democratic Party of Croatia–Party of Democratic Reform
Socijaldemokratska Partija Hrvatske–Stranka Demokratskih Promjena (SPH-SDP)
    Address. Prisavlje 14, 41000 Zagreb
    Telephone. (#385–41) 519490
    Fax. (#385–41) 518249
    Leadership. Ivica Račan (president)

The SPH-SDP is descended from the Croatian Communist Party (created in 1937 when Yugoslavia's Communist movement was reorganized by Tito) and from the succeeding League of Communists of Yugoslavia (LCY, created as the ruling party in 1952). Croatian elements were prominent in periodic attempts to liberalize and reform the LCY regime from within; but in the post-1989 move to independence and multi-partyism the Croatian LCY was rapidly sidelined by the rise of the new Croatian Democratic Union (HDZ). Seen as tainted with "Yugoslavism", the LCY lost much of its membership to the HDZ and other parties, failing to stem the outflow by changing its name to Party of Democratic Reform (SDP) and committing itself to democratic socialism and a market economy. In the 1990 pre-independence elections, the SDP trailed a poor second to the HDZ, winning 75 of the 349 legislative seats in its own right and a further 16 on joint lists with other parties. In further changes in 1991, the SPH title was adopted (the SDP rubric being retained as a suffix) and the party deferred to pro-independence sentiment by acknowledging Croatia as the "national state of the Croatian people", while stressing the need to accomodate non-Croat groups.

Advocating economic modernization combined with preservation of a welfare state, the SPH-SDP was reduced to 11 seats in the August 1992 lower house elections and failed to secure representation in its own right in the February 1993 upper house balloting, although it was allocated one seat by virtue of a pact with the Croatian Social Liberal Party. It performed better in the October 1995 lower house elections, winning nearly 9% of the vote and 10 seats.

Other Parties

Action of the Social Democrats of Croatia (*Akcija Socijal- Demokrata Hrvatske*, ASH), led by Miko Tripalo, founded in June 1994 by various small left-wing groupings, aiming to mount a credible electoral challenge independent of the ex-Communist Social Democratic Party of Croatia–Party of Democratic Reform, but won only 3.2% in the October 1995 elections.

Albanian Christian Democratic Party (*Albanska Demokrśćanska Stranka*, ADS), led by Marcel Gjoni, based in Croatia's Catholic ethnic Albanian community, linked to the party of the same name in the Federal Yugoslav province of Kosovo.

Christian National Party (*Krśćanska Narodna Stranka*, KNS), led by Zdravko Mršić, a right-wing grouping. *Address.* Degenova 7, 41000 Zagreb

Croatian Conservative Party (*Hrvatska Konzervativna Stranka*, HKS), won 0.2% of the vote in the 1995 lower house elections.

Croatian Democratic Party (*Hrvatska Demokratska Stranka*, HDS), led by Anto Kovačević, the rump formation remaining when then leader Marko Veselica led his supporters into the new Croatian Christian Democratic Union in December 1992. *Address.* Kralja Tomislava 14/1, 41000 Zagreb

Croatian Democratic Party of Rights (*Hrvatska Demokratska Stranka Prava*, HDSP), led Krešimir Pavelić, of similar far-right orientation as the Croatian Party of Rights.

Croatian Muslim Democratic Party (*Hrvatska Muslimanska Demokratska Stranka*, HMDS), led by Hasan Bosnić, founded in October 1989, a national Muslim formation eschewing purely religious identification, included in the ruling coalition prior to the 1992 elections. *Address.* Trnskog 8, 41000 Zagreb

Croatian Natural Law Party (*Hrvatska Stranka Naravnog Zakona*, HSNZ), led by Darko Peček, affiliate of the European Council of Natural Law Parties, won 0.3% in the 1995 elections.

Croatian Party (*Hrvatska Stranka*, HS), led by Hrvoje Šošić (an eminent economist), who is a member of the upper house nominated by the President.

Croatian Party of Rights 1861 (*Hrvatska Stranka Prava 1861*), launched in July 1995 by Dobroslav Paraga, former leader of the far-right Croatian Party of Rights, who had won 5.4 in the 1992 presidential election and who had been acquitted of terrorism and other charges in 1993; the new party won 1.3% in the October 1995 elections.

Croatian Social-Democratic Party (*Socijal-demokratska Stranka Hrvatske*, SDSH), led by Antun Vujić, founded in December 1989 as a revival of the pre-communist party of the same name, participated in the ruling coalition until August 1992, when its leader came last in the presidential elections with 0.7% of the vote.

Croatian Socialist Party (*Socijalistička Stranka Hrvatske*, SSH), led by Željko Mažar, successor to the communist-era front organization in Croatia (the Socialist League of the Working People), won three seats outright in the 1990 elections and 15 on a joint list with what became the Social Democratic Party of Croatia–Party of Democratic Reform, subsequently joining the government, but ceased to have Assembly representation in 1992.

Croatian Statehood Movement (*Hrvatski Državnotvorni Pokret*, HDP), led by Nikola Štedul, who in the communist era was the target of an assassination attempt by Yugoslav agents while living in exile in Scotland.

Green Action (*Zelene Akcija*, ZA-S), led by Nikola Visković (Split) and Dubravka Bacun (Zagreb), an environmentalist formation strong in Croatia's largest Adriatic port (Split), won one seat in 1990 on a joint list with what became the Social Democratic Party of Croatia–Party of Democratic Reform, but none in 1992. *Address.* Zrtava Fašizma 8, 58000 Split

Independent Party of Rights (*Nezavisna Stranka Prava*, NSP), splinter group of the far-right Croatian Party of Rights, won 0.3% in the 1995 elections.

Istrian People's Party (*Istarska Pučka Stranka*, IPS), led by Josip Fabris, a regionalist formation. *Address.* Trg. Revolucije 3, Pula

Liberal Party (*Liberalna Stranka*, LS), descended from the official communist-era League of Socialist Youth of Croatia.

Party of Democratic Action (*Stranka Demokratske Akcije*, SDA), Croatian section of the dominant party of the same name in Bosnia-Herzegovina.

Party of Serbs (*Stranka Srpski*, SS), led by Milorad Pupovać, founded in 1993 to represent ethnic Serbs.

Social Democratic Union of Croatia (*Socijaldemokratska Unija Hrvatske*, SDUH), led by Branko Horvat (a leading economist), won 3.2% in the 1995 lower house elections. *Address*. Tratinska 27, 41000 Zagreb

Transnational Radical Party (*Transnacionalna Radikalna Stranka*, TRS), led by Diana Rexhepi, originally founded in Rome, linked with the Radical Party of Italy.

Cuba

Capital: Havana

Population: 11,000,000 (1995E)

The Republic of Cuba, ceded by Spain to the United States following the Spanish-American war of 1898, became independent in 1902. The United States, however, retains the right to have military bases on the island (currently the Guantánamo naval base). Under the 1976 constitution (as modified in 1992) executive authority resides with the President of the Council of State, Dr Fidel Castro Ruz, who has held power since January 1959 (following the revolutionary overthrow of the government of Gen. Batista). Nominal legislative authority is vested in the unicameral National Assembly of People's Power (*Asamblea Nacional del Poder Popular*, ANPP), which holds twice-yearly ordinary sessions and elects a 31–member Council of State to represent it in the interim. Executive and administrative authority is held by a Council of Ministers, which is appointed by the ANPP upon the recommendation of the President. The majority of office-holders are members of the Communist Party of Cuba (PCC), the only authorized political party.

A PCC politburo was last elected in October 1991, as was a Council of State in March 1993. Direct municipal elections took place for the first time in December 1992, and the ANPP's 589 members were directly elected for a five-year term for the first time in February 1993 (although only PPC members were allowed to stand).

Communist Party of Cuba
Partido Comunista Cubano (PCC)
Address. c/o National Assembly of People's Power, Havana
Leadership. Fidel Castro Ruz (first secretary), Raúl Castro Ruz (second secretary)

The PCC was founded in 1961 as the Integrated Revolutionary Organizations (*Organizaciones Revolucionarias Integradas*, ORI), a coalition of the political and military groupings which had defeated the Batista dictatorship in the revolution of 1956–59. The components were Castro's rural guerrilla army, the July 26 Movement (*Movimiento 26 de Julio*); the communist Popular Socialist Party (*Partido Socialista Popular*, PSP); and the Revolutionary Directorate (*Directorio Revolucionario*, DR). No other political organizations were permitted to function after 1961. The ORI was transformed into the United Party of the Cuban Socialist Revolution in 1962, and adopted its present name in 1965.

The first PCC congress, held in 1975, approved a party constitution and programme, and the special status of the party as the leading force of society and the state was enshrined in the 1976 constitution. The second congress was held in 1980 and the third in 1986, at which time major changes in structure and personnel were approved. At its fourth congress in 1991, the PCC endorsed direct election to the ANPP, abolished the party secretariat, approved a substantially restructured politburo and removed the requirement that party members must be atheists.

Although regionally isolated, both diplomatically and economically (particularly by the United States), the PCC government supported numerous "anti-imperialist" revolutionary movements around the world in the 1960s and 1970s, and maintained close relations with the then Soviet Union and its allies until the demise of their communist regimes at the end of the 1980s.

The PCC has since reiterated its continuing hardline commitment to Marxist-Leninist ideology and the revolution.

Illegal Opposition Groups

Christian Democratic Party (*Partido Demócrata Cristiano*, PDC), led by José Ignacio Rasco, an affiliate of the Christian Democrat International

Cuban Council (*Concilio Cubano*, CC), a coalition of small and fragmented dissident groups formed in mid-1995.

Cuban Democratic Convergence (*Concertación Democrática Cubana*, CDC), an alliance of

opposition organizations formed in 1991 in support of political pluralism and economic reform.

Cuban Democratic Party (*Partido Democrático Cubano*, PDC), led by Ignacio Castro and Salvador Ramani, reportedly founded inside Cuba in 1990.

Cuban Democratic Platform (*Plataforma Democrática Cubana*, PDC), an exile organization.

Cuban Liberal Union (*Unión Liberal Cubana*, ULC), led by Carlos Alberto Montaner, an affiliate of the Liberal International.

Social Democratic Party of Cuba (*Partido Socialdemócrata de Cuba*, PSDC), led by Enrique Baloyra.

Cyprus

Capital: Nicosia   **Population:** 780,000 (1995E, including TRNC)

The Republic of Cyprus achieved independence from the UK in 1960 on the basis of a power-sharing constitution as between the majority Greek Cypriots and the minority Turkish Cypriots. Guaranteed by the UK, Greece and Turkey, this arrangement broke down by 1964, amid an escalation of inter-communal conflict. In 1974 the resultant territorial division between the two communities was solidified by the military intervention of Turkey, whose forces facilitated the effective partition of the island into the Greek Cypriot sector and what in 1983 became the Turkish Republic of Northern Cyprus (TRNC), whose self-proclaimed "independence" in about 40% of the island's area has been recognized only by Turkey. UN-sponsored talks, aimed at producing a federal settlement which preserved Cyprus as one sovereign state, made little substantive progress over the succeeding two decades. Under the 1960 constitution, which the Greek Cypriots continue to observe where possible, the Republic of Cyprus has an executive President, who is directly elected for a five-year term, by compulsory universal suffrage of those aged 21 and over, and who appoints the government. Legislative authority is vested in a unicameral House of Representatives (*Vouli Antiprosópon/Temsilciler Meclisi*), which theoretically has 80 members elected for a five-year term by proportional representation, 56 by the Greek Cypriot community and 24 by the Turkish Cypriots. Since 1964, however, the Turkish Cypriot community has declined to participate in these arrangements and has set up its own political structures (see separate section below).

Political parties in the Republic of Cyprus are eligible for state financial support if they, alone or in coalition, receive at least 3% of the electoral vote. Of the total sum available, 40% (or CY£200,000 in 1994) is divided equally among qualifying parties or coalitions, while 60% (or CY£300,000 in 1994) is allocated to qualifying parties in proportion to the percentage vote received in the most recent parliamentary elections.

Elections on May 26, 1996, for the 56 Greek Cypriot seats in the House of Representatives resulted as follows: Democratic Rally (DISY) 20 seats (with 34.5% of the vote); Progressive

Party of the Working People (AKEL) 19 (33.0%); Democratic Party (DIKO) 10 (16.4%); Unified Democratic Union of Cyprus (EDEK Socialists) 5 (8.1%); Movement of Free Democrats 2 (3.7%). Greek Cypriot presidential elections held on Feb. 7 and 14, 1993, were won by Glafkos Clerides (DISY), who took 50.3% of the second-round vote.

Democratic Party
Dimokratiko Komma (DIKO)

Address. 50 Grivas Dighenis Ave, PO Box 3979, Nicosia

Telephone. (#357–2) 472002

Fax. (#357–2) 366488

Leadership. Spyros Kyprianou (president), Alexis Galanos (vice- president), Stathis Kittis (general secretary)

DIKO was founded in 1976 as the Democratic Front, a centre-right alliance supporting President Makarios's policy of "long-term struggle" against the Turkish occupation of northern Cyprus. It became the largest party in the 1976 parliamentary elections, winning 21 of the 35 available seats in a pro-Makarios alliance which included the (communist) Progressive Party of the Working People (AKEL) and the (socialist) Unified Democratic Union of Cyprus (EDEK). Having succeeded Makarios as President on the latter's death in August 1977, the DIKO leader was elected unopposed in his own right in January 1978 and re-elected in February 1983, when he received 56.5% of the first-round vote. Meanwhile, DIKO had been weakened by defections and its parliamentary representation had slumped to eight seats in the 1981 elections (held by proportional representation), when its vote share was 19.5%. Kyprianou nevertheless retained the reins of power, supported by AKEL until the latter ended the alliance in late 1984 because it objected to the President's alleged intransigence in inter-communal talks. In early elections in December 1985 DIKO increased its vote share to 27.7% and its seat total to 16 in a House enlarged to 56 Greek Cypriot members. But Kyprianou failed to obtain a third presidential term in February 1988, receiving only 27.3% in the first round of voting and being eliminated.

DIKO mounted strong opposition to the policies of the new AKEL-endorsed independent President, George Vassilou, particularly his handling of the inter-communal talks. It was strengthened in 1989 when it absorbed the small Centre Union party led by Tassos Papadopoulos. Nevertheless, in parliamentary elections in May 1991 DIKO remained the third party, falling to 11 seats and 19.5% of the vote. Thereafter it formed a tactical alliance with EDEK to oppose the 1992 UN plan for Cyprus, claiming that it formalized the island's partition. In the February 1993

presidential elections, DIKO and EDEK presented a joint candidate, Paschalis Paschalides, who obtained only 18.6% of the first-round vote and was eliminated. In the second round, official DIKO support was given to Glafcos Clerides of the Democratic Rally (DISY), who won a narrow victory over Vassiliou. In return for this support, President Clerides included five DIKO ministers in the new 11–member government. The party slipped further to 10 seats in the May 1996 elections.

Democratic Rally
Dimokratikos Synagermos (DISY)

Address. Corner Pindarou/Skokou Streets, PO Box 5305, Nicosia

Telephone. (#357–2) 449791

Fax. (#357–2) 442751

Leadership. Yiannakis Matsis (president), Nicos Anastasiades (deputy president), Dimitris Syllouris (general secretary)

DISY was founded in 1976 by Glafkos Clerides as a conservative, pro-Western union of elements of the former Progressive Front and United and Democratic National parties. Clerides had previously been acting President of Cyprus in the wake of the right-wing coup and the resultant Turkish invasion of mid-1974, until the return of Archbishop Makarios as head of state in December 1974. The new party won 27.5% of the vote in the 1976 parliamentary elections but failed to obtain a seat because of the constituency-based system then in force. In that contest DISY condemned the victorious alliance of the (centre-right) Democratic Party (DIKO), the (communist) Progressive Party of the Working People (AKEL) and the (socialist) Unified Democratic Union of Cyprus (EDEK) as being communist-inspired. Held under a proportional system, the 1981 parliamentary elections gave DISY 32% of the vote and 12 of the 35 available seats, while the 1983 presidential balloting resulted in Clerides winning 34% and being defeated by the DIKO incumbent, Spyros Kyprianou. During 1985 DISY attacked Presidnt Kyprianou for his alleged intransigence in the UN-sponsored negotiations on the status of Cyprus, combining with AKEL to force early parliamentary elections in December 1985. These resulted in DISY supplanting AKEL as the largest single party, its support increasing from 31.9% in 1981 to 33.6%, which gave it 19 seats in a House enlarged to 56 Greek Cypriot members.

In the presidential election of February 1988, Clerides was again defeated, winning 48.4% of the second-round vote against the victorious AKEL-supported independent candidate, George Vassiliou. In parliamentary elections in May 1991 DISY's share of the vote, on a joint list with the small Liberal Party (KTP), rose to 35.8%, which yielded 20 seats (of which one went to the KTP). Thereafter, DISY gave broad support to President Vassiliou's conduct of the inter-communal talks, including his acceptance of a new UN plan tabled in 1992 demarcating Greek Cypriot and Turkish Cypriot areas of administration in a federal state, whereas DIKO and EDEK contended that the plan would entrench the island's partition. In the February 1993 presidential elections, however, Clerides astutely distanced himself from the UN plan and emerged as the unexpected victor against Vassiliou, his narrow 50.3% winning margin in the second round being in part due to the transfer to him of DIKO and EDEK voting support. Six DISY and five DIKO ministers were included in the new government appointed by President Clerides, who stood down as DISY leader in light of his election. In further talks, Clerides reverted to broad acceptance of the UN plan and sought to use his longstanding personal relationship with the Turkish Cypriot leader, Rauf Denktash, to expedite a settlement, although to no avail as at end-1995. DISY remained the strongest party in the May 1996 elections, winning 20 seats in its own right.

DISY is affiliated to the Christian Democrat International and the International Democrat Union.

Democratic Socialist Reform Movement
Ananeotiko Dimokratiko Sosialistiko Kinima (ADISOK)

Address. 19 Nikitara Street, PO Box 3494, Nicosia

Telephone. (#357–2) 367345
Fax. (#357–2) 367611
Leadership. Costas Themistocleous (acting president)

ADISOK was founded in January 1990 by a dissident faction of the (communist) Progressive Party of the Working People (AKEL), including four of the 15 politburo members and five of the 15 AKEL deputies, whose proposals for more party democracy were opposed by the leadership majority. Advocating a Cyprus settlement on the basis of UN resolutions, the new party made little impact in the May 1991 parliamentary elections, winning 2.7% of the vote and no seats. It slipped to 1.4% in the May 1996 elections.

The Ecologists
Ecologi

Address. PO Box 9682, 1722 Nicosia
Telephone. (#357-2) 493827
Fax. (#357-2) 498972
Leadership. Georgios Perdikis (president)

Part of the European Green movement, the Ecologists were launched as a national political movement shortly before the May 1996 parliamentary elections, in which they won a 1% vote share and therefore failed to gain representation.

Liberal Party
Komma Ton Phileleftheron (KTP)

Address. Flat G1, Tryfonos Building, Eleftheria Square, Nicosia
Telephone. (#357-2) 452117
Fax. (#357-2) 368900
Leadership. Nicos Rolandis (president), Phivos Mavrovouniotis (general secretary)

The KTP was formed in September 1986 by Rolandis, who had been Foreign Minister from 1978 until resigning in September 1983 over policy differences with President Kyprianou on the conduct of the inter-communal talks. At first an extra-parliamentary organization, in the 1988 presidential elections the KTP endorsed the successful independent candidate, George Vassiliou (then backed by the Progressive Party of the Working People and later founder of the Movement of Free Democrats). For the May 1991 parliamentary elections, however, it formed an alliance with the Democratic Rally, winning one seat (taken by Rolandis) on a joint list with the latter. It continued the alliance in the May 1996 elections but this time failed to gain representation.

The KTP is an observer member of the Liberal International.

Movement of Free Democrats
Kinima Eleftheron Dimokraton (KED)

Address. 2 Omerou Avenue, PO Box 874, Nicosia
Telephone. (#357–2) 474460
Fax. (#357–2) 474757
Leadership. George Vassiliou (president), Frixos Kolotas (vice-president), Michaelis Michaelides (general secretary)

The KED was launched in April 1993 by ex-President Vassiliou following his unexpected failure to secure a second term in the February 1993 presidential elections. A wealthy businessman, he had been elected to the presidency in 1988 as an independent candidate with the backing of the (communist) Progressive Party of the Working People (AKEL), which had again supported him in 1993. The KED was described as a centre-left formation which aimed to contribute to "the struggle of our people to solve the national problem" and to promote the admission of Cyprus to the European Union. The party won two seats in the May 1996 elections, these going to Vassiliou and his wife Androulla.

New Horizons
Neoi Orizontes (NO)
> *Address.* Byzantiou 9, Strovolos, Nicosia
> *Telephone.* (#357-2) 475333
> *Fax.* (#357-2) 476044
> *Leadership.* Nicholaos Koutsou (chair)

The right-wing NO was founded in early 1996 by elements close to the Greek Orthodox Church. Its platform on the Cyprus question differed from those of other parties in that, while they all accepted the concept of a federal Cyprus, the NO argued in favour of a unitary state and a single government. It failed to gain representation in the May 1996 elections, taking only 1.7% of the vote.

Progressive Party of the Working People
Anorthotiko Komma Ergazomenou Laou (AKEL)
> *Address.* Akamantos Street, PO Box 1827, Nicosia
> *Telephone.* (#357–2) 441121
> *Leadership.* Dimitrios Christofias (general secretary), Andreas Christou (parliamentary spokesman)

AKEL is directly descended from the Communist Party of Cyprus, which held its first congress in 1926 but was declared illegal by the British authorities amid the political and social unrest of 1931. Reconstituted as AKEL in 1941, the party emerged after the war as an orthodox pro-Soviet Marxist-Leninist formation and was again banned by the British in 1955. Legalized again in December 1959, it consolidated its dominant position in the trade union movement after independence in 1960. In the 1976 parliamentary elections it was part of a victorious alliance with the (centre-right) Democratic Party (DIKO) and the (socialist) Unified Democratic Union of Cyprus (EDEK). Following the death of President Makarios in 1977, it gave general backing to the new government of President Kyprianou (DIKO) and headed the poll in the 1981 parliamentary elections, winning 32.8% of the vote and 12 of the 35 seats then available. The alliance with DIKO was terminated by AKEL in December 1984 on the grounds that the President was showing insufficient flexibility in inter-communal talks with the Turkish Cypriots. In the December 1985 parliamentary elections AKEL slipped to third place, winning 27.4% and 15 seats in a House enlarged to 56 Greek Cypriot members.

For the February 1988 presidential elections AKEL opted to endorse an independent candidate, George Vassiliou, who was elected in the second round by a narrow 51.6% margin over Glafkos Clerides of the Democratic Rally (DISY), receiving support from EDEK and many DIKO voters. In early 1990 AKEL appeared to be weakened by the formation of the breakaway Democratic Socialist Reform Movement (ADISOK), when the leadership majority declined to revise the party's Marxist-Leninist principles and mode of operations. Nevertheless, in the May 1991 parliamentary elections, AKEL increased its vote share to 30.6% and its representation to 18 seats (while ADISOK won none). AKEL again endorsed Vassiliou in the February 1993 presidential elections, but the opposition of DIKO and EDEK to his handling of the national question resulted in their supporters swinging behind Clerides (DISY) in the second round, in which Vassiliou was defeated by a 50.3% to 49.7% margin. Later in the year the ex-President launched the Movement of Free Democrats, but this centre-left formation was seen as more of a threat to DIKO and EDEK than to AKEL.

AKEL gained ground in the May 1996 elections, winning 19 seats, but failed in its aim of overtaking DISY as the largest party.

Unified Democratic Union of Cyprus (EDEK Socialist Party)
Ethniki Dimokratiki Enosi Kyprou (EDEK)
> *Address.* 2 Stasinou/Boumboulinas Street, PO Box 1064, Nicosia
> *Telephone.* (#357–2) 458617
> *Fax.* (#357–2) 458894
> *Leadership.* Vassos Lyssarides (president), Takis Hadjidemetriou (vice-president), Yiannakis Omirou (general secretary)

EDEK was founded in 1969 as a democratic socialist party and contested the 1970 parliamentary elections as the Democratic Centre Union, winning two seats. In the early 1970s it opposed both Greek interference in Cyprus and the Turkish invasion of the island of 1974, which some of its members actively resisted. It supported the return to power of President Makarios in late 1974 and in the 1976 elections participated in a pro-Makarios alliance with the (centre-left) Democratic Party (DIKO) and the (communist) Progressive Party of the Working People (AKEL), winning four seats. It fell back to three seats in 1981 campaigning independently, and in the 1983 presidential election Vassos Lyssarides, presented as the candidate of the broader National Salvation Front, took third place with 9.5% of the vote, despite having withdrawn from the contest at the last minute. EDEK increased its House representation to six seats in the 1985 elections, winning 11.1% of the vote against 8.2% in 1981. The party was at that time broadly supportive of President Kyprianou's tough line in the inter-communal talks.

Lyssarides stood again in the February 1988 presidential elections but was eliminated in the first round, with only 9.2% of the vote. In the second round EDEK transferred its support to the AKEL-backed independent candidate, George Vassiliou, who was elected by a narrow margin. But EDEK quickly came to oppose President Vassiliou's accomodating line in the inter-communal talks, making common cause on this issue with DIKO against AKEL and the (conservative) Democratic Rally (DISY). In the May 1991 parliamentary elections EDEK won 10.9% of the vote and seven seats. Thereafter it mounted strong opposition, with DIKO, to Vassiliou's acceptance of the UN plan demarcating Greek Cypriot and Turkish Cypriot areas of administration in a federal Cyprus, claiming that the proposals amounted to partition of the island.

In the February 1993 presidential elections, EDEK and DIKO presented a joint candidate, Paschalis Paschalides, who obtained only 18.6% in the first round and was eliminated. In the second round, EDEK gave its support to Glafkos Clerides of DISY, who was narrowly victorious over Vassiliou. In the May 1996 legislative elections EDEK fell back to five seats.

Turkish Republic of Northern Cyprus (TRNC)

The "independent" TRNC was proclaimed in November 1983 as successor to the Turkish Federated State of Cyprus (TFSC), itself created in February 1975 as successor to the Turkish Cypriot Autonomous Administration dating from December 1968. Under its 1985 constitution, the TRNC has an executive President directly elected for a five-year term by universal adult suffrage and a 50-member Assembly of the Republic (*Cumhuriyet Meclisi*), also elected for a five-year term. Assembly elections on Dec. 12, 1993, resulted as follows: National Unity Party 17 seats; Democratic Party 15; Republican Turkish Party 13; Communal Liberation Party 5. In presidential elections on April 15 and 22, 1995, Rauf Denktash (standing as an independent) was re-elected with 62.5% of the second-round vote.

The TRNC has been recognized by no government except that of Turkey. The Greek Cypriot government regards the TRNC government and Assembly as illegal, although it accepts the legitimacy of the political parties operating in the Turkish Cypriot sector.

Communal Liberation Party

Toplumcu Kurtuluš Partisi (TKP)

Address. 13 Mahmut Pasa Street, Lefkosa/Nicosia

Telephone. (#90–520) 72555

Leadership. Mustafa Akinci (leader), Hüseyin Angolemli (general secretary)

The left-of-centre TKP (sometimes known as the Socialist Salvation Party) was founded in 1976 and espoused the principles of Mustapha Kemal Atatürk, founder of the modern Turkish state. It won six Assembly seats in 1976 and 13 in 1981. In the latter year the TKP presidential candidate, Ziya Rizki, came second with 30.4% of the vote. The party fell back to 10 seats in the June 1985 Assembly elections (winning 16% of the vote) and its presidential candidate, Alpay Durduran, came third with 9.2% of the vote. It then joined a coalition government with the National Unity Party (UBP), but withdrew in August 1986 amid differences on economic policy. In 1989 the TKP absorbed the Progressive People's Party (AHP), itself the product of a 1986 merger between the Democratic People's Party (DHP) and the Communal Endeavour Party (TAP). Of these ingredients, the DHP had been founded in 1979 by two former UBP Prime Ministers, Nejat Konuk and Osman Örek, of whom the former had in 1983–85, by now an independent, again been Prime Minister of a coalition government. The centre-right TAP had been founded in 1984, and neither it nor the DHP had won representation in the 1985 Assembly elections.

In the 1990 elections, the TKP's seat tally slipped to seven. In those of December 1993, which it contested as part of the Democratic Struggle alliance with Republican Turkish Party and the New Dawn Party, it declined further to five seats. In the first round of TRNC presidential elections in April 1995, the TKP leader came in fourth place with 14.2% of the vote.

Democratic Party

Demokrat Partisi (DP)

Address. c/o Cumhuriyet Meclisi, Lefkosa/Nicosia

Telephone. (#90–520) 83795

Fax. (#90–520) 87130

Leadership. Hakki Atun (leader), Serdar Denktaš (secretary-general)

The DP was launched in mid-1992 by a dissident faction of the National Unity Party (UBP) which advocated a more conciliatory line in the inter-communal talks than that favoured by the then UBP Prime Minister, Derviš Eroglu. Backed by President Denktash (formerly a UBP member), the new party had the support of 10 of the 45 UBP Assembly deputies elected in 1990–91. In October 1992 it was formally joined by Denktash, who was precluded by the constitution from leading a political party or submitting to party discipline. In the December 1993 Assembly elections, the DP came close to surplanting the UBP as the leading party, winning 15 of the 50 seats against 17 for the UBP. The DP leader was then appointed Prime Minister of a majority coalition government embracing the Republican Turkish Party (CTP). The coalition policy agreement, while not following the pro-partition line of Eroglu, offered little accomodation on the Cyprus question, favouring joint sovereignty and a rotational presidency. The DP backed Denktash's successful re-election bid in April 1995, after which Hakki Atun was reappointed to the premiership of a further DP/CTP coalition. In November 1995 the CTP withdrew from the government, but the following month Atun formed another DP/CTP coalition.

National Unity Party
Ulusal Birlik Partisi (UBP)
> *Address.* 9 Atatürk Meydani, Lefkosa/Nicosia
> *Telephone.* (#90–520) 73972
> *Leadership.* Derviš Eroglu (leader), Olgun Pašalar (general secretary)

The centre-right UBP was founded in 1976 by Rauf Denktash, leader of the Turkish Cypriot community, and had its origins in an earlier National Solidarity (UD) movement. Espousing the political principles of Mustapha Kemal Atatürk, founder of the modern Turkish state, the party won three-quarters of the seats in the 1976 Turkish Cypriot Assembly elections. Its then general secretary, Nejat Konuk, became the first Prime Minister of the TFSC, but resigned in March 1978, as did his successor, Osman Örek. Both participated in the formation of the breakaway Democratic People's Party, which later became part of the Communal Liberation Party (TKP). Having been formally elected to the Turkish Cypriot presidency in 1976, Denktash was re-elected in 1981 as the UBP candidate with 51.8% of the vote. In the 1981 Assembly elections, the UBP was reduced to 18 deputies but remained the largest party and in August 1981 formed a new government, which fell on a no-confidence vote in December 1981, whereafter the the UBP formed a coalition with two other parties. Following the declaration of the TRNC in November 1983, the UBP continued as the main ruling party and increased its representation to 24 seats out of 50 in the June 1985 elections, with 37% of the vote. In the same month, Denktash was re-elected to the TRNC presidency as the UBP candidate, with 70.5% of the vote.

A new coalition government between the UBP and the TKP broke down when the latter withdrew in August 1986, to be replaced by the New Dawn Party. Standing this time as an independent,

Denktash was in April 1990 re-elected TRNC President with 66.7% of the vote. In the May 1990 Assembly elections, the UBP won an absolute majority of 34 of the 50 seats, increasing this tally to 45 in by-elections in October 1991. Strains then intensified between Denktash and the UBP Prime Minister, Derviš Eroglu, with the latter advocating the formal partition of Cyprus on the basis of the existing territorial division, whereas the President favoured further exploration of a bicommunal solution in the UN-sponsored talks. This divergence resulted in July 1992 in the formation of the breakaway pro-Denktash Democratic Party (DP), which included 10 former UBP deputies. The rump UBP, following Eroglu's pro-partition line, remained the largest single party in the early Assembly elections of December 1993, but with only 17 seats (and 29.6% of the vote) it was unable to prevent the formation of a coalition of the DP and the Republican Turkish Party. Eroglu came in second place in the first round of TRNC presidential elections in April 1995 (winning 24.2% of the vote), but was easily defeated in the second by Denktash.

Republican Turkish Party
Cumhuriyetçi Türk Partisi (CTP)
> *Address.* 99A Sehit Salahi Street, Lefkosa/Nicosia
> *Telephone.* (#90–520) 73300
> *Leadership.* Mehmet Ali Talat (chair), Alpay Avsaroglu (general secretary)

The CTP was founded in 1970 by Ahmed Mithat Berberoghlou as a Marxist-Leninist formation espousing anti-imperialiism, non-alignment and a settlement of the Cyprus question "on the basis of top-level agreements between the leaders of the two communities". In 1973 Berberoghlou stood unsuccessfully against Rauf Denktash, then of the National Unity Party (UBP), for the vice-presidency of (then undivided) Cyprus. He also contested the 1976 presidential election in the TFSR, again losing to Denktash, while the CTP won only two out of 40 Assembly seats. The party increased its representation to six seats in 1981, when the CTP leader came in third place in the presidential elections with 12.8% of the vote. In the June 1985 presidential contest, Özgür improved to second place with 18.4% of the vote, while in Assembly elections the same month the CTP won 12 out of 50 seats with 21% of the vote. In 1988 the CTP's financial viability came under serious threat when a TRNC court awarded President Denktash over £100,000 in damages for an alleged libel in the party newspaper.

The CTP did not contest the April 1990 presidential election, while in the May 1990 Assembly balloting it won only seven seats, standing as part of the Democratic Struggle alliance with the Communal Liberation Party and the New Dawn Party. Having eschewed Marxism-Leninism in favour of democratic socialism, the party recovered in the December 1993 Assembly elections, winning 13 seats standing in its own right. It subsequently entered a coalition government with the recently-formed pro-Denktash Democratic Party (DP). The CTP leader took third place in the April 1995 presidential elections (winning 18.9% of the vote), whereafter formed a new coalition government with the DP. This alliance collapsed in November 1995 when President Denktash vetoed two CTP-approved cabinet changes, but was re-established the following month. In January 1996 former deputy premier Özker Özgür was ousted as CTP leader.

Other Parties and Alliances

National Struggle Party (*Milli Mücadele Partisi*, MMP), alliance formed for the 1993 elections by the Free Democratic Party (*Hür Demokrat Partisi*, HDP) led by Ismet Kotak, the Homeland Party (*Anavatan Partisi*, AP) and the Nationalist Justice Party (*Midiyetçi Adalet Partisi*, MAP).

New Cyprus Party (*Yeni Kibris Partisi*, YKP), founded in 1989 by Alpay Durduran, who was the 1985 presidential candidate of the Communal Liberation Party and who won 1.8% of the first-round vote in the 1995 presidential contest standing for the YKP.

New Dawn Party (*Yeni Doguš Partisi*, YDP), led by Ali Özkan Altinišik and Vural Çetin, a centre-right formation founded in 1984 and mainly representing Turkish settlers, won four Assembly seats in 1985 and joined a coalition with the National Unity Party in 1986, declined to one seat in 1990 (within the opposition Democratic Struggle alliance) and failed to secure representation in 1993. *Address*. 1 Genghis Khan Street, Lefkosa/Nicosia

Social Democratic Party (*Sosyal Demokrat Partisi*, SDP), led by Ergün Vehbi, founded in 1985 and led until his death by Raif Denktash (son of the TRNC President).

Unity and Sovereignty Party (*Birlik ve Egemenlik Partisi*, BEP), led by Arif Salih Kirdag.

Czech Republic

Capital: Prague

Population: 10,400,000 (1995E)

The Czech Republic became independent on Jan. 1, 1993, as a result of the dissolution of the Czech and Slovak Federative Republic, which had been under Communist rule (under various names) from 1948 to 1989 and had then become a multi-party democracy. Under the Czech constitution of December 1992, legislative power is vested in a bicameral Parliament of the Czech Republic (*Parlament České Republiký*), of which the lower house is the 200–member Chamber of Deputies (*Sněmovna Poslancu*), elected by proportional representation for a four-year term by universal suffrage of those aged 18 and over. The threshold for representation is 5% of the national vote for single parties, 7% for coalitions of two or three parties and 10% for coalitions of four or more parties. Under constitutional implementing legislation enacted in September 1995, there is also an 81–member Senate (*Sénate*) as the upper house, whose members are directly elected from single-member constituencies for a six-year term, with one third being renewed every two years (although all 81 were elected in the inaugural poll in 1996). Executive power is vested primarily in the Council of Ministers responsible to parliament, although considerable authority resides in the President, who is elected for a five-year term by the members of the legislature.

Under a 1994 amendment to the 1990 Law on Political Parties, state financial support of 3 to 5 million koruna is available proportionally to each party which obtains at least 3% of the national vote and a further sum is payable to parties for each seat obtained in the national legislature. In 1994 the total amount allocated for such purposes was some 160 million koruna.

To assure the transition to separate sovereignty, the National Council elected in the Czech Lands on June 5–6, 1992, under the federation became the Chamber of Deputies of the independent Czech Republic. The first post-separation elections were held on May 31-June 1, 1996, and resulted as follows: Civic Democratic Party 68 seats (with 29.6% of the vote); Czech Social Democratic Party 61 (26.4%); Communist Party of Bohemia and Moravia 22 (10.3%); Christian Democratic Union-Czechoslovak People's Party 18 (8.1%); Association for the Republic-Czechoslovak Republican Party 18 (8.0%); Civic Democratic Alliance 13 (6.4%).

Association for the Republic–Czechoslovak Republican Party

Sdružení pro Republiku–Republikánská Strana Československa (SPR- RSČ)

> *Address.* Bělohorská 74, 16900 Prague 6
> *Telephone.* (#42–2) 354833
> *Fax.* (#42-2) 312-4392
> *Leadership.* Miroslav Sládek (chair)

The right-wing populist SPR-RSČ held its constituent congress in February 1990 and came out in favour of economic protectionism, drastic cuts in the state bureaucracy, military neutrality, non-participation in international organizations such as the IMF, measures against "inadaptable" minorities such as Gypsies and the reintroduction of capital punishment. Obtaining its main support in northern Bohemia, the party won 14 seats in the 200–member Czech National Council in June 1992 (with 6% of the vote); its also secured representation in both houses of the then Federal Assembly. At that stage the SPR-RSČ supported the preservation of Czechoslovakia and urged the recovery of the country's original 1918 borders, i.e. including Transcarpathian Ruthenia, which was annexed by the USSR in 1945 and today forms part of Ukraine. The party's retention of "Czechoslovak" in its sub-title indicates a continuing preference for broader state boundaries.

Following the inauguration of the independent Czech Republic in January 1993, the party experienced serious dissension within its parliamentary group, whose membership had fallen to six deputies by mid-1995 as a result of defections. Some of these were to the Patriotic Republican Party launched in August 1995. In December 1995 Sládek received a suspended prison sentence for an assault on a policeman. In the 1996 lower house elections, however, the SPR-RSČ staged a recovery, winning 18 seats.

Christian Democratic Union-Czechoslovak People's Party

Křestánskodemokratická Unie-Československá Strana Lidová (KDU- ČSL)

> *Address.* Revoluční 5, 11015 Prague 1
> *Telephone.* (#42–2) 2481–0794
> *Fax.* (#42–2) 2481–2114
> *Leadership.* Josef Lux (chair), Milan Barot (general secretary)

The KDU-ČSL is descended from the Czechoslovak People's Party founded in 1918 as the new state's main Catholic formation and represented in most inter-war governments until it was dissolved in late 1938 in the aftermath of the Munich crisis. Revived as a component of the Communist-dominated National Front in 1945, the People's Party was allowed to continue in existence as a Front party after the Communists took sole power in 1948. From late 1989 it sought to free itself from its recent history as a satellite of the outgoing Communist regime, undertaking personnel and policy changes designed to re-establish itself as an independent pro-democracy formation. Having joined the broad-based coalition government appointed in December 1989, the People's Party in June 1990 removed Josef Bartončik as party chair amid allegations that he had been secret police informer. The party contested the elections of the same month in an alliance with other groups called the Christian and Democratic Union, which won nine of the 101 Czech seats in the federal lower house (with 8.7% of the vote), six of the 75 Czech seats in the federal upper house (with 8.8% of the vote) and 19 seats in the 200–member Czech National Council (with 8.4% of the vote).

Included in the post-1990 Czech coalition government, the Christian and Democratic Union was weakened in late 1991 by the departure of the Christian Democratic Party (KDS) to form an alliance with the new Civic Democratic Party (ODS). In April 1992 the remaining constituents officially became the KDU-ČSL, which in the June 1992 elections won 15 seats in the Czech National Council (with 6.3% of the vote) as well as seven and six of the Czech seats in the federal lower and upper houses respectively. The party became a member of the ODS-led Czech coalition government which took the republic to independence in January 1993, after which it no longer advocated autonomy for Moravia, where it had its strongest popular support. A residual hankering after old borders is apparent in the party's retention of "Czechoslovak" in its sub-title.

Following the separation, the KDU-ČSL came out in favour of a free enterprise system and Czech membership of Western economic and security structures. In late 1995 its parliamentary party was strengthened by the defection to it of five KDS deputies opposed to their party's decision to merge with the ODS. In the 1996 lower house elections the KDU-ČSL won 18 seats on a vote share of 8.1% and was included in another ODS-led government, now with minority status.

The KDU-ČSL is an affiliate of the Christian Democrat International and the International Democrat Union.

Civic Democratic Alliance

Občanská Demokratická Aliance (ODA)

Address. Rytířská 10, 11000 Prague 1

Telephone. (#42–2) 2421–4134

Fax. (#42–2) 2421-4390

Leadership. Jan Kalvoda (chair), Josef Reichman (general secretary)

The right-wing ODA was launched in December 1989 and contested the June 1990 multi-party elections as part of the victorious Civic Forum (*Občanské Fórum*, OF), becoming a member of both the federal and the Czech republican governments. Set up as an independent party on the fracturing of the OF in early 1991, the ODA contested the June 1992 elections its own right, winning 14 of the 200 Czech National Council seats (with 5.9% of the vote) but none in either house of the Federal Assembly. As a member of the subsequent Czech coalition government headed by the Civic Democratic Party (ODS), it supported the creation of a separate Czech Republic from January 1993. Its pro-market policy line was very similar to that of the ODS, the main differentiation lying in its greater emphasis on regional self-government and on the need for a reduction of the state's role. A hiccup in the ODA's participation in the generally stable Czech coalition occurred in January 1995, when party leader Kalvoda claimed that state security agents were illegally gathering information about political parties for use against them. The ODA won 13 lower house seats in the 1996 elections, on a 6.4% vote share, and continued as a government coalition partner.

The ODA is a member of the International Democrat Union.

Civic Democratic Party

Občanská Demokratická Strana (ODS)

Address. Sněmovní 3, 11800 Prague 1

Telephone. (#42–2) 311–9764

Fax. (#42–2) 311–8273

Leadership. Václav Klaus (chair), Petr Čermák (vice-chair)

The ODS came into being in early 1991 as a result of a split in the original pro-democracy Civic Forum (*Občanské Fórum*, OF), which had been launched in November 1989 by various anti-communist groups, notably the Charter 77 movement, under the acknowledged leadership of dissident playwright Václav Havel. Together with its Slovak counterpart, the OF had then brought about the "velvet revolution", quickly forcing the then regime to give up sole state power. In December 1989 Havel had been elected President by a federal parliament still dominated by Communists, while the OF itself had triumphed in the Czech Lands in the June 1990 Czechoslovak elections, winning 68 of the 101 Czech seats in the 150–member federal lower house (with 53.2% of the Czech vote) and 127 of the 200 seats in the Czech National Council (with 49.5% of the vote). It had then entered a federal coalition government with other pro-democracy parties (in which Klaus became Finance Minister) and had headed the Czech government in the person of Petr Pithart. In October 1990 Klaus had been elected as first official chair of the OF, announcing his intention to steer the movement to the right.

Once in power, the OF had experienced the inevitable internal strains between its disparate components. In February 1991 Klaus and his supporters formally launched the ODS, while elements preferring the maintenance of a broad-based movement converted the OF into the Civic Movement (*Občanské Hnutí*), which later became the Free Democrats, which in turn became the Free Democrats–Liberal National Social Party (SD-LSNS). A third OF breakaway party was the Civic Democratic Alliance (ODA). The ODS quickly built a strong organization and concluded an electoral alliance with the Christian Democratic Party (KDS). In the June 1992 elections the ODS/KDS combination became the leading formation both at federal level (with 48 of the 99 Czech seats in the lower house and 33.9% of the Czech vote) and in the Czech National Council (with 76 of the 200 seats and 29.7% of the vote). The resultant Czech-Slovak federal coalition was headed by Jan Stráský (ODS), while Klaus preferred to take the Czech premiership at the head of a coalition of the ODS, the KDS, the ODA and the Christian Democratic Union-Czechoslovak People's Party (KDU-ČSL).

In dominant governmental authority, the ODS moved swiftly to implement its programme of economic reform, including wholesale privatization of the state sector, especially in the Czech Lands. But its main immediate concern was the constitutional question and in particular the gulf between the Slovak demand for sovereignty within a federation and the Czech government view that preservation of the federation only made sense if it had a real role. Opinion polls at that stage showed that a majority of both Czechs and Slovaks favoured a continued federal structure. But the failure of Václav Havel to secure re-election as President in July 1992, due to Slovak opposition in the federal legislature, served to harden attitudes.

The upshot, probably desired more by the Czechs than by the Slovaks, was a formal separation as from the beginning of 1993, when the Czech coalition headed by the ODS became the government of the independent Czech Republic, with Klaus as Prime Minister.

In January 1993 Havel was elected President of the new Republic on the proposal of the ODS and its government allies, although foreign policy differences between the (non-party) head of state and the ODS emerged subsequently. Whereas the former promoted the Visegrad Group (with Hungary, Poland and Slovakia) as a central European framework of economic reform and progress, the Klaus government saw speedy integration with Western economic and security structures as the priority. In 1994-95 the Klaus government remained the most stable in ex-communist Europe. In local elections in November 1994 the ODS headed the poll, with 28.7% of the vote.

In November 1995 the ODS voted in favour of a formal merger with the KDS (under the ODS party name), although the decision of half of the 10-strong KDS parliamentary party to join the KDU-ČSL rather than the ODS reduced the impact of the merger. The KDS had originated in the mid-1980s as an unofficial ecumenical Christian group calling for party pluralism and had been established as a distinct political party in December 1989. It espoused family values and strong local government, opposed abortion and easy divorce, and favoured a market economy and integration with Western Europe. At first a component of the broad pro-democracy Civic Forum (*Občanské Fórum*, OF), the KDS had left the OF to contest the June 1990 elections within the broader Christian and Democratic Union. Included in the post-election Czech government headed by the OF, the KDS had opted in late 1991 to form an electoral alliance with the new ODS, while its erstwhile partners had later become the KDU-ČSL. Having won 10 seats in the 1992 Czech National Council elections, the KDS had been included in the consequential Czech coalition headed by the ODS. The KDS had held its first post-independence congress in December 1993, when party chair Václav Benda had been succeeded by the younger Ivan Pilip, who had become Education Minister the following year.

Despite the merger with the KDS, the ODS lost ground in the 1996 lower house elections, winning only 68 seats on a 29.6% vote share. Klaus was nevertheless reappointed Prime Minister of a further coalition with the KDU-ČSL and the ODA, now with minority status and dependent on the qualified external support of the Czech Social Democratic Party.

The ODS is affiliated to the International Democrat Union, as was the KDS, which had also been affiliated to the Christian Democrat International.

Communist Party of Bohemia and Moravia
Komunistická Strana Čech a Moravy (KSČM)
   Address. Politických Vězňu 9, 11100 Prague 1
   Telephone. (#42–2) 2421–0172
   Leadership. Miroslav Grebeníček (chair)
Founded under its present name in March 1990, the KSČM is directly descended from the Communist Party of Czechoslovakia (KSČ), which was founded in 1921 by the pro-Bolshevik wing of the Czech Social Democratic Party. The KSČ won nearly a million votes in the 1925 elections and was the only East European communist party to retain legal status in the 1930s, under the leadership of Klement Gottwald. It was eventually banned, as a gesture of appeasement to Nazi Germany, in the authoritarian aftermath of the 1938 Munich agreement, its leaders mostly taking refuge in Moscow. They returned at the end of World War II in the wake of the victorious Red Army as the dominant element of a National Front of democratic parties and in the 1946 elections became the largest party in the Czech Lands and the second strongest in Slovakia. Gottwald became Prime Minister and Communists thereafter used their control of the security apparatus to eliminate serious opposition to the party's designs. A government crisis of February 1948 enabled it to assume sole power, although most other Front parties were allowed to remain in existence in a subservient role throughout the subsequent 40 years of Communist rule (the exception being the Social Democrats, who were obliged to merge with the KSČ). Elections in May 1948 were held on the basis of a single National Front list controlled by the Communists, after which Gottwald took over the Czechoslovak presidency.

Purges of the KSČ leadership in 1951 in the wake of the Soviet-Yugoslav breach led to show trials and the execution of 11 prominent Communists in 1952, among them Rudolf Slánský, who had succeeded President Gottwald as party leader. They had been found guilty of being "Trotskyist-Titoist-Zionist-bourgeois-nationalist traitors". Following Gottwald's sudden death in 1953 (from pneumonia contracted at Stalin's funeral in Moscow), Antonín Novotný was elected to the revived post of party leader and later became President. Khrushchev's denunciation of Stalin in 1956 resulted in the rehabilitation of most of those executed in Czechoslovakia in 1952 (posthumously) and also of those imprisoned in that era, including Gustáv Husák. But no serious attempt was made to introduce political reform, pressure for which grew in the 1960s within and outside the party. Major economic reforms in 1967, largely inspired by Prof. Ota Šik, were aimed at decentralization and the creation of a "socialist market economy" but failed to stem the tide in favour of change. In January 1968 Novotný was replaced as KSČ leader by Alexander Dubček and as President by Gen. Ludvík Svoboda. Hitherto Slovak Communist leader, Dubček initiated what turned out to be the short-lived Prague Spring.

In April 1968 the KSČ central committee elected a new presidium dominated by reformers and also adopted an "action programme" promising democratization of the government system (although not party pluralism), freedom of assembly, the press, foreign travel and religion, curbs on the security police, rehabilitation of previous purge victims, and autonomy for Slovakia. Inevitably, this policy of "socialism with a human face" seriously alarmed the Soviet leadership and its Warsaw Pact satellites. Increasing pressure on the Prague reformers culminated in the military occupation of Czechoslovakia in August 1968 by forces of the USSR, East Germany, Poland, Hungary and Bulgaria (although not of Romania), on the stated grounds that they had been invited in by KSČ leaders, including Husák, who believed that the reform movement was out of control. Dubček and his immediate supporters were taken to Moscow as prisoners. They were quickly released on the insistence of President Svoboda, but the reform movement was effectively over. After anti-Soviet riots in early 1969, Husák replaced Dubček as party leader and initiated a major purge of reformist elements which reduced KSČ membership from 1,600,000 to 1,100,000. Those expelled from the party included Dubček and other leaders of the Prague Spring.

Over the following two decades, Husák combined rigorous pro-Soviet orthodoxy and repression of political dissidents with a measure of economic liberalization. Having become President in 1975, Husák in December 1987 surrendered the party leadership to Miloš Jakeš, another political hardliner. But the post-1985 Gorbachev reform programme in the USSR had its inevitable impact in Czechoslovakia, with the complication that the party leadership could not easily subscribe to reforms which they had been brought into power to eradicate. The upshot was that the Communist regime crumbled with remarkable rapidity following the opening of the Berlin Wall in early November 1989, amid an upsurge of massive popular protest. At the end of November Jakeš was replaced as KSČ leader by Karel Urbánek and the following month Husák resigned as President, having sworn in the first government with a non-Communist majority for over four decades, although it was led by a KSČ member. After Dubček had been elected chairman of the Federal Assembly (as a co-opted member), Husák was succeeded by the dissident playwright Václav Havel, who was elected head of state by a parliament still dominated by KSČ deputies. In late December 1989 an extraordinary KSČ congress elected Ladislav Adameć to the new post of party chair and issued a public apology for the party's past actions.

The Czech component of the KSČ responded to events by relaunching itself as the KSČM in March 1990, with Jiří Svoboba as leader and with a socialist rather than a Marxist-Leninist orientation. Hitherto, the KSČ had embraced the Communist Party of Slovakia but had had no Czech counterpart to that organization. In the June 1990 multi-party elections, the Czech Communists took second place in the Czech National Council, winning 32 of the 200 seats with 13.2% of the vote; they were also runners-up in the Czech balloting for the Federal Assembly, winning 15 of the 101 Czech lower house seats (with 13.5% of the vote) and 12 of the 75 Czech upper house seats (with 13.8%). The Communists then went into opposition for the first time since 1945, amid a continuing exodus of party members. In October 1990 the KSČM declared itself independent of the federal KSČ, shortly before the passage of a law requiring the KSČ to hand over to the government all of its assets at end-1989. In mid-1991 the KSČ was officially dissolved, but both the KSČM and its Slovak counterpart remained "Czechoslovak" in orientation.

In the June 1992 elections, the KSČM headed the Left Bloc Party, which included the Democratic Left Movement, the Left Alliance and the Movement for Social Justice. The Bloc won 35 of the 200 Czech National Council seats (with 14.1% of the vote) as well as 19 of the 99 Czech seats in the federal lower house and 15 of the 75 Czech seats in the upper house. Still in opposition, the KSČM mounted ultimately abortive resistance to the dissolution of the federation. Following the creation of the independent Czech Republic in January 1993, the party experienced much internal strife, including the resignation of Jiří Svoboda as leader over the rejection of his proposal to drop "Communist" from the party's title. He was replaced in June 1993 by the conservative Miroslav Grebeníček, whose election precipitated the formation of the breakaway Democratic Left Party. A further split in December 1993 resulted in the creation of the Left Bloc. These secessions meant that the KSČM had lost the majority of its deputies elected in 1992; it had also ceased to be supported by the former party newspaper *Rudé Právo* (which now favoured the Social Democrats and later dropped "*Rudé*", meaning "Red", from it masthead).

The KSČM nevertheless retained substantial core membership and organizational strength, as well as a significant public following for its advocacy of a "socialist market economy" based on economic democracy and co-operatives and for its opposition to NATO membership and to absorption into the "German sphere of influence". In local elections in November 1994 it won a creditable 13.4% of the overall vote. In the 1996 parliamentary elections it took 10.3% of the national vote and 22 lower house seats, effectively becoming the main opposition to a further coalition headed by Civic Democratic Party, given that the Czech Social Democratic Party offered the new government qualified support.

Czech-Moravian Centre Union
Českomoravská Unie Středu (ČMUS)
    Address. Františkánská 1–3, 60200 Brno
    Telephone. (#42–5) 4221–5279
    Fax. (#42–5) 4221–5276
    Leadership. Jan Kryčer, František Trnka
The ČMUS was created in February 1996 as a formal merger of the Bohemian-Moravian Centre Party (ČMSS), the Liberal Social Union (LSU) and the Agrarian Party (ZS). The three parties had been allied under the ČMUS rubric since December 1994, supporting pro-market economic policies but also urging the retention of the communist-era welfare state. Part of the motivation for the merger was the electoral rule specifying that party alliances required a higher share of the national vote to gain seats than did single parties. In the event, the ČMUS won only 0.5% of the vote in the 1996 elections, failing to gain representation.

The ČMSS had been derived from the Movement for Self-Governing Democracy–Association for Moravia and Silesia (HSD-SMS), founded in April 1990 in support of a demand that the historic province of Moravia-Silesia should have equivalent political status to Bohemia and Slovakia. In the June 1990 elections the HSD-SMS had taken third place in the Czech National Council, winning 22 of the 200 seats (with 10% of the vote); it had also secured nine of the 101 Czech seats in the federal lower house (with 7.9% of the vote) and seven of the 75 Czech seats in the upper house (with 9.1%). It had performed less well in June 1992, falling to 14 seats in the Czech National Council (with 5.9% of the vote) and failing to win federal representation. Thereafter strains had developed between a liberal faction emphasizing parliamentary work and a radical faction favouring extra-parliamentary action. On the creation of the independent Czech Republic in January 1993, the HSD-SMS had changed its name to the Movement for Moravian and Silesian Self-Governing Democracy, this

precipitating a split in its parliamentary group. In January 1994 the Movement had turned itself into a political party called the ČMSS, the new title indicating its intention to extend its activities to Bohemia.

The LSU had first appeared in May 1991 as a proclaimed alliance of the Agrarian Party (then led by Trnka), the then Czechoslovak Socialist Party (ČSS) and the Green Party (SZ). Its programme had called for a socially-responsible market economy, attention to environmental problems and local self-government. In the June 1992 elections the LSU had narrowly failed to obtain seats in the federal lower house but had won five of the 75 Czech seats in the upper house (with 6.1% of the vote). In the simultaneous Czech National Council elections, it had taken 16 of the 200 seats (with 6.5% of the vote). Due to internal tensions, however, the LSU had quickly ceased to function as a single entity, important factions of its constituent parties being re-established in their own right. Of these, the ČSS had, by stages, become the Free Democrats–Liberal National Social Party, while the rump LSU had in January 1994 transformed itself into a single party with individual membership.

Czech Social Democratic Party
Česká Strana Sociálně Demokratická (ČSSD)
    Address. Hybernská 7, 11000 Prague 1
    Telephone. (#42–2) 2421–9911
    Fax. (#42–2) 2422–6222
    Leadership. Miloš Zeman (chair)
Founded in 1878 as an autonomous section of the Austrian labour movement, the ČSSD became an independent party in 1911. Following the creation of Czechoslovakia after World War I, it won 25.7% of the vote in the 1920 elections (an inter-war record) but was weakened by the exodus of its pro-Bolshevik wing in 1921. Strongly supportive of the post-1918 political system (and a member of various coalitions), in 1938 the party was obliged to become part of the newly-created National Labour Party under the post-Munich system of "authoritarian democracy". Following the further dismantling of Czechoslovakia by Hitler in March 1939, the party went underground. It was a member of the government-in-exile in London during World War II, after which it participated in the Communist-dominated National Front, winning 37 of the 231 Czech seats in the May 1946 elections. The Social Democrats then came under mounting pressure from the Communists, who used the state security apparatus in a campaign to eliminate their main political rivals. Following a political crisis in February 1948, the ČSSD was forced to merge with the Communist Party and thereafter maintained its existence in exile.

Following the collapse of Communist rule in late 1989, the ČSSD was officially re-established in Czechoslovakia in March 1990, aspiring at that stage to be a "Czechoslovak" party appealing to both Czechs and Slovaks. It failed to secure representation in the June 1990 elections, after which its Czech and Slovak wings in effect became separate parties, although "Czechoslovak" remained its official descriptor. In the June 1992 elections the ČSSD won 16 seats in the 200–member Czech National Council (with 6.5% of the vote) and also secured representation in the Czech sections of both federal houses. It then mounted strong opposition to the proposed "velvet divorce" between Czechs and Slovaks, arguing in favour of a "confederal union", but eventually accepted the inevitability of the separation which duly came into effect at the beginning of 1993. At its first post-independence congress in February 1993, the party formally renamed itself the "Czech" SSD and elected a new leadership under Miloš Zeman, who declared his aim as being to provide a left-wing alternative to the neo-conservatism of the government in power, while at the same time ruling out co-operation with the Communist Party of Bohemia and Moravia.

The ČSSD made a major advance in the 1996 parliamentary elections, winning 61 of the 200 lower house seats on a 26.4% vote share and becoming the second strongest party. It opted to give qualified external support to a new centre-right coalition headed by the Civic Democratic Party, on the basis that privatization of the transport and energy sectors would be halted and that a Social Democrat would become chairman of the new lower house.

The ČSSD is a member party of the Socialist International.

Free Democrats–Liberal National Social Party
Svobodní Demokraté–Liberálni Národně Sociální Strana (SD-LNSS)

Address. Jungmannovo nám. 9, 11000 Prague
Telephone. (#42-2) 2422-6626
Fax. (#42-2) 2422-6568
Leadership. Jiří Dienstbier and Vavrinec Bodenlos (co-chairs)

The SD-LNSS was formed in late 1995 as a merger of the SD and the LNSS, although most LNSS deputies rejected the union and later founded the Civic National Movement. The LNSS had claimed descent from the National Socialist Party (founded in 1897), which had played a dominant role in the inter-war period and had been a member of the post-war National Front, becoming the Czechoslovak Socialist Party (ČSS) on the Communist takeover in 1948, after which it had been allowed to exist as a Front party. The ČSS had been unsuccessful in the 1990 elections

because of its pro-Communist past and in 1991 had joined the broader Liberal Social Union (LSU), which had won 16 Czech National Council seats in the 1992 elections but had thereafter suffered dissension, most of the old ČSS component eventually opting in June 1993 to form the independent LNSS with a centrist orientation.

The SD had been derived from the liberal wing of the original pro-democracy Civic Forum, which, following the secession of the Civic Democratic Party in early 1991, had become the Civic Movement (*Občanské Hnutí*, OH). After the OH had failed to secure representation in the 1992 elections (with 4.6% of the Czech vote), Dienstbier and his faction had in October 1993 launched the SD as a party, which became an observer member of the Liberal International.

In the 1996 parliamentary elections the SD-LNSS achieved only 2.1% of the national vote, failing to gain representation.

Other Parties

Association of Social Democrats (*Asociace Sociálních Demokratú*, ASD), led by Rudolf Battek, founded in May 1991 by a social democratic faction of the pro-democracy Civic Forum derived from the Charter 77 movement, unsuccessful in the 1992 elections as part of the broader Democratic Bloc. *Address.* Navratilova 2, 11200 Prague 1

Club of Committed Non-Party Members (*Klub Angažovaných Nestraníku*, KAN), led by Emil Dejmek, originally founded during the 1968 Prague Spring, re-established in 1990 as a conservative formation, failed to win representation in the 1992 elections (with 2.7% of the Czech vote), co-operated closely with the Christian Democratic Party prior to the latter's merger with the Civic Democratic Party. *Address.* Štefánikova 17, 15000 Prague 5

Civic National Movement (*Občanská Národne Hnutí*, ONH), led by Tomás Sterba, launched in February 1996 by most of the deputies of the former Liberal National Social Party (LNSS), who had opposed the creation of the merged Free Democrats–Liberal National Social Party the previous year.

Democratic Left (*Demokratická Levice*, DL), led by Lotar Indruch, founded in 1990 to promote left unity, contested the 1992 elections as part of the Left Bloc headed by the Communist Party of Bohemia and Moravia, lost part of its membership to the Democratic Left Party launched by reform Communists in mid-1993. *Address.* Mariánské Nám. 2, 60200 Brno

Democratic Left Party (*Strana Demokraticé Levice*, SDL), led by Josef Mečl, founded in June 1993 by a reformist faction of the Communist Party of Bohemia and Moravia after the latter had declined to change its name, embraced part of the Democratic Left, advocates a revival of socialism in a modern interpretation, but won only 0.1% of the vote in 1996. *Address*. Žitná 49, Prague 2

Democratic Union (*Demokratická Unie*, DEU), led by Alena Hromádková, a right-wing formation founded in June 1994, backed by the *Český Denik* newspaper, critical of the ruling Civic Democratic Party for emphasizing economic reform at the expense of law and order, described by Prime Minister Klaus as "a party of fundamentalist anti-Bolsheviks with no positive programme"; won 2.8% of the vote in 1996. *Address*. Kotlaska 5/64, 18000 Prague 8

Green Party (*Strana Zelených*, SZ), led by Jaroslav Vlček and Roman Haken, originally founded in 1989 and prominent in the "velvet revolution", but failed to win representation in the 1990 elections, and so for the 1992 elections joined the broader Liberal Social Union (LSU), which won 16 seats in the Czech National Council; amid subsequent tensions, the SZ opposed the conversion of the LSU into a unitary party and reverted to independent status in November 1993 (the LSU later becoming part of the Czech-Moravian Centre Union); the SZ was barred from the 1996 elections because it could not pay the required deposits. *Address*. Jandova 2, 19000 Prague 9

Left Bloc Party (*Strana Levého Bloku*, SLB), led by Marie Stiborová and Zdenek Mlymar, founded in December 1993 by a faction of the Communist Party of Bohemia and Moravia (KSČM) which opposed the latter's new conservative leadership; won only 1,4% of the vote in the 1996 elections.

Liberal Democratic Party (*Liberalné Demoktayické Strana*, LDS), led by Vojtéch Pruša, founded in 1989, represented in federal parliament in 1990-92 as part of the Civic Forum.

Moravian National Party (*Moravská Národni Strana*, MNS), led by Ivan Dřímal, a small formation advocating independence, or at least autonomy, for Moravia; won a 0.3% vote share in 1996. *Address*. Křenová 61, Brno

Movement for Self-Governing Moravia and Silesia– Moravian Association of National Unity (HSMA-MNSJ), won 0.4% of the national vote in the 1996 elections.

Party of Czechoslovak Communists (*Strana Československych Komunista*, SČK0, led by Miroslav Stepan, who founded the party in March 1995 on being released from prison for having, as Prague Communist Party boss in the late 1980s, ordered the security forces to break up pro-democracy demonstrations; although proclaiming itself the successor of the former ruling party, the SČK was not banned, but was barred from the 1996 elections because it could not pay the required deposits.

Party of Entrepreneurs and Farmers (*Strana Podníkatelu a Rolníku*, SPR), led by Rudolf Baránek, founded in February 1992 to promote the interests of small and medium-sized businessmen and farmers, won 3.2% of the vote in the 1992 Czech National Council elections. *Address*. Rašínovo 54, 12801 Prague 2

Patriotic Republican Party (*Vlástenecka Republikanska Strana*, VRS), far-right grouping founded in August 1995 as a merger of the National Democratic Unity (NDJ) and dissident members of the Association for the Republic–Czech Republican Party.

Pensioners for a Secure Life (*Duchodci za Životní Jistoty*, DZJ), led by Josef Koniček, founded in December 1989 to promote the interests of pensioners in the post-communist era, obtained 3.8% of the vote in the 1992 Czech National Counmcil elections and 3.1% in 1996. *Address*. Sudoměřská 32, 13000 Prague 3

Radical Czech Democratic Party, led by Milan Garncars, an agrarian party established in 1993.

Romany Civic Initiative (*Romanská Občanská Iniciativa*, ROI), a right-wing party promoting the interests of Gypsies in the Czech Republic.

Romany National Congress (*Romský Národní Kongres*, RNK), a left-wing party promoting the interests of Gypsies in the Czech Republic.

Denmark

Capital: Copenhagen   **Population:** 5,200,000 (1995E)

Under its 1953 constitution the Kingdom of Denmark is a democratic, multi-party monarchy in which legislative power is vested in the unicameral *Folketing*, whose members are elected under a highly complex proportional system for a four-year term (subject to dissolution) by universal suffrage of those aged 18 years and above. Of the 179 *Folketing* members, 135 are elected by proportional representation in 17 metropolitan districts, with 40 additional seats being divided to achieve overall proportionality among parties that have secured at least 2 percent of the vote nationally. In addition, the Faroe Islands and Greenland are allotted two representatives each (see separate sections below).

Under legislation enacted in December 1986, state funding is available to parties represented in the *Folketing* in approximate proportion to their number of members and to parties and candidates contesting national, regional or local elections on the basis of the number of votes received in the previous election (subject to a minimum requirement of 1,000 votes). The total amount available in 1996 was DKr80.9 million (about $16.5 million), of which, for example, the Social Democratic Party was eligible to receive DKr22.1 million (about $4.7 million) as the largest parliamentary party.

In general elections on Sept. 27, 1994, the Social Democratic Party won 62 of the 175 metropolitan seats (with 34.6% of the vote); the Liberal Party 42 (23.3%); the Conservative People's Party 27 (15.0%); the Socialist People's Party 13 (7.3%); the Progress Party 11 (6.4%); the Radical Liberal Party 8 (4.6%); the Red-Green Unity List 6 (3.1%); the Centre Democrats 5 (2.8%); Party of the Consciously Workshy 1. One of the two deputies elected from the Faroes joined the Liberal parliamentary group and the other the Conservative People's group; of the two Greenland deputies, one joined the Social Democratic group and the other the Liberal group. In October 1995 the Progress Party was reduced to seven seats as a result of the formation of the breakaway Danish People's Party.

Centre Democrats
Centrum-Demokraterne (CD)

Address. Vesterbrogade 62/3 sal., 1620 Copenhagen V

Telephone. (#45-31) 237115

Fax. (#45-31) 145420

Leadership. Mimi Stilling Jakobsen (leader), Inger Boriis (chair), Peter Duetoft (parliamentary group chair), Yvonne Herloev Andersen (secretary-general)

The CD was established in November 1973 by right-wing dissidents of the Social Democratic Party (SD) led by Erhard Jakobsen, who objected to the "increasingly leftist course" of the then SD government, particularly its plans for increased taxation. Favouring a mixed economy and rejecting "socialist experiments", the new party won 13 seats and 7.8% of the vote in the December 1973 elections, but fell back to three seats and 2.2% in 1975. Recovery in 1977 to 10 seats and 6.4% was

followed by a further setback in the 1979 elections, in which the CD tally was six seats and 3.2%. The 1981 contest yielded the CD's best result to date (15 seats and 8.3%), with the result that in September 1982 the party entered a four-party non-socialist coalition headed by the Conservative People's Party (KFP). Cut back to eight seats and 4.6% in 1984, the CD was the only coalition party to gain in the 1987 elections (to nine seats and 4.8%); it almost held its ground in the 1988 contest (nine seats and 4.7% vote) but went into opposition to a three-party coalition headed by the KFP. Under the new leadership of Mimi Jakobsen (a former Social Affairs Minister), the CD retained nine seats in the 1990 elections (with 5.1% of the vote).

Following the resignation of the centre-right coalition in January 1993, the CD joined a four-party centre-left administration headed by the SD. Strongly pro-European, the CD was a party to the "national compromise" which secured referendum approval of the Maastricht Treaty at the second attempt in May 1993. In the June 1994 European Parliament elections, the CD slumped to 0.9% and lost its two existing seats. It partially recovered to 2.8% and five seats in the September 1994 national elections, joining a three-party centre-left coalition again headed by the SD.

Christian People's Party
Kristeligt Folkeparti (KrFP)
Address. Bernhard Bangs Allé 23, 2000 Frederiksberg
Telephone. (#45-38) 885152
Fax. (#45-38) 883115
Leadership. Jann Sjursen (chair), Nils Chresten Andersen (general secretary)

The KrFP was founded in April 1970 as an inter-denominational formation of Christian groups opposed to abortion on demand, pornography and the permissive society in general. The party achieved representation in the *Folketing* for the first time in 1973, winning seven seats and 4.0% of the vote. It advanced to nine seats and 5.3% in 1975 but lost ground in subsequent elections, taking only four seats and 2.3% in 1981. In September 1982 it was allocated two portfolios in a centre-right coalition headed by the Conservative People's Party (KFP), but left the government after the 1988 elections, in which it just attained the 2% minimum required for representation and retained four seats. It again won four seats in the 1990 contest (on a 2.3% vote share) and in January 1993 was allocated two portfolios in a centre-left coalition headed by the Social Democratic Party. The KrFP slipped to 1.1% in the June 1994 European Parliament elections (insufficient for representation) and took only 1.8% in the September 1994 national elections, thus exiting from both the *Folketing* and the government.

The KrFP is affiliated to the Christian Democrat International.

Conservative People's Party
Konservative Folkeparti (KFP)
Address. Nyhavn 4, Postboks 1515, 1020 Copenhagen K
Telephone. (#45-33) 134140
Fax. (#45-33) 933773
Leadership. Torben Rechendorff (chair), Hans Engell (parliamentary group chair), Peter Sterup (secretary-general)

The KFP was founded in February 1916 by progressive elements of the old *Hoejre* (Right) grouping that had been represented in the *Folketing* since 1849 but had lost its traditional dominance with the rise of the Liberal Party (*Venstre*) and the Social Democratic Party (SD). The new party

abandoned the reactionary stance of the old *Hoejre*, adopting a programme featuring support for proportional representation and social reform. It provided parliamentary support for three *Venstre* governments in the 1920s but was in opposition from 1929 until joining a national unity coalition during World War II. After the war it maintained its pre-war electoral strength of 16-20% in most elections up to 1971 before falling to under 10% in the 1970s (and to a low of 5.5% and only 10 seats in 1975). It was in opposition to centre-left coalitions or minority SD governments for most of the period to 1982, the exceptional years being 1950-53, when it governed with the *Venstre*, and 1968-71, when it was in coalition with the Radical Liberal Party (RV) and the *Venstre*. The KFP strongly backed Denmark's entry into the European Community in 1973 and also remained a staunch supporter of Danish membership of NATO.

Under the leadership of Poul Schlüter, the KFP recovered to 12.5% and 22 seats at the 1979 elections and to 14.5% and 26 seats in 1981, with the result that in September 1982 Schlüter became the first Conservative Prime Minister since 1901, heading a four-party centre-right coalition with the *Venstre*, the Centre Democrats (CD) and the Christian People's Party. Committed to reducing the role of the state, the Schlüter government was to remain in office for more than a decade, albeit with changes in its party composition in 1988 and 1990. A further KFP advance to a high of 23.4% and 42 seats in 1984 was followed by a decline to 20.8% and 38 seats in 1987 and to 19.3% and 35 seats in the 1988 snap elections, called by Schlüter after the government had been defeated on an opposition motion that visiting warships should be informed of Denmark's nuclear weapons ban. He was nevertheless able to form a new minority government, this time consisting of the KFP, the *Venstre* and the RV. The KFP fell back to 16.0% and 30 in the December 1990 elections, after which Schlüter was obliged to form a minority two-party coalition with the *Venstre* because the other centre-right parties declined to participate. In June 1992 the government was severely embarrassed when Danish voters disregarded its advice by narrowly rejecting the Maastricht Treaty on European Union.

The KFP participated in the seven-party "national compromise" of October 1992 establishing the terms of joint support for the Maastricht Treaty in a further referendum. Before it could be held, the "Tamilgate" scandal, relating to the exclusion of relatives of Tamil refugees in the late 1980s, unexpectedly brought about the downfall of the Schlüter government in January 1993 and the installation of a majority coalition (the first since 1971) headed by the SD. In opposition, the KFP in September 1993 elected Hans Engell, a former Defence and Justice Minister, to succeed Schlüter as party chair. The party won 17.7% of the vote in the June 1994 European balloting, increasing its representation from two to three seats. It slipped to 15.0% percent and 27 seats in the September national elections, remaining in opposition.

Claiming a membership of 40,000, the KFP is a member of the International Democrat Union and the European Democrat Union; its European Parliament representatives sit in the European People's Party group.

Danish People's Party

Dansk Folkeparti (DF)
   Address. Christiansborg, 1240 Copenhagen K
   Leadership. Pia Kjaersgaard

The DF was launched in October 1995 by four disaffected deputies of the right-wing Progress Party (FP), including Pia Kjaersgaard, who had been ousted as FP leader earlier in the year. The DF espoused the same policies as the FP but was regarded as being to the right of the parent party.

Liberal Party

Venstre (V)
   Address. Soelleroedvej 30, 2840 Holte
   Telephone. (#45-42) 802233
   Fax. (#45-42) 803830
   Leadership. Uffe Ellemann-Jensen (chair), Anders Fogh Rasmussen (vice-chair), Ivar Hansen (parliamentary group chair), Claus Hjort Frederiksen (secretary-general)

The *Venstre* (literally "Left", although the party has long opted for the rubric "Liberal") was founded in June 1870 as Denmark's first organized party, derived from the Friends of the Peasants (*Bondevennerne*) and drawing its main support from small independent farmers (and later from sections of the urban middle class) opposed to the conservatism and political hegemony of the old *Hoejre* (Right), forerunner of the present-day Conservative People's Party (KFP). It became dominant in the then lower house by the 1880s but remained in opposition due to *Hoejre* control of the upper house. In 1901, however, what was then called the *Venstre* Reform Party formed a majority government under Johan Henrik Deuntzer, who was succeeded as Prime Minister by Jens Christian Christensen in 1905. The party was weakened in the latter year by the formation of the breakaway Radical Liberal Party (RV) but recovered partially in 1910 when it reunited with the small Moderate *Venstre* faction under the simple title *Venstre*. The party remained dominant until the 1924 elections, when it was replaced as

Denmark's leading political formation by the Social Democratic Party (SD), although it was again in power in 1926-29.

In opposition through the 1930s, *Venstre* experienced electoral decline, to 17.8% of the vote in 1935 compared with a high of 47.9% in 1903. After participating in the World War II national unity government, it rose to 23.4% in 1945 and formed a minority government under Knut Kristensen. Despite improving to 28.0% in 1947, *Venstre* went into opposition until 1950, when it formed a coalition with the KFP under the premiership of Erik Eriksen, who oversaw the introduction of the 1953 constitution. It then remained in opposition for 15 years, during which it support declined from 25.1% in 1957 to 18.5% in 1968, when it entered a centre-right coalition with the RV and KFP. This coalition lasted until 1971, but the watershed December 1973 elections, yielding fragmentation of the party structure (and only 22 seats for the *Venstre* on a 12.3% vote share), resulted in a highly minority *Venstre* government under Poul Hartling. Despite almost doubling its support to 23.3% and 42 seats in 1975, the *Venstre* went into opposition and slumped to 12.0% and 21 seats at the 1977 elections.

In August 1978 the *Venstre* entered its first-ever formal peace-time coalition with the SD, but this collapsed a year later, precipitating elections in which the *Venstre* obtained 12.5% and 22 seats. Having slipped to 11.3% and 21 seats in the 1981 elections, in September 1982 it joined a four-party centre-right government headed by Poul Schlüter of the KFP and also including the Centre Democrats (CD) and the Christian People's Party (KrFP). The KFP/*Venstre* tandem was to survive for over a decade, creating an all-time longevity record for a non-socialist government, although the CD and KrFP were replaced by the RV in 1998-90, after which the KFP and the *Venstre* formed a two-party coalition that lasted until January 1993. During this period *Venstre* electoral support improved to 12.1% and 22 seats in 1984, slipped to 10.5% and 19 seats in 1987, rose to 11.8% and 22 seats in 1988 and rose again to 15.8% and 29 seats in 1990.

As a pro-European party, the *Venstre* shared in the Schlüter government's embarrassment over the electorate's rejection of the EU's Maastricht Treaty in June 1992. In October 1992 it participated in the seven-party "national compromise" establishing the terms of joint support for the treaty in a second referendum. Before it was held, the Schlüter government resigned in January 1993 over the "Tamilgate" affair, so that the *Venstre* returned to opposition. Under the new leadership of Uffe Ellemann-Jensen (former Foreign Minister), the party headed the poll in the June

1994 European Parliament elections, winning 19.0% and four of Denmark's 16 seats. In September 1994 it was the principal victor in general elections, receiving its highest vote share (23.3%) for two decades and 42 seats. During the campaign Ellemann-Jensen controversially proposed the formation of a centre-right coalition that would for the first time include the populist Progress Party.

Claiming a membership of some 80,000, the *Venstre* is a member party of the Liberal International and of the European Liberal, Democratic and Reformist Group.

Progress Party
Fremskridtspartiet (FP)

Address. Christiansborg, 1240 Copenhagen K
Telephone. (#45-33) 374699
Fax. (#45-33) 151399
Leadership. Kirsten Jacobsen (leader), Kim Behnke (parliamentary group chair), Johannes Soerensen (secretary-general)

The FP was launched in August 1972 by Mogens Glistrup, a tax lawyer, who advocated the abolition of income tax, the dismissal of most civil servants and a major reduction of the state's role in the economy. The resultant increase in consumer demand would, he envisaged, yield more revenue from value-added tax (VAT), sufficient to cover drastically reduced government expenditure. More idiosyncratically, he also urged the abolition of Denmark's defence forces and the replacement of the Defence Ministry by a telephone answering machine with the message "We surrender" in Russia. The party caught a populist tide in the watershed 1973 general elections, contributing to the fragmentation of the party system by winning 28 seats and 15.9% of the vote, so that it became the second strongest party in the *Folketing*. It fell back to 24 seats and 13.6% in 1975, recovered to 26 seats and 14.6% in 1977 and then declined progressively to 20 seats (11.0%) in 1979, 16 seats (8.9%) in 1981 and six seats (3.6%) in 1984.

Meanwhile, Glistrup's parliamentary immunity was regularly suspended so that he could face charges of tax fraud in what turned out to be the longest trial in Danish history. Finally convicted in 1983 and sentenced to three years' imprisonment, he was expelled from the *Folketing*, re-elected in the 1984 elections (on temporary release from prison) and again expelled soon afterwards and returned to prison (from which was released in March 1985). Meanwhile, the FP's slump in the 1984 elections had exacerbated internal party dissension over his leadership style, resulting in the election of a new leadership under Pia Kjaersgaard and the moderation of the FP's more controversial policies. In particular, it now endorsed Denmark's continued membership of NATO and

the preservation of the welfare state. On the other hand, it took a strong anti-immigration stance, seeking to articulate growing public concern on the issue.

The FP advanced slightly in the 1987 elections (to nine seats and 4.8%), before becoming the main victor in the 1988 poll (rising to 16 seats and 9.0%). It fell back to 12 seats and 6.4% in the 1990 contest, prior to which Glistrup was expelled from the FP *Folketing* group for indiscipline. The FP was the only parliamentary party that opposed Danish ratification of EU's Maastricht Treaty in both the 1992 and the 1993 referendums, its lack of Euro-enthusiasm producing a slump in its vote to 2.9% in the June 1994 European Parliament elections. It recovered its 1990 share of 6.4% in the September 1994 national elections, although its representation slipped to 11 seats. During the campaign the Liberal Party leader caused controversy by publicly envisaging the formal inclusion of the FP in a future centre-right coalition.

Internal divisions in the FP in 1995 resulted in the ousting of Pia Kjaersgaard as leader and her replacement by Kirsten Jacobsen, following which a dissident faction including four FP deputies broke away to form the Danish People's Party.

Radical Liberal Party
Det Radikale Venstre (RV)

Address. Christiansborg, 1240 Copenhagen K
Telephone. (#45-33) 374747
Fax. (#45-33) 137251
Leadership.. Marianne Jelved (leader), Margrethe Vestager (chair), Hans Skov Andersen and Kirsten Groenborg (vice-chairs), Joergen Estrup (parliamentary group chair), Britta Nielsen (secretary-general)

Preferring the inaccurate English title "Social Liberal Party", the RV dates from 1905 as a left-wing splinter group of the historic Liberal Party (*Venstre*) inspired by the example of the Radical Party of France. Its original Odense Programme called for Danish neutrality in war, constitutional reform (including universal adult suffrage), a secret ballot, democratic local elections, provision for referendums on major issues, progressive taxation and land reform. Progress towards these aims was achieved by all-RV governments that held office in 1909-10 and 1913-20 (under the premiership of Carl Theodor Zahle, and more especially by the 1929-40 coalition between the RV and the now dominant Social Democratic Party (SD). Having participated in the World War II national unity government and the post-war all-party administration, the RV returned to coalition with the SD in 1957-64 (with the Single-Tax Party participating in 1957-60). During this period the party share of the vote rose from 8.1% in 1945 to 8.6% in 1953 but slipped to 5.3% by 1964, in which year it won only 10 *Folketing* seats out of 175.

Having recovered to 7.3% and 13 seats in 1967, the RV made a major advance in January 1968, to 15.0% and 27 seats, under the leadership of Hilmar Baunsgaard, who became Prime Minister of a non-socialist coalition that also included the *Venstre* and the Conservative People's Party (KFP). This lasted until 1971, when the RV slipped to a vote share of 14.3% (retaining 27 seats) and went into opposition; the next three elections also yielded major setbacks, to 11.2% and 20 seats in 1973, 7.1% and 13 seats in 1975, and 3.6% and six seats in 1977. Recovering to 5.4% and 10 seats in 1979, the RV slipped to 5.1% and nine seats in 1981 and remained outside the KFP-led centre-right coalition formed in September 1982. It improved to 5.5% and 10 seats in 1984 and to 6.2% and 11 seats in 1987, after which contest RV leader Niels Helveg Petersen rebuffed the SD's attempt to form a centre-left coalition and thereafter gave external support to a further centre-right government.

Having slipped to 5.6% and 10 seats in the 1988 elections, the RV accepted five cabinet posts in a new KFP-led coalition, but withdrew from participation in 1990 over its opposition to the latest austerity budget. In the December 1990 elections it slumped to a post-war low of 3.5% and seven seats, but nevertheless entered the SD-led centre-left coalition formed in January 1993, receiving three portfolios. In the June 1994 European Parliament balloting, the RV was the only government party to increase its vote share, to 8.5% (yielding one of the 16 seats). In the September 1994 national elections it scored 4.6% and increased its seat total to eight, thereafter joining another SD-led coalition that also included the Centre Democrats.

The RV is a member party of the Liberal International and of the European Liberal, Democratic and Reformist Group.

Red-Green Unity List
Enhedslisten-de Roed-Groenne (ELRG)
   Address. Studiestraede 24, 1455 Copenhagen K
   Telephone. (#45-33) 933324
   Fax. (#45-33) 320372
   Leadership. 21-member collective; Jette Gottlieb (parliamentary group chair), Keld Albrechtsen (secretary)

The ELRG was established in 1989 as an alliance of three parties of leftist and/or environmentalist orientation. Strongly opposed to Danish membership of NATO and the European Community (later Union), it was part of the campaign against Danish ratification of the Maastricht Treaty (successful in Denmark's first referendum in June 1992, but unsuccessful in the

second in May 1993). It achieved a breakthrough in the September 1994 general elections, winning 3.1% of the vote and six seats. Thereafter, its external support was important for the survival of the centre-left coalition government headed by the Social Democratic Party.

Social Democratic Party
Socialdemokratiet (SD)
   Address. Thorvaldsenvej 2, 1780 Copenhagen V
   Telephone. (#45-31) 391522
   Fax. (#45-31) 394030
   Leadership. Poul Nyrup Rasmussen (chair), Birte Weiss and Ole Stavad (deputy chairs), Pia Gjellerup (parliamentary group chair), Steen Christensen (general secretary)

Founded in 1871 to represent the emerging industrial working class, the SD first won seats in the *Folketing* in 1884 and in 1913-20 supported a minority government of the Radical Liberal Party (RV). It became the strongest parliamentary party (with 55 out of 148 seats) in 1924, in which year it formed its first government under the premiership of Thorvald Stauning. In opposition from 1926, the party returned to government in 1929 under Stauning, who headed a coalition with the RV until the German occupation in May 1940 and thereafter, until his death in May 1942, a national unity government. Having achieved its its highest voting support to date in the 1931 elections (46.1%), the SD was instrumental in the 1930s in introducing advanced welfare state legislation and other social reforms on the Scandinavian model.

The SD continued to be the predominant party after World War II, although it has never won an overall majority and has averaged about a third of the vote in recent elections. Stauning's successor as Prime Minister and SD leader, Vilhelm Buhl, headed the immediate post-war all-party coalition formed in May 1945, but the party lost support in the October 1945 elections and went into opposition. Talks with the Danish Communists on the creation of a broad Labour Party came to nothing. The SD returned to power in November 1947 as a minority government under Hans Hedtoft until his death in January 1955 and then under Hans Christian Hansen. In May 1957 the SD formed a majority coalition with the RV and the Single-Tax Party, under the premiership of Hansen until his death in February 1960 and then under Viggo Kampmann. After improving to 42.1% and 76 seats in the November 1960 elections (its best post-war result), the party formed a two-party coalition with the RV, under Kampmann until he was succeeded as party leader and Prime Minister by Jens Otto Krag in September 1962.

Krag reverted to a minority SD government after the September 1964 elections (in which the party slipped to 41.9% but retained 76 seats);

however, after losing ground in the next two elections, the party was in opposition from January 1968 until, following SD gains in the September 1971 elections (to 37.3% and 70 seats), Krag was able to form a new minority government the following month. Immediately after the October 1972 referendum decision in favour of European Community membership, Krag unexpectedly resigned in January 1973 and was succeeded by trade union leader Anker Joergensen. Later that year the SD was weakend by the formation of the Centre Democrats by a right-wing splinter group which claimed that the party was moving too far to the left. Heavy SD losses in the December 1973 elections (to 25.6% and 46 seats, its worst result in half a century) sent the party into opposition; but a partial recovery in the January 1975 contest (to 30.0% and 53 seats) resulted in an SD minority government under Joergensen. Following a further SD recovery in the February 1977 elections (to 37.0% and 65 seats), Joergensen in August 1978 negotiated the SD's first-ever formal coalition with the *Venstre* Liberals in peace-time. However, after another SD advance in the September 1979 elections (to 38.3% and 68 seats), Joergensen formed an SD minority government.

The SD suffered a setback in the 1981 elections, falling to 59 seats and 32.9% of the vote. It nevertheless remained in office until September 1982, when Joergensen resigned and was replaced by Denmark's first Prime Minister from the Conservative People's Party since 1901. The SD lost further ground at the January 1984 and September 1987 elections (to 56 seats and 31.6%, then to 54 seats and 29.3%), by which time the party had experienced its longest period of opposition since the 1920s. After unsuccessfully seeking to form a coalition with the RV and the Socialist People's Party (SFPP), Joergensen resigned as SD chair after the 1987 elections and was succeeded (in November 1987) by Svend Auken. But a lacklustre SD performance in further elections in May 1988 (to 55 seats and 29.9%) kept the party in opposition. It improved sharply at the next contest in December 1990 (to 69 seats and 37.4%), but remained in opposition, with the eventual result that in April 1992 Auken was replaced as party chair by Poul Nyrup Rasmussen. Two months later the SD shared in the embarrassment of the pro-European government parties when Danish voters narrowly rejected the Maastricht Treaty of the new European Union (EU).

The SD participated in the seven-party "national compromise" of October 1992 establishing the terms of joint support for the Maastricht Treaty in a further referendum. Before it could be held, the "Tamilgate" scandal unexpectedly brought about the downfall of the centre-right coalition in January 1993 and the installation of a majority coalition (the first since 1971) headed by the SD and including the RV, the Centre Democrats (CD) and the Christian People's Party. The Maastricht Treaty was duly approved at the second time of asking in May 1993, but a significant minority of SD activists and voters remained in the "no" camp. The party's difficulties over the EU were apparent in the June 1994 European Parliament elections, when the SD managed only 15.8% of the vote and three of the 16 Danish seats. In the September 1994 national elections, however, the party recovered to 34.6%, yielding 62 seats and enabling Rasmussen to form a three-party minority coalition with the RV and the CD.

Claiming a membership of 100,000, the SD is a member party of the Socialist International and of the Party of European Socialists.

Socialist People's Party
Socialistisk Folkeparti (SFP)

    Address. Christiansborg, 1240 Copenhagen K
    Telephone. (#45-33) 374480
    Fax. (#45-33) 147010
    Leadership. Holger K. Nielsen (chair), Steen Gade (parliamentary group chair), Asbjoern Agerschou (secretary-general)

The SFP was founded in November 1958 by a dissident faction of the Communist Party of Denmark (DKP) led by former DKP chair Aksel Larsen, following the latter's expulsion from the party for praising Titoism in Yugoslavia and criticizing the Soviet Union's suppression of the 1956 Hungarian Uprising. The new party advocated left-wing socialism independent of the Soviet Union, unilateral disarmament, Nordic co-operation, and opposition to NATO and to Danish accession to the European Community (EC). It won 11 seats and 6.1% of the vote at its first elections in 1960, fell back slightly in 1964 but advanced to 20 seats and 10.9% in 1966. Apart from that of 1971, the next five elections brought a gradual decline for the SFP, to a low of six seats and 3.9% in 1977, in part because of competition from the new Left Socialist Party, founded by SFP dissidents in 1967. In 1972 the SFP took a leading role in the unsuccessful "no" campaign in the Danish referendum on EC entry, acting in this as on other issues as an unofficial left wing of the Social Democratic Party (SD). During the 1970s the SFP usually gave external support to the SD-led minority governments characteristic of the decade.

The four elections from 1979 yielded an SFP resurgence, to an all-time high of 27 seats and 14.6% in 1987, when it was the only party to make significant gains and became the third strongest parliamentary party. Prior to the 1987 elections the SFP had stated its minimum conditions It remained in opposition to the Schlüter centre-right government and lost ground in the 1988 contest, falling to 24 seats and 13.0%. SD gains in the 1990 elections further reduced the SFP tally, to 15 seats and 8.3%. The party campaigned on the "no" side in the June 1992 referendum in which Danish voters narrowly rejected the Maastricht Treaty on European Union, although it no longer advocated Denmark's withdrawal. In October 1992, after some agonizing, the KFP joined the seven-party "national compromise" that set new terms for approval of the treaty, which was given by voters in May 1993. In June 1994 the SFP won 8.6% in European Parliament polls, thus retaining the one seat won in 1989. It declined to 13 seats and 7.3% in the September 1994 general elections (partly because of a rise in support for the Red-Green Unity List), thereafter pledging conditional support for the reconstituted SD-led coalition.

Claiming a membership of 8,000, the SFP maintains contact with other left-socialist parties in Europe. Its European Parliament representative sits in the Green Group.

Other Parties and Movements

Common Course (*Faelles Kurs*, FK), led by Preben Moeller Hansen (a trade union leader and former Communist), founded in 1986 as a left-wing populist party opposed to immigration, NATO and the European Community (later Union); won four *Folketing* seats in 1987 but lost them in 1988 and has not been represented since.

Communist Party of Denmark (*Danmarks Kommunistiske Parti*, DKP), led by Ole Sohn (chair) and Anne-Marie Joergensen (general secretary), founded in 1919 and represented in the *Folketing* from 1932, participated in the immediate post-war coalition government, winning 18 seats in 1945 but declining steadily thereafter to nil in 1960, having been weakened by the formation of the Socialist People's Party; re-entered the *Folketing* in 1973 with six seats, rising to seven in 1975 and 1977, but unrepresented since 1979. *Address*. Dr Tvaergade 3, 1302 Copenhagen K

Communist Workers' Party of Denmark (*Danmarks Kommunistisk Arbejderparti*, DKAP), a small Maoist grouping.

The Greens (*De Groenne*), sub-titled **Realistic-Ecological Alternative** (*Oekoloisk-Realistik Alternativ*), which has remained small because of the strong environmentalist current in several mainstream parties and also because of the recent success of the Red-Green Unity List.

Growth Party (*Vaekstparti, VP*), founded in November 1990 by Mogens Glistrup following his expulsion from the Progress Party.

Humanistic Party (*Det Humanistiske Parti*), led by Christian Adamsen, espousing non-violence.

June Movement (*Juni Bevaegelsen*), anti-EU formation led by Jens-Peter Bonde and named after the month of the initial Danish referendum rejection of the Maastricht Treaty, won 15.2% and two seats in the 1994 elections to the European Parliament, where its members sit in the Nations of Europe group.

Left Socialist Party (*Venstresocialisterne*, VS), founded in December 1967 by a left-wing dissidents of the Socialist People's Party (SFP), won four *Folketing* seats in 1968, lost them in 1971, regained them in 1975, reached high point of six seats in 1979, falling to five in 1981 and 1984, but weakened thereafter by factionalism and retro-defections to the SFP, unrepresented since 1987, much of its natural support switching to the Red-Green Unity List.

Party of the Consciously Workshy, a highly "alternative" party led by the comedian Jacob Haugaard, who in September 1994 was elected to the *Folketing* with a large vote in Jutland on a platform that included support for "a following wind on all cycle paths". *Address*. Christiansborg, 1240 Copenhagen K

People's Movement against the European Union (*Folkesbevaegelsen mod EF-Union*), founded to articulate rank-and-file feeling in officially pro-European parties, won 18.9% and four seats in the 1989 European Parliament elections, falling to 10.3% and two seats in 1994 (when it faced competition from the June Movement); its members sit in the Nations of Europe group at Strasbourg.

Schleswig Party (*Schleswigsche Partei*), led by Peter Bieling, founded in August 1920 following the incorporation of former German northern Schleswig into Denmark; representing the German minority, it had one *Folketing* seat until 1964 and in 1973-79, latterly in alliance with the Centre Democrats. *Address*. Vestergade 30, 6200 Abenraa

Single-Tax Party, also known as the **Justice Party** (*Retsforbund*), led by Poul Gerhard C. Kristiansen, founded in 1919 to propagate the theories of US economist Henry George, won between two and four *Folketing* seats in 1930s and 1940s, rising to 12 in 1950 but falling unevenly to nil in 1960, following participation in a coalition government headed by the Social Democratic Party from 1957; re-entered *Folketing* in 1973 with five seats, lost them all in 1975, won six seats in 1977 and five in 1979, but unrepresented since 1981. *Address.* Lyngbyvej 42, 2100 Copenhagen.

Danish Dependencies

Faroe Islands

Capital: Tórshavn

Population: 48,000 (1995E)

Under the 1993 Danish constitution the Faroe Islands are an internally self-governing part of the Kingdom of Denmark, whose government retains responsibility for their foreign affairs, defence, judiciary and monetary affairs. Executive power is formally vested in the Danish monarch, who is represented in Tórshavn by a High Commissioner, but actual authority for Faroese affairs (including fisheries) is exercised by a government (*Landsstyret* or *Landsstyrid*) headed by a chief minister (*Loegmadur* or *Lagmand*). Legislative authority is vested in a Faroes parliament (*Lagting* or *Loegting*), 27 of whose seats are filled by direct proportional election under universal adult suffrage and up to five more by distribution to party lists under an equalization system. Two representatives from the Faroes are elected to the *Folketing* in Copenhagen in Danish national elections. The Faroe Islands remained outside the European Community (later Union) when Denmark joined in 1973 but later signed a special trade agreement with the grouping.

Elections to the Faroes parliament on July 7, 1994, resulted in the following seat distribution: Union Party 8 (23.4% of the vote); People's Party 6 (16.0%); Social Democratic Party 5 (15.4%); Republican Party 4 (13.7%); Workers' Front 3 (9.5%); Christian People's Party/Faroes Progressive and Fishing Industry Party 2 (6.3%); Centre Party 2 (5.8%); Self-Government Party 2 (5.6%). The September 1994 elections to the Danish *Folketing* resulted in the return of candidates of the Union and People's parties.

Centre Party
Midflokkurin (Mfl)
Address. PO Box 3237, 110 Tórshavn
Leadership. Tordur Niclasen (chair)

The Mfl was founded in 1991 in opposition to the then coalition government of the Social Democratic and People's parties. It won two seats out of 32 in the July 1994 election and continued in opposition.

Christian People's Party/Faroes Progressive and Fishing Industry Party
Kristiligi Fólkaflokkurin/Framburds- og Fiskivinnuflokkurin (KF/FFF)
Address. Brekku 5, 700 Klaksvík
Telephone. (#298) 55324
Fax. (#298) 57581
Leadership. Rev. Niels Poul Danielsen (chair), Olavur Petersen

The KF/FFF was formed prior to the 1978 elections as an alliance of the centrist Progressive Party (which had been in coalition government in 1963-66) and centre-oriented fishing industry elements. Favouring increased self-government for the Faroes, it won two seats in 1978, 1980 and 1984, subsequently entering a centre-left coalition headed by the Social Democratic Party. It again won two seats in 1988, switching to the resultant centre-right coalition headed by the People's Party, but withdrawing in June 1989. It retained two seats in the 1990 and 1994 elections.

People's Party
Fólkaflokkurin (Fkfl)
Address. Aarvegur, PO Box 208, Tórshavn
Leadership. Anfinn Kallsberg (chair)

The moderate conservative and pro-autonomy Fkfl was founded in 1940 as a merger of a right-wing faction of the Self-Government Party Sjfl) and the small Commerce Party (*Vinnuflokkur*). It first entered a coalition government in 1950, with the Union Party (Sbfl) until 1954 and thereafter with the Sjfl until 1958. In 1963–66 its then leader, Jógvan Sundstein, headed a coalition with the

Republican Party (Tjfl), the Christian People's Party/Progressive and Fishing Industry Party (KF/FFF) and the Sjfl. The party was again in opposition from 1966 to 1974, when it joined a centre-left coalition with the Social Democratic Party (Jvfl) and the Tjfl, this alliance being continued after the 1978 election. In 1981 it entered a centre-right coalition with Sbfl and the Sjfl, becoming the second strongest parliamentary party in the 1984 elections with seven seats, but nevertheless going into opposition. It became the strongest party, with eight seats, in the 1988 election, after which Sundstein formed a centre-right coalition with the Tjfl, the Sjfl and the KF/FFF. This gave way to a Fkfl/Tjfl/Sbfl governing alliance in mid-1989, but the Fkfl's two new partners withdrew support in October 1990, precipitating an early election the following month in which the Fkfl slipped to seven seats. In January 1991 the party became the junior partner in a coalition with the Jvfl but withdrew in April 1993 over a fisheries policy disagreement. It declined to six seats in the July 1994 election, after which it remained in opposition.

The Fkfl won one of the two Faroes seats in the Danish elections of September 1994, its deputy joining the Liberal Party parliamentary group. The Fkfl is affiliated to the International Democrat Union.

Republican Party

Tjódveldisflokkurin (Tjfl)
   Address. Villingadalsvegi, 100 Tórshavn
   Telephone. (#298) 14412
   Leadership. Finnbogi Isakson

Its title meaning literally "Party for People's Government", the Tjfl was founded in 1948 as a left-wing party advocating secession from Denmark, citing as justification a 1946 plebiscite in which 48.7% had voted for independence and 47.2% for home rule under Danish sovereignty. Having won two seats in 1950, it improved sharply to six in 1954 and subsequently participated in centre-left coalitions in 1963-66, 1974-80 and 1985-88. It again won six seats in the 1988 election and joined a coalition headed by the People's Party, but this finally collapsed in October 1990. The Tjfl fell back to four seats in the November 1990 election and was in opposition until joining a coalition headed by the Social Democratic Party in April 1993. It again won four seats in the July 1994 election, after which it went into opposition.

Self-Government Party

Sjálvstýrisflokkurin (Sjfl)
   Address. Aarvegur, PO Box 208, 110 Tórshavn
   Leadership. Helena Dam A. Neystaboe
   Also known in English as the Home-Rule Party,

the Sjfl was founded in 1906 by the poet Joannes Patursson to campaign for real powers for the Faroes parliament (which then had a consultative role) and the preservation of the Faroese language. Opposing the pro-Danish line of the Union Party (Sbfl), it won 51.7% of the popular vote in 1916 (but not a parliamentary majority) and 49.8% in 1918, when it obtained an absolute majority of seats for the first (and so far only) time. Following the defection of its left wing to the Social Democratic Party (Jvfl) in 1928, a right-wing faction broke away in 1940 to join the People's Party (Fkfl), leaving the rump Sjfl as a centrist party. Having fallen to 16.7% and four seats in 1940, the Sjfl was unrepresented from 1943 to 1946, when it regained two seats in an electoral alliance with the Jvfl.

From the granting of home rule to the Faroes in 1948, the party was a partner in coalition governments in 1948-50 and 1954-75 and was then opposition until until January 1981, when it joined a centre-right coalition with the Union Party (Sbfl) and the Fkfl. Having slipped to one seat in 1966, the Sjfl recovered to two in 1974 and went up to three in 1980. After losing one seat in the 1984 election (on a slightly higher vote share), it entered a centre-left coalition headed by the Jvfl. After retaining two seats in the November 1988 election, it joined a centre-right coalition headed by the Fkfl but withdrew in June 1989. In early elections in November 1990 it moved back to three seats but remained in opposition until April 1993, when it joined another centre-left coalition. The party slipped back to two seats in July 1994, but nevertheless joined a four-party coalition headed by the Sbfl.

Social Democratic Party

Javnadarflokkurin (Jvfl)
   Address. Argjavegur 26, 160 Argir
   Telephone. (#268) 11820
   Fax. (#298) 14720
   Leadership. Marita Petersen (chair)

Its Faroese title meaning "Equality Party", the Jvfl dates from 1925 and first gained representation in 1928, when it was strengthened by the adhesion of a splinter group of the Self-Government Party (Sjfl). After making a breakthrough to six seats in 1936, it was a member of the first home rule government in 1948-50 and in 1958 became the strongest parliamentary party, winning eight seats out of 30 and forming a coalition with the Sjfl and the Union Party (Sbfl) under the premiership of Peter Mohr Dam. It was to retain a narrow plurality until 1978, although 27.6% was its highest vote share. In opposition from 1962, the Jvfl returned to government in 1966 and was continuously in office until 1980, providing the Prime Minister in 1966-68 and in 1970-80, latterly in the person of Atli Dam. After four years in opposition, the Jvfl again became the largest party in 1984, with eight seats out of 32, enabling Atli Dam to form a centre-left coalition with the Sjfl, the Republican Party (Tjfl) and the Christian People's Party/Progressive and Fishing Industry Party (KF/FFF).

A shift to the right in the 1988 election reduced the Jvfl to seven seats and consigned it to opposition. An early election in November 1990 restored the Jvfl to plurality status, with 10 seats, so that in January 1991 Atli Dam formed a two-party coalition with the People's Party (Fkfl). In April 1993 Atli Dam was succeeded as Jvfl leader and Prime Minister by Marita Petersen, but in October 1993 the Fkfl withdrew from the government and was replaced by the Tjfl and the Sjfl. In the July 1994 election the Jvfl went down to a heavy defeat, winning only five seats (and 15.4% of the vote), partly because of competition from the new Workers' Front (Vf). It nevertheless joined a new coalition headed by the Sbfl and including the Sjfl and the Vf.

Union Party
Sambandsflokkurin (Sbfl)

Address. Aarvegur, PO Box 208, Tórshavn
Leadership. Edmund Joensen (chair)

The conservative Sbfl was founded in 1906 in support of the maintenance of close relations between the islands and the Danish Crown and therefore in opposition to the Self-Government Party (Sjfl). It won 62.4% of the vote in its first election in 1906 and 73.3% in 1910, remaining the majority parliamentary party until 1918, when it was overtaken by the Sjfl. It recovered its dominance in the 1920s, but the advent of the Social Democratic Party (Jvfl) heralded increasing fragmentation of the party structure. In 1936 the Sbfl vote dropped sharply to 33.6% and since 1943 the party has never exceeded a 30% share. Following the introduction of home rule in 1948, the Sbfl provided the Faroes' Prime Minister until 1958: Andreas Samuelsen headed a coalition of the Jvfl and the Sjfl in 1948-50, while Kristian Djurhuus led one with the People's Party (Fkfl) in

1950-54 and another with the Fkfl and the Sjfl in 1954-58. It continued in government in 1958-62, but went into opposition after the 1962 election, in which it won only six seats and 20.5% of the vote.

Although it remained at six seats in the 1966 election, it entered a coalition with the Jvfl and the Sjfl that lasted until 1974, with then party leader Pauli Ellefsen holding the premiership in 1968-70. Having slipped to five seats and 19.1% in the 1974 election, the Sbfl won a narrow plurality in 1978 (eight seats and 26.3% of the vote) but remained in opposition. It retained eight seats on a 23.9% vote share in the 1980 contest, following which Ellefsen formed a coalition with the Fkfl and the Sjfl that lasted until 1984. In the latter year it slipped to seven seats (and 21.2%) and reverted to opposition status, subsequently registering an identical electoral result in 1988. In June 1989 the Sbfl joined a coalition headed by the Fkfl and including the Republican Party (Tjfl), but this collapsed in October 1990, causing an early election the following month in which the Sbfl won six seats. After four years in opposition, the Sbfl became the largest party in the July 1994 election, with eight seats, and subsequently formed a coalition with the Jvfl, the Sjfl and the new Workers' Front under the premiership of Edmund Joensen.

The Sbfl won one of the two Faroes seats in the September 1994 Danish elections, its deputy opting to join the Conservative People's Party parliamentary group.

Workers' Front
Verkmannafylkingin (Vf)

Address. Aarvegur, PO Box 208, 110 Tórshavn
Leadership. Oli Jacobsen

The Vf was founded in 1994 by left-wing dissidents of the Social Democratic Party (Jvfl) in alliance with some trade union leaders unhappy with the recent performance of the Jvfl in government. In its first election in July 1994 the Vf won three seats and obtained one portfolio in a coalition government headed by the right-wing Union Party and also including the Jvfl and the Self-Government Party.

Greenland

Capital: Nuuk (Godthaab)   **Population:** 56,000 (1995E)

The arctic island of Greenland is a part of the Kingdom of Denmark but has had internal self-government since May 1979, as approved by referendum in January 1979 by 70.1% of participating voters. Greenland accordingly has its own 31-member parliament (*Landsting*), which is popularly elected by proportional representation, and a government (*Landsstyre*) with responsibility for internal economic and social affairs, while the Danish government retains responsibility for foreign affairs, defence and monetary policy. Greenland entered the European Community (later Union) in 1973 as part of Denmark, but withdrew with effect from Feb. 1, 1985, on the strength of a local referendum decision against membership in February 1982.

Elections to the *Landsting* on March 5, 1995, resulted as follows: Forward (*Siumut*) 12 seats (with 38.5% of the vote); Community (*Atassut*) 10 (29.7%); Eskimo Brotherhood (*Inuit Ataqatigiit*) 6 (20.3%); Centre Party (*Akulliit Partiiat*), 2; independent 1.

Centre Party
Akulliit Partiiat (AP)
  Address. c/o Landsting, 3900 Nuuk
  Leadership. Bjarne Kreutzmann (chair)
  The liberal pro-market AP was formed prior to the 1991 Greenland election, in which it won two seats in the *Landsting*. It retained two seats in the March 1995 election and remained in opposition.

Community Party
Atassut
  Address. PO Box 399, 3900 Nuuk
  Telephone. (#299) 23366
  Fax. (#299) 25840
  Leadership. Daniel Skifte
  The centrist *Atassut* was founded in 1978 and achieved official status as a political party in 1981 under the leadership of Lars Chemnitz, who was chairman of the pre-autonomy Greenland council. In the April 1979 election preceding the move to autonomy it was defeated by the Forward party and went into opposition, from where it campaigned in favour of Greenland remaining in the European Community in the 1982 referendum—unsuccessfully as it turned out. *Atassut* retained opposition status after the 1983 election despite winning a larger popular vote than Forward, which got the same number of seats. Chemnitz resigned the party leadership in March 1984 and *Atassut* lost ground in the June 1984 election, therefore remaining in opposition. In the May 1987 election *Atassut* again overtook Forward in popular vote terms but won the same number of seats (11) and therefore continued in opposition. Its status was not changed by the 1991

contest, in which it fell back to eight seats, but in March 1995 *Atassut* won 10 seats (out of 31) and accepted participation in a coalition headed by Forward.

Eskimo Brotherhood
Inuit Ataqatigiit (IA)
  Address. PO Box 321, 3900 Nuuk
  Telephone. (#299) 23702
  Leadership. Josef Motzfeldt (chair)
  The IA was founded in 1978 by a group of Marxist-Leninists who had been active in the Young Greenland Council in Copenhagen and who opposed the home rule arrangements then being negotiated, advocating instead Greenland's "total independence from the capitalist colonial power". The new party also urged that Greenland citizenship should be restricted to those with at least one Eskimo parent and that the US military base at Thule should be closed. Having failed to persuade Greenlanders to vote against home rule in the January 1979 referendum, the IA failed to obtain representation in the April 1979 election, but was on the winning side in the 1982 referendum in which Greenlanders voted to leave the European Community. Having effectively absorbed the small Wage-Earners' Party (*Sulissartut*), the IA won two seats in the 1983 Greenland election. It increased to three seats in the next contest in 1984, when it joined a coalition government headed by the Forward (*Siumut*) party. The coalition collapsed in March 1987 after the then IA leader, Aqqaluk Lynge, had accused the *Siumut* prime minister of being "totally passive" in the face of the US government's enhancement of the Thule base.

Having improved to four seats in the resultant May 1987 election, the IA joined another coalition with *Siumut* with increased ministerial responsibilities, but again withdrew in 1988. The IA moved up to five seats in the March 1991 election and again formed a coalition with *Siumut*, under a new prime minister. In the March 1995 election the IA made further progress, to six seats (out of 31), but went into opposition after failing to persuade *Siumut* to take up its revived demand for complete independence for Greenland.

Forward
Siumut
> *Address.* PO Box 357, 3900 Nuuk
> *Telephone.* (#299) 22077
> *Fax.* (#299) 22319
> *Leadership.* Lars Emil Johansen (chair)

The socialist *Siumut* party was founded in July 1977, derived from earlier pro-autonomy groups and the political review *Siumut*. Having supported the autonomy arrangements approved by referendum in January 1979, *Siumut* won an absolute majority of 13 seats (out of 21) in the April 1979 election and formed Greenland's first home rule government under the premiership of Jonathan Motzfeldt. Opposed to Greenland's membership of the European Community, *Siumut* campaigned successfully for a vote in favour of withdrawal in the 1982 referendum. In the April 1983 election the party slipped to 11 seats (out of 24) but continued as a minority government until another election in June 1984, when it again won 11 seats (out of 25) and formed a majority coalition with the small Eskimo Brotherhood (IA). The coalition collapsed in March 1987, amid dissension over the status of the US military base at Thule, and *Siumut* retained 11 seats (out of 27) in the resultant May 1987 election, whereupon Motzfeldt sought to negotiate a "grand coalition" with the Community (*Atassut*) party. This provoked opposition from within *Siumut*, the eventual outcome being a further left-wing coalition with the IA.

Triggered by allegations of corruption among government ministers, an early election in May 1991 resulted in *Siumut* again winning 11 seats (out of 27) and forming a new coalition with the IA, although Motzfeldt was obliged, in view of the scandal, to vacate the premiership and *Siumut* leadership in favour of Lars Emil Johansen. In the next election in March 1995 *Siumut* won 12 seats (out of 31), but attempts to reconstitute the *Siumut*/IA combination foundered on the IA's revived demand for complete independence for Greenland. The outcome was the formation of a "grand coalition" between *Siumut* and *Atassut* committed to maintaining Greenland's autonomous status.

An affiliate of the Socialist International, *Siumut* has consistently returned one of Greenland's two members of the *Folketing* in Copenhagen, where its deputy usually sits in the parliamentary group of the Social Democratic Party.

Polar Party
Issittrup Partii (IP)
> *Address.* c/o Landsting, 3900 Nuuk
> *Telephone.* (#299) 25988
> *Fax.* (#299) 25899
> *Leadership.* Nikolaj Heinrich

Representing Greenland's business sector, the IP was formed prior to the May 1987 election on the initiative of Heinrich as president of the Federation of Fishermen and Trawlermen. Opposing the "anti-business" policies of the incumbent left-wing government headed by Forward (*Siumut*), it called in particular for the privatization of the state-owned fishing fleet. It won one seat (out of 27) in 1987, retaining it in 1991, but did not obtain representation in the March 1995 election.

Djibouti

Capital: Djibouti   **Population:** 710,000 (1995E)

The Republic of Djibouti (formerly the French Territory of the Afars and the Issas) has been ruled by President Hassan Gouled Aptidon since independence in 1977. The Popular Rally for Progress (RPP) was the ruling party in a single-party system from October 1981 until a referendum in September 1992 which produced an overwhelming vote in favour of a multi-party constitution. Under the new text, executive power is vested in the President who is elected for a six-year term. Legislative power is vested in a 65–member Chamber of Deputies (*Chambre des Députés*), which is elected for a five-year term. A total of four parties may compete for

Chamber seats, although for the December 1992 poll only three were registered, one of which (the National Democratic Party) withdrew before balloting began. Of the two that remained, the RPP eclipsed the Party of Democratic Renewal, taking all 65 seats. In the presidential election on May 7, 1993, Hassan Gouled Aptidon (RPP) was re-elected for a fourth term of office, obtaining just over 60 per cent of the vote.

Front for the Restoration of Unity and Democracy
Front pour la Restauration de l'Unité et de la Démocratie (FRUD)
   Leadership. Ali Mohamed Daoud (president), Ahmed Ougoureh Kifle (secretary-general)

The FRUD was formed in 1991 by the merger of three Afar groups: Action for the Revision of Order in Djibouti (*Action pour la Révision de l'Ordre à Djibouti*, AROD), the Front for the Restoration of Right and Equality (*Front pour la Restauration du Droit et l'Egalité*, FRDE) and the Djibouti Patriotic Resistance Front (*Front de la Résistance Patriotique de Djibouti*, FRPD). Advocating fair representation in government of Djibouti's different ethnic groups, the FRUD began an armed insurgency against the ruling regime in late 1991.

Factional divisions in the organization led in the first half of 1994 to the emergence of a new leadership, under Ali Mohamed Daoud, favouring negotiations with the government to end the civil war. This culminated in a peace agreement in December 1994, providing for an immediate ceasefire and revision of the constitution and of electoral lists before the next elections. It also provided for an alliance between the FRUD led by Daoud and the ruling Popular Rally for Progress for "the management of affairs", perhaps heralding the possible inclusion of FRUD members in the government. The agreement was condemned by the faction of the ousted former FRUD leader, Ahmed Dini Ahmed, as a "betrayal" of the organization's aims.

Movement for Unity and Democracy
Mouvement pour l'Unité et la Démocratie (MUD)
   Leadership. Mohammed Moussa Ali Tourtour

The MUD was set up in 1990 to campaign in favour of a pluralist democratic system. It has called for a national conference to arrange for a transition to multipartyism. The party leader, who was held in detention in 1991, was an unsuccessful candidate in the 1993 presidential election, taking fourth place.

Party of Democratic Renewal
Parti du Renouveau Démocratique (PRD)
   Leadership. Mohamed Djame Elabe (president)
   The PRD was formed in September 1992 to succeed the Movement for Peace and Reconciliation, which had been launched six months earlier by Mohamed Djama Elabe. Advocating the establishment of democratic parliamentary government, the PRD was the only opposition party to take part in the 1992 legislative elections, but was not awarded any seats despite being credited with about a quarter of the vote. Djama Elabe was the runner-up in the 1993 presidential election, with a 22 per cent share of the poll.

Popular Rally for Progress
Rassemblement Populaire pour le Progrès (RPP)
   Address. c/o Chamber of Deputies, Djibouti
   Leadership. Hassan Gouled Aptidon (chair), Moumin Bahdon Farah (secretary-general)

The RPP was set up in 1979, its main component being the African People's League for Independence (*Ligue Populaire Africaine pour l'Indépendance*, LPAI), which was a primarily Issa-supported organization prior to the country's accession to independence in 1977. The RPP was the ruling party under the single-party system from 1981, and was the first political group to be legalized under the pluralist constitution of 1992. Maintaining its grip on political power, the party took all the seats in the December 1992 elections to the Chamber of Deputies, and in the following year Gouled Aptidon was re-elected President of the Republic for a third six-year term.

Union of Democratic Movements
Union des Mouvements Démocratiques (UMD)
   Leadership. Aden Robleh Awaleh (chair)

The UMD was established as an umbrella organization of opposition groupings, including the National Democratic Party (PND). The PND had been founded in 1992 by Aden Robleh Awaleh, a former cabinet minister and vice-president of the ruling Popular Rally for Progress, who, from exile, was active in anti-government groupings from 1986. The PND withdrew from the December 1992 legislative elections and subsequently appealed for the formation of a transitional government of national unity to supervise the implementation of democratic reforms. Robleh Awaleh came third in the May 1993 presidential election, attracting about 12 per cent of the vote. In November 1995 he received a one-month suspended prison sentence for illegally organizing an opposition demonstration; he was reported at the time to be on hunger strike in support of a demand for the release of several UMD colleagues who had been arrested with him.

United Opposition Front of Djibouti

Front Uni de l'Opposition Djiboutienne (FUOD)
Leadership. Mohamed Ahmed Issa ("Cheiko")
The FUOD was created in mid-1992, bringing together internal opposition groups including some former members of the Gouled Aptidon government and encompassing the Front for the Restoration of Unity and Democracy.

Other Groups

Afar Masses Organization (*Organisation des Masses Afar*, OMA), launched in October 1993 under the chairmanship of Ahmed Malco.

Centrist and Democratic Reforms Party (*Parti Centriste et des Réformes Démocratiques*, PCRD), formed in late 1993 by a breakaway faction of the FRUD and led by Hassan Abdallah Watta.

Democratic Movement of Djiboutian Youth (*Mouvement Démocratique de la Jeunesse Djiboutienne*, MDJD), formed in 1991 and led by Aboulkarim Ali Amarkak.

Democratic Union for Djiboutian Justice and Equality (*Union Démocratique pour la Justice et l'Egalité Djiboutienne*, UDJED), launched in 1988, with a multi-ethnic executive committee headed by Abdallah Deberkaleh Ahmed and Idriss Ismail Ahmed.

Djibouti Democratic Union (*Union Démocratique Djiboutienne*, UDD), a primarily Gadabursi (ethnic) party formed in January 1992 under the leadership of Mahdi Ibrahim God and Mohamed Moussa Ainache.

Djibouti People's Party (*Parti Populaire Djiboutien*, PPD), organized in 1981 and composed largely of Afars.

Djiboutian National Movement (*Mouvement National Djiboutien*, MND), Issa-supported and led by Sallam Mahmoud and Mohamed Hussein Hassan.

Front for the Liberation of the Somali Coast (*Front pour la Libération de la Côte des Somalis*, FLCS), an Issa-supported group, under the chairmanship of by Abdallah Waberi Khalif, urging that Djibouti be incorporated into a greater Somalia.

Front of Democratic Forces (*Front des Forces Démocratiques*, FFD), an Issa group led by Omar Elmi Kairem.

Movement for Salvation and Reconstruction (*Mouvement pour le Salut et la Reconstruction*, MSR), a largely Arab grouping led by Galal Abdourahman Ahmed.

Parliamentary Opposition (*Opposition Parlementaire*, OP), an opposition grouping in the Chamber of Deputies headed by Kamil Ali Mohammed.

Social Democratic Union (*Union Social-Démocrate*, USD), led by Abdillahi Elmi.

Dominica

Capital: Roseau

Population: 70,000 (1995E)

The Commonwealth of Dominica gained independence from the United Kingdom as a republic in 1978. Executive authority is nominally vested in the President (who is elected by the legislature for not more than two five-year terms in office), although in practice the President acts as a constitutional head of state. The President appoints the Prime Minister and Cabinet from among the members of the unicameral House of Assembly, which has 21 elected members and nine appointed senators and which sits for five years.

In the general election of June 12, 1995, the Dominica United Workers' Party won 11 of the 21 elected seats in the Assembly, the Dominica Freedom Party 5 and the Labour Party of Dominica 5.

Dominica Freedom Party (DFP)

Address. 5 Cross Street, Roseau
Telephone. (#1-809) 448-2104
Fax. (#1-809) 448-6184
Leadership. Brian Alleyne (leader)

The right-wing DFP came to power, under the leadership of its founder Dame Eugenia Charles, in an overwhelming election victory in 1980. The party retained office (although with decreasing electoral majorities) until the June 1995 poll when it secured only five seats in the legislature, despite drawing almost 36% of the total vote. Dame Eugenia thereupon relinquished the premiership and party leadership and retired from politics. The DFP is affiliated to the Christian Democrat International and the International Democrat Union.

Dominica United Workers' Party (DUWP)

Address. c/o House of Assembly, Roseau
Leadership. Edison James (leader)

The DUWP was established in 1988 and became the official opposition following the 1990 election when it came second to the DFP winning six seats in the House of Assembly. Having increased its representation in a by-election in mid-term, the party secured a narrow majority in the legislative elections in June 1995 and formed a new government, with Edison James as Prime Minister.

Labour Party of Dominica (LPD)

Address. c/o House of Assembly, Roseau
Leadership. Rosie Douglas (leader)

The left-wing LPD was formed in 1985 by the merger of the United Dominica Labour Party (UDLP, set up in 1981), the Dominica Liberation Movement Alliance (DLMA, established in 1979) and the Dominica Labour Party (DLP). The DLP had been the dominant party after the 1975 election, but was seriously weakened in 1979 by the defection of Oliver Seraphine and others (who formed the Dominica Democratic Labour Party, DDLP) and the controversial leadership of Patrick John. The DLP and DDLP went into opposition following their defeat in the 1980 elections, but then reunited (retaining the DLP title) in 1983, with Seraphine as leader and John as deputy leader. Following the DLP-UDLP-DLMA merger, the new formation (under the leadership of Michael Douglas) contested the 1985 elections and secured five seats. In the 1990 and 1995 polls the party won four and five seats respectively. Rosie Douglas assumed the party leadership from his brother in 1992.

Dominican Republic

Capital: Santo Domingo   **Population**: 7,350,000 (1995E)

A Spanish colony until 1821, the Dominican Republic was subjugated in 1822 by neighbouring Haiti before achieving its independence in 1844. Having been occupied by the United States from 1916 to 1924, the country was then dominated by Gen. Rafael Trujillo from 1930, when he overthrew the elected President, until his assassination in 1961. The United States again intervened militarily in 1965 to suppress a popular rebellion against a regime which had assumed power following a military coup 1963. In 1966, following fresh elections, a new constitution was promulgated. Under its provisions, legislative power is exercised by a bicameral National Congress (*Congreso Nacional*) consisting of a 30–member Senate (*Senado*) and 120–member Chamber of Deputies (*Cámara de Diputados*). Members of both houses are elected for four years by universal adult suffrage. Executive power lies with the President, who is also elected by direct popular vote for four years (except for the truncated two-year term imposed in 1994 – see below).

Presidential and legislative elections held in May 1994 were acknowledged to be highly irregular. Joaquín Balaguer of the Christian Social Reform Party (PRSC) was nevertheless sworn in as President for a seventh term, reduced to two years, in August. Balaguer had initially concluded a "pact for democracy" with the Dominican Revolutionary Party (PRD) and the Dominican Liberation Party (PLD) to foreshorten the presidential term to 18 months (with consecutive presidential terms being ended). However, the PLD subsequently joined with the PRSC in endorsing a two-year term, prompting the PRD to withdraw from the congressional session and to boycott Balaguer's inauguration.

Fresh presidential elections were held May-June 1996, resulting in a narrow second-round victory for the PLD candidate, Leonel Fernandez.

Democratic Unity

Unidad Democrática (UD)

Address. c/o Congreso Nacional, Santo Domingo

Leadership. Fernando Alvarez Bogaert (leader)

The UD fought the May 1994 elections in coalition with the Dominican Revolutionary Party (PRD). This alliance won 57 seats in the Chamber of Deputies, of which the UD secured seven, and 15 in the Senate, of which the UD held three. In the subsequent political crisis surrounding the disputed election results, the UD did not support the congressional boycott imposed by the PRD in August.

Dominican Liberation Party

Partido de la Liberación Dominicana (PLD)

Address. Avda. Independencia 401, Santo Domingo

Telephone. (#1–809) 685-3540

Leadership. Leonel Fernandez (leader)

Juan Bosch Gaviño, the founder of the Dominican Revolutionary Party (PRD), led a breakaway group from that party to form the left-wing PLD during the 1974 election campaign. The PLD secured congressional representation in all elections from 1982, although in May 1994 it retained only 13 of the 44 seats in the Chamber of Deputies which it had won in the 1990 polling. An earlier serious factional split in 1992 had resulted in the defection of a large number of left-wing party members who subsequently formed the Alliance for Democracy (APD). As the PLD presidential candidate, Bosch came third in the 1978, 1982 and 1986 elections, before running a very close second to incumbent President Balaguer in 1990. Having then come a distant third in the 1994 polling, he resigned as PLD president.

In the first round of the presidential election in May 1996 the party leader, Leonel Fernandez, took second place with almost 39% of the vote; he narrowly won the second round on June 30, by virtue of attracting support from other parties against the PRD candidate.

Dominican Revolutionary Party

Partido Revolucionario Dominicano (PRD)

Address. Avda. Bólivar, Casi esquina Dr Delgado, Santo Domingo

Telephone. (#1–809) 688-9735

Fax. (#1–809) 688-2753

Leadership. José Francisco Peña Gómez (leader), Hatuey de Camps Jiménez (general secretary)

The left-of-centre PRD was founded in 1939 by Juan Bosch Gaviño who, having been in exile throughout the Trujillo dictatorship, returned to win the presidential election in December 1962. He was deposed in a military coup in mid-1963, and in 1965 the PRD led an insurrection against the new regime that resulted in armed intervention by the United States. Having lost the subsequent elections in 1966 to the Social Christian Reformist Party (PRSC), the PRD remained in opposition for the following 12 years. During that period Bosch resigned to form the Dominican Liberation Party (PLD).

In 1978 the PRD's candidate, Silvestre Antonio Guzmán, became President in the country's first peaceful and constitutional transfer of power. His party colleague, Jorge Salvador Blanco, was elected his successor in 1982 when the party also secured an absolute majority in both houses of Congress. During the Blanco regime the PRD experienced internal divisions between a pro-government bloc and rival centre-right and centre-left factions led respectively by Jacobo Majluta Azar and José Fransisco Peña Gómez. Majluta registered his faction of the PRD (*La Estructura*) as a separate political party in 1985, but nevertheless secured the PRD's nomination as presidential candidate in the 1986 contest (which he lost), while Peña Gómez succeeded him as PRD president.

In 1994 a revived PRD, in coalition with Democratic Unity (UD), won 15 seats in the Senate and 57 in the Chamber of Deputies, while Peña Gómez took second place by a very narrow margin in the presidential race—results which prompted accusations by the PRD of widespread irregularities and which led to the party boycotting Congress from August 1994. In the first round of fresh presidential elections in May 1996, Peña Gómez led his PLD and PRSC rivals with about 46% of the vote; but he was narrowly defeated by the PLD candidate in the second round on June 30.

The PRD has been a member of the Socialist International since 1966.

Social Christian Reformist Party

Partido Reformista Social Cristiano (PRSC)

Address. Avenida San Cristobal, Ensanche La Fe, Apdo 1332, Santo Domingo

Telephone. (#1–809) 566 7089

Leadership. Joaquín Balaguer, Jacinto Peynado Garrigoza (leaders)

The centre-right PRSC was founded in 1964 by Joaquín Balaguer, who had been Vice-President and then President of the Republic (under the Trujillo dictatorship) between 1957 and 1962. He returned to presidential office in elections in 1966 (after the US military intervention of 1965), in which the PRSC also won a majority of seats in both houses of the new National Congress. Balaguer served three consecutive terms until his electoral defeat in 1978, when the PRSC became the main opposition party to the Dominican Revolutionary Party (PRD). Having lost the 1982 elections, Balaguer narrowly regained the presidency and the PRSC won control of both congressional houses in the 1986 polls. In 1990 Balaguer retained office but the PRSC lost its majority in the Chamber of Deputies.

Although most elections since the 1960s had been marked by accusations of fraud, the outcome in May 1994 sparked a political crisis. Balaguer was awarded a disputed victory by a margin of less than 1% over his PRD rival, while the PRSC took 14 of the 30 Senate seats and 50 of the 120 seats in the Chamber of Deputies. Under the terms of an accord signed by all major parties in August 1994 to end the crisis, a fresh presidential election was to be held in November 1995 (subsequently rescheduled for May 1996 despite the opposition of the PRD) and re-election of a President to a consecutive term would be prohibited. With Balaguer barred from standing again, the PRSC nominated Jacinto Peynado as its presidential candidate. In the first round of the election in May 1996 Peynaldo trailed in third place with less than 18% of the vote and was eliminated from the second round runoff held at the end of June.

The PRSC is affiliated to the Christian Democrat International.

Other Parties

Alliance for Democracy (*Alianza por la Democracia*, APD), formed in 1992 by a dissident breakaway group of the Dominican Liberation Party, splitting the following year into two factions led respectively by Max Puig and Nélsida Marmolejos.

Christian Popular Party (*Partido Popular Cristiano*, PPC).

Constitutional Action Party (*Partido Acción Constitucional*, PAC), a far-right formation.

Democratic Integration Movement (*Movimiento de Integración Democrática*, MID or MIDA), a centre-right party led by Fransisco Augusto Lora.

Dominican Communist Party (*Partido Comunista Dominicano*, PCD), formed in 1944 and outlawed from the early 1960s until 1977. It is led by José Israel Cuello and Narciso Isa Conde.

Dominican Popular Movement (*Movimiento Popular Dominicano*, MPD), a left-wing group formed in the mid-1960s but denied legal status, led by Julio de Peña Valdés.

Dominican Workers' Party (*Partido de los Trabajadores Dominicanos*, PTD), founded in 1979 and led by José González Espinosa.

Ecologist Party (*Partido Ecologista*, PE), led by Aristides Fiallo.

Independent Revolutionary Party (*Partido Revolucionario Independiente*, PRI), evolved from Jacobo Majluta Azar's centre-right *La Estructura* faction of the Dominican Revolutionary Party, registered as a separate political party in 1985.

Liberal Party for Restructuring (*Partido Liberal por la Estructura*, PLE), led by Andres van der Horst, an affiliate of the Liberal International.

Movement of National Conciliation (*Movimiento de Conciliación Nacional*, MCN), a centre party established in 1969 and led by Jaime M. Fernández.

New Power Movement (*Movimiento Nuevo Poder*, MNP), led by Antonio Reynoso.

Progressive National Force (*Fuerza Nacional Progresista*, FNP), a right-wing group headed by Marino Vinicio Castillo.

Quisqueyan Democratic Party (*Partido Quisqueyano Demócrata*, PQD), a right-wing party founded in 1968 by Gen. Elías Wessin y Wessin, who had led the military coup in 1963 which ousted the Dominican Revolutionary Party government; Wessin y Wessin ran a distant fourth in the 1982 presidential election, after which the PQD allied itself with Balaguer's Social Christian Reformist Party.

Revolutionary Social Christian Party (*Partido Revolucionario Social Cristiano*, PRSC), a small democratic leftist party formed in 1961 and led by Claudio Isidoro Acosta.

Social Democratic Alliance (*Alianza Social Demócrata*, ASD), headed by José Rafael Abinader.

Ecuador

Capital: Quito   **Population:** 11,500,000 (1995E)

The Republic of Ecuador achieved independence from Spain in 1822 as part of Gran Colombia and became a separate republic in 1830. Its first 120 years were marked by frequent changes of government, particularly the period from 1925 to 1948, during which 22 heads of state held office. In 1963 the Liberal government of President Velasco was toppled by a military coup. Velasco was reinstalled in 1968 for a fifth term and from 1970 assumed dictatorial powers. He was ousted by the military in 1972 and a civilian democratic government was not restored until 1979. During the mid-1980s the conservative government of President León Febres Cordero was openly challenged by military nationalists led by Gen. Frank Vargas Pazzos. The election of 1988, however, was won by the centre-left Democratic Left (ID) candidate Rodrigo Borja Cevallos. The ID government prided itself in being the only administration in South America not to opt for the wholesale privatization of state enterprises. However, lower international oil prices in the aftermath of the Gulf war in early 1992 led to a slowing of the economy, and an austerity policy failed to halt spiralling inflation, high unemployment and widespread poverty. In the May 1992 presidential and congressional elections, the ID was heavily defeated by right-wing parties.

Under the 1979 constitution Ecuador has an executive President who is assisted by a Vice-President and a Cabinet. He appoints the ministers and governors of Ecuador's 20 provinces, including the Galapagos Islands. Legislative power is exercised by the National Congress which sits for a 60-day period from Aug. 10 of every year. Special sessions of the National Congress may be called. Congress is required by the Constitution to set up four full-time Legislative Commissions to consider draft laws when the House is in recess.

The President is directly elected together with a Vice-President for a four-year term and is precluded from seeking re-election. If no candidate wins an absolute majority, there follows a run-off election between the two best-placed candidates. The National Congress has 65 members elected on a provincial basis every two years, and 12 members elected for a four-year term on a national basis.

No single party won an overall majority in the congressional elections held on May 17, 1992, but right-wing parties gained the majority of the seats. In congressional elections on May 1, 1994, the right-wing Republican Unity Party (PUR) alliance with the Ecuadorian Conservative Party (PCE) obtained only seven of the 65 seats being contested, compared with 23 won by the Social Christian Party (PSC). This left the PUR-PCE with a total of nine seats in the 77-member Congress now dominated by the PSC with a total of 26 seats. Presidential elections on May 17 and July 5, 1992, were won by the PUR candidate, Sixto Duran Ballen, and he took office on Aug. 10, 1992. The entire Cabinet tendered its resignation on Oct. 13, 1995 (after Vice-President Alberto Dahik Garzoni had resigned and fled to Costa Rica), but remained in office pending the announcement of a new Cabinet.

In the first round of Ecuador's presidential elections, held on May 19, 1996, the poll was headed by Jaime Nebot, candidate of the Social Christian Party, who took more than 29% of votes, while Abdalá Bucaram of the Roldosista Party won 23.5%. In the second round on July 7 Abdalá Bucaram was elected with 54.5% of the vote.

Alfaroist Radical Front
Frente Radical Alfarista (FRA)

Address. G. Moreno y Gómez Rendón (esquina), Guayaquil

Leadership. Carlos Julio Emanuel (1988 presidential candidate)

The party was founded in 1972 as an addition to the Ecuadorian political centre-left. The party, named after the leader of the 1895 Liberal Revolution, Eloy Alfaro, was formed by Abdón Calderón Muñoz and a dissident faction from the Radical Liberal Party (PLR). The former Liberal Party (PL) faction leader won nine per cent of the national vote in the 1978 presidential election and in December of the same year he was assassinated by political opponents.

In the June 1986 mid-term congressional elections, the party held on to only two provincial seats and became the election's most prominent casualty. Its fortune did not improve in the January 1988 general election, when the FRA presidential candidate Carlos Julio Emanuel Morán came eighth and the party's representation in Congress remained at two deputies, one provincial and one national. In the presidential second round in May the FRA supported Rodrigo Borja of the Democratic Left (ID) but on his inauguration, the party went into opposition. The FRA won one seat in the May 17, 1992, congressional elections and held it in the 1994 polls.

Concentration of Popular Forces
Concentración de Fuerzas Populares (CFP)

Address. Boyacá entre Sucre y Colón, Guayaquil

Leadership. Averroes Bucaram Saxida (1992 presidential candidate), Dr Galo Vayas (director)

This centre-right populist party was founded in 1946 and has enjoyed varying fortunes since then.

The party was formed as the Popular Republican Union and changed to its current name two years later. Carlos Guevara Moreno, the party's leader until 1961, was elected mayor of Guayaquil in 1951. Although the party won the highest percentage of votes in the 1956 elections of any single party, it was defeated by a Conservative coalition. The party's fortunes nevertheless did not improve when in 1960 it formed an electoral alliance with the Socialist Party (PS) and the Ecuadorean Communist Party (PCE). In 1962 the mayorship of Guayaquil, by then the CFP's stronghold, went to the party's new leader Asaad Bucaram.

His substitute in the elections of 1978-79 was his niece's husband Jaime Roldós Aguilera, who with the additional backing of the Christian Democrats won both rounds and was sworn in as President in August 1979.

After the deaths of Asaad Bucaram and Roldós in 1981, the CFP moved to the right under the leadership of Averroes Bucaram Záccida, the former leader's son. It supported the government of the Christian Democrat Osvaldo Hurtado until 1984, when its representation in Congress was reduced to eight seats.

In May 1987 the party's presidential candidate Angel Duarte Valverde, who was widely thought to be the right's favoured candidate, came only fifth and the CFP advised its supporters to spoil their ballot papers in the presidential run-off. Although the party's seats were halved in the June 1990 elections, Averroes Bucaram was elected president of Congress the following August and almost immediately tried to stage a constitutional coup against the Borja government by impeaching several ministers who were subsequently dismissed by Congress.

His impeachment of President Borja, however, failed to be ratified by Congress and Bucaram subsequently lost his post. In 1991 Bucaram was selected as the CFP's presidential candidate for the May 17, 1992, elections and received a negligible percentage of the vote. The party won one seat in the Congress.

The party won one seat in the congressional elections of 1992, which it proceeded to lose in 1994.

Democratic Popular Movement
Movimiento Popular Democrático (MPD)

Address. 10 de Agosto y Riofrío, Quito

Leadership. Jaime Hurtado González

This left-wing and reputedly pro-Chinese party was founded in 1978 and aims to base any revolutionary government upon well-grounded socialist programmes. The MPD was formed by the pro-Chinese Ecuadorean Communist Party, Marxist-Leninist (PCE-ML) as an electoral vehicle. The party's then leader Jaime Hurtado González became a deputy in 1979 and stood as the MPD's presidential candidate in the elections of 1984 in which he won 6.1% of the poll. Hurtado was again selected as the party's presidential candidate in the 1988 elections and was also backed by the Broad Left Front (FADI) and the Ecuadorean Socialist Party (PSE) with which the MPD had formed an electoral alliance. The party held on to the four seats it had won in the 1986 mid-term elections but although the MPD opposed the Borja government, it lost three seats in the 1990 congressional elections. Fausto Moreno Ordóñez was the candidate in the presidential elections of May 17, 1992, and received a negligible percentage of the vote. In the concurrent congressional elections, the party won four seats.

Democratic Left
Izquierda Democrática (ID)

Address. Polonia 161, entre Vancouver y Eloy Alfaro, Quito

Telephone. (#593-2) 564 436

Fax. (#593-2) 564 860

Leadership. Rodrigo Borja Cevallos (former President of the Republic); Jorge Gallardo (national director)

Founded in 1970 the Democratic Left is a social democratic party on paper but in office has proved to be rather conservative and neo-liberal in its economic policies.

The party was formed by a faction of the Radical Liberal Party (PLR) led by Rodrigo Borja Cevallos opposed to President Velasquez, together with some independents and dissident members of the Ecuadorean Socialist Party (PSE). The 1988 general election brought the ID to power, Borja having won the first round of the presidential elections with 20% and the second round on May 8 with 47.4%.

Rodrigo Borja was inaugurated as President of Ecuador on Aug. 10, his government based on a pro-government alliance consisting of 30 ID Congressmen and 13 from the People's Democracy (DP-UDC) and other parties. His first task was to deal with Ecuador's economic problems which he did by implementing highly unpopular austerity measures, which, although modest in comparison to other shock measures in other Latin American countries, lost the ID the 1990 mid-term legislative elections and 13 seats in the Congress. In an attempt to boost the ID's elections prospects in the May 1992 general election, Borja submitted a letter of intent to the IMF in January proposing higher levels of public spending and the increased availability of credit to the private sector. The ID's candidate in the May 17, 1992, was Raúl Baca Carbo, the former president of Congress, thought to be too closely linked to the Borja government to have a chance of winning. He came a poor fourth with 8.4% of the vote and the party won seven seats in the Congress.

The party is a full member of the Socialist International.

Ecuadorian Conservative Party

Partido Conservador Ecuatoriano (PCE)

Address. Leonidas Plaza 1067 entre Baquerizo y Lizardo García, Quito

Telephone. (#593-2) 505061

Leadership. Alberto Dahik Garzoni (leader)

This party of right-wing traditionalists was founded in 1855, making the PCE Ecuador's oldest political party.

The PCE was founded by Gabriel García Moreno who was assassinated in 1875 after ruling the country as a dictator for 15 years. Traditionally the party represented the country's oligarchy, the church and the army, and its ideology has remained unchanged despite major reorganizations of the party in 1925 and 1989.

In the 1984 general election the PCE joined the National Reconstruction Front coalition supporting the victorious presidential candidate León Febres Cordero of the PSC and was given a cabinet post in his government. In the 1986 congressional elections the PCE's two seats were reduced to one which it retained in the general elections two years later.

Despite internal upheavals resulting in the reorganization of the party, the PCE managed to increase its parliamentary representation to three seats in the 1990 mid-term elections. In the May 17, 1992, congressional elections, the party won six seats. These six seats were retained in 1994.

Ecuadorian Roldosist Party

Partido Roldosista Ecuatoriano (PRE)

Address. Urdaneta y Escobedo, Guayaquil

Leadership. Abdalá Bucaram Ortiz (1992 presidential candidate)

The party was founded by Abdalá Bucaram Ortiz and was named after his brother-in-law, President Jaime Roldós Aguilera (see Concentration of Popular Forces and People, Change and Democracy—PCD). It started as a movement within the PCD and registered as a party in its own right after Roldós' death in 1981.

The party's strong opposition to the Borja government paid dividends in the 1990 congressional elections when the PRE increased its representation to 13 seats. The party joined forces with the Social Christian Party (PSC) and, as the dominant congressional block, caused the Borja government serious problems. Abdalá Bucaram was selected again as PRE candidate for the May 1992 presidential election. However, it was feared, in view of his past adverse comments about the army, that if he were elected there might be a military coup. He came third with 20.7% of the vote and the party won 13 seats in the Congress.

Ecuadorian Socialist Party

Partido Socialista Ecuatoriano (PSE)

Address. Pasaje San Luis No. 340, Quito

Telephone. (#593-2) 570065

Leadership. Enrique Ayala Mora

The party was formed by Richardo Paredes who together with other pro-Moscow members split away from the PSE a year later and in 1931 formed the Ecuadorean Communist Party (PCE). The mid-term elections of 1986 increased the Socialist seats to six and the PSE's Enríque Ayala Mora won the congressional vice-presidency. In September 1987 the PSE entered into a coalition with the National Liberation Party (PLN) and the Ecuadorean Popular Revolutionary Action (APRE).

The alliance's presidential candidate and leader

of an unsuccessful military rebellion against the Febrero government in 1987, Gen. Frank Vargas Pazzos (see People's Patriotic Union—UPP) fought the 1988 presidential elections with Enrique Ayala Mora of the PSE as his running-mate and came fourth. The PSE declared that it wanted nothing to do with the Democratic Left (ID) government before President Borja was sworn in, and in 1989 went into outright opposition.

This reflected on the party who in the 1990 legislative elections increased its number of deputies from three to eight. The PSE stood alone again in the May 17, 1992, elections and fielded León Roldós Aguilera as its presidential candidate, who received a negligible percentage of the vote.

In 1994 the party retained the two legislative seats won in 1992.

Popular Democracy—Christian Democrat Union
Democracia Popular—Unión Demócrata Cristiana (DP)
Address. Casilla 17-11, 5087 Quito
Telephone. (#593-2) 54 73 88
Fax. (#593-2) 50 29 95
Leadership. Osvaldo Hurtado Larrea (president), Pedro Pinto (secretary-general)

Founded in 1978, the DP is a centre-left party which has consistently campaigned on the issues of communal socialism, democracy and Latin American nationalism.

The DP-UDC had its origins in the Christian Democratic Party (PDC), formed in 1964, which merged with the progressive faction of the Ecuadorian Conservative Party (PCE) led by Julio César Trujillo in 1978. In 1979 Osvaldo Hurtado Larrea (formerly PDC leader) was elected Vice-President to President Jaime Roldós of the Concentration of Popular Forces (CFP) and after his death in 1981 assumed the presidency.

Hurtado's DP-UDC government became unpopular with the left for his policy of reducing state spending and the austerity measures which were introduced in 1983, but also with the right who opposed any state intervention in the running of the economy. The DP-UDC formed an alliance with the Democratic Left (ID) and the CFP after People, Change and Democracy (PCD), (a party formed by Roldós during his presidency) went into opposition in January 1982.

In 1989, the DP-UDC announced that it wished to retain only a congressional alliance with the ID but remain independent from the government so that it could present its own candidate in the 1992 presidential elections. In November of the same year, the DP-UDC withdrew completely from the alliance, following disagreements over the government's vegetable oil price rises. This distancing from the government saved the DP-UDC from suffering the fate of the ID (whose seats were

nearly halved), and the party managed to retain its seven seats. The party leader Vladimiro Alvarez Grau was the DP-UDC's presidential candidate in the May 17, 1992, elections and received a fraction of the overall vote. The party won five seats in the congress.

It did fractionally worse in the 1994 legislative polls, holding only four seats in the chamber. The DP is the Ecuadorian affiliate of the Christian Democrat International.

Radical Liberal Party
Partido Liberal Radical (PLR)
Address. Rábida 417 y La Niña, Quito
Leadership. Miguel Albornez (1988 presidential candidate); Dr Carlos Julio Plaza (director)

Founded on Oct. 10, 1991, the PLR is a centre-right grouping in Ecuadorian politics. The PLR is a direct descendant of the Liberal Party which had held continuous office from its foundation in 1895 to 1944. The PLR emerged after the Liberal Party fragmented into different groups in 1944 and was registered under its present name three years later. The party itself has suffered several splits. In 1970 a dissident group which disagreed with the party's support of the Velasco government left to found the Democratic Left (ID). In 1972 a further faction, led by Abdón Calderón Muñoz, broke away to form the Alfaroist Radical Front (FRA).

The June 1986 congressional election reduced the PLR's seats to three and in October of the same year the party went into opposition which caused internal dissent. The party's candidate in the 1988 elections, Miguel Albornoz, won only a small percentage of the ballot and the party retained only two seats in Congress. Further arguments within the party ensued. The party's congressional representation increased to three seats in the June 1990 election. Bolívar Chiriboga was the candidate of the PLR in the presidential election of May 17, 1992. He won a negligible percentage of the vote and in the simultaneous congressional elections, the party won two seats.

After the 1994 elections, the PLR managed to hold on to only one legislative seat.

Republican Unity Party
Partido Unidad Republicano (PUR)
Address. Rbida 417 y La Niña, Quito
Leadership. Sixto Durán-Ballén Córdobez, Abraham Romero

The party was founded on Oct. 10, 1991, by dissidents from the Social Christian Party (PSC). It began as a centre-right alternative to the main parties but soon became a vehicle for the presidential aspirations of Sixto Durán-Ballén Córdobez. The party was formed by dissidents from the Social Christian Party (PSC) led by Sixto

Durán Ballén Cordovez. As the PSC's presidential candidate Ballén came third with 13% of the poll in the January 1988 election. Public opinion polls before the May 17, 1992 elections suggested that he would be elected President and he duly won in the first round of voting with 36.1% of the vote, gaining most votes in the highlands and significant support in the western coastal regions. He faced Jaime Nebot Saadi in a run-off on July 5 and was expected to pick up the votes of the dispersed left-wing. In the simultaneous congressional elections, the party won 12 seats.

In the second round of voting Durán Ballén's victory became a formality and his inauguration was a great success for the party. However, amid internal claims that the party lacked leadership and direction, the PUR only held three legislative seats after the May 1994 poll.

Social Christian Party
Partido Social Cristiano (PSC)
    Address. Carrión 548 y R. Victoria, Quito
    Telephone. (#593-2) 544536
    Fax. (#593-2) 568562
    Leadership. Jaime Nebot Saadi (president)
The PSC was formed as the Social Christian Movement to support Camilo Ponce Enriquez who was, until 1952, Minister of Government in the third Velasco government and served as President of Ecuador in 1956-60. The party adopted its present name in 1967 and the following year Ponce's presidential candidacy attracted the support of the Conservative Party (PC) but he failed to be elected. The party continued to operate during the 1972-79 military dictatorship, but after Ponce's death in 1976 the party went through a temporary crisis.

The election campaign for the January 1988 election was adversely affected by the track record of the Febres administration, which was criticized for human rights violations in relation to its counter-insurgency campaign and for its failure in turning the economy round despite the high level of social sacrifice it had exacted from the population.

The PSC's presidential candidate Sixto Durán Ballén (see Republican Unity Party), came third with 15.6% of the vote and the party was reduced to only six deputies in Congress.

This, however, did not diminish the PSC's success in the June 1990 mid-term elections in which the party won 16 seats, making it the largest party in Congress. The PSC entered into a parliamentary alliance with the Ecuadorean Roldósist Party (PRE) and together they controlled Congress. Jaime Nebot Saadi was the presidential candidate in the May 17, 1992, presidential elections, and came second to the PUR's Sixto Dúran Ballén with 26.2% of the vote, forcing a second round

run-off scheduled for July 5. Nebot appealed for support from the third place candidate Abdalá Bucaram Ortíz but such a right-wing populist alliance was considered unlikely.

In the simultaneous congressional elections the PSC won 21 seats, making it the largest party bloc.

The party was again the only conspicuous winner in the 1994 polls with 26 seats.

Other Parties and Movements

Broad Left Front
Frente Amplio de Izquierda (FADI)
    Address. Huancavilca 416 y Chimborazo, Guayaquil
    Leadership. Gustavo Iturralde (1992 presidential candidate); Dr René Mauge Mosquera (secretary-general)
This left-wing alliance was formed in 1977 as an attempt to unite the splintered and weak left in the country. The alliance was a successor to the left-wing Popular Democratic Union (UDP) founded in 1966 and included a large proportion of the old alliance's member parties, such as the Ecuadorean Communist Party (PCE), the Ecuadorean Revolutionary Socialist Party (PSRE) and the Revolutionary Movement of the Christian Left (MRIC).

In August 1987 FADI had formed the United Front of the Left electoral alliance with the Popular Democratic Movement (MPD) and the Ecuadorean Socialist Party (PSE) which unsuccessfully fielded the MPD leader Jaime Hurtado in the presidential elections of January 1988. The simultaneous congressional election resulted in one provincial and one national seat for FADI.

In the congressional elections of June 17, 1990, FADI could not increase its parliamentary representation and retained its two seats. Its presidential candidate in the May 17, 1992, elections was Gustavo Iturralde who received a negligible percentage of the vote.

Confederation of Ecuadorian Indigenous Nationalities
Confederación de Nacionalidades Indígenas del Ecuador (CONIAE)
    Leadership. Luis Macas (president)
This indigenist organization campaigns for the return of traditional community-held lands, the payment by petrol companies of compensation to tribes for environmental damage and for the recognition of Quechua as an official Ecuadorean language. CONIAE co-ordinated a march on Quito in May 1990 of about 1,000 people to submit a petition for the recognition of their land rights. In June of the same year CONIAE organized an uprising by indigenous people spanning

seven provinces in which members of the army were held hostage in order to force President Borja to negotiate. The organization is supported by the major trade union confederation United Workers' Front (FUT) with whom it launched a joint campaign in January 1991, after which Borja accused CONIAE of wanting to set up a state within a state. CONIAE called on its members to boycott the May 17, 1992, presidential and congressional elections.

Montoneros Free Fatherland
Montoneros Patria Libre (MPL)
Leadership. Patricio Baquerizo

Montoneros Free Fatherland are the only guerrilla group remaining in Ecuador after the disbanding of the "Alfaro Lives, Dammit!" (*Alfaro Vive, Carajo!*—AVC) in 1991 (see Democratic Left). The MPL was formed by a small splinter group of the above guerrillas. Its first action, in January 1986, was to capture a military museum in Quito. Soon after, several MPL members were captured and given prison sentences for kidnapping a magistrate. The MPL subsequently held President Febres' representative on the Constitutional Guarantees Tribunal in an unsuccessful attempt to force Febres to stand trial for failing to implement his election promises. In 1988, in order to denounce the newly elected ID government's economic policy as a continuation of Febres', the MPL seized and held four media employees. Although the MPL were the initiators of a dialogue between the Borja government, the AVC and themselves in October 1988, the group later announced that it wanted no part in the ensuing peace agreement between the government and the AVC. The MPL has since turned to violent action and bank robberies, whose proceeds are believed to be used for arms purchases.

Patriotic Peoples' Union
Unión del Pueblo Patriótico (UPP)
Leadership. Lt.-Gen. (retd.) Frank Vargas Pazos (1992 presidential candidate)

The party was founded in 1987 and attracted a section of the Broad Left Front (FADI) after it decided to field Lt.-Gen. Frank Vargas Pazzos in the presidential election of January 1988. His candidacy was also supported by an alliance of several other parties which included the National Liberation Party (PLN), the Socialist Party (PSE) and the Ecuadorean Popular Revolutionary Action (APRE). Vargas had been forced to retire as chief of staff of the armed forces in 1986 and shortly after led two military rebellions in March 1986 forcing the resignation of the Minister of Defence and an army commander. Lt.-Gen. Vargas was amnestied in January 1987 in return for the release of President Febres Cordeo who was kidnapped by rebel air force officers (see PSC). Lt.-Gen. Vargas joined APRE in 1989 after having won a significant share of the presidential vote in the 1988 elections, coming fourth. The UPP did not win any congressional seats.

The party has won no seats since then.

People, Change and Democracy
Pueblo, Cambio y Democracia (PCD)
Address. 9 de Octobre 416 y Chile, Ed. Chile Bank, 8vo. Piso, Guayaquil
Leadership. León Roldos Aguilera (1992 presidential candidate)

The PCD was founded in 1980 by supporters of President Roldós within the Concentration of Popular Forces (CFP) and was joined by 12 CFP deputies. After his death in May 1981 the party had disagreements with his successor President Hurtado of the People's Democracy—Democratic Christian Union and went into opposition. The party lost all its seats in the 1984 election and apart from one seat gained in 1986 it has not since been represented in Congress. Although Aquiles Rigail of the PCD obtained the Social Health portfolio in the right-wing Social Christian Party (PSC) Febres Cordero Cabinet in 1987, the PCD discussed a possible merger with the Democratic Left (ID). In the 1988 presidential elections the PCD advocated a vote against the ID or Ecuadorean Roldosist Party candidate. Since 1988 the party has been led by Julián Palacios Cevallos.

It has won no seats since 1988.

Egypt

Capital: Cairo

Population: 59,000,000 (1995E)

The Arab Republic of Egypt achieved full independence in 1936, initially as a monarchy, which was overthrown in 1952. Following several experiments with single-party structures, the last and most durable being the Arab Socialist Union (ASU), a limited multi-party system evolved from 1976 which has been dominated by the National Democratic Party (NDP). Under the 1971 constitution, legislative power is exercised by the unicameral People's Assembly (*Majlis al-Shaab*) of 444 elective and 10 appointed members, which is elected for a five-year term by universal adult suffrage (of those aged 18 years and over). The Assembly nominates the President, who is confirmed by popular referendum for a six-year term and who appoints a Council of Ministers. There is also a Consultative Council with advisory powers; two-thirds of its 210 members are popularly elected and the other third are appointed by the President.

In elections to the People's Assembly on Nov. 29 and Dec. 6, 1995, the NDP was officially stated to have won 317 of the 444 elective seats, "independents" 114, the New Wafd Party 6, the National Progressive Unionist Party 5, the Liberal Socialist Party 1 and the Nasserite Party 1. Of the 114 "independent" deputies, 99 quickly declared their allegiance to the NDP. A further 10 members of the Assembly were appointed by the President.

Liberal Socialist Party (LSP)
Hizb al-Ahrar al-Ishtiraki

   Address. c/o Majlis al-Shaab, Cairo

   Leadership. Mustapha Kamal Murad

The main objective of the LSP, a small party originally formed in 1976 from the right wing of the then ruling Arab Socialist Union, is to secure a greater role for private enterprise within the Egyptian economy. The party's representation in the People's Assembly fell progressively from 12 seats to none in elections between 1976 and 1984. It then recovered some ground as the junior partner in an alliance with the Socialist Labour Party (SLP) which also unofficially included the Muslim Brotherhood (MB). Within this framework, three of its candidates were elected to the Assembly in 1987. The party boycotted the 1990 polling, and subsequently discontinued its alliance with the SLP and the MB. It won one seat in the 1995 Assembly elections.

National Democratic Party (NDP)
Hizb al-Watani al-Dimuqrati

   Address. Corniche al-Nil Street, Cairo

   Telephone. (#20–2) 575-7450/1/2

   Fax. (#20–2) 360-7681

   Leadership. Mohammed Hosni Mubarak (chair), Dr Yusuf Amin Wali (secretary-general)

The NDP was organized by the late President Anwar Sadat in July 1978 as the party of government in succession to the Arab Socialist Party (ASP), a pro-government centrist party set up in 1977 when the Arab Socialist Union was dissolved in favour of component groupings which had been designated the previous year. Having formally absorbed the ASP in October 1978, the NDP confirmed its dominance of the legislature with an overwhelming majority at the 1979 Assembly elections and in all subsequent polls (although the opposition has been increasingly critical of an electoral system which it regards as biased in the NDP's favour). On President Sadat's assassination in October 1981, Vice-President Mubarak succeeded to the presidency of both the country and the ruling party. He was sworn in for his third six-year term in October 1993. Following the NDP's customary victory in the November-December 1995 legislative elections, President Mubarak appointed Kamal el-Ganzouri as Prime Minister in succession to Atef Sidki, who had held the post for nine years.

The NDP is an affiliate of the Socialist International.

National Progressive Unionist Party (NPUP)
Hizb al-Tajammu al-Watani al-Taqaddumi al-Wahdawi

   Address. 1 Karim al-Dawla Street, Talaat Harb, Cairo

Telephone. (#20–2) 575-9281/9152
Fax. (#20–2) 578-6298
Leadership. Khaled Mohieddin (chair)

The NPUP was created in 1976 from the left-wing component of the Arab Socialist Union, advocating state ownership of industry and the exclusion of foreign investment. It claims to have suffered harassment and repression by the government, particularly in the late 1970s because of its antipathy (alone among the main parties) towards the Egyptian-Israeli peace process. Having failed to win any seats in the elections of 1979, 1984 and 1987, the party decided not to support the electoral boycott by other opposition parties in 1990, and secured six seats in the Assembly.

The NPUP led domestic opposition to the decision to participate in the US-led coalition which fought Iraq in the 1991 Gulf war. The party also opposed the passage of legislation in 1992 aimed primarily at combating Islamic fundamentalists, which gave the authorities greater internal security powers (in addition to those under emergency laws in force since 1981). The NPUP won five Assembly seats in the 1995 legislative elections.

New Wafd Party (NWP)
Hizb al-Wafd al-Gadid
   Address. 1 Bolis Hanna Street, Dokki, Cairo
   Telephone. (#20–2) 348-0830/1375
   Fax. (#20–2) 360-2007
   Leadership. Fuad Serageddin (chair)

The original Wafd had been a popular liberal and nationalist movement in the 1920s, but had been dissolved after the 1952 revolution. The NWP won the legal right in October 1983 to contest Assembly elections, having emerged initially in February 1978. In alliance with a number of Islamic groups, most notably the Muslim Brotherhood, the NWP won 58 seats with 15 per cent of the vote in May 1984, so becoming the only opposition party with parliamentary representation. Although strengthened by absorbing the small National Front Party led by Mahmoud al-Qadi, the NWP lost 23 of its seats in the 1987 election, the Muslim Brotherhood having entered into a de facto coalition with the Socialist Labour Party (SLP) and Liberal Socialist Party (LSP). As part of the general opposition campaign for reform of the electoral system, the NWP supported the 1990 Assembly election boycott, although party members running as independents retained at least 14 seats.

The NWP was the only opposition party to support President Mubarak's commitment of troops to Saudi Arabia during the Gulf crisis of 1990–91, a position which prompted widespread internal dissension and the defection of an influential leading member, Naaman Gomaa. The NWP was officially credited with only six seats in the Assembly elections of late 1995.

Socialist Labour Party (SLP)
Hizb al-Amal al-Ishtiraki
   Address. 313 Port Said Street, Sayyida Zeinab, Cairo
   Telephone. (#20–2) 390-9261/9761
   Fax. (#20–2) 390-0283
   Leadership. Ibrahim Shukri (chair)

The SLP was officially organized in November 1978 to provide "loyal and constructive opposition" to the ruling National Democratic Party (NDP). While affirming the need for Islamic precepts to serve as the basis of Egyptian legislation, the party advocated a democratic regime with a more equal sharing of wealth between urban and rural areas. Although the largest opposition party after the 1979 elections, the SLP lost ground at the expense of the New Wafd Party in the early 1980s, failing to secure any elective Assembly seats in May 1984. The party made a comeback in the 1987 elections, which it contested in alliance with the Liberal Socialist Party (LSP) on a joint list which unofficially included candidates of the (formally proscribed) Muslim Brotherhood. This alliance became the principal opposition force, winning 60 seats (20 of which the SLP held in its own right). The SLP boycotted the 1990 Assembly election, claiming that President Mubarak's government was insufficiently committed to democracy; however, eight party members running as independents reportedly won seats.

In the build-up to the 1991 Gulf war, the SLP was a vocal critic of the government's alignment with the US-led coalition against Iraq, a campaign which led to some arrests and judicial actions against party members for inciting unrest. Anti-government articles in the party newspaper in late 1993 and early 1994 led to the brief detention of several SLP members and accusations of defamation against the party chairman.

Other Parties

Centre Party (CP), led by Abul Ella Madi, launched in early 1996 by a youthful faction of the Muslim Brotherhood, including some Christian Copts as well as Muslim trade unionists.

Democratic Unionist Party (DUP), a centre-right party, recognized by the Political Parties Tribunal in April 1990, led by Mohammed Abd al-Munim al-Turk.

Green Party (*Hizb al-Khudr*), under the presidency of Hassan Ragab, was also recognized by the Political Parties Tribunal in April 1990.

Nasserite Party (NP), led by Farid Abdel Karim, won one seat in the 1995 Assembly elections, having been refused legalization in 1990 because it allegedly advocated a return to totalitarianism.

National Party (*Hizb al-Umma*), a small Muslim organisation, led by Ahmad al-Sabahi Awadallah, with ties to the supporters of former Sudanese Prime Minister Sadiq al-Mahdi.

Party of Social and Democratic Construction (PSDC), founded in 1986 as a moderate left-wing grouping by Sami Mubarak (brother of the President of the Republic), who had been elected to the People's Assembly in 1984 as a candidate of the New Wafd Party.

Young Egypt Party (*Misr al-Fatah*), founded and recognized in 1990, apparently reviving a party which had existed in the 1930s, with Ali Aldin Salih as its chair.

Illegal Groups

Egyptian Communist Party (*Hizb al-Shuyui al-Misri*), has been banned since 1925, subsequently experiencing numerous ideological schisms and breakaways which have yielded many communist splinter groups.

Egypt's Revolution (*Thawrat Misr*), a left-wing group inspired by the policies of former President Abdel Gamal Nasser, allegedly financed by his son Khaled Abdel Nasser, and led by Mahmud Nur al-Din.

Holy War (*Jihad*), a secret organization of militant Muslims who had reportedly split from the Muslim Brotherhood in the second half of the 1970s because of the latter's objection to the use of violence. The group was blamed for the assassination of President Sadat in 1981. In 1993 a number of *Jihad* supporters were imprisoned in

1993 on charges of plotting to overthrow the government, and a car bomb attack aimed at the Prime Minister was attributed to a splinter group variously referred to as New *Jihad*, the Vanguards of Conquest, and the Assassination Group.

Islamic Group (*Gamaat i-Islami*), emerged in the 1970s as the student wing of the Muslim Brotherhood, subsequently breaking away and aligning (until the mid-1980s) with Holy War (*Jihad*) in seeking to overthrow the government. It serves as a loose-knit, but very militant umbrella organization for many smaller groups, and has been accused of spearheading attacks on the security forces, government officials and tourists since 1992. The spiritual leader of the Islamic Group is believed to be Sheikh Omar Abdel Rahman, a blind theologian, whose extradition from detention in the United States is sought by the Egyptian authorities.

Muslim Brotherhood (*Ikhwan al-Muslimin*), established in 1928 to promote the creation of a pan-Arab Islamic state, and declared an illegal organisation in 1954. Although still technically banned, the Brotherhood has enjoyed de facto recognition since entering into coalition politics under President Mubarak's regime. It secured indirect Assembly representation in 1984 by running a number of its candidates under New Wafd Party auspices, and in the 1987 elections it joined forces with the Socialist Labour Party and Liberal Socialist Party, winning 37 of the coalition's 60 seats. The Brotherhood, which boycotted the 1990 elections in co-operation with other opposition parties, is still considered to have the largest following and financial resources among Egypt's Islamic organisations, despite the recent emergence of more radical groups. The movement's spiritual leader is Mustafa Mashhur, who succeeded Hamid Abu al-Nasr following the latter's death in January 1996; Mamoun al-Hudaiby is its secretary-general.

El Salvador

Capital: San Salvador

Population: 5,800,000 (1995E)

The Republic of El Salvador was ruled by Spain until 1821 and only finally gained full independence in 1839. Throughout its history, military dictatorships have either ruled directly or dominated the civilian administrations nominally in power, frequently intervening in the electoral process to choose a president suitable to the requirements of the current dictatorship and of the country's rich and powerful oligarchy. The elections since 1982 relied on substantial political, financial and practical support from the United States in an effort to combine stability with a degree of respectability. Against current trends, this secured the victory of the US-favoured Christian Democratic Party in the 1984 presidential elections, a victory which the oligarchy, though still dependent on US military aid, reversed with the victory of the Nationalist Republican Alliance (Arena) in the 1989 presidential elections.

Under the 1983 constitution, legislative power is vested in a unicameral Legislative Assembly (which replaced the National Constituent Assembly in 1985), enlarged to 84 seats in 1991. Executive power rests with the President, who appoints a Council of Ministers and is assisted by a Vice-President. Every two years, the legislature appoints three substitute Vice-Presidents to assume the presidency in the case of the Vice-President being unable to do so.

The President and Vice-President are elected nationally by universal adult suffrage for a five-year term and may not stand for immediate re-election. The members of the Legislative Assembly are elected for three-year terms.

Suffrage is universal for nationals over 18 years of age, except for members of the armed forces, who are not permitted to vote. Elections are regulated by the electoral law of 1961 which established the electoral council as a supervisory body for all elections.

In elections to the Legislative Assembly on March 20, 1994, the right-wing Nationalist Republican Alliance (Arena) won 39 seats, the Farabundo Martí National Liberation Front (FMLN) 21, the Christian Democratic Party (PDC) 18, the right-wing National Conciliation Party (PCN) 4, and the Democratic Convergence (CD) and evangelical Movement of Unity (MU) one each. In the first round of voting for presidential elections also held on March 20, 1994, Armando Calderon Sol, the Arena candidate, narrowly failed to win an outright majority, but he won the second round on April 24 with 68.2% of the vote, and took office on June 1.

Authentic Christian Democratic Movement
Movimiento Auténtico Demócrata Cristiano (MADC)

Leadership. Julio Adolfo Rey Prendes (1989 presidential candidate)

The party was founded in 1988 by Julio Adolfo Rey Prendes as a new centre-right party again populated by PDC dissidents. In the March 1991 Legislative Assembly elections the party won one seat.

Christian Democratic Party
Partido Demócrata Cristiano (PDC)

Address. 3ra Calle Poniente No. 924, San Salvador

Telephone. (#503) 221815

Fax. (#503) 230558

Leadership. Fidel Chavez Mena (1994 presidential candidate), Carlos Claramount (secretary-general)

Founded in 1960, the PDC originally claimed to be seeking a "third way" between capitalism and communism but years of co-habitation with the military during the 1980's shifted the party to the right, especially in the late 1980's when it called for the "reprivatisation" of the economy.

The PDC was founded by José Napoleón Duarte who was elected mayor of El Salvador in 1964. Although it contested National Assembly and presidential elections in 1964 and 1967 respectively, it was not until the 1970s that it made a significant political impact. In 1972 and 1977 the PDC led an opposition electoral alliance, the National Opposition Union (UNO) backing Duarte's candidacy for the presidency. Duarte was elected President in 1972 but was forced to flee the country following a military coup. He returned from exile in 1979 to join the "government junta" formed after the overthrow of the Romero military regime and in December was appointed President, the first civilian to hold the post in almost 50 years.

The PDC remained in two more national junta governments until 1982, relying on a tacit pact with the military following the departure of former allies like the MDN and UNO and at the price of a split within its own ranks. A left-wing faction led by Rubén Zamora broke away to form the Popular Social Christian Movement (MPSC). Right-wing parties controlled the National Assembly following the 1982 elections but the PDC's 24 seats legitimized its participation in a government of national unity. Duarte's victory in the presidential elections of March 1984 was widely believe to have been reliant on US assistance.

211

The outcome, however, ensured that the existing "unity Cabinet" was replaced by a PDC one. The party consolidated its hold on power in the March 1985 elections in which it won 33 Assembly seats and gained control of the majority of local councils. PDC members were elected as president and vice-president of the Legislative Assembly.

The Duarte government was involved in intermittent efforts to negotiate a peace settlement with the Farabundo Martí National Liberation Front (FMLN) but was constrained by the aggressive hardliners in the military high command opposed to any major concessions. It retained the support of the US administration under President Reagan whose financial aid permitted the quadrupling of the army and the intensification of the civil war against the guerrillas. The PDC's political support also drained away, especially among the poor affected by 60% unemployment, and among the rich after they were threatened with special taxes, which were subsequently ruled unconstitutional. A serious political split over the PDC presidential nomination for the 1989 elections also debilitated the party and led to the PDC's loss of control of the Legislative Assembly in 1988 when it won only 25 seats. Fidel Chávez Mena, known to be favoured by the private sector and the US administration, won the nomination forcing Julio Adolfo Rey Prendes, a proponent of Duarte's centre-right line, to break away to form, with the small right-wing Stable Centrist Republican Movement (MERECENO, the Authentic Christian Democratic Movement (MADC).

Chávez Mena shifted the party appreciably to the right and promoted liberal economic policies but was comfortably defeated in the first round of the 1989 presidential elections by Alfredo Cristiani Burkard of the Republican Nationalist Alliance (Arena).

In elections to an enlarged 84-seat Legislative Assembly in March 1991, the PDC won 26 seats, coming second to Arena which failed to win an overall majority.

In the run-up to the 1994 presidential elections there were two leading factions sparring for the party's nomination. Chávez Mena, the 1989 nominee, won the 1994 nomination against his rival Abraham Rodríguez, and subsequently finished third in the national poll. The battle between the two competing factions over the nomination finally came to a head with 11 dissident *abrahamistas*, supporters of Rodríguez, left the party to form the Renewal Social Christian Movement.

The PDC is the national representative to the Christian Democrat International.

Democratic Action
Acción Democrática (AD)

Leadership. René Fortin Magaña (1984 presidential candidate); Ernesto Allwood

Founded in 1981, the AD is ostensibly liberal and in favour of a mixed economy, the party achieved modest representation in the National Assembly in 1982 and 1985, a faction led by González supporting the Christian Democrat Party (PDC) government until December 1987. Since then its fortunes have declined markedly and in the March 1991 legislative elections it failed to win a single seat, and its future legal status as a party was in doubt.

Democratic Convergence
Convergencia Democrática (CD)

Leadership. Mario Reni Roldan (PSD); Rubén Ignacio Zamora Rivas (MPSC); Juan José Martel (secretary-general)

Founded in November 1987, the social democratic CD emerged from the experience of the Democratic Revolutionary Front (*Frente Democratico Revolucionario*, FDR), itself an umbrella organization representing upwards of 30 professional and labour organizations and formally structured around an alliance of five Marxist parties and the National Revolutionary Movement (MNR) and Popular Social Christian Movement (MPSC), the latter two providing the focus and direction. The FDR, formed in April 1980, became the spearhead of civilian opposition to the military-backed regimes and allied itself to the then recently formed Farabundo Martí National Liberation Front (FMLN). In January 1981, the FDR established a diplomatic political commission, in exile, in Mexico City which was recognized by the Mexican, French and Dutch governments as a representative political force.

In the mid-1980s the FDR's future was placed in doubt by FMLN plans to create a single vanguard party and by moves by the MNR and the MPSC to re-enter the political arena.

The subsequent alliance of the MNR and MPSC with the Social Democrat Party (*Partido Social Demócrata*, PSD), founded 1987, gave birth to the CD, which campaigned for an end to US military intervention, a ceasefire in the civil war and free elections.

The then MNR leader Guillermo Ungo and the PSD's Mario Reni Roldán were the CD's candidates for the presidency and vice-presidency in the presidential elections held on March 19, 1989. They received only 3.9% of the vote, a cause of much resentment in the alliance and directly attributed to the FMLN's call for an election boycott.

Undaunted, the CD decided to participate for the first time in the legislative elections held in

March 1991 because, in the words of Ungo, the social situation was desperate due to the civil war.

This time, the FMLN did not disrupt the elections and the CD took 12.2% of the vote and won eight Assembly seats.

The CD's subsequent promotion of the UN-sponsored peace process meant that with the formal signing of a peace treaty in January 1992, it was well placed to play a leading role in a re-alignment of the opposition in preparation for the 1994 general election.

A major set-back was faced in early 1992 when Víctor Manuel Valle of the MNR announced his party's withdrawal from the CD alliance over various internal leadership rivalries. In 1993 the alliance was once again strengthened by the addition of the Democratic Nationalist Union (*Unión Demócrata Nacionalista*, UDN), the former legal front of the Salvadoran Communist Party. In September of the same year the CD announced its intention to form itself as a unified party ending six years as a coalition.

In October 1994, Juan José Martel was nominated as the successor to Zamora Rivas as secretary-general of the party.

Democratic Party
Partido Democrática (PD)
   Leadership. Joaquín Villalobos

The PD was launched in March 1995 following the partial break-up in the FMLN (see above). The ERP and RN (see below) left the Front in late 1994 and moved almost immediately to form the PD with the MNR (see also below) and a number of dissidents from the mainstream Christian Democratic Party (PDC).

The members of the new PD grouping are National Resistance, the National Revolutionary Movement and People's Renewal Expression.

Farabundo Martí National Liberation Front
Frente Farabundo Martí para la Liberación Nacional (FMLN)
   Leadership. Salvador Sanchez Cerén (general co-ordinator)

Founded in 1980, the FMLN was originally left-wing, but the leadership, especially during the peace process, has increasingly distanced itself from a Marxist-Leninist perspective, seeing the FMLN, on a return to the political mainstream, to be a party attractive not only to the bulk of the "dispossessed" in the town and country (since they believe the working class to be in a minority) but also to liberal elements in the middle class and the Catholic church.

Four guerrilla organizations (the FPL, ERP, FARN and the PCS), formed the Unified Revolutionary Directorate (*Directorio Revolucion-*

ario Unificado, DRU) in June 1980. It was replaced in October by the FMLN, which took its name from a Communist Party leader of the 1932 peasant revolt. The FARN, which had temporarily broken away, rejoined along with the PRTC.

Under the FMLN, the 15-strong DRU co-ordinated the work of the five component groups whose individual leaders formed an executive commission charged with overall command. The FMLN maintained direct links with its political arm, the Democratic Revolutionary Front (FDR, see Democratic Convergence) via a political and diplomatic commission on which both were represented.

The FMLN launched a general offensive in January 1981, during which it secured strongholds in many areas. From the mid-1980s onwards, the FMLN was almost as active on the diplomatic front as it was militarily, proposing various power sharing solutions to end the civil war and it appeared ready to accept an electoral solution. Sustained violence from the right, however, blocked this path but the guerrillas claimed that the 53% abstention rate in the 1989 general election justified its struggle for radical political reforms.

Subsequently, the FMLN saw its task as making the country ungovernable so long as the ruling Arena party resisted a negotiated settlement. It launched large-scale military offensives in May and November 1990, both of which penetrated into the capital, San Salvador, to strengthen its position in UN-sponsored peace talks with the government.

A breakthrough occurred in September 1991 but the resultant peace agreement, formally signed in January 1992, was already under strain by March 1992. Then, in May 1992, without prior discussion with the Cristiani government who did not welcome the decision, the FMLN announced that it intended to form itself into a political party. The party was recognised by the Supreme Electoral Court on Dec. 15, 1992.

At the party's first national convention in September 1993, the FMLN endorsed Rubén Zamora of the CD as its 1994 presidential candidate. This did not, however, heal party differences and in December 1994 a majority of both the Peoples' Renewal Expression (ERP) and the National Resistance (RN) left the Front.

Nationalist Republican Alliance
Alianza Republicana Nacionalista (Arena)
   Address. Calle el Progreso 3210, San Salvador
   Leadership. Juan José Domenech (president), Armando Calderón Sol (honorary president)

Founded in 1981, Arena is an ultra-right party split between hard-liners standing for nationalism, law and order and against any accommodation with left-wing guerrillas, and modernisers who, however reluctantly, supported the peace process ending the 11-year civil war in return for economic and social stability.

Arena was founded by Roberto D'Aubuisson Arrieta, a former major and once head of the intelligence section of the notoriously brutal National Guard. This complemented his involvement during the 1970s in the National Democratic Organization (Orden), a mass-based paramilitary organization linked to the security forces and the White Warriors Union, one of several right-wing death squads. Trained in the art of political warfare in police academies in Washington and Taiwan, D'Aubuisson modelled Arena on the Chinese nationalist Kuomintang which had its own military wing. Arena quickly became a leading political force, winning 19 seats in the 1982 elections to the National Assembly, of which D'Aubuisson was elected president, while retaining its close associations with the death squads. D'Aubuisson was accused of personally organizing political killings from an office in the Assembly, the most notorious of which was the assassination in March 1980 of Monsignor Oscar Arnulfo Romero, Archbishop of San Salvador and a fierce critic of state violence.

Long associated with right-wing Republican politicians in the USA, D'Aubuisson had been shunned by the Carter administration but was rehabilitated by President Ronald Reagan as part of his administration's anti-communist cold war stance towards Central America. However, D'Aubuisson's continued association with the death squads meant that the USA did not endorse his candidacy for President in 1984 but instead supported, and some said "engineered", the victory of José Napoleon Duarte of the Christian Democrats. The defeat provoked the first split in Arena, D'Aubuisson's vice-presidential running mate Hugo Barrera breaking away in May 1985 to form the Liberation Party (PL).

Eager for increased influence and respectability, Arena's September 1985 national general assembly accepted D'Aubuisson's resignation as secretary-general and elected him as honorary life president. Under Alfredo Cristiani Burkard, Arena presented a more moderate image, especially to the USA, and won the 1988 presidential elections on a programme that offered the prospect of national reconciliation. To retain the support of the landed ruling class and to increase Arena's middle class support, Cristiani promised to reverse the Christian Democrats' land reforms and to liberalize the economy by removing state control over trade and banking. In an effort to placate the opposition he promised to increase state welfare provision, reform the administration of justice and open a

dialogue with the guerrillas to end the 11-year civil war.

In the March 1991 legislative elections, the party lost its overall majority in the Legislative Assembly, and although it remained the country's largest party, the result encouraged moderate elements to pursue a course of political consensus.

Tentative peace negotiations with the Farabundo Martí National Liberation Front (FMLN), which hardline elements in both the army and Arena tried to sabotage, began in April 1990 under UN auspices; a peace treaty was formally signed in January 1992 and a ceasefire established in February 1992. D'Aubuisson, who died of throat cancer in February 1992, adopted an increasingly "pragmatic" approach to the peace process and was judged to have played a crucial role behind the scenes in keeping Arena's most fundamentalist anti-communist factions behind Cristiani.

The party's legislative representation was unchanged in 1994, although Armando Calderón Sol defeated Rubén Zamora Rivas by a better than two-to-one margin in the second round of the presidential campaign.

National Conciliation Party
Partido de Conciliación Nacional (PCN)
Address. Calle Arce No. 1128, San Salvador
Leadership. Rutilio Aguilera and Hernán Contreras (joint secretaries general)

The right-wing PCN was founded in September 1961 as a social reform party. The PCN, the direct successor of the now defunct Revolutionary Party of Democratic Unification, was the ruling party from 1961 to 1979 until a coup overthrew President Carlos Humberto Romero in October 1979. The party was a vehicle for a succession of fraudulently elected military presidents, supported by the elite families, and which also used patronage to maintain the loyalty of civilian officials.

In the 1982 elections the PCN obtained 14 seats in the 60-seat Constituent Assembly and received four cabinet posts in a government of national unity, despite the party's strong anti-reformist bias and remaining close ties with the military. The party, however, split in the same year, with the right-wing, including nine Assembly delegates, forming the Authentic Institutional Party (PAISA). In 1985, the PCN, as a junior partner in a alliance with the Nationalist Republican Alliance (Arena) party, won 12 seats in the 1985 elections, a short-lived partnership ending when the party expelled three leaders who had colluded with the Arena to get the elections declared void. In 1987, in an attempt at political rehabilitation, the party claimed to have rediscovered its "social democratic" roots and opposed the Christian Democrat Party (PDC) government's austerity package, including a war tax. The manoeuvre produced scant reward, the party winning only seven seats in the March 1988 legislative elections and its candidate in the 1989 presidential election received a modest 4.9% of the vote. In July 1989 the party temporarily joined an alliance with the PDC and the Democratic Convergence (DC), claiming to be interested in promoting dialogues with the Farabundo Martí National Liberation Front (FMLN). In the lead up to the March 1991 legislative elections, the party had clear problems deciding where to locate itself on the political spectrum, one leader claiming that the party was "to the left of Arena and to the right of the PDC". It chose not to ally itself with Arena and came third after the PDC, winning nine per cent of the vote and nine seats.

National Resistance
Resistencia Nacional (RN)
Leadership. Eduardo Sancho (secretary-general)

The RN was a key member of the original FMLN, under the name of the Armed Forces of National Resistance (*Fuerzas Armadas de Resistencia Nacional*, FARN). Alongside the ERP, the RN left the FMLN in December 1994, and joined the Democratic Party in March 1995.

National Revolutionary Movement
Movimiento Nacional Revolucionario (MNR)
Leadership. Eduardo Calles; Jorge Antonio Pino (secretary-general)

The oldest and most established of the parties in the PD alliance, the MNR was founded in 1968 and is a social democratic grouping that advocates radical social reforms and a modernised, mixed economy. The MNR emerged from the fusion of the Radical Democratic Party and other groups. It was led initially from exile in the early 1970s by the writer Italo López Vallecillos whose successor Guillermo Ungo saw fit to join the civilian-military junta set up after the overthrow of the Romero regime in 1979 (see Christian Democrat Party). Ungo resigned in 1980, however, in protest at the government's "swing to the right", one consequence of which was the escalation in the activities of right-wing death squads who killed many MNR activists. The entire party leadership was forced into exile, where it remained until the end of 1987.

In April 1980, the MNR had joined with the MPSC to form the Salvadorean Democratic Front (FDS) which later in 1980 allied itself with five Marxist parties to form the Democratic Revolutionary Front (FD—see Democratic Convergence), the effective political wing of the

FMLN guerrillas. Ungo was elected FDR president in January 1981 and from exile in Panama achieved international status as the main spokesman and negotiator for the extra-parliamentary opposition and the various rebel groups. He returned to the country in 1984 and in late 1987 to test the political climate and concluded that the MNR could not operate in safety. This was enough to convince the MNR leadership to join with the Popular Social Christian Movement (MPSC) and the Social Democrat Party (PSD, see CD) in the formation of the Democratic Convergence (CD) in a bid to create a new national initiative for peace and free elections. Ungo died in Mexico city in February 1991.

The MNR withdrew from the Democratic Convergence (CD) in early 1992 and jointly established the Democratic Party in March 1995.

Peoples' Renewal Expression
Expresión Renovadora del Pueblo (ERP)
Leadership. Juan Ramón Medrano; Joaquín Villalobos (secretary-general)

The ERP was formerly known as the People's Revolutionary Army (*Ejercito Revolucionario del Pueblo*) and was the second largest grouping within the FMLN. The new name was chosen in late 1993 (still with the ERP initials) at the same time as the party ditched its long-standing commitment to Marxism-Leninism. In its new social democratic guise the ERP withdrew from the FMLN in December 1994, and in March 1995 joined the new Democratic Party.

Renewal Social Christian Movement
Movimiento Renovación Social Cristiano (MRSC)
Leadership. Abraham Rodríguez; Miguel Espinal Lazo (secretary-general)

The MRSC was founded in December 1994 by a pro-Rodríguez faction within the Christian Democratic Party (PDC). This defection amounted to half the PDC's Legislative Assembly representation.

Salvadoran Communist Party
Partido Comunista Salvadoreño (PCS)
Leadership. Schafik Jorge Handal (secretary-general)

A member of the FMLN (see above), the PCS now fulfils a major role within the Front. In the early 1980's the party assumed a more militant posture but gave this up to become a member of the FMLN.

Other Parties

Free People (*Pueblo Libre*, PL) gained enough of a mandate to be re-legalised in 1993. The party is a democratic pluralist party and is led by Will Bendeck.

Liberal Democratic Party (*Partido Liberal Democrático*, PLD) was launched in October 1994 by the party leader, Kirio Waldo Salgado, who accused the government of links to organised crime.

National Solidarity Movement (*Movimiento de Solidaridad Nacional*, MSN) was founded in 1993 as a Christian Evangelical party. It is led by Edgardo Rodríguez.

Unity Movement (*Movimiento de Unidad*, MU) is led by Jorge Martinez Mendénez (the 1994 presidential candidate and secretary-general of the party) and was launched in 1993 as a free enterprise party.

Equatorial Guinea

Capital: Malabo

Population: 400,000 (1995E)

The Republic of Equatorial Guinea gained independence from Spain in 1968. The current President, Brig.-Gen. Teodoro Obiang Nguema Mbasogo, seized power from the dictatorship of Francisco Macias Nguema in a coup in 1979. Ruling through a Supreme Military Council (composed of both military and civilians from December 1981), the regime banned all political parties until mid-1987, when the President announced the formation of a single "party of government" called the Democratic Party of Equatorial Guinea (PDGE). Constitutional amendments, approved by referendum in 1982, extended the President's term of office for a further seven years, and provided for the holding of presidential and legislative elections in a gradual transition from military to civilian rule. President Obiang Nguema secured another seven-year term when he was elected unopposed in June 1989. A new constitution, providing for the introduction of multi-party politics, was adopted by referendum in November 1991. It also provided for the separation of powers between the President and Prime Minister, and gave the President protection from impeachment, prosecution and subpoena before, during and after his term of office. The constitution also provides for a unicameral House of People's Representatives (*Cámara de Representantes del Pueblo*) of 80 members. who are directly elected for a five-year term by universal adult suffrage

The first multi-party legislative elections, held on Nov. 21, 1993, but boycotted by some opposition parties, resulted in the PDGE winning 68 seats, the Social Democratic and Popular Convention 6, the Social Democratic Union 5 and the Liberal Democratic Convention 1. In presidential elections on Feb. 25, 1996, President Obiang Nguema was re-elected with 99% of the vote, in a contest described by opposition groups and international observers as "a farce".

Coordinating Board of Opposition Democratic Forces
Junta Coordinadora de las Fuerzas de Oposición Democrática
Leadership. Teodoro Mackuandji Bondjale Oko (president)

This organization was set up in opposition to President Obiang Nguema in 1983 by mainly Spanish-based exile groupings, then including the Progress Party of Equatorial Guinea. The other participants were the National Alliance for the Restoration of Democracy (*Alianza Nacional de Restauración Democrática*, ANRD), founded in

1974 and led by Martin Nsomo Okomo; the Movement for the Liberation and Future of Equatorial Guinea (*Movimiento de Liberación y Futuro de Guinea Ecuatorial*, MOLIFUGE); the Liberation Front of Equatorial Guinea (*Frente de Liberación de Guinea Ecuatorial*, FRELIGE); and Democratic Reform (*Reforma Democrática*).

Democratic Party of Equatorial Guinea
Partido Democrático de Guinea Ecuatorial (PDGE)
Address. c/o Cámara de Representantes del Pueblo, Malabo

Leadership. Brig.-Gen. Teodoro Obiang Nguema Mbasogo (chair)

The PDGE was launched as the sole legal political party by President Obiang Nguema in October 1987. Shortly afterwards, a law was passed requiring all wage earners and public employees to contribute 3% of their income to the new government party. In response to increasing pressure for greater pluralism, party delegates at an extraordinary congress in August 1991 urged the regime to establish a framework for the legalization of other political parties. A new constitution, approved in November 1991, abolished the PDGE's sole party status and legislation permitting the formation of other parties, although very restrictive in its application, was adopted in early 1992. The party maintained its dominance in the legislative elections in November 1993, taking 68 of the 80 seats, and was the only party represented in the government appointed the following month. In October 1994 two prominent members of the PDGE resigned from the party in protest against the government's alleged human rights violations and its obstruction of the democratic process. The official results giving the PDGE victory in the September 1995 municipal elections were contested by the opposition, as was the official outcome of the presidential elections in February 1996 giving Obiang Nguema a 99% victory.

Joint Opposition Platform

Plataforma de la Oposición Conjunta (POC)

Leadership. Tomás Macheba, Severo Mota Nsa (leaders)

The POC was set up in 1992 as a coalition of parties opposed to the Obiang Nguema regime. The government rebuffed the coalition's electoral reform demands, and many POC members boycotted the November 1993 elections. The principal POC parties are the Progress Party of Equatorial Guinea (PPGE), the Liberal Democratic Convention (CLD) and the Social Democratic Union (UDS). Its six other affiliates were the Popular Union (*Unión Popular*, UP), legally recognized in May 1992 and led by Eusebio Eboga; the Socialist Party of Equatorial Guinea (*Partido Socialista de Guinea Ecuatorial*, PSGE), led by Tomás Mecheba Fernández; the Social Democratic Party (*Partido Social Demócrata*, PSD), led by Marcellino Mangue Mba; the Social Democratic Coalition Party (*Partido de Coalición Social Demócrata*, PCSD); the National Democratic Union (*Unión Nacional Democrática*, UND); and the Convergence for Social Democracy (*Convergencia para la Democracia Social*, CPDS), led by Placido Mico Abogo.

Liberal Democratic Convention

Convención Liberal Democrática (CLD)

Address. c/o Cámara de Representantes del Pueblo, Malabo

Leadership. Santos Pascual Bokomo Nanguande (chair)

Legalized in May 1992, the CLD was credited with winning one legislative seat in the November 1993 elections. In January 1994 the authorities prevented it from holding its first congress, apparently because Bokomo Nanguande had criticized the conduct of the elections.

Opposition Coordination of Equatorial Guinea

Coordinación Oposición de Guinea Ecuatorial (COGE)

This opposition grouping was formed in Gabon in 1991, and its six constituent parties signed an agreement in March 1992 committing them to work together for the establishment of democratic rule in Equatorial Guinea. The signatories were the Socialist Party of Equatorial Guinea (which subsequently joined the Joint Opposition Platform) and the following five parties: the Union for Democracy and Social Development (*Unión para la Democracia y el Desarrollo Social*, UDDS), led by Antonio Sibacha Bueicheku; the Party of Reunification (*Partido de Reunificación*, PR); the Movement for the National Unification of Equatorial Guinea (*Movimiento para la Unificación Nacional de Guinea Ecuatorial*, MUNGE); the Republican Party of Equatorial Guinea (*Partido Republicano de Guinea Ecuatorial*, PRGE); and the National Movement for the Reliberation of Equatorial Guinea (*Movimiento Nacional para la Reliberación de Guinea Ecuatorial*, MNRGE).

Progress Party of Equatorial Guinea

Partido del Progreso de Guinea Ecuatorial (PPGE)

Address. C/Nigeria 24, Malabo

Telephone. (#240) 9-2054

Leadership. Severo Moto Nsa (leader), José Luis Jones (secretary-general)

The PPGE was formed by Mota Nsa, a former minister, in exile in Spain in 1983. He and other PPGE leaders returned to Equatorial Guinea in 1988, apparently expecting reconciliation with the ruling regime. However, a petition for legal recognition of the party was denied by the government. This was followed by a further period of exile for Moto and brief imprisonment for José Luis Jones on coup plot charges. Moto returned again in May 1992, and the following October the PPGE was granted legal recognition. The PPGE became a prominent member of the Joint Opposition Platform (POC) and was one of the POC parties that boycotted the November 1993 legislative elections. In April 1995 Mota and others were convicted and sentenced by a military court on charges related to an alleged coup plot. However, they were all unexpectedly pardoned by President Obiang Nguema in August.

The PPGE is an affiliate of the Christian Democrat International.

Social Democratic and Popular Convention
Convención Social Demócrata y Popular (CSDP)
   Address. c/o Cámara de Representantes del Pueblo, Malabo
   Leadership. Secundino Oyonoh Agiaong, Rafael Obiang
   Confused in some sources with the Convergence for Social Democracy (a component of the Joint Opposition Platform, POC), the CSDP has been split on whether to participate in available political processes. A faction led by Obiang followed the POC in boycotting the November 1993 legislative

elections and the February 1996 presidential polling. A faction led by Oyonoh Agiaong participated in the 1993 elections, winning six seats in the House of People's Representatives, and Oyonoh Agiaong was nominated as a candidate for the 1996 presidential contest, withdrawing so late that his name appeared on the ballot paper.

Social Democratic Union
Unión Democráta Social (UDS)
   Address. c/o Cámara de Representantes del Pueblo, Malabo
   Leadership. Angel Miko Alo Nchama (leader)
   Formerly an opposition grouping based in Gabon, the UDS achieved legal recognition in October 1992 under the leadership of Carmelo Modu Akuse. Akuse was then expelled from the party in November 1992 and replaced by Angel Miko Alo Nchama. The UDS won five seats in the November 1993 legislative elections.

Eritrea

Capital: Asmara

Population: 3,275,000 (1995E)

A former Italian colony, Eritrea was a British protectorate from 1941 to 1952, when it became federated with Ethiopia by decision of the United Nations. It was annexed by Ethiopia in 1962. Following the fall of the government of Mengistu Haile Mariam in Ethiopia in 1991, Eritrea functioned as an autonomous region with the Eritrean People's Liberation Front (EPLF), now the People's Front for Democracy and Justice (PFDJ), establishing a provisional government. The Republic of Eritrea was declared in May 1993 following a referendum, bringing to an end a 30–year struggle for independence. A transitional government was established to administer the country for a maximum of four years pending the drafting of a constitution and multi-party elections. Legislative power is vested in a unicameral National Assembly, comprising 75 members of the central committee of the PFDJ, plus an equal number of elected members. The National Assembly elects the President, who is in turn its Chairman. Executive power is vested in the 24–member State Council, which is appointed and chaired by the President.

People's Front for Democracy and Justice (PFDJ)
   Leadership. Issaias Afewerki (chair)
   The PFDJ's predecessor, the Eritrean People's Liberation Front (EPLF), was originally founded in 1970 as a left-wing breakaway group from the traditionalist Eritrean Liberation Front, in pursuit of Eritrean independence. It latterly moved away from a Marxist stance. For much of its pre-independence existence the EPLF controlled large areas of the Eritrean countryside. By 1989 it

claimed to control 90 per cent of the province, completing its dominance thereafter with the fall of the Mengistu regime in 1991. The EPLF converted itself from a national liberation movement into a political party, taking the PFDJ designation, at a congress in February 1994.

Other Groups

Democratic Movement for the Liberation of Eritrea (DMLE), an anti-EPLF organization.

Eritrean Liberation Front (ELF), mainly Muslim and formed in the late 1950s to pursue Eritrean autonomy. It initiated anti-Ethiopian guerrilla activity in the early 1960s, but its influence later declined as it was increasingly marginalized by the breakaway Eritrean People's Libera- tion Front (which later became the People's Front for Democracy and Justice). Various ELF factions have since surfaced, but the Front had no recognized presence in the Eritrean provisional government formed by the EPLF in 1991.

Estonia

Capital: Tallinn   **Population:** 1,495,000 (1995E)

The full sovereignty of the Republic of Estonia was declared on Aug. 20, 1991 (and recognized by the USSR State Council on Sept. 6, 1991), following the Estonian legislature's repudiation in March 1990 of the absorption of Estonia by the USSR in August 1940. A new constitution approved by referendum in June 1992 provided for a parliamentary system combined with a strong presidency. The President is elected for a five-year term by secret ballot of members of the legislature and nominates the Prime Minister, who forms a Council of Ministers. The government must command the support of the 101-member unicameral Parliament (*Riigikogu*), itself popularly elected for a four-year term by a system of proportional representation. The franchise is vested in those possessing Estonian citizenship.

In parliamentary elections held on March 5, 1995, the Coalition and Rural People's Union won 32.2% of the vote and 41 seats, of which the Estonian Coalition Party took 18, the Estonian Rural People's Party (EME) 9, the Estonian Rural Union 8 and the Estonian Pensioners' and Families' League 6; the Estonian Reform Party 19 (16.2%); the Estonian Centre Party 16 (14.2%); the Pro Patria National Coalition/Estonian National Independence Party 8 (7.8%); the Moderates 6 (6.0%); Our Home is Estonia 6 (5.9%); and the Republican and Conservative People's Party (Right-Wingers) 5 (5.0%).

The presidential election on Sept. 20, 1992, was held under previous rules providing for direct popular voting in one round, with the legislature choosing between the two leading contenders if no candidate received an overall majority of votes cast by the electorate. In that contest Lennart Meri (Pro Patria) came second in the popular vote with 29.8% but was elected President by the *Riigikogu* on Oct. 5 by 59 votes to 31 for Arnold Rüütel (then Secure Home, later leader of the EME), who had won 42.2% of the popular vote.

Coalition and Rural People's Union
Koonderakonna ja Maarahva Ühendus (KMÜ)
    Address. c/o Riigikogu, Tallinn
    Leadership. The KMÜ is directed by "coalition council" of representatives of constituent parties.

The KMÜ alliance was created for the 1995 parliamentary elections, embracing the Estonian Coalition Party (EK), the Estonian Rural People's Party, the Estonian Rural Union, the Estonian Pensioners' and Families' League and the Farmers' Assembly. Broadly conservative in orientation and containing many former Communists, it is descended from the Secure Home (*Kindel Kodu*) coalition which in September 1992 backed the unsuccessful presidential candidacy of Arnold Rüütel and won 17 legislative seats with 13.6% of the vote. In March 1995 the KMÜ alliance headed the poll with an aggregate vote share of 32.2% and 41 seats on a platform promising agricultural subsidies and increased social expenditure. The following month it formed a coalition government with the Estonian Centre Party (EKe) under the premiership of Tiit Vähi of the EK. In October 1995, however, the EKe was replaced in the government by the Estonian Reform Party.

Development Party
Arengupartei (AP)
    Address. c/o Riigikogu, Tallinn
    Leadership. Andra Valdemann (chair)
    The AP was launched in May 1996 by a dissident faction of the Estonian Centre Party (EKe) led by

Valdemann, who had replaced Edgar Savisaar as EKe leader in October 1995 on the party's exit from government. She had then faced growing internal party opposition orchestrated by Savisaar, who had been re-elected EKe leader in late March 1996. Accordingly, she and six other EKe decided the found the AP, which was identified as being somewhat to the right of the parent party.

Estonian Centre Party
Eesti Keskerakond (EKe)
  Address. PO Box 3737, Tallinn 0090
  Telephone. (#372-2) 499304
  Fax. (#372-2) 493881
  Leadership. Edgar Savisaar (chair)
  The EKe was founded in October 1991, being an offshoot of the Estonian Popular Front (*Eestimaa Rahvarinne*, ER) that had spearheaded the post-1988 independence movement but had split into various parties after independence was achieved. As ER chair, Edgar Savisaar had been Prime Minister from April 1990 to January 1992, having previously been chairman of the Estonian branch of the Soviet-era Planning Committee (Gosplan). The EKe used the ER designation in the September 1992 parliamentary and presidential elections, winning 15 seats (with 12.2% of the vote) and achieving third place (with 23.7%) for its presidential candidate, Rein Taagepera. The EKe absorbed the Estonian Entrepreneurs' Party (*Eesti Ettevtjate Erakond*, EEE) prior to the March 1995 parliamentary elections, in which it won 16 seats with 14.2% of the vote. In April 1995 it joined a coalition government with the Coalition and Rural People's Union, obtaining four portfolios, including that of Internal Affairs for Savisaar.
  The dismissal of Savisaar in October 1995 for alleged involvement in a phone-tapping scandal caused the collapse of the government, and the EKe was not included in the succeeding coalition. Shortly before its formation Savisaar was replaced as EKe leader Andra Valdemann and announced his retirement from politics. However, in early 1996 he took the leadership of an anti-Valdemann group within the party, of which he was re-elected leader in March. The response of Valdemann and her supporters was to found the breakaway Development Party, which attracted seven of the 16 EKe deputies.

Estonian Coalition Party
Eesti Koonderakond (EK)
  Address. Kuhlbarsi 1-203, Tallinn 0104
  Telephone. (#372-2) 446746
  Fax. (#372-2) 314161
  Leadership. Tiit Vähi (chair), Riivo Sinijärv, Siiri Oviir and Endel Lippmaa (deputy chairs)
  The EK was founded in December 1991, its leader becoming caretaker Prime Minister in January 1992. In the September 1992 elections the party was part of the nationalist Secure Home coalition, which formed the main parliamentary opposition until 1995. The EK headed the Coalition and Rural People's Union (KMÜ) in the March 1995 election, winning 18 of the 41 alliance seats in its own right. The following month Tiit Vähi was appointed Prime Minister of a coalition government between the KMÜ and the Estonian Centre Party (EKe), the EK obtaining four portfolios in addition to the premiership. A political crisis in October 1995 resulted in the exit of the EKe from the government and its replacement by the Estonian Reform Party, under the continued premiership of Vähi.

Estonian Pensioners' and Families' League
Eesti Pensionäride ja Perede Liit (EPPL)
  Address. Sakala 3, Tallinn 0001
  Telephone. (#372-2) 446746
  Leadership. Harri Kärtner (chair)
  The EPPL is derived from the Estonian Democratic Justice Union/Pensioners' League (EDO/PÜ), which was not represented in the legislature elected in 1992. As a component of the victorious Coalition and Rural People's Union (KMÜ) in the March 1995 elections, it obtained six seats in its own right.

Estonian Reform Party
Eesti Reformierakond (ER)
  Address. Suur-Karja 13, Tallinn 0001
  Telephone. (#372-2) 443721
  Fax. (#372-2) 316191
  Leadership. Siim Kallas (chair)
  The ER was launched by Siim Kallas after he had been instrumental, as president of the Bank of Estonia, in the downfall of Prime Minister Mart Laar (Pro Patria National Coalition) in September 1994 but had then failed to secure legislative endorsement as Laar's successor in the premiership. Described as "liberal-rightist" in orientation, the ER includes the Estonian Liberal Democratic Party (*Eesti Liberaaldemokraatlik Partei*, ELDP) led by Paul-Eerik Rummo, which had contested the 1992 election as part of the winning Pro Patria coalition but had withdrawn from the latter in June 1994 in protest against Maar's leadership style. Using the unofficial designation "Liberals", the ER took second place in the March 1995 parliamentary elections, winning 19 seats and 16.2% of the vote. Having thus effectively become leader of the opposition, Kallas resigned from his post at the Bank of Estonia. Six months later, in November 1995, he became Deputy Premier and Foreign Minister when the ER joined a new government coalition

headed by the Estonian Coalition Party and including five other ER ministers.

Through the ELDP, the party is an observer member of the Liberal International.

Estonian Rural Centre Party
Eesti Maa-Keskerakond (EMK)
  Address. Rahukohtu 1-15, Tallinn 0100
  Telephone. (#372-2) 446815
  Fax. (#372-2) 449865
  Leadership. Vambo Kaal (acting chair)

The EMK was founded in 1990 to represent those in Estonia's farming community who favoured transition to a market economy. It entered into the Moderates coalition with the Estonian Social Democratic Party (ESDP) for the 1992 legislative elections, securing 12 seats in aggregate. It maintained the alliance with the ESDP in the March 1995 elections, in which the aggregate return was only six seats. During the campaign the EMK claimed that the agrarian parties in the Coalition and Rural Peoples's Union were dominated by former Communists.

Estonian Rural People's Party
Eesti Maarahva Erakond (EME)
  Address. Lai 39/41 ruba 201, Tallinn 0001
  Telephone. (#372-2) 609515
  Leadership. Arnold Rüütel (chair)

The EME was founded in September 1994 on the initiative of Rüütel, who had been Chairman of the Estonian Supreme Soviet in the latter years of Soviet rule but had supported moves to throw off rule from Moscow, becoming independent Estonia's first head of state in 1991. He headed the popular poll in the September 1992 presidential elections as the Secure Home candidate, winning 42.2% of the vote, but lost to the Pro Patria nominee in the decisive legislative balloting. In joining the Coalition and Rural People's Union (KMÜ) for the March 1995 parliamentary elections, the EME was instrumental in attracting agrarian support to the alliance. After the elections the EME formed a nine-member parliamentary group with the Farmers' Assembly (PK), whose deputies had been elected under the EME banner, and also established formal links with the Estonian Pensioners' and Families' League. In April 1995 it joined the new coalition government headed by the Estonian Coalition Party, but was reduced to seven deputies in February 1996 when the two PK members opted for independence.

Estonian Rural Union
Eesti Maaliit (EM)
  Address. Rahukohtu 1-9, Tallinn 0100
  Telephone. (#372-2) 443065
  Leadership. Arvo Sirendi (chair)

Founded in March 1991, the EM contested the 1992 parliamentary elections as part of the Secure Home coalition. For the March 1995 contest it was a member of the Coalition and Rural People's Union, winning eight seats in its own right.

Estonian Social Democratic Party
Eesti Sotsiaaldemokraatlik Partei (ESDP)
  Address. PO Box 3437, Tallinn 0090
  Telephone. (#372-2) 443038
  Fax. (#372-2) 444902
  Leadership. Eiki Nestor (chair), Ulo Laanoja and Mikhel Pärnoja (deputy chairs), Lembit Lutz (secretary-general)

The ESDP is descended from the historic Social Democratic Party founded in 1905 (when Estonia was part of the Russian Empire) and was maintained in exile during the post-1945 Soviet era. Relaunched in Estonia in 1990, the party became part of the independence movement, its firm anti-communism facilitating participation in right-oriented post-independence governments. It contested the 1992 parliamentary elections in the Moderates alliance with the Estonian Rural Centre Party (EMK); in the post-1992 coalition government headed by Pro Patria the ESDP sought to preserve a social welfare dimension to pro-market reforms. In the March 1995 elections the Moderates alliance of the ESDP and EMK retained only six seats.

The ESDP is a member party of the Socialist International.

Farmers' Assembly
Põllumeeste Kogu (PK)
  Address. PO Box 543, Tallinn 0001
  Telephone. (#372-2) 437733
  Leadership. Eldur Parder

Founded in 1992, the PK was a component of the victorious Coalition and Rural People's Union in the March 1995 elections. Its candidates stood under the banner of the Estonian Rural People's Party, with which it formed a joint parliamentary group. In February 1996, however, the two PK deputies withdrew their support from the government (effectively becoming independents) on the grounds that it had given insufficient attention to the needs of farmers.

Fatherland Union
Isamaaliit (IL)
  Address. Mustamäe tee 4, Tallinn 0006
  Telephone. (#372-2) 532628
  Fax. (#372-2) 394036
  Leadership. Toivo Jürgenson (chair)

The centre-right IL was created in December 1995 as a merger of the Fatherland (or "Pro Patria") National Coalition (*Rahvuslik Koondera-*

kond Isamaa, RKI) and the Estonian National Independence Party (*Eesti Rahvusliku Sõtumatuse Partei*, ERSP). Then the dominant government formations, these two parties had contested the March 1995 elections in alliance but had retained only eight seats with 7.9% of the vote, thereafter going into opposition.

The RKI had been formed in early 1992 as an alliance of several Christian democratic and other centre-right parties seeking to make a decisive break with the Soviet era. Led by Mart Laar, it won an indecisive plurality of 29 seats in the September 1992 elections (with 22% of the vote), its deputies combining the following month with those of the ERSP and others to elect Lennart Meri as President despite his having come second in the popular balloting with 29.8% of the vote. Laar then engineered the conversion of the RKI into a unitary formation and was named to head a coalition government. But he was eventually ousted as Prime Minister in September 1994, in part because of his self-confessed "dictatorial" methods.

The ERSP had been founded in August 1988, being then the only organized non-communist party in the whole of the USSR. Although centrist in orientation, it was consistently more anti-communist than other pro-independence formations, declining to participate in the 1990 Estonian Supreme Soviet elections and instead organizing the alternative "Congress of Estonia". Following independence in 1991, the ERSP became Estonia's strongest party, but was eclipsed by the RKI in the September 1992 elections, when the then ERSP chair, Lagle Parek, took fourth place in the presidential contest with only 4.3% of the vote. Thereafter the ERSP became a junior coalition partner in the government headed by the RKI.

The RKI was a member of the Christian Democrat International and of the International Democrat Union.

Moderates
Mõõdukad

> *Address.* c/o Riigikogu, Tallinn
> *Leadership.* Vambo Kaal (EMK), Eiki Nestor (ESDP)

Mõõdukad was launched in 1990 as an electoral alliance of the Estonian Rural Centre Party (EMK) and the Estonian Social Democratic Party (ESDP). The alliance won 12 seats in the 1992 parliamentary elections, becoming a member of the resultant government headed by the Pro Patria National Coalition. In the March 1995 elections the Moderates slumped to six seats, despite receiving endorsement from the then Prime Minister, Andres Tarand.

Our Home is Estonia
Meie Kodu on Eestimaa (MKE)

> *Address.* Mere pst 5-303, Tallinn 0001
> *Telephone.* (#372-2) 440421
> *Fax.* (#372-2) 441237
> *Leadership.* Viktor Andreev (EÜR), Sergei Kuznetsov (VEE)

The MKE was launched prior to the March 1995 election as an alliance of ethnic Russian parties, including the Estonian United People's Party (*Eestimaa Ühendatud Rahvapartei*, EÜR) and the Russian Party in Estonia (*Vene Erakond Eestis*, VEE). The grouping strongly opposed the 1993 Estonian citizenship law, which defined ethnic Russians and other Soviet-era settlers as foreigners and set exacting conditions for their naturalization. The fact that only Estonian citizens were entitled to vote prevented the alliance from obtaining a higher share in the 1995 elections among the estimated 30% ethnic Russian component of the population. The six elected MKE deputies formed a parliamentary group called the Russian Faction.

Republican and Conservative People's Party
Vabariiklaste ja Konservatiivide Rahvaerakond (Parempoolsed)

> *Address.* Rahukohtu 1-33, Tallinn 0090
> *Telephone.* (#372-6) 316602
> *Fax.* (#372-6) 316606
> *Leadership.* Karin Jaani (chair), Ulo Nugis (deputy chair)

Officially preferring to be called "The Right-Wingers" in English, Parempoolsed was launched in September 1994 as a merger of the Republican and Conservative parties. Its leader, Karin Jaani, had taken the Republican faction out of the then ruling Pro Patria alliance in June 1994, receiving the public support of Indrek Kannik, who had resigned as Defence Minister the previous month. The grouping won only five seats in the March 1995 elections (on a 5% vote share) and subsequently, in February 1996, entered into a cooperation agreement with the Fatherland Union.

Other Parties and Alliances

Better Estonia and Estonian Citizens (*Parem Eesti ja Eesti Kodanik*), an unsuccessful 1995 right-wing electoral alliance embracing the **Estonian National Progressive Party** (*Eesti Rahvuslik Eduerakond*) led by Ants Erm, the **Estonian National Party** (*Eesti Rahvuslik Erakond*) led by Elmut Laane, the **Estonian National Protection Party** (*Eesti Rahva Jäägerpartei*) led by Asso Kommer, and the **Estonian Home** (*Eesti Kodu*) led by Kalju Poldvere. *Address.* Rahnkohtu 1, Tallinn 0100

Estonian Blue Party (*Eesti Sinine Erakond*, ESE), led by Neeme Kuningas, unsuccessful in the 1995 elections. *Address.* Uus 3, Tallinn 0001

Estonian Democratic Labour Party (*Eesti Demokraatlik Tööpartei*, EDT), led by Vaino Valjas and Hillar Eller, set up in 1992 by elements of the former ruling Estonian Communist Party, now proclaiming a democratic socialist orientation; the EDT unsuccessfully contested the 1995 elections within the Justice (*Õiglus*) alliance, which also included the Party for Legal Justice. *Address.* Kentmanni 13, Tallinn 0001

Estonian Democratic Union (*Eesti Demokraatlik Liit*, EDL), led by Miina Hint, unsuccessful in the 1995 elections. *Address.* Sütiste 34-6, Tallinn 0034

Estonian Farmers' Party (*Eesti Talurahva Erakond*, ETE), led by Jaak-Hans Kuks, unsuccessful in the 1995 elections. *Address.* Rouge vald, Vorumaa 2741

Estonian Greens (*Eesti Rohelised*, ER), led by Jüri Liim, founded in 1991, won one legislative seat in 1992, but failed to win representation in 1995 as part of the Fourth Force (*Neljas Jud*, NJ) coalition with the Estonian Royalist Party. *Address.* PK 318, Tartu 2400

Estonian National League (*Eesti Rahvulaste Keskliit*, ERK), led by Tiit Madisson, unsuccessful in the 1995 elections. *Address.* Rataskaevu 6-12, Tallinn 0001

Estonian Royalist Party (*Eesti Rojalistlik Partei*, ERP), led by Kalle Kulbok; founded in 1989, the ERP won eight legislative seats in 1992 but lost them all in 1995 standing as part of the Fourth Force (*Neljas Jud*, NJ) alliance with the Estonian Greens; seeking a candidate to head an Estonian constitutional monarchy, the party at one stage proposed Prince Edward of England, before endorsing a Swedish prince with better credentials. *Address.* Lossi plats 1A, Tallinn 0100

Forest Party (*Metsaerakond*), led by Vello-Taivo Denks, won no seats in the 1995 elections. *Address.* Alexandri 14-19, Tartu 2400

The Future's Estonia Party (*Tuleviku Eesti Erakond* TEE), led by Jaanus Raidal, unsuccessful in the 1995 elections. *Address.* Toomkooli 7-11, Tallinn 0100

Northern Estonian Citizens' Party (*Põhja-Eesti Kodanike Partei*, PEKP), led by Karli Eskusson, won no seats in 1995. *Address.* Vana-Viru 9, Tallinn 0001

Party for Legal Justice (*Õigusliku Tasakaalu Erakond*, OTE), led by Peeter Tedre, contested the 1995 elections within the unsuccessful Justice (*Õiglus*) alliance, which also included the Estonian Democratic Labour Party. *Address.* Nunne 8, Tallinn 0001

Southern Estonian Citizens' Party (Lõuna-Eesti Kodanike Erakond, LEKE), led by Alar Sepp, won no seats in 1995. *Address.* Aardla 108-44, Tartu 2400

Ethiopia

Capital: Addis Ababa

Population: 57,000,000 (1995E)

What is now the Federal Democratic Republic of Ethiopia was a monarchy under the Emperor Haile Selassie until the 1974 revolution, after which there was military rule until the introduction of the 1987 constitution proclaiming the People's Democratic Republic of Ethiopia. Rebel forces under the Ethiopian People's Revolutionary Democratic Front (EPRDF) took control of Addis Adaba in May 1991, and Lt.-Col. Mengistu Haile Mariam, who had come to power after an internal struggle within the military leadership in 1977, fled the country. In July 1991 an 87–member Council of Representatives, elected at a multi-party conference, confirmed the leader of the EPRDF, Meles Zenawi, as transitional President. In December 1994 a new constitution was adopted, restructuring Ethiopia into nine ethnically-based federal states and providing for a parliamentary system of government centred on a bicameral parliament.

In elections to the 548-member Council of People's Representatives held on May 5, 1995, but boycotted by many opposition parties, the EPRDF won a landslide victory, consolidating its hold on power. Also assembled was a 117-member Federal Council to form a second chamber representing ethnic minorities and professional groups. In August 1995 the Federal Democratic Republic of Ethiopia was proclaimed.

Ethiopian People's Democratic Movement (EPDM)

Leadership. Tamirat Layne (secretary-general)

Founded in 1980 and principally Amhara in membership, the EPDM was one of the two original components of the Ethiopian People's Revolutionary Democratic Front set up in May 1988. EPDM forces had emerged as a military element in the anti-Mengistu insurgency in the mid-1980s, particularly in Wollo province. Following the Mengistu's overthrow, the EPDM became the largest Amhara-based element in the transitional government, its leader assuming the post of Prime Minister.

Ethiopian People's Revolutionary Democratic Front (EPRDF)

Address. c/o Council of People's Representatives, Addis Ababa

Leadership. Meles Zenawi (secretary-general), Tamirat Layne

The EPRDF was set up in May 1988 at the initiative of the Tigre People's Liberation Front (TPLF), in alliance with the Ethiopian People's Democratic Movement (EPDM). The organization was subsequently widened to embrace the Oromo People's Democratic Organization (OPDO), the Ethiopian Democratic Officers' Revolutionary Movement (EDORM), the Afar Democratic Union and the Afar Democratic Association. Although the TPLF had long subscribed to Marxist-Leninist ideology, an EPRDF congress in early 1991 endorsed an expansion of private enterprise and the introduction of market mechanisms in small-scale agriculture. Although advocating a united Ethiopia, the congress also accepted Eritrea's right to self-determination.

In military co-operation with the Eritrean People's Liberation Front (EPLF) and the Oromo Liberation Front (OLF), the EPRDF led the march on Addis Adaba which toppled the Mengistu regime in May 1991. Meles Zenawi became interim President and from that time the EPRDF has dominated the political scene at the centre. The Front's constituent elements accounted for 32 of the 87 on the Council of Representatives formed in July 1991, and won convincing victories in constituent assembly elections in 1994 and in national and regional elections in mid-1995.

Oromo Liberation Front (OLF)

Leadership. Gelassa Dilbo (secretary-general)

Although the OLF represents the largest ethnic group in Ethiopia, its military contribution to the struggle against the Mengistu regime was small in comparison to that of Eritrean forces or the Tigre People's Liberation Front (TPLF). Mutual antipathy between the OLF and TPLF led to the creation, under the latter's auspices, of the rival Oromo People's Democratic Organization (OPDO) in 1990. Initially committed to an independent Oromo state, the OLF said in June 1991 that it was prepared to accept substantial regional autonomy within a federal Ethiopia. Subsequent friction between the OLF and the ruling Ethiopian People's Revolutionary Democratic Front has persisted. The OLF boycotted regional elections in 1992 and the constituent assembly elections in 1994.

Oromo People's Democratic Organization (OPDO)

Leadership. Kuma Demeksa

The OPDO was set up in 1990 under the direction of the Tigre People's Liberation Front (TPLF) as the Oromo ethnic element in the Ethiopian People's Revolutionary Democratic Front. Its creation was regarded as a hostile act by the major Oromo organization, the Oromo Liberation Front (OLF), and has remained a source of friction between the OLF and the TPLF.

Tigre People's Liberation Front (TPLF)

Leadership. Meles Zenawi (chair)

Formed in 1975, the Marxist-Leninist TPLF pursued a separatist goal for Tigre Province until the late 1980s. It then moderated its ideological stance and its objective became an overall change of regime in Ethiopia as a federal entity. Having achieved dominance over Tigre province through its military insurgency, the TPLF initiated the establishment of the Ethiopian People's Revolutionary Democratic Front in 1988, precipitating the overthrow of the Mengistu regime in May 1991 and the assumption of power in the name of the EPRDF by TPLF chairman, Meles Zenawi.

Other Groups

Among the very large number of other parties and movements listed as being in existence in Ethiopia, those covered below appear to be among the more significant.

Afar People's Democratic Organization (APDO), led by Sultan Ahmed Ali Mirah, formed in 1975 as the Afar Liberation Front and generally thought to be the most important of the ethnic Afar groups; involved, along with Eritrean forces, in the struggle against the Mengistu regime; its leader returned to Ethiopia from prolonged exile in Saudi Arabia in 1991.

Coalition of Ethiopian Democratic Forces (COEDF), launched in April 1991 in the United States and bringing together groups which had opposed the Mengistu regime but which also opposed the ruling Ethiopian People's Revolutionary Democratic Front (EPRDF); its initial components included the Ethiopian People's Revolutionary Party, the All-Ethiopia Socialist Movement (Meison), the Ethiopian Democratic Union, the Tigre People's Democratic Movement and elements of the Ethiopian People's Democratic Alliance (EPDA)--the last three of which reportedly left the coalition in the same year.

Ethiopian Democratic Union (EDU), a conservative formation whose military activities against the Mengistu regime in northern provinces were reportedly supported by some Arab Gulf countries, but which ceased to be a significant force by the early 1980s; initially a part of the Coalition of Ethiopian Democratic Forces (COEDF) formed in 1991F.

Ethiopian Democratic Unity Party (EDUP), formerly the Workers' Party of Ethiopia (WPE) and the sole legal party under the Mengistu regime, name changed in 1990 as the party abandoned its Marxist-Leninist ideology and tried to broaden its support base in the face of the accelerating insurgency; banned following the overthrow of Mengistu in 1991.

Ethiopian People's Revolutionary Party (EPRP), founded in the mid-1970s by left-wing intellectual opponents of the military regime, committed to the overthrow of Mengistu but hostile to the dominant Ethiopian People's Revolutionary Democratic Front; following the rebel victory in 1991, it became the main component of the Coalition of Ethiopian Democratic Forces (COEDF) opposing the EPRDF's political dominance.

Fiji

Capital: Suva   **Population:** 750,000 (1995E)

Formerly a British colony, Fiji became an independent state within the Commonwealth in 1970. The constitution provided that the head of state was the British sovereign, represented by a Governor-General, who would appoint the Prime Minister and Cabinet in accordance with the wishes of the bicameral Fijian parliament.

The moderate Alliance Party, defending the constitutional and legal rights of the indigenous Fijian (Melanesian-Polynesian) population, ruled the country from independence until its defeat in the general election of April 1987 (after which it effectively ceased to operate). A new government was then formed from a coalition of the Fiji Labour Party (FLP) and the National Federation Party (NFP), which largely drew support from the population of Indian descent. However, in May 1987 a military coup was staged by the army commander, Sitiveni Rabuka. Although civilian government was subsequently restored with the establishment of an interim administration by the Governor-General (Ratu Sir Penaia Ganilau), Rabuka staged a second coup in September 1987. The following month he announced that the 1970 constitution had been revoked and declared Fiji a republic. The British sovereign ceased to be the head of state upon the resignation of the Governor-General, and Fiji's membership of the Commonwealth lapsed. The country was returned nominally to civilian rule in December 1987 when Ratu Ganilau accepted the presidency of the republic and a Fijian-dominated Cabinet (including Rabuka as minister for home affairs) was appointed.

A new constitution, promulgated in 1990, guaranteed the political dominance of the indigenous Fijian community within a bicameral parliament. The elected House of Representatives (*Vale*) has 70 seats, of which 37 are reserved for ethnic Fijians, 27 for ethnic Indians, five for other races, and one seat for the island of Rotuma. In the 34-member Senate (*Seniti*), appointed by the President, 24 seats are reserved for ethnic Fijians, nine for Indians and other races, and one for the inhabitants of Rotuma.

Executive authority is vested in the President who is appointed by the Great Council of Chiefs for a five-year term. In most cases the President is guided by the Cabinet, which conducts the government of the republic and which is led by the Prime Minister (who must be an ethnic Fijian).

The Fijian Political Party, under Rabuka's leadership, emerged from both the May 1992 and February 1994 general elections as the dominant party in the House of Representatives, and formed governments which included two General Voters' Party representatives on both occasions.

In June 1994 Prime Minister Rabuka announced that a commission would conduct a review of the ethnically-biased provisions of the 1990 constitution.

Fiji Labour Party (FLP)

Address. GPO Box 2162, Government Buildings, Suva

Telephone. (#679) 305811

Fax. (#679) 305808

Leadership. Jokapeci Koroi (president), Mahendra Pal Chaudhry (secretary-general)

The leftist FLP was formed in 1985 as a multiracial party, although it has drawn most of its support from the Indian community. It came to power briefly, in coalition with the National Federation Party (NFP), in the April 1987 general election, but the administration was overthrown the following month in a military coup. In 1991 the FLP broke with the NFP over the former's decision (which was ultimately reversed) to boycott the 1992 general election. Of the 13 (Indian-reserved) seats gained by the FLP in the 1992 election, only seven were retained in the balloting on Feb. 18 and 25, 1994.

Fijian Association Party (FAP)

Address. c/o Vale, Suva

Leadership. Josevata Kamikamica (president), Adi Kuini Speed (chair)

The Fijian Association was formed prior to the February 1994 general election by a breakaway faction of the Fijian Political Party, whose opposition to the 1994 budget caused the defeat of the government in the legislature in November 1993. In the election the new party won only five of the seats reserved for ethnic Fijians in the House of Representatives. In 1995 the Fijian Association merged with the All Nationals Congress—which had been formed in 1991 and whose leadership had subsequently been assumed by Adi Kuini Speed, a former president of the Fijian Labour Party.

Fijian Political Party

Soqosoqo ni Vakavulewa ni Taukei (SVT)

Address. c/o Vale, Suva

Leadership. Sitiveni Rabuka (president)

The Fijian Political Party was launched in 1991, drawing support predominantly from ethnic Fijians. In October of that year the party presidency was secured by Sitiveni Rabuka (the then Deputy Prime Minister who had led the two military coups in 1987). In the 1992 and 1994 general elections the party won the largest number of seats in the House of Representatives (30 of the Fijian-reserved seats in May 1992 and 31 in February 1994). It formed governments on both occasions under Rabuka's premiership, including members of the General Voters' Party (although the GVP withdrew from the administration in October 1995).

General Voters' Party (GVP)

Address. c/o Vale, Suva

Leadership. Leo Smith (leader)

Formed in 1990, the GVP represents the interests of those citizens not belonging to either the ethnic Fijian or Indian communities (collectively classified as General Electors under the 1990 constitution). In the May 1992 general election the party won five seats in the House of Representatives and joined in a coalition government led by the Fijian Political Party. In the February 1994 polling, the GVP retained four seats. It remained in the ruling coalition until October 1995, when it withdrew from ministerial participation (following the earlier dismissal of the party leader from the Cabinet).

National Federation Party (NFP)

Address. POB 13534, Suva

Telephone. (#679) 665633

Leadership. Jai Ram Reddy (leader), Balwant Singh Rakka (president)

The democratic socialist NFP was established in the early 1960s and has predominantly drawn its support from the Indian community. Weakened by factionalism in the late 1970s and early 1980s, the party then won power, in coalition with the Fiji Labour Party (FLP), in the April 1987 general election. The new government was promptly ousted in a military coup the following month. The alliance with the FLP ended in 1991 when the NFP voted not to join the FLP in its decision (which was subsequently reversed) to boycott the 1992 general election. Having won 14 of the 27 seats reserved for ethnic Indians in that election, the NFP increased its representation to 20 seats in the February 1994 polling.

Other Parties

Fiji Christian Party, formed in 1995 by the Methodist Church to oppose legislation to repeal the Sunday observance law (imposed after the 1987 coups).

Fiji Indian Congress Party, launched in 1991 and led by Vijay Raghwan.

Fiji Indian Liberal Party, formed in 1991 to represent the interests of the Indian community, particularly sugar-cane workers and students.

Fiji Muslim League, representing the Muslim minority among Fiji's ethnic Indian population.

Fijian Conservative Party, formed in 1989 and led by Isireli Vuibau.

Fijian Nationalist United Front Party, an anti-Indian communal organization which was launched in 1974 as the Fijian Nationalist Party and reorganized in 1992. A more extreme nationalist vehicle than the Fijian Political Party, the organization won five seats in the House of Representatives in the 1992 general election, but lost them all in the 1994 balloting.

National Democratic Party, led by Atunaisa Lacabuka.

New Labour Movement, under the leadership of Michael Columbus.

Taukei Solidarity Movement, an extreme right-wing indigenous Fijian nationalist group formed after the 1987 military takeover.

Western United Front, a mainly Fijian organization led by Ratu Osea Gavidi.

Finland

Capital: Helsinki

Population: 5,140,000 (1995E)

Under its 1919 constitution as amended, the Republic of Finland is a democratic parliamentary state with a President elected for a six-year term by universal adult suffrage in two rounds of voting if no candidate obtains an absolute majority in the first. The President has considerable executive powers (particularly in the foreign policy sphere) and appoints a Council of Minister under a Prime Minister which must enjoy the confidence of the 200-member unicameral Diet (*Eduskunta*) elected for a four-year term by universal adult suffrage. Parliamentary elections are held under a system of proportional representation in 15 electoral districts, with the number of seats being allocated according to the most recent population census figures. One of the electoral districts is formed by the autonomous Aaland Islands (inhabited mainly by ethnic Swedes), which returns one deputy to the Finnish Diet.

The state contributes to the financing of the national and international activities of political parties represented in the Diet in proportion to their number of seats. In 1994 the total amount paid was FM64.2 million (about $13.5 million), of which, for example, the Centre Party of Finland (then having the most seats) obtained FM17,660,251 (about $3,725,000).

Presidential elections held on Jan. 16 and Feb. 4, 1994, resulted in the candidate of the Finnish Social Democratic Party (SSDP), Martti Ahtisaari, winning in the second round with 53.9% of the votes cast. Parliamentary elections on March 19, 1995, resulted as follows: SSDP 63 seats (with 28.3% of the vote); Centre Party 44 (19.9%); National Coalition 39 (17.9%); Left-Wing Alliance 22 (11.2%); Swedish People's Party 12 (5.1%); Green Union 9 (6.5%); Finnish Christian Union 7 (3.0%); Progressive Finnish Party (Young Finns) 2 (2.8%); Finnish Rural Party 1 (1.3%); Ecological Party 1 (0.3%).

Centre Party of Finland
Suomen Keskusta (KESK)

Address. Pursimiehenkatu 15, 00150 Helsinki
Telephone. (#358-0) 172721
Fax. (#358-0) 653589
Leadership. Esko Aho (chair), Aapo Saari (parliamentary group chair), Paavo Väyrynen (1994 presidential candidate), Pekka Perttula (secretary-general)

The Centre Party was founded in 1906 as the Agrarian Union, committed to improving the lot of Finland's large rural population and also to national independence, social justice and democracy. Its chief ideologue was Santeri Alkio (1862-1930), who wrote the first detailed Agrarian programme. Following Finland's declaration of independence in 1917, the Agrarians were part of the successful opposition to right-wing attempts to install a monarchy, while welcoming the victory of the anti-Bolshevik Whites in the 1918 civil war. On the declaration of a republic in 1919, the party increased its electoral support to 19.7% and began its long career in government. Of the 63 governments formed since independence, 48 have included the Agrarian/Centre Party, which has provided the Prime Minister on 20 occasions, as well as three Presidents, namely Lauri Kristian Relander (1925-32), Kyösti Kallio (1937-40) and Urho Kekkonen (1956-81).

The Agrarians reached an inter-war electoral peak of 27.3% in 1930, but were usually the second party after the Finnish Social Democratic Party (SSDP), with which they formed a "red-green" coalition from 1937. The Agrarians subsequently shared government responsibility for Finland's hostilities with the USSR in 1939-40 and 1941-44, resulting in the loss of a tenth of Finnish territory. Under the leadership of V.J. Sukselainen, the party took 21.4% of the vote in the 1945 elections and became the third largest party in the Diet. Rising to 24.2% in 1948, it became the largest parliamentary party and retained this status in the 1951 and 1954 elections. Kekkonen held the premiership in five out of the seven governments formed between 1950 and 1956. Elected President in 1956, he was to complete four consecutive terms before resigning during his fifth (in October 1981) because of ill-health. His main contribution in the foreign policy sphere was to refine the so-called "Paasikivi-Kekkonen line", involving preferential relations with the USSR in the context of neutrality and non-alignment. By this strategy, he hoped to secure the return of the Finnish territories ceded during World War II, but faced a firm Soviet refusal to consider territorial change.

The Agrarians fell back to third position in the 1958 elections and were weakened by the formation in 1959 of the Finnish Rural Party (SMP) by right-wing Agrarian dissidents. They nevertheless continued to play a pivotal role in successive coalitions and in 1962 recovered a Diet plurality, winning 53 seats and 23.0% of the vote. In November 1963 Ahti Karjalainen (Agrarian) formed the first non-socialist government since World War II, the other participants being the conservative National Coalition (KOK), what became the Liberal People's Party (LKP) and the Swedish People's Party (RKP/SFP). It resigned the following month and was eventually succeeded in September 1964 by one of the same party composition but headed by the Agrarian leader, Johannes Virolainen. In 1965 the Agrarians followed the Scandinavian trend by changing their name to Centre Party, aiming to broaden its support beyond the declining rural population. In the 1996 elections, however, the party slipped to 49 seats and 21.2% and joined a centre-left coalition headed by the SSDP. Because of competition from the SMP, KESK lost further ground in the next two elections, falling to 37 seats and 17.1% in 1970 and to 35 seats and 16.4% in 1972. Karjalainen was nevertheless again Prime Minister in 1970-71 and the party participated in subsequent centre-left combinations.

Having recovered to 39 seats and 17.6% in 1975, KESK provided the Prime Minister (Martti Miettunen) of centre-left coalitions in office until 1977, when it switched to a subordinate ministerial role. It slipped back to 36 seats and 17.3% in the 1979 elections (which it fought in alliance with the LKP), thereafter participating in SSDP-led coalitions until 1987. In 1980 Paavo Väyrynen was elected KESK chair at the age of 34. In 1982 the LKP became a constituent organization of KESK, which inched up to 38 seats and 17.6% in the 1983 elections. In 1986 the LKP reverted to independent status; but its support remained with KESK, which improved to 40 seats and 17.6% (again) in the 1987 elections, after which the party had the unusual experience of being in opposition for a whole parliamentary term. Its reward in the 1991 elections was a surge to a plurality of 55 seats and 24.8%, enabling it to form a centre-right coalition with KOK, the RKP/SFP and the Finnish

Christian Union (SKL), with KESK leader Esko Aho (37) becoming the youngest Prime Minister in Finnish history.

Contending with deepening economic recession, the Aho government also faced dissent within the coalition parties on its aim of accession to the European Union (EU), not least within KESK itself. An additional farm support package served to defuse opposition to the entry terms in KESK rural ranks, and accession was duly approved in the October 1994 referendum, although not before the anti-EU SKL had withdrawn from the coalition. Meanwhile, former KESK leader Väyrynen had been placed third in the first round of presidential elections in January 1994, winning only 19.5 of the vote. In the March 1995 legislative elections, moreover, KESK was the main loser, falling to 44 seats and 19.9%, and went into opposition to a five-party coalition headed by the SSDP.

KESK is an affiliate of the Liberal International and its European Parliament representatives sit in the European Liberal, Democratic and Reformist Group.

Ecological Party
Ekologinen Puolue (EP)
　　Address. c/o Eduskunta, Helsinki
　　Leadership. Eugen Parkatti (chair), Pertti Virtanen (parliamentary leader)

The EP was founded in 1990 as a populist formation aiming to provide a "non-ideological" alternative to the left-leaning Green Union. It failed to win representation in the 1991 Diet elections, but secured one seat on a 0.3% vote share in March 1995.

Finnish Christian Union
Suomen Kristillinen Liitto (SKL)
　　Address. Mannerheimintie 40, 00100 Helsinki
　　Telephone. (#358-0) 407477
　　Fax. (#358-0) 440450
　　Leadership. C.P. Bjarne Kallis (chair), Jouko Jääskeläinen (secretary)

The SKL is an evangelical party founded in 1958 to propagate Christian values in public life and to resist secularization. It won its first Diet seat in 1970 on a 1.1% vote share, advancing to four seats and 2.5% in 1972 and to nine seats and 3.3% in 1975 (when it benefited from the electoral slump of the Finnish Rural Party (SMP). After SKL candidate Raino Westerholm had won a respectable 9% of the vote in the 1978 presidential elections, the party retained nine seats on a 4.8% vote share in the 1979 Diet elections. It slipped back to three seats and 3.0% in 1983, while in 1987 its reduced share of 2.6% gave it five seats on the strength of local electoral alliances with the Centre

Party of Finland (KESK) and the Liberal People's Party (LKP). It advanced again in 1991, to eight seats and 3.1%, and opted for its first taste of government, joining a non-socialist coalition headed by KESK and including the conservative National Coalition and the Swedish People's Party. Opposed to Finnish accession to the European Union (as supported by its coalition partners), the SKL withdrew from the government in June 1994. In the March 1995 Diet elections it slipped to seven seats and 3.0% of the vote, remaining in opposition.

The SKL is affiliated to the Christian Democrat International.

Finnish Rural Party
Suomen Maaseudun Puolue (SMP)
   Address. Hämeentie 157, 00560 Helsinki
   Telephone. (#358-0) 790299
   Fax. (#358-0) 790299
   Leadership. Raimo Vistbacka (chair), Timo Soini (secretary)

The SMP is derived from the Finnish Smallholders' Party, which was launched in 1959 by a dissident faction of what later became the Centre Party of Finland (KESK). Led by the charismatic Veikko Vannamo, the breakaway party took an anti-establishment, "Poujadist" line, defending the rights of "forgotten Finland" and claiming that the parent party had neglected the interests of small farmers and small businessmen. Renamed the SMP after obtaining negligible support in the 1962 and 1966 elections, the party came to prominence in 1968 when Vennamo won over 11% in challenging incumbent Urho Kekkonen (KESK) for the presidency. It achieved a breakthrough in the 1970 parliamentary elections, winning 10.5% and 18 seats (mainly as the expense of KESK), and retained 18 seats in 1972, although it support slipped to 9.2%.

The SMP was then weakened by splits arising from criticism of Vennamo's authoritarian leadership style and right-wing opposition to his willingness to co-operate with parties of the left. In the 1975 elections the rump SMP slumped to two seats and 3.6%, recovering only partially to seven seats and 4.5% in 1979, in which year Vennamo stood down as leader and was succeeded by his son Pekka. The 1983 elections yielded another breakthrough for the SMP, which won 17 seats and 9.7% of the vote and thereafter entered government for the first time as part of a coalition headed by the Finnish Social Democratic Party (SSDP) and including KESK and the Swedish People's Party (RKP/SFP). In the 1984 municipal elections the SMP obtained over 600 council seats.

The SMP fell back to nine seats and 6.3% in the 1987 elections but nevertheless joined a four-party coalition headed by the conservative National Coalition and including the SSDP and the RKP/SFP. It withdrew from the coalition in August 1990 in protest against new pensions proposals, but lost further support to a resurgent KESK in the 1991 elections, falling to seven seats and 4.8% and remaining outside the resultant non-socialist coalition headed by KESK. Having been part of the unsuccessful opposition to Finnish accession to the European Union, the SMP almost disappeared from the Diet in the March 1995 elections, winning only one seat on a 1.3% vote share.

Finnish Social Democratic Party
Suomen Sosiaalidemokraattinen Puolue (SSDP)
   Address. Saariniemenkatu 6, 00530 Helsinki
   Telephone. (#358-0) 77511
   Fax. (#358-0) 712752
   Leadership. Paavo Lipponen (chair), Antero Kekkonen and Liisa Jaakonsaari (deputy chairs), Matti Puhakka (parliamentary group chair), Markku Hyvärinen (general secretary)

The party was founded in 1899 as the Finnish Workers' Party to represent the growing ranks of organized labour as well as landless labourers, adopting its present name in 1903, when Finland was still part of the Russian Empire. The advent of universal suffrage in 1906 enabled the SSDP to become the largest parliamentary party (with 37% of the vote in that year), but its reforms were blocked by the Tsar. Following Finland's declaration of independence in 1917, radical Social Democrats fought on the losing Red side in the 1918 civil war (and later founded the Finnish Communist Party), whereas the non-revolutionary majority led by Vainö Tanner made its peace with the victorious Whites and embarked on a reformist path in the independent Finnish Republic declared in 1919. Despite electoral competition from Communist-front formations and the powerful Agrarians, the Social Democrats were usually the strongest party in the inter-war period, but managed only one period of minority government (in 1926-27) before entering a "red-green" coalition with the Agrarians in 1937. The SSDP vote rose to 39.8% in 1939, whereupon Tanner not only backed Finland's losing popular cause in the 1939-40 Winter War with the USSR but also supported Finnish participation in Nazi Germany's invasion of the USSR in 1941 with the aim of recovering lost territory. The SSDP leadership rejected adhesion to the Communist-led Finnish People's Democratic League (SKDL) formed in 1944, but many pro-Soviet party sections defected to the new organization. Finland's defeat in 1944, combined with post-war Soviet regional ascendancy, resulted in Tanner being imprisoned in 1946-48 for wartime pro-German activities.

Having won only 25.1% of the vote in the 1945 elections, the SSDP remained in a coalition government with the SKDL and the Agrarians (later called the Centre Party, KESK), but internal strife between pro-Soviet left and anti-communist right was to fester for more than two decades. With its vote share remaining stable at around 26% in successive elections, the party participated in coalition governments in 1951 and 1954-57, the latter a centre-left combination with the Agrarians. In the 1956 presidential elections Karl-August Fagerholm of the SSDP was narrowly defeated by Urho Kekkonen (Agrarian). In 1957 Fagerholm was also defeated (by one vote) for the SSDP chair, the victor being a rehabilitated Tanner, whose return provoked a new phase of internal party strife. In the 1958 elections the SSDP lost its customary status as the biggest parliamentary party (and declined further in 1962). In 1959 left-wing dissidents broke away to form what became the Social Democratic League of Workers and Smallholders (TPSL), which won seven seats in the 1966 election in alliance with the SKDL. But the same contest yielded a major recovery for the SSDP to 27.2% of the vote, well ahead of its rivals. Moreover, the TPSL failed to win seats in the 1970 and 1972 contests, while successive SSDP-led centre-left coalitions--under Rafael Paasio (who had succeeded the 82-year-old Tanner as party leader in 1963), Mauno Koivisto and Kalevi Sorsa--confirmed the ascendancy of the SSDP's moderate wing. The party headed the poll in all four elections of the 1970s, but had fallen to 23.9% by 1979.

In January 1982 Koivisto was elected President of Finland as the SSDP candidate and a new centre-left coalition was formed under Sorsa's premiership. A strong SSDP advance in the 1983 elections, to 26.7%, enabled Sorsa to form another government embracing KESK, the Finnish Rural Party (SMP) and the Swedish People's Party (RKP/SFP). The March 1987 elections produced a setback for the SSDP, to 24.1% and 56 seats, only just ahead of the conservative National Coalition (KOK), which became the lead party in a new coalition that included the SSDP. At the 34th SSDP congress in June 1987 Sorsa was succeeded as party chair by Pertti Paasio (son of Rafael). The same congress adopted a new programme which defined the party's six central aims as being a world of co-operation, peace and freedom; coexistence with nature; the transfer of power from capital owners to working people; a shift from representative democracy to "an active civil state"; a culturally equal society; and a vigorous process of social reform. In February 1988 President Koivisto was elected to a second six-year term as candidate of the SSDP.

The March 1991 elections ended a quarter century of continuous SSDP government office,

the party slipping to 22.1% and 48 seats and going into opposition to a centre-right coalition. Having replaced Paasio as SSDP chair in November 1991, Ulf Sundqvist (an ethnic Swede) himself resigned the leadership in February 1993 over allegations of financial impropriety in his previous post as executive director of the STS-Bank. He was succeeded by Paavo Lipponen, who steered the party into supporting Finnish accession to the European Union in the October 1994 referendum, although rank-and-file SSDP opposition was considerable. In March 1995 Lipponen led the party to a major victory in legislative elections, its vote share rising to a post-1945 high of 28.3%, which yielded 63 seats out of 200. In April 1995 Lipponen formed a five-party "rainbow" coalition that included the RKP/SFP, KOK, the Left-Wing Alliance and the Green Union. Meanwhile, in Finland's first direct presidential elections in January-February 1994, SSDP candidate Martti Ahtisaari had won a second-round victory with 53.9% of the vote, having headed the first-round voting with 25.9%.

The SSDP is a member of the Socialist International and of the Party of European Socialists.

Green Union
Vihreä Liitto (VL or VIHR)
Address. Eerikinkatu 24/A7, 00100 Helsinki
Telephone. (#358-0) 693-3877
Fax. (#358-0) 693-3799
Leadership. Pekka Haavisto (chair), Tuija Brax (parliamentary group chair), Sirpa Kuronen (secretary)

The VL was formed in February 1987 as a co-operative body for various existing local and national environmentalist organizations, the latter including the Green Parliamentary Group (*Vihreä Eduskuntaryhmä*), which had won two seats in 1983. Presenting a mainstream environmentalist platform, the Greens increased to four seats in the March 1987 elections and to 10 in March 1991. They fell back to nine seats on a 6.5% vote share in March 1995 but nevertheless took ministerial office for the first time the following month, when Pekka Haavisto became Environment Minister in a five-party "rainbow" coalition headed by the Finnish Social Democratic Party.

Left-Wing Alliance
Vasemmistoliitto (VAS)
Address. Siltasaarenkatu 6/7krs, 00530 Helsinki
Telephone. (#358-0) 774741
Fax. (#358-0) 7747-4200
Leadership. Claes Andersson (chair), Katja Syvärinen and Kari UOTILA (vice-chairs), Esko Helle (parliamentary group chair), Ralf Sund (secretary)

VAS was launched in April 1990 at a Helsinki congress of representatives of the leading Communist and left-socialist groups, who took cognizance of the collapse of East European communism then in progress. Following the congress, the Finnish Communist Party (*Suomen Kommunistinen Puolue*, SKP) and its electoral front organization, the Finnish People's Democratic League (*Suomen Kansan Demokraattinen Liitto*, SKDL), voted to disband in favour of the new party, which adopted a left-socialist programme and declared its opposition to Finnish membership of the European Community, later Union (EC/EU), as favoured by most other parties.

The SKP had been founded in 1918 by the pro-Bolshevik wing of the Finnish Social Democratic Party (SSDP) and had remained banned until 1944, when Finland accepted its second military defeat in five years by the USSR. Reflecting Moscow's new influence in internal Finnish affairs, the SKDL front was created in 1944 and established a sizeable electoral constituency, winning 23.5% of the vote in 1945, becoming the largest parliamentary party in 1958-62 and participating in various centre-left coalitions until 1982. Meanwhile, the SKP had in 1969 split into majority "revisionist" and minority "Stalinist" wings, the latter being formally ousted from the party in 1984 and two years later launching its own Democratic Alternative (*Demokraattinen Vaihtoehtoe*, DEVA) electoral front, which achieved little more than to weaken the SKDL, whose electoral support slumped to 9.4% in 1987 against 4.2% for DEVA.

In its first general elections in March 1991, VAS won 10.2% of the vote and 19 seats, thereafter forming part of the opposition to the 1991-95 centre-right government. It was prominent in the unsuccessful "no" campaign in the October 1994 referendum on EU accession, acting as a focus for considerable anti-EU sentiment among SSDP activists. In a swing to the left in the March 1995 parliamentary elections, VAS advanced to 11.2% and 22 seats, subsequently being allocated two portfolios in a five-party "rainbow" coalition headed by the SSDP and also including the conservative National Coalition, the Swedish People's Party and the Green Union.

The party's single representative in the European Parliament sits in the Confederal European United Left group.

Liberal People's Party
Liberaalinen Kansanpuolue (LKP)
    Address. Frederikinkatu 58A/6, 00100 Helsinki
    Telephone. (#358-0) 440227
    Fax. (#358-0) 440771
    Leadership. Pekka Rytilä (chair), Kaarina Talola (general secretary)

The LKP was launched in 1965 as a merger of the Finnish People's Party (*Suomen Kansanpuolue*, SKP) and the Liberal Union (*Vapaamielisten Liitto*, VL), both descended from the pre-independence liberal movement by way of the National Progressive Party (*Kansallinen Edistyspuolue*), which had a significant following in the inter-war years (and provided two Finnish Presidents). Post-war divisions and electoral weakness led in 1950 to the formation of the SKP, which recovered some support and participated in various coalition governments in the 1950s and early 1960s. The more conservative VL, dating from 1951, obtained negligible electoral support prior to the 1965 merger creating the LKP.

The LKP won nine seats and 6.5% of the vote in 1966, but its support gradually declined in subsequent elections, to four seats and 3.7% in 1979. During this period it participated in many coalition governments of the centre-left parties. At a national congress in June 1982, the LKP voted to become a constituent group of the much larger Centre Party of Finland (KESK), while retaining its own identity. However, an unhappy experience in the 1983 elections impelled the LKP to resume independent status in June 1986, whereafter it won only 1.0% of the vote in 1987 and failed to gain representation. It was no more successful in 1991 and 1995 (when its share of the vote was 0.6%).

The LKP is a member party of the Liberal International.

National Coalition
Kansallinen Kokoomus (KK/KOK)
    Address. Kansakoulukuja 3, 00100 Helsinki
    Telephone. (#358-0) 69381
    Fax. (#358-0) 694-3702
    Leadership. Sauli Ninistoe (chair), Ben Zyskowicz (parliamentary group chair), Pekka Kivelä (secretary-general)

The moderate conservative KOK was founded in December 1918 following the victory of the anti-Bolshevik Whites in the civil war that ensued after the end of Russian rule. Although monarchist in sympathy, the new party reconciled itself with the republic declared in 1919 and participated in several inter-war coalitions, averaging around 15% of the vote. In the early 1930s it gravitated towards the semi-fascist Lapua rural movement, but KOK leader J.K. Paasikivi later broke with the far right. KOK participated in all five governments in office from 1939 to 1944 (providing the Prime Minister on two occasions) and thus shared responsibility for the conduct of the 1939-40 Winter War against the USSR and for Finland's participation in Nazi Germany's invasion of the USSR in 1941.

KOK was in opposition to successive centre-left coalitions from 1944 to 1958, its vote share fluctuating from a high of 17.3% in 1948 to a low of 12.8% in 1954. On the other hand, Paasikivi served in the powerful post of President from 1946 to 1956 and was instrumental in establishing a consensus on Finland's post-war policy of good relations with the USSR, as continued by his successor, Urho Kekkonen of what became the Centre Party (KESK), and therefore known as the "Paasikivi-Kekkonen line". Between 1958 and 1966 KOK participated in several coalition governments, including the first completely non-socialist administration since the war, formed in 1963 and headed by KESK. Having slipped to 13.8% in the 1966 elections, KOK reverted to opposition status and was to remain out of office for over two decades. Under the successive chairmanships of Juhta Rihtniemi (1965-71) and Harri Holkeri (1971-79), the party moved to a more centrist position, notably by endorsing the "Paasikivi-Kekkonen line". One consequence was the departure of traditionalist elements in 1973 to join the Constitutional Party of the Right. But KOK compensated by attracting additional support in the centre, rising steadily to 22.1% of the vote in 1983 and establishing itself as the second strongest party after the Finnish Social Democratic Party (SSDP).

KOK made another advance in the 1987 elections (to 23.1% and 53 seats) and proceeded to form a four-party coalition with the SSDP, the Swedish People's Party (RKP/SFP) and the Finnish Rural Party (SMP), with Holkeri becoming Finland's first KOK Prime Minister since 1944. The coalition was weakened by the withdrawal of the SMP in August 1990 and also faced sharply deteriorating economic conditions. In the March 1991 elections KOK slipped to 19.3% and 40 seats (the third largest contingent) and was obliged to accept a subordinate role in a four-party non-socialist coalition headed by KESK and also including the RKP/SFP and the Finnish Christian Union (SKL). In presidential elections in January 1994 the KOK candidate, Raimo Ilaskivi, came in fourth place in the first round with 15.2% of the vote. KOK strongly backed Finland's accession to the European Union, although internal strains were apparent when Deputy Prime Minister Pertti Salolainen resigned as KOK chair in June 1994 after some party members had criticized his role in the accession negotiations.

The general elections of March 1995 brought a further setback to KOK, which fell to 17.9% and 39 seats. It nevertheless opted to join a "rainbow" coalition headed by the SSDP and also including the RKP/SFP, the Left-Wing Alliance and the Green Union.

KOK is affiliated to the Christian Democrat International and the International Democratic Union; its representatives in the European Parliament are members of the European People's Party.

Progressive Finnish Party

Nuorsuomalainen Puolue (NSP)
  Address. c/o Eduskunta, Helsinki
  Leadership. Risto E.J. Penttilä (chair), Jukka Tarkka (parliamentary group chair)

Known popularly as the "Young Finns", the NSP was founded in 1994 as a radical pro-market party arguing that Finland needed a deregulated economy to compete in the European Union following accession at the beginning of 1995. In its first parliamentary elections in March 1995 it won two seats on a 2.8% vote share.

Swedish People's Party

Ruotsalainen Kansanpuolue/Svenska Folkpartiet (RKP/SFP)
  Address. Gräsviksgatan 14, PO Box 282, 00181 Helsinki
  Telephone. (#358-0) 694-2322
  Fax. (#358-0) 693-1968
  Leadership. Ole Norrback (chair), Elisabeth Rehn (1994 presidential candidate), Haakan Malm and Margareta Pietikäinen (deputy chairs), Eva Biaudet (parliamentary group chair), Peter Stenlund (secretary)

The RKP/SFP was founded in 1906, when Finland was still a duchy of the Russian Empire, to represent the political and social interests of the ethnic Swedish population, which was then economically dominant. Being ethnically based, the party has traditionally encompassed a wide spectrum of ideological preferences, although it is usually characterized as centrist with progressive leanings. Its share of the overall vote has shown a gradual decline over recent decades (from 8.4% in 1945 to 5.1% in 1995), in line with the falling proportion of ethnic Swedes in the population; but its post-war representation in the Diet has remained rather more constant (the 1995 tally being 12 seats, compared with a high of 15 in 1951 and a low of 10 in the elections of the 1970s). The RKP/SFP's parliamentary contingent customarily includes the single deputy returned by the ethnic Swedish inhabitants of the autonomous Aaland Islands, where the main local parties, modelled on those of Sweden, form the Aalands Coalition for Finnish national elections.

The RKP/SFP has been in government more often than it has been in opposition, having participated in about two-thirds of all Finnish coalitions formed since 1906, including centre-left, centre-right and ideologically-mixed combinations. The pattern after 1945 was RKP/SFP participation in successive centre-left coalitions headed by the Finnish Social Democratic Party (SSDP) or the Centre Party (KESK), although in 1963-66 it was a member of the first entirely non-socialist governments since the war. Subsequent centre-left combinations also included the RKP/

SFP as a pivotal member, while in 1987 it joined a four-party coalition headed by the conservative National Coalition (KOK) and also including the SSDP and the Finnish Rural Party (SMP). Having slipped from 13 to 12 seats in the 1991 elections, the RKP/SFP joined another non-socialist coalition, this time headed by KESK and including KOK and the Finnish Christian Union.

For the January-February 1994 presidential elections the RKP/SFP candidate was Defence Minister Elisabeth Rehn, who surprised many (given her ethnicity and gender) by taking second place in the first round, with 22% of the vote, and thus going forward to the second round, in which she was defeated by the SSDP candidate but won a creditable 46.1% of the vote. The RKP/SFP supported Finland's accession to the European Union (as approved in the October 1994 referendum) and was allocated one of Finland's 16 seats in the European Parliament. Having retained 12 seats in the March 1995 parliamentary elections, it accepted two portfolios in a five-party "rainbow" coalition headed by the SSDP and also including KOK, the Left-Wing Alliance and the Green Union.

The RKP/SFP is affiliated to the International Democrat Union and the Liberal International; its representative in the European Parliament sits in the European Liberal, Democratic and Reformist Group.

Other Parties

Alliance for Free Finland (*Vapaan Suomen Liitto*, VSL), which won 1.0 percent of the vote in 1995.

Communist Workers' Party (*Kommunistinen Työväenpuolue*, KTP), led by Timo Lahdenmäki and Heikki Männikö, founded in 1988 by a Stalinist faction of the Democratic Alternative (later part of the Left-Wing Alliance), contested the 1991 and 1995 elections under the slogan "For Peace and Socialism", winning only 0.2% of the vote on the latter occasion.

Constitutional Party of the Right (*Perustuslaillinen Oikkeistopuolue*, POP), founded in 1973 by right-wing dissidents of the National Coalition and the Swedish People's Party, opposed to the then established Finnish foreign policy of close relations with the USSR, won single seats in 1975 and 1983, unrepresented in the Diet since then.

Finnish Pensioners' Party (*Suomen Eläkeläisten Puolue*, ELÄK), led by Erkki Pulli and Saara Mölsä, launched in 1986, with minimal electoral impact, winning 0.1% of the vote in 1995).

Joint Responsibility Party (*Yhteisvastuu Puolue*, YVP), which won 0.1% in the 1995 elections.

Natural Law Party (*Luonnonlain Puolue*, LLP), the Finnish branch of the world-wide natural law political movement, took 0.3% in the 1995 elections.

Women's Party (*Naisten Puolue*, NP), which won 0.3% in the 1995 elections.

France

Capital: Paris   **Population:** 58,350,000 (1995E)

The French Republic has one of the world's most developed multi-party systems that is perpetually fluid but essentially unchanging in its broad ideological structure. Under the 1982 constitution of the Fifth Republic as amended, an executive President, who appoints the Prime Minister, is elected for a seven-year term by universal suffrage of citizens above the age of 18 years, the requirement being an absolute majority of the votes cast either in the first round of voting or, if necessary, in a second. Legislative authority is vested in a bicameral Parliament (*Parlement*) consisting of (i) a 321-seat Senate (*Sénat*) whose members are indirectly elected for a nine-year term (a third being renewed every three years), 309 by electoral colleges of national and local elected representatives in the metropolitan and overseas departments/ territories and 12 by the *Conseil Supérieur des Français de l'Étranger* to represent French citizens living abroad; and (ii) a 577-member National Assembly (*Assemblée Nationale*) directly elected for a five-year term by universal adult suffrage. For the March 1986 Assembly elections the then Socialist-led government introduced a system of department-based proportional representation for the first time under the Fifth Republic; however, the incoming centre-right administration enacted legislation providing for a return to the previous system of majority voting in two rounds in single-member constituencies.

Under laws enacted in March 1988 and January 1990, state funding is payable to (i) political parties with parliamentary representation, in proportion to the size of their respective groups; (ii) all accredited presidential candidates (with the two reaching the second round receiving additional sums), according to a complex formula for the reimbursement of varying proportions of the ceilings set for campaign expenses; and (iii) Assembly election candidates who receive at least 5% of the first-round vote, at a rate equivalent to 10% of the applicable expenses ceilings. The total amount disbursed in 1990 under category (i) was FF260,267,857 (about $51 million), of which, for example, the Socialist Party, then substantially the largest Assembly party, received FF95,530,134 (about $18.8 million).

Assembly elections held on March 21 and 28, 1993, resulted as follows: Rally for the Republic (RPR) 247 seats (with 20.4% of the first-round vote); Union for French Democracy 213 (19.1%); Socialist Party (PS) 54 (17.6%); French Communist Party 23 (9.2%); Left Radical Movement 6 (0.9%); various right 24 (4.9%); various left 10 (3.6%). Presidential elections on April 23 and May 7, 1995, resulted in Jacques Chirac of the RPR being elected in the second round with 52.6% of the votes cast, against 47.4% for the PS candidate.

Democratic Force

Force Démocrate (FD)

Address. 133bis rue de l'Université, 75007 Paris

Telephone. (#33-1) 4555-7575

Fax. (#33-1) 4551-8953

Leadership. François Bayrou (president), Pierre Méhaignerie (honorary president), Dominique Baudis (executive president), Jean Arthuis (vice-president), Philippe Douste-Blazy (secretary-general)

The FD was launched at a conference held in Lyons in November 1995 as the successor of the Centre of Social Democrats (*Centre des Sociaux Démocrates*, CSD). The centrist, Christian democratic and pro-European CDS was founded in May 1976, although its constituent elements had their roots in a 19th-century movement aimed at reconciling Catholics with the Third Republic (1871–1940). After World War II these forces were represented by the Popular Republican Movement (*Mouvement Républicain Populaire*, MRP) led by Georges Bidault and other wartime resistance leaders, which was the strongest parliamentary party until the 1951 elections and took part in most Fourth Republic governments until its demise in 1958. Bidault was himself Prime Minister in 1946 and 1949–50; other MRP premiers were Robert Schuman (1947–48) and Pierre Pflimlin (1958). The immediate antecedents of the CDS were the Democratic Centre (*Centre Démocrate*, CD) and the Democracy and Progress Centre (*Centre Démocratie et Progrès*, CDP), both of which emerged under the Fifth Republic.

The CD had been launched in March 1966 by Jean Lecanuet, who had scored 15.9% in the 1965 presidential elections. In the 1969 contest most CD elements had backed Alain Poher (who received 23.3% in the first round and 41.8% in the second), although some had supported the successful Gaullist candidate, Georges Pompidou, thus abandoning the previous centrist policy of acting as a balancing force between the right-wing "majority" parties and the left-wing opposition. The CDP had been founded after the 1969 elections by centrist supporters of President Pompidou, notably Jacques Duhamel, Joseph Fontanet and René Pleven. In the 1973 Assembly elections the CD and the CDP had returned 24 and 34 deputies respectively, the former as part of the Reformers' Movement (created in 1971 by various centrist groups then outside the government "majority") and the latter in alliance with the ruling Gaullists and Independent Republicans. In the first round of the 1974 presidential elections the CDP had supported Jacques Chaban-Delmas (Gaullist) and the CD Valéry Giscard d'Estaing (Independent Republican), but both parties had contributed to the victory of the latter in the second round. Both parties had joined the resultant centre-right government headed by Jacques Chirac and had been prominent in further moves towards greater cohesion of the centre, notably the six-party Federation of Reformers created in June 1975, prior to the launching of the CDS in May 1976 under the presidency of Lecanuet.

For the 1978 Assembly elections the CDS joined with other non-Gaullist "majority" parties to form the Union for French Democracy (UDF), as part of which it returned 35 of the 124 UDF deputies and continued to participate in centre-right coalitions that included the Gaullist Rally for the Republic (RPR). In 1981 it backed Giscard d'Estaing's unsuccessful re-election bid and was reduced to 25 seats in the June 1981 Assembly elections won by the Socialist Party (PS). In opposition, the CDS elected Pierre Méhaignerie (a former Agriculture Minister) to succeed Lecanuet in March 1982, after which the party sought to establish a more autonomous identity within the UDF. In the 1986 Assembly elections the CDS participated in the victory of the centre-right parties, being rewarded with seven portfolios in the "cohabitation" government formed by Chirac.

In the first round of the 1988 presidential elections the CDS backed Raymond Barre, but the former Prime Minister managed only third place (with 16.5%) and was eliminated, whereafter the CDS endorsed Chirac in his losing contest with incumbent François Mitterrand (PS) in the second round. In the June 1988 Assembly elections the CDS shared in the defeat of the centre-right alliance, although its individual seat tally of 49 out of 129 for the UDF showed electoral resilience. The CDS was then in opposition for five years, during which it established an independent Assembly identity as the *Union du Centre* (UDC) and presented its own list in the 1989 European Parliament elections, winning seven seats. In the 1993 Assembly elections the CDS declined to give automatic support to better-placed centre-right candidates in the second round, although it remained a UDF component and increased its seat tally to 57 in the centre-right landslide. Included prominently in the further "cohabitation" government headed by Edouard Balladur (RPR), the CDS returned fully to the UDF fold in the 1994 European elections, winning four seats on a joint UDF/RPR list.

In the absence of a UDF candidate in the 1995 presidential elections, the CDS initially backed Balladur as the more centrist of the two RPR contenders. After Balladur had been eliminated in the first round, the CDS supported the victorious candidacy of Chirac in the second, being rewarded with a strong ministerial presence in the resultant centre-right government, including the portfolios of Education (François Bayrou), Labour (Jacques Barrot) and Economic Development (Jean Arthuis). In September 1995 Arthuis was appointed to the more important post of Economy and Finance Minister following the dismissal of Alain Madelin of the Popular Party for French Democracy. In the new government appointed in November the new FD held four ministerial posts.

The CDS is affiliated to the Christian Democrat International and its four members of the European Parliament sit in the European People's Party group.

Ecology Generation
Génération Écologie (GE)
    Address. 3 rue Roquépine, 75008 Paris
    Telephone. (#33-1) 4494-3006
    Fax. (#33-1) 4494-3014
    Leadership. Brice Lalonde

The GE was established in 1990 by Brice Lalonde, a presidential candidate for Friends of the Earth (*Amis de la Terre*) and other groups in 1981 (when he received 3.9% of the first-round vote) and subsequently Environment Minister in the 1991-92 government led by Édith Cresson of the Socialist Party (PS). Then more sympathetic to the Socialists than the rival Greens, the GE nonetheless refused to enter the subsequent Bérégovoy administration headed by the PS. The GE won 7% of the vote at the March 1992 regional elections, before slipping to less than 1% in the 1993 Assembly elections, despite a reciprocal support agreement with the Greens. Contesting the June 1994 European Parliament poll as an independent list, the GE recovered to just over 2% of the vote, without winning a seat. Following the victory of Jacques Chirac of the Rally for the Republic in the April-May 1995 presidential elections, a former GE member, Corinne Lepage, accepted appointment as Environment Minister in the new centre-right government.

French Communist Party
Parti Communiste Français (PCF)
    Address. 2 place du Colonel Fabien, 75940 Paris
    Telephone. (#33-1) 4040-1212
    Fax. (#33-1) 4040-1356
    Leadership. Robert Hue (national secretary), Alain Bocquet (National Assembly group president), Hélène Luc (Senate group president)

The PCF came into being in December 1920 when a majority of delegates at the Tours congress of the Socialist Party (then the SFIO) voted to join the Soviet-run Communist International (Comintern), whereas the anti-Bolshevik minority opted to maintain the SFIO. From 1921 to 1933 the PCF pursued a hardline policy of class war and opposition to all "bourgeois" parties, including the SFIO. From 1934, however, it gave priority to the struggle against fascism and supported (without joining) the 1936-38 Popular Front government headed by the Socialists. The PCF approved the August 1939 non-aggression pact between Nazi Germany and the USSR, but reverted to anti-fascist mode following the German invasion of the USSR in June 1941, its activists subsequently playing a prominent role in the French Resistance. The party joined the post-liberation government formed by Gen. de Gaulle in 1944, although it was denied any powerful portfolios. With the onset of the Cold War, it was excluded from the 1947 government headed by Paul Ramadier (SFIO) and was to remain in opposition for 34 years.

Strongly based in the General Confederation of Labour (the largest trade union body), the PCF outvoted the SFIO in most elections under the Fourth Republic, winning 25-29% of the vote. Having opposed the creation of the Fifth Republic in 1958, the PCF saw its vote fall to 18.9% in Assembly elections later that year but recovered to 20-22% in the contests of the 1960s and 1970s. In December 1966 the then PCF leader, Waldeck Rochet, signed an agreement with the Socialist-led Federation of the Democratic and Socialist Left (FGDS) providing for reciprocal voting support in the March 1967 Assembly elections. The arrangement resulted in PCF representation almost doubling, to 73 seats, although this tally was reduced to 34 in elections held in June 1968 in the aftermath of the "May events" that nearly toppled President de Gaulle. The PCF repudiated the Soviet-led military intervention that suppressed the 1968 "Prague Spring" in Czechoslovakia, although it remained in most respects an orthodox Marxist-Leninist party aligned to Moscow and opposed to French membership of NATO and the European Community. In 1969 the Communist presidential candidate, Jacques Duclos, came a creditable third in the first round, with 21.3% of the vote.

Following the election of François Mitterrand as leader of the new Socialist Party (PS) in 1971, the PCF signed a common programme with the PS and the Left Radical Movement (MRG) in 1972. The union yielded major left-wing gains in the March 1973 Assembly elections, which restored Communist representation to 73 seats. From 1974, however, serious strains developed within the alliance, not least because the steady growth of Socialist strength was viewed by the PCF as imperilling the union's equilibrium and as encouraging the PS to revert to a centre-left strategy. At its 22nd congress in February 1976 the PCF repudiated the thesis of the dictatorship of the proletariat and came out in favour of a specifically French model of socialism. The party nevertheless kept its distance from the revisionist "Eurocommunist" line then being advanced by the Italian Communists. Mainly because of PS and MRG resistance to further PCF nationalization proposals, no agreement was reached on a revised common programme for the March 1978 Assembly elections, in which the PCF presented its own manifesto. Second-round reciprocal support nevertheless applied, with the result that the PCF rose to 86 seats amid a left-wing advance that fell short of an overall majority.

The PCF candidate in the watershed May 1981 presidential elections was the then party leader, Georges Marchais, who obtained 15.4% of the first-round vote, whereafter the PCF swung behind Mitterrand in the second round and contributed to the PS leader's victory. In the resultant Assembly elections of June 1981, second-round support arrangements among the left-wing parties yielded most benefit to the Socialists, who won an absolute majority, while the PCF fell to 44 seats. The French Communists nevertheless entered government for the first time since 1947, obtaining four portfolios in the new PS-led administration. But strains quickly developed between the PS and PCF in government, notably over the latter's refusal to condemn the imposition of martial law in Poland and its opposition to deployment of new US nuclear missiles in Europe. In the European Parliament elections of June 1984 the PCF took only 11.2% of the vote, less than in any election since 1932. When Laurent Fabius of the PS formed a new government in July 1984, the Communists refused to participate, on the grounds that he was equivocal on giving priority to economic expansion and job-creation. In September 1984 the PCF deputies broke with the PS-led Assembly majority and voted against the government for the first time in the budget debate of December 1984.

At the PCF congress of February 1985 the party leadership under Marchais firmly resisted the demand of a "renovator" group for changes in policy and for greater internal party democracy. The Assembly elections of March 1986 produced a further setback for the PCF, which slipped to 35 seats and 9.8% of the vote (in part because some of its working-class support in areas of high immigrant population switched to the far-right National Front). Further internal strains and defections served to harden the Marchais line, which prevailed at the PCF conference in Nanterre in June 1987, when hardliner André Lajoinie was adopted as PCF presidential candidate. Prior to its 26th congress in December 1987, the PCF central committee expelled Pierre Juquin for having announced his presidential candidacy as a Communist "renovator". In the first round of the April-May 1988 presidential contest that saw the re-election of Mitterrand, Lajoinie recorded the PCF's lowest-ever national vote share (6.8%), while Juquin got 2.1%. In the June 1988 Assembly elections the PCF recovered somewhat to 11.3% in the first round, but slipped to representation of 27 seats.

Still resisting pressure for change in the PCF, Marchais responded to the collapse of East

European communism in 1989-90 and of the USSR in 1991 by claiming that he had been "duped" by his erstwhile comrades in that part of the world. The party suffered a further setback, to 9.2% of the first-round vote, in the March 1993 Assembly elections which brought the right back to governmental power, but displayed resilience in its strongholds by retaining 23 seats. Avowedly because of ill-health, Marchais formally vacated the PCF leadership at the party's 28th congress in January 1994 and was succeeded by Robert Hue, who was assigned the title "national secretary" as part of a decision to abandon "democratic centralism" in party decision-making. The Communist list won only 6.9% of the vote in the June 1994 European Parliament elections (and seven of the 87 French seats). In the April-May 1995 presidential elections, Hue took fifth place in the first round with 8.6% of the vote, whereupon the PCF backed the unsuccessful candidacy of Lionel Jospin (PS) in the second round.

The Greens
Les Verts

Address. 107 ave Parmentier, 75011 Paris
Telephone. (#33-1) 4355-1001
Fax. (#33-1) 4908-9744
Leadership. Dominique Plancke (national secretary), Dominique Voynet (1995 presidential candidate)

The Greens were organized as a unified mainstream environmentalist party in January 1984, officially embracing the suffix Ecologist Confederation-Ecologist Party (*Confédération Écologiste-Parti Écologiste*). This cumbersome nomenclature reflected the complexities of the movement's evolution since it fielded René Dumont for the presidency in 1974 and received 1.3% of the first-round vote. In the 1978 Assembly elections the earlier movement presented 200 candidates under the banner *Écologie 78*, winning 2.1% of the vote, while the *Écologie Europe* list took 4.4% in the 1979 European Parliament elections. Encouraged by that relative success, the movement in February 1980 joined with other groups to create the *Mouvement d'Écologie Politique* (MEP), which in 1981 backed the presidential candidacy of Brice Lalonde, then leader of Friends of the Earth and later founder of Ecology Generation (GE). As Ecology Today (*Aujourd'hui l'Écologie*), the MEP presented 82 candidates in the 1981 Assembly elections, winning 1.2% of the first-round vote (and no seats). In November 1982 the MEP became a political party called *Les Verts-Parti Écologiste* (VPE), which won some 6% of the overall vote in the 1983 municipal elections and elected several dozen councillors. The adoption of the longer title referenced above occurred at a Clichy congress (in January 1984) which achieved a merger of the VPE with various other environmentalist groups.

Standing as *Les Verts-Europe Écologie*, the formation again failed to win representation in the 1984 European Parliament elections, when its vote fell to 3.4%, and was no more successful in the 1986 Assembly elections, when it managed only 1.1% of the first-round vote. Subsequent internal divisions were reflected in the rejection by a Paris general assembly in September 1986 of a policy paper presented by the movement's four spokesmen urging rapprochement with like-minded groups. Four new spokesmen were elected from among the "fundamentalist" wing, one of whom, Antoine Waechter, stood in the 1988 presidential elections, winning 3.8% of the vote. The Greens declined to present official candidates for the June 1988 Assembly elections in protest against the return to constituency-based polling as opposed to the proportional system used in 1986. Returning to the electoral fray, they polled strongly in the 1989 European Parliament elections on a joint list with other groups, winning 10.6% of the vote and nine seats.

The 1993 Assembly elections yielded a 4% first-round vote for the Greens but no seats, despite an agreement with the GE not to run competing candidates. At their annual conference in November 1993 the Greens moved sharply to the left, electing Dominique Voynet as 1995 presidential candidate, while the disaffected Waechter later broke away to form the Independent Ecological Movement. Standing separately in the 1994 European Parliament elections, neither the Greens nor the GE gained sufficient support to win seats. Standing as the sole Green candidate in the 1995 presidential contest, Voynet was placed eighth of nine candidates, taking 3.3% of the first-round vote.

Left Radical Movement
Mouvement des Radicaux de Gauche (MRG)

Address. 3 rue la Boétie, 75008 Paris
Telephone. (#33-1) 4742-2241
Fax. (#33-1) 4742-8293
Leadership. Jean-Michel Baylet (president)

The MRG originated in July 1972 as a left-wing faction of the historic Radical Party which endorsed the common programme issued the previous month by the Socialist Party (PS) and the French Communist Party (PCF), whereas the Radical majority then led by Jean-Jacques Servan-Schreiber declined to join the new Union of the Left. Initially organized as the Radical-Socialist Study and Action Group, the left-wing faction was expelled in October 1972 and contested the March 1973 Assembly elections on a joint list with the PS called the *Union de la Gauche Socialiste et*

Démocrate, taking 11 of the 100 seats won by the alliance. The faction formally constituted itself as the MRG in December 1973 under the presidency of Robert Fabre, taking as its watchword the famous Radical slogan "*Pas d'ennemi à gauche*".

In contentious negotiations on revision of the common programme for the March 1978 Assembly elections, the MRG caused the first formal breakdown of talks in September 1977, when Fabre rejected the extensive nationalization programme demanded by the PCF. In the 1988 elections the MRG presented its own policy platform which differed from those of the PS and PCF in important respects, but the electoral alliance with the PS was maintained, and reciprocal support arrangements between the PS/MRG and the PCF again came into play in the second round. The result was that the MRG took 10 of the 113 seats won by the PS/MRG alliance. Immediately after the polling, Fabre repudiated the original common programme of the left and resigned the MRG presidency. He was succeeded by Michel Crépeau, who favoured the continuation of left-wing union, whereas the MRG right advocated reversion to a centre-left orientation and eventually, for the most part, rejoined the parent Radical Party or other centre-left groupings.

Crépeau stood as the MRG candidate in the first round of the 1981 presidential elections, winning only 2.2% of the vote. In the second round the MRG backed François Mitterrand of the PS, whose victory resulted in the appointment of a left-wing government in which Crépeau obtained a ministerial portfolio. In the June 1981 Assembly elections the MRG increased its seat tally to 14 by virtue of a further alliance with the victorious PS. Thereafter, the MRG participated in the PS-led government throughout its five-year tenure, while regularly seeking to assert its distinct political identity. In the 1984 European Parliament elections, for example, it was the principal component of a centre-left/ecological list called *Entente Radicale Écologiste pour les États-Unis d'Europe*, which secured 3.3% of the vote and no seats. The MRG also contested the 1986 Assembly elections in its own right (the move to proportional representation obviating the need for a joint list with the PS), but mustered only 0.4% of the total vote and two seats. The party nevertheless maintained a significant presence in local and regional government.

In opposition in 1986-88, the MRG experienced much internal agonizing about whether to maintain its leftward orientation or to turn to the centre. In the event, it was again allied with the PS in the 1988 Assembly elections held after the re-election of

Mitterrand to the presidency. With majority voting by constituency having been reinstated, the MRG obtained nine seats and was allocated three ministerial posts in the resultant PS-led coalition. It remained in government for the next five years, but had little success in its attempts to build a "second force" within the then "presidential majority". In the March 1993 Assembly elections the MRG shared in the heavy defeat of its Socialist allies, although left-wing voting discipline and the MRG's resilience in its remaining strongholds enabled the party to retain six seats with a first-round vote share of 0.9%.

Again in opposition, the MRG was temporarily strengthened by the adhesion of controversial businessman Bernard Tapie, who had served two brief spells as a minister in 1992-93 and had been elected as a "presidential majority" candidate in the 1993 Assembly elections. In the June 1994 European Parliament elections Tapie headed the MRG's *Énergie Radical* list, which won 13 seats on an impressive vote share of 12.1%, while the PS under the new leadership of Michel Rocard performed so badly that Rocard had to resign. Having backed Rocard's efforts to build a broader social democratic party, the MRG was much less enthusiastic about his left-wing successor, Henri Emmanuelli, and initially announced that its leader, Jean-François Hory, would contest the 1995 presidential elections with the aim of rallying the centre-left opposition. In the event, the selection of Lionel Jospin as the PS candidate served to restore the PS/MRG axis, in that Hory withdrew his candidacy and the MRG contributed to Jospin's powerful, albeit losing, performance in the presidential contest. Shortly after the second-round polling (in May 1995), the MRG's "Tapie era" finally ended when the former tycoon (by now bankrupt) was sent to prison after being convicted of attempted match-fixing when he owned Marseilles football club.

Hory resigned as MRG president in October 1995 and was succeeded by Jean-Michel Baylet in January 1996, when a party congress also elected six vice-presidents. These included the former Socialist minister, Bernard Kouchner, whose Reunite (*Réunir*) grouping, founded in November 1994, was merged into the MRG. With a view to sharpening its public image, the party decided to adopt the one-word title "Radical" for campaigning purposes, thereby creating much scope for confusion as between it and the historic Radical Party. In March 1996 a Paris court ordered it to revert to the MRG name within four months.

The MRG's 11 representatives in the European Parliament are the largest contingent in the European Radical Alliance group.

Movement for France

Mouvement pour la France (MPF)

Leadership. Philippe de Villiers

The MPF was created in November 1994 as the successor to The Other Europe (*L'Autre Europe*), which had been created to contest the June 1994 European Parliament election, principally on the initiative of the French-British financier, Sir James Goldsmith. Opposed to the Maastricht process of European economic and monetary union, it also condemned the 1993 GATT world trade liberalization agreement, arguing that Western Europe needed to protect its industry and employment levels from Asian competition based on cheap labor. In the European poll The Other Europe list obtained 12.4% of the vote and 13 of the 87 French seats. In the 1995 presidential elections, MPF leader Philippe de Villiers (a former member of the Union for French Democracy) was placed seventh out of nine first-round candidates, winning 4.7% of the vote.

National Centre of Independents and Peasants

Centre National des Indépendants et Paysans (CNIP)

Address. 146 rue de l'Université, 75007 Paris

Telephone. (#33-1) 4062-6364

Fax. (#33-1) 4556-0263

Leadership. Jean-Antoine Giansily (president), Pierre Olivier Mahaux (secretary-general)

The CNIP is derived from the *Centre National des Indépendants (CNI)*, which was formed in July 1948 on the initiative of Roger Duchet and René Coty and quickly succeeded in federating most independent parliamentarians of the moderate right. The CNI became the CNIP in January 1949 when it absorbed the small peasant-based *Parti Républicaine de la Liberté*. Between 1951 and 1962 the CNIP took part in various coalition governments, with party members Antoine Pinay being Prime Minister in 1952 and Coty serving as President in 1952-59. In July 1954 the CNIP was joined by Gaullist dissidents of the *Action Républicaine et Sociale* who had supported the Pinay government. In 1958 the CNIP supported the return to power of Gen. de Gaulle and the creation of the Fifth Republic, reaching its electoral peak in the November 1958 Assembly elections, in which it won 22% of the vote and 132 seats. One of these was filled by Jean-Marie Le Pen, who was later to become leader of the far-right National Front (FN).

The CNIP's influence declined in the 1960s. Deeply divided over de Gaulle's policy of withdrawal from Algeria, it finally broke with him in October 1962. In Assembly elections the following month it lost almost all its representation, as its outgoing deputies either were defeated or transferred to the "majority" camp as Independ-ent Republicans (later the nucleus of the Republican Party). In 1967-68 the CNIP was in alliance with Jean Lecanuet's *Centre Démocrate*, but proposals for a formal merger came to nothing. Although nominally an opposition leader during this period, CNIP honorary president Pinay declined invitations to stand against de Gaulle and Georges Pompidou in the presidential elections of 1965 and 1969 respectively. In 1974 the CNIP supported the successful presidential candidacy of Valéry Giscard d'Estaing (Independent Republican) and thereafter became one of the four main parties of the "presidential majority", being represented from 1976 in successive governments headed by Raymond Barre.

The CNIP contested the March 1978 Assembly elections in alliance with other non-Gaullist "majority" parties (winning nine seats), although it did not join the Union for French Democracy formed on the eve of the poll. Having backed Giscard d'Estaing's unsuccessful re-election bid in 1981, the CNIP was reduced to five seats by the Socialist landslide in the June 1981 Assembly elections, despite an electoral pact with the other centre-right parties. Another pact for the 1986 Assembly elections brought the CNIP a similar level of representation as a component of the victorious centre-right front, although its influence was further eroded by the Socialist victory in the 1988 presidential and Assembly elections. Through this period the CNIP maintained a significance presence in the Senate, where its representatives sat in broader centre-right groups. Continuance of the relationship in the 1993 Assembly elecions was impaired by the CNIP's public support for the anti-immigration policies of the FN.

National Front

Front National (FN)

Address. 8 rue du Général Clergerie, 75116 Paris

Telephone. (#33-1) 4727-5666

Fax. (#33-1) 4755-9667

Leadership. Jean-Marie Le Pen (president), Bruno Gollnisch (secretary-general)

The right-wing populist FN was founded in October 1972 on an anti-immigration, law and order, and strongly pro-market platform, bringing together various groups and personalities of the far right. The party has consistently denied that it is racist, pointing to the presence of French Afro-Caribbeans in its ranks and claiming that it welcomes non-whites provided they fully embrace French culture and civilization. Its founder and leader, Le Pen, had served in the elite Parachute Regiment and had been a National Assembly deputy in 1956-62, initially as a member of the *Union de Défense des Commerçants et Artisans* (UDCA) led by Pierre Poujade and later under the auspices of the National Centre of Independents and Peasants (CNIP), and had been closely identified with the *Algérie Française* movement. The FN made little impact in the 1970s, winning only 2.5% of the vote in the 1973 Assembly elections and 3% in 1978, while Le Pen took only 0.7% in the first round of the 1974 presidential contest and was unable to stand in 1981 because he could not obtain the required sponsorship of at least 500 national or local elected representatives.

The return to national power of the left in 1981 and increasing public concern about immigration yielded a surge of support for the FN, which successfully repackaged itself as a legitimate force on the right of the centre-right opposition. This approach brought the first far-right electoral success in 25 years when, in the March 1983 municipal elections, an FN candidate was returned to one of the new district councils in the Paris region, while later in the year the then FN secretary-general, Jean-Pierre Stirbois, won 16.7% of the first-round vote in a local by-election in Dreux, thus bringing about a second-round alliance between the FN and the Gaullist Rally for the Republic (RPR). The FN's major breakthrough came in the European Parliament elections of June 1984, when to the surprise of many observers it won 10.9% of the French vote and 10 seats. In the March 1985 regional elections it slipped to 8.7% of the first-round vote, and was weakend in late 1985 by a split which produced the rival *Front d'Opposition Nationale*. However, in the March 1986 Assembly elections (held under proportional representation), it secured 35 of the 577 seats, winning some 2.7 million votes (9.7%), many of them in working-class areas of high immigrant population where previously the French Communist Party had held sway. As a result of simultaneous regional elections, several RPR regional presidents were elected or re-elected with FN support.

Although the FN initially decided to support Jacques Chirac (then RPR Prime Minister) in the 1988 presidential elections, in May 1986 it withdrew its backing because of Chirac's insistence on abandoning proportional representation for Assembly elections. In January 1987 Le Pen announced his own presidential candidacy, thereby generating dissension within the RPR between those who rejected any co-operation with the far right and those who recognized that the centre-right candidate might need FN backing in the second round. In September 1987 Le Pen caused a major controversy when he publicly referred to Nazi extermination camps as a "detail" of the history of World War II, although he later expressed regret for the remark. The episode did him little damage in the 1988 presidential elec-

tions, in which he took fourth place in the first round with 14.4% of the vote (and declined to give endorsement to Chirac in the second). However, in Assembly elections in June 1988 (for which constituency-based majority voting again applied), the FN lost all but one of its seats despite achieving a first-round vote share of 9.7%. The successful FN candidate was Yann Piat (in the Var), but she was expelled from the FN in October 1988, whereafter she joined the Republican Party (and was assassinated in 1994).

The FN regained an Assembly seat in a by-election for Dreux in December 1989, when Marie-France Stirbois (widow of Jean-Pierre, who had died in a car crash in November 1988) won 61.3% of the second-round vote. Le Pen acclaimed the result as demonstrating public support for the FN's opposition to immigration and to "French decadence", and called for the repatriation of all foreigners who had come to France since 1974. While not opposing French membership of the European Union (EU), the FN strongly endorsed the old Gaullist concept of a "Europe of nation states" and therefore was part of the opposition to the EU's Maastricht Treaty on closer union, which obtained wafer-thin referendum endorsement by French voters in September 1992. In the March 1993 Assembly elections, the FN failed to win representation, despite a national first-round vote share of 12.4% and an election campaign in which the "respectable" centre-right parties took up many of the FN's concerns about immigration and the rule of law.

In the June 1994 European Parliament elections the FN slipped back to 10.5% (winning 11 of the 87 French seats). In the 1995 presidential elections, however, Le Pen took fourth place in the first round with an all-time FN voting high of 15.0% (4,573,202 votes). He again declined to give endorsement to Chirac of the RPR in the second round, announcing that he would cast a blank ballot in protest against "a detestable choice between two left-wing candidates". The FN continued its advance in municipal elections in June 1995, trebling its complement of councillors to 1,075 and winning control of three substantial southern towns (Toulon, Orange and Marignane). According to a post-election statement by Le Pen, the FN would apply "national preference" in the municipalities under its control, so that immigrants and foreigners would no longer get equal treatment in the allocation of subsidized housing, welfare benefits and public-sector jobs.

The FN maintains contact with other European parties of the radical right. Its representatives in the European Parliament are the largest component of the "unattached" contingent.

Popular Party for French Democracy
Parti Populaire pour la Démocratie Française (PPDF)

   Address. 259 blvd Saint Germain, 75007 Paris
   Telephone. (#33-1) 4222-6951
   Fax. (#33-1) 4222-5949
   Leadership. Hervé de Charette and Jean-Pierre Raffarin (joint chairs)

The PPDF was created in July 1995 from the Perspectives and Realities Clubs (*Clubs Perspectives et Réalités*, CPR) grouping, which had opted to convert itself into a political party. Founded in 1965 by Jean-Pierre Fourcade, the CPR had acted as a "think tank" for the broad Union for French Democracy (UDR), providing a political home for centrist intellectuals reluctant to join a traditional political party. Many of its leading members were associated with the Republican Party component of the UDF, notably its chair from 1982 to 1984, Jean-François Deniau, who had been a minister and European commissioner under the presidency of Valéry Giscard d'Estaing (1974–81). Having lost the French presidency in 1981, Giscard d'Estaing himself took the chairmanship of the CPR until 1989. Following the centre-right victory in the 1993 Assembly elections, the CPR obtained ministerial representation, Hervé de Charette being Foreign Minister at the time of the formation of the PPDF. Another PPDF minister, Alain Madelin, was dismissed from the government in August 1995 after failing to persuade Prime Minister Juppé (of the Gaullist Rally for the Republic) of the need for drastic measures to curb the budget deficit.

Radical Party
Parti Radical

   Address. 1 place de Valois, 75001 Paris
   Telephone. (#33-1) 4261-5632
   Fax. (#33-1) 4261-4965
   Leadership. André Rossinot (president), Aymeri de Montesquieu (secretary-general)

Founded in 1901 from pre-existing Radical groups sharing a commitment to anti-clericalism and the separation of Church and State, the Radicals are the oldest of the current crop of French parties. Their rarely-used full title is Radical Republican and Radical-Socialist Party (*Parti Républicain Radical et Radical-Socialiste*, PRRRS), reflecting the party's history as the mainstay of the Third Republic (1871–1940) and its frequent co-operation with the real left-wing parties under both the Third and Fourth Republics. The party is also often referred to as the *Parti Valoisien* after its headquarters address in Paris, from where it provided many Prime Ministers up to and after World War I, including Georges Clemenceau in 1906-09 and 1917-19. Its celebrated slogan was "*Pas d'ennemi à gauche*" ("No enemy to the left"),

on which basis it participated in the anti-fascist Popular Front government formed in 1936 under the leadership of what was then the SFIO and much later became the Socialist Party (PS). Despite a post-war electoral decline, the Radicals remained a focal point in the frequent coalition building of the Fourth Republic until its demise in 1958, providing the Prime Ministers of no less than 12 governments.

Traditionally eschewing rigid structures, the Radical Party suffered a series of splits in 1954-56, when Pierre Mendès-France moved the party to the left and tried to impose more internal discipline. By late 1958 Mendès-France and his left-wing followers had become the minority and subsequently broke away to participate in the formation of the Unified Socialist Party (PSU), part of which later joined the PS. During the first decade of the Fifth Republic (1958-68) the rump Radicals under the leadership of René Billères participated in moves towards union of the non-Communist left, joining the Federation of the Democratic and Socialist Left (FGDS) in 1965 and participating in the FGDS advance in the 1967 Assembly elections. After the May 1968 political and social crisis, however, Maurice Faure moved the party back to a centrist posture, which was consolidated following the election of Jean-Jacques Servan-Schreiber to the party presidency in 1971. The Radical majority's refusal to subscribe to a new union of the left involving the Socialists and the French Communist Party (PCF) caused the exit of the left-wing minority in 1972 to form what became the Left Radical Movement (MRG).

In the 1974 presidential elections the Radicals backed the successful candidacy of Valéry Giscard d'Estaing (Independent Republican), but only after the first round and in return for specific policy commitments. Under the Giscard d'Estaing presidency the Radicals were included in successive centre-right coalitions, although their initial return to government was controversial: appointed Minister of Reforms, Servan-Schreiber was dismissed within a fortnight for criticizing the proposed resumption of French nuclear tests in the Pacific. Pursuing attempts to forge greater unity among the smaller centrist and centre-left parties, the Radicals in July 1977 absorbed the Movement of Social Liberals (*Mouvement des Sociaux Libéraux*, MSL), which had been formed earlier in the year by Gaullist dissidents led by Olivier Stirn. Shortly before the March 1978 Assembly elections the Radicals joined the Union for French Democracy (UDR), returning seven deputies under the UDF banner. Shortly after their 79th annual conference in October 1979 the Radical Party was rejoined by an MRG dissident group opposed to the union of the left strategy.

The Radicals backed Giscard d'Estaing in his failed attempt to secure re-election in 1981 and won only two seats amid the PS landslide in the June 1981 Assembly elections. In October 1981 Stirn relaunched the MSL as a separate group, while declaring that he continued to regard himself as a Radical. In 1984 the MSL was again dissolved, although Stirn himself opted to form the Centrist and Radical Union (*Union Centriste et Radicale*, UCR). In the March 1986 Assembly elections (held under proportional representation) the Radicals recovered to seven seats as a component of the UDF and subsequently obtained three ministerial posts in the new centre-right coalition headed by Jacques Chirac of the Gaullist Rally for the Republic (RPR). However, the 1988 Assembly elections that followed the re-election of Mitterrand to the presidency reduced Radical representation to three seats and the party to opposition status.

A convinced pro-European party, the Radicals backed ratification of the Maastricht Treaty on European union in the September 1992 referendum. The party returned to government as a result of the centre-right victory in the March 1993 Assembly elections, again forming part of the UDF alliance and being allocated ministerial responsibilities as a consequence. In June 1994 the Radicals contested the European Parliament elections on the joint UDF/RPR list, winning one seat. In the 1995 presidential elections the party initially preferred Edouard Balladur (RPR) over Jacques Chirac (also RPR), but swung behind the victorious Chirac in the second round. It was rewarded with one portfolio in the subsequent Juppé government. In March 1996 Rossinot came third in the contest to succeed Giscard d'Estaing as UDF leader.

Through the UDF, the Radical Party is affiliated to the International Democrat Union. Its member of the European Parliament sits in the European Liberal, Democratic and Reformist Group.

Rally for the Republic
Rassemblement pour la République (RPR)
Address. 123 rue de Lille, 75007 Paris
Telephone. (#33-1) 4955-6300
Fax. (#33-1) 4551-4479
Leadership. Alain Juppé (president), Jean-François Mancel (secretary-general)

Although established under its present name in December 1976, the broadly conservative RPR is directly descended from the *Rassemblement du Peuple Français* (RPF) established in April 1947 by Gen. Charles de Gaulle, who had been head of the London-based Free French forces during World War II and then Prime Minister of the first post-liberation government (1944-46). Formed

with the central objective of returning de Gaulle to power, the RPF became the strongest Assembly party in 1951 (with 118 seats), but was weakened in 1952 by the creation of the dissident *Action Républicaine et Sociale* (ARS). When members of the rump RPF accepted ministerial posts in 1953, de Gaulle severed his links with the party, which was dissolved as a parliamentary group. Gaullist deputies then created the *Union des Républicains d'Action Sociale* (URAS), which became the *Centre National des Républicains Sociaux* (CNRS) in February 1954. Following de Gaulle's return to power in mid-1958 amid the collapse of the Fourth Republic, the movement was reconstituted for the November 1958 Assembly elections as the *Union pour la Nouvelle République* (UNR), which won a plurality of 188 seats. Inducted as President of the Fifth Republic in January 1959, de Gaulle appointed Michel Debré (UNR) as his Prime Minister.

Under the right-oriented Debré premiership a left-wing Gaullist faction formed the *Union Démocratique du Travail* (UDT), which was reunited with the UNR following the replacement of Debré by the technocratic Georges Pompidou in April 1962. In the November 1962 Assembly elections the UNR-UDT increased its dominance by winning 219 seats. In December 1965 de Gaulle won popular election for a second presidential term, comfortably defeating left-wing candidate François Mitterrand in the second round with 55.2% of the vote. For the March 1976 Assembly elections the UNR-UDT adopted the title *Union des Démocrates pour la Cinquième République* (UDCR), which slipped to 200 seats and henceforth relied on Valéry Giscard d'Estaing's Independent Republicans for a parliamentary majority. In November 1967 the UDCR title was formally adopted by the party, which at the same time absorbed a faction of the (Christian democratic) *Mouvement Républicain Populaire* (MRP) and other groups further to the left. In the wake of the May 1968 national crisis, the Gaullists registered a landslide victory in Assembly elections in June, winning 292 seats under the designation *Union pour la Défense de la République* and continuing in office under the reformist premiership of Maurice Couve de Murville. The new parliamentary group preferred the slightly different title *Union des Démocrates pour la République* (UDR), which was subsequently applied to the party as a whole.

De Gaulle resigned in April 1969 after unexpectedly being denied referendum approval of constitutional and regional reform proposals. He was succeeded in June elections by Pompidou, who won a comfortable 57.6% victory over a centrist candidate in the second round. The new Gaullist Prime Minister was Jacques Chaban-Delmas, seen as representative of the UDR's modernist wing, but corruption charges and other difficulties resulted in his replacement by the orthodox Pierre Messmer in July 1972. In the Assembly elections of March 1973 the UDR slumped to 183 seats, but Messmer continued as Prime Minister at the head of a coalition with centrist parties. Pompidou's death in office in April 1974 precipitated presidential elections in May, when Chaban-Delmas as the UDR candidate was eliminated in the first round (with only 14.6% of the vote). Many Gaullist voters preferred the more dynamic Giscard d'Estaing (Independent Republican), who won a narrow second-round victory over Mitterrand and proceeded to appoint Jacques Chirac (UDR) to head a government with strong centrist representation. Increasing strains between President and Prime Minister yielded Chirac's resignation in August 1976, whereupon the Gaullists ceased to hold the premiership but continued as part of the ruling coalition. In December 1976 Chirac engineered the conversion of the UDR into the RPR, which became his power base in increasingly acrimonious competition between the Gaullist and Giscardian wings of the "majority". In March 1977 Chirac was elected mayor of Paris, defeating the centrist candidate backed by the President.

After Chirac had failed to create a "majority" alliance for the March 1978 Assembly elections, the RPR slipped to 154 seats, against 124 for the new Union for French Democracy (UDF), grouping the Giscardian centrist parties. In the June 1979 European Parliament elections the RPR list (called *Défense des Intérêts de la France*, reflecting traditional Gaullist doubts about the European idea) managed only 16.3% (and fourth place) as against the UDF's 27.6%. In the 1981 presidential elections, moreover, Chirac took a poor third place in the first round (with 18% of the vote) and was eliminated; although he said that he would personally vote for Giscard d'Estaing in the second round in May, his failure to urge RPR supporters to do likewise was seen as contributing to the incumbent's narrow defeat by Mitterrand. In the resultant Assembly elections in June the RPR shared in the centre-right's decimation by the Socialist Party, slumping to 88 seats notwithstanding the presentation of single centre-right candidates in over three-quarters of the metropolitan constituencies under the banner of the *Union pour la Majorité Nouvelle* (UMN).

In opposition from 1981 to 1986, the RPR launched an internal modernization and rejuvenation programme, with Chirac bringing forward a new generation of leaders more favourable to European integration and more in tune with the changing social composition of France. On the basis of a declaration signed in April 1985, the RPR and the UDF presented a joint manifesto in the March 1986 Assembly elections as well as single candidates for many seats. In the resultant centre-right victory, the RPR emerged with 155 deputies in the new 577-seat Assembly elected by proportional representation, ahead of the UDF, so that Chirac was again appointed Prime Minister of a coalition government in which the RPR held 21 posts and the UDF parties 17. During the ensuing two years of "cohabitation" between a Socialist President and a Gaullist Prime Minister, the RPR experienced internal divisions about how to respond to the growing strength of the far-right National Front (FN) led by Jean-Marie Le Pen, with some Gaullists rejecting any links with the FN and others arguing that the party could not be ignored, especially since the FN was making inroads into RPR support. The debate intensified in January 1987 when Le Pen announced his own candidacy in the 1988 presidential elections, having previously indicated that the FN would support Chirac. After some equivocation, the RPR leader announced in May 1987 that there would be no national alliance between the RPR and the FN, while not prohibiting the informal RPR/FN voting co-operation that was already a factor in some localities and regions.

In his second tilt at the presidency in April-May 1988, Chirac took second place in the first round (with 19.9% of the vote) and thus went forward to the second against Mitterrand, losing to the incumbent by 45.98% to 54.02%. The relatively wide margin of the RPR candidate's defeat was attributed in part to the refusal of Le Pen to instruct his four million first-round supporters to vote for Chirac in the second. Assembly elections in June 1988 (held by constituency-based majority voting) were contested by the RPR in an alliance with the UDF called the *Union du Rassemblement et du Centre* (URC), but not only did the centre-right parties lose their majority but also the RPR for the first time returned fewer deputies (127) than the UDF (129). In opposition over the next five years, the RPR and UDF contested the 1989 European Parliament on a joint list (winning 28.9% of the vote) and in June 1990 announced the creation of yet another alliance, called the *Union pour la France* (UPF), amid much talk about the need for a unified party in the next legislative elections and a single presidential candidate. In reality, the RPR and the UDF continued their long struggle for supremacy on the centre-right, with the added spice of resumed personal rivalry between Chirac and Giscard d'Estaing. Also divisive in this period was the Maastricht Treaty on European union, which was supported wholeheartedly by the UDF, whereas important sections of the RPR (although not Chirac himself) campaigned for a "no" vote in the September 1992 referendum that yielded a very narrow majority for French ratification.

As widely forecast, the Assembly elections of March 1993 produced a landslide victory for the RPR/UDF alliance, which won 80% of the seats on a 40% first-round vote share. Crucially, the RPR emerged with 247 of the 577 seats, against 213 for the UDF parties, so that Chirac was able to nominate the new Prime Minister. His choice fell on Edouard Balladur, a former RPR Finance Minister and supposedly a Chirac loyalist, who was charged with running the government while the RPR leader concentrated on mounting a third attempt on the presidency. A leading RPR campaigner against the Maastricht Treaty, Philippe Séguin, was elected president of the National Assembly in April 1993. In the event, Balladur became so popular as Prime Minister that he was persuaded to renege on a pledge not to enter the presidential race. The upshot was that both Chirac and Balladur contested the 1995 elections, with the latter securing backing from within the UDF (which did not put up a candidate). Meanwhile, the RPR/UDF alliance was maintained for the June 1994 European Parliament elections, in which their combined vote slipped to 25.6%, yielding 28 of the 87 French seats.

After a slow start, Chirac's campaigning skills and command of the powerful RPR party machine, plus a late-breaking phone-tapping scandal in which Balladur was implicated, took the RPR leader to second place in the first round of the presidential balloting in April 1995 (with 20.8% of the vote), behind the Socialist candidate but ahead of Balladur (18.6%). Chirac therefore went into the second round in May and was at last victorious with 52.6% of the vote, despite again being denied second-round endorsement by the FN. Pledging himself to restoring "social cohesion", Chirac named Foreign Minister Alain Juppé (who had been the new President's campaign manager in his role as RPR secretary-general) to head a new coalition government maintaining approximate balance between the RPR and the UDF. At a party congress in October 1995 Juppé was formally elected to the RPR presidency in succession to Chirac, receiving 93% of the ballots in an uncontested election.

Claiming a membership of some 400,000, the RPR is a member of the International Democrat Union and of the European Democrat Union. Its representatives in the European Parliament sit in the Union for Europe group, the biggest component of which is *Forza Italia*.

Republican Party
Parti Républicain (PR)
  Address. 105 rue de l'Université 75007 Paris
  Telephone. (#33-1) 4062-3030
  Fax. (#33-1) 4555-9276
  Leadership. François Léotard (president), José Rossi (secretary-general)

The centrist PR was formed in May 1977 as a merger of the National Federation of Independent Republicans (*Fédération Nationale des Républicains Indépendants*, FNRI), the Social and Liberal Generation (*Génération Sociale et Libérale*, GSL), Act for the Future (*Agir pour l'Avenir*) and various support committees which had backed Valéry Giscard d'Estaing in his successful bid for the presidency in 1974. The PR's social liberal and strongly pro-European orientation was closely based on the theses advanced by Giscard d'Estaing his 1977 book *Démocratie Française*.

The FNRI had been established in June 1966 by Giscard d'Estaing as leader of a modernizing faction that had broken away from the National Centre of Independents and Peasants (CNIP) in 1962 in order to be able to criticize government policy while remaining part of the ruling "majority". On founding the FNRI Giscard d'Estaing himself had left the government of Georges Pompidou (although other FNRI representatives had continued to participate) and had led the new party to significant advances in the 1967 and 1968 Assembly elections (to 42 and 61 seats respectively) on the basis of his celebrated "*Oui, mais*" ("Yes, but") line of qualified support for the Gaullist-led government. In April 1969 Giscard d'Estaing had effectively supported the winning "no" side in the constitutional referendum which had yielded the resignation of President de Gaulle, whereupon the FNRI had backed the victorious Pompidou in the June 1969 presidential elections. The FNRI leader had then resumed his former post as Economy and Finance Minister, retaining it in successive Gaullist-led governments under the Pompidou presidency, while the FNRI had slipped to 55 seats in the 1973 Assembly elections.

Following Pompidou's death in office in April 1974, Giscard d'Estaing had been elected President in May as candidate of the FNRI and other centrist formations, taking second place in the first round (with 32.9% of the vote) and winning a narrow 50.7% victory in the run-off against François Mitterrand of the Socialist Party (PS). He had proceeded to appoint Jacques Chirac (Gaullist) to head a government with strong centrist representation, including his principal FNRI lieutenant, Michel Poniatowski, at the powerful Interior Ministry. Growing strains between the Giscardian and Gaullist wings of the "majority" from 1975 had resulted in Chirac's resignation in August 1976 and his replacement by a non-Gaullist (Raymond Barre), whereafter Chirac had relaunched the Gaullist party as the Rally for the Republic (RPR). The superior organization of the new RPR over the FNRI and other centrist parties (and the challenge to presidential authority which the RPR represented) had been highlighted in March 1977 when Chirac had defeated a candidate backed by the President in elections for the important post of mayor of Paris.

Seeking to build an effective counterweight to the RPR for the 1978 Assembly elections, the new PR participated in the formation of the broader Union for French Democracy (UDF), winning 71 of the 124 UDF seats. PR representatives took prominent portfolios in the reconstituted Barre government, but suffered from association with scandals such as the De Broglie Affair. In 1981 the PR and the rest of the UDF endorsed Giscard d'Estaing's re-election bid, although the President chose to stand as a "citizen-candidate" without specific party attribution. Following his narrow defeat by Mitterrand in the second round, the PR shared in the decimation of the UDF in the June 1981 Assembly elections, retaining only 32 seats. After five years in opposition, however, the PR shared in the centre-right's victory in the March 1986 Assembly elections, winning 59 seats in its own right and accordingly taking a prominent role in the resultant centre-right "cohabitation" government headed by Chirac of the RPR.

In mid-1987 the then PR president and government minister, François Léotard, disappointed Chirac by announcing that the PR would not support the RPR leader in the first round of the 1988 presidential elections, but rather would put up its own candidate. After speculation that Léotard would run himself, in September 1987 the PR gave its backing to Barre (not a PR member). However, the former Prime Minister managed only third place in first round of voting in April 1988 (with 16.5%) and was eliminated, whereafter the PR backed Chirac in his losing contest with Mitterrand in the second round. In the June 1988 Assembly elections the PR shared in the defeat of the centre-right alliance, although its individual seat tally of 58 out of 129 for the UDF showed electoral resilience. The PR was then in opposition for five years, during which it established itself as the organizational core of UDF, although the traditional reluctance of the centrist parties to develop party structures outside parliament continued to be apparent.

In the landslide victory of the RPR/UDF alliance in the March 1993 Assembly elections, the PR took 104 of the 213 seats won by the UDF and was accordingly allocated important portfolios in the new centre-right "cohabitation" government headed by Edouard Balladur of the RPR. The PR was subsequently tainted by a series of corruption scandals that necessitated the resignations of several of its ministers, including in October 1994 the then PR president and Industry and Foreign Trade Minister, Gérard Longuet, amid allegations of irregular party financing activities. The February 1994 murder of PR deputy Yann Piat (once a member of the far-right National Front) added to the party's poor public image. The decision of Giscard d'Estaing (by now heading the UDF) not to contest the 1995 presidential elections deprived the PR of its obvious candidate, with the result that the party opted for Balladur as the more centrist of the two RPR contenders. After Balladur had been eliminated in the first round, the PR supported the victorious candidacy of Chirac in the second, being rewarded with a strong ministerial presence in the resultant centre-right government, including the portfolios of Defence (Charles Millon), Agriculture (Philippe Vasseur) and Small Businesses (Jean-Pierre Raffarin). In June 1995 François Léotard was elected to resume the PR presidency in succession to Longuet.

The PR's five members of the European Parliament sit in the (Christian democratic) European People's Party group.

Social Democratic Party
Parti Social-Démocrate (PSD)
    Address. 191 rue de l'Université, 75007 Paris
    Telephone. (#33-1) 4753-8441
    Fax. (#33-1) 4705-7553
    Leadership. Philippe Déchâtre, (president), André Santini (secretary-general)

The PSD was established in December 1973 as the Movement of Democratic Socialists of France (*Mouvement des Démocrates Socialistes de France*, MDSF) by a faction of the Socialist Party (PS) opposed to the common programme issued by the PS and the French Communist Party in 1972. Claiming to enshrine the authentic socialist tradition of Jean Jaurès and Léon Blum, the MDSF advocated centrist unity and joined both the Reformers' Movement and the Federation of Reformers in the mid-1970s. The first MDSF vice-president, Émile Muller, won 0.7% of the vote in the first round of the 1974 presidential elections, whereafter the MDSF backed the successful candidacy of Valéry Giscard d'Estaing in the second. Having shortened its name to Movement of Democratic Socialists (MDS), the party joined the broader Union for French Democracy (UDF) created in 1978, as part of which it returned four deputies in the 1978 Assembly elections. It lost them all in the landslide to the PS in the 1981 elections which followed the election of François Mitterrand (PS) to the presidency.

The MDSF transformed itself into the PSD in

October 1982, at the same time absorbing some other social democratic elements. It regained representation in the 1986 Assembly elections as part of the UDF, being allocated one portfolio in the resultant "cohabitation" government headed by Jacques Chirac of the (Gaullist) Rally for the Republic (RPR). In the 1988 presidential elections the PDS backed the unsuccessful candidacies of Raymond Barre in the first round and of Chirac in the second, being reduced to three seats in the ensuing Assembly elections and going into opposition. Still part of the UDF, it increased to seven seats in the landslide to the centre-right in the 1993 Assembly elections and was part of the joint UDF/RPR list in the 1994 European Parliament elections, being allocated one seat. In the 1995 presidential elections it supported Edouard Balladur as the more centrist of the two RPR candidates in the first round, switching to the victorious Chirac in the second.

The PSD member of the European Parliament sits in the (Christian democratic) European People's Party group.

Socialist Party
Parti Socialiste (PS)

Address. 10 rue de Solférino, 75007 Paris

Telephone. (#33-1) 4556-7700

Fax. (#33-1) 4556-7874

Leadership. Lionel Jospin (first secretary), Pierre Moscovici (secretary)

The party was founded in April 1905 as the French Section of the Workers' International (*Section Française de l'Internationale Ouvrière*, SFIO), being a merger of the Socialist Party of France (inspired by Jules Guesde) and the French Socialist Party (led by Jean Jaurès). The SFIO sought to rally pre-1914 labour opposition to war within the Second International, but a majority of the party regarded World War I as one of French national defence (one notable exception being Jaurès, who was assassinated in July 1914 by a nationalist fanatic). At its December 1920 congress in Tours the SFIO was split when a majority of delegates voted for membership of the Communist International (Comintern) and thus founded the French Communist Party (PCF), while the minority maintained the SFIO as a non-revolutionary party. Having supported Radical Party administrations from 1924, the SFIO became the largest party in the 1936 elections under the leadership of Léon Blum, who formed a Popular Front government with the Radicals, supported externally by the PCF. In opposition from 1938, the "reconstituted" SFIO went underground following the French surrender to Nazi Germany in 1940; it played an active part in the resistamce and also participated in the Algiers Committee set up by Gen. de Gaulle as leader of the Free French.

Following the liberation of France in 1944, the SFIO joined a provisional government headed by de Gaulle, becoming the third largest Assembly party in the 1945 elections with 139 seats, behind the PCF and the (Christian democratic) Popular Republican Movement, and retaining this ranking in both 1946 elections, although its representation fell to 93 seats. Eschewing alliance with the PCF in favour of centre-left co-operation, the SFIO headed the first two Fourth Republic governments (under Blum in 1946-47 and Paul Ramadier in 1947), instituting an extensive nationalization programme. In 1947 Vincent Auriol of the SFIO was elected President of France, and in the 1951 Assembly elections the SFIO recovered to 104 seats. Although it fell back to 95 seats in the 1956 elections, in 1956–57 the then SFIO leader, Guy Mollet, was Prime Minister of the Fourth Republic's longest-lasting government, playing a major role in the creation of the European Economic Community. However, internal dissension and defections over the role of the Mollet government in the 1956 Suez crisis and over the SFIO's support for a French-ruled Algeria were intensified by the participation of Mollet and other SFIO ministers in the national unity government formed by de Gaulle on the collapse of the Fourth Republic in mid-1958. In Assembly elections in November 1958 the SFIO slumped to 40 seats, following which the party leadership supported the installation of de Gaulle as President of the Fifth Republic. The SFIO nevertheless refused to participate in the Gaullist-led government formed in January 1959 and was to remain in opposition for over two decades.

Having recovered somewhat to 66 seats in the 1962 Assembly elections, the SFIO in September 1965 joined with the Radicals and the small Convention of Republican Institutions (CIR) to form the Federation of the Democratic and Socialist Left (*Fédération de la Gauche Démocratique et Socialiste*, FGDS). Elected president of the FGDS was the CIR leader, François Mitterrand, who as leader of the former Democratic and Social Union of the Resistance (*Union Démocratique et Sociale de la Résistance*, UDSR) had participated in successive Fourth Republic governments and had opposed Gen. de Gaulle's return to power in 1958. As candidate of the FGDS, and supported by the PCF and other left-wing formations, Mitterrand took de Gaulle to the second round in the 1965 presidential elections (held by direct suffrage), winning 44.8% of the vote. In the 1967 Assembly elections the FGDS benefited from a second-round support pact with the PCF, winning a total of 121 seats. However, in further elections held in June 1968 in the wake of the May "events" the FGDS retained only 57 seats, amid a landslide to the Gaullists. This defeat heightened disagreements among the FGDS constituent groupings, in light of which Mitterrand resigned from the presidency in November 1968, shortly before the Radicals decided against joining a unified party based on the FGDS.

Notwithstanding the effective collapse of the FGDS, the SFIO pursued the goal of a broader "new" socialist party on the basis of a merger with Mitterrand's CIR and the Union of Clubs for the Renewal of the Left (*Union des Clubs pour le Renouveau de la Gauche*, UCRG). On the eve of the May 1969 presidential elections an intended founding congress of the new party was held at Alfortville, but the CIR refused to back the presidential candidacy of SFIO right-winger Gaston Defferre (mayor of Marseilles), who went on to score an ignominious 5% of the vote in the first round. Subsequently, the CIR did not participate when a new Socialist Party was proclaimed at the Issy-les-Moulineaux congress of July 1969, as a merger of the SFIO and the UCRG, whose leader, Alain Savary, was elected PS first secretary (and Mollet bowed out after 23 years as SFIO leader). However, renewed efforts to bring the CIR into the new party reached a successful conclusion in June 1971 with the holding of a "congress of socialist unity" at Epinay, with Mitterrand being elected first secretary of the enlarged PS.

Under Mitterrand's leadership, the PS adopted a strategy of "union of the left", signing a common programme with the PCF and the Left Radical Movement (MRG) in June 1972 that featured wide-ranging nationalization plans. On the basis of the programme, the left made major gains in the Assembly elections of March 1973, when the PS and the MRG (standing as the Union of the Socialist and Democratic Left) jointly returned 102 deputies, including 89 Socialists. The following year Mitterrand contested presidential elections as the agreed candidate of virtually the entire left in both rounds of voting, but was narrowly defeated by Valéry Giscard d'Estaing (Independent Republican) in the second round, receiving 49.2% of the vote. In 1975 the PS was further enlarged when it was joined by the minority wing of the Unified Socialist Party (*Parti Socialiste Unifié*, PSU) led by Michel Rocard and also by a "third component" consisting mainly of affiliated members of the Socialist-led CFDT trade union federation. However, the steady growth of PS strength engendered serious strains in the party's alliance with the PCF, culminating in the failure of the left to agree on a revised common programme for the March 1978 Assembly elections. In that contest reciprocal support arrangements were operated by the left-wing par-

ties in the second round, but the PS tally of 103 seats (plus 10 for the MRG) was disappointing, even though the PS could claim to have become the strongest single party with around 23% of the first-round vote.

Standing as the PS candidate in the May 1981 presidential elections, Mitterrand obtained 25.9% in the first round, which was also contested by PCF and MRG candidates; backed by the entire left in the second round, he defeated incumbent Giscard d'Estaing by 51.8% to 48.2%, thus becoming President at his third attempt. Assembly elections in June 1981 gave the Socialists their first-ever absolute majority, of 285 seats out of 491. The new PS-led government, which included MRG and PCF ministers, was headed by Pierre Mauroy, while Lionel Jospin succeeded Mitterrand as PS first secretary. The Mauroy government proceeded to implement extensive nationalization measures, but was quickly obliged to abandon plans for state-led economic expansion in the interests of containing inflation and preventing currency depreciation. The PCF withdrew from the government in July 1984 when Mauroy was replaced as Prime Minister by Laurent Fabius, who faced considerable unrest in the party and country over the government's switch to orthodox economic policies. In the Assembly elections of March 1986 (held under proportional representation) the PS lost its absolute majority, although it remained the largest party with 206 seats and 31.6% of the vote. It accordingly went into opposition to a centre-right coalition headed by Jacques Chirac of the (Gaullist) Rally for the Republic (RPR), with whom President Mitterrand was obliged to govern in uneasy political "cohabitation".

In opposition, the PS undertook a reassessment of its economic policies, including its traditional commitment to nationalization, and advocated a broad alliance of "progressive" forces against the centre-right. But the party's relations with the PCF remained badly strained, not least because of the growing influence of the "moderate" PS faction led by Rocard, who favoured realignment towards the centre. In the 1988 presidential elections Mitterrand was opposed in the first round by two Communist candidates (one official) as well as by Chirac for the RPR and Raymond Barre for the centrist Union for French Democracy (UDF). He headed the poll with 34.1% of the vote, whereupon all the left-wing parties backed him in the second round, in which he easily defeated Chirac by 54.01% to 45.98%. In new Assembly elections in June 1988 (for which constituency-based majority voting was reinstated), the PS increased its representation to 260 seats out of 577, short of an overall majority but sufficient to underpin a PS-led government headed by Rocard that included the MRG and independent centrists. Immediately after the presidential contest, former Prime Minister Mauroy succeeded Jospin as PS first secretary.

Legislative setbacks and disagreements with Mitterrand provoked Rocard's resignation in May 1991 and his replacement by Édith Cresson (PS), who became France's first woman Prime Minister. She failed to stem plummeting support for the government and was replaced in April 1992 by Pierre Bérégovoy, a Mitterrand loyalist and hitherto Finance Minister. In January 1992, moreover, former Prime Minister Fabius, also a Mitterrand loyalist, was elected to succeed Mauroy as PS first secretary, following an extraordinary party congress in December 1991 at which delegates had accepted that only free-market policies could achieve economic growth. The Bérégovoy government had some success in restoring stability, and in September 1992 secured referendum approval of the controversial Maastricht Treaty on European union, albeit by a very narrow majority. But public disquiet at continuing economic recession was aggravated by a series of corruption and other scandals involving prominent PS politicians. Particularly damaging to the party was the allegation that during his premiership Fabius and other ministers had allowed the dissemination of HIV-contaminated blood for transfusion to haemophiliacs.

The PS went down to a widely-predicted heavy defeat in the March 1993 Assembly elections, retaining only 54 seats on a 17.6% first-round vote share and going into opposition to another "cohabitation" government of the centre-right. In the immediate aftermath, Rocard took over the PS leadership from Fabius and embarked upon an attempt to convert the party into a broader-based social democratic formation oriented towards the centre. However, unresolved internal party divisions contributed to a poor performance in the June 1994 European Parliament elections, in which the PS list managed only 14.5% (and 15 of the 87 French seats), compared with 23.6% in the 1989 contest. Rocard immediately resigned as party leader and was succeeded by Henri Emmanuelli, a former National Assembly president identified with the traditional PS left. Straitened financial circumstances, necessitating the sale of the PS headquarters building in Paris, and the implication of PS officials in further corruption cases added to the party's problems in the run-up to the 1995 presidential elections.

An attempt to draft the outgoing president of the European Commission, Jacques Delors, as the PS presidential candidate was rebuffed by Delors himself in December 1994. In February 1995 a special PS congress in Paris endorsed former party leader Jospin as presidential candidate, on the basis of a primary election among party members in which the former Education Minister had easily defeated Emmanuelli, winning 66% of the votes. Closely supported by Delors, Jospin confounded the pundits by mounting an impressive presidential campaign and heading the first-round voting in April 1995, with 23.3% of the vote. He was defeated by Chirac of the RPR in the second round, but his tally of 47.4% as the candidate of the left served to restore Socialist morale after two years of turmoil. In June 1995 Jospin replaced Emmanuelli as PS first secretary and declared his intention to carry out a complete reform of party structures and policies before the Assembly elections due in 1998. The previous month Emmanuelli had received a suspended one-year prison sentence for receiving illicit campaign contributions as PS treasurer in the 1980s. Seven months after leaving office, Mitterrand died in January 1996 at the age of 79.

The PS is a member party of the Socialist International; its representatives in the European Parliament sit in the Party of European Socialists group.

Union for French Democracy

Union pour la Démocratie Française (UDF)
  Address. 12 rue François I, 75008 Paris
  Telephone. (#33-1) 4359-7959
  Fax. (#33-1) 4225-0381
  Leadership. François Léotard (president), Pierre Calzat (secretary-general)

The centre-right UDF was launched in February 1978 as an electoral alliance of the non-Gaullist "majority" (i.e. ruling) parties, namely the Republican Party (PR), what in 1996 became the Democratic Force and was then called the Centre of Social Democrats (CDS), the Radical Party, what later became the Social Democratic Party and the *Clubs Perspectives et Réalités* (which in 1995 became the Popular Party for French Democracy, PPDF). Its creation a month before the March 1978 Assembly elections was inspired in part by the decision of the (Gaullist) Rally for the Republic (RPR) to withdraw from first-round electoral pacts with the PR and CDS on the grounds that negotiation by these two parties of separate first-round agreements with the Radicals (the most left-wing of the "majority" parties) had violated the terms of the RPR/PR/CDS agreement.

The UDF was backed from the outset by President Giscard d'Estaing (after whose 1977 book *Démocratie Française* the alliance was named) and by his Prime Minister, Raymond Barre. Its creation therefore heightened tensions between the Giscardian and Gaullist wings of the "majority", the former viewing it as an attempt to engineer electoral superiority. In the 1978 elections the UDF parties won increased aggregate representation of 124 seats (compared with 154 for the RPR), assisted by the operation of reciprocal voting support arrangements with the RPR in the second round. Immediately after polling the UDF council formally elevated the alliance to the status of a federation of its constituent parties, under the presidency of Jean Lecanuet (leader of the CDS). In the June 1979 elections to the European Parliament the strongly pro-European UDF list (*Union pour la France en Europe*) came top of the poll with 27.6%.

The UDF was the mainstay of Giscard d'Estaing's bid for a second presidential term in 1981 as a "citizen-candidate" rather than as the nominee of any party. Following his narrow second-round defeat by François Mitterrand of the Socialist Party (PS), the UDF formed an electoral alliance with the RPR for the June 1981 Assembly elections, called the *Union pour la Majorité Nouvelle* (UMN) and providing for single first-round candidates in 385 of the 474 metropolitan constituencies as well as reciprocal voting support for the best-placed second-round candidate in the others. The UDF nevertheless shared in the rout of the centre-left by the PS, retaining only 63 Assembly seats on a first-round vote share of 19.2%. It therefore went into opposition for the next five years, the UMN alliance lapsing in 1983.

In April 1985 the UDF signed a new co-operation agreement with the RPR, with which it drew up a joint manifesto for the March 1986 Assembly elections (in which proportional representation applied). Presenting some candidates jointly with the RPR and others in its own right, the UDF increased its representation to 131 seats out 577, thus playing its part in the defeat of the PS-led government. In the succeeding centre-right coalition headed by the RPR, the UDF parties received 17 ministerial posts out of 41. But the fragility of the alliance became apparent in 1987 when the PR leader, François Léotard, announced that he would not support the RPR leader (and Prime Minister), Jacques Chirac, in the first round of the 1988 presidential elections, because the PR would present its own candidate. When it was announced in September 1987 that Barre (a centrist without formal party affiliation) would be a candidate, the PR and other UDF components declared their support for him. In the event, Barre came in third place in the first round in April 1988 with 16.5% of the vote, whereupon the UDF gave second-round support to Chirac in his unsuccessful attempt to deny Mitterrand a second term.

New Assembly elections held in June 1988 (by constituency-based majority voting) were contested by the UDF in an alliance with the RPR called the *Union du Rassemblement et du Centre* (URC). Not only did the centre-right parties lose their majority, but also the UDF for the first time returned more deputies (129) than the RPR (127). Immediately after the elections, Giscard d'Estaing replaced Lecanuet as president of the UDF. In opposition over the next five years, the UDF and RPR contested the 1989 European elections on a joint list (winning 28.9% of the vote) and in June 1990 announced the creation of the *Union pour la France* (UPF), amid much talk about the need for a unified party. In reality, the UDF and the RPR continued their long struggle for supremacy on the centre-right, with the added ingredient of resumed rivalry between Giscard d'Estaing and Chirac. Also divisive was the Maastricht Treaty on European union, which was supported wholeheartedly by the UDF, whereas important sections of the RPR campaigned for a "no" vote in the September 1992 referendum that yielded a narrow majority for French ratification.

As widely anticipated, the Assembly elections of March 1993 produced a landslide victory for the UDF/RPR alliance, which won 80% of the seats on a 40% first-round vote share. Crucially, the RPR emerged with 247 of the 577 seats, against 213 for the UDF parties, thus effectively dashing Giscard d'Estaing's further presidential ambitions. The UDF parties were allocated important portfolios in the new "cohabitation" government headed by Edouard Balladur of the RPR, and Giscard d'Estaing headed another joint UDF/RPR list in the European Parliament elections of June 1994, when the alliance's vote slipped to 25.6%. But the UDF was weakened by a series of corruption scandals that yielded the resignations of several ministers in 1994, with the result that both Giscard d'Estaing and Barre announced that they would not stand in the 1995 presidential elections. In the absence of a candidate from their own ranks, most UDF components initially supported Balladur as the more centrist of the two RPR contenders. After Balladur had been eliminated in the first round, however, the UDF officially swung behind the victorious candidacy of Chirac in the second (in May 1995), being rewarded with a strong ministerial presence in the resultant centre-right government headed by Alain Juppé of the RPR. In an apparent reconciliation of their longstanding personal rivalry, Giscard d'Estaing was invited to give "elder statesman" advice to the newly-installed President Chirac.

Giscard d'Estaing stood down as UDF leader in March 1996 (to devote himself to founding a centrist think tank) and indicated his preference that the succession should go to Alain Madelon (now of the PPDF and formerly a vice-president of the PR), who had the previous August been dismissed as Economy and Finance Minister after falling out with Juppé. However, UDF constituents preferred the PR leader, François Léotard, who secured 57.4% of delegates' vote at national council meeting in Lyons on March 31.

In addition to the parties referenced above, the UDF structure includes the Association for Management of Direct Adherents (*Association de Gestion des Adhérents Directs*, AGAD), which was established in 1990 with the aim of achieving grass-roots unity of the smaller UDF parties traditionally focused in their parliamentary groups. Particular targets of the unity movement were the Radical Party and the PSD, although the most prominent UDF minister involved in the initiative after the 1993 elections was Charles Millon (Defence), who was associated with the PR.

The UDF is affiliated to the International Democrat Union and the European Democrat Union; 13 of its 14 members of the European Parliament sit in the (Christian democratic) European People's Party, while the one Radical Party representative is a member of the European Liberal, Democratic and Reformist Group.

Workers' Struggle
Lutte Ouvrière (LO)
   Address. BP 233, 75865 Paris
   Leadership. Arlette Laguiller

Descended from a Trotskyist group which in 1940 rejected membership of the French Committees for the Fourth International, the LO was founded in June 1968 as the direct successor to *Voix Ouvrière* following the banning of the latter and other student-based Trotskyist organizations in the wake of the May 1968 "events". It contested the 1973 Assembly elections jointly with the Communist League (itself later succeeded by the Revolutionary Communist League, LCR), but the two groups put up separate candidates in the 1974 presidential elections, in which Arlette Laguiller of the LO won 2.3% in the first round. Having failed to return any of its 470 candidates in the 1978 Assembly elections on a platform that featured robust condemnation of the common programme of the mainstream left, the LO reverted to alliance with the LCR for the 1979 European Parliament elections, their joint list (*Pour les États-Unis Socialistes d'Europe*) winning 3.1% of the vote but no seats.

Laguiller again won 2.3% in the first round of the 1981 presidential contest and all 158 LO candidates were again unsuccessful in the ensuing Assembly elections. Standing on its own, the LO slipped to 2.1% in the 1984 Euro-elections, while Laguiller managed only 1.99% in the first round of the 1988 presidential contest and her party failed to win representation in either the 1988 or the 1993 Assembly elections. In her fourth presidential bid in 1995, however, Arguiller had her best result to date, winning 1,616,566 votes (5.3%) in the first round.

Other Parties and Alliances

Anarchist Federation (*Fédération Anarchiste*), umbrella organization of local anarchist cells, rejects electoral politics, has occasionally been linked with acts of violence by extremist groups.

Bonapartist Party (*Parti Bonapartiste*, PB), led by Emmanuel Johans, founded in 1993 to promote the ideas and achievements of Emperor Napoleon Bonaparte.

Citizens' Movement (*Mouvement des Citoyens*, MdC), won a National Assembly by-election in December 1995.

Communist Committees for Self-Management (*Comités Communistes pour l'Autogestion*, CCA), a small Trotskyist formation.

Communist Organization of France–Marxist-Leninist (*Organisation Communiste de France–Marxiste-Léniniste*, OCF-ML), led by Jacques Lucbert, a Maoist group rejecting electoral politics as "bourgeois trickery".

Democrats for the United States of Europe (*Démocrates pour les États-Unis d'Europe*, DEUE), led by Armand Touati, contested 1994 Euro-elections without success.

Employment First (*L'Emploi d'Abord*), led by Gérard Touati, contested 1994 Euro-elections without success.

Europe Begins at Sarajevo (*L'Europe Commence à Sarajevo*), led by Léon Schwartzenberg, a list presented in 1994 Euro-elections in opposition to Western policy on Bosnia, won 1.6% even though it withdrew from the campaign before polling.

Europe for All (*Europe pour Tous*), led by Jean Ailaud, contested 1994 Euro-elections without success

Federation for a New Solidarity (*Fédération pour une Nouvelle Solidarité*, FNS), a rightist formation derived from the European Labour Party (*Parti Ouvrier Européen*, POE), created by Argentine-born Jacques Chéminade to support his candidacy in the 1995 presidential elections, in which he finished last of nine first-round candidates, with only 0.3% of the vote.

For the Europe of Workers and Democracy (*Pour l'Europe des Travailleurs et de la Démocratie*), led by Daniel Gluckstein, contested 1994 Euro-elections without success.

French and European Nationalist Party (*Parti Nationaliste Français et Européen*, PNFE), a far-right group led by Claude Cornilleau.

French Democratic Party (*Parti Démocrate Française*, PDF), a centrist formation led by Guy Gennesseaux.

French Nationalist Party (*Parti Nationaliste Français*, PNF), far-right grouping formed in 1983 by a faction of the National Front opposed to the leadership of Jean-Marie Le Pen.

French Royalist Movement (*Mouvement Royaliste Français*, MRF), led by Jean de Beauregard, anti-left grouping aiming to restore a French monarchy.

Hunting, Fishing, Nature, Traditions (*Chasse, Pêche, Nature, Traditions*, CPNT), led by André Goustat, contested 1994 Euro-elections without success.

Independent Ecological Movement (*Mouvement Ecologiste Indépendant*, MEI), led by Antoine Waechter, the 1988 presidential candidate of the Greens, from which he broke away in 1993.

International Communist Party (*Parti Communiste Internationaliste*, PCI), led by Pierre Lambert, Trotskyist grouping founded in 1944, subsequently undergoing various name changes, broke with Fourth International in 1952 and helped to found the rival Fourth International–International Centre of Reconstruction, embraced electoral politics in the 1980s, with minimal impact.

Left Reform Movement (*Mouvement de la Gauche Réformatrice*, MGR), led by Aymar Achille-Fould.

Marxist-Leninist Communist Party (*Parti Communiste Marxiste-Léniniste*, PCML), a Maoist formation led by Jacques Jurquet.

Movement of Communist Renovators (*Mouvement des Rénovateurs Communistes*, MRC), led by Claude Llabrès, a reformist splinter group of the French Communist Party.

Natural Law Party (*Parti de la Loi Naturelle*, PLN), led by Benoît Frappé, contested 1994 Euro-elections without success.

New Forces Party (*Parti des Forces Nouvelles*, PFN), led by Félix Busson, a far-right formation founded in 1974 but eclipsed in the 1980s by the National Front.

Policy of Life for Europe (*Politique de Vie pour l'Europe*, PVE), led by Christian Cotten, contested 1994 Euro-elections without success.

National Restoration (*Restauration Nationale*, RN), led by Guy Steinbach, right-wing pro-monarchy formation supporting the claim of the Count of Paris, weakened in 1971 by a breakaway that led to the creation of New Royalist Action.

New Royalist Action (*Nouvelle Action Royaliste*, NAR), led by Bertrand Renouvin, founded in 1971 as a splinter group of National Restoration, advocating the restoration of a progressive monarchy with the Count of Paris as king.

The Other Politics (*L'Autre Politique*), led by former Socialist Party minister Jean-Pierre Chévènement, contested 1994 Euro-elections without success.

Popular Alliance (*Alliance Populaire*, AP), a far-right party led by Jean-François Touze.

Popular Gaullist Movement (*Mouvement Gaulliste Populaire*, MGP), led by Jacques Débu-Bridel and Pierre Dabezies, left-wing splinter group of the Rally for the Republic, founded in 1982 as a merger of earlier dissident Gaullist factions.

Progressive Union of Gaullist and Republican Democrats (*Union des Démocrates Gaullistes et Républicains de Progrès*, UDGRP), led by Jean-Pierre Cevaer.

Rally of Overseas and Minorities (*Rassemblement de l'Outre-mer et des Minorités*, ROM), led by Ernest Moutoussamy, contested 1994 Euro-elections without success.

Red and Green Alternative (*Alternative Rouge et Verte*, ARV), founded in November 1989 as a merger of the rump Unified Socialist Party (*Parti Socialiste Unifié*, PSU) and the New Left (*Nouvelle Gauche*, NG), espousing anarcho-syndicalism, internationalism, environmentalism and feminism; dating from 1960, the PSU had remained in existence when a minority faction led by Michel Rocard had joined the Socialist Party in 1975, while the NG had been founded in 1987 by an expelled "renovator" of the French Communist Party, Pierre Juquin, who won 2.1% in the 1988 presidential elections.

Reformers' Movement (*Mouvement des Réformateurs*, MR), led by Jacques Pelletier, launched in October 1992 as a new centre-left formation aligned with the Socialist Party, taking the name of the main centrist umbrella organization of the 1970s, sought without success to attract centrist voters from the Union for French Democracy in the 1993 Assembly elections.

Regionalist and Federalist List–Regions and Peoples in Solidarity (*Liste Régionaliste et Fédéraliste–Régions et Peuples Solidaires*), led by Max Siméoni, contested 1994 Euro-elections without success.

Revolutionary Communist League (*Ligue Communiste Révolutionnaire*, LCR), led by Alain Krivine, a Trotskyist party founded in 1973 as successor to the Communist League, as whose candidate Krivine won 1.1% in the 1969 presidential elections; contested Assembly and European elections of the 1970s in alliance with Workers' Struggle (LO), which emerged as the stronger of the two; Krivine on his own won 0.4% in the 1974 presidential contest, while in 1988 the LCR backed Pierre Juquin of the New Left (which later joined the Red and Green Alternative).

Revolutionary Marxist-Leninist Communist Party (*Parti Communiste Révolutionnaire Marxiste-Léniniste*, PCRML), led by Max Cluzot, a Maoist group founded in 1974 from earlier dissident Marxist-Leninist factions, has put up electoral candidates, without success.

Union of Libertarian Communist Workers (*Union des Travailleurs Communistes Libertaires*, UTCL), extreme leftist formation founded in 1978 by anarchist elements, rejects electoral politics.

Regional Parties

Breton Democratic Union (*Unvaniezh Demokratei Breizh/Union Démocratique Breton*, UDB), a socialist-oriented party founded in 1964 in quest of autonomy for Brittany by non-violent means, has obtained representation in most large city councils in Brittany, but remains a regional minority party.

Union of the Corsican People (*Unione di u Populu Corsu*, UPC), led by Edmond Siméoni, legal pro-autonomy movement which has obtained minority representation in the Corsican assembly, sometimes in alliance with more militant nationalist groups.

French Overseas Possessions

Overseas Departments

Under decentralization legislation enacted in 1982 by the then Socialist-led government in Paris, the four French overseas departments (*départements d'outre-mer*) of French Guiana, Guadeloupe, Martinique and Réunion each have the additional status of a region of France. Each therefore has a regional council (*conseil régional*) that is directly elected for a six-year term from party lists by proportional representation and has increased powers as compared with the previous indirectly-elected bodies. At the same time, the traditional departmental council (*conseil général*) remained in being in each overseas department, these bodies also being directly elected for a six-year term but by majority voting over two rounds in constituent cantons. Each overseas department elects representatives to the National Assembly and the Senate in Paris according to the procedures applicable in metropolitan France (the precise number depending on size of population). Political parties active in the overseas departments include local sections of metropolitan parties as well as a number of formations specific to particular departments.

French Guiana

Capital: Cayenne

Population: 121,000 (1995E)

Situated on the northern South American littoral between Suriname and Brazil, French Guiana has been under French control since the 17th century and a recognized French possession since 1817, being accorded departmental status in 1946. Elections to the 31-member regional council on March 22, 1992, resulted as follows: Guianese Socialist Party 16 seats (39.5% of the vote), Guianese Democratic Forces 10 (23.3%), Rally for the Republic 2 (5.8%), others 3 (31.3%).

Democratic Socialist Union (*Union Socialiste Démocratique*, USD), led by Théodore Roumillac.

Guianese Democratic Action (*Action Démocratique Guyanaise*, ADG), led by André Lecante, left-wing pro-independence party founded c.1981, represented in the regional council in 1986-92. *Address.* ave d'Estrées, Cayenne

Guianese Democratic Forces (*Forces Démocratiques Guyanaises*, FDG), led by Georges Othily, founded in 1989 by a dissident faction of the Guianese Socialist Party, became second-largest party in the regional council in 1992. *Address.* c/o Conseil Régional, Cayenne

Guianese National Popular Party (*Parti National Populaire Guyanais*, PNPG), led by José Dorcy, leftist party supportive of independence for French Guiana, was represented in the regional council in the 1980s. *Address.* BP 265, Cayenne

Guianese Socialist Party (*Parti Socialiste Guyanais*, PSG), led by Léone Michotte, Antoine Karam and Stéphan Phinéra-Horth, founded in 1956, consistently the strongest party in the department, for long led by Elie Castor, once officially the departmental section of the metropolitan Socialist Party, now autonomous and supportive of autonomy for French Guiana leading to full independence; provides the presidents of both the regional council and the general council, but lost its National Assembly seat to an independent leftist in 1993. *Address.* 1 cité Césaire, Cayenne

Movement for Decolonization and Social Emancipation (*Mouvement pour la Décolonisation et l'Émancipation Sociale*, MDES), led by Maurice Pindard, advocates independence for French Guiana.

Rally for the Republic (*Rassemblement pour la République*, RPR), led by Roland Ho-Wen-Sze, departmental section of the metropolitan RPR, supports the constitutional status quo, took a distant third place in the 1992 regional council elections, but retained its National Assembly seat in 1993. *Address.* 84 ave Léopold Héder, Cayenne

Socialist Party (*Parti Socialiste*, PS), led by Pierre Ribardière, departmental section of the metropolitan party, but eclipsed locally by the autonomous Guianese Socialist Party.

Union for French Democracy (*Union pour la Démocratie Française*, UDF), led by R. Chow-Chine, departmental section of the metropolitan party, has made little electoral impact despite essaying alliance with the local Rally for the Republic.

Walawari, led by Christiane Taubira-Delannon, left-wing movement emphasizing non-French aspects of departmental society.

Guadeloupe

Capital: Basse-Terre

Population: 400,000 (1995E)

A group of islands located in the Caribbean south-east of Puerto Rico, Guadeloupe has been a French possession since the 17th century and was annexed in 1815. Elections to the 41-member regional council on March 22, 1992, resulted as follows: Guadeloupe Objective (OG) 15 seats (29.3% of the vote), Socialist Party 9 (17.5%), dissident Socialists 7 (15.4%), Guadeloupe Progressive Democratic Party 5 (10.8%), Guadeloupe Communist Party 3 (5.8%), Popular Union for the Liberation of Guadeloupe 2 (5.5%). These results were later annulled because of irregularities, the re-run elections on Jan. 31, 1993, giving the OG an overall majority of 22 seats.

Guadeloupe Communist Party (*Parti Communiste Guadeloupéen*, PCG), led by Christian Céleste, founded in 1944 as the departmental section of the French Communist Party, became independent in 1958, for long favoured retention of departmental status, moved to cautious support for eventual independence in the 1980s as it steadily lost former electoral dominance; weakened by the formation of the Guadeloupe Progressive Democratic Party, it managed only fifth place in the 1992 regional coucil elections. *Address.* 119 rue Vatable, Pointe-à-Pitre

Guadeloupe Objective (*Objectif Guadeloupe*, OG), led by Lucette Michaux-Chevry, an eventually victorious centre-right alliance formed for the 1992 regional council elections, consisting of the departmental Rally for the Republic, Union for French Democracy and other conservative elements.

Guadeloupe Progressive Democratic Party (*Parti Progressiste Démocratique Guadeloupéen*, PPDG), led by Henri Bangou and Daniel Genies, founded in 1991 by dissident members of the Guadeloupe Communist Party (PCG) and others, outpolled the PCG in the 1992 regional council elections but took only fourth place.

Popular Movement for an Independent Guadeloupe (*Mouvement Populaire pour une Guadeloupe Indépendante*, MPGI), led by Simone Faisans-Renac, founded in 1982 as a radical pro-independence movement, later handicapped by the imprisonment in 1985 of then leader Luc Reinette, who was implicated in violent activities (and who later escaped).

Popular Union for the Liberation of Guadeloupe (*Union Populaire pour la Libération de la Guadeloupe*, UPLG), led by Lucien Perrutin, founded in 1978 as a semi-underground pro-independence movement, later operating legally in favour of greater autonomy, took a poor sixth place in the 1992 regional council elections.

Rally for the Republic (*Rassemblement pour la République*, RPR), led by Lucette Michaux-Chevry and Aldo Blaise, departmental federation of the metropolitan party, supportive of French status, suffered electorally from the defection of the RPR regional council president to the Union for French Democracy in 1986, but recovered in 1992 as the leading component of the Guadeloupe Objective alliance, which won a narrow overall majority in re-run elections in January 1993, although the party took only one of Guadeloupe's four National Assembly seats in March 1993. *Address.* 1 rue Baudot, Basse-Terre

Socialist Party (*Parti Socialiste*, PS), led by Georges Louisor, departmental federation of the metropolitan party, held the presidency of the regional council from 1986, but was split into two factions for the 1992 elections, the main party winning nine seats and a dissident group led by Dominique Larifla seven; went into regional council opposition after the December 1993 re-run election, but returned one National Assembly deputy (out of four) in March 1993 and retained its dominance of the general council in March 1994 elections. *Address.* résidence Collinette 801, Grand Camp, Les Abymes

Union for French Democracy (*Union pour la Démocratie Française*, UDR), led by Marcel

Esdras, departmental section of the centre-right metropolitan formation; after serious strains in the 1980s it resumed alliance with the Rally for the

Republic for the 1992 regional council elections, participating in the eventual victory of the Guadeloupe Objective alliance.

Martinique

Capital: Fort-de-France

Population: 400,000 (1995E)

Located in the Caribbean, Martinique came under French control in the 17th century and was annexed in 1790, achieving departmental status in 1946. Elections to the 41-member regional council on March 22, 1992, resulted as follows: Union for a Martinique of Progress 16 seats (25.9% of the vote), Independent Martinique Movement-Martinique Patriots 9 (16.0%), Martinique Progressive Party 9 (15.8%), For a Martinique of Labour 4 (6.8%), New Socialist Generation 3 (6.2%).

For a Martinique of Labour (*Pour une Martinique au Travail*), 1992 regional council electoral list of the Martinique Communist Party.

Independent Martinique Movement (*Mouvement Indépendantiste Martiniquais*, MIM), led by Alfred Marie-Jeanne, pro-independence formation that once aimed to seize power through a revolution, obtained increasing support through the 1980s, taking second place in the 1992 regional council election campaigning as the **Martinique Patriots** (*Patriotes Martiniquais*). *Address.* Mairie de Rivière-Pilote, Martinique

Martinique Communist Party (*Parti Communiste Martiniquais*, PCM), led by Armand Nicolas, founded in 1957 when the departmental federation of the French Communist Party split and the socialist pro-autonomy Martinique Progressive Party (PPM) was formed, later itself favouring autonomy, especially after its pro-independence wing broke away in 1984; from 1974 co-operated with the PPM and other left-wing parties, often in government in the department; shared in the electoral decline of French communism in the 1980s, taking fourth place in the 1992 regional council election standing as For a Martinique of Labour; nevertheless, left-wing voting discipline secured the election of Émile Capgras of the PCM as council president. *Address.* rue Émile Zola, Fort-de-France

Martinique Progressive Party (*Parti Progressiste Martinique*, PPM), led by Aimé Césaire and Camille Darsières, founded in 1957 by a splinter group of the Martinique Communist Party, eventually overtaking the parent party, Césaire

being elected president of the first directly-elected regional council in 1983, retaining the post in 1986; dissension between the PPM pro-autonomy and pro-independence wings weakened the party thereafter, third place being achieved in the 1992 regional council elections; won one of Martinique's four National Assembly seats in 1993, although it gained a plurality in general council polling in March 1994. *Address.* rue André Aliker, Fort-de-France

New Socialist Generation (*Nouvelle Génération Socialiste*, NGS), 1992 regional council electoral list of the Socialist Federation of Martinique.

Rally for the Republic (*Rassemblement pour la République*, RPR), led by Stephen Bagoe, departmental federation of the metropolitan party and of similar conservative persuasion, consistently the strongest single party in Martinique but usually in opposition to left-wing alliances; allied with the Union for French Democracy in the 1992 regional council elections, their Union for a Martinique of Progress list winning a substantial plurality, although not enough to obtain the council presidency; won two of the four Martinique National Assembly seats in 1993.

Socialist Federation of Martinique (*Fédération Socialiste de Martinique*, FSM), led by Jean Crusol, departmental section of the metropolitan Socialist Party, but consistently surpassed electorally by other left-wing parties, securing a poor fifth place for its New Socialist Generation list in the 1992 regional contest. *Address.* cité la Meynard, Fort-de-France

Socialist Revolution Group (*Groupe Révolution Socialiste*, GRS), led by Gilbert Pago, pro-independence Trotskyist formation founded in 1973, has made little electoral impact despite seeking to build a regional alliance against "colonialist represssion".

Union for a Martinique of Progress (*Union pour une Martinique de Progrès*, UMP), also referenced as the **Union for France**, consisting of the 1992 electoral alliance of the departmental Rally for the Republic and Union for French Democracy, which won a plurality on the regional council, although it failed to obtain the council presidency.

Union for French Democracy (*Union pour la Démocratie Française*, UDF), led by Jean Maran, departmental federation of the centre-right metropolitan formation, junior partner to the Rally for the Republic (RPR), with their combined forces consistently proving inferior to those of the Martinique left, as after the 1992 regional council elections, despite the RPR/UDF Union for a Martinique of Progress list heading the poll; the UDF took one of the four Martinique seats in the 1993 French National Assembly elections.

Réunion

Capital: Saint-Denis

Population: 605,000 (1995E)

The Indian Ocean island of Réunion has been a French possession since the 17th century and an overseas department since 1946. Re-run elections to the 45-member regional council on June 25, 1993, resulted as follows: Union for France 17 seats, FreeDOM 13, Réunion Communist Party 9, Socialist Party 6.

FreeDOM, led by Camille Sudre (formerly a member of the Socialist Party) and Marguerite (Margie) Sudre, pro-autonomy but conservative movement whose use of English in its title raises eyebrows in Paris; polled strongly in the 1991 general council and 1992 regional council elections, Camille Sudre (a medical doctor and well-known pirate broadcaster) being elected president of the latter body but later being obliged to face new elections in 1993 because of illegal broadcasts; again returned as the largest single party, FreeDOM secured the election of Margie Sudre (wife of Camille) as regional council president, to which post she added that of metropolitan State Secretary for Francophone Affairs following the advent of a centre-right government in Paris in 1995.

Left Radical Movement (*Mouvement des Radicaux de Gauche*, MRG), led by Jean-Marie Finck, departmental section of the metropolitan party, supportive of independence for Réunion (unlike the other main left-wing parties).

National Front (*Front National*, FN), led by Alix Morel, departmental section of the radical right-wing metropolitan party.

Rally for the Republic (*Rassemblement pour la République*, RPR), led by André-Maurice Pihouée

and Tony Manglou, departmental section of the conservative metropolitan party, favouring retention of French status, for long the leading electoral formation in alliance with the Union for French Democracy (UDF), but in local opposition in the 1980s to the combined forces of the left; lost ground in the 1992 and 1993 regional council elections to the new FreeDOM movement, and to the left in the 1994 general council elections; returned one of Réunion's five National Assembly deputies in 1993. *Address.* 23 rue Victor MacAuliffe, Saint-Denis

Réunion Communist Party (*Parti Communiste Réunionnaise*, PCR), led by Paul Vergès and Elie Hoarau, founded as an autonomous party in 1959 by the departmental branch of the French Communist Party, disavowed pro-Soviet orthodoxy of metropolitan party, has consistently been the leading left-wing electoral force in Réunion, but has not held council presidencies in the 1990s, supporting the successful Socialist Party candidate for general council president in 1994; returned one of Réunion's five National Assembly deputies in 1993. *Address.* 21bis rue de l'Est, Saint-Denis

Socialist Party (*Parti Socialiste*, PS), led by Jean-Claude Fruteau and Christophe Payet, departmental federation of the metropolitan Socialist Party, supports retention of departmental status, consistently allied with the stronger Réunion Communist Party (PCR) against the departmental right, Payet being elected general council president in 1994 with PCR support; returned one of Réunion's five National Assembly deputies in 1993. *Address.* 85 rue d'Après, Saint-Denis

Union for France (*Union pour la France*, UPF), 1992-93 joint electoral list of the departmental Rally for the Republic and the Union for French

Democracy; one of the department's five National Assembly deputies was returned under the UPF label in 1993.

Union for French Democracy (*Union pour la Démocratie Française*, UDF), led by Gilbert Gérard, departmental section of the centre-right metropolitan formation, favouring retention of French status, has been allied with the larger Rally for the Republic (RPR) in recent elections.

Overseas Territories and Territorial Collectivities

The French overseas territories (*territoires d'outre-mer*, TOM), namely French Polynesia, the French Southern and Antarctic Territories (with no permanent population), New Caledonia and the Wallis and Futuna Islands, are regarded as integral parts of the French Republic under present arrangements, the three with permanent populations electing representatives to the National Assembly and Senate in Paris. They differ from the overseas departments in that their representative body is the territorial assembly (*assemblée territoriale*) elected by universal adult suffrage) and that they have a greater, although varying, degree of internal autonomy. Also covered below are the two French overseas territorial collectivities (*collectivités territoriales*), namely Mayotte and St Pierre and Miquelon, whose status is explained in the relevant introductions.

French Polynesia

Capital: Papeete, Tahiti

Population: 200,000 (1995E)

French Polynesia consists of some 120 South Pacific islands, including Tahiti, which became a French protectorate in 1847 and a colony in 1860, with the other island groups being annexed later in the 19th century. The territory includes the former French nuclear testing site of Mururoa Atoll. Elections to the 41-member territorial assembly on March 17, 1991, resulted as follows: People's Front/Rally for the Republic 18 seats, Polynesian Union 14, New Land 5, Liberation Front of Polynesia 4.

Autonomous Patriotic Party (*Pupu Here Ai'a Te Nuina'a Ia Ora*), pro-autonomy rural party formed in 1965 by John Téariki, who was succeeded as leader in 1983 by Jean Juventin (mayor of Papeete); contested 1991 assembly elections as part of the Polynesian Union, by the end of the year joining the territorial government; won one of the two French Polynesia seats in the National Assembly in 1993. *Address.* BP 3195, Papeete, Tahiti

Free Tahiti Party, led by Charlie Ching, a pro-independence party which has not so far secured election to representative bodies.

Liberation Front of Polynesia (*Front de Libération de la Polynésie*, FLP), led by Oscar Temaru, pro-independence movement known locally as *Tavini Huiraatira*, won four seats in 1991 assembly elections.

New Land (*Ai'a Api*), led by Émile Vernaudon, centrist pro-autonomy party founded in 1982, was briefly in territorial government with the People's Front in 1991, having taken third place in that year's territorial elections. *Address.* BP 11055, Mahina, Tahiti

People's Front (*Tahoeraa Huiraatira*, TH), led by Gaston Flosse and Jacques Teuira, territorial branch of the conservative Rally for the Republic (RPR), founded in 1971 as a merger of various groups; under assorted names led the territorial government through most of the 1970s and early 1980s, in opposition from 1986, but returned to office on winning a plurality in 1991, first with the support of New Land and then backed by the Autonomous Patriotic Party (also linked with the RPR), whose leader became president of the territorial assembly; Flosse survived a 1992 conviction for illegal use of authority, being re-elected to the National Assembly in 1993. *Address.* BP 471, Pepeete

Polynesian Union (*Union Polynésienne*, UP), 1991 electoral alliance of the Autonomous Patriotic Party and *Te Tiaraama* formations.

Power to the People (*Ia Mana Te Nunaa*), led by Jacques Drollet, leftist pro-independence party founded in 1976, represented in the territorial assembly in the 1980s.

Rally of Liberals (*Rassemblement des Libéraux/ Pupu Taina*), led by Michel Law, favouring the retention of French status. *Address.* BP 169, Papeete, Tahiti

Taatiraa Polynesia, led by Arthur Chung and Robert Tanseau, a local formation whose political stance has not penetrated to the outside world. *Address.* BP 2916, Papeete, Tahiti

Te Tiaraama, led by Alexandre Léontieff, founded in 1987 by a faction of the People's Front, contested the 1991 territorial elections as part of the Polynesian Union headed by the Autonomist Patriotic Party.

Mayotte

Capital: Dzaoudzi   **Population:** 78,000 (1995E)

The Indian Ocean island of Mayotte or Mahoré has been a French possession since the mid-19th century, remaining such when the other Comoro Islands declared independence from France in 1975. In two referendums in 1976 its mainly Christian population opted for maintenance of the French connection rather than incorporation into the Muslim-dominated Comoros, being granted the special status of "territorial collectivity" pending possible elevation to that of a French overseas department. The island's representative body is its 19-member general council, elections to which in March 1994 gave the Mahoré People's Movement 12 seats, the Rally for the Republic 4 and independents 3.

Mahoré People's Movement (*Mouvement Populaire Mahorais*, MPM), led by Younoussa Bamana (president of the Mayotte general council) and Marcel Henry (member of the French Senate), articulated majority resistance to incorporation into a Comoro state in the mid-1970s, favours permanent overseas departmental status; consistently dominant in the local general council, although the island's seat in the French National Assembly was retained by the Union for French Democracy in 1993.

Party for the Mahoran Democratic Rally (*Parti pour le Rassemblement Démocratique des Mahorais*, PRDM), led by Darouèche Maoulida,

founded in 1978, favours Mayotte's incorporation into the Comoro Republic, finding little local support for this aim.

Rally for the Republic (*Rassemblement pour la République*, RPR), led by Mansour Kamardine, local federation of the conservative metropolitan party, favouring departmental status.

Union for French Democracy (*Union pour la Démocratie Française*, UDF), led by Henri Jean-Baptiste, local section of the centre-right metropolitan formation, unrepresented in the island's general council, but has returned Mayotte's National Assembly deputy in recent elections.

New Caledonia

Capital: Nouméa

Population: 172,000 (1995E)

The New Caledonia archipelago of Pacific islands has been a French possession since 1853. In recent years local politics have been dominated by a demand for the severance of the French connection by groups representing indigenous Melanesians (Kanaks), forming about 45% of the population, and the equally insistent demand of French and other settler groups that French status should be retained. Under complex and frequently changing arrangements instituted to accommodate local aspirations, there are currently three autonomous provincial assemblies (North, South and Loyalty Islands), whose members make up an overall territorial congress. Elections on July 9, 1995, resulted in the 54 seats in the latter body becoming distributed as follows: Rally for Caledonia in the Republic 22 (39.5% of the vote), Kanak Socialist National Liberation Front 12 (20.8%), A New Caledonia for All 7 (12.8%), National Union for Independence 5 (10.7%), Develop Together to Construct the Future 2 (3.8%), National Front 2 (3.6%), Rally for Caledonia in France 2 (3.5%), Kanak Future 1 (3.0%), Front for the Development of the Loyalty Islands 1 (2.3%).

A New Caledonia for All (*Une Nouvelle Calédonie pour Tous*, NCPT), led by Didier Leroux, founded in 1995 to support retention of French status on the basis of reconciliation of competing aspirations, took second place in South province elections of July 1995 and third place overall.

Develop Together to Construct the Future (*Développer Ensemble pour Construire l'Avenir*, DEPCA), pro-reconciliation grouping that won two seats in North province in 1995.

Front for the Development of the Loyalty Islands (*Front pour le Développement des Îles Loyautés*, FDIL), won one seat in Loyalty Islands province in 1995 elections.

Kanak Socialist Liberation (*Libération Kanak Socialiste*, LKS), led by Nidoish Naisseline, pro-independence Melanesian grouping based in the Loyalty Islands, where it won one seat in 1995 on a list called Kanak Future.

Kanak Socialist National Liberation Front (*Front de Libération Nationale Kanak Socialiste*, FLNKS), led by Paul Neaoutyine and Rock Wamytan, established in 1984 by radical elements of a pre-existing Independence Front, including the Caledonian Union (UC) and Kanak Liberation Party (PALIKA), prominent in pro-independence agitation in late 1980s and early 1990s, helped to secure restoration of New Caledonia to UN list of non-self-governing territories in 1986; accepted 1988 proposals of Socialist government in Paris for New Caledonia to be divided into three autonomous regions (two dominated by Kanaks), but assassination in 1989 of then FLNKS leader Jean-Marie Tjibaou and his deputy by a Kanak militant demonstrated perils of compromise; called in 1993 for immigration controls to prevent further dilution of Melanesians in advance of status referendum scheduled for 1998; won pluralities in North and Loyalty Islands provinces in 1995 elections, but dominance of the Rally for Caledonia in the Republic in the populous South province confined the FLNKS to second place in territorial congress.

National Front (*Front National*, FN), led by Guy George, territorial section of radical right-wing metropolitan party, won two South province seats in 1995.

National Union for Independence (*Union Nationale pour l'Indépendance*, UNI), pro-independence competitor of the Kanak Socialist National Liberation Front in North province, where it won five seats in July 1995 elections.

Rally for Caledonia in France (*Rassemblement pour une Calédonie dans la France*, RCF), strongly supportive of French status, won two South province seats in 1995.

Rally for Caledonia in the Republic (*Rassemblement pour la Calédonie dans la République*, RPCR), led by Jacques Lafleur and Pierre Frogier, territorial section of the conservative metropolitan Rally for the Republic, allied with local branches of component parties of centre-right Union for French Democracy, represents both *caldoches* (established settlers) and *métros* (recent immigrants), favours retention of French status, has consistently been the leading electoral force, currently providing not only the territorial congress president but also the islands' representatives in the French National Assembly and Senate. *Address.* BP 306, Nouméa

United Kanak Liberation Front (*Front Uni de Libération Kanak*, FULK), led by Yann Céléné Uregei, activist wing of the Melanesian liberation movement, associated with numerous acts of violence, rejected 1988 accord with Paris government establishing provincial structure; in 1992 launched Popular Congress of the Kanak People (*Congrès Populaire du Peuple Kanak*, CPPK) in quest for complete independence for New Caledonia.

St Pierre and Miquelon

Capital: Saint-Pierre   **Population:** 6,500 (1995E)

St Pierre and Miquelon are a group of eight islands off the Canadian Newfoundland coast that have been French possessions since the 17th century and have a population of French stock. Their elevation in 1976 from the status of overseas territory to that of overseas department generated a local campaign for reversion to territorial status with special elements, leading to legislation in 1984 converting the islands into an overseas territorial collectivity with effect from June 1985. Under these arrangements the islands' 19-member general council is the principal representative body, its members also serving as the territorial assembly. Elections on March 20, 1994, ended the long dominance of the local Socialist Party, with allied centre-right lists headed by the Union for French Democracy winning 15 seats.

Rally for the Republic (*Rassemblement pour la République*, RPR), led by Victor Reux, local section of conservative metropolitan formation, participated in victorious centre-right coalition in March 1994 elections; Reux won the islands' seat in French Senate in 1995.

Socialist Party (*Parti Socialiste*, PS), led by Marc Plantagenest, local section of the metropolitan Socialist Party, for long the majority party in the general council, led the successful campaign against departmental status; but in March 1994 its SPM 2000 list in Saint-Pierre and the allied Future Miquelon (*Miquelon Avenir*) list led by Jean de Lizarraga won only four general council/territorial assembly seats and went into opposition.

Union for French Democracy (*Union pour la Démocratie Française*, UDF), led by Gérard Grignon, local section of centre-right metropolitan formation, for long overshadowed electorally by the local Socialist Party, turned the tables in March 1994 with its Archipelago Tomorrow (*Archipel Demain*) list in Saint-Pierre, which together with the allied Miquelon Objectives (*Objectifs Miquelonnais*) list won 15 of the 19 council/assembly seats; elected president of the council, Grignon resigned in June 1996 and was succeeded by Bernard Le Soavec, defined politically as "various right"; the UDF has held the islands' National Assembly seat since 1986, Grignon being the deputy.

Wallis and Futuna Islands

Capital: Mata-Utu   **Population:** 14,500 (1995E)

Situated in the Pacific Ocean north of Fiji and west of Western Samoa, the Wallis and Futuna Islands became a French protectorate in 1842 but were never formally annexed. The islands are governed by a French administrator assisted by a 20-member territorial assembly elected by universal adult suffrage for a five-year term. There are also three traditional kingships, of Wallis, Sigave and Alo, exercising limited local powers. Assembly elections on Dec. 1, 1994, resulted in the Rally for the Republic winning 10 seats, the Union for Wallis and Futuna 7 and independents 3.

Left Radical Movement (*Mouvement des Radicaux de Gauche*, MRG), led by Kamilo Gata, territorial section of the centre-left metropolitan party, holds the islands' seat in the French National Assembly.

Rally for the Republic (*Rassemblement pour la République*, RPR), led by Clovis Logologofolau and Sosefo Makape Papilio, territorial section of the conservative metropolitan formation, dominant in recent territorial elections, although it holds only the French Senate seat for the islands and not the National Assembly seat.

Union for French Democracy (*Union pour la Démocratie Française*, UDF), territorial section of metropolitan centre-right party, known locally as *Luakaetahi*.

Union for Wallis and Futuna (*Union pour Wallis et Futuna*, UWF), alliance of Bright Future (*Taumu'a Lelei*) led by Soane Mani Uhila and the Local Popular Union (*Union Populaire Locale*, UPL) founded in 1985 by Falakiko Gata (hitherto a member of the territorial Union for French Democracy and before that of the territorial Rally for the Republic).

Gabon

Capital: Libreville   **Population:** 1,240,000 (1995E)

The Gabonese Republic achieved independence from France in 1960. Executive power is vested in the President, who is elected for a seven-year term and who appoints the Prime Minister and the Council of Ministers. Legislative power is vested in the 120–member National Assembly (*Assemblée Nationale*), which has a normal term of five years. The Gabonese Democratic Party (PDG) was the only legal political party from 1968 to 1990, when a national conference in March-April approved the introduction of a pluralist system and opposition parties were legalized.

In multi-party legislative elections held in September-November 1990 the PDG retained an overall majority in the National Assembly, although seven opposition parties gained representation. The results of the elections in five constituencies were subsequently annulled, and by-elections were held in March 1991 resulting in a redistribution of seats mainly in favour of the ruling party.

The re-election of Omar Bongo as President for the fourth time in December 1993 was disputed by the opposition and resulted in months of political unrest. An agreement between the government and opposition was negotiated in Paris in September 1994 whereby a transitional coalition government was to be installed, with local government elections scheduled to take place in 12 months and legislative elections six months later; also, the electoral code was to be revised. In October 1994 a new government was appointed in which six portfolios were allocated to opposition parties. In a referendum in July 1995, voters overwhelmingly approved the full implementation of the constitutional changes envisaged in the Paris agreement.

African Forum for Reconstruction

Forum Africain pour la Réconstruction (FAR)
   Address. c/o Assemblée Nationale, Libreville
   Leadership. Prof. Léon Mboyebi, Jean-Pierre Zongue-Nguema, Vincent Essolomongeu

Also identified as the Action Forum for Renewal (*Forum d'Action pour la Renouveau*), the FAR was created in early 1992 by a merger of the following three formations: the Movement for National Regeneration–Originals (*Mouvement de Redressement National*, MORENA-*Originels*), the original MORENA faction which won seven seats in the 1990 legislative elections; the Gabonese Socialist Union (*Union Socialiste Gabonais*, USG), which initially won four seats in the elections but subsequently lost one in the March 1991 by-elections; and the Gabonese Socialist Party (*Parti Socialiste Gabonais*, PSG), an extra-parliamentary party. MORENA had been set up in 1981 in clandestine opposition to the then single-party Bongo regime. By early 1990 the party had given rise to dissident factions, the most important of which was what later became the

Rally of Woodcutters. In the December 1993 presidential elections, Prof. Mboyebi polled less than 2% of the votes cast.

Gabonese Democratic Party

Parti Démocratique Gabonais (PDG)
   Address. BP 268, Libreville
   Telephone. (#241) 703121
   Fax. (#241) 703146
   Leadership. Jacques Adiahenot (secretary-general)

Founded in 1968 by President Bongo, the PDG was the ruling and sole legal party until early 1990, when a national political conference, convened in the light of growing pressure for democratization and widespread unrest, resulted in the acceptance by the President of a multi-party system. In April 1990 President Bongo announced his intention to place himself above party politics. In the legislative elections in the latter part of 1990, the PDG won a majority with 63 seats (subsequently increased to 66 seats following the by-elections in March 1991). In December 1993 Bongo was

263

re-elected as President, despite opposition claims of irregularities, with just over 51% of the vote.

Gabonese Progress Party
Parti Gabonais du Progrès (PGP)
    Address. c/o Assemblée Nationale, Libreville
    Leadership. Pierre-Louis Agondjo-Okawe (president), Anselme Nzoghe (secretary-general)
    Established as an opposition party in early 1990, the PGP won 18 seats in the National Assembly in the legislative elections later that year—a total subsequently increased to 19 following the March 1991 by-elections. Party leader Pierre-Louis Agondjo-Okawe contested the presidential election in December 1993 but, despite achieving third place, gained less than 5% of the votes cast.

Rally of Woodcutters
Rassemblement des Bûcherons
    Leadership. Fr. Paul M'Ba Abessole (leader), Pierre-André Kombila Koumba (secretary-general)
    The party name was adopted in February 1991 by what had been the Woodcutters (*Bûcherons*) faction of the Movement for National Regeneration (MORENA) in an effort to more clearly distinguish itself from the parent organization (the original rump of which later joined the African Forum for Reconstruction). The formation emerged from the 1990 legislative elections as the largest single opposition party, initially with 20 of the 120 seats. Despite its success, the party accused the government of electoral fraud and called for the holding of fresh elections under international supervision. The party boycotted the March 1991 by-elections which led to a reduction in its representation to 17 seats.
    In the December 1993 presidential election Fr. M'Ba Abessole was the runner-up to President Bongo, securing 26.5% of the votes cast—a result disputed by the opposition on the grounds of alleged electoral malpractice by the government.

Other Parties

Association for Socialism in Gabon (*Association pour le Socialisme au Gabon*, APSG), won six legislative seats in the 1990 elections.

Circle for Renovation and Progress (*Cercle pour le Renouveau et le Progrès*, CRP), gained one seat in the 1990 National Assembly elections.

Circle of Liberal Reformers (*Cercle des Liberaux Reformateurs*), formed in late 1992 and led by Jean-Boniface Assele.

Gabonese People's Union (*Union du Peuple Gabonais*, UPG), an opposition party whose then leader, Pierre Mamboundou, was allowed to return from exile in November 1993 but was prevented from contesting the presidential elections the following month; in September 1995 Sebastien Mamboundou Mouyama was elected chairman of the UPG.

National Front (*Front National*, FN), a right-wing party launched in 1991 under the leadership of Martin Efayong.

Social Democratic Party (*Parti Social-Démocrate*, PSD), formed in 1991; party leader Pierre Claver Maganga-Moussavou contested the December 1993 presidential election, achieving fourth place but attracting less than 4% of the votes cast.

Union for Development and Democracy (*Union pour la Démocratie et le Développement*, UDD), secured one seat in the 1990 legislative elections.

The Gambia

Capital: Banjul
                                                  Population: 1,100,000 (1995E)

The Republic of The Gambia achieved independence from Britain in 1965 and became a republic in 1970. Under the 1970 constitution, executive power was vested in the President, elected by universal suffrage for a five-year term. Legislative power was vested in a unicameral 50–member House of Representatives, comprising 36 members directly for a five-year term, five indirectly elected chiefs, eight non-voting members and the Attorney-General.

In July 1994 Sir Dawda Kairaba Jawara, then President of the Republic and leader of the ruling People's Progressive Party, was overthrown in a bloodless coup by young army officers led by Capt. Yahya Jammeh, who became head of state. An Armed Forces Provisional Ruling Council (AFRPC) was established, the constitution suspended, the House of Representatives dissolved and all political activity banned. Two failed coup attempts against the new regime were reported in November 1994 and January 1995. According to a programme published in February 1995, the restoration of elected organs of state was scheduled for July 1996.

July 22 Movement

Address. c/o Government Offices, Banjul

Leadership. Capt. Yahya Jammeh (president), Musa Bittaye (vice-president)

The Movement was created by Capt. Jammeh to provide a political power base following his coup of July 1994, after which the established Gambian parties were effectively banned. In February 1996 the Movement's vice-president was appointed Minister of Justice.

Unauthorized Parties

Throughout the post-independence period, until the July 1994 military coup, the Gambia had preserved a multi-party system in which the organizations listed below were active.

Gambia People's Party (GPP)

Leadership. Assan Musa Camara (leader)

The socialist GPP was established in 1986 by a dissident faction of former People's Progressive Party members. In the 1992 elections the party secured two seats in the House of Representatives, its leader finishing a distant third in the presidential vote.

People's Progressive Party (PPP)

Address. 21 OAU Boulevard, Banjul

Leadership. Sir Dawda Kairaba Jawara (secretary-general), I. A. A. Kelepha Samba (president)

Founded in 1958 under British colonial rule, the moderate centre-left PPP held a dominant position as the ruling party between independence in 1965 and July 1994. In the most recent legislative and presidential elections in April 1992 the party won 25 of the 36 directly elected seats in the House of Representatives and President Jawara was elected for a sixth term of office with over 58 per cent of the votes cast. After the military coup Jawara fled the country.

National Convention Party (NCP)

Address. 4 Fitzgerald Street, Banjul

Leadership. Sherif Mustapha Dibba (leader)

The NCP was formed in 1975, advocating social reform and a more equitable distribution of national wealth. In the 1992 elections the party won 6 legislative seats, and the Sherif Mustapha Dibba came second in the presidential poll with 22 per cent of the votes cast.

Other Parties

Gambia Socialist Revolutionary Party (GSRP), banned between November 1980 and November 1992.

Movement for Justice in Africa (MOJA), a party of the radical left which was formed in the late 1970s but banned until November 1992.

People's Democratic Organization for Independence and Socialism (PDOIS), a leftist grouping formed in 1986 and led by Sidia Jatta, who was an unsuccessful presidential candidate in 1992, and Halifa Salla.

People's Democratic Party (PDP), launched in 1991 and advocating agricultural self-sufficiency, mass education and development of the country's infrastructure, led by Dr. Momodou Lamin Bojang, who was an unsuccessful candidate in the 1992 presidential election.

Georgia

Capital: Tbilisi

Population: 5,500,000 (1995E)

The Republic of Georgia replaced the Georgian Soviet Socialist Republic in August 1990 and declared independence from the USSR in April 1991, achieving full sovereignty on the demise of the USSR in December 1991, although it did not join the Commonwealth of Independent States (CIS) until March 1994. A new constitution promulgated in October 1995 renamed the country Georgia and provided for an executive President, who is directly elected for a five-year term (once renewable) by universal adult suffrage and who appoints and presides over a Council of Ministers. The constitution provides for a bicameral parliament when conditions permit; in the interim legislative authority is vested in a unicameral parliament elected for a four-year term and consisting of 150 deputies returned by a system of proportional representation subject to a 5% threshold and a further 85 elected from single-member constituencies by simple plurality. The constitution maintains the autonomous status under Georgian sovereignty of Abkhazia, South Ossetia and Adzharia (each containing either a dominant or a significant Muslim population), this provision being specifically rejected by the parliament of the self-proclaimed sovereign republic of Abkhazia.

In presidential elections on Nov. 5, 1995, Eduard Shevardnadze of the Citizens' Union of Georgia (SMK) was re-elected with the support of 76.8% of those voting. Legislative elections on Nov. 5 and 19 and Dec. 3, 1995, resulted in 231 of the 235 seats being filled, with the SMK achieving dominance in an Assembly in which 10 other parties secured representation.

All-Georgian Union for Revival
Sruliad Sakartvelos Aghordzinebis Kavshiri (SSAK)

    Address. Sakartvelos Parlamenti, Tbilisi
    Leadership. Aslan Abashidze (chair)

    Founded in 1992 to represent Muslims in the autonomous republic of Adzharia, the SSAK contested the 1992 elections within the broad-based Peace Bloc (which won a narrow plurality). Standing on its own, the party came in third place in the 1995 parliamentary elections, winning a 6.8% vote share and a total of 31 seats.

Citizens' Union of Georgia
Sakartvelos Mokalaketa Kavshiri (SMK)

    Address. c/o Office of the President, Tbilisi
    Leadership. Eduard (Georgi) Shevardnadze (chair), Zurab Zhvania (general secretary)

    The SMK was established in November 1993 by President Shevardnadze, who had assumed power in March 1992 with the assistance of a Military Council that had ousted Zviad Gamsakhurdia two months earlier. In the Soviet era Shevardnadze had been first secretary of the Georgian Communist Party for 13 years until being appointed USSR Foreign Minister and a full CPSU politburo member in 1985; a leading reformer and close associate of Mikhail Gorbachev, he had resigned from both posts in 1990, warning that "dictatorship is coming". Shevardnadze told the SMK's founding congress that the formation would be an alliance of parties retaining their individual policy programmes, but would act together on legislative issues. The SMK quickly attracted support from other pro-democracy and pro-market formations, including the Green Party of Georgia (*Sakartvelos Mtsvaneta Partia*, SMP), whose leader became general secretary of the new formation.

    The Georgian Greens had originated in 1988 as a section of the All-Georgian Rustaveli Society, an anti-Soviet cultural formation then headed by Tengiz Sigua, who later founded the National Liberation Front. As in other parts of the then USSR, concern for environmental questions in Georgia was equivalent to being against the centralized Soviet regime. The Greens won 11 seats in the October 1992 legislative elections.

    In November 1995 Shevardnadze was re-elected President by an overwhelming popular majority, while in concurrent legislative elections the SMK became the dominant party in the new Assembly with 107 out of 231 seats.

Georgian Social Democratic Party

Sakartvelos Sotsial-Demokratiuli Partia (SSDP)
    Address. Tskhra Aprilis 2, 380018 Tbilisi
    Telephone. (#995-32) 999550
    Fax. (#995-32) 987389
    Leadership. Guram Muchaidze (secretary-general)

The SSDP is descended from a pre-Soviet Menshevik grouping (founded in 1893) which was dissolved in 1921 after the republic had been incorporated into the USSR. Revived in 1990, the party adopted a cautious approach to the independence issue, supporting the abortive new Union Treaty proposed by Soviet leader Gorbachev in 1991. Following independence, the SSDP won only two seats in the October 1992 parliamentary elections and subsequently aligned itself with President Shevardnadze's Citizens' Union of Georgia.

Lion All-Georgian Political Association

Lemi Sruliad Sakartvelos Politikuri Gaertianeba
    Address. Sakartvelos Parlamenti, Tbilisi
    Leadership. Akaki Gasviani (chair)

Founded in 1989, *Lemi* is based in the mountain district of Svaneti and advocates the transfer of resources to that region. It won one seat in the 1995 parliamentary elections.

National Democratic Party

Erovnul Demokratiuli Partia (EDP)
    Address. Rustaveli 21, 380008 Tbilisi
    Telephone. (#995-32) 990453
    Fax. (#995-32) 999616
    Leadership. Irina Sarishvili (leader), Ivane (Mamuka) Giorgadze (political secretary)

Descended from a pre-Soviet party of the same name, the EDP was re-established in 1988 as a pro-independence grouping with a Christian democratic orientation and favouring restoration of the monarchy as a means of national unification. Allied with the secular Democratic Party, it won 32.6% of the vote in the 1990 republican elections; after independence, however, it took only 12 seats in the 1992 parliamentary elections. Having initially supported Shevardnadze's assumption of power in March 1992, the EDP became critical of his policy of rapprochement with Moscow and also opposed Georgian accession to the Commonwealth of Independent States (CIS) in March 1994.

In December 1994 EDP leader Georgi Chanturia was assassinated when gunmen opened fire on his car in Tbilisi, the EDP subsequently blaming "Russian imperialist forces" and organized criminals for the murder. Chanturia's wife, Irina Sarishvili (a former Deputy Prime Minister), was seriously injured in the attack, but recovered sufficiently to assume leadership of the EDP. In the November 1995 legislative elections the EDP came in second place, winning 7.9% of the proportional vote and 31 seats. In January 1996 the EDP deputies failed in their bid to block ratification of the 1994 friendship treaty with Russia.

The EDP is affiliated to the Christian Democrat International.

National Liberation Front

Erovnuli Gantavisuplebis Pronti (EGP)
    Leadership. Tengiz Sigua and Tengiz Kitovani (joint chairs)

The EGP was founded in 1993 by Tengiz Sigua (a former head of state and government) and Tengiz Kitovani, who had both been instrumental in overthrowing the Gamsakhurdia regime in January 1992 but had fallen out with President Shevardnadze after his return to power in March 1992, being opposed to any concessions to Abkhazian separatism. In February 1994 it was announced that Kitovani's *Mkhedrioni* (Horsemen) paramilitary force had been dissolved and incorporated into the regular Georgian army. In January 1995, however, Kitovani mustered a 350-strong EGP force which marched to "liberate" Abkhazia before being intercepted by government troops. The episode resulted in Kitovani being arrested and the EGP banned. A further crackdown on the *Mkhedrioni* followed the assassination attempt of President Shevardnadze in August 1995.

Peace Bloc

Mshvidoba
    Leadership. Eldar Shengelaya (DS), Temur Zhorzholiani (SMP)

The conservative Peace Bloc won 29 seats in the October 1992 parliamentary elections, making it the biggest single grouping. The alliance embraced the pro-market Democratic Georgia Union (*Demokratiuli Sakartvelo*, DS) led by Shengelaya, the Georgian Monarchists' Party (*Sakartvelos Monarchistuli Partia*, SMP) led by Zhorzholiani, the Georgian Agrarian Union (*Sakartvelos Agraruli Kavshiri*, SAP), the Union of Social Justice of Georgia (*Sakartvelos Sotsialuri Samartlianobis Kavshiri*, SSSK) and the Georgian League of Economic and Social Revival (*Sakartvelos Economikuri da Sotsialuri Progresis Liga*, SESPL). None of these parties won representation in 1995.

Progress Bloc

Bloki Progresi (BP)
    Address. c/o Sakartvelos Parlamenti, Tbilisi
    Leadership. collective

Formed for the 1995 parliamentary elections,

the centrist, cautiously pro-reform Bloc embraced the Democratic Union of Georgia (*Sakartvelos Demokratiuli Kavshiri*, SDK) led by Avtandil Margiani (a former Deputy Premier); the Political Union of Young Democrats–Our Choice (*Politikuri Gaertianeba Akhalgazrda Demokratta Kavshiri–Chveni Archevani*) led by Mamuka Gachechiladze and Zurab Tsereteli; and the Georgian Proprietors' Political Association (*Sakartvelos Mesakutreebi Politikuri Gaertianeba*) led by Nika Tsilosani, Beso Tsilosani and Gia Zhorzholiani. Favouring the maintenance of close economic relations with Russia, the BP won four seats in the 1995 elections.

Reformers' Union of Georgia–National Concord

Sakartvelos Reformatorta Kavshiri–Erovnuli Tankhmoba (SRK-ET)

Address. c/o Sakartvelos Parlamenti, Tbilisi
Leadership. Bakur Gulua (chair)

The liberal centrist SRK-ET dates from the foundation of the SRK in 1993 under the leadership of Gulua (a Deputy Premier). Standing on a platform of pro-market reform and close relations with Russia in the 1995 elections, the broader SRK-ET included the Sportsmen's Union of Georgia (*Sakartvelos Sportsmenta Kavshiri*, SSK) led by Edisher Machaidze and the Kolkheti Georgian Citizens' Political Association (*Sakartvelos Mokalaketa Politikuri Gaertianeba Kolkheti*) led by Miron Subeliani. The alliance took only 2.9% of the vote in the party list section but won two single-member seats.

Solidarity Bloc

Tanadgoma

Address. c/o Sakartvelos Parlamenti, Tbilisi
Leadership. Vakhtang Goguadze, Otar Patatsia

Tanadgoma was founded in July 1995 by some 20 parliamentary deputies, the leadership of Goguadze (Speaker of the legislature) and Patatsia (Prime Minister) making it a government formation. Standing on a pro-market, pro-Russian platform, it slumped to three seats in the subsequent parliamentary elections.

Socialist Party of Georgia

Sakartvelos Sotsialisturi Partia (SSP)

Address. c/o Sakartvelos Parlamenti, Tbilisi
Leadership. Temur Gamtsemlidze (chair)

The SSP was founded in 1995 on a moderate left-wing programme and joined with the dominant Citizens' Union of Georgia in endorsing to candidacy of Eduard Shevardnadze in the November 1995 presidential election. In the simultaneous parliamentary contest the SSP, with 3.8% of the vote, failed to achieve the 5% minimum required for proportional representation but won four constituency seats.

Union for a Law-Governed State

Sakhelmtsipoebriv Samartlebrivi Gaertianeba (SSG)

Address. c/o Sakartvelos Parlamenti, Tbilisi
Leadership. Shalva Natelashvili (chair)

Founded in August 1995 on a centrist platform, the SSG won one constituency seat in the parliamentary elections towards the end of the year. Its leader was chairman of the previous legislature's legal committee.

Union of Georgian Traditionalists

Kartvel Traditsionalistta Kavshiri (KTK)

Address. c/o Sakartvelos Parlamenti, Tbilisi
Leadership. Akaki Asatiani (chair)

The right-wing opposition KTK won seven seats in the 1992 elections. In the 1995 parliamentary elections it failed to cross the 5% proportional threshold (winning 4.2% of the vote) but returned two constituency-based deputies.

United Communist Party of Georgia

Sakartvelos Ertiani Komunisturi Partia (SEKP)

Address. c/o Sakartvelos Parlamenti, Tbilisi
Leadership. Maj.-Gen. Paneleimon Giorgadze (first secretary)

The SEKP was launched in June 1994 as an attempted merger of various factions that claimed descent from the Soviet-era Georgian Communist Party (GCP). As the ruling party during the Soviet era, the GCP had been less enmeshed in corruption and abuse of power than its counterparts in other Soviet republics. It had nevertheless been dissolved in August 1991 in the wake of the failed hardliners' coup in Moscow, and its leaders had shifted their support to other parties. Following independence, Communist organizational structures were maintained by the Communist Workers' Party and the Alliance of Communists of Georgia. Despite the creation of the SEKP, unity of former GCP elements proved difficult to achieve. Standing on a conservative/nationalist platform, the SEKP leader, Maj.-Gen. Giorgadze, came fourth in the November 1995 presidential elections with only 0.5% of the vote, whereas the former GCP first secretary, Dzhumber Patiashvili, came second with 19.5%. In the parliamentary elections a list called the "United Communists and Social Democrats" failed to win representation.

United Republican Party

Gaertianebuli Respublikuri Partia (GRP)

Address. c/o Sakartvelos Parlamenti, Tbilisi
Leadership. Nodar Natadze (chair)

The GRP was founded in 1995 as a merger of the Georgian Popular Front (GPF) led by Natadze, the Charter 1991 Party and the Republican Party. The GPF had been launched in 1989 to work toward "a free and democratic society and the restoration of Georgia's complete state independence", its leader heading the parliamentary group which opposed President Gamsakhurdia prior to his ejection in January 1992. In the October 1992 legislative elections the GPF had formed part of the October 11 Bloc (which won 27 seats), subsequently giving qualified support to President Shevardnadze. In the 1995 parliamentary elections the GRP failed to surmount the 5% barrier for proportional seats, but won one constituency seat. It later joined in opposition demands for the withdrawal of Russian troops from Georgian territory (including Abkhazia).

Other Parties and Alliances

Agrarian Party of Georgia (*Sakartvelos Agraruli Partia*, SAP), founded in 1994 under the leadership of Roin Liparteliani, who came last in the 1995 presidential elections with 0.4% of the vote.

Christian Democratic Union of Georgia, led by Irakli Shengelaya, affiliated to the Christian Democrat International, a strong advocate of private ownership and political pluralism; formed part of October 11 Bloc in the 1992 legislative elections.

Highlanders' Political Union, won one seat in the 1992 elections, which it contested in alliance with the National Unity Party of Georgia.

Ilia Chavchavadze Society, founded in 1987, named after an aristocratic Georgian nationalist of the late Tsarist period, won seven seats in the 1992 elections.

Motherland Revival Society, won one seat in the 1992 elections.

National Independence Party (*Erovnuli Damoukideblobis Partia*, EDP), led by Irakli Tsereteli, founded in 1988, obtained 32.6% of the vote in the last Soviet-era elections in 1990, but declined to four seats in October 1992.

National Unity Party of Georgia, won one seat in the 1992 elections in alliance with the Highlanders' Political Union.

People's Friendship and Justice Party, won two seats in the 1992 elections.

People's Socialist Party of Georgia, led by Giorgi Khachapuridze, founded in April 1995, advocates a "socially organized market economy".

Radical Monarchist Union of Georgia, won one seat in the 1992 elections.

Round Table–Free Georgia, formed by supporters of ex-President Gamsakhurdia.

Social Justice Union of Georgia, won two seats in the 1992 elections.

Social Labour Party of Georgia, won four seats in the 1992 elections.

State Party–National Unity of Georgia, won one seat in the 1992 elections.

Union of National Reconstruction and Revival, led by Valerian Advadze, who came a poor third in the May 1991 direct presidential elections; having backed Shevardnadze's assumption of power in March 1992, it advocated close economic links with other ex-Soviet republics and won four seats in the October 1992 parliamentary elections.

Union of the Children of God, won two seats in the 1992 elections.

Unity Bloc (*Ertoba*), formed in 1992 under the leadership of Mikheil Naneishvili, encompassing the Liberal Democratic Party (*Liberalur Demokratiuli Partia*, LDP) and the All-Georgian Party of Peace and Freedom (*Sruliad Sakartvelos Mshvidobisa da Tavisuplebis Partia*, SSMTP); the alliance won 14 seats in the October 1992 parliamentary elections.

Workers' Union of Georgia, led by Vakhtang Gabunia.

Germany

Capital: Berlin   **Population:** 82,000,000 (1995E)

The Federal Republic of Germany (FRG) was established in 1949 in the three Western zones of post-World War II occupation (British, US and French), achieving full sovereignty in May 1955. The FRG's Basic Law (constitution) defined it as "a democratic and social federal state" with a bicameral parliament consisting of (i) a lower house (*Bundestag*) directly elected for a four-year term by universal adult suffrage, and (ii) an upper house (*Bundesrat*) indirectly constituted by representatives of the legislatures of the FRG's constituent states (*Länder*). Executive power is vested in the federal government headed by a Chancellor elected by the *Bundestag*, while the largely ceremonial President (head of state) is elected for a five-year term by a Federal Assembly (*Bundesversammlung*) made up of the *Bundestag* deputies plus an equal number of delegates nominated by the *Länder* parliaments. The reunification of Germany in October 1990 was achieved by the FRG's absorption of the five eastern *Länder*, created in the former Soviet-occupied and Communist-ruled German Democratic Republic, and also of Berlin (previously under four-power administration). The post-1990 FRG thus consists of 16 *Länder*, with a federal structure still governed by the 1949 Basic Law, under which each *Land* has a parliament exercising substantial powers in the economic and social fields.

The *Bundestag* is formed by a combination of direct elections from 328 single-member constituencies and the proportional allocation of a theoretically equal number of seats to party lists according to their share of the vote. Proportional seats are only allocated to parties winning at least 5% of the national vote or to those returning three deputies directly in any one electoral district (i.e. *Land*). In the 1994 *Bundestag* elections the 328 directly-elected seats were supplemented by 344 proportional seats (for a total complement of 672), the 16 additional "supra-proportional" mandates being required to achieve overall proportionality.

Under legislation enacted in July 1967, political parties are defined as being a constitutionally necessary element of a free democratic order and as contributing to the formation of the national political will, by influencing public opinion, encouraging participation in public life and training citizens for public office. On these grounds, state funding is granted to political parties or independent candidates obtaining at least 0.5% of the national vote or 10% in any electoral district, payable retrospectively in the next electoral period. Under an amendment to the 1967 law effective from January 1994, parties and independent candidates receive DM1.30 per annum for each vote received up to 5 million votes and DM1 for each additional vote above that figure. They are also allocated DM0.50 to match every DM1 that they receive from members' contributions or donations.

Elections to the *Bundestag* on Oct. 16, 1994, resulted as follows: Social Democratic Party of Germany (SPD) 252 seats (with 36.4% of the vote); Christian Democratic Union (CDU) 244 (34.2%); Christian Social Union (CSU) 50 (7.3%); Alliance 90/The Greens 49 (7.3%); Free Democratic Party (FDP) 47 (6.9%); Party of Democratic Socialism (PDS) 30 (4.4%).

Each of the 16 *Länder* has its own parliament (*Landtag*, or *Bürgerschaft* in the case of Bremen and Hamburg), normally elected for a four-year term, the most recent results to mid-1996 being as follows:

Baden-Württemberg (March 24, 1996)—CDU 69, SPD 39, Greens 19, FDP 14, Republicans 14.
Bavaria (Sept. 25, 1994)—CSU 120, SPD 70, Greens 14.
Berlin (Oct. 22, 1995)—CDU 87, SPD 55, PDS 34, Greens 30.
Brandenburg (Sept. 11, 1994)—SPD 52, CDU 18, PDS 18.

270

Bremen (May 14, 1995)—SPD 37, CDU 37, Greens 14, Work for Bremen 12.
Hamburg (Sept. 19, 1993)—SPD 58, CDU 36, Greens 19, Instead of a Party 8.
Hesse (Feb. 19, 1995)—CDU 45, SPD 44, Greens 13, FDP 8.
Lower Saxony (March 13, 1994)—SPD 81, CDU 67, Greens 13.
Mecklenburg-West Pomerania (Oct. 16, 1994)—CDU 30, SPD 23, PDS 18.
North Rhine–Westphalia (May 14, 1995)—SPD 108, CDU 89, Greens 24.
Rhineland-Palatinate (March 24, 1996)—SPD 43, CDU 41, FDP 10, Greens 7.
Saarland (Oct. 16, 1994)—SPD 27, CDU 21, Greens 3.
Saxony (Sept. 11, 1994)—CDU 77, SPD 22, PDS 21.
Saxony-Anhalt (June 26, 1994)—CDU 37, SPD 36, PDS 21, Greens 5.
Schleswig-Holstein (March 24, 1996)—SPD 33, CDU 30, Greens 6, FDP 4, South Schleswig
    Voters' Union 2.
Thuringia (Oct. 16, 1994)—CDU 42, SPD 29, PDS 17.

Alliance 90/The Greens
Bündnis 90/Die Grünen

Address. Baunscheidtstrasse 1A, 53113 Bonn
Telephone. (#49–228) 9166-131
Fax. (#49–228) 9166-234
Leadership. Krista Sager and Jürgen Trittin (spokespersons), Christa Nickels (leader of 1994 candidates' list), Heide Rühle (general secretary)

The Greens first emerged in West Germany in the 1970s at state and local level. A number of these disparate groups came together at a Frankfurt conference in March 1979 to form the Alternative Political Union, The Greens (*Sonstige Politische Vereinigung, Die Grünen*), which was given a federal structure under the rubric The Greens at a Karlsruhe congress in January 1980. A programme adopted in March 1980 called for a worldwide ban on nuclear energy and on chemical and biological weapons, the non-deployment of nuclear missiles in Europe, unilateral disarmament by West Germany, the dismantling of NATO and the Warsaw Pact, and the creation of a demilitarized zone in Europe. It also advocated the dismantling of large economic concerns into smaller units, a 35-hour week and recognition of the absolute right of workers to withdraw their labour.

Having taken only 1.5% of the vote in the 1980 federal elections, the Greens broke through to representation in 1983, winning 5.6% and 27 lower house seats. They progressed to 8.2% in the 1984 European Parliament elections and to 8.3% in the 1987 federal elections, winning 42 seats. Prominent in the Greens' rise was Petra Kelly, whose charismatic leadership attracted national publicity and acclaim. However, opposition within the party to "personality politics" contributed to her departure from the joint leadership in April 1984, together the other two members. (Some years later, in October 1992, Kelly and her partner, former army general turned pacifist Gert Bastian, were found dead in their Bonn apartment; according to

the German police, Kelly had been shot by Bastian, who had then killed himself.)

Divisions also surfaced between the Greens' "realist" wing ("*Realos*"), favouring co-operation with the Social Democratic Party of Germany (SPD), and the "fundamentalists" ("*Fundis*"), who rejected any compromises with other formations. In December 1985 the "realist" Greens of Hesse joined a coalition government with the SPD (the first such experience for both parties), but this collapsed in February 1987 after the Green environment minister, Joschka Fischer, had unsuccessfully demanded that the state government should halt plutonium processing at a plant near Frankfurt. The Hesse experience strengthened the "fundamentalist" wing at the Greens' annual congress in May 1987, when it obtained eight of the party's 11 executive seats. By 1989, however, the *Realos* had regained the initiative, in alliance with a "Fresh Start" (*Aufbruch*) group led by Antje Vollmer which had sought to mediate between the contending factions.

In late 1989 a Green Party (*Grüne Partei*) was launched in East Germany, being at that stage opposed to German reunification. It joined with the Independent Women's League (*Unabhängige Frauenbund*) in contesting the March 1990 *Volkskammer* elections, winning 2.2% of the vote and eight seats. Unwilling to join forces with the West German Greens, the eastern Greens instead joined Alliance 90, which had been founded in February 1990 by a number of East German grass-roots organizations, including the New Forum (*Neues Forum*) and Democracy Now (*Demokratie Jetzt*), on a platform urging "restructuring" of the GDR along democratic socialist lines, rather than German unification or the importation of capitalism. In the all-German *Bundestag* elections of December 1990 Alliance 90 secured eight seats by surmounting the 5% threshold in the former GDR, even though its overall national vote was only 1.2%. In contrast, the western Greens, with

271

an overall 3.9% share, failed to retain representation.

With German reunification a fact, the western Greens and Alliance 90 gradually resolved their differences, until parallel congresses in Hannover in January 1993 voted to unite under the official name Alliance 90 but with the suffix "The Greens" being retained for identification purposes. The merger was formalized at a Leipzig congress in May 1983. The Greens' Mannheim congress in February 1994 opted in principle for a "red-green" coalition with the Social Democrats at federal level, although without modifying policies (such as opposition to NATO membership) that were unacceptable to the SPD leadership. In the June 1994 European Parliament elections the Green list took third place with a 10.1% vote share, winning 12 of the 99 German seats. In the October 1994 *Bundestag* elections the Greens achieved a further federal advance, to 7.3% and 49 seats. The new parliamentary arithmetic precluded a coalition with the SPD, but the Green presence was acknowledged by the election of a Green deputy (Antje Vollmer) as one of the *Bundestag*'s four vice-presidents.

In 1995 the Greens registered significant advances in *Länder* elections in Hesse (February), North Rhine–Westphalia and Bremen (May) and Berlin (October), winning a vote share of 10–13% in the four contests. As at mid-1996 the state governments of Hesse, North Rhine–Westphalia, Saxony–Anhalt and Schleswig-Holstein were SPD/Green coalitions. At a Green party conference in Bremen in December 1995, a majority of delegates endorsed the party's traditional opposition to any external military role for Germany, although an unprecedented 38% backed a motion by Joschka Fischer (by now a leading Green deputy in the *Bundestag*) to the effect that German troops could be deployed on UN peacekeeping missions.

The German Greens maintain links with like-minded parties in Europe and the wider world. The party's representatives in the European Parliament are substantially the largest component of the Green Group.

Christian Democratic Union

Christlich-Demokratische Union (CDU)

Address. Konrad-Adenauer-Haus, Friedrich-Ebert-Allee 73–75, 53113 Bonn

Telephone. (#49–228) 5440

Fax. (#49–228) 544216

Leadership. Helmut Kohl (chair), Wolfgang Schäuble (parliamentary group chair), Peter Hintze (general secretary)

The moderate conservative CDU was established in October 1950 as a federal organization uniting autonomous groups of Christian Democrats (both Catholic and Protestant) which had re-emerged in all parts of Germany after World War II, descended in part from the Centre Party founded in the 19th century and prominent in the pre-Hitler Wiemar Republic. Following a strong showing in the first *Länder* elections held in West Germany in 1947, an alliance of these groups, including the Christian Social Union (CSU) of Bavaria, had become the strongest element in the first *Bundestag* elections in 1949 under the leadership of Konrad Adenauer, who became the first West German Chancellor. On the formation of the CDU in 1950, the CSU remained a separate though allied party in Bavaria, and has generally been regarded as the more right-wing of the two.

The CDU remained in government until 1969, presiding over the blossoming of the "German economic miracle" under the successive chancellorships of Adenauer (until 1963), Ludwig Erhard (1963–66) and Kurt-Georg Kiesinger (until 1969). From 1959, moreover, Heinrich Lübke of the CDU served two five-year terms in the federal presidency. During this period the CDU–CSU tandem was in coalition with the Free Democratic Party (FDP) until 1957, governed with an absolute *Bundestag* majority until 1961, returned to a coalition with the FDP in 1961–66 and then formed a "grand coalition" with the Social Democratic Party of Germany (SPD). Having slipped to 46.1% in the 1969 elections, the CDU–CSU went into opposition to an SPD/FDP coalition that was to endure until 1982. The CDU–CSU share of the vote fell to 44.9% in 1972, rose to 48.6% in 1976 and then fell to 44.5% in 1980, when a joint electoral list was headed by Franz-Josef Strauss of the CSU, who had threatened a rupture with the CDU unless he was accepted as the alliance's candidate for the chancellorship. Meanwhile, Karl Carstens of the CDU had been elected President of West Germany in May 1979.

The FDP's desertion of the SPD-led coalition in October 1982 enabled the CDU–CSU to form a new government with the FDP under the leadership of Helmut Kohl. In *Bundestag* elections in March 1983 the CDU advanced strongly to 38.2% and 191 seats (and the CSU also gained ground), so that the CDU–CSU/FDP coalition continued in office. In May 1984 Richard von Weizsächer of the CDU, a former mayor of West Berlin, was elected to succeed Carstens as President. In the January 1987 lower house elections the CDU declined to 34.5% and 174 seats (and the CSU also lost ground), but gains by the FDP enabled Kohl to continue as Chancellor with the same coalition partners. Criticism of Kohl's leadership surfaced at the CDU's congress of November 1987, when he was re-elected chair (as the only candidate) by his lowest ever number of delegates' votes. In the June 1989 European

Parliament elections the CDU slipped to 29.5% of the national vote.

Confidence in Kohl's leadership was restored by his performance as government leader through the process of German reunification in 1990, which served to make his position in the CDU unassailable. In the all-German elections of December 1990 the CDU won 36.7% of the vote overall and took 268 seats in the enlarged 662-member *Bundestag*. Although the combined CDU–CSU share of the vote was the lowest since 1949, an SPD decline enabled Kohl to form a further CDU–CSU/FDP coalition. In the 1990 contest the CDU was confirmed as the strongest party in the eastern *Länder*, although it later lost ground because the Kohl government was blamed for the problems of economic transition. As a dedicated pro-European party, the CDU strongly supported German ratification of the Maastricht Treaty on European union (which was finally completed in October 1993); it also backed moves to amend the German constitution so that German forces could be deployed on UN-approved peacekeeping missions outside the NATO area. In May 1994 Roman Herzog of the CDU was elected President, while in the following month's European Parliament elections the CDU registered 32.0% of the vote, winning 39 of the 99 German seats.

In the October 1994 federal lower house elections the CDU slipped to 34.2% and 244 seats (out of 672), sufficient to underpin a further CDU–CSU/FDP coalition under the continued chancellorship of Kohl (who was re-elected CDU chair in November 1994 with over 94% of delegates' votes at a special congress). However, CDU setbacks in *Länder* elections in 1993–94 meant that the SPD established a majority in the indirectly-elected *Bundesrat* (federal upper house). As of April 1996 only Saxony was governed by the CDU alone (and the CSU was in power in Bavaria), while CDU/SPD coalitions ruled in Baden-Württemberg and Bremen and in the eastern Länder of Berlin, Mecklenburg-West Pomerania and Thuringia.

The CDU is a member of the Christian Democrat International and the International Democrat Union; its European Parliament representatives sit in the European People's Party group.

Christian Social Union
Christlich-Soziale Union (CSU)

Address. Nymphenburger Strasse 64-66, 80335 Munich

Telephone. (#49–89) 12431

Fax. (#49–89) 1243-274

Leadership. Theodore Waigel (chair and parliamentary leader), Edmund Stoiber (minister-president of Bavaria), Bernhard Protzner (general secretary)

The CSU was established in Bavaria in January 1946 by various Catholic and Protestant political groups with the aim of rebuilding the economy on the basis of private initiative and property ownership and of restoring the rule of law in a federal Germany. Led by Josef Müller, it won an absolute majority in the first Bavarian *Landtag* elections in December 1946 (with 52.3% of the vote), although the emergence of the separatist Bavaria Party in the 1950 elections reduced the CSU to a relative majority, obliging it to form a coalition with the state Social Democratic Party of Germany (SPD). The CSU continued in being on the formation of the Christian Democratic Union (CDU) in October 1950, it being agreed that the CSU would be the CDU's sister party in Bavaria and that neither would oppose the other at elections. While both parties have espoused essentially the same policies, the CSU is generally reckoned to be more conservative than the CDU. It is also less enthusiastic than the CDU leadership about plans for European monetary union and favours retention of the Deutschmark for the foreseeable future rather than German participation in a single European currency.

The post-war CSU/SPD coalition in Bavaria lasted until 1954, when the CSU went into opposition to a four-party government headed by the SPD. Under the leadership of Hanns Seidel, the CSU returned to office in 1957 at the head of a three-party coalition and in 1962 regained an absolute majority in the Bavarian *Landtag*, which it has held ever since. Seidel was succeeded as CSU leader by Franz-Josef Strauss in 1961 and as Bavarian minister-president by Alfons Goppel, who held office from 1962 until 1978. Strauss became the CSU's dominant figure in the CDU-led federal government, serving as Defence Minister from 1956 until being forced to resign in 1963 over the *Spiegel* affair. He returned to government as Finance Minister in the 1966–69 "grand coalition" between the CDU, the CSU and the SPD, but in 1978 opted to become head of the CSU government of Bavaria. Strauss was the unsuccessful CDU–CSU candidate for the chancellorship in the 1980 *Bundestag* elections, in which the CSU vote slipped to 10.3% (from 10.6% in 1976) and its seat total to 52.

Having been in federal opposition since 1969, the CSU returned to government in 1982 as part of a coalition headed by the CDU and including the Free Democratic Party (FDP). In the 1983 *Bundestag* elections that confirmed the coalition in power the CSU improved to 10.6% and 53 seats, although two CSU deputies later departed to join the far-right Republicans. In the 1987 elections the

CSU slipped to 9.8% and 49 seats but continued its participation in the federal government. Strauss died in October 1988 and was succeeded as CSU leader by Theo Waigel and as Bavarian minister-president by Max Streibl. In the June 1989 European Parliament elections the CSU list took 8.2% of the overall West German vote. In Bavarian state elections in October 1990 the CSU maintained its absolute majority, winning 54.9% of the vote and 127 of the 204 seats.

As Germany moved towards reunification in 1990 the German Social Union (DSU) was set up in the re-established eastern *Länder* as a would-be sister party of the CSU. However, in the all-German *Bundestag* elections of December 1990 the DSU made minimal impact, while the percentage vote of the Bavaria-based CSU inevitably fell, to 7.1% (8.8% in western Germany), yielding 51 seats out of 662 and enabling the CSU to continue as part of the federal coalition. In the June 1994 European Parliament elections the CSU list took 6.8% and eight of the 99 German seats, while in the Bavarian *Landtag* elections of September 1994 the party won its customary overall majority, although its seat total slipped to 120 and its vote share to 52.8%. The party therefore suffered little from a corruption scandal which had caused the resignation of Steibl as Bavarian minister-president in May 1993 and his replacement by Edmund Stoiber. The CSU improved its vote share slightly to 7.3% in the October 1994 *Bundestag* elections (although its representation fell to 50 seats) and obtained three portfolios in the re-formed CDU/CSU/FDP federal coalition.

The CSU is affiliated to the Christian Democrat International and the International Democrat Union. Its representatives in the European Parliament sit in the European People's Party group.

Free Democratic Party
Freie Demokratische Partei (FDP)
Address. Thomas-Dehler-Haus, Adenauerallee 266, 53113 Bonn
Telephone. (#49–228) 5470
Fax. (#49–228) 547298
Leadership. Wolfgang Gerhardt (chair), Hans-Dietrich Genscher, Otto Graf Lambsdorff and Walter Scheel (honorary chairs), Hermann Otto Solms (parliamentary chair), Guido Westerwelle (secretary-general)
Strongly based in the farming community, the centrist and secular FDP was founded in December 1948 at a conference in Heppenheim (near Heidelberg) as a fusion of various liberal and democratic *Länder* organizations descended from the German State Party (*Deutsche Staatspartei*) and the more right-wing German People's Party (*Deutsche Volkspartei*, DVP) of the Weimar Republic (1918–33), and more distantly from the

People's Party (*Volkspartei*) founded in 1866. The DVP had been revived in Baden-Württemberg in 1945 under the leadership of Reinhold Maier (who became the state's first premier and was later FDP leader in 1957–60) and Theodor Heuss (who became the first FDP leader and was then West Germany's first President, from 1949 until 1959). An attempt in 1947 to create an all-German liberal party had foundered on the opposition of the East German Communists to the participation of the Berlin-based Liberal Democratic Party (LDP), whose enforced support for socialism impelled prominent members, notably Hans-Dietrich Genscher, to flee to the West to join the FDP.

The FDP secured representation in the first West German *Bundestag* elected in 1949, with an 11.9% vote share, and joined a coalition government headed by what became the Christian Democratic Union (CDU) and also including the Bavarian Christian Social Union (CSU). It slipped to 9.5% in the 1953 elections and was in opposition in 1956–61, declining further to 7.7% of the vote in the 1957 federal elections. A major advance in 1961, to 12.8%, brought it back to office in a new coalition with the CDU–CSU that lasted until 1966, when the FDP again went into opposition, this time to a "grand coalition" of the CDU–CSU and the SPD. Having declined to 9.5% in the 1965 elections, FDP fell back sharply to 5.8% in 1969, but nevertheless joined a centre-left coalition with the SPD. Having succeeded Erich Mende as FDP chair in 1968, Walter Scheel served as Vice-Chancellor and Foreign Minister from 1969 until being elected West German President in 1974. During this period opposition within the party to the government's *Ostpolitik* caused several FDP deputies, including Mende, to desert to the opposition Christian Democrats. Scheel was succeeded in his party and government posts by Genscher, under whose leadership the FDP slipped to 7.9% in the 1976 elections (from 8.4% in 1972), before recovering to 10.6% in 1980.

The SPD–FDP federal coalition finally collapsed in September 1982 when the Free Democratic ministers resigned rather than accept the proposed 1983 budget deficit. The following month the party joined a coalition with the CDU–CSU, this switch to the right causing internal dissension and the exit of some FDP left-wingers. The party slumped to 6.9% in the 1983 federal elections and failed to secure representation in the 1984 European Parliament elections, its problems including the steady decline of its traditional farming constituency. The election of Martin Bangemann as FDP chair in 1985 in succession to Genscher (who nevertheless remained Foreign Minister) resulted in the party taking a more conservative tack, on which basis it revived to 9.1% in the 1987 *Bundestag* elections and continued its coalition with the CDU–CSU. In 1988 Bangemann opted to become a European commissioner and was succeeded as FDP chair by Count Otto Lambsdorff, who won a tight party election despite having been forced to resign from the government in 1984 after being convicted of illegal party financing activities. Having recovered some ground in state elections in the late 1980s, the FDP regained representation in the European Parliament in 1989 (winning 5.6% of the German vote).

On the collapse of Communist rule in East Germany, an eastern FDP sister party was formally established in February 1990. In the East German elections of March 1990 this party was part of the League of Free Democrats (together with the Communist-era LDP under new leadership and the German Forum Party), which took a 5.3% vote share. On the reunification of Germany in October 1990 these eastern elements were effectively merged into the western FDP, enabling the party to make a major advance in the all-German *Bundestag* elections in December 1990, to 11.0% of the overall vote and 79 seats out of 662. Maintaining its federal coalition with the CDU–CSU, the FDP showed electoral buoyancy in 1991 but encountered new difficulties following Genscher's resignation from the government in April 1992, as highlighted by the enforced resignation in January 1993 of the FDP Vice-Chancellor and Economics Minister, Jürgen Möllemann, over a corruption scandal.

In June 1993 Genscher's successor as Foreign Minister, Klaus Kinkel, replaced Lambsdorff as FDP chair, but he failed to halt a series of electoral failures at state level, while the party slumped to 4.1% in the June 1994 Euro-elections and thus failed to win any seats. Kinkel obtained a reprieve when the FDP unexpectedly retained a *Bundestag* presence in the October 1994 federal elections, winning 47 out of 672 seats on a 6.9% vote share. Despite previous strains over issues such as overseas German troop deployment (which the FDP opposed), the party opted to continue the federal coalition with the CDU–CSU and was rewarded with further electoral failures in Bremen and North Rhine–Westphalia in May 1995, whereupon Kinkel vacated the FDP leadership while remaining Foreign Minister. Elected as his successor at a special party congress in June, Wolfgang Gerhardt distanced himself from Chancellor Kohl on various policy issues, but a further FDP failure in Berlin elections in October 1995 served to intensify internal divisions on the party's future course. In December 1995 the FDP Justice Minister, Sabine Leutheusser-Schnarrenberger resigned after her party colleagues had backed a government plan to institute electronic surveillance of suspected criminals.

After relaunching itself with a more right-wing orientation in January 1996, the FDP polled strongly in state elections in Baden-Württemberg, Rhineland-Palatinate and Schleswig-Holstein in March, winning representation in all three contests. Nevertheless, apart from its federal government participation, in April 1996 the FDP held office at state level only in Rhineland-Palatinate (in coalition with the SPD). The FDP is a member party of the Liberal International.

German People's Union
Deutsche Volksunion (DVU)
   Address. c/o Landtag, Kiel, Schleswig-Holstein
   Leadership. Gerhard Frey

The extreme right-wing DVU claims not to be a neo-fascist party but has been prominent in anti-foreigner and anti-immigration agitation, contending that the majority of Germans want a "racially pure" country. In 1987 Frey launched a DVU/List D movement (the D signifying *Deutschland* as an electoral alliance which included elements of the National Democratic Party and which won one seat in the Bremen state elections of September 1987. In January 1990 the DVU participated in the creation of the German Social Union in East Germany, although with minimal lasting electoral impact. Following unification the DVU increased its Bremen representation to six seats in September 1991 (with 6.2% of the vote) and also won six seats in Schleswig-Holstein in April 1992 (with 6.3%).

The DVU backed the unsuccessful Republicans in the October 1994 federal elections in the wake of reports that the two groups might overcome their longstanding rivalry for the far-right vote. In the May 1995 Bremen elections the DVU declined to 2.5% and lost its representation in the state assembly. It also failed to retain any seats in the Schleswig-Holstein state election on March 1996, taking only 4.3% of the vote.

Instead of a Party
Statt-Partei (SP)
   Address. c/o Bürgerschaft, Hamburg
   Leadership. Markus Ernst Wegner, Mike Bashford

The SP was set up in July 1993 with the aim of promoting "a different kind of politics", including a reduction in government bureaucracy, the introduction of popular referendums and more voting according to conviction rather than by party discipline. The party's main founder, the lawyer Markus Ernst Wegner, had previously been a member of the Christian Democratic Union (CDU) and attracted support not only from

Hamburg CDU branches but also from other parties. In the September 1993 Hamburg elections the SP won 5.6% of the vote and eight seats (out of 121) and entered into a "co-operation" agreement with the new minority government formed by the Social Democratic Party of Germany. The SP obtained 0.01% of the vote in October 1994 federal elections.

Party of Democratic Socialism
Partei der Demokratischen Sozialismus (PDS)

Address. Karl-Liebknecht-Haus, Kleine Alexanderstrasse 28, 10178 Berlin

Telephone. (#49–30) 284090

Fax. (#49–30) 2814-169

Leadership. Lothar Lisky (chair), Hans Modrow (honorary chair), Sylvia-Yvonne Kaufmann (deputy chair), Gregor Gysi (parliamentary leader), Wolfgang Gehrcke (general secretary)

The PDS was established under its present name in February 1990 amid the collapse of Communist rule in East Germany, being descended from the former ruling Socialist Unity Party of Germany (*Sozialistische Einheitspartei Deutschlands*, SED), although it sought to throw off this provenance by espousing a commitment to multi-party democracy. The SED itself had been created in April 1946 as an enforced merger of the East German Social Democratic Party of Germany (SPD) with the dominant Soviet-backed Communist Party of Germany (*Kommunistische Partei Deutschlands*, KPD). The KPD had been founded in December 1918 by the left-wing minority of the SPD and other leftist elements and had played an important opposition role in the inter-war Weimar Republic, usually in conflict with the SPD, until being outlawed on the advent to power of Hitler's Nazi regime in 1933. During the Third Reich many German Communists had taken refuge in Moscow, returning to Germany at the end of World War II to assume power in the eastern Soviet-occupied zone.

In what became the German Democratic Republic (GDR), the SED was effectively the sole ruling party for over four decades, operating through the familiar device of a National Front that included four other "democratic" parties supportive of socialism, namely the Christian Democratic Union, the Democratic Farmers' Party, the Liberal Democratic Party and the National Democratic Party. Walter Ulbricht was elected SED leader in 1950, in which year several leading party members were expelled in the wake of Yugoslavia's break with the Cominform; other were purged in consequence of the major anti-government uprising in East Berlin in 1953. Some of these expellees were rehabilitated in 1956, but further purges followed the Hungarian Uprising later that year. Economic difficulties and the nationalization of agriculture served to increase the exodus of East Germans to the West, to staunch which the authorities erected the Berlin Wall in 1961, extending it along the entire length of the border with West Germany. In August 1968 East German troops participated in the Soviet-led military intervention that crushed the "Prague Spring" in Czechoslovakia.

In May 1971 Ulbricht was replaced as SED leader by Erich Honecker, under whom East Germany normalized its relations with West Germany in 1972 and became a UN member in 1974. In the 1980s Honecker maintained rigid orthodoxy, showing no enthusiasm for the post-1985 reform policies of Mikhail Gorbachev in the USSR. In 1989, however, a rising tide of protest and renewed flight of East German citizens to the West via Hungary resulted in Honecker being replaced in October by Egon Krenz, who himself resigned in December after the historic opening of the Berlin Wall on Nov. 9 had unleashed irresistible pressure for change. Later in December an emergency SED congress abandoned Marxism, added the suffix Party of Democratic Socialism to the party's name and elected Gregor Gysi as leader. A government of national responsibility appointed in February 1990 contained a minority of Communists for the first time in East Germany's history, although Hans Modrow of the SED-PDS retained the premiership. Having dropped the SED component from its name, the PDS polled better than expected in multi-party elections in March 1990 (winning 16.4% of the vote), assisted by the personal standing of Modrow. It nevertheless went into opposition to a broad coalition of parties committed to German reunification.

In the all-German *Bundestag* elections of December 1990 the PDS won only 2.4% of the overall vote but scored 11.1% in the eastern *Länder* and was therefore allocated 17 of the 662 seats by virtue of the separate application of the 5% threshold rule to the two parts of Germany. Thereafter the PDS suffered from a tide of disclosures about the evils of the former SED regime, but retained a substantial following among easterners disadvantaged by rapid economic and social change. In February 1993 Gysi was succeeded as PDS leader by Lothar Bisky, under whom the party polled strongly in elections in the eastern *Länder* in 1993–94. Although the PDS failed to win representation in the June 1994 Euro-elections, in the October 1994 federal elections it increased its national vote share to 4.4% and its eastern share to around 18%, being allocated 30 *Bundestag* seats from the proportional pool by virtue of having returned three candidates in a single electoral district (Berlin).

In January 1995 a PDS congress endorsed a

"left-wing democratic" programme and voted down the party's Stalinist faction led by Sarah Wagenknecht. In June 1995 the PDS received a financial boost when an independent commission agreed that it could retain a proportion of the former SED's assets. In Berlin legislative elections in October 1995 the PDS advanced to 14.6% of the vote (yielding 34 of the 206 seats), mainly at the expense of the SPD. Whereas the SPD's then leader, Rudolf Scharping, had consistently rejected any co-operation with the PDS, his successor elected in November 1995, Oskar Lafontaine, envisaged building a broad progressive front, including the PDS, to challenge the Kohl government in the next federal elections. The PDS was the only major party to oppose the proposed merger of Berlin and Brandenburg, which voters of the latter rejected in a referendum in May 1996.

The Republicans
Die Republikaner

Address. Sandstrasse 41, 81678 Munich
Leadership. Rolf Schlierer (federal chair)

The far-right anti-immigration Republicans were established as a party in November 1983 by two former *Bundestag* deputies of the Bavarian Christian Social Union (CSU) who had criticized the alleged dictatorial style of the then CSU leader, Franz Josef Strauss, particularly as regards the latter's involvement in developing relations with East Germany in contravention of CSU policy. Standing for German reunification, lower business taxes and restrictions on foreigners, the new party was also joined by the small Citizens' Party (*Bürgerpartei*) of Baden-Württemberg. Having won only 3% in their first electoral contest, for the Bavarian *Landtag* in 1986, the Republicans did not contest the 1987 federal elections. Under the leadership of former SS officer Franz Schönhuber, however, the party won 7.5% and 11 seats in the January 1989 Berlin legislative elections. It also did well in the June 1989 European Parliament elections, winning 7.1% and six seats (on a platform of opposition to the European Community).

Amid the progression to reunification in 1990, the Republicans' electoral appeal waned. They obtained less than 2% in state elections in North Rhine-Westphalia and Lower Saxony in May 1990, whereupon Schönhuber was briefly ousted from the party chairmanship, recovering the post in July. In the December 1990 all-German elections the party managed only 2.1% (and no seats), while in simultaneous polling it lost its representation in Berlin, falling to 3.1%. The party made a comeback in the Baden-Württemberg state elections in April 1992, winning 10.9% of the vote and 15 seats. In May 1993, moreover, it secured *Bundestag* representation for the first time when

it was joined by a right-wing deputy of the Christian Democratic Union (CDU), Rudolf Krause. In June 1994, however, it failed to retain its European Parliament seats (falling to a 3.9% vote share), while in the October 1994 *Bundestag* elections the Republicans won only 1.9% (and no seats). Prior to the federal polling Schönhuber was again deposed as leader, officially because of an unauthorized meeting with the leader of the German People's Union, but also because of his negative media image. In state elections in March 1996, the Republicans again polled strongly in Baden-Württemberg, winning 9.1% and 14 seats, while in Rhineland-Palatinate they improved to 3.5%, without gaining representation.

Social Democratic Party of Germany
Sozialdemokratische Partei Deutschlands (SPD)

Address. Ollenhauerstrasse 1, 53113 Bonn
Telephone. (#49-228) 5321
Fax. (#49-228) 532410
Leadership. Oskar Lafontaine (chair), Rudolf Scharping (deputy chair and parliamentary leader), Herta Däubler-Gmelin, Johannes Rau, Wolfgang Thierse and Heidemarie Wiczorek-Zeul (deputy chairs), Franz Münterfering (general secretary)

The origins of the SPD lie in the reformist General Association of German Workers (*Allgemeiner Deutscher Arbeiterverein*, ADA) founded by Ferdinand Lassalle in 1863 and the Social Democratic Labour Party (*Sozialdemokratische Arbeiterpartei*, SDAP) founded by the Marxists Wilhelm Liebknecht and August Bebel in 1869. In 1875 these two forerunners merged to form the Socialist Labour Party of Germany (*Sozialistische Arbeiterpartei Deutschlands*, SAPD), which was outlawed from 1878 under Chancellor Bismarck's anti-socialist laws. Relegalized in 1890, the SAPD became the SPD at the 1891 Erfurt congress, when the party reaffirmed its Marxist belief in inevitable socialist revolution, although in practice it was already following the reformist line advocated by Eduard Bernstein. Representing the rapidly expanding industrial working class and benefiting from universal manhood suffrage, the SAPD became the largest party in the *Reichstag* in 1912, although it played no part in Germany's unrepresentative government before 1914.

Ideological divisions within the SPD were intensified by World War I, during which the party split into a "majority" reformist wing supportive of the German war effort and the anti-war "Independent Social Democrats" led by Liebknecht and Rosa Luxemburg. Most of the latter faction joined the Communist Party of Germany founded in December 1918, while the main SPD became a key supporter of the post-war Weimar Republic, of which party leader Friedrich Ebert was the first Chancellor and the first President

277

(from 1919 to 1925). SPD participation in most Weimar coalition governments was accompanied by theoretical criticism of capitalism, notably in the Heidelberg Programme of 1925, but thereafter the party was identified as a defender of the status quo against Soviet-backed Bolshevism on the left and the rising tide of fascism on the right. In the July 1932 elections the SPD was overtaken as the largest party by Hitler's National Socialist German Workers' Party (the Nazis), the latter winning 37.4% and the SPD 24.3%. In further elections in November 1932 the Nazis fell back to 33.2% and the SPD to 20.7%, while the Communists increased from 14.3% to 17%. Nevertheless, Hitler was appointed Chancellor in January 1933 and was granted emergency powers following the burning of the *Reichstag* in February. In new elections in March 1933 the Nazis won 43.9% against 18.3% for the SPD and 12.1% for the Communists, whereupon an enabling act approved by the non-Nazi centre-right parties (but not by the SPD) gave Hitler absolute power to ban his political opponents, including the SPD.

After World War II the SPD was re-established in both the Western and the Soviet occupation zones, headed in the former by Kurt Schumacher and in the latter by Otto Grotewohl. The East German SPD was quickly constrained to merge with the Communists in the Socialist Unity Party of Germany (SED), founded in April 1946. In the first elections to the West German *Bundestag* in August 1949 the SPD came a close second to the Christian Democrats, with a 29.2% vote share, and was the principal opposition party until 1966, under the leadership of Schumacher until his death in 1952, then of Erich Ollenhauer and from 1958 of Willy Brandt (the mayor of West Berlin). During this opposition phase, the SPD's federal vote slipped to 28.8% in 1953 but then rose steadily, to 31.8% in 1957, 36.2% in 1961 and 39.3% in 1965. Faced with the evidence of West Germany's economic miracle of the 1950s, the SPD in 1959 adopted its celebrated Godesberg Programme, which jettisoned Marxist theory, embraced private ownership within the context of an equitable social order and industrial co-determination (*Mitbestimmung*), and reversed the party's previous opposition to NATO and the European Community.

In October 1966 the SPD entered a West German federal government for the first time, in a coalition headed by the Christian Democratic Union (CDU) and the Bavarian Christian Social Union (CSU). Brandt became Vice-Chancellor and Foreign Minister, in which capacity he pursued an *Ostpolitik* seeking normalization of relations with the Communist-ruled East European states, including East Germany. In March 1969

Gustav Heinemann became West Germany's first SPD President, elected with the backing of the Free Democratic Party (FDP). In the September 1969 federal elections the SPD at last broke the 40% barrier, winning 42.7% of the vote and forming a centre-left coalition with the FDP. Brandt became West German Chancellor and led the SPD to a further advance in the 1972 *Bundestag* elections, to a post-war high of 45.8% of the vote. Brandt continued as head of an SPD/FDP coalition until 1974, when the discovery that a close aide was an East German spy forced him to resign. He was succeeded as Chancellor by Helmut Schmidt (although Brandt remained SPD chair) and the SPD/FDP coalition under Schmidt's leadership continued in power through the 1976 and 1980 federal elections, in which the SPD vote was 42.6% and 42.9% respectively.

The SPD/FDP government finally collapsed in September 1982, when the FDP withdrew and opted to join a coalition headed by the CDU–CSU. The SPD remained in opposition after the March 1983 and January 1987 *Bundestag* elections, in which its support fell back to 38.2% and 37.0% respectively, eroded in particular by the advancing Greens. Brandt finally resigned as SPD chair in March 1987, when the party objected to his appointment of a non-SPD Greek lady as his spokesperson. He was succeeded by Hans-Jochen Vogel, a prominent SPD moderate, who launched a major reappraisal of the party's basic policy programme, although without achieving a definitive resolution of the vexed question of whether the SPD should formally commit to a future federal coalition with the Greens. In the latter context, however, the "red–green" coalition formed in 1985 between the SPD and the Greens in the state of Hesse set a trend of co-operation between the SPD and what was later named the Alliance 90/The Greens.

The sudden collapse of East European communism from late 1989 caught the opposition SPD on the back foot, with the result that it tended to follow in the wake of events leading to German reunification in October 1990. Launched in October 1989, an East German SPD led by Ibrahim Böhme won 21.9% of the vote in multi-party elections in March 1990 and joined an eastern "grand coalition" government. Böhme quickly resigned on being found to have been a Stasi agent and was succeeded by Markus Meckel (then East German Foreign Minister), who was himself replaced by Wolfgang Thierse in June 1990. In September 1990 the East and West German SPDs were merged, but the party found it difficult to recover its pre-war strength in the east. Oskar Lafontaine was the SPD's Chancellor-candidate in the December 1990 all-German *Bundestag* elections, in which the party won only 33.5% of the overall vote (35.7% in the western *Länder*, 24.3% in the east), which yielded 239 of the 662 seats.

The SPD therefore continued in opposition and Vogel immediately resigned as SPD chair, being succeeded by Bjoern Engholm, then premier of Schleswig-Holstein. In November 1992 a special SPD conference endorsed a leadership recommendation that the party should give qualified backing to government-proposed constitutional amendments which would end the automatic right of entry to asylum-seekers and would allow German forces to be deployed outside the NATO area on UN-approved peacekeeping missions. Damaged by the revival of an old political scandal, Engholm resigned as SPD leader in May 1993 and was succeeded by Rudolf Scharping (then premier of Rhineland-Palatinate). In the June 1994 European Parliament elections the SPD slipped to 32.2% of the vote (from 37.3% in 1989) and won 40 of the 99 German seats. Scharping then led the SPD to its fourth successive federal election defeat in October 1994, although its share of the vote improved to 36.4% and its representation in the *Bundestag* rose to 252 seats out of 672. Concurrent SPD advances at state level gave it a majority in the *Bundesrat* (upper house), although in May 1995 the party lost ground in North Rhine-Westphalia and Bremen, and in October went down to a heavy defeat in Berlin (once an SPD stronghold).

In November 1995 an SPD conference in Mannheim elected Oskar Lafontaine (the party's 1990 Chancellor-candidate and still premier of Saarland) as SPD chair in succession to Scharping, who remained the SPD leader in the *Bundestag*. Located ideologically on the SPD left, Lafontaine had opposed the Maastricht Treaty on European union, on the grounds that it contained inadequate provisions for real political union, and was also an advocate of political alliance between the SPD, the Greens and the (ex-communist) Party of Democratic Socialism. He subsequently took the SPD into a stance of opposition to any speedy adoption of a single European currency and to the automatic granting of citizenship to ethnic German immigrants from Russia; but the party suffered further setbacks in three state elections in March 1996. At mid-1996 the SPD was in sole control in the states of Brandenburg, Hamburg, Lower Saxony and Saarland; in coalition with the Greens in Hesse, North Rhine–Westphalia, Saxony–Anhalt and Schleswig-Holstein; in coalition with the CDU in Baden-Württemberg, Berlin, Bremen, Mecklenburg-West Pomerania and Thuringia; and in coalition with the FDP in Rhineland–Palatinate.

The SPD is a member party of the Socialist International and its European Parliament representatives sit in the Party of European Socialists group.

Other Parties

Animal Protection Party (*Tierschutz Partei*, TP), won 0.2% of the vote in the 1994 federal elections.

Bavaria Party (*Bayernpartei*, BP), founded in 1946 to seek the restoration of an independent Bavarian state, represented in the *Bundestag* in 1949–53 (but not since) and influential in the Bavarian *Landtag* until the mid-1960s, won 0.1% in the 1994 federal elections.

Democratic Party of Germany (*Demokratische Partei Deutschlands*, DPD), led by Sedat Sezgin, founded in October 1995 to represent foreigners in Germany and to oppose racism, based in the two-million-strong Turkish immigrant community (most of whom do not have German citizenship and are therefore not entitled to vote).

Democratic Republicans of Germany (*Demokratische Republikaner Deutschlands*, DRD), a splinter group of the far-right Republicans founded in Hannover in mid-1989.

Ecological Democratic Party (*Ökologisch–Demokratische Partei*, ÖDP), won 0.4% in both the 1990 and the 1994 federal elections.

German Communist Party (*Deutsche Kommunistische Partei*, DKP), founded in West Germany in 1969 some 13 years after the banning of its predecessor, for long led by Herbert Mies, had close links with the then ruling Socialist Unity Party of East Germany, but lost any impetus on the collapse of the East German regime in 1989; Mies resigned in October 1989 and was replaced by a four-member council at the party's 10th congress in March 1990.

German Social Union (*Deutscher Sozialer Union*, DSU), led by Roberto Rink, launched in East Germany in January 1990 as an umbrella organization of 12 conservative groups including the far-right German People's Union, then allied with the Christian Social Union (CSU) of West Germany; won only 0.2% in December 1990; its decision in April 1993 to campaign throughout Germany caused a breach with the CSU.

The Greys (*Die Grauen*), led by Trude Unruh, formerly a pensioners' group within the West German Greens, became a separate party in mid-

1989 to represent the interests of older citizens; it won 0.8% of the federal vote in 1990 and 0.5% in 1994.

League of Free Citizens (*Bund der Freie Bürger*, BFB), led by Manfred Brunner, a right-wing party founded in 1994 to oppose further moves towards European political and economic union; its leader was formerly *chef de cabinet* to one of Germany's European Union commissioners.

National Democratic Party (*Nationaldemokratische Partei Deutschlands*, NPD), led by Günter Deckert, far-right formation founded in 1964, reached a high of 4.3% in the 1969 federal elections and won seats in several state parliaments in the late 1960s, but declined thereafter, being supplanted by the Republicans; in April 1995 Deckert received a prison sentence for incitement to racial hatred and other offences.

Natural Law Party (*Naturgesetz Partei*, NP), the German branch of a worldwide network of such parties, won 0.2% in the 1994 federal elections.

Party of Bible-Believing Christians (*Partei der Bibeltreuen Christen*, PBC), won 0.1% in the 1994 federal elections.

South Schleswig Voters' Union (*Südschleswigscher Wählerverband*, SSW/*Sydslesvig Vaelgerforening*, SSV), led by Wilhelm Klüver, representing ethnic Danes in Schleswig-Holstein, won one seat in the 1992 state elections with 1.9% of the vote (being exempt from the 5% threshold rule), increasing to two seats in 1996 (with 2.5%).

Work for Bremen (*Arbeit für Bremen*, AfB), a left-wing splinter group of the Social Democratic Party of Germany, formed prior to the May 1995 state elections, in which it won 10.7% and 12 seats.

Ghana

Capital: Accra

Population: 17,000,000 (1995E)

The Republic of Ghana achieved independence from Britain in 1957. Since the overthrow of the country's first President, Kwame Nkrumah, in 1966, Ghana has experienced long periods of military rule interspersed with brief spells of civilian government. The most recent military regime, dating back to December 1981, relinquished power in January 1993 under a civilian constitution which was approved in a referendum in April 1992. The constitution provides for a directly elected 200–member House of Parliament, and an advisory Council of State with 25 members appointed by the President. The ban on the operation of political associations imposed in 1982 was lifted in May 1992. Presidential and legislative elections were held in November and December 1992 respectively, as a prelude to the inauguration of the Fourth Republic in January 1993. Flt.-Lt. (retd) Jerry Rawlings, who had come to power as a result of the coup in December 1981, was elected President with over 58% of the votes cast. His National Democratic Congress also won an overwhelming victory in the simultaneous legislative polls, which were boycotted by the opposition parties.

EGLE (Every Ghanaian Living Everywhere) Party
Address. c/o House of Parliament, Accra
Leadership. Owurako Amofa (chair)
The party evolved from the Eagle Club formed in 1991, which was effectively a pro-Rawlings grouping rather than a support organization for the military government as a whole. It secured one seat in the December 1992 legislative polls.

National Convention Party (NCP)
Address. c/o House of Parliament, Accra
Leadership. Kow Nkensen Arkaah (leader)

Established in 1992 as a pro-government party, the NCP contested the legislative elections in December 1992, winning eight seats on a platform virtually identical with that of the National Democratic Congress (NDC). Kow Nkensen Arkaah of the NCP was inaugurated as Vice-President in January 1993 and the party was allocated one portfolio (Justice) in the government headed by the NDC, although the resignation of its holder in October 1993 signalled increasing strains in the ruling coalition. In December 1995 the NCP formally abrogated its alliance with the

NDC, having the previous month announced a merger with the People's Convention Party and the People's National Convention to form a united "Nkrumahist" party bearing the historic title Convention People's Party. At the end of December 1995 Vice-President Arkaah claimed that President Rawlings had physically assaulted him during a cabinet meeting.

National Democratic Congress (NDC)

Address. c/o House of Parliament, Accra

Leadership. Flt.-Lt. (retd) Jerry Rawlings (leader), Issifu Ali (chair)

The NDC was launched formally in June 1992, following the legalization of political parties, as a coalition of pro-government organizations. Opposition groups charged the NDC with intimidation during the presidential election in November 1992, won by Flt.-Lt. Rawlings, and staged a boycott of the legislative elections the following month. Consequently, the NDC won 189 of the 200 parliamentary seats, with another nine seats going to its electoral allies campaigning as the Progressive Alliance.

New Patriotic Party (NPP)

Leadership. Peter Ala Adjetey (chair), Agyenim Boateng (secretary-general)

The NPP announced its formation in June 1992, advocating the protection of human rights and the strengthening of democracy. Its candidate in the November 1992 presidential election, Albert Adu Boahen, was the closest challenger to Jerry Rawlings, polling just over 30% of the votes cast. The NPP's decision in August 1993 not to contest the results of the December 1992 legislative elections created friction with other opposition partners.

People's Convention Party (PCP)

Leadership. Alhaji Asuma Banda (leader)

Descended indirectly from the former ruling Convention People's Party of Kwame Nkrumah, the PCP was established in December 1993 by the following groupings: the National Independence Party and the People's Heritage Party (which both put forward unsuccessful candidates in the November 1992 presidential poll), the People's Party for Democracy and Development, and a faction of the People's National Convention (PNC). The PCP replaced the opposition Inter-Party Co-ordinating Committee (ICC), which had itself superseded the Co-ordinating Committee of Democratic Forces of Ghana, formed in 1991. In November 1995 the creation of a unified "Nkrumahist" party, to be called by the historic title of Convention People's Party, was announced by the PCP, the rump of the PNC and the National Convention Party.

People's National Convention (PNC)

Leadership. Hilla Limann, John Ndeburge (leaders)

The "Nkrumahist" PNC was set up in May 1992 by former President Hilla Limann, who trailed in third place in the presidential election in November. Dr. Limann's antipathy towards opposition party unity talks in late 1993 (leading to the establishment of the People's Convention Party, PCP), provoked divisions within the PNC, a number of whose members subsequently broke away to join the PCP. In November 1995, however, the rump of the PNC opted to merge with the PCP and the National Convention Party to form a unified "Nkrumahist" party bearing the historic title Convention People's Party.

Other Parties

Campaign for Democracy in Ghana (CDG), opposition grouping.

Free Democrats' Union, opposition grouping.

Ghana Democratic Movement (GDM), opposition grouping.

Ghana Democratic Republican Party (GDRP), formed in 1992 and led by Kofi Amoah.

United Revolutionary Front (URF), a coalition of Marxist-Leninist groups.

Greece

Capital: Athens

Population: 10,500,000 (1995E)

Officially called the Hellenic Republic, Greece is a parliamentary democracy with a largely ceremonial President as head of state, elected by vote of the parliamentary deputies for a five-year term. Predominant executive power resides in the Prime Minister and members of the Cabinet, who must enjoy the confidence of the 300-member unicameral Parliament (*Vouli*). The latter is elected for a four-year term by universal adult suffrage under a system of proportional representation based on electoral constituencies returning between one and 26 deputies depending on their population size. Voting is compulsory for citizens aged 18 years and over (unless they are ill or incapacitated). By-elections are held to fill any vacancies, except during the final year of a parliamentary term. Political parties are required by the 1975 constitution to "serve the free functioning of democratic government".

A law of May 1984 provides for public funding of political parties to cover organizational and electoral campaigning expenses, an amount equivalent to 0.001% of the national income being allocated for this purpose. Eligible parties are those with parliamentary representation which have obtained at least 3% of the total vote in the most recent election and which have presented lists in at least two-thirds of the electoral constituencies. Coalitions of parties are also eligible, those of two parties requiring 5% of the vote to qualify and those of three or more 6%. Of the total annual subsidy available, 10% is shared equally between the qualifying parties and the other 90% is allocated in proportion to the total votes received by each party at the most recent election.

Parliamentary elections held on Oct. 10, 1993, resulted as follows: Pan-Hellenic Socialist Movement 170 seats (with 46.9% of the vote); New Democracy 111 (39.3%); Political Spring 10 (4.9%); Communist Party of Greece 9 (4.5%).

Communist Party of Greece

Kommounistiko Komma Elladas (KKE)
  Address. Leoforos Irakliou 145, 14231 Athens
  Telephone. (#30–1) 252–3543
  Fax. (#30–1) 251–1998
  Leadership. Aleka Papariga (general secretary), Harilaos Florakis (honorary president)

For long known as the "exterior" Communist Party because many of activists were forced into exile after World War II, the present KKE is directly descended from the Socialist Workers' Party of Greece (SEKE) founded in November 1918, which joined the Communist International (Comintern) in 1924 and changed its name to KKE. The party secured its first parliamentary representation in 1926 and in 1936 held the balance of power between the Monarchists and the Liberals, the resultant deadlock provoking a military coup by Gen. Metaxas in August 1936, following which all political parties were banned. During World War II popular resistance to the occupying Axis powers was organized by the Communists in the National Liberation Front (EAM) and the guerrilla Greek People's Liberation Army (ELAS), which gained control of the countryside. Following the liberation, however, ELAS was suppressed by British (and later US) troops after civil war had broken out between the Communists and centre-right forces favouring restoration of the monarchy. The KKE was officially banned in July 1947 and by 1949 had been defeated, its leadership and thousands of members fleeing to Communist-ruled countries.

The banned KKE became the dominant force within the Democratic Party (which won 9.7% of the vote in 1950) and then within the legal United Democratic Left (EDA), which won 10.4% of the vote in 1951, rising to 24.4% and 79 seats in 1958, before falling back to 11.8% and 22 seats in the the 1964 elections won by the centre-left Centre Union. During this period the KKE remained an orthodox Marxist-Leninist party whose pro-Soviet line was unaffected by the suppression of the Hungarian Uprising in 1956. In 1967–74 the

KKE took a leading role in the opposition to the Greek military junta, but factional conflict not only within the exiled party but also between it and Communist forces in Greece culminated in a decision by the latter in February 1968 to form an independent "interior" KKE. The "exterior" KKE's support for the Soviet-led suppression of the Czechoslovak "Prague Spring" later in 1968 and the gravitation of the KKE "interior" towards reformist Eurocommunism served to widen the ideological gap between the two factions. Accused of prime responsibility for the split, the KKE "exterior" leader, Constantine Kolliyannis, was replaced by Harislaos Florakis in 1973.

Legalized after the fall of the military regime in mid-1974, the KKE "exterior" contested the November elections as part of the EDA, which also included the "interior" Communists, winning five of the EDA's eights seats. Standing on its own in subsequent elections, the KKE "exterior" advanced to 11 seats in 1977 (with 9.4% of the vote) and to 13 in 1981 (10.9%), when it also secured three of the 24 Greek seats in the European Parliament (with a 12.8% vote share). After its overtures for representation in the new government of the Pan-Hellenic Socialist Movement (PASOK) had been rejected, the KKE "exterior" subsequently adopted a critical attitude towards PASOK, accusing it of betraying its election promises, notably its pledge to take Greece out of the European Community and NATO. For its part, the PASOK government allowed tens of thousands of KKE supporters, exiled since the late 1940s, to return to Greece. Concurrently, the party's rigid pro-Moscow orthodoxy, which included support for the Soviet intervention in Afghanistan, caused some internal dissension and defections. In the 1984 Euro-elections the KKE "exterior" vote slipped to 11.6% (although it again won three seats), while in the June 1985 national elections it achieved 9.9% of the vote and 12 seats. On the latter occasion the deputies elected on the KKE "exterior" list included a former PASOK Finance Minister and nominees of the Agrarian Party (AKE) and the United Socialist Alliance of Greece (ESPE), the latter launched by PASOK dissidents in 1984. In the October 1986 municipal elections the KKE "exterior" withheld crucial second-round support from PASOK candidates, thus ensuring their defeat in Athens, Piraeus and Salonika (the three largest cities).

Influenced by the formation of the Greek Left Party (EAR) by the KKE "interior" the previous month, the 12th congress of the KKE "exterior" in May 1987 issued a call for a new left-wing alliance committed to socialism. The eventual result was the Progressive Left Coalition (*Synaspismos*) between the KKE "exterior", the EAR (including the KKE "interior") and other groups, the alliance winning 28 seats in the June 1989 general elections on a 13.1% vote share. In simultaneous European Parliament elections a joint Communist list won 14.3% and four seats. However, the subsequent participation of *Synaspismos* in two temporary governments, the first with the conservative New Democracy (ND) and the second with ND and PASOK (after further elections in November 1989 in which the Coalition slipped to 21 seats and 11.0%), generated unrest in the KKE "exterior", leading to some defections. The party remained in *Synaspismos* for the April 1990 elections, in which the alliance fell back to 19 seats and 10.2% of the vote. However, the 13th KKE "exterior" congress in February 1991 resulted in the party's orthodox wing narrowly gaining control and in the election as general secretary of Aleka Papariga, who in June 1991 took the party out of *Synaspismos*. By then the "exterior" suffix was no longer required as an identifier, in that the "interior" party had ceased to be a distinct formation.

Having opted for independence, the KKE experienced further internal turmoil, involving the expulsion or departure of various elements that preferred the reformist line of *Synaspismos*. In the October 1993 elections, however, the KKE retained appreciable support, winning 4.5% of the vote and nine seats, whereas *Synaspismos* failed to obtain representation. In the June 1994 Euro-elections it advanced to 6.3%, yielding two of the 25 Greek seats, and thereafter maintained a critical stance on the policies of the PASOK government.

The KKE's representatives in the European Parliament sit in the Confederal European United Left group.

New Democracy
Nea Demokratia (ND)
    Address. Odos Rigillis 18, 10674 Athens
    Telephone. (#30–1) 724–2824
    Fax. (#30–1) 721–4327
    Leadership. Miltiades Evert (president), Ioannis Varvitsiotis (vice-president), Antonis Sgardelis (director)

The moderate conservative ND was founded in October 1974 by Constantine Karamanlis, who had been Prime Minister in 1956–63 as leader of the National Radical Union (ERE) and had opposed the colonels' regime of 1967–74 from exile in Paris. The new party won an absolute majority in the November 1974 elections, securing 220 of the 300 seats on a 54.4% vote share. It was confirmed in power in the November 1977 elections, although it slipped to 172 seats and 41.8% of the vote, with Karamanlis continuing as Prime Minister until being elected President in May 1980, when he was succeeded as government and party leader by George Rallis. In January 1981 a key ND policy aim was achieved when Greece became a member of the European Community, but in the October 1981 elections the party was heavily defeated by the Pan-Hellenic Socialist Movement (PASOK), retaining only 115 seats and 35.9% of the vote.

In the wake of ND's 1981 defeat Rallis was ousted as leader and replaced by right-winger Evangelos Averoff-Tossizza, but the latter resigned in August 1984 following the ND's poor showing in the European Parliament elections two months earlier. He was succeeded by the moderate Constantine Mitsotakis, who led ND to another election defeat in June 1985, although it improved to 126 seats and 40.8% of the vote. Mitsotakis's leadership then came under strong criticism from "new right" elements led by Constantine Stephanopoulos, who in September 1985 broke away to form the Democratic Renewal Party (DIANA). Mitsotakis reasserted his authority at a February 1986 ND congress, when "new right" policy theses were rejected, and in October 1986 the party made significant gains in municipal elections, taking control from PASOK in the three largest cities (Athens, Piraeus and Salonkia). Nevertheless, internal strains resurfaced in May 1987 when Rallis resigned from the party in protest against the earlier expulsion of his son-in-law for criticizing the ND leadership for its alleged departure from the policies of Karamanlis.

ND won a relative majority of 145 seats in the June 1989 general elections, the parliamentary arithmetic obliging it to form a temporary coalition with the Progressive Left Coalition (*Synaspismos*). Another election in November 1989 produced another stalemate, with ND representation edging up to 148 seats (on a 46.2% vote share), so that a temporary three-party coalition of ND, PASOK and *Synaspismos* representatives plus non-party technocrats was formed. Yet more general elections in April 1990 gave ND exactly half the seats (150) with 46.9% of the vote, so that Mitsotakis was able to form a single-party government with the external support of the single DIANA deputy. In May 1990 Karamanlis was returned for another term as President, securing parliamentary election as the ND candidate although at 82 he was no longer a party politician.

Amid a deteriorating economic situation, the Mitsotakis government experienced growing internal rifts in 1992–93, culminating in the formation of the breakaway Political Spring (PA) in June 1993. Deprived of a parliamentary majority, Mitsotakis resigned in September 1993, precipitating early elections in October, in which ND was heavily defeated by PASOK, falling to 111 seats and 39.3% of the vote. Mitsotakis immediately resigned as ND leader and was succeeded by

Miltiades Evert, who had been dismissed from the ND government in October 1991 for criticizing its free-market policies. ND took second place in the June 1994 European Parliament elections, winning 32.7% of the vote and nine of the 25 Greek seats, one of which went to the singer Nana Mouskouri despite (or perhaps because of) her self-admitted ignorance of politics. In October 1994 the ND candidate registered a notable victory in the Athens mayoral contest, while remaining much weaker than PASOK in local government.

In January 1995 the Greek parliament voted to drop phone-tapping and various corruption charges against Mitsotakis arising from his term as Prime Minister; the former ND leader complained that the decision denied him the opportunity of proving his innocence in court. In March 1995 the ND candidate, Athanasios Tsaldaris, failed to secure parliamentary election as President, being defeated by Constantine Stephanopoulos, who was nominated by the PA (and backed by PASOK in the interests of avoiding a general election), having disbanded his DIANA party following its failure in the 1994 Euro-elections.

ND is a member party of the Christian Democrat International, the International Democrat Union and the European Democrat Union. Its members of the European Parliament sit in the European People's Party group.

Pan-Hellenic Socialist Movement
Panellenio Sosialistiko Kinema (PASOK)

Address. Odos Charilaou Tricoupi 50, 10680 Athens

Telephone. (#30–1) 360–9831

Fax. (#30–1) 364–3664

Leadership. Kostas Simitis (president), Kostas Skandalidis (general secretary)

PASOK was founded in 1974, being derived from the Pan-Hellenic Liberation Movement (PAK) created by Andreas Papandreou in 1968 to oppose the military dictatorship which held power in Greece from 1967 to mid-1974. Having worked in the USA as an economics professor (and become a US citizen), Papandreou had returned to Greece in 1959 and had held ministerial office in pre-1967 Centre Union governments headed by his father George. Briefly imprisoned after the 1967 colonels' coup, he had been allowed to go into exile and had founded PAK, becoming convinced of the need for an unequivocally socialist party that would follow a "third road" distinct from West European social democracy and East European communism. According to Papandreou, the absence of a socialist tradition in Greece meant that PASOK had its roots in the wartime resistance and in the post-war National Liberation Front (EAM), which had been Communist-led, with a later centre-left admixture deriving from the Centre Union. PASOK was originally committed to the socialization of key economic sectors and also to withdrawal from the European Community (EC) and NATO, but was later to revise such policies when it came into government.

PASOK emerged from the November 1974 elections as the third strongest party, with 12 of 300 seats and 13.6% of the vote. In the November 1977 elections it became the strongest opposition party, with 93 seats and 25.3%, and in October 1981 it won an absolute majority of 170 seats (with 48.1% of the vote) and formed its first government under Papandreou's premiership. Four years later, in June 1985, PASOK was returned for a second term, although with its representation reduced to 161 seats on a 45.8% vote share. Prior to the 1985 contest, the PASOK candidate, Christos Sartzetakis, had been elected President in acrimonious parliamentary balloting in March. In office, PASOK experienced considerable internal divisions over the government's foreign and economic policies, including a new five-year agreement signed in September 1983 allowing US bases to remain in Greece, the dropping of opposition to EC and NATO membership, and the introduction of an economic austerity programme in 1985. Various critics of the leadership were expelled from PASOK in the 1980s and a number of breakaway groups were formed, although none had any enduring impact. In the October 1986 municipal elections PASOK suffered sharp reverses, losing the three largest cities to the conservative New Democracy (ND), although it remained by far the strongest party at local level.

In the June 1989 parliamentary elections PASOK was damaged by the Koskotas affair, involving financial malpractice in the Bank of Crete, and by Papandreou's extramarital affair with a young air hostess called Dimitra Liani, with whom he later contracted his third marriage. The party's representation slumped to 125 seats (on a 39.2% vote share) and it went into opposition to a temporary coalition between ND and the Progressive Left Coalition (*Synaspismos*). Further elections in November 1989 produced another statemate, with PASOK improving slightly to 128 seats and 40.7% of the vote, well behind ND, although the latter's lack of an overall majority dictated the formation of another temporary coalition, this time of the three main parties (but not including their leaders). Meanwhile, Papandreou had been indicted on corruption charges arising from the Koskotas affair. Greece's third general elections in less than a year, held in April 1990, broke the deadlock, with PASOK slipping to 123 seats and 38.6% and going into opposition to an ND government.

Continuing divisions within PASOK were highlighted during its second congress in September 1990, when Papandreou's nominee for the new post of party general secretary, Akis Tsochatzopoulos, was approved by a bare one-vote majority. Papandreou nevertheless remained unchalleneged as PASOK leader, and in January 1992 was finally acquitted of the various corruption charges against him. In the October 1993 elections PASOK stood on a manifesto which jettisoned much of the left-wing rhetoric of the 1980s and instead professed a "social democratic" identity, supportive of EC and NATO membership and of good relations with the USA. It won an overall majority of 170 seats (on a 46.9% vote share) and returned to government with Papandreou once again Prime Minister. Also reappointed (as Minister of Culture) was the famous actress and 1967–74 pro-democracy campaigner Melina Mercouri, although she was to die in office in March 1994. In the June 1994 European Parliament elections PASOK headed the poll, winning 37.6% of the vote and 10 of the 25 Greek seats. In October 1994 PASOK maintained its dominance in local elections, although losing the Athens mayoral contest to an ND candidate.

Growing unrest within PASOK over the ageing Papandreou's continued leadership and the undisguised political ambitions of his wife Dimitra developed into a fullscale succession struggle when the Prime Minister fell seriously ill in November 1995. Papandreou eventually resigned in January 1996 and was succeeded as PASOK political leader and Prime Minister by Kostas Simitis, who defeated acting Prime Minister Apostolos Tsokhatzopoulos in a runoff ballot of PASOK deputies by 86 votes to 75. Simitis had resigned from the government in September 1995 in protest against alleged sabotage of his reform plans by the PASOK hierarchy. Following the death of Papandreou on June 22, 1996, Simitis prevailed over strong internal opposition by securing election to the PASOK presidency at a special party congress at the end of the month.

PASOK is a member party of the Socialist International; its representatives in the European Parliament sit in the Party of European Socialists group.

Political Spring
Politiki Anixi (PA)

Address. c/o Vouli, Athens

Leadership. Antonis Samaras (president)

The right-wing populist PA was established in June 1993 by Antonis Samaras, a dissident member of the then ruling New Democracy (ND) who had been dismissed as Foreign Minister in April 1992 because Prime Minister Mitsotakis had objected to his hardline approach to the question of recognition of the ex-Yugoslav republic of Macedonia. (The party is often referred to in non-Greek sources by the acronym POLA, but in Greece this somewhat pejorative designation is used only by its opponents.) The new party attracted three other ND deputies into defection, so that the government lost its narrow parliamentary majority and was forced to resign. In early general elections in October 1993 Samaras (42) campaigned for an end to rule by the "dinosaurs" (i.e. Mitsotakis and Andreas Papandreou, leader of the Pan-Hellenic Socialist Movement, PASOK) and opposed any concessions by Greece that would allow Macedonia to use that word in its official title. The party won 10 seats with a vote share of 4.9%, becoming part of the parliamentary opposition to the new PASOK government. In the European Parliament elections of June 1994 the PA advanced to 8.7% of the vote, giving it two of the 25 Greek seats. In March 1995 the PA successfully nominated the veteran conservative politician Constantine Stephanopoulos as President, his election to the post by parliament in preference to an ND candidate being achieved on the basis of PASOK support.

The PA's representatives in the European Parliament sit in the Union for Europe group, the main national component of which is the radical right Forza Italia of Italy.

Progressive Left Coalition

Synaspismos tis Aristeras kai tis Proodou
   Address. Plateia Eleftherias 1, 10553 Athens
   Telephone. (#30–1) 321–7064
   Leadership. Nikos Constantopoulos (president)

Synaspismos was created prior to the June 1989 general elections as an alliance of the orthodox Communist Party of Greece (KKE) "exterior", the Greek Left Party (*Elleniki Aristera*, EAR) and a number of minor leftist formations. The EAR had been launched in April 1987 by the majority wing of the KKE "interior", itself founded in 1968 by resident Greek Communists opposed to the pro-Soviet orthodoxy of the exiled leadership of the KKE, which became known as the "exterior" party. Following the restoration of democracy in 1974, the Eurocommunist KKE "interior" had been part of the United Democratic Left (EDA), then including the KKE "exterior", and had won two of the EDA's eight seats in the November 1974 elections. In 1977 it had obtained one of the two seats won by an Alliance of Progressive and Left Forces (the precursor of *Synaspismos*), but had failed to win representation in 1981, before regaining one seat in 1985, when its share of the vote was 1.8%. In the 1984 European Parliament

elections the KKE "interior" had again won one seat, on a 3.4% vote share.

Reuniting the various Greek Communist factions, *Synaspismos* polled strongly in the June 1989 national elections, winning 28 seats out of 300 and 13.1% of the vote. In concurrent Euro-elections a *Synaspismos* list won four of the 24 Greek seats with 14.3% of the vote. However, the decision of the *Synaspismos* leadership to join a temporary coalition government with the conservative New Democracy (ND) generated rank-and-file unrest, with the result that the alliance fell back to 21 seats and 11.0% in November 1989 elections. The subsequent participation of *Synaspismos* in another temporary coalition, this time with ND and the Pan-Hellenic Socialist Movement (PASOK), was also controversial, and the alliance slipped again in the April 1990 elections, to 19 seats and 10.2% of the vote. The upshot was that in February 1991 the orthodox faction regained control of the KKE "exterior", which in June 1991 withdrew from *Synaspismos* and expelled elements that opted to remain in the alliance. The following month the prominent Communist reformer Maria Damanaki was re-elected *Synaspismos* chair.

In opposition to an ND government, *Synaspismos* endeavoured to transform itself into a unified party, to which end the EAR was dissolved in June 1992. However, the local organizational strength of the KKE (now the sole Communist Party) proved decisive in the October 1993 general election, in which *Synaspismos* failed to win representation (on a 2.9% vote share), whereas the KKE won nine seats. Damanaki thereupon resigned as *Synaspismos* leader and was succeeded by Nikos Constantopoulos. In the June 1994 European Parliament elections *Synaspismos* recovered to 6.3% (only narrowly behind the KKE) and took two of the 25 Greek seats.

The *Synaspismos'* members of the European Parliament sit in the Confederal European United Left group.

Other Parties

Christian Democracy (*Christianiki Democratia*, CD), left-leaning Christian party led by Nikolaos Psaroudakis, who was elected a deputy in 1985 on the list of the Pan-Hellenic Socialist Movement, opting to sit as an independent.

Communist Party of Greece–Renovating Left (*Kommunistiko Komma Ellados–Ananeotiki Aristera*, KKE-AA), led by Yiannis Banias, created in 1987 by a minority faction of the "interior" Communist Party opposed to the majority's decision to join a broader Greek Left Party (which later became part of the Progressive Left Coalition).

Democratic Socialist Party (*Komma Dimokratikou Sosialismou*, KODISO), centre-left formation founded in 1979, led by Charalambos Protopapas, who was elected a deputy in 1985 on the list of New Democracy, opting to sit as an independent.

Green Party of Greece, led by Nicos Galatis.

Hellenic Liberal Party, mainstream liberal formation led by Nikitas Venizelos, grandson of former Prime Minister Eleftherios Venizelos (1864–1936), from whose historic Liberal Party (founded 1910) the present party claims direct descent.

National Political Union (*Ethniki Politiki Enosis*, EPEN), led by Chryssanthos Dimitriades, far-right party founded in 1984, at first led by ex-Col. George Papadopoulos (military dictator in 1967–73), held one European Parliament seat in 1984–89.

Olympianism Party, pacifist grouping led by George Zoe.

Pan-Hellenic Unaligned Party of Equality (PAKI), founded in 1988, led by Charalambos Aloma Tamontsides.

Revolutionary Communist Party of Greece (EKKE), a Maoist formation dating from 1970.

Union of the Democratic Centre (*Enosi Dimokratikou Kentrou*, EDIK), led by Ioannis G. Zighdis, centre-left formation founded in 1974 as a merger of pre-1967 parties (including the Centre Union), won 60 seats in 1974, 15 in 1977 and none in 1981 (suffering from the left-right polarization of Greek politics); its leader was elected a deputy in 1985 with the backing of the Pan-Hellenic Socialist Movement.

United Socialist Alliance of Greece (*Eniaea Sosialistiki Parataxi Ellados*, ESPE), left-wing party founded in 1984 by Stathis Pagagoulis, previously a deputy minister in the government of the Pan-Hellenic Socialist Movement, who was elected a deputy in 1985 on the list of the Communist Party of Greece.

Grenada

Capital: St George's   **Population:** 97,000 (1995E)

A former British dependency, Grenada became a fully independent member of the Commonwealth in 1974. The head of state is the British sovereign represented by a Governor-General. The right-wing Grenada United Labour Party (GULP) government, headed by Sir Eric Gairy, was overthrown in 1979, when the socialist New Jewel Movement (formed in 1973) established a People's Revolutionary Government under the leadership of Maurice Bishop. Factional conflict within the new government led to the murder of Bishop during a coup in October 1983, prompting international intervention by United States-led military forces. A general election was held in December 1984 and a phased withdrawal of US forces was completed by June 1985.

Under the terms of the 1974 independence constitution, executive power is exercised by the Prime Minister who appoints the Cabinet. Legislative power is vested in a bicameral parliament, comprising a 13–member Senate and a 15–member House of Representatives. Members of the House of Representatives are elected for up to five years by simple majority in single-member constituencies. The Prime Minister, who is majority leader in the House of Representatives, directly appoints seven members of the Senate; three others are chosen on the advice of the Leader of the Opposition and the remaining three by the Prime Minister (but this time after consulting various interests).

A general election on June 20, 1995, resulted in the New National Party winning 8 seats in the House (with 32.7% of the vote), the National Democratic Congress 5 (31.1%) and the GULP 2 (26.8%).

Grenada United Labour Party (GULP)

Address. c/o House of Representatives, Church Street, St George's

Leadership. Sir Eric Gairy (president), Joseph McGuire (general secretary)

The right-wing GULP was formed in 1950 and held a majority of the elective seats in the then colony's legislature from 1951 to 1957 and from 1961 to 1962. The party regained power in 1967 with Gairy as Premier, and was returned to office in 1972 and 1976 (Grenada becoming independent and Gairy becoming Prime Minister in 1974). Regarded by the opposition as corrupt and authoritarian, Gairy was overthrown by the New Jewel Movement's bloodless coup in 1979 and went into exile, returning in 1984 following the US invasion. Subsequent efforts to re-establish the GULP as the major party were unsuccessful. It secured four seats in the House of Representatives in the 1990 general election (having had no representation in the previous parliament), but won only two seats in the 1995 polling.

National Democratic Congress (NDC)

Address. c/o House of Representatives, Church Street, St George's

Telephone. (#1-809) 440-3769

Leadership. George Brizan (leader), Kenny Lalsingh (chair)

The centrist NDC was launched in 1987 by George Brizan following his resignation as a minister in the then New National Party (NNP) government in protest at the policies and allegedly authoritarian style of the Prime Minister, Herbert Blaize. The new party was joined by a variety of opposition figures, including Marcel Peters (who had formed the Grenada Democratic Labour Party in 1985 after his expulsion from the Grenada United Labour Party) and Kenny Lalsingh (who had left the NNP in 1985 and established the Democratic Labour Congress the following year). In 1989 Brizan stepped down as opposition leader in favour of Nicholas Braithwaite, who had led an interim government for 13 months after the US invasion in 1983. Following the 1990 general election, in which the NDC won seven parliamentary seats, Braithwaite became Prime Minister and formed a new administration. Brizan replaced Braithwaite as NDC leader in 1994 and as Prime Minister in February 1995. In the June 1995 general election the party retained only five legislative seats and moved into opposition.

National Party (NP)

Leadership. Ben Jones (leader), George McGuire (chair)

The NP was organized in July 1989 by the then Prime Minister, Herbert Blaize, following his deposition as leader of the New National Party. Blaize died in December 1989 and the Governor-General appointed Deputy Prime Minister Ben Jones as his acting successor pending the March 1990 general election, in which the NP retained only two seats. It briefly participated in the subsequent National Democratic Congress administration before moving into opposition in early 1991. The party did not win any seats in the 1995 poll.

New National Party (NNP)

Address. c/o House of Representatives, Church Street, St George's

Leadership. Keith Mitchell (leader)

The NNP was created in August 1984 by the merger of the conservative Grenada National Party (GNP), led by Herbert Blaize; the centrist National Democratic Party (NDP), formed earlier in 1984 and then led by George Brizan; and the right-wing Grenada Democratic Movement (GDM), dating from 1983 and led by Francis Alexis. Although a part of the initial formation, the Christian Democratic Labour Party withdrew a month later. The GNP, which had been set up in 1956, held a majority of the elective seats in the colonial legislature from 1957 to 1961 and from 1962 to 1967, when Blaize was Chief Minister. It was in opposition from 1967 to 1979 and was largely inactive during the New Jewel revolutionary regime. In the December 1984 general election the NNP had a massive victory, winning 14 of the 15 legislative seats, and Blaize became Prime Minister. However, the party subsequently suffered internal divisions and was in serious disarray by April 1987, when Brizan and Alexis left the government and moved into opposition. In January 1989 Keith Mitchell defeated Prime Minister Blaize for the party leadership, prompting the latter to form a new organization, the National Party. Having secured only two seats in the 1990 general election, the NNP revived in the June 1995 polls, winning eights seat and a majority in the House of Representatives. Mitchell thereupon became the new Prime Minister.

Other Parties

Good Old Democracy (GOD), led by Justin McBurnic.

Grenada People's Movement (GPM), launched in 1989 by Rafael Fletcher (a former deputy leader of the Grenada United Labour Party).

Maurice Bishop Patriotic Movement (MBPM), set up in 1984 by former members of the New Jewel

Movement who had supported Bishop against the radical military faction responsible for his murder the previous year; led by Terry Marryshow and Einstein Louison.

United Republican Party (URP), formed in 1993 by Grenadians residing in New York in the United States; contested the 1995 general election without success.

Guatemala

Capital: Guatemala City

Population: 10,600,000 (1995E)

Guatemala's modern political history has been very unstable. Three separate constitutions have been promulgated since 1955 and there have been four successful military coups (1957, 1963, 1982 and 1983) and two failed coups (in May and December 1988). Left-wing political parties are illegal and a 30-year civil war by left-wing guerrillas has yet to break the monopoly on power held by a small ruling class and the military. Peace talks aimed at national reconciliation, the expansion of democracy, the ending of gross human rights abuses and the demilitarization of the country, are currently proceeding between the government, moderate sections of the army and the guerrillas.

Under its 1985 constitution, which came into effect in January 1986, the Republic of Guatemala has a unicameral National Congress of 116 members, 87 of whom are directly elected and 29 are elected on the basis of proportional representation. Both President and congressional deputies are elected for a five-year term. The President may not be re-elected. If in the presidential elections none of the candidates secures an absolute majority, a second round between the two leading candidates takes place. The President is assisted by a Vice-President and an appointed Cabinet. Voting is compulsory for those 18 years of age and older who can read and write but is optional for illiterates from the same age group. Non-voting is punishable by a small fine. The police and active duty military personnel are not allowed to vote.

On June 6, 1994, Ramiro de Leon Carpio (non-party) was elected President by the National Congress to succeed Jorge Serrano Elias, of the right wing Social Action Movement (MAS), who had been ousted from power on June 1 before completing his term of office which began in January 1991. A new national unity Cabinet was appointed between mid-June and early July and served until fresh presidential and legislative elections were held on Nov. 12, 1995. These proved inconclusive and Alvaro Arzu of the National Advancement Party (PAN) with 36.56% of the vote and Alfonso Portillo of the Guatemalan Republican Front with 22.08% were to contest a second round run-off on Jan. 7, 1996. Elections to the National Congress were also held on Nov. 12, 1995, and won by the PAN with 43 seats. The Guatemalan Republican Front won 21 seats, the New Guatemala Democratic Front six, the Christian Democratic Party four, the Union of the National Centre three, the Democratic Union two and the National Liberation Movement one.

Democratic Institutionalist Party
Partido Institucional Democrático (PID)

Address. 2a Calle 10-73, Zona 1, Guatemala City

Leadership. Donaldo Alvárez Ruíz; Oscar Humberto Rivas Garcia (secretary-general)

Founded in 1965, the PID is a right-wing party that is a firm believer in free enterprise. The party was formed by the leader of the 1963 coup and then dictator Col. Enrique Peralta Azurdia together with businessmen, leading propertied families and members of the army. It met with defeat in the 1966 presidential election despite being the "official" party. Thereafter the PID mostly fought elections in alliance with other parties (1970 and 1974 with the extreme right-wing National Liberation Movement (MLN); 1978 with the centre-right Revolutionary Party (PR); and 1982 within the centrist Popular Democratic Front (PDF), made up of the PID, PR and the Front for National Unity (FUN)) and enjoyed 12 years in government. The PID's fourth term in government was cut short by a military coup in March 1982, soon after Gen. Aníbal Guevara became President. Modest results were achieved in the two elections following the counter-coup of 1983. In 1984 the PID won five seats in the Constituent Assembly and in 1985, in coalition with the MLN, one seat in the Congress. In the 1990 elections, the party joined the FUN and the Guatemalan Republican Front (FRG) in the "No Sell-Out Platform" (PNV) supporting the former dictator Gen. (retd) Efraín Ríos Montt, who was generally thought to be the most likely victor in the presidential race before he was barred from standing. The coalition nevertheless won 12 seats in the Constituent Assembly.

Following the deregistration of the party in the wake of the demise of the PNV alliance, the party's legislative members aligned themselves with the MLN. The party however managed to gain no congressional representation in 1994.

Democratic Party of National Co-operation
Partido Democrático de Cooperación Nacional (PDCN)
   Leadership. José (Pepé) Fernandez (1990 presidential candidate), Rolando Baquiax Gómez (secretary-general)
   The PDCN is a centre-right party founded in 1983 by Acisclo Valladares Molina and, after failing to win a seat in the 1984 Constitutional Assembly elections, re-organized by Jorge Serrano Elías (see Solidarity Action Movement, MAS). The PDCN fought the 1985 general election in alliance with the Revolutionary Party (PR) and together they won 11 seats. Serrano left the party soon after coming third in the presidential race. Between 1986 and 1990 the PDCN supported the ruling Guatemalan Christian Democracy Party (DCG), but for the November 1990 general election campaign it entered into a coalition with the PR. However, this coalition was dissolved when the candidate, Fernando Andrade Díaz Durán, withdrew and the PR entered its own candidate.

Democratic Union
Unión Democrática (UD)
   Leadership. José Luis Chea Urruela
   This relatively new right-wing party was launched prior to the 1994 general election and campaigned on a platform of being a party with no historical baggage. However, despite this it could only gain one congressional seat at the election.

Emergent Movement of Harmony
Movimiento Emergente de Concordia (MEC)
   Leadership. Benedicto Lucas (1990 presidential candidate)
   The MEC is a right-wing party founded in 1983 by Col. Francisco Luis Gordillo Martínez, who was a member of Ríos Montt's junta in 1982. The MEC unsuccessfully fought the 1984 Constituent Assembly election and the 1985 and 1990 general elections. The party supported Serrano Elías of the Solidarity Action Movement (MAS) in the 1991 presidential run-off.

Guatemalan Christian Democratic Party
Democracia Cristiano Guatemalteca (DCG)
   Address. Av. Elena 20—66 Zona 3, Guatemala City
   Telephone. (#502-2) 84988
   Fax. (#502-2) 323743
   Leadership. Mario Vinicio Cerezo Arévalo (former President), Francisco Villagran Kramer (leader of the right-wing faction), René de Leon Schlotter (leader of the left-wing faction), Alfonso Cabrera Hidalgo (secretary-general)
   Founded in August 1955, the DCG is a centre-right party which, despite its reformist rhetoric has been decidedly conservative when in office. The DCG came out of an anti-Communist tradition and was founded with the help of the Roman Catholic Church in the belief that a Christian approach to politics would prevent reformist governments that held power in 1944-54, which they classified as left-wing. The DCG's policy was to oppose violence and promote social justice through direct church assistance while at the same time closing ranks with the extreme right-wing National Liberation Movement (MLN) in 1958. The contradictions within the DCG came to a head during the Peralta regime (1963-1966), when an anti-Communist faction accepted 10 seats in Congress while the majority of the party campaigned in opposition for basic social welfare and reforms of the army. After the expulsion of the right-wing faction, the party gained considerable support from students, trade unionists and rural communities during the unrest and repression of the 1960s.

Following attacks by right-wing paramilitaries and the murder of several of its leaders, the DCG went underground in June 1980 but re-emerged for the 1982 election campaign as a partner of the National Renewal Party in the National Opposition Union (UNO). The alliance won three seats in Congress and the PNR presidential candidate came third with 15.6%. The DCG initially supported the 1982 coup led by Ríos Montt who promised to put an end to violence and corruption but distanced itself from the regime when it became an open dictatorship. The DCG gained the reputation of being the party least involved in repression and corruption and the one most likely to promote social reforms. In the 1984 constituent elections it won the most seats (20 out of 88). This paved the way for the resounding victory in the November 1985 general election.

The Cerezo government, which took office on 14 January 1986, proved to be a conservative one. The government nevertheless suffered three coup attempts and a number of coup plots by the extreme right wing and sections of the army between 1987 and 1989.

The DCG attempted to recreate its progressive image by forging an alliance with the Democratic Convergence (DC), but this could not counteract the worsening effects of the economy, the allegations of corruption levelled against the party's leadership and the general disillusionment with the DCG.

The party managed to muster only 27 seats in the November 1990 congressional elections, and Alfonso Cabrera, unable to campaign through illness, came third in the presidential contest with 17.3% of the votes. In 1994, the party's representation fell from 28 to 13 seats.

After the party had joined the National Front alliance in April 1995, a number of disgruntled DCG deputies resigned their party memberships and set up a defiant independent bloc in Congress.

The party is a full member of the Christian Democrat International.

Guatemalan Republican Front

Frente Republicano Guatemalteco (FRG)
  Address. 6A avda A/3-18, Zona 1, Guatemala City
  Telephone. (#502-2) 501778
  Leadership. Gen. (retd.) Efraín Rios Montt (former President), Teresa Sosa de Rios (1995 presidential candidate)

A party that was formed as a vehicle for former President of the Republic Gen. (retd.) Efraín Rios Montt, the FRG was a key participant in the 1990 "No Sell-Out Platform" (*Plataforma No Venta*, PNV). This electoral grouping was an alliance between the FRG, the Democratic Institutionalist Party (*Partido Institucional Democrático*, PID) and the National Unity Front (*Frente de Unidad Nacional*, FUN), and was extreme right-wing and populist, standing for strict law and order. Montt was an extremely unpopular man, having staged a military coup in 1982 and assumed dictatorial powers.

Largely due to the unpopularity of Montt, the alliance was deregistered after the 1990 poll on the dubious legal grounds that heads of state who participated in coups are banned from running for the presidency. In 1993 the party again failed to regain legislative approval.

The FRG was similarly affected by this ban, but in the 1994 legislative contest staged an impressive come-back winning 32 of the available seats, a result that gained Montt the presidency of Congress. The former president's wife is currently the FRG's presidential election candidate.

National Advancement Party

Partido por el Adelantamiento Nacional (PAN)
  Address. 6A Calle 7-70, Zona 9, Guatemala City
  Telephone. (#502-2) 317431
  Leadership. Alvaro Enrique Arzu Irigoyen (president), Luis Flores (secretary-general)

Founded in 1989, the PAN is a centre-right grouping and currently the second force in Guatemalan politics. The party's founder, Alvaro Arzú Irigoyen, gained his reputation as an efficient administrator during his years as mayor of the capital, Guatemala City (1985-1990). He resigned from his mayoral post and formed the PAN to contest the 1990 general election. His candidature was regarded favourably by the business community and the US government. Arzú came fourth in the first round of the presidential elections with 17.3% of the vote, and the PAN obtained 12 seats in the Congress. A PAN member, Oscar Berger, with 34% of the vote was elected mayor of Guatemala City. In return for supporting the victorious presidential candidate Jorge Serrano of the Solidarity Action Movement (MAS), Arzú was named as Foreign Minister in the new government and the PAN was also given the communications, transport and public works portfolio. However, it became clear during the Mexico peace talks with the Guatemalan National Revolutionary Unity (URNG) guerrillas in May 1991, to which Arzú was not invited, that Serrano would not allow him a major role in government. Arzú resigned as Foreign Minister in September 1991 in protest at Serrano's decision to establish diplomatic relations with Belize, sovereignty over which had long been claimed by Guatemala.

The party was runner-up to the FRG in the 1994 elections, winning 24 congressional seats to the FRG's 32.

National Front

Frente Nacional (FN)
  Leadership. Fernando Andrade Díaz Durán (1995 presidential candidate)

The FN was launched in April 1995 as an electoral coalition of the Guatemalan Christian Democratic Party, the Union of the National Centre and the Social Democratic Party. Its presidential candidate polled 12.9% in the first round in November 1995.

National Liberation Movement
Movimiento de Liberación Nacional (MLN)

Address. 5a Calle 1-20, Zona 1, Guatemala City

Leadership. Mario Sandoval Alarcón (president), Alfredo Castillo Corado (1995 presidential candidate), Edgar Antonio Figueroa Muñoz (secretary-general).

Founded in 1960, the MLN is an extreme right-wing party that is strongly opposed to negotiations with guerrilla groups and traditionally has represented agrarians (especially coffee growers) and industrial élites.

The self-proclaimed "party of organized violence" was founded by Mario Sandóval Alarcón as the successor of Col. Castillo Armas' National Democratic Movement (MDN) which, with US backing, overthrew the reformist Arbenz government in 1954. The MLN staged the 1963 coup led by Col. Peralta Azurdia (see Democratic Institutional Party—PID) and formed a government with the Revolutionary Party (PR) until it was itself overthrown in 1964. The MLN's presidential candidate came third in the 1966 elections, but from 1970 the party was in government for eight years, its leader Col. Carlos Araña Osorio was President from 1970-74, and in 1974-1978 Gen. Kjell Laugerud presided over an MLN-PID government, with Sandóval as acting Vice-President. The 1970s also saw the height of the activity of MLN-linked death squads. For the July 1984 constituent elections the MLN entered into a coalition with the Authentic Nationalist Central (CAN) and won most of the coalition's 23 seats which made it the largest block in the Constituent Assembly. It entered into another coalition with the PID before the November 1985 general elections.

In the presidential race, Sandóval came fourth with 12.6% of the vote, and both MLN and PID won six seats each in the Congress. The MLN secretary-general, Héctor Aragón Quiñonez, and his supporters, subsequently left the party. The MLN strongly opposed the policies of the new DCG government and in particular its position of support for the Central American peace process, accusing it of being Marxist.

The MLN had also strongly condemned the government's efforts to end the 30-year war with left-wing guerrillas but, by early 1990, their attitude to the peace process had mellowed. In response to the opening of peace talks with the Guatemalan National Unity Movement (URNG) guerrillas in the Norwegian capital Oslo, the MLN supported the eventual incorporation of the URNG into the political mainstream. In the November 1990 general election, the MLN, in coalition with the National Advancement Front

(FAN), won a mere four seats in the Congress and their presidential candidate Col. Luis Ernesto Sosa came fifth in the first round of the presidential contest, receiving 17.3% of the vote.

The party secured two seats in its own right in 1994.

National Renewal Party
Partido Nacionalista Renovador (PNR)

Leadership. Fernando Leal (1990 presidential candidate), Renán Quiñonez Sagastume (secretary-general)

The PNR is a right-of-centre party founded in August 1979. Its leader and former National Liberation Movement (MLN) member Alejandro Maldonado Aguirre stood for President for the National Opposition Union (UNO) coalition in 1982 and came third. In the July 1984 the PNR won five seats in the Constituent Assembly elections but in the 1985 general election won only one seat in the Congress.

Fernando Leal stood in the 1990 presidential elections with negligible results. The party currently has no representation in Congress.

National Unity Front
Frente de Unidad Nacional (FUN)

Address. 6A avda 5-18, Zona 12, Guatemala City

Telephone. (#502-2) 714048

Leadership. Col. Enrique Peralta Azurdia (former President), José Alejandro Gramajo (1995 presidential candidate)

The FUN was originally set up as a coalition of the Christian Democrats, the Authentic Revolutionary Party (PRA) and the Popular Participation Front (FPP) in the run-up to the 1978 elections. Having supported other party candidates since then, the FUN is currently not represented in Congress.

Nationalist Authentic Central
Central Auténica Nacionalista (CAN)

Address. 15A avda 4-31, Zona 1, Guatemala City

Telephone. (#502-2) 512992

Leadership. Mario David García (1985 presidential candidate), Jorge Roberto Arana España (secretary-general)

The CAN is a right-wing party founded in 1980 as the successor of the *Central Arañista Organzado* (itself founded in 1979 by supporters of Gen. (retd) Carlos Manuel Araña Osorio, President 1970-1974). The CAN was in favour of a military coup following the March 1982 elections but by September called for free elections. The party reached its peak in 1984, as the junior partner in the alliance with the National Liberation Movement (MLN) which, with 23 seats, became the largest bloc in the Constituent Assembly. Since the dissolution of the coalition in 1985 the CAN only managed to win a single seat in Congress in the 1985 elections. It did not participate in the 1990 elections.

New Guatemala Democratic Front
Frente Democrático de Nueva Guatemala (FDNG)

Leadership. Jorge Luis Gonzalez del Valle (1995 presidential candidate)

The FDNG is a left-wing alliance that was formed in 1995 as offering a broad range of political movements from which to chose. It was formed as an alliance between the Social Christian Party (PSC) and the Social Reformist Union (URS), which quickly threw the electoral prospects of the group into doubt following their withdrawal from the alliance a few months later.

Revolutionary Party
Partido Revolucionario (PR)

Leadership. Angel Lee (1990 presidential candidate), Mario Fuentes Pieruccini (secretary-general)

Founded in 1957, the Revolutionary Party is technically reformist, but has in the past wavered between centre-right and right-wing positions. The PR started life as a left-wing party, formed by veteran supporters of the 1944 progressive government of President Juan José Arevalo Bermejo. At the 1959 party convention, however, most of the radical wing was expelled. In 1966 general election, Julio César Méndez Montenegro was elected President and the party captured 30 out of 55 seats in the Congress. The victory was attributed partly to a secret pact with the army, which then constantly hampered Méndez Montenegro's reformist plans. In the 1970 elections the PR lost power to the right-wing National Liberation Movement (MLN), and the party plunged into a protracted turmoil which caused two splits. In 1974 the left of the party split away to found the United Front of the Revolution (FUR) with the remainder in the PR going to the right by forming an alliance with the Institutional Democratic Party (PID).

For the 1985 general election, however, the PR began to swing to the left and entered into a coalition with the Democratic Party of National Co-operation (PDCN) on a programme promising agricultural and administration reforms. The PR-PDCN presidential candidate, Jorge Serrano Elías (see Solidarity Action Movement and PDCN), came third and the coalition together won 11 congressional seats. Following four years in opposition, the PR's presidential candidate José

Angel Lee obtained a mere 2.15% of the vote in the November 1990 general election, ending up in seventh place, and the party won two seats in the Congress. In the second round of the presidential elections, the PR supported the victor, Serrano.

The party lost its one member of Congress in 1994.

Social Christian Party
Partido Social Cristiano (PSC)

Leadership. Alfonso Alonzo Barillas (secretary-general)

The PSC was a brief founder member of the New Guatemala Democratic Front electoral alliance before withdrawing in late 1995. The PSC itself was formed in 1983 and is currently without congressional representation.

Social Democratic Party
Partido Social Demócrata (PSD)

Address. 12 Calle 10-37 Zona 1, Apartado Postal 1279, 01901 Guatemala City

Telephone. (#502-2) 539477

Fax. (#502-2) 539477

Leadership. Carlos Gallardo Flores (president), Sergio Alejandro Flores (secretary-general)

Founded in 1978, the PSD is nominally centre-left but its determination to secure an expanding role in the political mainstream led it to join in government with the right-wing government of Jorge Serrano Elías.

The PSD went underground and its leaders into exile in 1980 following the shooting of some of its leading members by right-wing death squads. From their Costa Rican exile the PSD leaders joined other opposition groups in the Guatemalan Committee of Patriotic Unity (founded February 1982) in denouncing the 1982 elections, marred by violence and fraud, and endorsing the Guatemalan National Revolutionary Unity guerrilla coalition's "popular revolutionary war" as the only way forward. The PSD boycotted the 1984 elections, but in early 1985, with the prospect of relatively free and fair elections, its leaders returned to Guatemala and re-registered the party. The United Revolutionary Front centre-left coalition, of which the PSD was a leading member, gained two seats in Congress. For the November 1990 elections the PSD joined forces with the Popular Alliance 5 (AP5) and went ahead with their election campaign despite threats by right-wing paramilitaries to their candidates and the killing of a regional party secretary. The PSD-AP5 won one seat in the Congress and the PSD secretary-general, Mario Solórzano was made Labour Minister in the new government.

Its credibility dented by its collaboration with the Serrano Elías government, the PSD failed to secure legislative representation in 1994.

The party is a full member of the Socialist International.

Social Reformist Union
Unión Reformista Social (URS)

Leadership. Alfonso Fuentes Soria (1995 presidential candidate), Marcos Emilio Recinos Alvarez (secretary-general)

The URS was a brief founder member of the New Guatemala Democratic Front electoral alliance before withdrawing along with the PSC in late 1995. The party's 1995 presidential candidate is a former rector of the State University.

Solidarity Action Movement
Movimiento de Acción Solidaria (MAS)

Leadership. Jorge Serrano Elías (former President, currently in exile), José Eduardo Rottman Ruiz (secretary-general)

Founded in 1986, the MAS is a right-wing grouping that represents mainly business interests and believes in the deregulation of the economy. The party was formed by Jorge Serrano Elías, a businessman, evangelical Christian, veteran anti-Communist and former president of the Council of State created under Gen. Ríos Montt's military junta in 1982. He stood as the presidential candidate for the Revolutionary Party—Democratic Party of National Co-operation (PR-PNDC) coalition in the 1985 general election and after coming third with 13.8% of the vote, left the PDCN. In the November 1990 elections, Serrano campaigned on a platform of law and order, respect for human rights and "total peace" with the guerrillas (he had been a member of the National Reconciliation Commission in peace negotiations with the Guatemalan National Revolutionary Unity (URNG) guerrillas.

In the second round, backed by the Emergent Movement of Harmony (MEC), National Liberation Movement (MLN), PNV and especially the National Advancement Party (PAN), Serrano was swept to power with 68.1% of the vote. He rewarded the PAN for its support as soon as he was sworn in on Jan. 6, 1991, by forming a MAS-PAN alliance and appointing two leading PAN members to his Cabinet.

Serrano agreed a four-point framework peace agreement with the URNG guerrillas in July 1991. The party failed to gain representation in the 1995 congressional elections.

Union of the National Centre
Unión del Centro Nacional (UCN)

Address. 12 Calle 2-45 Zona 1, Guatemala City
Telephone. (#502-2) 2918
Fax. (#502-2) 536216
Leadership. Sidney Shaw (director), Juan Ayerdi Aguilar (secretary-general)

Founded in 1983, the UCN claims to be a "stabilizing centrist" party, although Carpio surrounded himself with conservative economists during the 1990 election campaign and his running-mate came from the extreme right. Election promises included greater efficiency in agriculture and in the collection of taxes, but offered no promise of social reforms. The UCN was formed by Carpio, a newspaper publisher, as a vehicle for his presidential aspirations. At first the party adopted an anti-Communist stance, but at times it attempted to project a left-wing image. It fought the 1984 Constituent Assembly elections with a lavish media campaign never seen in Guatemala and reaped instant success, winning 21 seats and became the biggest single party bloc in the Constituent Assembly. In the 1985 general elections, Carpio was favoured by sections of the army, and like his direct opponent, the Guatemalan Christian Democracy Party's (DCG) Vinicio Cerezo, was also supported by the US administration. He came second with 31.6% in the second round of voting and his party gained 22 congressional seats. The UCN acted as leader of the parliamentary opposition between 1986-1990, generally supporting the government's foreign policy but criticizing its excessive spending and, at times, condemning its domestic policies as being right wing. In the November 1990 general election, the UCN won a convincing victory, winning 41 of the 116 congressional seats and a clear majority of mayoral representations. Carpio, standing as the UCN presidential candidate, came first with 25.7% of the vote, but because he did not get an overall majority he had to contest a second round. He managed to win the backing of the DCG, but nevertheless came only second to the surprise winner, Jorge Serrano of the Solidarity Action Movement. The new government, along with the DCG, National Advancement Party and Guatemalan Republican Front ensured that the UCN was completely excluded from cabinet posts and congressional commissions. Carpio Nicolle was tragically assassinated on July 3, 1993. This significant loss was largely responsible for the collapse of UCN congressional representation to eight in 1994.

The UCN is a full member of the Liberal International.

United Revolutionary Front
Frente Unido Revolucionario (FUR)

Leadership. Leonel Hernandez (1990 presidential candidate), Edmundo Lopez Duran

The FUR came into being as the successor to the Revolutionary Democratic Union (URD) of the early seventies. It is a left-wing party founded by Marco Tulio Collado and Humberto González Gamarra. Both left the FUR to found the

Democratic Revolutionary Unity (URD) in mid-1990 and were murdered by right-wing death squads, Collado in January 1990 and Gamarra in October 1990.

Other Parties and Movements

Civic Democratic Front (*Frente Cívico Democrático*, FCD) is led by Danilo Barillas and is an offshoot of the Guatemalan Christian Democratic Party (DCG).

Citizens for Democracy (*Ciudadanos por Demócracia*, CPD) was launched in 1993 and is a small left-wing founded and led by Miguel Angel Albizurez.

Democratic Alliance (*Alianza Democrática*, AD) is a minor centre-left party that is led by its founder Leopoldo Urrutia.

Guatemalan Committee of Patriotic Unity (*Comité Guatemalteco de Unidad Patriótica*, CGUP) is an alliance of three smaller parties: the Democratic Front Against Oppression (FDCR); the January 31 Popular Front (FP-31); and the Committee for Peasant Unity (CUC). All three have allegiance to far-left guerrilla groups and are believed to be the political wings of the ORPA and the EGP (see below). The CGUP is led by Luís Tejera Gómez.

Guatemalan Labour Party—National Leadership Nucleus
Partido Guatemalteco del Trabajo
(PGT)—Nucleo de Dirección Nacional (LN)
   Leadership. Carlos Gonzalez (general secretary), Mario Sanchez (PGT-LN faction)
   The PGT and its LN internal faction is in reality the *de facto* communist party of Guatemala and has been banned since 1954. Its current incarnation was founded after a split in the old Guatemalan Labour Party in 1978. Formerly allied to the URNG, the PGT withdrew in 1987 in preparation for an abortive cease-fire agreement with the government.

Guatemalan National Revolutionary Unity
Unidad Revolucionaria Nacional Guatemalteca (URNG)
   Leadership. Raúl Molina Mejía
   Founded in 1979, the URNG alliance is nominally Marxist but its programme calls for social reforms, increased democracy and the demilitarisation of the country. It relies mainly upon spectacular actions damaging to the economic infrastructure.
   The URNG is an umbrella organization consist-ing of the following guerrilla groups: the Armed People's Organization (*Organización del Pueblo en Armas*, ORPA), founded in 1972 by a group of ex-Rebel Armed Forces (FAR) members, based mainly among the rural Indian population; the Guerrilla Army of the Poor (*Ejército Guerrillero de los Pobres*, EGP); founded in the late 1960s by ex-FAR members in exile; follows the ideas of Che Guevara; the Rebel Armed Forces (*Fuerzas Armadas Rebeldes*, FAR) founded in 1962 as an alliance of the Guatemalan Labour Party (PGT), the November 13 Revolutionary Movement of Radical Officers (MR13) and students, although the PGT and MR13 broke away in the mid-1960s; and the Urban Revolutionary Command (*Comando Urbano Revolucionario*, CUR); a small Guatemala City-based group which joined the URNG in 1989.

The URNG was formed by the EGP, FAR and PGT (ORPA joined a year later) in order to present a unified front against the army offensives. The framework for a central military command was set up in early 1982, but until the late 1980s the individual member groups continued to operate separately. The new period of civilian rule which began in 1986 encouraged the guerrillas to seek an agreement with the government and army that would allow the URNG to enter the political mainstream. Guerrilla activities were scaled down until October 1987, when peace talks with the Guatemalan Christian Democratic Party (DCG) government proved unproductive and the army went on a renewed offensive. While the government, intimidated by a series of army coup plots, continued to postpone further talks, the URNG stepped up their activities again in 1989. Semi-official peace talks with the National Reconciliation Commission (CNR) (made up of representatives from Guatemalan political parties and "notable citizens") started in Norway in March 1990 and resulted in the Oslo Accords, which set a rough timetable for peace negotiations. In June peace talks in the Spanish capital Madrid the URNG agreed not to disrupt the forthcoming November general election. Meetings between the URNG, the CNR and representatives of the Guatemalan business community followed in August in Ottawa, Canada, and in November in Metepec, Mexico. A major breakthrough in the peace process came in the Mexico City talks of April 1991 when, for the first time, representatives of the Guatemalan armed forces agreed to attend. In July 1991, a framework peace was agreed upon as a basis for future negotiations.

In 1995, for the first time in its history, the URNG urged Guatemalans to participate in national elections but only in support of so-called "alternative candidates", although such candidates were never named.

Guinea

Capital: Conakry

Population: 6,200,000 (1995E)

The Republic of Guinea gained independence from France in 1958. The first President, Ahmed Sekou Touré, dominated the political stage for the next quarter of a century, pursuing a policy of socialist revolution and internal suppression. After his death in March 1984, the armed forces staged a coup, forming a Military Committee for National Recovery (CMRN) under the leadership of Maj.-Gen. Lansana Conté. The 1982 constitution was suspended after the takeover, as was the Democratic Party of Guinea, which had been the ruling and sole legal political party. A new constitution was approved by referendum in December 1990; in early 1991 the CMRN was dissolved and a mixed military and civilian Transitional Committee of National Recovery was set up as the country's legislative body. In April 1992 legislation providing for the legalization of political parties came into effect.

President Conté was confirmed in office in December 1993 in Guinea's first multi-party elections. In legislative elections in June 1995, the Party of Unity and Progress, led by the President, won a majority of the seats in the new 114–seat National Assembly (*Assemblée Nationale*). Some 850 candidates representing 21 out of 46 legalized parties participated in the elections. Opposition parties challenged the results, claiming electoral malpractice, and announced that they would would boycott the new parliament.

Democratic Party of Guinea–African Democratic Rally

Parti Démocratique de Guinée–Rassemblement Démocratique Africain (PGG-RDA)

Address. c/o Assemblée Nationale, Conakry

Leadership. Ismael Mohamed Gassim Gushein

President Touré's former ruling Democratic Party of Guinea, which had been dissolved in 1984, was revived in 1992 as the PDG-RDA. Following the 1993 presidential election, in which the PDG-RDA leader, Ismael Mohamed Gassim Gushein, secured less than 1% of the vote, the party split, with dissidents forming the Democratic Party of Guinea–Renewal (PDG-R). Each faction won one National Assembly seat in the 1995 legislative elections.

Democratic Party of Guinea–Renewal

Parti Démocratique de Guinée–Renouvellement (PDG-R)

Address. c/o Assemblée Nationale, Conakry

The PGC-R was formed after the 1993 presidential election by a dissident faction of the Democratic Party of Guinea–African Democratic Party. Like its parent party, it won one seat in the 1995 National Assembly elections.

National Union for Prosperity in Guinea
Union Nationale pour la Prospérité de la Guinée (UNPG)

Address. c/o Assemblée Nationale, Conakry

Leadership. Faciné Touré (leader)

The UNPG was formed in August 1993. Faciné Touré contested the presidential election later that year but achieved less than 1.5% of the votes cast. In the 1995 poll the UNPG gained legislative representation with two seats.

Party of Renewal and Progress

Parti pour le Renouveau et le Progrès (PRP)

Address. c/o Assenblée Nationale, Conakry

Leadership. Siradiou Diallo (leader)

The PRP's candidate for the 1993 presidential election, Siradiou Diallo, took fourth place in the poll with almost 12% of the votes cast. In the June 1995 legislative elections the party secured nine seats.

Party of Unity and Progress

Parti de l'Unité et le Progrès (PUP)

Address. c/o President's Office, Conakry

Leadership. Maj.-Gen. Lansana Conté (leader)

Acting as the core of an informal coalition supporting the ruling regime, the PUP nominated

Maj.-Gen. Conté as its candidate for the December 1993 presidential poll, in which he won nearly 52% of the votes cast. In the 1995 legislative elections the PUP won an absolute majority with 71 seats.

Rally of the Guinean People
Rassemblement du Peuple Guinéen (RPG)
   Address. c/o Assemblée Nationale, Conakry
   Leadership. Alpha Condé, Tidiane Cisse (leaders)

The RPG leader, Alpha Condé, had been a prominent exiled opponent of former President Touré and the subsequent military regime until his eventual return to Guinea in May 1991. The RPG was one of the first parties registered under the new parties law in 1992. In the December 1993 presidential election, Condé took second place with a 19.5% share of the vote. In the 1995 legislative elections, the RPG won the most seats among the opposition parties with 19.

Union for the New Republic
Union pour la Nouvelle République (UNR)
   Address. c/o Assemblée Nationale, Conakry
   Leadership. Mamadou Boye Ba (leader)

Party leader and presidential candidate, Mamdou Boye Ba, took third place in the December 1993 ballot with just over 13% of the vote. The UNR won nine seats in the 1995 elections to the National Assembly.

Other Parties

Democratic Union of Guinea (*Union Démocratique de Guinée*, UDG).

Djama Party (*Parti Djama*), secured one seat in the National Assembly poll in 1995.

Guinean Ecologist Party (*Parti Guinéen Ecologiste*, PGE).

Guinean Progress Party (*Parti du Progrès Guinéen*, PPG).

Guinean Rally for Development (*Rassemblement Guinéen pour le Développement*, RGD).

National Democratic Union of Guinea (*Union Nationale Démocratique de Guinée*, UNDG), led by Issiaga Mara.

Union for the Progress of Guinea (*Union pour le Progrès de Guinée*, UPG), led by Jean-Marie Dore, who contested the 1993 presidential election but won less than 1% of the votes cast.

Union of Democratic Forces of Guinea (*Union des Forces Démocratiques de Guinée*, UFDG).

Guinea-Bissau

Capital: Bissau   **Population:** 1,050,000 (1995E)

The Republic of Guinea-Bissau achieved independence from Portugal in 1974. Its first President, Luis Cabral, was overthrown in a coup in 1980 by the present head of state, Brig.-Gen. João Bernardo Vieira. The African Party for the Independence of Guinea and Cape Verde (PAIGC) continued to be the sole ruling party after the 1980 coup, although the Cape Verdian branch broke away from the Guinea-Bissau branch in 1981. In a constitution adopted in 1984 Guinea-Bissau was declared to be an anti-colonialist and anti-imperialist republic and a state of revolutionary national democracy, with the PAIGC as the leading force in society and the State. In January 1991 the PAIGC formally approved the introduction of multi-party democracy, and in May legislation legalizing political activity by opposition parties was adopted. The first political parties were recognized in November 1991. The revised constitution provided for the direct election of the President and a 100–member National People's Assembly (*Assembléia Nacional Popular*).

 Multi-party legislative elections took place in July 1994, resulting in a victory for the PAIGC which secured an absolute majority of seats. In presidential elections, which were conducted over two rounds in July and August 1994, President Vieira was returned to office, with just over 52% of the vote in the second ballot. In October 1994 the secretary-general of the PAIGC was appointed as Prime Minister.

African Party for the Independence of Guinea and Cape Verde
Partido Africano da Independência da Guiné e Cabo Verde (PAIGC)
  Address. CP 106, Bissau
  Leadership. Brig.-Gen. João Bernardo Vieira (president), Manuel Saturnino da Costa (secretary-general)
  The PAIGC was founded in 1956 and engaged in armed struggle against Portuguese colonial rule from the early 1960s. From independence in 1974 it was the sole and ruling party. It had been initially a joint Guinea-Bissau and Cape Verde organization with a bi-national leadership, but the Cape Verde branch broke away from the mainland organization following the November 1980 coup in Guinea-Bissau. While retaining a leftist stance, the PAIGC at the beginning of the 1990s endorsed the establishment of a new multi-party system. In legislative elections in July 1994 the PAIGC won 62 of the 100 seats in the National People's Assembly, with 46% of the votes cast. The simultaneous presidential polls produced no outright winner in the first round, but incumbent President Vieira was returned in the second round run-off against the Social Renewal Party candidate in August.

Front of Struggle for the Liberation of Guinea
Frente da Luta para a Liberaçao da Guiné (FLING)
  Address. c/o Assembléia Nacional Popular, Bissau
  Leadership. François Mendy Kankoila
  The FLING claims to trace its organization back to the initiation of armed struggle against Portuguese colonial rule, opposing the unification of Cape Verde with the mainland. In 1981 it was announced that it had been dissolved into the ruling African Party for the Independence of Guinea and Cape Verde, although remnants of the organization continued to be active in exile. It was legalized in its present form in May 1992. FLING won a single seat in the 1994 legislative elections; its leader contested the presidential poll, but achieved less than 3% of the first ballot vote.

Guinea-Bissau Resistance–Bafata Movement
Resistência da Guiné-Bissau–Movimento Bafatà (RGB-MB)
  Address. c/o Assembléia Nacional Popular, Bissau
  Leadership. Domingos Fernandes Gomes (chair)
  Founded in Portugal in 1986 and legalized in December 1991, the party came second to the ruling African Party for the Independence of Guinea and Cape Verde in the 1994 legislative elections, winning 19 seats. In the presidential poll Fernandes Gomes took third place in the first round with just over 17% of the votes cast.

Social Democratic Front
Frente Democrática Social (FDS)
  Leadership. Rafael Barbosa
  The FDS was among the first groups to emerge openly in opposition to the Vieira regime, and was the first to announce its formation as an opposition party. It was legalized in December 1991. Party leader Barbosa had been one of the founders of the PAIGC, but was subsequently purged and imprisoned before being formally amnestied in 1987. Factional strife within the FDS has led to several defections by members to launch other groups, including the United Social Democratic Party, the Social Renewal Party and the National Convention Party.

Social Renewal Party
Partido para a Renovação Social (PRS)
  Address. c/o Assembléia Nacional Popular, Bissau
  Leadership. Koumba Yalla (leader)
  The PRS was set up in January 1992 by defectors from the Social Democratic Front, and was legalized the following October. In the 1994 legislative elections it secured 12 seats in the National People's Assembly. Having come second to President Vieira in the first round of the presidential poll, party leader Yalla was narrowly defeated in the second round run-off with nearly 48% of the vote, despite being endorsed by all opposition parties.

Union for Change
União para a Mudança (UM)
  Address. c/o Assembléia Nacional Popular, Bissau
  Leadership. Rafael Barbosa (leader)
  The UM was set up as an opposition coalition to contest the July 1994 elections. It won six seats in the National People's Assembly, but its presidential candidate, Bubakar Djalo, attracted less than 3% of the vote in the first ballot. The six parties forming the UM were the Democratic Front, the Democratic Party of Progress, the Guinea-Bissau League for the Protection of the Ecology, the Party of Renovation and Development, the Social Democratic Front and the United Democratic Movement.

United Social Democratic Party
Partido Unido Social Democrático (PUSD)
  Leadership. Vítor Saude Maria
  The PUSD was formed by a splinter group of the Social Democratic Front in July 1991. Its leader, Saude Maria, had earlier been a Prime Minister under the Vieira regime until March 1984 when he left the ruling African Party for the Independence of Guinea and Cape Verde. The

party won no seats in the National People's Assembly in 1994, and Saude Maria secured only 2% of the vote in the presidential election.

Other Parties

Democratic Front (*Frente Democrática*, FD), led by Marcelino Batista, left-of-centre party formed in 1990, initially refused legalization in August 1991, but then granted legal status (the first opposition party to be registered) in November 1991.

Democratic Party of Progress (*Partido Democrático do Progresso*, PDP), led by Amine Michel Saad, launched in December 1991 and granted legal status in August 1992.

Guinea-Bissau League for the Protection of the Ecology (*Liga da Guiné-Bissau para a Proteção da Ecologia*), an environmentalist party dating from 1993.

Guinean Civic Forum (*Foro Cívico da Guiné*, FCG), whose candidate for the 1994 presidential election, Antonieta Rosa Gomes, won 1.8% of the vote.

National Convention Party (*Partido da Convenção Nacional*, PCN), formed in May 1993 by a dissident faction of the Social Democratic Front and led by Djibril Balde.

Party of Democratic Convergence (*Partido da Convergência Democrática*, PCD), led by Vítor Mandinga, won 5.3% of the votes cast in the 1994 legislative polls but no seats; its candidate took fourth place in the first ballot of the presidential election.

Party of Renovation and Development (*Partido da Renovação e Desenvolvimento*, PRD), led by João da Costa and Manuel Rambout Barcelos, legalized in October 1992 and initially known as the "Group of 121", formed by dissidents of the ruling African Party for the Independence of Guinea and Cape Verde who advocated more rapid democratization.

United Democratic Movement (*Movimento da Unidade Democrática*, MUDE), legalized in August 1992, led by Filinto Vaz Martins, who was Education Minister in the early 1980s and then lived in Portugal until returning to Guinea-Bissau in November 1991.

Guyana

Capital: Georgetown

Population: 820,000 (1995E)

Guyana (formerly British Guiana) became independent in 1966 and the Co-operative Republic of Guyana was formally proclaimed within the Commonwealth in 1970. Under the 1980 constitution legislative power is held by the 65–member unicameral National Assembly (53 elected for five years by universal suffrage, on the basis of proportional representation, and 12 regional representatives). Executive power is held by the President and his government. The President appoints a First Vice-President and Prime Minister (who must be an elected member of the National Assembly) and a Cabinet which may include non-elected members and is collectively responsible to the legislature.

On Oct. 9, 1992, Cheddi Jagan, veteran leader of the People's Progressive Party (PPP), was sworn in for a five-year as the new President, following the PPP's first post-independence electoral victory on Oct. 5. He received 52.3% of the vote compared with 43.6% for incumbent President Hugh Desmond Hoyte of the People's National Congress (PNC), which had been in power since 1964. In simultaneous Assembly elections, the PPP obtained 35 seats, the PNC 27, the Working People's Alliance 2 and the United Force 1.

People's National Congress (PNC)
Address. Congress Place, Sophia, POB 10330, Georgetown
Telephone. (#592–2) 57850

Leadership. Hugh Desmond Hoyte (leader)
The PNC was founded in 1957 by Forbes Burnham, formerly chairman of the People's Progressive Party (PPP). It was the main opposi-

tion party after the 1957 and 1961 elections, but in 1964, after a change in the electoral system, it joined the United Force (UF) in a coalition government which led British Guiana to independence in 1966. Drawing most of its support from the African-descended population, the party won all subsequent elections (which were widely regarded as rigged) until October 1992, when it was runner-up to the PPP, winning 27 Assembly seats with 43.6% of the vote.

The PNC initially followed a moderate socialist line with emphasis on co-operative principles, but took a swing to the left in the 1970s before adopting a more pragmatic approach under the leadership of Hugh Desmond Hoyte (who took over the presidency on Forbes's death in 1980). The party experienced severe internal divisions both prior to, and after, the 1992 elections, with former Prime Minister Hamilton Green being expelled in 1993. In 1994 a new party constitution was adopted that ceased to refer to the PNC as a socialist movement.

People's Progressive Party (PPP)

Address. 41 Robb Street, Georgetown
Telephone. (#592–2) 72095
Leadership. Cheddi Jagan (general secretary)

The left-wing PPP was formed by Cheddi Jagan in 1950 as an anti-colonial party speaking for the lower social classes, although it has since drawn its support almost exclusively from the Indian-descended community. In 1957 the PPP gained an absolute majority in the Assembly and Jagan became the first Chief Minister. In 1961, when internal autonomy had been conceded by the British authorities, the party again won a majority and Jagan became Prime Minister. In the 1964 elections, held under a British-imposed proportional representation system, the PPP won the most votes but less than half of the Assembly seats, thereby losing power to the coalition headed by the People's National Congress. The party denounced most subsequent elections as fraudulent until October 1992, when it regained power, winning 35 seats with 52.3% of the vote. Prior to the election, Jagan softened the party's previously hard-line insistence on state ownership.

United Force (UF)

Address. 96 Robb Street, Georgetown
Telephone. (#592–2) 62596
Leadership. Manzoor Nadir (leader)

The conservative UF was formed in 1961. Advocating racial integration and a mixed economy, it has drawn much of its support from White, Amerindian and other minority communities. The party joined a coalition government with the People's National Congress in 1964 but withdrew in 1968 in protest at the enfranchisement of the many emigrant Guyanese. In the first post-independence elections in 1968, UF representation fell was reduced to four Assembly seats. It failed to win any seats in the 1973 election but was creditied with two seats in both the 1980 and 1985 polls. In October 1992 the party retained only one seat.

Working People's Alliance (WPA)

Address. Walter Rodney House, Croal Street, Stabroek, Georgetown
Telephone. (#592–2) 56624
Fax. (#592-2) 53679
Leadership. Eusi Kwayana and Rupert Roopnaraine (co-chairs)

The WPA was formed in the mid-1970s as an alliance of left-wing groups that included the African Society for Cultural Relations with Independent Africa (ASCRIA), Indian Political Revolutionary Associates (PIRA), *Ratoon* (a student group) and the Working People's Vanguard Party (which left before the WPA constituted itself as a political party in 1979). In 1980 one of its leaders, Walter Rodney, was killed by a bomb explosion, an incident for which the PNC was widely believed to be have been responsible. Having boycotted the 1980 elections, the WPA won one seat in 1985 and two in 1992. The party is affiliated to the Socialist International.

Other Parties

Al-Mujahidden Party, representing Guyana's Muslim population and led by Hoosain Ganie.

Democratic Labour Movement (DLM), a centrist organization established in 1982, led by Paul Nehru Tennassee, who stood unsuccessfully in the 1992 presidential election.

Good and Green for Guyana (GGG), formed by Hamilton Green as the Good and Green for Georgetown to contest the September 1994 municipal elections in the capital (after which the broader party title was adopted); Green had been expelled from the People's National Congress in 1993.

Guyana Labour Party (GLP), formed in early 1992 by Nanda K. Gopaul who urged supporters to back the People's Progressive Party in the October elections of that year.

Guyana Republican Party (GRP), a right-wing organization formed in 1985 and led from the United States by Leslie Prince.

Guyanese Action for Reform and Democracy (GUARD), organized in 1989 as a civic movement campaigning for constitutional and electoral reforms.

National Republican Party (NRP), formed by Robert Gangadeen in 1990 following his split from the United Republican Party.

People's Democratic Movement (PDM), a centrist group formed in 1973 and led by Llewellen John.

People's Labour Movement (PLM), affiliated to the Christian Democrat International.

Union of Guyanese International (UGI), headed by Lindley Geborde.

United Republican Party (URP), a right-wing group whose leader, Leslie Ramsammy, stood unsuccessfully in the 1992 presidential election.

United Workers' Party (UWP), led by Winston Payne.

Haiti

Capital: Port-au-Prince

Population: 7,200,000 (1995E)

The Republic of Haiti became independent from France in 1804. Between 1957 and 1986 its rulers were President for Life François "Papa Doc" Duvalier and, from 1971, his son Jean-Claude. The latter years of Jean-Claude "Baby Doc" Duvalier's rule were marked by prolonged popular unrest, and he fled abroad in February 1986. A new constitution, which was drawn up in late 1986 and overwhelmingly approved in a referendum in March 1987, provided for a bicameral legislature made up of a 27–member Senate (*Sénat*) and a Chamber of Deputies (*Chambre des Députés*) of at least 70 members (currently 83). Repeated military intervention, however, prevented the creation of stable civilian government. The President elected in December 1990, Jean-Bertrand Aristide, was deposed and forced into exile by a military coup in September 1991 led by Gen. Raoul Cédras. In September 1994 US troops began occupying the country following an agreement allowing the military junta members to leave the country. President Aristide returned in October and a new government was sworn in the following month.

Elections for the Chamber of Deputies and for partial renewal of the Senate were held in June 1995, repeated in August due to logistical problems and violence, and finally completed by a second round run-off in September. The overall outcome was that the populist, pro-Aristide Lavalas Political Organization (OPL) won substantial majorities in both the Senate and the Chamber of Deputies. In presidential elections held in December 1995 the Lavalas candidate, René Préval, secured a landslide victory (albeit in a low turnout) against 13 other candidates. The inauguration of Préval in February 1996 marked the first peaceful handover by one elected President to another in 192 years of independence.

Lavalas Political Organization
Organisation Politique Lavalas (OPL)

Address. c/o Chambre des Députés, Port-au-Prince

Leadership. Gérard Pierre-Charles (leader)

The centrist *Lavalas* (variously translated as "waterfall", "flood" or "avalanche") was organized in 1991, subsequently becoming the dominant pro-Aristide political formation. In the 1995 legislative elections held between June and September, *Lavalas* was endorsed by President Aristide and won a commanding victory, taking 17 of the 27 seats in the Senate and 66 of the 83 seats in the Chamber of Deputies. In the December 1995 presidential election, the OPL candidate, René Préval, received 87.9% of the vote.

Movement for the Installation of Democracy in Haiti
Mouvement pour l'Instauration de la Démocratie en Haïti (MIDH)

Leadership. Marc Bazin (leader)

The centre-right MIDH was founded in 1986 by Marc Bazin, who had briefly served in 1982 as Finance Minister in a Duvalier cabinet. In the December 1990 election, Bazin was the presidential candidate of the National Alliance for Democracy and Progress (*Alliance Nationale pour la Démocratie et le Progrès*, ANDP), which the MIDH had established the previous year with the Revolutionary Progressive Nationalist Party. In that contest Bazin was runner-up to Jean-Bertrand Aristide, receiving just over 14% of the vote. In the simultaneous legislative elections the ANDP came second to the National Front for Change and Democracy. Bazin endorsed the coup which deposed Aristide in 1991 and was Prime Minister under the subsequent military regime from June 1992 to June 1993. The MIDH boycotted the 1995 legislative elections.

National Front for Change and Democracy
Front National pour le Changement et la Démocratie (FNCD)

Leadership. Evans Paul (leader)

The FNCD, a coalition of centre-left organizations, was formed in late 1990, initially in support of Jean-Bertrand Aristide's successful presidential election campaign. It emerged from the December 1990–January 1991 legislative elections as the strongest party (although without an overall majority in the Senate or Chamber of Deputies). In 1995, however, the FNCD was no longer linked to President Aristide (who gave his endorsement to the Lavalas Political Organization candidate) and was defeated. The FNCD leader also heads a grouping of popular organizations, the Democratic Unity Confederation (*Confédération d'Unité Démocratique/Kovansyon Inite Demokratik*, CUD/KID), which had been formed in 1987.

Party of the National Congress of Democratic Movements
Parti du Congrès National des Mouvements Démocratiques (CNMD)
Pati Kongrè Nasyonal Mouvman Demokratik Yo (KONAKOM)
   Leadership. Victor Benoît (general secretary)
   The social democratic KONAKOM was founded in 1987 by delegates from an array of political groups, trade unions, peasants' and students' organizations, and human rights associations.

Rally of Progressive National Democrats
Rassemblement des Démocrates Nationaux Progressistes (RDNP)
   Leadership. Leslie Manigat (secretary general)
   The RDNP is a centrist party, described as "noiriste", or appealing to the Black majority rather than to the established mulatto elite. Its leader was elected to the presidency of the republic in January 1988, but was ousted in a military coup the following June. Although allowed to return from exile in 1990, Manigat's presidential candidacy in the 1990 election was declared invalid. In the December 1990–January 1991 legislative elections, the party won a handful of seats in the Chamber of Deputies.

Revolutionary Progressive Nationalist Party
Parti Nationaliste Progressiste Révolutionnaire (PANPRA)
   Leadership. Serge Gilles (leader)
   The social democratic PANPRA was formed in 1986 and is a member of the Socialist International. In 1989 PANPRA and the Movement for the Installation of Democracy in Haiti (MIDH) established the National Alliance for Democracy and Progress (*Alliance Nationale pour la Démocratie et le Progrès*, ANDP), which was the runner-up to the National Front for Change and Denocracy (FNCD) in elections in December 1990 and January 1991. PANPRA opposed the military coup in September 1991, and in June 1993 withdrew its support in the legislature for the government formed the previous year by Marc Bazin, the MIDH leader.

Other Organizations

Alliance for the Liberation and Advancement of Haiti (*Alliance pour la Libération et l'Avancement d'Haïti*, ALAH), led by Reynold Georges.

Front Against Repression (*Front Contre la Répression*), formed in 1989 as a coalition of groups including Haiti's leading trade union federation.

Haitian Christian Democratic Party (*Parti Démocratique Chrétien d'Haïti*, PDCH), founded in 1979 by Silvio Claude; a frequent political detainee under the Duvalier regime who unsuccessfully contested the 1990 presidential election as an anti-Aristide candidate and was then killed in the violence associated with the 1991 military coup; the current leader is Marie-France Claude.

Haitian Moderate Republican Party (*Parti Républicain Modéré Haïtien*, PRMH), led by Nicolas Estiverne.

Haitian National Popular Party (*Parti Populaire National Haïtien*, PPNH), headed by Bernard Sansaricq, a right-wing anti-Duvalierist.

Movement for National Development (*Mouvement pour le Développement National*, MDN), a centre-right formation led by Hubert de Ronceray, who came second in the presidential election in January 1988 and who supported the deposition of President Aristide in 1991.

Movement for National Reconstruction (*Mouvement pour la Reconstruction Nationale*, MRN), set up in 1991 by René Théodore of the Unified Party of Haitian Communists (*Parti Unifié Communiste Haïtien*, PUCH); excluded from the 1995 elections, the MRN called for the annulment of the results.

Movement for the Liberation of Haiti/Revolutionary Party of Haiti (*Mouvement pour la Libération d'Haïti/Parti Révolutionnaire d'Haïti*, MLH/PRH), led by François Latortue.

Movement for the Organization of the Country (*Mouvement pour l'Organisation du Pays*, MOP), a centre party led by Gérard Philippe August, who unsuccessfully contested the presidential election in 1988.

National Agricultural and Industrial Party (*Parti Agricole et Industriel National*, PAIN), a conservative organization formed by Louis Déjoie II, the son of the candidate who lost the last free elections (in 1957) to François "Papa Doc" Duvalier; Dejoie took third place in the 1990 presidential election.

National Front for Concerted Action (*Front National de Concertation*, FNC), established in 1987 as a focus of centre-left opposition groupings and led by Gérard Gourgue, a lawyer and human rights activist.

National Kombit Movement (*Mouvement Koumbite National*, MKN), under the leadership of Volvick Rémy Joseph.

National Party of Labour (*Parti National du Travail*, PNT), formed in 1986 and headed by Thomas Desulme.

National Patriotic Movement (*Mouvement National Patriotique*, MNP), led by Déjean Belizaire.

Party for National Unity and Development (*Parti pour l'Unité Nationale et le Développement*, PUND).

Rally of Democrats for the Republic (*Rassemblement des Démocrates pour la République*, RDR), a neo-Duvalierist formation launched in 1993.

Revolutionary Front for the Advancement and Progress of Haiti (*Front Révolutionnaire pour l'Avancement et le Progrès d'Haïti*, FRAPH), founded in 1993 as a neo-Duvalierist party in opposition to any attempt to reinstate President Aristide.

Union of Democratic Patriots (*Union des Patriotes Démocratiques*, UPD).

Honduras

Capital: Tegucigalpa

Population: 5,700,000 (1995E)

The Republic of Honduras gained its independence from Spain in 1821. The country was ruled by the conservative National Party of Honduras (PNH) from 1933 to 1957, a period which marked the political ascendancy of the army which used the party as a vehicle to legitimize its hold on power. A series of military coups, however, in 1956, 1963 and 1972, were needed to ensure this control was maintained. In an interlude of civilian government, a series of moderate social and political reforms were introduced by the Liberal Party of Honduras (PLH), in office from 1957 to 1963, which included a programme of land reform and the establishment of the state social security system. The military ruled from 1963 to 1980, except for a short period under PNH government in 1971-72, before the PLH was returned to power in 1980. Even then, the military still wielded great influence. The PLH won the presidential election of 1985 but lost power to the PNH in November 1989.

Under the 1982 constitution, there is a 130-member unicameral National Assembly. Executive power rests with the President. The President is in theory elected for a four-year term by a simple majority of votes, although at the presidential and legislative elections on Nov. 24, 1985, the PLH candidate, who had received the most votes, was appointed President. The 128-member National Assembly is elected for a four-year term on the basis of proportional representation. Men and women over 18 are eligible to vote and registration and voting are compulsory until the age of 60.

In presidential elections held on Nov. 28, 1993, Carlos Roberto Reina of the centre-right PLH emerged as the winner with 52.36% of the vote, defeating the candidate of the ruling PNH who received 40.74%. Simultaneous congressional elections were also won by the PLH. A new government took office on Jan. 27, 1994.

Christian Democratic Party of Honduras

Partido Demócrata Cristiano de Honduras (PDCH)

Address. Colonia San Carlos, 2da. Av. Atras de los Castanos No. 204, Apartado postal 1387, Tegucigalpa

Telephone. (#504) 323139

Fax. (#504) 326060

Leadership. Orlando Iriarte (1993 presidential candidate), Celo Mendez Segunda (secretary-general)

Founded in 1980, the PDCH is a Christian democratic party which boasts both progressive and conservative wings and is a full member of the Christian Democrat International. The party performed poorly in presidential and legislative elections in 1981 and 1985, receiving less than 2% in the presidential race and no more than two seats in the Congress.

In July 1986, the party joined the Innovation and Unity Party (PINU), the Honduran Patriotic Front (FPH) and the Revolutionary Democratic Liberal Movement (MLDR or M-*lider*—see Liberal Party of Honduras) faction of the ruling PLH in an opposition coalition concerned particularly with promoting the neutrality of the country in the region's conflicts. In October 1986, Palma replaced the more conservative Efraín Diáz Arrivillaga as party president and this more moderate stance led the party in September 1990 to urge the PNH government to modify its IMF-approved economic austerity plan in order to avoid "confrontation between the public and the dominant class". A PDC member, Juan Ramón Martínez, was appointed to the Cabinet as Head of the National Agrarian Institute (INA), an agency in charge of agrarian reform.

In 1993 the party could only muster 1.1% of the vote.

Liberal Party of Honduras

Partido Liberal de Honduras (PLH)

Address. Col. Miramontes, Detras del Supermercado, 'La Colonie', Tegucigalpa DC

Telephone. (#504) 320520

Fax. (#504) 320797

Leadership. Rafael Pineda Ponce (president), Gloria Oqueli de Macoto (secretary-general)

Founded in 1890 the party was split between conservative and more progressive wings both of which have proceeded to be conservative in office. The oldest active party, the PLH has since 1970 been in effect a coalition of disparate tendencies, each with its own leadership and structure, overlaying the traditional divide between the conservative rural and the more reformist urban wings of the party. The party held power in 1929-22 and then in 1957-63 before being deposed by the military, an experience which did not prevent it in 1980 from being the main force in an interim government under the then military President Gen. Policarpo Paz Garcia. The party then won the subsequent November 1981 general election, winning an absolute majority in the National Assembly. Its leader from 1979, Roberto Suazo Córdova, a pro-USA right-winger and head of the conservative *rodista* faction of the party, was installed as President in January 1982, formally ending 18 years of almost uninterrupted military rule, although the armed forces retained extensive legal and de facto powers.

In January 1983 the PLH almost lost its legislative majority when Suazo Córdova's *rodistas* clashed with the Popular Liberal Alliance (ALIPO) faction of the party, led by the brothers Carlos Roberto and Jorge Arturo Reina, who were subsequently driven out and in February 1984 established the Revolutionary Democratic Liberal Movement (MLDR or M-*lider*). The *rodistas* in turn split in 1985, with competing factions backing Oscar Mejía Arellano and José Azcona Hoyo for the presidency. Azcona had resigned from Suazo Córdova's government in 1983 and subsequently accused the regime of corruption. Azcona won the presidency in alliance with ALIPO and after having agreed a power-sharing National Unity Pact (PUN) with the National Party (PNH), the second since 1971, giving the PNH two cabinet posts and control of the Supreme Court and other important political and administrative posts.

While Azcona's government was pre-occupied with issues arising from the Nicaraguan conflict, not least the presence in the country of some 20,000 US-backed right-wing *contra* rebels, the battle for the PLH presidential election ensued, eventually won in December 1988 by Flores Facussé, a former minister in the Suazo Córdova government, who had forged a surprise alliance with the dissident M-*lider* movement. Flores Facussé, however, lost the 1989 presidential election but the party received two posts in the new PNH cabinet.

The Liberals under Carlos Reina won handsomely in the presidential elections of 1993 against former Supreme Court president Oswaldo Ramos of the National Party and in the subsequent legislative balloting again defeated the Nationalists by 71 seats to 55.

Technically a part of the PLH, the Popular Liberal Alliance (ALIPO) faction maintains its own distinct organizational structure. It is led by Carlos and Jorge Reina.

The PLH is a full member of the Liberal International.

National Innovation and Unity Party

Partido de Innovación Nacional y Unidad (PINU)

Address. Apartado Postal No. 105, 2a Av. Calle Real No. 912, Frente a Hiasa, Camayaguela DC

Leadership. German Leitzelar (president), Olban Valladares (1993 presidential candidate)

Founded in 1970 the PINU has since 1986 claimed to be social democratic and to have links with the German Social Democratic Party (SPD). The party, whose support comes mainly from professionals and some rural workers' groups, was not afforded legal recognition until 1978. In 1981 it secured only 2.5% of the vote and three of the 82 seats in the National Assembly, one of which was won by Julín Méndez, the first *campesino* (peasant) leader ever to sit in the legislature. Despite an enlarged Assembly, the party's number of seats fell to two in the 1985 general election and Aguliar gained only 1.6% of the vote in the presidential race.

The party retained its two legislative seats in 1993 with a vote share of 2.8%.

National Party of Honduras

Partido Nacional de Honduras (PNH)

Address. Case del Partido, Paseo El Obilisco, Camayaguela DC

Leadership. Rafael Leonardo Callejas Romero; Oswaldo Ramos Soto (1993 presidential candidate and leaders of the *Oswaldista* movement); Roberto Martinez Lozano (leader of the *Roma* movement); Carlos Kattan Salem (secretary-general)

Founded in 1923, the PNH is a traditionally conservative party which now promotes neo-liberal economic measures. Traditionally the party of large landowners, the party has also been closely identified with the military. It held power from 1933 to 1957, including the dictatorship of Gen. Tiburcio Carías Andino (1939-49) and in 1971-72 and 1985-87 when it participated with the Liberal Party of Honduras (PLH) in short-lived National Unity (PUN) governments.

The PNH, like the PLH, is the product of various factions, including the Movement for Nationalist Democratization (MDN), the Movement for Unity and Change (MUC) and the Nationalist Labour Tendency (TNL). The ruling PLH government (1981-85) encouraged PNH in-fighting by using the then PLH dominated Supreme Court and the National Electoral Tribunal (TEN) to support the pro-government MUC in its claim to control the party. This decision was reversed by the military in 1985 when it supported the accession of the newly-created MONARCA faction led by Rafael Leonardo Callejas. The MONARCA won all 63 of the PNH's 134 seats in the 1985 general election and as part of the subsequent PUN government, where it controlled the foreign and labour ministry portfolios, forced the PLH to give it control of the Supreme Court, the TEN and an important role in the administration of the legislature.

Callejas was the party's unopposed candidate in the 1989 presidential elections, which he won comfortably. On taking office, the government restored relations with the IMF and other creditors and implemented a package of IMF-approved neo-liberal economic measures which included the wholesale dismissal of thousands of public sector workers (many of whom were PLH supporters), the privatization of state-owned agencies, the abolition of price controls on basic essentials and the devaluation of the currency. The measures caused continuous and widespread social unrest throughout 1990-91 despite Calleja's periodic promises to increase social sector spending. Anti-government protest was increasingly repressed by the security forces and the armed forces leading to international protests at the high level of systematic human rights abuses.

The party subsequently lost the 1993 presidential elections under the candidature of former Supreme Court president Oswaldo Ramos Soto. Following this defeat, internal divisions within the party crystallized and by the end of 1995 there were eight distinct dissident factions within the party, the most important of these being the *Oswaldista* and *Roma* movements.

Other Parties and Movements

Democratic Action Party (*Partido de Acción Democrática*, PAD) is a centrist party founded in 1986 and led by its founder Gen. (retd.) Walter Lopez Reyes.

Democratic Unification Party (*Partido de Unificación Democrática*, PUD) was launched in 1993 as the public wing of a number of former elements of the MRH, a clandestine guerrilla alliance (see below). Led by Gustavo Garcia España the group is banned from democratic participation until at least 1997.

Honduran Social Democratic Party (*Partido Socialista Democrático de Honduras*, PSDH), a social democratic grouping again founded in 1986 and led by Jorge Illescas Oliva.

National Unified Directorate—Movement of Revolutionary Unity

Directorio Nacional Unificado—Movimiento de Unidad Revolucionario (DNU-MUR)

Leadership. Mario Sosa Navarro (Communist Party), Raul Lopez (MPL), Efraín Duarte (FPR-LZ), Gustavo Garcia España (FMLH)

Also known as the Honduran Revolutionary Movement (*Movimiento Revolucionario Hondureño*, MRH), the DNU-MUR was formed in 1983 as an umbrella organization in an attempt to co-ordinate the efforts of the militant left to form a single army under one command to conduct a guerrilla war and to "play an active part in the event of a regionalization of the Central America crisis". Founding members included the Communist Party of Honduras; the Social Action Party of Honduras; the Central American Workers' Revolutionary Party (PRTC, founded 1975); the Lorenzo Zelaya Popular Revolutionary Forces (FPR-LZ, founded by students at the National Autonomous University in 1980-71); the Revolutionary Unity Movement (MUR); the Cinchonero Popular Liberation Movement (MPL Cinchoneros, founded 1981); the Morazanista Front for the Liberation of Honduras (FMLH, founded in 1979). All member groups of the DNU-MUR took advantage of a general amnesty approved by the National Assembly in June 1991, although some rebels made it known that they intended to continue fighting. Four leaders of the Chinchoneros had announced their willingness to lay down arms in May 1991 and the FPR-LZ was the last group to disarm in October 1991.

The FMLH members of the newly-styled MRH staged an attack in June 1991 against a UN peace-keeping office in the capital, following this with a parcel-bomb attack against the Economic Ministry in August 1994.

Hungary

Capital: Budapest

Population: 10,250,000 (1995E)

After four decades of Communist rule in the People's Republic of Hungary, in January 1989 the National Assembly legalized freedom of assembly and association. A month later the then ruling Hungarian Socialist Workers' Party (MSMP) approved the formation of independent parties, some of which had begun organizing on an informal basis the previous year. In September formal sanction was given to multi-party participation in national elections, the People's Republic giving way the following month to the revived Hungarian Republic. The President as head of state is indirectly elected for a five-year term by the unicameral National Assembly (*Országgyülés*), which is elected for a four-year term by universal adult suffrage in two rounds of voting, its 386 members including eight providing ethnic minority representation. The extremely complex electoral system, involving the election of 210 deputies from regional and national lists by a form of proportional representation and the other 176 from single-member constituencies, has a basic threshold for the attainment of Assembly representation of 5% of the vote, so that only eight parties won seats in 1994 out of some 40 parties which presented candidates and well over 100 registered with the authorities.

The Assembly elections of May 8 and 29, 1994, resulted as follows: Hungarian Socialist Party 209 seats (with 32.9% of the regional-list vote), Alliance of Free Democrats 69 (19.8%), Hungarian Democratic Forum 37 (11.7%), Independent Smallholders' Party 26 (8.9%), Christian Democratic People's Party 22 (7.1%), Federation of Young Democrats 20 (7.0%), Agrarian Union 1 (2.1%), Liberal Citizens' Alliance 1 (0.7%), Party of the Republic 1 (0.6%).

Agrarian Union
Agrárszövetsége (ASz)
 Address. 10 Arany János u., Budapest V
 Telephone. (#36–1) 131–0953

Fax. (#36–1) 111–2663
 Leadership. Tamás Nagy (chair), Tibor Nagy-Husszein (deputy chair)
 The ASz was founded in December 1989 as a

307

merger of leftist agrarian groups opposed to the land privatization policies of the Independent Smallholders' Party. It was allocated one Assembly seat in May 1994 on the basis of a 2.1% vote share.

Alliance of Free Democrats
Szabad Demokraták Szövetsége (SDS)
  Address. Mérleg u. 6, 1051 Budapest V
  Telephone. (#36–1) 117–6911
  Fax. (#36–1) 118–7944
  Leadership. Iván Peto (president), Gábor Kuncze (parliamentary leader), Ferenc Wekler (secretary-general)

The SDS began life in March 1988 as the Network of Free Initiatives, representing the centre-left "urban" rather than the "populist" strand in the opposition, many of its members being lapsed Marxists. The grouping was reorganized as a political party in November 1988 and held its first general assembly in March 1989. It won 91 Assembly seats in 1990 on a vote share of 21.4%, becoming the leading opposition party of the post-Communist era. Factional strife between "pragmatists" and "ideologues" appeared to be healed in November 1992 by the election of Iván Peto as party president. Despite initial hopes of a major breakthrough, the party slipped to 70 seats in the May 1994 Assembly elections, its first-round voting share falling to 19.8%. It decided to enter a centre-left coalition with the Hungarian Socialist Party, its presidential nominee, Arpád Göncz, being elected President of Hungary by the Assembly in June 1995.

The SDS is affiliated to the Liberal International.

Christian Democratic People's Party
Kereszténydemokrata Néppárt (KDNP)
  Address. 5 Nagy Jenö u., 1126 Budapest XII
  Telephone. (#36–1) 175–0333
  Fax. (#36–1) 155–5772
  Leadership. György Giczi (president), Béla Csepe (parliamentary leader), György Rubovszky (secretary-general)

Located ideologically on the right of centre, the KDNP claims to be a revival of the Popular Democratic Party, the leading opposition formation in the immediate post-World War II period. The party won 21 Assembly seats in 1990 on a 6.5% vote share. It thereupon opted to join a three-party coalition government headed by the Hungarian Democratic Forum (MDF). Avoiding the MDF's rout in the May 1994 elections, the KDNP improved to 22 seats with a 7.1% share of the popular vote.

Federation of Young Democrats–Hungarian Civic Party
Fiatal Demokraták Szövetsége–Magyar Polgari Párt (FIDES-MPP)
  Address. 28 Lenday u., 1062 Budapest VI
  Telephonr. (#36–1) 269–5353
  Fax. (#36–1) 269–5343
  Leadership. Viktor Orban (president), László Kövar (parliamentary leader), János Ader (general secretary)

Then known simply as the Federation of Young Democrats, this right-wing grouping came in fifth place in the 1990 Assembly elections, winning only 20 of 378 elective seats on a 7.0% vote share, although later that year it won elections for mayor in nine of the country's largest cities. In the May 1994 general elections, its national representation declined further to 20 seats and it remained an opposition party. A 35–year age limit on membership was abandoned in April 1993, paving the way for the adoption of the FIDES-MPP designation two years later.

The party is an affiliate of the Liberal International.

Hungarian Democratic Forum
Magyar Demokrata Fórum (MDF)
  Address. 3 Bem József tér., 1027 Budapest II
  Telephone (#36–1) 212–4601
  Fax. (#36–1) 156–8522
  Leadership. Sándor Lezsák (president)

A centre-right party of populist/nationalist orientation, the MDF was founded in September 1988 with the avowed purpose of "building a bridge between the state and society". It held its first national conference in Budapest in March 1989, when it demanded that Hungary should again become "an independent democratic country of European culture". In the April 1990 Assembly election the party won a plurality of 165 of 378 elective seats, on a first-round vote of 24.7%. The result was an MDF-led coalition headed by József Antall, also including the Christian Democratic People's Party (KDNP) and the Independent Smallholders' Party.

In January 1993 Antall survived a challenge to his MDF leadership the party's nationalist right, led by István Csurka. In early June Csurka and three parliamentary colleagues were expelled from the party, promptly forming the Hungarian Justice and Life Party. Antall died in December 1993 and was succeeded, on a temporary basis, by Sandor Lezsák, who was named chairman of the MDF executive committee in February 1994, after resigning from the party presidency in favour of the then Defence Minister, Lajos Für.

The May 1994 Assembly elections delivered a major rebuff to the MDF, which slumped to 37 seats on a vote share of only 11.7% and went into opposition. As a result Lezsák withdrew completely from the leadership at the beginning of June, being succeeded by the former Finance Minister, Iván Szabo as parliamentary leader. On being confirmed as MDF president in September, Für ruled out a merger with the KDNP "for the time being". Various problems contributed to FÜR's decision early in 1996 to vacate the leadership, which returned to Lezsák, who faced major opposition within the party. An anti-Lezsák group immediately formed the breakaway Hungarian Democratic People's Party, the rump MDF being reduced to some 20 Assembly members.

The MDF is affiliated to both the Christian Democrat International and the International Democrat Union.

Hungarian Democratic People's Party

Magyar Demokrata Néppárt (MDNP)
  Address. c/o Országgyülés, Budapest
  Leadership. Iván Szabo

The MDNP was launched in March 1996 by Szabo after he had been rebuffed in a challenge for the presidency of the Hungarian Democratic Forum, of which he was then leader in the National Assembly. The new party attracted the adherence of over a dozen centre-leaning MDF deputies.

Hungarian Socialist Party

Magyar Szocialista Párt (MSP)
  Address. 26 Köztársaság tér., 1081 Budapest VIII
  Telephone. (#36–1) 210–0081
  Fax. (#36–1) 210–0011
  Leadership. Gyula Horn (president), György Janosi, Imre Szekeres and Ferenc Baja (deputy presidents), Zoltan Gal (Assembly leader)

The MSP is the successor to the former ruling (Communist) Hungarian Socialist Workers' Party (MSMP), which had been created under an earlier designation by the June 1948 merger of Hungary's Communist and Social Democratic parties. The original Hungarian Communist Party was founded in November 1918 and took a leading role in the short-lived Republic of Councils (soviets) declared in Hungary in March 1919, its leading activists going underground during the succeeding "White Terror" and Horthy dictatorship. Many prominent Communists took refuge in Moscow and towards the end of World War II (during which Hungary was allied to the Axis powers) the entry into Hungary of Soviet forces was followed by the establishment of a provisional government comprising Communists, Smallholders, Social Democrats and the National Peasant Party. Although the Smallholders obtained an absolute majority (57%) in elections held in November

1945, the coalition was continued, with a Communist as Interior Minister. Two years later, in the elections of August 1947, the Communists emerged as the strongest single party (with 22% of the vote), ahead of the Smallholders, while the combined share of the Communists, Social Democrats and National Peasant Party was 45%. Under the leadership of Mátyás Rákosi, the Communists then effectively eliminated their coalition partners as independent political forces and in June 1948 the Social Democratic Party was merged with the Communist Party to form the Hungarian Workers' Party (HWP) many Social Democrats who opposed the merger going into exile.

In elections held in May 1949 the HWP presented an unopposed joint list with four other parties called the People's Independence Front (PIF) and of the 402 elective seats in Parliament over 70% were allotted to the HW. In August 1949 a new constitution was adopted similar to those of other East European "people's democracies" and in the elections of May 1953 the HWP was the only party to be mentioned in the manifesto of the PIF, which in October 1954 was replaced by the broader-based Patriotic People's Front (*Hazafiás Népfront*).

Meanwhile, former Social Democrats were gradually eliminated from the HWP leadership and purges conducted by the Rákosi "Muscovites" against the "home Communists", notably László Rajk, who was executed in October 1949 after a show trial, and János Kádár, who spent several years in prison. Following Stalin's death in March 1953 Rákosi resigned from the premiership (although continuing as party leader), in which post he was succeeded in July 1953 by Imre Nagy, who embarked on a "new course" economic policy involving the halting of compulsory collectivization, greater emphasis on the production of consumer goods, the release of political prisoners and greater cultural freedom. However, in early 1955 the HWP central committee condemned the new policies as "right-wing" and "opportunist", with the result that Nagy was removed from the premiership and dismissed from his party posts in April 1955.

Following Khrushchev's denunciation of Stalin at the 20th congress of the Soviet Communist Party in February 1956, Rákosi was obliged to resign from the Hungarian party leadership in July 1956. Thereafter, widespread opposition built up to Rákosi's successor, Ernö Gerö (another hardliner), culminating in the reappointment of Nagy to the premiership in October 1956 amid violent clashes between Hungarian demonstrators and Soviet forces (which were then withdrawn from the country). Nagy announced a new programme, including free elections, Hungary's withdrawal from the Warsaw Pact and a policy of permanent neutrality, and formed a national coalition administration including non-Communist representatives. Gerö was succeeded as party secretary by János Kádár, who initially supported Nagy's programme but who in early November 1956 formed an alternative "revolutionary workers' and peasants' government". At the invitation of the latter, Soviet forces then returned in strength and crushed Hungarian resistance over several days of heavy fighting.

Nagy and his associates were executed as traitors and Kádár was confirmed as leader of the party, which was reconstituted as the Hungarian Socialist Workers' Party (HSWP). After a period of severe reprisals, Kádár instituted a policy of reconciliation and limited liberalization, which was only partly tarnished Hungary's participation in the Soviet-led intervention in Czechoslovakia in 1968.

Economic, social and cultural liberalization was followed in 1983 by a partial democratization of the political process, involving in particular a choice of candidates in national and local elections, although still within a framework of HSWP supremacy. These and other Hungarian initiatives were specifically acknowledged by the new post-1985 Soviet Communist Party leadership as having furnished some guidelines for the Soviet Union's own reform programme under Mikhail Gorbachev.

At an extraordinary party congress in October 1989, the MSMP renounced Marxism in favour of democratic socialism, adopted its current name and appointed Rezsö Nyers to the newly-created post of presidium president. Chosen to succeed Nyers in May 1990, Gyula Horn led the party to an overall majority in the May 1994 Assembly elections, with a tally of 209 seats on a 32.6% first-round vote share. Nevertheless, mainly for purposes of international respectability, Horn brought the centrist Alliance of Free Democrats into a new coalition. Horn was re-elected party president in March 1996, when approval was also given to a reduction of the size of the MSP presidium.

The MSP is an observer member of the Socialist International.

Independent Smallholders' Party
Független Kisgazda Párt (FKP)
    Address. 24 Belgrád rakpárt, 1056 Budapest V
    Telephone. (#36–1) 118–2855
    Fax. (#36–1) 118–1824
    Leadership. József Torgyán (president), Sándor Kavassy (deputy president), Geza Gyimothy (general secretary)

Its main policy plank being the return of collectivized land to former owners, the FKP was founded in November 1989 as a revival of the party that emerged as the strongest from Hungary's first post-war election in 1945. Deep internal divisions on the desirability and extent of reparations for property lost during the Communist era came to a head in December 1989. A group of dissidents led by Imre Boros resigned from the FKP to form the National Smallholders' and Bourgeois Party, which developed no taste for life on the outside and rejoined the parent party in August 1991. Meanwhile, the FKP had won 44 seats and 11.7% of the vote in the 1990 Assembly elections and had joined a centre-right coalition government headed the Hungarian Democratic Forum (MDF).

In February 1992 FKP leader József Torgyán announced that the party was withdrawing from the government coalition because the MDF had denied it an opportunity to influence policy. This decision was accompanied by the expulsion of 33 of the FKP's 45 Assembly deputies, who launched the Smallholders' Party–Historical Section in order to support the MDF-led Antall government. In the May 1994 general elections the rump party recovered somewhat by winning 26 seats on an 8.9% vote share. It then experienced a surge in popular support in the polls, as expressions of extreme nationalist sentiment emanated from Torgyán. The party became embroiled in fierce conflict over government moves to produce a new constitution to replace the much-amended Communist-era text, one FKP proposal being that the President should be directly elected, with enhanced powers, on the expiry of the five-year term of Arpád Göncz (Alliance of Free Democrats) in August 1995. Seeking to force a referendum, the FKP collected well over the number required for a popular consultation, but the ruling MSP contended that such a change would generate political instability. As a consequence of the MDF scission of March 1996, the FKP became the largest single opposition party in the Assembly.

The FKP is affiliated to the Christian Democrat International.

Liberal Citizens' Alliance
Liberális Polgari Szövetseg (LPS)
    Address. c/o Országgyülés, Budapest
    Leadership. Péter Zwack (chair), Ferenc Kiss (honorary chair)

The LPS was launched in 1989 as the Entrepreneurs' Party to promote a market economy and low taxation for the country's emerging entrepreneurs. It adopted its present name in June 1990 but failed to secure representation in the 1990 elections. It was credited with one constituency seat in 1994.

Party of the Republic
Köztársaság Párt (KP)

Address. 8 Szentkirály u., 1088 Budapest VIII
Telephone. (#36–1) 138–3744
Fax. (#36–1) 138–4642
Leadership. János Palotas (chair), András Veer (deputy chair), László Takacs (secretary-general)

The pro-market KP was founded in 1992 on the initiative of János Palotas, a colourful entrepreneur who had been elected to the Assembly in 1990 as a candidate of the Hungarian Democratic Forum (MDF) but had quickly become alienated from that party. The KP won a parliamentary by-election in April 1993, in alliance with the Agrarian Union. It managed only 2.5% of the national vote in the May 1994 Assembly elections, but was allocated one seat by virtue of a local alliance with the MDF.

United Smallholders' Party–Historical Section
Egyesült Kisgazda Párt–Töténelmi Tagozat (EKP-TT)

Address. 34 Jókai u., 1065 Budapest VI
Telephone. (#36–1) 132–2900
Leadership. János Szabo (chair), István Boroczs (deputy chair), Antal Bélafi (secretary-general)

The TKP-TT came into being as a result of the February 1992 decision of the leadership of the Independent Smallholders' Party (FKP) to leave the government coalition, this move being opposed by three-quarters of the 44 FKP Assembly deputies. Claiming to represent continuity with established FKP policies, the EKP-TT remained a part of the then ruling coalition headed by the Hungarian Democratic Forum, but failed to secure representation in May 1994.

Other Parties

Hungarian Independence Party (*Magyar Függetlenség Pártja*, MFP), led by Tibor Hornyak, right-wing formation launched in April 1989 as a revival of a post-war group of the same name. *Address.* 97 Arany János u., 7400 Kaposvár

Hungarian Justice and Life Party (*Magyar Igazság es Elet Párt*, MIEP), led by István Csurka and Lajos Horvath, extreme right-wing grouping launched in June 1993 by dissidents of the then ruling Hungarian Democratic Forum (MDF) after Csurka had unsuccessfully challenged József Antall for the MDF leadership; overtly anti-semitic, the party contends that national revival is being thwarted by a "Jewish-Bolshevik-liberal conspiracy" and advocates the recovery of Hungary's pre-1914 borders; its original Assembly contingent of about 10 fell to zero when it secured only 1.6% of the vote in the May 1994 Assembly elections. *Address.* 3 Akadémia u., 1054 Budapest V

Hungarian People's Party (*Magyar Néppárt*, MNP), led by János Marton, centrist grouping founded in 1989 as successor to pre-war National Peasant Party (*Nemzeti Parasztpárt*, NPP), which title it uses as a suffix; won less than 1% of the vote in 1990 and failed to place any candidates on the ballot in 1994. *Address.* 61 Baross u., 1082 Budapest VIII

Hungarian Social Democratic Party (*Magyarországi Szociáldemokrata Párt*, MSzDP), led by László Kapolyi, revival of the party forced to merge with Hungary's Communist Party in 1948; split in 1989 into "historic" and "renewal" wings, reunited in October 1993; secured less than 1% in the May 1994 general election; an observer member of the Socialist International. *Address.* 76 Dohány u., 1074 Budapest VII

Hungarian Workers' Party (*Magyar Munkáspárt*, MMP), led by Gyula Thürmer, derived from pro-reform decisions taken at the October 1989 congress of the then ruling Hungarian Socialist Workers' Party (MSMP), when a group of hard-line Communists opposed to conversion into the Hungarian Socialist Party launched the "János Kádár Society" as the "legal heir" to the MSMP; using the MSMP title, it won only 3.7% in 1990 (and no seats); adopted its present name prior to the 1994 election, at which it slipped to 3.3%. *Address.* 61 Baross u., 1082 Budapest VIII

Hungary's Green Party (*Magyarországi Zöld Párt*, MZP), led by Zoltán Medvecziki, launched in 1989, took only 0.4% of the vote in 1990 and half of that in 1994. *Address.* 3 Kiskorona u., Budapest

Lungo Drom Alliance, led by Florian Farkas, representing Hungary's Gypsies (*Roma*), dominant party in 53–member National Autonomous Authority of the Romany Minority, elected in April 1995.

Movement for Hungarian Unity, led by Imre Pozsgay (1990 presidential candidate of the Hungarian Socialist Party and the first prominent Hungarian Communist to acknowledge that the 1956 uprising had been a popular revolt), launched in 1995 as successor to National Democratic Federation, which had won no seats in 1994.

World National Party for People's Party (*Vilánemzeti Népuralmista Párt*, VNP), extreme right-wing grouping led by Albert Szabo, a Hungarian-born Australian national.

Iceland

Capital: Reykjavík   **Population:** 265,000 (1995E)

The Republic of Iceland was established in 1944 (having previously been a Danish possession), with a democratic parliamentary system of government. Under the 1944 constitution as amended, the President is directly elected as head of state for a four-year term (renewable without restriction), although real executive power resides in the cabinet headed by the Prime Minister. Legislative authority is vested in the unicameral parliament (*Althing*) of 63 members, also elected for four years (subject to dissolution) by a mixed system of proportional and direct representation. The *Althing* divides itself by election into an Upper House (*Efri Deild*) of a third of its members and a Lower House (*Nedri Deild*) of the remaining two-thirds.

Icelandic parties are eligible for subventions from state funds, to finance research on political questions, in proportion to the number of *Althing* seats held plus one. In 1994 the total paid out was Kr36 million (about US$600,000), of which, for example, the Independence Party received Kr14.3 million.

Elections to the *Althing* on April 8, 1995, resulted as follows: Independence Party 25 seats (with 37.1% of the vote), Progressive Party 15 (23.3%), the People's Alliance 9 (14.3%), Social Democratic Party 7 (11.4%), People's Movement/Awakening of the Nation 4 (7.2%), Women's Alliance 3 (4.9%). A presidential election on June 29, 1996, resulted in victory for Olafur Ragnar Grímsson of the People's Alliance, who received 40.9% of the popular vote.

Independence Party (IP)
Sjálfstaedisflokkurinn
   Address. Háaleitisbraut 1, 105 Reykjavík
   Telephone. (#354) 515–1700
   Fax. (#354) 515–1717
   Leadership. Davíd Oddsson (chair), Geir Haarde (leader in the *Althing*), Kjartan Gunnarsson (secretary-general)

The IP is a liberal conservative party, advocating Iceland's continued membership of NATO and the retention of the existing US base in Iceland. It was established in 1929 by a merger of conservative and liberal groups favouring Iceland's independence from Denmark (achieved in 1944). Having consistently been the strongest party in the *Althing* (although never with an absolute majority), it has taken part in numerous coalition governments–with the Social Democratic Party (SDP) and a Communist-led left-wing front in 1944–46, with the Progressive Party (PP) and the SDP in 1947–49, with the PP in 1950–56, with the SDP in 1959–71 and with the PP in 1974–78 and 1983–87. Meanwhile, in 1980–83 dissident IP deputies had participated in a coalition with the PP and the People's Alliance.

In the April 1987 elections the IP suffered a major setback (principally because of the impact of a breakaway Citizens' Party), winning only 27.2% of the vote and 18 of 63 seats (as against 38.7% and 23 of 60 seats in 1983). It nevertheless continued in government as the head of a "grand coalition" with the PP and the SDP, the IP leader, Thorsteinn Pálsson becoming at 39 Iceland's youngest-ever Prime Minister.

Pálsson stepped down as Prime Minister in September 1988 because of a dispute over economic policy, being succeeded as party chair in March 1991 by Davíd Oddsson, who formed a government following an election in which the IP consolidated its position as the largest party, rising from 18 to 26 seats. Only one of these was lost in the 1995 election, in which the IP took 37.1% of the vote. However, because of losses by its Social Democratic Party coalition partner, it felt obliged to form a new centre-right coalition with the Progressive Party in order to secure parliamentary stability and majority government.

The IP is affiliated to the International Democrat Union.

People's Alliance (PA)
Althdubandalagid
   Address. Laugavegi 3, 101 Reykjavík
   Telephone. (#354) 521–7500
   Fax. (#354) 531–7599

Leadership. Margrét Frímannsdóttir (chair), Svavar Gestsson (leader in the *Althing*), Kristján Valdimarsson (general secretary)

Strongly based in the Icelandic trade union movement, the PA describes itself as a "socialistic" party of "leftists who want to defend and strengthen the independence of the Iceland people, protect the interests of the working class, and ensure progress at all levels in the country on the basis of democratic socialism and co-operation". The formation, which advocates withdrawal from NATO and the closure of the US base in Iceland, is commonly referred to as "Communist-led" or "Communist-dominated", but the PA itself rejects such descriptions and does not regard itself as part of any international communist movement.

The origins of the PA can be faced to the formation of the Communist Party of Iceland in 1930 following a split in the Social Democratic Party (SDP). Having joined the Comintern, the Icelandic Communists first obtained representation in the *Althing* in 1937 (with three seats). Although a proposal for reunification was rejected by the SDP in 1938, left-wing Social Democrats joined with the Communists to form the United People's Party–Socialist Party (SA-SF), which left the Comintern and in 1942 won seven parliamentary seats. When Iceland became independent in 1944, the SA-SF entered a coalition government with the SDP and Independence Party, but withdrew in 1946 mainly over its opposition to a US military presence in Iceland.

For the 1956 elections, the SA-SP combined with the small National Defence Party and a left-wing faction of the SDP to form the People's Alliance, which won eight seats and joined a coalition with the SDP and the Progressive Party (PP) which lasted until 1958. Having been essentially an electoral alliance, the PA converted itself into a single political party in 1968, whereupon the non-Marxist section broke away to form the (now defunct) Union of Liberals and Leftists, claiming that the PA had become "the Communist Party under another name". At the same time, the PA denounced the Soviet-led military intervention in Czechoslovakia and thereafter adopted a "Eurocommunist" orientation.

After winning 10 seats in the 1971 elections, the PA joined a coalition with the PP and the Union of Liberals and Leftists, which resigned in 1974. The PA won 14 seats in the 1978 elections and formed a coalition with the PP and the SDP. After new elections the following year, in which its representation fell to 11 seats, it entered a coalition with the PP and dissident Independence Party members early in 1980. However, it fell back to 10

seats in 1983 and went into opposition. In the April 1987 elections the PA was for the first time overtaken in terms of votes and representation by the Social Democrats and remained in opposition.

The PA's representation in the *Althing* rose to nine seats in 1991, this level being maintained in 1995 on a slightly reduced vote share of 14.3%. It remained in opposition through both elections, being active in the opposition to government economic austerity measures. Former Finance Minister Ólafur Ragnar Grímsson vacated the PA leadership in late 1995 in order to stand for the Icelandic presidency, to which in June 1996 he was elected by a comfortable relative majority over three other candidates.

People's Movement
Thjódvaki

Address. c/o Althing, Reykjavík
Leadership. Jóhanna Sigurdardóttir (chair), Svanfrídur Jonasdóttir (leader in the *Althing*)

Also known for campaigning purposes as "Awakening of the Nation", *Thjódvaki* was launched for the 1995 *Althing* elections by Jóhanna Sigurdardóttir, who as deputy chair of the Social Democratic Party (SDP) had unsuccessfully sought the chairmanship in June 1994, after which she had resigned as Social Affairs Minister and left the party. Proclaiming a left-of-centre orientation, the new formation secured an impressive 7.2% vote share in the April 1995 elections, giving it four parliamentary representatives. Somewhat unexpectedly, these found themselves co-operating closely with the SDP in opposition to the post-election centre-right government.

Progressive Party (PP)
Framsóknarflokkurinn

Address. Hafnarstraeti 20, 101 Reykjavík
Telephone. (#354) 562–4480
Fax. (#354) 562–3325
Leadership. Halldór Asgrímsson (chair), Valgerdur Sverrisdóttir (leader in the *Althing*), Egill Heldar Gíslasson (secretary-general)

The PP's principal aim is to safeguard the Icelandic nation's economic and cultural independence on the basis of a democratic and parliamentary system, with emphasis on the freedom of the individual. The party also stands for basing the national economy on private initiative, with state intervention remaining exceptional. The party has favoured Iceland's continued membership of NATO but has called from the withdrawal of NATO forces from the country.

The party was established in 1916 to represent farming and fishing interests and the co-operative movement in these sectors. Usually the second largest party in the *Althing*, the PP has taken part in various coalition governments–with the Independence Party (IP) and the Social Democratic Party (SDP) in 1946–49, with the IP in 1950–56, with the SDP and the People's Alliance (PA) in 1956–58, with the PA and the Union of Liberals and Leftists in 1971–74, with the IP in 1974–78, with the SDP and the PA in 1978–79, with the PA and dissident IP members in 1980–83, with the IP in 1983–87 and with the IP and the SDP since July 1987.

The 1983–87 period of coalition with the IP resulted in both parties losing ground in the April 1987 elections, in which PP slipped from 14 to 13 seats, although its share of vote increased from 18.5 to 18.9%. Three months later the PP entered a "grand coalition" headed by the IP and also including the Social Democrats.

The party was awarded four ministries in this government, with Hermannsson returning as Prime Minister of a three-party coalition in September 1988.

The PP went into opposition following the election of April 1991, at which its parliamentary representation was unchanged. It returned to government after the 1995 contest, in which it advanced to 23.3% of the vote, as the junior partner in a centre-right alliance with the Independence Party.

The PP is a member party of the Liberal International.

Social Democratic Party (SDP)
Althýduflokkurinn
  Address. Hverfisgätu 8–10, 101 Reykjavík
  Telephone. (#354) 552-9244
  Fax. (#354) 562-9155
  Leadership. Jón Baldvin Hannibalsson (chair), Rannveig Gudmundsdóttir (leader in the *Althing*), Sigurdur Tomas Björgvinsson (general secretary)

Founded in 1916 as a trade union party, the SDP became organizationally independent in 1940 but was weakened by the defection of its left-wing faction to the Communist-dominated United People's Party–Socialist Party (see under entry for People's Alliance). Over the following three decades the SDP remained the fourth strongest party in a stable four-party system, usually polling around 15% in general elections, and participated in five coalition governments, the longest-lived being one with the Independence Party (IP) in 1959–71; it also briefly formed a minority SDP government in 1958–59.

Amid decreasing political stability in the 1970s and early 1980s, the SDP experienced shifting fortunes and was mostly in opposition (although it participated in a centre-left coalition in 1978–79 and then formed another interim minority government). Competition from short-lived alternative social democratic parties resulted in electoral setbacks for the SDP, notably in 1983 when the impact of a left-wing dissident Social Democratic Federation reduced the SDP to only six seats and 11.7% of the vote.

Under the new leadership of Jö Baldvin Hannibalsson, however, the SDP was reinvigorated, and strengthened by the return of most of the Federation dissidents in 1986. In the April 1987 elections its share of the vote increased to 15.2% and its representation to 10 seats (out of 63), giving it the status of third-strongest party, ahead of the People's Alliance for the first time. The SDP thereupon entered a "grand coalition" headed by the Independence Party and also including the Progressive Party.

The SDP retained 10 seats in the 1991 elections, after which it joined a coalition with the Independence Party. Internal party unrest over government austerity measures culminated in an unsuccessful challenge to the leadership of Hannibalsson (then Foreign Minister) in June 1994 and the formation of the breakaway People's Movement. In the 1995 *Althing* elections the Social Democrats fell back to fourth place, winning only 11.4% of the vote and going into opposition.

The SDP is a member party of the Socialist International.

Women's Alliance (WA)
Samtök um Kvennalista
  Address. Laugavegi 17, 101 Reykjavík
  Telephone. (#354) 551-3725
  Fax. (#354) 552-7560
  Leadership. Collective; Kristín Asgeirsdóttir (leader in the *Althing*)

The Alliance was launched in March 1983 as an explicitly feminist party, believing the improvement of the condition of women to be "imperative" and also that "the experience, values and perspectives of women are urgently needed to influence the decision-making processes of our society". Rejecting classification on the left/right spectrum, the Alliance also advocates decentralization of local and national government, the transfer of economic and administrative power to the people, an end to the arms race and the abolition of all military alliances.

Possibly given additional credibility by the fact that Iceland elected a woman President in 1980, the Women's Alliance was successful in its first general election contest in April 1983, winning 5.5% of the vote and three of the 60 *Althing* seats. It made further significant progress in the April 1987 elections, when it took 10.1% of the vote and doubled its representation to six seats (out of 63). In post-election coalition negotiations with other parties, the Alliance refused to compromise on its basic policy principles and accordingly remained in opposition.

The Alliance fell back to five seats in the 1991 *Althing* elections, remaining in opposition. More evidence of the ebbing of the feminist tide came in the 1995 elections, when the WA slipped further to three seats on a 4.9% vote share, apparently losing support to the new People's Movement under its charismatic female leadership.

India

Capital: New Delhi   **Population**: 950,000,000 (1995E)

The Republic of India gained independence from the United Kingdom in 1947, when the sub-continent was divided into the new states of India and Pakistan. It is a secular and democratic republic, comprising 25 self-governing states and seven union territories. Executive power is vested in the President, who is elected for a five-year term by an electoral college consisting of elected members of the upper and lower houses of parliament (respectively the *Rajya Sabha* and the *Lok Sabha*) and of state legislative assemblies. The President appoints a Prime Minister and, on the latter's advice, a Council of Ministers, all of whom are responsible to parliament. Most of the 245 members of the *Rajya Sabha* are indirectly elected by the state assemblies (one-third being replaced every two-years), while all but two of the 545 members of the *Lok Sabha* are directly elected for a five-year term by universal adult suffrage. Legislative responsibility is divided between the Union and the states, the former possessing exclusive powers to make laws in the realm of foreign affairs, defence, citizenship and overseas trade.

In the general elections of April-May 1996 the ruling Indian National Congress–Congress (I), having been dominant for most of the period since independence, was heavily defeated, obtaining only 136 of the 534 seats declared, while the Hindu fundamentalist *Bharatiya Janata* Party (BJP) achieved plurality status by winning 161 seats. The BJP's subsequent attempt to sustain a minority administration was not successful, whereupon a multi-party United Front alliance, commanding the support of some 180 *Lok Sabha* members, formed a minority government under the premiership of Deve Gowda of the *Janata Dal*.

All-India Dravidian Progressive Federation
All-India Anna Dravida Munnetra Kazhagam (AIADMK)
    Address. 175 Avvai Shanmugam Salai Royapet-tah, Madras 600014
    Leadership. Jayalalitha Jayaram (leader)
    The AIADMK, which reflects Tamil national-ist sentiment, was formed in 1972 by a breakaway faction of the Dravidian Progressive Federation (DMK), and became the dominant regional party in Tamil Nadu state from 1977. Its DMK rival was briefly the ruling party from 1989 until 1991, when the AIADMK was again swept back to power with 163 seats. Controversy attached thereafter to the AIADMK leader and chief minister of Tamil Nadu, universally known as Jayalalithia, who in September 1995 was accused by opposition par-ties of allocating huge state resources to finance her foster-son's wedding. In state and national elections in April-May 1996, the AIADMK resumed its earlier alliance with the Indian National Congress–Congress (I) but was decimated, retaining only four seats in the state legislature and going into opposition to a govern-ment of the DMK. Unrepresented in the *Lok Sabha*, the AIADMK nevertheless held 15 *Rajya Sabha* seats as at July 1996.

All-India Forward Bloc (AIFB)
    Address. 66 North Avenue, New Delhi 110001
    Telephone. (#91–11) 379-2514
    Leadership. Chitta Basu (leader)
    The leftist AIFB is based mainly in West Bengal, where it is a constituent of the Left Front state administration led by the Communist Party of India-Marxist. In the general election in April-May 1996 the party won three *Lok Sabha* seats, declaring its support for the United Front federal government inaugurated in June 1996. The AIFB also held two *Rajya Sabha* seats as at July 1996.

All-India Indira Congress–Tiwari

Address. c/o *Lok Sabha*, New Delhi 110001

Leadership. Narain Dutt Tiwari (leader)

Amid growing divisions within the then ruling Indian National Congress–Congress (I), a dissident faction claimed in May 1995 to have elected Narain Dutt Tiwari as party president in place of P.V. Narasimha Rao. Tiwari was subsequently expelled from Congress (I). His faction won four *Lok Sabha* seats in the April-May 1996 general election and was allocated one portfolio in the United Front government inaugurated in June 1996.

Assam People's Council

Asom Gana Parishad (AGP)

Address. 213 V.P. House, New Delhi 110001

Telephone. (#91–11) 371-8242

Leadership. Prafullo Kumar Mohanta (president)

The AGP won power in Assam in 1985, the year of its foundation. However, in 1989 the federal government imposed President's rule in the state as a result of the activities of separatist groups. The party was subsequently defeated by the Indian National Congress–Congress (I) in fresh state elections in 1991. It emerged from the April-May 1996 general election with five *Lok Sabha* seats (having won only two in 1991) and obtained two ministerial posts in the United Front national government inaugurated in June 1996. In simultaneous state elections, an AGP-led alliance secured a majority in the Assam legislative assembly, regaining power from Congress (I). As of July 1996 the AGP held one seat in the *Rajya Sabha*.

Bahujan Samaj Party (BSP)

Address. C-I/11 Humaun Road, New Delhi 110001

Telephone. (#91–11) 4631353

Leadership. Kanshi Ram (leader)

The BSP represents India's Harijans or "untouchables". Following the 1993 state elections in Uttar Pradesh, the party joined a governing coalition led by the *Samajwadi* Party. It then withdrew from the coalition in June 1995 and formed a new government itself, with the aid of opposition parties. However, on the resignation of the BSP chief minister in October 1995, President's rule was imposed in the state (and remained in force in mid-1996 pending fresh elections). The BSP is also represented in the Punjab and Madhya Pradesh legislative assemblies. In the general election in April-May 1996 the party won 10 federal seats in the *Lok Sabha*, principally in constituencies in Uttar Pradesh and Punjab. It subsequently ruled out alignment with any central

governing party or coalition. As at July 1996 it held one seat in the *Rajya Sabha*.

Bharatiya Janata Party (BJP)

Address. 11 Ashoka Road, New Delhi 110001

Telephone. (#91–11) 382234

Fax. (#91–11) 378-2163

Leadership. Atal Behari Vajpayee (leader)

The *Bharatiya Janata* ("Indian People's") Party was formed in 1980 as a breakaway group from the *Janata* Party, establishing itself as a radical, right-wing Hindu nationalist organization. Its influence as a national party rose dramatically in the 1989 general election, when it won 88 *Lok Sabha* seats (compared with only two in 1984). Having increased its legislative representation to 119 seats in 1991, it became the main opposition to the Indian National Congress–Congress (I) government. It was associated in this period with many actions by militant Hindus opposed to Muslim influence and establishments in the "Hindu belt" of central-northern India.

In the April-May 1996 general election the BJP emerged as the largest single party, winning at least 161 seats and commanding the support of about another 35 *Lok Sabha* deputies from other parties. In mid-May party leader Vajpayee was invited to form a new BJP minority federal government (including *Shiv Sena* representation); however, his administration could not muster sufficient parliamentary support to secure a vote of confidence, with the result that his government resigned after only 13 days in office.

At state level, as at June 1996, the BJP was the ruling party in Delhi, Gujarat and Rajasthan, and was part of the governing coalition (with *Shiv Sena*) in Maharashtra. In the *Rajya Sabha* it held 40 seats as at July 1996.

Communist Party of India (CPI)

Address. Ajay Bhavan, 15 Kotla Marg, New Delhi 110002

Telephone. (#91–11) 331-5546

Fax. (#91–11) 331-5543

Leadership. Indrajit Gupta (general secretary)

Founded in 1925, the CPI split in 1964 when the rival Communist Party of India-Marxist (CPI-M) was formed. From the end of the 1970s the CPI maintained a policy of opposition to the political dominance of the Indian National Congress–Congress (I), working closely with the CPI-M and other left-wing parties. In the general election in April-May 1996 the CPI won 12 seats in the *Lok Sabha* (compared with 13 in 1991). An important national component within the United Front (UF) alliance of centrist, leftist and regional parties, being awarded two portfolios in the new UF federal government (which replaced the short-lived, post-election BJP administration) but undertook to give it parliamentary support. As of July 1996 the party held five seats in the *Rajya Sabha* and participated in the leftist coalitions governing in Kerala and West Bengal.

Communist Party of India–Marxist (CPI-M)

Address. AK Gopalan Bhavan, 27–29 Bhai Vir Singh Marg, New Delhi 110001
Telephone. (#91–11) 344165
Fax. (#91–11) 374-7483
Leadership. Jyoti Basu (leader), Harkishen Singh Surjeet (general secretary)

The CPI-M was created in 1964 by dissident members of the Communist Party of India (CPI) favouring a more radical leftist line. Originally pro-Chinese, the party declared its independence of China in 1968. Although a national party, the CPI-M's main support has traditionally come from West Bengal, Kerala and Tripura. In federal and state elections in April-May 1996 the party secured 32 seats in the *Lok Sabha* (having won 35 in 1991), retained control of the state government in West Bengal and regained power (heading a leftist coalition) in Kerala. Although one of the main constituents of the United Front (UF) alliance, the CPI-M decided that it would not join the new UF federal government inaugurated in June but would give it external support. At at July 1996 the CPI-M held 15 seats in the *Rajya Sabha*.

Dravidian Progressive Federation

Dravida Munnetra Kazhagam (DMK)

Address. Anna Arivalayam, Teynampet, Madras 600018
Leadership. Muthuvel Karunanidhi (leader), E.G. Sugavanam (president)

A Tamil communalist party founded in 1949, the DMK urges full autonomy for the state of Tamil Nadu within the Indian Union and opposes the retention of Hindi as an official language. In 1977 it lost power in Tamil Nadu to the All-India Dravidian Progressive Federation (AIADMK), which had earlier broken away from the parent party. The rump DMK was briefly returned as the ruling party from 1989 until 1991, but after a period of President's rule its AIADMK rival was swept back to power with a large majority in the state legislature. Assisted by various government scandals and a split in the Tamil Nadu Indian National Congress–Congress (I) which produced the pro-DMK Tamil Maanila Congress, the DMK turned the tables in the 1996 state elections, winning 172 seats and forming a government on May 13 under veteran leader Muthuvel Karunanidhi. The DMK also formed a new administration in the union territory of Pondicherry.

Having won no seats in the *Lok Sabha* in the 1991 general election, the DMK returned 17 representatives from Tamil Nadu constituencies in the April-May 1996 national poll. The party joined the United Front federal government inaugurated in June 1996, being allocated the industry portfolio in the new administration.

Indian National Congress–Congress (I)

Address. 24 Akbar Road, New Delhi 110001
Telephone. (#91–11) 301-9606
Fax. (#91–11) 301-7701
Leadership. P.V. Narasimha Rao (president), Madhav Sinh Solanki, Sudhakarrao Naik, Buddha Priya Maurya, Ahmed Patel, Jarardhana Poojari (secretaries)

The Indian National Congress, dating from 1885 and traditionally committed to democracy, socialism and secularism, has been India's ruling formation for most of the five decades since it led India to independence in 1947 under Jawaharlal (Pandit) Nehru. In 1969, three years after Nehru's daughter, Indira Gandhi, had acceded to the leadership, the party split into two groups when an anti-Gandhi conservative faction—the Indian National Congress-Organization (INC-O)—became India's first recognized opposition party. Having aroused widespread opposition by governing under emergency powers from 1975, the Congress government was defeated in the March 1977 general elections, going into opposition for the first time since independence. Further splits resulted in Mrs Gandhi forming the mainstream Congress (I), which returned to power with an overwhelming majority in the elections of early 1980. Her new government's more pro-market orientation contributed to the formation of the breakaway Indian National Congress (Socialist) in 1981. In July 1981 the Supreme Court ruled that Congress (I) was the authentic heir of the historic Congress party, although the Congress (I) designation continued in universal usage.

Indira Gandhi was assassinated by Sikh militants in October 1984 and was succeeded as Prime Minister and party leader by her son, Rajiv Gandhi. Rajiv led the party to a convincing general election victory in 1984–85 but substantial opposition to his leadership subsequently developed, leading to expulsions and resignations from the party, including the exit of V.P. Singh, who in 1987 formed the *Jan Morcha* anti-corruption movement which heralded the establishment of the opposition *Janata Dal*. As a result of the November 1989 general elections, Congress (I) was forced into opposition by a National Front alliance dominated by *Janata Dal*.

During the next election campaign, Rajiv was assassinated by Sri Lankan Tamil militants in May 1991, but Congress (I) regained power and formed a government under the premiership of the party's new president, P.V. Narasimha Rao. By early 1996, however, Rao's administration was deeply unpopular, its political standing having been badly damaged by alleged involvement in the country's largest corruption scandal and by related ministerial resignations. In the April-May 1996 elections Congress (I) returned only about 140 members to the *Lok Sabha*, representing a loss of nearly half of its previous representation. The party was also voted out of power in the states of Assam and Kerala. Despite the poor electoral performance and loss of power, Rao was re-elected as party leader. Having manoeuvred to deny a parliamentary vote of confidence to the minority government formed in May by its principal electoral rival, the Bharatiya Janata Party, Congress (I) gave its tacit support to the United Front administration inaugurated in June. As at July 1996 Congress (I) held 85 seats in the *Rajya Sabha*.

Janata Dal (JD)

Address. Sardar Patel Bhawan, 7 Jantar Mantar Road, New Delhi 110001

Telephone. (#91–11) 332-5886

Leadership. H.D. Deve Gowda (leader), Lalu Prasad Yadav (president), Ramvilas Paswan (secretary-general)

The *Janata Dal* ("People's Party") was formed in 1988 as a merger of the *Jan Morcha* ("Popular Front") dissident faction of the Indian National Congress–Congress (I), the *Lok Dal* and other outgrowths of the old *Janata* Party. It advocates non-alignment, the eradication of poverty, unemployment and wide disparities in wealth, and protection of minorities. The JD contested the 1989 general election as the dominant component of an opposition National Front, winning 141 of the Front's 144 seats. With the support of the *Bharatiya Janata* Party (BJP) and the communist parties, the National Front formed a fragile new government, ousting Congress (I) from power.

A split in the JD in late 1990 resulted in the creation of the breakaway *Janata Dal* (S), which subsequently evolved into the *Samajwadi* Party. This instability led to an early general election in 1991, in which the official JD won only 55 *Lok Sabha* seats and Congress (I) was returned to power. A further party split in 1994 saw the establishment of a separate parliamentary group which subsequently adopted the *Samata* Party designation.

For the April-May 1996 general elections the JD was the largest constituent in a leftist United Front, but was itself reduced to some 45 seats in the *Lok Sabha*. Following the elections, the Front commanded the support of about 180 lower house deputies, so that it was eventually able to form a new government under the premiership of the H.D. Deve Gowda of the JD. At that point the

JD was also the ruling party in the states of Bihar and Karnataka and held 23 seats in the *Rajya Sabha*.

Revolutionary Socialist Party (RSP)

Address. c/o *Lok Sabha*, New Delhi 110001

Leadership. Tridib Chowdhury (general secretary)

In the general elections of April-May 1996 the Marxist-Leninist RSP won five seats in the *Lok Sabha*, all from West Bengal, as part of the United Front (UF) alliance, but did not join the subsequent UF government. The party held one seat in the *Rajya Sabha* as at July 1996 and has also won representation in a number of state legislative assemblies, including West Bengal, Tripura and Kerala.

Samajwadi Party (SP)

Address. 227 North Avenue, New Delhi 110001

Telephone. (#91–11) 379 2783

Leadership. Mulayam Singh Yavda (leader)

Inaugurated at a convention in 1992, the SP derives from a dissident faction of the *Janata Dal* (JD). Following the 1993 state elections in Uttar Pradesh, the SP formed a governing coalition with the *Bahujan Samaj* Party (BSP). However, the coalition collapsed in June 1995 and President's rule was imposed in the state the following October pending fresh elections. In the general elections of April-May 1996 the SP won 17 *Lok Sabha* seats, almost all from Uttar Pradesh. Declaring its support for the United Front federal government inaugurated in June 1996, the SP was allocated the defence portfolio in the new administration. As at July 1996 it held five seats in the *Rajya Sabha*.

Samata Party

Address. 13 Balwant Rai Mehta Lane, New Delhi 110001

Telephone. (#91–11) 3782614

Leadership. George Fernandes (president)

The *Samata* ("Equality") Party derives from a factional split in the *Janata Dal* (JD) in early 1994, its president being a veteran socialist and trade union leader. The new grouping contested the general elections of April-May 1996, winning six *Lok Sabha* seats in the state of Bihar, but surprisingly was not part of the victorious United Front alliance.

Shiromani Akali Dal (SAD)

Address. c/o *Lok Sabha*, New Delhi 110001

Leadership. Prakash Singh Badal (president)

The SAD is the main political organization of India's Sikh community, which is concentrated in Punjab. In support of its demands for Sikh self-determination, the SAD became increasingly militant in the early 1980s and has since been subject to factional rivalry and division. In the general elections of April-May 1996 the party won eight of Punjab's 13 *Lok Sabha* seats.

Shiv Sena

Address. c/o *Lok Sabha*, New Delhi 110001
Leadership. Bal Thackeray (leader)

Founded in 1967 and based in Maharashtra, *Shiv Sena* is an extreme right-wing Hindu communalist party allied to the *Bharatiya Janata* Party (BJP) at state government and federal parliamentary levels. In the general elections of April-May 1996 the party won 15 seats in the *Lok Sabha* and supported the subsequent short-lived BJP federal administration. As at July 1996 it held three seats in the *Rajya Sabha*.

Sikkim Democratic Front (SDF)

Address. c/o Legislative Assembly, Gangtok, Sikkim
Leadership. Pawan Kumar Chamling (leader)

The SDF became the ruling party in Sikkim on winning about 60% of the legislative assembly seats in state elections in December 1994. In the April-May 1996 general election the party won Sikkim's single *Lok Sabha* seat.

Sikkim Revolutionary Forum

Sikkim Sangram Parishad (SSP)

Address. c/o Legislative Assembly, Gangtok, Sikkim
Leadership. Nar Bahadur Bhandari (president)

The SSP lost its majority in the Sikkim legislature to the Sikkim Democratic Front in state elections in December 1994. In the April-May 1996 general election the party lost Sikkim's single *Lok Sabha* seat. As of June 1996 the party held one seat in the *Rajya Sabha*.

Tamil Maanila Congress (TMC)

Address. c/o *Lok Sabha*, New Delhi 110001
Leadership. G.K. Moopanar (leader)

The TMC is a breakaway faction of the Indian National Congress–Congress (I) in Tamil Nadu. Its leaders were formally expelled from the parent party in April 1996, prior to the general election in which the TMC secured 20 of Tamil Nadu's 39 seats in the *Lok Sabha*. At state level it was allied with the victorious Dravidian Progressive Federation (DMK), winning 39 legislative assembly seats in its own right. The party was a leading component of the United Front federal government inaugurated in June 1996, being awarded the finance portfolio and four other posts in the new administration.

Telugu Desam Party (TDP)

Address. 5 Parliament House, New Delhi 110001
Telephone. (#91–11) 303 4783

Leadership. Chandrababu Naidu, Lakshmi Parvati (factional leaders)

Founded in 1982 as an Andhra Pradesh-based leftist party by N.T. Rama Rao, the TDP was the ruling party in the state from 1983 to 1989. In 1994 it regained power from the Indian National Congress–Congress (I) in a convincing victory in the state elections, Rao becoming chief minister again. Political divisions within the party resulted in a split in 1995 between those state assembly deputies supporting Rao and those supporting Chandrababu Naidu. In August Rao resigned the premiership and was replaced by Naidu in September. On Rao's death in January 1996, leadership of his faction was taken over by his wife, Lakshmi Parvati. In the general election of April-May 1996, the TDP–Naidu faction won 16 seats in the *Lok Sabha* (and the Parvati faction none), being allocated four posts in the subsequent United Front federal government formed in June 1996. As at July 1996 the TDP held one seat in the *Lok Sabha*.

United Front (UF)

Address. c/o *Lok Sabha*, New Delhi 110001
Leadership. Deve Gowda (leader), Ram Vilas Paswan (parliamentary leader in the *Lok Sabha*), I.K. Gujaral (parliamentary leader in the *Rajya Sabha*)

Officially called the National Front–Left Front for the April-May 1996 general elections, the UF consists of a loose alliance of 13 broadly leftist and regional organizations dominated by three national parties, namely the *Janata Dal* (JD), the Communist Party of India-Marxist (CPI-M) and the Communist Party of India (CPI), and also including the All-India Forward Bloc, the All-India Indira Congress–Tiwari, the Assam People's Council, the Dravidian Progressive Federation (DMK), the Karnataka Congress Party, the Madhya Pradesh Vikas Congress, the Maharastrawadi Gomantak, the Revolutionary Socialist Party, the Samajwadi Party, the Tamil Maanila Congress and the Telugu Desam Party–Naidu.

Upon the demise of the short-lived post-election government of the Bharatiya Janata Party at the end of May 1996, the UF parties, with the support of about 180 members in the *Lok Sabha* and the acquiescence of the Indian National Congress–Congress (I) deputies, formed a new federal administration under the premiership of Deve Gowda (JD) which won a parliamentary vote of confidence the following month. The CPI-M opted not to take ministerial portfolios, while continuing to be a member of the Front, which advocates the preservation of national unity, social and economic equality, and commitment to secularism and federalism.

319

Other Parties

All-India Hindu Association (AIHA), a right-wing Hindu party led by Shive Saran.

All-India Majlis-e-Ittehadul Muslimeen (AIMEIM), a Muslim-based party led by Sultan Salahuddin Owaisi, secured representation in the *Lok Sabha* in a 1994 by-election; declared its support for the United Front central government inaugurated in June 1996.

Autonomous State Demand Committee (ASDC), led by Jayanta Rongpi, secured representation in the *Lok Sabha* in a 1994 by-election.

Communist Party of India–Marxist-Leninist (CPI-ML), founded in 1969 by Maoists expelled from the Communist Party of India-Marxist (CPI-M); banned between 1975 and 1977, after which it adopted less radical policies but failed to gain national or state representation.

Haryana Vikas Party (HVP), returned three *Lok Sabha* members from Haryana constituencies in April-May 1996, supported short-lived government of the *Bharatiya Janata* Party.

Hill People's Union (HPU), founded in 1985 to represent the interests of the tribal hill peoples of Meghalaya state, secured eight of the 60 seats in the 1993 state assembly elections.

Hill State People's Democratic Party (HSPDP), advocating the preservation of the distinct identity of the tribal peoples of Meghalaya state and the protection of their interests within the Indian Union; emerged from the 1993 state elections as the second largest party after the Indian National Congress–Congress (I).

Indian National Congress (Socialist)–Congress (S), founded in 1981 as a breakaway faction from the Indian National Congress–Congress (I) and led by Sarat Chandra Sinha; retained one *Lok Sabha* seat in the 1991 general election.

Indian Union Muslim League (IUML), a remnant of the pre-independence Muslim League, aiming to represent the interests of the Muslim ethnic and religious minority; has attracted support mainly in southern India, particularly in Kerala state.

Jammu and Kashmir National Conference (JKNC), a state-based party, opposed to Hindu communalism and advocating the maintenance of Jammu and Kashmir's status as an integral part of the Indian Union but with internal autonomy and self-government; was the dominant party in Kashmir for most of the period from independence until 1990, when communal violence led to the imposition of President's rule in the state until the JKNC won state elections in 1996.

Janata Party (JP), briefly in power at the federal level from March 1977 until January 1980, after which it fragmented and the rump party's influence declined; led by Subrahmaniam Swamy.

Jharkhand Mukti Morcha (JMM), founded in 1980 to represent the interests of the tribal people of the state of Bihar, where it won about 5% of the seats in the 1995 legislative assembly; also represented in the Orissa state assembly; won a handful of seats in 1996 general elections to the *Lok Sabha*.

Karnataka Congress Party (KCP), an autonomous state party that won one *Lok Sabha* seat in 1996 as part of the United Front coalition.

Kerala Congress (KC), a participant in the Left Democratic Front coalition government, headed by the Communist Party of India-Marxist (CPI-M), which came to power in Kerala in May 1996 following state elections.

Madhya Pradesh Vikas Congress (MPVC), formed early in 1996 by Madhya Pradesh dissidents of the Indian National Congress–Congress (I), won two lower house seats in the subsequent general elections, declared support for the United Front government inaugurated in June 1996.

Maharashtrawadi Gomantak Party (MGP), a Hindu-dominated party that has long competed for control of the Goan legislative assembly with the Indian National Congress–Congress (I), to which it came second in the December 1994 state elections; won one *Lok Sabha* seat in 1996 as part of the United Front coalition.

Manipur People's Party (MPP), the second largest party in the Manipur legislative assembly after the Indian National Congress–Congress (I).

Mizo National Front (MNF), legalized in 1986 (upon the conferment of statehood on Mizoram), having earlier waged an underground campaign for national self-determination; in state elections in 1993 became the second largest party with 14 of the 40 seats in the legislative assembly.

Nagaland People's Council (NPC), the second largest party in the Nagaland legislative assembly; failed to retain the state's single *Lok Sabha* seat in the 1996 general election; as of June 1996 it held one seat in the *Rajya Sabha*.

Peasants' and Workers' Party of India (PWPI), a Marxist party led by Dajiba Desai, operates primarily in the state of Maharashtra.

Republican Party of India (RPI), committed to the egalitarian aims and objectives set out in the preamble to the 1950 Indian constitution, led by C.M. Armugham.

United Goans Party (UGP), a small regional party which won three seats in the legislative assembly in Goa in state elections in 1994.

Indonesia

Capital: Jakarta

Population: 196,000,000 (1995E)

The Republic of Indonesia, comprising mainly some 13,700 islands, was known until 1949 as the Netherlands East Indies; since 1976 it has also included East Timor (effectively annexed as the 27th Indonesian province after the withdrawal of Portuguese troops, although this act has never been officially recognized by the United Nations). Following a brief period as a federation, Indonesia became in 1950 a unitary state in which executive power resides in the President (a position held since 1967 by Gen. Suharto), who governs with the assistance of an appointed Cabinet. The President is elected for a five-year term by a 1,000–member People's Consultative Assembly (*Majelis Permusyarwaratan Rakyat*), described in the constitution as the embodiment of the whole Indonesian people. Of the Assembly's members, 500 are from the legislative House of Representatives (*Dewan Perwakilan Rakyat*), to which 400 are elected for a five-year term by direct universal adult suffrage, the remaining 100 being appointed by the President. The Assembly's other 500 members are government appointees, delegates of the regional assemblies and representatives of parties and groups (appointed in proportion to their elective seats in the House of Representatives).

The dominant political organization, the Joint Secretariat of Functional Groups (GOLKAR), was brought under government control at the end of the 1960s to provide a civilian vehicle for President Suharto's military regime. In 1973 nine other existing political organizations were ordered by the government to fuse into two new parties—the Indonesian Democratic Party (PDI) and the United Development Party (PPP)—creating a three-party system which was consolidated by legislation in 1975. Political parties are obliged under a law of 1984 to adopt the *pancasila* creed enshrined in the 1945 constitution (enjoining monotheism, humanitarianism, national unity, democracy by consensus and social justice) as their sole ideological foundation.

GOLKAR retained power in elections to the House of Representatives held in June 1992, winning 282 of the 400 elective seats, against 62 for the PPP and 56 for the PDI. The People's Consultative Assembly re-elected Suharto for a sixth term as President in March 1993.

Indonesian Democratic Party
Partai Demokrasi Indonesia (PDI)
  Address. Jalan Diponegoro 58, Jakarta 10310
  Telephone. (#62–21) 336331
  Leadership. Megawati Sukarnoputri (chair)
  The PDI was created by the merger in 1973 of three nationalist and two Christian-based political parties. It advocates the restoration of full civilian rule, but has remained largely supportive of the Suharto regime. In the general election held in June 1992 the party increased its representation from 40 to 56 seats, attracting about 15% the vote.

In January 1995 it was reported that some 300 members of the PDI were to be investigated for alleged links to the attempted communist coup in 1965.

Joint Secretariat of Functional Groups
Sekretariat Bersama Golongan Karya (GOLKAR)
  Address. Jalan Anggrek Nelimurni, Jakarta 11480
  Telephone. (#62–21) 548-1618

Leadership. Gen. Suharto (president), Harmoko (chair)

Originally formed in 1964, GOLKAR is a government-sponsored amalgamation of groups representing farmers, fishermen and the professions, and including members of the Indonesian armed forces. It has been the dominant political force under Suharto's military regime, for which it provides a civilian basis. In successive elections to the House of Representatives since 1971 GOLKAR has achieved a substantial majority, most recently in June 1992 when it secured 282 seats with just over 68% of the votes cast.

In March 1995 GOLKAR expelled one of its members from the House of Representatives (Bambang Warih Koesoemo), in what appeared to be part of an extensive clampdown on dissent.

United Development Party

Partai Persatuan Pembangunan (PPP)
  Address. Jalan Diponegoro 60, Jakarta 10310
  Telephone. (#62–21) 356381
  Leadership. Ismael Hassan Metareum (president)

The PPP, like the Indonesian Democratic Party, was created in 1973 as a result of the Suharto regime's pressure on political organizations to "simplify" the party system. Four Islamic groups merged initially to form the party, although the *Nahdatul Ulama* faction withdrew in 1984, after which support for the PPP fell considerably. In the balloting in June 1992 the party won 62 of the 400 elective seats in the House of Representatives, gaining 17% of the vote.

Other Groupings

Association of Indonesian Muslim Intellectuals (*Ikatan Cendikiawan Muslim Indonesia*, ICMI), formed in 1990 with government support, and led by Bacharuddin Jusuf Habibie.

Democracy Forum, launched in 1991 to promote national political political dialogue by Abdurrahman Wahid, chair of *Nahdatul Ulama*, which had been a constituent of the moderate Islamic United Development Party until 1984, when it withdrew to devote itself to social and religious works.

Indonesian United Democratic Party, launched in May 1996 by Sri Bintang Pamungkas shortly after he had been sentenced to 34 months' imprisonment after been found guilty of insulting President Suharto.

Banned Organizations

Communist Party of Indonesia (*Partai Komunis Indonesia*, PKI), banned since 1966 following an abortive coup attempt the previous year; in April 1996 the government restored the voting rights of over a million people disenfranchised for involvement in the failed coup, while maintaining the electoral exclusion of 20,000 others.

Free Papua Movement (*Organisasi Papua Merdeka*, OPM), seeking the integration of Irian Jaya into neighbouring Papua New Guinea, responsible for the taking of Western hostages in January 1996.

National Liberation Front of Aceh (NLFA), formed in 1989 to press for independence for the north Sumatran state of Aceh.

Revolutionary Front for an Independent East Timor (*Frente Revolucionário do Este Timor Independente*, FRETILIN), the main pro-independence grouping in East Timor, formed in 1974 under Portuguese rule and subsequently the main channel of local opposition to Indonesia's annexation of the territory in 1975–76; following the capture and imprisonment of José Alexandre ("Xanawa") Gusmão, led since November 1993 by Konis Santana.

Iran

Capital: Tehran

Population: 60,000,000 (1995E)

The Islamic Republic of Iran was proclaimed in 1979 after the overthrow of the monarchy. Overall authority is exercised by the *Wali Faqih*, the country's spiritual leader. The state President and the 270–member legislature, the *Majlis-e-Shoura-e-Islami* (Islamic Consultative Assembly), are elected by universal suffrage every four years on a non-party basis. The *Majlis* approves the appointment of all members of the Council of Ministers and may request their resignation. The post of Prime Minister was formally abolished in July 1989. An Assembly of

Experts is elected, also by universal suffrage, to decide issues such as succession to the position of *Wali Faqih*. It is composed entirely of clerics. Ayatollah Ruhollah Khomeini, Iran's *Wali Faqih* since 1979, died in June 1989, and the Assembly of Experts elected Ayatollah Sayed Ali Khamenei as his successor. A 12–member Council of Constitutional Guardians made up of experts in Koranic law and up to six civil lawyers supervises elections and examines legislation adopted by the *Majlis* to ensure its conformity to the principles of religious law and the constitution.

In June 1993 Hojatolislam Ali Akbar Hashemi Rafsanjani was re-elected President for a second successive four-year term. A general election held in April and May 1992 strengthened the position of supporters of Rafsanjani's reformist policies (espousing economic liberalization and openness in foreign relations).

There are no officially recognized political parties, although the 1979 constitution does not restrict their formation provided they do not contravene national sovereignty or unity or the principles of Islam. The Islamic Republican Party (IRP), which became the ruling party after the revolution in what was effectively a one-party state, was officially disbanded in June 1987 by Ayatollah Khomeini on the grounds that it was in danger of becoming "an excuse for discord and factionalism". Some of the opposition organizations which have operated since 1979— including clandestine, guerrilla and separatist groups—are listed below.

Communist Party of Iran, established in 1979 as an alternative to the pro-Soviet stance of Party of the Masses (*Tudeh*).

Feyadeen-e-Khalq, a Marxist and secular guerrilla organization.

Kumelah, a Kurdish wing of the Communist Party of Iran has also fought for Kurdish autonomy.

Kurdish Democratic Party of Iran (KDPI), a separatist group which campaigns for Kurdish autonomy and which has been outlawed since 1979. Members of its guerrilla wing are often referred to as *peshmergas*.

Liberation (or Freedom) Movement of Iran (*Nezhat-e-Azadi-e-Iran*), established in 1961 by Mehdi Bazargan. The organization supported the anti-Shah demonstrations of 1978 and Dr Bazargan became the first Prime Minister under the Islamic regime in February 1979. However, he resigned over the seizure of the US embassy in Tehran in November of that year, and thereafter remained one of the most outspoken critics tolerated by the government. The movement boycotted the 1984 and 1988 legislative elections, and Dr Bazargan claimed that it was not allowed to participate freely in the 1992 campaign.

Mujaheddin-e-Khalq, a leftist but Islamic guerrilla organization led by Massoud Rajavi and operating mainly from Iraq.

National Democratic Front (*Jebhe-e-Democratic-e-Melli*), an offshoot of the National Front and led, from exile, by Hedayatollah Matine-Daftari, who founded the organization in 1979.

National Front (*Jebhe-e-Melli*), established in 1977 as a largely secular coalition of nationalist factions and led, from exile, by Karim Sanjabi.

National Movement of Iranian Resistance, based in France, two of whose leaders—Abdol-Rahman Boroumand and former Prime Minister Dr Shapour Bakhtiar—were assassinated in 1991.

National Resistance Council, established in October 1981 in France by Abolhassan Bani-Sadr (deposed as President of Iran earlier that year) and the Council's current leader, Massoud Rajavi of the Mujaheddin-e-Khalq. In 1984 the Council comprised some 15 opposition groups, operating either clandestinely in Iran or from exile abroad. Bani-Sadr left the Council in that year because of his objection to Rajavi's growing links with the Iraqi government.

Party of the Masses (*Tudeh*), communist and traditionally pro-Soviet from its formation in 1941. Having been banned in 1949, the party came into the open in 1979 but was banned again in 1983 by the Islamic regime. Dissident party members reportedly founded the Democratic Party of the Iranian People in France in 1988.

Iraq

Capital: Baghdad

Population: 19,500,000 (1995E)

The Republic of Iraq was declared in 1958 following the overthrow of the monarchy. Power is wielded in the main by the minority Sunni Muslims and is concentrated in the hands of the Revolutionary Command Council (RCC), which elects the President by a two-thirds majority from among its own members. The RCC is appointed by the President, who also appoints the Council of Ministers. Legislative authority is shared between the RCC and the 250–member National Assembly, the latter elected by universal adult suffrage under a system of proportional representation. A leading role is also played by the 17–member "regional command" of the dominant Baath Arab Socialist Party, which itself dominates the broader state-sponsored National Progressive Patriotic Front (NPPF).

In September 1991 President Saddam Hussein nominally ended *de facto* one-party rule by the Baath Party by approving a measure authorizing the creation of political parties outside the NPPF framework. However, there have been no reports of the formation of such groups in areas under government control. In May 1994 President Hussein assumed the additional post of Prime Minister. The official results of Assembly elections held on March 24, 1996, gave no details of the party affiliation of those elected, although the Baath Party announced that it remained the dominant political force. All of the 689 candidates for the 220 seats at issue were approved by the NPPF, the other 30 (for Kurdish-controlled regions) being filled by presidential nomination.

An Iraqi Kurdistan National Assembly was elected in May 1992 in the Kurdish-inhabited areas of Iraq. It was not recognized by the Iraqi regime, which had set up a Kurdish Legislative Council under earlier and now effectively defunct "autonomy" arrangements. The Democratic Party of Kurdistan (DPK) and the Patriotic Union of Kurdistan (PUK) filled 50 seats each following the elections to the new Assembly, with four being awarded to the Assyrian Democratic Party and one to the (Assyrian) Christian Union.

Baath Arab Socialist Party
Hizb al-Baath al-Arabi al-Ishtiraki

Address. PO Box 6012, al-Mansour, Baghdad

Leadership. Saddam Hussein (secretary-general of regional command), Izzat Ibrahim (deputy secretary-general)

The Baath (Renaissance) stands for secular pan-Arabism, socialism, anti-imperialism and anti-Zionism. It is historically (but now only theoretically) a regional party of which the Iraqi party is one "regional command", others being in Lebanon and Syria. Founded originally in Syria in the latter part of the 1940s, the Baath has held power in Iraq since July 1968, when it was the leading force in the Revolutionary Command Council which overthrew the Aref military regime. The party had previously been part of the group which overthrew the dictatorship of President Kassem in February 1953, but was then itself deposed in a military coup in November of the same year.

In 1973 the Baath was instrumental in setting up an umbrella National Progressive Front with the aim of securing the co-operation of other political forces. This organization was renamed the National Progressive Patriotic Front following the outbreak of war with Iran in 1980. Saddam Hussein has held the party leadership (as well as the Iraqi presidency) since 1979. There have been periodic purges in which critics of his leadership have been removed.

Kurdistan Democratic Party (KDP)
Hizb al Dimuqraati al-Kurdi

Address. Aqaba bin Nafis Square, Baghdad

Leadership. Muhammad Said al-Atrushi (secretary-general)

This small Kurdish formation has participated

in the Baath-led National Progressive Patriotic Front since 1974.

Kurdistan Revolutionary Party (KRP)

Address. c/o National Assembly, Baghdad
Leadership. Abd al-Sattar Tahir Sharif (secretary-general)

The KRP, founded in 1972, has consistently been a pro-regime participant in the National Progressive Patriotic Front since 1974.

National Progressive Patriotic Front (NPPF)

Address. c/o National Assembly, Baghdad
Leadership. Naim Haddad (secretary-general)

Formed in 1973 as the National Progressive Front (the addition of the word Patriotic in the early 1980s indicating the need for national solidarity in the war with Iran), this Baath-dominated organization serves in practice as little more than a mechanism for compiling and endorsing lists of electoral candidates. Initially it included the Iraqi Communist Party (ICP), subsequently incorporating compliant Kurdish groups in 1974. The ICP recognized the privileged role of the Baath Arab Socialist Party, which was to have a majority in the Front and the National Assembly. However, relations between the Baath and the Communists deteriorated in the late 1970s, with the result that in March 1979 the ICP withdrew from the Front.

Illegal Opposition Groups

Democratic Party of Kurdistan (DPK), an insurgent Kurdish organization led by Masoud Barzani; the DPK controlled the largest rebel force during the unsuccessful 1991 uprising against Saddam Hussein.

Iraqi Communist Party (ICP), led by Aziz Muhammad, allied with the Kurdish opposition since the party's suppression at the end of the 1970s.

Iraqi National Congress (INC), launched in 1992, aiming to unite the various Kurdish, Sunni and Shia factions of the opposition, and headed by a three-member presidential council comprising Masoud Barzani of the Democratic Party of Kurdistan, Hassan al-Naqib and Muhammad Bahr al-Eloom; the participants committed themselves to the overthrow of Saddam Hussein and the establishment of a federal system permitting a substantial degree of ethnic autonomy without partition of the country.

Iraqi National Joint Action Committee (INJAC), a 17–member opposition grouping launched in Syria in 1990 and encompassing Shia, Kurdish and other organizations.

Nation Party (*Hizb al-Umma*), established in 1982 and led by Saad Saleh Jabr.

Patriotic Union of Kurdistan (PUK), a major Kurdish insurgent group, a rival to the Democratic Party of Kurdistan, led by Jalal Talabani.

Supreme Assembly of the Islamic Revolution of Iraq (SAIRI), formed in 1982 by Shia Muslim opponents of the Sunni-based ruling regime, and chaired by Ayatollah Muhammad Bakr al-Hakim; it includes guerrilla groups such as Voice of Islam and Holy Warriors (*Mujaheddin*).

Ireland

Capital: Dublin   **Population:** 3,600,000 (1995E)

The Irish Republic's 1937 constitution expressly applies to the whole of Ireland (Éire) and therefore contains an implicit claim to sovereignty over the six counties of Northern Ireland, which are under UK sovereignty. Pending "the reintegration of the national territory", the government's authority extends only to the 26 counties of the Republic. The Irish parliament (*Oireachtas*) consists of (i) the President (*Uachtará na hÉireann*) directly elected for a seven-year term (once renewable); (ii) a 166–member lower house (*Dáil Eireann*) elected by universal adult suffrage for a five-year term); and (iii) a 60–member indirectly-elected Senate (*Seanad*), including 11 prime ministerial appointees, with power to delay, but not to veto, lower house legislation. The cabinet, which is responsible to the *Dáil*, is headed by a Prime Minister (*Taoiseach*), who is the leader of the majority party or coalition. Members of the *Dáil* are elected by the single transferable vote (STV) version of proportional representation, from multi-member constituencies.

Under legislation governing the remuneration of public representatives, leaders of parties which have seven or more seats in the *Dáil* are eligible for allowances from public funds to help them carry out their parliamentary duties.

Elections to the *Dáil* on Nov. 25, 1992, resulted as follows: *Fianna Fáil* 68 seats (with 39.1% of first-preference votes), *Fine Gael* 45 (24.5%), Labour Party 33 (19.3%), Progressive Democrats 10 (4.7%), Democratic Left 4 (2.8%), others 6.

Democratic Left (DL)

Address. 69 Middle Abbey Street, Dublin 1

Telephone. (#353–1) 872–9550

Fax. (#353–1) 872–9700

Leadership. Proinsías de Rossa (president), Catherine Murphy (executive committee chair), John Gallagher (general secretary)

The DL was launched by a reformist faction of the Workers' Party which broke away in February 1992. Committed to democratic socialism, the DL won four *Dáil* seats in November 1992 (when the parent party failed to win representation). In December 1994 the DL agreed to join a coalition government with *Fine Gael* and the Labour Party, its leader becoming Minister of Social Welfare.

Fianna Fáil (FF)

Address. 13 Upper Mount Street, Dublin 2

Telephone. (#353–1) 676–1551

Fax. (#353–1) 678–5690

Leadership. Bertie Ahern (leader), Pat Farrell (general secretary)

Republican, nationalist and populist, *Fianna Fáil* seeks the peaceful reunification by consent of Ireland, national self-sufficiency, social justice and the preservation of the Irish language and culture. It strongly supports the European Union's common agricultural policy but opposes any extension of the powers of the European Parliament. It favours nuclear disarmament and wants all of Ireland to be a nuclear-free zone.

Fianna Fáil (literally "Warriors of Destiny", but officially known in English as The Republican Party) was founded in 1926 by Éamon de Valera, who was the sole surviving leader of the 1916 rebellion, and the leading opponent of the 1921 treaty with Britain, boycotted the Free State *Dáil* (because of a required oath of allegiance to the British monarch) until 1927; in 1932 it came to power in general elections. De Valera then became *Taoiseach* (and was President of Ireland from 1959 until his death in 1973).

Fianna Fáil remained in government until 1948, introducing the autonomist (and strongly Catholic) constitution of 1937 and maintaining neutrality during World War II. The party was again in power in 1951–54, 1957–73, 1977–81 and in 1982. His ministerial career having survived gun-running allegations in 1970, Charles Haughey became party leader and *Taoiseach* in 1979. The party has

usually been the largest in the *Dáil*, but has only once (in 1965) had an overall majority; it had 75 TDs elected in November 1982, with 47.3% of the vote, and 81 in 1987 when it won 44.1%.

Haughey returned as Prime Minister after the latter election, but after the next, in June 1989, FF parliamentary strength had been reduced to 77 seats. The result was the first really serious political impasse in independent Ireland's history. It was resolved by Haughey agreeing the following month to the inclusion of the PDs in *Fianna Fáil*'s first-ever experience of coalition government. Subsequently, the FF deputy leader and Defence Minister, Brian Lenihan, began as favourite to win the November 1990 presidential election, but lost public confidence when he was dismissed from the government a month before voting over a scandal, the consequence being that he was heavily defeated by Mary Robinson.

Haughey finally bowed out in January 1992, being succeeded as *Fianna Fáil* leader and therefore as Prime Minister by his old party adversary, Albert Reynolds. In November 1992 the party experienced its poorest election result since World War II (its *Dáil* representation falling to 68 seats), but Reynolds managed to entice the resurgent Labour Party into a majority coalition. Less than two years later, however, the coalition collapsed over the affair of the allegedly paedophile Catholic priest, which forced Reynolds's resignation in November 1994. *Fianna Fáil* then went into opposition to a coalition headed by *Fine Gael*, although it remained the largest parliamentary party under the new leadership of Bertie Ahern.

The seven FF members of the European Parliament elected in 1994 (with 35% of the vote) sit in the Union for Europe group, the largest components of which are *Forza Italia* and the French Rally for the Republic.

Fine Gael (FG)

Address. 51 Upper Mount Street, Dublin 2

Telephone (#353–1) 676–1551

Fax. (#353–1) 660–9168

Leadership. John Bruton (leader), Kay Brophy (chair), Jim Miley (general secretary)

Of Christian democratic orientation, *Fine Gael* supports free enterprise, social justice, decentralization, reconciliation with the North, participative democracy, tax equity and the maintenance or improvement of education and welfare provision. It supports an active Irish role in strengthening the European Union and the constructive use of Irish neutrality in addressing international issues including peace, disarmament, human rights and self-determination for peoples.

Fine Gael (literally "Tribe of the Gael", but officially known in English as the United Ireland Party) was created in 1933 by the merger of *Cumann na nGaedhale* ("Society of the Gaels"), the ruling party of the Irish Free State in 1923–32, with the Centre Party and the fascist "Blueshirt" movement of Gen. Eoin O'Duffy, who briefly led the new party. Although it was the main party in favour of the treaty which established the state, *Fine Gael* supported the 1949 declaration of a republic, and has retained nationalist ideals. Since the 1970s it has been involved in efforts to make Irish society more pluralistic, supporting the lifting of the constitutional prohibitions on divorce and abortion.

The party ruled through coalitions, all involving Labour, in 1948–51, 1954|7, 1973–77, June 1981 to February 1982, and November 1982 to February 1987, and was the main opposition party outside those periods. Its leader since 1977, the outgoing *Taoiseach* Dr Garret FitzGerald, resigned when the February 1987 elections reduced the FG share of the vote to 27.1%, and its *Dáil* seats to 51 (from 37.3% and 70 in November 1982). The new leader, Alan Dukes, maintained the party's strong commitment to the 1985 Anglo-Irish Agreement whereby the Republic's government recognized partition but secured a consultative role in the administration of the North.

In the June 1989 elections *Fine Gael* increased its parliamentary representation to 55, but remained in opposition. In November 1990 Dukes resigned as party leader and was replaced by his more right-leaning deputy, John Bruton. In the November 1992 *Dáil* elections, however, *Fine Gael* slumped to 45 seats, its worst showing since 1948. Nevertheless, a political crisis in late 1994 resulting in the resignation of the *Fianna Fáil* Prime Minister enabled Bruton to form a three-party coalition government with Labour and the Democratic Left.

Fine Gael is affiliated to the Christian Democrat International. Its four members of the European Parliament (elected in 1994 on a 24.3% vote share) sit in the European People's Party group.

The Green Party
Comhaontás Glas
    Address. 5A Upper Fownes Street, Dublin 2
    Telephone. (#353–1) 677–1436
    Fax. (£353-1) 679–7168
    Leadership. Mary Bowers (co-ordinator)
The party stands for a globally-sustainable economic system, with, on a national level, a basic income for all citizens, the phasing out of monopoly capitalism and its replacement by an economy based on workers' co-operatives and small family businesses. It was established in 1981 with support from the Ecology Party of the United Kingdom (now the Green Party) and from members of anti-nuclear and environmental protection groups in Ireland.

The party won its first *Dáil* seat in the June 1989 election, retaining it in 1992. Like other Green parties in the European Union, it made a much greater impact in the June 1994 European Parliament elections, winning two of Ireland's 15 seats with 7.9% of the vote.

The Labour Party
Páirtí Lucht Oibre
    Address. 17 Ely Place, Dublin 2
    Telephone. (#353–1) 661–2615
    Fax. (#353–1) 661–2640
    Leadership. Dick Spring (leader), Ruairí Quinn (deputy leader), Jim Kemmy (chair), Ray Kavanagh (general secretary)
The social democratic Labour Party seeks the peaceful transformation of Irish society into a socialist republic. It calls for the resolution of the economic crisis by means which would not impoverish weaker sections of the community, including public-sector job creation and taxation equity between wage-earners and the self-employed, especially farmers. It supports the 1985 Anglo-Irish Agreement and aspires to the reunification of Ireland by consent. It also advocates strict neutrality.

The Labour Party, founded in 1912 by James Connolly and Jim Larkin, was the main opposition party in the *Dáil* of the Irish Free State in 1922–26, and became independent of the trade union movement in 1930. It supported the *Fianna Fáil* minority government under Éamon de Valera in 1932–33 but opposed the 1937 constitution (although supporting its main effect, which was to create a republic outside the British Empire). It participated in coalition governments in 1948–51 with four other parties, in 1954–57 with *Fine Gael* and a farmers' party, *Clann na Talmhan* and with *Fine Gael* alone in 1973–77, 1981–82 and from December 1982 to January 1987–providing the *Tánaiste* (Deputy Prime Minister) in all these governments.

The party withdrew from government in 1987 in opposition to proposed cuts in the health budget, thus precipitating a general election in which it won 12 seats (as against 16 in November 1982). The party decided in 1986 to end its participation in coalitions, a strategy which had consistently been opposed by its own left wing.

Labour steadily lost support, its share of the general election vote fell from 17% in 1969 to 9.1% in 1982 and 6.5% in 1987.

Labour's recovery began at the June 1989 elections, when it increased its *Dáil* representation from 12 to 15 seats. The following year it joined with the Workers' Party in backing the successful presidential candidacy of Mary Robinson, who had twice been a Labour parliamentary candidate but was no longer a party member. In the November 1992 elections Labour achieved its best election result to date, more than doubling its *Dáil* representation to 33 seats after a campaign focusing on the shortcomings of the FF government. Nevertheless, in January 1993 the party entered into a majority coalition with FF, which lasted until November 1994, when Labour ministers took exception to FF conduct in the case of a Catholic priest accused of paedophilia. The party promptly rediscovered its sympathies with *Fine Gael*, joining a three-party coalition which also included the Democratic Left.

The Labour Party is a member of the Socialist International. Its single member of the European Parliament (elected in 1994 on a party vote share of 11%) sits in the Party of European Socialists group.

Progressive Democrats (PDs)

Address. 25 South Frederick Street, Dublin 2
Telephone. (#353–1) 679–4399
Fax. (#353–1) 679–4757
Leadership. Mary Harney (parliamentary leader), Garvan McGinley (general secretary)

The PDs are a centre-right grouping calling for reduced government spending, privatization, a secular state and acceptance of the reality of partition.

The PD party was founded in December 1985, following a split in the opposition *Fianna Fáil* (FF), by four FF TDs including Desmond O'Malley, a former cabinet minister, as leader. The PDs have campaigned mainly for fiscal responsibility, to which end they have supported what they regarded as "essential and balanced" measures by successive governments (including the cuts proposed in the first budget of the new *Fianna Fáil* government in 1987), while opposing those which they have seen as "ill-thought-out and unjust" (such as primary teaching cuts and the abolition of the National Social Services Board).

In its first electoral test, in February 1987, the PDs secured 210,587 votes (11.8%) and 14 seats in the *Dáil*, thus displacing Labour as the third party. It appeared to draw more support away from the traditional right-wing party, *Fine Gael*, than from FF.

The PDs then experienced the loss of initial momentum familiar to most new parties, falling to only six seats at the 1989 election, after which the party opted to join a coalition government headed by *Fianna Fáil*. Its withdrawal three years later precipitated the November 1992 *Dáil* elections, in which PD representation rose to 10 seats. O'Malley resigned as PD leader in October 1993 and was succeeded by the first female head of a significant Irish party.

Sinn Féin (SF)

Address. 44 Parnell Square, Dublin 1
Telephone. (#353–1) 872–6100
Fax. (#353–1) 873–3411
Leadership. Gerry Adams (president)

Republican, revolutionary and nationalist, *Sinn Féin* (literally "Ourselves") supports the Irish Republican Army (IRA) campaign in Northern Ireland, and seeks the establishment of a unitary democratic socialist state. It was founded in 1905 by Arthur Griffith as a nationalist party and was radicalized by the 1916 rebellion. In 1918 it won, but did not take up, 72 of the 105 Irish seats in the UK House of Commons; instead, it formed *Dáil*, and Northern loyalists organized to resist independence. After a three-year guerrilla war a treaty in 1922 partitioned the country into the autonomous Irish Free State, in 26 countries, and Northern Ireland (still in the UK) in the other six. The anti-treaty *Sinn Féin* under Éamon de Valera supported the IRA in a civil war with Free State forces. De Valera left in 1926 to form *Fianna Fáil*; *Sinn Féin* was left on the margin of Southern politics, supporting IRA campaigns conducted mainly in Britain and on the Northern border. It won (but did not occupy) four seats in the *Dáil* in 1957, but lost them in 1961.

The movement split in 1969–70; the left wing evolved into the Workers' Party while the nationalist faction became known (and is still often referred to) as Provisional *Sinn Féin*, and had as its military wing the Provisional IRA ("the Provos"). By the 1980s *Sinn Féin* had become involved in community and electoral politics in the South, and won seats on some local councils, but not in the *Dáil*. A younger, more radical leadership was elected in 1983. In 1986 it ended the policy of abstention from the *Dáil* and registered for the first time as a political party, but in the 1987 elections it won only 1.9% of the vote.

The policy change in favour of *Dáil* participation proved to be somewhat academic. *Sinn Féin* continued to be signally unsuccessful in Irish Republic elections, winning no seats in 1987, 1989 or 1992.

The Workers' Party (WP)

Pairtí na nOibri

Address. 28 Gardiner Place, Dublin 1

Telephone. (#353–1) 874–0716

Fax. (#353–1) 874–8702

Leadership. Marion Donnelly (chair), Pat Quearney (general secretary)

The Independent Marxist WP stands for a united democratic socialist republic in which the working classes control industry and resources. The party supports Irish neutrality and nuclear disarmament. Its economic programme calls for full employment and growth of 5% per year.

Founded in 1905.

The WP is derived from *Sinn Féin*, which was from the 1920s the political counterpart of the illegal Irish Republican Army (IRA). *Sinn Féin* developed in a socialist direction in the 1960s, but split in 1969–70 as a result of events in the North, between the nationalist Provisionals and the socialist Official *Sinn Féin*, whose military wing was the Official IRA (known as "the Stickies" from self-adhesive badges worn at Easter by supporters). In 1972 the Official IRA announced the cessation of its activities apart from "defence and retaliation". After feuds with the Irish National Liberation Army in 1975 and 1977, and with the Provisional IRA in 1977, it was said to have disbanded in line with the party's adoption in 1971 of a parliamentary strategy.

In 1977 the party changed its name to *Sinn Féin* The Workers' Party (SFWP)–although its Northern Ireland section (see separate UK chapter) had a different name. It ran unsuccessful candidates in 16 *Dáil* constituencies, but was represented at local government level. One member was elected to the *Dáil* in June 1981, when the party became (as it remains) the only all-Ireland party with parliamentary representation. In April 1982 it dropped the *Sinn Féin* prefix, becoming the WP; it won three seats in the June general elections, but lost one in November despite increasing its overall vote to 2.3%. In February 1987 it won 3.8%, giving it three Dublin seats and one in Cork. Tomás MacGiolla retired in 1988 after 28 years as party president.

At the 1989 elections the WP had a major success when it increased its *Dáil* representation to seven seats. In February 1992, however, six of these seven deputies, including its leader, Proinsías de Rossa, resigned after their proposal to abandon Leninism in favour of democratic socialism had been narrowly rejected at a party conference, the result being the Democratic Left. The rump group failed to secure parliamentary representation in November 1992.

Other Parties

Christian Solidarity Party (CSP), led by Gerard Casey (chair) and Micheál Ó Searcóid (secretary).

Communist Party of Ireland (CPI), led by James Stewart (general secretary) and Eugene McCartan (chair), all-Ireland formation founded in 1921 by Roddy Connolly, reestablished in 1933, split during the World War II over a 1941 decision to suspend activities in the Republic with reunification of its southern and northern elements not occurring until 1970; staunchly pro-Soviet right up to the demise of the USSR (though harbouring a reformist minority), it has never won a *Dáil* seat and has only limited industrial influence.

Independent Fianna Fáil, formed in 1970 and led by Neil Blaney, who was dismissed as *Fianna Fáil* Agriculture Minister in 1970 because of his strong anti-partition views. Blaney remained a TD, and was elected to the European Parliament, but the party (which exists almost exclusively in his Donegal constituency) has had no other TDs since 1977.

Irish Republican Socialist Party (IRSP–*Pairtí Poblachtach Sóisialach na hÉirean*), formed in December 1974 by left-wing militarist members of Official *Sinn Féin* (now the Workers' Party) and the Official IRA, and led initially by Seamus Costello (who was assassinated by the Official IRA in 1977). The IRSP functioned as the political wing of the Irish National Liberation Army (INLA). It never gained *Dáil* representation in its own right, although two members imprisoned in the North were elected as candidates of the ephemeral H-Block–Armagh Committee in 1981 (in the context of the hunger strikes and other protests by paramilitary prisoners). The IRSP has virtually ceased to exist following feuding in 1986–87 between INLA factions after the decision of one faction to disband both the INLA and the party.

Republican Sinn Féin, an ultra-nationalist faction which broke away from Provisional *Sinn Féin* in 1986 in protest at that party's decision to take up any seats it won in future *Díl* elections. Presenting itself as the legitimate successor to the original (abstentionist) *Sinn Féin*, this small organization is led by "old guard" Provisionals of the early 1970s.

World Socialist Party of Ireland, based in Belfast (Northern Ireland) but also active in the South; part of the world Socialist Movement.

Israel

Capital: Jerusalem (not recognized by UN)   **Population:** 5,400,000 (1995E)

The State of Israel declared its independence in 1948, following the end of the British mandate to administer what was then Palestine. The existence of numerous parties within a proportional representation system (currently giving parliamentary seats to parties securing at least 1.5% of the national vote) has meant that no one party has ever secured an overall parliamentary majority. In consequence, the country has been governed by a succession of coalitions. The President (in a largely ceremonial role) is the constitutional head of state and is elected for a five-year renewable term by the unicameral 120-seat parliament (*Knesset*), itself elected for a maximum term of four years. Constitutional changes enacted in 1992 provided for the direct election of the Prime Minister with effect from the 1996 general elections, in which voters therefore had two ballots, one for the prime ministerial contest and the other for the party election.

In elections on May 29, 1996, Binyamin Netanyahu (*Likud*) won the prime ministerial contest with 50.4% of the vote against 49.5% for Shimon Peres of the Israel Labour Party (ILP). Simultaneous elections to the 14th *Knesset* resulted in the ILP winning 34 seats (with 26.8% of the vote), *Likud* 32 (25.1%), the Sephardic Torah Guardians (*Shas*) 10 (8.5%), the National Religious Party 9 (7.8%), *Meretz* 9 (7.4%), the Movement for Israel and Immigration 7 (5.7%), the Democratic Front for Peace and Equality (*Hadash*) 5 (4.2%), United Torah Judaism 4 (3.2%), Third Way 4 (3.1%), the United Arab List 4 (2.9%) and *Moledet* 2 (2.3%).

Note. For political movements in the Gaza Strip and West Bank, see separate chapter headed "Palestinian Entity".

Democratic Front for Peace and Equality (Hadash)

Address. PO Box 26205, 3 Rehov Hashikma, Tel Aviv

Telephone. (#972–3) 827492

Leadership. Hashem Mahameed (leader), Meir Vilner (secretary-general)

The largely Arab-supported *Hadash* party was established in its present form prior to the 1987 elections, its main component being the pro-Soviet New Communist Party (*Rakah*). It won three seats in the 1992 elections, increasing to five in 1996.

Gesher

Address. c/o Knesset, Jerusalem

Leadership. David Levi (leader)

Meaning "bridge", the Gesher party was launched in February 1996 by Levi, a former Deputy Prime Minister and Foreign Minister. Hitherto a prominent member of the right-wing *Likud*, he had broken with the party after being defeated by Binyamin Netanyahu in a leadership contest in March 1993. Based in the Sephardic Jewish population (which provides the bulk of

Likud's electoral support), *Gesher* proclaimed its aim to "build a social bridge between the different classes in society and a political bridge between left and right". The new party opted to contest the May 1996 *Knesset* elections in alliance with *Likud* and *Tzomet*, and Levi was eventually persuaded not to stand as a prime ministerial candidate. He was rewarded by being appointed Deputy Prime Minister and Foreign Minister in the resultant government formed by Netanyahu.

Israel Labour Party (ILP)

Mifleget Avoda Hayisraelit

Address. PO Box 3263, Tel Aviv 69302

Telephone. (#972–3) 527-2315

Fax. (#972–3) 527-1744

Leadership. Shimon Peres (chair), Nissim Zvili (general secretary)

Affiliated to the Socialist International, the ILP is a Zionist and democratic socialist party, which supports territorial compromise as a means of achieving peace with Israel's Arab neighbours. It was formally established in 1968 through a merger of the traditional *Mapai* Labour Party (the leading party of coalition governments since 1948) and two other factions (*Rafi* and *Achdut Ha'avoda*). Its unbroken hold on power ended with the electoral defeat of 1977. The party remained in opposition to *Likud*-led coalitions until the 1984 elections, which resulted in neither of the opposing political blocs being able to command a parliamentary majority. The ILP thereupon became a partner in a 'rotating premiership' national unity coalition with *Likud*, this decision prompting the United Workers' Party (*Mapam*) to withdraw from its longstanding electoral alignment with Labour.

Following the 1988 elections the ILP formed another national unity coalition with Likud, but this collapsed in 1990. In February 1992 the former Labour Prime Minister, Yitzhak Rabin, regained the party leadership from Shimon Peres. In *Knesset* elections in June the ILP emerged as the largest party with 44 seats, so that Rabin became Prime Minister. He led the subsequent ILP-dominated government which negotiated the historic peace agreement between Israel and the Palestine Liberation Organization in September 1993, until his assassination by a right-wing Jewish fanatic in November 1995. He was succeeded as party chair and Prime Minister by Peres, who vowed to continue the Middle East peace process. In April 1996 an ILP convention adopted a new programme which withdrew the party's opposition to the creation of a Palestinian state. In elections the following month, however, Peres narrowly lost the prime ministerial contest to the *Likud* leader, while in the *Knesset* balloting the ILP slumped to 34 seats and went into opposition.

Likud

Address. 38 Rehov King George, Tel Aviv 61231
Telephone. (#972–3) 563-0666
Fax. (#972–3) 528-2901
Leadership. Binyamin Netanyahu (leader)

Its title meaning "consolidation" or "unity", Likud is identified with the claim to indivisible sovereignty over the whole of the biblical Land of Israel (including the West Bank and Gaza). Economically, its constituent groups favour a liberal and free enterprise philosophy. The bloc was originally formed in 1973, under the leadership of Menachem Begin, as a parliamentary alliance between *Herut* (Freedom), the Liberal Party of Israel, the *Laam* (For the Nation) grouping (which formally merged with *Herut* in 1985), and Hillel Seidel's one-man *Ahdut* faction. On coming to power in 1977, *Likud* was joined by Ariel Sharon's *Shlomzion* group, while two further groups were absorbed prior to the 1988 elections.

The *Likud*-dominated governments of 1977–84, first under Begin and then under Yitzhak Shamir, spanned the period of the historic peace agreement with Egypt (and the return of Sinai captured by Israel in 1967) and the controversial Israeli invasion of Lebanon in 1982. Having reached an all-time high of 48 seats in 1981, *Likud* fell back to 41 seats in the 1984 elections and was obliged to enter into a 'rotating premiership' arrangement with the Israel Labour Party. This national unity coalition was continued after a further *Likud* decline in the 1988 poll (to 39 seats), until finally breaking down in 1990. The immobility of the subsequent Shamir government, which was critically dependent on a number of small right-wing parties, was regarded as an important factor in Likud's electoral defeat in the June 1992 elections, when its representation fell to 32 seats.

In March 1993 the relatively youthful and telegenic Binyamin Netanyahu was elected leader of *Likud* in succession to Shamir. His acrimonious relationship with his leadership rival, David Levi, led to a split in early 1996, when Levi announced the formation of the Gesher party, although the latter quickly opted for an electoral alliance with *Likud*, as did the *Tzomet* grouping. Backed by all of the secular and religious right, Netanyahu narrowly defeated Peres in the May 1996 direct elections for the premiership, although in the simultaneous *Knesset* contest *Likud* and its allies remained at 32 seats. Netanyahu was therefore obliged to form a coalition which included not only *Gesher* and *Tzomet* ministers but also representatives of the Sephardic Torah Guardians (*Shas*), the National Religious Party, the Movement for Israel and Immigration and Third Way.

Meretz

Address. c/o Knesset, Jerusalem
Leadership. Yosi Sarid (leader)

Meretz (meaning "vitality" or "power") was formed in early 1992 as an alliance of three parties of the left: the Civil Rights and Peace Movement (*Ratz*) led by Shulamit Aloni (a former member of the Israel Labour Party); the United Workers' Party (*Mapam*), which had formerly been in an alignment with the Israel Labour Party (ILP) until 1984; and Change (*Shinui*) led by Amnon Rubinstein. The alliance stands for civil rights, equal status for women, electoral reform and religious pluralism. It also advocates a phased peace settlement with the Palestinians and Israel's Arab neighbours by way of interim agreements and guarantees for security and demilitarization. In the 1992 *Knesset* elections *Meretz* secured 12 seats and thereafter served as a coalition partner in ILP-led governments. In February 1996 Aloni was succeeded as *Meretz* leader by Yosi Sarid, then Environment Minister. The formation's representation slipped to nine seats in the May elections, after which it went into opposition.

Moledet

Address. 14 Rehov Yehuda Halevi, Tel Aviv
Telephone. (#972-3) 654580
Leadership. Gen. Rechavam Ze'evi (leader)

An ultra-Zionist secular party, *Moledet* (or "Homeland") was formed in 1988. It has called for the annexation of the occupied territories and the expulsion of their Arab inhabitants. *Moledet*'s withdrawal from the *Likud*-led coalition in early 1992, along with the right-wing *Tehiya* faction (with which it subsequently merged in 1994), fatally undermined the government's working majority. In the consequent elections in June 1992, *Moledet* increased its *Knesset* representation from two to three seats, although in November 1995 one of the three broke away to form Yamin Yisrael. In the May 1996 elections *Moledet* retained two seats and undertook to give external support to the new *Likud*-led coalition.

Movement for Immigration and Israel

Yisrael Ba-aliya
Address. c/o Knesset, Jerusalem
Leadership. Natan Sharansky (leader), Yuli Edelstein (deputy leader)

Originally founded in 1992 as an immigrants' rights movement, based in the 500,000-strong Russian Jewish immigrant community, *Yisrael Ba-aliya* achieved a high profile through the media skills and charismatic leadership of Natan Sharansky, the well-known former Russian Jewish dissident and political prisoner (then called Anatoly Shcharansky) who had been allowed to emigrate to Israel under a Soviet-Western exchange of 1986. Having previously supported *Likud*, Sharansky launched *Yisrael Ba-aliya* as a political party in June 1995, on a platform advocating higher government priority for the absorption of immigrants and limited Palestinian autonomy. It won an impressive seven seats in the May 1996 *Knesset* elections and was awarded two portfolios in the subsequent *Likud*-led coalition government, with Sharansky becoming Industry and Trade Minister and Yuli Edelstein Absorption Minister.

National Religious Party (NRP)

Hamiflaga Hadatit Leumit
Address. 166 Ibn Gavirol Street, Kastel Building, Tel Aviv
Telephone. (#972-3) 544-2151
Fax. (#972-3) 546-8942
Leadership. Zevulun Hammer (leader)

The NRP was founded in 1956 and stands for strict adherence to Jewish religion and tradition, although in a more accomodating way than the ultra-orthodox parties. Having participated in governments headed by the Israel Labour Party up to 1977, the party was represented in *Likud*-led coalitions from 1986 (when its leader became Religious Affairs Minister) and gained a second portfolio in June 1990. The NRP went into opposition following the June 1992 elections, in which it secured six *Knesset* seats, but returned to government (with two portfolios) after increasing its representation to nine seats in May 1996.

Sephardic Torah Guardians (Shas)

Shomrei Torah Sephardim
Address. Beit Abodi, Rehov Hahida, Bene Baraq
Telephone. (#972-3) 579776
Leadership. Aryeh Deri (leader), Rabbi Eliezer Shach (spiritual leader)

Shas is an ultra-orthodox religious party, formed in 1984 as a splinter group from *Agudat Yisrael* (which later became part of the United Torah Judaism). *Shas* retained its six seats in the 1992 legislative elections and, although previously allied with the right-wing bloc in the *Knesset*, joined the coalition formed by the Israel Labour Party and *Meretz* in July of that year. However, it withdrew from the government in September 1993 and announced its formal return to opposition status in February 1995. *Shas* increased its representation to 10 seats in the May 1996 elections, subsequently being allocated two portfolios in the new government headed by *Likud*.

Third Way

Derech Hashlishi
Address. c/o Knesset, Jerusalem
Leadership. Avigdor Kahalani (leader)

The Third Way party was launched prior to the May 1996 elections by a faction of the Israel Labour Party opposed to the then Peres government's readiness make territorial concessions in order to secure a peace agreement with Syria. Strongly opposed to any Israeli withdrawal from the Golan Heights (but very adjacent to Labour on economic and social issues), the new party won a creditable four seats in its first electoral outing and was included in the subsequent coalition government headed by *Likud*, its leader becoming Public Security Minister.

Tzomet

Address. 22 Rehov Huberman, Tel Aviv
Telephone. (#972-3) 204444
Leadership. Rafael Eitan (leader)

Tzomet (meaning "crossroads") is a right-wing, nationalist group formed prior to the 1988 elections by the defection of its leader from the *Tehiya* party (which itself later merged with *Moledet*). In 1992 the party won eight *Knesset* seats, but split in 1994 when two parliamentary members defected to form a separate faction which took the name

Yi'ud. Tzomet contested the May 1996 elections in alliance with *Likud*, its leader being appointed Agriculure Minister in the resultant Netanyahu government.

United Torah Judaism

Address. c/o Knesset, Jerusalem
Leadership. Meir Porush, Rabbi Avraham Ravitz (leaders)

The United Torah Judaism was formed prior to the 1992 elections as a coalition of the ultra-orthodox *Agudat Yisrael* and the *Degel Hatora* (the latter having been formed in 1988 by dissidents of the former), together with two smaller formations (*Poale Agudat Yisrael* and *Moria*). The coalition won four seats in the 1992 polling, retaining them in 1996.

United Workers' Party (Mapam)

Mifleget Hapoalim Hameuchedet
Address. PO Box 1777, Tel Aviv 61016
Telephone. (#972-3) 697-2111
Fax. (#972-3) 691-0504
Leadership. Chanan Eeres (chair), Victor Blit (secretary-general)

The left-wing *Mapam* was founded in 1948 by socialist Zionist groups based in the kibbutz movement, the trade unions and the intelligentsia; it was also the only Zionist party to include Arabs in its membership. In 1969 *Mapam* became aligned with the Israel Labour Party (ILP), contesting elections jointly with the ILP while maintaining an autonomous organization and its own programme. However, when Labour opted to join a national unity coalition with Likud in 1984, *Mapam* withdrew from the alignment to operate as an independent party. Prior to the 1992 election, *Mapam* joined with two other left-orientated and pro-peace parties to form the *Meretz* alliance, which subsequently joined a Labour-led coalition government but went into opposition after the May 1996 elections.

Like the ILP, *Mapam* is a full member party of the Socialist International.

Other Parties and Movements

Arab Democratic Party (ADP), led by Abd al-Wahab Darawshah, founded in 1988, committed to international recognition of the Palestinian people's right to self-determination and civil equality between Arab and Jewish citizens of Israel; won two *Knesset* seats in the June 1992 elections.

Gush Emunim ("Bloc of the Faithful"), engaged in the unauthorized establishment of Jewish settlements in the occupied territories.

Kahane Lives (*Kahane Chai*), a right-wing religious nationalist party named after Rabbi Meir Kahane, the Jewish-American leader of the extremist *Kach* movement who was assassinated in New York in 1990; led by Rabbi Binyamin Zeev Kahane (son of the late leader), Kahane Lives advocates the expulsion of all Arabs from Israel and the occupied territories; it was banned in 1994.

New Liberal Party (NLP), formed in 1987 as an alliance of the Independent Liberal Party, a centrist faction of *Likud* and other elements; led by Yitzhak Berman and Nissim Eliad, the NLP failed to win *Knesset* representation in 1992 and 1996.

Progressive List for Peace (PLP), a Jewish-Arab movement dating from the early 1980s and led by Muhammad Miari; advocating the establishment of a Palestinian Arab state coexisting with Israel, it lost its small *Knesset* representation in 1992.

United Arab List, led by Abdul Maduh Dahamshe, seeks a Palestinian state with east Jerusalem as its capital, won four seats in the 1996 *Knesset* elections.

Yamin Yisrael (usually rendered as "Israel's Right"), led by Shaul Gutman, a right-wing party formed in November 1995 by one of the three *Knesset* deputies of the *Moledet* party; opposed to the then Labour-led government's peace process with the Palestinians, and more particularly to withdrawal from the West Bank.

Yi'ud, launched in June 1994 by two dissident deputies (Gonen Segev and Alex Goldfarb) of the ultra-nationalist *Tzomet*; in December 1994 it entered the then coalition government led by the Israel Labour Party.

Italy

Capital: Rome

Population: 58,000,000 (1995E)

Under its 1948 constitution, Italy is "a democratic republic founded on work", with a system of parliamentary democracy. The head of state is the President, who is elected for a seven-year term by an electoral college of the two houses of parliament (plus delegates named by the regional assemblies) and who appoints the Prime Minister and, on the latter's recommendation, other ministers. The President has the important power of being able to dissolve parliament at any time except in the last six months of its full term. Legislative authority and government accountability are vested in a legislature of two houses with equal powers, namely (i) the upper 315–member Senate of the Republic (*Senato della Repubblica*), whose members are directly elected for a five-year term on a regional basis, except that life senators (numbering nine in mid-1996) may be appointed by the President; and (ii) the lower 630–member Chamber of Representatives (*Camera dei Deputati*), which is also directly elected for a five-year term subject to dissolution. Under electoral system modifications approved by referendum in April 1993, proportional representation by share of vote gave way to a predominantly "first-past-the-post" system for both houses. In the case of the Chamber, 475 of its 630 members are elected by plurality voting in constituencies and the other 155 by a system of proportional representation, subject to a requirement that at least 4% of the national vote must be won to obtain seats.

Italian parties have been eligible for state financial subventions for two decades, a referendum on the issue in 1976 having produced a 56.4% majority in favour of parties being subsidized from public funds. There are two state funds on which parties can draw, one relating to campaign expenses in an election year and the other for defraying ongoing organizational costs. From the first fund some Lit30,000 million (about US$19 million) is distributed to parties that win at least one parliamentary seat. From the second a total of some Lit90,000 million (about $57 million) is distributed annually, of which three-quarters is allocated to parties in proportion to their seat totals, just under a quarter equally to parties that presented candidates in at least two-thirds of constituencies in the most recent election, and 2% equally to all represented parties.

The established post-war party structure came under increasing challenge in the 1980s, before effectively disintegrating in the early 1990s amid a torrent of scandals concerning illegal party financing and other graft. The party establishments reacted by creating new party names and alliances, thus giving a new facade to Italian party politics while maintaining underlying orientations. Elections to the Chamber of Representatives on April 21, 1996, resulted as follows: Olive Tree 284 seats (with 34.8% of the vote), Freedom Alliance 246 (44%), Northern League-Federal Italy 59, (10.1%), Communist Refoundation Party 35 (8.6%), others 6 (2.5%). At the time of the elections the main components of the centre-left Olive Tree (*Ulivo*) alliance were the Democratic Party of the Left, the Democratic Union, the Green Federation, the Italian Popular Party, Italian Renewal, the Italian Socialists, the Movement for Democracy and the South Tyrol People's Party.

Christian Democratic Centre
Centro Cristiana Democratica (CCD)
   Address. c/o Camera dei Deputati, Rome
   Leadership. Clemente Mastella (president)
   The CCD was established by a right-wing group of the former ruling Christian Democratic Party

when the majority wing of the latter opted to become the Italian Popular Party in January 1994. As a member of the victorious Freedom Alliance (PL) coalition in the March 1994 election, the CCD was allocated one portfolio in the short-lived Berlusconi government. Remaining part of the

PL, it contested the April 1996 parliamentary elections in close alliance with the United Christian Democrats, their joint list taking a 5.8% vote share.

Communist Refoundation Party

Partito della Rifondazione Comunista (PRC)
 Address. 131 viale Policlinico, 00163 Rome
 Telephone. (#39–6) 441821
 Fax. (#39–6) 4423–9490
 Leadership. Fausto Bertinotti (secretary-general), Armando Cossuta (president)

The PRC came into being at a session held in Rome in February 1991 of dissident members of the Italian Communist Party (PCI) opposed to the latter's majority preference for conversion into the democratic socialist Democratic Party of the Left (PDS). After legal proceedings, the PRC was awarded the right to use the traditional hammer and sickle symbol of the PCI and was formally launched at a Rome conference in May 1991. Having won 5.6% of the vote in the 1992 general elections, the PRC advanced to 6.0% in 1994, when it was part of the left-wing Progressive Alliance (AP) headed by the PDS. Subsequently distancing itself from the PA, the PRC increased its support marginally to 6.1% in the June 1994 European Parliament elections, winning five seats, while the April-May 1995 regional elections yielded an 8.4% vote share.

In June 1995 the PRC was weakened by the defection of 14 of its 35 lower house deputies in protest at the alleged "isolationism" of the party leadership. Undeterred, the rump PRC contested the April 1996 parliamentary elections independently and increased its vote share to 8.6%, which restored its Chamber representation to 35 seats. Although it had, by mutual agreement, remained outside the centre-left Olive Tree coalition, the PRC opted after the elections to give qualified parliamentary backing to the new Olive Tree government.

The PRC's representatives in the European Parliament sit in the Confederal European United Left group.

Democratic Alliance

Alleanza Democratica (AD)
 Address. 35 via Belsiana, 00187 Rome
 Leadership. Willer Bordon (president)

The AD was founded in October 1992 by dissidents of the then Christian Democratic Party (later the Italian Popular Party) aspiring to combat political corruption by providing a broadly-based "honest Italy" alternative to the existing parties. Its first leader was Mario Segni, who spearheaded the campaign for reform of the Italian political system, but who subsequently launched the Segni Pact as a separate formation. In the March 1994 elections the AD consisted of the Italian Republican Party and elements of the Italian Socialist Party (PSI, later the Italian Socialists), winning 1.2% of the national vote as a component of the left-wing Progressive Alliance (AP). In the June 1994 European Parliament elections a joint AD/PSI list won three seats on a 1.8% vote share. For the April 1996 general elections, the AD became part of the Democratic Union component of the victorious centre-left Olive Tree alliance.

Democratic Party of the Left

Partito Democratico della Sinistra (PDS)
 Address. 4 via delle Botteghe Oscure, 00186 Rome
 Telephone. (#39–6) 671–155311
 Fax. (#39–6) 679–8376
 Leadership. Massimo D'Alema (general secretary)

The PDS is directly descended organizationally, but not ideologically, from the Italian Communist Party (*Partito Comunista Italiano*, PCI), delegates to the March 1990 extraordinary congress of which voted to abandon the traditional name of the PCI. Formal adoption of the new title followed in February 1991, at a final congress (*ultimo congresso*) of the PCI.

Formed as a result of the split in the Italian Socialist Party at the 1921 Livorno congress, the PCI went underground during the Mussolini period, its then leader, Palmiro Togliatti, escaping to Moscow, where he worked for the Comintern until his return to Italy in 1944. In the early 1940s the PCI played a leading role in the struggle against the fascist regime and the German Nazi occupation forces.

Under Togliatti's leadership the PCI participated in the post-war coalition government until being excluded in May 1947, after which it mounted a violent campaign of political and industrial opposition. Following the decisive election victory of the Christian Democrats in April 1948 the PCI took the road of democratic opposition and subsequently developed into the largest and most influential non-ruling Communist party in Europe. Throughout the post-war period the PCI was consistently the second strongest party (after the Christian Democrats) in terms of both votes and seats in parliament.

From 1975 the PCI governed a large number of regions, provinces and municipalities, (particularly in the "red belt" of Emilia-Romagna, Umbria and Tuscany), usually in coalition with other left-wing parties. At national level, the PCI's claims for admission to government responsibility were resisted, although following the sharp increase in the party's vote in the June 1976 elections (to over 34%) successive Christian Democrat-led governments accepted parliamentary support from the PCI, initially through abstention and subsequently, from March 1978, on the basis of the PCI being included in the official parliamentary majority. The PCI withdrew from this arrangement in January 1979 and reverted to a position of full opposition; in the elections of that year its vote share fell to 30.4%.

In 1980 the PCI adopted a new strategy of "democratic alternative" based on an alliance with the Socialists, but the latter remained committed to centre-left coalitions. In the 1983 general elections the PCI again lost ground, winning 198 seats and 29.9% of the vote, although in the June 1984 European Parliament elections it emerged as the largest party for the first time in its history, winning 33.3% of the vote.

Under the new leadership of Alessandro Natta (who had succeeded Enrico Berlinguer on the latter's death in June 1984), the PCI was strengthened in November 1984 by absorbing the Party of Proletarian Unity for Communism (originally founded in 1972). However, it lost ground in the May 1985 regional and local elections (surrendering Rome to the Christian Democrats) and suffered a further setback in the June 1987 general elections, when its Chamber representation fell to 177 seats and its share of the vote to 26.6%. A post-election reorganization of the PCI leadership bodies included the appointment of Achille Occhetto as deputy general secretary and thus as potential successor to Natta.

Meanwhile, Natta had paid an official visit to Moscow in January 1986 (the first by a PCI leader since 1978) and had reportedly healed the breach caused by Verlinguer's outspoken criticism of the Soviet role in Afghanistan and Poland. Nevertheless, the 17th PCI congress in April 1986 reaffirmed the party's rejection of the Soviet model and its identity as part of the European democratic left.

In June 1988 Natta was succeeded as PCI leader by Achille Occhetto, who promised a "new course" for Italian communism. This process turned out to be the abandonment of much of the traditional party line and the transformation of the PCI into the PDS in February 1991, with a democratic socialist orientation. Having won 16.1% of the national vote in the 1992 elections, the PDS advanced to 20.4% in the March 1994 contest, although it failed to make the hoped-for breakthrough to political power as a member of the left-wing Progressive Alliance. In the June 1994 European Parliament elections PDS support slipped to 19.1%, which gave the party 16 seats. This setback precipitated the resignation of Occhetto as general secretary and the succession of Massimo D'Alema. In late 1994 and April-May

1995 the PDS made major advances in local and regional elections, on the latter occasion heading the poll with 24.6% of the vote.

In July 1995 the PDS took the momentous decision to enter a structured centre-left alliance, called the Olive Tree, which registered a major victory in the April 1996 parliamentary elections, with the PDS securing 21.1% of the vote in its own right. The PDS was awarded nine posts in the resultant centre-left government.

The PDS is affiliated to the Socialist International; its representatives in the European Parliament sit in the Party of European Socialists group.

Democratic Union
Union Democratica (UD)
Address. c/o Camera dei Deputati, Rome
Leadership. Antonio Maccanico (president)

A former cabinet minister and proponent of institutional reform, Maccanico launched the UD prior to the April 1996 general elections, in which it formed part of the victorious Olive Tree alliance. In January 1996 Maccanico had been designated Prime Minister after the fall of the Dini government, but had failed to obtain sufficient party backing even though he claimed that a parliamentary majority existed for his reform proposals. In the post-election Olive Tree minority government, Maccanico was awarded the post and telecommunications portfolio.

Federation of Italian Liberals
Federazione dei Liberali Italiani (FLI)
Address. via Frattina, 00187 Rome
Telephone. (#39–6) 679–6951
Leadership. Raffaello Morelli

The FLI acts as the umbrella body of liberalism in Italy following the effective demise of the old Italian Liberal Party (*Partito Liberale Italiano*, PLI) amid the corruption scandals of the early 1990s.

Founded in 1848, the PLI had its roots in the 19th-century liberal movement. Founded by Count Camillo di Cavour (the diplomatic architect of Italian unification), it was a strong proponent of Italian unity. In the period following World War II it increased its representation in the Chamber of Deputies from 13 members in 1953 to 39 in 1963; thereafter it declined to five seats in 1976, although it won nine seats in June 1979 and 16 in June 1983. In June 1987 it slipped to 11 seats and 2.1% of the vote.

The PLI participated in several post-war coalition governments, including the Socialist-led Cabinet of 1983–87 and its successor headed by a Christian Democrat. In November 1987 the PLI caused a brief crisis by withdrawing from the government in protest against the 1988 draft budget, but after five days the coalition was reconstituted with identical composition.

In the April 1996 parliamentary elections the Liberal remnants formed part of the new Democratic Union, itself part of the victorious Olive Tree alliance of centre-left parties.

Forza Italia (FI)

Address. 48 via dell'Umiltà, 00187 Rome
Telephone. (#39–6) 67311
Fax. (#39–6) 5994–1315
Leadership. Silvio Berlusconi (president)

The FI was launched in January 1994, its Italian title being variously translated into English as "Go Italy" and "Come On Italy", as being the English equivalent of the traditional chant of supporters of the Italian football team which provided the party's title. The FI was created by Berlusconi, Italy's most powerful media tycoon (and owner of the leading Milan football club), who identified the prevention of an electoral victory by the ex-Communist Democratic Party of the Left (PDS) as the new formation's principal objective. To this end, it organized the Freedom Alliance right-wing front, which secured an absolute parliamentary majority of 366 seats in the March 1994 general elections and accordingly formed a new government.

In the June 1994 European Parliament elections the PL won a narrow majority of 44 of Italy's 87 seats, 27 of which were credited to the FI. However, growing strains between the coalition parties culminated in the collapse of the Berlusconi government in December as a result of the withdrawal of the Northern League. There followed strong FI pressure for fresh general elections, despite disappointing local election results for the party in late 1994 and April-May 1995. Berlusconi had greater success in a multiple referendum exercise in June 1995, when there were majorities for propositions which would maintain the dominance of his media interests. But the FI leader was increasingly tainted by financial corruption allegations in the run-up to the April 1996 general elections. He led the FI to a retained vote share of 21% within a reduced PL alliance, but it was not enough to prevent the centre-left from coming to power.

The party's representatives in the European Parliament form the largest national contingent of the Union for Europe group, the second biggest being the French Rally for the Republic members.

Freedom Alliance

Polo delle Libertà (PL)
Address. c/o Camera dei Deputati, Rome
Leadership. Silvio Berlusconi (*Forza Italia*) and Gianfranco Fini (National Alliance)

The PL was formed in 1994 as effectively the umbrella of two alliances of right-wing parties, namely the main Freedom Alliance, consisting of *Forza Italia* and the Northern League (LN) in the north, and the Good Government Alliance (*Polo del Buon Governo*, PBG), encompassing National Alliance (AN) and the Christian Democratic Centre in the south. Loosely, however, all four, plus the Radical Party, regarded themselves as components of the overarching PL. Having taken power after the March 1994 general elections under the premiership of Silvio Berlusconi, the component PL parties quickly experienced dissension, which resulted in the exit of the LN in December and the resultant collapse of the PL government.

When the LN renamed itself the Northern League–Federal Italy in February 1995, a pro-Berlusconi faction formed the breakaway Italian Federal League. The aggregate PL vote in regional elections in April-May 1995 slipped to 40.7%, from 43% in the 1994 parliamentary elections. The PL structure remained largely in place for the April 1996 general elections, although personal rivalry and public disputation between Berlusconi and AN leader Fini did the alliance little good in the further general elections held in April 1996. Although the PL's overall share of the proportional vote rose to some 44% (about 10% higher than that obtained by the centre-left Olive Tree alliance), the latter's relative majority of seats meant that the PL parties became the principal opposition to the new Prodi government.

Green Federation

Federazione dei Verdi
Address. 1A via Catalana, 00186 Rome
Telephone. (#39–6) 6880–2879
Fax. (#39–6) 6880–3023
Leadership. Carlo Ripa Di Meana (spokesman), Sergio Andreis (secretary)

Officially called the National Federation for the Green List, the Italian branch of the European Green movement was founded as a national electoral movement at a constituent assembly held in Florence in December 1984 (attended by representatives of numerous existing groups), the Italian Greens won some 1.8% of the vote overall in regional and local elections held in May 1985 (when they were supported by the Radical Party, which had declined to present candidates itself). In the July 1987 general elections the Greens made a significant breakthrough, winning 2.5% of the vote and returning 13 members to the Chamber of Deputies and one to the Senate.

They improved further in 1992, winning four Senate and 16 Chamber seats on a vote share of 2.8%. For the 1994 general elections the Greens joined the Progressive Alliance, headed by the

Democratic Party of the Left (PDS), their vote share slipping to 2.7%. In a recovery in the June 1994 European Parliament elections, the Greens won three seats on a 3.2% vote share. Joining the centre-left Olive Tree alliance for the April 1996 parliamentary elections, the Greens won 2.5% of the proportional vote and had the satisfaction of seeing party member Edo Ronchi appointed Environment Minister in the new Olive Tree government.

The Italian Greens in the European Parliament are members of the Green Group.

Italian Democratic Socialist Party

Partito Socialista Democratico Italiano (PSDI)
 Address. c/o Fondazione Turati, 00186 Rome
 Telephone. (#39–6) 474–4198
 Fax.·(#39–6) 474–3406
 Leadership. Gianfranco Schietroma (national secretary)

The party dates from a split in the Italian Socialist Party at the January 1947 Rome congress, when an important section led by Giuseppe Saragat opposed the Pietro Nenni Socialists' popular front policy (involving an alliance with the Communists). Originally formed as the Workers' Socialist Party (PSLI), it merged with other factions in 1952 to become the PSDI.

During 1947–62 the Democratic Socialists took part in coalition governments of the centre (with Christian Democrats, Liberals and Republicans) and in 1963–74 in centre-left governments (with Christian Democrats, Socialists and Republicans). During this period there was an ultimately abortive attempt at reunification between the Democratic Socialists and the Socialists.

In 1974–76 the PSDI supported Christian Democratic governments sustained from outside by centre-left parties and in 1976–79 Christian Democratic governments supported by the Republicans, Communists and Socialists. In August 1979 the PSDI joined a coalition with the Christian Democrats and Liberals. From October 1980 the PSDI took part in all coalition governments which took included the Socialist Party, most recently in the Socialist-led government of Bettino Craxi (1983–87) and in its successor headed by a Christian Democrat.

Having improved slightly in the June 1983 Chamber elections (from 3.8 to 4.1% and from 20 to 23 seats), the PSDI slipped to 3% and 17 seats in June 1987. Prior to the elections a PSDI congress in January 1987 had voted in favour of a radical common platform with the Socialists with the aim of achieving a left-wing government excluding the Christian Democrats.

The PSDI won 17 lower house seats on a 2.7% vote share in the 1992 elections. All were lost in the 1994 contest, although the party succeeded in

retaining three Senate seats on the latter occasion with only 0.2% of the popular vote. In the European Parliament elections of June 1994 it won one seat with 0.7% support. For the April 1996 parliamentary elections it formed part of the victorious centre-left Olive Tree coalition, putting aside its original *raison d'être* by co-operating closely with the ex-Communist Democratic Party of the Left.

The PSDI is an affiliate of the Socialist International, although its representative in the European Parliament is "unattached" rather than a member of the Party of European Socialists group.

Italian Federal League

Lega Federale Italiano (LFI)
 Address. c/o Camera dei Deputati, Rome
 Leadership. Roberto Maroni (president)

The LFI was founded in February 1995 by a dissident group of the Northern League (LN) opposed to the party's withdrawal from the Berlusconi government in December 1994. The faction also rejected the conversion of the LN into the LN–Federal Italy. LFI leader Maroni had been Deputy Prime Minister and Interior Minister in the recent government. His new party was not prominent in the 1996 election campaign.

Italian Popular Party

Partito Popolare Italiano (PPI)
 Address. 46 piazza de Gesù, 00186 Rome
 Telephone. (#39–6) 67751
 Fax. (#39–6) 6775–3951
 Leadership. Giovanni Bianchi (president), Gerardo Bianco (secretary-general)

The PPI is the successor to the post-war Christian Democratic Party (DC), for long Italy's dominant formation, which in January 1994, beset by corruption scandals, reverted to the PPI title of an earlier age. The PPI had been founded by Don Luigi Sturzo before World War I and had functioned as Italy's Catholic party until the rise of fascism in 1922. It was revived as the DC towards the end of World War II, taking part in January 1944 in the first congress of (six) democratic parties for over 20 years (in Bari). It participated in coalition governments from April 1944 and in the formation of the National Consultative Council in 1945. Its post-war leader, Alcide De Gasperi, was Prime Minister from December 1945 until August 1953, overseeing the post-war reconstruction programme with considerable success.

In general elections to a Constituent Assembly in June 1946 the DC emerged as the strongest party with 35.2% of the votes and 207 (out of 556) seats. In elections to the Chamber of Deputies held in

April 1948 it gained 48.7% of the votes and 307 (out of 574) seats, but in June 1953 the DC's strength in the Chamber was reduced to 262 seats (based on 40.1% of the votes). From August 1953 onwards the DC continued in office either as the sole government party or in coalition, at first with Liberals and Democratic Socialists, and later also with Republicans. In the 1958 elections it obtained 42.2% of the votes and 273 seats in the Chamber. In elections held after 1963 the DC maintained its position as the strongest party until the 1990s.

At a congress in Naples early in 1962 the DC had approved a policy of "opening to the left" (*apertura a sinistra*) involving the formation of administrations relying on Socialist support. The DC formed coalition governments including Socialists from July 1964 to June 1968 and from December 1968 to July 1969; it accepted other coalition partners between March 1970 and February 1971 and from June 1972 to July 1973. Thereafter it again included Socialists in its government from July 1973 to November 1974, when it formed a coalition with Republicans only. From July 1976 onwards it was in power as a minority government.

However, in March 1977 the DC concluded an agreement with five other parties, including the Communist Party (PCI), which undertook to give external support to the DC government. In March 1978 the DC entered into a limited policy agreement with the PCI, but the latter withdrew from both agreements in January 1979, whereupon the DC formed a coalition government with the Democratic Socialists and Republicans. This administration fell at the end of March 1979 after losing a confidence vote, whereupon premature elections in June 1979 resulted in the DC retaining its position as the largest parliamentary party (although its percentage declined slightly). In August 1979 the DC formed a coalition with the Democratic Socialists and Liberals under the premiership of Francesco Cossiga.

There followed further DC-led coalition governments until June 1981, when the DC joined a coalition headed by Giovanni Spadolini of the Italian Republican Party, the first non-Christian Democrat to head a post-war Italian administration. In December 1982 the DC resumed the leadership of a coalition government, but after the June 1983 general elections in which the DC's representation in the Chamber of Deputies was reduced from 262 to 225 members, it agreed to join the first coalition government to be led by a Socialist (Bettino Craxi).

After lasting for an unprecedented four years, the Craxi government ended in March 1987 amid recriminations from the DC that the PSI leader was reluctant to honour a pact of August 1986 specifying that a DC Prime Minister should take over early in 1987. An "institutional" DC government followed until early general elections in June 1987, when the DC increased its representation in the Chamber to 234 seats. The party accordingly resumed the government leadership, forming a five-party coalition with the Socialist, Republican, Democratic Socialist and Liberals parties, with Giovanni Goria as Prime Minister followed by Ciriaco De Mita from March 1988.

De Mita resigned in May 1989 and was succeeded as DC Prime Minister by the indispensable Andreotti, who formed another five-party centre-left coalition government. In July 1990 the coalition was rocked by the resignations of five ministers from the De Mita DC faction, but Andreotti survived until the Socialists withdrew from the government in March 1991. But he bounced back yet again to form his seventh centre-left cabinet headed by the DC, this one including three other parties. The DC then became a leading victim of the political corruption cases which resulted in a melt-down of the Italian party system, the most prominent DC casualty being Andreotti himself, who was accused of maintaining links with the Mafia (and later brought to trial on such charges). It slumped to a post-war low of 29.7% and 206 seats in the April 1992 parliamentary elections, being obliged therefore to cede the premiership to a Socialist, although it remained a government party.

The DC's plummeting fortunes were revealed in local elections in June 1993, when only one of 47 DC candidates prevailed in mayoral contests. Having reverted to the historical PPI name in January 1994, the party contested the March 1994 general elections as part of a centrist alliance called the Pact for Italy (*Patto per l'Italia*, PI), which had been launched in January by Mario Segni, leader of the Segni Pact. As the leading component of the PI, the PPI won only 11.1% of the vote in the March 1994 general election, slipping further to 10% in the June elections to the European Parliament, in which the party took only eight of Italy's 87 seats.

In opposition, the PPI experienced deep divisions over whether to form an alliance with Silvio Berlusconi's then ruling Freedom Alliance. The controversy resulted in an open split in March 1995, when the anti-Berlusconi "Democratic" wing elected Gerardo Bianco as PPI leader in the absence of the previously dominant right-wing faction, which disputed the election's legitimacy. In local elections in April-May 1995 the two factions competed separately, the "Democrats" winning 6% and the pro-Berlusconi faction 3%. In July 1995 the pro-Berlusconi faction finally broke away, forming the United Christian Democrats, while the remaining PPI became the second largest component of the victorious centre-left Olive Tree alliance in the April 1996 general elections, its list of candidates featuring Olive Tree leader Romano Prodi. The PPI accordingly obtained substantial representation in the resultant Prodi government.

The PPI is a member of the Christian Democrat International and the International Democrat Union. Its representatives in the European Parliament sit in the European People's Party group.

Italian Republican Party

Partito Repubblicano Italiano (PRI)
    Address. 70 piazza dei Caprettari, 00186 Rome
    Telephone. (#39–6) 683–4037
    Leadership. Bruno Visentini (president), Giorgio La Malfa (secretary)

Founded as such in 1894, the PRI has its origins in the *Fiovine Italia* of 1831, who was republicans fought, under the leadership of Giuseppe Mazzini, for national unity and independence. The PRI was dissolved by the Facist regime and reconstituted in 1943, taking part in the Resistance. Under the republican constitution introduced in January 1948 the PRI was a partner in numerous coalition governments led by Christian Democrats from 1948 to 1981.

In June 1981 the then PRI leader, Giovanni Spadolini, became the first non-Christian Democrat to head an Italian government since the war, forming a five-party centre-left Cabinet which lasted until November 1982. In the June 1983 Chamber elections the PRI's vote increased to 5.1% and its representation to 29 seats, however, in those of June 1987 it fell back to 3.7% and 21 seats. Meanwhile, the PRI had participated in the Socialist-led centre-left coalition of 1983–87, while after the 1987 elections it joined a similar coalition headed by the Christian Democrats.

Thereafter the PRI continued its participation in centre-left coalitions until going into opposition in April 1991. Then a PRI member, Antonio Maccanico accepted the post of Cabinet Secretary in the Ciampi government formed in May 1993, although the party itself remained in opposition. Having won 4.4% of the national vote in 1992, the PRI contested the March 1994 poll as a member of the Democratic Alliance (AD), and thus also of the broader Progressive Alliance (AP). In the June 1994 European balloting a specifically PRI list secured 0.7% of the vote, its one seat going to Giorgio La Malfa. Having resigned the party leadership in 1988 and been reinstated in January 1994, La Malfa again resigned in October 1994 and was again reinstated in March 1995. The PRI contested the April 1996 general elections as part of Maccanico's new Democratic Union, although in the Italian way participation in a broader grouping did not mean that the PRI ceased to exist.

The single PRI representative in the European Parliament sits in the Europeam Liberal, Democratic and Reformist Group.

Italian Renewal

Rinnovamento Italiano (RI)
    Address. c/o Camera dei Deputati, Rome
    Leadership. Lamberto Dini (president)

Dini announced the formation of the RI in February 1996, a month after the fall of his year-old government of technocrats. It formed part of the victorious Olive Tree alliance in the April 1996 elections, obtaining three cabinet posts in the new Prodi government, with Dini becoming Foreign Minister.

Italian Social Movement

Movimiento Sociale Italiano (MSI)
    Address. c/o Camera dei Deputati, Rome
    Leadership. Pino Rauti (president)

The MSI name was retained in January 1995 by the minority pro-fascism faction of the former Italian Social Movement-National Right (MSI-DN), as the latter formally converted itself into the National Alliance.

Italian Socialists

Socialisti Italiani (SI)
    Address. 26 piazza San Lorenzo in Lucina, 00186 Rome
    Telephone. (#39–6) 6830–7666
    Fax. (#39–6) 6830–7659
    Leadership. Enrico Bosselli (general secretary), Ottaviano Del Turco (president)

The SI designation was adopted by the Italian Socialist Party (PSI) in 1994. Founded in 1892, the PSI suffered three major splits. In 1921 a group broke away to found the Italian Communist Party; in 1947 the Saragat Democratic Socialists opposed to an alliance with the Communists broke away from the Pietro Nenni wing and eventually formed the Italian Democratic Socialist Party (PSDI); and a merger in 1966 of the PSI and the PSDI was followed in 1969 by the latter breaking away again.

The PSI was strongly represented in the Chamber of Deputies from 1953, with the number of seats held by it rising to 87 in 1963 (while in 1968 the combined PSI and PSDI, known as the *Partito Socialista Unificato*, gained 91 seats in the Chamber). After the 1963 "opening to the left", the PSI. After repeatedly co-operated with the Christian Democrats either by joining in coalition governments or by giving external support.

After it had for many years been a member of coalition governments led mainly by the Christian Democrats, the PSI resigned from the Fanfani government in April 1983. In the ensuing general elections of June 1983 it increased its representation in the Chamber of Deputies from 62 to 73 members, and in June 1983 the PSI leader, Bettino Craxi, formed Italy's first Socialist-led government, based on a coalition of Christian Democrats, Democratic Socialists, Republicans and Liberals.

The Craxi administration lasted for nearly four years (unprecedented for a post-war Italian government), eventually resigning in March 1987 amid a dispute with the Christian Democrats over the application of a rotation pact of August 1986 under which a Christian Democrat was to take over the premiership early in 1987. In the June 1987 elections the PSI further increased its strength, to 94 seats and 14.3% of the vote. It subsequently entered a further five-party centre-left coalition headed by the Christian Democrats.

In the April 1992 parliamentary elections the PSI slipped to 13.6% of the popular vote, but remained in the government coalition. Craxi then came under judicial investigation on numerous charges of financial corruption and illegal party funding, with the consequence that he resigned as party leader in February 1993, having served 17 years in the post. In the wake of charges against many other PSI representatives, the party slumped to 2.2% in the March 1994 general elections, which some PSI elements contested under the banner of the Democratic Alliance, doing the same in the European Parliament elections in June. The following month 1994 Craxi received a long prison sentence, and still faced other charges, along with several dozen other former PSI officials.

Seeking to recover its former constituency, the PSI transformed itself into the SI in November 1994, believing that dropping the discredited descriptor "party" from its title would improve its public image. In the April 1996 parliamentary elections the SI was a component of the victorious Olive Tree alliance, in close alliance with the new Italian Renewal formation.

The SI is a member party of the Socialist International, its representatives in the European Parliament sitting in the Party of European Socialists group.

Movement for Democracy
Movimento per la Democrazia (MpD)
Address. 3 Lungotevere Marzio, 00186 Rome
Telephone. (#39–6) 6830–0447
Fax. (#39–6) 6830–0446
Leadership. Leoluca Orlando

This anti-Mafia movement was founded as *La Rete* (The Network) at Palermo, Sicily, in 1991 and became the city's leading party in the 1992 general elections, winning three Senate and 12 Chamber seats. As a member of the left-wing Popular Alliance in the March 1994 elections it won 1.9% of the national vote. In the June European Parliament poll it obtained one seat on a 1.1% vote share.

By now preferring the MpD label, the party contested the April 1996 general elections as part of the victorious Olive Tree alliance.

The party's representative in the European Parliament sits in the Green Group.

National Alliance
Alleanza Nazionale (AN)
Address. 39 via della Scrofa, 00186 Rome
Telephone. (#39–6) 6880–3014
Fax. (#39–6) 654–8256
Leadership. Gianfranco Fini (secretary-general), Maurizio Gaspari (co-ordinator)

The radical right-wing AN is the direct descendant of the post-war Italian Social Movement (MSI), which was founded in 1946 as a successor to the outlawed Fascist Party of the late dictator Benito Mussolini. The MSI first contested parliamentary elections in 1948, winning six seats in the Chamber of Deputies. Between 1953 and 1972 its representation in the Chamber fluctuated between 29 and 24 members. It contested the 1972 general elections in an alliance (*Destra Nazionale*, DN) with the Italian Democratic Party of Monarchical Unity, and this alliance gained 56 seats in the Chamber. The two parties formally merged as the MSI-DN in January 1973, but in the 1976 elections the new party obtained only 35 seats in the Chamber.

The MSI-DN did not rule out the use of violence in its activities, and its extremist members were involved in numerous clashes and other acts of violence, which were not approved by the party as a whole. In December 1976 a total of 26 MSI-DN parliamentarians (17 deputies and nine senators) broke away from the party to form a group known as *Democrazia Nazionale* (DN), which was led by Ernesto De Marzio, it repudiated all fascist tendencies and announced that it would support the Christian Democrats. However, in the 1979 elections this group won no seats, while the rump MSI-DN retained 30 seats in the Chamber of Deputies.

In the 1983 elections the party made significant gains both at national and at regional and provincial level, gaining 42 seats in the Chamber of Deputies (with 6.8% of the vote). In the June 1987 elections, however, it slipped back to 35 seats (5.9% of the vote).

The party's veteran leader, Giorgio Almirante (who had been a member of Mussolini's government), retired in December 1987 and was succeeded by Gianfranco Fini, regarded as a representative of the young "new face" of the party. Meanwhile, the party had decided in October 1987 to mount an active campaign in South Tirol/Bolzano in support of the Italian speaking minority and against the political aspirations of the German-speaking majority.

In the 1992 parliamentary elections the MSI-DN slipped to 34 Chamber seats and 5.4% of the vote, one of the party's successful candidates in Naples being Alessandra Mussolini, grand-daughter of the former dictator. It then sought to capitalize on the massive corruption scandals that engulfed the centre-left parties so long in government. The AN designation was used by the MSI-DN from January 1994 as part of a strategy to attract support from former Christian Democrats and other right-wing groups, including Italian monarchists, and the party joined the Freedom Alliance (PL) of conservative parties headed by Silvio Berlusconi's new *Forza Italia* party, becoming the leading force in the PL's southern arm, designated the Good Government Alliance (*Polo del Buon Governo*). In the March 1994 elections the AN advanced strongly to 13.5% of the proportional vote as part of the PL, its support being concentrated in southern Italy. Six AN ministers were included in the Berlusconi government appointed in May 1994. In the following month's European Parliament elections the AN won 12.5% of the vote and 11 seats. The party's first post-war experience of national office ended with the collapse of the Berlusconi government in December 1994.

The AN title was officially adopted by the party in January 1995 at a Rome congress which also decided to delete most references to fascism in basic AN policy documents. Thereafter party spokesmen became even more insistent in rejecting the "neo-fascist" label commonly appended by the media and others, especially since a hardline minority which saw no discredit in the term "fascist" had in effect broken away by opting to maintain the Italian Social Movement in being. The regional elections of April-May 1995 showed a modest increase in the AN vote to 14.1%, which rose appreciably to 15.7% in the April 1996 general elections, for which the AN remained within the PL alliance. In the latter contest Fini added to his reputation as a keen debater and effective campaigner, rather overshadowing Berlusconi.

The AN's representatives in the European Parliament are "unattached" to any of the formal political groups.

Northern League–Federal Italy

La Lega Nord–Italia Federale (LN-IF)
 Address. 63 via Arbe, 20125 Milan
 Telephone. (#39–2) 607–0379
 Fax. (#39–2) 6680–2766
 Leadership. Umberto Bossi (secretary-general), Franco Roccetta (president)

The LN-IF is the renamed Northern League (LN), itself created in February 1991 as a federation of the Lombardy League (*Lega Lombarda*, LL) and fraternal parties in Emilio Romagna, Liguria, Piedmont, Tuscany and Venice. The LL had been launched in 1979, named after a 12th-century federation of northern Italian cities. It had achieved prominence in the 1980s as the most conspicuous of several regional groups to challenge the authority of the government in Rome, in particular its use of public revenues to aid the impoverished south. Adopting the same stance, the LN called at its foundation for a move to a federal system with substantial regional autonomy in most areas except defence and foreign policy. Party leaders subsequently denied that the LN's attitude to southern Italians was tantamount to racism but made no apology for the League's advocacy of a strong anti-immigration policy, including resolute action against illegal immigrants and against criminality in immigrant communities.

Having won 8.7% of the national vote and 55 Chamber seats in the 1992 general elections, the LN made political capital out of popular disgust over the bribery scandals engulfing Italy's political establishment, winning a record 40% of the vote in the Milan mayoral election of June 1993. For the March 1994 parliamentary elections the LN joined the Freedom Alliance (PL), winning 8.4% of the national vote; in June 1994 it won six European Parliament seats on a 6.6% vote share. Having joined the Berlusconi government in May, the LN withdrew in December because of chronic policy and personal differences with other PL components, notably with Berlusconi's *Forza Italia* party. In February 1995 the League relaunched itself outside the PL, adding "Federal Italy" to its title to convey its basic message. A small pro-Berlusconi faction remained part of the PL, founding the Italian Federal League.

The LN-IF contested the April 1996 general elections independently, increasing its share of the national vote to 10.1% and becoming the strongest single party in northern Italy. In opposition to the resultant centre-left government in Rome, the LN-IF convened a "parliament" in Mantua in May 1996, when party leader Umberto Bossi reasserted the League's secessionist objective and announced the creation of a "Committee for the Liberation of Padania"—a reference to the lands north of the River Po. However, such schemes received a knock in local elections the following month, when the LN-IF polled poorly throughout "Padania" and managed only third place in Mantua, seat of its "parliament".

The LN-IF's six members of the European Parliament sit, somewhat controversially, in the European Liberal, Democratic and Reformist Group, mainly consisting of members of the Liberal International, to which the LN-IF is not affiliated.

Proletarian Democracy

Democrazia Proletaria (DP)

Address. 62 via Farini, 00184 Rome

Leadership. Russo Spena (secretary)

The name "Proletarian Democracy" was originally used by an electoral alliance formed for the 1976 elections (in which it gained six Chamber seats) by the Party of Proletarian Unity (PdUP), Continuous Struggle (LC) and the pro-Chinese Workers' Vanguard, all Marxist formations somewhat to the left of the Italian Communist Party. The PdUP, which consisted of former Socialists and former Communists, split in 1977, when the former Socialist faction merged with the Workers' Vanguard to form the Proletarian Democracy party. Having unsuccessfully contested the 1979 Chamber elections in a New United Left alliance with the LC, DP fought the 1983 elections on its own and won seven seats with 1.5% of the vote. In July 1987 it increased its representation to eight seats, with 1.7% of the vote.

Thereafter the DP became less noticeable at elections, preferring to work within the broader left-wing alliances that were formed in the 1990s.

Radical Party

Partito Radicale (PR)

Address. 76 via di Torre Argentina, 00186 Rome

Telephone. (#39–6) 689791

Fax. (#39–6) 6880–5396

Leadership. Marco Pannella (president)

The PR was founded in December 1955 on a platform of non-violence, anti-militarism, human and civil rights, and the construction of a "socialist and democratic society". It has also campaigned for women's and homosexual rights, against nuclear energy and against "extermination by famine" in the Third World.

Originally formed by a left-wing faction of the Italian Liberal Party, the PR became concerned with civil rights from 1962 and in 1970 sponsored the divorce law and subsequently campaigned against the use of the referendum to change the law. It successfully supported legislation on conscientious objection, the lowering of the age of majority to 18 years, more liberal laws on drug offences and family relations and the partial legalization of abortion. The Radicals were the first Italian party to have a woman secretary (in 1977–78).

Having obtained four Chamber seats in 1976, the Radicals achieved a significant success in the 1979 elections in which they won 18 Chamber seats (3.4% of the vote) and two in the Senate. In 1983 the party announced at first that it would not take part in the general elections and later that it would campaign for the casting of blank or invalid ballot papers. In the event 11 members of the party were elected to the Chamber by 2.2% of the voters.

At its annual congresses in 1985 and 1986 the PR considered a proposal that the party should be disbanded, in protest against the "autocracy" of the larger parties. However, the congress in late 1986 decided against dissolution provided that paid-up membership rose to at least 15,000 by January 1987. Although this target was apparently not achieved, the party remained in being and in the July 1987 elections increased its Chamber representation to 13 seats and its share of the vote to 2.6%. Prominent among the new PR deputies was Ilona Staller, a pornographic film actress better known as Cicciolina.

A further congress in Bologna in January 1988 rejected proposals by the party's former leader, Marca Pannella, that the PR should convert itself into a transnational European party and also that its symbol of a fist holding a rose should be abandoned in favour of a representation of Mahatma Gandhi. The same congress decided that the party would not take part in any future Italian elections.

Meanwhile, in November 1979 the then PR secretary-general, Jean Fabre (a French national), had been sentenced by a Paris court to a month in prison for evading conscription. More serious was the 30–year prison sentence passed in 1984 on a PR deputy, Antonio Negri, following his conviction for complicity in terrorist acts, although he and seven others were acquitted in January 1986 of being "moral leaders" of extremist groups such as the Red Brigades.

Pannella's return to the PR leadership in 1992 served to end the electoral non-participation policy and also shifted the party to the right. Contesting the March 1994 elections as part of the Freedom Alliance, the PR presented a Pannella List but won no seats in its own right. Running as Pannella Reformers in the June 1994 European Parliament elections, it won two seats with a 2.1% vote share. In June 1995 referendum approval was given to three out of four proposals presented by the PR leader with the aim of restricting trade union powers.

The formation's representatives in the European Parliament sit in the European Radical Alliance group.

Segni Pact

Patto Segni (PS)

Address. Largo del Nazareno, 00187 Rome

Leadership. Mario Segni

The PS leader, Mario Segni, had been a leading anti-corruption campaigner within the then Christian Democratic Party, later the Italian Popular Party (PPI), until breaking away in 1992 to advocate reform of the Italian political system, initially within the Democratic Alliance. For the March 1994 general elections he launched the Pact for Italy, drawing in the PPI to assume the dominant role. Having received only only 4.6% of the national vote in March, the PS fell back to 3.3% in the June 1994 European Parliament election, in which it won three seats. In the April 1996 general elections the Segni forces, like the PPI, formed part of the victorious Olive Tree alliance.

The Pact's three representatives in the European Parliament sit in the European People's Party group.

South Tyrol People's Party
Südtiroler Volkspartei (SVP)
Address. 7A Brennerstrasse, 39100 Bozen/ Bolzano
Telephone (#39–471) 974484
Fax. (#39–471) 981473
Leadership. Siegfried Brugger (president), Hartmann Gallmetzer (general secretary)

The SVP is a Christian democratic party of the German-speaking population of Bolzano province (South Tirol). From 1948 onwards it consistently held three seats in the Italian Chamber of Deputies (and from 1979 one directly-elective seat in the European Parliament). The party's struggle for equal rights for the German-speaking and Ladin-speaking population of South Tirol led to Austro-Italian agreements on the status of the province in 1969–71 and a new statute for the Trentino-Alto Adige region in 1971. The SVP has been the strongest in the South Tirol *Landtag* and the second-strongest (after the Christian Democrats) in the regional council of Trentino-Alto Adige, winning 22 seats out of 70 in November 1983.

Normally securing representation in the Rome parliament thereafter, the SVP won one seat in the June 1994 European Parliament elections. For the April 1996 general elections it was part of the victorious centre-left Olive Tree alliance.

The SVP is affiliated to the International Democrat Union; but its European Parliament representative sits in the European People's Party group.

Union of the Democratic Centre
Union delle Centro Democratico (UCD)
Address. c/o Camera dei Deputati, Rome
Leadership. Raffaele Costa and Francesco d'Onofrio

The UCD was formed by right-wing elements of the Italian Liberal Party prior to the March 1994 general elections, which it contested as part of the Freedom Alliance. The two UCD leaders were both awarded ministerial portfolios in Berlusconi government of May-December 1994.

United Christian Democrats
Cristiani Democratici Uniti (CDU)
Address. c/o Camera dei Deputati, Rome
Leadership. Rocco Buttiglione (president)

The CDU was launched in July 1995 by a right-wing minority group of the Italian Popular Party (the former Christian Democratic Party) which favoured participation in the Freedom Alliance (PL) rather than the centre-left Olive Tree coalition. As part of the PL, the CDU contested the proportional section of the April 1996 parliamentary elections in close co-operation with the Christian Democratic Centre, their joint list securing 5.8% of the vote.

Other Regional Parties

Fatherland Front (*Heimatbund*), militant South Tyrol ethnic German formation, founded in 1971 by Hans Stieler and later led by Eva Klotz, advocates a South Tyrol "free state" able to opt for union with Austria; has mounted an electoral challenge in recent contests to the dominant South Tyrol People's Party.

For Trieste (*Per Trieste*), led by Manlio Cecovini, founded in opposition to the 1975 Osimo Treaty settling the Trieste territorial dispute between Italy and the then Yugoslavia, autonomist group advocating special status for Trieste within the special statute region of Friuli–Venezia Giulia.

Lombard Alpine League (*Lega Alpina Lombarda*, LAL), seeks to articulate local aspirations in Italy's border regions in the Alps, won one Senate seat in March 1994 and 0.3% of the vote in the June 1994 European Parliament elections.

Sardinian Action Party (*Partito Sardo d'Azione*, PSA), favouring autonomy for the island of Sardinia, obtained 12.3% of the vote in the Sardinian regional elections of June 1989.

Southern League (*Lega Meridionale*, LM), a *Mezzogiorno* formation, won 0.7% in June 1994 European Parliament elections.

Valdostan Union (*Union Valdôtaine/Union Valdostana*), a pro-autonomy grouping representing the French-speaking minority in the special statute region of Val d'Aosta, represented in the regional assembly from 1959, usually the region's strongest party and usually represented in the national parliament.

Jamaica

Capital: Kingston

Population: 2,400,000 (1995E)

A former British dependency, Jamaica became a fully independent member of the Commonwealth in 1962. The head of state is the British sovereign, represented by a Governor-General. Legislative power is vested in a bicameral parliament consisting of a 60–member House of Representatives, which is popularly elected for up to five years, and a 21–member appointed Senate (normally 13 on the advice of the Prime Minister and eight on that of the Leader of the Opposition). The Prime Minister and Cabinet are responsible to parliament and are appointed to office by the Governor-General acting on its advice. The Prime Minister is leader of the majority party in the House.

In general elections on March 30, 1993, the People's National Party retained power with 52 seats against the Jamaica Labour Party's 8.

Jamaica Labour Party (JLP)

Address. PO Box 536, Kingston 10
Telephone. (#1-809) 929-2457
Fax. (#1-809) 922-9002
Leadership. Edward Seaga (leader), Edmund Bartlett (general secretary)

The conservative JLP advocates private enterprise, foreign investment and economic growth, and has generally pursued a pro-Western foreign policy (backing the US invasion of Grenada in 1983). Founded in 1943 as the political wing of the Bustamente Industrial Trade Union, it was the ruling party from 1944 to 1955, from 1962 (when it led Jamaica to independence) to 1972, and again from 1980 to 1989 under Edward Seaga's premiership. Defeat in the 1989 polling was followed by further electoral losses in March 1993, when the party secured only eight seats in the House of Representatives. Seaga retained the leadership of the JLP (which he first assumed in 1974) despite considerable opposition to his stewardship from party dissidents. A former party chairman, Bruce Golding, left the party and formed the National Democratic Movement (NDM) in late 1995.

The JLP is affiliated to the International Democrat Union.

National Democratic Movement (NDM)

Leadership. Bruce Golding (leader)

Golding launched the NDM in November 1995, having earlier resigned as chairman of the Jamaica Labour Party. The new party called for constitutional reforms, advocating a clear separation of powers between the central executive and elected representatives.

People's National Party (PNP)

Address. 89 Old Hope Road, Kingston 6
Telephone. (#1–809) 927-7805
Fax. (#1–809) 927-4389
Leadership. Percival J. Patterson (president), Maxine Henry-Wilson (general secretary)

Formed in 1938 as a democratic socialist party, the PNP has more recently pursued a centrist line, drawing its main support from middle class and urban elements. Its founder, Norman Manley, led the party until 1969, during which time it won the 1955 and 1959 elections. Norman Manley was succeeded by his son, Michael, who became Prime Minister following the PNP's first post-independence electoral success in 1972. Projecting a radical socialist image, the Manley government retained power until its decisive defeat in the 1980 general election, after which the party distanced itself from the Workers' Party of Jamaica (WPJ). Having boycotted the 1983 polls, the PNP campaigned extensively outside parliament and made substantial gains in municipal elections in 1986. The party was returned to power with almost 57% of the vote in the 1989 general election, and further consolidated its position in early balloting in March 1993 when it won 52 of the 60 seats in the House of Representatives. Veteran leader Michael Manley resigned in 1992 and was replaced by Percival J. Patterson.

Other Parties

Christian Conscience Party (CCP), formed in 1983 when it unsuccessfully participated in the general election.

Jamaica American Party (JAP), launched in 1986 by James Chisholm with the aim of making Jamaica the 51st state of the USA, but with negligible public support.

Jamaica Communist Party (JCP), led by Chris Lawrence.

Revolutionary Marxist League (RML), a Trotsky-ist party.

United Progressive Movement (UPM), formed in 1993.

Workers' Party of Jamaica (WPJ), led by Trevor Munroe, formed as a communist group in 1978, initially allied with the left-wing of the then ruling People's National Party, which later severed all links; failed to win representation in the 1989 or 1993 elections.

Japan

Capital: Tokyo   **Population:** 125,500,000 (1995E)

Under its constitution adopted in 1947, Japan is a constitutional monarchy. Legislative authority is vested in a popularly-elected bicameral Diet (*Kokkai*), which is composed of a 511–member House of Representatives (*Shugiin*), elected for up to four years, and a House of Councillors (*Sangiin*), whose 252 members are elected for six years, half being due for re-election every three years. In 1994 legislation was enacted to the effect that from the elections due 1997 the lower house would have 500 members, of which 300 would be elected from single-member constituencies and 200 by proportional representation, the latter from 11 electoral districts rather than from national lists as originally envisaged.

The new legislation imposed a qualified ban on private donations to individual politicians for electoral purposes, allowing them to set up fund-raising organizations to receive corporate donations of up to 500,000 yen a year from any one company, although a five-year term was placed on such practice. As finally enacted, the legislation provided for an annual state subsidy to parties of 30,900 million yen (about $310 million), to be distributed to individual parties according to their Diet representation and percentage share of the vote in the most recent election.

The Liberal Democratic Party (LDP) was in office from its formation in 1955 until 1993 when, undermined by a series of scandals and splits, it lost its lower house majority in a general election on July 18, the outcome being as follows: LDP 223 seats (36.6% of the vote); Social Democratic Party of Japan (SDPJ) 70 (15.4%); Japan Renewal Party (*Shinseito*) 55 (10.1%); Clean Government Party (*Komeito*) 51 (8.1%); Japan New Party (JNP) 35 (8.1%); Japan Communist Party 15 (7.7%); Democratic Socialist Party 15 (4.8%); New Party Harbinger (*Sakigake*) 13 (2.6%); United Social Democratic Party (*Shaminren*) 4 (0.7%); independents 30. A new government was formed by a coalition of seven former opposition parties under the premiership of Morihiro Hokosawa (JNP), who was replaced in April 1994, amid a continuing process of political realignment and change, by Tsutomu Hata (*Shinseito*). Two months later the Hata government fell and was replaced by a coalition headed by Tomiichi Murayama of the SDJP but dominated by the LDP and also including *Sakigake*. In partial elections to the upper house in July 1995, the government lost ground but retained its overall majority. Meanwhile, most of the non-LDP and non-SDPJ parties now in opposition had come together to form the New Frontier Party (*Shinshinto*). Murayama resigned as Prime Minister in January 1996 and was replaced by Ryutaro Hashimoto of the LDP.

Japan Communist Party (JCP)

Nihon Kyosanto

Address. 4–26–7, Sendagaya, Shibuya-ku, Tokyo 151

Telephone. (#81–3) 3403–6111

Fax. (#81–3) 3746–0767

Leadership. Kenji Miyamoto (central committee chair)

Founded in 1922 but not legalized until 1945, the JCP has in recent decades presented itself as a democratic party independent of external influences, following its own programme of "scientific socialism" (having abandoned the theory of the dictatorship of the proletariat in 1976). Its share of the vote in the 1980s was consistently some 9% and its lower house representation around 30 seats. In the July 1993 lower house elections the party won 15 seats with a total vote share of 7.7 per cent. In the House of Councillors the party's representation increased to 14 seats in the July 1995 polling.

Liberal Democratic Party (LDP)

Jiyu-Minshuto

Address. 1–11–23, Nagata-cho, Chiyoda-ku, Tokyo 100

Telephone. (#81–3) 3581–6211

Fax. (#81-3) 3503-4180

Leadership. Ryutaro Hashimoto (president), Hiroshi Mitsuzuka (secretary-general)

The conservative LDP favours private enterprise, a continuing close relationship with the United States, and an expansion of Japanese interests in Asia. It was formed in 1955 by a merger of the Liberal and Democratic parties. Both of these constituent elements were composed of factions based around individuals, and this characteristic became an enduring feature of the LDP and its leadership succession. The LDP remained the ruling party until 1993 when, weakened by corruption scandals and defections, it was forced from office at the general election in July (gaining 223 of the 511 seats, with less than 37 per cent of the vote). In June 1994 the party returned to government in an unlikely coalition with the Social Democratic Party of Japan and the New Party Harbinger, and in January 1996 the LDP president, Ryutaro Hashimoto (who had assumed the party leadership in September 1995) took over the premiership. In the July 1995 upper house elections the LDP increased its plurality to 110 seats.

New Clean Government Party

Komeishinto

Address. 17 Minami-Motomachi, Shinjuku-ku, Tokyo 160

Telephone. (#81–3) 3353–0111

Leadership. Tomio Jujii (chair)

The original Clean Government Party (*Komeito*) was organized as a political party in 1964 with Buddhist affiliations, following a largely centrist ideology based on respect for humanity. Having won 51 seats in the House of Representatives in the 1993 elections, the party participated in the Hokosawa and Hata non-LDP coalition governments before going into opposition in June 1994. In December 1994 it split into two groups, one of which (encompassing about half of the *Komeito* members in the House of Councillors and all of its lower house representatives) entered the new New Frontier Party (NFP), while the other— renamed *Komeishinto* or *Komei* New Party— remained a separate entity, retaining 11 upper house seats following the July 1995 elections.

New Frontier Party (NFP)

Shinshinto

Address. c/o House of Representatives, Tokyo

Leadership. Ichiro Ozawa (president)

Shinshinto was formally inaugurated in December 1994 as an amalgamation of the following non-communist parties in opposition to the ruling coalition: the Japan New Party (JNP), which was formed in 1992 by Morihiro Hokosawa (Prime Minister from July 1993 to April 1994 in the first government since 1948 that excluded the Liberal Democratic Party, LDP) and which absorbed the small United Social Democratic Party (*Shaminren*) in May 1994; the Democratic Socialist Party (DSP), which had been set up in 1961 by right-wing dissidents from the then Japan Socialist Party (later the Social Democratic Party of Japan); the Japan Renewal Party (*Shinseito*), launched just before the 1993 lower house elections by LDP dissidents, including Ichiro Ozawa, who was seen as the main guiding hand in the radical changes in Japan's party structure); the bulk of the Clean Government Party (*Komeito*); and a number of smaller formations. The new party displayed a broad ideology, spanning a range from right-wing conservative to social democrat. The JNP, DSP, JRP and Komeito had won 35, 15, 55 and 51 seats respectively in the lower house elections in July 1993; by the end of 1995 Shinshinto adherents numbered about 170 in the House of Representatives and 68 in the House of Councillors. Ichiro Ozawa was elected party president in December 1995, replacing Toshiki Kaifu (a former LDP leader and Prime Minister from 1989 to 1991).

New Party Harbinger

Sakigake

Address. 2–17–42, Akasaka, Minato-ku, Tokyo 107

Telephone. (#81–3) 5570–1341

Leadership. Masayoshi Takemura (leader)

Sakigake was formed in June 1993 by a breakaway faction of the Liberal Democratic Party (LDP). The party won 13 seats in the July 1993 lower house elections, subsequently joining the two successive non-LDP coalitions. On the collapse of the second in June 1994 it opted to remain in government as a coalition partner of the SDPJ and LDP.

Second Chamber Club
Ni-In Club
  Address. 1015, 5–52–15, Nakano, Nakano-ku, Tokyo 164
    Telephone. (#81–3) 3508–8629
    Leadership. Yukio Aoshima (secretary)
  The Ni-In Club is a latter-day remnant of the Green Wind Club (*Ryukufukai*) of the late 1940s, the advantages of incumbency enabling a handful of Ni-In representatives to secure re-election over subsequent decades. In the July 1995 upper house elections, however, the Ni-In Club retained only two of the five seats it had secured in 1992.

Social Democratic Party of Japan (SDPJ)
Nihon Shakai Minshuto
  Address. 1–8–1, Nagata-cho, Chiyoda-ku, Tokyo 100
    Telephone. (#81–3) 3580–1171
    Fax. (#81–3) 3580–0691
    Leadership. Tomiichi Murayama (party head), Kanjyu Sato (general secretary)
  Founded in 1945, the formation was known until 1991 as the Japan Socialist Party (JSP), which was briefly in power in 1947–48 as part of a broad coalition and thereafter perpetually in opposition until 1993. A radical party platform was adopted in the mid-1960s (advocating non-alignment, a non-aggression pact among the great powers and a democratic transition from capitalism to socialism), but from the mid-1980s the party began to abandon much of its Marxist ideology in favour of democratic socialism on the West European model. This process was accelerated by the party's heaving defeat in the 1986 lower house elections, following which Takako Doi was elected party chair, becoming the first woman to head a major Japanese party, although she resigned after another setback for the SDPJ in the 1991 local elections.

In the July 1993 lower house elections, the SDPJ's representation fell sharply from 136 to 70 seats, but it remained the second largest party and was subsequently a partner in a coalition excluding the hitherto-dominant Liberal Democratic Party.

On Jan. 5, 1996, Murayama resigned from the post of Prime Minister in the ruling coalition and was replaced by the leader of the dominant LDP, although the SDPJ obtained six posts in the new government. Ten days later Murayama was re-elected as SDPJ leader, defeating Tadatoshi Akiba by a 5 to 1 margin in a ballot of party members. On Jan. 19 an SDPJ convention formally approved the change of the party's Japanese name to Social Democratic Party and adopted a new platform which incorporated liberal aims and values in place of the leftist orientation which the party had maintained on paper but had repudiated in practice.

Sports Peace Party
Supotsu Heiwato
  Address. c/o House of Councillors, Tokyo
  Leadership. Kenji Inoki (leader)
  Founded by a former professional wrestler with the aim of promoting world peace by the application of the sporting ethos to international relations, the party won two upper house seats in the elections of 1992 but was reduced to one seat in the July 1995 balloting.

Other Parties

Communitarian Democratic Power, led by Peter Safa F. Sawada, an affiliate of the Christian Democrat International.

Pensioners' Party (*Nenkinto*), led by Toru Takaku, won two upper house seats in 1989.

Progressive Party (*Kakushinto*), led by Seiichi Tagawa, founded in 1987 by members of the New Liberal Club opposed to the latter's majority decision to rejoin the Liberal Democratic Party.

Salarymen's New Party (*Sarariman Shinto*), led by Shigeru Aoki, launched in 1983 to seek tax reforms in the interests of salaried workers; held two upper house seats in the late 1980s.

Tax Party (*Zeikinto*), which held two upper house seats in the late 1980s.

Welfare Party (*Fukushito*), led by Eita Yashiro, seeking improved social services; won one upper house seat in 1983.

Jordan

Capital: Amman

Population: 4,700,000 (1995E)

The Hashemite Kingdom of Jordan attained independence in 1946. It is a constitutional monarchy in which the King, as head of state, appoints a Prime Minister, who in turn selects a Council of Ministers in consultation with the monarch. The Council is responsible to the bicameral National Assembly (*Majlis al-Umma*), comprising the 80–member lower House of Representatives (*Majlis al-Nuwwab*), which is elected for a four-year term, and the upper House of Notables (*Majlis al-Ayaan*), whose 40 members are appointed by the King. In April 1992 King Hussein ibn Talal formally abolished all martial law provisions introduced after the 1967 Arab-Israeli War (in which Israel had occupied the West Bank of the Jordan), and in July 1992 legislation was passed lifting the ban on political parties. Under current regulations, parties are not allowed to receive funding from abroad and are required to undertake to work within the constitution.

Multi-party elections to the House of Representatives were held on November 8, 1993. With the exception of the Islamic Action Front, most political parties had a low profile in the elections and the majority of candidates were returned as independents.

Arab Islamic Democratic Movement
Haraki al-Arabiyya al-Islamiyya al-Dimaqrati (Du'a)

Leadership. Yusuf Abu Bakr (secretary-general)

The party is a liberal Islamist grouping, highly critical of the Islamic Action Front's "regressive" interpretation of the Koran. As an "inter-faith" movement it aims to reinforce the relationship between Muslims and Christians. Both women and Christians were included in the party's initial temporary executive committee.

Communist Party of Jordan
Hizb al-Shuyui al-Urduni

Leadership. Yaqub Zayadin (secretary-general)

Banned since 1957, the Communist Party applied for legal status in October 1992. Authorization was initially denied because the party's manifesto was deemed to be at odds with the Jordanian constitution. However, recognition was granted in early 1993 on the condition that the phraseology of party philosophy was amended. The organization stands for Arab nationalism, with strong adherence to Marxist-Leninist ideology.

Future Party
Hizb al-Mustaqbil

Address. c/o Majlis al-Nuwwab, Amman

Leadership. Suliman Arrar (secretary-general)

Recognized in late 1992, the party is conservative in nature. It espouses pan-Arab principles and is a strong proponent of Palestinian rights. In the 1993 elections it won one seat in the House of Representatives.

Homeland Party
Hizb al-Watan

Address. c/o Majlis al-Nuwwab, Amman

Leadership. Akif al-Fayiz (secretary-general)

The Homeland Party, recognized in June 1993, is described as conservative, with strong tribal affiliation. Two members were successful in the November 1993 elections, and the party subsequently participated with other centrist organizations in forming the Jordanian National Front.

Islamic Action Front (IAF)

Address. c/o Majlis al-Nuwwab, Amman

Leadership. Ishaq Farhan (secretary-general)

The IAF, a broad-based Islamic coalition but dominated by the Muslim Brotherhood, was formed and registered in late 1992. It advocates the establishment of a *sharia*-based Islamic state, with the retention of the monarchy, and believes in the equal rights of women with men in all aspects. The Front is generally perceived as hostile to peace talks with Israel. In the November 1993 elections to the House of Representatives, the IAF emerged as the largest single party with 16 seats. In municipal elections in July 1995 the IAF was heavily defeated as traditional tribal community leaders won majorities in most constituencies.

Jordanian Arab Democratic Party (JADP)
Hizb al-Arabi al-Dimaqrati al-Urduni
  Address. c/o Majlis al-Nuwwab, Amman
  Leadership. Muniz Razzaz (secretary-general)
Most members of the leftist JADP are former Baathists and pan-Arabists. The party was recognized in July 1993 and gained two seats in the House of Representatives the following November. The two elected members subsequently joined a parliamentary bloc of leftists, Arab nationalists and liberal deputies known as the Progressive Democratic Coalition.

Jordanian Arab Socialist Baath Party (JASBP)
Hizb al-Baath al-Arabi al-Ishtiraki al-Urduni
  Address. c/o Majlis al-Nuwwab, Amman
  Leadership. Taysir Homsi (secretary-general)
Because of apparent ties with its Iraqi counterpart, the party was initially denied legal status. This decision was reversed in January 1993 following assurances of the organization's independence and a change of name from the "Baath Arab Socialist Party in Jordan" to the JASBP. One member was returned to the House of Representatives in the 1993 elections.

Jordanian National Alliance (JNA)
Hizb al-Tajammu al-Watani
  Address. c/o Majlis al-Nuwwab, Amman
  Leadership. Mijhim al-Khreisheh (secretary-general)
Recognized in December 1992, the JNA is a nationalist and pro-establishment group of tribal leaders from the south and central parts of Jordan. Four members were elected to the House of Representatives in November 1993, after which the party joined with three other centrist groups to form the Jordanian National Front, primarily a parliamentary bloc.

Jordanian People's Democratic Party
Hizb al-Shaab al-Dimaqrati (Hashd)
  Address. c/o Majlis al-Nuwwab, Amman
  Leadership. Taysir al-Zibri (secretary-general)
The leftist Hashd was set up in 1989 by the Jordanian wing of the Democratic Front for the Liberation of Palestine, a component of the Palestine Liberation Organization (PLO). It was recognized in January 1993 after initial concerns over its independence, and won one seat in the elections the following November.

Jordanian Pledge Party
Hizb al-Ahd al-Urduni
  Address. c/o Majlis al-Nuwwab, Amman
  Leadership. Abd al-Hadi al-Majali (secretary-general)

The party, recognized in December 1992, is centrist in outlook, supporting political pluralism, democracy and a free market economy. It emphasises the development of a national Jordanian identity, with a clear distinction between the Jordanian and Palestinian political entities. Two members, including the secretary-general, were elected to the House of Representatives in 1993. Although the party initially called for the creation of a common front among centrist parties, it did not align after the elections with those parties in the Jordanian National Front, but rather with a group of independent deputies in a National Action Front.

Jordanian Progressive Democratic Party
Hizb al-Taqaddumi al-Dimaqrati al-Urduni
  Address. c/o Majlis al-Nuwwab, Amman
  Leadership. Ali Abd al-Aziz Amer (secretary-general)
The party was originally formed as a merger of three leftist groups—the Jordanian Democratic Party, the Jordanian Party for Progress (which later withdrew) and the Palestinian Communist Labour Party Organization. It was the first leftist party to attain legal status (in mid-January 1993), having deleted references to its socialist objectives from the party manifesto, and secured one seat in the November 1993 elections. The secretary-general and several other party figures are former members of the Palestinian National Council, as well as of the 13

Jordanian Socialist Democratic Party (JSDP)
Hizb al-Dimaqrati al-Ishtiraki al-Urduni
  Address. c/o Majlis al-Nuwwab, Amman
  Leadership. Isa Madanat (secretary-general)
Established by former members of the Communist Party of Jordan, the leftist JSDP achieved legal status in January 1993 despite refusing a government request to delete the word 'socialism' from its party platform. One member holds a seat in the House of Representatives.

Reawakening Party
Hizb al-Yaqtha
  Address. c/o Majlis al Nuwwab, Amman
  Leadership. Abd al-Rauf al-Rawabda (secretary-general)
The organization was recognized in February 1993. Two members, including the secretary-general, were returned to the House of Representatives in the 1993 elections, following which the party joined in the formation of the centrist Jordanian National Front.

Unionist Arab Democratic Party (The Promise)
Hizb al-Wahdawi al-Arabi al-Dimaqrati al-Waad
  Leadership. Anis Muasher, Muhammed Uran, Talal al-Umar (leaders)

This centrist party—formed in early 1993 from a merger of the Democratic Unionist Alliance, the Liberal Unionist Party and the Arab Unionist Party—advocates a free market economy and the need to attract foreign investment in Jordan. The issue of party leadership has caused internal dissension, and the post of secretary-general has rotated among the three heads of the constituent political groups.

Other Parties

Arab Baath Party for Progress (*Hizb al-Baath al-Arabi al-Taqaddumi*), a leftist and pro-Syrian grouping legalized in April 1993, led by Mahmud al-Maayta.

Arab Democratic Party of the Masses (*Hizb al-Jamahir al-Arabi al-Dimaqrati*), an Arabist and leftist in orientation, led by Abd al-Khaliq Shatat.

Freedom Party (*Hizb al-Huriyya*), led by Fawwaz al-Zubi, a former member of the Communist Party of Jordan, reported to be "trying to combine Marxist ideology with Islamic tradition and nationalist thinking"; legalized in February 1993.

Jordanian Arab Partisans' Party (*Hizb al-Ansar al-Arabi al-Urduni*), led by fnmMuhammed Fay-sal al-Majali, legalized in December 1995.

Jordanian Democratic Popular Unity Party (*Hizb al-Wihda al-Shabiyya al-Dimaqrati al-Urduni*), led by Azmi al-Khawaja, formed by Jordanian leftist supporters of the Popular Front for the Liberation of Palestine opposed to peace negotiations with Israel; attained legal status in February 1993.

Popular Unity Party (*Hizb al-Wihda al-Shabiyya*), a centrist and nationalist party recognized in late 1992 and led by Talal al-Ramahi.

Progress and Justice Party (*Hizb al-Taqaddumi wa al-Adl*), led by Ali al-Saad, a nationalist and moderate formation advocating a free market economy.

Kazakhstan

Capital: Almaty **Population:** 17,000,000 (1995E)

Having been a constituent republic of the USSR for over half a century, Kazakhstan was one of the last group of Soviet republics to declare their independence on the demise of the USSR in December 1991. The constitution approved by referendum on Aug. 30, 1995, was independent Kazakhstan's third in less than four years, a Soviet-era text having been replaced in January 1993 by a post-Soviet version that was eventually thought to be deficient. The 1995 constitution of the Kazakh Republic (hitherto Republic of Kazakhstan) provides for an executive President with substantial authority, popularly elected for a five-year term, with powers to appoint the Prime Minister and other ministers and to dissolve the legislature (*Kenges*). The latter body is bicameral, consisting of (i) a Senate (*Senat*) of 47 members, of whom 40 are indirectly elected for a four-year term by the councils of the country's 19 regions and the capital, while seven are appointed by the President; and (ii) an Assembly (*Majlis*) of 67 members also elected for a four-year term from single-seat constituencies.

Elections for both houses in December 1995, with run-off balloting for Assembly seats continuing into February 1996, resulted in the lower house seats being distributed as follows (according to unofficial calculations): People's Union of Kazakhstan Unity (SNEK) 24, December National Democratic Party 12, Kazakhstan Agrarian Union 5, Confederation of Kazakh Trade Unions 5, Communist Party of Kazakhstan 2, independents and unfilled seats 19. In a presidential election on Dec. 1, 1991, Nursultan Nazarbayev was returned for a five-year term as the sole candidate. On April 29, 1995, he secured referendum approval for the extension of his term to the year 2000 without need of further popular consultation.

Citizen
Azamat

Address. c/o Kenges, Almaty

Leadership. Murat Auezov, Petr Svoik and Turegeldy Sharmanov (co-chairs)

Azamat was founded in April 1996 as an opposition alliance that called for a government of "honest and competent" people. It was the first opposition formation including eminent public figures, its three co-chairs having each held senior posts in the Soviet-era bureaucracy (one of them being the leader of the Socialist Party of Kazakhstan).

Communist Party of Kazakhstan
Kommunisticheskaya Partiya Kazakhstana (KPK)

Address. c/o Kenges, Almaty

Leadership. Serikbolsin Abdildin (chair)

The KPK was maintained in being when a faction of the old ruling party opposed its conversion into the Socialist Party of Kazakhstan in September 1991; it eventually achieved legal registration in March 1994. The party advocates close economic ties with other ex-Soviet republics, retention of state ownership of strategic sectors of the economy, universal welfare provision and equality of ethnic groups. The KPK was credited with winning two seats in the parliamentary elections of late 1995–early 1996. In April 1996 the procurator-general requested the Justice Ministry to ban the KPK, on the grounds that it had "a pro-communist ideology" and had organized anti-government demonstrations.

December National Democratic Party
Natsionalnaya Demokraticheskaya Partiya–Jeltogsan (NDP-Jeltogsan)

Address. c/o Kenges, Almaty

Leadership. Hasen Kozhakhmetov

Jeltogsan was founded in 1990 as a pro-independence movement, named after the month of anti-government riots in the capital in 1986 (in the Soviet era), after which its leader, a well-known composer, was imprisoned. A Kazakh/Turkic nationalist movement, *Jeltogsan* advocates close links with Turkey and Iran, and in 1992 announced the sending of party volunteers to assist Azerbaijan in its conflict with Armenia. In 1995 its leader was prominent in the opposition to the presidential constitution adopted in August.

Freedom Civil Movement of Kazakhstan

Grazhdanskoye Dvizhenie Kazakhstana–Azat (GDK-Azat)

Address. c/o Kenges, Almaty

Leadership. Mikhail Isinaliyev

The Kazakh nationalist *Azat* was founded in 1990 to promote Kazakhstan's independence, on the achievement of which it lost ground to other political forces. In October 1992 it joined with the December National Democratic Party and the Republican Party of Kazakhstan to form the Republican Party *Azat*, but the merger quickly broke down over policy and personal differences.

Kazakhstan Agrarian Union

Address. c/o Kenges, Almaty

Based in Kazakhstan's vast rural areas, this peasant-based formation was credited with winning five Assembly seats in the 1995-96 general elections.

People's Congress of Kazakhstan

Narodnyi Kongress Kazakhstana (NKK)

Address. c/o Kenges, Almaty

Leadership. Olzhas Suleymenov (chair)

The NKK was founded in October 1991, deriving from a well-supported anti-nuclear movement and smaller intellectual groups; it included ecological and internationalist aims in its platform. The party initially appeared to have the backing of President Nazarbayev, and so attracted support in the state bureaucracy. Gravitating to opposition, the party won nine seats in the 1994 election. In August 1995 its chairman was appointed as Kazakhstan's ambassador to Italy.

People's Union of Kazakhstan Unity

Soyuz Narodnoye Edinstvo Kazakhstana (SNEK)

Address. Room 501, 13 pl. Respubliki, 480013 Almaty

Telephone. (#7–3272) 637789

Leadership. Nursultan Nazarbayev (leader), Kuanysh Sultanov (chair), Serik Abdrakhmanov (chair of political board)

The SNEK was launched as a "presidential" formation in February 1993, its leadership composed primarily of former Communist officials and inheriting much of the organization of the former ruling party. The party advocates gradual economic reform and political pluralism, also laying stress on the need to reduce ethnic difference, while opposing the concept of dual citizen-

ship and language rights for ethnic Russians. In the March 1994 parliamentary elections the SNEK became the largest grouping (amid claims of electoral fraud). It was formally constituted as a political party in February 1995, thereafter giving support to President Nazarbayev in his conflict with the Constitutional Court. SNEK remained the dominant party following general elections in December 1995 and early 1996.

Republic Co-ordinating Council of Public Associations

Koordinatsionnyi Sovet Obshestvennyih Obyedinenyi Respublika (KSOOR)

Address. c/o Kenges, Almaty

Leadership. Serikbolsin Abdildin (co-ordinator)

The formation of the KSOOR was announced in May 1994, principally on the initiative of the Socialist Party of Kazakhstan (SPK), as a "constructive opposition bloc" of several parties and movements. In addition to the SPK, it included the Communist Party of Kazakhstan (whose leader became its co-ordinator), the People's Congress of Kazakhstan, the Freedom Civil Movement of Kazakhstan, the December National Democratic Party, the Republican People's Slavic Movement–Harmony and the *Tabigat* (Nature) Ecological Party. Its non-party components included the Confederation of Kazakh Trade Unions (which won 11 seats in its own right in the 1994 election and five in 1995–96) and the Democratic Committee on Human Rights.

Republican Party of Kazakhstan

Respublikanskaya Partiya Kazakhstana (RPK)

Address. c/o Kenges, Almaty

Leadership. Sabetkazy Akatayev

Formed prior to Kazakhstan's post-Soviet independence, the RPK entered into an unsuccessful merger with the Freedom Civil Movement of Kazakhstan (*Azat*) and the December National Democratic Party in October 1992, after the collapse of which it generally supported the government.

Republican People's Slavic Movement–Harmony

Respubliukanskoye Obshestvennoye Slavyanskoye Dvizhenie–Lad

Address. 85 Vinogradova, kv. 408, 480012 Almaty

Leadership. Alexandra Dokuchaeva (chair)

Founded in mid-1993, *Lad* is the largest ethnic Russian movement in Kazakhstan, also drawing support from other Russian-speaking groups such as Tatars, Germans and Koreans. Advocating close relations with Russia, dual citizenship for ethnic Russians and equal status for the Russian language, it won only four seats in the 1994 election. Many ethnic Russians did not have the right to vote on that occasion.

Socialist Party of Kazakhstan
Sotsialisticheskaya Partiya Kazakhstana (SPK)
    Address. c/o Kenges, Almaty
    Leadership. Petr Svoik (chair)

The SPK was born a month after the abortive August 1991 coup by hardliners in Moscow, being the new name of the then ruling Communist Party of Kazakhstan (KPK). Then led by the eminent writer Anuar Alimzhanov, the SPK adopted a programme of political pluralism and cautious economic reform. President Nazarbayev (the former KPK leader) withdrew from the SPK before his re-election in December 1991, subsequently launching the People's Union of Kazakhstan Unity as the government party. The opposition SPK won only eight seats in the 1994 legislative elections and was not credited with any in December 1995. In April 1996 the SPK leader (a former head of the State Committee on Prices and Anti-Monopoly Measures) became a co-chair of the new Citizen movement, although the SPK retained its individual identity.

Other Parties

Alash National Freedom Party (*Partiya Natsionalynoi Svobody Alash*), a Kazakh nationalist, Islamist and pan-Turkic grouping named after a legendary founder of the Kazakh nation, led by Aron Atabek and Rashid Nutushev.

Russian Centre (*Rossiiskaya Centrum*, RC), led by Nina Sidorova, based in the ethnic Russian community, denied registration for the 1995 elections, after which it leader was charged with contempt of court for filing a legal suit against President Nazarbayev on the grounds that he had defamed the RC.

Social Democratic Party of Kazakhstan (*Sotsial-Demokraticheskaya Partiya Kazakhstana*, SDPK), founded in May 1990, led by Dos Kushimov.

Society for Assistance to the Cossacks of Semirechye (*Obshchestvo Sodeistviia Semerechenskim Kazakan*), led by Nikolay Gunkin, ethnic Russian formation registered in July 1994 but suspended four months later for allegedly seeking links with Cossacks in Russia; claims that Kazakhstan is a "fascist" state bent on the elimination of ethnic Russians.

Unity Movement (*Dvizheniye Edinstvo*), led by Yuri Startsev.

Kenya

Capital: Nairobi   **Population:** 32,200,000 (1995E)

Kenya achieved independence from the United Kingdom in 1963 and was proclaimed a republic the following year. In 1964 the ruling Kenya African National Union (KANU) became effectively the sole legal party, and it was not until December 1991 that President Daniel arap Moi, faced with increasing internal and external pressure, approved constitutional amendments establishing a multi-party system. The central legislative authority is the unicameral National Assembly, with 188 directly-elected representatives and 12 members nominated by the President. It has a five-year mandate. Executive power is vested in the President, Vice-President and Cabinet. Both the Vice-President and the Cabinet are appointed by the President, who is elected for a five-year term by universal adult suffrage. Presidential elections take place in one round, with only a relative majority being required for election.

In multi-party elections held on Dec. 29, 1992, President Moi was re-elected, as the KANU candidate, with only 36% of the popular vote. The disputed results of simultaneous legislative elections gave KANU 100 of the 188 elective seats, the Forum for the Restoration of Democracy–Asili 31, the Forum for the Restoration of Democracy–Kenya 31, the Democratic Party of Kenya 23 and other parties 3.

Democratic Party of Kenya (DP)

Address. PO Box 56395, Nairobi

Leadership. Mwai Kibaki (leader)

The DP emerged at the beginning of 1992 as a result of the departure by former Kenya African National Union members from the ruling party to join the opposition. Its leader Mwai Kibaki, who had been a longstanding government figure until his resignation in December 1991, attacked widespread official corruption and declared the new party's commitment to democracy, open government and free enterprise. In the December 1992 elections, which were denounced as rigged and fraudulent by the opposition, Kibaki took third place in the presidential balloting with almost 20 per cent of the votes cast, while DP candidates secured 23 seats in the National Assembly.

At the end of November 1995 it was announced that the DP and the other main opposition parties had agreed to forge a unified front against the ruling KANU regime and to establish a new democratic order in Kenya.

Forum for the Restoration of Democracy-Asili (FORD-Asili)

Address. PO Box 72695, Nairobi

Leadership. Stephen Musila (chair), Kimani Wanyoike (secretary-general) [*Note.* On being ousted from these posts in March 1996, George Nthenge and Martin Shikuku disputed the legitimacy of their respective successors.]

FORD was formed by prominent opposition politicians in August 1991, attracting immediate government hostility. The most high-profile figure at this stage was Oginga Odinga, a Vice-President of Kenya in the 1960s and a former member of the ruling party. The government's repressive response to the FORD pro-democracy campaign drew international condemnation, threatening Kenya's relations with crucial aid donors. The party was registered immediately following the regime's acceptance of multi-partyism at the end of 1991. From mid-1992, however, FORD was weakened by mounting internal divisions and rivalry over the selection of the party's presidential election candidate; this resulted in a split into two opposing factions—FORD-Asili under Kenneth Matiba and FORD-Kenya led by Odinga—which were registered as separate political parties in October 1992.

In the December 1992 elections, in which the party claimed that gross irregularities took place, Matiba finished second to President Moi with 26 per cent of the vote, while FORD-Asili candidates won 31 seats in the National Assembly (although one representative subsequently defected to KANU in June 1993). Divisions within FORD-Asili emerged in November 1994 when the party's national executive committee reportedly suspended Matiba and secretary-general Shikuku for six months, and Salim Ndamwe was named as acting chair. The suspensions were rejected by Matiba and Shikuku as unconstitutional. Further internal turmoil ensued, with new party officers appointed in March 1996 failing to obtain support from their predecessors.

Together with the other main opposition parties, FORD-Asili agreed in November 1995 to join in a new alliance to oust President's Moi's KANU government.

Forum for the Restoration of Democracy-Kenya (FORD-Kenya)

Address. PO Box 72595, Nairobi

Telephone. (#254-2) 226931

Fax. (#254-2) 544357

Leadership. Kijana Wamalwa (chair)

FORD-Kenya was one of the two main rival elements to emerge from the original FORD opposition movement. The party was registered in October 1992, initially under the leadership of Oginga Odinga, who achieved fourth place in the presidential election December 1992, with almost 17.5 per cent of the votes cast. In the simultaneous legislative elections FORD-Kenya tied for second place with FORD-Asili, winning 31 National Assembly seats. FORD-Kenya subsequently joined the opposition alliance to challenge the validity of election results. In June 1993 Odinga assumed the leadership of the official opposition in the National Assembly. However, in January of the following year he died and was succeeded as chair of FORD-Kenya by Michael Wamalwa, hitherto the party's vice-president.

In June 1995 secretary-general Munyua Waiyaki resigned his party membership, announcing that he was joining a new party. At the end of November 1995 it was reported that Wamalwa had been ousted as chair of FORD-Kenya by Raila Odinga (a son of the late leader), reflecting factional rivalries within the party. However, the following month the High Court confirmed Wamalwa as party chair, restraining Odinga from taking over the leadership.

At a meeting of representatives of the main opposition parties in late November (attended by Wamalwa), a new alliance was launched to confront the KANU regime. FORD-Kenya has observer status in the Liberal International.

Kenya African National Union (KANU)

Address. PO Box 72394, Nairobi

Leadership. Daniel arap Moi (president)

KANU was established in 1960 espousing centralized government, "African socialism" and racial harmony. It has been the ruling party since

1964, and between 1982 and 1991 its status as the sole legal political organization was embodied in the constitution. Daniel arap Moi succeeded Jomo Kenyatta as President and party leader in 1978. In December 1990, following President Moi's lead, KANU delegates voted to retain the one-party system. However, the sustained pro-democracy campaign and international pressure for reform made this position increasingly untenable, and in December 1991 the party endorsed Moi's abrupt decision to introduce multi-partyism. KANU subsequently suffered a number of defections to new opposition parties.

In the December 1992 elections, Moi retained the Presidency with just over 36 per cent of the votes cast, the opposition vote having been split between the leaders of three opposition parties. In the legislative elections KANU secured a majority with 100 of the elective National Assembly seats, although many sitting KANU members were defeated including 15 cabinet ministers.

In December 1995 KANU reportedly outlined a new strategy to revitalize and strengthen the party in the run-up to the 1997 general elections.

Kenya National Congress (KNC)
Address. c/o Electoral Commission, Nairobi
Leadership. Chilube wa Tsuma (leader)
The KNC was launched in September 1992, ostensibly presenting itself as a means to restore unity between the rival factions of the Forum for the Restoration of Democracy. The party won a single seat in the 1992 National Assembly elections; its presidential candidate, Chilube wa Tsuma, gained under 0.2 per cent of the vote.

Kenya National Democratic Alliance (KENDA)
Address. PO Box 39695, Nairobi
Leadership. Mukaru Ng'ang'a (chair)
Legalized in early 1992, KENDA focused on criticizing of the human rights record of President Moi's regime. The party did not win any National Assembly representation in 1992 and its leader came last in the presidential election.

Kenya Social Congress (KSC)
Address. PO Box 55318, Nairobi
Leadership. George Anyona (leader)
Founded and legalized in 1992, the KSC secured one seat in the 1992 legislative elections. Party leader Anyona received less than 0.3 per cent of the presidential poll.

Party of Independent Candidates of Kenya (PICK)
Address. c/o Electoral Commission, Nairobi
Leadership. John Harun Mwau (leader)
The party gained one National Assembly seat in the 1992 elections, its leader coming second to last in the presidential contest.

Safina Party
Leadership. Richard Leakey, Paul Muite (leaders)
In May 1995 the internationally-recognized conservationist and palaeontologist, Richard Leakey, announced that he was joining Paul Muite and other members of the Mwangaza Trust (the charitable status of which had been revoked by the government in January 1995) in the formation of a new opposition party. The following month the party name, Safina ("Noah's Ark"), was announced and an application for registration was made. A party statement proposed the building, with other opposition groups, of a viable alternative to the ruling KANU regime, stressing a rejection of tribalism and racism. Leakey's move into politics was condemned by President Moi, and by the end of November 1995, when a new alliance of opposition of parties including Safina was announced, the government had not agreed to the registration of the new party.

Other Parties

Islamic Party of Kenya (IPK), formed in 1992 but denied legal status.

National Development Party (NDP), formed in 1994. People's Union of Justice and New Order (PUJNO), led by Wilson Owili.

Rural National Democratic Party (RNDP), supporting farmers interests. Social Democratic Party (SDP), formed in 1992 by Johnstone Makau.

United Muslims of Africa (UMA), based in the Muslim population concentrated in orthern Kenya and coastal towns.

Rebel Group

February 18 Movement, alleged by the government in February 1995 to be a subversive organization planning to destabilize the country and maintaining guerrilla camps in a neighbouring country.

Kiribati

Capital: Tarawa   **Population:** 77,000 (1995E)

Kiribati (the former Gilbert Islands) became an independent republic in 1979. Under the constitution, legislative power is vested in a unicameral 41-seat House of Assembly (*Maneaba ni Maungatabu*). This comprises 39 popularly elected members, one nominated representative of the displaced Banaban community (resident since the 1950s in Fiji because of the environmental degradation of their island by phosphate mining), and the Attorney General (as an *ex-officio* member, unless already elected). An executive President (known as the *Beretitenti*), who is popularly elected from amongst members of the Assembly, governs with the assistance of an appointed Cabinet and is empowered to dissolve the Assembly and to call general elections. Both President and Assembly serve a four-year term.

Traditionally there have been no formally organized political parties in Kiribati. Loose associations of individuals have tended to form in response to specific issues or in support of particular individuals. In the most recent legislative elections, held between July 21-29, 1994, two such groupings, the Maneaban Te Mauri (MTM) and the National Progressive Party (NPP), secured 13 and seven seats respectively. The other 19 elective seats in the Assembly were won by independents, the majority of whom gave their support to the MTM. Subsequent presidential elections held on September 30 1994 resulted in a decisive victory for Teburoro Tito of the MTM over the incumbent, Teatao Teannaki. The latter had been elected in 1991 (replacing Ieremia Tabai, who had been President since independence in 1979).

North Korea

Capital: Pyongyang   **Population:** 24,000,000 (1995E)

Liberated in 1945 from Japanese colonial rule, the Korean peninsula was occupied by Soviet troops in the north and by US forces in the south. In 1948 separate states were established on either side of the 38th parallel (the north becoming the Democratic People's Republic of Korea, commonly known as North Korea), each of which reflected the ideology of its respective super-power and each of which claimed jurisdiction over the entire peninsula. In 1950 the communist North invaded the South and was resisted by US-led United Nations forces. The Korean War was ended by an armistice in 1953, with the ceasefire line (which became the new *de facto* border) straddling the 38th parallel.

Under the terms of North Korea's 1972 constitution, nominal political authority is held by a unicameral Supreme People's Assembly (SPA), the 687 members of which are supposed to be elected every four years, although no election has been held on schedule since 1972. The SPA elects a standing committee to represent it when not in session. It also elects a President who, in addition to being head of state, holds executive power and governs in conjunction with a Central People's Committee and an appointed Administration Council (Cabinet). Actual political control is exercised by the communist Korean Workers' Party (KWP), which was dominated throughout the post-war period by Kim Il Sung, as party leader and head of state, until his death in July 1994. Also known as the Great Leader, Kim was the object of an extravagant personality cult, and spent his last two decades in power preparing the way for the succession of his son, Kim Jong Il (known as the Dear Leader).

Elections to the SPA were last held in April 1990, from a single list of KWP or KWP-approved candidates. The late Kim Il Sung was re-elected President of the Republic in May 1990.

Korean Workers' Party (KWP)
Chosun No-Dong Dang

Address. c/o Supreme People's Assembly, Pyongyang

Leadership. The post of general secretary has remained vacant since the death of Kim Il Sung in July 1994.

Originating at the end of World War II, the KWP became the sole ruling force in the Democratic People's Republic of Korea established in 1948, and has since maintained control of all political activity within the state. Under Kim Il Sung's undisputed leadership, the party adhered to the concept of *Juche* (variously defined as involving political independence, economic self-reliance and national self-defence) as the ideological foundation for North Korean communism.

Having in 1961 again recognized the Communist Party of the Soviet Union as "the vanguard of the world communist movement", the KWP moved to a pro-Chinese line from 1963 and later to an independence stance on the ideological competition between Moscow and Beijing. The rapid post-1989 collapse of communism in Eastern Europe and of the Soviet Union itself in 1991 did not appear to shake the KWP's certainty about its right to rule. With communist regimes becoming an endangered species, the KWP inevitably drew closer to Beijing, although there was no inclination in Pyongyang to follow the Chinese lead in combining communist rule with economic liberalization.

The death of the Kim Il Sung in July 1994 generated much external expectation that the forces of political reform would be unleashed in North Korea. In the event, nothing changed in the system of KWP rule, at least on the surface.

Although groomed for succession, Kim Jong Il had not formally assumed his late father's party and state titles by mid-1996, amid continuing speculation about a power struggle within the ruling elite.

Other Approved Formations

Chondoist Chongu Party
Leadership. Ryu Mi Yong (chair)

Descended from an anti-Japanese religious nationalist movement of the pre-war period, this party enjoyed a measure of independence until the Korean War, following which it became a subservient appendage of the ruling Korean Workers' Party within the Democratic Front for the Reunification of the Fatherland.

Democratic Front for the Reunification of the Fatherland (DFRF)
Leadership. Chong Du Hwan (chair)

The DFRF is an umbrella grouping comprising the dominant Korean Workers' Party and two minor political parties, together with several mass working people's organizations.

Korean Social Democratic Party (KSDP) Chosun Sahoeminjudang
Leadership. Kim Byong Sik (chair)

Founded as the Democratic Party in 1945, the KSDP initially attracted substantial middle-class and peasant support until its original leaders either fled to the south or were liquidated in 1946. Since then it has been under the effective control of the Korean Workers' Party within the Democratic Front for the Reunification of the Fatherland.

South Korea

Capital: Seoul   **Population:** 46,000,000 (1995E)

Liberated in 1945 from Japanese colonial rule, the south of the Korean peninsula was occupied by United States troops and the north by Soviet forces. In 1948 separate states were established on either side of the 38th parallel (the south becoming the Republic of Korea), each of which reflected the ideology of its respective super-power, and each of which claimed jurisdiction over the entire peninsula. In 1950 South Korea was invaded by the communist North, but was saved from defeat by a US-led United Nations military intervention. The Korean War was ended by an armistice in 1953, with the ceasefire line (which became the new de facto border) straddling the 38th parallel.

There were frequent constitutional revisions as South Korea evolved through five republics between 1948 and 1987, brief experiments with democracy being invariably undermined by military intervention in the political process. The Sixth Republic was proclaimed in February 1988, following a revision of the constitution the previous October in the face of massive popular unrest. Under the current constitution, executive power is held by the President who is popularly elected for a single five-year term and who governs with the assistance of an appointed State Council (Cabinet) led by a Prime Minister. Legislative authority rests with a unicameral National Assembly (*Kuk Hoe*), serving a four-year term. Of the 299 Assembly seats, 253 are filled by constituency-based direct election and 46 on the basis of proportional representation.

In legislative elections in March 1992 the ruling Democratic Liberal Party (DLP)—renamed the New Korea Party (NKP) in December 1995—narrowly lost its overall majority, while remaining the largest single party in the National Assembly. In the presidential poll in December 1992, Kim Young Sam of the DLP was elected as Roh Tae Woo's successor and was inaugurated in February 1993. Considerable party political realignment occurred both before and after the 1992 elections. In further legislative elections on April 11, 1996, the NKP again failed to win an overall majority, although its plurality of 139 seats out of 299 confirmed it in power.

Democratic Party (DP)

Minju Dang

Address. 51–5 Yonggang-dong, Mapo-ku, Seoul 121–070

Telephone. (#82–2) 711-2070

Fax. (#82–2) 711-3328

Leadership. Chang Chun Ik (secretary-general)

The Democratic Party was organized in early 1990, largely by dissident members of the Reunification Democratic Party who opposed absorption into the Democratic Liberal Party (later the New Korea Party). In September 1991 the DP was substantially expanded by merger with the Kim Dae Jung's New Democratic Party, although Kim subsequently withdrew from politics (until 1995) following his defeat by Kim Young Sam of the (then) DLP in the 1992 presidential election. Having emerged from the March 1992 legislative elections with 97 seats, the DP remained the main opposition party until September 1995, when a majority of DP Assembly members defected to the new National Congress for New Politics (launched by Kim Dae Jung on his return to the political stage).

National Congress for New Politics (NCNP)

Sae Jungchi Kukmin Hoiee

Address. c/o National Assembly, Seoul

Leadership. Kim Dae Jung (leader)

The NCNP was formally inaugurated in September 1995 following the return to politics of Kim Dae Jung, who had been a major opposition figure in the 1980s but had been defeated in the 1992 presidential election. His new party attracted a sufficient number of defecting Democratic Party deputies to make it the largest opposition group in the National Assembly. In the April 1996 legislative elections, however, it failed to achieve its target of at least 100 seats, winning only 79 and thus remaining in opposition.

New Korea Party (NKP)

Address. 14–8 Yoido-dong, Yongdeungpo-ku, Seoul 150–010

Telephone. (#82–2) 783 9811

Fax. (#82–2) 780 5920

Leadership. Kim Young Sam (president), Lee Hong Koo (chair)

Formerly the Democratic Liberal Party (DLP), the ruling NKP assumed its current name at the end of 1995. The party had been launched as the DLP in 1990 by the merger of (then) President Roh Tae Woo's Democratic Justice Party with two groups previously in opposition – Kim Jong Pil's New Democratic Republican Party and Kim Young Sam's Reunification Democratic Party. Upon its formation the DLP controlled over two-thirds of the 299 seats in the National Assembly. However, in the March 1992 legislative elections the party's fortunes declined to one seat less than a majority. In August 1992 Roh Tae Woo resigned the party leadership in favour of Kim Young Sam who, as the DLP candidate, narrowly won the presidential election the following December with about 42 per cent of the vote. In early 1995, after a dispute with President Kim, Kim Jong Pil resigned as DLP chair and then left the party, subsequently forming the United Liberal Democratic Party. The DLP's fortunes sank further in June 1995 when it was severely defeated in local elections, losing in 10 of the 15 key metropolitan and provincial centres.

The party's change of name in December 1995 was seen as an attempt to signal a clear break with the legacy of corruption that had enveloped former senior party figures. The move yielded some benefit in the April 1996 legislative elections, in which the party again failed to win an overall majority but nevertheless consolidated its position as substantially the largest party, with 139 seats in its own right. The following month an NKP convention elected former Prime Minister Lee Hong Koo as party chair on the proposal of President Kim, his elevation signalling the importance placed by the government on the goal of Korean reunification, seen as essential if the country was to become one of the world's leading powers in the 21st century. Shortly after the convention the NKP acquired a legislative majority (of 150 seats) as a result of defections from other parties and the adhesion of independents.

United Liberal Democrats (ULD)
Jayu Minju Yonmaeng
   Address. c/o National Assembly, Seoul
   Leadership. Kim Jong Pil (leader)

The conservative ULD was established in March 1995 by Kim Jong Pil and other defectors from the ruling Democratic Liberal Party (renamed the New Korea Party in December 1995). In May it effectively absorbed the small New People's Party.

Kuwait

Capital: Kuwait City   **Population:** 1,700,000 (1994E)

Kuwait is an hereditary monarchy. It is governed by the Amir, who is chosen by and from the royal family. He appoints the Prime Minister and the Council of Ministers. The 1962 constitution provides for an elected legislature. However, following the dissolution of the National Assembly in 1986, the Amir ruled by decree without reference to any legislative body until 1990, when a National Council (partly elected and partly appointed) was created. This body was superseded in 1992 by a new National Assembly (*Majlis al-Umma*) consisting of 50 members elected by direct (but restricted) adult male suffrage and 25 appointed by the Amir. Elections to the Assembly were held on Oct. 5, 1992, on a non-party basis. No political parties as such have been formed in Kuwait, although a number of political "tendencies" have been permitted to function since the 1992 elections.

Constitutional Alliance, a moderate pro-market grouping supported by the merchant class.

Islamic Constitutional Movement, a moderate, Sunni Muslim organization led by Ismael al-Shatti; several members won seats in the 1992 National Assembly elections.

Islamic Popular Group, also Sunni Muslim, but smaller and more conservative than the Islamic Constitutional Movement.

Kuwait Democratic Forum, a secular, liberal grouping, several of whose members were elected to the National Assembly in 1992; led by Abdallah Nibari. The KDF was instrumental in the growth of the pro-democracy movement following the end of the Gulf crisis in 1991.

National Islamic Coalition, representing Kuwait's Shia Muslims.

Salafeen, an Islamic fundamentalist organization.

Kyrgyzstan

Capital: Bishkek   **Population:** 4,700,000 (1995E)

Having been a constituent republic of the USSR since December 1936, the independent Republic of Kyrgyzstan was proclaimed in December 1990 and became a sovereign member of the Commonwealth of Independent States later the same month. Under the post-Soviet constitution of May 1993, as amended significantly by referendum in February 1996, the President is popularly elected for a five-year term and appoints and dismisses the Prime Minister (subject to parliamentary endorsement). The Soviet-era unicameral legislature was replaced in 1995 by a bicameral Supreme Council (*Zhorgorku Kenesh*), consisting of the 70–member Assembly of People's Representatives as the upper house and a 35–member Legislative Assembly as representing the people as a whole, both also elected for five-year terms.

Elections to both houses on Feb. 5 and 19, 1995, were contested by over 1,000 candidates from 12 parties, a total of 29 lower house seats being filled, with pro-government candidates reportedly predominating. In a presidential election on Dec. 24, 1995, Askar Akayev was re-elected for a second a five-year term with around 72% of the vote.

Democratic Movement of Kyrgyzstan
Demokraticheskaya Dvizhenie Kyrgystana (DDK)
    Address. c/o Zhorgorku Kenesh, Bishkek
    Leadership. Zh. Zheksheyev (chair)

Founded in May 1990, the DDK served as an umbrella for a number of pro-democracy and pro-independence groups, including the Mutual Help Movement (*Ashar*), Truth (*Aqi*) and the Osh Region Union (*Osh Aymaghi*). Following Kazakhstan's declaration of independence from the Soviet Union in December 1990, several components broke away to launch independent formations, leaving the rump DDK with a more nationalist identity. The DDK backed the election of Askar Akayev to the presidency in October 1991, but later withdrew its support because it opposed his policies of equal rights for all ethnic groups. It formally constituted itself as a political party in June 1993.

Democratic Party of Free Kyrgyzstan
Demokraticheskaya Partiya Erkin Kyrgyzstan (ErK)
    Address. c/o Zhorgorku Kenesh, Bishkek
    Leadership. Topchubek Turganaliyev (chair)

The ErK (an acronym meaning "Will") was founded in 1991 as a splinter group of the DDK on a platform of moderate nationalism and support for a liberal market economy. It was weakened in 1992 by the secession of the more nationalist Fatherland group, after which its attempts to build a pro-democracy alliance made little progress.

National Unity Democratic Movement
Demokraticheskaya Dvizhenie Narodnoye Edinstvo (DDNE)
    Address. c/o Zhorgorku Kenesh, Bishkek
    Leadership. Yury Razgulyayev (chair)

The DDNE was launched in October 1991, in the aftermath of Kyrgyz/Uzbek inter-ethnic strife, principally on the initiative of then Vice-President German Kuznetsov, who returned to his native Russia in July 1993. Advocating co-operation between ethnic groups and a mixed economy, the party won representation in the February 1995 general elections.

Party of Communists of Kyrgyzstan
Partiya Kommunistov Kyrgyzstana (PKK)
    Address. c/o Zhorgorku Kenesh, Bishkek
    Leadership. Absamat Masaliyev (first secretary)

The PKK was launched in June 1992 as the successor to the former ruling Kyrgyz Communist Party, which had been disbanded in August 1991. Registered in September 1992, the PKK attracted significant support and won representation in the February 1995 general elections.

Social Democratic Party of Kyrgyzstan
Partiya Sotsial-demokraticheskaya Kyrgyzstana (PSDK)
    Address. c/o Zhorgorku Kenesh, Bishkek
    Leadership. Zh. Ibramov, A. Atambayev and A. Maryshev (joint chairs)

The PSDK was launched in July 1993 with the political endorsement of President Akayev. Supporting the government's reformist, pro-market line, it won representation in the February 1995 legislative elections.

Other Parties

Accord Slavic Association (*Soglasiye*), an ethnic Russian formation, led by Anatoly Bulgakov and Anatoly Sorokin.

Agrarian Labour Party, led by Usun Sadykov, founded in June 1995 to represent agro-industrial workers.

Agrarian Party of Kyrgyzstan, led by A. Aliyev, founded in 1993 and generally supportive of land privatization although opposing the government's land reform programme as "unviable".

Banner National Revival Party (*Partiya Natsionalnovo Vozrozhdeniya Asaba*), named after a Kyrgyz military banner and launched in November 1991 by a nationalist faction of the Democratic Movement of Kyrgyzstan, led by Ch. Bazarbayev and Asan Ormushev.

Ecological Movement of Kyrgyzstan, led by T. Chodurayev.

Fatherland (*Alta-Mekel*), led by Omurbek Tekebayev, founded in 1992 by a Kyrgyz nationalist faction of the Democratic Party of Free Kyrgyzstan.

Republican Popular Party of Kyrgyzstan, founded in May 1993 by scientists and academics under the leadership of Zh. Sharshenaliyev

Unity Party of Kyrgyzstan, led by A. Muraliyev.

Uzbek Justice (*Uzbek Adalet*), based in the Uzbek-populated Osh region.

Laos

Capital: Vientiane   **Population:** 4,900,000 (1995E)

The Lao People's Democratic Republic (LPDR) was proclaimed in 1975 following military victory by the communist Lao Patriotic Front in a 25–year civil war. A President, Council of Ministers and Supreme People's Assembly (SPA) were installed, but effective political power has since been exercised by the leadership of the sole legal political organization, the Lao People's Revolutionary Party (LPRP). The LPDR's first constitution was unanimously endorsed by the SPA in August 1991. Under its terms the LPRP is defined as the "leading nucleus" of the political system. The President (the head of state) is elected by the National Assembly for a five-year term. Members of the National Assembly are elected for a period of five years by universal adult suffrage. The Prime Minister and Council of Ministers are appointed by the President with the approval of the National Assembly (also for a five-year tenure).

Nouhak Phoumsavan was elected as state President at a special session of the SPA held in November 1992 following the death of the previous President, Kaysone Phomvihane. A general election to the new 85–member National Assembly (created as a replacement for the SPA as laid down in the 1991 constitution) was held on Dec. 20, 1992. All candidates were approved by the Lao Front for National Construction, an umbrella organization of various political and social groups which had succeeded the Lao Patriotic Front in 1979. The LPRP remained the dominant force in the new Front, which was charged, like its predecessor, with promoting national solidarity and socialist economic development.

Lao People's Revolutionary Party (LPRP)
Address. c/o National Assembly, Vientiane

Leadership. Gen. Khamtay Siphandone (president)

Founded in 1955 as the Lao People's Party, the communist LPRP assumed its present name in 1972. It was the leading force in the Lao Patriotic Front, whose military victory in the civil war heralded the establishment of the Lao People's Democratic Republic in 1975. The LPRP has since maintained its political supremacy, although in the mid-1980s it initiated a programme of economic restructuring and reform.

Dissident Groups

Ethnics Liberation Organization of Laos, led by Pa Kao Her.

Free Democratic Lao National Salvation Force, which has been active in the north-east of the country.

United Front for the Liberation of Laos, led by Phoungphet Phanareth.

United Lao National Liberation Front, a coalition of mainly rightist and tribal groups led by Vang Shur.

Latvia

Capital: Riga

Population: 2,500,000 (1995E)

Independent from 1920, Latvia was effectively annexed by the Soviet Union in August 1940 but repudiated its Soviet status in May 1990 and gained Soviet endorsement of its resumption of sovereignty in September 1991 as the Republic of Latvia. Reactivated in 1990, Latvia's 1922 constitution was fully restored in 1993, confirming the Republic as a parliamentary democracy in which the sovereign power of the people is exercised through a directly-elected unicameral Parliament (*Saeima*). The head of state is the President, who is elected for a four-year term by the *Saeima*, an absolute majority of the total complement of 100 deputies being required. The appointment and continuance in office of the Prime Minister and other ministers is also subject to the *Saeima*'s consent. Members of the *Saeima* are elected from five electoral districts for a three-year term by universal, equal, direct and secret suffrage of those aged 18 and over, on the basis of proportional representation but subject to at least 5% of the vote being obtained.

Elections to the *Saeima* on Sept. 30–Oct. 1, 1995, resulted as follows: Master Democratic Party 18 seats (with 15.1% of the vote), Latvia's Way Union 17 (14.6%), Popular Movement for Latvia-Zigerists Party 16 (14.9%), Fatherland and Freedom Union 14 (11.9%), Latvian Farmers' Union 8 (6.3%), Latvian Unity Party 8 (7.1%), Latvian National Conservative Party 8 (6.3%), National Harmony Party 6 (5.6%), Latvian Socialist Party 5 (5.6%).

Fatherland and Freedom Union
Apvieniba Tevzemei un Brvibai (TUB)
   Address. 10 Kaleju iela, Riga 1050
   Telephone. (#371–7) 325041
   Fax. (#371–7) 229575
   Leadership. Maris Grinblats (chair), Janis Straume (chair of *Saeima* group)
   The TUB is an alliance of several groups of the far right, reportedly in contact with right-wing extremists in Germany. It is also viewed as having been the party of the Waffen SS at the time of the German occupation during World War II. The TUB won 5.4% of the vote and six seats in 1993, this tally rising to 11.9% and 14 seats in the 1995 elections. It thus became the strongest single party within the National Bloc alliance of conservative parties founded in September 1994. After TUB leader Grinblats had tried and failed to build a viable coalition government, the TUB joined a broad centre-right coalition headed by a non-party Prime Minister, with party leader Grinblats becoming a Deputy Prime Minister and Education Minister.

Latvian Christian Democratic Union
Latvijas Kristigo Demokratu Savieniba (LKDS)
   Address. 28 Jekaba iela, Riga 1811
   Telephone. (#371–7) 323534
   Fax. (#371–7) 830333

   Leadership. Paulis Kalviņš (chair)
   Founded in March 1991 and descended from pre-war parties of similar orientation that had substantial parliamentary representation, the LKDS is a Catholic group which has received strong support from the local religious establishment. Having won six seats and 5% of the vote in 1993, the LKDS was allied with the Latvian Farmers' Union in the autumn 1995 elections, in which the alliance took eight seats and 6.3% of the vote. An LKDS representative obtained a junior ministerial post in the subsequent centre-right coalition government.
   The LKDS is affiliated to the Christian Democrat International.

Latvian Farmers' Union
Latvijas Zemnieku Savieniba (LZS)
   Address. 2 Republikas laukums, Riga 1010
   Telephone. (#371–7) 327163
   Leadership. Andris Rozentals (chair), Pauls Putniņš (chair of *Saeima* group)
   The LZS is the modern descendant of a similarly-named organization founded in 1917 and prominent in the inter-war period until banned in 1934. As suggested by its name, it is primarily devoted to defending rural interests taking a somewhat conservative position on the nationality issue. The party won 12 seats in the

June 1993 general elections (with 10.6% of the vote), following which Guntis Ulmanis (a former chairman of the Latvian Supreme Soviet) was the successful LZS candidate in the July parliamentary election of a new President of Latvia. Having in September 1994 joined the National Bloc of opposition parties, for the autumn 1995 elections the LZS entered into alliance with the Latvian Christian Democratic Union and the Democratic Party of Latgale, winning eight seats on a 6.3% vote share. It subsequently joined a broad centre-right coalition government under a non-party Prime Minister but dominated by the Master Democratic Party. In June 1996 Ulmanis was re-elected President with the backing of most of the coalition parties.

Latvian Green Party
Latvijas Zala Partija (LZP)
   Address. c/o Saeima, 11 Jekaba iela, Riga 1811
   Leadership. Olegs Batarevskis, Peteris Jansons and Juris Zvirgzds (co-chairs)
   Founded in 1990, the LZP endorsed a Green List at the 1993 election, which captured only 1.2% of the vote. Despite his party's lack of parliamentary representation, an LZP member was named Minister of State for the Environment in the government headed by the Latvia's Way Union. The Greens also obtained representation at junior ministerial level in the broad centre-right coalition government formed after the 1995 elections, which it had contested in alliance with the Latvian National Conservative Party.

Latvian National Conservative Party
Latvijas Nacionala Konservativa Partija (LNNK)
   Address. 23 Elizabetes, Riga 1050
   Telephone. (#371–7) 320436
   Fax. (#371–7) 320451
   Leadership. Andrejs Krastiņš (chair), Aleksandrs Kiršteins (chair of *Saeima* group)
   The former Latvian National Independence Movement (*Latvijas Nacionala Neatkaribas Kustiba*, LNNK), launched in 1988, adopted its present name in June 1994, but retained the familiar LNNK abbreviation. Ultra-nationalist and anti-Russian, the party advocates that welfare benefits should be limited to ethnic Latvians and that no more than 25% of non-Latvians should be accorded Latvian citizenship. It also favours Latvian membership of the European Union. In the 1993 general elections the party won 15 seats on a 13.6% vote share; but its image was tarnished by association with the campaign rhetoric of a far-right party member of German origin, Joahims Zigerists, who was later expelled from the LNNK and formed the Popular Movement for

Latvia-Zigerists Party. On the President's invitation, Andrejs Krastiņš (then the party's associate chair) attempted to form a right-wing government in August 1994, but was rebuffed by the *Saiema*.
   The LNNK was a member of the opposition National Bloc launched in September 1994. However, for the autumn 1995 parliamentary elections it formed an unlikely alliance with the Latvian Green Party, winning eight seats on a 6.3% vote share. It subsequently joined a broad centre-right coalition government under a non-party Prime Minister but dominated by the Master Democratic Party, in which Krastiņš (by now LNNK chair) became a Deputy Prime Minister and Defence Minister.

Latvian Socialist Party
Latvijas Socialistiska Partija (LSP)
   Address. c/o Saeima, 11 Jekaba iela, Riga 1811
   Leadership. Sergejs Dimanis (chair), Alfreds Rubiks (former chair)
   The LSP was created in 1995 as successor to the Equal Rights Party (commonly known as Equality), which had been founded in 1993 to represent the interests of the non-Latvian population and had advocated the adoption of Russian as Latvia's second official language. At the time of the June 1993 general elections (in which it won seven seats on a 5.8% vote share), the party's most prominent figure, Alfreds Rubiks, was in prison awaiting trial for supporting the abortive August 1991 coup by hardliners in Moscow (and his credentials as an elected deputy were rejected by the new *Saiema*. In July 1995 Rubiks was sentenced to eight years' imprisonment for conspiring to overthrow the government in 1991. He was nevertheless placed at the head of the candidates' list of the new LSP for the autumn 1995 elections, in which the party won five seats on a 5.6% vote share. Still in prison, Rubiks was a candidate in the June 1996 *Saeima* elections for a new President, receiving five votes.

Latvian Unity Party
Latvijas Vienibas Partija (LVP)
   Address. c/o Saeima, 11 Kekaba iela, Riga 1811
   Leadership. Alberis Kauls (chair), Roberts Dilba (deputy chair), Edgar Bans (chair of *Saeima* group)
   The LVP was established in 1994 by a group of orthodox Communists opposed to rapid economic and social change, inclining to a populist mode of propagating its theses. Its 7.1% and eight seats in the 1995 parliamentary elections gave it a pivotal role in the formation of a broadly conservative coalition dominated by the Master Democratic Party. Appointed a Deputy Prime Minister and Agriculture Minister, LVP leader Alberis Kauls lasted only eight months in the government, being

forced to resign in May 1996 over his persistent criticism of the coalition agricultural policy. But the party continued in the government, with deputy leader Roberts Dilba replacing Kauls.

Latvia's Way Union

Savieniba Latvijas Cels (SLC)
    Address. 4–9 Terbatas, Riga 1011
    Telephone. (#371–7) 224162
    Fax. (#371–7) 821121
    Leadership. Valdis Birkavs (chair), Andrejs Pantelejevs (chair of *Saeima* group)

The SLC originated as a loose grouping of well-known personalities, sponsored by the World Federation of Free Latvians and the influential Club 21 network, who came together prior to the 1993 parliamentary elections. Although evincing a centre-right political stance and a liberal-conservative socio-economic approach, the party has been viewed by many Latvians as rooted in the ways of the Soviet era because of the earlier careers of many of its leading members. Nevertheless, its pivotal parliamentary position enabled it to lead successive post-independence coalition governments, its 32.4% vote share in 1993 making it the largest party in the *Saeima*, with 36 seats. Paying the democratic penalty for government incumbency in difficult times, it slumped to 17 seats and 14.6% in the 1995 elections, although it continued in government in a broad centre-right coalition in which the Master Democratic Party had the dominant position, with Maris Gailis of the SLC becoming a Deputy Prime Minister and Environment and Regional Development Minister.

The SLC is an observer member of the Liberal International.

Master Democratic Party

Demokratiska Partija Saimnieks (DPS)
    Address. 9 Valnu iela, Riga 1050
    Telephone. (#371–7) 216754
    Leadership. Ziedonis Cevers (chair), Ivars Kezbers (chair of *Saeima* group)

The DPS is descended from the pre-war Democratic Centre Party (*Demokratiska Centra Partija*, DCP), which was relaunched in 1992 and won five seats on a 4.8% vote share in 1993. It subsequently became simply the Democratic Party before merging with another group in 1994 under the *Saimnieks* label, a Latvian term denoting a traditional source of authority (sometimes rendered in English as "In Charge"). Taking a pro-market position on economic issues and exhibiting a moderate national policy orientation, *Saimnieks* was initially linked with the Political Union of Economists for the 1995 general elections but later opted to present candidates independently. Having become the largest single

party with 15.1% of the vote and 19 seats, it sought to form a coalition including the far-right Popular Movement for Latvia–Zigerists Party, but presidential opposition thwarted the plan. It settled for participation, as the strongest party, in a broad centre-right coalition headed by a non-party Prime Minister.

Subsequent tensions between *Saimnieks* and its coalition partners were apparent in the party's decision to nominate Ilga Kreituse (DPS Speaker of the *Saeima*) as its presidential candidate, in opposition to incumbent Guntis Ulmanis of the Latvian Farmers' Union. In the parliamentary voting in June 1996 she was runner-up with 25 votes. The following month *Saimnieks* was strengthened by an agreement that it would absorb the small Republican Party (led by Andris Plotnieks) and by the decision of two deputies of the National Harmony Party to defect into its ranks.

National Harmony Party

Tautas Saskanas Partija (TSP)
    Address. 60 Lačpleša iela, Riga 1010
    Telephone (#371–7) 289913
    Fax. (#371–7) 281619
    Leadership. Janis Jurkans (chair)

The TSP consists of the residue of the Harmony for Latvia–Rebirth (*Saskaņa Latvijai–Atdzimana*) grouping following the split in 1994 which led to the creation of the Political Union of Economists. It won six seats on a 5.6% vote share in the autumn 1995 elections, on a platform advocating harmony between Latvians and non-Latvians with guaranteed rights for minorities. In July 1996 the TSP *Saeima* contingent was reduced to four (one below the number required for official recognition as a group) by the decision of two members to join the Master Democratic Party.

Political Union of Economists

Tautsaimnieku Politiska Apvieniba (TPA)
    Address. 13 Jauniela, Riga 1970
    Telephone. (#371–7) 213859
    Leadership. Edvins Kide (chair)

The TPA was launched in March 1994 by four of the 13 *Saeima* delegates elected in 1993 by the Harmony for Latvia–Rebirth (the rump of which became the National Harmony Party). In distinct contrast to right-wing parties such as the Latvian National Conservative Party, Harmony had called for the coexistence of Latvians and non-Latvians, with entrenched rights for minority groups. In September 1994 it joined a coalition government headed by the Latvia's Way Union. For the autumn 1995 general elections the TPA considered an alliance with the Master Democratic Party, but eventually opted to stand independently and failed to win a seat.

Popular Movement for Latvia–Zigerists
Party Tautas Kustiba Latvijai–Zigerists Partija (TKL-ZP)
Address. c/o Saeima, 11 Jekaba iela, Riga 1811
Leadership. Joahims Zigerists (chair)

The radical right-wing TKL-ZP, commonly referred to as *Latvijai*, was founded in 1995 by Joahims Zigerists, who had been elected to the *Saeima* in 1993 as a candidate of the Latvian National Conservative Party (LNNK) but had later been expelled from the LNNK after a court conviction in Germany for incitement to racial hatred. Zigerists had been born and brought up in Germany (as Joachim Siegerist) but claimed Latvian nationality through his father, an ethnic German who had fled from Latvia as the Red Army approached at the end of World War II. In August 1995 Zigerists was expelled from the *Saeima* for poor attendance and was also barred from standing in the autumn 1995 general elections because of his inability to speak much Latvian. His party nevertheless took an impressive third place, winning 14.9% of the vote and 16 *Saeima* seats. A post-election move by the Master Democratic Party to draw the TKL-ZP into a government coalition was successfully resisted by President Ulmanis.

In *Saeima* elections for the state presidency in June 1996, the TKL-ZP candidate, Imants Liepa, took third place with 14 votes. In the same month the TKL-ZP parliamentary group was weakened by the departure of six deputies on the grounds that the party had become "undemocratic".

Other Parties

Christian People's Party (*Kristigo Tautas Partija*, KTP), led by Uldis Augstkalns, formed in February 1996 as successor to the residue of the Latvian Popular Front (*Latvijas Tautas Fronte*, LTF), which had led Latvia's independence campaign but had failed to win seats in the 1993 and 1995 elections.

Labour and Justice Coalition (*Koalcija Darbs un Taisngums*, KDT), formed for the 1995 parliamentary elections.

Latvian Liberal Party (*Latvijas Liberala Partija*, LLP).

Latvian National Democratic Party (*Latvijas Nacionali Demokratiska Partija*, LNDP).

Latvian Social Democratic Party (*Latvijas Social-Demokratiska Partija*, LSDP), led by Juris Bojars, founded in 1995 as successor to the Latvian Democratic Labour Party, itself formed in 1990 by a dissident minority of the former ruling Latvian Communist Party.

Latvian Social Democratic Workers' Party (*Latvijas Socialdemokratiska Stradnieku Partija*, LSDSP), led by Janis Dinevics and affiliated to the Socialist International, had been Latvia's leading party in the 1920s, but won under 1% of the vote in 1993 and failed to make a breakthrough in 1995.

Latvians' Independence Party (*Latvieu Neatkarbas Partija*, LNP), contested 1995 elections in alliance with the Political Union of the Disadvantaged (*Maznodroinato Politiska Apvieniba*, MPA).

Party of Our Land (*Partija Musu Zeme*, PMZ), contested 1995 elections in alliance with the Anti-Communist Society (*Pretkomunistu Apvieniba*, PA).

Russian Citizens of Latvia Party (*Latvijas Krievu Pilsonu Partija*, LKPP).

Lebanon

Capital: Beirut

Population: 3,000,000 (1995E)

The Republic of Lebanon became fully independent from France in 1944. A "National Covenant", agreed in 1943, determined that power should be allocated between the country's main religious communities on the basis of their relative numerical strength according to a 1932 census. The President is by convention a Maronite Christian, the Prime Minister a Sunni Muslim and the Speaker of the (unicameral) National Assembly (*Majlis al-Umma/Assemblée Nationale*) a Shia Muslim. Between 1975 and 1990 civil war conditions prevailed in Lebanon with varying degrees of intensity. Rooted in traditional inter-communal rivalries and exacerbated by foreign political and military interventions, the conflict undermined central government authority and enhanced the power of contending militias and paramilitary factions.

Constitutional amendments approved in September 1990—in the framework of the 1989 Taif Accord on the restoration of civil peace—upgraded the executive powers of the Prime Minister and the Cabinet and reduced the powers of the President. The reforms also provided for an increase in the number of seats in the National Assembly, to achieve equal representation of the Christian and Muslim communities (rather than the previous ratio of 6:5 in favour of the Christians).

The subsequent gradual return of relative peace to most of Lebanon, with a strong Syrian military presence and the disarming of militia groups, created conditions under which general elections could be held for the first time in 20 years. Voting for the 128–member Assembly was conducted in stages between August and October 1992, although many Christians refused to participate. The elections resulted in 34 seats being won by Maronite Christian representatives, 27 by Sunni Muslims and 27 by Shia Muslims, these communal identifiers being more important than party attribution. The rest of the seats were shared among smaller religious denominations. The President of the Republic, Elias Hrawi, was elected for a six-year term by the National Assembly in November 1989.

Amal

Leadership. Nabi Berri

Amal ("Hope") was founded by Imam Musa Sadr, an Iranian. Although a part of the Muslim leftist and Palestinian alliance in the post-1975 civil war, *Amal* subsequently became increasingly militant on behalf of Lebanon's Shia Muslims, clashing during the 1980s with pro-Palestinian Muslims, the Palestinians themselves, and the Christian right. At the same time, the leadership aligned itself with Syria. Nabi Berri was reconfirmed as Amal leader at a congress in February 1992. In October 1992, following the legislative elections in which Amal made an impressive showing in the south of the country, he was elected as Speaker of the National Assembly.

Baath Arab Socialist Party

Hizb al-Baath al-Arabi al-Ishtiraki

Leadership. Abd al-Majid Rafii (secretary-general of pro-Iraqi wing); Abdullah al-Amin (secretary-general of pro-Syrian wing)

Originally established as the Lebanese regional command of the pan-Arab Baath, the Lebanese branch became divided into competing pro-Iraqi and pro-Syrian factions, and has not attained the degree of influence exercised by the party in Iraq or Syria. In the post-1975 civil war and its aftermath the party formed part of the left-wing National Movement, which sought constitutional changes to the advantage of the Muslim community, and in 1984 was a founder member of a new Muslim leftist National Democratic Front. The pro-Syrian wing has maintained dominance over the pro-Iraqi element on the strength of backing from Syrian forces stationed in Lebanon.

Lebanese Communist Party

Hizb al-Shuyui al-Lubnani
Parti Communiste Libanais

Address. POB 633, rue al-Hout, Beirut

Leadership. Faruq Dahruj (secretary-general)

The Lebanese Communist Party dates from 1924 but was legalized only in 1970. Primarily Christian during the first 50 years of its existence (drawing support from the Greek Orthodox community in particular), the party participated in leftist Muslim fronts in the post-1975 civil war, although it has come into conflict with the Shia *Amal* movement. The party's long-time secretary-general, George Hawi, resigned in 1992 and was succeeded by his deputy, Faruq Dahruj.

National Bloc

Kutla al-Wataniyah
Bloc National

Address. rue Pasteur, Gemmayze, Beirut

Telephone. (#961–1) 584585

Fax. (#961–1) 584591

Leadership. Raymond Eddé

A right-wing Maronite Christian party set up in 1943, the National Bloc has opposed any basic changes in the country's traditional power structure. It also advocates the exclusion of the military from politics.

National Liberal Party

Hizb al-Ahrar al-Watani
Parti National Libéral (PNL)

Address. rue du Liban, Beirut

Leadership. Dory Chamoun

Founded in 1958 by Camille Chamoun at the end of his term as President of Lebanon, the PNL lost ascendancy among Maronite Christians to its

Phalangist Party rivals in the late 1970s. Having assumed the party leadership from his father in the mid-1980s, Dany Chamoun was assassinated in 1990 (for which murder the then Phalangist militia leader was convicted in June 1995). He was succeeded by his brother, Dory, in May 1991. The party has pressed for the withdrawal of Syrian forces from the country and has argued in recent years that a federal system is the only way to preserve a single Lebanese state.

Party of God
Hizb Allah

Leadership. Sheikh Hassan Nasrallah (secretary-general)

Hizb Allah (or Hezbollah)—a militant, pro-Iranian Shia Muslim group—emerged after 1982 as an anti-Israeli and anti-Western movement, involved in numerous kidnappings and other violence. Its continuing pursuit of confrontation with Israel provoked a cross-border strike by Israeli forces in February 1992 in which the group's former secretary-general, Sheikh Abba Musawi, was killed. The organization participated for the first time as an electoral party in the 1992 elections, contributing, with *Amal*, to the significant Shia representation in the National Assembly.

Phalangist Party
Kata'eb
Phalanges Libanaises

Address. POB 992, place Charles Hélou, Beirut
Telephone. (#961–1) 338230
Leadership. Georges Saade (president)

The Phalangist Party, a right-wing Maronite Christian organization, was founded in 1936 by Pierre Gemayel, who remained its dominant figure until his death in 1984. Gemayel was succeeded as party leader by his vice-president, Elie Karameh, who was himself replaced by the present leader in 1986. From the early 1970s the party took the lead among Christian organizations in building up militia forces to counter the growing strength and militancy of Lebanese Muslim leftists and Palestinian groups. Phalangists spearheaded the Christian side in clashes leading to the outbreak of civil war in 1975 and, following subsequent rivalry with the National Liberal Party (PLN), emerged at the end of the decade as the dominant Christian formation.

Georges Saade played an important role in the negotiations leading to the Taif Accord on national reconciliation in 1989, although the party supported the boycott of the 1992 elections observed by many Maronite Christians, principally on the grounds that a Syrian troop withdrawal from Lebanon should precede such a poll. In March 1994 the government proscribed the Phalangist militia, the Lebanese Forces, led by Samir Geagea. The latter was arrested the following month in connection with the assassination in 1990 of Dany Chamoun, leader of the PLN, and eventually sentenced to life imprisonment in June 1995.

Progressive Socialist Party (PSP)
Hizb al-Taqaddumi al-Ishtiraki
Parti Socialiste Progressiste (PSP)

Address. POB 14-5287, Beirut
Telephone. (#961-1) 861758
Fax. (#961-1) 312336
Leadership. Walid Jumblatt (president), Sharif Fayad (general secretary)

Founded in 1949 and a member of the Socialist International, the PSP is a largely Druze (Muslim) group advocating democratic socialism. Following the outbreak of civil war in 1975, the PSP initiated the creation of the National Movement of Muslim leftists and Palestinians against the Phalangists and other right-wing Christian formations. Walid Jumblatt assumed the leadership on the assassination of his father Kamal in 1977. The PSP fought against the Israeli invasions of 1978 and 1982, then consolidated its own control of the Chouf mountains, the heartland of the Druze sect, while participating in a series of opposition fronts. It also became increasingly hostile to the Shia *Amal* movement, with which PSP forces engaged in heavy fighting in 1987.

The PSP participated in the 1992 National Assembly elections (in which Druze candidates achieved eight seats), its leader continuing to be a member of the government.

Other Groupings

Arab Democratic Party, a pro-Syrian Alawite group based in Tripoli.

Arab Nationalist Movement (*Haraka al-Qawmiyya al-Arabiyya*), an Arab nationalist organization with Marxist tendencies, established in 1948 by militant Palestinian leader Georges Habash.

Armenian Revolutionary Federation (*Parti Tachnag*), founded in 1890 and socialist in ideology, principal representative of the Armenian community in Lebanon.

Constitutional Party (*Dustur*), a business-oriented party, which played a leading part in the struggle against the French mandate and in drafting the 1943 National Covenant; led by Michel Bechara al-Khouri.

Democratic Party (*Parti Démocrate*, PD), a secular group, formed in 1969, and led by Emile Bitar, strongly supportive of private enterprise.

Independent Nasserite Movement (*Murabitun*), founded in 1958 as a socialist party and the largest of extant Nasserite groups in Lebanon; led by Ibrahim Qulayat, it draws its main support from among the Sunni Muslim community.

Islamic Unification Movement, a Sunni Muslim group formed in 1982, led by Sheikh Said Shaban.

Lebanese Christian Democratic Union (*Union Chrétienne Démocrate Libanaise*, UCDL), a member party of the Christian Democrat International, led by George Jabre.

Organization of Communist Action in Lebanon (*Organisation de l'Action Communiste du Liban*, OCAL), founded in 1970 by the merger of two left-wing groups, led by Muhsin Ibrahim.

Parliamentary Democratic Front (*Jabha al-Dimuqratiyah al-Barlamaniyah*), mainly supported by Sunni Muslims, advocating maintenance of traditional power-sharing between Christians and Muslims.

Popular Nasserite Organization, absorbed the Arab Socialist Union in 1987.

Syrian Social National Party (*Parti Socialiste Nationaliste Syrien*, PSNS), organized in 1932 and banned between 1962 and 1969, led by Dawoud Baz, advocates a "greater Syria" embracing Lebanon, Syria, Iraq, Jordan and Palestine.

Union of Working People's Forces, a leftist party led by Kamal Shatila.

Waad Party, formed in 1991 by members of the Lebanese Forces Maronite militia and led by Elie Hobeika.

Lesotho

Capital: Maseru   **Population:** 2,000,000 (1995E)

The Kingdom of Lesotho became an independent hereditary monarchy in 1966. Between 1970, when the constitution was suspended, and the beginning of 1986 the country was ruled by a Council of Ministers headed by Chief Leabua Jonathan, and the power of the King was considerably eroded. In January 1986 the armed forces staged a bloodless coup, executive and legislative powers being conferred upon the King, although a Military Council became the effective ruling body. In March 1986 all political activity was banned. In March 1990 the chairman of the Military Council removed executive and legislative powers from King Moshoeshoe II, who went into exile. His son, Letsie III, was elected as King by an assembly of chiefs.

Following changes in the military leadership in April 1991 a new constitution was instituted, providing for the re-establishment of a bicameral parliament consisting of a directly-elected 65–member National Assembly and a Senate made up of chiefs and nominated members. Executive power is vested in the Prime Minister, as leader of the majority parliamentary party, and the Cabinet appointed by the Prime Minister. In multi-party elections held in March 1993 the Basotho Congress Party (BCP) won all the seats in the National Assembly. The following month the BCP leader, Ntsu Mokhehle, was sworn in as Prime Minister and the Military Council was dissolved.

In August 1994 King Letsie III suspended the constitution, dissolving the National Assembly and dismissing the BCP government. He attempted to install a non-elected transitional council but, following the intervention of South Africa and other regional powers, then agreed to restore the elected government. Following Letsie's voluntary abdication, Moshoeshoe II was restored to the throne in January 1995 but was killed in a car accident in January 1996, Crown Prince Mohato being named as his successor.

Basotho Congress Party (BCP)

Address. POB 111, Maseru

Leadership. Ntsu Mokhehle (president)

The BCP was formed as a pan-Africanist and left-wing party in the early 1950s. Its refusal to co-operate with the government of Chief Jonathan following the suspension of the 1970 constitution led to a factional split. One wing of the party, led by Gerard Ramoreboli, accepted seats in an appointed interim National Assembly. The main branch, led from exile by Dr Mokhehle, continued to oppose the Jonathan regime, launching numerous armed attacks on pro-government targets, allegedly with South African support. Dr Mokhehle was allowed by the Military Council to return to Lesotho in the late 1980s. The BCP won a landslide victory in the multi-party elections in March 1993, securing all 65 seats in the National Assembly, and the military regime relinquished power to a civilian government headed by Dr Mokhehle.

Basotho National Party (BNP)

Address. POB 124, Maseru

Leadership. Retselisitsoe E. Sekhonyana (leader)

The BNP was founded in the late 1950s as the Basutoland National Party (changing its name at independence in 1966) by Chief Leabua Jonathan, who was Prime Minister from 1965 until the military coup in January 1986. During his premiership Chief Jonathan wrested executive control from the King, suspending the 1970 constitution and increasing his power over the country. Following the overthrow of the BNP government, supporters of Chief Jonathan (who died in 1987) were barred from political activity. With the legalization of political parties in May 1991, the BNP emerged as one of the leading parties. However, this was not reflected in the results of the March 1993 legislative polls, prompting BNP accusations of electoral malpractice by the Basotho Congress Party.

Other Parties

The large number of other registered parties in Lesotho include those listed below.

Basotho Democratic Alliance (BDA)

Address. Fairways Centre Building, POB 2239, Maseru

Leadership. S. C. Ncojane (president)

An anti-communist and pro-South African party, the BDA was established in 1984.

Communist Party of Lesotho (CPL)

Address. POB 441, Maseru

The CPL was set up in the early 1960s, operating legally until it was banned in 1970. This ban was only partially lifted in 1984, and not until 1992 did the party begin operating in the open. The CPL has drawn its support mainly from Basotho migrant workers in South Africa.

Democratic Movement for Reconstruction (DMR)

Address. POB 310, Roma, 180

Leadership. Khauta Khasu (leader)

The party was established in early 1992 by former prominent Basotho Congress Party figures.

Kopanang Basotho Party

Address. Lithoteng Private Centre, Maseru P/B 133

Leadership. Limakatso Ntakatsane (leader)

Launched in 1992, the party campaigns for women's rights, protesting against what it terms repressive and discriminatory laws against women in Lesotho.

Marematlou Freedom Party

Address. POB 65, Maseru 100

Leadership. Vincent Malebo (leader)

Founded in 1962, the party is conservative and royalist, promoting the extension of the authority of the King.

United Democratic Party (UDP)

Address. POB 776, Maseru 100

Leadership. Ben L. Shea (chairman), Charles Mofeli (leader)

The UDP was formed in 1967. In the 1980s the party favoured closer ties with South Africa and advocated the expulsion from Lesotho of all South African political refugees. Party leader Mofeli was a vocal critic of the government of Chief Jonathan and of the successor military regime.

Liberia

Capital: Monrovia

Population: 2,750,000 (1995E)

The Republic of Liberia, an independent state from 1847, was founded by freed black slaves from the United States of America. In September 1990 Gen. Samuel Kanyon Doe, who had seized power in a military coup in 1980 and had been elected President in 1985, was deposed and killed as rival rebel groups struggled with government forces for control. The Economic Community of West African States (ECOWAS), which had sent a peacekeeping force to Liberia in August 1990, backed the nomination of Amos Sawyer as Interim President, and in January 1991 an Interim Government of National Unity (IGNU) was appointed. Civil war, however, continued.

In July 1993 a UN-sponsored peace agreement was signed by the IGNU, the National Patriotic Front of Liberia (NPFL) and the United Liberation Movement for Democracy in Liberia (ULIMO). It provided for a ceasefire, the encampment of troops and the formation of a transitional civilian administration. A five-member Council of State and 35–member Transitional Legislative Assembly were installed in March 1994, while the National Transitional Government met for the first time two months later. As a result of further peace talks involving all the main factions, it was agreed in December 1994 that a new Council of State should be appointed which would hand over to an elected government on 1 January 1996 following multi-party elections in November 1995. However, negotiations on the composition of the Council were stalled until August 1995 when a new peace accord was brokered. In September the Council was inaugurated, a new 16–member transitional government was formed and elections were rescheduled for August 1996. The posts in the transitional government were shared among the organizations listed below, their cooperation becoming increasingly national as further heavy fighting erupted in Monrovia April 1996.

Armed Forces of Liberia (AFL)

Leadership. Gen. Hezekiah Bowen

The leader of the AFL was appointed as Minister of Defence in the transitional government announced in September 1995.

Central Revolutionary Council-NPFL

Leadership. Tom Woeweiyu

Formed in September 1994 by dissidents of the National Patriotic Front of Liberia (NPFL) who sought to depose Charles Taylor as leader, the organization is in coalition with the Liberia Peace Council and the Armed Forces of Liberia, with representation in the transitional government formed in September 1995.

Liberia Peace Council (LPC)

Leadership. George Boley (chair)

Formed in 1993, the LPC engaged in numerous clashes during the civil war with forces of the National Patriotic Front of Liberia (NPFL) in south-eastern Liberia. In coalition with the Central Revolutionary Council-NPFL and the Armed Forces of Liberia, the LPC is represented in the Council of State by its leader, George Boley, and holds posts in the transitional government.

Lofa Defence Force (LFD)

Leadership. François Massaquoi

This regional organization was formed in 1993, being based in the Lorma ethnic group.

National Patriotic Front of Liberia (NPFL)

Leadership. Charles Taylor

Heading the NPFL, former government minister Charles Taylor launched the armed rebellion that led to the collapse of the Doe regime in September 1990 and embroiled the country in protracted civil war. In September 1994 dissidents forming the Central Revolutionary Council-NPFL tried unsuccessfully to depose Taylor. Following the peace accord reached in August 1995, Taylor assumed a seat on the new six-member Council of State, and the NPFL was allocated the key portfolios of foreign affairs, interior and justice in the new transitional government formed in September 1995.

United Liberation Movement for Democracy in Liberia (ULIMO)
    Leadership. Alhaji G. Kromah
    ULIMO was formed by supporters of the Doe regime after the former President's death, and has been a major protagonist in the civil war. Alhaji G. Kromah represents ULIMO on the Council of State inaugurated in September 1995, and the organization's portfolios in the new transitional government include that of finance.

Libya

Capital: Tripoli

Population: 4,000,000 (1995E)

Libya became independent in 1951 under a monarchy which was subsequently overthrown in 1969 by a military coup led by Col. Moamer al Kadhafi. Kadhafi himself is referred to as "the leader of the revolution", wielding considerable power but holding no official post. Initial moves by the regime towards a one-party structure were superseded when the 1977 constitution of the Socialist People's Libyan Arab Jamahiriyah was introduced. Officially, under the constitution, authority is vested in the Libyan people, with local "basic people's congresses" forming an indirect electoral base for the General People's Congress (or parliament), which is serviced by a Secretariat and which appoints the General People's Committee (broadly equivalent to a Council of Ministers). There are no political parties and no opposition groups have been able to emerge within the country itself.

Expatriate Opposition

Co-operation Bureau for Democratic and National Forces, an anti-Kadhafi umbrella organization led by Abd al-Munim al-Huni.

Libyan Alliance, an anti-Kadhafi front which emerged in the late 1980s.

Libyan National Liberation Army (LNLA), a paramilitary unit organized in Chad with covert US backing in 1988 to destabilize the Libyan regime, but dispersed after the fall of the Chadian government in 1990; the LNLA severed its earlier links with the National Front for the Salvation of Libya in early 1994.

National Front for the Salvation of Libya (NFSL), formed in Sudan in 1981, now operating out of Egypt and the United States, and at the forefront of recent efforts to co-ordinate anti-Kadhafi activity among other opponents of the regime.

Liechtenstein

Capital: Vaduz

Population: 31,000 (1995E)

The Principality of Liechtenstein is an hereditary monarchy in the male line which has maintained an independent existence since the Middle Ages under a system that is still feudal in many respects, although the country is essentially a parliamentary democracy. Under its constitution of 1921, the Prince exercises legislative power jointly with a unicameral Diet (*Landtag*) of 25 members, who are elected every four years by universal adult suffrage under a proportional representation system based in the Principality's two constituencies and subject to a minimum requirement that 8% of the vote must be obtained. The Chief of Government is appointed by the sovereign from the majority party or group in the Diet, while the Deputy Chief of Government is also appointed by the sovereign from the Diet's leading minority party.

Having been introduced for most local elections in 1977, female suffrage at national level was narrowly approved by referendum in July 1984 (of male voters), the first elections in which women could vote being held in February 1986.

At the *Landtag* elections of Oct. 24, 1993, the Fatherland Union (VU) won 13 seats (with a vote share of 50.1%), the Progressive Citizen's Party (FBP) 11 (44.2%) and the Free List 1 (8.5%). In accordance with the constitution, the VU and the FBP have formed a coalition government since 1938.

Fatherland Union

Vaterländische Union (VU)

Address. 13 Fürst Franz Josef Strasse, 9490 Vaduz

Telephone. (#41–75) 232–0832

Fax. (#41–75)·232–9192

Leadership. Oswald Kranz (chair), Mario Frick (parliamentary leader), Magda Batliner (secretary)

Considered the more liberal of the two major parties, the VU favours a constitutional monarchy, democracy and social progress. It was founded at the end of World War I as the People's Party (*Volkspartei*, VP), which attracted substantial working-class support (particularly anong returning emigrant workers) for its programme of economic union with Switzerland and a constitution according rights to the people. After winning a majority in the 1918 elections, the party formed the government for the decade 1918–1928, during which the aforementioned policies were implemented. In 1936 the VP merged with the *Heimatdienst* movement to create the VU, which served as the junior coalition partner of the Progressive Citizens' Party (FBP) from 1938 to 1970, when it became the senior partner. It lost its coalition seniority to the FBP in 1974 but regained it in 1978, holding the government leadership until the elections of February 1993, when the FBP gained the advantage. However, unprecedented second elections the same year re-established the VU as the leading government party under the premiership of Mario Frick.

The VU is a member party of the European section of the International Democrat Union (as is the FBP).

Free List

Freie Liste (FL)

Address. Postfach 177, 9494 Schaan

Leadership. Paul Volk (parliamentary spokesman), Christel Hilti, Hansjörg Hilti, Helen Marxer, Hugo Risch and Margrit Wille (council members)

Less conservative than the two traditional parties, the environmentalist FL was formed prior to the 1986 election, at which it became the first challenger to the ruling coalition since 1974 but narrowly failed to secure the 8% vote share necessary for parliamentary representation. It again fell short in 1989, in part because 3.2% of the vote went to a new Liechtenstein Non-Party List (*Überparteiliche Liste Liechtensteins*, ÜLL), which did not long endure. The FL's two seats in February 1993 were reduced to one in October, although the party remained an important alternative presence.

Progressive Citizens' Party

Fortschrittliche Bürgerpartei (FBP)

Address. 5 Feldkircher Strasse, 9494 Schaan

Telephone. (#41–75) 233–3531

Fax. (#41–75) 232–2912

Leadership. Norbert Seeger (chair), Thomas Büchel (parliamentary leader), Heidi Kindle (secretary)

Founded in 1918 as the conservative Citizens' Party (*Bürgerpartei*), what subsequently became the FBP held a majority of Diet seats from 1928 to 1970 and in 1974-78 and therefore headed the government in those periods. Since 1938 it has participated with the Fatherland Union (VU) in Europe's longest-serving government coalition, being the junior partner in 1970-74 and from 1978 until it regained the advantage in the elections of February 1993. However, the incoming FBP Chief of Government, Markus Büchel, quickly alienated his own party and lost a confidence vote (tabled by the FBP) in September 1993, whereupon another general election in October, in which the FBP list was headed by Josef Biedermann, reduced the FBP to junior status in the ruling coalition.

The FBP is a member party of the European section of the International Democrat Union (as is the VU).

Lithuania

Capital: Vilnius   **Population:** 3,650,000 (1995E)

The Republic of Lithuania was independent from the end of World War I until being absorbed by the Soviet Union in August 1940, an action that was repudiated by the Lithuanian legislature in March 1990, following which the country's full independence was recognized by the USSR State Council in September 1991. Its 1992 constitution provides for an executive President who is directly elected for a five-year term and who appoints the Prime Minister and other ministers, subject to parliamentary approval. Legislative authority is vested in a Parliament (*Seimas*) of 141 members also serving four-year terms, of whom 71 are elected from constituencies by majority voting and 70 by proportional representation. Under changes to the electoral law given parliamentary approval in June 1996, the threshold for obtaining proportional seats was raised from 4% to 5% (and previous concessions on the threshold rule for minority parties were abolished), while voters became entitled to record a preference for individual candidates on party lists.

Parliamentary elections held on Oct. 25 and Nov. 15, 1992, resulted as follows: Lithuanian Democratic Labour Party 74 seats (with 42.6% of the national vote), Lithuanian Reform Movement (later the Homeland Union) 29 (20.5%), Lithuanian Christian Democratic Party and allies 18 (12.2%), Lithuanian Social Democratic Party 8 (5.9%), Lithuanian Polish Union 4 (2.1%), Lithuanian National Union and allies 4 (1.9%), Lithuanian Centre Movement 2, others 2.

Homeland Union

Tevynes Santara
   Address. 1–302 Gedimino pr., Vilnius 2001
   Telephone. (#370–2) 224747
   Fax. (#370–2) 224555
   Leadership. Vytautas Landsbergis (chair), Gediminas Vagnorius (executive chair)

Also known as the Lithuanian Conservative Party (*Lietuvos Conservative Partija*, LCP), the Homeland Union was launched in May 1993 as successor to the remnants of the Lithuanian Reform Movement (*Sajudis*), which had spearheaded the independence campaign. Under the leadership of Vytautas Landsbergis, the broadly-based *Sajudis* had been the leading formation in the 1990 elections, but in the face of economic adversity had suffered a heavy defeat in the 1992 contest, winning only 20.5% of the popular vote. The new Homeland Union proclaimed a centre-right orientation, while announcing that its ranks were open to former Communists.

Lithuanian Centre Movement

Lietuvos Centro Judejimas (LCJ)
   Address. Literatu 8, Vilnius 2001
   Telephone. (#370–2) 613655

   Leadership. Romualdas Ozoldas (chair)

Registered in August 1992, the LCJ contested the autumn 1992 parliamentary elections on a pro-market, pro-decentralization platform, winning two seats.

Lithuanian Christian Democratic Party

Lietuvos Krikcioniu Demokratu Partija (LKDP)
   Address. 36/2 Pylimo, Vilnius 2001
   Telephone. (#370–2) 227387
   Fax. (#370–2) 227387
   Leadership. Algirdas Saudargas (chair), Povilos Katilius (executive chair), Kazimieras Kryževičius (secretary-general)

The LKDP was launched in 1989 as the revival of a pre-Soviet party dating from 1905, adopting a Christian democratic programme on the West European model. The party's third-place vote share of 12.2% and 18 seats in the 1992 parliamentary elections was achieved in co-operation with *Sajudis* (later the Homeland Union) and on a joint list with the Lithuanian Democratic Party and a pressure group representing former political prisoners and deportees.

The LKDP is affiliated to the Christian Democrat International.

Lithuanian Christian Democratic Union
Lietuvos Krikstiones Demokratu Unija (LKDU)
Address. 35/8 Pylimo, Vilnius 2001
Telephone. (#370-2) 624008
Leadership. Victoras Petkus (chair)
The small LKDU, an offshoot of the Lithuanian Christian Democratic Party and also affiliated to the Christian Democrat International, obtained one *Seimas* seat in the 1992 elections.

Lithuanian Democratic Labour Party
Lietuvos Demokratines Darbo Partijos (LDDP)
Address. 1 B. Radvilaites, Vilnius 2600
Telephone. (#370-2) 615420
Fax. (#370-2) 611770
Leadership. Česlovas Juršenas (chair)
Following a March 1990 constitutional revision revoking the monopoly of the Lithuanian Communist Party (LCP), the LDDP was launched in December by a pro-reform and pro-independence faction of the party. (The LCP was banned in August 1991 and its property confiscated.) The LDDP registed an unexpected victory in the 1992 parliamentary elections, winning an overall majority of seats with 42.6% popular vote on a platform of gradual transition to a market economy. The then LDDP leader, Algirdas Mykolas Brazauskas, was accordingly elected to the chair of the *Seimas* and thus to the position of head of state. In the latter capacity he received popular endorsement in a presidential election in February 1993, following which Adolfas Šleževičius was appointed Prime Minister of an LDDP government. Disclosures that Šleževičius might have used confidential government information for personal financial benefit forced his resignation in February 1996, the new LDDP Prime Minister being Laurynas Mindaugas Stankevičiius. In May 1996 the LDDP opted to detach the premiership from the party chairmanship, Česlovas Juršenas being elected to the latter post. But the signs were that the divisions in the ruling party over the Šleževičius affair and attendant evidence of corruption in high places had damaged the LDDP in advance of parliamentary elections in October 1996.

Lithuanian Democratic Party
Lietuvos Demokratu Partija (LDP)
Address. 34/9 Gedimino, Vilnius 2001
Telephone. (#370-2) 626033
Fax. (#370-2) 479275
Leadership. Saulius Pečeliunas (chair)
Descended from a party of the same name founded in 1902, the LDP was re-established in 1989 and formed part of the pro-independence movement under the umbrella of *Sajudis* (later the Homeland Union). In the 1992 parliamentary elections the LDP presented a joint list with the

Lithuanian Christian Democratic Party, winning four of the coalition's tally of 18 seats.

Lithuanian Independence Party
Lietuviu Nepriklausomybes Partija (LNP)
Address. 38/1 Pylimo, Vilnius 2600
Telephone. (#370-2) 614721
Fax. (#370-2) 223639
Leadership. Valentinas Šapalas (chair)
Founded in 1990, the LNP suffered an early setback in April 1992 when its then leader, Virgilius Čepaitis, was convicted by the Supreme Court of having "deliberately co-operated" with the Soviet-era KGB. In the 1992 parliamentary elections it was allied with the Lithuanian National Union, winning one of the joint list's four seats.

Lithuanian National Union
Lietuviu Tautininku Sajunga (LTS)
Address. 22 Gedimino pr., Vilnius 2600
Telephone. (#370-2) 624935
Fax. (#378-2) 617310
Leadership. Rimantas Smetona (chair)
The LTS was launched in April 1989 as a revival of the party of the same name founded in 1924 and subsequently prominent in inter-war Lithuanian politics. The party's 1992 election list, which incorporated the Lithuanian Independence Party, won four seats on a 1.9% share of the national vote.

Lithuanian Polish Union
Lietuvos Lenku Sajunga (LLS)
Address. 40 Didžioji, Vilnius 2001
Telephone. (#370-2) 223388
Leadership. Rychard Maceikianec (chair), Zbignev Semionovicz (parliamentary chair).
Founded in 1992 to represent Lithuania's ethnic Poles (about 8% of the total population), the LLS won four *Seimas* seats in 1992, with a 2.1% vote share. Its programme envisages the "national rebirth" of Lithuanian Poles, through the promotion of Polish education within the context of a commitment to the present Lithuanian state.

Lithuanian Social Democratic Party
Lietuvos Socialdemokratu Partija (LSDP)
Address. 16/5 J. Basanavičius, Vilnius 2009
Telephone. (#370-2) 652380
Fax. (#370-2) 652157
Leadership. Aloyzas Sakalas (chair), Alvydas Akstinavičius (general secretary)
Directly descended from the original party founded in 1896 and prominent in the inter-war period of independence, the LSDP was revived in 1989 with a social democratic platform on the West European model. Having formed part of the broad pro-independence movement under the umbrella of *Sajudis* (later the Homeland Union), the party

contested the 1992 parliamentary elections independently, winning 5.9% of the vote and eight seats. It subsequently formed part of the parliamentary opposition to the ruling Lithuanian Democratic Labour Party.

The LSDP is a member of the Socialist International.

Other Parties

Lithuanian Centre Union, led by Romualdas Ozolas.

Lithuanian Conservative Union, formed in 1992 by a dissident faction of the Lithuanian Independence Party after charges of pro-Soviet collaboration had been preferred against its then leader.

Lithuanian Economic Party, led by Klemensas Seputis.

Lithuanian Farmers' Party (*Lietuvos Ukininkija Partija*, LUP), established in 1905 as the Lithuanian Farmers' Union, revived in 1990, adopted present name in 1994, led by Albinas Vaižmužis.

Lithuanian Green Party (*Lietuvos Žalias Partija*, LŽPP), led by Rimantas Astraukas, mainstream ecological grouping launched in 1992.

Lithuanian Liberal Union, chaired by Ginutis Vencius.

Lithuanian New Social Liberal Party, established in 1994 by Algis Klimaitis-Urbonavičius.

Lithuanian Republican Party, led by Kazimieras Petraitis.

Lithuanian Russians' Union, led by Sergei Dmitriyev.

Lithuanian Socialist Party, led by Albinas Visockas.

Lithuanian Women's Party (Lietuvos Moteru Partija, *LMP*), founded in February 1995 on the initiative of Kazimiera Prunskiene, a former Prime Minister (1990–91) and former head of the (Soviet-era) Association of Women of Lithuania, who rejected the Supreme Court's ruling in 1992 that she had knowingly collaborated with the KGB.

National Progress Party, led by Ecidijus Klumbys.

Union of Political Prisoners, led by A. Stasiskis, not to be confused with the similarly-named organization associated with the Lithuanian Christian Democratic Party.

Luxembourg

Capital: Luxembourg-Ville   **Population:** 405,000 (1995E)

Fully independent since 1867, the Grand Duchy of Luxembourg is, under its 1868 constitution as amended, a constitutional hereditary monarchy in which the head of state (the Grand Duke) exercises executive power through a government headed by a Prime Minister and accountable to the legislature. The latter is the Chamber of Deputies (*Chambre des Dáputás*), whose 60 members are elected for a five-year term by citizens aged 18 and over (voting being compulsory). A system of proportional representation is based on four electoral districts, in which each voter has the same number of votes as there are seats and may cast them all for a single party list or may select candidates of more than one party. There is also an advisory Council of State, whose 21 members are appointed for life, seven directly by the Grand Duke and the other 14 by him on the recommendation of the Council itself or of the Chamber of Deputies.

Since political parties in Luxembourg do not have a legal personality, there is no law providing for state funding of parties. However, groups represented in the Chamber of Deputies receive subsidies from public funds according to their size for the purposes of financing their parliamentary activities.

Elections to the Chamber of Deputies on June 12, 1994, resulted as follows: Christian Social People's Party 21 seats (with 31.4% of the vote); Luxembourg Socialist Workers' Party 17 (24.8%), Democratic Party 12 (18.9%), Action Committee for Democracy and Justice 5, Green Alternative 5.

Action Committee for Democracy and Justice

Aktiounskomitee fir Demokratie a Gerechtegkeet (ADR)
Comité d'Action pour la Dámocratie et la Justice (CADJ)

Address. BP 365, L-4004 Esch sur Alzette
Telephone. (#352) 463742
Fax. (#352) 463745
Leadership. Robert Mehlen (president)

The ADR was launched in March 1987 as the "Five-Sixths Action Committee" to campaign for universal entitlement to pensions worth five-sixths of final salary. Benefiting from the increasing number of pensioners on electoral rolls, the formation won four Chamber seats in the 1989 elections and five in 1994.

Christian Social People's Party

Chrëschtlech-Sozial Vollekspartei (CSV)
Parti Chrétien Social (PCS)

Address. 4 rue de l'Eau, BP 826, L-2018 Luxembourg
Telephone. (#352) 225731
Fax. (#352) 472716
Leadership. Jean-Claude Juncker (leader), Erna Hennicot-Schoepges (president), Claude Wiseler (secretary-general)

Committed to the promotion of "a policy of solidarity and social progress under the guidance of Christian and humanist principles" and the preservation of the constitutional status quo, the CSV has long been Luxembourg's strongest party, drawing its support from the conservative middle class, Catholic workers and the farming community. The party is a keen proponent of European economic and monetary union via the European Union (EU), with the proviso that Luxembourg's special banking secrecy laws must be maintained against any EU encroachment.

Founded as the *Parti de la Droite* the CSV adopted its present name in December 1914. Since 1919 the party has taken part in coalition government with various other parties and has supplied Prime Ministers as follows: Emile Reuter (1919–25), Joseph Bech (1926–37), Pierre Dupong (1937–53), Joseph Bech (1953–58), Pierre Frieden (1958–59), Pierre Werner (1959–74 and 1979–84), Jacques Santer (1984–94) and Jean-Claude Juncker (from 1995).

The party formed a coalition with the Luxembourg Socialist Workers' Party (LSAP) following the June 1984 elections, prior to which it had been in coalition with the Democratic Party. Its share of the vote in June 1984 was 34.9%, while in simultaneous elections to the European Parliament it retained three of Luxembourg's six seats.

In the June 1994 elections the CSV's Chamber representation fell back to 21 seats (with 31.4% of the vote), while in simultaneous European Parliament elections it lost one of its three seats. Having formed another coalition with the LSAP, CSV Prime Minister Santer was unexpectedly appointed president of the European Commission from January 1995. He was succeeded as head of the Luxemboury government and CSV leader by Juncker, hitherto Finance Minister.

The CSV is a member of the Christian Democrat International and the International Democrat Union. Its two representatives in the European Parliament sit in the European People's Party group.

Communist Party of Luxembourg

Kommunistesch Partei vu Letzeburg (KPL)
Parti Communiste Luxembourgeois (PCL)

Address. 18 rue Christophe Plantin, L-2339 Luxembourg
Telephone. (#352) 492095
Fax. (#352) 493747
Leadership. Aloyse Bisdorff (president)

Formed as a result of a split in the Luxembourg Socialist Workers' Party (LSAP) at the 1921 Differdange congress, the KPL first obtained a seat in the Chamber of Deputies in 1934 but the result was annulled by the Chamber majority. A proposal to ban the party was defeated in a referendum in 1937, and the KPL was represented in the Chamber of Deputies from 1945, the number of seats held by it fluctuating between three in 1954–64 and six in 1968–74, and declining to two in 1979. The PCL took part in the national unity government of 1845–47, after which it went into opposition, but co-operated with the LSAP at local level. In the June 1979 elections the KPL obtained 5.8% of the vote (compared with 10.4% in 1974), while in 1984 its share fell to 5.0%.

The KPL's representation fell to a single seat in the 1989 elections. The death the following year of its veteran leader, René Urbany (son of the previous leader), was a further blow, as was the demise of the Soviet Union in 1991. In the 1994 elections the KPL experienced its first post-1945 failure to win Chamber representation.

Democratic Party

Demokratesch Partei (DP)
Parti Démocratique (PD)

Address. 46 Grand'rue, L-1660 Luxembourg
Telephone. (#352) 221021
Fax. (#352) 221013
Leadership. Lydie Würth-Polfer (president), Henri Grethen (secretary-general)

Dating from the origins of parliamentarism in Luxembourg in the 1840s, the DP was an established formation in the 19th century, resisting the introduction of universal suffrage and suffering a major defeat in 1919 in consequence. After a process of readaptation, the party became one of the three national parties represented in the post-1945 Chamber, where its representation has fluctuated between 11 and 15 seats.

The PD has taken part in coalition governments:

in the national unity administration of 1945–47, in coalition with the Christian Socials in 1947–51 (when the PD was known as the *Groupement Patriotique et Démocratique*), in 1959–64 and in 1968–74, with the Luxembourg Socialist Workers' Party in 1974–79 and with the Christian Socials in 1979–84. In the June 1984 elections it slipped to 14 seats (and from 21.3 to 18.7% of the vote) and went into opposition to a coalition of the Christian Socials and Socialists. Also in June 1984, it retained one of Luxembourg's six seats in the European Parliament.

The DP remained in opposition after the 1989 and 1994 elections, in which it improved from 11 to 12 seats, taking 18.9% of the vote on the latter occasion and retaining its European Parliament seat on both occasions.

The DP is affiliated to the Liberal International, its member of the European Parliament sitting in the European Liberal, Democratic and Reformist Group.

The Green Alternative

Di Gráng Alternativ (GA)
Parti Vert-Alternatif (PVA)
  Address. 13 marchá aux Herbes, BP 454, L-2014 Luxembourg
  Telephone. (#352) 463740
  Fax. (#352) 463743
  Leadership. Abbès Jacoby and Fálix Braz (joint secretaries)

This organization was founded in June 1983 by a number of individuals and groups, including free radio and youth groups, environmentalists and former Socialists. It won two seats (out of 64) and 5.2% of the vote in the June 1984 national elections, while in European Parliament elections the same month it achieved 6.1% without winning representation. In accordance with the "rotation principle" established by the German Greens, the party's two elected deputies were replaced by alternatives half way through the parliamentary term.

The GA again won two seats in the 1989 elections (for a Chamber reduced in size), before making a major advance in the 1994 contest, to five seats. Concurrent elections to the European Parliament were contested jointly with the Green Ecologist Initiative List, tiny Luxembourg's second ecology party, espousing a less radical environmentalist vision than the GA. This stratagem yielded 10.9% of the vote and one of the Grand Duchy's six Euroseats, but a reported imminent union between the two remained unconsummated as of mid-1996.

Green Ecologist Initiative List

Gráng Lëscht Ekologesch Initiativ (GLEI)
Initiative Vert Ecologiste (IVE)
  Address. 10 rue Schrobilgen, L-2526 Luxembourg
  Telephone. (#352) 448806
  Fax. (#352) 463741

Leadership. Jup Weber

Founded in 1989, the GLEI won two Chamber seats in that year's elections, on a platform assessed as being more conservative than that of the Green Alternative (GA). It lost both of them in the June 1994 contest, but a joint GLEI/GA list for the simultaneous European Parliament elections attracted 10.9% of the vote and returned Jup Weber as the Grand Duchy's first Green MEP.

Luxembourg Socialist Workers' Party

Lëtzebuerger Sozialistesch Arbechterpartei (LSAP)
Parti Ouvrier Socialiste Luxembourgeois (POSL)
  Address. 16 rue de Crácy, L-1364 Luxembourg
  Telephone. (#352) 455991
  Fax. (#352) 456575
  Leadership. Ben Fayot (president), Jacques Poos and Lise Linster (deputy presidents), Raymond Becker (secretary-general)

Founded in 1902 as the Luxembourg Social Democratic Party, the party made little earlier progress because of the qualified franchise. After a minority had broken away in 1921 to form the Communist Party, the party first took part in government from the end of 1937, after which the Socialist ministers laid the basis for modern social legislation. During the Nazi occupation the party was dismembered, but after World War II it re-emerged under its present name and took part in a government of national union until 1947, when it returned to opposition. Following renewed government participation in 1951–59 and 1964–68, the party was defeated in the 1968 legislative elections, whereafter its right wing formed the breakaway Social Democratic Party (which later became defunct).

The LSAP was later reconstructed and made gains in the elections of 1974, after which it joined a coalition government with the Democratic Party. It returned to opposition after losing ground in the June 1979 elections but returned to government (in coalition with the Christian Socials) after making a major advance in the June 1984 national elections, in which it rose from 14 to 21 seats and from 24.3 to 33.6% of the vote. In European Parliament elections the same month the LSAP retained two of the six Luxembourg seats.

The LSAP won 18 seats (25.5% of the vote) in a smaller Chamber in 1989 and slipped to 17 (24.8%) in 1994, retaining two European Parliament seats on both occasions and continuing as the junior coalition partner.

The LSAP is a member party of the Socialist International, its two representatives in the European Parliament being members of the Party of European Socialists group.

Macedonia

Capital: Skopje

Population: 2,000,000 (1995E)

A former constituent republic of the Socialist Federal Republic of Yugoslavia, Macedonia declared independence under its November 1991 constitution, as approved by referendum two months earlier. The constitution defines Macedonia as a democratic, pluralist state based on citizenship, not ethnicity, and specifically rules out any territorial claims on neighbouring countries. It provides for an executive President who is directly elected for a five-year term and a Cabinet, headed by a Prime Minister, accountable to the legislature. The latter is the unicameral Assembly (*Sobranje*) of 120 members, who are elected for a four-year term by those aged 18 and over under a constituency-based system of majority voting over two rounds.

The objection of Greece to "Macedonia" being used in the official title of another state prevented the new country's admission to the United Nations until April 1993, under the interim designation "Former Yugoslav Republic of Macedonia" (FYROM). An agreement of September 1995 on related issues concerning Macedonia's flag and constitution left the "Macedonia" dispute unresolved, so the FYROM designation remained the country's name under international law as at mid-1996.

Assembly elections on Oct. 16 and 30, 1994, and some re-runs on Nov. 13 resulted in the following seat distribution: Social Democratic Union of Macedonia (SDSM) 58, Liberal Party of Macedonia 29, Party for Democratic Prosperity 10, Socialist Party of Macedonia 8, National Democratic Party 4, Democratic Party of Macedonia 1, Social Democratic Party of Macedonia 1, Democratic Party of Turks in Macedonia/Party of Democratic Action–Islamic Way 1, Party for the Total Emancipation of Romanies in Macedonia 1, independents 7. A presidential election on Oct. 16, 1994, resulted in Kiro Gligorov (SDSM), standing as the candidate of the Union of Macedonia, being re-elected with 78.4% of the valid votes against one other contender.

Democratic Party of Turks in Macedonia
Demokratska Partija na Turcite vo Makedonija (DPTM)

Address. c/o Sobranje, Skopje

Leadership. Erdogan Sarach, Mubdil Bejazil

Based in Macedonia's small ethnic Turk community, the DPTM contested the 1994 Assembly elections in alliance with the Party for Democratic Action–Islamic Way (*Partija zá Demokratska Akcija–Islamska Svetlost*, PDA-IS) led by Mazlam Kenan, winning one seat.

Internal Macedonian Revolutionary Organization–Democratic Party for Macedonian National
Unity Vnatrešna Makedonska Revolucionerna Organizacija–Demokratska Partija za Makedonsko Nacionalno Edinstvo (VMRO-DPMNE)

Address. 36 Petar Drapšin br., 91000 Skopje

Telephone. (#389–91) 211586

Fax. (#389–91) 111441

Leadership. Ljupo Georgievski (president), Boris Zmejkovski (secretary)

The nationalist VMRO was named after an historic movement (founded in 1893 by Goce Delčev) which had fought for independence from the Turks. The DPMNE, established by Macedonian migrant workers in Sweden, merged with the VMRO in June 1990 to create a party describing itself as being of the "democratic centre" and favouring a revival of Macedonian cultural identity. The VMRO-DPMNE became the largest single party in the 1990 Assembly elections (with 38 seats) and formed the core of the resultant "government of experts" which asserted Macedonia's independence. However, a mid-1992 government crisis resulted in the party going into opposition, from where it failed to gain representation in 1994. The party condemned an assassination attempt on President Gligorov in October 1995 but was suspected in some quarters of having been involved, in light of its vehement opposition to concessions made by the government the previous month to secure recognition by Greece.

Liberal Party of Macedonia
Liberalnata Partija na Makedonija (LPM)
  Address. 12 Ilindenska bb, 91000 Skopje
  Telephone. (#389–91) 233944
  Fax. (#389–91) 228004
  Leadership. Stojan Andov (president)

The LPM was founded in 1989 as the Alliance of Reform Forces of Macedonia (*Sojuz na Reformskite Sili na Makedonija*, SRSM), which was an affiliate of the federal Alliance of Yugoslav Reform Forces (*Savez Reformskih Snaga Jugoslavije*, SRSJ), led by Ante Marković. In the 1990 elections it was allied in some areas with the Young Democratic Progressive Party (*Mlas Demokratska Progresivna Partija*, MDPS), which it later absorbed. The alliance won only six seats in 1990, but SRSM representatives were included in the resultant coalition government. In 1992 the SRSM adopted the name Reform Forces of Macedonia–Liberal Party and used the shorter LPM designation in the 1994 elections, when as part of the Union for Macedonia it won 29 Assembly seats and continued to be a component of the government coalition headed by the Social Democratic Union of Macedonia (SDSM). However, increasing dissension with the SDSM culminated in the LPM being dropped from the government in February 1996, whereupon party leader Stojan Andov resigned as Speaker of the Assembly (in which capacity he had recently served as acting President during the recuperation of President Gligorov from an assassination attempt. Having become the largest single opposition party in the Assembly, the LPM launched a campaign for early elections, but without success. The party was not assisted by SDSM allegations that, as Speaker, Andov had accumulated substantial personal wealth from the privatization of state assets.

The LPM is an observer member of the Liberal International.

Macedonian Democratic Party
Demokratska Partija Makedonije (DPM)
  Address. 89 Partizanski od., 91000 Skopje
  Telephone. (#389–91) 363099
  Fax. (#389–91) 222710
  Leadership. Tomislav Stojanovski (president)

The centrist DPM was founded in June 1993 on the initiative of Petar Gošev, who had been a member of the Communist-era Macedonian presidency and had later headed the Social Democratic Union of Macedonia (SDSM). In the mid-1992 government crisis he had refused to become Prime Minister of an SDSM-led coalition and had spent a year in the political wilderness before leaving the SDSM to set up the DPM, which drew in four minor parties. In the 1994 Assembly elections, however, the DPM won only one seat.

National Democratic Party
Narodna Demokratska Partija (NDP)
  Address. Gorna Čaršija bb, 94000 Tetovo
  Telephone. (#389–94) 24604
  Leadership. Ilijaz Halili (president)

An ethnic Albanian party, the NDP was originally founded in 1990 and merged with the Party for Democratic Prosperity (PDP) after the 1990 Assembly elections. It re-established itself as an independent party in February 1994 in opposition to the PDP's participation in the government coalition. In the 1994 elections the NDP became the largest non-government party, winning four seats, although it lost this status when the Liberal Party of Macedonia was ousted from the ruling coalition in February 1996.

Party for Democratic Prosperity
Partija za Demokratski Prosperitet (PDP) Partia per Prosperitet Demokratik (PPD)
  Address. 62 Karaorman, 94000 Tetovo
  Telephone. (#389–94) 21380
  Leadership. Abdurahman Aliti (president), Mithat Emini (honorary president), Naser Ziberi (general secretary)

The PDP is the main party of Macedonia's ethnic Albanians, constituting about a quarter of the country's population, organizing only in areas with substantial Albanian population. Subsequent to the 1990 election (in which it won 25 seats) it absorbed the smaller ethnic Albanian National Democratic Party (NDP) led by Ilijas Halili. After joining the government in 1992, the PDP underwent a split in February 1994 between pro-government moderates led by Dzeladin Murati and anti-government Albanian nationalists led by Halili, who opted to re-establish the NDP as an independent party. Claiming to be the "party of continuity", the rump PDP came into sharp conflict with its government coalition partners in mid-1994 over the conviction of a group of alleged Albanian separatists, including PDP honorary president Mithat Emini, on subversion charges. The party fell back sharply to 10 seats in the 1994 Assembly elections but continued to be a member of the government coalition headed by the Social Democratic Union of Macedonia. From February to July 1995 its deputies boycotted the Assembly in protest against a new law banning the use of Albanian in official identity documentation. This phase was marked by the defection of another anti-government PDP faction, which formed the Party for Democratic Prosperity of Albanians in Macedonia.

Party for Democratic Prosperity of Albanians in Macedonia

Partija za Demokratski Prosperitet na Shqiptare vo Makedonija (PDPSM)

Address. c/o Sobranje, 91000 Skopje

Leadership. Arben Xhaferi (president)

The ethnic Albanian PDPSM was formed in April 1995 by a dissident faction of the Party for Democratic Prosperity opposed to the latter's participation in the coalition government in Skopje. The split occurred amid a boycott of parliamentary proceedings by ethnic Albanian deputies in protest against recent legislation perceived as discrimating against ethnic Albanians.

Party for the Total Emancipation of Romanies in Macedonia

Partija za Celosna Emancipacija na Romite vo Makedonija (PCERM)

Address. Orizari bb, 91000 Skopje

Telephone. (#389–91) 612726

Leadership. Faik Abdić (president)

Concerned to promote the interests of the estimated 57,000 Roma (Gypsies) in Macedonia, the PCERM won one Assembly seat in 1990 in alliance with the Socialist Party of Macedonia, retaining it in 1994.

Social Democratic Party of Macedonia

Socijaldemokratska Partija na Makedonija (SDPM)

Address. 20 J.H. Konstantinov, 91000 Skopje

Telephone. (#389–91) 334207

Leadership. Tihomir Jovanovski (president)

The SDPM was founded in March 1990 by Prof. Slavko Milosavljevski, who had been prominent in Communist-era dissent in Macedonia and had been expelled from the then ruling League of Communists in 1972. Advocating social democracy on the West European model, the party failed to gain representation in the 1990 Assembly elections, but won one seat in 1994.

Social Democratic Union of Macedonia

Socijaldemokratski Sojuz na Makedonija (SDSM)

Address. 8 Bihačka, 91000 Skopje

Telephone. (#389–91) 321371

Fax. (#389–91) 221071

Leadership. Branko Crvenkovski (parliamentary leader), Blagoj Handziski (secretary)

The SDSM is directly descended from the former ruling League of Communists of Macedonia (*Soyuz na Komunistite na Makedonija*, SKM), which in 1989 attempted a relaunch by adding "Party of Democratic Change" (*Partija za Demokratska Preobrazba*, PDP) to its title. Under the SKM-PDP designation it came second in the

1990 Assembly elections, with 31 seats; but its nominee, Kiro Gligorov, was elected head of state by the Assembly in January 1991 and it became the leading component of a coalition government formed in mid-1992. The party describes itself as standing in the "European democratic tradition", favouring an effective market economy and the "transformation" of property relations and a multi-cultural society. In 1994 it was confirmed in power in both presidential and Assembly elections (winning 58 seats in the latter), heading the Union of Macedonia (SM) alliance with the Liberal Party of Macedonia (LPM) and the Socialist Party of Macedonia. Reappointed SDSM Prime Minister in December 1994 at the head of a coalition of the SM parties and the ethnic Albanian Party for Democratic Prosperity, Branko Crvenkovski carried out a major government reshuffle in February 1996 in which the LPM ceased to be a member of the ruling coalition.

Socialist Party of Macedonia

Socijalistika Partija na Makedonija (SPM)

Address. Ilindenska bb, 91000 Skopje

Telephone. (#389–91) 228015

Fax. (#389–91) 220025

Leadership. Kiro Popovski (president), Zejnel Begović (secretary)

Previously known as the Socialist Alliance–Socialist Party of Macedonia and registered in September 1990, the SPM is the successor to the Macedonian branch of the Socialist Alliance of the Working People of Yugoslavia, the front organization of the Communist era. For the 1990 elections the SPM formed an alliance with the Party for the Total Emancipation of Romanies in Macedonia, winning four Assembly seats on a platform advocating the creation of a "politically free, economically effective, ecologically responsible and socially just state". In the 1994 contest it formèd part of the victorious Union of Macedonia headed by the Social Democratic Union of Macedonia, doubling its representation to eight seats and being included in the resultant government.

Union of Macedonia

Sojuz na Makedonija (SM)

Address. c/o President's Office, Skopje

Leadership. Kiro Gligorov

The SM was established in the run-up to the October 1994 elections as an alliance of the three non-Albanian parties of the post-1992 coalition government, namely the Social Democratic Union of Macedonia, the Socialist Party of Macedonia and the Liberal Party of Macedonia (LPM). It not only won over three-quarters of the Assembly seats but also secured the re-election of President

Gligorov by a massive 78.4% of the 52.4% turnout. The ejection of the LPM from the government in February 1996, reportedly against the advice of Gligorov, left the remaining two SM parties with a much narrower parliamentary majority of 66 seats.

Other Parties

Democratic Alliance of Serbs in Macedonia (*Demokratski Sojuz na Srbite vo Makedonija*, DSSM), led by Borivoje Ristić.

Democratic Party of Serbs in Macedonia (*Demokratska Partija na Srbite vo Makedonija*, DPSM), led by Dragiša Miletić.

Democratic Party of Yugoslavs of Macedonia (*Demokratska Partija Jugoslovena Makedonije*, DPJM), led by Zivko Leksoski, founded in June 1990 to represent those defining themselves as "Yugoslavs".

Movement for Pan-Macedonian Action (*Dvizenje za Semakedonska Akcija*, MAAK), led by Ante Popovski, founded in March 1990 and the main early political vehicle of Macedonian national aspirations, but later eclipsed by other formations.

Party of Yugoslavs in the Republic of Macedonia (*Stranka na Jugosloveni vo Republika Makedonija*, SJRM), led by Voislav Karastojanovski.

Union of Ethnic Croats (*Sojuz na Ethniki Hrvatski*, SEH), led by Marija Damjanovska.

Workers' Party (*Rabotnicka Partija*, RP), led by Krste Jankovski.

Madagascar

Capital: Antananarivo   **Population:** 12,700,000 (1995E)

The Republic of Madagascar became fully independent from France in 1960. Post-independence politics were dominated by President Philibert Tsiranana and his Malagasy Social Democratic Party until 1972, when the military took control. In 1975 Didier Ratsiraka assumed the presidency, his regime retaining power until a new multi-party constitution heralded a decisive opposition victory in presidential and legislative elections in 1993. Under the new constitution, which was approved in a referendum in August 1992, the Prime Minister is head of government and exercises virtually all executive power. The President, as head of state, is directly elected for a five-year term. The bicameral legislature comprises a Senate (*Sénat*) and a directly-elected 138–member National Assembly (*Assemblée Nationale*). Two-thirds of the members of the Senate are selected by an electoral college for a term of four years, the remaining one-third being appointed by the President.

In presidential elections held over two rounds in November 1992 and February 1993 Albert Zafy, representing an alliance of opposition forces launched in 1991, defeated the incumbent President Ratsiraka, taking nearly 67 per cent of the vote in the second ballot. In legislative elections in June 1993, political groupings supporting President Zafy secured a majority in the National Assembly with over 70 of the 138 seats (with some 20 parties winning representation of some sort).

In a constitutional referendum in September 1995, voters decided that the President, rather than the National Assembly, should have the power to appoint or dismiss the Prime Minister. The following month the leader of the National Union for Development and Democracy was appointed Prime Minister.

Association of United Malagasys–Famima
    Address. c/o National Assembly, Antananarivo
    Attracting supporters of former President Ratsiraka, *Famima* won 11 seats in the 1993 legislative poll.

Committee for the Support of Democracy and Development in Madagascar
Comité de Soutien à la Démocratie et au Développement de Madagascar (CSDDM)
    Address. c/o National Assembly, Antananarivo

Leadership. Francisque Ravony (leader)

The CSDDM was formed at the end on 1992, supporting Albert Zafy's presidential candidacy. Two representatives were returned to the National Assembly in June 1993.

Congress Party for Madagascar Independence-Renewal (AKFM-Fanavaozana)

Address. c/o National Assembly, Antananarivo
Leadership. Rev. Richard Andriamanjato (leader)

AKFM-*Fanavaozana* was launched by a breakaway faction of the Congress Party for Madagascar Independence (AKFM) in 1989. A pro-Zafy group, it took five seats in the 1993 legislative elections, while the pro-Ratsiraka AKFM rump won none.

Fihaonana

Address. c/o National Assembly, Antananarivo
Leadership. Guy Razanamasy (leader)

Also referred to as the Confederation of Civil Societies for Development, the pro-Zafy *Fihaonana* was launched in 1993 and secured eight seats in that year's legislative elections.

Living Forces Rasalama

Forces Vives Rasalama
Address. c/o National Assembly, Antananarivo
Leadership. Alain Ramaroson (president)

The principal element in the coalition of groups opposed to the Ratsiraka regime from 1991, *Forces Vives Rasalama* supported Albert Zafy's successful presidential candidacy and subsequently won 47 seats in the legislative elections in June 1993, giving it the largest representation in the National Assembly.

Militant Party for the Development of Madagascar

Parti Militant pour le Développement de Madagascar (PMDM)
Address. c/o National Assembly, Antananarivo
Leadership. Manandafy Rakotonirina (president)

The party was formed in 1972 as the Movement for Proletarian Power, originally with radical left-wing credentials but latterly with an increasingly liberal outlook. A significant opposition group by the end of the 1980s, it was the second largest party in the National Assembly following legislative elections in 1989. The organization changed its name in 1990, although it retained its earlier Malagasy initials (MFM). Party leader Rakotonirina, who stood as a first-round presidential candidate in November 1992 (taking third place with just over 10 per cent of the vote) supported Albert Zafy in the second ballot. However,

following the June 1993 legislative elections, in which it won 15 National Assembly seats, the party went into opposition.

National Movement for the Independence of Madagascar

Movement National pour l'Indépendance de Madagascar (MONIMA)
Leadership. Monja Jaona (leader)

MONIMA's longstanding leader contested the 1982 presidential election as Didier Ratsiraka's only competitor, winning 20 per cent of the vote. The party subsequently performed poorly in the 1989 presidential and legislative elections, and was further weakened in 1990 by the defection of a faction which became the Democratic Party for the Development of Madagascar. Another setback was the serious wounding of Jaona during a clash with soldiers at a demonstration in March 1992. The party failed to win representation in the 1993 elections.

National Union for Development and Democracy

Union Nationale pour le Développement et la Démocratie (UNDD)
Address. c/o National Assembly, Antananarivo
Leadership. Emmanuel Rakotovahiny (leader)

The UNDD was founded by Albert Zafy in 1991 as an element of the opposition coalition launched against President Ratsiraka. Following his election to the presidency of the Republic in February 1993 Zafy resigned his party position, being accorded the title of honorary UNDD president. In the June 1993 legislative elections the UNDD won seven seats, five of which were linked to Living Forces Rasalama. In October 1995 party leader Rakotovahiny was appointed Prime Minister.

Popular Impulse for National Unity

Elan Populaire pour l'Unité Nationale
Vonjy Iray Tsy Mivaky (VITM)
Address. BP 1069, Antananarivo 101
Telephone. (#261-2) 29694
Leadership. Dr. Jérôme Marojàma Razanabahiny (leader)

Social democratic in orientation (and affiliated to the Socialist International), *Vonjy* functioned through the late 1970s and 1980s within the political structure established by the Ratsiraka regime, securing a small number of seats in legislative elections up to 1989. In the early 1990s the party suffered from defections and allegations of corruption in the leadership, and in the June 1993 elections to the National Assembly it won only one seat.

Rally for Socialism and Democracy
Rassemblement pour le Socialisme et le Démocratie (RPSD)
    Address. c/o National Assembly, Antananarivo
    Leadership. Evariste Marson (leader)
    The RPSD leader came fourth in the first ballot of the presidential election in November 1992 with 4.6 per cent of the vote. The party switched allegiance to Albert Zafy in the second round but then, having won eight National Assembly seats in the June 1993 legislative elections, went into opposition.

Vanguard for Economic and Social Recovery
Avant-Garde pour le Redressement Economique et Social (ARES)
    Leadership. Didier Ratsiraka (leader)
    Launched by Ratsiraka following his unsuccessful bid for re-election in 1993, ARES superseded the Vanguard of the Malagasy Revolution (*Avant-Garde de la Révolution Malgache*, AREMA) which the former President had organized in 1976 and through which he maintained power. AREMA had been the dominant element of a coalition front, known as the National Front for the Defence of the Revolution (FNDR), within which all political formations were required to conduct their activity. From March 1990 participation in the FNDR ceased to be obligatory for political parties, and the FNDR was itself restyled as the Militant Movement for Malagasy Socialism (MMSM). It was as the candidate of the MMSM that Ratsiraka failed to secure re-election to the presidency in the November 1992 and February 1993 ballots.

Other Parties

Accord, an acronym of the French version of its full title (Christian Action by Regional Cadres and Businessmen for Development), supported the presidential bid of Albert Zafy and won two seats in the legislative elections in June 1993.

Acting Together (*Farimbona*), a pro-Zafy organization, secured two Assembly seats in June 1993.

Action and Reflection Group for the Development of Madagascar (*Groupe d'Action et Réflexion pour le Développement de Madagascar*, GRAD), led by Tovonanahary Rabetsitonja, part of the anti-Ratsiraka opposition alliance, won one seat in the June 1993 ssembly elections.

Christian Democratic Movement of Madagascar (*Mouvement des Démocrates Chrétiens de Malgaches*, MDCM), led by Jean-Jacques Rakotoniaina, an affiliate of the Christian Democrat International.

Christian Democratic Party of Madagascar (*Parti Démocrate Chrétien de Madagascar*, PDCM), led by Alexis Bezaka, an affiliate of the Christian Democrat International.

Democratic Party for the Development of Madagascar (*Parti Démocratique pour le Développement de Madagascar*, PDDM), led by René Ranaivosoa, formed in 1990 by a dissident group of the National Movement for the Independence of Madagascar.

Progress (*Fivoarana*), won two National Assembly seats in 1993.

Malagasy Christian Democratic Union (*Union Démocratique Chrétien Malgache*, UDECMA), led by Solo Norbert Andriamorasata, an affiliate of the Christian Democrat International.

Torch (*Fanilo*), as one of the anti-Zafy groupings returned 13 representatives to the National Assembly in the 1993 elections.

Weights and Measures (*Vatomizana*), part of the pro-Zafy majority in the National Assembly following the 1993 polls, holds one seat.

Malawi

Capital: Lilongwe

Population: 10,000,000 (1995E)

The former British protectorate of Nyasaland achieved independence as Malawi in 1964, becoming a one-party republic under a new constitution two years later. The authoritarian regime of President Hastings Banda and his Malawi Congress Party (MCP) retained power from that time until widespread popular protest in the early 1990s led to constitutional amendments introducing multi-party democracy in 1993. An interim constitution, drafted by a National Consultative Council and approved in May 1994, provided for a directly elected executive President and 177–member National Assembly, both serving five-year terms.

Multi-party legislative and presidential elections were held in May 1994, resulting in victory for the United Democratic Front and its leader Bakili Muluzi, who formed a new government including representatives of other former opposition parties.

Alliance for Democracy (AFORD)
Address. Private Bag 28, Lilongwe
Telephone. (#265) 743166/269
Fax. (#265) 743170
Leadership. Chakufwa Chihana (president)
AFORD was launched in September 1992 to secure democratic reforms in Malawi. Later that year the government declared membership of the group illegal, and its leader was subsequently imprisoned until mid-1993 when the party was legalized. In March 1993 AFORD absorbed the membership of the former Malawi Freedom Movement, an organization founded by Orton Chirwa who had been a minister in the Banda regime in the 1970s before being arrested and imprisoned for treason in 1981.

In the multi-party legislative elections in May 1994 AFORD won 36 National Assembly seats. In the presidential poll, Chakufwa Chihana came third with 18.6% of the votes cast. Subsequent talks to bring AFORD into the coalition government led by the United Democratic Front broke down, and in June 1994 the party declared that it had signed a memorandum of understanding with the defeated Malawi Congress Party. However, in September 1994, Chihana and five other AFORD politicians joined the Cabinet, and the party's alliance with the MCP was terminated the following January.

In July 1995 the number of AFORD ministers in the Cabinet was cut from six to two in a reshuffle, but the party's ties with the UDF were strengthened by the signature of a formal coalition agreement. In May 1996 Chihana resigned as Second Vice-President and Minister of Irrigation in order to spend more time on party work, although AFORD continued to be a government party.

Malawi Congress Party (MCP)
Address. Private Bag 388, Lilongwe 3
Telephone. (#265) 783322
Leadership. Lovemore Mulo (secretary-general)
Under the leadership of President Hastings Banda, the traditionalist and conservative MCP was the sole legal party from 1966 until 1993, when multi-party democracy was introduced in the wake of growing popular demands for political reform.

In the legislative elections in May 1994 the MCP took second place with 55 National Assembly seats (subsequently winning an additional seat in re-run elections in two constituencies). Dr Banda conceded defeat in the presidential election, coming second to the UDF candidate with 33.6% of the vote.

In early January 1995 Dr Banda, his closest aide John Tembo, and two former senior police officers were arrested on charges of murder relating to the deaths of four politicians in 1983. Following the arrests, Lovemore Mulo was named as MCP secretary-general. The trial of the accused began in July and resulted in their acquittal at the end of the year.

Also in January 1995, the alliance between the MCP and AFORD, which had been announced in June 1994, was ended by the latter.

Malawi Democratic Party (MDP)
Address. PO Box 30891, Lilongwe
Telephone. (#265) 720680
Leadership. Kampelo Kalua (leader)
The MDP performed poorly in the 1994 elections, attracting less than 1% in both the legislative and presidential contests. Kampelo Kalua, the party's presidential candidate, was briefly arrested in September 1995 but was acquitted the following month.

Malawi National Democratic Party (MNDP)
Address. PO Box 30548, Lilongwe
Telephone. (#265) 784766
Fax. (#265) 781387
Leadership. Tim Mangwazu (leader)
Although the MNDP did not win any seats in the 1994 legislative elections, party leader Mangwazu was awarded a portfolio in the Cabinet formed by President Muluzi at the end of May 1994. He was not, however, reappointed to the new Cabinet named in July 1995.

United Democratic Front (UDF)
Address. PO Box 856, Blantyre
Telephone. (#265) 677135
Fax. (#265) 677013
Leadership. Bakili Muluzi (president)
The UDF was formed in 1992 by former officials of the Malawi Congress Party to campaign for a multi-party democracy, and emerged from the elections in May 1994 as the leading political force. The party won 84 seats in the National Assembly (later increased to 85 following re-run

elections in two constituencies), and Bakili Muluzi secured the Presidency with 47.3 per cent of the votes cast. UDF members have predominated in the appointment of subsequent Cabinets.

United Front for Multi-Party Democracy (UFMD)

Address. PO Box 30761, Lilongwe
Telephone. (#265) 744208
Leadership. Edmund Jika (leader)

The UFMD was launched in 1992, achieving legal status in mid-1993. It did not secure any seats in the 1994 National Assembly elections, and backed the winning candidate of the United Democratic Front (UDF) for the presidency. The party was represented in the UDF-led Cabinet, with a single portfolio, until July 1995.

Other Parties

Christian Democratic Party (CDP), led by Harry Chiume, did not contest the 1994 elections. *Address.* PO Box 2476, Blantyre

Congress for the Second Republic (CSR), led by Kanyama Chiume, made a negligible impact in the 1994 National Assembly elections, its small share of the vote being restricted to the northern area of the country. *Address.* PO Box 30700, Lilongwe; PO Box 30285, Blantyre

Malawi Democratic Union (MDU), led by James Mkumba, polled the lowest number of votes in the 1994 National Assembly elections. *Address.* PO Box 515, Blantyre.

Malayasia

Capital: Kuala Lumpur

Population: 20,000,000 (1995E)

The Federation of Malaysia consists of the 11 states of Peninsular Malaysia and the two states of Sarawak and Sabah situated on the northern coast of the island of Kalimantan (Borneo). It gained independence from the United Kingdom in 1957, subsequently merging with the self-governing state of Singapore and the former British crown colonies of Sarawak and Sabah in 1963. Singapore's inclusion was terminated in 1965. The constitution codifies a federal system of government under an elective constitutional monarchy. The nine hereditary Malay rulers of Peninsular Malaysia (but not the heads of the states of Malacca, Penang, Sarawak and Sabah) elect a Supreme Head of State (*Yang di-Pertuan Agong*) every five years from among their own number. The *Yang di-Pertuan Agong* appoints a Cabinet headed by a Prime Minister. The bicameral legislature consists of a partially elected Senate (*Dewan Negara*) and a fully elected (by universal adult suffrage) 192–member House of Representatives (*Dewan Rakyat*). The administration of the 13 states is carried out by rulers or governors and each state has its own constitution and a unicameral state assembly which shares power with the federal parliament.

The major political force in Malaysia is the National Front (*Barisan Nasional*), a coalition of parties representing the country's major ethnic groups (Malay, Chinese and Indian). In elections to the House of Representatives on April 24-25, 1995, the National Front, dominated by the United Malays National Organization (UMNO), was returned to power with 162 seats, the other 30 seats being distributed as follows: Democratic Action Party 9, Sabah United Party 8, Pan-Malaysian Islamic Party 7, Spirit of '46 6. It was similarly successful in simultaneous elections to the 11 state assemblies of Peninsular Malaysia (winning control of 10).

National Front Parties

The **National Front** (*Barisan Nasional*) is the governing multi-racial coalition, comprising 14 parties at the time of the 1995 elections, as covered below. Launched in 1973, it superseded the earlier Alliance Party which had been founded in 1952 and held power from independence in 1957. The coalition contests state and federal elections as a single political body, with candidates of the constituent parties agreeing not to stand against each other. It has remained in power since its foundation, winning a majority of seats in six consecutive general elections. In the 1995 federal elections, with an unprecedented 62 per cent of the popular vote, the Front won 162 of the 192 seats in the House of Representatives. In simultaneous elections to the 11 state assemblies of Peninsular Malaysia, the Front won all but 55 of the 394 seats, failing only to wrest control of Kelantan. As of mid-1996 it also controlled the state administrations of Sabah and Sarawak.

Liberal Democratic Party (LDP)
Address. c/o State Assembly, Kota Kinabalu, Sabah
Leadership. Chong Kah Kiet (president)
The LDP is a Chinese-dominated grouping based in Sabah. It joined the ruling federal National Front coalition in 1991.

Malaysian Chinese Association (MCA)
Address. Wisma MCA, 8th Floor, 163 Jalan Ampang, POB 10626, 50720 Kuala Lumpur
Telephone. (#60–3) 261-8044
Fax. (#60–3) 261-9772
Leadership. Datuk Seri Dr Ling Liong Sik (president)
More conservative than the Chinese-based opposition Democratic Action Party, the MCA was formed in 1949 to support the interests of the Chinese community in Malaysia. It withdrew from the National Front coalition in 1969 in protest against the government's response to violent communal rioting in which many Chinese were killed, and did not rejoin until 1982. In the 1995 elections the party increased its parliamentary representation from 18 to 30 seats as part of the coalition.

Malaysian Indian Congress (MIC)
Address. Menara Manickavasagam, 6th Floor, 1 Jalan Rahmat, 50350 Kuala Lumpur
Telephone. (#60–3) 442-4377
Leadership. Dato Seri S. Sami Vellu (president), Dato G. Vadiveloo (secretary-general)
The MIC, founded in the mid-1940s, is the main representative of the Indian community in Malaysia and is a member of the ruling National Front coalition, for which it secured seven seats in the House of Representatives in the 1995 federal elections.

Malaysian People's Movement (MPM)
Gerakan Rakyat Malaysia (Gerakan)
Address. 10–12 Jalan 1/77B, off Changkat Thambi Dollah, 55100 Kuala Lumpur
Telephone. (#60–3) 241-7855
Fax. (#60–3) 248-5648
Leadership. Dato Seri Dr Lim Keng Yaik (president), Dato Chan Choong Tak (secretary-general)

Founded in 1968 and based in Penang, *Gerakan* is a social democratic party which largely attracts the support of Chinese intellectuals. The party won seven seats in the 1995 federal elections as part of the National Front.

People's Justice Movement
Angkatan Keadilan Rakyat (AKAR)
Address. Paramount Industrial Centre, Lot 3, Ground Floor, Kolombong Rd, 88100 Kota Kinabalu, Sabah
Telephone. (#60–88) 428779
Leadership. Dato Mark Koding (leader)
AKAR was established in 1989 by former Sabah United Party members. It has been a constituent party of the ruling National Front since 1991.

People's Progressive Party (PPP)
Address. 43 Jalan Station, Ist Floor, 3000 Ipoh, Perak
Telephone. (#60–5) 518837
Leadership. Mak Hon Kam (president)
Founded in the mid-1950s, the left-wing PPP draws its support mainly from the Chinese community around Ipoh, the capital of the north western state of Perak, and is a member of the National Front coalition.

Sabah Democratic Party
Parti Demokratik Sabah (PDS)
Address. c/o State Assembly, Kota Kinabalu, Sabah
Leadership. Datuk Bernard Dompok (leader)
The PDS, a component of the ruling National Front, was organized in 1994 by defectors from the Sabah United Party.

Sabah Progressive Party (SAPP)
Address. c/o State Assembly, Kota Kinabalu, Sabah
Leadership. Datuk Yong Teck Lee (leader)
The SAPP is a Chinese-dominated grouping within the National Front which, like the Sabah Democratic Party, was set up in 1994 as a breakaway faction from the Sabah United Party. In May 1996 the SAPP leader was appointed Chief Minister of Sabah.

Sarawak National Action Party (SNAP)
Address. 304–5 Mei Jun Bldg, Rubber Rd, POB 2960, 93758 Kuching, Sarawak
Telephone. (#60–82) 254244
Leadership. Datuk Amar James Wong Kim Min (president)
Supported largely by the Iban population (ethnic Dayaks) of Sarawak, the SNAP is a member not only of the federal National Front but also of the state-level ruling Front of Three

Bavisan Tiga), with the United Traditional Bumiputra Party and the Sarawak United People's Party. The SNAP won six of the 56 state assembly seats in the elections of September 1991.

Sarawak Native People's Party
Parti Bansa Dayak Sarawak (PBDS)
    Address. c/o State Assembly, Kuching, Sarawak
    Leadership. Dato Leo Moggie anak Irok (president)
    The PBDS was set up in 1983 by a breakaway group from the Sarawak National Action Party. The following year it was accepted as a National Front partner and formed a coalition state government with the United Traditional Bumiputra Party, the SNAP and the Sarawak United People's Party. In 1987, having been dismissed from the state (but not the federal) National Front grouping, the PBDS emerged from state elections as the largest single party with 15 seats. However, it suffered a resounding defeat in the state poll in 1991, being reduced to seven seats.

Sarawak United People's Party (SUPP)
    Address. 7 Central Rd West, POB 454, 93710 Kuching, Sarawak
    Telephone. (#60–82) 246999
    Leadership. Tan Sri Datuk Amar Wong Soon Kai (president)
    The centre-left Chinese-based SUPP is a member not only of the federal ruling National Front but also of the state-level Front of Three (*Bavisan Tiga*) coalition, which was returned to power in the 1991 state elections, in which the SUPP won 16 of the coalition's 49 seats.

United Malays National Organization (UMNO)
Pertubuhan Kebangsaan Melayu Bersatu
    Address. Menara Dato' Onn, 38th Floor, Jalan Tun Dr Ismail, 50480 Kuala Lumpur
    Fax. (#60–3) 4420273
    Leadership. Dato'Seri Mahathir bin Mohamad (president), Mahmud Zhudi (secretary-general)
    Founded in 1946, UMNO supports the interests of the numerically dominant Malay population, while also promoting the right of all Malaysians to participate in the political, social and economic life of the nation. The party has been the dominant political organization since the attainment of national independence in 1957, and is the leading component of the ruling National Front. Following the 1986 elections, UMNO experienced unprecedented internal conflict, Prime Minister Mahathir in 1987 only narrowly defeating a challenge for the party presidency by one of his key ministers, Tengku Razaleigh Hamzah. The intraparty strife culminated in 1988 in the organization of the "New" UMNO (UMNO-*Baru*) by the pro-

Mahathir faction, while Razaleigh and his dissident supporters formed the rival Spirit of '46 party. Despite the period of discord, Mahathir led the party (reverting to its original name) to another election success in 1990 and was subsequently reconfirmed as party president. In the 1995 federal elections UMNO secured 88 of the National Front's 162 seats in the House of Representatives.

United Sabah People's Party
Parti Bersatu Rakyat Sabah (PBRS)
    Address. c/o State Assembly, Kota Kinabalu, Sabah
    Leadership. Datuk Joseph Kurup (leader)
    The party was formed in 1994 as a breakaway faction of the Sabah United Party and is a member of the ruling National Front.

United Traditional Bumiputra Party
    Parti Pesaka Bumiputra Bersatu (PPBB)
    Address. Jalan Satok/Kulas, 93400 Kuching, Sarawak
    Leadership. Tan Sri Datuk Patinggi Amar Haji Abdul Taib Mahmud (president)
    The PPBB is not only a member of the federal National Front but is also the dominant partner in the ruling Front of Three (*Bavisam Tiga*) coalition in Sarawak state, with the Sarawak National Action Party and the Sarawak United People's Party. In the 1991 state elections the party secured 27 of the coalition's 49 assembly seats.

Non-Front Parties

Democratic Action Party (DAP)
    Address. 24 Jalan 20/9, Petaling Jaya, Selangor
    Telephone. (#60–3) 757-8022
    Fax. (#60–3) 757-5718
    Leadership. Lim Kit Siang (secretary-general)
    The DAP, founded in 1966 as the Malaysian offshoot of the People's Action Party (PAP) of Singapore, is a predominantly Chinese party with a democratic socialist orientation. Contesting its first general elections in May 1969 in alliance with the Malaysian People's Movement (*Gerakan*), it made a political breakthrough for non-Malays, winning 13 federal and 31 state assembly seats. This success precipitated a wave of serious communal violence and the detention of leading DAP members, including Lim Kit Siang. Thereafter the DAP's activities were circumscribed by various internal security measures. It nevertheless remained the main opposition party at the national level in the 1970s and 1980s, although its representation in the House of Representatives dropped sharply in the April 1995 federal elections from 20 seats

to nine. In the state elections held at the same time the party secured 11 seats overall. The DAP is a member of the Socialist International.

Malaysian Islamic Council Front
Barisan Jama'ah Islamiah SeMalaysia (Berjasa)

Leadership. Dato Haji Wan Hashim bin Haji Wan Achmed (president)

Berjasa is a Kelantan-based moderate pro-Islamic party formed in 1977. In 1980 it joined the National Front coalition, but withdrew in 1989 to join the loose opposition Muslim Unity Movement alliance. In the 1995 elections the party failed to win any representation at federal or state level.

Muslim Front of Malaysia
Hizbul Muslimin Malaysia (Hamim)

Leadership. Datuk Haji Asri Muda (president)

Hamim was formed in 1983 by Asri Muda as a breakaway faction of the Pan-Malaysian Islamic Party, of which he had been president. Asri Muda had opposed efforts to transfer powers held by the party leadership to a Council of Theologians. The party contested the 1995 federal and state elections as part of the opposition Muslim Unity Movement (which it had joined on the latter's formation in 1989), but won no seats.

Pan-Malaysian Islamic Party
Parti Islam SeMalaysia (PAS)

Address. Markaz Tarbiyyah PAS Pusat, Lorong Haji Hassan, off Jalan Batu Geliga, Kuala Lumpur

Telephone. (#60–3) 689-5612

Leadership. Fadzil Nor (president), Halim Arshat (secretary-general)

Founded in the early 1950s, the fundamentalist PAS seeks the establishment of the Islamic system in society and the state. It joined the ruling National Front in 1973, but has been in opposition to the governing coalition since 1977. Contesting the 1990 and 1995 elections as part of the Muslim Unity Movement (formed in 1989 as a loose opposition alliance), the PAS won seven seats in the federal House of Representatives on both occasions. In the 1995 state assembly elections the party won control of Kelantan, its stronghold, taking 24 of the 43 seats, enabling Datuk Haji Nik Abdul Aziz Nik Mat to form a PAS government. It also won nine seats in two other assemblies (in Kedah and Trengganu), making it the most successful of the opposition parties at state level.

Sabah People's Union
Bersatu Rakyat Jelata Sabah (Berjaya)

Address. c/o State Assembly, Kota Kinabalu, Sabah

Leadership. Haji Mohamed Noor Mansoor (president)

Founded in 1975, *Berjaya* controlled the Sabah state assembly from 1976 until 1985, subsequently being weakened by defections and having little electoral success either at federal or state level. *Berjaya* was a member of the federal ruling National Front until withdrawing shortly before the 1986 elections.

Sabah United Party
Parti Bersatu Sabah (PBS)

Address. c/o State Assembly, Kota Kinabalu, Sabah

Leadership. Datuk Joseph Pairin Kitingan (president)

The PBS was founded by Pairin and other dissidents from the Sabah People's Union in 1985, and won a majority of state assembly seats that year. It was admitted to the federal ruling National Front in 1986 but withdrew into opposition in 1990. The party suffered damaging defections in 1989 and again in early 1994, forcing it to relinquish the state administration to the National Front.

Spirit of '46
Semangat '46

Address. c/o House of Representatives, Kuala Lumpur

Leadership. Tengku Razaleigh Hamzah (president), Datuk Suhaimi Kamaruddin (secretary-general)

Spirit of '46 was formed in 1988 by dissidents from the United Malays National Organization (UMNO) who had supported Razaleigh Hamzah's narrowly unsuccessful challenge for the UMNO presidency the previous year. The grouping's name referred to the year of the original foundation of UMNO. In 1989 it was instrumental in the formation of the Muslim Unity Movement opposition coalition which, headed by the Pan-Malaysian Islamic Party (PAS), took control of Kelantan in the 1990 state elections. In the 1995 federal elections the party's representation in the House of Representatives fell from eight to six seats. In the state elections the group won 11 seats in Kelantan, taking second place to the PAS.

In May 1996, following his first face-to-face meeting with Prime Minister Mahathir for seven years, Razaleigh Hamzah announced his intention to rejoin UMNO. No date for the reversion was specified, reportedly because Razaleigh wanted to ensure that he took the rest of his party with him.

Other Parties

Communist Party of Malaya (CPM), led by Chin Peng, officially banned since 1948, opposed to the

Malaysian Federation, agreed to terminate its insurgency in 1989, but remained essentially an underground organization.

Malayan Communist Party (MCP), led Ah Leng, urban-based illegal grouping formed in 1989 by hardline Marxist-Leninist revolutionaries, accepts Malaysian Federation while aspiring to overthrow its government and economic system.

Malaysian Nationalist Party (*Parti Nationalis Malaysia*, PNM or NasMa), an opposition multi-racial grouping launched in 1985 and led by Zainab Yang.

Malaysian People's Party (*Parti Rakyat Malaysia*, PRM), a left-wing grouping under the presidency of Syed Husin Ali.

Sabah People's Party (*Parti Rakyat Sabah*, PRS), founded in 1989 and led by Datuk James Ongkili.

Social Justice Party (*Parti Keadilan Masyarakat*, Pekemas), set up in 1971 by a splinter group of the Malaysian People's Movement.

United Malaysian Indian Party (UMIP), led by Kumar Manoharan.

Maldives

Capital: Malé   **Population:** 250,000 (1995E)

There are no political parties in the Republic of Maldives, a former British protectorate until independence in 1965. There is a 48–member Citizens' Assembly (*Majlis*), 40 members of which are elected for five years, with the remaining eight appointed by the President. The Citizens' Assembly designates the President for a five-year term, but the action must be confirmed by popular referendum. The President appoints, and presides over, the Cabinet.

President Mamoun Abdul Gayoom first took office in 1978. His re-election for a fourth term was confirmed in October 1993 after he won an overwhelming majority of votes cast in a national referendum. Non-party elections to the Citizens' Assembly were held in December 1994.

Mali

Capital: Bamako   **Population:** 9,000,000 (1995E)

Mali was under French rule until it achieved independence with Senegal as the Federation of Mali in June 1960. The Federation, formed the previous year, was dissolved in August 1960 when Senegal withdrew, the title of the Republic of Mali then being adopted. Following a coup in 1968, the country was ruled until 1991 by a Military Committee for National Liberation with Gen. Moussa Traoré as executive President, head of state and government, and (from 1979) secretary-general of the sole legal political party, the Mali People's Democratic Union. In March 1991 the regime was overthrown in a coup and replaced by a transitional military-civilian administration (the Transition Committee for the Salvation of the People, CTSP). A new constitution establishing multi-party rule was approved in a referendum in January 1992. It provides for a directly elected executive President, with a five-year term of office, and a National Assembly (*Assemblée Nationale*) of 129 members (13 of whom represent the interests of Malians resident abroad), who also serve for five years.

In multi-party legislative elections on March 8, 1992, the Alliance for Democracy in Mali–Pan-African Party for Liberty, Solidarity and Justice (ADEMA-PPLSJ) secured a majority of seats in the National Assembly. A presidential election held on April 12 and 26, 1992, was won by the ADEMA-PPLSJ leader, Alpha Oumar Konare, who formed a new civilian government.

Alliance for Democracy in Mali–Pan-African Party for Liberty, Solidarity and Justice
Alliance pour la Démocratie au Mali–Parti Pan-Africain pour la Liberté, la Solidarité et la Justice (ADEMA-PPLSJ)

Address. BP 1791, Bamako

Telephone. (#233) 220368

Leadership. Alpha Oumar Konare and Ibrahim Boubacar Keita (leaders), Aly Nouhoun Diallo (political secretary)

ADEMA was a principal element in the pro-democracy campaign launched in 1990 against the Moussa Traoré regime and was represented in the Transition Committee (CTSP) set up after the March 1991 coup. The organization, having registered for legal status in April 1991 under the ADEMA-PPLSJ rubric, won substantial majorities in the municipal, legislative and presidential elections the following year. In the National Assembly elections in March 1992 ADEMA-PPLSJ candidates took 76 seats (subsequently reduced to 74, amid allegations of irregularities), while in April Alpha Oumar Konare captured the presidency with almost 70% of the second-round vote. The party's political secretary was elected as president of the National Assembly in July 1992. Governments headed by the ADEMA-PPLSJ remained in power thereafter, the party retaining its dominance despite the formation in 1994 of the breakaway Movement for African Independence, Rebirth and Integration.

Front to Safeguard Democracy
Front Sauvegarde de la Démocratie (FSD)

Address. c/o Assemblée Nationale, Bamako

The formation of the FSD by 13 parties opposed to the ruling Alliance for Democracy in Mali–Pan-African Party for Lberty Solidarity and Justice (ADEMA-PPLSJ) was announced in May 1992. Participants included the Sudanese Union–African Democratic Rally, the Rally for Democracy and Progress, the Union of Democratic Forces for Progress and the Union for Democracy and Development.

Malian Union for Democracy and Development
Union Malienne pour la Démocratie et le Développement (UMDD)

Address. c/o Assemblée Nationale, Bamako

Leadership. Nansat Katia Seydou

Formed in April 1991, the UMDD won a single seat in the National Assembly elections in March 1992.

Movement for African Independence, Rebirth and Integration
Mouvement pour l'Indépendance, la Renaissance et l'Intégration Africaines (MIRIA)

Address. c/o Assemblée Nationale, Bamako

Leadership. Mohamed Lamine Traoré, Mohamedoun Dicko

MIRIA was launched in September 1994 by a dissident faction of the dominant Alliance for Democracy in Mali–Pan-African Party for Liberty, Solidarity and Justice after a period of internal strife over the role and structure of the ruling party, also involving conflicts of personal ambition.

National Congress for Democratic Initiative
Congrès National d'Initiative Démocratique (CNID)

Address. c/o Assemblée Nationale, Bamako

Leadership. Mountaga Tall (chair), Amida Diabate (secretary-general)

The CNID, launched in 1990 as part of the pro-democracy campaign, was part of the Transition Committee (CTSP) formed after the March 1991 coup. It achieved legal status in May 1991. Deriving support mainly from the younger electorate, the party won nine National Assembly seats in the March 1992 legislative elections, becoming the second largest group, although well behind the Alliance for Democracy in Mali–Pan-African Party for Liberty, Solidarity and Justice (ADEMA-PPLSJ). Party leader Mountaga Tall contested the first round of April 1992 presidential election, finishing third with about 11.4% of the vote. Members of the CNID and the Rally for Democracy and Progress were included in a new government appointed by President Konare in April 1993, but both parties withdrew from the coalition in February 1994. A serious split in the CNID was reported in March 1995 when a number of members of the governing committee were suspended.

Party for Democracy and Progress
Parti pour la Démocratie et le Progrès (PDP)

Address. BP 1823, Bamako

Telephone. (#233) 226452

Leadership. Idrissa Traoré (leader)

The PDP won two National Assembly seats in the 1992 legislative elections and subsequently participated in the coalition government until withdrawing in February 1994 (although the PDP Minister for Youth and Sports refused to resign his cabinet post and remained as an independent). Party leader Idrissa Traoré received about 4% of the votes cast in the first round of the presidential election in April 1992.

Popular Movement for Development and the United Republic of West Africa
Mouvement Populaire pour le Développement et la République Unie de l'Afrique de l'Ouest (MPDRUAO)

> *Address.* c/o Assemblée Nationale, Bamako
> *Leadership.* Boubou Sall (leader)

This organization, formally registered in July 1991 and promoting the idea of regional federation in West Africa, won six seats in the National Assembly elections in March 1992.

Rally for Democracy and Labour
Rassemblement pour la Démocratie et le Travail (RDT)

> *Address.* c/o Assemblée Nationale, Bamako
> *Leadership.* Amadou Ali Niangadou (leader)

Formed in May 1991, the RDT won three seats in the legislative elections in March 1992. The party leader finished seventh in the presidential election with 4% of the votes.

Rally for Democracy and Progress
Rassemblement pour la Démocratie et le Progrès (RDP)

> *Address.* BP 2110, Bamako
> *Telephone.* (#233) 223092
> *Fax.* (#233) 226795
> *Leadership.* Almamy Sylla (leader)

The RDP was formed in 1990 and registered in April the following year. In 1992 it secured four seats in the National Assembly elections, and party leader, Almamy Sylla, took fourth place in the first ballot for the presidency with nearly 10% of the vote. In May 1992 Sylla was a leading participant in the formation of a 13-party opposition coalition, the Front to Safeguard Democracy. The RDP was included in a new government in April 1993 but withdrew from the coalition in February 1994.

Sudanese Progress Party
Parti Soudanais du Progrès (PSP)

> *Address.* c/o Assemblée Nationale, Bamako
> *Leadership.* Sekene Mody Cissoko (leader)

The PSP was awarded two seats in the National Assembly following legal action over irregularities in the March 1992 legislative elections.

Sudanese Union–African Democratic Rally
Union Soudanaise–Rassemblement Démocratique Africain (US-RDA)

> *Address.* c/o Assemblée Nationale, Bamako
> *Leadership.* Mamadou Bamou Touré (secretary-general)

Formed as the national wing of a broader independence movement in French-ruled Africa, the US-RDA was the sole legal political party from independence in 1960 until the military coup in 1968. Revived in 1991, it won eight seats in the 1992 legislative elections, the third largest complement. The party's performance in the presidential election was adversely affected by a split over the selection of a candidate. The initial nomination of Tiéoulé Mamadou Konate was repudiated by a faction of the party leadership, which instead selected Baba Hakib Haidara. Ultimately both stood as candidates, Konate coming second and Haidara fifth in the first round ballot. Konate was then defeated by the candidate of the Alliance for Democracy in Mali–Pan-African Party for Liberty, Solidarity and Justice (ADEMA-PPLSJ) in the run-off, winning about 30% of the vote. Konate was prominent in the establishment of the opposition Front to Safeguard Democracy in May 1992.

Union for Democracy and Development
Union pour la Démocratie et le Développement (UDD)

> *Address.* c/o Assemblée Nationale, Bamako
> *Leadership.* Moussa Balla Coulibaly

The UDD, whose leader was a former official of President Moussa Traoré's ruling party, was formed in 1991. It won four seats in the March 1992 National Assembly elections and was among those parties which subsequently announced the formation of the opposition Front to Safeguard Democracy.

Union of Democratic Forces for Progress
Union des Forces Démocratiques pour le Progrès (UFDP)

> *Address.* c/o Assemblée Nationale, Bamako
> *Leadership.* Col. Youssouf Traoré

The UFDP was formed in 1991 by a former supporter of President Moussa Traoré who had broken with the regime around 1980. The UFDP won three seats in the National Assembly elections in March 1992 and was involved in the formation of the opposition Front to Safeguard Democracy.

Tuareg Groups

Azawad Liberation Front (*Front pour la Libération de l'Azaouad*, FLA), which serves as an umbrella organization for the following insurgent Tuareg groups: the **Arab Islamic Front of Azawad** (*Front Islamique Arabe de l'Azaouad*, FIAA); the **Popular Front for the Liberation of Azawad** (*Front Populaire de Libération de l'Azaouad*, FPLA); the **Popular Movement of Azawad** (*Mouvement Popu-*

laire de l'Azaouad, MPA); and the **Revolutionary Army for the Liberation of Azawad** (*Armée Révolutionnaire de Libération de l'Azaouad*, ARLA). A

peace process was initiated in 1992 with the signing of a national pact between rebel groups and the government.

Malta

Capital: Valletta

Population: 368,000 (1995E)

Malta was granted independence from Britain in 1964 as a member of the Commonwealth and declared itself a Republic in 1974. Its 1964 constitution as amended in 1974 defines Malta as a parliamentary democracy, with a largely ceremonial President elected for a five-year term by the legislature. Executive power resides in the Cabinet headed by the Prime Minister, chosen from and responsible to the unicameral House of Representatives currently of 65 members elected for a five-year term (subject to dissolution) by universal suffrage of those aged 18 and over. Members are returned from multi-seat electoral divisions by proportional representation, a degree of overall proportionality being ensured under a 1987 constitutional amendment which specifies that a party winning a majority of the popular vote should be awarded "bonus" seats if such are needed to give it a parliamentary majority. Another amendment adopted at the same time, also by agreement between the two main parties, gave constitutional force to Malta's status as a neutral state.

Elections to the House of Representatives on Feb. 22, 1992, resulted as follows: Nationalist Party 34 seats (51.8% of the vote), Malta Labour Party 31 (46.5%).

Malta Labour Party (MLP)
Partit tal-Haddiema
 Address. Centra Nazzjonali Laburista, Triq Milend, Hamrun HMR 02
 Telephone. (#356) 249900
 Fax. (#356) 244204
 Leadership. Alfred Sant (leader), Mario Vella (president), Jimmy Magro (general secretary)

The MLP was founded in 1920 as a trade union party and played an important role in the 1921–30 period of internal self-government. In the first elections to a Maltese Legislative Assembly held in October 1947 under a new constitution restoring self-government, the MLP, then led by Dr Paul Boffa, won 24 out of the Assembly's 40 seats. A government formed by Dr Boffa was in office until September 1950. In October 1949, however, the MLP was split, with Dr Boffa founding a (moderate) Independent Labour Party, which gained 11 seats in the 1950 Assembly elections, seven (as the Malta Workers' Party) in 1951 and three in 1953, whereafter it contested no further elections.

The MLP first gained a majority of seats (23 out of 40) in the Assembly in 1955 and was thereafter in power under Dom Mintoff until 1958, when his government resigned over a dispute with Britain on Malta's constitutional future. In the 1962

general election the MLP was defeated, gaining only 16 out of 42 seats in parliament, after the Roman Catholic Church hierarchy had called on the electorate not to vote Labour. It was not returned to power until 1971 (under the leadership of Dom Mintoff) when it won 28 out of the 55 seats in the House of Representatives. In May 1978 it was officially amalgamated with the (36,000-strong) General Workers' Union.

Returned to power with an increased majority of 34 out of 65 seats in 1976, the MLP achieved the same result in the December 1981 elections, but came under severe criticism from the opposition Nationalist Party for achieving a parliamentary majority on the strength of fewer popular votes than the Nationalists. After a lengthy constitutional crisis, during which the Nationalists boycotted the House of Representatives for 15 months, the constitution was amended so that a party winning a majority of votes would if necessary be given additional seats to enable it to govern. This happened in the May 1987 elections, when the MLP retained 34 seats of the Nationalists 31, but the latter won 50.9% of the votes and were therefore allocated four additional seats. Labour thus went into opposition under Karmenu Mifsud Bonnici (who had succeeded Mintoff in December 1984).

The MLP's decline continued in the 1992

general elections, to 46.5%, so that it remained in opposition and Mifsud Bonnici gave way to Alfred Sant as party leader. The latter initiated a modernization of Labour's programme and organization (including completing a palatial new party headquarters), while maintaining the party's policy of clear neutrality in international relations and opposition to membership of the European Union. In October 1994 Labour's institutional ties with the trade union movement were apparent in its backing for a one-day general strike called in protest against the government's economic policies.

The MLP is a member party of the Socialist International.

Nationalist Party (NP)
Partit Nazzjonalista (PN)
   Address. Dar Centrali PN, Pietà
   Telephone. (#356) 243641
   Fax. (#356) 242886
   Leadership. Edward Fenech Adami (leader), Guido de Marco (deputy leader), Austin Gatt (general secretary)

Dating from 1880, the NP has its origins in the wave of nationalism which swept Europe in the 19th century and it fought successfully for Malta's self-government and later independence. Between 1887 and 1903, when Malta had representative government, the party held all elective seats in the Council of Government. After a period of colonial rule representative government was re-introduced in 1921 and the party held a majority of seats until 1927 (when the Constitutional Party and the Malta Labour Party (MLP) formed an alliance). When the NP regained a majority in 1933, the self-governmennt constitution was revoked.

During World War II several leaders of the party were detained or exiled, but from 1950 to 1955 the party was in government in coalition with the Workers' Party. It later held office from 1962 to 1971 (during which period Malta became independent in 1964).

The party was narrowly defeated by the MLP

in 1971 and again in 1976. In the elections of December 1981 the party gained 50.9% of the vote but only a minority of seaats in the House of Representatives. The party subsequently started a civil disobedience campaign and boycotted sessions of the House until March 1983. However, following constitutional amendments ensuring proportionality between votes obtained and representation, the NP obtained a majority in May 1987 (31 elective seats and four "bonus" seats) and formed a government.

The NP retained a majority in the February 1992 general elections and therefore continued in office. The NP government's main priority externally was to expedite Malta's application to become a full member of the European Union (submitted in 1990). It also signed up for NATO's Partnership for Peace programme in 1995, while pledging to uphold the 1987 constitutional guarantee of neutrality.

The NP is affiliated to the Christian Democrat International and the International Democrat Union.

Other Parties

Communist Party of Malta (*Partit Komunista Malti*, PKM), led by Anthony Vassallo (general secretary) and Charles Zammit (chair), founded in 1969 as orthodox pro-Soviet party by former members of the Malta Labour Party, to which it gave unofficial support in the Mintoff era by not contesting elections; achieved minimal support in 1987 and 1992 elections.

Democratic Alternative (*Alternizza Demokratika*, AD), led by Wenzu Mintoff and Saviour Balzan, environmentalist party formed prior to 1992 elections, in which it obtained 1.7% of the vote and no seats.

Malta Democratic Party (*Partit Demokratiko Malti*, PDM), led by Michael Vella and Lino Briguglio, founded in 1986 on a platform of decentralization and environmentalism.

Marshall Islands

Capital: Dalap-Uliga-Darrit (Majuro atoll)   **Population:** 56,000 (1995E)

The Marshall Islands comprise a double chain of atolls in the Pacific region of Micronesia. From 1947, as part of the UN Trust Territory of the Pacific, they were administered by the United States government. In 1979 a new constitution was adopted, and in 1982 the Republic of the Marshall Islands signed a comtract of free association (implemented in 1986) under which the United States recognized the territory as a fully sovereign and independent state, while retaining authority in regard to defence. In December 1990 the United Nations Security Council approved the termination of the Trusteeship in relation to the Marshall Islands, and the country joined the UN the following year.

The Marshall Islands has a 12-member Council of Chiefs (the *Iroij*), composed of traditional leaders, with consultative authority on matters relating to custom. Legislative authority resides in a 33-member legislature (the *Nitijela*), which is elected for four years and which chooses a President from among its members. The President is both head of state and head of government and appoints the Cabinet.

Traditionally there have been no formal political parties in the islands. President Amata Kabua was returned to office for a fifth successive term in November 1995, having been chosen by members of the new *Nitijela* which had been elected earlier that month. Kabua has been opposed by a grouping formed in 1991 led by Tony DeBrum.

Mauritania

Capital: Nouakchott

Population: 2,300,000 (1995E)

The Islamic Republic of Mauritania achieved independence from France in 1960 as a one-party state under the Mauritanian People's Party. Following a coup in 1978, the constitution was suspended and the National Assembly and former government and ruling party dissolved. The Military Council of National Salvation (CMSN) ruled until 1992.

In July 1991 a new constitution was approved, providing for the election of a President by universal suffrage for a six-year term and for the appointment of a Prime Minister. Legislative power is vested in a 79–member National Assembly (*Assemblée Nationale*), directly elected for five years, and a 56–member Senate, indirectly elected for a six-year term. At the same time legislation allowing the formation of political parties was approved by the CMSN.

Multi-party presidential and legislative elections were held in early 1992. On Jan. 24, 1992, President Moaouia Ould Sid'Ahmed Taya was returned to office for a further term with nearly 63 per cent of the votes cast, defeating three other candidates. On March 6 and 13, 1992, Taya's Democratic and Social Republican Party won an overwhelming victory in the National Assembly elections, although they were boycotted by opposition groups. The same party also won control of the Senate in inaugural indirect elections on April 3 and 10, 1992, its dominance being confirmed at the first biennial replenishment on April 15, 1994.

Democratic and Social Republican Party
Parti Républicain Démocratique et Social (PRDS)
    Address. c/o Assemblée Nationale, Nouakchott
    Leadership. Cheikh Sid'Ahmed Ould Baba (leader)
    The centre-left PRDS was formed soon after the legalization of multi-partyism in 1991 in support of President Taya, on whose behalf it successfully campaigned in the January 1992 presidential election. In the National Assembly elections in March 1992 the PRDS took 67 of the 79 seats. The following month it was one of only two parties to contest the Senate elections in which it won 36 seats (17 of the remaining 20 seats going to independent candidates and three to representa-

tives of Mauritanians resident abroad). In March 1995 it was announced that the Movement of Independent Democrats (*Mouvement des Démocrats Indépendants*, MDI), hitherto a constituent of the opposition Union of Democratic Forces, had joined the PRDS.

Mauritanian Renewal Party
Parti Mauritanien pour le Renouvellement (PMR)
    Address. c/o Assemblée Nationale, Nouakchott
    Leadership. Moulaye al-Hassan Ould Jeydid (leader)
    Registered in 1991, the centrist PMR won a single seat in the March 1992 National Assembly

elections but joined the general opposition boycott of the Senate elections the following month.

National Vanguard Party
Parti Nationale de l'Avant-Garde (PNAG)
Leadership. Khattry Ould Taleb Jiddou

Legalized in late 1991, the PNAG was one of the few parties not to join the boycott of the National Assembly elections in March 1992 and was the only party apart from the Democratic and Social Republican Party to contest the Senate elections in April 1992. It failed to win any seats in either case, but its leader was given a junior ministerial post. He was dismissed in January 1994, the party thereafter coming under pressure from the authorities because of its alleged links with the ruling Baath Arab Socialist Party of Iraq. In December 1995 Jiddou and other PNAG members were among over 50 alleged pro-Baath activists put on trial for forming an illegal organization, although those sentenced was acquitted on appeal the following month.

Rally for Democracy and National Unity
Rassemblement pour la Démocratice et l'Unité Nationale (RDUN)
Address. c/o Assemblée Nationale, Nouakchott
Leadership. Ahmed Moktar Sidi Baba (leader)

The centre-right RDUN was the main party to contest the dominance of the PRDS in the March 1992 legislative elections in view of the boycott by other opposition groups. However, it won only one seat in the National Assembly, and subsequently took no part in the Senate elections in April.

Socialist and Democratic Popular Union
Union Populaire Socialiste et Démocratique (UPSD)
Leadership. Mohamed Mahmoud Ould Mah (leader)

Recognized in September 1991, the UPSD contested the January 1992 presidential election, but party leader, Ould Mah, came fourth the poll with 1.36 per cent of the votes cast. The party boycotted the subsequent legislative elections.

Umma Party
Leadership. Ould Sidi Yayia (leader)

An influential Islamic fundamentalist organization, Umma was formed in 1991 but not allowed to register formally as a legal political party because of the constitutional ban on parties based on religion.

Union for Democracy and Progress
Union pour la Démocratie et le Progrès (UDP)
Leadership. Hamdi Ould Mouknass (president)

The UDP was legalized in 1993, its ranks reportedly including former prominent members of the Union of Democratic Forces.

Union of Democratic Forces
Union des Forces Démocratique (UFD)
Leadership. Ahmed Ould Daddah (leader)

Legalized in October 1991 and generally considered the strongest opposition formation, the UFD supported the (second-placed) presidential candidacy of Ahmed Ould Daddah in January 1992, but then led the opposition boycott of the subsequnent legislative elections. In March 1995 an important element of the UFD, the Movement of Independent Democrats (*Mouvement des Démocrats Indépendants*, MDI), announced that it had joined the ruling Democratic and Social Republican Party.

Other Parties

Action for Change (*Action pour Changement*), reportedly granted recognition in August 1995 and led by Messaoud Ould Boulkheir.

Democratic and Social Union (*Union Démocratique et Sociale*, UDS), established in early 1992.

Democratic Centre Party (*Parti du Centre Démocratique*, PCD), registered in 1991.

Democratic Justice Party (*Parti pour la Justice Démocratique*, PJD), legalized in September 1991.

National Party for Unity and Democracy (*Parti National pour l'Unité et la Démocratie*, PNUD), formed in the first half of 1992.

Progressive People's Party (*Parti Populaire du Progrès*, PPP), founded in 1991 and led by Taleb Ould Jiddou.

Socialist and Democratic Unity Party (*Parti Unitaire Démocratique et Socialiste*, PUDS), legalized in August 1995.

Clandestine Groups

African Liberation Forces of Mauritania (*Forces de la Libération Africaine de Mauritanie*, FLAM), formed in 1983 and engaged in guerrilla activity from 1989 in response to perceived government oppression of Black inhabitants.

Rally for the Rebirth of Black Africans (*Rassemblement pour la Renaissance des Noirs Africans de Mauritanie*), established in 1989 in the wake of ethnic confrontation and violence.

United Front for Armed Resistance in Mauritania (*Front Uni pour la Résistance Armée en Mauritanie*), a hardline Black resistance group launched in Senegal in 1990.

Mauritius

Capital: Port Louis

Population: 1,125,000 (1995E)

A former British colony, Mauritius achieved independence in 1968. The British monarch remained as head of state until the country became a republic in March 1992. The post of President is a largely ceremonial role, executive power being vested in the Prime Minister who is leader of the majority parliamentary party. The President, elected for a five-year term by the National Assembly, appoints the Council of Ministers on the recommendation of the Prime Minister. There is a unicameral National Assembly, 62 of whose members are elected by universal adult suffrage for a term of five years, while up to eight seats are allocated under a "best loser" system.

A political crisis in November 1995 provoked the dissolution of the National Assembly and the holding of early elections on Dec. 21, 1995. The ruling coalition was trounced by an alliance of the Labour Party and Mauritian Militant Movement (MMM), which made a clean sweep of the 60 elective Mauritius parliamentary seats. The Organization of the People of Rodriguez (OPR) won the two elective seats of the island of Rodriguez, while "best loser" seats were allocated to the Rodriguez Movement (2), the Mauritian Social Democratic (Gaëtan Duval) Party (1) and Hizbullah (1).

Labour Party

Parti Travailliste

    Address. 7 Guy Rozement Square, Port Louis

    Telephone. (#230) 212-6691

    Fax. (#230) 696-1982

    Leadership. Navin Ramgoolam (leader)

The Labour Party led Mauritius to independence in 1968 under the premiership of Sir Seewoosagur Ramgoolam but lost all of its elective seats in 1982. Recovering some ground in the 1983 contest, it was a constituent of the subsequent governing coalitions led by the Mauritian Socialist Movement (MSM). In September 1990 it moved into opposition as a consequence of an electoral alliance forged between the MSM and the Mauritian Militant Movement (to promote constitutional measures that would allow Mauritius to become a republic). The Labour Party contested the 1991 general election in an opposition alliance with the Mauritian Social Democratic Party, but won only a handful of seats. In April 1994 it signed an electoral pact with the MMM, and in the December 1995 general election this alliance defeated the ruling coalition, taking all the elective seats for the main island. Labour leader Navin Ramgoolam (son of Sir Seewoosagur) was sworn in as the country's new Prime Minister at the end of December. He stated that his government would continue the pro-market economic policies of its predecessor but with more emphasis on equal opportunities and welfare for the poor.

The Labour Party is a full member of the Socialist International.

Mauritian Militant Movement

Mouvement Militant Mauricien (MMM)

    Address. c/o National Assembly, Port Louis

    Leadership. Paul Bérenger (leader)

The socialist MMM was founded in 1969 with a substantial trade union following. Briefly in government from 1982, the party split in 1983 when the then MMM president and Prime Minister, Sir Aneerood Jugnauth, was expelled from the party and thereupon formed the Mauritian Socialist Movement (MSM). In the 1991 general election an alliance of the MMM, the MSM and the Democratic Labour Movement won a large parliamentary majority, and the MMM gained substantial representation in the new coalition government which transformed the country into a republic in 1992. Disputes between the MMM and the MSM during 1993 led to the dismissal of the MMM leader, Paul Bérenger, from the Council of Ministers and the subsequent departure, in mid-1994, of the pro-coalition faction within the party to form the Mauritian Militant Renaissance. In April 1994 the MMM signed an electoral pact with the Labour Party, and in the December 1995 general election this alliance ousted the ruling coalition.

Bérenger opined that the alliance's victory was because the Prime Minister and the MSM had lost touch with their rural base and the urban poor.

Mauritian Social Democratic Party

Parti Mauricien Social-Démocrate (PMSD)
  Address. PO Box 599, Port Louis
  Leadership. Xavier Luc Duval (leader)

The conservative PMSD originated in the pre-independence period, mainly representing the French-speaking and Creole middle classes. Under the leadership of Gaëtan Duval, the party increased its representation to 23 seats in 1967 and took part in the 1969-73 national unity government led by the Labour Party, with Duval as External Affairs Minister. Its departure in December 1973 was because of Labour opposition to Duval's policy of dialogue with South Africa. The PMSD was again in coalition with Labour in 1976-82, while from 1983 until 1988 it was a junior member of coalition headed by the alliance of Labour and the Mauritian Socialist Movement (MSM). Although the PMSD fought the 1991 election in an opposition alliance with Labour, it agreed to enter the governing coalition led by the MSM in February 1995. Meanwhile, Sir Gaëtan (as he now was) had secured the succession to the party leadership on his son, Xavier Luc. Tarred by the government's unpopularity and despite standing as the "Gaëtan Duval Party", the PMSD failed to win an elective seat in the December 1995 contest, although it was awarded one "best loser" seat. Sir Gaëtan Duval died in May 1996.

Mauritian Socialist Movement

Mouvement Socialiste Mauricien (MSM)
  Address. c/o Sir Aneerood Jugnauth, La Caverne, Vacoas
  Leadership. Sir Aneerood Jugnauth (leader)

Formed in 1983 by Sir Aneerood Jugnauth, following his expulsion from the Mauritian Militant Movement, the MSM was the dominant party in subsequent coalition governments until the general election in December 1995 when, in alliance with the Mauritian Militant Renaissance, it failed to retain any seats in the National Assembly.

Organization of the People of Rodrigues

Organization du Peuple Rodriguais (OPR)
  Address. c/o National Assembly, Port Louis
  Leadership. Louis Serge Clair (leader)

Seeking to represent the interests people of the island of Rodrigues, the OPR has consistently held the two elective seats for Rodriguez in the National Assembly and was included in successive government coalitions until the elections in December 1995, when it went into opposition.

Other Parties

Democratic Labour Movement (*Mouvement des Travaillistes Démocrates*, MTD), led by Anil Kumar Baichoo, held two seats in the National Assembly and one post in the Mauritian Socialist Movement-led coalition government until its electoral failure in the December 1995 polls.

Hizbullah, an Islamic fundamentalist formation that obtained sufficient support in the December 1995 elections to be awarded one "best loser" seat.

Mauritian Democratic Union (*Union Démocratique Mauricienne*, UDM), led by Guy Ollivry, founded by former members of the Mauritian Social Democratic Party, has not attracted any significant electoral support; affiliated to the Christian Democrat International.

Mauritian Militant Renaissance (*Renouveau Militant Mauricien*, RMM), led by Paramhansa Nababsing, was formed in mid-1994 by a dissident faction of the Mauritian Militant Movement, which had chosen to remain within the governing coalition following the dismissal of MMM leader, Paul Bérenger, from the Council of Ministers in August 1993; the RMM fought the December 1995 elections in alliance with the Mauritian Socialist Movement, but failed to secure any seats in the National Assembly.

Mauritian Socialist Party (*Parti Socialiste Mauricien*, PSM), led by Harish Boodhoo, originally a breakaway faction from the Labour Party, absorbed into the Mauritian Socialist Movement in 1983, but reconstituted as a separate party in 1988 by its former leader.

Muslim Action Committee (*Comité d'Action Musulman*, CAM), led by Youssouf Mohammed, has drawn support from among the Indo-Mauritian Muslim community since its formation in 1958.

Mexico

Capital: Mexico City   **Population:** 93,700,000 (1995E)

Mexico achieved independence from Spain in 1821. The iron rule of Porfirio Díaz, President from 1876 to 1911 (known as the *Porfiriato*), except for the period 1880-84, ended the political instability of earlier years but precipitated the violent revolution of 1910-20 which produced such leaders as Emiliano Zapata and Francisco "Pancho" Villa. Since 1929 one party, renamed the Institutional Revolutionary Party (PRI) in 1946, inherited the mantle of the revolution and has held political power ever since, although opposition parties have consistently accused the PRI of serious electoral malpractice. In addition, the PRI's vote in presidential elections has continued to decline, falling from 95% in 1976 to 74% in 1982 and 50.36% in 1988 under the combined weight of the foreign debt burden, subsequent economic austerity policies, large-scale corruption and human rights violations.

Under the 1917 constitution (as amended) a bicameral Congress is made up of a 64-member Senate, elected every six years (two from each state and two from the Federal District), and a 500-member Federal Chamber of Deputies. Executive power rests with the President, who appoints a Cabinet, including the governor of the Federal District.

The President is elected for a six-year term, known locally as the *sexenio*, as are the 64 senators. The 500 deputies are elected every three years, 300 by majority vote in single-member constituencies and the remaining 200 by proportional representation of parties winning at least 1.5% of the national vote. Each state has its own constitution and is administered by a governor, who, with the exception of the governor of the Federal District, is elected for a six-year term. All elections, both national and state, are held on the basis of universal adult suffrage. All Mexican citizens 18 years of age and older are required to vote, although the law is rarely enforced.

The PRI extended its unbroken 65-year period in power when Ernesto Zedillo Ponce de Léon was elected President on Aug. 21, 1994, and in simultaneous congressional elections the PRI won 300 of the 500 seats in the Chamber of Deputies and 95 of the 128 Senate seats. The new 56th legislature was installed on Nov. 1, a new Cabinet named on Nov. 30, and Zedillo took office on Dec. 1, 1994.

Institutional Revolutionary Party
Partido Revolucionario Institucional (PRI)
Address. Insurgnetes Norte 61, 06350 México DF
Fax. (#52-5) 535-3116
Leadership. Santiago Oñate Laborde (president), Fernando Ortiz Arana (chair of executive), Humberto Roque Villanueva (leader in the Chamber)

The PRI was founded in 1929 as the National Revolutionary Party (*Partido Nacional Revolucionario*, PNR). The party inherited a general populist and symbolic tradition from the Mexican Revolution which gave it room to manoeuvre in practice, uniting disparate political tendencies from socialism and social democracy through to right-wing conservatism. Its current belief in a market-led economy and the conservatism of its foreign policy, points to a clear move to the right.

Following a period of violent revolutionary struggle between 1910 and 20, the PRI emerged to dominate the country's political life, first as the National Revolutionary Party, founded by President Plutarco Elías Calles, which was renamed the Party of the Mexican Revolution in 1938 before taking its present name in 1946.

Of the many PRI Presidents, the most radical and most influential was probably Gen. Lázaro Cárdenas (1934-40), whose re-organization of the party led to the PRI becoming a huge network for social control and patronage, incorporating labour and peasant unions and popular organizations for civil servants, professional groups and the army. Cárdenas nationalized the oil industry in 1938 and introduced significant land reforms through the *ejido* common land system.

The authoritarian face of the party was shown most forcibly during the presidencies of Gustavo Díaz Ordaz (1964-70) and Luis Echeverría Alvárez (1970-76), when student unrest was violently repressed. President José López Portillo (1976-82) headed another conservative regime but in foreign policy it supported the 1979 Nicaraguan revolution and permitted the legalization of several left-wing parties.

President Miguel de la Madrid (1982-88), from the right of the party, gave effect to the party's anti-corruption rhetoric by bringing charges of corruption against the head of the state oil company and the chief of the Mexico city police.

The 1988 election victory of President Carlos Salinas de Gortari, by the smallest margin in the PRI's history, was one of the most controversial ever, opposition leaders being united in their claim that the PRI had been involved in widespread fraud. In July 1989 the PRI conceded victory to the National Action Party candidate in the governorship election in Baja California, its first electoral defeat in 60 years.

To restore its image at home and abroad, the PRI proposed electoral laws, passed by the Congress in July 1990, which the opposition Party of the Democratic Revolution opposed, claiming that they would preserve PRI majorities in the Chamber of Deputies and the Senate. Internal unrest also surfaced within the PRI as dissidents in the Critical Current faction (*Corriente Crítica*) and the Movement for Democratic Change (*Movimiento por el Cambio Democratico*, MCD) objected to the lack of internal democracy and the continuation of the *dedazo* system whereby the party's elite hand-picked election candidates and delegates to the PRI's national assembly.

The Salinas regime set out to improve the country's image and pledged itself to root out official corruption and to promote human rights. It established a pact for economic solidarity and growth (PECE) to contain wage and price increases in 1989 and initiated an ambitious programme to deregulate and liberalize the economy and privatize the state sector, most notably state banks nationalized in 1982. Negotiations were also begun in 1990 to conclude a North American Free Trade Agreement (NAFTA) with the USA and Canada. This became the centre-piece of the government's strategy to modernize the country and extricate it from a decade of debt-ridden stagnation. Critics also contended that it was designed to maintain the PRI's hold on power.

In a final split with the republican and revolutionary past, Salinas in November 1991 proposed that the 1917 constitution be altered to allow for the radical reform of the agriculture sector and the education system, and that official recognition, denied since the 1857 constitution, be conferred on the Roman Catholic Church. The proposals became law in February 1992.

In March 1993, controversy over donations from private businesses to the PRI led to the replacement of Gennaro Borrego Estrada as party chair by Fernando Ortiz. The run-up to the 1994 presidential elections was similarly torrid for the party following the assassination of the party's preferred candidate, Luis Colosio, in March 1994. He was replaced by Ernesto Zedillo as PRI candidate and was duly elected on Aug. 21, 1994, albeit with a record low share of the vote (50.18%). He took office on Dec. 1.

The PRI is a consultative member of the Socialist International.

Labour Party
Partido del Trabajo (PT)

Leadership. Alberto Anaya Gutierrez (president), Cecilia Soto González (1994 presidential candidate)

Founded in preparation for the 1991 congressional elections, the moderate PT won 1.2 percent of the vote in that election. In the 1994 presidential elections, the PT placed itself in direct competition with the left-wing Party of the Democratic Revolution this time gaining 2.82% of the national vote. Ten PT candidates were successfully elected to the Chamber of Deputies.

Mexican Socialist Party
Partido Mexicana Socialista (PMS)

Leadership. Herberto Castillo (PMT), Gilberto Rincon Gallardo (secretary-general)

The PMS, founded in March 1987 following a merger of various large and small left-wing groups, and was at one time, Mexico's third largest party. It was made up of the Mexican Workers' Party (*Partido Mexicano de los Trabajadores*, PMT); the Union of the Communist Left (*Unidad de la Izquierda Comunista*, UIC); the Trotskyist Workers' Revolutionary Party (*Partido Revolucionario de los Trabajadores*, PRT); the Patriotic Revolutionary Party (*Partido Patriótico Revolucionario*, PPR); and the People's Revolutionary Movement (*Movimiento Revolucionario del Pueblo*).

The largest PMS component was the Unified Socialist Party of Mexico (*Partido Socialista Unificado de México*, PSUM), which itself had been the product of a merger in November 1981 of the following parties: the Mexican Communist Party (*Partido Comunista Mexicano*, PCM); the

Popular Action Movement (*Movimiento de Acción y Unidad Socialista*, MAUS); the Mexican People's Party (*Partido del Pueblo Mexicana*, PPM); and the Revolutionary Socialist Party (*Partido Socialista Revolucionario*, PSR).

In May 1989 the PMS became a constituent element of the Party of the Democratic Revolution.

National Action Party
Partido Acción Nacional (PAN)

Address. Angel Urraza 812 esq. López Cotilla Colonia del Valle, 03109 México DF

Telephone. (#52-5) 559-6300

Fax. (#52-5) 559-0925

Leadership. Felipe Calderón Hinojosa (president), Diego Fernandez de Cevallos (1994 presidential candidate), Enrique Gabriel Jimenez Remus (leader of the *Neopanista* faction), Felipe Calderon Hinojosa (secretary-general)

Founded in 1939, the PAN is a right-wing social Christian party, with close associations with the Roman Catholic Church, which has highlighted human rights and social welfare abuses and advocated a government of national reconciliation.

Since its founding, the party has been the major opposition grouping and has stood against the Institutional Revolutionary Party (PRI) in congressional elections since 1943, in local elections since 1946 and most presidential elections since 1952. Internal disputes prevented it from presenting a presidential candidate in 1976. In 1982, its then leader, Pablo Emilio Madero, was accorded 16.4 per cent of the vote and the party won 55 seats in the Chamber of Deputies, reduced to 41 in the 1985 elections.

Together with the Authentic Party of the Mexican Revolution (PARM), the PAN was long regarded as a fairly benign opposition permitted to win a limited number of seats in order to give a pluralist credibility to a fairly monolithic system dominated by the PRI. However, during 1984-86, PAN supporters accused the PRI of blatant electoral fraud and were involved in numerous and occasionally violent protests, mainly in the relatively prosperous northern states where the party draws much of its support. Alvárez, who played a prominent part in the protests by staging a 40-day hunger strike, was narrowly elected party leader in 1987 as the representative of the northern radical conservative faction, the *neopanists,* opposed to the moderate traditionalist Madero grouping, the *Foro Democrático y Doctrinario* who were more disposed to work with the PRI. In July 1989, the party inflicted the first electoral defeat on the PRI in 60 years when the PAN candidate Ernesto Ruffo Appel won the governorship of the state of Baja California.

In August 1991, following complaints of blatant electoral malpractice, President Carlos Salinas de Gotari intervened and decided that the PAN's Carlos Medina Plascencia should replace the PRI hardliner Ramón Aguirre Veláquez as the governor-elect for the state of Guanajuato. The decision strengthened the hand of the party's leadership who were already disposed to a conciliatory approach to the government, especially in support of new electoral laws, a position endorsed by the national committee, which voted in September 1991 against the *Forista* faction who were opposed to such conciliation.

The change in mood was due in part to the tangible rewards that the PRI's liberal economic policies had given to some party members coupled with a growing belief throughout the party that a viable opposition movement to the government had diminished with the emphatic electoral defeat of the Party of the Democratic Revolution (PRD) in the August 1991 congressional elections, when the PAN's own total representation in the Congress was cut from 102 to 89 seats.

After the disappointing results in the 1991 elections, dramatic improvements began to take place in the PAN. In early 1992 the party captured the gubernatorial seat of Guanajuato followed by a notable victory over the PRI for the governorship of Chihuahua in July 1992. In the August 1994 presidential balloting, the PAN came second to the PRI with 25.9% of the popular vote whilst also taking the party's chamber representation above its 1991 level by winning 119 seats. It also took 25 seats in the newly enlarged Senate.

More significant still was the winning of the governorship of Jalisco state in February 1995, as well as the Guadalajara mayoralty and a majority of state legislative seats for the first time.

Party of the Democratic Revolution
Partido de la Revolución Democrática (PRD)

Leadership. Porfirio Muñoz Ledo (chair), Mario Saucedo (secretary-general)

Originally founded in October 1988, the social democratic PRD was established by a group of left-wing dissidents of the ruling Institutional Revolutionary Party (PRI) led by Cuauhtémoc Cárdenas, the son of President Lázaro Cárdenas (1934-40), a revered figure in post-revolutionary history.

Cárdenas, as head of the Democratic Current faction (CD), was expelled from the PRI in 1987. He then accepted the presidential nomination of the Authentic Party of the Mexican Revolution (PARM) until he brought together several parties to form an electoral coalition, the National Democratic Front (*Frente Democrático Nacional*, FDN), to back his candidacy in the July 1988 presidential election. Including the PARM, these were the Popular Socialist Party (PPS), the Mexican Socialist Party (PMS), the right-wing Mexican Democratic Party (PDM) and the Socialist Workers Party (*Partido Socialista de los Trabajadores*, PST).

The FDN claimed that the subsequent PRI victory was a "massive fraud", Cárdenas contending that he had won a clear majority. The FDN parties, however, still managed to stun the PRI by taking over 31% of the vote and receiving between them a total of 139 seats in the Congress owing to a low direct vote being boosted by seats awarded by proportional representation.

Of the FDN parties, only the PMS merged into the newly-formed PRD in October 1988 and the FDN itself became effectively defunct.

The PRD was the most forceful opposition voice in its condemnation of electoral laws, finally passed by the Congress in July 1990, stating that they would preserve PRI majorities in the Chamber of Deputies and the Senate. One of the reforms had the effect of banning electoral alliances and coalitions, thus outlawing a future FDN-like electoral formation.

The party participated, however, in the November 1990 state and local elections in the state of Mexico, winning no seats outright but being allocated eight by proportional representation. Along with the PAN, the PRD stated the elections had been a "scandalous fraud".

The PRD expressed its vigorous opposition to the PRI's reform of the 1917 constitution in December 1991 but in late February 1992, Senator Porfirio Muñoz Ledo, considered as the party's second leading figure, stated the conditions existed for a dialogue between Cárdenas and Salinas. In state legislature and local government elections held in the state of Jalisco in February 1992, the PRD received 3.6% of the vote, compared to 31.5% for the PAN and 50.5% for the PRI.

In the August 1994 presidential elections, the PRD candidate Cuauhtémoc Cardenas Solórzano came third with an increased 16.6% of the vote, while PRD representation in the Chamber rose to 71 seats and to eight in the enlarged Senate.

The PRD is a full member party of the Socialist International.

Other Parties

Mexican electoral law dictates that parties must gain at least 1.5% of the total vote in a national election in order to maintain their electoral registrations and continue to legally participate in the democratic process. A majority of the parties listed below are affected by this ruling.

Cardenista National Reconstruction Party

Partido del Frente Cardenista de Reconstruction Nacional (PFCRN)

Address. 199 avda México, Col. Hipódromo Condesa, 06170 México DF

Leadership. Rafael Aguilar Talamantes (president and 1994 presidential candidate), Graco Ramirez Abreu (secretary-general)

Formerly the Workers' Socialist Party (PST), the new designation PFCRN was taken in 1988 prior to the balloting of that year. In its early period it was sometimes seen as the Marxist-Leninist wing of the ruling Institutional Revolutionary Party (PRI), but it very much had its own flavour. Becoming increasingly independent, the PST's own candidate in the presidential elections of 1982, Candido Diaz gained only 1.5% of the cast vote.

In 1988, the PFCRN took part in the election as part of the National Democratic Front (FDN) alliance with the PRD (see above), and took 23 proportional Chamber seats. Things slumped for the party in 1994 when its candidate gained only 0.9% of the national vote with the party obtaining no congressional representation.

Green Ecologist Party of Mexico

Partido Verde Ecologista de México (PVEM)

Leadership. Jorge Gonzalez Torres (President of the Party and 1994 presidential candidate)

Mexico's Greens formerly entered the political arena in 1987 gaining a 1.4% share of the vote in the 1991 elections. However, according to electoral law this was not sufficient to gain the party full legal status. Jorge Gonzalez obtained 0.9% of the vote in the August 1994 presidential election while in the simultaneous balloting for the Federal District Assembly it took a significantly higher 4% share for two of the 66 available seats.

Mexican Democratic Party

Partido Demócrata Mexicano (PDM)

Address. Edison 89, 06030 México DF

Telephone. (#52-5) 592-5688

Fax. (#52-5) 535-0031

Leadership. Marcelo Gaxiola Félix (president), Gumersindo Magaña Negrete (1988 presidential candidate)

The PDM is a right-wing conservative party founded in May 1971, modelled as a successor to the *Unión Sinarquista Nacional* (UNS), a neo-fascist and ultra-Catholic movement which had attracted a large popular following in the late 1930s. It received a total of 12 seats following the 1982 congressional elections, reduced to eight in 1985 and by the 1988 elections, when it joined the FDN (see Party of the Democratic

Revolution), it had lost all congressional representation. The party allied itself temporarily with the National Action Party in 1983 as the short-lived Democratic Action for Electoral Rescue (ADRE).

Having obtained no congressional representation in either 1988 or 1991, it endorsed Pablo Madero of the National Opposition Union (UNO) as its 1994 presidential candidate while he himself waited for his party to be formerly recognised. Madero gained 0.9% of the vote in the subsequent August election.

Popular Socialist Party
Partido Popular Socialista (PPS)
Address. Av. Alvaro Obregón 185, Colonia Roma, 06977 México DF
Leadership. Marcela Lombardo Otero (1994 presidential candidate), Jorge Cruikshank García (secretary-general)

Founded in June 1948 as the Popular Party (PP), the party has been known as the PPS since 1960. The PPS is actually a centrist party which, prior to the collapse of the Eastern bloc, had pro-Soviet foreign policies and on the domestic front has cultivated a left of centre populist and nationalist image opposed to "North American imperialism and the oligarchic bourgeoisie".

Although founded by the socialist trade union leader Vicente Lombardo Toledano, a close confidant of President Lázaro Cárdenas (see Institutional Revolutionary Party), the party consistently belied its left-wing credentials, being long considered a "loyal opposition" party, along with the PARM and PAN, and duly "rewarded" by the ruling Institutional Revolutionary Party (PRI) with seats in the Congress. Between 1963 and 1985 it endorsed every PRI presidential candidate but saw its representation in the Congress increase from only 10 to 11 seats. Jorge Cruickshank, the party's secretary-general, sat in the Senate from 1976-82, as the only opposition senator elected since 1929.

The party broke with the PRI in 1988 over its choice of Carlos Salinas de Gotari as its presidential candidate and joined the National Democratic Front to support the candidacy of the PARM's Cuauhtémoc Cárdenas Solórzano (see Party of the Democratic Revolution). In the August 1991 congressional elections, none of its candidates were directly elected, but it received 12 seats in the Chamber of Deputies by proportional representation.

The party was not prominent in the opposition to the PRI's November 1991 reforms to the 1917 constitution, chief amongst which was the official recognition of the Roman Catholic Church. This contrasted with Ortiz Mendoza's protests during the Papal visit in May 1990 when he accused Pope John Paul II of making "political speeches" and recommended that he be expelled from the country and that governors who had welcomed him should be impeached for flouting the constitutional provision separating church and state.

In August 1994 the party received only 0.5% of the vote and failed to gain any congressional representation.

Revolutionary Workers' Party
Partido Revolucionario de los Trabajadores (PRT)
Leadership. Rosario Ibarra de la Piedra (1988 presidential candidate), Pedro Peñaloza (co-ordinator)

The PRT is a Trotskyist party which contested the 1982 presidential and congressional elections without success, but won six of the proportionally distributed seats in 1985.

Standing aloof from the National Democratic Front (FDN) coalition in the 1988 elections, it received no seats. In April 1991 the PRT joined the Revolutionary Socialist Current (*Corriente Revolucionario Socialista*, CRS), the People's Front (*Frente del Pueblo*, FDP) and the Independent Democratic Alliance (*Alianza Democrática Independiente*, ADI), to form the Socialist Electoral Front (*Frente Electoral Socialista*, FES), led by Raúl Jordan, who said that the aim of the FES was to regroup in Mexico those who "still consider socialism a valid option".

In the national elections of 1991 the party came in last with 0.6% of the valid vote.

Minor Parties

Authentic Party of the Mexican Revolution (*Partido Auténtico de la Revolución Mexicana*, PARM) was founded in 1951 and is similar in outlook to the PRI. It is led by Jésus Guzman Rubio and gained 0.6% of the vote in 1994.

Movement Towards Socialism (*Movimiento al Socialismo*, MAS) is led by Adolfo Gilly and was part of the FDN in 1988.

Nava Political Party (*Nava Partido Politico*, NPP) is a regional party strong in the state of San Luis Potosí and is led by Concepción Nava Calvillo.

Guerrilla and Paramilitary Groups

Aside from the now rather venerable Army of the Poor (EP), the majority of the current guerrilla groups have sprung up in the last two years or so following the January 1994 uprising in Chiapas state.

Mexican Peasant Worker Front of the South-east (*Frente Campesino Obrero Mexicano del Sureste*, FCOMS), grew from the Chiapas uprising.

Popular Movement of National Liberation (*Movimiento Popular de Liberación Nacional*, MPLN), similarly grew from the events of early 1994.

Zapatista National Liberation Army
Ejército Zapatista de Liberación Nacional (EZLN)
   Leadership. "Subcomandante Marcos"
   Instrumental in the Chiapas rising of January 1994, the EZLN are reported to number in excess of 1,000 men. It's main campaign is for economic relief for an impoverished region and also for Mexico's indigenous peoples.

Federated States of Micronesia

Capital: Palikir   **Population:** 115,000 (1995E)

The Federated States of Micronesia (FSM), comprising more than 600 islands, occuping the archipelago of the Caroline Islands in the western Pacific Ocean. From 1947, as part of the UN Trust Territory of the Pacific, they were administered by the United States government. In 1979 a new constitution was adopted, and in 1982 the FSM signed a compact of free association (implemented in 1986) under which the United States recognized the territory as a fully sovereign and independent state, while retaining authority in regard to defence. In December 1990 the United Nations Security Council approved the termination of the Trusteeship in relation to the FSM, and the republic joined the UN the following year.

The four constituent states of the FSM are the island groups of Chuuk (formerly Truk), Kosrae, Pohnpei and Yap, each of which have elected governors and legislatures. Federal authority is vested in a President who is elected by the unicameral federal Congress. The Congress comprises 14 senators, of whom four (one from each state) are elected for a four-year term and 10 for a two-year term. There are no formal political parties in the FSM.

Following a general election in March 1991, Bailey Olter was unanimously elected President the following May. He was re-elected on May 11, 1995, and inaugurated on June 9.

Moldova

Capital: Chişinău   **Population:** 4,500,000 (1995E)

The Moldavian Soviet Socialist Republic declared independence from the USSR in August 1991 as the Republic of Moldova, becoming a sovereign member of the Commonwealth of Independent States (CIS) in December 1991. A new constitution which entered into force in August 1994 describes Moldova as a "presidential, parliamentary republic" based on political pluralism and "the preservation, development and expression of ethnic and linguistic identity", in which context special autonomous status is conferred on the Transdnestr and Gagauz regions, respectively of predominantly ethnic Russian and ethnic Turk population. Other clauses proclaim Moldova's permanent neutrality and ban the stationing of foreign troops on Moldovan territory. Executive power is exercised by the President, who is directly elected for a five-year term, and by the Prime Minister and other ministers. Legislative authority is vested in the unicameral Parliament of 104 members, who are elected by universal adult suffrage for a four-year term by a system of proportional representation requiring lists to obtain at least 4% of the vote to gain representation.

The country's first multi-party parliamentary elections on Feb. 27, 1994, resulted as follows: Agrarian Democratic Party of Moldova (PDAM) 56 seats (with 43.2% of the vote), Socialist Party/Unity Movement bloc 28 (22.0%), Peasants and Intellectuals bloc (which later became the Party of Democratic Forces) 11 (9.2%), Christian Democratic Popular Front, 9 (7.5%). In a presidential election on Dec. 8, 1991, the incumbent head of state from the Soviet era, Mircea Snegur, was re-elected unopposed, drawing his main support from the PDAM but later founding the Party of Revival and Accord of Moldova.

Agrarian Democratic Party of Moldova
Partidul Democrat Agrar din Moldova (PDAM)
Address. Bdul Stefan cel Mare 162, et. 4, Chişinău
Telephone. (#373–2) 246144
Leadership. Dumitru Motpan (chair), Petru Lucinschi (parliamentary chair)

Established in November 1991 by Soviet-era agrarian forces, the PDAM at first provided political support for President Snegur and was the core of the government of national unity formed in mid-1992. Favouring continued Moldovan independence and participation in CIS economic structures (although not in CIS military or political integration), it won a narrow overall parliamentary majority in 1994, with 43.2% of the popular vote. In April 1995 the PDAM took almost half the seats in country-wide local elections. But the party was weakened three months later by Snegur's decision to launch the rival Party of Revival and Accord of Moldova. As a result, the PDAM lost its parliamentary majority, although remaining (at least for the time being) the dominant political grouping.

Christian Democratic Popular Front
Frontul Popular Cretin-Democrat (FPCD)
Address. Str. Nicolae Iorga 5, Chişinău
Telephone. (#373–2) 234547
Fax. (#373–2) 234480
Leadership. Iurie Rosca (chair)

The FPCD was launched in March 1992 as the successor of the radical pan-Romanian wing of the Popular Front of Moldova, which had been the dominant political grouping at the time of the eclipse of the Communist Party in mid-1991. Preferring to call Moldova by the historic name Bessarabia, the FPCD saw independence as the first step towards the "sacred goal" of reunification with Romania, although it toned down its pan-Romanian rhetoric when that goal receded as a practical proposition. In May 1993 the FPCD executive appointed Iurie Rosca as party chair in place of Mircea Druc, a former Prime Minister who had gone to live in Romania and had become a Romanian citizen. In the 1994 Assembly elec-

tions the FPCD won nine seats on a vote share of 7.5%.

Party of Democratic Forces
Partidul Fortelor Democratice (PFD)
Address. Str. Mitr. Dosoftei 68, et. 7, Chişinău
Telephone. (#373–2) 222782
Leadership. Valeriu Matei (chair)

Founded in October 1995, the PFD is a merger of the components of the United Democratic Congress (*Congresul Democrat Unit*, CDU), which itself had been launched in June 1994 as an alliance of moderate pan-Romanian parties, including the Congress of Intellectuals (*Congresul Intelectualitatji*, CI), the Democratic Party (*Partidul Democrat*, PD) and the Christian Democratic Party (*Partidul Cretin-Democrat*, PCD). These formation were derived from the Popular Front of Moldova, which had been dominant through the achievement of independence, when reunion with Romania had seemed a realistic proposition.

Of the CDU components, the CI and the PCD had contested the 1994 elections within the Peasants and Intellectuals bloc, which also embraced the Alliance of Free Peasants (*Aliana Taranilor Liberi*, ATL) and the National Liberal Party (*Partidul Naional Liberal*, PNL). Not least because the ATL consists mainly of agricultural sector bureaucrats rather than actual peasants, the bloc failed to make great inroads into the rural support of the Agrarian Democratic Party of Moldova, winning only 11 seats on a 9.2% vote share. In the same elections the PD had been allied with the anti-separatist Gagauz People's Party (*Partidul Popular Gagauz/Gagauz Halk Partisi*, PPG/GHP), but the alliance failed to reach the 4% threshold for representation.

Party of Revival and Accord of Moldova
Partidul Renasterii si Concilierii din Moldova (PRCM)
Address. c/o President's Office, Chişinău
Leadership. Mircea Snegur (chair), Nicolae Andronić (deputy chair)

The PRCM was established in July 1995 by President Snegur, who had announced his resignation from the Agrarian Democratic Party of Moldova because it had opposed his policies, particularly the economic reform programme. Joined by 11 of the 56 PDAM deputies, the PRCM declared itself to be "a mass party of the centre" aspiring to bring together "all the healthy political forces in the country" on the basis of a presidential rather than a parliamentary system of government. The new party also provided backing for the President's cautious line on possible reunification with Romania, stressing the essentially Romanian identity of Moldova but concerned not to provoke secession by non-Romanian regions such as Russian-populated Transdnestr. These objectives formed the core of Snegur's campaign for re-election in November 1996 as candidate of the PRCM.

Socialist Party
Partidul Socialist (PS)
Address. Str. Cosmonautilor 6, cam. 408, Chişinău
Telephone. (#373–2) 723237
Leadership. Valeriu Senic, Valentin Krylov, Veronica Abramciuc The PS was founded in August 1992 as a pro-Russian successor to the former ruling Communist Party (which had been suspended a year earlier), advocating full membership of all CIS structures, government regulation of the economy and an independent multi-ethnic state. The registration in September 1993 of the Party of Communists of the Moldovan Republic provided the PS with some competition on the conservative wing of politics. In the February 1994 parliamentary elections, however, the PS and the allied Unity Movement took an impressive second place by winning 28 seats on a 21.8% vote share.

Unity Movement
Micarea Unitatea–Edinstvo (UE)
Address. Str. Hînceşti 35, cam. 12, Chişinău
Telephone. (#373–2) 731296
Leadership. Petr Shornikov (chair) The UE originated in 1989 as part of a broader movement opposed to a Romanian nationalist orientation for Moldova and prepared to make concessions to the ethnic Russians of the Transdnestr region. The UE leader, Petr Shornikov, was barred from standing in the 1994 parliamentary elections because he was thought to have supported the Dnestr Republic separatists. The UE was allied with the Socialist Party in that contest, the joint list winning 28 seats.

Other Parties

Association of Victims of the Totalitarian Communist Regime (*Asociatja Victimelor Regimului Totalitar Comunist*, AVRTC), led by Mihail Moroanu, obtained 0.9% in 1994 elections

Association of Women (*Asociatja Femeilor*, AF), led by Liudmila Scalnii, took a creditable 2.8% vote share in 1994.

Democratic Labor Party (*Partidul Democrat al-Muncii*, PDM), led by Alexandru Arseni, also obtained 2.8% in 1994 elections.

Ecological Party/Green Alliance (*Partidul Ecologist/ Aliana Verde*, PE/AV), led by Mircea Ciuhrii, won 0.4% in 1994.

National Christian Party (*Partidul Natjonal Cretin*, PNC), led by Vladimir Nicu, a pan-Romanian nationalist formation, obtained only 0.3% of the vote in 1994, suspended by the Justice Ministry in September 1994 for contravening law on parties.

Party of Communists of the Moldovan Republic (*Partidul Comunistilor din Republica Moldova*, PCRM), led by Vladimir Voronin, legalized in September 1993, would-be successor to Soviet-era Communist Party banned in August 1991.

Party of Reform (*Partidul Reformei*, PR), led by Stefan Gorda, founded in 1993 to advocate a free-market independent Moldova, won only 2.4% of the vote in 1994, subsequently sought to build a broader alliance of pro-reform forces.

Republican Party (*Partidul Republican*, PR), led by Victor Puca, won 0.9% in 1994.

Social Democratic Party (*Partidul Social Democrat*, PSD), led by Oazu Nantoi, narrowly failed to surmount 4% barrier in 1994, winning 3.7%.

Socialist Action Party (*Partidul Actiunea Socialista*, PAS), founded in May 1996 by Aurel Cepoi, hitherto a deputy of the Socialist Party, favouring a socially responsible pro-market strategy.

Transdnestr and Gagauz Parties

Dignity (*Demnitatea*), also known as the Left-Bank Democratic Movement (*Mişcarea Democratică din Stînga Nistrului*), anti-separatist Transdnestr formation.

Union of Patriotic Forces, leading Transdnestr separatist movement, led by Igor Smirnov (president of "Dnestr Republic") and Vasily Yakovlev.

Democratic Party of the Gagauz, led by G. Savostin.

Motherland Party (*Vatan*), the leading formation in the ethnic Turk Gagauz region, led by Stepan Topol and Andrei Cheshmeji.

Monaco

Capital: Monaco-Ville

Population: 32,000 (1995E)

The Principality of Monaco is an hereditary monarchy dating from the 13th century in which constitutional limitations on the monarch's powers have been in force since 1911. The 1962 constitution vests executive authority in the Prince, who governs through a Minister of State selected from a list of three French civil servants submitted by the French government, assisted by government councillors and palace personnel. Legislative authority is vested in the Prince and the National Council (*Conseil National*) of 18 members, who are elected by citizens aged 21 and over for a five-year term. There are no formal political parties in Monaco, the following listing being of informal groupings that have appeared in recent years.

Campora List (*Liste Campora*), led by Anne-Marie Campora (mayor of Monaco-Ville), whose candidates in the 1991 elections were designated *Evolution Communale*, won 15 of the 18 seats in 1993.

Médecin List (*Liste Médecin*), led by Jean-Louis Médecin (former mayor of Monaco-Ville), who had headed a list called *Action Communale* in 1991, won two seats in 1993.

National and Democratic Union (*Union Nationale et Démocratique*, UND), formed in 1962 as a merger of the National Union of Independents (*Union Nationale des Indépendants*) and the National Democratic Entente (*Entente Nationale Démocratique*), won all 18 National Council seats in the elections of 1968, 1978, 1983 and 1988; thereafter superseded by more politically focused lists.

Mongolia

Capital: Ulan Bator

Population: 2,400,000 (1995E)

The state of Mongolia was, until January 1992, called the Mongolian People's Republic (MPR), which had been proclaimed as the world's second socialist state in 1924 after the (communist) Mongolian People's Revolutionary Party (MPRP) had established control over the country. Constitutional changes in May 1990 ended the one-party system in force since the foundation of the MPR, while in February 1992 a new constitution entered into force permitting private ownership and establishing Mongolia as a democratic parliamentary state with a directly elected President. The legislature, the 76–member unicameral Mongolian Great Hural, is directly elected for a four-year term by all citizens over 25 years of age and itself elects a Prime Minister who appoints a Cabinet.

Legislative elections on June 28, 1992, returned the MPRP to power with an overwhelming majority of 71 seats. Four years later, however, elections on June 30, 1996, resulted in a heavy defeat for the MPRP at the hands of the opposition Democratic Union (embracing most of the non-MPRP parties listed below), which won 50 seats. The first direct presidential election was held on June 6, 1993, resulting in victory for the incumbent, Punsalmaagiyn Ochirbat, who had been elected as President by the legislature in 1990 as a representative of the ruling MPRP but who had switched allegiance to the opposition in April 1993.

Mongolian National Democratic Party (MNDP)

Address. Chingisiyn Orgon Choloo 1, Ulan Bator

Telephone. (#976-1) 324221

Fax. (#976-1) 325170

Leadership. Davaadorjiyn Ganbold (president)

The MNDP was created in late 1992 by the merger of four groups in opposition to the then government of the Mongolian People's Revolutionary Party (MPRP), namely the Mongolian Democratic Party (formed in 1990 as the political arm of the anti-MPRP Mongolian Democratic Union); the Mongolian National Progress Party (launched in 1990 to advocate prompt transition to a market economy); the Mongolian United Party (itself the product of a merger in early 1992 of the Republican Party and the Free Labour Party); and the Mongolian Renewal Party (set up in 1991 by a reformist faction of the MPRP). Although the new party commanded only four legislative seats following the June 1992 elections, it joined with the Mongolian Social Democratic Party in supporting the 1993 re-election of President Ochirbat (on behalf of the opposition), which denied the ruling MPRP control of all the centres of power. In the June 1996 legislative elections it formed a key element of the Democratic Union alliance which unexpectedly inflicted a decisive defeat on the MPRP.

Mongolian People's Revolutionary Party (MPRP)

Address. Baga Toyruu 37/1, Ulan Bator 11

Telephone. (#976-1) 323245

Fax. (#976-1) 320368

Leadership. Budragchaagiyn Dash-Yondon (secretary-general)

Founded in 1921 (initially as the Mongolian People's Party), the MPRP was the country's only authorized political formation from 1924 until 1990. During that time it was organized along communist lines with a tightly centralized structure, its policies frequently reflecting its close links with the Soviet Communist Party. In March 1990, influenced by the collapse of East European communist regimes and by domestic opposition, the People's Great Hural voted to remove the constitutional article guaranteeing the MPRP's leading role in the government of Mongolia. The following month an extraordinary MPRP congress approved policies intended to separate the powers of state and party and to promote internal party democracy, and also endorsed the adoption of a multi-party system, a mixed economy and an independent non-aligned foreign policy.

Having secured a victory in the first multi-party legislative elections in July 1990, with 60% of the vote, the MPRP adopted a new party programme in early 1992 in which it distanced itself from socialist and communist ideology. In further legislative elections in June 1992 the party convincingly retained its position as the ruling party, gaining 71 of the 76 seats in the renamed Mongolian Great Hural. However, in the first direct presidential election held in June 1993, the MPRP candidate, Lodongiyn Tudev, was runner-up to the opposition-backed incumbent with 38.7 per cent of the vote. In the June 1996 legislative elections, moreover, the MPRP went down to a heavy defeat, having been damaged by popular resentment at the government's failure to deal with inflation and unemployment.

Mongolian Social Democratic Party (MSDP)

Address. POB 578, Ulan Bator 210611

Telephone. (#976-1) 329469

Fax. (#976-1) 322055

Leadership. Radnaasumbereliyn Gonchigdorj (chair), Yadamin Balgansuren (general secretary)

An affiliate of the Socialist International, the MSDP was founded in March 1990, pledging itself to the promotion of a mixed economy and neutrality in foreign affairs. In the 1992 elections the party won just over 10 per cent of the vote but gained only one legislative seat. In the 1993 presidential poll, the party supported the re-election of incumbent President Ochirbat, who contested the election on behalf of the parties opposed to the ruling MPRP. In the June 1996 legislative elections it formed part of the victorious Democratic Union alliance.

Other Parties

Mongolian Green Party, organized in 1990 as the political wing of the Mongolian Alliance of Greens.

Mongolian People's Party, formed in 1991 to forestall plans by the restructured Mongolian People's Revolutionary Party to revert to its original name.

Religious Democratic Party, centred on Buddhist philosophy and led by Tseren Bayarsuren, registered in 1991.

United Heritage Party, formed in 1993 by an amalgamation of four small groupings supporting national independence, small business and private ownership.

Morocco

Capital: Rabat

Population: 27,000,000 (1995E)

The Kingdom of Morocco was established in 1957 (the former French and Spanish protectorates having joined together as an independent sultanate the previous year). It became a constitutional monarchy under the 1962 constitution, with the Prime Minister and Cabinet appointed by the King. Legislative authority is vested in a unicameral Chamber of Representatives (*Majlis al-Nuwwab*) of 333 members, 222 of whom are directly elected by universal adult suffrage and the remainder by an electoral college composed of government, professional and labour representatives. In September 1992 the electorate accorded approval to a revised constitution giving greater powers to the government and the Chamber of Representatives.

Nine years after the previous ballot, direct elections to the Chamber were held in June 25, 1993, and indirect elections on Sept. 17, 1993. The outcome was that loyalist parties of the National Entente (*Entente Nationale*) together with the allied National Rally of Independents secured 195 seats in the new Chamber, while the opposition parties of the Democratic Bloc (*Bloc Démocratique*) 114, Bloc-affiliated labour organizations 6 and others 18.

Constitutional Union
Union Constitutionelle (UC)
   Address. 4 ave Bin el Ouidane, Rabat
   Telephone. (#212–7) 76935
   Leadership. Maati Bouabid (leader)
   Founded in 1983 and supporting the constitutional status quo, the centre-right UC became the dominant element in the government coalition formed after the 1984 elections, participating in the National Entente of pro-government parties. In the 1993 parliamentary elections the party's representation in the Chamber fell significantly to 54 seats.

Independence Party
Istiqlal
   Address. 4 charia Ibnou Toumert, Rabat
   Telephone. (#212–7) 730951
   Fax. (#212–7) 725354
   Leadership. Mohamed Boucetta (secretary-general)
   The party was founded in 1943 and was the leading political force prior to Moroccan independence. In 1959 the party split, its left-wing faction subsequently forming the National Union of Popular Forces. Originally a firm supporter of the monarchy, it has adopted a reformist and critical stance, stressing the need for better living standards and equal rights for all Moroccans. A member of the Democratic Bloc, the party took 50 seats in

the Chamber of Representatives at the 1993 elections.

National Democratic Party
Parti National Démocratique (PND)
   Address. 18 rue de Tunis, Rabat
   Telephone. (#212–7) 30754
   Leadership. Mohammed Arsalane al-Jadidi (secretary-general)
   The PND, established in 1981 by disaffected members of the National Rally of Independents, was one of the smaller parties in the centre-right coalition government formed after the 1984 parliamentary elections. As a National Entente party, it maintained its Chamber representation in the 1993 elections, winning 24 seats.

National Rally of Independents
Rassemblement National des Indépendants (RNI)
   Address. rue Erfour, Rabat
   Telephone. (#212–7) 65418
   Leadership. Ahmed Osman (president)
   Essentially a political vehicle for King Hassan, the royalist RNI was established in 1978 to give cohesion to the group of independents which was then numerically dominant in the Chamber. Even after a number of independents had defected to the National Democratic Party in 1981, the RNI was able to emerge as the second strongest party after the 1984 legislative elections, continuing its

government participation. Its parliamentary representation fell to 41 seats in the 1993 elections.

National Union of Popular Forces

Union Nationale des Forces Populaires (UNFP)

Address. 28 rue de Magellan, BP 747, Casablanca

Telephone. (#212–2) 302023

Leadership. Moulay Abdallah Ibrahim (leader)

The UNFP was formed in 1959 by the breakaway progressive left wing of the Independence Party. It subsequently split in 1972 between the Rabat and Casablanca sections of the party, the former reorganizing itself in 1974 as the Socialist Union of Popular Forces. Having boycotted earlier legislative elections, the UNFP contested the 1993 poll as part of the opposition Democratic Bloc but won no seats.

Organization of Democratic and Popular Action

Organisation de l'Action Démocratique et Populaire (OADP)

Address. BP 15797, Casablanca

Telephone. (#212–2) 278442

Leadership. Mohamed Ben Said (secretary-general)

The OADP was formed in 1983. It is a member of the Democratic Bloc and won two seats in the 1993 legislative elections.

Party of Renewal and Progress

Parti du Renouveau et du Progrès (PRP)

Address. 32 rue Lédru Rollin, BP 13152, Casablanca

Telephone. (#212–2) 222238

Leadership. Ali Yata (secretary-general)

Recognized in 1974 (as the Party of Progress and Socialism, until it changed its name in 1994), the party was the successor to the banned Moroccan Communist Party. It advocates nationalization and democracy as part of its left-wing orientation, and joined in the formation of the opposition Democratic Bloc in 1992. In the 1993 elections the party took 10 seats in the Chamber of Representatives.

Popular Movement

Mouvement Populaire (MP)

Address. 12 rue Marinin Hassan, Rabat

Telephone. (#212–7) 730808

Fax. (#212–7) 200165

Leadership. Mohammed Tensar (secretary-general)

The centre-right MP was set up in 1957, its support coming principally from the Berber population. It was a participant in government coalitions from the early 1960s, and was the third strongest party in the Chamber of Representatives following the 1984 elections. The party's founder,

Mahjoubi Aherdane, was ousted as MP secretary-general in October 1986 and later set up the breakaway Popular National Movement. Contesting the 1993 elections as a National Entente party, the MP secured 51 seats in the Chamber.

Popular National Movement

Mouvement National Populaire (MNP)

Address. c/o Majlis al-Nuwwab, Rabat

Leadership. Mahjoubi Aherdane (leader)

The Popular National Movement was set up in 1991 by Mahjoubi Aherdane, former leader of the Popular Movement. Contesting the 1993 elections as a National Entente party, the MNP won 25 seats in the Chamber.

Socialist Union of Popular Forces

Union Socialiste des Forces Populaires (UNSP)

Address. 17 rue Oued Souss, Agdal, Rabat

Telephone. (#212-7) 773905

Fax. (#212-7) 772901

Leadership. Abderrahmane Youssoufi (first secretary), Mohamed el-Yazghi (deputy first secretary)

Originally the Rabat section of the National Union of Popular Forces, and temporarily suspended by the government in 1973, the party was formed separately with its current name the following year. The left-wing progressive UNSP, which is linked with the prominent Democratic Confederation of Labour trade union group and is affiliated to the Socialist International, has called for political democratization and been critical of government economic policy. A member of the Democratic Bloc, the party increased its representation in the Chamber to 52 seats in the 1993 legislative elections.

Other Parties

Action Party (*Parti de l'Action*, PA), led by Abdallah Senhaji, formed in 1974 to advocate democracy and progress, won two legislative seats in 1993.

Constitutional and Democratic Popular Movement (*Mouvement Populaire Constitutionnel et Démocratique*, MPCD), a breakaway group from the Popular Movement, led by Abdelkarim Khatib.

Democratic Party for Independence (*Parti Démocratique pour l'Indépendance* PDI), led by Thami el-Ouazzani, set up in the 1940s, won nine seats in the 1993 elections.

Liberal Progressive Party (*Parti Libéral Progressiste*, PLP), led by Aknoush Ahmadou Belhaj, advocates individual freedom and free enterprise.

National Party for Unity and Solidarity (*Parti Nationale pour l'Unité et la Solidarité*, PNUS), led by Muhammed Asmar.

Party of the Democratic and Socialist Vanguard (*Parti de l'Avant-garde Démocratique et Socialiste*,

PADS), an offshoot of the Socialist Union of Popular Forces, legalized in 1992.

Social Centre Party (*Parti du Centre Social*, PCS), a centre-left grouping.

Mozambique

Capital: Maputo

Population: 18,000,000 (1995E)

The Republic of Mozambique gained independence from Portugal in June 1975 after a 10–year armed struggle by the Marxist-Leninist Front for the Liberation of Mozambique (FRELIMO). A one-party system was established with FRELIMO as the sole legal party, but a continuing rebellion was waged against the regime by the anti-communist Mozambique National Resistance (RENAMO). After FRELIMO had in 1989 abandoned Marxist-Leninist ideology in favour of democratic socialism, the following year a new constitution came into effect heralding a multi-party system, direct elections and a free market economy. Under the constitution, the President was to be elected by universal adult suffrage for a five-year period, and might be re-elected on only two consecutive occasions. Legislative authority was to be vested in the Assembly of the Republic (*Assembléia da República*), similarly elected for a five-year term.

Negotiations between the FRELIMO government and RENAMO to end the protracted civil war culminated in the signing of a peace accord in October 1992. Because of delays in the implementation of the peace plan, presidential and legislative elections did not take place until October 1994. These resulted in victory for incumbent President Joaquim Chissano and for FRELIMO, which won 129 of the 250 seats in the Assembly, against 112 for RENAMO and nine for the Democratic Union. Eleven of the 14 groups contesting the Assembly elections failed to win representation.

Democratic Congress Party
Partido do Congresso Democrático (PACODE)
  Address. 333 rua Valentim Siti, Maputo
  Telephone. (#258–1) 401357
  Leadership. Vasco Campiro Momboya (president)
  Favouring decentralization, equality, respect for human rights, and a market economy combined with workers' rights, PACODE came tenth in the October 1994 legislative elections with 1.1% of the vote. Party leader Momboya took sixth place in the presidential poll.

Democratic Party of Mozambique
Partido Democrático de Moçambique (PADEMO)
  Address. Rua C 419, 1st Floor, Maputo
  Telephone. (#258–1) 492041
  Leadership. Wehia Ripua (president)
  Legally recognized in June 1993 and strongly federalist in outlook, PADEMO secured less than 1% of the vote in the 1994 Assembly elections,

while its candidate in the presidential contest was a distant third.

Democratic Union
União Democrática (UD)
  Address. c/o Assembléia da República, Maputo
  A coalition comprising the Liberal and Democratic Party of Mozambique, the National Democratic Party and the National Party of Mozambique, the UD won nine seats in the 1994 Assembly elections making it the only grouping other than FRELIMO and RENAMO to secure representation.

Front for the Liberation of Mozambique
Frente de Libertação de Moçambique (FRELIMO)
  Address. Rua Pereira do Lago 3, Maputo
  Telephone. (#258–1) 490181/9
  Leadership. Joaquim Chissano (president)
  FRELIMO was founded in 1962 by the merger of three nationalist organizations. It fought

against Portuguese rule from 1964 until 1974, when agreement on independence was reached, thereafter assuming the status of the sole legal party until 1990. Although initially committed to a Marxist-Leninist ideology, FRELIMO abandoned the doctrine in 1989 (subsequently embracing democratic socialism), at the same time calling for a negotiated settlement with the Mozambique National Resistance (RENAMO), against which it had been fighting a protracted civil war. In the October 1994 elections, consequent upon the peace process dating from the 1992 accord, FRELIMO retained power. President Chissano won the presidential election with 53% of the votes cast, while the party secured 129 of the 250 seats in the Assembly of the Republic.

Independent Party of Mozambique

Partido Independente de Moçambique (PIMO)
    Address. Av do Trabalho 1A, Maputo
    Telephone. (#258–1) 401438
    Leadership. Yaqub Sibindy (president)
    PIMO gives priority in its policies to moral education and peace, land privatization and job creation for demobilized soldiers, but won only just over 1% of the vote in both the presidential and legislative polls in 1994.

Liberal and Democratic Party of Mozambique

Partido Liberal e Democrático de Moçambique (PALMO)
    Address. Av Olof Palme 956, 3rd floor, Maputo
    Telephone. (#258–1) 424422
    Leadership. Martins Bilal (president)
    Founded in 1990, PALMO has been particularly critical of what it regards as the economic domination of the country by the non-indigenous population. The party fought the 1994 Assembly elections as a coalition member of the Democratic Union, which won nine seats.

Mozambique National Movement

Movimento Nacionalista Moçambicano (MONAMO)
    Address. Av Mao Tse Tung 230, 1st Floor, Maputo
    Telephone. (#258–1) 422781
    Leadership. Maximo Dias (leader)
    The social democratic MONAMO, in an electoral alliance with the Patriotic Action Front, took fourth place in the 1994 legislative balloting, but with less than 2% of the vote. Party leader Dias came fifth in the presidential contest.

Mozambique National Resistance

Resistência Nacional de Moçambique (RENAMO)
    Address. Av Ahmed Sekou Touré 657, Maputo
    Telephone. (#258–1) 422617
    Leadership. Afonso Dhlakama (president)
    Reportedly with foreign support, RENAMO was in military conflict with the FRELIMO government from 1976 until the peace process launched by the October 1992 accord. It registered as a political party in August 1994, and was the principal opponent and the runner-up to FRELIMO in the elections the following October. Afonso Dhlakama was the closest contender after FRELIMO's Chissano for the presidency, with almost 34% of the vote, while RENAMO candidates secured 112 seats in the Assembly of the Republic.

Mozambican National Union

União Nacional de Moçambicana (UNAMO)
    Address. Av 25 de Setembro 1123, Maputo
    Telephone. (#258–1) 424804
    Leadership. Carlos Reis (president)
    UNAMO was formed in 1987 by a breakaway faction of the Mozambique National Resistance (RENAMO). A federalist and social democratic organization, it was the first opposition party to be granted legal status. UNAMO fared poorly in the 1994 legislative elections, taking 13th place. Carlos Reis was fourth in the presidential poll, although he attracted less than 3% of the vote.

Mozambique People's Progress Party

Partido do Progresso do Povo Moçambicano (PPPM)
    Address. Av 25 de Setembro 1123, Maputo
    Telephone. (#258–1) 426925
    Leadership. Padimbe Kamati Andrea (president)
    The PPPM was legalized at the end of 1992, subsequently suffering a split when a faction withdrew to the form the Labour Party. Promoting federalism and the development of agriculture among its policies, the party achieved only 10th place in the 1994 Assembly elections.

National Democratic Party

Partido Nacional Democrático (PANADE)
    Address. c/o Assembléia da República, Maputo
    Leadership. José Massinga (leader)
    Supporting a market economy, better education and training, and incentives to private investment, PANADE was legalized in 1993. It contested the 1994 Assembly elections as a coalition member of the Democratic Union, which won nine seats.

National Party of Mozambique

Partido Nacional de Moçambique (PANAMO)
    Address. c/o Assembléia da República, Maputo
    Leadership. Marcos Juma (president)
    In alliance with the Liberal and Democratic Party of Mozambique and the National

Democratic Party, PANAMO contested the 1994 elections as a constituent of the Democratic Union, which won nine seats.

Social, Liberal and Democratic Party
Partido Social, Liberal e Democrático (SOL)
  Leadership. Casimiro Nhamithambo (president)
  Formed by a breakaway faction of the Liberal and Democratic Party of Mozambique, SOL was legally recognized in 1993. The party campaigned on a platform of equality, a market economy and decentralization, taking fifth place in the 1994 Assembly elections with nearly 1.7% of the vote (but no seats).

United Front of Mozambique
Frente Unida de Moçambique (FUMO)
  Address. Av Mao Tse-tung 230, Maputo
  Leadership. Domingos Arouca (president)
  In the 1994 elections FUMO's stance included the defence of human rights, the privatization of all state-owned companies, a market economy and denationalization of land. The party took 1.4% of the legislative vote, achieving eighth place in the presidential contest.

Other Parties

Democratic Confederation of Mozambique (*Confederação Democrático de Moçambique*, CODEMO).

Democratic Party for the Liberation of Mozambique (*Partido Democrático de Libertação de Moçambique*, PADELIMO).

Democratic Renewal Party (*Partido Renovador Democrático*, PRD), led by Maneca Daniel, obtained legal status in 1994, managing only 11th place in that year's legislative elections.

Democratic Union of Mozambique (*União Democrática de Moçambique*, UDEMO).

Independent Congress of Mozambique (*Congresso Independente de Moçambique*, COINMO).

Labour Party (*Partido Trabalhista*, PT), led by Simbene Mabote, formed in 1993 by a breakaway faction of the Mozambique People's Progress Party; decentralist and mildly socialist, the party came last in the 1994 legislative elections.

Liberal Federal Progressive Party of Mozambican Relgious Communities (*Partido Progressivo e Liberal Federalista das Comunidadaes Religiosas de Moçambique*, PPLFCRM).

Mozambique Agrarian Party (*Partido Agrário de Moçambique*, PAM).

Mozambique Communist Party (*Partido Comunista de Moçambique*, PACOMO).

Mozambique Democratic Alliance (*Aliança Democrática de Moçambique*, ADM).

Mozambique Internationalist Democratic Party (*Partido Internationalista Democrático de Moçambique*, PIDEMO).

National Convention Party (*Partido de Convenção Nacional*, PCN), led by Lutero Simango, obtained legal status in 1992, favours market economy, support for agriculture and respect for human rights, won about 1.3% of the vote in 1994 Assembly elections, did not contest presidential poll.

Patriotic Action Front (*Frente de Ação Patriótica*, FAP), led by João Palaso, founded in 1991, fought the 1994 Assembly elections in alliance with the Mozambique National Movement, taking fourth place.

Patriotic Alliance (*Aliança Patriótica*, AP), formed alliance with the Mozambique National Movement and the Patriotic Action Front in 1994, winning nearly 2% of the vote in 1994 legislative elections.

Revolutionary Party of the United Socialist People of Mozambique (*Partido Revolucionário do Povo Socialista Unido de Moçambique*, PREPSUMO).

Myanmar (Burma)

Capital: Yangon (Rangoon)   **Population:** 45,000,000 (1995E)

The Union of Myanmar (known as Burma until an official change of name in 1989) achieved independence from the United Kingdom in 1948. The first constitution of the new state created a parliamentary system of government, but a military coup in 1962 brought the country's democratic experience to an end. The ruling military junta (the Revolutionary Council), under the leadership of Ne Win, established the Burma Socialist Programme Party (BSPP) as the country's sole, legal, political organization. In September 1988, after two months of continuous mass protest centred on the capital (Yangon) which had effectively rendered the country ungovernable, there was a further coup by the armed forces, which abolished all state organizations and established in their place a military council and a Cabinet (the latter also consisting almost entirely of members of the military). Under new legislation announced the following month, the State Law and Order Restoration Council (SLORC, the ruling junta) and the government became the principal organs of power.

Political organizations were permitted to function (over 230 having registered by early 1989) and multi-party elections to a Constituent Assembly were held in May 1990, resulting in an overwhelming victory for the opposition National League for Democracy (NLD). However, the SLORC prevented the Assembly from convening, withdrawing recognition from most opposition parties, and the country has since remained under military control. Seven parties (listed immediately below) were invited by the SLORC to participate in the January 1993 launching of a national convention to co-ordinate the drafting of a new constitution.

Khami National Solidarity Organization (KNSO)
Leadership. U San Tha Aung (leader)

Founded in 1988 (and also known as the Mro National Solidarity Organization), the party won a single seat in the May 1990 Constituent Assembly elections.

Lahu National Development Party (LNDP)
Leadership. U Daniel Aung (leader)

The LNDP is based in the Lahu tribe of eastern Shan state. Its leader has called for the granting of local autonomy to all national minorities.

National League for Democracy (NLD)
Address. 97B West Shwegondine Road, Bahan Township, Yangon
Leadership. Daw Aung San Suu Kyi (leader)

The pro-democracy NLD was founded soon after the military takeover in September 1988 by three prominent opposition figures (Aung Gyi, Tin U and Daw Aung San Suu Kyi) as a broad-based coalition to unite the country's various anti-regime factions. Aung Gyi left the party in December 1988 to form the Union National Democracy Party. Although Aung San Suu Kyi

and Tin U were arrested in July 1989 and declared ineligible to compete in the May 1990 balloting, the NLD nevertheless won a massive victory in the elections, taking 392 of the 485 contested seats with about 60% of the total votes. However, the SLORC subsequently rendered the Constituent Assembly powerless and effectively nullified the NLD victory. In September 1990 the party's two other principal leaders, Kyi Maung and Chit Khaing, were arrested, and the following April the SLORC announced that the NLD's central committee had been "invalidated", thus removing the four leading figures from their party positions. Furthermore, during 1991 and 1992, the regime took steps to annul the election of numerous NLD Assembly members and to effect the expulsion of Aung San Suu Kyi, who remained under house arrest, from the party.

NLD representatives participated from January 1993 in sessions of the national convention charged with drawing up a new constitution, rallying considerable opposition to the military's draft proposals. Having released Tin U and Kyi Maung from prison in March 1995, the SLORC unexpectedly freed Aung San Suu Kyi from house arrest in July. She was reinstated as the general secretary of the NLD in October 1995, although the official electoral commission overruled the appointment. The following month, after NLD delegates withdrew from the latest session of the national convention, the regime responded by formally expelling the party for non-attendance.

National Unity Party (NUP)

Address. 93C Windermere Rd, Kamayut, Yangon

Leadership. U Tha Kyaw (chairman)

The NUP was launched as the successor to the former ruling Burma Socialist Programme Party (BSPP) in the aftermath of the September 1988 military coup. However, unlike the BSPP, NUP membership has not been open to members of the armed forces. In the Constituent Assembly elections in May 1990, the party gained about 21% of the vote but won only 10 seats. In September 1993 the NUP was reportedly being superseded by the Union Solidarity and Development Association as the civilian front through which the armed forces could exercise political control.

Shan Nationalities League for Democracy (SNLD)

Leadership. U Khun Tun Oo (leader)

Founded in 1988, the opposition SNLD was the runner up to the National League for Democracy in the May 1990 elections, winning 23 seats in the Constituent Assembly.

Shan State Kokang Democratic Party (SSKDP)

Leadership. U Yan Kyin Maw (leader)

The party, set up in 1988, won a single seat in the May 1990 elections.

Union Pa-O National Organization (UPNO)

Leadership. U San Hla (leader)

Based in west-central Shan state, the organization secured three Constituent Assembly seats in May 1990.

Other Parties

The following parties also contested the May 1990 elections to the Constituent Assembly (the individual seat tallies, where applicable, being given in parentheses).

Anti-Fascist People's Freedom League.

Arakan League for Democracy (11 seats)

Chin National League for Democracy (3 seats)

Democracy Party (1 seat)

Democratic Organization for Kayan National Unity (2 seats)

Graduates' and Old Students' Democratic Association (1 seat)

Kachin State National Congress for Democracy (3 seats)

Kamans National League for Democracy (1 seat)

Karen State National Organization (1 seat)

Kayah State Nationalities League for Democracy (2 seats)

League for Democracy and Peace.

Lisu National Solidarity Party (1 seat)

Mara People's Party (1 seat)

Mon National Democratic Front (5 seats)

National Democratic Party for Human Rights (4 seats)

National Hill Regional Progressive Party (2 seats)

Party for National Democracy (3 seats)

Patriotic Old Comrades' League (1 seat)

People's Democratic Party.

Ta-ang (Palaung) National League for Democracy (2 seats)

Union Danu League for Democracy Party (1 seat)

Union National Democracy Party (1 seat)

United Nationalities League for Democracy (1 seat)

Zomi National Congress (2 seats)

Illegal Groups

Most ethnic opposition to the SLORC regime came to an end in 1995. The most powerful of the country's insurgent groups, the **Karen National Union (KNU)**, lost its last remaining strongholds to government forces at the beginning of the year, and a major offensive was launched from March against the **Mong Tai Army (MTA)**, an ostensibly Shan nationalist group.

Namibia

Capital: Windhoek   **Population:** 1,600,000 (1995E)

Having been under South African control from 1915, the Republic of Namibia achieved independence in March 1990. South Africa's mandate to rule the territory was terminated by the United Nations in 1966, but it continued its occupation until final agreement was reached at the end of 1988 on the implementation of a UN-sponsored independence plan. Under the 1990 multi-party constitution, executive power is vested in the President and the Cabinet. The President, as head of state and government, is directly elected by universal adult suffrage, and must receive more than 50% of the votes cast. One person may not hold the office of President for more than two five-year terms. The legislature consists of the National Assembly and the National Council. The National Assembly, with a five-year mandate, has 72 directly-elected members and up to six non-voting members nominated by the President. The indirectly-elected and mainly advisory National Council, consisting of two members from each region, has a six-year term of office.

The first post-independence presidential and legislative elections were held on Dec. 7-8, 1994, resulting in incumbent President Sam Nujoma of the South West Africa People's Organiza-tion of Namibia (SWAPO) being returned for a second term and SWAPO winning a major-ity of 53 seats in the National Assembly.

Democratic Coalition of Namibia (DCN)

Address. c/o National Assembly, Windhoek
Leadership. Moses Katjiuongua (leader)

The DCN was formed in 1994, initially bring-ing together three parties, namely the South West African National Union (SWANU), the National Patriotic Front (NPF) and the German Union (GU) faction of the Action Christian National (ACN). The grouping stressed the importance of action to combat crime, streamline the civil service and army, develop the economy, and improve basic services. SWANU withdrew from the coalition prior to the December 1994 elections, in which the DCN gained one seat in the National Assembly.

Democratic Turnhalle Alliance of Namibia (DTA)

Address. PO Box 173, Windhoek
Telephone. (#264–61) 238530
Fax. (#264–61) 226494
Leadership. Mishake Muyongo (leader)

Founded in 1977 as a multiracial coalition, the DTA was the majority political formation in the South African-appointed transitional govern-ment prior to independence and was supported by South Africa. Following Constituent Assembly elections in 1989 (organized under the UN-sponsored independence plan) it became the main opposition grouping. Having been revamped as a single party in November 1991, the DTA contested the legislative and presidential elections in 1994, focusing on the issues of unemployment, rising crime and corruption. In the presidential poll, party leader Muyongo came second to incumbent President Nujoma of the South West Africa People's Organization (SWAPO) with nearly 24% of the votes cast. In the National Assembly the party secured 15 seats with a 20.8% vote share, trailing SWAPO by a considerable margin.

Monitor Action Group (MAG)

Address. PO Box 354, Windhoek
Telephone. (#264–61) 226159
Fax. (#264–61) 229242
Leadership. Kosie Pretorius (leader)

The MAG, set up during 1994 by the former leader of the predominantly white Action Christian National (ACN), defines itself as a pressure group for "principle politics" rather than a political party as such. It aims to promote "a Christian outlook and standpoint" and advocates the removal of the "secular concept" from the Namibian constitution. In the elections to the National Assembly in December 1994 the MAG won a single seat.

South West Africa People's Organization of Namibia (SWAPO)

Address. PO Box 1071, Windhoek
Telephone. (#264–61) 38364
Fax. (#264–61) 32368
Leadership. Sam Nujoma (president), Moses Garoëb (secretary-general)

SWAPO was established in 1958 as the Ovamboland People's Organization, adopting its present name in 1968. It was the principal liberation movement in the pre-independence period, having launched an armed struggle in 1966. From 1973 it was recognized by the UN General Assembly as "the authentic representative of the people of Namibia". In the pre-independence Constituent Assembly elections in 1989, SWAPO won a majority. In February 1990 the Assembly adopted the new constitution and elected SWAPO leader Sam Nujoma to be Namibia's first President. Following independence, SWAPO formed the government, advocating national reconciliation, economic development, and an improvement in the basic conditions of life for the majority.

In December 1991 the organization held its first congress since its inception. The constitution and political programme were amended to transform SWAPO from a liberation movement to a mass political party. In the December 1994 elections Nujoma retained the presidency, winning just over 76% of the vote, while SWAPO candidates secured 53 of the 72 elective seats in the National Assembly. This was a sufficient majority to amend the constitution framed by the Constituent Assembly in the run-up to independence.

United Democratic Front (UDF)

Address. c/o Private Bag 13323, Windhoek
Telephone. (#264–61) 288-0111
Fax. (#264–61) 226899
Leadership. Justus Garoëb (president)

Founded as a centrist alliance of eight ethnic parties, the UDF won four seats in the 1989 Constituent Assembly elections, subsequently reorganizing itself as a unitary party in October 1993. Although in third place in the December 1994 legislative poll, the party attracted only 2.7% of the vote and won only two National Assembly seats.

Other Parties

Christian Democratic Action for Social Justice (CDA), led by Rev. Peter Kalangula.

Federal Convention of Namibia (FCN), led by J. Diergaardt, an alliance of ethnically-based parties, including the NUDO-Progressive Party *Jo'Horongo* and the Rehoboth Free Democratic Party (or Liberation Front), opposed to a unitary form of government for Namibia; won only a marginal vote in the December 1994 legislative balloting.

Namibia National Democratic Party (NNDP), led by Paul Helmuth.

Namibia National Front (NNF), a coalition of leftist nationalist groups.

South West Africa National Union (SWANU), led by Hitjevi Veii, joined the Democratic Coalition of Namibia in 1994 but withdrew later that year; took only some 0.5% of the vote in the December 1994 elections and gained no representation.

Workers' Revolutionary Party (WRP), led by Werner Mamugwe, a leftist organization formed in 1989, was the least successful party in the 1994 National Assembly elections, winning less than 0.2% of the vote.

Nauru

Capital: Domaneab

Population: 11,000 (1995E)

Nauru achieved independence in 1968, having previously been a United Nations Trust Territory administered by Australia. Under the constitution legislative power is vested in an 18-member unicameral Parliament, elected for up to three years, which selects a President from among its members. The President, who is head of state, governs with the assistance of an appointed Cabinet. Nauru's first President, Hammer DeRoburt, who had dominated the political structure of the island since independence, was forced to resign in August 1989 after a vote of no confidence. Following a general election in December 1989 Bernard Dowiyogo was elected President. He was re-elected in November 1992 but, after the next general election in November 1995, was voted out by Parliament and replaced by Lagumot Harris. Nauru politics tend to operate on family rather than party lines, although a political organization called the Democratic Party of Nauru has been in existence since 1987.

Nepal

Capital: Kathmandu   **Population:** 20,000,000 (1995E)

Following the overthrow of the ruling Rana family in a popular revolt in 1950, the King of Nepal resumed an active political role. In 1959 the country's first constitution was promulgated and a parliament was elected. However at the end of the following year the King dissolved parliament and dismissed the government. All political parties were banned in 1961 and for the next 30 years Nepal experienced direct rule by the monarchy, although a tiered, party-less system of *panchayat* (council) democracy was introduced under a new constitution in 1962. In February 1990 a series of peaceful demonstrations in support of the restoration of democracy and human rights escalated into full-scale confrontation with the government. The following April the ban on political parties was rescinded, restrictions on the press lifted and constitutional reform promised. A new constitution guaranteeing parliamentary government and a constitutional monarchy was proclaimed in November 1990. It provides for a bicameral legislature comprising a popularly-elected 205–member House of Representatives (*Pratinidhi Sabha*) and a National Council (*Rashtriya Sabha*) of 60 members, of whom 10 are nominees of the King, 35 are elected by the House of Representatives and 15 are elected by an electoral college.

The first multi-party general election was held in May 1991 and resulted in a victory for the Nepali Congress Party (NCP). In further elections on Nov. 15, 1994, the United Communist Party of Nepal (UCPN) became the largest party with 88 seats against 83 for the NCP, with the National Democratic Party (RPP) winning 20, the Nepal Workers' and Peasants' Party 4, the Nepal Goodwill Council (NSP) 3 and independents 7. The UCPN leader, Man Mohan Adhikari, was accordingly sworn in as the country's first communist Prime Minister at the end of the month.

A political crisis arose in June 1995 when Adhikari recommended the dissolution of parliament by King Birendra and a fresh general election, apparently to avoid losing an imminent vote of no confidence. The Prime Minister's decision, and his appointment as head of a caretaker government pending elections scheduled for November, were challenged by opposition parties which, in August, won a ruling from the Supreme Court reinstating the existing parliament. In September Adhikari resigned after losing a parliamentary vote of no confidence and was replaced as Prime Minister by Sher Bahadur Deuba of the NCP. A new coalition government led by the NCP and including the RPP and the NSP then took office.

National Democratic Party
Rashtriya Prajatantra Party (RPP)
   Address. c/o House of Representatives, Kathmandu
   Leadership. Lokendra Bahadur Chand, Surya Bahadur Thapa (leaders)
   The right-wing, monarchist RPP is composed of two principal factions, led by former Prime Ministers Chand and Thapa respectively. In the November 1994 elections the party secured 20 seats in the House of Representatives, joining the NCP-led coalition government which replaced the communist administration in September 1995.

Nepal Goodwill Council
Nepal Sadhbhavana Parishad (NSP)
   Address. c/o House of Representatives, Kathmandu
   Leadership. Gajendra Narayan Singh (president), Hridayesh Tripathi (general secretary)
   This small party promotes the rights of the

Madhesiya Indian community of the Terai region of Nepal. In November 1994 it won three seats in the elections to the House of Representatives. Its president was awarded a portfolio in the NCP-led coalition government formed in September 1995.

Nepal Workers' and Peasants' Party
Nepal Mazdoor Kisan Party (NMKP)

Address. c/o House of Representatives, Kathmandu

Leadership. Narayan Man Bijukche (chair)

The pro-Chinese communist NWPP won four seats in the House of Representatives in the 1994 elections.

Nepali Congress Party (NCP)
Address. New Baneshwor, Kathmandu

Telephone. (#977–1) 227748

Fax. (#977-1) 227747

Leadership. Sher Bahadur Deuba (leader), Krishna Prasad Bhattarai (president), Mahendra Narayan Nidhi (general secretary)

Founded in the late 1940s as Nepal's wing of the Indian National Congress, with a socialist but pro-monarchist orientation, the NCP came to government in 1959 but was ejected by the monarch a year later and banned along with other political parties from 1961. Over the following two decades many NCP activists were detained or restricted, while the exiled leadership campaigned for the restoration of democracy. The party achieved a measure of official acceptance through the 1980s, although various moves to reach a political accord with the King were inconclusive amid periodic repressive action by the authorities.

Following the widespread popular agitation that began in early 1990, the NCP president was appointed by the King to lead a coalition government pending multi-party elections in May 1991, in which the NCP won an overall majority of 110 seats. In further elections to the House of Representatives in November 1994 (brought about by a vote of no confidence in the NCP government), the party won only 83 of the 205 seats and relinquished power to the United Communist Party of Nepal (UCPN). However, following the

resignation of the UCPN administration in September 1995, the NCP formed a new coalition under the premiership of Sher Bahadur Deuba.

United Communist Party of Nepal (UCPN)
Address. POB 5471, Kathmandu

Telephone. (#977–1) 223639

Leadership. Man Mohan Adhikari (leader)

The UCPN was formed in early 1991 by the merger of the Marxist and Marxist-Leninist factions of the Communist Party of Nepal. In the May 1991 elections it won the second highest number of seats (69) in the House of Representatives, thereby becoming the official opposition. Although the party was left short of a workable majority in the November 1994 elections (from which it emerged as the largest party with 88 seats), the UCPN leader, Man Mohan Adhikari, was invited to form a new government. However, his controversial efforts to maintain his administration ended with his resignation as Prime Minister in September 1995 and the party's return to opposition status.

Other Parties

Communist Party of Nepal (Democratic/ *Manadhar*), a communist faction which contested the May 1991 elections, winning two seats.

National People's Council (*Rashtriya Janata Parishad*, RJP), formed in 1992 by Maitrika Prasad Koirala and Kirti Nidhi Bista, both former Prime Ministers seeking a non-radical alternative to the Nepali Congress Party.

National People's Liberation Forum, a left-wing formation which opposes the 1990 constitution.

Nepal People's Council (*Nepal Praja Parishad*, NPP), led by Ram Hari Sharma.

Nepal People's Party (*Nepal Janata Dal*, NJP), led by Hari Prasad Pokharel, linked with the *Janata Dal* of India.

Netherlands

Capital: Amsterdam
Seat of Government: The Hague   **Population:** 15,500,000 (1995E)

The Kingdom of the Netherlands (consisting of the Netherlands in Europe and the Caribbean territories of Aruba and the Netherlands Antilles) is a constitutional and hereditary monarchy whose two non-European parts enjoy full autonomy (see next section). Under its 1815 constitution as amended, the Netherlands in Europe has a multi-party parliamentary system of government employing proportional representation to reflect the country's religious and social diversity. Executive authority is exercised on behalf of the monarch by a Prime Minister and other ministers, who are accountable to the States-General (*Staten-Generaal*). The latter consists of (i) the 75–member First Chamber (*Eeerste Kamer*) elected by the members of the country's 12 provincial councils for a four-year term; and (ii) the 150–member Second Chamber (*Tweede Kamer*), also elected for a four-term but by universal suffrage of those aged 18 and over. Under a draft constitutional amendment approved by the government in October 1995, the existing Second Chamber election system of pure proportional representation is to be replaced by a mixed system whereby half the seats will be filled from electoral districts and half from national party lists.

While political parties in the Netherlands have traditionally relied on members' subscriptions and donations, since 1972 state funding has been available for policy research and educational foundations attached to parties represented in the Second Chamber. Parties also receive certain concessions to defray expenses during election campaigns, including a limited amount of free media access.

Elections to the Second Chamber on May 3, 1994, resulted as follows: Labour Party 37 seats (with 24.0% of the vote), Christian Democratic Appeal 34 (22.2%), People's Party for Freedom and Democracy 31 (19.9%), Democrats 66 24 (15.5%), General Union of the Elderly 6 (3.6%), Green Left 5 (3.5%), Centre Democrats 3 (2.5%), Reformational Political Federation 3 (1.8%), State Reform Party 2 (1.7%), Reformed Political Association 2 (1.3%), Socialist Party 2 (1.3%), 55+ Union 1 (0.9%).

Centre Democrats

Centrumdemocraten (CD)

Address. PO Box 84, 2501 CB The Hague

Telephone. (#31-70) 346-9264

Leadership. Hans Janmaat (chair and parliamentary leader), W.B. Schuurman (secretary)

The radical right-wing CD was created in 1986 by the majority "moderate" wing of the Centre Party (CP), the residue of which became the Centre Party 86. Established on an anti-immigration platform mainly by former members of the ultra-nationalist Dutch People's Union (NVU), the CP had succeeded in attracting significant support among white working-class voters in inner city areas with heavy immigrant concentrations. In the 1982 Second Chamber elections it had obtained over 68,000 votes (0.8%) and one seat, while in the 1984 local elections it won 10% of the vote in Rotterdam and eight seats on the city council. Violent incidents occurred at several CP meetings prior to the May 1986 Second Chamber elections, in which the party failed to secure representation. Eight days before polling the CP had been declared bankrupt by a Dutch court after failing to pay a fine of 50,000 guilders imposed for forgery of election nominations. It later re-emerged as the CF.

Having regained one Second Chamber seat in 1989, the CD advanced to three seats in May 1994, winning 2.5% of the vote. In the following month's European Parliament elections it registered only 1% and failed to win representation.

Christian Democratic Appeal
Christen-Democratisch Appèl (CDA)

Address. 5 Dr. Kuyperstraat, 2514 BA The Hague

Telephone. (#31–70) 342–4888

Fax. (#31–70) 364–3417

Leadership. Ennëus Heerma (parliamentary leader), H. Helgers (chair), Cees Bremmer (general secretary)

The right-of-centre, Christian-inspired CDA was founded in April 1975 as a federation of (i) the Anti-Revolutionary Party (*Anti-Revolutionaire Partij*, ARP) founded in 1878 by Abraham Kuyper; (ii) the Christian Historic Union (*Christelijk-Historische Unie*) established by ARP dissidents in 1908; and (iii) the Catholic People's Party (*Katholieke Volkspartij*) dating from 1928 and given its present name in 1945. The new formation represented an attempt by these confessional parties to reverse the steady decline in their vote since 1945. The CDA was constituted as a unified party in October 1980, after a five-year preparatory phase. It gained 49 seats in the Second Chamber in 1977, 47 in 1981 and 45 in 1982.

From 1977 the CDA headed several coalition governments—with the People's Party for Freedom and Democracy (VVD) until September 1981, with the Labour Party and the Democrats 66 until May 1982, with the Democrats 66 only until November 1982, and with the VVD after that under Ruud Lubbers.

Having slipped from 48 to 45 Second Chamber seats in the September 1982 elections, the CDA subsequently experienced some internal dissension over the government's economic and defence policies. Nevertheless, in May 1986 it staged a sharp recovery, to 54 seats, and continued in government with the VVD.

The CDA retained 54 seats in the 1989 Second Chamber elections (with 35.3% of the vote), after which it formed a centre-left coalition with the PvdA, under the continued premiership of Lubbers, who became the Netherlands' longest-serving post-war Prime Minister. In advance of the May 1994 election, however, Lubbers announced his retirement from Dutch politics, with the result that the CDA campaigned under the new leadership of Elco Brinkman, amid difficult economic and social conditions. The outcome was that the party suffered its worst-ever electoral defeat, losing a third of its 1989 support and slumping to 22.2% and 34 seats, three less than the PvdA. The CDA recovered somewhat in the June 1994 European Parliament elections, to 30.8%, which yielded 10 of the 31 Dutch seats; nevertheless, Brinkman resigned as CDA leader in August, as the party went into opposition to a PvdA-led coalition.

The CDA is a member of the Christian Democrat International. Its representatives in the European Parliament sit in the European People's Party group.

Democrats 66
Democraten 66 (D66)

Address. 10 Noordwal, 2513 EA The Hague

Telephone. (#31–70) 385–8303

Fax. (#31–70) 385–8183

Leadership. Hans A.F.M.O. van Mierlo (leader), W. Vrijhoef (chair), Gerrit-Jan Wolffensperger (parliamentary leader), Guus Faasen (general secretary)

Founded in 1966 with "a commitment to change inspired by a sense of responsibility for the future" and its first aim being "the democratization of certain constitutional laws", D66 obtained representation in the Second Chamber with seven seats in 1967 and 11 seats in 1971, but only six seats in 1973 and eight in 1977. In 1981 D66 increased its electoral support significantly, gaining over 11% of the vote and 17 seats in the Second Chamber. A downward trend reappeared in 1982, when the party was reduced to six seats. However, in May 1986 it recovered to nine seats and 6.1% of the votes.

D66 has usually regarded the Labour Party as its most obvious partner for participation in government and with that party (and three others) took part in a coalition government in 1973–77. It subsequently participated in coalitions with the Christian Democratic Appeal (CDA) in 1982. This last experience of government was seen as contributing to the party's setback in the September 1982 elections, in light of which Jan Terlouw resigned as leader and was eventually replaced by his predecessor, Hans van Mierlo.

D66 lower house representation rose from nine seats in 1986 to 12 in 1989, the latter tally being doubled in a major advance in May 1994 on a vote share of 15.5%, on the basis of which the party joined a coalition government with the PvdA and the People's Party for Freedom and Democracy (VVD). In the June European Parliament elections D66 slipped back to 11.7%, taking four of the 31 Dutch seats. A key condition of D66 participation in the government was that the constitution should be amended to make provision for "corrective referendums" in which parliamentary legislation on some subjects could be overturned by the people. After VVD ministers had opposed the proposal and Labour had expressed doubts, the version given cabinet approval in October 1995 extended the list of excluded subjects.

D66 is a member party of the Liberal International. Its representatives in the European Parliament sit in the European Liberal, Democratic and Reformist Group.

General Union of the Elderly

Algemeen Ouderen Verbond (AOV)

Address. 12 Louis Kookenweg, 5624 KW Eindhoven

Telephone. (#31-40) 433961

Fax. (#31-40) 124765

Leadership. Martin Batenburg (chair), H.M. (Jet) Nijpels-Hezemans (parliamentary leader)

Formed as a union of several pensioners' movements, the AOV is pledged to opposing cuts in the state pension and other benefits for the elderly. It won a creditable 3.6% of the vote in the May 1994 Second Chamber elections, giving it six seats. The AOV was then damaged by a fierce internal dispute, as a result of which three lower house deputies broke away or were expelled from the group.

Green Left

Groen Links (GL)

Address. PO Box 700, 1000 AS Amsterdam

Telephone. (#31-20) 620-2212

Fax. (#31-20) 625-1849

Leadership. A. Harrewijn (chair), Paul Rosenmuller (parliamentary leader)

The GL was founded prior to the 1989 Second Chamber elections as an alliance of the Evangelical People's Party (*Evangelische Volkspartij*, EVP), the Radical Political Party (*Politieke Partij Radikalen*, PPR), the Pacifist Socialist Party (*Pacifistisch Socialistische Partij*, PSP) and the Communist Party of the Netherlands (*Communistische Partij van Nederland*, CPN). It became a unitary party in 1991, when each of its constituent groups voted to disband.

Of the component parties, the EVP had been formed in 1978 and had held one seat in the 1982-86 Second Chamber. The PPR had been founded in 1968 by a left-wing faction of the Catholic People's Party (later the mainstay of the Christian Democratic Appeal), had won seven seats in 1972 and had participated in a centre-left coalition in 1973-77. The PSP had dated from 1957 and had won between one and four seats in subsequent elections. The CPN had been founded in 1918 by left-wing Social Democrats, had held 10 seats in post-1945 Second Chamber but had steadily declined to zero representation in 1986.

Having won six seats and 4.1% of the vote in its first contest in 1989, the GL slipped to five seats and 3.5% in May 1994. In the following month's European Parliament elections it recovered slightly to 3.7%, retaining one of the two seats it had won in 1989.

Labour Party

Partij van de Arbeid (PvdA)

Address. 30 Nicolaas Witsenkade, 1017 ZT Amsterdam

Telephone. (#31-20) 551-2155

Fax. (#31-20) 551-2330

Leadership. Willem (Wim) Kok (leader), Fálix Rottenberg (chair), Jacques Wallage (parliamentary leader), Alard Beck (general secretary)

The PvdA was founded in 1946 as the post-war successor to the Social Democratic Workers' Party, founded in 1894 by P.J. Troelstra and other dissidents of the Social Democratic Union (created by F.D. Nieuwenhuis in 1881). From its establishment in 1946 as a broader-based party including many former liberals, the PvdA engaged in the reconstruction of the Netherlands after the German occupation. Its leader, Willem Drees, was Prime Minister of a Labour-Catholic coalition government from 1948 to 1958, whereafter the PvdA was in opposition for 15 years—except briefly in 1965–66, when it took part in a coalition government with the Catholic People's Party (KVP) and the Anti-Revolutionary Party (ARP).

The PvdA was weakened in 1970 by a right-wing breakaway by followers of Dr Willem Drees (son of Willem), who formed the "Democratic Socialists 1970" (DS-70) party. Although DS-70 gained eight seats in the 1971 elections, thereafter its representation declined and the party was dissolved in January 1983.

In 1971 and 1972 the PvdA contested elections on a joint programme with the Democrats 66 (D66) and the Radical Political Party, and in 1973 it formed a coalition government with these parties and also the KVP and the ARP, with the then PvdA leader, Joop den Uyl, becoming Prime Minister. This was the first Dutch government with a left-wing majority of ministers. However, after the 1977 elections, in which the PvdA increased its seats in the Second Chamber from 43 to 53, it went into opposition to a centre-right government led by the Christian Democratic Appeal (CDA). From September 1981 to May 1982 the party took part in a coalition government with the CDA and D66.

The PvdA was then in opposition, despite achieving a significant advance in the May 1986 Second Chamber elections, from 47 to 52 seats. Following those elections, Wim Kok (hitherto leader of the Netherlands Trade Union Confederation) became PvdA leader in succession to Joop den Uyl (who died in December 1987).

Although it fell back to 49 seats on a 31.9% vote share, the PvdA returned to government after the 1989 elections, as junior coalition partner to the CDA. In August 1991 Marjanne Sint resigned as PvdA chair because of the party's acceptance of cuts in the state social security system, introduced by the CDA-PvdA coalition. In the May 1994 lower house elections the PvdA slipped again, to

24.0%, but overtook the CDA as the largest party and therefore became the senior partner in a new three-party coalition, this time with the People's Party for Freedom and Democracy and D66. In the June 1994 elections to the European Parliament, support for Labour declined further, to 22.9%, giving it eight of the Netherlands' 31 seats.

The PvdA is a member party of the Socialist International. Its European Parliament representatives sit in the Party of European Socialists group.

People's Party for Freedom and Democracy
Volkspartij voor Vrijheid en Democratie (VVD)
  Address. PO Box 30836, 2500 GV The Hague
  Telephone. (#31–70) 361–3061
  Fax. (#31–70) 360–8276
  Leadership. Hans F. Dijkstal (leader), Willem Hoekzema (chair), Frits Bolkestein (parliamentary leader), Nico van Batenburg (general secretary)

Founded in 1948, the VVD is descended from the group of liberals led by J.R. Thorbecke who inspired the introduction of constitutional rule in 1848. Organized as the Liberal Union from 1885, the Dutch liberals (like their counterparts elsewhere in Europe) lost influence as the move to universal suffrage produced increasing electoral competition on the left, with the result that after World War II many liberals joined the new Labour Party. However other liberal elements under the leadership of P.J. Oud founded the VVD, which remained in opposition to Labour-Catholic coalitions until 1959, when an electoral advance enabled the party to join a coalition with the Catholics.

After languishing electorally in the 1960s, the VVD made steady advances in the 1970s under the leadership of Hans Wiegel, winning 28 seats in the Second Chamber in 1977 and joining a coalition headed by the new Christian Democratic Appeal (CDA). Reduced to 26 seats in 1981 the VVD went into opposition, but under the new leadership of Ed Nijpels made a big advance to 36 seats the following year and joined a further coalition with the CDA. This was continued after the 1986 elections, although the VVD slipped back to 27 seats and from 23.1 to 17.4% of the vote.

The VVD lost ground in both the 1986 and 1989 elections, on the latter occasion going into opposition for the first time since 1982. In the May 1994 contest, however, the VVD made a major advance by Dutch standards, from 14.6 to 19.9% of the vote, while the June European Parliament elections gave it a 17.9% tally and six of the 31 Dutch seats. In August 1994 the VVD returned to government, joining a coalition with the PvdA and Democrats 66. In provincial elections in March 1995 the VVD struck a popular chord with its tough policy prescriptions on immigration and asylum seekers, overtaking the CDA as the strongest party at provincial level and therefore increasing its representation in the First Chamber to 23 seats. Within the national government, VVD ministers urged cuts in government spending to reduce the deficit to the Maastricht criterion for participation in a single European currency, thereby coming into conflict with the PvdA, which preferred to raise taxes.

The VVD is a member of the Liberal International. Its European Parliament representatives sit in the European Liberal, Democratic and Reformist Group.

Reformational Political Federation
Reformatorische Politieke Federatie (RPF)
  Address. PO Box 302, 8070 AH Nunspeet
  Telephone. (#31-341) 256744
  Fax. (#31-341) 260348
  Leadership. A. van den Berg (chair), Leen C. van Dijke (parliamentary leader), W. van Grootheest (secretary)

Founded in March 1975, the RPF seeks a reformation of political and social life in accordance with the Bible and Calvinistic tradition and creed. The party was formed by the National Evangelical Association, dissenters from the Anti-Revolutionary Party (ARP) and Associations of Reformed (Calvanist) Voters. In 1981, and again in 1982, it won two seats in the Second Chamber (with 108,000 votes in 1981 and 125,000 in 1982). In 1982 it also obtained 10 seats in provincial elections and about 100 in municipal elections. In 1986 it was reduced to one seat in the Second Chamber, winning 83,269 votes.

The RPF again won one seat in 1989, but trebled this tally in May 1994 on a 1.8% vote share. For the following month's European Parliament elections the RPF presented a joint list with the Reformed Political Association (GPV) and the State Reform Party, which took a 7.8% vote share and elected two members (neither from the RPF).

Reformed Political Association
Gereformeerd Politiek Verbond (GPV)
  Address. PO Box 439, 3800 AK Amersfoort
  Telephone. (#31-33) 461-3546
  Fax. (#31-33) 461-0132
  Leadership. J.C. Cnossen (chair), Gert J. Schutte (parliamentary leader)

On its creation in April 1948, the founders of the GPV claimed to represent the continuation of the ideas of the Dutch national Calvinists of the 16th and 17th centuries, but on the basis of recognition of the separation of Church and State and of spiritual and fundamental freedoms. Before World War II the Anti-Revolutionary Party had claimed to represent these ideas, but the founders of the Association objected to the "partly liberal and partly socialistic" tendencies which they believed to be developing in that party. The GPV has never held more than two seats in the Second Chamber, winning one in 1986 with some 88,000 votes.

The GPV recovered to two seats in 1989, retained in May 1994 with 1.3% of the vote. For the following month's European Parliament elections the GPV presented a joint list with the Reformational Political Federation (RPF) and the State Reform Party (SGP), which took a 7.8% vote share and two seats (one for the GPV and one for the SGP). The two elected members sit in the anti-EU Nations of Europe group.

Socialist Party
Socialistische Partiji (SP)
    Address. 65 Vijverhofstraat, 3032 SC Rotterdam
    Telephone. (#31-10) 467-3222
    Fax. (#31-10) 467-3558
    Leadership. J.G.C.A. Marijnissen (chair and parliamentary group)
    The left-wing SP derives from a Maxist-Leninist party founded in 1971 and has latterly obtained electoral support from former adherents of the Communist Party of the Netherlands, which disbanded in 1991 to become part of the Green Left. The SP increased its vote share from 0.4% in 1989 to 1.3% in the May 1994 Second Chamber elections, returning two deputies.

State Reform Party
Staatkundig Gereformeerde Partij (SGP)
    Address. 165 laan van Meerdervoort, 2517 AZ The Hague
    Telephone. (#31-70) 346-8688
    Fax. (#31-70) 365-5959
    Leadership. Rev. D.J. Budding (chair), B.J. van der Vlies (parliamentary leader), A. de Boer (secretary)
    Founded in 1918, the right-wing Calvinist SGP bases its political and social outlook on its own interpretation of the Bible. It advocates strong law enforcement, including the use of the death penalty, and is opposed to supranational government on the grounds that it would expose the Netherlands to corrupting influences. It has consistently attracted somewhat under 2% of the vote, which gave it three Second Chamber seats through the 1980s, slipping to two in May 1994. For the following month's European Parliament elections the SGP presented a joint list with the

Reformed Political Association (GPV) and the Reformational Political Federation (RPF), which took a 7.8% vote share and two seats (one for the SGP and one for the GPV). The two elected members sit in the anti-EU Nations of Europe group.

55+ Union
Unie 55+
    Address. PO Box 111, 7450 AC Holten
    Telephone. (#31-548) 362422
    Fax. (#31-548) 363422
    Leadership. J.H.C. Goeman (chair), H.A. Heerkens (parliamentary leader)
    The 55+ Union is the smaller of two main Dutch pensioners' parties, being more inclined to radicalism than the General Union of the Elderly. It obtained 0.9% of the vote and one Second Chamber seat in the May 1994 elections.

Other Parties

Anti-Unemployment Party (*Anti-Werkloosheid Partij*, AWP), led by A.A. Wissink.

Bierman List (*Lijst Bierman*, LB), led by M. Bierman, who was elected to the First Chamber in May 1995.

Centre Party 86 (*Centrumpartij 86*), extreme right-wing formation, being the rump left when the old Centre Party became the Centre Democrats in 1986.

Great Alliance Party (*Grote Alliance Partij*, GAP), led by J.A. Geiger.

The Greens (*De Groenen*), led by Kirsten Kuipers, founded in 1984 as a conservative church-oriented party, won one upper house seat in March 1995.

National Socialist Action Front (*Aktiefront National Socialisten*, ANS), led by Eite Homann, a far-right formation.

Political Party of the Elderly (*Politieke Partij voor Ouderen*, PPO), led by K. Blokker.

Socialist Labour Party (SAP), a Trotskyist formation, led by H.E.W. Lindelauff.

Women's Party (*Vrouwenpartij*, VP), led by P.A. Roggeband-Baaij and Lottie Schenk.

Netherlands Dependencies

The Kingdom of the Netherlands incorporates two Caribbean territories which became Dutch possessions in the 17th century, namely Aruba and the Netherlands Antilles, both of which exercise full autonomy in domestic affairs and have flourishing multi-party systems. Unlike those in French dependencies in the same region, political parties in Aruba and the Netherlands Antilles have little direct connection with or derivation from metropolitan parties.

Aruba

Capital: Oranjestad   **Population:** 77,000 (1995E)

Located off the north-east coast of Venezuela, the island of Aruba was part of the Netherlands Antilles until it secured self-government (*status parte*) on Jan. 1, 1986. It has an appointed Governor representing the Dutch sovereign and a 21–member legislature (*Staten*) elected for a four-year term, to which the Prime Minister and Council of Ministers are accountable for their executive authority (which excludes external relations and defence). Elections to the *Staten* on July 29, 1994, resulted as follows: Aruban People's Party/Christian Democracy 10 seats, People's Electoral Movement 9, Aruban Liberal Organization 2.

Aruban Democratic Party (*Partido Democratico Arubano*, PDA), led by Léonard Berlinski, founded in 1983, anti-independence formation, won two seats in 1985 elections, joined post-separation coalition headed by Aruban People's Party/ Christian Democracy, but withdrew later in 1986, failed to gain representation in 1993 and 1994 elections.

Aruban Liberal Organization (*Organisacion Liberal Arubano*, OLA), led by Glenbert F. Croes, moderate party founded in 1991, won two seats in 1994 elections and joined coalition headed by Aruban People's Party/Christian Democracy. *Address.* c/o Staten, Oranjestad, Aruba

Aruban Patriotic Party (*Partido Patriótico Arubano*, PPA), led by Benedict (Benny) J.M. Nisbett, founded in 1949, anti-independence grouping, won two seats in 1985 elections, joined post-separation coalition headed by Aruban People's Party/Christian Democracy (1986–89), then coalition headed by People's Electoral Movement (1989–93), meanwhile being reduced to one seat in 1993 elections, which it lost in 1994.

Aruban People's Party/Christian Democracy (*Arubaanse Volkspartij/Democracia Cristiana*, AVP/ DC), led by Jan Henrik (Henny) A. Eman, founded by him in 1942, advocated separation from Netherlands Antilles (but not full independence), on achievement of which Eman became Prime Minister of Aruba, heading four-party coalition with Aruban Patriotic Party, Aruban Democratic Party (which quickly withdrew) and National Democratic Action; in opposition after 1989 and 1993 elections, but confirmed as leading party in 1994 elections (with 10 of 21 seats), after which Eman formed coalition with Aruban Liberal Organization; affiliated to Christian Democrat International. *Address.* c/o Staten, Oranjestad, Aruba

National Democratic Action (*Acción Democratico Nacional, ADN)*, led by Pedro P. Kelly, founded in 1985, participated in first post-separation coalition in 1986–89 headed by Aruban People's Party/Christian Democracy, then in coalition headed by People's Electoral Movement (1989– 94), meanwhile winning only one seat in 1993 elections, which it lost in 1994.

New Patriotic Party (*Partido Patriótico Nobo*, PPN), led by Eddy Werleman, founded in 1987 by dissident faction of Aruban Patriotic Party, won one seat in 1989 elections, which it lost in 1993.

People's Electoral Movement (*Movimento Electoral di Pueblo*, MEP), led by Rudy Croes, founded in 1971 by Gilberto (Betico) François Croes, was leading proponent of Aruba's separation from Netherlands Antilles and eventual full independence (not least to have benefit of offshore oil reserves), in opposition on achieve-ment of separate status in 1986, returned to power after 1989 elections under Nelson Oduber, with Oduber heading coalition with National Democratic Action and Aruban Patriotic Party; then backtracked on aim of full independence in 1996, accepting continued Dutch sovereignty; coalition collapsed in 1994, causing new elections in which the MEP took second place and went into opposition to a coalition headed by Aruban People's Party/Christian Democracy; affiliated to Socialist International. *Address*. 84 Cumana, Oranjestad, Aruba

Netherlands Antilles

Capital: Willemstad, Curaçao

Population: 200,000 (1995E)

Consisting of the Caribbean islands of Curaçao, Bonaire, St Maarten, St Eustatius (or Statia) and Saba, the Netherlands Antilles have an appointed Governor representing the Dutch sovereign and a 22–member legislature (*Staten*) elected for a four-year term, to which the Prime Minister and Council of Ministers are responsible. Elections on Feb. 25, 1994, gave some comfort to a large number of parties on the different islands, as follows: Restructured Antilles Party 8 seats, National People's Party 3, New Antilles Movement 2, St Maarten Patriotic Alliance 2, Democratic Party-Bonaire 2, Democratic Party-Curaçao 1, Democratic Party-St Maarten 1, Bonaire Patriotic Union 1, Windward Islands People's Movement 1, Democratic Party-Statia 1. *Note* The foreign-language party names given below are thought to be those most commonly used of the Spanish, Dutch and Papiamento (local dialect) versions.

Bonaire Patriotic Union (*Unión Patriótico Bonairiano*, UPB), led by Rudi Ellis, represented in the *Staten* since 1977, won one seat in 1985, three in 1990 and one in 1994; affiliated to Christian Democrat International. *Address*. PO Box 55, Kralendijk, Bonaire

Democratic Party-Bonaire (*Democratische Partij-Bonaire*, DP-B), led by Jopie Abraham, centrist party founded in 1954 as autonomous island party linked with other Antilles Democratic parties, won control of island council in 1984 and two *Staten* seats in 1985, joined Antilles coalition headed by New Antilles Movement, failed to win represeen-tation in 1990 *Staten* elections, regained two seats in 1994, joined coalition headed by Restructured Antilles Party. *Address*. 13A Kaya America, Kralendijk, Bonaire

Democratic Party-Curaçao (*Democratische Partij-Curaçao*, DP-C), led by Raymond Bentoera, centrist party founded in 1944 and linked with other Antilles Democratic parties, was in Antilles coalition governments in 1958–73, 1977–79, 1981 and 1985–90, latterly headed by National People's Party, reduced to only one *Staten* seat by 1994. *Address*. 28 Neptunusweg, Willemstad, Curaçao

Democratic Party-St Eustatius (DP-SE), led by Kenneth van Putten, English-speaking centrist autonomous island party linked with other Antilles Democratic parties, dominant party on mainly Catholic St Eustatius (Statia), won one *Staten* seat in 1985, 1990 and 1994 (when it joined coalition headed by Restructured Antilles Party).

Democratic Party-St Maarten (DP-SM), led by Sarah Wescott-Williams, English-speaking centrist autonomous island party linked with other Antilles Democratic parties, joined coalition headed by National People's Party from 1984 and by New Antilles Movement from 1985, won two *Staten* seats in 1990, weakened thereafter by splits, reduced to one seat in 1994. *Address*. PO Box 414, Philipsburg, St Maarten

Independent Social (*Sochal Independiente*, SI), led by George Hueck, Curaçao-based grouping formed in 1986 by dissident faction of National People's Party.

National People's Party (*Partido Nashonal di Pueblo*, PNP), led by Maria Ph. Liberia-Peters, Christian democratic party founded in 1948 and based on Curaçao, headed Antilles coalition 1988–93, defeated in November 1993 referendum on whether Curaçao should seek Aruba-style separate status (which it favours), reduced from seven to three *Staten* seats in 1994 elections; affiliated to Christian Democrat International. *Address.* 54 Penstraat, Willemstad, Curaçao

New Antilles Movement (*Movementu Antiá Novo*, MAN), led by Dominico (Don) F. Martina, pro-independence social democratic party founded in 1979 by non-Marxist faction of Workers' Liberation Front; headed coalition governments in 1982–84 and 1985–88, reduced to two *Staten* seats in 1990, again won two in 1994, when it joined coalition headed by Restructured Antilles Party, also part of the Curaçao island government; affiliated to Socialist International. *Address.* Landhuis Morgenster, Willemstad

Progressive Democratic Party (PDP), led by Millicente de Weever, formed in 1991 by dissident faction of Democratic Party-St Maarten, became member of St Maarten government coalition.

Restructured Antilles Party (*Partido Antía Restrukturá*, PAR), led by Miguel A. Pourier, Christian social Curaçao-based formation founded in 1993, became leading Antilles party in 1994 elections, thereafter heading government coalition with five other parties, also leading party in Curaçao island council. *Address.* 3/26 Fokkerweg, Curaçao

Saba Democratic Labour Party (SDLP), led by Steve Hassell, became ruling party on mainly English-speaking Saba in May 1995, winning three of the five island council seats.

St Maarten Patriotic Alliance (SPA), led by Vance James, founded in 1990 in opposition to the then dominant Democratic Party-St Maarten, became leading St Maarten party in 1991 island council elections, won two Antilles seats in 1994, joining coalition headed by Restructured Antilles Party. *Address.* 69 Frontstraat, Philipsburg, St Maarten

Serious Alternative People's Party (SAPP), led by Julian Rollocks, won one seat on St Maaarten island council in May 1995, entering island coalition with Democratic Party-St Maarten.

Windward Islands People's Movement (WIPM), led by Will Johnston, based in mainly English-speaking and Catholic Saba and St Eustatius (Statia), dominant party in Saba until 1995, won one *Staten* seat in the 1985 and 1990 elections, and again in 1994, when it joined coalition headed by Restructured Antilles Party; affiliated to Christian Democrat International. *Address.* PO Box 525, Saba

Workers' Liberation Front of May 30 (*Frente Obrero Liberashon 30 di Mei*, FOL), led by Wilson Godett, Stanley Indersen and Tolinchi Pietersz, pro-independence socialist grouping dating from 1969, usually represented in Curaçao island council, held one *Staten* seat in 1985–90.

New Zealand

Capital: Wellington

Population: 3,500,000 (1995E)

New Zealand has as its head of state the British sovereign, represented locally by a Governor-General. Legislative authority is vested in a unicameral House of Representatives which consists of 99 members elected by universal adult suffrage for up to three years. A new system of proportional representation for elections to an expanded 120-member House comes into effect at the elections due in October 1996. The Prime Minister and Cabinet are responsible to the legislature and are appointed by the Governor-General acting upon its advice.

In the general election on November 6, 1993, the National Party led by Jim Bolger was returned to power, but with only a one-seat majority. This was subsequently eroded by defections and a general splintering of political groupings, so that by June 1995 New Zealand had its first minority government since the 1920s. In February 1996 the National Party government signed a formal coalition agreement with the United New Zealand Party.

The Alliance

Leadership. Sandra Lee (leader)

The Alliance was launched in 1991 advocating the preservation of the welfare state and an end to free-market policies. It is a centrist coalition of five parties—the Green Party of Aotearoa, the Liberal Party, the New Labour Party (NLP), the New Zealand Democratic Party (NZDP) and the New Zealand Self-Government Party (*Mana Motuhake o Aotearoa*). In the November 1993 general election the coalition won two seats in the House of Representatives with over 18% of the vote. Sandra Lee, parliamentary leader of the New Zealand Self-Government Party, assumed the leadership of the Alliance in November 1994 upon the resignation of Jim Anderton, the coalition's other member of parliament and leader of the New Labour Party.

Green Party of Aotearoa,

Address. POB 11-652, Wellington

Telephone. (#64-4) 520 5656

Fax. (#64-4) 520 5649

Leadership. Vivienne Stephens (general secretary)

The party was founded as the New Zealand Values Party in 1972, adopting its present name in 1988. It is a leftist ecologist group and a constituent party of the Alliance coalition which was launched in 1991 and which won two parliamentary seats in the November 1993 election.

Liberal Party

Leadership. Malcom Wright (president)

Formed in 1991 by dissident members of the National Party (NP), the Liberal Party is a constituent of the Alliance coalition.

National Party (NP)

Address. 14th Floor, Willbank House, 57 Willis Street, POB 1155, Wellington 1

Telephone. (#64-4) 472 5211

Fax. (#64-4) 478 1622

Leadership. Jim Bolger (leader), Geoff Thompson (president)

The conservative National Party was established in the 1930s by the merger of the Reform and Liberal parties. It has traditionally stood for private enterprise, competitive business and personal freedom, drawing most of its support from rural and suburban areas.

The party first came to power in 1949, remaining in office until 1957. Having regained a majority in the 1960 general election, it then held power for all but three years (1972-75) until 1984. Following the general election defeat in that year, the NP's leader (since 1974) and former Prime Minister, Sir Robert Muldoon, was replaced by his deputy, John McLay. He in turn was replaced by Jim Bolger in 1986 following intraparty dissent. In the same year the NP merged with the libertarian New Zealand Party, which had been formed as a rival organization in 1983.

Having suffered a further electoral defeat in 1987, the NP returned to office with a landslide victory in October 1990. However, subsequent internal divisions led to the breakaway in early 1993 of Winston Peters, a charismatic former NP minister, who formed an opposition New Zealand First Party. Although returned to power in the November 1993 general election, the NP retained only 50 legislative seats. This bare majority was cancelled out in September 1994 when a NP member of parliament defected to form the Right of Centre Party (ROC), with which Prime Minister Bolger was then obliged to form a coalition. In June 1995 the NP's parliamentary strength was further eroded when four NP members defected to form the United New Zealand Party; however, in February 1996, the NP government signed a formal coalition agreement with the new party, so restoring its slim majority.

New Labour Party (NLP)

Address. Private Bag 5, Newton, Auckland

Telephone. (#64-9) 360 1918

Fax. (#64-9) 360 0744

Leadership. Jim Anderton (leader)

The NLP was formed by Jim Anderton in 1989 upon his resignation from the New Zealand Labour Party (NZLP). In the 1990 general election the party secured one seat, attracting 6% of the vote. Anderton retained the seat in the November 1993 polling, which the NLP contested as a constituent party of the Alliance coalition. In November 1994 Anderton resigned his position as leader of the Alliance but remained an influential figure within the coalition.

New Zealand Democratic Party (NZDP)

Address. 2 Gillies Ave, POB 9967, Auckland 2

Telephone. (#64-9) 523 1888

Fax. (#64-9) 524 0798

Leadership. John Wright (leader)

Founded in 1953 as the Social Credit Political League, the NZDP adopted its present name in 1985. It is a constituent party of the Alliance coalition.

New Zealand First Party

Address. c/o House of Representatives, Wellington

Leadership. Winston Peters (leader)

New Zealand First is a conservative and populist group which was set up in 1993 by former

National Party (NP) members. In the November 1993 general election the party secured two parliamentary seats with just over 8% of the vote. It has adopted an anti-immigration stance.

New Zealand Labour Party

Address. Fraser House, 162 Willis Street, PO Box 784, Wellington

Telephone. (#64-4) 384 7649

Fax. (#64-4) 384 8060

Leadership. Helen Clark (leader)

Founded in 1916, the Labour Party first held power from 1935-49, during which time it developed an advanced welfare state system. It has since been in office for shorter periods from 1957-60, 1972-75 and, most recently, from 1984-90. Having for long been committed to a socialist programme, the Labour administration formed under the premiership of David Lange after the general election victory in 1984 introduced sweeping changes in the form of economic deregulation and reduction of government subsidies. The party maintained its opposition, however, to nuclear weapons and nuclear energy; legislation in 1985 prohibiting the use of the country's ports and waters by nuclear warships created friction with New Zealand's allies, particularly the United States.

In 1987 the Labour Party retained its legislative majority, but divisions subsequently emerged among the leadership leading to Lange's resignation and replacement as Prime Minister by Geoffrey Palmer in 1989. Palmer was succeeded in September 1990 by Mike Moore; however, this change could not reverse Labour's serious decline in popularity and in a general election the following month the National Party (NP) was swept back into office with a large majority. Despite its failure to regain power in the November 1993 election, Labour revived to win 45 of the 99 legislative seats, restricting the National Party to a one-seat majority. In December 1993 Moore was replaced as party leader by Helen Clark. During 1994 and 1995 several Labour members of parliament defected to the Right of Centre Party (ROC) and the United New Zealand Party.

The New Zealand Labour Party is affiliated to the Socialist International.

New Zealand Self-Government Party

Mana Motuhake o Aotearoa

Address. c/o House of Representatives, Wellington

Leadership. Sandra Lee (leader), Peter Moeahu (president)

The party is a pro-Maori grouping which was formed in 1981. It contested the November 1993 general election as a constituent of the Alliance coalition, and its leader, Sandra Lee, was returned to the House of Representatives as one of two successful Alliance candidates. In November 1994 she assumed the leadership of the Alliance.

Right of Centre Party (ROC)

Address. c/o House of Representatives, Wellington

Leadership. Ross Meurant (leader)

The ROC was created in September 1994 by Ross Meurant upon his resignation from the National Party (NP). He continued to support the Bolger government in the House of Representatives, however, and retained his junior ministerial position in the administration.

United New Zealand Party

Leadership. Clive Matthewson (leader)

The United New Zealand Party was established in June 1995 by a group of seven parliamentarians—four National Party (NP) defectors and three former New Zealand Labour Party members (one of whom, Peter Dunne, had already left the party in mid-1994 to form the Future New Zealand Party). In February 1996 the National Party government signed a formal coalition agreement with the United New Zealand Party.

Other Parties

ACT New Zealand, set up in 1994 as the political arm of the Association of Consumers and Taxpayers. It campaigns for a flexible education system, reform of the tax system and better hospital care. The party is led by Sir Roger Douglas (a former member of the New Zealand Labour Party and finance minister), Rodney Hide and Derek Quigley.

Ethnic Minority Party, formed in April 1996 as the country's first racially based party appealing to Asian immigrants.

Socialist Unity Party (SUP), formed in 1966 by dissident members of the Communist Party of New Zealand (CPNZ). It has little popular support but exerts considerable industrial influence. The SUP is led by George Jackson and Ken Douglas.

Socialist Workers' Organization (SWO), formed in 1995 through a merger of the Communist Party of New Zealand (CPNZ) and the International Socialist Organization (ISO). Its national organizer is Barry Lee.

New Zealand's Associated Territories

Cook Islands

Capital: Avarua (on Rarotonga)   **Population:** 20,000 (1995E)

Since 1965 the Cook Islands have been a self-governing territory in free association with New Zealand which, in addition to providing economic assistance, has responsibility for the territory's defence and foreign policy. The Parliament of the Cook Islands comprises 25 members (10 representing the main island of Rarotonga, 14 representing constituencies on other islands, and one representing the many Cook Islanders resident in New Zealand), sitting for up to five years. It chooses a Prime Minister from among its members who then appoints a Cabinet. In general elections held on March 24, 1994, the ruling Cook Islands Party (CIP) was returned to power, securing 20 seats in the legislature. The Democratic Party (DP) won three seats and the Alliance Party took two.

Alliance Party

Address. c/o Parliament, Rarotonga
Leadership. Norman George (leader)

The centrist Alliance Party was established in 1992 by Norman George, a former member of the Democratic Party (DP). Advocating government spending cuts and education and tax reform, the party won two legislative seats in the March 1994 elections.

Cook Islands Party (CIP)

Address. c/o Parliament, Rarotonga
Leadership. Sir Geoffrey Henry (leader)

The first formally constituted political party in the islands, the CIP was the ruling party from the introduction of associated statehood in 1965 until 1978 when the Chief Justice ruled that the results of elections in March of that year had been distorted by corrupt practices. The CIP consequently lost its majority, with power in the legislature shifting in favour of the Democratic Party (DP). The party leader and former premier, Albert Henry, was convicted of fraud in 1979 and was subsequently succeeded by his kinsman, Geoffrey Henry. In elections in March 1983 the CIP won a slim majority, but the administration formed by Henry was undermined by the death of one CIP member of parliament and the defection of another to the DP. Henry resigned and a further election was held in November 1983, which was won by the DP. The CIP was returned to power under Henry's premiership following elections in 1989, and retained office with an overwhelming majority in the March 1994 general election.

Democratic Party

Address. POB 492, Rarotonga
Leadership. Terepai Maoate (leader)

The DP was formed in 1971 with the main aim of countering the personalised rule of Albert Henry of the Cook Islands Party (CIP). The DP was in opposition to the CIP until a legal ruling in 1978 gave it a parliamentary majority, and its founder, Sir Thomas Davis, became Prime Minister. The government fell in the elections of March 1983 but was returned to power the following November in fresh polling. In August 1984 Davis appointed several CIP members to his government, but most withdrew their support in mid-1985. He experienced an increasing decline in popularity during 1986 and was forced to resign as Prime Minister in July 1987, Pupuke Robati being designated his successor. In the wake of its election defeat by the CIP in 1989 the DP suffered defections and Robati resigned the leadership to make way for Terepai Maoate. The party's fortunes slumped further in the March 1994 election when it secured only three legislative seats.

Other Parties

Cook Islands Labour Party, formed in 1988 and led by Rena Ariki Jonassen.

Cook Islands People Party, launched in 1988 under the leadership of Sadaraka Sadaraka.

Democratic Tumu Party, led by Vincent Ingram.

Niue

Capital: Alofi   **Population**: 2,500 (1995E)

The island of Niue has since 1974 had self-government in free association with New Zealand, which manages Niue's defence and external affairs in consultation with the Niue government. Executive authority is exercised by a Premier and three other ministers drawn from, and answerable to, the 20-member Niue Assembly (14 village representatives and six elected on a common roll). The most recent general election was held on February 16, 1996, after which the incumbent Premier, Frank Lui, was narrowly voted back into office by members of the new legislature. Lui had replaced Sir Robert Rex in early 1993, the latter having served as the island's Premier from 1974 until his death in December 1992. Although the Niue political system is not based on formal political organizations, the Niue People's Party, led by Young Vivian, functions as a loose opposition grouping.

Other Territories

New Zealand's other associated territories are the Ross Dependency, in Antarctica, which has no permanent population, and Tokelau (population, 1,500). Executive and administrative authority on Tokelau is vested in an appointed administrator, who is responsible to New Zealand's Minister of Foreign Affairs and Trade (although in May 1996 the New Zealand parliament approved legislation giving the territory's national representative body, the General Fono, subordinate legislative powers). There are no political parties.

Nicaragua

Capital: Managua   **Population:** 4,400,000 (1995E)

The Republic of Nicaragua achieved independence in 1838 but was subjected to US military intervention in 1912-25 and 1927-33. The country was subsequently left in the control of the Somoza family until the overthrow of the right-wing dictatorship of Gen. Anastasio Somoza Debayle by a popular revolutionary movement, the Sandinista National Liberation Front (*Frente Sandinista de Liberación Nacional*, FSLN) in 1979. Far-reaching economic and social reforms were introduced despite attempts by conservative groups and US-backed right-wing *contra* rebels to destabilize the government. The FSLN won the presidential and legislative elections in November 1984 with 67% of the vote but lost the next election in 1990 to the National Opposition Union (*Unión Nacional Opositora*, UNO). The 1984 elections were the first to be held in the country since 1974.

War fatigue among the population and a decade of economic austerity were instrumental factors in the FSLN's unexpected and heavy electoral defeat in February 1990 (although it remained the country's largest party), the victorious right-wing UNO alliance promising to end the civil war, promote national reconciliation and attract foreign aid and investment. The UNO presidential candidate, Violeta Barrios de Chamorro, emerged as the clear winner with 54.7% of the vote. In simultaneous legislative elections, UNO won 51 seats to the FSLN's 39, five seats short of an overall majority. Chamorro took office on April 25, 1990.

Under the 1987 constitution, executive power rests with the President, who is head of state and commander-in-chief of the Defence and Security Forces and governs with the assistance of a Vice-President and an appointed Cabinet. Both the President and Vice-President are directly elected for a six-year term, consecutive terms of office being permitted. A unicameral National Assembly is made up of 92 representatives (each with an alternative representative), who are directly elected for a six-year term by a system of proportional representation. Also returned as members of the Assembly are those unelected presidential and vice-presidential candidates (as representatives and alternates respectively) who receive nationally at least as many votes as the average winning percentages in each of the 143 regional electoral districts. Men and women over 16 are eligible to vote.

Centre Group
Grupo del Centro (GC)
Leadership. Sergio Mendietta (PIAC), Frank Duarte (PANC), Gustavo Tablada (PSN)

The GC was formally established early in 1993 by elements of the centre-right National Opposition Union (UNO) which, having backed the successful presidential candidacy of Violeta de Chamorro in 1990, later gravitated to a centre-left alignment with the former ruling Sandinistas. Supportive of President Chamorro (although she eschewed party identification), the GC/Sandinista alliance thereafter effectively became the government coalition, while the conservative UNO formations reorganized as the Opposition Political Alliance (APO).

The components of the GC were the Central American Intregrationist Party (*Partido Integra-ciónalista de la América Central*, PIAC); the Conservative National Action Party (*Partido de Acción Nacional Conservador*, PANC), founded in 1989; and the Nicaraguan Socialist Party (*Partido Socialista Nicaraguense*, PSN), dating from 1937 and in recent years of social democratic orientation.

Communist Party of Nicaragua
Partido Comunista de Nicaragua (PCdeN)
Leadership. Eli Altamirano Pérez (general secretary)

The PCdeN was formed in 1970 by a group of pro-Chinese dissidents from the Nicaraguan Socialist Party (PSN). For the 1996 elections the PCdeN joined the National Project alliance.

Conservative Party of Nicaragua
Partido Conservador de Nicaragua (PCN)
Address. Colegio Centroamérica, 500 m al Sur, Managua
Telephone. (#505-2) 670484

Address. Costado Sur de la Diplotienda, Managua
Leadership. Fernando Aguero Rocha (president); Eduardo Molina (1990 presidential candidate)

The PCN is effectively the former Democratic Conservative Party of Nicaragua (PCDN) in a new guise. In 1992 it entered into a merger with the much smaller Conservative Social Party (PSC) and the Conservative Party of Labour (PCL).

Launched in 1979, the PCDN was a right-wing party formed by three factions of the traditional Conservative Party (PC), which had been the main legal opposition during the Somoza era. It inherited the radical middle class tradition of Pedro Joaquín Chamorro Cardenal, the anti-Somoza owner of the daily *La Prensa* newspaper and husband of the current President Violeta Chamorro de Barrios, who was assassinated in 1978. It supported the 1979 revolution but baulked at Sandinista reforms.

The party suffered a serious split in 1984 on the question of whether or not to participate in the general election. One wing opposed to participation, led by Miriam Arguello and Mario Rappaccioli, broke away to form the Nicaraguan Conservative Party (PCN), which in turn joined the anti-Sandinista opposition grouping, the Nicaraguan Democratic Co-ordinator (CDN), which included business groups and two trade unions in favour of an electoral boycott. The remaining wing, the PCDN, fielded Clemente Guido for the presidency, won 14% of the vote and, with 14 seats, emerged as the largest opposition party in the National Assembly. Another debilitating split within the PCDN led to the departure of Enrique Sotelo Borgen, whose PCDN "non officialist" faction forged a pact with the Independent Liberal Party (PLI).

Although vice president of the National Assembly, Guido refused to sign the 1987 constitution, although his deputy did so, along with 11 Conservative delegates. This provoked a leading conservative Córdova Rivas to stage a week-long hunger strike in the name of party unity. Factionalism continued however, one led by Eduardo Molina and another by Hernaldo Zúñiga, who went onto form the Conservative National Alliance Party (PANC). The PCDN stood alone in the 1990 general election, with Molina as its presidential candidate. The PANC, still to be legally recognized, joined the victorious UNO coalition. Arguello's PCN itself split into the National Conservative Party (PNC) and Arguello's own Conservative Popular Alliance Party (PAPC). Both joined the UNO alliance and Arguello was elected leader of the National Assembly after the 1990 elections.

Independent Liberal Party
Partido Liberal Independiente (PLI)
Address. Cuidad Jardín, F29 frente a Óptica Selecta, Managua.
Leadership. Wilfredo Navarro Moreira (president), Virgilio Godoy Reyes (secretary-general)

Founded in 1946, the PLI has been the focus of the UNO/APO opposition to any accommodation of the Sandinistas. The PLI was formed by a dissident faction of intellectuals of Somoza's National Liberal Party who were opposed to the extension of the dictatorship's powers and who subsequently boycotted rigged elections. It welcomes the 1979 revolution and joined both the Revolutionary Patriotic Front and the Council of State. Godoy served as Minister of Labour in the Sandinista-led government. Opposed to restrictions placed on campaign activities, it called for a boycott of the 1984 elections shortly before the poll but won nine seats in the National Constituent Assembly. In March 1985 the PLI joined other centre-right opposition groups in the externally based Nicaraguan Democratic Co-ordinator (CON) alliance and was one of six opposition parties to campaign for new elections, a ceasefire in the civil war and the depoliticization of the army, a general amnesty and the return of seized lands to their original owners.

It refused to sign the 1987 constitution and joined the UNO alliance of parties which won the 1990 presidential election. Godoy was named Vice-President but quickly became a figurehead for the majority of UNO deputies, mayors of local councils, the organization of private business (Cosep) and the hierarchy of the Roman Catholic church, ideologically opposed to the government. Godoy demanded the resignation of the Presidency Minister Antonio Lacayo, the perceived architect of a policy of close collaboration with the Sandinistas, and the dismissal of Gen. Humberto Ortega Saavedra, the former Sandinista leader retained as Commander-in-Chief of the armed forces. He also called on Chamorro to honour her pledge of land and credits made to the *contras* before their demobilization in June 1990. These demands, which were ignored, were identical to those of re-armed *contra* rebels, known as *recontras*. Apart from a rising in November 1990 when right-wing mayors and supporters took temporary control of Region V of the country, the Godoy faction had little political success.

Having endorsed Godoy Reyes as its 1996 presidential candidate, the PLI was the only liberal group not to join the Liberal Alliance (AL), preferring to remain in the Opposition Political Alliance (APO).

Liberal Alliance
Alianza Liberal (AL)
Leadership. Arnoldo Aleman Lacayo (1996 presidential candidate)

This alliance of four of the five small liberal parties in Nicaraguan politics was formed in December 1994 to support the 1996 presidential bid of Arnoldo Aleman Lacayo. Its members are the Nationalist Liberal Party (*Partido Liberal Nacionalista*, PLN) led by Arnoldo Aleman Lacayo and re-founded in 1988; the Constitutional Liberal Party (*Partido Liberal Constitutionalista*, PLC) led by Leopold Navarro and founded in 1968; the Liberal Party (*Partido Liberal*, Pali) led by Ricardo Vega García and formed in 1983 by PLI dissidents; and the Independent Liberal Party of National Unity (*Partido Liberal Independiente de Unidad Nacional*, PLIUN), led by Eduardo Coronado Pérez and founded in 1988 by another group of PLI defectors.

National Action Party
Partido de Acción Nacional (PAN)
Address. 4C Puente La Reynaga, Abajo, c. al Lago, Managua
Telephone. (#505-2) 496868
Leadership. Guilio Baltodano (president)

The small PAN was formed in 1988 by disaffected members of the Nicaraguan Social Christian Party, later becoming part of the National Project alliance.

National Conservative Party
Partido Nacional Conservador (PNC)
Leadership. Silviano Matamoros Lacayo (president)

Formed in 1990, the right-wing PNC believes in a free market and is the most direct descendent of the original Conservative Party of Nicaragua (PCN), although the latter again exists in a new guise.

A splinter group of the former Democratic Conservative Party of Nicaragua and a member of the National Opposition Coalition (UNO) that came to power in 1990, the PNC submitted a controversial draft bill in June 1990 calling on the National Assembly to rescind the *piñata* laws 85 and 86 passed by the outgoing Sandinista government which had formalized the distribution of state property, mostly confiscated from political opponents, among Sandinista supporters. The laws were signed by UNO representative Antonio Lacayo Oyanguren, the Presidency Minister, and by army commander in chief and former FSLN leader Gen. Humberto Ortega Saavedra in March 1991 as part of the transition agreements between governments.

National Project

Proyecto Nacional (PN)

Leadership. Antonio Lacayo Oyanguren (1996 presidential candidate)

The PN was launched in April 1995 as a presidential vehicle for the group's leader, Antonio Lacayo Oyanguren, being in effect a working coalition of most of the Centre Group together with the Nicaraguan Social Christian Party, the Social Democratic Party and the Nicaraguan Democratic Movement.

Nicaraguan Democratic Movement

Movimiento Democrático Nicaragüense (MDN)

Address. Casa L-39, Ciudad Jardín Bnd, 50m al Sur, Managua

Telephone. (#505-2) 43898

Leadership. Roberto Urroz Castillo

A small, left-of-centre party formed in 1978, the MDN was initially a backer of the Sandinistas then moving over to the *contra* side under the leadership of Alfonso Robelo Callejas. In 1995 it became a member of the National Project alliance of parties headed by the Nicaraguan Social Christian Party.

Nicaraguan Social Christian Party

Partido Social Cristiano Nicaragüense (PSCN)

Address. Cindad Jardín, P. María, 1 calle al Lago, Managua

Telephone. (#505-2) 22026

Leadership. Germán Alfaro Ocambo (president)

Founded in 1957 and opposed to the Somoza dictatorship, it survived splits in 1976 and 1979. After the 1979 revolution it joined the Council of State, from which it resigned in November 1980. In 1981 it was a founder member of the Nicaraguan Democratic Co-ordinator (CDN), a right-wing coalition of parties opposed to the Sandinistas. In November 1981 it expressed itself open to negotiations with the FSLN and did not follow other parties, such as the Nicaraguan Democratic Movement (MDN) and a right-wing PSC offshoot, the Christian Democratic Solidarity Front (FSDC), in establishing bodies supportive of the armed activities of right-wing *contra* rebels.

It was banned as a party by the FSLN government following its support of the CDN's boycott of the 1984 elections. Ramírez had opposed the decision and relations with other CDN parties became increasingly soured. In 1985 it co-founded a Costa Rican-based alliance, the Co-ordinator of the Nicaraguan Opposition (CON) alliance with the MDN, PSD, the Independent Liberal Party (PLI) and the Democratic Conservative Party (PCD). In February 1987 it was one of five parties calling for a ceasefire and fresh elections. Internal strife ensued and in mid-1987 a right-wing faction led by PSC secretary-general Agustín Jerk Anaya and Eduardo Rivas Gasteazoro left the party. This faction subsequently subdivided itself into the National Confidence Democratic Party (PDCN) and the National Action Party (PAN).

In November 1987 Ramírez was one of eight members appointed by the FSLN to a National Reconciliation Commission established under the Arias peace plan for the Central American region. In the 1990 elections, the PSC joined the UNO opposition alliance, winning a single seat in association with an electoral ally, the Yatama, a right-wing *contra* rebel organization formed in 1987 from indigenous Atlantic coast political rebel groups. The Yatama disbanded along with other *contra* groups in mid-1990.

The party is currently in a period of "restructuring" under the auspices of the Christian Democrat International.

Opposition Political Alliance

Alianza Politica Opositora (APO)

Leadership. Virgilio Godoy Reyes, Guilio Baltodano (head of political council)

The anti-Sandinista APO was launched in 1989 as the National Opposition Union (*Unión Nacional Opositora*, UNO), a US-supported electoral bloc of 14 parties, including left-wing and right-wing parties formed to support the candidacy of Violeta Chamorro de Barrios in the 1990 presidential elections.

After Chamorro took office in April 1990, pre-electoral differences deepened and the UNO split into two factions, eight parties following Vice-President Virgilo Godoy's Independent Liberal Party (PLI) in opposing policies masterminded by Presidency Minister Antonio Lacayo Oyanguren. Chamorro's inner circle of advisors showed themselves to be astute and adept although lacking a strong political, economic and military base in a sharply polarized society. They had to rely on the support of a "pragmatic" FSLN leadership and the Sandinista People's Army (EPS) to maintain a modicum of political and military stability.

The government, however, managed to end the 11-year civil war and disarm and demobilize right-wing *contra* rebels while simultaneously working to create a national consensus for a radical free market reform programme. Such reforms were vigorously resisted by Sandinista mass organizations fighting public-sector cuts, privatizations and low pay. They were also criticized as insufficient by the hostile UNO right-wing factions, supported by business groups, who accused the government of allowing the FSLN to dictate the pace of change. This UNO right-wing criticism reached a crescendo in September 1991 when Chamorro partially vetoed the decision of the National Assembly to nullify previous FSLN legislation granting property rights to Sandinista supporters.

Despite the fact that the country at times appeared to be ungovernable, the government used alternate policies of confrontation and conciliation to guarantee a gradual shift away from the legacy left by FSLN.

Whereas the UNO had been an alliance of 14 groups, the APO established in February 1993 embraced only four parties, namely the Independent Liberal Party, the National Conservative Party, the National Action Party and (interestingly) the pro-Chinese Communist Party of Nicaragua.

Sandinista National Liberation Front
Frente Sandinista de Liberación Nacional (FSLN)

Address. Costado Deste, Parque El Calmen, Managua

Telephone. (#505-2) 660845

Fax. (#505-2) 661560

Leadership. Daniel Ortega Saavedra (general secretary); Tomás Borge (deputy general secretary)

The social democratic FSLN was founded in 1961 and is named after the national hero Agusto César Sandino, was founded by a small group of intellectuals, including former Nicaraguan Socialist Party (PSN) member Carlos Fonseca Amador and Thomas Borge Martínez, and began guerrilla activity against the US-backed Somoza regime in 1963. After suffering a series of defeats, it abandoned all military activity from 1970 to the end of 1974.

Fonseca, the FSLN's leading theoretician, was killed in action in 1976, and after 1975 disagreements on strategy split the movement into three factions. The Protracted People's War (GPP) group, led by Borge, favoured the creation of

liberated zones on the Chinese and Vietnamese model, which would provide bases from which to attack towns; the Proletarian Tendency (PT), led by Jaime Wheelock, maintained that the FSLN should concentrate on winning the support of the urban working class; and the third way group (*terceristas*), led by Daniel Ortega Saavedra, advocated a combination of an armed offensive and broad political alliances with other opposition organizations, which would lead to a general insurrection.

A synthesis of all three strategies was finally agreed upon but with the *terceristas* the dominant tendency, and in March 1979 a national directorate was formed, consisting of the three main leaders of each faction. After intensified fighting, Gen. Anastasio Somoza Debayle was overthrown in the popular revolution of July 1979.

The FSLN's decisive role in the overthrow of the Somoza dictatorship inevitably made it the dominant political force after the revolution, although it shared power initially with anti-Somoza forces in the FSLN-led Patriotic Revolutionary Front (FPR) and with elements of the conservative middle class, in a Council of State. This Council was superseded in 1984 when Daniel Ortega was elected President and the FSLN secured a clear majority in a new National Assembly.

Initially, Sandinista measures to combat illiteracy and improve primary health care were very successful but eventually half the national budget came to be devoted to the war against US-backed right-wing *contra* rebels who had initiated in 1981 a guerrilla war to destabilize the government. US trade and investment embargoes led to greater reliance on Soviet-bloc aid, until 1987, when the Soviet Union began to scale down its oil supplies.

In 1987, the emphatic opposition of the FSLN to direct negotiations with the *contras* was modified when it welcomed peace plans devised by the Contadora group and by President Arias of Costa Rica which took shape in the Guatemala region peace accords. The Sandinistas made major concessions to their critics in the hope of achieving peace; these included an end to the state of emergency, a readiness to talk to the contras, an amnesty of prisoners and an end to bans on the media. In December 1989, the FSLN signed a regional agreement calling for the demobilization of the Salvadoren guerrillas in the expectation that other governments would finally act to dismantle contra camps in Honduras.

After their surprise defeat in the 1990 presidential elections, the Sandinistas vowed to defend the "fundamental conquests of the revolution", such as nationalization of banks and foreign trade, state farms and the rights and freedoms contained in the 1987 constitution.

After the elections, however, the FSLN lost both its discipline and unity. Grass-root members became increasingly alienated from the leadership which was criticized for collaborating too much with the Chamorro government in the name of a responsible opposition. This gulf deepened when the leadership interposed itself between the UNO government and the mass Sandinista organizations during the 1990 strikes against cuts in jobs and services. Accusations that the FSLN leadership had personally benefited from laws allowing for the disposal of state property and land before the Sandinistas relinquished power (known locally as the *piñata* after a children's game where everyone rushes to grab what they can) also left their mark on rank-and-file supporters. However, when the UNO right-wing parties in the National Assembly repealed the laws in June 1991, which had also given land to *campesinos* (peasants), all 39 FSLN delegates withdrew from the Assembly indefinitely. Sandinista mass organizations rallied to their defence and in September Chamorro partially vetoed the Assembly's decision.

Following an extraordinary party congress in May 1994, three distinct factions emerged within the FSLN: an 'orthodox' faction headed by Ortega; a moderate 'renewalist' faction headed by former Nicaraguan Vice-President Sergio Ramírez Mercado; and a centrist 'unity' grouping headed by Henry Ruiz Hernández. At the congress, the Ortega faction proved victorious (although Ramírez gained for himself the role of Ortega's alternate). He was ousted from this post by Ortega in September 1994 at which point the FSLN delegation elected a moderate, Doria María Téllez, as its new leader rather than Ortega.

In early 1995 the disagreement came to a head with Ramírez, Téllez and 75% of the *Sandinista* legislative delegation withdrawing from the FSLN to form a new party, the Sandinista Renewal Movement (see below).

Sandinista Renewal Movement
Movimiento de Renovación Sandinista (MRS)
   Address. 1c Tienda Katty, Abaja, Apdo 24, Managua
   Telephone. (#505-2) 780279
   Fax. (#505-2) 780268
   Leadership. Sergio Ramírez Mercado, Dora María Téllez, Fernando Silva.
   At an extraordinary party congress of the Sandinista National Liberation Front (FSLN) in May 1994, the Daniel Ortega faction within the party proved dominant, at the expense of Sergio Ramirez Mercado in particular. He was ousted by Ortega in September 1994, at which point the FSLN membership elected the moderate Doria

María Téllez as its new leader rather than Ortega.

In January 1995 the disagreement came to a head with Ramírez, Téllez and three-quarters of the Sandinista Assembly deputies withdrawing from the FSLN to form a new party, the MRS, which was in opposition to the government.

Social Democratic Party
Partido Social Demócrata (PSD)
   Address. Frente al Teatro Aguerri, Managua
   Telephone. (#505-2) 281277
   Leadership. Adolfo Jarquin Ortez (president)
   Founded in 1979 as a break-away from the Nicaraguan Social Christian Party (PSCN), the PSD was previously in alliance with the Nicaraguan Democratic Movement in backing the candidature of Antonio Lacayo before joining in the larger National Project.

Minor Parties

Central American Unionist Party (*Partido Unionista Centroamericano*, PUCA) is a regionalist integrationist grouping led by Blanca Rojas Echaverry.

Christian Democratic Union (*Unión Demócrata Cristiana*, UDC) was formed in early 1993 by a merger of two further former UNO members, the Social Christian Popular Party (PPSC) and the Democratic Party of National Confidence (PDCN). It is led by Dr Luis Humberto Guzman (a former president of the National Assembly).

Movement of Revolutionary Unity (*Movimiento de Unidad Revolucionaria*, MUR) is a vaguely radical party made up of former Sandinista members and secured one percent of the vote in 1993. It is led by Moisés Hassan Morales.

National Democratic Party (*Partido Conservador de Nicaragua*, PCN) was formed in 1994 as an off-shoot from the PSD (see above) and is led by Alfrédo César Aguirre.

Nicaraguan Marxist-Leninist Party (*Partido Marxista-Leninista de Nicaragua*, PMLN) is led by Isidro Tellez Toruño.

Nicaraguan Resistance Party (*Partido de la Resistencia Nicaragüense*, PRN) was formed in late 1992 by former *contra* commanders and registered in 1993. It is led by Héctor Sanchez amongst others.

Popular Conservative Alliance (*Alianza Popular Conservadora*, APC) was formerly a member of the UNO (alongside the PLC, Pali, UDC, MDN and PSD), the APC was founded in 1985. It is led by Francisco Anzoategui Lacayo.

Workers' Revolutionary Party (*Partido Revolucionario de los Trabajadores*, PRT), a Trotskyite party led by Bonafacio Miranda.

Major Guerrilla Groups

Democratic Forces of National Salvation
Fuerza Democrática por la Salvación Nacional (FDSN)

Leadership. José Angel Moran Flores (alias *El Indomable*)

The FDSN was founded in 1991 from the ranks of 20,000 *contra* rebels who had demobilized in June 1990 after 10 years fighting the FSLN government with US support, renewed hostilities as *recontras* (re-armed ex-*contras*), primarily in the north-western departments, particularly the mountainous Jinotega province. In tune with right-wing parties in the UNO coalition (see PLI), they accused the government of colluding with the FSLN and failing to guarantee them land and security. They demanded the removal of Presidency Minister Antonio Lacayo and of Army Commander-in-Chief and former Sandinista leader Humberto Ortego Saavedra, the break-up of the army, and a general purging of Sandinistas from the state security forces. In a communiqué of Dec. 14, 1991, they said they had withdrawn from peace talks and would conduct military operations throughout the country if the government did not respond constructively to their basic demands.

The *recontras* renewed hostilities in January 1992. Further fighting was reported in January 1993.

Revolutionary Alliance of Workers and Peasants
Frente Revolucionario de Obreras y Campesinos (FROC)

Leadership. Víctor Manuel Gallegos (alias *Pedro el Honduran*)

The FROC was founded November 1991 as an umbrella organization with the aim of co-ordinating the actions of re-armed left-wing Sandinistas, *recompas*, who were committed to fighting the *recontras* and defending the social changes introduced by the 1979 Sandinista revolution. Known *recompa* groups include: Guerrilla Organization 91, Danto-19 ("death to the revengers"), the Altamirano Sandinista Movement, the Property Self Defence Group, the Armed Insurrectional Revolutionary Front, and the Nora Astorga Front, the last a group of 200 armed women, formed in March 1992 and active in the north and who were also campaigning against the government for child care programmes and free medicine. The group pillaged the town of Estrelí in July 1993.

Niger

Capital: Niamey   **Population:** 9,100,000 (1995E)

The Republic of Niger attained independence from France in 1960. Following a coup in 1974, the military took control and set up a Supreme Military Council, under Lt.-Col. Seyni Kountché, which ruled the country for the next 15 years. After Kountché's death in 1987, the Council appointed Brig. Ali Saibou as his successor. The National Movement for a Development Society (*Mouvement National pour une Société de Développement*, MNSD) was formed as the sole legal political party in August 1988 with Saibou as its chairman. In May 1989 Saibou was named as head of the country's new ruling body, a joint military-civilian Higher Council for National Orientation, which superseded the Supreme Military Council. A national conference held between July and November 1991 suspended the constitution, took over executive authority from Saibou and then appointed a transitional Prime Minister. In a referendum in December 1992, voters approved a new multi-party constitution. This provided for a directly elected President with a five-year term (once renewable) and for a similarly elected 83–member National Assembly (*Assemblée Nationale*), also with a five-year mandate.

Multi-party legislative elections in February 1993 were won by the Alliance of Forces for Change (AFC), a coalition of parties opposed to the MNSD. The following month, in the second round of a presidential election, Mahamane Ousmane of the Democratic and Social Convention, an AFC party, was elected President. In further legislative elections on Jan. 12, 1995 (brought about by a party defection from the AFC and a subsequent vote of no confidence against the government), the opposition MNSD and its allies won a small majority over AFC parties. Relations between President Ousmane and the new Prime Minister, Hama Amadou of the MNSD, deteriorated seriously during 1995 over the issue of their respective powers. At the end of January 1996, President Ousmane was overthrown in an army coup led by Col. Ibrahmim Barre Mainassara, the constitution being suspended and parties banned. In May 1996, however, a new constitution based on that of 1992 was promulgated, following its approval by referendum, and the ban on political parties lifted. The following party entries reflect the political position immediately prior to the military takeover.

Alliance of Forces for Change (AFC)
Alliance des Forces de Changement (AFC)
   Address. c/o Assemblée Nationale, Niamey
   The AFC was formed at the time of the February 1993 legislative elections by parties opposing the ruling National Movement for a Development Society (MNSD), in response to the early indications of a victory by the former sole legal party. By combining as a coalition, the AFC controlled a majority of seats in the National Assembly, and in March 1993 secured the presidential election of Mahamane Ousmane ahead of his MNSD rival. In September 1994 the Niger Party for Democracy and Socialism withdrew from the AFC, the parliamentary strength of which was further weakened prior to the January 1995 legislative elections by the defection of the Niger Progressive Party–African Democratic Rally. In the elections the AFC took 40 seats, but lost its majority in the 83–member National Assembly.

Democratic and Social Convention–Rahama
Convention Démocratique et Social–Rahama (CDS-Rahama)
   Address. c/o Assemblée Nationale, Niamey
   Leadership. Mahamane Ousmane (leader)
   A member party of the Alliance of Forces for Change, the CDS-*Rahama* won 22 seats in the February 1993 legislative elections, and its leader secured the presidency of the Republic the following month with about 55% of the vote. In the January 1995 National Assembly elections the party increased its number of seats to 24. However, other AFC parties did not secure sufficient additional seats to retain the coalition's majority over the National Movement for a Development Society (MNSD) and its allies.

National Movement for a Development Society
Mouvement National pour une Société de Développement (MNSD)
   Address. c/o Assemblée Nationale, Niamey
   Leadership. Tandja Mamadou (chair), Hama Amadou (secretary-general)

The MNSD was formed by the military regime in 1988 as the sole legal political party. In March 1991 the process of transition to multi-partyism was endorsed by the MNSD, which participated in the July-November 1991 national conference which took over the presidential executive authority and appointed a new administration to supervise the transition to democracy. Although the MNSD won 29 seats in the February 1993 legislative elections (seven more than its nearest rival), the formation of the Alliance of Forces for Change (AFC) coalition relegated it to minority status. In the subsequent presidential election, MNSD candidate Tandja Mamadou led in the first ballot but lost the second round run off with a 45% vote share. In the January 1995 elections the MNSD again won 29 seats, securing, with other opposition parties, a three-seat majority over AFC members. Following a controversy over the President Ousmane's initial appointment of a new Prime Minister, the MNSD secretary-general, Hama Amadou, assumed the post in February 1995 and named a new Cabinet. Serious tensions between the President and Prime Minister over their respective powers had arisen by the end of August 1995.

Niger Alliance for Democracy and Social Progress–Zaman Lahiya
Alliance Nigérienne pour la Démocratie et le Progrès Social–Zaman Lahiya (ANDPS-Zaman Lahiya)
   Address. c/o Assemblée Nationale, Niamey
   Leadership. Moumouni Djermakoye (leader)
   A constituent group of the Alliance of Forces for Change (AFC), the ANDPS won 11 National Assembly seats in February 1993. In the first round of the presidential poll, party leader Djermakoye came fourth with 15% of the vote, his supporters subsequently backing the successful candidacy of Democratic and Social Convention (CDS-*Rahama*) leader Ousmane in the second round. In the January 1995 elections the party's representation slipped to nine seats.

Niger Party for Democracy and Socialism

Parti Nigérien pour la Démocratie et le Socialisme (PNDS)

   Address. c/o Assemblée Nationale, Niamey

   Leadership. Mahamadou Issoufou (general-secretary)

PNDS general-secretary Issoufou was appointed Prime Minister after the elections in early 1993, holding the post until September 1994, when the PNDS withdrew from the ruling Alliance of Forces for Change. This move led to early legislative elections in January 1995, in which the party took third place with 12 seats. The following month Issoufou was elected Speaker of the National Assembly.

Niger Progressive Party–African Democratic Rally

Parti Progressiste Nigérien–Rassemblement Démocratique Africain (PPN-RDA)

   Address. c/o Assemblée Nationale, Niamey

   Leadership. Dandiko Dankoulodo (chair)

The PPN-RDA has represented itself as the heir to the party of the same name which had been Niger's sole and ruling party from 1960 until the 1974 coup. In 1993 it joined in the formation of the Alliance of Forces for Change (AFC), but defected just before the January 1995 legislative elections, in which it secured a single seat.

Niger Social Democratic Party–Alheri

Parti Social Démocrate Nigérien–Alheri (PSDN-Alheri)

   Address. c/o Assemblée Nationale, Niamey

   Leadership. Kazelma Oumar Taya (leader)

PSDN-*Alheri* leader Taya contested the first ballot of the 1993 presidential election but secured less than 2% of the vote. In the January 1995 elections, as a constituent of the Alliance of Forces for Change, the PSDN won two National Assembly seats.

Party for National Unity and Development–Salama

Parti pour l'Unité Nationale et le Développement–Salama (PUND-Salama)

   Address. c/o Assemblée Nationale, Niamey

The PUND-*Salama* won three seats in the National Assembly in the January 1995 elections, as a component of the Alliance of Forces for Change.

Union for Democracy and Social Progress–Amana

Union pour le Démocratie et le Progrès Social–Amana (UDPS-Amana)

   Address. c/o Assemblée Nationale, Niamey

As a member of the Alliance of Forces for Change, the party took two legislative seats in the January 1995 elections.

Union of Democratic and Progressive Patriots

Union des Patriotes Démocratiques et Progressistes (UPDP)

   Address. c/o Assemblée Nationale, Niamey

   Leadership. André Salifou (leader)

The UPDP's candidate in the first round of the 1993 presidential election, Illa Kane, was eliminated with only about 2.5% of the votes cast. Contesting the January 1995 elections in opposition to the Alliance of Forces for Change, the party secured a single National Assembly seat.

Union of Popular Forces for Democracy and Progress–Sawaba

Union des Forces Populaires pour la Démocratie et le Progrès–Sawaba (UPFDP-Sawaba)

   Leadership. Djibo Bakary

Party leader Bakary won about 1.7% of the first-round vote in the 1993 presidential election.

Tuareg Groups

Organization of the Armed Resistance (*Organisation de la Résistance Armée*, ORA), launched in March 1995 upon the disintegration of the Co-ordination of the Armed Resistance, which had previously represented Tuareg rebels in negotiations with the government. In April 1995 an agreement to end the four-year insurgency was signed, and in June the National Assembly approved an amnesty bill. The ORA includes the **Front for the Liberation of Air and Azawad** (*Front de Libération de l'Air et l'Azaouad*, FLAA) and the **Front for the Liberation of Tamoust** (*Front pour la Libération de Tamoust*, FLT). The FLT leader (and overall ORA leader), Mano Dayak, was killed in December 1995 when his aircraft exploded on take-off from a northern Niger airstrip.

Nigeria

Capital: Abuja   **Population:** 96,000,000 (1995E)

Nigeria attained independence from the United Kingdom in 1960, becoming a federal republic within the Commonwealth in 1963. A series of coups have punctuated the post-independence politics of the country, resulting in long periods of military rule. Having come to power in 1985, the regime of Gen. Ibrahim Babangida promised a return to pluralist politics by 1992. The handover was delayed, although in 1989 two political parties were created by the regime, namely the Social Democratic Party (SDP) to represent centre-left opinion and the National Republican Convention (NRC) to represent the conservative spectrum, with no regional, religious or tribal politics being permissible. In presidential elections eventually held on June 12, 1993, the SDP candidate, M.K.O. Abiola, was widely believed to have defeated the NRC candidate, but the regime aborted the contest amid legal wrangling. In August 1993 Babangida stepped down as President, transferring power to a non-elected Interim National Government under Chief Ernest Aedgunle Shonekan. The term of office of the new administration was to run until the end of March 1994, during which time fresh presidential elections were to be organized. However, in November 1993 Defence Minister Gen. Sanni Abacha seized power in a bloodless coup. The existing organs of the state were dissolved and political activity was prohibited. The two official political parties created in 1989 were proscribed. At the same time, a Provisional Ruling Council (PRC) was established with Gen. Abacha as chairman.

A government-sponsored National Constitutional Conference (NCC), inaugurated in June 1994 to consider the political future of the country, proposed in December that military rule should continue until 1 January 1996. In April 1995, however, as it formally adopted a draft constitution, the NCC declared that a transition to civilian rule could not be achieved within that time. In June 1995 Abacha lifted the ban on political activity, and then announced in October 1995 that the military government would remain in office for a further three years. He asserted that by October 1998 democratic reforms would be completed in readiness for elections.

In addition to facing internal opposition from human rights organizations, notably the Campaign for Democracy (CD), the Abacha regime has incurred widespread international hostility, in particular for the execution in November 1995 of the leader of the Movement for the Survival of the Ogoni People (MOSOP), Ken Saro-Wiwa. As a direct consequence, Nigeria's membership of the Commonwealth was suspended later the same month.

In addition to the CD and MOSOP, other active pro-democracy political organizations as of mid-1996 included the National Democratic Coalition (NADECO), founded in 1994 to back M.K.O. Abiola's claim to the presidency, and the National Liberation Council (NLC), founded in exile in 1995 by Nobel laureate Wole Soyinka. Also active was the National Democratic Alliance (NDA) led by former head of state Gen. Babangida, advocating a gradual return to democratic rule.

Norway

Capital: Oslo

Population: 4,350,000 (1995E)

Norway achieved independence from Sweden in 1905 on the basis of the 1814 Eidsvold Convention, which as subsequently amended provides for a constitutional and hereditary monarchy, with the King exercising authority through a Council of State (government) headed by a Prime Minister. The government is accountable to the unicameral legislature (*Storting*) of 165 members, who are elected for a four-year term by universal suffrage of citizens aged 18 and over on the basis of proportional representation in 19 electoral districts. The *Storting* divides itself by election into an upper house (*Lagting*) of a quarter of its members and a lower house (*Odelsting*) of the remaining three-quarters, with each house being required to consider and vote on legislative proposals. In the event of a disagreement between the houses, a bill requires approval by a majority of two-thirds of the *Storting* as a whole. An important feature of the constitution is that the *Storting* cannot be dissolved between elections and that any vacancies are filled from party lists rather than by-elections. If the government falls on a vote of no confidence, the leader of the opposition party holding the next highest number of seats is asked to form a new government.

Norwegian political parties receive funds from the public purse in proportion to their electoral support in the most recent general elections, the official purpose of such subsidies being to assist parties in their educational activities.

Parliamentary elections on Sept. 13, 1993, resulted as follows: Norwegian Labour Party 67 seats (with 36.9% of the vote), Centre Party 32 (16.7%), Conservative Party 28 (17.0%), Socialist Left Party 13 (7.9%), Christian People's Party 13 (7.9%), Progress Party 10 (6.3%), Liberal Party 1 (3.6%), Red Electoral Alliance 1 (1.1%).

Centre Party

Senterpartiet (SP)

Address. 7b Kristian Augustsgt., 0130 Oslo
Telephone. (#47) 2298-9600
Fax. (#47) 2220-6915
Leadership. Anne Enger Lahnstein (chair), Johan J. Jakobsen (parliamentary leader), Steinar Ness (secretary-general)

Originating from the agrarian trade union, the party was founded in 1920 as the Agrarian Party with the object of gaining greater political and parliamentary influence for those working in rural occupations and of raising them to the level of other occupations. Since 1931, when co-operation with the agrarian trade union was ended, the party has been independent and has worked for society in general, changing its name to Centre Party in 1959, thus emphasizing its position between the right-wing and left-wing parties.

In 1931–33 the party formed a minority government. After unsuccessful efforts to work with the Conservatives and Liberal parties, the party, in 1935, entered into a "crisis compromise"

with the Norwegian Labour Party, which was then in power for 30 years. In 1963 the party entered into a brief minority coalition with other non-socialist parties; from 1965 to 1971 it headed a majority non-socialist government; and in 1972–73 participated in a minority government with the Liberals and the Christian People's Party.

The Party was in opposition to minority Labour governments from 1973 to September 1981, when it gave its general support to a minority Conservative administration. In June 1983 it entered a majority three-party centre-right government headed by the Conservatives, which continued until in May 1986 it was replaced by a further minority Labour administration. Meanwhile, the Centre Party had won 12 seats and 6.7% of the vote in the September 1985 elections, as against its earlier high-point of 20 seats and 11% in 1973.

Having slipped from 12 to 11 seats in the 1989 elections (on a 6.5% vote share), the SP joined another centre-right coalition headed by the Conservatives but withdrew in October 1990 in protest against government policy on foreign

442

financial interest. This caused the coalition's collapse and the formation of a minority Labour government in November 1990 to which the SP gave qualified parliamentary support. Campaigning on a strongly anti-EU platform, the SP made major gains in the September 1993 general elections, overtaking the Conservatives by increasing its representation to 32 seats on a 16.7% vote share (a post-war high). It subsequently played a prominent role in the successful "no" campaign for the November 1994 referendum on EU accession.

Christian People's Party

Kristelig Folkeparti (KrF)
    Address. 18-20 Øvre Slottsgt., 0105 Oslo
    Telephone. (#47) 2241-1180
    Fax. (#47) 2242-3207
    Leadership. Valgerd Svarstad Haugland (chair and parliamentary leader), Gunnar Husan (secretary-general)

Founded in 1933 as a non-socialist Christian-oriented formation, the party had one member elected to the *Storting* in 1933 and two in 1936. Established at national level by 1945, it gained eight seats and later steadily increased its parliamentary representation, winning 22 seats in 1977 and thus becoming the country's third strongest party (although in 1981 it retained only 15 seats). It has taken part in majority coalition governments in 1965-71 (with the Conservative, Liberal and Centre parties) and in a minority coalition government with the Centre and Liberal parties in 1972-73 under the premiership of Lars Korvald. In June 1983 it entered a centre-right government with the Conservatives and the Centre Party, but went into opposition in May 1986 to a minority administration of the Norwegion Labour Party. In the September 1985 elections the party had won 16 seats and 8.3% of the vote, retaining its position as the third strongest formation.

The KrF slipped to 14 seats in the 1989 elections (8.5%), after which it joined a centre-right coalition with the Conservative and Centre parties that lasted only a year. It fell again to 13 seats (7.9%) in the September 1993 contest, its advocacy of the popular cause of opposition to EU membership doing it little good, as non-socialist voters of that persuasion opted for the SP.

The KrF is a member of the Christian Democrat International.

Communist Party of Norway

Norges Kommunistiske Parti (NKP)
    Address. PO Box 3634, Oslo 1
    Leadership. Ingve Iversen (chair), Gunnar Wahl (secretary)

The NKP was founded in November 1923 by left-wing members of the Norwegian Labour Party after the latter had withdrawn from the Comintern, which it had joined in 1919. During the Nazi occupation (1940–45) the party continued to work underground, and in the 1945 general elections it won 11 seats. However, in the 1949 elections the party lost all these seats and its central committee thereupon purged the party of "Trotskyist, bourgeois-nationalist and Titoist" elements, becoming an orthodox pro-Soviet party. In 1953 the party gained three seats in the *Storting*, and in 1957 only one, which it lost in 1961.

Having not been represented in parliament since 1961, the party in 1973 joined a Socialist Election Alliance (comprising also the Socialist People's Party and other left-wing groups), which won 16 seats in the 1973 elections to the *Storting*. In November 1975, however, the party decided not to dissolve itself in order to merge in the new Socialist Left Party but to continue as a Communist Party—thus conforming to advice from the Communist Party of the Soviet Union stating that "a homogeneous Marxist-Leninist party" was "necessary" and that "all manifestations of opportunism of the right and left" should be rejected. In the September 1985 elections the party won 0.2% of the vote.

The NKP contested the 1989 elections on a joint list with the Red Electoral Alliance, without success. It did not put up candidates for the 1993 elections.

Conservative Party

Høyre (H)
    Address. 20 Stortingsgt., 0117 Oslo
    Telephone. (#47) 2282-9090
    Fax. (#47) 2282-9080
    Leadership. Jan Petersen (chair), John Bernander (deputy chair), Anders Talleraas (parliamentary leader), Svein Grønnern (secretary-general)

Since its foundation in 1884, the Conservative Party has participated in over a dozen governments, most of them coalitions with other non-socialist parties. The party's electoral support varied from about 50% in 1894 to around 20% in the years after 1933 and to around 30% in the 1980s. On the basis of the substantial gains made by the party in the September 1981 elections, the Conservative leader, Kåre Willoch, formed a one-party minority administration. In June 1983 this was transformed into a three-party government when both the Centre and Christian People's parties accepted cabinet membership. However, this government fell in April 1986 and was replaced by a minority administration of the Norwegian Labour Party. In August 1986 Willoch was succeeded as party leader by Rolf Presthus, but the latter died unexpectedly in January 1988.

Although the party's representation declined to 37 seats in 1989 (on a 22.2% vote share), it succeeded in forming a minority centre-right coalition with the Centre (SP) and Christian People's parties under the premiership of Jan P. Syse. This collapsed a year later upon the withdrawal of the SP, giving way to a minority government of the Norwegian Labour Party. In the September 1993 *Storting* elections the Conservatives slumped to 28 seats (16.9%), being damaged by their strong advocacy of Norwegian membership of the European Union (EU). The party accordingly remained in opposition.

The Conservative Party is affiliated to the International Democrat Union.

Liberal Party

Venstre (V)

Address. 16 Møllergt., 0179 Oslo

Telephone. (#47) 2242-7320

Fax. (#47) 2242-4321

Leadership. Odd Einar Dørum (chair), Lars Sponheim (parliamentary leader), Hans Antonsen (secretary-general)

Founded in 1884, the *Venstre* held 23 seats in the *Storting* in 1936, but its parliamentary representation after World War II was consistently lower than that figure (its 21 seats gained in 1949 being reduced to 14 by 1961, though rising to 18 in 1965). Of its 13 members elected in 1973, a majority supported the projected entry of Norway into the European Community (EC); after such entry had been rejected in the referendum of September 1972, the anti-EC minority participated in a coalition government with the Christian People's and Centre parties, while the pro-EC Liberals subsequently formed the Liberal People's Party (DLF). The Liberal Party was thus left with only four seats in the *Storting*, and this number was reduced to two in the elections held in September 1973. It retained two seats in 1977 and 1981, but failed to secure representation in 1985, when its share of the vote fell to 3.1%. The party nevertheless retained considerable strength at local level.

In June 1988 the DLF rejoined the parent party, which nevertheless failed to regain *Storting* representation in 1989, when its vote share was 3.2%. In the September 1993 contest, however, Liberals took one seat with 3.6% of the vote.

Norwegian Labour Party

Det Norske Arbeiderparti (DNA)

Address. PO Box 8734 Youngstorget, 0028 Oslo

Telephone. (#47) 2294–0600

Fax. (#47) 2294–0601

Leadership. Gro Harlem Brundtland (leader), Thorbjørn Jagland (chair), Dag Terje Andersen (general secretary)

Descended from a rural socialist movement of the mid-19th century, the DNA was established in 1887 amid a rapid growth of urban trade unionism in the 1880s. By the end of the 19th century the party had 17,000 members and commanded 24,000 votes. In 1904 it won four seats in Parliament, and by 1915 the party had 62,000 members and gained 198,000 votes (32% of the total electorate). In 1918 the party's leadership was taken over by its left wing, largely under the influence of the Russian revolution, but disagreements ensued over membership of the Third International (Comintern). In 1921 dissenters formed the Social Democratic Party and in 1923 the Communist Party was formed; but in 1927 a basis was found for the reunification of the Norwegian Labour Party and the Social Democratic Party, with some Communists also joining the reunified party, which in that year obtained 368,000 votes (or 36.8% of the total vote) and established itself as the country's strongest party. After a short-lived first Labour minority government in 1927, it won 40% of the vote in 1933 and two years later formed its second government, which was to last for 30 years almost without interruption.

Under Nazi occupation during World War II the party was illegal and its leaders went into exile or were sent to German concentration camps. At the end of the war, the party's chairman, Einar Gerhardsen, formed a broad coalition government, and in October 1945 it obtained a majority in Parliament, whereupon a Labour government was formed, remaining in office until 1965 except for a brief interval in 1963.

The party was again in power from 1971 to 1972, when the government resigned on being defeated in a referendum rejecting Norway's membership of the European Community. During the 1973–81 period the party formed minority governments, but went into opposition following its setback in the September 1981 elections. However, the Conservative-led non-socialist coalition collapsed in April 1986 and was replaced by a further minority Labour government under Gro Harlem Brundtland. Meanwhile, the DNA had won 71 seats and 41.2% of the vote in September 1985, an improvement on its 27.1% share in 1981 but significantly below the levels regularly obtained up to 1969.

The DNA went in opposition after the September 1989 elections, in which it lost eight seats. A year later, however, Brundtland formed her third minority government, with the parliamentary backing of the Centre Party. In November 1992, following the death of her son, she resigned as party chair, while continuing as Prime Minister. In the September 1993 elections Labour rose to 67 seats on a 36.9% vote share, so that Brundtland formed her fourth minority government. In June 1994 delegates at a special DNA conference decided by a two-to-one majority to support Norwegian accession to the European Union (EU) in the forthcoming national referendum, although substantial rank-and-file opposition to membership contributed to the decisive 52.2% "no" vote in November. Unlike her Labour predecessor in 1972, and despite having strongly favoured a "yes" vote, Brundtland did not resign over an acknowledged major defeat. Instead she stressed the need for continuity and for negotiations to clarify Norway's relationship with the EU as a non-member.

The DNA is a member party of the Socialist International.

Progress Party
Fremskrittspartiet (FrP)
 Address. PO Box 8903 Youngstorget, 0028 Oslo
 Telephone. (#47) 2241-0769
 Fax. (#47) 2242-3255
 Leadership. Carl I. Hagen (chair and parliamentary leader), Hans A. Limi (secretary-general)

The FrP was established in 1973 as Anders Lange's Party for a Strong Reduction in Taxation and Public Intervention, its founder being a well-known dog-kennel owner who had become a national celebrity as a result of his political comments in a dog-breeding magazine which he edited. Following Lange's death in 1974, the party took its present name in January 1977. In the 1973 general elections it gained four seats in the *Storting* but lost all these in the 1977 elections. It returned to the *Storting* in the 1981 elections, when it gained four seats and 4.5% of the vote. In September 1985, however, it slipped to two seats and 3.7%.

The FrP became the third strongest parliamentary party in the September 1989 elections, winning 22 seats and 13.0% of the vote. Four years later, however, it experienced a major electoral reverse, winning only 10 seats and 6.3% of the vote.

Red Electoral Alliance
Rød Valgallianse (RV)
 Address. 27 Osterhausgt., 0183 Oslo
 Telephone. (#47) 2298-9050
 Fax. (#47) 2298-9055

Leadership. Jørn Magdahl (parliamentary leader)

The RV is derived from the electoral front of the (Maoist) Workers' Communist Party (founded in 1972) and later attracted independent socialist elements, including left-wing members of the Norwegian Labour Party. For the 1989 elections it joined with the Communist Party of Norway to present the Local List for the Environment and Solidarity (*Fylkeslistene for Miljø og Solidaritet*, FMS), which failed to made an impact. Standing on its own in the September 1993 contest, the RV won one seat on a 1.1% vote share.

Socialist Left Party
Sosialistisk Venstreparti (SV)
 Address. (#47) 45 Storgt., 0185 Oslo
 Telephone. (#47) 2220-6979
 Fax. (#47) 2220-0973
 Leadership. Kjellbjørg Lunde (chair and parliamentary leader), Per Eggum Mauseth (deputy chair), Hilde Vogt (secretary)

The formtion of the SV in March 1975 preceded by the establishment of the Socialist Electoral Alliance by three groups—the Communist Party of Norway, the Socialist People's Party and the Left Social Democratic Organization; in the 1973 elections the Alliance gained 16 seats in the *Storting* (and 11.2% of the votes cast) on an anti-EC, anti-NARO and strongly socialist platform.

Following the conversion of the Alliance into the Socialist Left Party in March 1975, the Communist Party decided in November 1975 not to dissolve itself in order to join the new party, and in the general election of September 1977 the SV gained only 4.1% of the votes and two seats. However, in 1981 it gained four seats in the *Storting* (with 5% of the votes), while in September 1985 it progressed further to six seats and 5.4%.

The SV made a major advance in the 1989 elections, to 17 seats on a vote share of 10.1%. In the September 1993 contest, however, it fell back to 13 seats (7.9%). It subsequently played a prominent part in the successful campaign against Norwegian accession to the EU.

Oman

Capital: Muscat   **Population:** 2,200,000 (1995E)

The Sultanate of Oman is ruled by decree, with the Sultan taking the advice of an appointed Cabinet and Consultative Council (*Majlis al-Shura*). The Consultative Council replaced the former Consultative Assembly in December 1991. On the completion of its first term in December 1994, the Council's membership increased from 59 to 80 and women were allowed to stand as candidates in the capital Muscat. There are no recognized political parties.

Pakistan

Capital: Islamabad

Population: 130,000,000 (1995E)

The Islamic Republic of Pakistan was proclaimed in March 1956, Pakistan having been granted independence as a Commonwealth dominion following the partition of the British Indian Empire in August 1947. Military governments have largely dominated the political stage since independence, the most recent headed by Gen. Zia ul-Haq who was killed in an air crash in August 1988. The constitution promulgated in 1973 provides for a parliamentary system with a bicameral federal legislature (*Mijlis-e-Shoora*) consisting of a 237–member National Assembly, which serves a five-year term and in which 217 seats (207 Muslim and 10 non-Muslim) are directly elected and 20 reserved for women, and an 87–member upper house (Senate), about half of whose members are elected every three years for a six-year term. The President, who is elected by the federal legislature for a (renewable) term of five years, is empowered under the constitution to dismiss the Prime Minister and dissolve parliament.

Following National Assembly elections in 1988, Benazir Bhutto of the Pakistan People's Party (PPP) became Prime Minister, but her government was dismissed by President Ghulam Ishaq Khan in August 1990. Fresh elections in October 1990 resulted in victory for the right-wing Islamic Democratic Alliance (IDA) headed by Mian Mohammad Nawaz Sharif, who formed a coalition administration. Subsequently, the IDA fell into disarray, and political paralysis led to the resignations of both President Khan and Prime Minister Nawaz Sharif in July 1993. As a result of further National Assembly elections held on Oct. 9, 1993, the PPP returned to power as the largest single party, its share of the elective seats rising to 98 (including those won in by-elections held on Dec. 2, 1993). Elections to 37 seats in the Senate were held in March 1994, as a result of which the PPP held a plurality of 23 seats in the upper chamber.

In simultaneous provincial assembly elections, the PPP won an outright majority in Sindh and also took control of the Punjab provincial government in a coalition. An alliance headed by the opposition Pakistan Muslim League (Nawaz group) initially formed a government in North West Frontier Province, but federal rule was imposed in February 1994 and a PPP administration assumed power the following April. The elections in Baluchistan resulted in no visible edge for any single party.

Awami National Party (ANP)

Address. c/o National Assembly, Islamabad
Leadership. Ajmal Khattak (president)

The ANP was formed in 1986 by a merger of a number of left-wing groups, including the People's Movement (*Awami Tehrik*), the National Democratic Party, the bulk of the Workers' and Peasants' (*Mazdoor Kissan*) Party (an element of which joined the National Democratic Alliance, NDA) and a dissident faction of the Pakistan National Party (PNP) opposed to the incorporation of the PNP into the NDA. Having won six National Assembly seats in the 1990 federal elections, the ANP secured only three in the October 1993 polls (although it emerged as the second strongest party in the North-West Frontier Province assembly). The party holds one ministerial appointment in the Pakistan People's Party-led government.

Justice Movement (JM)

Address. c/o Imran Khan's Residence, Lahore
Leadership. Imran Khan (leader)

The Justice Movement was founded in April 1996 by Imran Khan, the former Pakistan cricket captain, who declared that its aim was to "bring about a change in the country by demanding justice, honesty, decency and self-respect". At a launch press conference in Lahore, Khan accused the incumbent government of the Pakistan People's Party (PPP) of corruption and of leading Pakistan to "the brink of disaster" and near-certain bankruptcy. The launch of the JM came a fortnight after a bomb explosion had killed seven patients at a Lahore cancer hospital which Khan had founded. His announcement followed long speculation about his political ambitions, given the veneration in which he was held by the Pakistani public for his former cricketing prowess. His recent marriage to an English heiress of Jewish ancestry had at first appeared to dent his image in a devoutly Muslim country, where PPP circles in particular sought to depict Khan as a "playboy" who had been seduced by the West. In the event, his new wife's enthusiastic adoption of the Islamic faith did much to quell doubts among the general public.

Muhajir National Movement

Muhajir Qaumi Mahaz (MQM)

Address. c/o Senate, Islamabad

Leadership. Altaf Hussain, Afaq Ahmed, Imran Farooq

Founded in 1981, the MQM advocates the recognition of Urdu-speaking Muslim migrants to Pakistan (Muhajirs), mostly from India at the time of partition, as the 'fifth nationality' of the country. The party won 15 seats in the National Assembly elections in 1990 and was represented in the Sharif coalition government until its withdrawal in mid-1992. Divided into two main factions, the MQM did not contest the National Assembly in the 1993 elections, but retained substantial support in the Sindh province assembly poll. MQM militants and the government held talks during 1995 in an attempt to end serious fighting and civil disorder in areas of Sindh, especially in Karachi. Little progress was made, however, and the death toll in 1995 approached 2,000. Renewed violence in December 1995 followed the discovery on the outskirts of Karachi of the bullet-riddled bodies of two relatives of the main MQM leader, Altaf Hussain. By then the MQM was split into at least two factions.

National Democratic Alliance (NDA)

Address. c/o National Assembly, Islamabad

Leadership. Nawabzada Nasrullah Khan (leader)

The NDA was set up in 1992 as a coalition of formations including the National People's Party (NPP), the left-wing Pakistan National Party (PNP), the (Islamic) Pakistan Democratic Party, the *Awami Jamhoori* Party (AJP), the *Jamhoori Wattan* Party (JWP) and the North-West Frontier Province branch of the Workers' and Peasants' (*Mazdoor Kissan*) Party. The alliance won a single seat in the October 1993 National Assembly elections, while two of its constituent groupings (the NPP and the JWP) also secured separate representation.

National People's Party (NPP)

Address. c/o National Assembly, Islamabad

Leadership. Ghulam Mustafa Jatoi (chair)

Formed in 1986 by a breakaway faction from the Pakistan People's Party (PPP), the NPP was a member of the Sharif coalition government from 1990 until its expulsion in March 1992. Although a constituent of the National Democratic Alliance (NDA), the NPP won a seat in its own right in the 1993 National Assembly elections.

Pakistan Islamic Assembly

Jamaat-e-Islami-e-Pakistan (JIP)

Address. c/o National Assembly, Islamabad

Leadership. Amir Qazi Hussain Ahmad (chair)

The JIP is a right-wing Sunni fundamentalist group which was organized in 1941. It participated in the formation of the Islamic Democratic Alliance (IDA) in 1988 and in the 1990 elections won eight National Assembly seats. However, in May 1992 the party withdrew from the IDA, alleging that the alliance had failed to implement the process of Islamization that had been part of its election manifesto. In 1993 it was instrumental in launching the Pakistan Islamic Front (PIF), which contested the October 1993 elections and won three National Assembly seats.

Pakistan Muslim League (PML)

Address. c/o National Assembly, Islamabad

Leadership. Mian Mohammad Nawaz Sharif (leader of Nawaz group), Hamid Nasir Chattha (leader of Junejo group)

The PML, established in 1962 as the successor to the pre-independence All-India Muslim League, has long been beset by evolving factional rivalries and divisions. As of end-1995, the PML (Nawaz group) was the largest factional element, headed by former Prime Minister Nawaz Sharif who had been instrumental in the formation of the Islamic Democratic Alliance which had won the 1990 federal elections. Following the October 1993 elections, in which it secured 73 National Assembly seats, the PML (Nawaz) formed the core of the parliamentary opposition to the Pakistan People's Party (PPP) administration.

The PML (Junejo group), headed by Hamid Nasir Chatta, won six seats in the 1993 federal polling and joined the PPP-led government in coalition.

Pakistan People's Party (PPP)

Address. House 1, Street 85, Old Embassy Road, G-6-4 Islamabad

Telephone. (#92-51) 210686

Fax. (#92-51) 223124

Leadership. Benazir Bhutto (chair), Rafiq Ahmed Sheikh (general secretary)

447

The PPP was formed in 1967, advocating Islamic socialism, democracy and a non-aligned foreign policy. Its founder, Zulfikar Ali Bhutto, was executed in 1979 by Gen. Zia ul-Haq's military regime, the party leadership being assumed by his widow, Begum Nasrat, and by his daughter, Benazir. In the November 1988 National Assembly elections, after Gen. Zia's death, the PPP became the largest single party (although without an overall majority) and Benazir Bhutto was designated Prime Minister. The party lost power with the dismissal of her government in August 1990, after which, in elections the following October, its legislative strength was more than halved. The party returned to power in the October 1993 elections, winning 89 of 206 contested National Assembly seats and assuming control (by April 1994) of three of the country's four provincial assemblies. In a presidential election in November 1993, the federal parliamentary deputies elected Farooq Leghari, the PPP nominee.

In December 1993 the PPP hierarchy ousted the Prime Minister's mother as party co-chair, reflecting the estrangement between Benazir and both her mother and her brother, Murtaza Bhutto, who announced the formation of a breakaway faction of the PPP in March 1995.

The PPP is a consultative member of the Socialist International.

Other Parties

All Pakistan Jammu and Kashmir Conference, founded in 1948 and advocating the settlement of the status of Jammu and Kashmir by means of a plebiscite, led by Sardar Sikandar Hayat Khan, president of the Pakistani-administered region.

Assembly of Islamic Clergy (*Jamiat-ul-Ulema-e-Islam*, JUI), favouring constitutional government based on Sunni Islamic principles; won six National Assembly seats in 1990 elections but none in 1993.

Assembly of Pakistani Clergy (*Jamiat-ul-Ulema-e-Pakistan*, JUP), a progressive Sunni Muslim formation led by Maulana Shah Ahmed Noorani Siddiqui, which was represented in the Sharif coalition government following the October 1990 elections; failed to gain representation in 1993.

Baluchistan National Alliance (BNA), led by Nawab Mohammad Akbar Bugti.

Baluchistan National Movement (BNM), Hayee group, led by Abdul Hayee Balluch, won one seat in October 1993 Assembly elections.

Baluchistan National Movement (BNM) Mengal group, won one seat in October 1993 Assembly elections.

Gharib Awami Party (GAP), contested October 1993 Assembly elections, without success.

Gharib Ittehad Party (GIP), contested October 1993 Assembly elections, without success.

Gharib Qaumi Movement (GQM), contested October 1993 Assembly elections, without success.

Holy War (*Hizbe Jihad*), a grouping that formed part of the Islamic Democratic Alliance until its expulsion in September 1991, led by Murtaza Pooya.

Islami Jamhoori Mahaz (IJM), won four seats in October 1993 Assembly elections.

Jamhoori Wattan Party (JWP), won two seats in October 1993 Assembly elections.

Jamiat Mashaikh Mahaz (JMM), contested October 1993 Assembly elections, without success.

Mutahidda Deeni Mahaj (MDM), won two seats in October 1993 Assembly elections.

Pakhtoon Khawa Milli Awami Party (PKMAP), won three seats in October 1993 Assembly elections.

Pakhtoon Khawa Qaumi Party (PKQP), won one seat in October 1993 Assembly elections.

Pakistan Jafari Movement (*Tehrik-e-Jafariya-e-Pakistan*, TJP), a Shia grouping organized as a political party in 1987, led by Allama Sajid Ali Naqvi.

Pakistan Labour Party (PLP), contested October 1993 Assembly elections, without success.

Pakistan Saraiki Party (PSP), contested October 1993 Assembly elections, without success.

People's Leadership Party (PLP), launched in 1995 and chaired by Aslam Beg.

Punjabi-Pakhtoon Alliance (*Punjabi Pakhtoon Ittehad*, PPI) formed in 1987 to represent the interests of Punjabis and Pakhtoons, led by Malik Mir Hazar Khan.

Service Movement (*Khaksar Tehrik*, KT), a right-wing Islamic party advocating universal military training, led by Mohammad Ashraf Khan.

Sindh National Alliance (SNA), a nationalist group formed in 1988 advocating a separate homeland for the Sindhis.

Sindh National Front (SNF), led by Mumtaz Ali Bhutto (an uncle of the former Prime Minister), advocating broad autonomy for the four provinces of Pakistan.

Sipah-Sahaba Pakistan (SSP), a Sunni extremist breakaway faction from the Assembly of Islamic Clergy, led by Maulana Tariq Azam.

Solidarity Movement (*Tehrik-e-Istiqlal*), a democratic Islamic movement led by Ashraf Vardag.

Unity Movement (*Tehrik-e-Ittehad*), founded in 1995 and led by a retired general, Hameed Gul.

Palau

Capital: Koror

Population: 17,000 (1995E)

The Republic of Palau (also known as Belau) comprises a chain of islands and islets in the western Pacific Ocean. From 1947, as part of the UN Trust Territory of the Pacific, they were administered by the United States government. At the beginning of 1981 a popularly approved constitution came into force which prohibited the stationing of US nuclear weapons and the storage of nuclear waste in Palau. However, the following year Palau and the United States signed a compact of free association under which the US granted internal sovereignty and economic aid in return for continuing control of Palau's defence. From 1983 onwards, a succession of referendums to override the constitutional ban on the transit and storage of nuclear materials and enable the compact to come into effect failed to gain the required 75%majority. In 1992 the approval requirement was lowered to that of a simple majority, and in a referendum the following year the compact was accepted. On October 1, 1994, Palau became a sovereign and independent state, and the UN Trust Territory of the Pacific was terminated.

Under the 1981 constitution, executive authority is vested in a President, who is directly elected for a four-year term. Legislative authority is exercised by the National Congress (*Olbiil era Kelulau*), a bicameral body consisting of a 16-member House of Delegates (one member from each of Palau's constituent states) and a 14-member Senate. The constitution also provides for a Council of Chiefs to advise the President on matters relating to tribal laws and customs. There are no formal political parties, although two broad tendencies have emerged in local politics—the Coalition for Open, Honest and Just Government, which opposes the compact of free association, and the Ta Belau Party, which defends it.

In the most recent presidential election on November 4, 1992, the incumbent Vice-President, Kuniwo Nakamura, polled 50.7%of the vote to narrowly defeat Johnson Toribiong.

Palestinian Entity

Government centre: Jericho

Population: n.a.

Of the Arab territories captured by Israel in the Six-Day War of 1967, the Gaza Strip, the West Bank and East Jerusalem contained a substantial Palestinian Arab population, whose resistance to continued Israeli occupation and increasing Jewish settlement of these areas was led for the next 25 years by the Palestine Liberation Organization (PLO), which had been founded in 1964. A peace process started in October 1991 led to the signing in September 1993 of a declaration of principles on interim arrangements for Palestinian self-rule. Under this agreement the PLO renounced terrorism and recognized Israel's right to exist within secure borders, while Israel recognized the PLO as the legitimate representative of the Palestinian people. The declaration of principles established a timetable for progress towards a final settlement, certain important stages of which, although delayed, had been achieved by the beginning of 1996. These included Israeli military withdrawal from the Gaza Strip and most of the Arab towns and villages in the West Bank (although the numerous Jewish settlements remained in place under Israeli military protection); the interim transfer of powers to a "Palestinian authority", designated the "Palestine National Authority (PNA)" by the PLO; and elections for a new 86-member Palestinian Council (to replace the PNA) and a President.

Held on Jan. 20, 1996, the Palestinian elections drew the participation of over 750,000 voters out of an electorate of 1,013,235 and resulted in the PLO chairman, Yassir Arafat, being returned as President by an overwhelming majority (against one other candidate) and his *Fatah* grouping and allied groups winning a decisive majority in the Palestinian Council. The electoral process gave some impetus to the evolution of the PLO factions into political movements, although "rejectionist" groups both within and outside the PLO refused to take part, notably the Islamic Resistance Movement (*Hamas*). Another threat to the peace process was the victory of the right-wing parties in the Israeli general election in May 1996 and the advent of a government which, while undertaking to honour international treaties entered into by its predecessor, opposed any further Israeli withdrawal from the West Bank.

PLO Groups

Al-Fatah (the reverse acronym of the Arabic for Palestine Liberation Movement), established in 1959 and the core component of the PLO, of which *Fatah* leader Yassir Arafat was elected chairman in 1969, thereafter remaining the dominant political figure on the Palestinian stage. Despite resistance from "rejectionist" PLO factions, Arafat facilitated negotiations with Israel that were to lead, in 1993, to mutual recognition and the beginning of Palestinian self-rule in the occupied territories. In the January 1996 elections for a Palestinian Council exercising some powers of self-rule, *Fatah* candidates won 55 of the 86 seats and "independent *Fatah*" candidates a further seven, while Arafat was popularly elected to the Council's presidency with 88.1% of the vote.

Arab Liberation Front (ALF), regarded as Iraqi-backed, reported in 1995 to be split between "rejectionist" elements and those favouring the peace process.

Democratic Front for the Liberation of Palestine (DFLP), formed in 1969 as a splinter from the Popular Front for the Liberation of Palestine; the principle of PLO concessions to Israel caused divisions within the DFLP, the main faction under Nayif Hawatmeh declaring its opposition to the peace accord in 1993.

Palestine Liberation Front (PLF), led by Muhammad (Abdul) Abbas, originally Iraqi-backed, later split into various factions and associated with terrorist attacks (notably the *Achille Lauro* hijacking in 1985); reported to be more united in the early 1990s.

Palestine National Salvation Front (PNSF), an umbrella organization formed in 1985, opposed to the concessionary policies of PLO chairman Arafat; by 1991 represented only the Popular Front for the Liberation of Palestine–General Command (an offshoot of the main PFLP), *Al-Saiqi* (a pro-Syrian faction) and *Fatah* Uprising (a *Fatah* splinter group).

Palestine People's Party (PPP), led by Bashir al-Barghutti, formed in 1982 as the Palestine Communist Party, assuming its present name in 1991; backed the 1993 Israel-PLO peace accord.

Palestine Popular Struggle Front (PPSF), an offshoot of the Popular Front for the Liberation of Palestine, created during the early period of the Lebanese civil war, later split into factions, with the mainstream endorsing the 1993 Israel-PLO peace accord.

Popular Front for the Liberation of Palestine (PFLP), established in 1967 and the second largest PLO faction; under the leadership of Georges Habash, the PFLP has maintained its opposition to the Arafat policy of negotiation with Israel, condemning the peace accord of September 1993 and urging instead an intensification of the armed struggle for an independent Palestinian state.

Revolutionary Council of Fatah (also known as the **Abu Nidal Group**), an anti-Arafat guerrilla organization which has been responsible for numerous terrorist incidents around the world over the last 20 years.

Revolutionary Palestinian Communist Party (RPCP), led by Abdullah Awwad, founded in the late 1980s by a faction of what became the Palestine People's Party, supportive of the *intifada* in the occupied territories and critical of the subsequent Israel-PLO peace process.

Other Groups

Islamic Holy War (*Al-Jihad al-Islami*), militant fundamentalist and anti-Israeli group, responsible for suicide bombing attacks on Israeli military and civilian targets in the 1990s, opposed to the Israel-PLO peace process; its secretary-general,

Fathi Shqaqi, was shot dead in Malta in October 1995, probably by Israeli agents.

Islamic Resistance Movement (*Hamas*), a vehemently anti-Israeli, Islamic fundamentalist movement in the occupied territories which rose to prominence from 1989; frequently in conflict with mainstream PLO groups, *Hamas* did not put up candidates in the January 1996 elections to the Palestinian Council; led by Sheikh Ahmed Yassin (in prison), Mousa Mohamed Abu Marzouk (based in Syria) and Ibrahim Ghawshah

Palestinian Democratic Union (PDU), led by Zuheira Kamal and Jamil Salhut, identified with the Democratic Front for the Liberation of Palestine, supportive of the Israel-PLO peace process.

Panama

Capital: Panama City

Population: 2,600,000 (1995E)

The Republic of Panama seceded from Colombia in 1903. Its modern history has been marked by the considerable influence exercised by the United States on the country's internal affairs, especially in relation to the control of the Panama Canal. Elected governments were overthrown in 1941, 1949, 1951 and 1968, usually after disputed elections, and there were serious constitutional crises in 1918, 1948, 1955 and 1968. In the 1972 and 1978 elections to the then National Assembly of Community Representatives, no candidate was allowed to represent a political party. A tentative return to democratic government in the early 1980s was overshadowed by the presence of the National Guard, whose commander, Gen. Manuel Antonio Noriega Morena, effectively ruled the country and annulled the result of the May 1989 presidential election, which provoked the US military invasion in December of the same year.

Nicolás Ardito Barletta of the Democratic Revolutionary Party (PRD), the winner of the May 1984 presidential election, was initially favoured by the military and his election campaign was supported by a centre-right coalition of six parties, the now defunct National Democratic Union (UNADE). He was forced to resign by the military in September 1985 when he announced that he would investigate charges that Noriega had ordered the killing of a political opponent, Hugo Spadáfora. Barletta's successor Eric Arturo Delvalle was forced to flee the country after an abortive attempt to dismiss Noriega but still claimed to be president from exile. An interim President, Manuel Solis Palma, was then appointed by the military.

Domestic and international pressure, especially from the US, for the removal of Noriega, who had also been implicated in drug smuggling, continued to mount. His attempt to deny the Civic Opposition Democratic Alliance (ADOC) victory in the May 1989 presidential and legislative elections, by annulling the result, led to his overthrow following a US military invasion in December. The results of the May elections which had been held in safe keeping by the Roman Catholic Church, were then declared valid on Dec. 27 but were incomplete and covered only 64% of voters. Guillermo Endara Galimany was duly sworn in as "constitutional President" to head a democratic government of reconstruction and national reconciliation.

Ernesto Pérez Balladares of the PRD won the presidential elections held on May 8, 1994, with 33.3% of the vote. In simultaneous legislative elections, the PRD emerged as the largest single party, with 21 out of 72 seats. Pérez Balladares took office on Sept. 1, including in his Cabinet independents and members of the Arnulfista Party (PA) and Christian Democrat Party (PDC).

Constitutional reforms adopted in April 1983 established a unicameral Legislative Assembly (which replaced the National Assembly of Community Representatives in 1984) consisting of 67 members. Executive power rests with the President, assisted by two elected Vice-Presidents, who appoints a Cabinet.

Deregistration of parties in Panamanian politics occurs at the comparatively high cut-off point of 5% of the vote. Those who fail to gain this minimum level of support in an election (providing legislative representation) are subsequently banned from the electoral process.

Arnulfista Party

Partido Arnulfista (PA)

Address. 37-41 Avenida Perú y Calle 38 Este, Casa la Esperanza, Panamá

Telephone. (#507) 222-1267

Leadership. Mireya Moscoso de Gruber (president and 1994 presidential candidate), Carlos Young Adames (secretary-general)

Only founded in 1990, the PA is the main right-wing grouping in Panama. It was established by a faction of the now defunct Authentic Panameñista Party (*Partido Panameñista Auténtico*, PPA) led by the late veteran politician Arnulfo Arias Madrid, President of Panama in 1940-41, 1949-51 and for an 11-day period in 1968 as the successful candidate of the five-party Opposition National Union (UNO) before being deposed in a coup d'état. The PPA itself had been launched in 1984 as the "*authentic*" *panameñista* party, as distinct from the renegade Panameñista Party (PP) set up by Alonso Pinzón and Luis Suárez to contest the 1980 legislative elections, against Arias's wishes.

The PPA, along with MOLIRENA and the Christian Democrat Party (PDC), joined the Civic Opposition Democratic Alliance (ADOC) to back Arias's fifth presidential campaign in 1984 against the military's choice, Nicolas Ardito Barletta of the National Democratic Union (UNADE), whose victory they later claimed was fraudulent. The opposition also refused to accept the official results which gave ADOC only 27 of the 67 seats in the Legislative Assembly.

The PPA, which gradually lost the leadership of the ADOC to the PDC, itself split in August 1988 following Arias's death. One faction, again taking the party's original name (PP) and willing collaborate with the military-backed regime, nominated Hildebrando Nicosia as their candidate in the May 1989 presidential elections. The other faction, however, received ADOC's endorsement of its presidential candidate, PA leader Guillermo Endara, who was judged to have won the election, despite the result being annulled by the military, but who nevertheless, following the US invasion of December 1989, was installed in office. To confirm a break with the past, Endara supporters then established the PA, which was legalized in May 1990.

The ruling ADOC coalition government weathered massive public opposition to its October 1990 austerity policies only to face sustained protests by the trade unions, especially public sector workers, in the new year. Internal divisions and evidence of official corruption and drug-related scandals, some involving Endara's own law firm, severely damaged Endara's reputation. In April 1991, he dismissed five PDC cabinet ministers who he accused of "disloyalty and arrogance", leaving the *Arnulfistas* without an assured majority in the Legislative Assembly. The PDC had 28 seats to the 16, seven and four respectively of the remaining ADOC members, MOLIRENA, the AP and the PLA.

Endara was also increasingly accused of sacrificing national sovereignty by being subservient to the US government, especially in his harsh public criticism of Cuba and most controversially in agreeing to the radical reform of the country's banking secrecy laws in July 1991, which critics said would do little to stop drug trafficking and drug laundering but would drain the country of foreign exchange. Critics, led by the PDC, also accused the government of fomenting military coup scares in order to keep the country in a perpetual state of emergency.

This, they alleged, allowed state security forces more effectively to quell opposition protest. Endara was also blamed for not pressing the US government for adequate compensation for the civilian victims of the December 1989 military invasion, and for not placing imprisoned military associates of Noriega on trial.

In September 1991 Endara's choice for Legislative Assembly president was defeated when Marco Ameglio, a PLA member, aligned himself with the opposition.

The widow of former President Arias Madrid stood as the party's presidential candidate in the 1994 elections, which she lost to the PRD.

Authentic Liberal Party

Partido Liberal Auténtico (PLA)

Address. 46 via España y Calle, frente Clínica Arrocha, Panamá

   Telephone. (#507) 227-1041

   Fax. (#507) 227-4119

   Leadership. Arnulfo Escalona Riós (president)

The PLA was founded by Escalona, the former leader of the National Liberal Party (PLN) who resigned in 1987 in protest at the support offered by the party's president to Gen. Manuel Noriega. The PLN was a member of the ruling National Democratic Union (UNADE) but the newly formed PLA joined the Civic Opposition Democratic Alliance (ADOC) and supported a faction which backed Guillermo Endara, later leader of the PA (see above), who was subsequently adopted as ADOC candidate in the ultimately abortive presidential poll of May 1989. The PLA, individually, won four Legislative Assembly seats in concurrent legislative elections, finally confirmed in February 1990, and Escalona was named the Assembly's Vice-President.

However, association with the increasingly unpopular Endara government damaged the party and led to internal divisions. A PLA dissident, Marco Ameglio, sided with the opposition in September 1991 to defeat Escalona in the election for the presidency of the Legislative Assembly.

Christian Democratic Party

Partido Demócrata Cristiano (PDC)

Address. Av. Peru, frente a Plaza Porras, Edf. PDC, Apartado 6322, Panamá 5

   Telephone. (#507) 273204

   Fax. (#507) 273944

   Leadership. Ricardo Arias Calderón (president), Eduardo Vallarino (1994 presidential candidate), H. L. Camilo Brenes (secretary-general)

Founded in 1960, the centre-right PDC is a full member of the Christian Democrat International. The PDC had its origins in the student National Civic Union (1957-1960), where the tradition of European Christian democratic parties was assimilated. Middle-class professionals, intellectuals and students swelled its ranks but the Federation of Christian Workers (FTC) was also an early

affiliate. The PDC contested the 1964 and 1968 presidential elections without much success and during the period when party politics were effectively banned by the military (1968-1978), the party reorganized itself, winning 20% of the vote in the 1980 legislative elections and taking 19 of the 56 seats in the newly formed National Legislative Council (the other 37 being filled by nominees of a non-party National Assembly of Community representatives established in 1972). In 1984, the PDC was part of the Civic Opposition Democratic Alliance (ADOC) which lost the presidential and legislative elections following suspected widespread fraud by the military.

During 1987, the PDC became increasingly involved in confrontations with the government, openly campaigning through strikes (supported mainly by businesses rather than trade unions) and street demonstrations (which were violently suppressed) for the resignation and removal of Gen. Manuel Noriega who was accused of drug-trafficking, electoral fraud, corruption and murder. The PDC was again part of the ADOC electoral alliance in May 1989 which supported the presidential candidacy of the Guillermo Endara (see Arnulfista Party, AP) and, following the official ratification of the results following the US military invasion in December became the largest party in the Legislative Assembly with 28 of the 67 seats. Its subsequent withdrawal from the ADOC coalition government in April 1991, when Endara dismissed five PDC cabinet ministers, caused a predictable political crisis. This had followed months of in-fighting and Arias Calderón had publicly described Endara's economic programme, which advocated severe austerity measures and the privatization of state enterprises, as "senseless". Although Arias Calderón was stripped of his Interior and Justice Ministry post he won in the May 1989 election annulled by Noriega.

In succeeding months, the PDC became the leader of the opposition, to such an extent that it was exerting strong influence within such organizations as the Civic Crusade, an organization from which Endara had drawn his strongest support and which in June called for a plebiscite to decide on the desirability of Endara remaining in office. In September 1991, the PDC was judged firmly to have secured its political influence on parliamentary committees as a direct result of facilitating the victory of a dissident PLA candidate in the election of a new president of the Legislative Assembly.

First Vice-President of the Republic Arias Calderón, resigned from this post in December 1992 in a move designed to distance himself from President Endara in the run-up to the May 1994 presidential election. However, the party managed to gain only one seat in the legislative elections.

Civilist Renovation Party

Partido Renovación Civilista (PRC)

Address. 1a/Of.4 Edif. Casa Oceánica, Avenida Aquilino de la Guardia, Panamá

Telephone. (#507) 263-8971

Fax. (#507) 263-8975

Leadership. Tomás Herrera (president), Carlos Harris (secretary-general)

Registered in 1992 shortly after the 1991 elections, the PRC is an anti-military grouping that succeeded in winning three legislative seats in the 1994 elections.

Democratic Revolutionary Party

Partido Revolucionario Democrático (PRD)

Address. 35-02 Avenida 7a Central, Area del casino, apartado 2650, Panamá 9A

Telephone. (#507) 225-1050

Leadership. Ernesto Pérez Balladares (president), Tomás Aldamirrano Duque (First Vice-President).

Founded in September 1979, the PRD was originally populist and dedicated to the nationalist revolutionary ideals of Gen. Omar Torrijos Herrera, Commander-in-Chief of the National Guard who led a coup in October 1968 allegedly against imperialism and the oligarchy and in favour of a progressive and multi-class alliance to defend national independence and promote self-determination and integrity. The party subsequently in the 1980s became a vehicle for Gen. Manuel Noriega and is now characterized by its critics as the mainstay of the right-wing Noriega tradition.

The PRD was the product of the radical Torrijos years (1968-79) dominated by extensive reforms, notably in land distribution, the creation of a non-party National Assembly of Community Representatives (est. 1972) to replace a dissolved National Assembly, and the signing, in 1977, of treaties whereby the US government agreed to hand over control of the Canal Zone in the year 2000.

Formally created in 1979 by Torrijos supporters, who included businessmen, Christian Democrats and Marxists, the party retained its progressive image until the death of Torrijos in an air crash in July 1981. The military continued the tradition of Torrijos, albeit manipulating political power from the right of the political spectrum. By the time of the May 1984 presidential and legislative elections, the PRD-led National Democratic Union (UNADE) coalition was a tool of the military and was duly declared the clear winner despite evidence of widespread fraud. The lack of PRD political autonomy was amply demonstrated when the Unade President Nicolás Ardito Barletta was forced to stand down by the military in 1985 after indicating his intention of investigating allegations that Noriega was implicated in the murder of an opposition candidate Hugo Spadáfora. Well-publicized allegations in 1985-88 of Noriega's involvement in murders, drug-dealing, money-laundering, gun-running and espionage for and against the United States did not deflect PRD support for the military.

The party was a member of the Coalition of National Liberation (COLINA) alliance in the May 1989 presidential and legislative alliance and served as apologists for Noriega's annulment of the result until the US military invasion in December. Subsequently, in pursuit of a popular grass-roots base, it allied itself with domestic groups demonstrating for adequate compensation from the US government for civilians killed and property destroyed during the invasion, and with popular protests against corruption in the government and against its austerity policies. In July it opposed government moves to abolish the army, stating that it was needed to guarantee the security of the Panama Canal, and also spearheaded opposition to US demands that Panama's banking secrecy laws be repealed to assist in the detection of drug traffickers and money launderers.

In early 1990 a new group of PRD leaders emerged, distancing themselves from General Noriega and declaring themselves for democracy. Although loyal in opposition to the Endara regime (the Arnulfista Party leader and former president), they blamed it for the US invasion in 1989. In the elections of 1994 the PRD finally took power with a plurality of 31 seats in the legislature and 33.2% victory for Pérez Balladares.

Labour Party

Partido Laborista (PALA)

Address. Transística, Edif. Inversiones Cali, Urb. Orillac, Panamá

Telephone. (#507) 261-4174

Leadership. Carlos Lopéz Guevara, Arturo Dietz, Azael Vargas.

PALA was founded in September 1982 as an extreme-right wing group in Panamanian politics. It was the product of several attempts by Vargas to establish a strong party on the extreme right. He split from the now defunct Agrarian Labour Party (PLA), co-founded the National Renovation Movement (MNR)—which in 1982 became the Conservative Party (now defunct) before founding the PALA. The party's hostility to organized labour attracted the support of the country's ruling class, and PALA's then president Carlos Eleta Almarán was prepared to endorse the presidential candidacy of Gen. Ruben Darío Paredes, Chief of the National Guard, in 1984 but for the latter's withdrawal. PALA then joined the National Democratic Union (UNADE) and supported its candidate Nicolás Ardito Barletta, whose subsequent victory was felt to have been heavily dependent on the military's ability to rig the results. PALA accepted three cabinet posts but its clientist relationship with the military hindered its further development, a factor behind the ousting of Eleta Almarán as a president who was known to favour a more independent line of development. A member of UNADE's successor, the National Liberation Coalition (COLINA), which contested the abortive presidential and legislative elections of May 1989 and supported Gen. Noriega, PALA received one seat in the Legislative Assembly as a result of partial legislative elections held on Jan. 29, 1991, covering nine seats unaccounted for in the May 1989 results.

Motherland Movement
Movimiento Papa Egoró
Address. 3° Edif. Avon, Via España/Rey Kung, Panamá
Telephone. (#507) 269-8003
Leadership. Fernando Manfredo Bernal (president), Raúl Alberto Leis (secretary-general)

This initially small and rather curious party rapidly grew from inauspicious beginnings in November 1991 to being the third placed grouping in the 1994 presidential elections. The party's founder was the film star, singer and sometime lawyer, Rubén Blades, who in both 1992 and 1993 was quoted in opinion polls as being the favourite for the presidency in 1994. Blades, however, found it hard to shake off the rumours that his nomination in 1993 was no more than a stunt to advance his career, especially in the United States.

After the May 1994 elections, Blades returned to California to resume his show business career, leaving the party to its current leader Fernando Manfredo. The party's future thus appeared to be unsure.

National Renovation Movement
Movimiento de Renovación Nacional (MORENA)
Leadership. Pedro Vallarino Cox (president), Demetrio Decerega (secretary-general)

Founded and registered in 1993, MORENA gained one legislative seat in the 1994 elections.

Nationalist Republican Liberal Movement
Movimiento Liberal Republicano Nacionalista (MOLIRENA)
Address. Apartado 7468, Zona 5, Panamá City
Telephone. (#507) 251596
Fax. (#507) 251177
Leadership. Rubén Dario Carles (1994 presidential candidate), Alfredo Ramírez (president), Luis Guillermo Casco Arias (secretary-general).

Founded in October 1981, *MOLIRENA* is ostensibly a right-wing party that preaches the principles of a free market. The party was established by breakaway groups of the now defunct Third Nationalist Party (TPN) and Republican Party (PR) and the Liberal Party (PL). Opposed to the military's hold on the country, it joined the Opposition Democratic Alliance (ADO) to contest the 1984 presidential and legislative elections and thereafter supported the campaign of the National Civic Crusade for the removal of the Commander of the Defence forces, Gen. Manuel Noriega. The party was a member of the Opposition Civic Democratic Alliance (ADOC) denied power by Noriega following the presidential and legislative elections of May 1989. Once the ADOC was installed in power following the US military invasion in December, the party received 15 seats in the Legislative Assembly. Ford was named as the Second Vice-President and Minister for Planning and Economic Policy. As such, he had a major say in defining the government's IMF-approved economic austerity programme and was the architect of a plan, presented in September 1991, for the wholesale privatization of the state sector, including, most controversially, social welfare agencies.

The party's electoral gains in 1991 were largely wiped out in the 1994 polls, their legislative representation falling from 15 to 5 seats.

MOLIRENA is a full member of the Liberal International.

Solidarity Party
Partido Solidaridad (PS)
Address. Edif. Plaza Balboa, Panamá
Telephone. (#507) 263-4097
Leadership. Samuel Lewis Galindo (president), Simón Tejeira Quiros (secretary-general)

Founded and registered in 1993 the PS managed, with a short run-up to the election, to win two Assembly seats in the May 1994 polls.

Other Parties

Agrarian Labour Movement (*Movimiento Laborista Agrario*, MOLA), led by Carlos Eleta.

Christian Social Movement (*Partido Social Cristiano*, MSC) was founded in September 1993 as a former PDC splinter leftist group led by Gloria Moreno de López.

Doctrinal Panamanian Party (*Partido Panemañista Doctrinario*, PPD), led by Salvador Muñoz.

Independent Democratic Union (*Unión Democrática Independiente*, UDI), led by Jacinto Cardenas.

National Integration Movement (*Movimiento de Integración Nacional*, MIN), led by Dr Arrigo Guardia.

National Liberal Party (*Partido Liberal Nacional*, PLN), led by Dr Roberto Aleman.

National Unity Mission (*Misión de Unidad Nacional*, MUN), led by José Paredes.

Popular Action Party (*Partido Acción Popular*, PAP), led by Juan Lombardi.

Popular Nationalist Party (*Partido Nacionalista Popular*, PNP), led by Jorge Flores.

Republican Liberal Party (*Partido Liberal Republicano*, *Libre*), led by Gonzalo Tapia Colante and Carlos Orrilac.

Papua New Guinea

Capital: Port Moresby

Population: 4,000,000 (1995E)

The head of state of Papua New Guinea, which achieved full independence in 1975, is the British sovereign represented by a locally-nominated Governor-General. Legislative power is vested in a unicameral National Parliament, the 109 members of which are elected for up to five years by universal adult suffrage. Executive power is exercised by a Prime Minister and a National Executive Council (Cabinet) who are responsible to Parliament and are appointed to office by the Governor-General acting upon its advice.

In the most recent general election in June 1992 the *Pangu Pati* secured the highest number of seats with 22, while the People's Democratic Movement (PDM) won 15. The PDM leader was elected Prime Minister by the legislature the following month, but was forced from office in August 1994 and replaced by Sir Julius Chan, the leader of the People's Progress Party (PPP) which had won 10 seats in the 1992 elections.

Black Action Party (BAP)

Leadership. Joseph Onguglu (leader)

The small BAP has ministerial representation in the coalition government formed by Sir Julius Chan of the People's Progress Party (PPP) in August 1994.

League for National Advancement (LNA)

Address. c/o National Parliament, Port Moresby

Leadership. Karl Stack (leader)

The LNA was formed in 1986 by a breakaway group of *Pangu Pati* members of Parliament. In the June 1992 general election the party secured five legislative seats, subsequently participating in the coalition government led by the People's Democratic Movement (PDM) until August 1994.

Melanesian Alliance (MA)

Address. c/o National Parliament, Port Moresby

Leadership. Fr. John Momis (chair)

Based on the island of Bougainville, the nationalist MA was established at the end of the 1970s by Fr. Momis, a former separatist leader, and John Kaputin. The party won six parliamentary seats in the 1987 general election, increasing its representation to nine seats in the June 1992 poll. Fr. Momis, who had been appointed to the coalition government formed in August 1994 by Sir Julius Chan of the People's

Progress Party (PPP), was dismissed from ministerial office in July 1995 for refusing to support legislation abolishing the country's system of provincial government.

Melanesian United Front

Address. c/o National Parliament, Port Moresby

Leadership. Utula Utuoc Samana (leader)

Founded in the early 1980s as the Morobe Independence Group, the Front adopted its current title in 1988, having secured four parliamentary seats in the general election held the previous year. In the June 1992 poll the party's legislative representation fell to a single seat.

National Party (NP)

Address. c/o National Parliament, Port Moresby

Leadership. Michael Mel, Paul Pora (leaders)

The National Party was organized by Iambakey Okuk in 1980, evolving from the People's United Front which had been formed two years earlier. In the 1992 general election the party won only two seats, its parliamentary representation falling sharply from the levels attained during the 1980s. NP leader, Paul Pora, who had been appointed to the coalition government formed in August 1994 by Sir Julius Chan of the PPP, was dismissed from ministerial office in July 1995 for refusing to support legislation abolishing the country's system of provincial government.

Pangu Pati

Address. c/o National Parliament, Port Moresby
Leadership. Chris Haiveta (leader)

The centre-left *Pangu Pati* was formed in 1967 by Michael Somare. In 1975 the campaign for independence for Papua New Guinea was successful and Somare became the country's first Prime Minister. He continued to lead a coalition government after the 1977 election, but suffered a parliamentary defeat in 1980 and was replaced by a new administration led by the People's Progress Party (PPP). The *Pangu Pati* regained power after the 1982 general election, in coalition with the United Party, but was seriously weakened in April 1985 by the defection of Paias Wingti and other party members to form the People's Democratic Movement (PDM); the government fell the following November. The party remained a significant parliamentary bloc, winning 26 seats in the 1987 election, and returned to power in mid-1988 in a coalition with several minor parties. Rabbie Namaliu, who had taken over the leadership from Somare, became Prime Minister. In the June 1992 election there was a considerable fall in support for the *Pangu Pati*; it emerged as the largest single party but with only 22 seats. The party remained in opposition until August 1994 when, under Chris Haiveta's leadership, it formed a new coalition government with the PPP.

People's Action Party (PAP)

Address. c/o National Parliament, Port Moresby
Leadership. Akoka Doi, Ted Diro (leaders)

The PAP was formed in December 1986 by Ted Diro, who at that time was a minister in the coalition government led by the People's Democratic Movement (PDM). Following the general election in mid-1987, in which the PAP won six seats, Diro was accused of corruption in his former ministerial post. Lengthy legal proceedings ensued and Diro was found guilty of misconduct in office in September 1991. The PAP was a member of the coalition administration formed in July 1988 by Rabbie Namaliu of the *Pangu Pati*, but has not been represented in government since the June 1992 election, in which it won 13 seats.

People's Democratic Movement (PDM)

Address. c/o National Parliament, Port Moresby
Leadership. Paias Wingti (leader)

The PDM was launched in March 1985 by Paias Wingti, formerly a leading member of the *Pangu Pati*. When the coalition government of Michael Somare fell on a vote of no confidence in November 1985, Wingti took office as Prime Minister of a new PDM-led coalition. He remained in office following the 1987 election, in which the PDM won 18 seats, but was defeated in Parliament

on a no-confidence motion in July 1988. The PDM remained in opposition until the June 1992 election when the party secured 15 seats and Wingti became Prime Minister at the head of a coalition comprising the PDM, People's Progress Party (PPP) and League for National Advancement (LNA). Political manoeuvring by Wingti in September 1993, involving his resignation and re-election as Prime Minister, was condemned by the parliamentary opposition as an abuse of the democratic process, and in August 1994 the Supreme Court upheld a constitutional challenge. Wingti was ousted from the premiership, and the PPP, having withdrawn from its coalition with the PDM, formed a new coalition with the *Pangu Pati*.

People's Progress Party (PPP)

Address. c/o National Parliament, Port Moresby
Leadership. Sir Julius Chan (leader)

Founded in 1970, the conservative PPP participated in the post-independence government until 1978, when it went into opposition. It formed the core of the coalition government that succeeded the Somare administration in March 1980, with Sir Julius Chan as Prime Minister, but reverted to opposition again in August 1982. In late 1985 the PPP joined the government formed by Paias Wingti of the People's Democratic Movement (PDM), which survived until July 1988. The party returned to office in the PDM-led coalition formed after the June 1992 general election (in which the PPP won 10 seats), but withdrew in August 1994 following a constitutional ruling against the PDM leader. Sir Julius Chan was subsequently elected Prime Minister of a new coalition administration comprising the PPP, *Pangu Pati* and the Black Action Party (BAP).

Other Parties

Christian Democratic Party, established in early 1995.

Movement for Greater Autonomy, formed in May 1995 by premiers of several of the country's northern provinces who opposed the abolition of the provincial government system.

Papua Party, a centrist and regionalist party organized in 1987. It participated in the coalition administration formed in July 1988 by Rabbie Namaliu of the *Pangu Pati*.

Papuan National Alliance, a regional group.

People's Christian Alliance, formed in 1981 and led by Tom Koraea.

People's National Party (PNP), launched in 1993 by a group of largely independent members of Parliament.

United Party (UP), a conservative, mainly highlands-based party founded in the late 1960s. Having been the main opposition grouping in the pre-independence House of Assembly, the UP lost ground in the 1977 elections. The following year the party split, with a large section leaving to form the People's United Front (which in 1980 reorganized as the National Party). Following the 1982 elections, in which it suffered substantial losses, the UP joined the *Pangu Pati* in a coalition, returning to opposition in April 1985. UP members were appointed to Paias Wingti's PDM-led administration in November 1985, but the party's fortunes declined further in the 1987 elections, and it failed to win any parliamentary seats in the June 1992 polling.

Separatist Group

Bougainville Revolutionary Party (BRA), a rebel group in armed conflict with the central government in support of its demands for independence for the island of Bourgainville.

Paraguay

Capital: Asunción

Population: 5,000,000 (1995E)

Paraguay achieved independence from Spain in 1811. Its first constitution was introduced in 1844 in order to legitimize the power of Carlos Antonio López, one of the three consecutive dictators to rule Paraguay up to the end of the war of the Triple Alliance in 1870, in which Paraguay's population was halved. Political forces subsequently developed into the Colorado and Liberal parties who have dominated Paraguayan politics since 1876. A three-year period of military rule, albeit by reformist officers, followed the 1933-35 second Chaco war with Bolivia. A new constitution introduced in 1940 failed to build a state-dominated society and after a succession of unstable governments Gen. Alfredo Stroessner took power in a military coup in 1954.

During Stoessner's 35-year rule Paraguay was under a permanent state of siege and all constitutional rights and civil liberties were suspended. The country's economic and political structure was nonetheless stabilized and its infrastructure greatly modernized. Stoessner was declared the winner of all eight elections which were held at five-year intervals. He was overthrown on Feb. 3, 1989, in a "palace coup" led by Gen. Andrés Rodríguez, who was sworn in immediately as interim President. The subsequent presidential and congressional elections which took place on May 1, 1989, in which Rodríguez and the Colorado Party won a sweeping victory, were considered to have been relatively free and open by international observers. Election to membership of the Group of Rio in October 1990 and entry into the Mercosur South American Common Market, with Argentina, Brazil and Uruguay, in March 1991 did much to restore the country's international credibility.

Under the 1992 constitution executive power is vested in the President, who is directly elected by simple plurality for a non-renewable five-year term and who governs with the assistance of a Council of Ministers. The 1992 text curtailed the previous powers of the President, which included the power to veto congressional legislation, to control foreign policy, and to declare a state of siege with the consequent suspension of all civil liberties. Legislative authority is vested in the bicameral National Congress.

Both the 45-member Senate and the 80-member Chamber of Deputies are directly elected for five-year terms (subject to dissolution by the President). The party receiving the largest number of votes is allotted two-thirds of the seats in both houses, with the remaining seats being divided among other parties according to their electoral strength. A political coalition is not allowed currently to put forward a presidential candidate or participate in the elections.

Voting is compulsory for all men and women of 18 years of age and older. Women have been allowed to vote since 1958.

In presidential elections held on May 9, 1993, Juan Carlos Wasmosy, the Colorado candidate, defeated Domingo Laíno, of the Authentic Radical Liberal Party (PLRA), and Guillermo Caballero Vargas, of the National Encounter coalition. In simultaneous elections for the Congress, the Colorados gained 42.99% of the vote, winning 20 seats in the Senate and 38 in the Chamber of Deputies, and thus lacked an overall majority in either house.

Authentic Radical Liberal Party
Partido Liberal Radical Auténtico (PLRA)
  Address. Mariscal Lopez 435, Asunción
  Telephone. (#595-21) 200299
  Fax. (#595-21) 200299
  Leadership. Juan Manuel Benitez Florentín (president), Domingo Laino (1993 presidential candidate)

This centrist party was founded in 1978 and has been the second party in Paraguayan politics since that time. The PLRA was formed by Domingo Laíno, president of the Radical Liberal Party (PLU, a splinter group from the PLR). The party was a founder member of the National Agreement (*Acuerdo Nacional, AN*), a coalition of four opposition parties with the aim of pressing for democratization and respect for human rights. Although the PLRA was the largest opposition party within Paraguay it was denied legal status. Under the Stroessner regime, it boycotted all elections and organized anti-government rallies.

The PLRA was legalized on March 8, 1989, a month after the military coup against Stroessner. The party unsuccessfully asked for elections to be postponed in order to give all opposition parties an opportunity to put their case and to draw up a new electoral register.

The PLRA convention of March 1989 decided to participate in the May elections despite the short notice, but its attempt to form a National Accord coalition was outlawed by the authorities. Undeterred, Laíno stood as the PLRA presidential candidate and the party came second in both the presidential and the congressional elections, winning the highest percentage of the opposition vote (although as expected its share of the vote was far smaller than that of the ruling Colorados). Laíno obtained 18% of the votes and the PLRA won 20.1%, giving it 19 seats in the Chamber and 10 seats in the Senate.

In the Constituent Assembly elections of Dec. 1, 1991, the PLRA again proved to be the strongest opposition party but ran a relaxed campaign, now convinced that the Colorados were a spent force. It won only 27% of the vote and obtained 57 seats in the 198-seat Assembly.

In May 1990 the remains of the electorally unsuccessful Liberal Party (PL) were merged with the PLRA, achieving the aforementioned results. In the 1993 presidential polls, Laíno came a creditable second with 32% of the vote, and the party itself achieved the same placing in both the Senate and the Chamber of Deputies contest.

The party is the Paraguayan affiliate of the Liberal International.

Christian Democratic Party
Partido Demócrata Cristiano (PDC)
  Address. Colón 871, Casilla 1318, Asunción
  Leadership. José Burro (president), Luis Manuel Andrada Nogués (general secretary)

The pro-free-enterprise, centrist PDC was founded in 1960 and has been the country's representative in the Christian Democrat International (although the latter is currently in a period of suspended reorganisation). Formed by Luis Alfonso Resck, the party was illegal from the outset although it obtained the right to hold meetings. The PDC consistently called for a boycott of elections and in 1978 joined three other opposition parties in the National Accord alliance (AN). Resck was charged with subversion in July 1981 and after a hunger strike and imprisonment, during which he was tortured, he went into exile. As a result of pressure from the West German government, Resck was permitted to return to Paraguay in April 1986.

The PDC was legalized following the February 1989 coup which toppled Stroessner, and was allowed to participate in the elections of May 1, 1989. It obtained one seat in the Chamber (with 1% of the vote). In the Dec. 1, 1991, Constituent Assembly elections, the party won only one of the 198 seats.

Constitution for All
Constitución Para Todos (CPT)
  Leadership. Carlos Alberto Filizzola Pallares

Founded in 1991, the CPT is an independent coalition supported by the Roman Catholic church and the CUT and CNT trade union federations. The CPT grew out of Asuncion for All (*Asunción para Todos*, APTO), a new radical and progressive movement which won the May 1991 municipal elections in the capital, with 35% of the vote, beating the ruling Colorado Party's candidate by 7% of the vote. APTO's victorious charismatic candidate, Carlos Filizzola, was the president of the Association of Physicians and led a widely-reported doctors' strike in 1986 which became a focus for the popular opposition to Stroessner.

The CPT, however, fared surprisingly badly in the Dec. 1, 1991, Constituent Assembly elections despite its important role in mobilizing popular support for constitutional reform. The CPT obtained only 11% of the vote and 16 seats, suffering a set-back even in Asunción, where it won only 23% of the poll.

Febrerist Revolutionary Party
Partido Revolucionario Febrerista (PRF)
Address. Casa del Pueblo, Manduvirá 552, Asunción
Tel. (#595-21) 494041
Fax. (#595-21) 493995
Leadership. Victor Sanchez Villagra (president), Ricardo Estigarribia Velásquez (secretary-general)

The social democratic PRF was founded in 1936 and is an affiliate of the Socialist International. The PRF was founded following the radical nationalist coup of Feb. 17, 1936, which inspired the party's name.

In 1983 the radical wing, led by Euclides Acevedo, gained control of the party and in February 1984 the PRF called the first demonstration against the government in 20 years. Although the centrist faction regained control of the party in 1985, the PRF continued to organize and participate in rallies, and its clear stance against the regime resulted in raids on its offices and arrests of PRF leaders.

The party participated again in elections after the coup against Stroessner in February 1989. Acevedo tried to persuade interim President Andrés Rodríguez to postpone the elections to enable opposition parties to organize their campaigns, but was informed that this would set a bad precedent and told to regard the elections as a "training" exercise. The PRF nonetheless ran candidates in the May 1, 1989, general election, obtaining an overall vote of 2.1% and was allocated two seats in the Chamber and one in the Senate. In the Dec. 1, 1991, elections to the Constitutional Assembly, the party gained only 1.2% of the vote.

National Encounter
Encuentro Nacional (EN)
Address. c/o Congrese Nacional, Asunción
Leadership. Guillermo Caballero Vargas (1993 presidential candidate)

The party was founded in 1992 as an electoral vehicle of Guillermo Vargas, an independent candidate who in fact led the 1993 opinion polls right up to the ballot at which point his support fell away. The grouping won eight seats in each house and entered into opposition with the Liberals.

National Republican Association—Colorado Party
Asociación Nacional Republicana—Partido Colorado (ANR-PC)
Address. 25 de Mayo 842 c/Tacuary, Asunción
Telephone. (#595-21) 444137
Fax. (#595-21) 444138
Leadership. Eugenio Sanabria Cantero (president)

The right-wing Colorado Party was founded in 1887 and has been the major force in Paraguayan politics ever since. The Colorado Party originated in a conservative faction created by Gen. Bernardino Caballero (President of Paraguay 1882-91) and it took its name from the faction's red banners.

The Colorados were in power from 1887 until 1904, remained in opposition to Liberal governments until 1940 and opposed Moríngo's pro-Axis regime. A Colorado/Febrerist Revolutionary Party (PRF) coalition government was installed in 1946 after the USA put pressure on the regime.

The military coup of May 5, 1954, marked the beginning of Gen. Alfredo Stroessner's 35-year dictatorship. Then an army commander, he was officially elected President in July 1954. In 1956 Stroessner reorganized the party after exiling his main Colorado rival, Epifanio Méndez Fleitas. The 1958 elections were, like all six later elections held under his rule, completely stage-managed. To give a semblance of democracy, two opposition parties were permitted to take part and win some seats in Congress from 1968. The manipulated results invariably showed overwhelming support for Stroessner, despite the reality of exile, arrests, long prison sentences and torture being meted out to his political opponents.

The violent coup of Feb. 3, 1989, which toppled Stroessner took place shortly before his former close ally, Rodríguez, was to be transferred from his top army position of First Army Commander to the passive role of Defence Minister. Rodríguez, as interim President, legalized most opposition parties and called a general election for May 1, 1989. As the Colorado's presidential candidate, Rodríguez won 78.18% of the valid vote and the party polled 72.8% of the vote in the congressional elections, giving it the two-thirds majority in Congress demanded by the constitution.

Rodríguez, promising that he would not stand for a second term, was sworn on May 15, 1989, and retained his interim Cabinet. The ensuing power struggle between the "traditionalists" and the newly-formed "democratic" wing led, however to a severe rift in the party. A Colorado Party convention, dominated by "traditionalists", went ahead in early December 1989 despite a court injunction brought by the "democratic" faction, led by Blas Riquelme, and said to be supported by Rodríguez. This was followed on Dec. 11, 1989, by the resignation of the whole Cabinet. The leader of the "traditionalists", the Foreign Minister José María Argaña whose influence had grown considerably since the February coup, was dismissed in mid-August 1990 after his public statement that the Colorados would never give up power (contrary to Rodríguez's pledge to hold elections in 1993).

At an extraordinary Colorado convention in February 1993 the military-backed Juan Carlos Wasmosy defeated Dr Argaña for the party's presidential nomination. Following this rejection, Argaña campaigned against Wasmosy in the May 1993 general elections. The split led to an even separation of votes between the factions.

Following the elections, Argaña set up a new break-away party called the National Reconciliation Movement (Movimiento Reconciliatión Nacional, MRN), which formed a rival legislative block with the PLRA and EN (see below). In late 1994 three generals accused Wasmosy of vote-rigging and officially called for his impeachment. This clash between the Colorado Party and the military continued into 1995 with General Ovieda leading the fight against Wasmosy. In the face of this a new party faction was launched, fuelled by Ovieda, which began making overtures to the exiled Albert Stroessner, prompting the possibility of a new *stronista* faction within the Colorado party.

In April 1995, a new majority anti-Ovieda Senate was elected, increasing the tension between the President and the General.

Paraguayan Communist Party

Partido Comunista Paraguayo (PCP)

Leadership. Ananías Maidana (general secretary)

Legalized in 1989, the PCP had been illegal since its foundation in 1928 apart from short periods in 1936 and in 1946-47. Various attempts to mount a guerrilla resistance to the Stroessner regime from 1959 onwards were completely suppressed by 1966 and many of PCP leaders and members were believed to have been imprisoned without trial and tortured to death. Despite democratization following the overthrow of Stroessner in February 1989, the PCP was not permitted to participate in the May 1, 1989, elections. PCP general secretary Antonio Maidana, however, who was released from prison in 1978 to be expelled from the country, returned from exile in December 1989.

Other Parties

Democratic and Social Assembly (*Concertación Democrática y Social*, CDS), led by Ricardo Canese.

Humanist Party (*Partido Humanista*, PH), won 0.3% or less in May 1, 1989, congressional elections.

Paraguayan Peasant Party (*Movimiento Paraguayo del Campesino*, MPC).

Peoples' Democratic Movement (*Movimiento Democrático del Pueblo*, MDP), led by Merceded Soler.

Socialist National Party (*Partido Nacional Socialista*, PNS), led by Juan Carlos Bader.

Workers' Party (*Partido de los Tradajadores*, PT), led by María Herminia Feliciangeli.

Peru

Capital: Lima

Population: 23,800,000 (1995E)

The Republic of Peru achieved independence from Spain in 1826. In the post-independence era up to the present, periods of civilian government have frequently alternated with the rule of military dictatorships, the last holding power in 1968-80. A move towards broad political alliances has characterized the recent activity of both left-wing and right-wing parties and the current President, Alberto Keinya Fujimori, had attempted to establish political consensus by forming a national unity government. Failing this, coupled with his deep distrust of the opposition and the judiciary, Fujimori staged an army-backed presidential coup in April 1992.

Under the 1980 constitution, a bicameral National Congress is made up of a 180-member Chamber of Deputies and Senate consisting of 60 elected members plus past Presidents who can sit for life. Executive power rests with the President, who appoints a Council of Ministers. The President, together with the two Vice-Presidents and the Congress, is elected nationally by universal adult suffrage for a five-year term. If in the presidential elections no candidate obtains at least 36% of the vote, a second round between the two leading candidates is contested. The President may not stand for a second term. The Senate is elected on a regional basis and the Chamber of Deputies, which can be dissolved by the President in exceptional circumstances, is elected regionally by party-list proportional representation, 40 members from the province of Lima and 140 representing the rest of the country. Men and women over 18 are eligible to vote and registration and voting is compulsory until the age of 60. Women gained the vote for the first time in 1956.

Alberto Keinya Fujimori of Change 90 (*Cambio 90*) was re-elected in the presidential election held on April 9, 1995, with 64.42% of the vote, defeating his closest rival, Javier Perez de Cuéllar of the Union for Peru (UPP) movement, who received 21.81%. In the simultaneous congressional elections, the New Majority-Change 90 (NM-C90) won 67 seats, with the UPP the next largest group with 17 seats. Fujimori was sworn in for a second consecutive five-year term on July 28 along with the majority of the previous Cabinet. In the Nov. 12, 1995, election for the mayorship of the capital, Lima, regarded as second in importance only to the presidency, the NM-C90 candidate was defeated by an independent.

American Popular Revolutionary Alliance—Peruvian Aprista Party

Alianza Popular Revolucionaria Americana (APRA)

Address. Avenida Alfonso Ugarte 1012, Lima 1

Tel. (#51-1) 440-6886

Fax. (#51-1) 445-2986

Leadership. Luis Alva Castro (secretary-general), Jorge del Castillo Gálvez (political commission president), Mercedes Cabanillas (1995 presidential candidate)

Founded in 1924, the highly influential APRA has historically been the leading centre-left force in Peruvian politics. Pledges in the mid-1980s to promote democracy and human rights, improve general living standards and to resist IMF-imposed austerity programmes gave the party a populist image but were largely unfulfilled. Faced with spiralling inflation and mounting guerrilla activity, the APRA government imposed its own economic austerity measures and extended states of emergency around the country, conferring increased powers on the security forces.

APRA, the oldest and most dominant party in Peru, started as a continent-wide anti-imperialist movement by Victor Raúl Haya de la Torre, a Peruvian Marxist in exile in Mexico. Its original purpose was politically to unite Latin America, obtain joint control of the Panama Canal and gain social control of land and industry. The Peruvian branch of APRA, the Peruvian Aprista Party (PAP), was founded in 1930 when Haya returned to Peru. As it became the sole surviving Aprista party, the PAP was increasingly referred to as APRA.

In 1981, a conservative faction led by Andrés Townsend Ezcurra split away to form the Hayista Base Movement (MBH), claiming that Haya's aims had been betrayed. Alan García Pérez took over as secretary-general in 1982 and led the party to victory in the April 1985 elections. APRA candidates won 107 seats in the 180-seat Chamber of Deputies and 32 gained seats in the Senate. García came first in the presidential elections but obtained only 21.3% of the vote. However, his direct opponent Dr Alfonso Barrantes Lingán of the Socialist Left (IS) withdrew before the June run-off election.

García, the first Aprista to be elected President, and youngest ever to hold the office, was sworn in on July 25, 1985. His principal election promises were to halt the country's economic decline by devoting no more than 10% of export earnings to service the huge foreign debt. In an attempt to address widespread and escalating guerrilla activity, he set up a Peace Commission. In June 1986, however, García ordered the quelling of mutinies in three different prisons, staged mainly by Shining Path guerrillas, as a result of which an estimated 254 guerrillas were killed by the security forces. All the members of the Peace Commission resigned in protest. In addition, accusations that the government was using the right-wing Commando Rodrigo Franco death squads to intimidate left-wing opponents dented APRA's liberal image.

In the April 1990 presidential and congressional elections, APRA won only 16 senatorial seats and 49 seats in the Chamber of Deputies, and its presidential candidate and secretary-general Luís Alvaro Castro, was beaten by two newcomers to politics, Mario Vargas Llosa of the Democratic Front (FREDEMO) coalition and Alberto Keinya Fujimori of Change 90. APRA supported the victorious Fujimori in the second round of the presidential election.

In the aftermath of the Fujimori's April 1992 presidential coup, García, elected secretary-general of the party in February, went into hiding from where he called for popular resistance to restore democratic rule.

In early 1993, an extradition request made to Colombia to hand over the exiled García was rejected. Following attempts by García to obtain Colombian citizenship, he was stripped of the secretary-generalship of the APRA and the current leadership was installed. The charges of corruption arrayed against him remained unanswered until secret bank accounts implicating the former President were discovered in August 1994.

The internal strife and unpopularity of the party led to it achieving a dismal 5% of the presidential vote in April 1995. For the first time this lead to the possibility of APRA losing its electoral base.

The party is a consultative member of the Socialist International.

Change 90—New Majority
Cambio 90—Nueva Mayoría (C-90-NM)
Address. c/o Congreso, Lima
Leadership. Alberto Keinya Fujimori (leader), Pablo Correa (C-90 secetary)

The centre-right grouping of the C-90 was founded in 1989 to help the presidential aspiration of Alberto Fujimori. *Cambio 90* was formed by a group of independents to fight the April 1990 elections. Their campaign slogan was "hard work, honesty and technology" which promoted the apolitical image of *Cambio's* presidential candidate, the agronomist Alberto Fujimori. Support from the evangelical churches alienated the Roman Catholic Church, despite Fujimori himself being a Roman Catholic. This, however, did not deter many workers and rural migrants in towns and cities and peasants in the Andes who, disillusioned with the major political parties and fearful of the Democratic Front's (FREDEMO) promised "austerity programme", were attracted to *Cambio*. In the first round of the presidential election held in April 1990, Fujimori came a close second with 24.6% of the vote, forcing a second round. Supported by APRA and all the left-wing parties, he won the June run-off election with 56.3% of the vote, defeating the FREDEMO candidate Mario Vargas Llosa. Fujimori became President in July and formed a "government of national unity" consisting of members from left-wing and right-wing parties, technocrats and members of the armed forces. The fact that *Cambio* was only the third-largest force in the Senate and Chamber of Deputies meant that Fujimori had to rely on the support of other parties. This was reduced as public opposition mounted to both the government's stern economic austerity measures, something which Fujimori had denounced during his election campaign, and the privatization of 230 of the 240 state-run companies. He also pledged to resume repayments on the foreign debt, halted since 1985.

In the belief that the Congress and judiciary were wilfully opposing his economic restructuring programme and impeding the war against the *Sendero Luminoso* (Shining Path) guerrillas, Fujimori suspended sections of the constitution in an army-backed coup in April 1992 and dissolved Congress and dismissed hundreds of judges. The coup, condemned internationally, struck, initially at least, a popular chord among the general public who had lost confidence in government institutions and wanted affirmative action at a time of extreme economic crisis and escalating violence. Fujimori promised plebiscites on his action and proposed constitutional reforms and announced that fresh congressional elections would be held by February 1993.

In 1995 Fujimori was re-elected with a vote share of 64.3%, while the ruling C-90 coalition won an overwhelming 51.4% of the vote.

Christian Democratic Party
Partido Demócrata Cristiano (PDC)
Address. Avenida España 321, Casilla 14.0422, Lima 1
Telephone. (#51-1) 423-8042
Fax. (#51-1) 441-8938
Leadership. Rolando Hinojosa Vásquez (president)
A member of the Christian Democrat International, the PDC is a centrist party founded in 1956 which has been without representation in Congress since a split in 1966 which led to the formation of the Popular Christian Party (PPC).

Civic Works Movement
Movimiento Obras Cívicas (MOC)
Address. c/o Congreso, Lima
Leadership. Ricardo Belmont
Another party organized in the run-up to the 1995 presidential elections, the MOC was a vehicle for the presidential aspirations of its leader, Ricardo Belmont, who in the end could only manage a fifth-place finish. The MOC's candidate took 2.58% of the vote.

Hayist Base Movement
Movimiento de Bases Hayistas (MBH)
Leadership. Vacant (following the death of Andrés Townsend Ezcurra in late 1994)
The MBH is a right-wing party named after the founder of APRA, Victor Raúl Haya de la Torre, and claiming to represent his populist theses. It was formed in 1981 by Andrés Townsend Ezcurra and other party dissidents after Townsend's expulsion from APRA. The MBH contested the 1985 elections with the Popular Christian Party (PPC) as the Democratic Convergence (CODE) on a platform of privatization and monetarism and jointly won 12 seats in the Chamber of Deputies and seven seats in the Senate. Since the dissolution of the alliance in 1986, the MBH has had only minor political impact.

Independent Moralizing Front
Frente Independiente Moralizador (FIM)
Address. c/o Congreso, Lima
Leadership. Fernando Olivera (leader)

A very new party, the FIM was launched prior to the 1995 presidential elections by Fernando Olivera, a former investigator for the State Prosecutor's Office who had pursued former President García on corruption charges. In the subsequent congressional elections the party won a very creditable six seats.

Liberal Party
Partido Liberal (PL)
Leadership. Miguel Cruchaga (secretary-general)
The PL is the new incarnation of the former Liberty Movement (*Movimiento Libertad*), becoming official from September 1993.
Libertad was formed by the internationally renowned novelist Mario Vargas Llosa in reaction to the APRA government's proposals to nationalize banks and other financial institutions. In early 1988 the organization joined forces with the Popular Action (AP) and the Popular Christian Party (PPC) and formed the Democratic Front (FREDEMO) with which *Libertad* won considerable successes but not the presidency. After the elections the coalition was disbanded and shortly afterwards its presidential candidate Vargas Llosa announced his resignation from *Libertad* on the grounds that he wished to devote more time to his writing. Vargas Llosa publicly denounced Fujimori's April 1992 army-backed presidential coup, claiming that his pledges of constitutional reforms and fresh elections were the classic justifications of dictators to legitimize their illegal actions. Other party spokesmen demanded that any reforms should be made in accordance with the 1979 constitution.
The PL, in its new separate formation, won no congressional representation in 1995.

Popular Action
Acción Popular (AP)
Address. Paseo Colón 218, Lima
Telephone. (#51-1) 423-4177
Leadership. Fernando Belaúnde Terry (leader), Raúl Diez Canseco (secretary-general and 1995 presidential candidate)
The right-wing AP was founded in 1956 and has recently been a vociferous proponent of free-market policies in place of state-led reforms. The party was founded in order to back Fernando Belaúnde Terry's candidacy in the elections of 1956, in which he came second. The party split almost immediately.
A renewed alliance with the Popular Christian Party and the small *Movimiento Libertad* (ML) in the Democratic Front (FREDEMO), formed in early 1988, gave the AP a much needed boost. Although FREDEMO ultimately did not win the

April 1990 elections, AP candidates took a large share of FREDEMO seats in both the Chamber and Senate. Belaúnde gave instructions that no AP member should join the Fujimori government but instead his party was to present itself as a "constructive opposition". Consequently Juan Carlos Hurtado Miller resigned from the party so that he could accept the post of Prime Minister and Economy Minister, resigning in February 1991 because of differences over economic policy. FREDEMO was dissolved in mid-1990, leaving the AP free to support new political initiatives, for example the 14-point agreement of the Socialist Left (IS).

Belaúnde Terry was among prominent politicians opposed to Fujimori's April 1992 army-backed presidential coup and was present to witness the swearing-in of Maximo San Román Cáceres as the alternative "constitutional" President.

Popular Christian Party
Partido Popular Cristiano (PPC)
    Address. Avenida Alfonso Ugarte 1406, Lima
    Telephone. (#51-1) 423-8723
    Fax. (#51-1) 423-6582
    Leadership. Luís Bedoya Reyes (president)
The conservative PPC came into being in 1966. The party was formed by a splinter group of the Christian Democratic Party (PDC) led by the mayor of Lima, Luís Bedoya Reyes. It kept a low profile during the period of military dictatorship (1968-80) but came to prominence once the democratic process was re-installed.

The PPC contested the 1985 general elections as part of the Democratic Convergence (CODE), an alliance with the small Hayista Base Movement (MBH), after failing to interest Popular Action (AP) in a joint campaign. Bedoya stood as the coalition candidate in the presidential elections and with 9.7% of the vote once again came third. In the Chamber of Deputies the CODE won 12 seats and in the Senate seven. The alliance was dissolved soon after the elections and in December 1986 the PPC underwent an internal reorganization which was to improve the party's electoral chances. Just over a year later the PPC joined the AP and the small Freedom Movement (*Libertad*) in the Democratic Front (FREDEMO) alliance.

As part of this alliance, the party helped win a plurality of one third of each house of Congress. In 1995 the party backed the UPP and Javier Pérez de Cuéllar, who achieved a distant second in the polls. In the most recent congressional elections the PPC could only retain three seats.

Union for Peru
Unión por el Perú (UPP)
    Address. c/o Congreso, Lima
    Leadership. Javier Pérez de Cuéllar (1995 presidential candidate)
The UPP was formed in August 1994 to facilitate the 1995 presidential nomination of former United Nations Secretary-General Javier Pérez de Cuéllar. Although achieving second place in the 1995 presidential elections, with only 21.8% of the vote he came a distant second.

Left-Wing Parties and Alliances

Nationalist Left Party
Partido de Izquierda Nacionalista (PIN)
    Leadership. Róger Caceres Velásquez (president)
The PIN was formed as a coalition of groups from the Puno department of Peru. In 1990 under the campaign name of the National Front of Workers and Peasants (*Frente Nacional de Trabajadores y Campesinos*, FNTC), the party retained its two congressional seats from 1985.

Peruvian Communist Party
Partido Comunista Peruano (PCP)
    Leadership. Julio Renan Raffo (secretary-general)
Founded in 1928, the PCP split in 1969 into two sections taking their names from their respective periodicals Red Flag and Red Fatherland. In 1970, a Maoist group which was to later form the Shining Path guerrilla group (*Sendero Luminoso*) broke away from the Red Flag. Unlike other left-wing parties, the PCP-BR has refused to enter the IS, IU or UNIR and in recent years abandoned its pro-Chinese stance for a pro-Albanian one. Nominally pro-Albanian before the major political unrest in Albania in late 1990 and early 1991, the PCP-BR advocates but does not practise armed struggle.

In November 1991, a significant meeting of the party national congress voted to remove its most prominent leader Jorge del Prado Chávez who had been party leader since 1965. Following this unanticipated move, the party voted to move into direct conflict with the Fujimori government which it declared was in danger of becoming a dictatorship. The PCP forms part of the broader United Left.

Popular Front of Workers, Peasants and Students
Frente Obrero, Campesino, Estudiantil y Popular (FOCEP)
    Leadership. Genero Ledesma Izquieta
FOCEP was formed in 1962 and was legalized in 1978 prior to the 1978 Constituent Assembly

election. Originally a nominal Trotskyite alliance, the group now operates as a single party and is an arm of the broader United Left alliance.

FOCEP was disqualified from participating in the congressional ballot of November 1992.

Popular Democratic Union
Unión Democrático Popular (UDP)

Leadership. Luis Benitez, Edmundo Murrugarra

Founded in 1978, the UDP was itself an alliance of 18 parties that could not agree upon a union with the Peruvian Communist Party. Instead it joined with UNIR. The party now occupies a position slightly left of the mainstream United Left, with reputed links with the Shining Path terrorist group.

Revolutionary Communist Party
Partido Comunista Revolucionario (PCR)

Leadership. Manuel Dammert (secretary-general)

Formed in 1974 as a hard-line Maoist grouping, the PCR is now a moderate party in its outlook. The party split from the Revolutionary Vanguard in 1974.

Revolutionary Socialist Party
Partido Socialista Revolucionario (PSR)

Leadership. Gen. (retd.) Leonidas Rodriguez Figueroa (president)

Founded in 1976, the party was inspired by the policies of Gen. Juan Velasco Alvarado (President from 1968-1975). The PSR stresses a sustained programme of reforms to establish socialism.

Socialist Accord
Acuerdo Socialista (ACSO)

Leadership. José Antonio Luna, Manuel Dammert

ACSO was launched in early 1989 by two parties that had been former parties to the IU alliance, namely the Revolutionary Socialist Party (PSR) and the Revolutionary Communist Party (PCR). The group supported Barrentes Lingán of the Socialist Left in the 1990 presidential election.

Socialist Confluence
Confluencia Socialista (CS)

Leadership. Collective

A left-wing alliance formed by a breakaway group from the United Left and made up of the Socialist Political Action (*Acción Política Socialista*, APS), the Socialist Action Movement (*Movimiento de Acción Socialista*, MAS), the Non-Partisan Movement (*Movimiento No Partidarizado*, MNP) and the Revolutionary Mariáteguist Party (*Partido Mariáteguista Revolucionario*, PMR).

Socialist Left
Izquierda Socialista (IS)

Address. Plaza 2 de Mayo 46, Lima 1

Leadership. Alfonso Barrantes Lingán (1990 presidential candidate)

The IS was formed in 1989 by a group of parties who believed in offering critical support to the government of President Alan García Pérez of APRA. This led to a split with the left in the United Left (IU) coalition. Barrantes subsequently came fifth as IS candidate in the April 1990 presidential elections with a mere 4.07% of the vote, but three IS candidates were elected to the Senate. IS support for Alberto Fujimori of Change 90 in the presidential run-off resulted in a small share of power, with the energy and mines portfolio being awarded to Fernando Sánchez Albavera. In late August 1990 Barrantes proposed to the government a 14-point economic "national agreement" which included suggestions for joint negotiation with labour and business organizations on wages and prices and a reform of the state to avert the turmoil and social upheaval of Peru's economic decline. The proposal was supported by the right-wing Popular Action (AP) and the Popular Christians (PPC).

Unified Mariáteguista Party
Partido Unificado Mariáteguista (PUM)

Leadership. Eduado Caceres Valdiva (general-secretary)

The PUM was formed in 1984 as an alliance of the Revolutionary Left Movement (MIR-Perú), the Revolutionary Vanguard (VR) and a section of the Revolutionary Communist Party (PCR). The PUM incorporates Maoist, Guevarist and Trotskyist traditions but is also influenced by the ideas of indigenous cultural revival championed by the founder of the Peruvian Communist Party (PCP), José Carlos Mariátegui. It forms part of the broader United Left alliance.

Union of the Revolutionary Left
Unión de Izquierda Revolucionaria (UNIR)

Leadership. Rolando Breña Pantoja (president), Jorge Hurtado Pozo (secretary-general)

UNIR was formed in 1979 by the Breña faction of the Communist Party of Peru-Red Fatherland (PCP-PR), the National Liberation Front (FNI) and the Movement of the Revolutionary Left-Peru (MIR-Perú). It was nominally Maoist but participated in the 1980 and 1985 legislative elections. Breña Pantojo paid an official visit to North Korea in February 1992.

United Left
Izquierda Unida (IU)

Address. Avenida Grau 184, Lima 23

Telephone. (#51-1) 427-8340

Leadership. Gustavo Mohome (leader), Augustin Hoya de la Torre (1995 presidential candidate)

Founded in 1980 the IU is a left-wing coalition advocating non-payment of the foreign debt, increased public ownership, nationalization of US-owned copper mines, exchange controls, a ban on remittances of profits abroad and the greater distribution of wealth to narrow the gap between rich and poor.

The IU was formed as a left-wing front in response to the poor results in the May 1980 general election caused by sectarianism among left-wing parties. Proof that a united left could be successful came almost immediately in the December 1980 municipal elections in which the IU captured six departmental capitals and came second in Lima.

In November 1983 IU president Alfonso Barrantes Lingán, a former APRA member and labour lawyer, was elected mayor of Lima and the IU gained 29% of the national vote in the municipal polls. Barrantes stood as the IU's presidential candidate in the 1985 elections and came a close second with 21.3% of the vote. Barrantes resigned from the IU soon after and formed the Socialist Left (IS) alliance with other breakaway parties. Despite the left being now officially split in two, the IU still managed to obtain 17% of the national vote in the local elections in November 1989. In April 1990, the IU fielded Henry Pease as the coalition's presidential candidate. He won 6.97% of the valid vote and came fourth. Like most left-wing parties, the IU encouraged its supporters to vote for Alberto Fujimori of Change 90 in the second round of the 1990 presidential elections. In return, President Fujimori appointed two IU members to his "national unity" Cabinet.

IU leader Mohome joined with the rest of the opposition in opposing Fujimori's army-backed coup in April 1992. With Augustin Hoya de la Torre as the IU candidate in 1995, the grouping could only manage 0.54% of the vote. Significant support, both within and outside the alliance, shifted to the campaign of Javier Pérez de Cuéllar of the Union for Peru.

In mid-1995 the IU embraced the Unified Mariáteguista Party and its components; the Popular Front of Workers, Peasants and Students; the Union of the Revolutionary Left; the Peruvian Communist Party; and the Workers' Revolutionary Party.

Workers' Revolutionary Party
Partido Revolucionario de los Trabajadores (PRT)
    Address. Plaza 2 de Mayo, Apdo 2449, Lima
    Leadership. Hugo Blanco Galdós

The PRT was founded in 1978 by several small Trotskyist groups and led by the former guerrilla leader Hugo Blanco Galdós, the PRT contested the constituent elections of that year as part of the Labour, Peasant, Student and People's Front. In 1980 the party gained registration and in an alliance with two other parties it won three seats in the Chamber and two in the Senate in the elections. Hugo Blanco Galdós left the PRT before the 1985 elections and the party's influence has declined ever since, although the party has remained a component of the United Left.

Other Minor Groupings

21st Century Harmony (*Armonia Siqlo XXI*) was launched in 1994 by Susana Higuchi, the estranged wife of President Fujimori. It was hoped that the group would spearhead her rival presidential campaign.

Democratic Co-ordination—Peru Possible Nation (*Coordinadora Democrática—Perú País Posible*, CODE), also sometimes referred to as the **Democratic Convergence**, Code was founded in 1992 by another ex-Apista Congressman, José Barba Caballero (party leader). Alejandro Toledo's *País Posible* merged with Code in 1995 and Toledo ran as the party's presidential candidate.

Independent Agricultural Movement (*Movimiento Independiente Agrario*—MIA) is a small group that achieved one congressional seat in 1995. It is led by former strip-tease artist, Suzy Diaz.

Renovation (*Renovación*), is an offshoot from the former Liberty Movement (PL) and is led by Rafael Rey. Its six members of Congress are currently in support of President Fujimori.

Socialist Party of Peru (*Partido Socialista del Perú*—PSP), led by María Cabredo de Castillo.

Socialist Workers' Party (*Partido Socialista de los Trabajadores*—PST), is led by Ricardo Napuri and is a Trotskyite party founded in 1982 by a merger of the former PST and the Marxist Workers' Party.

Solidarity and Democracy (*Solidaridad y Democracia*, SODE), led by a former Aprista congressman, Javier Silva Ruete. The party adheres to broad Christian Democrat principles.

Guerrilla Movements

Shining Path
Sendero Luminoso
    Leadership. Manuel Abimael Guzmán Reinoso (imprisoned); Oscar Ramirez Durand (*Sendero Rojo*)

Eschewing what they term as "parliamentary cretinism" and negotiations with the government, supporters claim that "Guzmán Thought" represents the "fourth sword" of communism after Marxism, Leninism and Maoism. *Sendero* holds to the classic Maoist dictum that peasant support bases must be formed in the countryside, after which cities, where political and economic power is concentrated, can be surrounded and overwhelmed. In recent years, however, its operations have spread to urban areas, especially to the capital, Lima.

Shining Path originated among a small group of intellectuals at the state university of San Cristobal de Huamanga, Ayacucho, in the southern Andes, who in 1970 had split away from the PCP-Red Flag. In May 1980, it launched its "people's war" which to date has claimed the lives of more than 25,000 people, placed 40% of the country under a perpetual state of emergency and has made *Sendero* a major threat to any government.

Despite army counter-insurgency measures, *Sendero*'s scope of operations has spread from the southern to the central Andes and, critically, to the eastern Amazonian Upper Huallaga valley region where it finances its guerrilla operations by acting as an intermediary between peasant cocoa farmers and drug traffickers.

The group's leader, Manuel Guzmán, was captured and imprisoned in September 1992, with his principle deputy, Edmundo Cox, being apprehended in August 1993. In January 1994 it

was reported that the Shining Path had split into two factions, one loyal to Guzmán and the other styling itself the Red Path (*Sendero Rojo*).

By March 1994 some 4,100 *senderistas* had surrendered under a 1992 amnesty law and guerrilla activity has consequently been reduced since.

Tupac Amarú Revolutionary Movement
Movimiento Revolucionario Tupac Amarú (MRTA)
Leadership. Néstor Serpa Cartolini

Deriving its name from Tupac Amarú, the leader of the 1781 Indian revolt against Spanish colonial rule, the MRTA was formed by groups who broke away from the Revolutionary Socialist Party (PRS) in 1983.

Unlike *Sendero Luminoso*, it has been less hostile towards the rest of the left-wing movement. In late 1987, an original urban guerrilla strategy was changed for that of open rural warfare with a base of operations in the northern Huallaga region, the country's chief drug producing region where it is now in direct competition with *Sendero* in extracting protection money from drug-traffickers and peasant growers of coca to finance its military activities. Since September 1990 the MRTA has been interested in peace talks leading to eventual political integration.

The MRTA's (then) leader, Victor Polay Campos, was captured by police in February 1989, escaped in July 1990, and was recaptured in June 1992.

Philippines

Capital: Manila

Population: 68,000,000 (1995E)

The Republic of the Philippines became independent from the United States in 1946. In 1965 Ferdinand Marcos became President, retaining power thereafter through the increasing use of political corruption and coercion. In an attempt to generate domestic support and to placate the US government, Marcos agreed to hold a presidential election in February 1986. He was opposed by Corazon Aquino (the widow of Benigno Aquino, the country's most prominent opponent of the Marcos regime until his murder in 1983). Although Marcos claimed victory, it was generally believed that Aquino had secured a greater number of votes. In the face of huge popular demonstrations in favour of Aquino, and a growing mutiny within the armed forces, Marcos fled the country and Aquino was declared President.

A new constitution was approved by referendum in February 1987. Under its terms, legislative authority is vested in a bicameral popularly-elected Congress, consisting of a 204–member House of Representatives (with provision for an additional 50 members to be appointed by the President to represent minority groups) elected for three years, and a 24–member Senate elected for six years (with half being due for re-election every three years). Executive power is in the hands of a directly-elected President and an appointed Cabinet.

The popular approval of the constitution was accepted as a *de facto* election of Corazon

Aquino as President. In a general election in May 1987 candidates endorsed by the President won a decisive victory in the new Congress. Presidential and legislative elections were next held on May 11, 1992, when Aquino's chosen successor and former Defence Secretary, Fidel Ramos, succeeded her as President, although his supporters failed to achieve an overall majority in the legislature. Further legislative elections on May 8, 1995, resulted in pro-Ramos majorities in both houses of the Congress.

Communist Party of the Philippines
Partido Komunista ng Pilipinas (PKP)
Leadership. Felicisimo Macapagal (president)
The PKP was founded in 1930 with a pro-Soviet stance and was illegal in 1932-38, 1942-45 and 1947-74. Since 1968, when a radical faction broke away to form the Communist Party of the Philippines–Marxist-Leninist (CPP-ML), the PKP has advocated political reform rather than violent change. Although it participated in the popular movement to oust President Marcos in 1986, it has little political influence, having been eclipsed by the CPP-ML as the country's primary focus for those interested in communist ideology.

Democratic Filipino People's Power
Laban ng Demokratikong Pilipino (LDP)
Address. c/o Congress of the Philippines, Metro Manila
Leadership. José Cojuangco (secretary-general)
The LDP was established in 1988 as an alliance of the Filipino Democratic Party–People's Power (*Partido Demokratikong Pilipino–Laban, PDP-Laban*), itself the product of a merger of the PDP and Benigno Aquino's *Laban* in 1983, and People's Struggle (*Lakas ng Bansa*), founded in 1987 by a nephew of Corazon Aquino. A faction of the PDP-*Laban*, led by Aquilino Pimentel, refused to enter the LDP and continued to function as a separate political movement. Having arisen as a vehicle for the pro-Aquino legislators elected in 1987, the party had an organizational rather than ideological basis and displayed frequent signs of instability. It emerged from the 1992 legislative poll as the largest party, but ran fourth in the presidential contest and was subsequently seriously weakened by defections.

In August 1994 the party formed an electoral alliance with People's Struggle–National Union of Christian Democrats (*Lakas*-NUCD), led by President Fidel Ramos. In the May 1995 elections this alliance secured 170 of the 201 proclaimed seats in the House of Representatives, also taking nine of the 12 contested Senate seats. However, the alliance fell into disarray in August 1995 when LDP senators split into opposing factions over the ousting of Edgardo Angara as Senate president.

Liberal Party (LP)
Address. 7 1st Street, Acacia Lane, Mandaluyong, Metro Manila
Telephone. (#63-2) 531-6748
Fax. (#63-2) 931-6649
Leadership. Jovito Salonga (leader), Raul Daza (president)
Dating from a split in the Nationalist Party in 1946 and affiliated to the Liberal International, the LP was revived as a political force in the mid-1980s, achieving significant congressional representation in the 1987 elections. However, the party then suffered numerous defections and its electoral performance has correspondingly declined. In the May 1992 presidential election, party leader Salonga took sixth place with about 10% of the vote.

National People's Coalition (NPC)
Address. c/o Congress of the Philippines, Metro Manila
Leadership. Ernesto Maceda (president)
The NPC was founded as a centre-right coalition shortly before the 1992 elections by elements of the historic Nationalist Party and the Liberal Party supporting the presidential ambitions of Eduardo Cojuangco, a wealthy businessman and former Marcos confidant. In the presidential contest he took third place with just over 18% of the vote, while the party also won five seats in the Senate and emerged as the third strongest group in the House of Representatives. In the May 1995 legislative elections the NPC secured 31 seats in the House, while its representation in the Senate fell to two.

Nationalist Party (NP)
Leadership. Salvador Laurel, Juan Ponce Enrile (factional leaders)
The NP, founded in 1907 and the country's oldest party (commonly known as the *Nacionalistas*), had been reduced by 1988 to a minor right-wing formation. Subsequent attempts to revive the party as a political force were hampered by factional rivalries over the party nomination for the 1992 presidential election. The party split into three wings—one supporting Salvador Laurel (who secured the nomination, but came seventh in the election with only 3.4% of the vote), another

backing Juan Ponce Enrile, and a third supporting Eduardo Cojuangco, which evolved into the National People's Coalition (NPC).

New Society Movement
Kilusan Bagong Lipunan (KBL)

Leadership. Vicente Mellora (secretary-general)

The KBL was organized in 1978 as a vehicle for the personal rule of former President Ferdinand Marcos. Although discredited after his overthrow in 1986, the party continued to exist in opposition to the Aquino government and supported the unsuccessful bid of his widow, Imelda Marcos, for the presidency in the May 1992 election.

People's Reform Party (PRP)
Address. c/o Congress of the Philippines, Metro Manila

Leadership. Miriam Defensor-Santiago

The opposition PRP was formed in 1991 by its leader to support her candidacy in the presidential election the following year. Campaigning on an anti-corruption platform, she achieved second place with almost 20% of the total vote. In the May 1995 elections Defensor-Santiago won a Senate seat for the PRP.

People's Struggle–National Union of Christian Democrats (*Lakas*-NUCD)
Address. 853 A. Armaiz Ave, Makati, Metro Manila

Telephone. (#63-2) 813-4179

Fax. (#63-2) 815-6095

Leadership. Fidel Ramos (leader), José Rufino (secretary-general)

Lakas was launched at the beginning of 1992 to support the presidential candidacy of Fidel Ramos, who left the Democratic Filipino People's Power (LDP) in November 1991 upon the designation of a rival as the LDP presidential nominee. The party fought the 1992 elections in coalition with the National Union of Christian Democrats (led by Raul Manglapus and affiliated to the Christian Democrat International) and with a Muslim formation. Having received the endorsement of Corazon Aquino, Ramos narrowly won the presidency with 23.6% of the vote. At the same time the coalition also secured two Senate seats and 51 seats in the House of Representatives. The ranks of *Lakas*-NUCD were subsequently inflated by defections from other parties, particularly the LDP, with which it concluded an electoral alliance in August 1994. In the May 1995 legislative polling this alliance won an overwhelming majority (170 seats) in the House of Representatives, as well as nine of the 12 Senate seats up for election (five of which were taken by *Lakas*-NUCD).

Other Parties

Mindanao Alliance, led by Homobono Adaza, formed in 1978, committed to the protection of civil and human rights and the economic development of the region of Mindanao.

People's Party (*Partido ng Bayan*), led by Fidel Agcaoli, formed in 1986 as a militant, nationalist, left-wing group.

Philippine Democratic Socialist Party (PDSP), led by Norberto Gonzales, formed in 1981.

Visayas Movement (*Pusyon Visaya*), led by Valentino Legaspi, founded in 1978, centred in the Visayas region of the central Philippines.

Women for the Mother Country (*Kababaihan Para Sa Inang Bayan*), led by Tarhata Lucman, established in 1986 as a militant feminist party.

Insurgent Movements

Abu Sayyaf, a radical Islamic group led by Abubakar Janjalani, active on the southern island of Basilan in the mid-1990s..

Communist Party of the Philippines–Marxist-Leninist (CPP-ML), founded in 1968 as a Maoist breakaway faction from the then pro-Soviet Communist Party of the Philippines (PKP), led by Benito E. Tiamzon and José Maria Sison; created National Democratic Front (NDF) in 1973 with the aim of uniting progressive forces; a guerrilla war launched in 1969 by its military wing, the New People's Army (NPA), continued sporadically in the mid-1990s, despite government efforts to negotiate a ceasefire.

Moro Islamic Liberation Front (MILF), a fundamentalist faction of the Moro National Liberation Front which split from the parent group in 1978; its military wing is known as the *Bangsa* Moro Islamic Armed Forces.

Moro National Liberation Front (MNLF), a guerrilla organization seeking autonomy for the Muslim communities in Mindanao.

Poland

Capital: Warsaw   **Population:** 38,500,000 (1995E)

The Communist-ruled People's Republic of Poland established in 1947 gave way in 1989 to the pluralist Polish Republic. Under its "small" constitution promulgated in December 1992 (pending the drafting of a comprehensive "large" text), there is a President who is popularly elected for a five-year term and who appoints the Prime Minister subject to parliamentary approval. Legislative authority is vested in a bicameral National Assembly (*Zgromadzente Narodowe*) elected by universal adult suffrage for a four-year term, consisting of (i) a directly-elected Senate (*Senat*) of 100 members, of whom 94 are returned from 47 two-member provinces and three each from Warsaw and Krakow provinces; and (ii) a National Assembly (*Sejm*) of 460 members, who are elected by a system of proportional representation that requires party lists (except those representing ethnic minority communities) to obtain at least 5% of the vote (and coalitions 8%). The 5% threshold rule was introduced because the parliamentary elections of October 1991 had produced a highly fragmented *Sejm* in which 29 parties or groups had representation.

Elections to the *Sejm* on Sept. 19, 1993, resulted as follows: Democratic Left Alliance (headed by Social Democracy of the Polish Republic, SRP) 171 seats (with 20.4% of the vote), Polish Peasant Party 132 (15.4%), Democratic Union 74 (10.6%), Union of Labour 41 (7.3%), Confederation for an Independent Poland 22 (5.8%), Non-Party Bloc for Reform 16 (5,4%), German Minority Socio-Cultural Associations 4 (0.6%). (The Democratic Union later became the broader Freedom Union.) Presidential elections held in two rounds on Nov. 5 and 19, 1995, resulted in the Democratic Left Alliance candidate, Aleksander Kwaśniewski (then leader of the SRP), winning in the second round with 51.7% of the vote.

Centre Alliance
Porozumienie Centrum (PC)
   Address. 47 ul. Zawojska, 02927
   Telephone. (#44–22) 642–8289
   Fax. (#44–22) 642–6987
   Leadership. Jaroslaw Kaczyński (chair)

The PC was founded in 1990 as an attempt to create a Polish version of the German Christian Social Union, i.e. a broad-based Christian-oriented party of the centre-right. It backed the successful 1990 presidential candidacy of Lech Walesa (of whom Kaczyski, who had been editor of Solidarity's weekly journal, was a close associate) and subsequently became the core component of the Centre Citizens' Alliance (*Porozumienie Obywatelskie Centrum*, POC), which won 44 *Sejm* seats (with 8.7% of the vote) in the October 1991 parliamentary elections, becoming the fourth largest grouping and providing the Prime Minister (Jan Olszewski) of the subsequent centre-right government. Following the collapse of the latter in June 1992 over its controversal decision to release Communist-era security files, a PC congress voted to expel Olszewski and other elements (later

regrouped in the Movement for the Republic and more recently in the Movement for the Reconstruction of Poland). After agreeing to join the seven-party coalition formed in July 1992 by Hanna Suckocka of the Democratic Union (later the Freedom Union), the PC unexpectedly withdrew its support later in the year to become part of the "soft" opposition. In the September 1993 parliamentary elections the PC obtained only 4.4% of the vote and therefore failed to win representation. In May 1994 the PC joined the Covenant for Poland alliance with four other centre-right parties. In November 1995 it supported President Walesa's unsuccessful re-election bid.

The PC is an affiliate of the Christian Democrat International and of the International Democrat Union.

Christian National Union
Zjednoczenie Chrzácijasko-Narodowe (ZChN)
   Address. 28 ul. Twarda, 00853 Warsaw
   Leadership. Marian Pilka (chair), Tomasz Szyszka (general secretary)

Opposed to abortion and on the conservative wing of Christian democraccy, the ZChN was founded in September 1989 as the party vehicle of a number of Catholic groups. Having backed the successful candidacy of Lech Walesa in the 1990 presidential elections, it contested the 1991 parliamentary elections as the main component of Catholic Electoral Action (*Wyborcza Akeja Katolicka*, WAK), which became the third strongest formation in a fragmented *Sejm* with 49 seats from a vote share of 8.7%. The ZChN participated in subsequent centre-right coalition governments, but was weakened in 1992 when its then leader (and Marshal of the *Sejm*), Wieslaw Chrzanowski, featured in a government list of alleged Communist-era collaborators published by the ZChN Interior Minister, Antoni Macierewicz. The latter was expelled from the party (which opposed disclosure of old secret service files on human rights grounds) and later founded the Christian National Union-Polish Action.

In the September 1993 parliamentary elections, the ZChN headed the Homeland (*Ojczyzna*) alliance, which included the Conservative Party (PK) and the Peasant Alliance (PL) but failed to win representation. In May 1994 the ZChN joined the Covenant for Poland alliance with four other centre-right parties. Chrzanowski vacated the ZChN chair in March 1995 and was succeeded by Ryszard Czarnecki, who himself quickly resigned after objecting to the party's decision to support Walesa in his (unsuccessful) re-election bid in November. He was succeeded in February 1996 by Marian Pilka, a 42–year-old historian.

Confederation for an Independent Poland

Konfederacja Polski Niepodleglej (KPN)

Address. 18/20 ul. Nowy Swiat, 00920 Warsaw
Telephone. (#48-22) 261043
Fax. (#48-22) 261400
Leadership. Leszek Moczulski (chair)

The nationalist KPN was founded in September 1979, becoming the first significant clandestine opposition party of the Communist era and enduring much attempted repression for that reason. Evoking the ideas of inter-war Polish leader Marshal Pilsudski, KPN candidate Leszek Moczulski obtained only 2.5% of the vote in the 1990 presidential election. In the 1991 parliamentary elections, the KPN won 46 lower house seats on a vote share of 7.5%, thereafter usually giving external support to the Olszewski government. Following the collapse of the latter in June 1992, it became part of the "hard" opposition to the successor administration headed by Anna Suchocka of the Democratic Union (later the Freedom Union). In the September 1993 parliamentary elections, the KPN fell back to 22 *Sejm* seats on a vote share of 5.8%. In opposition

to the subsequent government dominated by Social Democracy of the Polish Republic, the KPN in 1995 took a leading role in the creation of a "Patriotic Camp" alliance of right-wing parties that included the Non-Party Bloc for Reform and the Movement for the Republic.

Covenant for Poland

Przymierze dla Polski (PdP)

Address. c/o ZChN, 28 ul. Twarda, 00853 Warsaw
Leadership. Rotates every two months between leaders of constituent parties

The PdP was announced in May 1994 as a "confederation" of five parties of the centre-right, namely the Centre Alliance, the Christian National Union, the Conservative Party, the Movement for the Republic and the Peasant Alliance. None of these five had surmounted the 5% barrier to *Sejm* representation in the 1993 elections, although their combined vote share was 15%.

Democratic Left Alliance

Sojusz Lewicy Democratyczne (SLD)

Address. c/o Zgromadzente Narodowe, Warsaw
Leadership. Wlodzimierz Cimoszewicz, Józef Oleksy

The SLD was created prior to the 1991 elections as an alliance of Social Democracy of the Polish Republic (SRP) and the All-Poland Trade Unions' Federation (*Ogólnopolskie Porozumienie Zwiazków Zawodowych*, OPZZ), the latter derived from the official trade union federation of the Communist era. Having won 60 lower house seats in 1991, the SLD achieved a plurality of 171 in the September 1993 elections, forming a coalition government with the Polish Peasant Party (PSL). The PSL held the premiership until February 1995, when Józef Oleksy of the SLD/SRP took the post. The then SRP leader, Aleksander Kwaśniewski, was the successful SLD candidate in the November 1995 presidential elections, with the support of over 30 other groupings. In February 1996 Oleksy was replaced as Prime Minister by Wlodzimierz Cimoszewicz, an adherent of the SLD but not of any of its constituent parts.

Freedom Union

Unia Wolnósci (UW)

Address. 30 al. Jerozolimskie, 00024 Warsaw
Telephone. (#48-22) 275047
Fax. (#48-22) 277851
Leadership. Leszek Balcerowicz (chair), Donald Tusk (deputy chair), Jacek Kurón (1995 presidential candidate)

The UW was founded in April 1994 as a merger of the Democratic Union (*Unia Demokratyczna*, UD) and the smaller Liberal Democratic Congress

(*Kongres Liberalno-Demokratyczny*, KLD). The new formation declared itself to be strongly of the democratic social centre, favouring market-oriented reforms but urging sensitivity to resultant social problems.

Of the constituent parties, the UD had been created by members of the election committees set up by the Solidarity-affiliated Citizens' Movement for Democratic Action to support the 1990 presidential candidacy of the then Prime Minister, Tadeusz Mazowiecki, who in the event won only 18.1% of the first-round vote. In May 1991 the UD was joined by the left-of-centre Democratic Action Civic Movement-Democratic Social Movement (ROAD-RDS) and the right-of-centre Forum of the Democratic Right (FPD), although the latter later withdrew to join in forming the Conservative Party. The UD components were united in their opposition to President Walesa's "demagogic populism" and began to urge a deceleration of the pro-market reform programme, although in 1989–90 the UD had been closely identified with the "shock therapy" economic programme of Finance Minister Leszek Balcerowicz (later to become leader of the UW). In the October 1991 parliamentary elections the UD headed the list of 29 groups gaining representation, winning 62 *Sejm* seats on a 12.3% vote share. Its then leader, Bronislaw Geremek, tried and failed to form a government, so that the UD became the main opposition to the 1991–92 Olszewski government. Upon its fall in June 1992, Hanna Suchocka of the UD formed a seven-party coalition, becoming Poland's first female Prime Minister and quickly establishing a measure of order in government business. Her administration negotiated the passage of the "small" constitution, but it fell in May 1993 on losing key support in the *Sejm*. In the September 1993 elections the UD improved its representation to 74 seats, but fell back to 10.6% of the vote and third place in the parliamentary order, thus becoming the principal opposition to the new coalition government of Social Democracy of the Polish Republic and the Polish Peasant Party.

The other UW component, the KLD (an affiliate of the International Democrat Union), had been founded in February 1990 as the outgrowth of a post-1988 Gdánsk-based group led by journalist Donald Tusk, previously called the Congress of Liberals. Supported largely by white-collar and business sectors, it advocated the privatization of state enterprises and won 37 *Sejm* seats in 1991 on a vote share of 7.5%. In the September 1993 elections it failed to reach the 5% threshold for representation.

The UW candidate in the 1995 presidential elections was Jacek Kurón, who achieved a creditable third place in the first round with 9.2% of the national vote.

Movement for the Reconstruction of Poland
Ruch Odrodzenia Polski (ROP)
   Address. c/o Zgromadzente Narodowe, Warsaw
   Leadership. Jan Olszewski (chair)

The ROP was launched by Olszewski as a radical pro-market formation on the strength of his respectable fourth place (with 6.9% of the vote) in the first round of the November 1995 presidential election. Then identified with the Centre Alliance (PC), Olszewski had become Prime Minister in the wake of the 1991 parliamentary elections, heading a centre-right coalition which had eventually fallen in June 1992 in acrimonious circumstances related to the government's proposal to publish lists of Communist-era collaborators. Expelled from the PC, Olszewski had become leader of the more right-wing Movement for the Republic (RdR) but had been replaced in December 1993 following the general defeat of pro-market formations in the September 1993 parliamentary elections, although from April 1994 he became honorary chair of what was by then a deeply divided party.

Non-Party Bloc for Reform
Bezpartyjny Blok Wspierania Reform (BBWR)
   Address. c/o Sejm, Warsaw
   Leadership. Zbigniew Religa (chair), Stanislaw Kowolik (parliamentary leader)

The BBWR was founded in June 1993 in an attempt to provide a party political base for President Lech Walesa, the formation's initials being the same as those of the party established in 1928 by supporters of Marshal Pilsudski, the authoritarian inter-war Polish leader much revered by Walesa. Criticized by established parliamentary parties as a threat to the democratic system, the new grouping failed to generate much impetus and only just surmounted the 5% barrier to representation in the September 1993 parliamentary elections, winning 5.4% of the vote and 16 *Sejm* seats. President Walesa subsequently distanced himself from the BBWR, which became identified with the political ambitions of Zbigniew Religa, a member of the Senate. On June 1, 1994, Religa announced his resignation as BBWR chair because of differences with other leaders; he retracted his resignation later the same day. In 1995 the BBWR joined with the Confederation for an Independent Poland and other right-wing parties in creating a "Patriotic Camp" alliance in opposition to the coalition government dominated by Social Democracy of the Polish Republic (SRP). The

BBWR was not prominent in President Walesa's unsuccessful re-election bid in November 1995, when he won only 33.1% of the first-round vote (compared with 40% in 1990) and was defeated by the SRP leader in the second round.

Polish Peasant Party

Polskie Stronnictwo Ludowe (PSL)

Address. 4 ul. Grzybowska, 00131 Warsaw

Telephone. (#48-22) 206020

Leadership. Waldemar Pawlak (president), Bogdan Pek (vice-president), Gabriel Janowski (parliamentary leader)

The PSL was founded in 1945 by Stanislaw Mikolajczyk after the leadership of the historic Peasant Party (founded in Galicia in 1895) had opted for close co-operation with the Communists. In November 1949, after Mikolajczyk had been ousted by leftist PSL members, the two groups merged as the United Peasant Party (*Zjednoczone Stronnictwo Ludowe*, ZSL), which became part of the Communist-dominated National Unity Front. The ZSL was thus committed to the goal of transforming Poland into a socialist society, although private peasant ownership of land was guaranteed by the government from 1956 and by constitutional guarantee from 1983. ZSL representatives were consistently included in the government and other state bodies under Communist rule. In the 1980s the party sometimes criticized aspects of government policy affecting the agricultural sector. In 1987 it supported the broad government programme for the democratization of political life and introduction of market mechanisms, while supporting the maintenance of the existing power structure.

In August 1989 a group of rural activists revived the PSL on the basis of its 1946 programme, becoming known as the Polish Peasant Party-Wilnanóv (PSL-W). The following month the ZSL was included in the new Solidarity-led coalition government and in November relaunched itself as the Reborn Polish Peasant Party (PSL-O). Six months later, in May 1990, the PSL-O, PSL-W and some members of Rural Solidarity held a unification congress to constitute the present PSL, which aimed to establish itself as the "third force" in Polish politics. Thereafter the party experienced serious divisions over attempts by some members to secure the expulsion of ex-ZSL officials (who nevertheless remained entrenched).

In September 1990 the PSL withdrew its support from the Solidarity-led government, partly because it was deprived of the agriculture portfolio in a reshuffle and partly in disagreement with government agricultural policy. The then PSL leader, Roman Bartoszcze, received 7.2% of the vote in the first round of presidential elections in November 1990. Bartoszcze was replaced in June 1991 by Waldemar Pawlak, who restored unity to the party and led it to a creditable 8.7% of the vote and 48 seats in the October 1991 *Sejm* elections, in which it headed a Programmatic Alliance list. Although it broadly supported the subsequent centre-right Olszewski government, the PSL opposed its proposal to release secret police files to expose informers of the Communist era. This issue brought down the government in June 1992, whereupon Pawlak was endorsed by the *Sejm* as the new Prime Minister, but was unable to form a government.

Benefiting from rural disenchantment with economic "shock therapy", the PSL polled strongly in the September 1993 parliamentary elections, becoming the second largest party with 132 seats in the *Sejm* on an overall vote share of 15.4% (and a historically high 46% of the peasant vote). It then opted to join a coalition government with Social Democracy of the Polish Republic (SRP), the largest party, which agreed that Pawlak should be Prime Minister in light of lingering doubts about its Communist ancestry. The new coalition displayed tensions almost from the start, notably over government appointments, and in November 1994 the PSL deputy president was dismissed as chair of the *Sejm*'s privatization committee on the grounds that he had tried to block or slow down the sell-off of state enterprises. It also came into protracted conflict with President Walesa and the latter's concepts of presidential government, the eventual result being Pawlak's resignation in February 1995 and the appointment of an SRP Prime Minister, although the SRP/PSL coalition was maintained. In the November 1995 presidential elections Pawlak received a modest 4.3% of the first-round vote.

Social Democracy of the Polish Republic

Socjaldemokracja Rzeczpospolitej Polskiej (SRP)

Address. 44A ul. Rozbrat, 00419 Warsaw

Telephone. (#48-22) 621–0341

Fax. (#48-22) 621–6657

Leadership. Józef Oleksy (chair), Leszek Miller and Izabella Sierakowska (deputy chairs), Jerzy Szmajdzinski (general secretary)

The SRP was founded in January 1990 upon the dissolution of the former ruling (Communist) Polish United Workers' Party (*Polska Zjednoczona Partia Robotnicza*, PZPR), of which it is the organizational successor, but with a dedication to democratic socialism replacing previous theses. The PUWP was founded in December 1948 by a merger of the (Communist) Polish Workers' Party (PWP)—which had superseded the Communist Party of Poland established in 1918—and the Polish Socialist Party (after "deviationists" had been expelled from both these parties). The PWP had formed part of the Soviet-backed "Lublin Committee", which had declared itself the provisional government of Poland towards the end of 1944 and had later been the dominant force in the post-war coalition regime.

In 1956 the party's central committee removed from its political bureau all "Stalinist" elements and appointed as the party's first secretary Wladyslaw Gomulka (who had served five years in prison for "Titoism" and "nationalist deviationism"); he thereupon advocated the theory of "different roads to socialism" (i.e. not necessarily adherence to the Soviet model) and reversed a number of earlier repressive measures. In 1959, however, Gomulka emphasized the need to oppose "revisionism" which led to questioning the fundamentals of Marxism-Leninism, and in 1964 the PUWP firmly supported the USSR in the Sino-Soviet dispute. The party also supported the Soviet military intervention in Czechoslovakia in 1968, in which Polish troops participated.

Following riots caused by major increases in food and fuel prices Gomulka was in December 1970 replaced by Edward Gierek, who thereupon announced a price freeze, wage increases and other reforms. In September 1980 Gierek was replaced by Stanislaw Kania, who was faced with the fact that something like a quarter of the PUWP members had joined the Solidarity free trade union movement led by Lech Walesa. A party congress held in July 1981 was attended by many first-time participants and also by Solidarity members. However, in October 1981 Kania was replaced by Gen. Wojciech Jaruzelski, who was already Chairman of the Council of Ministers. Upon the imposition of martial law on Dec. 13, 1981, and the effective banning of Solidarity many leading party members were relieved of their posts and a number were detained for trial on various charges (among them Gierek). Serious industrial and social disturbances ensued in many parts of the country, but gradually the government was able to re-establish full control. In February 1983 Gen. Jaruzelski found it necessary to call on the PUWP to launch a campaign to eliminate "apathy" within the party.

The 10th PUWP congress was held on June 29–July 3, 1986, and was attended by 1,776 elected delegates and 107 foreign delegates. In his opening speech Gen. Jaruzelski said, with reference to the banned Solidarity and other dissident groups: "The situation in the country today is characterized by the spread of accord, the strengthening of public order and also the proceeding disintegration and social isolation of anti-state groups". He added that further measures would be taken "to pardon and soften the punishment of perpetrators of offences against the state and social order".

(Under a bill passed by the *Sejm* on July 17, 1986, an estimated 20,000 persons were, by Sept. 15, 1986, released from custody and/or pardoned.) The 10th congress was addressed by Mikhail Gorbachev, the General Secretary of the Communist Party of the Soviet Union, who endorsed the statements made by Gen. Jaruzelski.

Leadership changes resulting from the 10th congress meant that Gen. Jaruzelski was one of only two Politburo members remaining from the pre-1981 leadership. The purge process continued at central committee sessions in June and December 1988, more than half of the members of both bodies being replaced during 1988 alone. The new leadership strove to contain the political challenge posed by Solidarity, agreeing in April 1989 to partial democratization of the political process but then finding that the pro-democracy movement was uncontainable. After Solidarity had made a virtual clean sweep of unreserved seats in the June 1989 parliamentary elections, the following month Gen. Jaruzelski was elected to a redefined presidency by a bare minimum (50% plus one) of legislative ballots, vacating the post of PZPR first secretary in favour of the outgoing Prime Minister, Mieczyslaw Rakowski. Only four Communists were included in the Solidarity-led coalition government formed in September 1989, although by prior agreement their portfolios included interior and defence.

Constitutional amendments approved in December 1989 deleted reference to the PZPR's "leading role" in state and society and abandoned the goal of creating a "socialist economic system". The following month a PZPR special congress voted to disband the old party and to form the new SRP, abandoning Marxism-Leninism and embracing European democratic socialist principles. The SRP's successor status was acknowledged, not least by its laying claim to the PZPR's assets (many of which were, however, confiscated by the government on grounds of suspect legal title). Quickly forging an alliance with the All-Poland Trade Unions' Federation (OPZZ) which became the core of the Democratic Left Alliance (SLD), the SRP backed the candidacy of Wlodzimierz Cimoszewicz in the November-December 1990 presidential elections; but he came fourth in the first round, receiving only 9.2% of the vote.

Following Lech Walesa's victory in the second round, the SRP went into opposition and concentrated on maximizing its considerable organizational advantages. These yielded results in the October 1991 parliamentary elections, when the SRP-led SLD list took second place among 29 parties that obtained *Sejm* representation, winning 60 seats on a 12% vote share. Its deputies faced considerable hostility in the new legislature, but the party's image improved rapidly in the country as transition to a market economy took a social toll and the centre-right became increasingly fragmented. In the September 1993 parliamentary elections the SRP/SLD became the largest formation in the *Sejm*, winning 171 seats with 20.4% of the vote. Despite its seniority, the SRP opted to accept participation in a coalition headed by the more liberal Polish Peasant Party (PSL), being conscious of its need to prove its democratic credentials. The advent of the SRP/PSL coalition was seen as marking the end of the initial domination of post-Communist politics by Solidarity-inspired parties and a sign that the "successor" label was no longer an automatic barrier to political success.

The PSL held the premiership until February 1995, when Józef Oleksy of the SRP took the post, amid chronic strains between the government and President Walesa, who used his power of veto on a series of measures adopted by parliament. The SLD candidate in the November 1995 presidential elections was the then SRP leader, Aleksander Kwaśniewski, who headed the first-round polling with 35.1% of the vote and defeated Walesa in the second with 51.7%. Sworn in as President in December 1995, Kwaśniewski vacated the SRP chair, to which Oleksy was elected in January 1996, three days after his enforced resignation as Prime Minister over allegations (later discounted by the authorities) that he had been an informant of Moscow. Oleksy was replaced as Prime Minister by Wlodzimierz Cimoszewicz (the 1990 presidential candidate but not an SRP member), who headed a new coalition of the SRP and the PSL.

Solidarity
Solidarność

Address. c/o Zgromadzente Narodowe, Warsaw
Leadership. Marian Krzaklewski (chair)

The political grouping of the mid-1990s using the celebrated Solidarity title is a small descendant of the nation-wide free trade union movement of the 1980s that effectively brought about the downfall of Communist rule in Poland (and indirectly elsewhere in Eastern Europe). The recent history of Solidarity dates from Lech Walesa's resignation in 1990 as leader of the national trade union movement. Walesa failed to secure the election of his favoured successor, Leszek Kaczyński, and did not enjoy close relations with the new leader, Marian Krzaklewski. Under KrzaklewskiSolidarity decided to contest the parliamentary elections of October 1991, when it achieved an unexpectedly low 5.05% of the vote and 27 seats in the *Sejm*. Increasingly, tensions emerged between the union and its parliamentary representatives, who included prominent individuals such as Bogdan Borusewicz

and Jan Rulewski. The trade union became both more right-wing, reflected in its support for lustration and decommunization and its readiness to detect a resurgence of Communist forces, as well as more radical, with increasing propensity to industrial action and hostility to privatization policies. Significant elements of Solidarity also displayed animosity to its former leader, President Walesa, manifested at the Solidarity congress following the fall of the Olszewski government in June 1992 and in subsequent demonstrations supporting the unsubstantiated notion that Walesa had acted as a Communist collaborator.

However, Solidarity deputies proved instrumental in the negotiations leading to the formation of Hanna Suchocka's seven-party coalition in July 1992; although the grouping did not enter the coalition, it undertook to support it. Widespread strikes in the summer and autumn of 1992 appeared to threaten this agreement, but positive signs of a union-government accord then emerged, including negotiations (also undertaken with numerous other trade unions) for a corporatist-style package of legislation known as the Pact for Industry. Further strikes in the mining industry in December and a wave of strikes in the public sector in spring 1993 then brought relations to breaking point. The parliamentary group had by then divided, with some Solidarity deputies continuing to support the government, while others voted against it on the budget, public sector pay and pensions. It was Solidarity which tabled the successful vote of no confidence in Suchocka's government in May 1993, although it appeared that the leadership did not expect the motion to pass. As a result, a number of prominent parliamentarians withdrew (or were withdrawn) from political activity on Solidarity's behalf.

Few elements of Solidarity proved receptive to Walesa's call for a new Non-Party Bloc for Reform (BBWR) in June 1993 and Walesa clearly dissociated himself from the trade union, which retained a vocal anti-Walesa element. In the September 1993 elections some erstwhile deputies stood on the Democratic Union's list, but Solidarity again stood under its own banner, obtaining only 4.9% of the vote and no *Sejm* seats, although in simultaneous senate elections it took 13.3% and 10 seats. By the end of 1993 Solidarity was profoundly weakened, both as a direct political force and as a trade union. Solidarity backed President Walesa's unsuccessful re-election bid in November, although relations between the former Solidarity leader and the latter-day grouping of that name remained distant. Undaunted by recent setbacks, the eighth Solidarity congress in June 1996 resolved that the formation would contest the parliamentary elections due in 1997. A Solidarity Electoral Action organization was set up, the aim being to build a broad alliance of the centre-right to challenge the incumbent government dominated by Social Democracy of the Polish Republic.

Union of Labour
Unia Pracy (UP)

Address. 17 ul. Grójecka, Warsaw

Leadership. Ryszard Bugaj (parliamentary leader)

The UP was founded in June 1992 as a merger of two small parliamentary groupings of Solidarity provenance, namely Labour Solidarity (*Solidarność Pracy*, SP) and the Democratic Social Movement (RDS), plus elements of the divided Polish Socialist Party (PPS) and the Great Poland Social Democratic Union. A former underground Solidarity leader, Prof. Bugaj (the UP leader) had previously been prominent in the Democratic Action Civil Movement (ROAD)—later part of the Democratic Union, which became the Freedom Union—and had been an articulate critic of the economic "shock therapy" policies of the immediate post-Communist period. In the October 1991 parliamentary elections the SP had won four *Sejm* seats with a 2.1% vote share. Despite the paucity of its resources, the broader UP achieved an impressive 7.3% of the vote in the September 1993 parliamentary elections, winning 41 *Sejm* seats and becoming the main left-wing opposition to the new government dominated by Social Democracy of the Polish Republic but headed by the Polish Peasant Party (until 1995).

Other Parties and Groups

Of some 300 other political parties and movements in existence in Poland by mid-1996, the following is a listing of those perceived to be of some significance.

Christian Democratic Labour Party (*Chrzecijasko-Demokratyczne Stronnictwo Pracy*, CDSP), led by Tomasz Jackowski, founded in 1989 as successor to pre-Communist party banned in 1946, presented joint list with Christian Democratic Party in 1991 elections, winning 2.4% and five seats; unrepresented since 1993; affiliated to Christian Democrat International.

Christian Democratic Party (*Partia Chrzecijakich Demokratow*, PChD), led by Pawel Laczkowski, moderate Catholic grouping allied with Christian Democratic Labour Party in 1991 elections; affiliated to Christian Democrat International.

Christian National Movement-Polish Action (*Ruch Chrzecijansko-Narodowe-Akcja Polska*, RChN-AP), formed in February 1993 by Antoni Macierewicz, who as Interior Minister in the post-1991 Olszewski coalition had favoured publication of the files of Communist-era collaborators, bringing about the government's fall in June 1992 and his own expulsion from the Christian National Movement.

Christian Peasant Union (*Sojusz Ludowo-Chrzecijanski*, SLCh), led by Józef Slisz and Artur Balazs, contested 1991 elections within Peasant Alliance, re-established separate identity in 1992 prior to joining Suchocka coalition government, failed to win representation in 1993.

Conservative Liberal Movement (*Ruch Konserwatywno Liberalny*, RKL), led by Jan Krzysztof Bielecki (a former Prime Minister) and Andrzej Olechowski (a former Foreign Minister), launched in April 1995 on a platform placing more emphasis on conservatism than on liberalism.

Conservative Party (*Partia Konserwatywna*, PK), led by Aleksander Hall, formed in December 1992 as merger of several groups, including right-wing faction of Democratic Union (later Freedom Union); member of unsuccessful Homeland coalition with Christian National Union and Peasant Alliance in 1993 elections, joining five-party Covenant for Poland in May 1994.

Democratic Party (*Stronnictwo Demokratyczne*, SD), led by Zbigniew Adamczyk, founded in 1939, became Communist-era Front party for professionals and intellectuals, independent from mid-1989 and participated in Solidarity-led coalition, won one *Sejm* seat in 1991 (with 1.4%) and none in 1993.

German Minority Socio-Cultural Associations, led by Hans Krol, representing ethnic Germans in Upper and Lower Silesia, won seven *Sejm* seats in 1991, retained four in 1993 (being exempted from new 5% threshold rule).

Movement for the Republic (*Ruch dla Rzeczpospolitej*, RdR), led by Romuald Szeremietiew, founded in June 1992 as the Christian Democratic Forum (*Forum Chrzecijasko-Demokratyczne*, FChD) by dissidents of the Centre Alliance led by recently-ousted Prime Minister Jan Olszewski, became the RdR in September 1992 and was part of the "hard" opposition to the 1992–93 Suchocka government; failed to win seats in September 1993 elections, became badly divided after replacement of Olszewski in December 1993, joined Covenant for Poland in May 1994; affiliated to Christian Democrat International.

Party X (*Partia X*), founded in 1991 by Stanislaw (Stan) Tymiński (a Canadian Pole and distant runner-up to Lech Walesa in 1990 presidential election), named after "X" placed on ballot papers, favours rapid transition to market economy; most of its candidates declared ineligible for 1991 elections because of forged supporter lists, but still won three seats (and 0.5%), failed to retain any in 1993.

Peasant Alliance (*Porozumienie Ludowe*, PL), derived from Rural Solidarity version of Polish Peasant Party opposed to latter's Communist provenance, won 5.5% and 28 *Sejm* seats in 1991, thereafter in government until withdrawing in April 1993; participated in unsuccessful Homeland coalition with Christian National Union and Conservative Party in 1993 elections, joining Covenant for Poland in May 1994.

Polish Economic Programme (*Polski Program Gospodarczy*, PPG), led by Tomasz Bankowski, launched in 1992 by majority ("big beer") faction of Polish Party of the Friends of Beer, participated in 1992–93 Suchocka coalition; unrepresented and inactive since 1993.

Polish National Party-Polish National Commonwealth (*Polskie Stronnictwo Narodowe-Polska Wspolnota Narodowa*, PSN-PWN), led by Boleslaw Tejkowski, far-right formation linked with violence and intimidation directed against non-Poles.

Polish Socialist Party (*Polska Partia Socjalistyczna*, PPS), led by Jan Mulak, founded in 1892, operated underground during World War II, provided Poland's first post-war Prime Minister, obliged to merge with the Communists in 1948, but maintained by exiles in London and elsewhere; was revived in Poland in 1987 but constant internal divisions contributed to electoral failure in 1991 and 1993 (when one PPS faction joined the Democratic Left Alliance); in February 1996 the two main factions reunited under Mulak's leadership; affiliated to the Socialist International through the Socialist Union of Central and Eastern Europe.

Union of Political Realism (*Unia Polityki Realnej*, UPR), led by Janusz Korwin-Mikke, extreme right-wing formation embracing nationalism, antisemitism and Catholicism, won three *Sejm* seats in 1991 (with 2.3%), unsuccessful in 1993.

Portugal

Capital: Lisbon

Population: 9,800,000 (1995E)

Under Portugal's 1976 constitution as amended, legislative authority is vested in the unicameral Assembly of the Republic (*Assembláia da República*), currently consisting of 230 members elected for a four-year term (subject to dissolution) by universal adult suffrage of those aged 18 and over according to a system of proportional representation in multi-member constituencies. The head of state is the President, who is popularly elected for a five-year term (once renewable) by absolute majority, a failure to achieve which in a first round of voting requires the two leading candidates to contest a second round. The President appoints the Prime Minister, who selects his or her ministerial team, all subject to approval by the Assembly. There is also a Supreme Council of National Defence, a 13–member Constitutional Tribunal and an advisory Council of State chaired by the President.

Portuguese political parties and parliamentary groups are eligible for annual subsidies from public funds, on the following basis: (i) a sum equivalent to 1/225th of the minimum national salary is payable on each vote obtained at the most recent Assembly elections; (ii) a sum equivalent to four times the minimum salary, plus one-third of the minimum national salary multiplied by the number of deputies in an Assembly group, is payable to defray deputies' secretarial costs.

Elections to the Assembly on Oct. 1, 1995, resulted as follows: Socialist Party (PS) 112 seats (with 43.9% of the vote), Social Democratic Party (PSD) 88 (34.0%), Popular Party 15 (9.1%), United Democratic Coalition 15 (9.1%). A presidential election on Jan. 14, 1996, resulted in Jorge Sampaio (PS) winning a 53.8% first-round victory over Aníbal Cavaco Silva (PSD).

Popular Party

Partido Popular (PP)

Address. 5 largo Adelino Amaro da Costa, 1196 Lisbon

Telephone. (#351–1) 886–9735

Fax. (#351–1) 886–0454

Leadership. Manuel Fernando do Silva Monteiro (chair), Luis Felipe Paes Beiroco (secretary-general)

The conservative Christian democratic PP was established in 1974 as the Democratic Social Centre (*Centro Democrático Social*, CDS). It quickly began using the suffix "Popular Party" to distinguish itself from the main Social Democratic Party (PSD), being formally known as the CDS-PP until opting for the shorter PP title in the 1990s.

The CDS was founded on the basis of an earlier Manifesto Association, (*Associação Programa*) by Prof. Diogo Freitas do Amaral, who had been a member of the Council of State under the quasi-fascist Salazarist regime overthrown in 1974. The CDS was attacked by left-wing groups in 1974–75. In the April 1975 constituent elections, in which it allied with the Christian Democrats, it won 16 of the 250 seats. In 1976 it became the largest party in the new Assembly, with 15.9% of the vote and 42 of the 263 seats. The CDS joined a Socialist-led government in January–July 1978, but fought the 1979 and 1980 elections as part of the victorious Democratic Alliance, led by the Social Democratic Party (PSD); Freitas do Amaral became Deputy Prime Minister in the ensuing coalition government. The coalition ended in April 1983, and the CDS, standing alone, won only 12.4% and 30 seats in that month's Assembly elections; it then elected a new leader, Dr Francisco António Lucas Pires. In 1985 the CDS declined further, to 9.8% and 22 seats. The leadership of the CDS passed in 1985 to a former Salazarist minister, Prof. Adriano Alves Moreira.

Freitas do Amaral, endorsed by the CDS and PSD, narrowly lost the second round of the 1986 presidential elections to Mário Soares of the Socialist Party. The CDS continued to decline, securing only 4.4% and four seats in 1987, and Freitas do Amaral was re-elected leader at a congress in January 1988.

What was now known as the PP won only five Assembly seats in the 1991 elections (with a 4.4% vote share), after which Freitas do Amaral finally resigned the party leadership. In the European Parliament elections of June 1994, however, the party regained support, winning three of Portugal's 25 seats on a 12.5% vote share. This European success did not moderate the party's deep reservations about Portuguese membership of the European Union, which struck something of a chord in the October 1995 Assembly elections, when the PP advanced to 9.1% of the vote and 15 seats.

The PP is an affiliate of the Christian Democrat International, although its three European Parliament members sit in the Union for Europe group, the biggest components of which are the French Gaullist Rally for the Republic and *Forza Italia* of Italy.

Portuguese Communist Party

Partido Comunista Portugués (PCP)

Address. 1 rua Soeiro Pereira Gomes, 1699 Lisbon

Telephone. (#351–1) 793–6272

Fax. (#351–1) 796–9216

Leadership. Alvaro Barreirinhas Cunhal (president), Carlos Carvalhas (secretary-general)

The PCP was founded in March 1921 by the pro-Bolshevik wing of the Socialist Party (PS) and was banned from May 1926 until April 1974. Its leader since the 1940s has been Cunhal, a charismatic Stalinist who was imprisoned throughout the 1950s and was then in exile until 1974. The PCP took part in interim governments between May 1974 and July 1976. In April 1975 it won 30 seats (out of 250) in constituent elections, with 12.5% of the vote; in April 1976 it won 40 seats in the Assembly, with 14.6%, but in June its presidential candidate won only 7.6%. From 1979 to 1986 the PCP was in an electoral front—the Popular Unity Alliance (APU)—with the small Portuguese Democratic Movement (MDP/CDE). The PCP itself won 44 seats in the Assembly in 1979, 39 in 1980 and 44 in 1983. In 1985 the APU won 15.4% and 38 seats, almost all for the PCP. In the 1986 presidential elections the PCP at first backed Dr Francisco Salgado Zenha, but in the second round it reluctantly endorsed Mário Soares of the PS.

In 1987 the PCP formed a new front, the United Democratic Coalition (DCU), along with a minority section of the MDP known as the Democratic Intervention (ID), some independent left-wingers and the ecologist Greens. The CDU secured 31 seats with 12.1% of the vote, but the PCP-led parliamentary bloc rose from fourth to third place as a result of the eclipse of the Democratic Renewal Party (PRD); it also held its three seats in the simultaneous European Parliament elections. In early 1988 the PCP experienced internal divisions as it prepared for a congress, with some members calling for "democratization" and the Cunhal leadership insisting on maintaining rigid pro-Soviet orthodoxy.

In the event, the 12th PCP congress in December 1988 showed some awareness of developments in the Soviet Union by making a formal commitment to freedom of the press and multi-party politics.

Yet even as communism was collapsing all over Eastern Europe in 1989–90, the PCP majority maintained a hardline view of events, showing no sympathy with the popular aspirations to multi-party democracy. The electoral consequence was that the PCP-dominated CDU fell back to 17 seats (8.8% of the vote) in the 1991 elections and to 15 seats (8.6%) in October 1995.

Social Democratic Party
Partido Social Democrata (PSD)
Address. 9 rua de So Caetano, 1296 Lisbon
Telephone. (#351–1) 395–2140
Fax. (#351–1) 397–6967
Leadership. Marcelo Rebelo de Sousa (leader), Eduardo de Azevedo Soares (secretary-general)

Centre-right rather than social democratic in orientation, the PSD was founded in May 1974 as the Popular Democratic Party (*Partido Popular Democrático*, PPD) and adopted the PSD label in 1976, when the Portuguese political scene created by the 1974 revolution was heavily tilted to the left. The party took part in five of the first six provisional governments established after the April 1974 revolution. It was in opposition in June–September 1975 and from June 1976; it supported the election of Gen. António Ramalho Eanes as President in 1976. It was the second largest party in the April 1975 constituent elections, with 27% of the votes, and in the April 1976 legislative elections (24%).

The PSD supported the non-party government of November 1978–June 1979, and fought the 1979 elections along with the Democratic Social Centre (CDS, later the Popular Party, PP) as the Democratic Alliance, winning 79 seats for itself. The then PSD leader, Dr Francisco Sá Carneiro, became Prime Minister. Fresh elections in October 1980 increased the PSD total to 82 seats; Sá Carneiro died in December, and was succeeded by Dr Francisco Pinto Balsemão, co-founder of the PSD, who brought the Popular Monarchist Party (PPM) into the coalition in September 1981. The PSD held 75 seats in the April 1983 elections, which it fought alone, and in June it joined the Socialist Party (PS) in a new coalition government, with a new PSD leader, the former Prime Minister (1978–79) Carlos Mota Pinto, as deputy leader.

In October 1985 the PSD increased its vote to 29.9% and won 88 seats—the largest bloc—in the Assembly, allowing it to form a minority government under Aníbal Cavaco Silva, who had been elected party leader in May 1985. He subsequently strengthened his control over the party and after the presidential elections of 1986, in which the PSD endorsed the losing CDS candidate, he opposed all suggestions for alliance with other parties. On April 3, 1987, his government lost a vote of confidence concerning the integration of Portugal into the European Community in 1987.

In early elections in July 1987 the PSD secured a greatly increased vote—50.2%—and 148 seats, giving it the absolute majority which it had sought (the first in the Assembly since 1974). In simultaneous elections to the European Parliament, the nine PSD members appointed in January 1986 were replaced by 10 popularly-elected PSD members (from the total of 24 Portuguese representatives). In August Cavaco Silva was reappointed Prime Minister of an almost wholly PSD government.

The PSD retained governmental office in the October 1991 parliamentary elections, although with a slightly reduced majority of 135 of 230 seats on a 50.4% vote share. In the June 1994 European Parliament elections the party fell to 34.4%, taking only nine of the 25 Portuguese seats. This result and the PSD's negative opinion poll ratings impelled Cavaco Silva to resign from the party leadership in January 1995, although he remained Prime Minister until the October elections to prepare for a presidential challenge. Under the new leadership of Joaquim Fernando Nogueira, the PSD lost the October contest, although its retention of 88 seats on a 34% vote share was a better performance than many had predicted.

Cavaco Silva's presidential ambitions were also thwarted by the swing of the political pendulum to the left. Standing as the PSD candidate in January 1996, he was defeated by the Socialist candidate in the first voting round, winning only 46.2% of the vote. The PSD's somewhat drastic response to these twin setbacks was to elect a new leader, namely Marcelo Rebelo de Sousa, a popular media pundit who had never held ministerial office.

Of the PSD's nine European Parliament representatives, eight belong to the European Liberal, Democratic and Reformist Group (although the party is not a member of the Liberal International) and the other one to the European People's Party group (although the party is not a member of the Christian Democrat International either).

Socialist Party
Partido Socialista (PSP)
Address. 2 Largo do Rato, 1200 Lisbon
Telephone. (#351–1) 383–0376
Fax. (#351–1) 383–3845
Leadership. António Guterres (general secretary), Almeida Santos (chair)

Founded in 1875, the early Socialist Party was a member of the Second International and played a minor role in the first period of democratic government in Portugal (1910–26). Forced underground during the period of the fascistic "New State" (1928–74), Socialists were active in various democratic movements. In 1964 Dr Mário Alberto Nobre Lopes Soares and others formed Portuguese Socialist Action (*Accão Socialista Portuguesa*, ASP), which led to the reconstruction of the Socialist Party (PS) among exiles in West Germany in 1973.

Soares was repeatedly arrested and banished from Portugal, but the April 1974 revolution permitted his return and the PS took part in the coalition government formed in May. In April 1975 the party won 116 of the 250 seats in a Constituent Assembly which drew up a constitution aspiring to a "transition to socialism", although in July–September the PS was excluded from the government, along with other parties except the Portuguese Communist Party (PCP). In April 1976 the PS won 35% of the vote and 107 of the 263 seats in the new Assembly. In June it supported the successful presidential candidate, Gen. António Ramalho Eanes, who in July appointed Soares as Prime Minister of a minority PS government including independents and military men. That was followed in January–July 1978 by a coalition, also led by Soares, of the PS and the Democratic Social Centre (CDS, later the Popular Party, PP). The PS supported a government of independents formed in October 1978.

The PS later suffered numerous defections, was decisively defeated in the 1979 Assembly elections, and went into opposition. In June 1980 it formed the Republican and Socialist Front (*Frente Republicana e Socialista*, FRS) electoral coalition with the (now defunct) Independent Social Democratic Action party (ASDI) and the Left Union for a Socialist Democracy (UEDS, formed in 1978 by António Lopes Cardoso, a former PS Agriculture Minister). The FRS won 74 seats in the October 1980 Assembly elections. Reforms in 1981 (since reversed) increased the power of the PS general secretary, leading to dissent within the party.

In the April 1993 elections the PS gained 36.2% of the valid vote and 101 (out of 250) seats; it then formed a coalition government with the Social Democratic Party (PSD). In 1985 that government lost a vote of confidence and in the ensuing elections the PS fell to 20.7% and 57 seats. It was excluded from the minority government formed by the PSD. In February 1986, however, Soares was elected as the country's first civilian President in over 50 years, whereupon he resigned his PS posts. His 1986 opponents included two former PS ministers—Maria de Lourdes Pintasilgo, backed by the Popular Democratic Union (UDP) and Dr Francisco Salgado Zenha, backed by the PCP.

The sixth PS congress in June 1986 elected Manuel Vitor Ribeiro Constâncio (a former Finance Minister and central bank governor, regarded as a pragmatic left-winger) as party leader. It also significantly moderated the party's programme and altered its structure. A minority faction developed around Dr Jaime Gama, a former Foreign Minister close to Soares, but he was later reconciled with the leadership, whereafter the *soaristas* (who wanting more active opposition to the PSD, including co-operation with the Communists) were led by the President's son, João Soares.

Elections in July 1987 gave the PS 22.3% of the vote and 60 seats, so that it remained the leading opposition party. It also held its six European Parliament seats, which were subject to direct election for the first time. The October 1991 parliamentary elections resulted in the PS advancing to 72 seats (on a 30% vote share), but the party remained in opposition, with its leadership passing in February 1992 from Jorge Sampaio to António Gutterez, a young technocrat with a non-ideological approach to politics. The party achieved an all-time high national vote in the December 1993 local elections and again outpolled the ruling PSD in the June 1994 European Parliament elections, in which its vote share was 34.9% and its seat tally 10 of the 25 allocated to Portugal. In the October 1995 Assembly elections Gutterez led the PS back to governmental office, albeit in a narrow minority position in terms of strict parliamentary arithmetic, its seat tally being 112 out of 230 (on a 43.9% vote share). The new minority PS government, which was expected to obtain the external support of the United Democratic Left on most key issues, announced a programme of accelerated privatization of state enterprises, combined with introduction of a guaranteed minimum wage, social and educational improvements and regional devolution for mainland Portugal. In January 1996 Socialist political authority was consolidated when the PS presidential candidate Sampaio (who had become mayor of Lisbon) was elected to the top state post with a commanding 53.8% of the first-round vote.

The PS is a member of the Socialist International. Its representatives in the European Parliament sit in the Party of European Socialists group.

United Democratic Coalition

Coligação Democrático Unitária (CDU)

> *Address.* c/o Assembláia da República, Lisbon
> *Leadership.* Alvaro Barreirinhas Cunhal

The CDU is the electoral front organization of the Portuguese Communist Party (PCP), dating from prior to the 1979 Assembly elections, in which the PCP presented a joint list with the Portuguese Democratic Movement (MDP) called the United People's Alliance (APU). The APU won 47 seats in 1979, before falling to 41 in 1980 and to 38 in 1985, its constituent formations having campaigned separately in 1983. In the 1986 presidential election the APU backed the independent candidacy of former Prime Minister Maria de Lourdes Pintasilgo in the first round, switching with reluctance in the second to Mario Soares of the Socialist Party (PS). Following the MDP's withdrawal in November 1986, the pro-Soviet PCP converted the APU into the CDU, which also included a group of MDP dissidents, the Greens and a number of independent leftists.

The new CDU won 31 Assembly seats in 1987, seven less than the APU in 1985. In the October 1991 elections, with the Soviet Union in its death throes, CDU representation was further reduced to 17 seats (with 8.8% of the vote). In the June 1994 European Parliament elections the CDU list (in which Greens were prominent) improved to 11.2% and won three of Portugal's 25 seats. In the October 1995 Assembly elections the CDU slipped further to 15 seats (8.6% of the vote), thereafter offering qualified parliamentary backing to the new PS minority government.

The three CDU representatives in the European Parliament sit in the Confederal European United Left group.

Other Parties

Communist Party of Portuguese Workers (*Partido Comunista dos Trabalhadores Portugueses*, PCTP), led by Garcia Pereira, a Maoist faction.

Communist Party Reconstituted (*Partido Comunista Reconstruido*, PCR), led by Eduardo Pires.

The Greens (*Os Verdes*), led by Mario Tomá, left-leaning environmentalist party, participates in Communist-dominated United Democratic Coalition.

National Solidarity Party (*Partido Solidariedade Nacional*, PSN), led by Manuel Sergio, pensioners' party founded in 1990, won one Assembly seat in 1991, but none in 1995.

Popular Democratic Union (*Unio Democrática Popular*, UDP), Marxist-Leninist group, component of Movement for Popular Unity (MUP) that had one Assembly seat in late 1970s and early 1980s.

Popular Monarchist Party (*Partido Popular Monárquico*, PPM), led by Gonçalo Ribeiro Telles and Augusto Ferreira do Amaral, pro-market monarchist formation, won six Assembly seats in 1980, but none in subsequent elections.

Revolutionary Socialist Party (*Partido Socialista Revolucionário*, PSR), a Trotskyist group, whose then leader, Francisco Louca, was assassinated in October 1989.

Workers' Party of Socialist Unity (*Partido Operário de Unidade Socialista*, POUS), Trotskyist cell formed in 1979 by Socialist Party dissidents.

Macao

Capital: Macao

Population: 425,000 (1995E)

A Portuguese possession since the 16th century, the peninsula of Macao (or Macau) and two associated islands, located on the southern Chinese coast opposite Hong Kong, are administered as an autonomous "collective entity" of Portugal, but are scheduled to revert to Chinese sovereignty in December 1999. Executive authority is currently exercised by the Governor and an appointed government, with a legislative assembly having an advisory and consultative role. Of the assembly's 23 members, seven are appointed by the Governor, eight directly elected by universal adult suffrage and eight indirectly elected.

In the absence of political parties as such, elections for the directly-elected assembly seats in September 1992 were contested by a number of "civic associations", of which the pro-Chinese *União Promotora para o Progresso* (UNIPRO) and *Uniáo para o Desenvolvimento* (UPD) each won two seats, the others (one each) going to the *Associação de Novo Macau Democrático* (ANMD), the *Unidade para o Futuro de Macau* (UNIF), the *Associção de Amizade* (AMI) and *Solidariedade Laboral*.

Qatar

Capital: Doha   **Population:** 685,000 (1995E)

The state of Qatar has a Council of Ministers appointed by and presided over by the head of state (the Amir) and assisted by an appointed 30–member Consultative Council (*Majlis al-Shura*). There is no elected parliament and there are no political parties. The overthrow of Sheikh Khalifa ibn Hamad al-Thani by his son in June 1995 was seen by some as a harbinger of political reform. As of mid-1996, however, Qatar's established political system remained in place.

Romania

Capital: Bucharest   **Population:** 23,000,000 (1995E)

The Communist-ruled People's Socialist Republic of Romania became simply Romania in December 1989 on the violent overthrow of the Ceaușescu regime. A new constitution approved by referendum in December 1991 provided for a strong presidency, political pluralism, human rights guarantees and a commitment to the market economy. Under a law passed in early 1990 Romania opted for the French system of executive-legislative separation by barring members of parliament from holding ministerial posts and by according substantial powers to the President, who is directly elected for a four-year term in two rounds of voting if required and who appoints the Prime Minister and other ministers subject to approval by the legislature. The latter is bicameral, consisting of the 143–member Senate (*Senat*) and the 328–member Chamber of Deputies (*Cameră Deputatilor*), both elected for a four-year term by proportional representation on the basis of party lists, subject to a minimum of 3% of the national vote being obtained (an additional 1% being required for each member of an alliance of two or more parties up to a maximum of 8%). The threshold requirement presents no barrier to parties representing Romania's ethnic Hungarians winning national representation, since they are the largest national minority in any European country (making up about 8% of the population). For other minorities, up to 13 additional Chamber seats are available (10 being allocated after the 1992 elections).

Elections to the Chamber of Deputies on Sept. 27, 1992, resulted as follows: Democratic National Salvation Front (FNSD) 117 (27.7% of the vote), Democratic Convention of Romania 82 (20.0%), National Salvation Front (FSN) 43 (10.2%), Romanian National Unity Party 30 (7.7%), Hungarian Democratic Union of Romania 27 (7.5%), Greater Romania Party 16 (3.9%), Socialist Party of Labour 13 (3.0%), others 13 (20%). The FNSD subsequently became the Social Democracy Party of Romania (PDSR), while the FSN adopted the prefix Democratic Party. Presidential elections on Sept. 27 and Oct. 11, 1992, resulted in Ion Iliescu (then FNSD, later PDSR) being confirmed in office with 61.4% of the second-round vote.

Christian Democratic National Peasants' Party of Romania

Partidul National Tărănesc Cretin Democrat din România (PNTCDR)

Address. 34 bd. Carol I, sector 3, Bucharest

Telephone. (#40–1) 615–4153

Fax. (#40–1) 312–1303

Leadership. Ion Diaconescu (chair), Ion Ratiu and Ion Puiu (deputy chairs), Radu Vasile (secretary-general)

Founded in 1869, the National Peasants' Party (PNT) was of political importance in the inter-war period and was banned by the Communists in 1947. Revived in December 1989 under veteran leader Ion Puiu, the party refused to co-operate with the post-Communist National Salvation Front (FSN) because of the large number of former Communists within FSN ranks. Prior to the May 1990 elections the bulk of the "historic" PNT opted to merge with a younger group of Christian democratic orientation under the chairmanship of Corneliu Coposu, another veteran peasant leader who had served 17 years in prison under the Communist regime before becoming Prime Minister in its final phase. The result of the merger was the present PNTCDR, which favours a market economy and the recovery of Romanian-populated territories lost during World War II. Having won 12 Chamber seats in 1990, the PNTCDR, as a leading component of the Democratic Convention of Romania (CDR), advanced to 42 seats in September 1992, when it also won 21 Senate seats. Coposu died in November 1995.

The PNTCDR is affiliated to the Christian Democrat International.

Civic Alliance Party

Partidul Aliantei Civice (PAC)

Address. 5 bd. Natiunile Unite, sector 5, Bucharest

Telephone. (#40–1) 615–2163

Fax. (#40–1) 312–5035

Leadership. Nicolae Manolescu (PAC chair), Ana Blandiana (AC chair)

The Civic Alliance (AC) was founded in November 1990 by a group of intellectuals and trade unionists to provide an extra-parliamentary focus for post-Communist opposition groups. In July 1991 it decided to set up an electoral wing under the leadership of literary critic Nicolae Manolescu, the resultant PAC winning 13 Chamber and seven Senate seats in the September 1992 elections as part of the opposition Democratic Convention of Romania. In 1995 the PAC was weakened by the defection of a dissident group which later joined the National Liberal Party. In July 1996 the PAC joined a National Liberal Alliance with the Liberal Party 1993.

Democratic Agrarian Party of Romania

Partidul Democrat Agrar din România (PDAR)

Address. 45 al. Alexandru, sector 1, 71273 Bucharest

Telephone. (#40–1) 633–6672

Fax. (#40–1) 312–8763

Leadership. Victor Surdu (president), Ion Coja (vice-president)

Registered in January 1990, the centrist PDAR is based in the agricultural labouring and small peasant class, aiming to further the creation of a modern agricultural sector in Romania and also espousing a distinctly nationalistic platform. It failed to secure Chamber representation in the September 1992 elections but won five seats in the Senate on a 3.3% vote, subsequently becoming one of the "Pentagon" parties supporting the government headed by what became the Social Democracy Party of Romania. In April 1994, however, it withdrew support from the government in protest at a bill introducing an IMF-decreed land tax. Having nominated Ion Coja as its candidate for the November 1996 presidential elections, the PDAR undertook alliance-building initiatives with the aim of creating a viable electoral grouping.

Democratic Convention of Romania

Conventie Democrat din România (CDR)

Address. 5 splaiul Funirii, sector 3, 70001 Bucharest

Telephone. (#40–1) 312–4041

Fax. (#40–1) 312–4014

Leadership. Emil Constantinescu (chair)

The centre-right CDR was launched prior to the February 1992 local elections as an alliance of 18 parties and organizations, deriving from the eight-party Democratic Union (*Uniunea Demokratica*, UD) founded in 1990 in opposition to the National Salvation Front (FSN) government which had replaced the Ceaušescu regime in December 1989. The main components of the CDR were the Christian Democratic National Peasants' Party of Romania (PNTCDR), the Civic Alliance Party, the Romanian Social Democratic Party (PSDR), the Liberal Party 1993 and the Romanian Ecological Party. Other founding formations included the Democratic Unity Party, the Christian Democratic Union Party, the Association of Former Political Detainees of Romania, the December 21 Association, the Ecologist Federation of Romania, the Movement for Romania's Future, the Workers' and Peasants' Brotherhood, the Global Union of Free Romanians and the National Union of the Unemployed.

The CDR alliance took second place in the September 1992 parliamentary elections, winning 82 Chamber and 34 Senate seats on a vote share of 20%. In the concurrent presidential contest Emil Constantinescu of the CDR was runner-up, winning 31.2% in the first round and 38.6% in the second. Although affiliated to the CDR at that point, the Hungarian Democratic Union of Romania (UDMR) presented a separate list in the 1992 elections. In June 1995 the CDR rejected the UDMR's overtures for renewed co-operation, on the grounds that the UDMR had become too nationalistic. For the November 1996 presidential elections, Constantinescu was again the CDR candidate, his platform featuring a pledge to accelerate the privatization programme. Engineered by the PNTCDR, Constantinescu's candidacy was opposed by some CDR elements and was a factor in the decision of the PSDR to leave the alliance and to align itself with the Democratic Party-National Salvation Front.

Democratic Party-National Salvation Front
Partidul Democrat-Frótul Salváre Nationale (PD-FSN)
> *Address.* 1 allea Modrogan, sector 1, Bucharest
> *Telephone.* (#40–1) 679–3618
> *Fax.* (#40–1) 633–5332
> *Leadership.* Petre Roman (chair)

The original National Salvation Front (FSN) assumed governmental power following the overthrow of the Ceaušescu regime in December 1989, most of its leaders having previously been members of the Communist *nomenklatura*. Having taken on a party identity in February 1990, the FSN had a landslide victory in the May elections, winning 66.3% of the vote and 263 Chamber seats, while FSN leader Ion Iliescu was elected President with 85.1% of the vote. Iliescu thereupon vacated the FSN leadership (in compliance with a law barring the head of state from serving as the leader of a political party) and the Front became divided between those favouring rapid economic reform to create a market economy and those supporting the President's more cautious approach. In March 1991 the first FSN national conference, against the advice of the Iliescu faction, approved a radical free-market reform programme presented by then Prime Minister Petre Roman. The latter vacated the premiership in October 1991 and was re-elected FSN leader in March 1992, whereupon the Iliescu faction broke away to form the Democratic National Salvation Front (later to become the ruling Social Democracy Party of Romania).

The FSN candidate, Caius Dragomir, came a poor fourth in the autumn 1992 presidential election, winning only 4.8% of the first-round vote. The party fared better in the concurrent parliamentary elections, winning 43 Chamber and 18 Senate seats on a vote share of over 10%. The following year it adopted the "Democratic Party" prefix, often being known by that title thereafter.

In February 1996 Roman was nominated as the PD-FSN candidate for the presidential elections due in November and announced his intention to stand on a social democratic platform. The previous month the PD-FSN had formed the Social Democratic Union (*Uniunea Social Democrat*, USD) with the Romanian Social Democratic Party, although each formation remained an autonomous entity.

The Ecologists
Ecologistii
> *Address.* 11 Alexandru Phillippide, 70259 Bucharest
> *Telephone.* (#40–1) 641–2943
> *Fax.* (#40–1) 610–4858
> *Leadership.* Eduard-Victor Gugui (president)

The Ecologists were established in April 1996 as a merger of the Romanian Ecologist Movement (MER) and other rurally-based elements with a "green" orientation. Claiming some 60,000 members, the MER was Eastern Europe's largest environmentalist group and had polled creditably in the May 1990 parliamentary elections, winning 12 Chamber seats (with a 2.6% vote share) and becoming a government party in 1991–92. In the September 1992 contest some MER elements had participated in a joint list with the Romanian Ecological Party as part of the Democratic Convention of Romania, while the main MER had ceased to be represented as such.

Greater Romania Party
Partidul România Mare (PRM)
> *Address.* 39A calea Victoriei, 70101 Bucharest
> *Telephone.* (#40–1) 613–9796
> *Fax.* (#40–1) 615–0229
> *Leadership.* Corneliu Vadim Tudor (chair)

Registered in June 1991, the PRM is the political wing of the extreme nationalist Greater Romania movement, which advocates strong government in pursuit of Romanian nationalist interests, the recovery of Romanian-populated territories lost during World War II and recognition of war-time pro-fascist dictator Marshal Ion Antonescu as a great leader. Often accused of antisemitism, it also sees merit in the "patriotic achievements" of the Ceaušescu regime. The party won 16 Chamber and six Senate seats in the 1992 elections, on a vote share of 3.9%, and became one of the so-called "Pentagon" parties giving external support to the government of the Social Democracy Party of Romania (PDSR). Within parliament it formed joint groups with the Socialist Party of Labour and the Democratic Agrarian Party of Romania.

In 1995 party leader Vadim Tudor repeatedly urged the government to institute a clamp-down on the Hungarian Democratic Union of Romania (UDMR), which he accused of planning a Yugoslavia-style dismemberment of Romania. This and other differences resulted in the PRM withdrawing its support from the government in October 1995, with a political eye to the elections due a year later. Nominated as PRM presidential candidate, Vadim Tudor encountered problems in April 1996 when the Senate voted to withdraw his parliamentary immunity, thus exposing him to a range of legal actions, including some related to his extremist political views. Also in April 1996, a PRM congress endorsed a programme of action for the party in government, its proposed measures including the banning of the UDMR and restrictions on foreign investment in Romania. In September 1996 the PRM absorbed the small Romanian Party for a New Society (PRNS) led by Gen. Victor Voichita.

Hungarian Democratic Union of Romania
Uniunea Democrată Maghiară din România (UDMR) Romániai Magyar Demokraták Szövetsége (RMDSz)
Address. 13 str. Herăstrău, 71297 Bucharest
Telephone. (#40–1) 633–3569
Fax. (#40–1) 679–6675
Leadership. Béla Markó (president), Bishop László Tökes (honorary president), Geza Szocs (general secretary)

The principal political vehicle of Romania's ethnic Hungarian minority, the UDMR was registered in January 1990 with the aim of furthering ethnic Hungarian rights within the framework of a democratic Romania. It took 7.2% of the vote in the May 1990 parliamentary elections, winning 29 Chamber and 12 Senate seats, so that it became the largest single opposition formation. Despite being affiliated to the Democratic Convention of Romania (CDR), the UDMR contested the September 1992 elections separately, winning 7.5% of the vote and 27 Chamber seats, while again returning 12 senators. Following the resignation of Géza Domokos as UDMR president, the moderate Béla Markó was elected as his successor at a party congress in January 1993, after the more radical Bishop László Tökes (hero of anti-Ceaușescu protest actions in Timiçoara, Northern Transylvania, in the late 1980s) had withdrawn his candidacy to accept appointment as honorary president. The same congress called on the government to assist with the preservation of Hungarian language and culture, while calling for self-administration of majority Hungarian districts rather than full autonomy (as urged by some radicals). In mid-1995 the UDMR was rebuffed in its efforts to re-establish political co-operation with the CDR parties, whose spokesmen contended that it had become a party of extreme nationalism. In 1996 the UDMR came under increasingly fierce attack by the extreme nationalist Greater Romania Party, which called openly for the UDMR to be banned. For the November 1996 presidential election the UDMR candidate was Senator György Frunda.

The UDMR is an affiliate of the Christian Democrat International and of the International Democrat Union.

Liberal Party 1993
Partidul Liberal 1993 (PL-93)
Address. 133–135 cal. Victoriei, sector 1, 71101 Bucharest
Telephone. (#40–1) 659–5095
Fax. (#40–1) 650–3590
Leadership. Horia Rusu (president), Dinu Patriciu and Dinu Zamfirescu (vice-presidents), Ludovic Orban (secretary-general)

The PL-93 was registered in May 1993 as a merger of the Youth Wing and the Democratic Convention splinter groups of the National Liberal Party (PNL), which had remained in the Democratic Convention of Romania (CDR) when the main PNL withdrew in April 1992. In the September 1992 parliamentary elections, the PNL-Youth Wing had obtained 11 Chamber seats and the PNL-Democratic Convention two, their respective Senate tallies being one and four seats. In February 1993 a faction of the PNL-Youth Wing, calling itself the New Liberal Party, returned to the PNL fold. In July 1993 the new PL-93 absorbed a liberal faction of the Civic Alliance Party (PAC), following which it claimed the adherence of 25 Chamber deputies. In July 1996 the PL-93 became a member of a National Liberal Alliance with the PAC.

National Liberal Party
Partidul National Liberal (PNL)
Address. 21 bd. Nicolae Bălcescu, sector 1, 70112 Bucharest
Telephone. (#40–1) 614–3235
Fax. (#40–1) 615–7638
Leadership. Mircea Ionescu-Quintus (chair)

Dating from 1848 and founded as a party in 1875, the centre-right PNL suspended operations in 1947, so as not to expose members to Communist persecution, and was revived in January 1990. The party took third place in the May 1990 elections, winning 29 Chamber seats on a 6.4% vote share and 10 Senate seats, but was weakened by internal divisions that produced the breakaway Liberal Union. The PNL was a founding member of the Democratic Convention of Romania (CDR) but withdrew in April 1992 because of policy differences, although two PNL splinter groups refused to endorse the action and remained within the CDR, later becoming the Liberal Party 1993 (PL-93). A PNL congress in February 1993 approved a merger with the New Liberal Party (consisting of former PNL elements that had broken away from what became the PL-93) and elected Mircea Ionescu-Quintus as leader. The latter decision was contested by the previous leader, Radu Câmpeanu, who had been the PNL candidate in the 1990 presidential elections. Câmpeanu was reinstated by a Bucharest court in early 1994, but Ionescu-Quintus showed that he had majority support among party members. Merger with the New Liberals was finalized in May 1995, when the PNL also absorbed a faction of the Civic Alliance Party. It thus regained parliamentary representation of about a dozen deputies, who were technically classified as independents.

A feature of the PNL programme is its call for the restoration to the Romanian throne of the exiled King Michael, who had been deposed by the Communists in 1947. In 1992 the former monarch declined nomination as the PNL presidential candidate, having briefly visited Romania in April that year (but later being twice barred from entry). Complications ensued for Michael's claim to the throne when a Romanian court ruled in October 1995 that the first son of his father, the pre-war Carol II, was the rightful heir despite having been the product of a morganatic marriage.

Romanian Communist Party
Partidul Comunist Român (PCR)

Leadership. Victor Hancu (president)

The PCR was the ruling party in the post-war era, until the overthrow of Nicolae Ceaušescu in December 1989 and the advent of the National Salvation Front (FSN) government. Most of those associated with the Communist regime then switched their allegiance to other parties, especially to what later became the ruling Social Democracy Party of Romania (PDSR). But some elements retained allegiance to the PCR, contending that the post-Communist government had brought only hardship and humiliation to Romania.

The PCR was founded in May 1921 when the left-wing section of the Romanian Social Democratic Party broke away and joined the Communist International (Comintern). Banned in 1924, the party played an important role in organizing anti-fascist resistance, building a broad national front of democratic forces during World War II, when Romania was at first allied with the Axis powers. Following Romania's switch to the Allied side in 1944, the Communists came to power within alliances with other parties and in the first post-war Assembly elections (November 1946) obtained 73 of the 348 seats (out of 414) won by the People's Democratic Front (PDF), which included the Social Democrats and two smaller left-wing groups. In early 1948 the PCR merged with the pro-Communist Social Democrats to form the Romanian Workers' Party (RWP), following which the opposition Social Democrats and other non-Communist parties were gradually outlawed. By now firmly established in government, the Communist-dominated PDF was the only list presented in the November 1950 elections, a People's Republic having been declared a year earlier.

An internal power struggle in the early 1950s brought the Stalinist Gheorghe Gheorghiu-Dej to the RWP leadership in 1955, although from 1956, after the denunciation of Stalin by the Soviet Communists, the Romanian party increasingly asserted its independence of Moscow. Following the death of Gheorghiu-Dej in March 1965, Nicolae Ceaušescu was elected leader of the RWP, which in July that year reverted to the PCR title and was declared to be "the leading political force of the whole society" in the 1965 constitution. Ceaušescu added the state presidency to his party leadership in 1967. In 1968 the PCR supported the "Prague Spring" of the Czechoslovak Communists and condemned the Soviet-led military intervention which crushed it. Over the following two decades Ceaušescu remained in unchallenged power, combining an independent foreign policy with rigid orthodoxy at home, with his wife Elena taking an increasingly prominent role in the 1980s. At first untouched by the anti-Communist tide which swept through Eastern Europe in late 1989, the Ceaušescu regime in Romania ultimately experienced the bloodiest overthrow, involving heavy street fighting in Bucharest and other cities in December. Captured trying to flee the capital, Ceaušescu and his wife were summarily tried, found guilty of genocide and embezzlement of over $1,000 million, and executed (on Christmas Day).

Under the successor regime of the National Salvation Front (almost all of whose leaders had been active Communists) an initial proposal to ask the people in a referendum whether the PCR should be banned was quickly dropped as being "a political mistake". In fact, under subsequent legislation outlawing all groups that supported "totalitarianism, extremism, fascism or communism", the PCR effectively ceased to exist as an organized force. However, as economic and social conditions deteriorated in the early 1990s, attachment to the PCR and its supposed achievements became less unfashionable and some adherents began to work for a formal restoration. They were boosted in May 1994 by a Bucharest court decision authorizing the party's revival and registration. A month later, however, the Romanian

Supreme Court revoked the registration under the aforementioned legislation. During the hearing party leader Victor Hancu denied that the new formation was a continuation of the pre-1989 PCR, although an associate had stated that the PCR would decide at its "15th congress" whether to rehabilitate Ceaușescu (who had been re-elected party leader at the 14th PCR congress only a month before being overthrown).

Romanian Ecological Party

Partidul Ecologist Român (PER)

Address. 10A Stelea Spatarul Str., sector 3, 70476 Bucharest

Telephone. (#40–1) 615–8285

Leadership. Otto Weber (chair), Iustin Draghici (president)

The PER was registered in January 1990 and became the "green" wing of the post-Communist opposition Democratic Convention of Romania (CDR), although it remained substantially smaller in terms of membership than the more radical environmentalist movement which later became the Ecologists. Having won eight Chamber seats in May 1990 on a 1.7% vote share, the PER was reduced to four in September 1992.

Romanian National Unity Party

Partidul Unitaii Nationale Române (PUNR)

Address. 13/1 piata Amzei, sector 1, Bucharest

Telephone. (#40–1) 659–5256

Leadership. Gheorghe Funar (president)

The right-wing PUNR was founded in March 1990 as the political arm of the nationalist Romanian Hearth (*Vătra Româneasca*) movement, which aspires to the recovery of the "greater Romania" borders of the inter-war period and is strongly opposed to any special recognition of the rights of Romania's ethnic Hungarian minority. The party was fifth-placed in the September 1992 parliamentary elections, winning 30 Chamber and 14 Senate seats on a vote share of some 8%. In August 1994 it opted to join the government coalition headed by the Social Democracy Party of Romania (PDSR). In mid-1995 serious coalition tensions arose when the PUNR demanded the foreign affairs portfolio and asserted that too many concessions were being made by Romania in its quest for better relations with Hungary. However, after the PDSR had threatened either to continue as a minority government or to bring about an early election, the PUNR moderated its position and remained in the ruling coalition.

Underlying differences remained, however, and were sharpened in October 1995 by the decisions of the Socialist Party of Labour and the Greater Romania Party (PRM) to withdraw external sup-

port from the government. The dismissal of the PUNR Communications Minister in January 1996 caused a new crisis, in which the PUNR in March announced that it was definitely leaving the government. It was again persuaded to change its mind, although by then it had become an opposition party in all but ministerial status. An important factor at play was the party's desire to establish an independent image for the elections scheduled for November 1996, and in particular not to be outflanked on the nationalist right by the PRM. In the latter context, PUNR leader Gheorghe Funar (the party's 1996 presidential candidate) became a vocal critic of a draft treaty with Hungary tabled by the government in mid-1996, contending that its provisions on the rights of Romania's Hungarian minority amounted to a "national betrayal". One such outburst in early September 1996, in which he made a fierce personal attack on the President, finally brought matters to a head, the PUNR being ejected from the government by the Prime Minister (although one of the four PUNR ministers preferred to leave the party rather than give up his ministerial office).

Romanian Social Democratic Party

Partidul Social Democrat Român (PSDR)

Address. 9 Dem. I. Dobrescu str., sector 1, 70119 Bucharest

Telephone. (#40–1) 614–6110

Fax. (#40–1) 614–6089

Leadership. Sergio Cunescu (president), Constantin Avramescu (vice-president)

The PSDR is directly descended from the historic party founded in 1893 but forced to merge with the Romanian Communist Party in 1948, after which the authentic PSDR was maintained in exile. Following the overthrow of the Ceaușescu regime in December 1989, several groups claimed to be reviving the true PSDR, the confusion eventually being resolved by a court ruling awarding the PSDR designation to the main faction, which had Socialist International recognition. The party won only one Chamber seat in the May 1990 elections. As a component of the Democratic Convention of Romania (CDR) it improved to 10 Chamber seats in September 1992, when it also elected a member of the Senate. The PSDR withdrew from the CDR in January 1996, instead joining a new Social Democratic Union with the Democratic Party-National Salvation Front.

The PSDR is an affiliate of the Socialist International through the Socialist Union of Central-Eastern Europe.

Social Democracy Party of Romania

Partidul Democratiei Sociale din România (PDSR)

Address. 11 Atrena Str., sector 1, 71271 Bucharest

Telephone. (#40–1) 212–0695

Fax. (#40–1) 312–4655

Leadership. Oliviu Gherman (chair), Adrian Năstase (executive chair), Nicolae Văcăroiu (deputy chair), Miron Mitrea (secretary-general)

The PDSR was launched in July 1993 as a merger of the Democratic National Salvation Front (*Frontul Salváre Nationale Democrat*, FSND), the Romanian Socialist Democratic Party (*Partidul Socialist Democrat Român*, PSDR) and the Republican Party (*Partidul Republicán*, PR). Essentially a "presidential" formation designed to provide a party political base for President Iliescu, the PDSR defines itself as a social democratic, popular and national party of the centre-left, supportive of gradual transition to a market economy on the basis of social responsibility and desirous of reversing the post-Communist decline in industrial and agricultural production (over which it has presided).

The FSND had come into being in March 1992 when a group of pro-Iliescu deputies of the National Salvation Front (FSN) opposed to rapid economic reform withdrew from the parent party to form what was initially called the FSN-December 22 (the date of Ceaușescu's overthrow in 1989), which was registered as the FSND the following month. The FSND had won a relative majority of seats in both houses of parliament in the September 1992 elections, with around 28% of the vote, and had backed Iliescu's successful re-election bid in the concurrent presidential contest. Of the other PDSR components, the leftist PSDR (often confused with the separate and unrelated Romanian Social Democratic Party) had been closely allied with the FSN in the post-Ceaușescu period. Its first leader, Marian Circiumaru, had been expelled from the party in August 1990 for assorted alleged offences. The PR, a centrist pro-market party, had been founded in 1991 as a merger of the Republican Party and the Social Liberal Party-May 20.

Having formed a minority government in the wake of the 1992 elections, the PDSR in August 1994 entered into a coalition with the right-wing Romanian National Unity Party (PUNR), with external support from the even more right-wing Greater Romania Party (PRM) and the neo-Communist Socialist Party of Labour (PSM). By mid-1995, however, serious differences had developed between the government parties, with the result that the PRM and the PSM withdrew their support in late 1995, while the PUNR was finally ejected from the government in early September 1996. Technically, therefore, the PDSR was reduced to minority status in the Chamber, although it remained politically dominant in advance of elections scheduled for November 1996. Local elections in June 1996 yielded poor results for the PDSR, with former tennis champion Ilie Naștase failing to win election as mayor of Bucharest as a PDSR candidate. In July 1996 the PDSR nominated Iliescu as its presidential candidate, the nomination being formally accepted by the incumbent President the following month. By then incumbent Prime Minister Nicolae Văcăroiu, who had been appointed in November 1992 as a non-party technocrat, had announced his membership of the PDSR.

Socialist Party of Labour

Partidul Socialist al Muncii (PSM)

Address. 3 Neugustori Str., sector 3, 70481 Bucharest

Telephone. (#40–1) 312–0323

Leadership. Ilie Verdet (president), Adrian Paunescu (vice-president)

The PSM was founded in November 1990 as in some respects a successor to the former ruling Romanian Communist Party, although it renounced Marxism-Leninism and embraced democratic socialist principles, including a commitment to a mixed social market economy. Its principal founders were Communist-era Prime Minister Ilie Verdet and the elderly Constantin Pirvulescu, who had been involved in the creation of the PCR in 1921.

The PSM's stated aim of reviving socialism in Romania in order to restore stability after "almost a year of anarchy" provoked an immediate negative reaction in Bucharest, where there were street demonstrations in protest at what was seen as a desire to revert to the Communist-era system. In the September 1992 elections, the PSM received only 3% of the national vote, which yielded 13 Chamber and five Senate seats. In the new parliament, the party gave a pointer to its orientation by forming group alliances with the far-right Greater Romania Party (PRM) and the conservative Democratic Agrarian Party of Romania. After giving qualified support to the government headed by the Social Democracy Party of Romania, the PSM opted for outright opposition in October 1995. For the presidential elections due in November 1996, its candidate was Adrian Paunescu, a well-known poet who had been close to the Ceaușescu regime.

Other Parties

Among well over 100 other registered parties in Romania, those listed below appear to have some political significance.

Alternative Party of Romania (*Partidul Alternativa României*, PAR), led by Adrian Iorgulescu, founded in early 1996, believing that all established parties are self-serving and ineffective.

Christian Democratic Union (*Uniunea Democrat Cretina*, UDC), a left-of-centre formation.

Christian Republican Party (*Partidul Republicán Cretin*, PRC), a right-of-centre formation.

Democratic Front of Romania (*Fróntul Democratic Román*, FDR).

Democratic Party of Romania (*Partidul Democrat din România*, PDR).

Hungarian Christian Democratic Party of Romania (*Partidul Cretin Democrat Maghiár din România*, PCDMR).

Liberal Monarchist Party of Romania (*Partidul Liberal Monarhist din România*, PLMR), led by Dan Cernovodeanu, founded in 1990 to seek the restoration of the Romanian monarchy.

National Reunification Party (*Partidul Reunire National*, PRN), led by Mircea Druc (a former Prime Minister of Moldova, who left that country in 1993 to become a Romanian citizen).

Roma Party (*Partida Romilor*, PR), led by Gheorghe Raducanu, representing Romania's substantial Gypsy population.

Romanian Peasants' Party (*Partidul Taranesc Román*, PTR).

Romanian Socialist Party (*Partidul Socialist Román*, PSR), led by Tudor Mohora.

Romanian Workers' Party (*Partidul Muncitoresc Román*, PMR), led by Critian Nicolae, founded in March 1995 by former Communists who revered the memory of Ceaušescu:

Traditional Social Democratic Party of Romania (*Partidul Social Demokrat Traditional din România*, PSDTR), led by Eugen Branzan, founded in 1991 as a merger of the Traditional Social Democratic Party and the National Democratic Party (PND).

United Christian Party of Romania (*Partidul Uniúnii Cretine din România*, PUCR).

Russia

Capital: Moscow

Population: 153,500,000 (1995E)

The Russian Federation was formerly the Russian Soviet Federative Socialist Republic, the largest constituent republic of the USSR, and became a sovereign member of the Commonwealth of Independent States on Dec. 21, 1991. Approved by referendum in December 1993, its present constitution defines Russia as a democratic, pluralist federation headed by an executive President, directly elected for a four-year term (once renewable consecutively), who guides the domestic and foreign policy of the state, serves as commander-in-chief of the armed forces and nominates the Prime Minister and other ministers, subject to approval by the legislature. The latter body is the bicameral Federal Assembly (*Federalnoe Sobranie*), consisting of (i) the upper Federation Council (*Sovet Federatsii*) of 178 members, to which each of the Federation's 89 territorial entities sends two representatives; and (ii) the lower State Duma (*Gosudarstvennaya Duma*) of 450 members elected for a four-year term, half of whom are returned by proportional representation from party lists obtaining at least 5% of the vote and the other half from single-member constituencies on the basis of majority voting. The President may reject a first vote of no confidence by the legislature, but upon the repassage of such a measure within three months must either resign or dissolve the legislature and call new elections. A presidential veto on legislation may only be overridden by a two-thirds majority of the whole membership of the Federal Assembly. The President has considerable scope under the constitution to govern by the issuance of decrees.

Elections to the State Duma on Dec. 17, 1995, resulted as follows: Communist Party of the Russian Federation (KPRF) 157 seats (with 22.3% of the proportional vote), Our Home is Russia 55 (10.1%), Liberal Democratic Party of Russia 51 (11.2%), Yavlinsky-Boldyrev-Lukin Bloc (*Yabloko*) 45 (6.9%), Agrarian Party of Russia 20 (3.8%), Russia's Democratic Choice 9

(3.9%), Power to the People 9 (1.6%), Congress of Russian Communities 5 (4.3%), Women of Russia 3 (4.6%), Forward Russia 3 (1.9%), Ivan Rybkin Bloc 3 (1.1%), Pamfilova-Gurov-Lysenko Bloc 2 (1.6%), Workers' Self-Management Party 1 (4.1%), Common Cause 1 (0.7%), other parties 9, independents 77. (The Ivan Rybkin Bloc later became the Socialist Party of Russia. The Pamfilova-Gurov-Lysenko Bloc was presented by the Republican Party of the Russian Federation.)

A presidential election held in two rounds on June 16 and July 3, 1996, resulted in incumbent Boris Yeltsin, standing with endorsement from many centrist formations although not as a party candidate, being re-elected in the second round with 53.7% of the vote against Gennady Zyuganov of the KPRF.

Agrarian Party of Russia
Agrarnaya Partiya Rossii (APR)
Address. 1 Okhotnyi ryad, 121019 Moscow
Telephone. (#7–095) 292–8901
Leadership. Mikhail Lapshin (chair)

The APR was founded in February 1992 to provide political representation for collective and state farmers, as well as for agro-industrial workers and managers, on a platform opposed to the introduction of a free market in land. Its predominantly conservative constituent organizations included the Agrarian Union of Russia (*Agrarnyi Soyuz Rossii*, ASR) led by Vasily Starodubtsev, which had held its inaugural congress in June 1990. APR spokesmen made a point of stressing that the APR was not the agrarian branch of the Communist Party of the Russian Federation (KPRF). But in policy terms the two parties shared much common ground, notably a conviction that the free-market programme of the Yeltsin administration was damaging Russia. The APR took fourth place in the December 1993 State Duma elections, winning 7.9% of the popular vote and 47 seats (later increased by the adhesion of deputies elected as independents).

The APR subsequently aligned itself with the KPRF/nationalist opposition in the new parliament, even though the Agriculture Minister in a more conservative Yeltsin administration was identified with the APR. After much confusion, the party decided to remain outside an electoral bloc launched in June 1995 by the APR chairman of the State Duma, Ivan Rybkin (who later founded the Socialist Party of Russia). In the December 1995 parliamentary elections, the APR received only 3.8% of the party list vote, so that it did not qualify for proportional seats; but it won 20 seats in the constituency section (and had the unofficial support of some of the 77 deputies returned as independents). The APR backed the unsuccessful candidacy of the KPRF leader in the mid-1996 presidential elections and subsequently, without great enthusiasm, joined the new KPRF-inspired Popular-Patriotic Union of Russia.

Common Cause
Obshche Delo (OD)
Address. c/o Federalnoe Sobranie, Moscow
Leadership. Irina Khakamada

Common Cause was founded in 1995 as yet another formation of the liberal democratic pro-reform centre. In the December 1995 State Duma elections it obtained 0.7% of the national vote (well below the threshold for the allocation of proportional seats) but was the victor in one constituency contest.

Communist Party of the Russian Federation
Kommunisticheskaya Partiya Rossiiskoi Federatisii (KPRF)
Address. 8/7 B. Komsomolskii per., 101000 Moscow
Telephone. (#7–095) 206–8751
Fax. (#7–095) 206–8751
Leadership. Gennady Zyuganov (chair), Valentin Kuptsov (deputy chair)

The KPRF was registered in March 1993 after a Communist "revival/unification" congress had been held at Klyazm (near Moscow) the previous month, following a Constitutional Court ruling in December 1992 that the banning in November 1991 of the Communist Party of the Soviet Union (*Kommunisticheskaya Partiya Sovietskogo Soyuza*, KPSS) had been unconstitutional. The KPRF is therefore the self-proclaimed successor to the Russian branch of the KPSS (not least to its financial assets), albeit without those parts of the latter's Marxist-Leninist ideology which had underpinned 70 years of authoritarian one-party rule.

The KPSS was directly descended from Vladimir Ilyich Ulyanov Lenin's majority (Bolshevik) wing of the Russian Social Democratic Labour Party (itself established in 1898), which at the party's second congress held in London in 1903 out-voted the minority (Menshevik) wing on Lenin's proposal that in existing Russian conditions the party must become a tightly-disciplined vanguard of professional revolutionaries. In 1912 the Bolshevik wing established itself as a separate formation, which became a legal party in Russia following the overthrow of the Tsar in February 1917 and which in October 1917 seized power from the Mensheviks. The party changed its name to Russian Communist Party (Bolsheviks) in 1918, to All-Union Communist Party (Bolsheviks) in 1925 and to the KPSS designation in 1952.

Following Lenin's death in January 1924, Joseph Stalin (who had become general secretary of the central committee in April 1922) took full control over the party and government. He proceeded to eliminate all actual and potential rivals on the right and left of the party, notably Leon Trotsky (the architect of the Communist victory in the post-revolution civil war), who was expelled from the party in November 1927, exiled in January 1929 and finally murdered by Stalin's agent in his Mexican home in August 1940.

From October 1925 Stalin adopted the programme of the eliminated leftist opposition by launching the first five-year plan of rapid industrialization and forcible collectivization of agriculture (the latter involving the virtual elimination of the land-owning peasants, or *kulaks*, as a class). Between 1928 and 1938 total industrial output almost quadrupled, although agricultural output declined. The assassination of politburo member Sergei Kirov in December 1934 led to the great purges of the late 1930s, in which almost the entire generation of party activists formerly associated with Lenin disappeared. In December 1936 a new constitution was promulgated under which the Communist Party was enshrined as the leading force in the state.

After the interval provided by the August 1939 Stalin-Hitler pact, the German invasion of the Soviet Union in June 1941 coincided with Stalin's assumption for the first time of formal government responsibilities as Prime Minister and supreme commander of the Soviet armed forces. The eventual victory of the Red Army and its penetration into Eastern Europe led to the establishment of Soviet-aligned Communist regimes in a number of states, causing post-war tensions in relations with the Western powers which eventually deteriorated into the Cold War. During the post-war period Stalin remained in absolute control of the party and state apparatus and mounted further purges of suspected opponents.

Immediately after Stalin's death in March 1953 moves were initiated to reverse the Stalinist system and the cult of his personality. Stalin's secret police chief, Lavrenti Beria, was executed and Stalin's designated successor, Georgy Malenkov, was immediately ousted from the party leadership by Nikita Khrushchev and replaced as Prime Minister by Nikolai Bulganin in February 1955. Under

Khrushchev's leadership, the KPSS in 1955 re-established relations with the Yugoslav Communists (hitherto regarded as right-wing deviationists) and in his celebrated "secret" speech to the 20th party congress in February 1956 Khrushchev denounced the Stalinist terror.

Khrushchev's denunciation of Stalin triggered off serious challenges to the Communist regimes in Poland and also in Hungary, where orthodox Communist rule was re-established by Soviet military intervention in November 1956. In March 1958 Khrushchev added the premiership to his party leadership, but growing doubts within the KPSS hierarchy about his policies and style culminated in his removal from the party and government leadership in October 1964, in which posts he was succeeded by Leonid Brezhnev and Alexei Kosygin respectively.

Under Brezhnev's leadership the cautious liberalization policy of the Khrushchev era was largely halted or reversed. Although the Soviet government pursued a policy of détente with the West, its refusal to countenance deviation from Communist orthodoxy was demonstrated by the Soviet-led intervention in Czechoslovakia in 1968, following which Brezhnev enunciated his doctrine that Communist countries were entitled to intervene in other Communist countries if the preservation of socialism was deemed to be threatened. Having established a position of complete authority as party leader, Brezhnev was elected USSR head of state in June 1977.

However, the Brezhnev era was essentially a period of conservatism and stagnation, this being acknowledged by the party itself after his death in November 1982. He was succeeded as party leader by former KGB chief Yury Andropov, but he died in February 1984, and his successor, Konstantin Chernenko, lasted only a year before he too died in office. The party then opted for the relatively young Mikhail Gorbachev (54), who embarked upon a reform programme that was ultimately to lead to the demise of the Soviet Union.

At the April 1985 plenary meeting of the KPSS central committee and the 27th party congress in March 1986, Gorbachev advanced the concept of a "restructuring" (*perestroika*) of social relations based on "resolute efforts to overcome elements of stagnation and negative phenomena to accelerate the country's socio-economic development". At the same time, the party became committed to a new "openness" (*glasnost*) in public and media discussion of present and past conditions in the Soviet Union. Perhaps most controversially of all, Gorbachev proposed electoral reform, including the multiple choice of candidates and the introduction of secret ballots in the election of party secretaries; however, this proposal was not specifically endorsed in the central committee's resolution giving general formal backing to Gorbachev's plans.

In order to encourage the policy of *glasnost*, Gorbachev declared that the activities of state and public organizations should be more open to public scrutiny through the official media, and be more receptive to criticism. He also announced the preparation of a law on the procedure for filing a complaint against a party official who had infringed the rights of a citizen. (Such a law was passed by the Supreme Soviet on June 30, 1987, and came into effect on Jan. 1, 1988.)

Differences within the KPSS leadership over the desirable pace of reform were demonstrated by the dismissal of Boris Yeltsin as first secretary of the Moscow party committee on Nov. 11, 1987, as a direct consequence of a speech by him to the KPSS central committee the previous month in which he had accused other senior leaders of frustrating the *perestroika* process and had also criticized aspects of the present leadership style, including the high profile accorded to Gorbachev's wife Raisa. Formerly a close associate of the party leader, Yeltsin was in February 1988 dropped from alternate membership of the KPSS political bureau.

Yeltsin thereafter effectively ceased to be a KPSS member, becoming the leading advocate of democratization and economic liberalization in the Russian Federation, of which he was elected President in May 1990 (by a legislature itself elected competitively two months earlier).

Meanwhile, Gorbachev had succeeded Andrei Gromyko as USSR head of state in October 1988, subsequently introducing historic constitutional changes to allow for a multi-party system and private economic enterprise, although he himself remained a Communist, apparently convinced that the KPSS would retain its dominance in genuinely competitive elections. Others in the KPSS hierarchy did not share his confidence, nor his belief that the Soviet Union could be preserved as a voluntary association. Gorbachev's proposed new Union Treaty, envisaging an association of "sovereign" republics with extensive powers of self-government, was the final straw for his hard-line conservative opponents, who in August 1991 attempted to assume power in Moscow while Gorbachev was away on holiday. The coup attempt quickly crumbled, not least because of the courageous opposition displayed by Yeltsin; but it served to accelerate the unravelling of the Soviet system, in that most of the republican Communist parties withdrew from the KPSS while it was in progress, and were subsequently banned or suspended as the republics moved to independ-ence. In the Russian Federation both the KPSS and the KPRF were banned under the aforementioned presidential decree (issued on Nov. 6, 1991), their assets being declared state property.

The leadership of the revived KPRF elected at the Klyazm congress was headed by Gennady Zyuganov, a former Soviet apparatchik who had been co-chair of the National Salvation Front formed in October 1992 by Communists and Russian nationalists who deplored the passing of the supposed glories of the Soviet era. The KPRF was thus placed in uneasy spiritual alliance with the non-Communist nationalist right in opposition to the reformist forces of the centre in governmental power in Moscow, in particular to the Yeltsin presidency. The manifest negative effects of economic transition, including unemployment, inflation and rampant crime, provided the KPRF with powerful ammunition in its unaccustomed role as a party seeking electoral support in a multi-party system. In the State Duma elections of December 1993 it took third place with 65 seats and 12.4% of the proportional vote, thereafter becoming the principal focus of opposition to the Yeltsin administration. The appointment in January 1995 of an acknowledged Communist as Justice Minister did not mean that the KPRF had become a government party. Using the slogan "For our Soviet motherland", it contested the December 1995 State Duma elections on a platform promising the restoration of "social justice", its reward being a plurality of 157 seats, of which 99 came from a 22.3% share of the vote in the proportional half of the contest.

Remaining in opposition (although welcoming a more conservative government orientation), the KPRF presented Zyuganov as its candidate for the mid-1996 presidential election, on a platform condemning the devastation of Russia's industrial base by IMF-dictated policies and promising to restore economic sovereignty. He came a close second to Yeltsin in the first round of voting on June 16, winning 32.04%, but lost to the incumbent in the second round, when he won 40.4%. The KPRF thereupon initiated the launching in August 1996 of the Popular-Patriotic Union of Russia (*Narodno-Patrioticheskii Soyuz Rossii*, NPSR), which was designed to rally all anti-Yeltsin forces and which Zyuganov insisted, shortly before being elected as its leader, was not a Communist front organization.

Congress of Russian Communities
Kongress Russkikh Obshchin (KRO)

Address. c/o Federalnoe Sobranie, Moscow
Leadership. Dmitry Rogozin (chair), Gen. (retd.) Aleksandr Lebed (presidential candidate)

Founded in mid-1995, the moderately nationalist KRO stresses the need to preserve the unity of the Russian nation and has support in the Russian military for that and other reasons. The KRO was boosted when the controversial but popular former commander of Russia's 14th Army in Moldova's Transdnestr region, Gen. Aleksandr Lebed, agreed to take a prominent place on the KRO's list of candidates for the December 1995 elections, following his resignation from the armed forces in May 1995. The KRO also entered into an electoral alliance with the more centrist Democratic Party of Russia. However, favourable early opinion poll ratings for the KRO were not sustained in the actual voting, which gave it only 4.3% of the national vote (and therefore no proportional seats), its tally of five State Duma seats coming from the constituency contests.

Disappointed with the election outcome, delegates at a special KRO congress in late May 1996 ousted Yury Skokov from the leadership and replaced him with the more nationalistic Dmitry Rogozin. There was an immediate dividend for Lebed in the following month's presidential elections, when he came third in the first round on June 16 with 14.5% of the national vote and therefore became a very marketable political commodity. President Yeltsin speedily made him his National Security Adviser, thus securing his backing for a difficult second-round contest with the candidate of the Communist Party of the Russian Federation.

Forward Russia!

Vpered Rossiya!

   Address. c/o Federalnoe Sobranie, Moscow
   Leadership. Boris Fedorov
   Forward Russia! is the better-known electoral name of the Liberal Democratic Union (*Liberalno-Demokraticheskiy Soyuz*, LDS), which was founded in early 1994 by a dissident faction of what became Russia's Democratic Choice led by Boris Fedorov, a former reforming Finance Minister. The LDS declared its support for speedy transition to a market economy but called for observance of "traditional" social values as this was being accomplished. According to Fedorov, the new party's name was purposely selected with a view to rehabilitating the concept of liberal democracy after its misuse in the title of the extreme right-wing Liberal Democratic Party of Russia. Unlike some other centrist leaders, Fedorov supported the Russian military operation in Chechenya. In the December 1995 State Duma elections Forward Russia! failed in the proportional section with just under 2% of the national vote but won three constituency seats.

Liberal Democratic Party of Russia

Liberalno-Demokraticheskaya Partiya Rossii (LDPR)

   Address. 1 Rybnikov per., 103045 Moscow
   Telephone. (#7–095) 923–6370
   Fax. (#7–095) 975–2511
   Leadership. Vladimir Zhirinovsky (chair), Sergei Abeltsev (deputy chair)
   The right-wing nationalist LDPR was founded in March 1990 in the era of the Soviet Union, the borders of which it wishes to restore to Russian hegemony, although it does not favour the Communist economic system. Its leader, the controversial Vladimir Zhirinovsky, attracted 6,211,007 votes (7.8%) in the 1991 presidential poll on an openly xenophobic platform with racist and antisemitic overtones. Among his more extravagant proposals was one for a Russian reconquest of Finland (which had been part of the Tsarist empire until World War I). The party was technically banned in August 1992 on the grounds that it had falsified its membership records. However, it was allowed to contest the December 1993 parliamentary elections, in which it became the second strongest State Duma party with 64 seats and actually headed the proportional voting with 22.8% of the national poll.

Although forming the main parliamentary opposition to the Yeltsin administration, the LDPR lost momentum in 1994–95, as its leader made increasingly bizarre utterances and was shunned by other politicians close to him in the ideological spectrum. Zhirinovsky's decision to sign the April 1994 "treaty on civil accord" between Yeltsin and over 200 political and social groups did not increase his standing in the political class and served to alienate some of his natural supporters. In the December 1995 State Duma elections the LDPR again took second place with 51 seats, but slumped to 11.4% of the proportional vote. In the 1996 presidential elections, moreover, Zhirinovsky came a poor fifth in the first round, with only 5.7% of the vote.

Our Home is Russia

Nash Dom-Rossiya (NDR)

   Address. 12 pr. Akad. Sakharova, Moscow
   Telephone. (#7–095) 921–8815
   Fax. (#7–095) 923–0746
   Leadership. Viktor S. Chernomyrdin (chair)
   The centre-right NDR was launched in May 1995 mainly to provide a party political base for the cautious pro-market reform programme of Prime Minister Chernomyrdin and by extension for President Yeltsin, although the latter did not publicly endorse the new formation. Supported by most government ministers, the NDR was quickly branded by the more radical pro-market elements (and by the conservative/nationalist opposition)

as being funded by Gazprom, which Chernomyrdin (a former USSR Gas Minister) had run before joining the Russian government. In August 1995 the NDR was heavily defeated in its first important electoral contest, for the governorship of Yeltsin's home province of Sverdlovsk. In the December 1995 State Duma elections, it registered only 10.1% of the national vote, which yielded 45 proportional seats in addition to 10 won in constituency contests. But its organizational resources made a significant contribution to Yeltsin's second-round presidential victory in July 1996, after which Chernomyrdin was reappointed Prime Minister.

Power
Derzhava

Address. c/o Federalnoe Sobranie, Moscow

Leadership. Aleksandr Rutskoi, Viktor Kobelev, Konstantin Dushenov

Derzhava was launched in May 1994 by six State Duma deputies who had been elected in 1993 as candidates of the far-right Liberal Democratic Party of Russia (LDPR) in 1993 but wished to back the presidential aspirations of Aleksandr Rutskoi. The name of the group is an old Russian world signifying the authority of the state.

In securing election to the Russian vice-presidency in June 1991 (as Boris Yeltsin's running-mate), Rutskoi had founded the Democratic Party of Communists of Russia, which had later evolved into the People's Party of Free Russia (NPSR). Whereas the NPSR was originally part of the centrist and pro-reform Civic Union, Rutskoi sided with the anti-Yeltsin conservative camp in the 1993 power struggle between the State Duma majority and the President, his consequential suspension as Vice-President in early September leading directly to the violent confrontation of October 1993. Following the conservatives' defeat, Rutskoi was among those arrested and charged with subversion, while the NPSR was suspended. After being voted a parliamentary amnesty in February 1994, however, Rutskoi relaunched his party as the Russian Social Democratic People's Party (RSDNP) in May. His objective, he said, was to build a "social patriotic movement" embracing Communists and nationalists, with the particular aim of bringing the Russian-populated territories of neighbouring states into a "greater Russia". A power struggle ensued between Rutskoi and the RSDNP moderate faction led by Vasily Lipitsky, culminating in the latter being ousted as party chair in March 1995 and forming the centrist Russian Social Democratic Union the following month.

Having established control of the RSDNP, Rutskoi subsequently chose to pursue his political ambitions through the *Derzhava* grouping, which had meanwhile attracted considerable support in parliament and in the country. In the December 1995 State Duma elections, however, the "*Derzhava*-Rutskoi" list obtained only 2.6% of the national vote (and therefore no proportional seats) and also failed in the constituency contests (although *Derzhava* continued to have some support in the upper house of the Federal Assembly). Rutskoi claimed that his list had been the victim of massive electoral fraud. He registered as a preliminary candidate for the mid-1996 presidential elections but failed to collect the one million signatures needed to be declared an official candidate.

Power to the People
Vlast Narodu

Address. c/o Federalnoe Sobranie, Moscow

Leadership. Nikolai I. Ryzhkov, Sergei Baburin

Power to the People was created for the December 1995 parliamentary elections as an alliance of nationalist (but anti-fascist) formations, headed by the Russian All-People's Union (*Rossiiskii Obshchenarodnyi Soyuz*, ROS). It also included the Russian National People's Union (*Rossiiskii Obshchenatsionalnyi Soyuz*, RONS) led by populist Sergei Baburin, who had controlled the largest anti-Yeltsin formation in the State Duma prior to the December 1993 elections (which RONS was barred from contesting because it had participated in the parliamentary rebellion against President Yeltsin in September-October 1993). Headed by Nikolai Ryzhkov (a former Soviet Prime Minister), Power for the People called for a return to central economic planning, with rigid controls over energy supplies, food staples and consumer goods. Less specifically, it promised to restore "the great and indivisible Russia", thereby attracting support not only from right-wing groups but also from some latter-day Communists nostalgic for the certainties of the Soviet era. However, in the December 1995 elections it won only nine seats (all in the constituency section), its national vote share being an unimpressive 1.6%. Following the mid-1996 presidential elections, Ryzhkov participated in the launching of the Patriotic-Popular Union of Russia initiated by the Communist Party of the Russian Federation.

Republican Party of the Russian Federation
Respublikanskaya Partiya Rossiiskoi Federatsii (RPRF)

Address. 11/31–6 Siminovsky val, 109044 Moscow

Telephone. (#7–095) 298–1349

Leadership. Vladimir Lysenko (chair), Ella Pamfilova, Aleksandr Gurov

The centre-left RPRF was founded in 1990 by

former members of the Democratic Platform within the Communist Party of the Soviet Union. It was subsequently a component of the Russian Movement for Democratic Reform (RDDR) created in February 1992 and was also involved in the launching in July 1992 of the pro-Yeltsin Democratic Choice grouping, which later became Russia's Democratic Choice. Maintaining its own autonomy, the RPRF announced in June 1995 that the well-known former Social Security Minister, Ella Pamfilova, would head its list in the December State Duma elections. In the event, what was entitled the "Pamfilova-Gurov-Lysenko Bloc" obtained only 1.6% of the national vote (and therefore no proportional seats) and had to be content with winning two constituency seats (one of them going to Pamfilova).

Russia's Democratic Choice

Demokraticheskiy Vybor Rossii (DVR)
    Address. c/o Federalnoe Sobranie, Moscow
    Leadership. Yegor Gaidar (chair)

The DVR was originally founded in November 1993 as Russia's Choice (VR), deriving from the Bloc of Reformist Forces-Russia's Choice (*Blok Reformistkikh Sil-Vybor Rossii*, BRVR) created five months earlier by a group of radical pro-market reformers which included Yegor Gaidar and the then First Deputy Prime Minister, Vladimir Shumeiko. The BRVR was itself derived from the pro-Yeltsin Democratic Choice (*Demokraticheskii Vybor*, DV) bloc created by a large number of centre-right groups in July 1992. The new VR/DVR grouping was in part an attempt to provide a stable political framework for centre-right reformist forces hitherto operating under a host of different (and constantly changing) party or alliance labels. It had only limited success in achieving this objective.

Founding DVR parties included (i) Democratic Russia (*Demokraticheskaya Rossiya*, DR), led by Lev Ponomarev and Viktor Kurochkin, which had been launched in October 1990 as an anti-Communist movement of Christian democratic orientation and which had strongly backed President Yeltsin when Gaidar was in charge of economic policy; (ii) the Peasants' Party of Russia, led by Yury Chernichenko, which was strongly supportive of private land ownership; (iii) the Free Democratic Party of Russia, led by Marina Salye; (iv) the Free Labour Party, led by Igor Korovikov; (v) the Party of Constitutional Democrats, led by Vladimir Zolotarev; and (vi) the Party of Democratic Initiative.

Russia's Choice became the largest parliamentary grouping in the December 1993 State Duma elections, winning 76 seats and 15.4% of the national vote. But strong advances by anti-reform parties resulted in Gaidar and most other radical reformers being dropped from the government in January 1994. In April 1994, in securing Gaidar's signature of his "treaty on civil accord", President Yeltsin expressed a desire for close co-operation with the VR bloc, while explaining that he could not, as head of state, become an actual member. In June 1994 the VR formally established itself as a political party, adding "Democratic" to its title. Elected DVR chair by a large majority, Gaidar said that it would represent pro-Yeltsin opinion but would not be a "presidential" party in the accepted sense. Thereafter, mounting DVR criticism of the slow pace of economic reform under the Chernomyrdin government was unassuaged by the promotion of Anatoly Chubais (then of the DVR) to the rank of First Deputy Prime Minister in November 1994, although Chubais remained influential as the last radical reformer left in the government.

In March 1995 the DVR withdrew support from President Yeltsin in protest against the Russian military action in Chechenya. Two months later Chubais announced that he was suspending his DVR membership and giving his support to Chernomyrdin's new Our Home is Russia formation. The centre-right's incorrigible addiction to new nomenclature was displayed in June when the DVR launched the United Democrats (*Obyedinennyi Demokraticheskii*, OD) as its electoral bloc, which included the Russian Party of Social Democracy and was joined in September by the Congress of National Associations of Russia, representing over 20 ethnic minority groups. However, the December 1995 elections were dismal for the DVR/OD, which slumped to 3.9% of the national vote (and therefore failed to obtain any proportional seats) and won only nine constituency seats.

The Yeltsin administration's shift to an even more conservative posture as a result of the electoral verdict caused Yegor Gaidar to resign from the Presidential Advisory Council in January 1996 and to describe his breach with the President as "final and irrevocable". In the same month Chubais was dismissed from the government for disregarding presidential instructions. In June-July 1996 most DVR elements nevertheless backed President Yeltsin's successful re-election bid, although some preferred the candidacy of Grigory Yavlinsky of the Yavlinsky-Boldyrev-Lukin Bloc (*Yabloko*).

The DVR is affiliated to the International Democrat Union.

Socialist Party of Russia

Sotsialisticheskaya Partiya Rossii (SPR)
    Address. c/o Federalnoe Sobranie, Moscow
    Leadership. Ivan Rybkin (chair)

The left-of-centre SPR was launched by Ivan

Rybkin in April 1996 in an effort to provide a party framework for the support which a bloc headed by him had attracted in the December 1995 parliamentary elections. The core component of the bloc was Russia's Regions (*Regiony Rossii*, RR), consisting of agricultural organizations throughout Russia; it also included the Russian United Industrial Party, the Union of Realists, Future of Russia/New Names and Dignity and Charity. Rybkin was then chairman of the State Duma, having been elected in December 1993 as a candidate of the Agrarian Party of Russia, which had eventually, after much prevarication, decided against participation in the bloc. Featuring Col.-Gen. Boris Gromov, the last Soviet commander in Afghanistan and leader of the My Fatherland (*Moye Otechestvo*) movement, Rybkin's list attracted 1.1% of the national vote, thus failing by a wide margin to obtain proportional seats, although three of its candidates were elected to the State Duma in the constituency section.

Women of Russia
Zhenshchiny Rossii (ZR)
  Address. 6 ul. Nemirovich Danchenko, Moscow
  Telephone. (#7–095) 209–7708
  Fax. (#07–095) 200–0274
  Leadership. Alevtina Fedulova (chair), Yekaterina Lakhova (parliamentary leader)

  Led by a former official of the Communist Party of the Soviet Union, the ZR aspires to bring about the social and political equality of women. Placed on the centre-left of the post-Soviet political spectrum, it advocates a "humane" approach to economic transition, favouring the retention of a comprehensive social welfare system and of free state education. It is also strongly in favour of the maintenance of law and order. Having won 25 seats in the 1993 State Duma elections (with 8.1% of the vote), the ZR based its 1995 campaign on a demand that the legislature (and not the President) should have the right to nominate and dismiss government ministers. It was reduced to three seats won in the constituency section, having narrowly failed to surmount the 5% barrier to proportional representation. The movement endorsed President Yeltsin in his successful re-election bid in mid-1996.

Workers' Self-Management Party
Partiya Narodnogo Samoupravleniya (PNS)
  Address. c/o Federalnoe Sobranie, Moscow
  Leadership. Svyatoslav Fedorov (chair)

  The centrist PNS was founded in August 1994 by Svyatoslav Fedorov, a distinguished eye surgeon who had previously been prominent in the Party of Economic Freedom and later in the Russian Movement for Democratic Reform, which was one of the antecedents of Russia's Democratic Choice. Supportive of pro-market economic reform, the PNS seeks in particular to represent the interests of small and medium-sized businesses. It was allied with the Party of People's Conscience for the December 1995 elections, in which it registered a not insignificant 4.1% of the national vote but won only one constituency seat. In the mid-1996 presidential elections, Fedorov came sixth out of 10 candidates in the first round, winning 0.9% of the vote.

Yavlinsky-Boldyrev-Lukin Bloc (Yabloko)
  Address. 1 Okhotnyi ryad, 121019 Moscow
  Leadership. Grigory Yavlinsky, Yuri Boldyrev, Vladimir Lukin

  Yabloko was launched in October 1993 by the three personalities giving their names to the formation, who supported transition to a market economy but strongly opposed the "shock therapy" then being administered by the Yeltsin administration. Yavlinksy was a well-known economist, Boldyrev a scientist and Lukin a former ambassador to the United States. Having won 33 seats and 7.8% of the proportional vote in the December 1993 elections, Yabloko was one of the few State Duma groups which declined to sign the April 1994 "civic accord treaty" between the government and most political groupings, on the grounds that the initiative contravened constitutional provisions. *Yabloko* also condemned the Russian military operation in Chechenya launched in December 1994. In the December 1995 State Duma elections, *Yabloko* took a creditable fourth place, winning 45 seats on a proportional vote share of 6.9%. Its candidate in the 1996 presidential election was Yavlinsky, who came fourth in the first round with 7.3% and gave qualified support to incumbent Boris Yeltsin in the second.

Other Parties and Groupings

All-Union Communist Party of Bolsheviks (*Vsesoyuznaya Kommunicheskaya Partiya Bolshevikov*, VKPB), led by Nina Andreyeva, political home of the hardest Communist hardliners, favouring a complete reversion to the Soviet system.

Beer Lovers' Party (*Partiya Lyubitelei Piva*, PLP), led by Konstantin Kalachev and Dimtry Shestakov, "alternative" party opposed to corruption and bureaucracy.

Constructive Ecological Movement of Russia (*Konstruktivno-Ekologicheskoye Dvizheniye Rossii*, KEDR), led by Anatoly Panfilov, environmentalist group whose Cyrillic script acronym means "cedar" in Russian, obtained 0.8% of the vote in December 1993.

Democratic Alternative Party (*Partiya Demokrat-icheskaya Alternativa*, PDA), led by Vyacheslav Shostakovsky, founded in February 1995 by centrist elements favouring pro-market reform but opposing "shock therapy" policies.

Democratic Party of Russia (*Demokraticheskaya Partiya Rossii*, DPR), led by Sergei Grazyev, founded in May 1990 in support of an independent Russian state in voluntary association with other Soviet republics, joined centrist pro-reform initiatives in 1991–92, but opposed break-up of USSR and moved to a more conservative stance, amid much internal dissension and several splits; won 21 seats in the 1993 elections (with 5.5% of the vote); its controversial then leader, Nikolai Travkin, joined the Chernomyrdin government in May 1994, thereby provoking opposition from DPR deputies, who effectively ousted him in October; in the December 1995 elections it was allied with the right-wing Congress of Russian Communities, but the leadership's decision to back the presidential candidacy of Gen. Lebed in 1996 provoked the formation of a pro-Yeltsin DPR faction.

Dignity and Charity (*Dostoinstvo i Miloserdie*, DM), led by Vyacheslav Grishin, centrist group representing war veterans and invalids, won 0.7% of the vote in 1993; in the 1995 elections formed part of the centre-left bloc headed by Ivan Rybkin (later founder of the Socialist Party of Russia).

For an Honest Russia (*Za Chestnuyu Rossiyu*), led by Oleg Novikov, founded in mid-1995 as a pro-reform electoral bloc based on the Association of Privatized and Private Enterprises, urging that the fight against corruption and organized crime should become a top government priority.

Future of Russia/New Names (*Budushchee Rossii/ Novye Imena*, BR/NI), centrist pro-reform grouping led by Oleg Sokolov, won 1.25% of the vote in 1993; in the 1995 elections formed part of the centre-left bloc headed by Ivan Rybkin (later founder of the Socialist Party of Russia).

Movement for Russia's National Revival (*Dvizheniye za Natsionalnoye Vozrozhdeniye Rossii*, DNVR), led by Dimitry Vasilyev, founded in 1994 as political arm of radical nationalist *Pamyat* ("Memory") organization and other groups of similar orientation; former *Pamyat* leader Konstantin Smirnov-Ostashuili committed suicide in April 1991 six months after being sentenced to two years in a labour camp for inciting racial hatred.

Muslims of Russia (*Musulmani Rossii*), led by Mukkadas Bibarsov, registered in July 1996, following a split in the Union of Muslims of Russia over its leadership's decision to endorse Boris Yeltsin in the 1996 presidential elections.

My Motherland (*Moya Rodina*, MR), led by Viktor Mishkin (a former secretary of the Young Communist League), leftist formation founded in March 1995, receiving some support in unreconstructed trade union hierarchies.

National Republican Party of Russia (*Natsionalno Respublikanskaya Partia Rossii*, NRPR), led by Nikolai Lysenko, a nationalist group which has made little electoral headway against competing right-wing parties, although for the December 1995 election it raised the 200,000 signatures needed for inclusion on ballot papers.

National Salvation Front (*Front Natsionalnogo Spaseniya*, FNS), led by Valery Smirnov, descended from the FNS founded in October 1992 by neo-Communists and Russian nationalists but immediately banned by President Yeltsin on grounds that it was "designed to fuel national dissension" and posed "a real threat to the integrity of the Russian Federation and the independence of neighbouring sovereign states"; unbanned in February 1993 by Constitutional Court ruling that Yeltsin had acted unconstitutionally, but still denied registration for the December 1993 elections (having backed the losing conservative side in the October confrontation between parliament and President); in 1994 the then FNS leadership joined former Vice-President Rutskoi's right-wing Power (*Derzhava*) bloc, while a new FNS leadership contested the 1995 elections on a similar platform combining Russian nationalism with opposition to further privatization.

Party of Economic Freedom (*Partiya Ekonomicheskoi Svobogy*, PES), led by entrepreneur Konstantin Borovoi and Sergei Federov, founded in June 1992 to promote "shock therapy" economic reform, disqualified from December 1993 elections for breaking rules, did not feature in December 1995 election results.

Party of National Unity (*Partiya Natsionalnogo Edinstva*, PNE), led by Vladimir Danilov, right-wing nationalist formation, refuses to recognize the demise of the Soviet Union, which it seeks to restore under Russian leadership.

Party of People's Conscience (*Partiya Narodnoi Sovesti*, PNS), led by Alexei Kazannik (a former prosecutor-general), created in early 1995 as a centrist electoral bloc that included the People's Self-Government Party and the People's Party of

Russia led by Telman Gdlyan; opposed to the Chernomyrdin government, the PNS demanded official action to combat organized crime, high-level corruption and general lawlessness.

Party of Russian Unity and Accord (*Partiya Rossiiskogo Edinstva i Soglasiya*, PRES), founded by Sergei Shakhrai and Aleksandr Shokhin (both former Deputy Prime Ministers), claiming to represent Russia's regional governments, advocates economic reform by gradualism; won 6.8% and 27 seats in December 1993 elections, thereafter holding senior ministerial posts, although Shokhin resigned as Deputy Prime Minister in November 1994; from May 1995 eclipsed as the "government party" by Our Home is Russia (which was joined by Shokhin).

Russian Christian Democratic Movement (*Rossiiskoye Khristianskoye Demokraticheskoye Dvizheniye*, RKhDD), led by Viktor Aksyuchits, Gleb Anishchenk, Vyacheslav Polossin, founded in April 1990 to promote "a radical reconstruction of all spheres of life in the country based on the norms of Christian morality"; originally participated in what became Russia's Democratic Choice, but withdrew because of its radical economic line and secular orientation, later aligned itself with the right-wing Power (*Derzhava*) movement; affiliated to Christian Democrat International.

Russian Movement for Democratic Reform (*Rossiiskoe Dvizheniye Demokraticheskikh Reform*, RDDR), led by Gavriil Popov (former mayor of Moscow), centrist group founded in February 1992 by dissidents of the International Movement for Democratic Reforms (*Mezhdunarodnoe Drizhenie Demokraticheskikh Reform*, MDDR), whose leaders had included Stanislav Shatalin (author of the "500 days" economic reform plan), Eduard Shevardnadze (once Soviet Foreign Minister and later President of Georgia) and Aleksandr Yakovlev (later leader of the Russian Party of Social Democracy); the RDDR participated in the July 1992 meeting that led to the creation of what later became Russia's Democratic Choice, but did not join the grouping; deserted early in 1995 by prominent member Anatoly Sobchak (then mayor of St Petersburg but defeated in June 1996), the RDDR joined the Social Democratic Platform bloc headed by the Russian Social Democratic Union, but made little impact in the December 1995 elections.

Russian National Unity (*Russkoye Natsionalnoye Edinstvo*, RNE), led by Aleksandr Barkashov, openly antisemitic far-right formation, advocating a "greater Russia" including adjoining territories of ethnic Russian population and the expulsion of non-Russians, thought to have support in the upper ranks of the military, police and state bureaucracy; its paramilitary wing was prominent in the October 1993 confrontation in Moscow, fighting on the side of the anti-Yeltsin hardliners and suffering many casualties; did not contest the 1995 elections in its own right, although members featured in the lists of other right-wing groups.

Russian Party of Social Democracy (*Rossiiskaya Partiya Sotsialnoy Demokratii*, RPSD), led by Aleksandr Yakovlev (former adviser to President Gorbachev and reputed to be the originator of *glasnost*, later head of the Ostankino television station), founded in February 1995, allied with Russia's Democratic Choice for 1995 elections.

Russian People's Congress Party (*Partiya Russkogo Narodnogo Kongressa*, PRNK), led by Nikolai Stolyarov, centrist group founded in May 1995; Stolyarov had previously been prominent in the New Regional Policy (*Novaya Regionalnaya Politika*, NRP) bloc of State Duma deputies mostly elected as independents in December 1993.

Russian Social Democratic Union (*Rossiiskii Sotsial-Demokraticheskii Soyuz*, RSDS), led by Vasily Lipitsky, founded in April 1995 by moderate faction of the Russian Social Democratic People's Party (RSDNP) after Lipitsky had been ousted as RSDNP leader by Aleksandr Rutskoi (later leader of the right-wing Power bloc); for the 1995 elections the new RSDS constructed a broader alliance called the Social Democratic Platform, which made little impact on voters, perhaps because the party was known to have considered inviting former Soviet leader Mikhail Gorbachev to join its list.

Russian Socialist Party (*Rossiiskaya Sotsialisticheskaya Partiya*, RSP), announced in late April 1996 by millionaire presidential candidate Vladimir Bryntsalov, who came last of 10 candidates in the first round in June with 0.2% of the vote; aiming to provide "a truly Russian model of socialism", the RSP was the third socialist party to be launched in April 1996, after the Socialist Party of Russia and the Socialist People's Party of Russia (also founded by a presidential candidate).

Russian United Industrial Party (*Rossiiskaya Obyedinennaya Promyshlennaya Partiya*, ROPP), led by Arkady Volsky and Vladimir Shcherbakov, centrist grouping founded in April 1995; prominent industrialist Volsky had previously headed the

Civic Union for Stability, Justice and Progress (GSSSP), linking elements of the Democratic Party of Russia and the People's Party of Free Russia (NPSR); in the 1995 elections the new ROPP was part of the centre-left bloc headed by Ivan Rybkin (later founder of the Socialist Party of Russia).

Russia's Regions (*Regiony Rossii*, RR), led by Artur Chilingarov, consisting of agricultural organizations throughout Russia, many of them dating from the Soviet era of agricultural collectivization; for the 1995 elections was the core component of the centre-left bloc headed by Ivan Rybkin (later founder of the Socialist Party of Russia).

Social Democratic Party of the Russian Federation (*Sotsial-Demokraticheskaya Partiya Rossiiskoi Federatsii*, SDPRF), led by Anatoly Golov, founded in May 1990 by a breakaway faction of the pro-Union Social Democratic Association (itself launched a year earlier by over 100 socialist and social democratic groups in the then Soviet Union); for the December 1995 elections the SDPRF was part of the unsuccessful Social Democratic Platform bloc headed by the Russian Social Democratic Union.

Socialist People's Party of Russia (*Partiya Sotsialisticheskaya Narodnoi Rossii*, PSNR), led by Martin Shakkum, founded in April 1966 by presidential candidate Martin Shakkum, who came eighth in the first round in June 1996, with 0.4% of the vote.

Socialist Workers' Party (*Sotsialisticheskaya Rabochaya Partiya*, SRP), led by Lyudmila Vartazarova, small leftist grouping that mainly operates as a pressure group within the Agrarian Party of Russia and the Communist Party of the Russian Federation.

Transformation of the Fatherland (*Preobrazheniye Otechestva*), led by Eduard Rossel, won 0.5% of the vote in December 1995 on a platform urging decentralization of economic and political power to the regions.

Union of Communist Parties (*Soyuz Kommunisticheskikh Partii*, SKP), led by Oleg Shenin and Viktor Anpilov, umbrella body of some 20 unreconstructed Communist groups in Russia and neighbouring republics, including the Russian Communist Workers' Party (*Rossiiskaya Kommunisticheskaya Rabochaya Partiya*, RKRP), led by Viktor Tyulkin, and Anpilov's Workers' Russia (*Rabochaya Rossiya*, RR); also active in the National Salvation Front, Anpilov had been one of those arrested after the October 1993 confrontation between State Duma conservatives and the President; a "Communists-Workers' Russia-For the Soviet Union" list took 4.6% of the vote in December 1995 but no seats; Anpilov and other leftists were carefully excluded from the new Popular-Patriotic Union of Russia initiated by the Communist Party of the Russian Federation in mid-1996.

Union of Muslims of Russia (*Soyuz Musulman Rossii*, SMR), led by Ruslan Aushev (President of Ingushetia) and Akhmet Khalitov, founded in 1995 with the aim of representing the Russian Federation's 20 million Muslims, strongly opposed to Russian military action in Chechenya, based its (unsuccessful) 1995 election campaign on proposition that Russia should emulate the sultanate of Brunei in its social and economic arrangements; its leadership backed Yeltsin in the 1996 presidential elections, thereby provoking an anti-Yeltsin faction to form the separate Muslims of Russia.

Union of Realists (*Soyuz Realistov*, SR), led by Yury Petrov (a formmer chief of staff to President Yeltsin), founded in March 1995 as an alliance of some 20 centrist groupings; in the 1995 elections formed part of the centre-left bloc headed by Ivan Rybkin (later founder of the Socialist Party of Russia)

Rwanda

Capital: Kigali

Population: 7,500,000 (1995E)

The Republic of Rwanda achieved independence from Belgium in 1962. Following a military coup led by Gen. Juvénal Habyarimana in 1973, the Hutu-dominated regime created the National Republican Movement for Democracy and Development (MRNDD), which remained the sole legal political party until the adoption of a multi-party constitution in 1991. By then a rebellion had been launched by the predominantly Tutsi Rwandan Patriotic Front

(FPR), with which the government signed the Arusha Accord of August 1993 providing for the establishment of interim institutions in a transition period leading to multi-party elections. However, delays in the deployment of a UN observer force and divisions within various political parties led to the repeated postponement of the start of the transition period.

The fragile peace process ended abruptly in April 1994 when President Habyarimana was killed in a plane crash and mass violence of genocidal proportions ensued. Although generally presented as an ethnic conflict between the majority Hutu and minority Tutsi, the violence was also politically-motivated, in that supporters of the Habyarimana regime sought to eliminate all opposition, Tutsi and Hutu. The violence prompted the resumption of the rebellion by the FPR which, by July 1994, claimed military victory. In the same month Pasteur Bizimungu, a senior FPR figure, was inaugurated as President for a five-year term and the composition of a new government of national unity was announced. The majority of posts in the Council of Ministers were assigned to FPR members, while the remainder were divided among the Republican Democratic Movement (whose leader was appointed Prime Minister), the Liberal Party, the Social Democratic Party and the Christian Democratic Party. The new administration declared its intention to honour the terms of the 1993 Arusha Accord within the context of an extended period of transition (to June 1999). However, the MRNDD and the Coalition for the Defence of the Republic (CDR) were excluded from participation in the government.

A 70–member Transitional National Assembly was inaugurated in December 1994 (without benefit of election). In May 1995 it adopted a new constitution which brought together elements of the 1991 constitution, the 1993 Arusha Accord, the FPR's victory declaration of July 1994 and a protocol of understanding signed in November 1994 by political parties not implicated in the earlier massacres. Presidential and legislative elections were last held (on a single-party basis) in December 1988.

Christian Democratic Party

Parti Démocratique Chrétien (PDC)

Address. BP 2348, Kigali

Telephone. (#250) 76542

Fax. (#250) 72237

Leadership. Jean-Nepomucene Nayinzira (leader)

The PDC, established in 1990, holds one portfolio in the FPR-led administration that came to power in July 1994.

Coalition for the Defence of the Republic

Coalition pour la Défense de la République (CDR)

The CDR was formed in 1992, drawing support from uncompromising Hutu groups. In the mass violence between April and June 1994, its unofficial militia (*Impuza Mugambi*, or "Single-Minded Ones") was reported to have taken a leading role in the slaughter of Tutsis and moderate Hutus. CDR participation in the transitional government and legislature was subsequently proscribed by the new administration led by the Rwandan Patriotic Front.

Liberal Party

Parti Libéral (PL)

Address. BP 1304, Kigali

Telephone. (#250) 77916

Fax. (#250) 73838

Leadership. Prosper Higiro, Justin Mugenzi (leaders of opposing factions)

Affiliated to the Liberal International, the PL was formed in 1991 but split into two factions during late 1993 and early 1994. The faction led by Higiro joined the government installed by the Rwandan Patriotic Front following its military victory in July 1994.

National Republican Movement for Democracy and Development

Mouvement Républicain National pour la Démocratie et le Développement (MRNDD)

Address. BP 1055, Kigali

Telephone. (#250) 76086

Fax. (#250) 76174

Leadership. Mathieu Ngirumpatse (chair)

The MRNDD (formerly the National Revolutionary Movement for Democracy until 1991) was founded in 1975 by Gen. Juvénal Habyarimana as a single national party embracing both military and civilian elements. Of Catholic orientation, it has observer status in the Christian Democrat International. It remained the sole legal party until the promulgation of legislation authorizing the formation of political parties in June 1991. The party retained a strong presence in subsequent coalition governments, ensuring President Habyarimana's continuing powerful influence. In the carnage that followed the

President's death in April 1994, the MRNDD's large unofficial militia (*Interahamwe*, or "Those Who Stand Together") was reported to be extensively involved in Hutu atrocities. The party was consequently excluded from the transitional government formed in July 1994 following the defeat of government forces by the Rwandan Patriotic Front.

Republican Democratic Movement
Mouvement Démocratique Républicain (MDR)
    Leadership. Faustin Twagiramungu (leader)
    The current MDR, legalized in July 1991, stems from the *Parmehutu*-MDR which was the dominant party until 1973 when it was banned by the Habyarimana regime. The MDR led the campaign in late 1991 for the creation of a provisional government of all parties to manage the transition to pluralism and, from April 1992, headed successive coalition governments. The party was a signatory of the August 1993 Arusha Accord with the then rebel Rwandan Patriotic Front (FPR), and Faustin Twagiramungu (on the anti-Habyarimana wing of the party) became the agreed nominee of the pro-democracy parties for the premiership in the envisaged transitional government. Many MDR members were subsequently victims of Hutu extremism in the atrocities perpetrated from April 1994. Twagiramungu was appointed Prime Minister in the FPR-dominated administration formed in July 1994. However, in August 1995, he was dismissed by President Bizimungu and replaced by Pierre-Celestin Rwigyema.

Rwandan Patriotic Front
Front Patriotique Rwandais (FPR)
    Leadership. Col. Alex Kanyarengwe (chair)
    The largely Tutsi FPR launched an insurgency from Uganda against the Habyarimana regime in October 1990. By 1992, in the light of extensive territorial gains by the FPR in northern Rwanda, the government was obliged to enter into negotiations which, a year later in August 1993, culminated in the signing of the Arusha Accord. The peace process was shattered in April 1994 by the massacres of Tutsis and moderate Hutus which followed the death of President Habyarimana, as a consequence of which the FPR renewed the military offensive that brought it to power three months later.

Social Democratic Party
Parti Social-Démocrate (PSD)
    Address. c/o Ministry of Finance, Kigali
    Leadership. Marc Rugenera, Augustin Iyamuremye, Charles Ntakirutinka
    The PSD was one of the first three opposition parties to be recognized under the 1991 constitution, and participated in government coalitions from April 1992. The party's president and vice-president were both killed in the mass violence from April 1994, their bodies being discovered and identified in February 1995. The PSD holds three portfolios in the coalition government dominated by the Rwandan Patriotic Front.

Other Parties

Ecologist Party (*Parti Ecologiste*, PECO), which had made little political headway.

Islamic Democratic Party (*Parti Démocratique Islamique*, PDI), aiming to represent Rwanda's small Muslim community.

Labour Rally for Democracy (*Rassemblement Travailliste pour la Démocratie*, RTD), led by Emmnauel Nizeyimana.

Progressive Party of Rwandan Youth (*Parti Progressiste de la Jeunesse Rwandaise*, PPJR), led by André Hakizimana.

Rwandan Democratic Party (*Parti Démocratique Rwandais*, PADER).

Rwandan People's Democratic Union (*Union Démocratique du Peuple Rwandais*, UDPR), headed by Vincent Gwabukwisi.

Rwandan Republican Party (*Parti Républicain Rwandais*, PARERWA), led by Augustin Mutumba.

Rwandan Socialist Party (*Parti Socialiste Rwandais*, PSR).

Union of the Rwandan People (*Union du Peuple Rwandais*, UPR), led by Silas Majyambere.

St Christopher and Nevis

Capital: Basseterre (St Kitts) **Population:** 45,000 (1995E)

The former British dependency of St Christopher (St Kitts) and Nevis has been fully independent since 1983. Under its independence constitution, the head of state is the British sovereign, represented by a Governor-General. The unicameral National Assembly, which has a five-year legislative mandate, consists of a Speaker, three senators nominated by the Governor-General on the advice of the government and the opposition (four if the Attorney-General is not an elected representative) and 11 members popularly elected by universal adult suffrage. The Prime Minister and Cabinet are responsible to the Assembly and appointed to office by the Governor-General upon its recommendation. The island of Nevis has its own legislature (the Nevis Island Assembly, consisting of five elected and three nominated members) and executive, having exclusive responsibility for the island's internal administration. Nevis has the right to secede from the federation with St Kitts, subject to a referendum.

In the general election held on July 3, 1995, the St Kitts-Nevis Labour Party won seven of the 11 National Assembly seats, ending 15 years of rule by the People's Action Movement, which won only one seat. Of the three seats for constituencies on Nevis, two were retained by the Concerned Citizens Movement and one by the Nevis Reformation Party.

Concerned Citizens Movement (CCM)

Address. c/o Assembly, Charlestown, Nevis
Leadership. Vance Amory (leader)

The Nevis-based CCM first won representation in the Nevis Island Assembly in 1987, and gained one National Assembly seat in 1989. In June 1992 the party won control of the local Assembly (returning three of the five elected members), and the following year increased its National Assembly representation to two seats, both of which it retained in the July 1995 elections. As Premier of Nevis, CCM leader Vance Amory in June 1996 instructed his legal department to prepare a bill for the secession of Nevis.

Nevis Reformation Party (NRP)

Address. PO Box 480, Charlestown Nevis
Leadership. Joseph Parry (leader)

The NRP was formed in 1970, advocating the secession of Nevis from St Kitts. In 1980, having retained two National Assembly seats, the party formed a coalition government with the People's Action Movement which oversaw the independence of the federal state of St Kitts-Nevis. In August 1983 the NRP won all five elective seats on the Nevis Island Assembly, and the following year returned all three Nevis members to the National Assembly. From 1989 it lost ground to the Concerned Citizens Movement, retaining only one local Assembly seat in June 1992, and one National Assembly seat in both the 1993 and 1995 elections.

The NRP is an affiliate of the International Democrat Union.

People's Action Movement (PAM)

Address. PO Box 330, Cayon Street, Basseterre
Telephone. (#1-809) 465-4018
Fax. (#1-809) 465-1001
Leadership. Kennedy Alphonse Simmonds (leader)

The centrist PAM was formed in 1965. Campaigning in the 1980 elections on a platform of early independence, the party won three of the (then) nine elective seats, which with the two seats won by the Nevis Reformation Party (NRP) permitted the formation of a coalition government. The coalition led St Kitts-Nevis to independence in 1983, when Simmonds became the first Prime Minister. The PAM won an absolute majority of seats in both the 1984 and 1989 elections. In the 1993 poll, although finishing second in the popular vote and returning only four of the 11 National Assembly members, the PAM retained office as a minority government with the support of the NRP. In the subsequent atmosphere of increasing political instability, an early election was called for July 1995, in which the party lost all but one seat and was forced into opposition.

The PAM is affiliated to the Christian Democrat International and is linked to the International Democrat Union through the Caribbean Democrat Union.

St Kitts-Nevis Labour Party (SKNLP)

Address. Masses House, PO Box 550, Basseterre
Telephone. (#1–809) 465-5347
Fax. (#1–809) 465-8328
Leadership. Denzil D. Douglas (leader), Herbert Wycliff-Morton (chair), Joseph M. France (national secretary)

Founded in 1932 as a socialist organization, the Labour Party was the dominant party under the British colonial regime before 1980. Having lost power in the 1980 elections to a coalition of the People's Action Movement and the Nevis Reformation Party, the party opposed what it regarded as the disproportionate amount of power given to Nevis by the independence constitution of 1983. It remained in opposition (failing to persuade the Concerned Citizens Movement to form a coalition following the 1993 elections) until the July 1995 polls when it won a secure majority of National Assembly seats, and formed a new administration.

The SKNLP is a consultative member of the Socialist International.

Other Parties

People's Democratic Party (PDP), a Nevis-based organization led by Theodore Hobson.

Progressive Liberal Party (PLP), launched in 1988 in St Kitts and headed by James Sutton.

United National Movement (UNM), Nevis-based and under the leadership of Eugene Walwyn.

United People's Party (UPP), formed in 1993 in St Kitts and led by Michael Powell.

St Lucia

Capital: Castries

Population: 142,300 (1995E)

St Lucia became independent of the United Kingdom in 1979, remaining within the Commonwealth. The head of state is the British sovereign, represented by a Governor-General. Legislative power is vested in a bicameral parliament consisting of an appointed Senate, and a 17–member House of Assembly which is popularly elected for a five-year term. The Prime Minister and Cabinet are responsible to parliament and are appointed to office by the Governor General acting on its advice. In the general election on April 27, 1992, the ruling United Workers' Party (UWP) won a third consecutive term of office, obtaining 11 of the 17 seats against six for the St Lucia Labour Party.

Progressive Labour Party (PLP)

Address. 19 St Louis Street, Castries
Telephone. (#1–809) 452 2203
Leadership. George Odlum (chair)

The PLP was formed in 1981 by left-wing defectors headed by George Odlum from the then ruling St Lucia Labour Party (SLP). In the May 1982 general elections the party won only one seat, despite gaining just over 27% of the vote. In subsequent elections in 1987 and 1992 support for the PLP drastically declined and it did not win any parliamentary representation.

St Lucia Labour Party (SLP)

Address. PO Box 64, Castries
Telephone. (#1–809) 452-6032
Fax. (#1–809) 453-1977

Leadership. Julian R. Hunte (leader), Philip J. Pierre (chair), Oliver Scott (general secretary)

The SLP was formed in 1946 and, having won the first elections held under universal adult suffrage in 1951, held power in the then colony until 1964. It remained in opposition until the first post-independence election in 1979, when it won a majority and formed a new government. The party then suffered a period of internal disaffection, again going into opposition following an early election in May 1982. It recovered some support over the following years, winning eight of the 17 parliamentary seats in the two elections in April 1987 (following which there was another crucial defection), but secured only six seats in the 1992 elections.

The SLP is a consultative member of the Socialist International.

United Workers' Party (UWP)

Address. 1 Riverside Road, Castries
Telephone. (#1–809) 452-3438
Leadership. Vaughan Lewis (leader)

The right-wing UWP was formed in 1964, evolving from the National Labour Movement and People's Progressive Party of the 1950s. Under the leadership of John Compton, the party ruled from 1964 until 1979, when it was decisively beaten in the first post-independence election. Having joined a coalition government of national unity in the early months of 1982, the UWP then won over 56% of the vote in the May 1982 elections and was returned to power. The party has since retained a (sometimes slim) parliamentary majority, most recently winning 11 seats in the 1992 elections. In early 1996 John Compton retired as leader of the UWP (after 30 years) and as Prime Minister. He was replaced by Vaughan Lewis, who named his new Cabinet in early April and awarded Compton the honorary non-cabinet post of senior minister.

The UWP is linked to the International Democrat Union through its membership of the Caribbean Democrat Union.

St Vincent and the Grenadines

Capital: Kingstown

Population: 110,000 (1995E)

A former British dependency, St Vincent and the Grenadines became fully independent in October 1979. The head of state is the British sovereign, represented within the islands by a Governor-General. The unicameral House of Assembly, which serves a five-year term of office, comprises six appointed Senators (four by the government and two by the opposition) and 15 representatives popularly elected by universal adult suffrage. The Prime Minister and Cabinet are responsible to the Assembly and are appointed to office by the Governor-General acting upon its advice. The governing New Democratic Party won 12 National Assembly seats at the general election of Feb. 21, 1994, the remaining three going to a centre-left opposition electoral alliance that became the United Labour Party.

New Democratic Party (NDP)

Address. PO Box 1300, Kingstown
Telephone. (1-809) 456-1703
Fax. (#1-809) 475-2152
Leadership. Sir James Mitchell (president)

The conservative NDP was launched by the current party president in 1975, supporting political unity in the East Caribbean, social development and free enterprise. Having become the formal opposition party in 1979 and the ruling party in 1984, the NDP won all 15 elective seats in the House of Assembly in the 1989 polls, drawing two-thirds of the total vote. Although there was an appreciable drop in support (to about 54%) in the 1994 elections, the party retained power under Mitchell's continuing premiership.

The NDP is affiliated to the International Democrat Union.

People's Political Party (PPP)

Leadership. George Walker (leader)

The PPP was a significant political force from its foundation in 1952 until the late 1970s, became largely inactive in the 1980s but appeared to gain a new lease of life in the mid-1990s as a focus of opposition to corruption and incompetence in the established political class.

United Labour Party (ULP)

Address. PO Box 1491, Bay Street, Kingstown
Telephone. (#1–809) 457-2761
Fax. (#1–809) 457-2761
Leadership. Vincent Beache (leader), Louis Straker (chair), Julian Francis (general secretary)

The ULP was formally constituted in September 1994 by the merger of the St Vincent Labour Party (SVLP), formed in 1955 as a moderate, social democratic organization, and the more left-wing Movement for National Unity (MNU), founded in 1982 by Ralph Gonsalves upon his withdrawal from the United People's Movement. The SVLP, having won a solid electoral victory in 1974, led the country to independence in October 1979, and retained power in the first post-independence balloting the following December. In opposition from

1984, the party fought the February 1994 elections in alliance with the MNU, winning nearly 44% of the votes cast but only three seats.

The ULP is a consultative member of the Socialist International.

United People's Movement (UPM)
Leadership. Oscar Allen (leader)

The UPM was formed as a coalition of left-wing groups in August 1979, and unsuccessfully contested the elections at the end of that year. In 1982 the founder, Ralph Gonsalves, left the party to form the less radical MNU (later a component of the United Labour Party). The UPM failed to secure any legislative representation in the 1984, 1989 or 1994 elections.

San Marino

Capital: San Marino

Population: 24,500 (1995E)

The Most Serene Republic of San Marino, which traces its independent history back to 301 AD and its constitution to 1600, is a parliamentary democracy with a flourishing multi-party system. Legislative power is vested in the 60–member Grand and General Council (*Consiglio Grande e Generale*), which is directly elected by a system of proportional representation by citizens aged 18 and over, serving a five-year term subject to dissolution. A ten-member Congress of State (*Congresso di Stato*), or government, is elected by the Council for the duration of its term. Two members of the Council are designated for six-month terms as executive Captains Regent (*Capitani Reggenti*), one representing the city of San Marino and the other the countryside. An interval of three months must elapse before a councillor can be re-elected as a Captain Regent.

Elections to the Grand and General Council on May 30, 1993, resulted as follows: Christian Democratic Party of San Marino 26 seats (with 41.4% of the vote), Socialist Party of San Marino 14 (23.7%), Progressive Democratic Party 11 (18.6%), Popular Democratic Alliance 4 (7.7%), Democratic Movement 3 (5.3%), Communist Refoundation 2 (3.4%).

Christian Democratic Party of San Marino
Partito Democratico Cristiano Sammarinese (PDCS)
   Address. 6 via delle Scalette, 47031 San Marino
   Telephone. (#39-541) 991193
   Fax. (#39-541) 99269
   Leadership. Cesare Antonio Gasperoni (secretary-general)
   Founded in 1948, the PDCS was in opposition to a left-wing coalition until 1957, whereafter it headed centre-left coalitions until reverting to opposition in 1978. The party achieved narrow pluralities in successive Council elections, winning 25 seats in 1974, 26 in both 1978 and 1983 and 27 in 1988. The PDCS returned to power in July 1986, when the left-wing government collapsed and was replaced by San Marino's (and Europe's) first-ever coalition between Christian Democrats and Communists. This lasted until February 1992, when the PDCS opted to form a coalition with the Socialist Party of San Marino. The Christian Democrats retained their Council dominance in the 1993 elections, albeit with slightly reduced representation of 26 seats.

The PDCS is affiliated to the Christian Democrat International.

Communist Refoundation
Rifondazione Comunista (RC)
   Address. c/o Consiglio Grande e Generale, San Marino
   Leadershhip. Giuseppe Amichi, Renato Fabbri
   Following the example of the Communist Refoundation Party in Italy, the RC was founded by a minority Marxist-Leninist faction of the San Marino Communist Party which declined to accept the conversion of the latter into the democratic socialist Progressive Democratic Party in April 1990. The new formation won two Council seats on a 3.4% vote share in May 1993.

Democratic Movement
Movimiento Democratico (MD)
   Address. c/o Consiglio Grande e Generale, San Marino
   Leadership. Emilio Della Balda
   The MD was created prior to the 1993 election

as successor to the San Marino Social Democratic Party (PSDS), which had been founded in December 1975 by the more right-wing faction of the Independent San Marino Democratic Socialist Party (PSDIS), itself a right-wing breakaway from the San Marino Socialist Party (PSS). To complicate matters further, MD leader Emilio Della Balda had previously been leader of the more left-wing ex-PSDIS faction, namely the Unitarian Socialist Party (PSU), but had rejected the PSU's decision to rejoin the PSS in 1990.

The most moderate of tiny San Marino's three non-communist socialist parties, the PSDS had won two Council seats in the 1978 election and had joined the governing coalition in 1982–83, being reduced to one seat in the 1983 election and to none in 1988, although Della Balda was elected as a Socialist and therefore gave the MD parliamentary status at its formation. In the 1993 election the new MD won three seats.

Popular Democratic Alliance

Alleanza Democratica Popolare (ADP)

Address. c/o Consiglio Grande e Generale, San Marino

Leadership. Tito Masi

The centrist ADP emerged before the May 1993 Council elections, in which it took fourth place behind the three main parties, winning four seats.

Progressive Democratic Party

Partito Democratico Progressista (PDP)

Address. 1 via Sentier Rosso, San Marino

Telephone. (#39-541) 991199

Leadership. Stefano Macina (secretary-general)

The PDP was founded in April 1990 as successor to the San Marino Communist Party (PCS), in line with similar conversions to democratic socialism on the part of Communist parties elsewhere in Europe. Founded in 1941, the PCS had been an orthodox pro-Soviet party after World War II, being in government with the San Marino Socialist Party (PSS) until 1957. It had come back to government in 1978 in coalition with the PSS. Confirmed in office in 1983, the left-wing

government had collapsed in 1986 amid differences over foreign and domestic issues, being replaced by the first-ever coalition of the PCS and the San Marino Christian Democratic Party (PDCS). PCS Council representation had risen to 18 at the May 1988 elections. The new PDP was forced into opposition in February 1992 when the PDCS decided that the PSS was a more suitable partner.

Socialist Party of San Marino

Partito Socialista Sammarinese (PSS)

Address. 46 via G. Ordelaffi, Borgo Maggiore, 47031 San Marino

Telephone. (#39-541) 902016

Fax. (#39-541) 906438

Leadership. Marino Bollini (president), Maurizio Rattini (secretary-general)

The PSS was in coalition government with the Communists from 1945 until 1957 and then in opposition until 1973, when it entered a coalition with the Christian Democratic Party (PDCS). The Socialists were a distant second to the PDCS in successive Council elections, winning eight seats in 1974 against 25 for the PDCS. The PDCS/PSS coalition continued until November 1977, when the Socialists withdrew because of economic policy differences. The party retained eight Council seats in the 1978 elections, thereafter entering a left-wing coalition with the Communists and the Unitarian Socialists (PSU) which continued after the 1983 elections, in which the PSS advanced to nine seats. The left-wing coalition collapsed in mid-1986, when the PSS went into formal opposition for the first time since World War II. In 1990 the PSU (which had been formed in 1975 by a left-wing faction of the Independent Social Democrats, themselves originally a right-wing splinter of the PSS) merged with the PSS. The PSS revived its coalition with the PDCS in February 1992, continuing it after the May 1993 elections, when it advanced to 14 seats.

The PSS is affiliated to the Socialist International.

São Tomé and Príncipe

Capital: São Tomé

Population: 127,000 (1995E)

The Democratic Republic of São Tomé and Príncipe achieved full independence from Portugal in 1975. There was only one legal political party—the Movement for the Liberation of São Tomé and Príncipe–Social Democratic Party (MLSTP-PSD)—until August 1990, when a new constitution providing for a multi-party democratic system was approved by referendum. Under the constitution, executive power is vested in a directly-elected President who may serve for a maximum of two consecutive five-year terms. Legislative power is vested in a 55–member National Assembly (*Assembléia Nacional*) with a maximum four-year term. A regional government looks after the affairs of the island of Príncipe, which assumed autonomous status in April 1995.

Presidential elections in March 1991 were won by independent candidate Miguel Trovoada, who was supported by the Democratic Convergence Party–Reflection Group, which had defeated the ruling party in the first multi-party legislative elections two months earlier. Further legislative elections in October 1994 resulted in the MLSTP-PSD winning a plurality of 27 seats and regaining governmental power. In August 1995 a group of young army officers temporarily seized power in a bloodless coup. However, following mediation by Angolan representatives, the President and civilian government were restored to office.

In further presidential elections on June 30 and July 21, 1996, incumbent Miguel Trovoada (Independent Democratic Action) was re-elected in the second round with 52.7% of the vote. Another brief military takeover by young army officers followed in August, but President Trovoada was restored to power on Aug. 22.

Democratic Convergence Party–Reflection Group
Partido de Convergencia Democrática–Grupo de Reflexão (PCD-GR)
   Address. c/o Assembléia Nacional, São Tomé
   Leadership. Leonel Mario d'Alva (chair), João do Sacramento Bonfim (secretary-general)

Initially an underground opposition movement, the PCD-GR formally came into existence following the constitutional changes in 1990. In the January 1991 legislative elections the party won a majority with just over 54 per cent of the votes cast, and in March it supported the successful presidential candidacy of Miguel Trovoada. Relations between the PCD-GR and the President subsequently deteriorated, as did the party's popularity, culminating in defeat in the legislative elections in October 1994, in which its representation in the National Assembly fell from 33 to 14.

Independent Democratic Action
Ação Democrática Independente (ADI)
   Address. c/o Assembléia Nacional, São Tomé
   Leadership. Gabriel Costa (leader)

Founded in 1992 under the leadership of an adviser to President Trovoada, the centrist ADI won 14 of the 55 seats in the National Assembly in the 1994 elections, making it the joint runner-up with the Democratic Convergence Party–Convergence Group. In January 1996 the ADI accepted representation in a government of national unity headed by the Movement for the Liberation of São Tomé and Príncipe–Social Democratic Party. Trovoada was re-elected President in the second round of voting in July, having come a poor second in the first round with only 25% of the vote.

Movement for the Liberation of São Tomé and Príncipe-Social Democratic Party (MLSTP-PSD)
Movimento de Libertação de São Tomé e Príncipe-Partido Social Democrata (MLSTP-PSD)
   Address. c/o Assembléia Nacional, São Tomé
   Leadership. Carlos Alberto da Graça (secretary-general), Armindo Vaz de Almeida (deputy secretary-general)

The leftist MLSTP was formed in the early 1970s and became the driving force in the campaign against Portuguese rule. After independence it maintained its position as the sole legal political organization until the adoption of multi-partyism in 1990, at which point the Social Democratic Party designation was added to its title and the longstanding leader, Manuel Pinto da Costa, stood down. The party was defeated by the Democratic Convergence Party–Convergence Group in the January 1991 legislative elections and did not endorse any candidates in the presidential poll the following March. However, in the October 1994 legislative elections, the MLSTP-PSD was returned to power winning 27 of the seats in the 55–member National Assembly. The party's secretary-general, Carlos Alberto da Graça, was appointed Prime Minister of a Cabinet largely composed of MLSTP-PSD members. In December 1995, however, he was replaced by his party deputy, Armindo Vaz de Almeida, who formed a national unity government also including the Independent Democratic Alliance (ADI) and the extra-parliamentary Opposition Democratic Coalition. The MLSTP-PSD candidate in the mid-1996 presidential elections was da Costa, who headed the field in the first round with 40% of the vote but lost to the incumbent in the second round, when he received 47.3%.

Opposition Democratic Coalition
Coligação Democrática da Oposição (CODO)
 Leadership. Virgilio Carvalho (leader)

CODO had its beginnings in the the mid-1980s as an alliance of Portugal-based exile groups in opposition to the then single-party regime. Following the introduction of multi-partyism, it contested the January 1991 legislative elections winning a single seat. It failed to gain any representation in the October 1994 Assembly poll, but was nevertheless included in a national unity government formed in January 1996.

Other Parties

Christian Democratic Front (*Frente Democrata Cristã*, FDC), launched in late 1990, the small right-wing FDC failed to secure legislative representation in either the 1991 or the 1994 elections.

Popular Alliance (*Aliança Popular*, AP), led by Carlos Espírito Santo, a small Portugal-based expatriate party, recognized in 1993.

Saudi Arabia

Capitals: Riyadh (royal capital),
 Jeddah (administrative capital)

Population: 19,500,000 (1995E)

The Kingdom of Saudi Arabia is under the direct rule of the King, who is also the Prime Minister and who presides over a Council of Ministers. There is no parliament nor are there any legal political parties. A royal decree in March 1992 provided for the establishment of a Consultative Council, composed of 60 members and a chairman and appointed every four years in accordance with the Islamic principle of "consultation". The Consultative Council, which has only an advisory role, was inaugurated in December 1993. No details of its deliberations have been made public.

Senegal

Capital: Dakar

Population: 8,200,000 (1995E)

Senegal was under French rule until it achieved independence with Mali as the Federation of Mali in June 1960. The Federation, formed the previous year, was dissolved in August 1960 when Senegal withdrew. The following month the Republic of Senegal was proclaimed. Under its 1963 constitution as amended, executive power is vested in the President, who is directly elected by universal suffrage for a five-year term. The President, as head of state and head of government, appoints the Prime Minister who appoints the Council of Ministers in consultation with the President. Legislative power is vested in a bicameral parliament consisting of the 120–member National Assembly (*Asssemblée Nationale*), which is also directly elected for a five-year term, and a Senate (*Sénat*), the intention to establish the latter body being announced at the end of 1995.

In presidential elections on Feb. 21, 1993, President Abdou Diouf of the Senegal Socialist Party (PSS) won his third term of office, with 58.4% of the votes cast. In Assembly elections on May 9, 1993, the PSS obtained 84 seats (with 56.6% of the vote), the Senegalese Democratic Party 27 (30.2%) and four minor parties or alliances the other nine seats.

African Party for Democracy and Socialism/And Jëf

Parti Africain pour la Démocratie et le Socialisme/And Jëf (PADS/AJ)

   Address. BP 12025, Dakar

   Leadership. Landing Savane (secretary-general)

The progressive reformist PADS/AJ was formed in 1991 by a merger of the Revolutionary Movement for the New Democracy with two other left-wing groups. The party's leader, Landing Savane, took third place in the February 1993 presidential election but gained less than 3% of the votes cast. In May 1993 the party contested the legislative elections in an alliance with the National Democratic Rally and the Convention of Democrats and Patriots, which was called *Jappoo Liggeeyal* (Let Us Unite) and which won three National Assembly seats (and 4.9% of the vote). In February 1994 Savane and the leader of the Senegalese Democratic Party (PDS) were arrested and charged with provoking anti-government riots. The charges against them were dropped later in the year. It was reported in September 1994 that the PADS/AJ, the PDS and the Movement for Socialism and Unity had formed an opposition coalition called *Bokk Sopi Senegal* (Uniting to Change Senegal).

Convention of Democrats and Patriots

Convention des Démocrates et des Patriotes (CDP)

   Address. 96 rue 7, Bopp, Dakar

   Leadership. Iba Der Thiam (secretary-general)

The CDP was established in 1992 by Iba Der Thiam, a former government minister, who stood as a presidential election candidate in February 1993 but gained only 1.6% of the vote. The party contested the May 1993 Assembly election in an alliance with the African Party for Democracy and Progress/And Jëf and the National Democratic Rally.

Democratic League-Labour Party Movement

Ligue Démocratique-Mouvement pour le Parti du Travail (LD-MPT)

   Address. BP 10172, Dakar Liberté

   Leadership. Abdoulaye Bathily (secretary-general)

The Marxist LD-MPT was registered in 1981. Increasingly critical of the Diouf administration, party leader Bathily launched a campaign in 1990 for a "non-Diouf unity government". His unsuccessful presidential candidacy in February 1993 attracted only 2.4% of the votes cast, although the party secured three seats (and 4.1% of the vote) in the National Assembly elections the following May.

Independence and Labour Party

Parti de l'Indépendance et du Travail (PIT)

   Address. BP 5612, Dakar Fann

   Leadership. Amath Dansokho (secretary-general)

The communist PIT, formed by a dissident faction of the African Independence Party, was registered in 1981. Having co-operated with other opposition groups in the late 1980s, the party subsequently entered into negotiations with the ruling Senegal Socialist Party and, in 1991, secretary-general Dansokho joined the Diouf government. In May 1993 the PIT won two seats in the legislative elections, gaining just over 3% of the vote. The party's central committee issued a statement critical of the government in August 1995, and the following month Dansokho was dismissed from the government, together with Maguette Thiam, another senior PIT official.

Movement for Socialism and Unity

Mouvement pour le Socialisme et l'Unité (MSU)

   Address. Villa no 54, rue 4, Bopp, Dakar

   Leadership. Dia Mamadou (secretary-general)

The MSU was registered in 1981 as the *Mouvement Démocratique Populaire*, advocating socialist self-management for the economy. It did not contest the presidential or legislative elections in 1993, but was reported in September 1994 to have joined the African Party for Democracy and Socialism/And Jëf and the Senegalese Democratic Party in an opposition coalition.

National Democratic Rally

Rassemblement National Démocratique (RND)

   Address. Villa no 29, Cité de Professeurs, Fann Résidence, Dakar

Leadership. Madior Diouf (secretary-general)

The progressive RND was founded in 1976 by Cheikh Anta Diop (who died in 1986) but was not legalized until 1981. Secretary-general Madior Diouf stood in the February 1993 presidential election, taking sixth place with just under 1% of the vote. The party contested the National Assembly elections within the opposition *Jappoo Liggeeyal* (Let Us Unite) alliance with the African Party for Democracy and Progress/And Jëf and the Convention of Democrats and Patriots, which won three seats.

Party for the Liberation of the People

Parti pour la Libération du Peuple (PLP)
 Address. 4025 Sicap Amitié II, Dakar
 Leadership. Babacar Niang (secretary-general)

The anti-imperialist PLP was formed in 1983 by dissident National Democratic Rally members, who accused the party under Cheikh Anta Diop's leadership of becoming an ally of the government. Secretary-general Niang stood as a candidate in the February 1993 presidential election, taking eighth and last place with 0.8% of the vote.

Senegal Socialist Party

Parti Socialiste Sénégalais (PSS)
 Address. BP 12010, Dakar
 Telephone. (#221) 252232
 Fax. (#221) 258054
 Leadership. Abdou Diouf (secretary-general), Papa Amath Dieng (permanent secretary)

Founded in 1958 but descended from pre-war socialist movements in French West Africa, the democratic socialist PSS has been the ruling party in Senegal since independence in 1960, adopting its present name at the end of 1976, before which change it had been called the Senegalese Progressive Union (UPS). Although it was in effect the country's only legal party between 1964 and 1974 under the presidency of its founder, Léopold Sédar Senghor, the constitution continued to guarantee a plurality of political parties and in 1974 the Senegalese Democratic Party was officially recognized as an opposition party. A three-party system, introduced in 1976, was later extended to allow a multiplicity of parties. Abdou Diouf assumed the leadership of the PSS in 1981, after which new agricultural and industrial policies, intended to give a greater role to the private sector, were adopted.

The PSS has dominated all Senegalese elections, most recently in 1993, when Diouf retained the presidency of the Republic and the party won 84 seats in the 120–member National Assembly. The party is a member of the Socialist International

Senegalese Democratic Party

Parti Démocratique Sénégalais (PDS)
 Address. 5 blvd Dial Diop, Dakar
 Telephone. (#221) 257406
 Fax. (#221) 256177
 Leadership. Abdoulaye Wade (secretary-general)

Founded in 1974, the liberal democratic PDS was required by a constitutional amendment of March 1976 to adopt a formal political position to the right of the government party (in a three-party system which was later expanded to cover further parties). In successive legislative elections since 1978, it has been runner-up to, but some distance behind, the Senegal Socialist Party (PSS)—most recently in May 1993, when the party secured 27 seats in the National Assembly with 30.2% of the vote share. In presidential elections over the same period, party leader Wade has been similarly placed. In the February 1993 poll he gained just over 32% of the votes cast.

Although the PDS was the major element in the growing opposition movement at the end of the 1980s, the party was persuaded by early 1991 (like the Independence and Labour Party) to accept the government's offer of participation in a coalition administration. This continued until October 1992, when Wade and the other PDS members in the government resigned their posts. In May 1994 charges against Wade for his alleged role in the assassination of a member of the Constitutional Court in May 1993 were dismissed. Other charges, linked to anti-government rioting in February 1994, were similarly dropped later in the year. It was reported in September 1994 that the PDS had joined the African Party for Democracy and Socialism/And Jëf and the Movement for Socialism and Unity in an opposition coalition. In March 1995 the PDS resumed its participation in the PSS-dominated coalition government, being assigned five portfolios.

The PDS is a member of the Liberal International.

Senegalese Democratic Union-Renewal

Union Démocratique Sénégalais-Rénovation (UDS-R)
 Address. Villa no 272, Ouagou Niayes, Dakar
 Leadership. Mamadou Puritain Fall (secretary-general)

Defining itself as progressive-nationalist, the UDS-R was set up in 1985 by dissidents from the Senegalese Democratic Party. In the May 1993 legislative elections the party won a single seat in the National Assembly with 1.2% of the vote.

Other Parties

African Independence Party (*Parti Africain de l'Indépendance*, PAI), a Marxist-Leninist formation dating from 1957 which was legalized in 1976 within the then three-party system; dissident factions subsequently broke away, forming the Independence and Labour Party and the African Party for the Independence of the Masses.

African Party for the Independence of the Masses (*Parti Africain pour l'Indépendance des Masses*, PAI-M), a splinter group from the African Independence Party which was legalized in 1982.

Senegalese Democratic Party-Renewal (*Parti Démocratique Sénégalais-Rénovation*, PDS-R), a breakaway group from the Senegalese Democratic Party which was registered in 1987 under the leadership of Sérigne Diop.

Senegalese People's Party (*Parti Populaire Sénégalais*, PPS), registered in 1981 and following an independent Marxist line, led by Oumar Wone.

Separatist Groups

Men and Women Fighting for Truth (*Dahira Moustarchidine Oua Moustarchidate*), a radical Islamic group which was proscribed in February 1994.

Movement of Democratic Forces of Casamance (*Mouvement des Forces Démocratiques de la Casamance*, MFDC), an outlawed separatist group which has pursued armed resistance to the government in the southern province of Casamance; placed under house arrest in April 1995, the MFDC leader, Fr Diamakoune Senghor, called in a national broadcast in December 1995 for all MFDC activists to lay down their arms.

Seychelles

Capital: Victoria　　　　　　　　　　　　　　　　**Population:** 74,000 (1995E)

The Republic of Seychelles achieved independence from Britain in June 1976. President James Mancham, who at that time led the Seychelles Democratic Party, was ousted in a coup in 1977 by the present head of state, France-Albert René. René established a one-party state with the Seychelles People's Progressive Front (SPPF) as the sole legal party. Pressure for democratic reform was resisted until December 1991, when the SPPF endorsed a return to political pluralism. A new constitution, drafted by an elected constitutional commission, was approved in a popular referendum in June 1993. It provided for the simultaneous direct election for five-year terms of the President and unicameral National Assembly (with 11 of the Assembly's 33 seats allocated on a proportional basis to parties obtaining at least 9% of the total votes cast). The President may hold office for a maximum of three consecutive terms.

Multi-party Assembly elections on July 23, 1993, resulted in the SPPF obtaining 28 seats (with 57.5% of the proportional vote), the Democratic Party 4 (32.8%) and the United Opposition 1 (9.7%). In a simultaneous presidential contest, President René was re-elected with 59.5% of the vote..

Democratic Party (DP)
Address. POB 413, Mont Fleuri
Telephone. (#248) 224916
Fax. (#248) 224302
Leadership. Sir James Mancham (leader), Daniel Belle (secretary-general)

The DP was registered in March 1992 as a revival of the former Social Democratic Party, which had been effectively dissolved following the declaration of a one-party state in the late 1970s. Party leader and former President of the

Republic, Sir James Mancham, returned from exile in April 1992. In July 1992 the DP won eight of the 22 seats on the constitutional commission elected to draft a new constitution. In multi-party presidential elections held the following July, Mancham was runner-up to incumbent President René of the Seychelles People's Progressive Front, taking 36.7% of the vote. At the same time, in elections to the National Assembly, the DP obtained four seats allocated on a proportional basis.

National Alliance Party (NAP)

Address. 210 Victoria House, POB 673, Victoria
Telephone. (#248) 225562
Fax. (#248) 225626
Leadership. Philippe Boullé (leader)

Founded in 1992, the NAP contested the elections the following year within the United Opposition coalition, which secured only one proportionally allocated seat in the National Assembly. As the UO candidate in the presidential elections, NAP leader Boullé came in third place with only 3.8% of the vote.

Seychelles National Movement
Mouvement National Seychellois (MNS)

Address. c/o National Assembly, Victoria
Leadership. Gaby Hoarau (president)

The MNS was formed and originally based in Belgium in the 1980s. In 1993 it joined the United Opposition electoral coalition, which won just under 10% of the vote in the legislative elections of that year, gaining one seat.

Seychelles Party
Parti Seychellois
Parti Seselwa (PS)

Address. c/o National Assembly, Victoria
Leadership. Rev. Wavel Ramkalawan (leader)

Registered in January 1992 and a constituent party of the United Opposition, the PS has sought to win the support of the Creole community.

Seychelles People's Progressive Front (SPPF)
Front Populaire Progressiste des Seychelles (FPPS)

Address. PO Box 154, Victoria
Telephone. (#248) 224455
Fax. (#248) 225351
Leadership. France-Albert René (leader and secretary-general), James Michel (deputy secretary-general)

Founded in 1964 as the left-of-centre Seychelles People's United Party, the SPPF adopted its present name in 1978, a successful coup having been staged the previous year by party leader René, who was then Prime Minister. René assumed the presidency of the Republic and the SPPF became the sole legal party until December 1991, when the ban on political activity by other parties was suspended. In elections to the constitutional commission in July 1992, the SPPF won the majority of the votes cast and was awarded 14 of the 22 seats on the commission. In the presidential and legislative elections in July 1993, René and the SPPF won an emphatic victory. René retained the presidency with almost 59.5% of the vote, while the party won 28 seats (22 of them directly elected) in the National Assembly.

United Opposition (UO)

Address. PO Box 154, Victoria
Telephone. (#248) 224124
Fax. (#248) 225151
Leadership. Philippe Boullé (1993 presidential candidate)

Comprising the Seychelles Party, the National Alliance Party and the Seychelles National Movement, the UO was formed as an electoral coalition in 1993, opposing the adoption of the new constitution. NAP leader Philippe Boullé was the UO candidate in the presidential balloting, coming a distant third with less than 4% of the vote. In the legislative elections the group took only a single proportionally allocated seat.

Other Parties

Seychelles Christian Democrats, led by André Uzice, who had been a minister in the Mancham government before the 1977 coup.

Seychelles Liberal Party (SLP), founded in 1992 and led by Ogilvy Berlouis.

Seychelles Movement for Democracy (*Mouvement Seychellois pour la Démocratie*, MSD), under the leadership of Jacques Hodoul.

Sierra Leone

Capital: Freetown

Population: 4,700,000 (1995E)

The Republic of Sierra Leone achieved independence from the United Kingdom in 1961, originally as a constitutional monarchy. In 1971 a republican constitution was adopted and Siaka Stevens, leader of the All People's Congress (APC), became President. The APC was declared the sole legal party in 1978, and the country remained a one-party state until a referendum in 1991 endorsed the introduction of multi-party politics. General elections were arranged for the following year, but the process was curtailed in April 1992 by a military coup led by Capt. Valentine Strasser. Under the Strasser regime a National Provisional Ruling Council (NPRC) was set up in May 1992, the legislature was dissolved and all political activity suspended. In July 1992 the NPRC was designated the Supreme Council of State, and the Cabinet was reconstituted as the Council of State Secretaries, including civilian and military figures.

In 1993 the regime announced the adoption of a transitional programme envisaging a return to civilian government in early 1996 following multi-party elections. In April 1995 Strasser lifted the ban on political activity, stating that parties wishing to participate in elections should register with an Interim National Electoral Commission. These developments took place against a background of intensifying rebel activity by the Revolutionary United Front (RUF). In January 1996 Strasser was deposed by Brig. Julius Maada Bio, who became the new chairman of the NPRC and head of state. Nevertheless, elections went ahead as planned on Feb. 26-27 for a 68–member legislative assembly, with seats being awarded to parties securing 4.8% or more of the vote, as well as for the presidency, with a second round of voting being required for the latter on March 15. Both elections were contested by 13 parties and both resulted in victory for the Sierra Leone People's Party (SLPP).

All People's Congress (APC)

Address. 39 Siaka Stevens Street, Freetown

Leadership. Edward Mohammed Turay (1996 presidential candidate)

Established in 1960 by Siaka Stevens (who died in 1988), the leftist APC was the dominant party from 1968 and the sole authorized political formation between 1978 and 1991. In the 1996 legislative elections the party came in fourth place with less than 6% of the vote and only five seats. In the presidential poll the APC candidate finished fifth.

Democratic Centre Party (DCP)

Address. c/o Sierra Leone Assembly, Freetown

Leadership. Adu Aiah Koroma (1996 presidential candidate)

Following the February 1996 elections the DCP was awarded three assembly seats, having secured 4.8% of the vote. In the presidential poll the party's candidate took sixth place with a similar vote share.

National Unity Party (NUP)

Address. c/o Sierra Leone Assembly, Freetown

Leadership. John Karimu (1996 presidential candidate)

With 5.3% of the vote in both the legislative and presidential elections in February 1996, the NUP secured four seats in the 68–member assembly.

People's Democratic Party (PDP)

Address. c/o Sierra Leone Assembly, Freetown

Leadership. Thaimu Bangura (leader)

The PDP was first registered in 1991. In the February 1996 polling it took third place, securing 15.3% of the vote and 12 seats in the legislative election, while the party leader won 16.1% of the presidential vote.

Sierra Leone People's Party (SLPP)

Address. c/o Sierra Leone Assembly, Freetown

Leadership. Ahmad Tejan Kabbah (leader)

The SLPP was the dominant party at independence and the party of government until 1967. It was then banned in 1978 but resurfaced in 1991 under the leadership of Salia Jusu-Sheriff. In the February 1996 elections the party won the largest share of the votes in both the legislative and presidential polls (36.1% and 35.8% respectively), securing 27 assembly seats. The SLPP's presidential candidate, Ahmad Tejan Kabbah, won the second round runoff in March against his nearest rival from the United National People's Party (UNPP), taking about 60% of the vote.

United National People's Party (UNPP)

Address. Sierra Leone Assembly, Freetown

Leadership. John Karifa-Smart (presidential candidate)

The UNPP was runner-up to the SLPP in the 1996 elections, drawing 21.6% of the vote in the legislative poll (securing 17 assembly seats) and about 41% in the second round runoff of the presidential contest.

Other Parties

The following parties also contested the February 1996 elections but polled below the 4.8% voting threshold and so failed to win any representation:

People's National Convention (PNC)

People's Progressive Party (PPP)

National Alliance Democratic Party (NADP)

National Democratic Alliance (NDA)

National People's Party (NPP)

National Unity Movement (NUM)

Social Democratic Party (SDP)

Rebel Movement

Revolutionary United Front (RUF), engaged in armed conflict with the government since 1991 and linked to the National Patriotic Front of Liberia (NPFL); peace negotiations between the government and the rebels were initiated in February 1996.

Singapore

Capital: Singapore City

Population: 3,000,000 (1995E)

Singapore achieved internal self-rule from the United Kingdom in 1959, and four years later joined the Federation of Malaysia. On leaving the federation in 1965, the Republic of Singapore became an independent sovereign state. The legislature is a unicameral Parliament of 81 members elected by universal adult suffrage for five years. The President appoints a Cabinet, headed by a Prime Minister, which is collectively responsible to Parliament.

In legislative elections held on Aug. 31, 1991, the People's Action Party (PAP) (which has had a majority continuously since 1959) won 77 of the 81 seats. In a presidential election on Aug. 28, 1993, Ong Teng Cheong of the PAP became Singapore's first directly elected President (the post having previously been filled by legislative election).

Islamic Movement
Angkatan Islam
Leadership. Mohamed bin Omar (president)
A small party founded in 1958, the moderate Islamic Movement did not contest any seats in the 1991 legislative elections.

National Solidarity Party (NSP)
Leadership. Kum Teng Hock (president)
The centrist NSP was formed in 1986 with the aim of attracting the votes of young professionals. It contested eight constituencies in the 1991 elections and, although failing to win a parliamentary seat, attracted over 7% of total votes cast.

People's Action Party (PAP)
Address. 510 Thomson Rd, SLF Bldg 07–02, Singapore 1129
Telephone. (#65) 2589898
Fax. (#65) 2599222
Leadership. Goh Chok Tong (secretary-general)
The PAP, founded as a radical socialist party in 1954, has been Singapore's ruling party since 1959. After the defection of its more militant members to form the Socialist Front (*Barisan Sosialis*) in 1961, the PAP leadership effectively transformed the party into a moderate, anti-communist organization, supporting a pragmatic socialist programme emphasising economic development and social welfare. Despite its overwhelming legislative dominance, the PAP's share of the total vote has fallen steadily in elections since 1980 (down to 61% in 1991), and the opposition's capture of four parliamentary seats in the most recent poll represented a serious blow to the government.

Until the end of 1992 the party's secretary-general (i.e. leader) was Lee Kuan Yew, who was also Prime Minister from 1959 to 1990. He remains a senior figure in the party and in the current government led by his successor, Goh Chok Tong. Ong Teng Cheong, prior to his direct election as President of the Republic in August 1993, resigned as both chair and member of the PAP. He received about 59% of the votes cast in the election.

Singapore Democratic Party (SDP)
Address. 1 North Bridge Rd, 17–08 High Street Centre, Singapore 0617
Telephone. (#65) 3380378
Fax. (#65) 3383893
Leadership. Ling How Doong (chair)
The liberal and centrist SDP was founded in 1980 by Chiam See Tong in an attempt to create a credible opposition to the ruling People's Action Party, although its criticisms of government policies have been largely restricted to such issues as

515

housing, employment and industrial relations. In the 1991 elections the SDP was the most successful of the opposition parties, winning three of the nine parliamentary seats that it contested (Chiam See Tong retaining the seat he had held since 1984). In June 1993 Chiam resigned as secretary-general of the party, apparently as the result of an internal power struggle.

Singapore Justice Party (SJP)

Leadership. Muthusamy Ramasamy (secretary-general)

The SJP, established in 1972, has presented a small number of candidates in each general election but has yet to win a seat.

Singapore Malays National Organization

Pertubuhan Kebangsaan Melayu Singapura (PKMS)

Address. 218F Changi Rd, PKM Bldg, Fourth Floor, Singapore 1441

Telephone. (#65) 3455275

Fax. (#65) 3458724

Leadership. Mohammed Aziz Ibrahim (secretary-general)

The Singapore Malays National Organization (more commonly known as the PKMS) was founded as an affiliate of the United Malays National Organization in Malaysia in the early 1950s, assuming its present title in 1967. It seeks to advance the rights of Malays in Singapore, to safeguard and promote Islam, and to encourage racial harmony. The party has so far failed to gain parliamentary representation.

United People's Front (UPF)

Address. 715 Colombo Court, 7th Floor, Singapore 0617

Leadership. Ang Bee Lian (chair)

The UPF was formed in 1975 as a coalition of several small groups. It did not contest any constituencies in the 1991 elections.

Workers' Party (WP)

Address. 411B Jalan Besar, Singapore 0820

Telephone. (#65) 2984765

Leadership. J.B. Jeyaretnam (secretary-general)

The WP, originally founded in 1957, was revived by its present secretary-general in 1971. The party advocates the establishment of a democratic socialist government, with a constitution guaranteeing fundamental citizens' rights. In a by-election in 1981 Jeyaretnam became the first opposition member of Parliament since 1968, although he forfeited the seat in 1986 following a controversial conviction. In 1988 the WP merged with the left-wing Socialist Front (*Barisan Sosialis*), which had been established by People's Action Party dissidents in 1961, and with the Singapore United Front (dating from 1973). Although the party won no seats in the 1988 legislative elections, it attracted nearly 17% of the total votes cast. In the 1991 poll the WP contested 13 seats, won one and gained over 14% of the total vote.

Slovakia

Capital: Bratislava

Population: 5,300,000 (1995E)

The independent Slovak Republic came into being on Jan. 1, 1993, upon the dissolution of the Czech and Slovak Federative Republic, which had been proclaimed in April 1990 as successor to the (Communist-ruled) Czechoslovak Socialist Republic declared in 1960, itself successor to the People's Republic of Czechoslovakia established in 1948. Adopted in September 1992, its constitution vests supreme legislative authority in the unicameral National Council (*Národná Rada*) of 150 members, who are elected for a four-year term by citizens aged 18 and over. Elections are by a system of proportional representation under which single parties must obtain at least 5% of the national vote to be allocated seats, alliances of two or three parties at least 7% and alliances of four or more parties at least 10%. The National Council elects the President for a five-year term by secret balloting in which a three-fifths majority of all members is required.

National Council elections on September 30-October 1, 1994, resulted as follows: Movement for a Democratic Slovakia/Agrarian Party of Slovakia 61 seats (with 35.0% of the vote), Common Choice (consisting of the Party of the Democratic Left, the Green Party in Slovakia, the Social Democratic Party of Slovakia and the Farmers' Movement of Slovakia) 18

(10.4%), Hungarian Coalition (consisting of Coexistence, the Hungarian Christian Democratic Movement and the Hungarian Civic Party) 17 (10.2%), Christian Democratic Movement 17 (10.1%), Democratic Union of Slovakia 15 (8.6%), Association of Workers of Slovakia 13 (7.3%), Slovak National Party 9 (5.4%).

Agrarian Party of Slovakia
Rol'nícka Strana Slovenska (RSS)
   Address. 11 Magnelová, 83104 Bratislava
   Telephone. (#42–7) 215291
   Leadership. Pavol Delinga (chair)
   Founded in October 1990 to protect agricultural interests, the conservative RSS was allied with the Farmers' Movement of Slovakia in the 1990 local elections. Later it opted to ally itself with the ruling Movement for a Democratic Slovakia, thus becoming a government party, although without representation in the Cabinet.

Association of Workers of Slovakia
Zdruzenie Robotníkov Slovenska (ZRS)
   Address. 83 ul. Horná, 97401 Banská Bystrica
   Telephone. (#42–88) 742563
   Fax. (#42–88) 745596
   Leadership. Ján L'upták (chair)
   The ZRS was established as an independent party in April 1994, having previously been a trade union component of the (ex-Communist) Party of the Democratic Left, on whose list Ján L'upták (a former bricklayer) had won a parliamentary seat in 1992. Standing on a left-wing platform urging protection of workers' rights and neutrality in international relations, it obtained 7.3% of the vote and 13 seats in the autumn 1994 elections, subsequently opting to become a government party and to accept four portfolios (including privatization) in the new coalition government headed by the Movement for a Democratic Slovakia. In January the ZRS central council decided to close the party's Bratislava's branch, members of which had recently published an article criticizing L'upták for being subservient to Prime Minister Mečiar. Announcing the closure decision, the KRS leader said that there were no workers left in the branch, only intellectuals.

Christian Democratic Movement
Krest'ansko-demokratické Hnutie (KDH)
   Address. 2 Žabotova, 81104 Bratislava
   Telephone. (#42–7) 496308
   Fax. (#42–7) 496313
   Leadership. Ján Carnogurský (chair), Stanislav Vajcik (secretary-general)
   Founded in February 1990 under the leadership of Communist-era Catholic dissident Ján Carnogurský, the KDH began as the Slovak wing of the Czechoslovak Christian Democrats but presented its own list in Slovakia for the 1990 Council elections, coming in second place with 31 seats and 19.2% of the vote. Carnogurský became Prime Minister of Slovakia following the dismissal of Vladimír Mĕiar of the Movement for a Democratic Slovakia (HZDS) in April 1991. The party went into opposition after the June 1992 elections, in which it fell back to 18 seats with 8.9% of the vote. It returned to government in March 1994 in the centre-left coalition headed by what became the Democratic Union of Slovakia, but went into opposition again after the autumn 1994 Council elections. In that contest it was allied with the non-party Standing Conference of the Civic Institute, the combined list taking a creditable 10.1% vote share and 17 seats. The KDH subsequently rebuffed suggestions that it should join a government coalition with the HZDS.
   The KDH is affiliated to both the Christian Democrat International and the International Democrat Union.

Coexistence
Együttélés/Spolužitie/Wspoinota/Suzitie (ESWS)
   Address. 7 Pražská, 81409 Bratislava
   Telephone. (#42–7) 497877
   Fax. (#42–7) 497877
   Leadership. Miklós Duray (chair), Erzsébet Dolnik (secretary-general)
   Founded in March 1990, the liberal democratic ESWS is based in Slovakia's 600,000–strong ethnic Hungarian community, being committed to defending the rights of all minorities in Slovakia, including Poles, Ruthenians and Ukrainians. Allied with the Hungarian Christian Democratic Movement (MKdH/MKdM) in the 1990 and 1992 Council elections, it won nine of the alliance's 14 seats on the latter occasion. For the autumn 1994 elections the ESWS was part of the broader Hungarian Coalition (*Mad'arská Koalicia*, MK), including both the MKdH/MKdM and the Hungarian Civic Party, winning nine of the alliance's 17 seats. Thereafter ESWS leaders came increasingly into conflict with the populist policies of the Mečiar government seen as intended to impose an exclusively Slovak concept of national identity.
   The ESWS is a member of the Liberal International.

Democratic Union of Slovakia

Demokratická Únia Slovenska (DÚS)
   Address. 1 Pražská, 81104 Bratislava
   Telephone. (#42–7) 491208
   Fax. (#42–7) 496971
   Leadership. Jozef Moravčik (chair), Milan Kňažko (first deputy chair)

The centrist DÚS was founded in April 1994 as a merger of two elements of the coalition government which had come to power the previous month, namely: (i) the Democratic Union of Slovakia, led by then Prime Minister Jozef Moravčik, which had originated in February 1994 as the "Realistic Political Alternative" breakaway group of the then ruling Movement for a Democratic Slovakia (HZDS); and (ii) the Alliance of Democrats of the Slovak Republic (ADSR), another HZDS splinter group created in June 1993 by Milan Kňažko, who had been dismissed as Foreign Minister three months earlier. Commanding the support of 18 members of the National Council at the time of the merger, the DÚS subsequently failed in its aim of constructing a broad centrist alliance. The only significant grouping to come under its banner was a moderate splinter group of the right-wing Slovak National Party called the **National Democratic Party-New Alternative** (*Národna Demokratická Strana–Nová Alternatíva*, NDS-NA), led by L'udovit Černák. In the autumn 1994 elections the DÚS list came in fifth place with 8.6% of the vote and only 15 seats.

The DÚS is affiliated to the Liberal International.

Farmers' Movement of Slovakia

Hnutie Pol'nohospodárov Slovenska (HPS)
   Address. 18 Sama Chalúpku, 07101 Michalovce
   Telephone. (#42–7) 215291
   Leadership. Józef Klein (chair)

The left-leaning HPS established a political presence in the 1990 local elections but did not contest general elections until 1994, when it won one seat as part of the Common Choice (*Spoločná Vol'ba*, SV) alliance, which also included the (ex-Communist) Party of the Democratic Left, the Green Party in Slovakia and the Social Democratic Party of Slovakia.

Green Party in Slovakia

Strana Zelench na Slovenska (SZS)
   Address. 56 Palisády, 81106 Bratislava
   Telephone. (#42–7) 323231
   Fax. (#42–7) 364848
   Leadership. Józef Pokorny (chair)

Founded as a party in late 1989, the left-leaning SZS argues that "green philosophy" is a necessary ingredient of social democracy and that creation of a market economy is not an end in itself but rather the means of improving the quality of life. The party obtained six seats in the Slovak National Council in 1990, lost them all in 1992 and regained two in 1994. For the 1994 elections the SZS was part of a centre-left opposition alliance called Common Choice (*Spoločná Vol'ba*, SV), which also included the (ex-Communist) Party of the Democratic Left, the Social Democratic Party of Slovakia and the Farmers' Movement of Slovakia.

Hungarian Christian Democratic Movement

Mad'arská Krest'ansko-demokratické Hnutie (MKdH)
Magyar Keresztény-demokrata Mozgalom (MKdM)
   Address. 2 Žabotova, 81104 Bratislava
   Telephone. (#42–7) 495164
   Fax. (#42–7) 495264
   Leadership. Béla Bugar (chair)

More moderate in its representation of ethnic Hungarian interests than Coexistence (ESWS), the MKdH/MKdM was founded in March 1990 on a Christian-oriented, pro-market platform. It contested the 1990 and 1992 Council elections in alliance with the ESWS, winning five seats on the latter occasion. For the autumn 1994 elections it was part of the broader Hungarian Coalition (*Mad'arská Koalicia*, MK), also including the Hungarian Civic Party, and took seven of the alliance's 17 seats.

The party is affiliated to both the Christian Democrat International and the International Democrat Union.

Hungarian Civic Party

Mad'arská Obianská Strana (MOS)
Magyár Polgári Párt (MPP)
   Address. 2 Žabotova, 81101 Bratislava
   Telephone. (#42–7) 497684
   Fax. (#42–7) 495322
   Leadership. László Nagy (chair)

The liberal MOS/MPP was founded in February 1990 as the Hungarian Independent Initiative, which secured representation in 1990 on the pro-democracy Public Against Violence list. Renamed the MOS/MPP in January 1992, the party failed to achieve the 5% threshold in the June 1992 Slovak Council elections. Despite being less militant than Coexistence or even than the Hungarian Christian Democratic Movement, it joined these two parties in the Hungarian Coalition (*Mad'arská Koalicia*, MK) for the autumn 1994 elections, winning one of the alliance's 17 seats.

The party is affiliated to the Liberal International.

Movement for a Democratic Slovakia

Hnutie za Demokratické Slovensko (HZDS)

Address. 32A Tomášikova, 82369 Bratislava

Telephone. (#42–7) 231769

Fax. (#42–7) 224213

Leadership. Vladimír Mečiar (chair), Tibor Cabaj (parliamentary leader)

The populist HZDS was registered in May 1991 a month after Vladimír Mečiar (a former Communist) had been ousted from the premiership of Slovakia (then still part of Czechoslovakia) after coming into conflict with the mainstream leadership of the pro-democracy Public Against Violence (VPN). In an explicitly nationalist appeal called "For a Democratic Slovakia" and issued in April 1991, Mečiar had argued in favour of a diluted form of federalism providing greater protection for Slovak economic and political interests than was contemplated in Prague. The HZDS quickly confirmed that it was Slovakia's leading political formation, winning 74 of the 150 Slovak Council seats in the June 1992 elections. Restored to the premiership, Mečiar at first resisted Czech insistence that either the federation should have real authority at government level or the two parts should separate. By late 1992 Mečiar had embraced the latter option, leading Slovakia to sovereignty from the beginning of 1993 and forming a governmental coalition with the radical right-wing Slovak National Party (SNS).

The Mečiar government of independent Slovakia quickly came under attack for its perceived authoritarian tendencies and acceptance of the entrenched position of former Communists in the state bureaucracy. Policy and personal clashes precipitated a series of defections from the HZDS in 1993–94, while Mečiar's appointment of a former Communist as Defence Minister in March 1993 caused the SNS to leave the government, which was thus reduced to minority status. Having failed to persuade the (ex-Communist) Party of the Democratic Left (SDL') to accept ministerial office, Mečiar restored the coalition with the SNS in October 1993; but chronic divisions within the HZDS led to the Prime Minister's defeat on a no-confidence motion and reluctant resignation in March 1994. In opposition to a centrist coalition headed by what became the Democratic Union of Slovakia, the HZDS remained the country's strongest formation, with a strong following for its combination of economic conservatism and fiery nationalism.

Allied in the autumn 1994 elections with the small Agrarian Party of Slovakia, the HZDS won a decisive plurality of 61 seats (on a 34.9% vote share) and became the lead partner in a "red-brown" government coalition with the SNS and the left-wing Association of Workers of Slovakia.

Public commitments notwithstanding, the return of the HZDS to power meant a slow-down in the pace of transition to a market economy. It also revived earlier conflict between Mečiar and President Kováč, who had been elected by the legislature in February 1993 as candidate of the HZDS but who had subsequently distanced himself from the movement as he became embattled with the Prime Minister on a series of political issues. The tension flared in March 1995 when the President refused at first to sign a bill transferring overall control of the security services from the head of state to the government. Although he signed the measure the following month when the National Council had readopted it, HZDS deputies engineered passage of a vote of censure on the President (but well short of the two-thirds majority needed to remove him), while the HZDS executive called for his resignation and expulsion from the movement. Mečiar himself proposed a national referendum on whether the President should step down, making it clear what his recommendation would be. However, as of September 1996 Kováč remained in office, with the chasm between President and Prime Minister no nearer to being bridged.

Party of the Democratic Left

Strana Demokratickej L'avice (SDL')

Address. 12 Gonduličova, 81610 Bratislava

Telephone. (#42–7) 333617

Fax. (#42–7) 335574

Leadership. Józef Migas (chair), Pavol Kanis (deputy chair)

Somewhat paradoxically, the collapse of Communist rule in Czechoslovakia in late 1989 inspired the Slovak Communists to re-establish a separate Communist Party of Slovakia (KSS), in indirect succession to the KSS originally founded in 1939 but later absorbed into the Communist Party of Czechoslovakia (KSČ). In October 1990 the KSS majority wing adopted the new name "Communist Party of Slovakia-Party of the Democratic Left", which became simply "Party of the Democratic Left" later in the year. The SDL' emerged from the June 1992 general elections as the second largest party in the Slovak National Council, winning 29 seats on a 14.7% vote share. After the government of the Movement for a Democratic Slovakia (HZDS) had been reduced to minority status in March 1993, the SDL' rejected HZDS offers of ministerial status and instead became the leading party in a centre-left opposition alliance called Common Choice (*Spoločná Vol'ba*, SV), which also included the Social Democratic Party of Slovakia, the Green Party in Slovakia and the Farmers' Movement of Slovakia.

In the autumn 1994 general elections, however, the SDL' failed to emulate the recent success of other East European ex-Communist parties and alliances, falling back to 13 seats. Many commentators attributed this relative failure to voters' perception of the HZDS as being the real "party of continuity" with the Communist era. In 1995-96 the SDL' became increasingly divided over whether to accept persistent HZDS offers of coalition status, the election of the relatively unknown Józef Migas as leader in April 1996 being a compromise between the contending factions. During a major coalition crisis in June 1996 the SDL's decision to give qualified external support to the government attracted much criticism from other opposition parties.

Slovak National Party
Slovenská Národná Strana (SNS)
Address. 17 Vajanského nábrežie, 81499 Bratislava
Telephone. (#42–7) 325808
Fax. (#42–7) 325808
Leadership. Ján Slota (chair), Jozef Prokes (honorary chair), Anna Malikova (deputy chair)

The nationalistic and anti-Hungarian SNS was founded in December 1989 and registered in March 1990, its programme calling for the assertion of Slovak rights and the revival of national pride and patriotism. It advocates the establishment of Slovak-language schools in every district (including those with ethnic Hungarian majorities) and exclusive use of Slovak at all official levels. It obtained 13.9% of the vote in the 1990 Slovak National Council elections, but only 7.9% (and nine seats) in the June 1992 contest, after which it joined a coalition with the dominant Movement for a Democratic Slovakia (HZDS). It continued to support the government after the resignation of its sole minister in March 1993, and in October resumed formal coalition status, obtaining several key ministries.

In February 1994 the SNS was weakened by a split involving the defection of the party's "moderate" wing led by the then chair L'udovit Černák, this faction later joining the Democratic Union of Slovakia. The following month, on the fall of the HZDS government, the rump SNS went into opposition, whereupon the SNS central council decided in May that only ethnic Slovaks were eligible to be members of the party. In the autumn 1994 elections the SNS took only 5.4% of the vote (and nine seats), being nevertheless awarded two portfolios in a new HZDS-led coalition. Thereafter the party resolutely opposed the granting of any form of autonomy to ethnic Hungarian areas of Slovakia under the March 1995 Slovak-Hungarian friendship treaty, tabling proposed constitutional amendments in July 1996 whereby minorities would have not only the right but also the duty to master the state language (i.e. Slovak). It also promised to block Slovakia's entry into NATO (if such became a possibility), despite the goal of accession being official government policy.

Social Democratic Party of Slovakia
Sociálnodemokratická Strana na Slovensku (SDSS)
Address. 2 Zabotova, 81104 Bratislava
Telephone. (#42–7) 494700
Fax. (#42–7) 494621
Leadership. Jaroslav Volf (chair), Ján Sekaj (secretary)

The SDSS derives from the historic Czechoslovak Social Democratic Party, which was a leading formation in the inter-war period but was forcibly merged with the Communist Party in 1948, after which the authentic party was maintained by exiled groups in Britain and elsewhere. When the party was relaunched in post-Communist Czechoslovakia in February 1990, the Slovak branch quickly asserted its separate identity. The SDSS list in the June 1992 general elections was headed by the 1968 "Prague Spring" Communist leader, Alexander Dubček. It failed to win representation in either the federal or the Slovak lower chambers, but did obtain five seats in the federal upper chamber on a 6.1% share of the vote. Dubček died in November 1992 as a result of a road accident that many regarded as suspicious. The SDSS regained national representation in the autumn 1994 elections, winning two seats as a component of a centre-left opposition alliance called Common Choice (*Spoločná Vol'ba*, SV), which also included the (ex-Communist) Party of the Democratic Left, the Green Party in Slovakia and the Farmers' Movement of Slovakia. The party's participation in the SV was opposed by a minority faction styling itself "Revival of Social Democracy", under the leadership of Boris Zala.

The SDSS is a member party of the Socialist International.

Other Parties

Christian Social Union (*Krest'anská Socialná Unia*, KSU), led by Viliam Oberhauser, originating in March 1992 as a right-wing splinter group of the Christian Democratic Movement, failed to win representation in 1992 and 1994 elections, obtaining 2.1% in the latter.

Communist Party of Slovakia (*Komunistická Strana Slovenska*, KSS), led by Vladimír Dado, descended from the original Slovak Communist Party founded in 1939, now consisting of the Marxist-Leninist minority which rejected conversion into the democratic socialist Party of the Democratic Left in 1990; obtained 2.7% in the 1994 elections.

Democratic Party (*Demokratická Strana*, DS), led by Peter Osuský, conservative formation founded in 1944 but suspended in 1948, revived in 1989, joined Slovak government in 1990 but failed to win representation in 1992; absorbed several small centre-right groupings in 1994 but won only 3.4% in autumn Council elections on a joint list with the Party of Entrepreneurs and Tradesmen.

Party of Entrepreneurs and Tradesmen (*Strana Podnikatel'ov a Živnostnikov*, SP), led by Vladimír Randa, pro-market formation allied with the Democratic Party in autumn 1994 elections, without success.

Slovak Green Alternative (*Slovenská Zelench Alternativa*, SZA), led by Zora Lazarova,

conservative environmentalist formation, allied with Movement for a Democratic Slovakia in 1994 elections.

Parties aiming to represent Slovakia's Roma (Gypsy) minority include the **League of Romany Unity**, the **Party of Integration of Romanies in Slovakia**, the **Party of the Democratic Union of Romanies in Slovakia**, the **Romany Civic Initiative**, the **Romany National Congress** and the **Social Democratic Party of Romanies in Slovakia**. In September 1995 most of these parties agreed to contest the next elections on a joint list.

Slovenia

Capital: Ljubljana

Population: 2,000,000 (1995E)

Having been a constituent republic of the Communist-ruled Socialist Federal Republic of Yugoslavia since World War II, Slovenia declared independence in June 1991 on the basis of a referendum held in December 1990. Its constitution adopted in December 1991 provides for a multi-party democracy, in which the largely ceremonial President is directly elected for a five-year term and the head of government is the Prime Minister, who is designated by (and may be removed by) the legislature. The latter is a bicameral body, consisting of the (i) the upper National Council (*Državni Svet*), whose 40 members serve five-year terms, 22 being directly elected and 18 indirectly elected by socio-economic interest groups; and (ii) the lower National Assembly (*Državni Zbor*), whose 90 members are elected for a four-year term, 40 by constituency-based majority voting and 50 by proportional representation from party lists which obtain at least 3% of the vote. One seat each is reserved for Slovenia's Hungarian and Italian ethnic minorities.

Elections to the National Assembly on Dec. 6, 1992, resulted as follows: Liberal Democracy of Slovenia 22 seats (with 21.4% of the vote), Slovenian Christian Democrats 15 (13.9%), United List of Social Democrats 14 (12.1%), Slovenian People's Party 11 (8.9%), Slovenian National Party 11 (8.8%), Democratic Party of Slovenia 6 (4.4%), Greens of Slovenia 5 (3.3), Social Democratic Party of Slovenia 4 (3.1%), minority representatives 2. There was substantial realignment of party allegiance in the course of the subsequent parliamentary term.

Democratic Party of Slovenia
Demokratična Stranka Slovenije (DSS)
    Address. 5 Tomšičeva, 61000 Ljubljana
    Telephone. (#386–61) 261073
    Fax. (#386–61) 255077
    Leadership. Tone Peršak (president)
    The DSS is descended from the Slovene Democratic League (*Slovenska Demokratična Zveza*, SDZ), which registered as a party in March 1990. One of the leading proponents of secession from Yugoslavia, the SDZ contested the 1990 elections as a member of the victorious Democratic United Opposition (DEMOS) alliance. It stood on

its own in the December 1992 contest, winning six lower house seats with 3.1% of the vote, following which it absorbed a small social democratic faction to become the DSS. In March 1994 three of the DSS deputies joined the restructured Liberal Democracy of Slovenia, the leading government party. Of the other three, one became an independent and two opted to retain the DSS label.

Liberal Democracy of Slovenia
Liberalna Demokratča Slovenije (LDS)
    Address. 3 trg Republike, 61001 Ljubljana
    Telephone. (#386–61) 256106

Fax. (#386–61) 256150

Leadership. Janez Drnovšek (president), Gregor Golobić (general secretary)

The centre-left and staunchly secular LDS was founded in March 1994 as a merger of the ruling Liberal Democratic Party (LDS), itself derived from the Communist-era Federation of Socialist Youth of Slovenia (ZSMS), and three small formations, namely: (i) a moderate faction of the Democratic Party of Slovenia, including half of its Assembly contingent of six deputies; (ii) all five deputies of the Greens of Slovenia; and (iii) the Socialist Party of Slovenia (SSS), which was derived from the Communist-era front organization (and had no Assembly representation). A third of the deputies in the 90–member Assembly accepted the authority of the new formation, which espoused classical liberal principles regarding individual rights and liberties, also advocating decentralization of power and rapid transition to a market economy.

The former LDS came down the list of parties winning seats in the April 1990 Slovenian elections, which were the first multi-party contest in over half a century in what was then still Yugoslavia. Following the achievement of independence in 1991, however, LDS leader Janez Drnovšek became Prime Minister in April 1992, heading a centre-left coalition government committed to privatization of the economy. In the first post-independence elections in December 1992, the LDS became the strongest Assembly party, winning 22 seats on a 21.4% vote share. Drnovšek accordingly formed a new centre-left government that included the Slovenian Christian Democrats (SKD), the United List of Social Democrats (ZLSD) and the Social Democratic Party of Slovenia (SDSS). In March 1994 the SDSS left the ruling coalition in acrimonious circumstances, while SKD participation came under severe strain at regular intervals thereafter. In January 1996 the ZLSD withdrew from the coalition in advance of Assembly elections scheduled for November 1996.

The LDS is affiliated to the Liberal International.

Party of Democratic Reform

Stranka Demokratskih Reformi (SDR)

Address. 4 Subičeva st., 61000 Ljubljana

Leadership. Peter Bekes (president)

The SDR was created in February 1990 from the ruins of the former ruling League of Communists of Slovenia (*Zveza Komunista Slovenije*, ZKS). The parent party had embraced Eurocommunist principles in the 1970s, while Milan Kučan, its most prominent leader in the late 1980s, took a leading role in Slovenian opposition to the federal government in Belgrade. Elected president of the Slovenian republic as the ZKS candidate in 1990, Kučan stood as a nominal independent in December 1992, winning re-election with 64% of the vote. Whereas the SDR had taken second place in its own right in the 1990 legislative elections, it contested those of December 1992 as part of the United List of Social Democrats (ZLSD), although it subsequently declined to join in a formal merger of the ZLSD parties.

Slovenian Christian Democrats

Slovenski Křčanski Demokrati (SKD)

Address. 4 Beethovnova, 61000 Ljubljana

Telephone. (#386–61) 262179

Fax. (#386–61) 211738

Leadership. Lojze Peterle (president), Ignac Polajnar (Assembly leader), Vida Čadonič-Špelič (secretary-general)

Claiming descent from a pre-war Christian democratic party, the SKD was founded in March 1990 by a group of "non-clerical Catholic intellectuals" advocating the full sovereignty of Slovenia, gradual transition to a market economy and integration into European organizations, especially the European Union. For the April 1990 elections it was the largest component of the victorious Democratic United Opposition (DEMOS) alliance, winning 11 Assembly seats in its own right, so that SKD leader Lojze Peterle became Prime Minister and led Slovenia to the achievement of full independence in 1991. He remained Prime Minister despite the break-up of DEMOS at the end of 1991 but was forced to resign in April 1992 by a successful no-confidence motion criticizing the slow pace of economic reform. In the December 1992 Assembly elections the SKD advanced to 15 seats (on a 13.9% vote share), thereafter joining a new centre-left coalition headed by Liberal Democracy of Slovenia (LDS).

Within the post-1992 ruling coalition, strains in the SKD's relations with the LDS sharpened in 1994, leading to Peterle's resignation in September in protest against the induction of an LDS president of the National Assembly. The SKD remained a government party, but renewed coalition tensions in 1996 were highlighted by the support which SKD deputies gave to a motion of no confidence in the LDS Foreign Minister in May. The party opted nevertheless to remain in the ruling coalition pending general elections in December 1996.

The SKD is affiliated to the Christian Democrat International and to the International Democrat Union.

Slovenian National Party

Slovenska Narodna Stranka (SNS)

Address. 2 Kotnikova, 61000 Ljubljana

Telephone. (#386–61) 224241

Fax. (#386–61) 213294

Leadership. Zmago Jelinčič (president), Jure Jesenko (secretary-general)

Founded in 1991, the SNS is an extreme right-wing formation advocating a militarily strong Slovenia, revival of the Slovenes' cultural heritage and protection of the family as the basic unit of society. It is also strongly opposed to any consideration being given to Italian and Croatian irredentist claims on Slovenian territory or property. The party won 9.9% of the vote and 12 lower house seats in December 1992 but became deeply divided in 1993 after party leader Zmago Jelinčič was named as a federal Yugoslav agent. Also problematical for the party were reports that leading members were listed in security service files as having been informers in the Communist era. As a result of these and other embarassments, five SNS deputies formed an independent Assembly group that became the core of the breakaway Slovenian National Right.

Slovenian People's Party

Slovenska Ljudska Stranka (SLS)
    Address. 3 Zarnikova, 61000 Ljubljana
    Telephone. (#386–61) 301891
    Fax. (#386–61) 101871
    Leadership. Marjan Podobnik (president)
    Identifying its antecedents in a pre-war Catholic/populist party of the same name, the SLS was founded in May 1988 as the non-political Slovene Peasant League (*Slovenska Kmečka Zveza*, SKZ), which registered as a party in January 1990. It won 11 Assembly seats in 1990 as a member of the victorious Democratic United Opposition (DEMOS) alliance and adopted the SLS label in 1991. In the December 1992 elections it won 11 Assembly seats on the strength of 8.96% of the national vote.

Social Democratic Party of Slovenia

Socialdemokratična Stranka Slovenije (SDSS)
    Address. 11 Komenskega, 61000 Ljubljana
    Telephone. (#386–61) 314086
    Fax. (#386–61) 301143
    Leadership. Janez Janša (president), Barbara Medved (vice-president), Ivo Hvalica (parliamentary leader), Brane Grims (general secretary)
    Founded in February 1989, the SDSS seeks to be the authentic Slovenian party of European social democracy but has been obliged to compete for the left-wing vote with the organizationally powerful United List of Social Democrats. The party was a component of the victorious Democratic United Opposition (DEMOS) alliance in the 1990 elections. In December 1992 its presidential candidate took only 0.6% of the first-round vote, but the party won 3.1% and four seats in the simultaneous legislative elections, subsequently participating in the centre-left coalition government headed by Liberal

Democracy of Slovenia (LDS). In 1993 the SDSS Defence Minister and party leader, Janez Janša, became enmeshed in an arms-trading scandal, which led indirectly to his dismissal in March 1994, whereupon the SDSS joined the parliamentary opposition.
    The SDSS is an observer member of the Socialist International.

United List of Social Democrats

Združena Lista Socialnih Demokratov (ZLSD)
    Address. 15 Levstikova, 61000 Ljubljana
    Telephone. (#386–61) 254222
    Fax. (#386–61) 215855
    Leadership. Janez Kocijančič (president), Dusan Kumer (secretary)
    The left-wing conservative ZLSD was created prior to the December 1992 elections as an alliance of the following formations deriving from the former ruling League of Communists and its front organization: (i) the Slovenian Democratic Party of Pensioners (*Demokratska Stranka Upokojencev Slovenije*, DeSUS), also known as the "Grey Panthers"; (ii) the Social Democratic Union (*Socialdemokratska Unija*, SDU); (iii) the Workers' Party of Slovenia (*Delavska Stranka Slovenije*, DSS); and (iv) the Party of Democratic Reform (SDR). The 1992 electoral outcome was third place in the new Assembly, with 14 seats and 12.1% of the vote, on the strength of which the ZLSD joined a centre-left coalition government headed by Liberal Democracy of Slovenia (LDS). Of the four constituent groupings, the DeSUS, SDU and DSS formally merged in April 1993 to become the ZLSD, whereas the SDR preferred to maintain a separate identity. The ZLSD lasted as a coalition partner until January 1996, when the LDS Prime Minister's move to dismiss one of its four ministers caused the party to withdraw from the government.

Other Parties

The following is a selective listing of other parties which contested the 1992 Assembly elections or were formed subsequently.

Christian Social Union (*Unija Social-Křšcanski*, ZSK), led by Franc Miklavič, founded in early 1995 as a progressive Christian formation.

Greens of Slovenia (*Zeleni Slovenije*, ZS), led by Vane Gošnik, founded as a party in June 1989, member of the Democratic United Opposition (DEMOS) in 1990, elected five deputies in December 1992, all of whom joined the restructured Liberal Democracy of Slovenia in 1994, leaving the parent group without representation.

Istrian Democratic Assembly (*Istarski Demokratski Sabor*, IDA), Slovenian wing of a Croatian regional party.

Kramberger's United List, led by a wealthy entrepreneur who contested the 1992 presidential elections as an independent.

National Democratic Party (*Narodni Demokratska Stranka*, NDS), led by Marjan Vidmar, founded in 1994 by a right-wing splinter group of the Slovenian Christian Democrats.

Party of Citizens' Equality (*Stranka za Enakopravnost Občanov*, SEO).

Slovenian National Right (*Slovenska Nacionalna Desnica*, SND), led by Sašo Lap, founded in 1993 by a splinter group of the extreme right-wing Slovenian National Party.

Socialist Party of Slovenia (*Socialistična Stranka Slovenije*, SSS), represented in the 1990-92 Assembly.

Solomon Islands

Capital: Honiara

Population: 365,000 (1995E)

The Solomon Islands achieved internal self-government in 1976, and became independent in July 1978. The head of state is the British sovereign represented by a Governor-General. Legislative authority is vested in a unicameral National Parliament, the 47 members of which are popularly elected for up to four years. The Prime Minister (who is elected by members of Parliament from among their number) and an appointed Cabinet exercise executive power and are responsible to Parliament.

Solomon Mamaloni became Prime Minister in 1989 following the election victory of his People's Alliance Party (PAP). He resigned as party leader in October 1990 but remained as Prime Minister at the head of a coalition government of "national unity" (which became the basis of the National Unity and Reconciliation Progressive Party). Following a general election on May 26, 1993, the anti-Mamaloni parliamentary parties joined with independent members to form a government alliance—the National Coalition Partners (NCP)—and chose Francis Billy Hilly as Prime Minister. The administration lost its slim majority in October 1994, resulting in Hilly's resignation and the formation the following month of a new Mamaloni government.

National Action Party of the Solomon Islands (NAPSI)

Address. c/o National Parliament, Honiara
Leadership. Francis Saemala (leader)

NAPSI was formed prior to the 1993 general election by Francis Saemala, who had previously been an independent. In the election the party won five seats in the National Parliament, and subsequently participated in the National Coalition Partners administration.

National Unity and Reconciliation Progressive Party (NURPP)

Address. c/o National Parliament, Honiara
Leadership. Solomon Mamaloni (leader)

The NURPP was formed as the Group for National Unity and Reconciliation (GNUR) to contest the May 1993 general election. Under Mamaloni's leadership the organization secured the highest number of seats, winning 21, but failed to achieve the majority necessary to form a government. An alliance of anti-Mamaloni parties and independents formed a new administration and remained in power until October 1994 when it lost its slim parliamentary majority. The following month Mamaloni resumed the post of Prime Minister, forming a new administration, and the GNUR regrouped as the NURPP.

Nationalist Front for Progress (NFP)

Leadership. Andrew Nori (leader)

The NFP was formed in 1985 by Andrew Nori, who was previously a People's Alliance Party (PAP) member of Parliament. It aims to promote rural development and the settlement of land disputes. In the May 1993 general election the party was credited with one seat, its leader subsequently joining the National Coalition Partners administration.

People's Alliance Party (PAP)

Address. c/o National Parliament, Honiara
Leadership. Sir David Kausimae (leader)

The PAP was established through the merger in 1979 of the People's Progressive Party (PPP), led by Solomon Mamaloni, and the Rural Alliance Party (RAP), headed by David Kausimae. Having served as Prime Minister from 1981 to 1984, Mamaloni returned to the office in March 1989 following the PAP's general election victory. In October 1990 he resigned from the PAP to head a coalition administration, a move that effectively split the party. David Kausimae, who assumed the leadership, subsequently announced the expulsion from the party of those PAP members of Parliament serving in the Mamaloni government. The PAP won seven seats in the May 1993 general election, after which it participated in the National Coalition Partners administration.

Solomon Islands Labour Party

Address. c/o National Parliament, Honiara
Leadership. Joses Tuhanuku (leader)
Founded in 1988, the party secured two legisla-

tive seats in the 1989 general election and four seats in May 1993. It subsequently participated in the National Coalition Partners administration.

Solomon Islands Liberal Party

Leadership. Bartholomew Ulufa'alu (leader)
The party adopted its present name in 1986, having been formed in 1976 as the National Democratic Party. In the May 1993 election it failed to retain any of the four legislative seats it had won in 1989.

Solomon Islands United Party (SIUPA)

Address. c/o National Parliament, Honiara
Leadership. Ezekiel Alebua (leader)

The party was established by Sir Peter Kenilorea, who became the first Prime Minister of the Solomon Islands when the country achieved independence in 1978. Kenilorea's administration fell in 1981 and he was replaced by Solomon Mamaloni of the People's Alliance Party (PAP). Following the 1984 general election, SIUPA became the senior partner in a new coalition government. Forced to resign as Prime Minister in late 1986, Kenilorea was replaced by Ezekiel Alebua. SIUPA was defeated in the 1989 general election, securing only six legislative seats, and in the 1993 polling its representation fell again to two seats. The party was subsequently represented in the National Coalition Partners administration which was in office until October 1994.

Somalia

Capital: Mogadishu   **Population:** 9,000,000 (1995E)

The Republic of Somalia was formed by the unification of the British Somaliland Protectorate and the UN Trust Territory of Somalia at independence in 1960. In 1969 President Mohammed Siyad Barre seized power, and under his regime the Somali Revolutionary Socialist Party (SRSP) became the sole legal party. Siyad Barre was overthrown in a rebellion led by United Somali Congress (USC) guerrillas in January 1991. Ali Mahdi Mohamed was installed as Interim President and free elections were promised. In July 1991 the USC and five other groups agreed on the re-adoption of the constitution which had been in force from 1961 until Siyad Barre's coup. A Cabinet appointed in October 1991 represented an attempt to unite various groups behind the USC, but after fighting between opposing USC factions—one led by Ali Mahdi Mohamed and the other by Gen. Mohamed Farah Aidid—had broken out in Mogadishu in November 1991, the attempt to establish a national government was suspended. Other leading political groups subsequently split into pro-Aidid and pro-Mahdi factions.

In May 1991 the area which had formerly constituted the British Somaliland Protectorate, in the north, was proclaimed independent by the Somali National Movement (SNM), as the

Republic of Somaliland, with its capital at Hargeisa, but has received no international recognition.

A United Nations peace-keeping presence in Somalia between 1992 and March 1995, aiming to disarm warring factions and protect relief operations, was unable to restore order, and essentially anarchic conditions have persisted in the country. In mid-June 1995 factions allied with Gen. Aidid elected him President of the country, and the appointment of a Cabinet was subsequently announced.

The groupings listed below generally reflect membership of clans and sub-clans within Somalia.

Somali National Alliance (SNA)
Leadership. Osman Atto

The SNA was established by Gen. Mohamed Farah Aidid after his faction of the United Somali Congress split from the pro-Mahdi counterpart in 1992. Among the other affiliates are the pro-Aidid factions of the Somali Democratic Movement (SDM), the Somali Patriotic Movement (SPM) and the Somali Salvation Democratic Front (SSDF). The Southern Somali National Movement (SSNM) withdrew from the SNA in 1993.

In mid-June 1995 Gen. Aidid was reportedly removed from the chairship of the SNA and replaced by Osman Atto. At the same time it was reported that Aidid had been elected President of Somalia by loyal clan factions.

Somali Salvation Alliance (SSA)
Leadership. Ali Mahdi Mohamed

The SSA was set up in November 1993 as an alliance of the pro-Mahdi factions of the following affiliates: the United Somali Congress (USC), the Somali Democratic Movement (SDM), the Somali Patriotic Movement (SPM), the Somali Salvation Democratic Front (SSDF), the Southern Somali National Movement (SSNM), the United Somali Front (USF), the United Somali Party (USP), the Somali African Muki Organization, the Somali Democratic Front, the Somali National Democratic Union (SNDU) and the Somali National Union (SNU). The SNU was reported in May 1994 to have announced its intention to leave the alliance.

Somali Salvation Democratic Front (SSDF)
Leadership. Gen. Mohamed Abshir Musse (pro-Mahdi faction), Col. Abdullahi Yusuf Ahmed (pro-Aidid faction)

The SSDF was formed in the early 1980s, initially as the Democratic Front for the Salvation of Somalia, through a coalition of the Somali Salvation Front (SSF), the Somali Workers' Party (SWP) and the Democratic Front for the Liberation of Somalia (DFLS). In May 1993 Yusuf Ahmed concluded an accord with Gen. Aidid, provoking a split between his followers and the rump of the organization.

Somali Democratic Movement (SDM), led by Abdulkadir Mohamed Adan (pro-Mahdi faction) and Mohamed Nur Aliyow (pro-Aidid faction), based in the Rahanwin clan grouping.

Somali National Front (SNF), led by Gen. Mohamed Said Hersi ('Morgan'), founded in 1991, became an active guerrilla force in the south of the country, seeking the restoration of the former Somali Revolutionary Socialist Party government

Somali Patriotic Movement (SPM), led by Gen. Adan Abdullahi Noor ('Gabio') (pro-Mahdi faction) and Col. Ahmed Umar Jess (pro-Aidid faction), established in 1989 and representing Ogadenis in southern Somalia, split into rival factions after the ousting of the Siyad Barre regime, with the largest component supporting Gen. Aidid.

Somali Revolutionary Socialist Party (SRSP) led by Ahmed Suleiman Abdullah (assistant secretary-general), established in 1976 as the country's sole legal party, but effectively ceased to function with the collapse of the regime of Mohammed Siyad Barre; most of its top leadership posts are currently vacant.

Southern Somali National Movement (SSNM), led by Abd al-Aziz Sheikh Yusuf and Abdi Warsame Isaq, withdrew from the Somali National Alliance in August 1993, subsequently joining the pro-Mahdi Somali Salvation Alliance, although some members refused to endorse the change.

United Somali Congress (USC), founded in 1989, led the successful rebellion against Siyad Barre's regime, but divided in 1991 along sub-clan lines led by Interim President, Mahdi Mohamed, and Gen. Aidid respectively.

Somaliland Groupings
Somali National Movement (SNM)
Leadership. Abdel-Rahman Ahmed Ali ('Tur') (chair)

Formed in 1981 and drawing support mainly from the Isaq clan, the SNM conducted guerrilla operations against the Siyad Barre regime in the north and north-west of the country until early 1991. In May 1991 the organization proclaimed an independent Republic of Somaliland claiming jurisdiction over the area which had formerly constituted the British Somaliland Protectorate, including Hargeisa and the northern port of Berbera.

In 1994 the SNM split between President Mohamed Ibrahim Egal and his predecessor, Abdel-Rahman Ahmed Ali, who allied himself with the Somali National Alliance and called for the reincorporation of Somaliland into Somalia. Fighting between the two groups broke out in Hargeisa in November 1994, but forces loyal to President Egal remained in control.

Somali Democratic Alliance (SDA), led by Mohamed Farah Abdullahi, represents the Gad-

abursi ethnic grouping in the north-west, which opposes the Isaq-dominated Somali National Movement and its declaration of an independent Republic of Somaliland.

Somali Eastern and Central Front (SECF), led by Hirsi Ismail Mohamed, opposed to an independent Somaliland.

United Somali Front (USF), led by Abdurahman Dualeh Ali, formed in 1989 to represent the Issa community in the north-west of the country (Somaliland).

United Somali Party (USP), led by Mohamed Abdi Hashi, based in the north-west, opposed the Somali National Movement's declaration of independence for Somaliland in 1991.

South Africa

Capital: Pretoria (administrative),
Cape Town (legislative),
Bloemfontein (judicial)   **Population:** 41,900,000 (1995E)

The Republic of South Africa was established in 1961, evolving from the Union of South Africa which had been formed in 1910 and achieved independence from the United Kingdom in 1931. The National Party (NP), which was the ruling party from 1948 until May 1994, pioneered the system of apartheid under which the population was divided into four different racial categories (Whites, Coloureds, Indians and Africans), each entitled to varying degrees of political, social and economic rights. In practice, the system maintained the supremacy of the minority White (particularly Afrikaner) population. In the face of domestic and international pressure, the NP government in 1989 indicated a preparedness to negotiate an end to apartheid, the following year lifting restrictive measures against the African National Congress (ANC) and other proscribed organizations. Multi-party negotiations began in December 1991 and resulted in the adoption in November 1993 of an interim constitution, under which non-racial elections were to be held; it would remain in force until 1999, when elections under a final constitution agreed by a democratically elected parliament were scheduled. The interim constitution provides for a bicameral parliament consisting of a 400–member National Assembly, elected according to a system of proportional representation on national and regional party lists, and a Senate composed of 10 members from each of nine regional legislatures. Executive power is vested in a President (elected by the National Assembly) and Cabinet, or Government of National Unity. Parties achieving 20% of the national vote are entitled to nominate a Deputy President, while each party with at least 5% of the votes is entitled to a number of ministerial portfolios proportionate to the number of seats it holds. The interim constitution also provides for the re-incorporation of the 10 bantustans (Black homelands) into South Africa.

The first non-racial, multi-party legislative elections took place on April 26-29, 1994. They resulted in a decisive victory for the ANC, which had been in the forefront of the struggle against the apartheid regime. In May 1994 the ANC leader, Nelson Mandela, was elected

President of the Republic by the National Assembly, and the Government of National Unity assumed office.

The National Assembly and Senate sat jointly as a Constituent Assembly to draft a permanent constitution, a text of which was agreed on May 7, 1996, only hours before the specified deadline.

African Christian Democratic Party (ACDP)

Address. POB 348, Randpark Ridge 2156, Johannesburg

Telephone. (#27–11) 794–1654

Fax. (#27–11) 794–1624

Leadership. K. Meshoe (leader)

The ACDP won two National Assembly seats in the April 1994 elections, having campaigned for the social and economic transformation of the country based on a "moral, judicial and ethical system, open market economics and direct democracy". It also gained representation in three of the nine provincial assemblies.

African National Congress of South Africa (ANC)

Address. 51 Plein Street, Johannesburg 2001; POB 61884, Marshaltown 2107

Telephone. (#27–11) 330–7000

Fax. (#27–11) 330–8870

Leadership. Nelson Mandela (president), Thabo Mbeki (vice-president), Jacob Zuma (national chair)

Founded in 1912, the organization became the leading Black formation in South Africa. It was banned by the apartheid regime from 1960 to 1990, its most prominent figures being imprisoned (in particular, Nelson Mandela and Walter Sisulu) or exiled. From the late 1970s, as ANC guerrilla attacks within the country escalated, the South African armed forces increased counter-insurgency operations against the liberation movement's camps in neighbouring states.

While emphasising that it was prepared for an armed seizure of power in order to establish a non-racial political system, the ANC indicated that this position did not preclude a negotiated transition to democracy. ANC proposals, set out in 1989, argued that negotiations would only be possible in a free political climate. Having released Walter Sisulu from detention in October of that year, the National Party (NP) government then released Mandela in February 1990 and legalized all previously banned organizations. The ANC began the transformation from liberation movement to political party, suspending its armed struggle and engaging in constitutional talks with the government.

Substantive multi-party negotiations on a future constitution took place from 1991 to 1993,

although the process was frequently threatened by escalating political violence, for which the ANC blamed the Inkatha Freedom Party (IFP) and members of the state security forces.

Although the ANC had replaced its commitment to comprehensive nationalization with an emphasis on a mixed economy, the organization announced a radical plan in January 1994 to end the economic and social inequities of the apartheid era. This Reconstruction and Development Programme gave priority to housing, education, health improvement and economic growth.

The non-racial, multi-party legislative elections in April 1994 resulted in an overwhelming victory for the ANC, which secured 252 National Assembly seats with 62.6% of the vote and took control of seven of the nine provincial assemblies. The following month Nelson Mandela became President of the Republic. The new Cabinet was dominated by the ANC, but also included members of the NP and the IFP.

In December 1994 the First Deputy President, Thabo Mbeki, succeeded Walter Sisulu as ANC vice-president, thus becoming Mandela's heir apparent, although there were other aspirants to that accolade. The ANC consolidated its political dominance in November 1995 by winning about 66.4% of the votes cast in South Africa's first democratic local elections. In May 1996 the influential Cyril Ramaphosa (who had led the ANC team in the constitutional negotiations and was currently chairman of the Constitutional Assembly drafting a new constitution for South Africa) vacated the post of ANC secretary-general, having resigned from parliament the previous month to take up a senior post in a black-owned business conglomerate. In August 1996 President Mandela formally notified the ANC executive committee that he would not seek a second term in the presidential elections due in 1999 and that he would stand down from the ANC presidency at the party's next national conference, scheduled for 1997.

Democratic Party (DP)

Address. POB 8825, Johannesburg 2000

Telephone. (#27–11) 483–2743

Fax. (#27–21) 483–3401

Leadership. Tony Leon (leader)

The moderate, predominantly White DP was formed in 1989 (by the merger of the Progressive

Federal Party, the Independent Party and the National Democratic Movement), advocating the establishment of a democratic, non-racial society by peaceful means. Almost immediately, the new party was weakened by the defection of one of its founders, Willem de Klerk, who urged White voters to support the National Party which had earlier elected his brother, F.W. de Klerk, as its new leader. In 1992 the party lost five of its parliamentary representatives when they defected to the ANC. In the April 1994 elections the DP took fifth place, winning seven National Assembly seats with just over 1.7% of the votes cast.

Freedom Front
Vryheidsfront (VF)
Address. POB 74693, Lynnwood Ridge 0040, Pretoria
Telephone. (#27–12) 474477
Fax. (#27–12) 474387
Leadership. Gen. Constand Viljoen (leader)
The VF was launched by its leader in March 1994 following a rift in the Afrikaner People's Front over the issue of participation in the forthcoming April elections. Viljoen opted to register the new party in order to promote the objective of a confederal South Africa based on the right of self-determination for Afrikaners and all other groups. The VF was the only one of the White far-right parties to contest the elections, in which it secured nine National Assembly seats with almost 2.2% of the vote. In June 1995 the party welcomed President Mandela's willingness to consider a consultative referendum to gauge the views of Afrikaners on the concept of a separate homeland.

Inkatha Freedom Party (IFP)
Address. POB 4432, Durban 4000
Telephone. (#27–31) 307–4962
Fax. (#27–31) 307–4964
Leadership. Chief Mangosuthu Buthelezi (leader)
The IFP, formed originally as a liberation movement, was relaunched in 1990 as a multi-racial political party, although it remains a predominantly Zulu organization with its power-base in KwaZulu/Natal. Hostility between Inkatha and the ANC (which accused Inkatha of being an ally of the White minority regime) engendered serious political violence, particularly in the early 1990s, and major differences over constitutional and other issues continue. Having belatedly agreed to participate in the April 1994 elections, the IFP took third place with 43 National Assembly seats and about 10.5% of the votes cast. It also won a majority of seats in the

KwaZulu/Natal provincial assembly. The party was awarded three portfolios in the ensuing ANC-dominated Cabinet. However, the disaffection of the IFP and its Zulu supporters has continued, centring on the demand for separate status for KwaZulu/Natal. In April 1995 IFP members withdrew from the Constituent Assembly charged with the drafting of a permanent constitution.

National Party (NP)
Address. Private Bag X402, Pretoria 0001
Telephone. (#27–12) 324-5020
Fax. (#27–12) 344–6047
Leadership. F.W. de Klerk (chair), Roelf Meyer (parliamentary leader and secretary-general)
The conservative National Party came to power in 1948, and was the instigator of the system of apartheid in South Africa which was maintained repressively until the end of the 1980s. At that point the party, under the new leadership of F.W. de Klerk, abandoned its defence of apartheid in favour of reform of the political system, although it continues to advocate the constitutional protection of minority rights.

During the 1980s there were splits involving both the hardline and liberal wings of the party. In 1982 16 NP members of the House of Assembly who were opposed to any diminution of White supremacy were expelled from the party, another two resigning in sympathy. This faction subsequently formed the Conservative Party of South Africa which, following the 1987 elections, became the official opposition. Also in 1987, a number of liberal members defected from the NP as a result of their dissatisfaction with the lack of fundamental change.

Following his inauguration as State President in 1989, de Klerk implemented a number of dramatic measures, including the release of political prisoners and the legalization of banned organizations, as a prelude to substantive constitutional negotiations with anti-apartheid groups. South Africa's White population voted in support of continuing the reform process in a referendum in March 1992, after which de Klerk declared "today we have closed the book on apartheid'.

In the multi-party elections in April 1994 the NP was runner-up to the ANC, winning 82 National Assembly seats with just over 20 per cent of the votes cast. The party also won a majority of seats in the Western Cape regional assembly. De Klerk was subsequently named as one of two Executive Deputy Presidents in the new Mandela administration, which also included several other NP ministers. Following the advent of majority rule, the NP suffered a number of defections to the ANC. In February 1996 Roelf Meyer left the government of national unity to take up the new post of NP secretary-general, charged with charting a new future for the party and what de Klerk described as a "new spiritual trek towards an unknown political destination" In May 1996 de Klerk announced that the NP would withdraw from the government at the end of June, since the "development of a strong and vigilant opposition [was] essential for the maintenance of a genuine multi-party democracy".

Pan-Africanist Congress of Azania (PAC)

Address. POB 25245, Ferreirastown 2048, Johannesburg
Telephone. (#27–11) 337–8207
Fax. (#27–11) 337–7990
Leadership. Clarence Makwetu (president)

The PAC was formed in 1959 by a breakaway faction of the ANC which advocated the establishment of a democratic society through African, and not multi-racial, organizations. It rejected multi-racial co-operation on the grounds that it was a means of safeguarding White interests. Like the ANC, the PAC was banned by the apartheid regime between 1960 and 1990. Having announced in January 1994 that it was abandoning armed struggle, and claiming to be the authentic voice of the Black population, the PAC registered for the April elections in which it secured 1.25% of the vote and five National Assembly seats.

South African Communist Party (SACP)

Address. POB 1027, Johannesburg 2000
Telephone. (#27–11) 339–3621
Fax. (#27–11) 339–4244
Leadership. Raymond Mhlaba (acting chair)

The Communist Party of South Africa was formed in 1921 and refounded as the SACP in 1953. Banned until 1990, it has long co-operated closely with the ANC, some senior appointments within which have been held by SACP members. SACP candidates were included on the ANC list for the April 1994 elections after which the then party chairman, Joe Slovo (who died in January 1995), was appointed to President Mandela's new administration.

Other 1994 Election Participants

The following parties also contested the April 1994 elections but failed to secure any representation in the National Assembly (achieving collectively less than 1% of the vote).

African Democratic Movement (ADM), a Ciskei-based organization led by Brig. O.J. Gqozo.

African Moderates Congress Party, led by M. Phiri.

African Muslim Party, under the leadership of Dr. I. Sooliman.

Dikwankwetia Party of South Africa (DPSA), a Qwaqwa-based party.

Federal Party, committed to community empowerment and led by Frances Kendall.

Keep it Straight and Simple Party (KISS).

Luso-South African Party, with support among the country's Portuguese community.

Minority Front.

SOCCER (Sports Organization for Collective Contributuions and Equal Rights) Party.

Women's Rights Peace Party.

Workers' List Party.

Ximoko Progressive Party.

Other Groups

Afrikaner People's Front (Afrikaner Volksfront, AVF), founded in 1993 to oppose Black majority rule and linking over 20 rightist Afrikaner groups. The AVF boycotted the April 1994 elections.

Afrikaner People's Guard (Afrikaner Volkswag).

Afrikaner People's Union (Afrikaner Volksunie), chaired by G. Kruger.

Afrikaner Resistance Movement (Afrikaner Weerstandsbeweging, AWB), an extreme White right-wing paramilitary organization, formed in 1973, under the leadership of Eugene Terre'Blanche.

AWB Boer Commandoes (AWB Boerekommandos), led by Poon Jacobs.

Azanian People's Organization (AZAPO), launched in the late 1970s as a Black consciousness movement. It rejected constitutional negotiations with the White minority government and declared its opposition to the April 1994 elections. AZAPO excludes White members and is led by Mosibudi Mangena.

Boer Freedom Movement (Boer Vryheidsbeweging).

Boer Resistance Movement (Boere Weerstandsbeweging), a military wing of the Boer State Party.

Boer State Party (Boerestaat Party, BP), a far-right White group, formed in 1988, which seeks the establishment of an Afrikaner state.

Conservative Party of South Africa (Konsertwatiewe Party van Suid-Afrika), launched in 1982 by former National Party members who rejected any constitutional moves towards power-sharing with the non-White population. The party was runner-up to the National Party at the elections in 1987 and 1989. It unsuccessfully urged White voters to reject the reform process in the March 1992 referendum, thereafter insisting on the right to self-determination including the possibility of a White homeland. The party boycotted the April 1994 elections, subsequently mounting a campaign for the United Nations to classify Afrikaners as an oppressed indigenous people. Dr. Ferdinand Hartzenberg is party leader.

Islamic Party.

Merit Party.

National Front of South Africa, a neo-fascist Afrikaner organization.

New Afrikaner Resistance (New Afrikaner Weerstandsbeweging).

Northwest Democrats.

Reconstituted National Party (Herstigte Nasionale Party, HNP), founded in 1969 by extreme right-wing former members of the National Party. The HNP, advocating "Christian Nationalism" and strict apartheid, briefly held one parliamentary seat (following a by-election) between 1985 and 1987. It opposed the constitutional reform process and, like the Afrikaner People's Front of which it was briefly a member in 1993, boycotted the April 1994 elections. The party is led by J. Marais.

Rights Party.

South African Women's Party (SAWP).

United Christian Democratic Party (UCDP).

United People's Front (UPF).

Western Cape Federalist Party (Wes-Kaap Federaliste Party, WKFP)

White Liberation Movement (Blanke Bevrydingsbeweging, BBB), an extreme right-wing activist group led by Johan Schabort, which was banned between 1988 and 1990.

Workers' International to Rebuild the Fourth International.

World Apartheid Movement (Wereld Apartheidsbeweging).

Spain

Capital: Madrid

Population: 40,000,000 (1995E)

The Kingdom of Spain's 1978 constitution rescinded the "fundamental principles" and organic legislation under which General Franco had ruled as Chief of State until his death in 1975 and inaugurated an hereditary constitutional monarchy. Executive power is exercised by the Prime Minister and the Council of Ministers nominally appointed by the King but collectively responsible to the legislature, in which they must command majority support. Legislative authority is vested in the bicameral *Cortes Generales*, both houses of which are elected for four-year terms (subject to dissolution) by universal adult suffrage of those aged 18 and over. The upper Senate (*Senado*) currently has 256 members, of whom 208 were directly elected in 1996 (four from each of the 47 mainland provinces, six from Santa Cruz de Tenerife, five from the Balearic Islands, five from the Canary Islands and two each from the North African enclaves of Ceuta and Melilla), the other 48 senators being designated by the 19 autonomous regional legislatures. The lower Congress of Deputies (*Congreso de los Diputados*) consists of 350 deputies elected from party lists by province-based proportional representation, with each of the 50 provinces being entitled to a minimum of three deputies.

Pursuant to the constitutional description of political parties as the expression of pluralism and an essential instrument of political participation, subsidies are available from state funds for parties represented in the Congress of Deputies, in proportion to number of seats and votes obtained at the most recent general elections. Parties are also eligible for state subsidies to defray election campaign expenses, again in proportion to representation obtained, and to certain benefits during campaigns, such as free advertising space in the media. A separate channel of public subsidy is the entitlement of parliamentary groups in the national and regional legislatures to financial assistance according to their number of members.

Elections to the Congress of Deputies on March 3, 1996, resulted as follows: Popular Party 156 seats (with 38.9% of the vote), Spanish Socialist Workers' Party 141 (37.5%), United Left 21 (10.6%), Convergence and Union 16 (4.6%), Basque Nationalist Party 5 (1.3%), Canarian Coalition 4 (0.9%), Galician Nationalist Bloc 2 (0.9), United People 2 (0.7%), Catalan Republican Left 1 (0.7%), Basque Solidarity/Basque Left 1 (0.5%), Valencian Union 1 (0.4%).

Communist Party of Spain
Partido Comunista de España (PCE)

Address. 8 Marqués de Monteagudo, 28028 Madrid

Telephone. (#34–1) 356–9807

Fax. (#34–1) 534–3781

Leadership. Julio Anguita González (secretary-general), Fernando Perez Royo (parliamentary leader)

The PCE was founded in April 1920 by dissident members of the youth wing of the Spanish Socialist Workers' Party (PSOE) who wished to join the Third (Communist) International and who united in November 1921 with the *Partido Comunista Obrero Español* (PCOE), formed by further defections from the PSOE. The PCE held its first congress in 1922 but was forced underground by the Primo de Rivera dictatorship and had only 800 members by 1929. The party formed part of the republican Popular Front from January 1936, winning 17 seats in the Congress in that year. During the Francoist uprising the PCE policy was "victory first, then revolution", in contrast to the Trotskyists and anarcho-syndicalists. Under the subsequent Franco regime, the PCE was active in the clandestine resistance, its general secretaries (in exile) being Dolores Ibárruri Gómez ("*La Pasionaria*") in 1942–60 and Santiago Carrillo Solares from 1960 (when Ibárruri was appointed honorary president of the party). Undergoing various splits during the 1960s, the PCE developed links with the Italian Communist Party (PCI), sharing the latter's opposition to Moscow's leadership, notably the 1968 Czechoslovakian intervention, and its support for co-operation with other democratic parties. From 1968 a minority pro-Soviet faction, which broke away in 1970 reviving the name of the PCOE, was led by Enrique Lister, but it reunited with the PCE in April 1986.

In July 1974 the exiled PCE leadership joined other anti-Franco parties in the *Junta Democrática*, which in March 1976 joined the Socialist-led Democratic Platform to form the Democratic Co-ordination. Legalized in April 1977, when it had some 200,000 members, the PCE supported the restoration of a constitutional monarchy and won 20 seats in the Congress of Deputies elected in June 1977 (and three in the Senate). The ninth (1978) PCE congress was the first held in Spain for 46 years. The party's congressional strength increased to 23 in the elections of March 1979, but it becamde internally divided between two large and broadly Euro-communist factions and two smaller and broadly pro-Soviet factions. The weakened party was reduced to 4.1% of the vote and four deputies in the October 1982 elections, whereupon Carrillo resigned and was succeeded as PCE secretary-general (in November) by a more committed Euro-communist, Gerardo Iglesias Argüelles.

In local elections in May 1983 the PCE vote recovered to 7.9%, but in the following months it suffered a series of splits, mainly between "*gerardistas*" favouring a broad left alliance and "*carrillistas*" opposed to such a strategy. In March 1985 Carrillo was forced out of the PCE leadership, his supporters being purged from the central committee. In April 1986 the PCE was a founder-member of the United Left (IU), which secured 4.6% of the vote and seven lower house seats in the June general elections. The then deputy general secretary, Enrique Curiel, resigned in December 1987, and Iglesias himself resigned in February 1988 after losing the support of the large Madrid, Catalan and Andalusian sections. Later that month the 12th PCE congress elected Julio

Anguita (a former mayor of Córdoba) as his successor. Meanwhile, the PCE had become involved in sporadic efforts to reunify the Spanish communist movement following the establishment by Ignacio Gallego of the People's Communist Party of Spain (PCPE) and by Carrillo of what became the Workers' Party of Spain (PTE).

PCE president Dolores Ibárruri died in November 1989, whereafter the PCE continued its "broad left" strategy in the 1993 and 1996 elections, derving some benefit in terms of increased membership and votes from the troubles of the ruling Spanish Socialist Workers' Party (PSOE) and the broadly conservative policies of the González government.

Popular Party
Partido Popular (PP)
   Address. 13 Génova, 28004 Madrid
   Telephone. (#34–1) 319–4008
   Fax. (#34–1) 308–4618
   Leadership. José María Aznar López (president), Francisco Alvarez Cascos (secretary-general)

The moderate conservative PP was established in its present form in January 1989 as successor to the Popular Alliance (*Alianza Popular*, AP), which had been created in October 1976 as a distinctly right-wing grouping embracing the dominant political forces of the Franco era.

The AP was formed as a coalition of seven right-wing and centre-right parties: *Reforma Democrática* (RD), led by a former Francoist minister Manuel Fraga Iribarne; *Acción Regional* (AR), led by Laureano López Rodó; *Acción Democrática Española* (ADE), formed in 1976 and led by Federico Silva Muñoz; *Democracia Social* (DS), led by Licinio de la Fuente; *Unión del Pueblo Español* (UDPE), led by Cruz Martínez Esteruelas; *Unión Nacional Española* (UNE), led by Gonzalo Fernández de la Mora, and *Unión Social Popular* (USP), led by Enrique Thomas de Carranza. In March 1977 five of the parties merged as a single organization named the *Partido Unido de Alianza Popular* (PUAP) led by Fraga as secretary-general. The two non-participating parties were the ADE and the UNE, both led by former Francoist ministers, but they remained in alliance with the PUAP until late 1979.

In the June 1977 general elections the AP, then widely regarded as a Francoist grouping, won 8.2% of the vote, giving it 16 seats in the Congress of Deputies and two in the Senate. Divided over whether to endorse the 1978 constitution (which Fraga in the event supported), the AP lost support. In the March 1979 general elections the Democratic Coalition which it had formed with other right-wing groups, including *Acción Ciudadana Liberal*, the *Partido Popular de Cataluña*, *Renovación*

Española (RE) and the Popular Democratic Party (PDP), won only 6% of the vote, giving it nine seats in the Congress and three in the Senate. At the 1979 and 1980 party congresses, the AP leadership moved the party, with some difficulty, towards a mainstream conservative orientation, a leading advocate of which was Fraga, who was elected AP president in 1979. In mid-1980 the AP merged with the PDP and RE; the combined party, projecting a moderate image (and denouncing the 1981 coup attempt), doubled its membership in 1981–82.

The Galician elections of October 1981 enabled the AP to form a minority government in that region, where it secured a majority in 1983 by recruiting members of the by then dissolved Union of the Democratic Centre (UCD). Meanwhile, in the national parliamentary elections of October 1982 the AP-led bloc won 26.6% of the vote and 106 seats in the lower chamber (and 54 in the upper), so eclipsing the UCD and becoming the main opposition formation.

From 1983 the AP led a regional and national electoral alliance, the Popular Coalition (*Coalición Popular*, CP), including the PDP, the Liberal Union (UL) and regional formations such as the Union of the Navarrese People (UPN), the Aragonese Party and the Valencian Union. The CP came under severe strain following the June 1986 general elections, in which it secured 26% of the vote and 105 seats in the lower house (and 63 in the Senate). In July 1986 the PDP broke away. In December, after an electoral rout in the Basque Country, Fraga resigned as AP president. In January 1987 the national AP broke with the Liberal Party (PL, as the UL had become) although the AP-PL alliance remained in existence in some regions. The 8th AP congress, in February 1987, installed a new youthful party leadership headed by Antonio Hernández Mancha, who had been AP leader in Andalusía. During 1987 the AP contested elections at various levels, securing 231 seats in autonomous parliaments, over 13,000 local council seats and 17 seats in the European Parliament (for which its list was led by Fraga). However, by late 1987 defections resulting from chronic internal infighting had reduced the party's strength in the national Congress of Deputies to 67.

The conversion of the AP into the PP at a party congress in January 1989 reflected the wish of most AP currents to present a moderate conservative alternative to the ruling Spanish Socialist Workers' Party (PSOE) and to eschew any remaining identification with the Franco era. The congress was preceded by a power struggle between Hernández and Fraga, the latter having been persuaded by supporters that he should try to regain the leadership. In the event, Hernández opted out of the contest shortly before the congress, so that Fraga resumed the leadership of a more united party, which subsequently made particular efforts to build alliances with regional conservative parties. In the October 1989 general elections it advanced marginally to 106 seats and 30.3% of the vote, but remained far behind the PSOE. In December 1989 the PP won an absolute majority in the Galician assembly, whereupon Fraga became regional president, being succeeded as PP leader by José María Aznar López.

In the early 1990s the PP was not immune from scandals concerning irregular party financing, of the type affecting most of Latin Europe; but it remained relatively untarnished compared with the ruling PSOE. In general elections in June 1993 the party increased its Chamber representation to 141 seats and its vote share to 34.8%, less than four points behind the PSOE. Continuing in opposition, the PP registered major victories in the October 1993 Galician regional election and in the June 1994 European Parliament elections, on the latter occasion overtaking the PSOE by winning 40.6% of the vote and 28 of the 64 seats. Further advances followed in regional and local elections in May 1995, although in actual voting the PP failed to match its large opinion poll lead over the PSOE. Aznar's public standing was boosted by a car-bomb assassination attempt against him in Madrid in April 1995.

In early general elections in March 1996 the PP at last overtook the PSOE as the largest Chamber party, but its 156 seats (from 38.9% of the vote) left it well short of an overall majority. Aznar was accordingly obliged to form a minority government, which received qualified pledges of external support from the Catalan Convergence and Union, the Basque Nationalist Party and the Canarian Coalition in return for concessions to their regional agendas. His government programme promised urgent economic austerity measures to achieve the "national objective" of meeting the Maastricht treaty criteria for participation in a single European currency.

The PP is affiliated to the Christian Democrat International and the International Democrat Union. Its representatives in the European Parliament sit in the European People's Party group.

Spanish Socialist Workers' Party

Partido Socialista Obrero Español (PSOE)

Address. 70 Ferraz, Madrid 28008

Telephone. (#34–1) 582–0444

Fax. (#34–1) 582–0525

Leadership. Felipe González Márques (general secretary), Alfonso Guerra (deputy general secretary), Ramón Rubial Cavia (president)

Of social democratic orientation, the PSOE seeks a fairer and more united society based on social, economic and political democracy. It supports Spanish membership of the European Union (EU) and of the Atlantic Alliance, having opposed the latter until 1986. It defined itself as Marxist in 1976, but since 1979 has regarded Marxism as merely an analytical tool. It defends divorce and the decriminalization of abortion in certain circumstances.

Originally founded in 1879 from socialist groups in Madrid and Guadalajara, the PSOE held its first congress in 1888 and became a leading party of the Second International. It was allied with the Republicans from 1909, as a result of which its founder, Pablo Iglesias, was elected to the Congress of Deputies in 1910. The party had some 40,000 members when its left wing broke away in 1920–21 to form the Communist Party of Spain (PCE). The PSOE doubled its membership during the 1920s and returned about one third of the deputies in the Congress in 1931. It played an important role in the history of the Spanish Republic until the end of the Civil War in 1939, when it was banned by the Franco regime. The exiled leadership, based in Toulouse (France), refused to ally with other anti-Franco forces, but a more radical internally-based *"renovador"* faction began to organize in the late 1960s. The internal section gained control at a congress in Paris in 1972, and in 1974 it elected Felipe González as first secretary (although a rival "historico" faction survived in France and evolved into the Socialist Action Party). Both the PSOE and various regional socialist parties experienced rapid growth in Spain at about this time, partly due to the death of Franco.

In June 1975 the PSOE joined other non-Communist opposition parties in the *Plataforma Democrática* alliance, which in March 1976 merged with the PCE-led *Junta Democrática*. The latter had been created in 1974 and included the Popular Socialist Party (*Partido Socialista Popular*, PSP), which had been formed in 1967 as the *Partido Socialista del Interior* (PSI). The PSOE was also a component of the even broader *Coordinación Democratica*, which negotiated with the post-Franco government for the restoration of civil and political rights, regional autonomy and popular consultation on the future form of government. During 1976 the PSOE formed the *Federación de Partidos Socialistas* along with groups such as the Party of Socialists of Catalonia (PSC), *Convergencia Socialista Madrileña*, the *Partit Socialiste des Illes*, the *Partido Socialista Bilzarrea* and the Aragonese and Galician Socialist parties.

In December 1976 the PSOE, the largest socialist group with about 75,000 members, held its first congress inside Spain for 44 years. It was formally legalized on Feb. 17, 1977, along with a number of other parties. The PSOE participated in the June 1977 general elections together with the PSC and the Basque Socialist Party (PSE-PSOE), winning a total of 118 seats in the Congress of Deputies and 47 in the Senate. In February 1978 the PSC formally affiliated to the national party, as the PSC-PSOE, and in April the PSOE absorbed the PSP, which had six deputies and four senators. The Aragonese and Galician parties were similarly absorbed in May and July 1978. In the March 1979 general elections the PSOE, with its Basque and Catalan affiliates, won 121 seats in the Congress and 68 in the Senate, therefore remaining in opposition. At a centennial congress in May 1979 González unexpectedly stepped down as party leader after a majority of delegates refused to abandon a doctrinal commitment to Marxism. His control was re-established during a special congress in late September, the hard-liners being defeated by a 10 to 1 majority.

The PSOE made further gains in the October 1982 general elections, in which it won 48.7% of the vote (passing the 10 million mark for the first time) and gained an absolute majority in both chambers (with 202 of the 350 deputies and 134 of the 208 senators). A PSOE government was formed on Dec. 1, with González as Prime Minister; it subsequently negotiated Spain's entry into the European Communities (later the EU) with effect from Jan. 1, 1986. In January 1983 the PSOE absorbed the Democratic Action Party (*Partido de Acción Democráta*, PAD), which had been formed in March 1982 by centre-left defectors from the then ruling Union of the Democratic Centre (UCD). In 1985 the PSOE experienced serious internal divisions over the government's pro-NATO policy, which ran counter to the party's longstanding rejection of participation in any military alliance. The issue was resolved by a referendum of March 1986 which delivered a majority in favour of NATO membership on certain conditions, including reduction of the US military presence in Spain.

The PSOE retained power in the June 1986 general elections with a reduced vote share of 43.4% but a renewed majority of 184 lower house seats and 124 in the Senate. It thereafter pursued what were generally seen as moderate and somewhat conservative policies, particularly in the economic sphere. The PSOE's narrow loss of an overall majority in the October 1989 general elections (in which it slipped to 175 seats in the lower house on a 39.6% vote share) was attributed in part to internal divisions, highlighted by the prior emergence of the dissident Socialist Democracy splinter group and by the defection of a substantial PSOE group to the United Left (IU). In the early 1990s the PSOE's standing was damaged further by a series of financial scandals involving prominent party figures, combined with familiar left/right tensions. At the 32nd PSOE congress in November 1990 the left-leaning Deputy Prime Minister and deputy party leader, Alfonso Guerra, was able to block a move by the party's right to strengthen its base in leadership bodies. However, a corruption scandal involving his brother compelled Guerra to resign from the government in January 1991; although he remained deputy leader of the party, the PSOE right became increasingly dominant thereafter.

In early general elections in June 1993 the party retained a narrow relative majority of 159 Chamber seats (on a 38.7% vote share), sufficient for González to form a minority government with regional party support. Held amid further disclosures about irregular party financing, the 33rd PSOE congress in March 1994 resulted in the transfer of the party's controversial organization secretary, José María ("Txiki") Benegas to another post. In the June 1994 European Parliament elections PSOE support slumped to 31.1%, so that the party took only 22 of the 64 Spanish seats, while in simultaneous regional elections the PSOE lost overall control of its stronghold of Andalusia. Further setbacks followed in Basque Country elections in October 1994 and in regional/municipal polling in May 1995, although the PSOE retained control of Madrid and Barcelona.

The tide of corruption and security scandals rose inexorably through 1995, with the CESID phone-tapping disclosures in June causing the small Catalan Convergence and Union party to withdraw its external support from the PSOE government the following month. The eventual upshot was another early general election in March 1996 in which the PSOE finally lost power, although the margin of its defeat was less wide than many had predicted: it retained 141 seats with 37.5% of the vote, only slightly down on its 1993 showing and only 1.5% behind the Popular Party, which was therefore obliged to form a minority government.

The PSOE is a member party of the Socialist International and its European Parliament representatives sit in the Party of European Socialists group.

United Left
Izquierda Unida (IU)
  Address. 6 General Rodrigo, 28003 Madrid
  Telephone. (#34–1) 553–4909
  Fax. (#34–1) 534–9747
  Leadership. Julio Anguita González (co-ordinator)
  The radical left-wing (mainly Marxist) IU was founded in April 1986 as an electoral alliance,

originally consisting of the Communist Party of Spain (PCE), the Peoples' Communist Party of Spain (PCPE), the Progressive Federation (FP), the Socialist Action Party (PASOC), the Communist Union of Spain (UCE) and the Republican Left (IR). It was later joined by the Carlist Party and the Humanist Party (PH), although the latter quickly withdrew, and it formed a local alliance with the Unity of the Valencian People (UPV). The first president of the IU was the then PCE leader, Gerardo Iglesias.

In the June 1986 general elections the IU won seven seats in the Congress of Deputies and none in the Senate. The FP left the IU in late 1987, partly as a result of the unilateral decision of the PCE to sign a parliamentary accord against political violence without consulting the other IU parties. In December 1987 the IU leadership adopted a strategy seeking to make the IU a permanent rather than *ad hoc* alliance, and to broaden its base during 1988 beyond the member parties to incorporate independent left-wingers and pressure groups. The IU was expanded in 1988–89 to include the Republican Left (*Izquierda Republicano*, IR), led by Isabelo Herreros Martín-Maestro, and the Unitarian Candidature of Workers (*Candidatura Unitaria de Trabajadores*, CUT), led by Juan Manuel Sánchez Gordillo. In the October 1989 general elections the IU increased its lower house representation to 18 seats (on a 9.1% vote share) and also won one Senate seat.

Proposals for a formal merger between the IU parties caused dissension in 1991–92, the outcome being that component formations retained their autonomous identity. In the June 1993 general elections the IU made only marginal headway, again winning 18 lower house seats but with 9.6% of the vote. It fared substantially better in the June 1994 European Parliament elections, obtaining nine of the 64 Spanish seats on a 13.6% vote share. In simultaneous regional elections in Andalusia, it won 19.2% of the vote. In the March 1996 general elections the IU derived some benefit from the defeat of the Spanish Socialist Workers' Party, winning 10.6% of the national vote and 21 lower house seats (although none in the Senate).

The IU representatives in the European Parliament sit in the Confederal European United Left group.

Other National Parties

Carlist Party (*Partido Carlista*, PC), formed in 1934, a left-wing group which arose from a 19th-century Catholic monarchist movement; strongest in the north of Spain, the Carlists turned against the Franco regime after 1939 and many of its leaders were exiled; in the post-Franco era it became a component of the United Left alliance.

Centrist Union (*Unión Centrista*, UC), led by Fernando García Fructuoso, launched in early 1995 by elements that included former members of the Democratic and Social Centre (*Centro Democrático y Social*, CDS), which had been founded prior to the 1982 elections by Adolfo Suárez González, who had vacated the leadership of the Union of the Democratic Centre (*Unión de Centro Democrático*, UCD) on resigning as Prime Minister in January 1981 and had been rebuffed when he tried to regain the party leadership in July 1982; allied regionally and locally with the Popular Party (PP) and an affiliate of the Liberal International, the CDS had won 14 lower house seats and five European Parliament seats in 1989, although the resignation of Suárez González in September 1991 had heralded virtual extinction in the 1993 national and 1994 European elections; the new UC fared little better in the March 1996 general elections. *Address*. 30 Jorge Juan, 28001 Madrid

Feminist Party of Spain (*Partido Feminista de España*, PFE), led by Lidia Falcón O'Neill, founded in 1979, aiming to spread the gospel of women's liberation at the political and social levels, but not making much headway in Catholic and socially conservative Spain. *Address*. 29/1A Magdalena, 28012 Madrid

The Greens (*Los Verdes*), confederation resulting from ecologist conferences in Tenerife in May 1983 and in Malaga in June 1984, legally registered in November 1984, inaugurated at a congress in Barcelona in February 1985; the resultant Green Alternative (*Alternativa Verde*) electoral alliance won less than 1% of the vote in the 1986 general elections, and subsequent assorted electoral variants (sometimes simultaneous and competing) have made no further progress, although the movement has gained some representation at local level. *Address*. Apdo 565, 38400 Puerto de la Cruz, Tenerife

Humanist Party (*Partido Humanista*, PH), formed in 1984 and led by Rafael de la Rubia, a member of the United Left electoral coalition (IU) at the time of the 1986 general elections, subsequently independent.

Liberal Party (*Partido Liberal*, PL), led by José Antonio Segurado, founded in 1977, absorbed the small Liberal Union (*Unión Liberal*, UL) in 1985, closely allied with the Popular Party from 1989, although retaining independent party status. *Address*. 4 plaza de las Cortes, 28014 Madrid

National Front (*Frente Nacional*, FN), led by Blas Piñar López, far-right party founded in October 1986 aiming to rally Francoist forces against the then ruling Spanish Socialist Workers' Party.

Socialist Action Party (*Partido de Acción Socialista*, PASOC), led by Pablo Castellano and Alonso Puerta, founded in January 1983 by left-wing socialists who regarded the then ruling Spanish Socialist Workers' Party (PSOE) as having betrayed the working class; succeeded the PSOE *Histórico*, which arose from the 1974 split between the *renovadores* ("renewal") group based inside Spain (led by Felipe González) and the *historicos* loyal to the exiled leadership of Rodolfo Llopis; having absorbed some even smaller socialist formations, PASOC was a founder member of the United Left alliance in 1986, through which it gained representation at national, regional and European levels. *Address.* 5 Espoz y Mina, 28012 Madrid

Socialist Democracy (*Democracia Socialista*, DS), led by Ricardo García Damborenea, founded in 1990 by a left-wing dissident faction of the then ruling Spanish Socialist Workers' Party.

Spanish Falange (*Falange Española*), led by Carmen Franco and Diego Marquez Jorrillo, residual survival of the ruling formation of the Franco era, won one lower house seat in 1979 in a National Union (*Unión Nacional*) with other neo-fascist groups; other far-right formations appeared to supersede the Falange in the 1980s, notably the National Front; in the 1990s it has sought to articulate right-wing sentiment among those damaged by free-market government policies.

Regional Parties

As the leading national formations, the Popular Party (PP), Spanish Socialist Workers' Party (PSOE) and United Left (IU) are organized in most of Spain's autonomous regions, either under their own name or in alliance with autonomous regional parties. There are also many regional parties without national affiliation.

ANDALUSIA

Regional assembly elections on March 3, 1996, resulted as follows: PSOE 52 seats, PP 20, a joint list of the IU, Greens and local progressives (the *Convocatoria por Andalucía*) 13, Andalusianist Party 4.

Andalusianist
Party Partido Andalucista (PA)
  Address. 24 av. San Francisco Javier, Edificio Seville 1/9a-2, 41005 Seville
  Telephone. (#34–5) 422–6855
  Fax. (#34–5) 421–0446

  Leadership. Antonio Moreno (president), Antonio Ortega (secretary-general)
  The PA was founded in 1976 (as the Socialist Party of Andalusia) on a progressive nationalist platform, seeking self-determination for Andalusia on terms more concessionary than those of the 1981 autonomy statute. Legalized in 1977, the party fought the 1979 general elections on a moderate regionalist manifesto, securing five seats in the Congress of Deputies (which it failed to hold in 1982). It won two seats in the Catalan assembly in March 1980 and three seats in the Andalusian assembly in May 1982 (with 5.4% of the vote). The party adopted its present name at its fifth congress in February 1984. In the 1986 Andalusian elections it was reduced to two seats, but it slightly raised its vote in the 1987 local elections. The party regained national representation in 1989, winning two lower house seats, and advanced strongly to 10 seats in the Andalusian regional assembly in 1990. However, it lost its national seats in 1993 and fell back to three regional seats in 1994. In the 1996 contests it again failed at national level, while improving to four seats in the Andalusian assembly.

ARAGON

Regional assembly elections on May 28, 1995, resulted as follows: PP 27 seats, PSOE 19, Aragonese Party 14, IU 5, Aragonese Junta 2.

Aragonese Party
Partido Aragonés (PAR)
  Address. Paseo de Sagasta 20, 50006 Zaragoza, Aragon
  Telephone. (#34–76) 214127
  Fax. (#34–76) 237403
  Leadership. José Mur (president), Emilio Eiroa García (secretary-general)
  Officially called the Aragonese Regionalist Party (*Partido Aragonés Regionalista*) until 1990, the PAR was founded in January 1978 to campaign for greatly increased internal autonomy for the provinces of Aragon within the Spanish state. Having its main strength in Zaragoza, it secured one of the region's 13 seats in the national lower house in 1977, retaining it in 1979. In the 1982 general elections the PAR was allied with the conservative Popular Alliance (later the Popular Party) and lost its seat. It became the third-largest bloc in the regional assembly in the May 1983 elections, which gave it 13 seats. Standing alone in the 1986 national elections, it regained a lower house seat. After the 1987 regional elections, which produced no overall majority, the then PAR president, Hipólito Gómez de las Roces, was elected regional premier. The party retained its one national seat in 1989 and 1993, but lost it in 1996.

In the interim, it won 14 seats in the regional assembly in March 1995.

ASTURIAS

Regional assembly elections on May 28, 1995, resulted as follows: PP 21 seats, PSOE 17, IU 6, Asturianist Party 1.

Asturianist Party
Partiu Asturianista (PAS)
Address. c/o Regional Assembly, Oviedo, Asturias
Leadership. Xuan Xosé Sánchez Vicente (president)
Founded in 1986, the regionalist PAS has made little electoral progress, winning a single seat in 1995.

BALEARIC ISLANDS

Regional assembly elections on May 28, 1995, resulted as follows: PP 30 seats, PSOE 16, Socialist Party of Majorca-Nationalists of Majorca 6, IU 3, Majorcan Union 2, others 2.

Majorcan Union
Unio Mallorquina (UM)
Address. 1/3/3 av. de Joan March, 07004 Palma de Mallorca
Leadership. María Antonia Munar (president), Pablo Mosquera (secretary-general)
The regionalist UM has a centrist political orientation. It won six of the 52 regional assembly seats in 1983, so that it had the balance of power between the PP and the PSOE. By 1995, however, it had slipped to only two seats.

Socialist Party of Majorca-Nationalists of Majorca
Partit Socialista de Mallorca-Nacionalistes de Mallorca (PSM-NM)
Address. c/o Regional Assembly, Palma de Mallorca
The left-oriented "Majorcan nationalist" PSM-NM list won six out of 59 regional assembly seats in 1995.

BASQUE COUNTRY (EUSKADI)

Regional assembly elections on Oct. 23, 1994, resulted as follows: Basque Nationalist Party 22 seats, Basque Socialist Party-Basque Left 12, United People 11, PP 11, Basque Solidarity 8, IU 6, Alavan Unity 5.

Basque Left
Euskal Ezkerra (EuE)
Address. 5/1° Jardines, 48005 Bilbao, Euzkadi
Leadership. Xabier Gurrutxaga (secretary-general)
The EuE was formed by militant pro-independence elements of the previous Basque Left grouping who rejected the 1993 merger with the Basque federation of the Spanish Socialist Workers' Party to create the Basque Socialist Party-Basque Left. The militant rejectionists have a slightly different Basque title than that of the previous Basque Left, but it apparently translates the same in English. In the March 1996 national elections the EuE presented a joint list with Basque Solidarity, returning one deputy to the lower house.

Basque Nationalist Party
Partido Nacionalista Vasco (PNV) Euzko Alderdi Jeltzalea (EAJ)
Address. 16 Ibáñez de Bilbao, 48080 Bilbao, Euzkadi
Telephone. (#34–4) 424–4410
Fax. (#34–4) 423–0635
Leadership. Xabier Arzallus Antía (president), José Antonio Ardanza Garro (*lendakari*), Ricardo Ansotegui (secretary)
Dating from 1895, the Christian democratic PNV stands for an internally autonomous Basque region (including Navarra) within Spain and is opposed to the terrorist campaign for independence. It opposes unrestrained capitalism and supports a mixed economy. The PNV developed from the Basque Catholic traditionalist movement led by its founder, Sabino Arana y Goiri. It returned seven deputies to the Spanish *Cortes* in 1918, 12 in 1933 and nine in 1936, succeeding in the latter year in establishing an autonomous Basque government under José Antonio Aguirre. Allied with the republican regime in the Spanish civil war, its leadership was forced into exile by Gen. Franco's victory, and the party was suppressed throughout the Franco era. Aguirre died in 1960 and the Basque "government in exile" nominated Jesus María de Leizaola to succeed him as *lendakari* (president of the Basque government).

In the 1977 Spanish general elections the PNV won seven seats in the Congress of Deputies and eight in the Senate; its representatives abstained in the parliamentary vote on the 1978 constitution, and its supporters were among the 56% of voters in Guipúzcoa and Vizcaya (the two largest Basque provinces) who abstained in the ensuing referendum. It lost one of its seats in Congress in 1979, but in that year's elections to the Basque general junta the PNV won 73 of the 171 seats in the two main provinces, whereupon de Leizaola returned from France, ending the 43–year-old "government in exile". In the March 1980 elections to the new Basque parliament it won 37.6% of the vote and 25 of the 60 seats. The then PNV leader, Carlos Garaikoetxea, became *lendakari* of the autonomous Basque government in April 1980.

In 1982 the PNV secured eight seats in the Spanish Congress and nine in the Senate. In the February 1984 Basque elections it won 42% of the vote and 32 of the 75 seats. Garaikoetxea was forced to resign due to intra-party disputes in December 1984, and in February 1985 was succeeded as party leader by Xabier Arzalluz and as *lendakari* by José Antonio Ardanza Garro, a PNV member, who agreed a "pact of government" with the Basque Socialist Party (later the Basque Socialist Party-Basque Left, PSE-EE). In June 1986 the PNV's representation in the *Cortes* fell to six seats in the lower chamber and seven in the upper. The party split in September, with supporters of Garaikoetxea leaving to form Basque Solidarity (EA). In the Basque elections of November 1986 the PNV held only 17 of its seats and was again obliged to govern in coalition with the PSE (which won fewer votes but more seats than the PNV).

In January and March 1989 the PNV organized huge demonstrations in Bilbao calling upon separatist militants to end their armed struggle. However, subsequent efforts to form an electoral alliance with the EA and the Basque Left (EE) failed, with the result that in October 1989 the PNV's national representation fell to five Congress and four Senate seats, although it was confirmed as the largest party in the 1990 Basque parliament elections, with 22 seats. The PNV again won five lower house seats in the 1993 general elections, after which the PNV usually gave external support to the PSOE minority government. In the June 1994 European Parliament election the PNV headed a regional list which won 2.8% of the vote and two seats, one of which was taken by a PNV candidate. In regional elections in October 1994, the PNV won 22 of the 75 Basque parliament seats.

In the March 1996 national elections the PNV retained five lower house seats and improved from three to four in the Senate. The following month it joined with the Catalan Convergence and Union and the Canarian Coalition in undertaking to give external parliamentary support to a minority PP government, in exchange for certain concessions to its regionalist agenda.

The PNV is a member party of the Christian Democrat International and its European Parliament representative sits in the European People's Party group.

Basque Socialist Party-Basque Left Partido
Socialista de Euskadi-Euskadiko Ezkerra (PSE-EE)

Address. 3 plaza de San José, Bilbao 9, Euzkadi
Telephone. (#34–4) 424–1606
Leadership. Ramón Jaúregui (secretary-general)

The PSE-EE was created in March 1993 when the PSE (the autonomous Basque federation of the Spanish Socialist Workers' Party, PSOE) merged with the smaller and more radical EE. The merged party continued with the PSE's pro-autonomy line, whereas the Marxist EE had previously been committed to independence for the Basque provinces. That the latter was able to accept the PSE's stance for the merged party was in part because its militant pro-independence wing rejected the merger and broke away to maintain the Basque Left in being as an independent formation.

Founded in 1977, the PSE won seven seats in the Congress of Deputies in 1977, and five in 1979. It was in an autonomist pact until late 1979, when it parted company with the Basque Nationalist Party (PNV) over the latter's insistence on the necessity of including Navarra in the Basque autonomy statute. However, having won eight lower house seats in the 1982 national elections, the PSE from early 1985 agreed to support a PNV administration. In June 1986, for the first time, the PSE-PSOE won more seats in the Congress than any other party in the region, with seven deputies to the PNV's six, although the Socialist vote in the three provinces of the Basque autonomous region was the lowest anywhere in Spain, at around 25%. In November 1986, after a split in the PNV, the PSE was confirmed as the largest single party, winning 19 of the 75 seats in elections to the Basque parliament. Early in 1987 the PSE joined a coalition administration with the PNV, with a PSE member Jesus Eguiguren, being elected president of the parliament. In the 1990 Basque elections the PSE slipped to 16 seats.

The EE had been launched in 1976 as a pro-independence electoral alliance which had as its main component the Basque Revolutionary Party (*Euskal Iraultzarako Alderdia*, EIA), which had been formed by supporters of Mario Onaindía Machiondo, then a political prisoner, as a non-violent Marxist offshoot of the *Politico-Military* faction of the terrorist group, Basque Nation and Liberty (ETA). Onaindía was secretary-general of the EE for some ten years after its foundation. In June 1977 the EE secured one seat in each chamber of the Spanish parliament, both EE representatives subsequently voting against the 1978 constitution because of its limited provisions for Basque autonomy. The party lost its

Senate seat in 1979, but in the 1980 elections to the Basque parliament the EE won 9.7% of the vote and six seats (out of 60). The EIA dissolved itself in mid-1981, and the EE was reorganized shortly afterwards, incorporating Roberto Lertxundi Baraffano's faction of the Basque Communist Party (EPK). It was relaunched in March 1982, as the Basque Left-Left for Socialism alliance (EE-IS), and retained its Congress seat in October. A radical nationalist faction, the New Left (*Nueva Izquierda*), led by José Ignacio Múgica Arregui, broke away from the EE later in 1982; *Ezkerra Marxista*, a similar tendency formed in October 1983, sought to remain within the EE, but the leadership declared its intention to purge any dissident groups. The EE held its six Basque parliament seats in 1984, following which Onaindia resigned as general secretary in January 1985. In 1986 the EE won a second seat in the Congress, and nine in the Basque parliament. In the 1990 Basque elections the EE tally was again six seats.

The merged PSE-EE did not aggregate the two parties' previous electoral support, winning only 12 seats in the 1994 Basque parliament elections.

Basque Solidarity
Eusko Alkartasuna (EA)
   Address. 3 bajo San Prudencio, 01005 Vitoria
   Telephone. (#34–45) 232762
   Fax. (#34–45) 232953
   Leadership. Carlos Garaikoetxea (president), Inaxio Oliveri Vitoria-Gasteiz (secretary-general)

The EA is a radical nationalist (pro-independence), pacifist and social democratic movement, which rejects the revolutionary nationalism of United People (HB). Its various ideological tendencies include the social democratic majority, the anti-communist *Bultzagilleak* group from Guipúzcoa, the traditional nationalists known as *sabinianos* from the early nationalist leader Sabino Arana and the *abertzales* or patriots. The party was founded in October 1986 as the Basque Patriots (*Eusko Abertzaleak*), as a result of a split in the Basque Nationalist Party (PNV) which precipitated early elections to the Basque parliament the following month, when the EA won 14 seats against 17 for the parent party. Its first congress in April 1987 showed that it then had the support of several hundred mayors and local councillors. (Garaikoetxea, the then leader of the PNV, had become *lendakari*, or president of the Basque government, in April 1980, but had been forced to resign in December 1984.)

In January 1987 the EA agreed a joint programme for government with the Basque Left (EE/EuE), this document later applying to the EA's relations with the radical EuE following the main EE's decision to create the Basque Socialist Party-Basque Left. In June 1987 the EA contested the European Parliament elections as part of the autonomist Europe of the Peoples Coalition (EPC), Garaikoetxea winning a seat. In November the EA declined to sign an inter-party Basque accord against terrorism parallelling that signed by parties in the Spanish parliament; the EA stated that the accord did not address the fundamental issues of self-determination and national reintegration. It slipped to nine seats in the 1990 Basque parliament elections and to eight in 1994, but retained its single national lower house seat in the March 1996 elections on a joint list with the EuE.

United People
Herri Batasuna (HB)
   Address. 8/3° Astarioa, 48001 Bilbao, Euzkadi
   Telephone. (#34–4) 424–0799
   Fax. (#34–4) 423–5932
   Leadership. Jon Idigoras, Iñaki Esnaola

A Marxist-oriented Basque nationalist formation, HB calls for the withdrawal of "occupation forces", i.e. the Spanish military and police, and negotiations leading to the complete independence of Euzkadi, and is regarded as the closest of the main parties to the illegal terrorist group Basque Nation and Liberty (*Euzkadi ta Askatasuna*, ETA). It was founded in 1978 as an alliance of two legal Basque nationalist groups, the social democratic Basque Nationalist Action (*Accion Nacionalista Vasca*, ANV), formed in 1930, and the Basque Socialist Party (*Euskal Socialista Biltzarrea*, ESB), formed in 1976, with two illegal groups, the People's Revolutionary Socialist Party (HASI) and the Patriotic Workers' Revolutionary Party (LAIA). HASI and LAIA had formed the *Koordinadora Abertzale Sozialista* (KAS), which functioned in effect as the political wing of the main ETA faction, ETA *Militar*, and the KAS manifesto was adopted more or less in full by HB.

HB has contested Basque and Spanish elections since 1979, when it won three seats (which it refused to occupy) in the Spanish Congress of Deputies, one in the Senate and a total of 48 seats (out of 248) in the provincial assemblies of Guipúzcoa, Vizcaya and Navarra. In October 1979 HB called for abstention in the referendum on the creation of an autonomous Basque region excluding Navarra; in a 59% turnout the draft statute was supported by some 90.3% of voters. In March 1980 HB won 16.3% of the vote and 11 of the 60 seats in elections to the new Basque parliament, but it has consistently refused to take up its seats in assemblies above the level of *ayuntamientos* (local councils). Although it lost one of its Congress seats in the elections of October 1982, albeit with an increased vote, it won 12 seats (out of 75) in the Basque parliamentary elections of February

1984. Also in 1984 it won a High Court ruling obliging the Interior Ministry to recognize it as a party despite its alleged links with ETA.

In 1986 HB secured five seats in the Spanish Congress, one in the Senate and 13 in the Basque parliament. In February 1987 HB nominated one of its leaders, Juan Carlos Yoldi (then in prison charged with ETA activities), as its candidate for *lendakari* (Basque premier). Also in early 1987 HB called for the formulation of a joint nationalist strategy with the Basque Nationalist Party (PNV) and Basque Solidarity. In June an HB candidate was elected to the European Parliament (with 1.7% of the national vote). In January 1988 HB was the only one of the seven parties represented in the Basque parliament which was not invited to, and did not, sign a pact against terrorism.

In the 1989 national elections HB lost one lower house seat and surprised observers by announcing that it would occupy its four remaining seats, ending a decade-long boycott. However, on the eve of the opening of parliament, HB deputy-elect Josh Muguruza was killed and HB leader Iñaki Esnaola wounded in an attack apparently carried out by right-wing terrorists. Later the remaining HB deputies were expelled for refusing to pledge allegiance to the constitution. HB won two Congress seats and one in the Senate in the 1993 national elections, while the October 1994 Basque parliament balloting yielded 11 seats (two less than in 1990). Meanwhile, HB had lost its European Parliament seat in June 1994, its share of the national vote falling to 0.97%.

Alavan Unity

Unidad Alavesa (UA)

Address. c/o Basque Parliament, Vitoria, Euzkadi

Leadership. José Luis Añúa (president), Pablo Mosquera (secretary-general)

The UA is a Popular Party splinter group campaigning for recognition of the rights of the province of Alava within the Basque Country. It won three seats in the 1990 Basque parliament elections and five in 1994.

CANARY ISLANDS

Regional assembly elections on May 28, 1995, resulted as follows: Canarian Coalition 21 seats, PP 18, PSOE 16, Canarian Nationalist Party 4, Hierro Independent Grouping 1.

Canarian Coalition

Coalición Canaria (CC)

Address. 7–9 Galcerán, 38004 Santa Cruz de Tenerife

Leadership. Manuel Hermoso Rojas (chair)

Created prior to the 1993 general elections, the broadly centrist CC includes the following parties: (i) the Canarian Independent Groupings (*Agrupaciones Independientes de Canarias*, AIC) led by Manuel Hermoso Rojas and Paulino Rivero; (ii) the Canarian Independent Centre (*Centro Canario Independiente*, CCI) led by Lorenzo Olarte Cullén; (iii) the Canarian Initiative/Left (*Iniciativa/Izquierda Canaria*, ICAN) led by José Mendoza Cabrero and José Carlos Mauricio Rodríguez; and (iv) the Mazorca Assembly (*Asamblea Majorera*, AM) led by José Miguel Barragan Cabrera.

Of these components, the AIC was formed in 1985 as an alliance of Hermoso's *Agrupación Tinerfeña Independiente* (ATI) of Santa Cruz de Tenerife with the *Agrupación Palmera Independiente* (API) of Las Palmas and the *Agrupación Gomera Independiente* (AGI) of Tenerife. In the June 1986 general elections the AIC won about 60,000 votes, securing one seat in the Congress of Deputies and two in the Senate. The AIC retained one lower house seat in the 1989 general elections and was subsequently the only party to support Prime Minister González's re-election apart from his own Spanish Socialist Workers' Party (PSOE). In the 1991 Canaries regional elections the AIC, with 16 seats, took second place behind the PSOE and the AIC candidate, Manuel Hermoso Rojas, was elected to the island presidency with support from the ICAN (five seats), the AM (two) and other parties.

In the 1993 national elections the CC returned four deputies and six senators, who subsequently gave qualified support to the minority PSOE government. In June 1994 the CC captured one seat in elections to the European Parliament. In September 1994 the CC-led regional government lost its narrow majority when the Canarian Nationalist Party (PNC) left the alliance. In the May 1995 regional elections the CC obtained a plurality of 21 assembly seats out of 60 and continued to lead the islands' government. In the March 1996 national elections the CC retained four lower house seats but won only two of the directly elected Senate seats. It thereupon pledged qualified external support for a minority government of the centre-right Popular Party.

The CC's representative in the European Parliament sits in the European Radical Alliance group.

Canarian Nationalist Party (*Partido Canaria Nacionalista*, PCN), led by Bernardo Cabrera and Ernesto Lujan Ojeda, was original component of Canarian Coalition, but withdrew in 1994, won four seats in 1995 Canaries regional elections.

Hierro Independent Grouping (*Agrupación Herreña Independiente*, AHI), which won one regional assembly seat in 1995.

National Congress of the Canaries (*Congreso Nacional de Canarias*, CNC), led by Antoni Cubillo Ferreira, pro-independence group founded in 1986, favours leaving the EU and joining the OAU.

Regional assembly elections on May 28, 1995, resulted as follows: PP 13 seats, PSOE 10, Union for the Progress of Cantabria 7, Regionalist Party of Cantabria 6, IU 3.

Regionalist Party of Cantabria
Partido Regionalista Cántabro (PRC)
   Address. c/o Regional Assembly, Santander, Cantabria
   Leadership. Migel Angel Revilla (secretary-general)
   The centre-right PRC obtained two of the 35 seats in the May 1983 elections to the regional parliament. By the May 1995 elections it had improved to four seats out of 39.

Union for the Progress of Cantabria
Unión para el Progreso de Cantabria (UPCA)
   Address. c/o Regional Assembly, Santander, Cantabria
   Leadership. Juan Hormaechea Cazón (leader)
   The conservative UPCA contested the 1991 regional elections on the Popular Party (PP) list, winning 15 of that list's 21 seats (out of 39). In June 1993, however, the UPCA president of the regional government, Juan Hormaechea Cázon, broke with the PP, with the result that his party was reduced to seven seats in the May 1995 regional elections and lost the government presidency.

Regional assembly elections on May 28, 1995, resulted as follows: PP 50 seats, PSOE 27, IU 5, Union of the León People 2.

Democratic Liberal Party (*Partido Liberal Demócrata*, PLD), won a single seat (out of 84) in the 1983 regional elections.

Union of the León People (*Unión del Pueblo Leonés*, UPL), separatist formation that won two seats (out of 84) in the 1995 regional elections.

Regional assembly elections on May 28, 1995, resulted as follows: PSOE 24 seats, PP 22, IU 1.

Regional assembly elections on Nov. 19, 1995, resulted as follows: Convergence and Union 60 seats, Party of Socialists of Catalonia 34, PP 17, Republican Left of Catalonia 13, Initiative for Catalonia/Greens 11.

Convergence and Union
Convergència i Unió (CiU)
   Address. 231–6 Valencia, 08007 Barcelona, Catalunya
   Telephone. (#34–3) 487–0111
   Fax. (#34–3) 215–8428
   Leadership. Jordí Pujol i Soley (secretary-general)
   The pro-autonomy CiU was founded in 1979 as an alliance of the Democratic Convergence of Catalonia (*Convergència Democràtica de Catalunya*, CDC) and the Democratic Union of Catalonia (*Unión Democrática de Catalunya*, UDC), and later absorbed the small Catalan Democratic Left Party (*Esquerra Democrática de Catalunya*, EDC). The CDC and UDC had contested the 1977 general elections as part of a Democratic Pact (*Pacte Democràtic*), which obtained 11 seats in the Congress of Deputies (and voted for the 1978 constitution). In the 1979 elections the CiU won eight seats in the Congress and one in the Senate. In elections to the new Catalan parliament in March 1980 the CiU displaced the Catalan Socialist Party (PSC-PSOE) as the region's main political force, winning 28% of the vote and 43 of the 135 seats. Pujol was elected premier of the *Generalitat* (the Catalan administration) and formed a coalition with the local affiliate of the Union of the Democratic Centre, then the ruling party in Madrid, and a number of independents. In the October 1982 general elections the CiU increased its representation in the Spanish Congress to 12 members (and nine in the Senate). In the April 1984 Catalan elections the CiU won 46.8% of the vote and 72 seats, enabling it to form a majority administration.
   In the 1986 national elections the CiU returned 18 deputies and eight senators, thus becoming the fourth-largest party in the Spanish parliament. It was allied with the new liberal Democratic Reformist Party (PRD), which failed to win any seats, their joint candidate for Prime Minister having been Miquel Roca Junyent, the CiU parliamentary leader who had formed the PRD and was regarded as the national leader of the reformist-liberal bloc. The CiU obtained three seats in the 1987 European Parliament elections. In March 1992 the CiU confirmed its regional dominance by winning 71 of the 135 seats in the Catalan assembly, while national elections in June 1993 yielded 17 lower house and 14 Senate seats,

on a vote share of nearly 5%. The party thereafter gave qualified parliamentary support to the minority government of the Spanish Socialist Workers' Party (PSOE). In June 1994 the CiU retained three seats in the European Parliament elections with 4.7% of the vote.

The travails of the PSOE government in 1994–95 encouraged the CiU to attach more autonomist conditions to its continued support, beyond the original demand for greater transfer of tax receipts to the Catalan government. After much confusion, the CESID phone-tapping scandal of mid-1995 finally impelled the CiU into formal opposition and support for new general elections. This switch enabled the party to maintain its ascendancy in regional elections in Catalonia in November 1995, although it fell back to 60 seats (out of 135). The March 1996 national elections resulted in the CiU slipping to 16 lower house and eight Senate seats, with 4.6% of the overall vote. After protracted negotiations, the CiU agreed to give external support to a minority government of the anti-regionalization Popular Party (PP), which in return was obliged to swallow a dose of further devolution and to express admiration for Catalan culture. Featuring a doubling (to 30%) of tax receipt transfers from Madrid to Barcelona (and to the other autonomous regions), the deal with the PP was approved by the CiU executive in late April 1996 by 188 votes to 20 with 21 abstentions.

Of the CiU components, the UDC is affiliated to the Christian Democrat International. Of the three CiU European Parliament members, one sits in the European People's Party and two in the European Liberal, Democratic and Reformist Group.

Initiative for Catalonia

Iniciativa per Catalunya (IC)

Address. 7 Ciutat, 08002 Barcelona, Catalunya

Telephone. (#34–3) 302–7493

Fax. (#34–3) 412–4252

Leadership. Rafael Ribó Massó (president)

The IC was launched in 1986 as an alliance of Communist and other left-wing formations in Catalonia, headed by the Unified Socialist Party of Catalonia (*Partit Socialista Unificat de Catalunya*, PSUC) led by Ribó Massó and also including the Party of Communists of Catalonia (*Partit dels Comunistes de Catalunya*, PCC) and the Union of Left Nationalists (*Entesa des Nacionalistas d'Esquerra*, ENE).

Founded in 1936 by the merger of four left-wing groups, the PSUC took part in the government of Catalonia until 1939, when it was forced underground by the Francoist victory. Legalized again in 1976, it became a member of the provisional government of Catalonia. In the 1980 elections to the new Catalan parliament the PSUC

obtained 19% of the vote and 25 of the 135 seats; but in the 1984 elections it was reduced to six seats and 5.8% of the vote. In the June 1986 national elections the PSUC retained the single seat in the Congress of Deputies which it had won in 1982 (as against eight won in 1977 and 1979).

Contesting the 1992 regional and 1993 national elections as effectively the Catalan version of the national United Left, the IC made little impact. For the November 1995 regional elections it formed an alliance with the Catalan Greens (*Els Verds*), their joint list obtaining 11 of the 135 seats.

Party of Socialists of Catalonia

Partit dels Socialistes de Catalunya (PSC)

Address. 75–77 Nicaragua, 08029 Barcelona, Catalunya

Telephone. (#34–3) 321–0100

Fax. (#34–3) 439–7811

Leadership. Joan Reventós i Carner (president), Josep María (Raimon) Obiols i Germà (first secretary)

The PSC is affiliated to, but not formally part of, the Spanish Socialist Workers' Party (PSOE), pursuing similar economic and social policies but seeking the transformation of the current autonomist constitution into a federal one. The present party was founded in July 1978 as a merger of three pre-existing socialist formations, including the Catalan branch of the PSOE. After winning 15 lower house seats in the 1977 national elections, the following year the PSC affiliated to the PSOE, contesting subsequent national elections as a federation of the Spanish party.

In the 1979 general elections the PSC returned 17 lower house deputies, but was defeated by the centrist Convergence and Union (CiU) alliance in the 1980 elections to the Catalan parliament, obtaining 33 of the 135 seats. In the 1982 national elections the PSC won an absolute majority (25) of the Catalan seats in the lower house. In the 1984 Catalan elections it obtained 30% of the vote and 41 seats, while in the 1986 national elections it fell back to 21 seats but remained ahead of other Catalan parties. The same pattern of ascendancy in national contests and inferiority at regional level was apparent in subsequent elections. In the November 1995 Catalan elections the PSC won 34 seats (against 39 in 1992), again coming a distant second to the CiU.

Republican Left of Catalonia

Esquerra Republicana de Catalunya (ERC)

Address. 45 ent. carrer Villarroel, 08011 Barcelona, Catalunya

Telephone. (#34–3) 453–6005

Fax. (#34–3) 323–7122

Leadership. Heribert Barrera (president), Angel Colom i Colom (secretary-general)

Dating from 1931, the ERC was the majority party in the Catalan parliament of 1932 but was forced underground during the Franco era. Re-legalized in 1977, it adopted a moderate left-wing economic programme, also advocating Catalan self-determination and defining languages other than Catalan as foreign. It contested the June 1977 national elections along with the *Partido del Trabajo de España*, other groups and independent candidates in an alliance, the *Esquerra de Catalunya-Front Electoral Democràtic*, and elected one deputy. In 1979 the ERC allied with the *Front Nacional de Catalunya*, and won one seat each in the Spanish Congress of Deputies and the Senate. In elections for the new Catalan parliament in March 1980 the ERC gained 9% of the vote and 14 of the 135 seats. In the October 1982 Spanish elections it held its single seat in the Congress, and in the Catalan elections in April 1984 it won 4.4% and its strength was reduced to five members.

The ERC divided during the 1980s between a liberal wing, which favoured participation in the Catalan *Generalitat* (government), and the left, which favoured an independent line. The 15th (1985) ERC congress elected the liberal Joan Hortalà i Arau (the Catalan industry minister) as the party's leader, succeeding the more nationalistic Heribert Barrera i Costa. The 1986 elections deprived the ERC of its representation in the Madrid parliament, but in 1987 the party was part of the Europe of the Peoples Coalition (CEP) that secured a seat in the European Parliament (this being retained in 1989 but lost in 1994).

In 1991 the ERC absorbed the radical separatist Free Land (*Terre Lliure*) movement, the consequences being a switch from a pro-federalism line to advocacy of outright independence for Catalonia and the return of Barrera i Costa as party leader. The ERC retained its single seat in the national lower house in the 1993 and 1996 elections. In Catalonia, it won 11 of 135 regional parliament seats in 1992, rising to 13 in November 1995.

EXTREMADURA

Regional elections on May 28, 1995, resulted as follows: PSOE 31 seats, PP 27, IU 6, United Extremadura 1

United Extremadura

Extremadura Unida (Ex-U)
　Address. c/o Regional Assembly, Cáceres, Extremadura
　Leadership. Pedro Cañada Castillo (secretary-general)

The regionalist Ex-U obtained six seats in the Extremadura assembly in 1983, but had fallen to one (out of 65) by 1995.

GALICIA

Regional elections on Oct. 17, 1993, resulted as follows: PP 43, Party of Galician Socialists 19, Galician Nationalist Bloc 13.

Galician Nationalist Bloc

Bloque Nacionalista Galego (BNG)
　Address. c/o Regional Assembly, Santiago de Compostela, Galicia
　Leadership. Xosé Manuel Beiras (secretary-general)

Founded in 1983, the BNG advocates greater autonomy for Galicia and traditional left-wing economic policies. Its regional electoral support had risen steadily, from five seats in 1989 to 13 (out of 75) in 1993. In 1991 it absorbed the more centrist Galician National Party (*Partido Nacionalista Galego*, PNG) led by Pablo González Mariñas, which had been formed in 1986 by a progressive faction of the Galician Coalition.

Party of Galician Socialists

Partido dos Socialistas de Galicia (PSdG)
　Address. 1–9 Pino, 15704 Santiago de Compostela
　Telephone. (#34–81) 589622
　Leadership. Francisco Vázquez (secretary-general)

The PSdG is the autonomous regional federation of the Spanish Socialist Workers' Party (PSOE). It is the largest party in the region as regards national, but not regional, elections, having won 18 seats in the Congress of Deputies in 1982 and 15 in 1986. In 1981 it secured 17, and in 1985 22, of the 71 seats in the Galician parliament, control of the Xunta passing in 1985 to what became the Popular Party (PP), although in 1987 the PSdG-PSOE again established control briefly. Despite advancing to 28 seats in 1989, the party went into opposition to the PP. It slumped to 19 seats in the 1993 regional elections and continued in opposition.

Galician Coalition (*Coalición Galega*, CG), led by Xenén Bernardez Alvarez and Aniceto Núñez, centre-right regionalist grouping (also known as the Galician Centrists after one of its components, *Centristas de Galicia*, led by Victorino Núñez) was founded in December 1983 mainly by ex-members of the Galicianist Party (*Partido Galeguista*) and of the Union of the Democratic Centre (UCD), both of which were dissolved in 1983; the CG won 11 seats in the Galician parliament in 1985 (although five of its deputies subsequently defected) and one lower house seat in the 1986 general elections; split in 1986–87, with the Galician Nationalist Party (PNG) eventually breaking away (and later joining the Galician Nationalist Bloc); won only two regional seats in 1989 and none in 1993.

Galician Socialist Party-Galician Left (*Partido Socialista Galego-Esquerda Galega*, PSG-EG), led by Camilio Nogueira, left-wing regionalist grouping.

United Galicia (*Galicia Unida*), a centrist party formed in November 1986 by Xosé Luis Santos Lago.

MADRID

Regional elections on May 28, 1995, resulted as follows: PP 54 seats, PSOE 32, IU 17.

MURCIA

Regional elections on May 28, 1995, resulted as follows: PP 26 seats, PSOE 15, IU 4.

NAVARRA

Regional elections on May 28, 1995, resulted as follows: PP-Union of the Navarrese People 17 seats, Socialist Party of Navarra-PSOE 11, Convergence of Navarran Democrats 10, United People 5, IU 5, Basque Solidarity 2.

Socialist Party of Navarra
Partido Socialista de Navarra (PSN)
Address. c/o Regional Assembly, Pamplona, Navarra
Leadership. Javier Otano (president)
The PSN is the regional federation of the Spanish Socialist Workers' Party (PSOE). Formed in 1975 as the *Federación Socialista de Navarra*, it was integrated into the PSOE in 1982, although it retained its own identity and structure. Having won 19 of the 50 regional seats in 1991, the PSN was in opposition to the Union of the Navarrese People until the 1995 elections, in which it fell back to 11 seats but nevertheless secured the election of Javier Otano as regional premier by virtue of support from other parties.

Union of the Navarrese People
Union del Pueblo Navarro (UPN)
Address. 1/4° Plaza Príncipe de Viana, 31002 Pamplona, Navarra
Telephone. (#34–48) 227211
Fax. (#34–48) 210870
Leadership. Jesús Aizpun (president), Rafael Gurrea (secretary)
Founded in 1979, the conservative and Christian Democratic UPN won a single seat in the Congress of Deputies in 1979 but lost it in 1982. In the 1982 and 1986 national elections the UPN allied with the right-wing Popular Alliance, precursor of the Popular Party (PP); it also co-operated with the Popular Democratic Party (PDP) and the Liberal

Union (UL), now the Liberal Party. In the 1983 Navarra regional elections the UPN (then led by Javier Gomara) won 13 of the 50 seats, increasing to 14 in 1987 and to a plurality of 20 in 1991, when its candidate Juan Cruz Alli Aranguren was elected president of the regional government. It slipped to 17 seats in 1995 and went into opposition to a coalition headed by the Socialist Party of Navarra.

As Navarra is claimed by Basque nationalists as part of the historic territory of Euzkadi, the Basque Nationalist Party (PNV), Basque Solidarity (EA) and United People (HB) contest Spanish and regional elections there, with limited success. They secured none, three and six seats respectively in the 1995 regional elections.

LA RIOJA

Regional assembly elections on May 28, 1995, resulted as follows: PP 17 seats, PSOE 12, IU 2, Rioja Party 2.

Rioja Party
Partido Riojano (PR)
Address. 17/1° Portales, 26001 Logroño, La Rioja
Telephone. (#34–41) 254199
Fax. (#34–41) 254396
Leadership. Miguel González de Legarra (president), Alejandro Fernández de la Pradilla (secretary-general)
This small regionalist grouping has attempted, with little success, to challenge the dominance in the Rioja region of the national parties (mainly the PP and the PSOE, organized locally as the *Partido Socialista de La Rioja*). It has usually returned two successful candidates in regional elections, most recently in May 1995.

VALENCIA

Regional elections on May 28, 1995, resulted as follows: PP 42 seats, Socialist Party of Valencia-PSOE 32, IU/Greens 10, Valencian Union 5.

Socialist Party of Valencia
Partido Socialista del País Valenciano (PSPV)
Address. 3 Almirante, 46003 Valencia
Leadership. Antonio García Miralles (president), Joan Lerma Blasco (secretary-general)
The PSPV is a regional version of the Spanish Socialist Workers' Party (PSOE) and was the dominant Valencian party in regional and national elections of the 1980s and early 1990s. In the May 1995 regional elections, however, it came a poor second to the Popular Party, winning only 32 of the 89 seats.

Valencian Union

Unión Valenciana (UV)

Address. 16/2A avda de César Giorgeta, 46007 Valencia

Leadership. Vicente González Lizondo (president)

The centre-right regionalist UV was founded in 1982, describing itself as "progressive and independent, inter-classist and democratic". At first allied with national conservative parties, it stood on its own in the 1986 national elections and won one lower house seat, which it has retained in subsequent elections. At regional level it has maintained a small but significant presence, winning five seats in May 1995 and securing the election of its leader as president of the regional parliament.

Unity of the Valencian People (*Unitat del Poble Valencià*, UPV), led by Pere Mayor Penadés, founded in 1982 by two regionalist parties as a "democratic, left nationalist, egalitarian, ecologist and pacifist" formation; won two regional seats in 1987 in alliance with the United Left, but failed to win representation in 1995.

North African Sovereignties

Under legislation approved in September 1994 the North African enclaves of Ceuta and Melilla acquired full autonomous status as regions of Spain. Political life in both possessions is dominated by local branches of metropolitan formations, notably the Popular Party and the Spanish Socialist Workers' Party. Some local political movements are in existence, however.

Ceuta National Party (*Partido Nacional Ceuti*, PNC), led by José Infantes López.

Initiative for Ceuta (*Iniciativa por Ceuta*, IC), led by Ahmed Subair, leftist grouping formed in December 1990, based in the Muslim community and named after the Initiative for Catalonia.

Progress and Future of Ceuta (*Progreso y Futuro de Ceuta*, PFC), led by Francisco Fraiz Armada, supports continued Spanish status, won six Ceuta assembly seats in 1995, its leader being elected government president with support from other parties.

Party of Melilla Democrats (*Partido de los Demócratas Melillenses*, PDM), led by Aomar Muhammadi Dudú, founded in 1985 to advocate equal rights and opportunities for the Arab and European communities.

Spanish Nationalist Party of Melilla (*Partido Nacionalista Español de Melilla*, PNEM), also known as the Pro-Melilla Association (*Asociación Pro-Melilla*), led by José González Orell, founded in 1980 to support the maintenance of Spanish status.

Union of the Melilla People (*Unión del Pueblo Melillense*, UPM), led by José Imbroda Dominguez, right-wing group that favours independence for Melilla (but not union with Morocco).

Sri Lanka

Capital: Colombo

Population: 18,000,000 (1995E)

Ceylon gained its independence from the United Kingdom in 1948, and in 1972 was redesignated the Republic of Sri Lanka. Under the present constitution, promulgated in 1978, its name was changed again to the Democratic Socialist Republic of Sri Lanka, and a presidential form of government was adopted. The President, who is directly elected by universal suffrage for a six-year term, has the power to appoint or dismiss members of the Cabinet, including the Prime Minister, and to dissolve Parliament. The unicameral Parliament has 225 members, directly elected for a period of six years under a system of proportional representation which was first introduced in 1989.

In a general election held on Aug. 16, 1994, the United National Party (UNP), in power since 1977, was defeated by a left-wing coalition, the People's Alliance, which emerged as the largest grouping. Chandrika Bandanaraike Kumaratunga was sworn in as Prime Minister to head a coalition government dominated by her Sri Lanka Freedom Party (SLFP), and including the Lanka Equal Society Party (LSSP), the Democratic United National Front (DUNF), the Sri Lanka Muslim Congress (SLMC), the Communist Party of Sri Lanka (CPSL) and later, the Ceylon Workers' Congress (CWC).

On Nov. 12, 1994, Kumaratunga was elected President with 62.3% of the popular vote, being succeeded as Prime Minister by her mother, Sirimavo Bandaranaike. Kumaratunga had pledged to return the executive presidency to a largely ceremonial role.

Ceylon Workers' Congress (CWC)

Address. 19 St Michael's Road, POB 12, Colombo 3

Leadership. W.E.K.R. Savumyamoorthy Thondaman (president)

The CWC represents the interests of Tamil workers of Indian origin on tea plantations. The party president holds a post in the SLFP-dominated Cabinet formed after the August 1994 parliamentary elections.

Communist Party of Sri Lanka (CPSL)

Address. c/o Parliament, Colombo

Leadership. Pieter Keuneman (chair)

Formerly pro-Soviet, the CPSL has called for the nationalization of banks, estates and factories, and for the use of national languages (rather than English). Following the victory of the left-wing People's Alliance in the 1994 elections, the party secured one portfolio in the government led by the Sri Lanka Freedom Party.

Democratic People's Liberation Front (DPLF)

Address. c/o Parliament, Colombo

Leadership. Dharmalingam Sithadthan (leader)

The DPLF is the political wing of the Tamil separatist People's Liberation Organization of Tamil Eelam (PLOTE), and has operated as a national political party since 1988. In the 1994 legislative elections it secured three parliamentary seats.

Democratic United National Front (DUNF)

Address. c/o Parliament, Colombo

Leadership. G.M. Premachandra (general secretary)

The DUNF was formed in 1992 by a dissident group of United National Party (UNP) politicians. Following the electoral victory of the People's Alliance in the 1994 legislative polling, the party joined the coalition administration headed by the Sri Lanka Freedom Party.

Eelam People's Democratic Party (EPDP)

Address. c/o Parliament, Colombo

Leadership. Douglas Devananda (general secretary)

The EPDP is an unrecognized Tamil group, nine members of which secured parliamentary seats as independents from Jaffna in the 1994 legislative elections.

Lanka Equal Society Party

Lanka Sama Samaja Party (LSSP)

Address. 457 Union Place, Colombo 2

Leadership. Bernard Soysa (leader)

The Trotskyist LSSP dates from the 1930s. Upon the defeat of the United National Party by the left-wing People's Alliance in the August 1994 parliamentary elections, the LSSP leader joined the new coalition government headed by the Sri Lanka Freedom Party.

People's Alliance

Address. c/o Parliament, Colombo

Leadership. Chandrika Bandanaraike Kumaratunga (leader)

The People's Alliance was formed in 1993 as a coalition of left-wing groups dominated by the Sri Lanka Freedom Party (SLFP). In the 1994 legislative elections it secured 105 of the 225 seats, subsequently forming a new administration with the parliamentary support of moderate Tamil parties and the Sri Lanka Muslim Congress. In November 1994 Kumaratunga won the presidential election as the People's Alliance candidate, with 62.3% of the popular vote.

Sri Lanka Freedom Party (SLFP)

Address. 301 T.B. Jayah Mawatha, Colombo 10

Telephone. (#94–1) 696289

Leadership. Sirimavo Bandaranaike (president)

Founded in 1951, the SLFP campaigned for the attainment of republican status for Sri Lanka prior to adoption of the 1972 constitution. With a democratic socialist orientation, the party has advocated a non-aligned foreign policy, industrial development in both the state and private sectors, and certain safeguards for national minorities.

In August 1994 the SLFP was returned to power for the first time since its heavy electoral defeat in 1977. Heading the People's Alliance coalition, which emerged as the largest parliamentary grouping in the legislative elections with 49% of the vote, the party formed a new government under the premiership of Chandrika Bandanaraike Kumaratunga, who was subsequently elected President of the Republic in direct balloting the following November.

Sri Lanka Muslim Congress (SLMC)

Address. c/o Parliament, Colombo

Leadership. M.H.M. Ashraff (leader)

The SLMC was formed in 1980 to represent Muslim interests in the Tamil-dominated Eastern area, and has operated as a national political party since 1986. In the August 1994 elections the party won seven parliamentary seats, committing its support to the People's Alliance and securing a post in the new coalition Cabinet headed by the Sri Lanka Freedom Party.

Tamil United Liberation Front (TULF)
Address. 238 Main Street, Jaffna
Leadership. Murugesu Sivasithamraram (president)

The moderate TULF was formed in 1976 by a number of Tamil groups. It aims to establish a Tamil homeland (Tamil Eelam) in north-eastern Sri Lanka with the right of self-determination. In the August 1994 elections, its parliamentary representation fell from 10 to five seats.

United National Party (UNP)
Address. 400 Kotte Road, Pitakotte
Telephone. (#94-1) 865375
Leadership. Ranil Wickremasinghe (leader)

The UNP was formed in 1947. It adopted a democratic socialist programme in the late 1950s, but its policies in government from 1977 reflected its strong support in conservative landowning, business and professional circles. The party lost power in August 1994 when it secured only 94 of the 225 seats in Parliament. In the presidential election the following November the UNP contender, Srima Dissanayake (whose husband Gamini Dissanayake had been the party's first choice as candidate prior to his assassination in October), came second with about 35.9% of the vote.

Other Parties

Democratic Workers' Congress (DWC), led by Vythilingam Palanisamy, founded in 1978 on a moderate left-wing platform.

Liberal Party, led by Rajiva Wijesinha, closely aligned with Sri Lanka Freedom Party, a member of the Liberal International.

Muslim United Liberation Front (MULF), led by M.I.M. Mohideen.

New Equal Society Party (*Nava Sama Samaja Party*, NSS), formed by militant dissidents of the Lanka Equal Society Party, proscribed for seditious activities in 1983.

People's Liberation Front (*Janatha Vimukthi Peramuna*, JVP), a Sinhalese extremist group originally of Maoist orientation, attempted to overthrow government in 1971, later sporadically active in cells.

People's United Front (*Mahajana Eksath Peramuna*, MEP), led by Dinesh Gunawardena, a left-wing, strongly Sinhalese and Buddhist formation.

Sinhalese Freedom Front (*Singhalaye Nithahas Peramuna*, SNP), led by Arya Sena Tera, a Buddhist-centred nationalist group launched in 1994.

Sri Lanka Progressive Front (SLPF), won a single seat in the 1994 legislative polling.

Sri Lanka Mahajana (People's) Party (SLMP), led by Sarath Kongahage, left-leaning formation originally founded in 1984.

Militant Tamil Groups

Eelam National Democratic Liberation Front (ENDLF)

Eelam People's Revolutionary Liberation Front (EPRLF)

Liberation Tigers of Tamil Eelam (LTTE), the largest and most hardline of the militant Tamil separatist groups, has been fighting Sri Lankan forces for control of the Tamil majority areas in the north and east of the country since 1983; a major government offensive at the end of 1995 succeeded in capturing the main LTTE stronghold of Jaffna town.

People's Liberation Organization of Tamil Eelam (PLOTE)

Tamil Eelam Liberation Organization (TELO)

Sudan

Capital: Khartoum   **Population**: 26,000,000 (1995E)

The Republic of Sudan has, since its establishment in 1956, experienced political instability, north-south division and civil war. A period of transitional military rule followed the coup of 1985 in which the army seized power from President Jaafar al-Nemery, who had himself come to power in a coup in 1969 and who had established a one-party state. Power was transferred to a civilian regime in May 1986, and for three years a series of coalition governments held office, with Sadiq al-Mahdi as the most prominent political figure (as he had been in civilian administrations prior to the Nemery coup). In June 1989, another military coup installed a Revolutionary Command Council (RCC) led by Lt.-Gen. Omar Hassan Ahmad al-Bashir. Political parties have remained illegal since that time, although in practice the leaders and supporters of the National Islamic Front (NIF) have exerted substantial influence over the Bashir government.

In early 1992 Bashir announced the appointment of a 300–member Transitional National Assembly (including all the members of the RCC and a number of their advisers, all cabinet ministers and state governors, and representatives of the army, trade unions and former political parties) to serve for an indeterminate period pending the convening of an elected legislative body. In October 1993 the RCC dissolved itself and named Bashir as President of a new civilian government which included most ministers from the outgoing administration. In November 1994 the government inaugurated a "Supreme Council for Peace", including representatives from the south, to promote discussion on ending civil war in the country.

National Islamic Front (NIF)
Leadership. Dr Hassan Abdallah al-Turabi

The NIF, formed in the mid-1980s, is headed by one of the world's leading Islamic fundamentalist theoreticians, who has called for the creation of Islamic regimes in all Arab nations. Notwithstanding the formal ban on political parties, the NIF has established such a position of influence under the Bashir regime that observers consider it has become a de facto government party. NIF militants also reportedly direct the Islamic 'security groups' which have assumed increasing authority in dealing with government opponents.

Opposition Groups

Democratic Unionist Party (DUP), a right-of-centre group in exile led by Uthman al-Mirghani.

Sudanese Communist Party (SCP), led by Mohammed Ibrahim Nugud.

Sudanese People's Liberation Movement (SPLM), and its military wing, the Sudanese People's Liberation Army (SPLA), were formed in 1983 by Col. John Garang, under whose leadership the SPLA became the dominant southern rebel force. The SPLM has not advocated secession for the south, although it has reportedly endorsed the proposed division of Sudan into two highly autonomous, albeit still confederated states, with the south operating under secular law and the north under Islamic religious law. The SPLA has been weakened since 1991 by serious factional rivalries.

Umma (People's) Party (UP), a moderate Islamist centre party which continues to exist in exile, led by former Prime Minister Sadiq al-Mahdi.

Suriname

Capital: Paramaribo   **Population:** 400,000 (1995E)

Formerly Dutch Guiana, the Republic of Suriname achieved complete independence from the Netherlands in 1975. In February 1980 the government was overthrown in a military coup led by Sgt.-Maj. (later Lt.-Col.) Désiré "Desi" Bouterse, and after another coup in August a newly formed National Military Council (NMR) suspended the constitution and dissolved the legislature in August 1981. An interim President and a predominantly civilian Council of Ministers (presided over by a Prime Minister) was appointed in 1982. Real power, however, remained with the army. A National Assembly, consisting of 31 nominated members, was appointed in January 1985, and in November of the same year the ban on traditional political parties was lifted. A new constitution, approved by a national referendum, was inaugurated in September 1987. In January 1988 the Assembly elected Ramsewak Shankar as President.

A military coup of Dec. 22, 1990, deposed President Ramsewak Shankar, who formally "resigned" on Dec. 24 and handed power to provisional President Johan Kraag of the minority Suriname National Party (NPS), being widely considered to be a mouthpiece for Bouterse. In a subsequent general election held on May 25, 1991, the opposition coalition New Front (NF), consisting of the Suriname National Party (NPS), the Progressive Reform Party (VHP) and the Party for Unity and Harmony (KTPI), won an absolute majority of 30 seats in the National Assembly but failed to secure the necessary two-thirds majority to form a government. In the 817-member United People's Assembly, specially convened by the National Assembly in September 1991, Runaldo Venetiaan of the NF was finally elected as President with 645 votes, so that he was able to form a government (which also included some members of the Suriname Labour Party (SPA).

Under the 1987 constitution, ultimate authority rests with a 51-member National Assembly, which can amend any proposal of law by the government. Executive authority rests with the President, who is elected by the National Assembly for a five-year term. The President is head of state, head of government, head of the armed forces, chair of the Council of State and chair of the Security Council which, in the event of "war, state of siege or exceptional circumstances to be determined by law", assumes all government functions. The President is assisted by a Vice-President, who is also elected by the National Assembly, and a Cabinet appointed by the President and responsible to the Assembly. Constitutional amendments, unanimously approved by the National Assembly on March 25, 1992, restricted the role of the army to national defence and combating "organized subversion". Serving members of the armed forces were restricted from holding representative political office but not denied personal involvement in political activity.

The 51 members of the National Assembly are elected by direct universal suffrage for a five-year term. To designate a President a party has to have at least a two-thirds majority in the National Assembly, that is 34 seats. If none of the parties obtains such a majority, the National Assembly elects one of the parties' candidates. If there is still no consensus, the United People's Assembly, consisting of the National Assembly plus 700 municipal and district councillors, has the final vote.

Democratic Alternative '91

Democratische Alternatif '91 (DA '91)

Address. c/o National Assembly, Paramaribo

Leadership. Gerard Brunings (leader), Hans Prade (1991 presidential candidate)

Formed in March 1991, the DA'91 is a new, anti-military, centre-left grouping of parties in national politics. The alliance campaigns for a commonwealth relationship with the Netherlands, and for the constitutional exclusion of military from involvement the political process. It has taken a strong stand against corruption and claims not to co-operate with anyone involved in corruption.

The DA'91 consists of small anti-military parties, a coalition of dissidents who left the Front for Democracy and Development (FDO) critical of its alleged failure to curb the influence of the military. It contested the May 1991 general election, winning nine seats in the National Assembly with 16.7% of the vote. One seat was taken up by Winston Hesserun, brother of Artie Jesserun of the Suriname National Party (NPS) who lost his seat because two members of the same family, according to the constitution, were not allowed to sit simultaneously in the Assembly. In the final vote for the presidency, staged on Sept. 7, 1991, by an 817-member United People's Assembly (specially summoned by the National Assembly), Prade won 52 votes.

National Democratic Party

Nationale Democratische Partij (NDP)

Address. c/o National Assembly, Paramaribo

Leadership. Lt.-Col. Désiré Bouterse (former army commander)

Founded in 1987, the NDP is a prominent right-wing party which is backed by the Suriname military. The NDP was formed by *Standvaste.* the 25 February Movement under Lt.-Col. Désiré (Desi) Bouterse. In the November 1987 general election the NDP was shunned by the electorate as being Bouterse's political mouthpiece. Wijdenbosch resigned in January 1991 as chairman of the NDP to take the posts of Vice-President and Prime Minister in the army-backed provisional government of Johan Kraag following the December 1990 military coup. The party, which dominated Kraag's government, against expectations increased its vote to 21.8% in the May 1991 general election. Its number of seats in the National Assembly increased from three to 12, making it the joint largest single party with the Suriname National Party (NPS) and ensuring for it an influential role in the legislature. In the election for a new President in the 817-member United People's Assembly (specially summoned by the National Assembly), held in September 1991, Wijdenbosch came second with 120 votes.

National Republic Party

Partij Nationalistische Republiek (PNR)

Leadership. Robin Ravales

Founded in 1963, the party returned to political activities in 1987 to little success.

New Front

Nieuwe Front (NF)

Address. c/o National Assembly, Paramaribo

Leadership. Ronald Venetiaan (leader), Henck A. E. Arron (chair)

Founded in 1987, the NF alliance (sub-titled "for Democracy and Development" is a coalition of Indian, Javanese and mixed-race ethnic groups plus the Suriname Labour Party which seeks constitutional reform to reduce the involvement of army in internal affairs. It also seeks international military and technological aid to fight drug trafficking and advocates the renegotiation of bilateral links with the Netherlands and closer ties with Latin America and the Caribbean.

The New Front had its origins in the Front for Democracy and Development (*Front voor Demokratie en Ontwikkeling*, FDO) led by former President Henck Arron (toppled by the Bouterse-led army in 1980). In November 1987 the FDO won the election with an overwhelming 85% of the vote. Following the December 1990 military coup, dissident groups, critical of the NF's failure to curb military influence, left in March 1991 to form the Democratic Alliance (DA'91). The NF had its ranks swelled by the Suriname Labour Party (SLA), who joined shortly before the May 1991 general election which it convincingly won, taking 30 seats and 54.2% of the valid vote. This victory at a national level complemented the NF's control of a clear majority of local and regional councillors.

The NF government pledged to co-operate with international initiatives, especially in the United States, to fully investigate the army's alleged long-term involvement in gun running, cocaine processing, international drug trafficking, and money laundering. The Dutch government, which had suspended its development aid immediately after the December 1990 military coup, was sufficiently impressed by Venetiaan's pledges to agree in November 1991 to release 100 million guilders in development aid and 50 million guilders in transitional aid.

The main components of the NF are the Party of National Unity and Harmony, the Progressive Reform Party, the Suriname Labour Party and the Suriname National Party.

Party of Unity and Harmony

Kerukanan Tulodo Pranatan Ingil (KTPI)

Address. Weidestraat, Paramaribo

Leadership. Willy Soemita

Founded in 1947, the party has been the traditional protector and promoter of the interests of the ethnic Indonesian community and has switched its political allegiances to further this end. Formerly the Javanese Farmers' Party (*Kaum-Tani Persuatan Indonesia*), the KPTI is the oldest party in the country. In the 1970s, its leader, Willy Soemita, was convicted of corruption but made a successful comeback, the party being a founder member of the Front for Democracy and Development (FDO), later the New Front (NF).

Following the May 1991 general election, the KTPI's number of seats in the National Assembly fell from nine to seven. Soemita was appointed Minister of Social Affairs and Housing in the NF Cabinet and in March 1992 the KTPI's Soeratino Setrored was appointed to the portfolio of agriculture, animal husbandry and fishing, replacing party colleague Johan Sisal, whose subsequent appointment as Internal Affairs Minister provoked opposition from other NF parties.

Progressive Reform Party

Vooruuitstrevende Hervormings Partij (VHP)
   Address. c/o National Assembly, Paramaribo
   Leadership. Ramsewak Shankar
   Founded in 1949, the VHP is the leading left-wing party, a Hindustani-based grouping with its stronghold in Saramancca. A founder member of the Front for Democracy and Development (FDO), renamed for the May 1991 elections as the New Front, the party was the main loser in the elections, its representation in the National Assembly falling from 18 to nine seats.

Progressive Workers' and Farm Labourers' Union

Progressieve Arbeiders en Landbouwers Unie (PALU)
   Leadership. Ir Iwan Krolis (leader)
   Founded in the late 1970s, the PALU is a nominal socialist party which supported the Bouterse regime (1980-87) and in the November 1987 general election won four seats. It proceeded to lose these in the May 1991 general election.

Suriname Labour Party

Suriname Partij voor Arbeid (SPA)
   Address. c/o National Assembly, Paramaribo
   Leadership. Fred Darby
   The party, whose membership is predominantly Creole, joined the New Front (NF) just before the May 1991 general election and won two of its overall total of 30 seats. At the swearing-in of an NF government in September 1991, the SLP was given the defence, labour and transport portfolios in the new Cabinet. The party has links with the C-47 trade union.

Suriname National Party

Nationale Partij Suriname (NPS)
   Address. Wanicastraat, Paramaribo
   Leadership. Ronald Venetiaan (leader), Otmar Roel Rodgers (secretary)
   Founded in 1946, the party was a founder member of the Front for Democracy and Development (FDO) which changed its name to the New Front. Despite the NF's victory in the May 1991 general election, the NPS saw its representation in the National Assembly reduced from 13 to 12 seats; its deputy chairman Artie Jesserun giving his seat up to his brother Winston (see DA'91), because, according to the constitution, two family members could not simultaneously sit in the legislature, a check on the establishment of political dynasties. The NPS's Eddy Sedoc was named Finance Minister in March 1992.

Guerrilla Movements

Surinamese Liberation Army (Jungle Commando—SLA)

   Address. St Laurent du Maroni, French Guiana
   Leadership. Ronnie Brunswijk (leader), Johan "Castro" Wally (second-in-command)
   Founded in 1986, the SLA is a centre-left group which supports the rights of the Bush Negro community for self-determination.

   Founded by Ronnie Brunswijk and Max Belfort, the SLA undertook guerrilla raids on police posts and important parts of the infrastructure, operating from bases in neighbouring French Guiana to avoid army counterattacks.

   It signed a peace agreement in July 1989 with the Shankar government, the so-called "Kourou Accord" (because it was signed in Kourou in French Guiana), which was never implemented owing to pressure from the army commander in chief, Lt.-Col. Désiré "Desi" Bouterse.

   Another preliminary peace accord was signed with Bouterse in March 1991 under which the SLA would be integrated into Suriname police force and given special duties within the army.

   Progress towards a final peace agreement, however, remained stalled in April 1992, with the SLA remaining unwilling to be disarmed by the army, which it claimed was responsible for arming the Tucayana Amazonas, Mandela and Angula guerrilla groups.

   Finally, a suspension of hostilities was called on May 5, 1992, and the conclusion of a formal peace treaty came on August 1, 1992.

Angula (*Defiance*) Carlos Maassi (leader); a Saramaccaner based "Bush Negro" clan group formed in 1990. The main guerrilla group, the Surinamese Liberation Party (SLA), accuses it of being a front for the military.

Mahabini—Dead or Alive, first emerged in November 1991 when the group claimed responsibility for an attack on a police post in Moengo in which one policeman died. The group is suspected of having links with dissenting members of the SLA unhappy with the peace negotiations with the army.

Mandela Bush Negro Liberation Movement (BBM), Leendert Adams (alias "Biko") (leader); founded in 1989 by members of the Mataurier "bush negro" clan; it is opposed to the agreement between the military and the Surinamese Liberation Army (SLA) and supports the Tucayana. The SLA accuses it of being in receipt of guns from the army.

Tucayana Amazonas based in Bigi Poika, founded in 1989, "Commander Thomas" (leader); Alex Jubitana, Chair of the Tucayana Advisory Group; An Amerindian insurgent group which objected to the July 1989 Kourou Accord between the government and the Surinamese Liberation Army (SLA).

Union for Liberation and Democracy (UBD), Kofi Ajongpong (leader); based in Moengo and founded in 1989 by radical elements of the Surinamese Liberation Army (SLA).

Swaziland

Capital: Mbabane (administrative)
Lobamba (to be legislative capital)

Population: 920,000 (1995E)

The Kingdom of Swaziland achieved full independence from the United Kingdom in 1968. The country is ruled by a King (*Ngwenyama* or Paramount Chief) whose succession is governed by Swazi law and custom. The present King, Mswati III, acceded to the throne in 1986. Under the 1978 constitution considerable executive power is vested in the King and is exercised by a Cabinet appointed by him. The bicameral Parliament consists of a Senate and a House of Assembly, with limited powers. The House of Assembly has 65 members, 55 of which were directly elected for the first time in September-October 1993 (on a non-party basis), with voters electing one representative from each of the *Tinkhundla* (tribal assemblies). A further 10 members are appointed by the King. There are 30 members of the Senate, 20 of whom are nominated by the King and 10 elected by the House of Assembly. Party political activity, banned in 1973, was formally prohibited under the 1978 constitution. However, following indications that the constitution might be revised, a number of political associations have re-emerged in the 1990s.

Confederation for Full Democracy in Swaziland, formed in 1992 as an alliance of organizations advocating democratic reform, including the People's United Democratic Movement and the Swaziland Youth Congress (SYC).

Imbokodvo National Movement (INM), founded in 1964, a traditionalist and royalist organization, but also advocates policies of development and the elimination of illiteracy.

Ngwane National Liberatory Congress (NNLC), led by Ambrose Zwane, founded in 1962, emerging as a result of a split in the Swaziland Progressive Party; seeks an extension of democratic freedoms and universal suffrage.

People's United Democratic Movement (PUDEMO), led by Kislon Shongwe, emerged in the 1980s, circulating pamphlets critical of the King, thus attracting official hostility and suppression; campaigns for electoral reform, multi-party democracy and limits on the power of the monarchy.

Swaziland National Front (SWANAFRO), led by Elmond Shongwe.

Swaziland Progressive Party (SPP), led by J. J. Nquku, founded in 1929 as the Swazi Progressive Association, adopted present title in 1960, after which it suffered from factional divisions and defections.

Swaziland United Front (SUF), led by Matsapa Shongwe, founded in 1962 following a split within the Swaziland Progressive Party.

Swaziland Youth Congress (SYC), a constituent of the Confederation for Full Democracy in Swaziland; in February 1995 it reportedly claimed responsibility for an arson attack on the House of Assembly building in Mbabane.

Sweden

Capital: Stockholm

Population: 8,800,000 (1995E)

The Kingdom of Sweden is a parliamentary democracy in which the monarch has purely ceremonial functions as head of state. There is a Cabinet headed by a Prime Minister and responsible to a unicameral Parliament (*Riksdag*) of 349 members elected for a three-year term by universal adult suffrage of citizens above the age of 18 years under a system of proportional representation, with 310 seats being filled in 28 multi-member constituencies and the remaining 39 allocated to parties according to a complex formula. A party must obtain 4% of the national vote to qualify for a seat.

Since 1966 state subsidies have been paid to political parties which have at least one representative in the *Riksdag* or have obtained at least 2.5% of the national vote in either of the two most recent elections, with an additional "secretariat subsidy" being available for parties achieving 4% or more of the vote. The amount of the subsidies is related to party representation or voting strength, but "secretariat subsidies" are higher for opposition parties than for those in the government. Similar arrangements apply at the level of regional and local government. In the 1994/95 financial year the total amount allocated for party subsidies in the state budget was SKr127 million (about $17 million).

Parliamentary elections on Sept. 18, 1994, resulted in the following seat distribution and percentage shares of the vote: Social Democratic Labour Party 161 (45.3%), Moderate Alliance Party 80 (22.4%), Centre Party 27 (7.7%), Liberal People's Party 26 (7.2%), Left Party 22 (6.2%), Green Ecology Party 18 (5.0%), Christian Democratic Community Party 15 (4.1%).

Centre Party
Centerpartiet (CP)

Address. 7B Bergsgatan, PO Box 22107, 104 22 Stockholm

Telephone. (#46–8) 617–3800

Fax. (#46–8) 652–6440

Leadership. Olof Johansson (chair), Ake Pettersson (secretary-general)

The Centre Party works for a decentralized society with a social market economy, with all parts of the country having an equal chance to develop; for the protection of the environment; and for the use of technology not only for man's material welfare but also for his mental well-being. The party is strongly opposed to the development of nuclear energy capacity.

The party was founded in 1910 as the Farmers' Union Party for the purpose of representing the population in the country's rural areas; it has developed into one of the centre with supporters in both rural and urban districts. It first gained parliamentary representation in 1917 and formed its first government in June 1936. From October 1936 it co-operated in government with the Social Democratic Labour Party (SAP), and in 1939–45 in a national coalition government. In 1951–57 the party was again a partner with the SAP in a coalition government, at the end of which it changed its name to Centre Party-Farmers' Union Party (1957), shortening this to Centre Party a year later.

In 1976–78 the CP headed a three-party non-socialist government including also the Liberal People's (FP) and Moderate Alliance (MSP) parties, this coalition, led by Thorbjörn Fälldin, being re-established after the September 1979 elections. In elections to the *Riksdag* in September 1982 the CP obtained 15.5% of the valid votes and 56 (out of 349) seats and went into opposition. In the September 1985 elections, which it contested jointly with the Christian Democratic Community Party (KdS), the CP slipped to 12.4% and 44 seats (including one Christian Democrat) and continued in opposition. In view of this setback Fälldin resigned the party leadership in December 1985, having come under sharp criticism for his opposition to a rapprochement with the SAP, the party's traditional allies. He was replaced by Karin Söder (who became Sweden's first female party leader), but she resigned in January 1987 for health reasons and was succeeded by Olof Johansson.

The CP's decline continued in the 1988 and 1991 elections, to 42 and 31 seats respectively, but after the latter contest the party entered a centre-right coalition headed by the MSP. In June 1994 its participation was shaken by the resignation of party chairman Olof Johansson as Environment Minister, in opposition to the controversial Öresund Sound bridge project. In the September 1994 parliamentary elections the CP was further reduced to 27 seats (on a vote share of 7.7%) and again went into opposition. The CP supported Swedish accession to the European Union (EU), while advocating non-participation in a single European currency or in any EU defence co-operation.

The CP's two representatives in the European Parliament (one of them a critic of the EU), who were elected in September 1995 with 7.2% of the vote, sit in the European Liberal, Democratic and Reformist Group.

Christian Democratic Community Party
Kristdemokratiska Samhällspartiet (KdS)
   Address. 7 Malargatan, PO Box 451, 101 26 Stockholm
   Telephone. (#46–8) 243825
   Fax. (#46–8) 219751
   Leadership. Alf Svensson (chair), Sven Persson (secretary-general)
   The KdS has described itself as "the third alternative in Sweden, where all [other] parties are socialistic or non-socialistic". It propagates "a new way of life" and concentrates on social problems, calling for a review of the abortion law among other things. It also calls for a halt to the building of nuclear power stations. The party was founded in 1964 and obtained some 78,000 votes in its first general election in 1964. By 1982 this total had increased to 103,820 (1.9%). Having thus failed to pass the 4% barrier to representation in the *Riksdag*, in September 1985 it entered into an electoral pact with the Centre Party, winning some 2.6% of the vote in its own right and being allocated one of the Centre Party's 44 seats (Alf Svensson becoming the party's first representative in the *Riksdag*). Meanwhile, the party had established a significant local government presence, with almost 300 elected councillors by the mid-1980s.

Originally called the Christian Democratic Assembly (*Kristen Demokratisk Samling*), the party assumed its present name in 1987, when it also adopted a new programme. The KdS failed to secure representation in the 1988 parliamentary elections, but again came back strongly three years later, winning 26 *Riksdag* seats in 1991 (with 7.1% of the vote) and becoming a member of a centre-right coalition government. It slipped back in the 1994 contest, only just clearing the 4% barrier and winning 15 seats. It thereupon went into opposition to a minority government of the Social Democratic Labour Party. The KdS was strongly in favour of Swedish accession to the EU.

The KdS is affiliated to the Christian Democrat International.

Green Ecology Party
Miljöpartiet de Gröna
   Address. PO Box 16069, 103 22, Stockholm
   Telephone. (#46–8) 208050
   Fax. (#46–8) 201577
   Leadership. Marianne Samuelsson and Birger Schlaug (spokespersons)
   Founded in September 1981, the party stands for nature conservation, anti-pollution taxation and other measures, agricultural production to achieve national self-sufficiency in basic foodstuffs, the phasing-out of nuclear energy, support for the peace movement, the creation of nuclear-weapons-free zones in Scandinavia and Europe, a flexible retirement age and the ending of discrimination against immigrants. It has also called for a six-hour day, lower interest rates and reduced economic growth (this last goal being achieved in the early 1990s, although not quite in the way envisaged by the party).

In the 1982 and 1985 general elections the party fell well short of the 4% vote minimum required for representation in the *Riksdag*, not least because the major parties, particularly the Social Democratic Labour Party and the Centre Party, have incorporated a strong environmentalist strand in their platforms. On the other hand, it succeeded in obtaining representation in over 30% of local councils by 1988, in which year it became the first new party to enter the *Riksdag* for 70 years, winning 20 seats on a 5.5% vote share. It slumped to 3.4% in 1991 and so failed to gain representation; but in 1994 it recovered strongly to 5.0% and 18 *Riksdag* seats, thereafter giving qualified external support to the minority government of the Social Democratic Labour Party.

Opposed to Sweden's accession to the EU, the Greens were prominent in the "no" campaign for the November 1994 referendum on EU membership, finishing on the losing side. The party's four representatives in the European Parliament, elected in September 1995 on a greatly increased vote share of 17.2%, are members of the Green Group.

Left Party

Vänsterpartiet (VP)

Address. 84 Kungsgatan, PO Box 12660, 112 93 Stockholm

Telephone. (#46–8) 654–0820

Fax. (#46–8) 653–2385

Leadership. Gudrun Schyman (chair), Bertil Måbrink (parliamentary leader), Maggi Mikaelsson (secretary)

The VP is the latter-day successor to the historic Swedish Communist Party, which was founded as early as May 1917 under the name Left Social Democratic Party by the revolutionary wing of the Social Democratic Labour Party (SAP). It changed its name to Communist Party in 1921, having joined the Communist International (Comintern), to which it belonged until that organization's dissolution in 1943. In the post-1945 era, the party at first displayed pro-Soviet orthodoxy but in the 1960s embarked upon a revisionist course in line with "Eurocommunist" prescriptions. To signify the party's aim of becoming "a forum for the whole socialist left", the new designation Left Party-Communists (*Vänsterpartiet-Kommunisterna*, VPK) was adopted in 1967. This decision, combined with attendant policy evolution, generated much dissension within the party prior to the withdrawal of an orthodox faction in early 1977 to form the Communist Workers' Party. The suffix "Communists" was dropped from the party's title by a congress decision of May 1990.

The party has been represented in the *Riksdag* since its foundation, and for long periods minority SAP governments have relied on its support. In both the 1979 and 1982 general elections what was then the VPK obtained 20 seats and 5.6% of the valid votes, while in September 1985 it slipped to 5.4% and 19 seats (out of 349); but a concurrent SAP decline meant that VPK voting strength became crucial to the SAP government's survival in the late 1980s. The renamed VP won 16 seats in the 1991 general elections (on a vote share of 4.5%), thereafter going into full opposition to a centre-right coalition government. In a general swing to the left in September 1994, the VP achieved the party's best result since 1948, winning 6.2% of the vote and 22 seats.

The VP campaigned vigorously against Sweden's accession to the European Union (the only parliamentary party to do so), but was on the losing side in the November 1994 referendum. The party's three representatives in the European Parliament, elected in September 1995 with 12.9% of the vote, sit in the Confederal European United Left group.

Liberal People's Party

Folkpartiet Liberalerna (FPL)

Address. 66 Luntmakargatan, Box 6508, 113 83 Stockholm

Telephone. (#46–8) 674–1600

Fax. (#46–8) 673–4079

Leadership. Maria Leissner (chair), Ingemar Eliasson (parliamentary leader), Torbjörn Pettersson (secretary-general)

Although the present party dates from 1934, organized liberalism began in Sweden at the end of the 19th century with the objectives of social justice, universal suffrage and equality. After World War I a coalition government with the Social Democratic Labour Party (SAP), led by a Liberal Prime Minister, completed the process of democratization. At the same time, the introduction of universal suffrage reduced the party's influence, while between 1923 and 1934 the party was split over the issue of alcohol prohibition. Nevertheless, it formed governments in 1926–28 and 1930–32, and it took part in the national government during World War II.

In 1948 the party became the second strongest in the then lower chamber of the *Riksdag*, with 57 seats, but by 1968 its representation had declined to 34. In the unicameral *Riksdag* established in January 1971 the party won 58 seats in 1970, but only 34 in 1973 and 39 in 1976. It then took part in the first non-socialist government to be formed in Sweden for 44 years in coalition with the Centre and Moderate Alliance (Conservative) parties. The collapse of this coalition in October 1978 over the nuclear issue was followed by a year of minority Liberal rule under Ola Ullsten; but as a result of the September 1979 elections the three-party non-socialist coalition was re-established. However, the Conservatives left this government in 1981 after disagreements on taxation, and the Liberal and Centre parties formed a minority government until the September 1982 elections brought the Social Democrats back to power. In those elections the Liberal vote dropped to 5.9% and its representation to 21 seats.

The FPL staged a significant recovery in the September 1985 elections, winning 14.2% of the vote and 51 seats, but remaining in opposition. It fell back to 44 seats to 1988 (12.2%) and to 33 in 1991 (9.1%), when it joined a four-party centre-right coalition. Another setback followed in the September 1994 elections, which yielded only 7.2% and 26 seats, after which the party reverted to opposition status and party leader Bengt Westerberg gave way to Maria Leissner. The FPL was strongly in favour of Swedish accession to the EU in January 1995.

The FPL is a member of the Liberal International. Its single member of the European

Parliament, elected in September 1995 with 4.8% of the vote, sits in the European Liberal, Democratic and Reformist Group.

Moderate Alliance Party
Moderata Samlingspartiet (MSP)
Address. PO Box 1243, 111 82 Stockholm
Telephone. (#46–8) 676–8000
Fax. (#46–8) 216123
Leadership. Carl Bildt (chair), Gunnar Hök-mark (secretary-general)

The MSP combines a conservative heritage with liberal ideas to advocate a moderate, anti-socialist policy in favour of a free-market economy and individual freedom of choice. The party was originally founded in 1904 as the political expression of better-off peasants and the emerging industrial bourgeoisie, and participated in coalitions or formed minority governments several times before 1932; after which the Social Democratic Labour Party (SAP) was in almost uninterrupted power for 44 years (though during World War II all democratic parties took part in the government). The party increased its support during the 1950s, winning more than 20% of the vote in the 1958 general elections, but declined in subsequent contests, obtaining only 11.6% in the 1970 elections, prior to which it changed its name from Conservative to Moderate Alliance Party.

Later the party advanced again, gaining 15.6% of the vote in the 1976 elections whereupon it entered the first non-socialist coalition for 40 years (with the Centre and Liberal parties). This was dissolved in October 1978 but re-established after the September 1979 elections, in which the party made a significant advance, to 20.3% and 73 seats. It withdrew from the coalition in May 1981 amid disagreements over fiscal policy, although it generally gave external support to the government thereafter. In the elections of September 1982 the party gained further support (23.6% of the vote and 86 seats) and thus became the dominant non-socialist party in Sweden, although the Social Democrats were returned to power as a minority government. In the September 1985 elections the MSP slipped to 21.3% and 76 seats (out of 349) and continued in opposition. In light of this setback, Ulf Adelsohn resigned as party chairman in June 1986 and was succeeded by Carl Bildt (son-in-law of Adelsohn's immediate predecessor, Gösta Bohman).

A further decline in 1988 (to 18.3% and 66 seats) was followed by recovery in 1991 to 21.9% and 80 seats, enabling Bildt to form a four-party centre-right coalition with the Centre, Christian Democratic Community and Liberal People's parties. In the September 1994 elections the MSP again won 80 seats (and a slightly higher 22.4% vote share), but a general swing to the left resulted in a minority SAP government. Two months later the MSP warmly welcomed the referendum decision in favour of EU membership. Released of the burdens of government, Bildt accepted appointment as the EU's chief mediator in former Yugoslavia, while retaining the less taxing post of MSP chair.

The MSP is affiliated to the Christian Democrat International and to the International Democrat Union. Its five members of the European Parliament, elected in September 1995 with 23.2% of the vote, sit in the European People's Party group.

New Democracy
NyDemokrati (NyD)
Address. PO Box 1255, 111 82 Stockholm
Telephone. (#46–8) 786–5771
Fax. (#46–8) 204077
Leadership. Vivianne Franzén (chair)

New Democracy was founded in February 1990 on a populist platform of massive tax cuts, abolition of the welfare state, stringent curbs on immigration, opposition to EU membership and cheaper alcohol. It caused a sensation in the 1991 general elections, winning 24 *Riksdag* seats with a vote share of 6.7%. For most of the subsequent parliamentary term it gave often vital external voting support to the centre-right minority government. In March 1994, however, the resignation of its controversial leader, Count Ian Wachmeister (known as "the crazy count"), assisted a reorientation which resulted in the party joining the opposition. Having lost its early momentum, New Democracy fell well short of the 4% barrier to representation in the 1994 elections, taking only 1.2% of the vote.

Swedish Social Democratic Labour Party
Sveriges Socialdemokratiska Arbetareparti (SAP)
Address. Socialdemokraterna, 68 Sveavägen, 105 60 Stockholm
Telephone. (#46–8) 700–2600
Fax. (#46–8) 219331
Leadership. Göran Persson (chair), Ingela Thalen (general secretary)

The SAP seeks "to transform society in such a way that the right of decision over production and its distribution is placed in the hands of the entire nation"; to replace "a social order based on classes" by "a community of people in partnership on a basis of liberty and equality"; and to work for "Sweden's non-alignment and neutrality in war" and for "world peace on the basis of self-determination for every nation, of social and economic justice, of détente and disarmament and of international co-operation".

Founded in April 1889, the party sent its first

member to the *Riksdag* in 1896, namely Hjalmar Branting, who, after serving as Minister of Finance in 1917–18, became Prime Minister in Sweden's first Social Democratic government in 1920; he was Prime Minister again in 1921–23 and in 1924–25. The share of national vote gained by the party in elections rose from 28.5% in 1911 to 53.8% in 1940, whereafter it declined to 46.7% in 1944 and remained more or less stable until 1968, when it rose to 50.1%. In the four succeeding elections the SAP share fell to 42.9% in 1976, rose slightly to 43.3% in 1979 and to 45.6% in 1982, but slipped to 45.1% in September 1985, when it won 159 seats in the *Riksdag* (out of 349).

Except for a short interval in 1936, the party was in office from 1932 to 1976, in coalition with the Centre Party between 1936 and 1939 and between 1951 and 1957, in a four-party coalition during World War II, and at other times as a minority party requiring the support of one or more other parties on important issues. The party's 44 years of virtually uninterrupted power established the record for continuous governmental power by a social democratic party, and also resulted in Sweden becoming what was widely regarded as a model social democracy. In over 100 years of existence, the SAP has had only six leaders, namely Hjalmar Branting, Per-Albin Hansson, Tage Erlander, Olof Palme, Ingvar Carlsson and Göran Persson (since March 1996). Carlsson succeeded to the party leadership and premiership following the assassination of Palme on Feb. 28, 1986 (the responsibility and motives for which remained uncertain a decade later).

Having formed a minority government since 1982, the SAP went into opposition after the September 1991 elections, when its share of the vote fell from 43.2% in 1988 to 37.6% and its representation from 156 seats to 138. It recovered in a general swing to the left in the September 1994 elections, bringing it 45.3% of the vote and 161 seats and enabling it to form another minority government under Carlsson. For the November 1994 referendum on EU membership, the official government and party line was to favour a "yes" vote; but the extent of anti-EU opinion within SAP ranks compelled the leadership to allow the contrary case to be made within the party. In both the 1994 general elections and the September 1995 European Parliament polling anti-EU candidates were included on the SAP lists. The result on the latter occasion was that three of the seven Social Democrats elected (on a vote share of only 28%) were "Euro-sceptic" to a greater or lesser extent.

Meanwhile, Carlsson had surprised the political world by announcing in August 1995 that he intended to stand down as party leader and Prime Minister the following March, marking the 10th anniversary of his elevation. The initial favourite to succeed him was the Deputy Prime Minister, Mona Sahlin; but disclosures about irregularities in her financial affairs forced her not only to withdraw from the leadership race but also to resign from the government. Instead, the succession went to the current Finance Minister, Göran Persson, who was elected SAP chair unopposed at a special party congress on March 15, 1996, and appointed Prime Minister two days later.

The SAP is a member party of the Socialist International. Its seven European Parliament representatives are members of the Party of European Socialists group.

Other Parties

Centre Democrats (*Centrum-Demokraterna*, CD), led by Berndt Fredin, contested 1994 elections. *Address.* PO Box 278, 401 24 Göteborg

Communist Party of Marxist-Leninist Revolutionaries (*Kommunistiska Partiet Marxist-Leninisterna Revolutionärerna*, KPMLR), led by Frank Baude and Dan Ericsson, founded in 1970 as a pro-Albanian party, broke away from the Communist League of Marxist-Leninists (now the Communist Party of Sweden) and was originally known as the Communist League of Marxist-Leninist Revolutionaries; has contested elections, although with minimal support. *Address.* PO Box 31187, 400 32 Göteborg

Communist Party of Sweden (*Sveriges Kommunistiska Parti*, SKP), led by Roland Pettersson (chair) and Jan-Olof Norell (secretary), an independent communist party founded in 1967 by pro-Chinese elements of the old Communist Party, notably the Clarte League (named after the Clarte movement of Henri Barbusse in 1916); bases itself on the Swedish people's "tradition of rebellion", the European democratic tradition and the international Marxist/Maoist tradition; emphasizes that national independence and democratic freedom are essential for the working people to prevent decline into "a new brutal system of exploitation and oppression"; claimed to have influenced Sweden's foreign policy to shift from "informally US-allied to heavily pro-Vietnamese" during the Vietnam War; from 1974 the SKP campaigned strongly against the Soviet Union and what it regarded as the latter's growing influence on Sweden's public opinion; in its last electoral contest (1979) the party obtained 10,862 votes (0.2%).

Communist Workers' Party of Sweden (*Sveriges Arbetarepartiet Kommunisterna*, SAK), led by Rolf Hagel, founded in 1977 "based on the principles of Marxism-Leninism and proletarian internationalism" and rejecting the Euro-communist orientation of the main Left Party-Communists (VPK, later simply the Left Party), was joined by two of the 17 VPK members elected to the *Riksdag* in 1976, although neither was re-elected in September 1979, when the party obtained only 10,797 votes and failed to secure representation (as it did in subsequent elections).

European Labour Party (*Europeiska Arbetarpartiet*, EAP), led by Tore Fredin, contested 1994 elections. *Address.* PO Box 11918, 161 11 Bromma

Humanist Party (*Humanistiska Partiet*, HP), led by Bo Höglund, contested 1994 elections. *Address.* 46 Södermannagatan, 116 40 Stockholm

Socialist Party (*Socialistiska Partiet*, SP), a Trotskyist grouping founded in 1953 as the Communist Workers' League by dissidents of the main Communist Party (later the Left Party); took its present name in 1982; it has contested elections but with only minimal support.

Swedish Pensioners' Interests Party (*Sveriges Pensionärers Intressparti*, SPI), led by Nils-Olof Persson, contested 1994 elections. *Address.* PO Box 5187, 200 72 Malmö

World Socialist Group, Sweden (*Varldssocialistika Gruppen, Sverige*), led by Dag Nilsson, has links with the Socialist Party of Great Britain.

Switzerland

Capital: Bern   **Population:** 7,000,000 (1995E)

The Swiss Confederation is a republic in which power is held by the electorate (consisting of all citizens above the age of 20 years). The latter not only elects members of the Federal Assembly (*Bundesversammlung* or *Assemblée Fédérale*) and of cantonal and local councils but also has powers to vote on constitutional amendments or on other matters. Constitutional amendments may be enacted as a result of an initiative supported by at least 100,000 voters and either containing a draft amendment or proposing the substance of an amendment and leaving the drafting to Parliament. A referendum may be held on a matter already approved by Parliament. Constitutional amendments and the most important international treaties are subject to approval by popular vote and by the cantons in a "compulsory referendum". A national "facultative referendum" may be held on other matters of general validity (but not on the budget) already approved by Parliament if, within 90 days of parliamentary adoption, 50,000 voters or eight cantons request a vote on the specific act or decree.

The bicameral Federal Assembly consists of (i) a Council of States (*Standerat* or *Conseil des États*) consisting of two members for each of 20 cantons and one for each of six half-cantons, the electoral process being left to the decision of each of the cantons or half-cantons, and (ii) a 200–member National Council (*Nationalrat* or *Conseil National*) elected for a four-year term in proportion to the population of the cantons (each of the 20 cantons and six half-cantons being represented by at least one member). In all cantons and half-cantons the elections to the National Council are conducted under a list system and by proportional representation, with voters being able to cast preferential votes. In all but one canton and one half-canton a simple majority system applies for elections to the Council of States. The President of the Confederation, who is also President of the *Bundesrat* or *Conseil Fédéral* (seven-member government), is elected, together with a Vice-President, for a one-year term by the two houses of Parliament, which also elect the members of the government for a four-year term.

Elections to the National Council held on Oct. 22, 1995, resulted in the following seat distribution and percentage shares of the vote: Social Democratic Party of Switzerland 54 (21.8%), Radical Democratic Party of Switzerland 45 (20.2%), Christian Democratic People's Party of Switzerland 34 (17.0%), Swiss People's Party 29 (14.9%), Green Party of Switzerland 9 (5.0%), Freedom Party of Switzerland (Automobile Party) 7 (4.0%), Liberal Party of Switzerland 7 (2.7%), Swiss Democrats 3 (3.1%), Independents' Alliance 3 (1.8%), Evangelical People's Party of Switzerland 3 (1.8%), Swiss Party of Labour 3 (1.2%), Christian Social Party 1, Federal Democratic Union 1, Ticino League 1, Women Make Politics! 1. The outcome was a continuation of the existing government coalition of the four largest parties (first established in 1959).

Note. The non-English party titles given below begin with the one to which the party itself accords senior status, the official abbreviation of that version being used thereafter in entries. It will be noted that few parties have an official version of their title in all four official languages (German, French, Italian and Romansch)

Christian Democratic People's Party of Switzerland
Christlichdemokratische Volkspartei der Schweiz (CVS)
Parti Démocrate-Chrétien Suisse (PDC)
Partito Democratico-Cristiano Popolare Svizzero (PDC)
Partida Cristiandemocratica dalla Svizra (PCS)
   Address. 6 Klaraweg, Postfach 5835, 3001 Bern
   Telephone. (#41–31) 352–2364
   Fax. (#41–31) 352–2430
   Leadership. Anton Cottier (president), Peter Hess (parliamentary leader), Raymond Loretan (general secretary)
   The CVS is a mainstream Christian democratic party, advocating the encouragement of family life, a social market economy, peace in independence and freedom (i.e. maintenance of the country's armed forces) and solidarity with the Third World poor. The party also favours increased taxes on tobacco and alcohol. The party was founded in 1912 as the Swiss Conservative Party (*Parti Conservateur Suisse*), following the establishment of national (i.e. not cantonal) parties by Social Democrats in 1882 and Radicals in 1894 and a call for a Swiss Catholic party. By adopting the name Conservative Party, the founders emphasized the political rather than the religious (denominational) character of the new party, which was joined by representatives of Christian trade union parties in denominationally mixed cantons. Having in 1957 become the *Parti Conservateur Chrétien-Social Suisse*, the party took its present name in 1970, as that of a party organized at federal level and no longer a union of cantonal parties.
   The party has been represented by two members in the government since 1959 and in recent elections has won around one-fifth of the national vote. It was the strongest party in the *Nationalrat* between 1975 and 1983, falling to third place in the latter year but recovering to second place in 1987 (with 42 seats and 20% of the vote). It fell back to third place in 1991, with 36 seats and 18.3% of the vote) and slipped further in 1995 to 34 seats and 17.0%.
   The CVS is a member party of the Christian

Democrat International and the International Democrat Union.

Christian Social Party
Christlichsoziale Partei (CSP)
Parti Chrétien-Social (PCS)
   Address. 21 Hopfenweg, Postfach 5775, 3001 Bern
   Telephone. (#41–31) 370–2102
   Leadership. Hedy Jager (secretary)
   The small CSP stands on the progressive wing of Christian democracy, advocating that governments have important social responsibilities to which resources must be allocated. The party won one *Nationalrat* seat in the October 1995 general elections.

Evangelical People's Party of Switzerland
Evangelische Volkspartei der Schweiz (EVP)
Parti Évangelique Suisse (PES)
Partito Evangelico Svizzero (PES)
   Address. 32 Josefstrasse, Postfach 7334, 8023 Zurich
   Telephone. (#41–1) 272–7100
   Fax. (#41–1) 272–1437
   Leadership. Otto Zwygart (president), Daniel Reuter (secretary)
   Founded in 1919, the EVP is a centrist party based on Protestant precepts, advocating a social market economy, avoidance of damage to the environment, a restructuring of agriculture, land reform, strict control of traffic, civilian service for conscientious objectors and a halt to the construction of nuclear power stations. First represented in the *Nationalrat* in 1919, the party has maintained a small but consistent presence in the post-war era, winning three seats in 1991 (with 1.9% of the vote) but slipping to two seats in 1995 (with 1.8% of the vote). In the *Nationalrat* it has been closely aligned with the Independents' Alliance.
   The EVP is affiliated to the Christian Democrat International.

Federal Democratic Union
Eidgenössisch-Demokratische Union (EDU)
Union Démocratique Fédérale (UDF)
Unione Democratica Federale (UDF)
   Address. Postfach, 3607 Thun 7
   Telephone. (#41–33) 223637

Fax. (#41–33) 223744

Leadership. Waber Christian (president)

The EDU was founded in 1975 on a policy platform deriving from a conservative and fundamentalist interpretation of the Bible. The party was established by Max Wahl and other members of the (now defunct) Swiss Republican Movement, which had itself been created in 1971 by James Schwarzenbach, who had previously founded what later became the Swiss Democrats. Advocating restrictions on the permanent settlement of foreigners in Switzerland, the EDU won four *Nationalrat* seats in 1975 and one in 1983. It failed to win representation in the 1987 general elections, but gained one seat in 1991, which it retained in 1995.

Freedom Party of Switzerland

Freiheits Partei der Schweiz (FPS)

Address. Postfach, 4622 Egerkingen

Telephone. (#41–62) 612343

Fax. (#41–62) 612608

Leadership. Roland F. Borer (president)

The FPS is better known as the Automobile or Car Party, the name under which it was launched in March 1985 to represent motorists' "rights", to support the construction of motorways and the provision of parking facilities in towns, and to oppose increases in car tax or a levy on vehicles using motorways, as well as all limitations of the "freedom of car drivers". More broadly, the party espouses free enterprise and anti-state precepts, akin to those of the conservative wing of the Radical Democratic Party (of which its first leader, Michael Dreher, had been a member). The FPS title was adopted in 1994, by which time the party was combining concern for the interests of motorists with a demand for curbs on immigration.

The party won two *Nationalrat* seats at its first election in 1987 (with 2.6% of the vote). It advanced strongly to eight seats on a 5.1% vote share in 1991, but fell back to seven seats and 4.0% in October 1995.

Green Party of Switzerland

Grüne Partei der Schweiz (GPS)

Parti Écologiste Suisse (PES)

Partida Ecologica Svizra (PES)

Address. 21 Waisenhausplatz, 3011 Bern

Telephone. (#41–31) 312–6660

Fax. (#41–31) 312–6662

Leadership. Verena Diener (president), Cécile Bühlmann (parliamentary leader), Bernhard Pulver (general secretary)

The mainstream environmentalist GPS was founded in May 1983 as the Federation of Green Parties of Switzerland, embracing nine groupings, among them the *Groupement pour l'Environnement*

in the canton of Vaud (which had gained one seat in the *Nationalrat* in 1979), the *Parti Écologique* of Geneva, the *Mouvement pour l'Environnement* of Neuchâtel, the Green Party of Zurich and the Green Party of North-West Switzerland. In the 1983 general elections the federated party obtained 2.9% of the vote and three seats in the *Nationalrat*. After it had been joined by further groups, it changed its name to Green Party of Switzerland in 1985. Thereafter the Greens operated both as a federal party and as a collection of cantonal groups, which were free to make their own electoral alliances.

In the October 1987 federal elections the GPS obtained nine seats in the *Nationalrat* (and 4.8% of the vote), rather less than had been expected in view of public alarm over recent chemical pollution of the Rhine and also over the Chernobyl nuclear disaster in the then Soviet Union. Part of the reason was that some pro-ecology voting support went to the Progressive Organizations of Switzerland, which included left-oriented Greens. The mainstream GPS made a substantial advance in the 1991 elections, to 14 seats and 6.1% of the vote. But the tide of environmental concern receded by the time of the October 1995 federal elections, in which the Greens fell back to nine seats on a 5% vote share.

Independents' Alliance

Landesring der Unabhängigen (LdU)

Alliance des Indépendants (AdI)

Address. 9 Gutenbergstrasse, Postfach 7075, 3001 Bern

Telephone. (#41–31) 382–1636

Fax. (#41–31) 382–3695

Leadership. Monika Weber (president), Verena Grendelmeier (parliamentary leader), Rudolf Hofer (secretary)

The LdU was founded in 1936 to represent the interests of socially responsible citizens and consumers outside the conventional party framework. In the post-war era, operating very much like a conventional party, the formation achieved significant *Nationalrat* representation, of 10 seats between 1951 and 1967, when its tally rose to 16. Since then it has been in steady decline, in part because of the emergence of the Green Party of Switzerland and other formations representing particular interests. In the October 1995 elections the LdU/AdI won only three seats (with 1.8% of the vote), as compared with five seats (and 2.8%) in 1991.

Liberal Party of Switzerland

Liberale Partei der Schweiz (LPS)

Parti Libéral Suisse (PLS)

Partito Liberale Svizzero (PLS)

Address. 32 Spitalgasse, Postfach 7107, 3001 Bern

Telephone. (#41–31) 311–6404

Fax. (#41–31) 312–5474

Leadership. François Jeanneret (president), Jean-Michel Gross (parliamentary leader), Philippe Boillod (secretary)

The LPS stands for "the maintenance of federalism and of the market economy and the guaranteeing of individual freedom and responsibility, without ignoring the need for solidarity and the necessity of the functions of the state". It also calls for protection of the individual, the maintenance of an efficient defence force and of "armed neutrality", cooperation with the Third World, improvement of the quality of life, the use of natural gas and nuclear power as an alternative to oil, and freedom of information (but with state control over radio and television frequencies).

Descended from the liberal movement of the late 19th century, the LPS is based in the four mainly Protestant cantons of Geneva, Vaud, Neuchâtel and Basel-Stadt, where the party maintained an independent identity as liberals in other cantons were absorbed into the Radical Democratic and Christian Democratic People's parties. The party took its present name in 1977, having previously been the Liberal Democratic Union of Switzerland.

In the 1983 general elections the LPS retained eight *Nationalrat* seats on the basis of 2.8% of the vote, advancing in 1987 to nine seats (although with 2.7% of the vote). A further advance in 1991 to 10 seats and 3.0% was followed by a decline to seven seats and 2.7% of the vote in October 1995.

The LPS is a member of the Liberal International.

Radical Democratic Party of Switzerland

Freisinnig-Demokratische Partei der Schweiz (FDP)

Parti Radical-Démocratique Suisse (PRD)

Partito Liberale-Radicale Svizzero (PLR)

Address. 10 place de la Gare, CP 6136, 3001 Bern

Telephone. (#41–31) 311–3438

Fax. (#41–31) 312–1951

Leadership. Franz Steinegger (president), Pascal Couchepin (parliamentary leader), Christian Kauter (secretary-general)

The FDP claims to be "the founder of modern Switzerland" in that "after a confrontation with conservative forces in 1848 it laid the foundations for the Swiss federal state as it exists today". A Radical Democratic group was first established in the Federal Assembly in 1878, 16 years before the establishment of the party as such in 1894. The introduction of proportional representation in 1919 diminished the party's influence in the *Nationalrat*, but it held a dominant position in the federal government until 1959. In that year it

formed a coalition with the Social Democratic Party, the Christian Democratic People's Party and the Agrarians (later the Swiss People's Party), which has been maintained ever since.

The 1983 general elections resulted in the FDP becoming the country's strongest party, with 23.4% of the vote and 54 of the 200 *Nationalrat* seats. It remained so in 1987, with 51 seats and 22.9% of the vote, and in 1991, despite slipping to 44 seats and 21.0%. In the October 1995 elections, however, it yielded first place to the Social Democrats, despite improving marginally to 45 seats on a lower vote share of 20.2%.

The FDP is a member of the Liberal International.

Social Democratic Party of Switzerland

Sozialdemokratische Partei der Schweiz (SPS)

Parti Socialiste Suisse (PSS)

Partito Socialista Svizzero (PSS)

Address. 34 Spitalgasse, Postfach 7876, 3001 Bern

Telephone. (#41–31) 311–0744

Fax. (#41–31) 311–5414

Leadership. Peter Bodenmann (president), Ursula Mauch (parliamentary leader), André Daguet (secretary)

Founded as a federal party in 1888, the SPS quickly became a powerful political force in the country, particularly after the introduction of proportional representation in 1919. In the post-1945 period it has regularly obtained about 25% of the total vote and since 1959 has held two of the seven seats in a four-party coalition government also including the Radical Democratic, Christian Democratic People's and Swiss People's parties. During the 1970s "new left" elements were in the ascendancy within the party, which accordingly adopted more radical policies (although with little effect on governmental action). However, at a congress held in Lugano in November 1982 a new programme of basic principles was adopted by a large majority, confirming the reformist, social democratic character of the party and thus representing a defeat for the left wing, which had argued for a socialist programme based on the concept of self-management.

In the 1983 general elections the SPS was out-polled by the Radical Democratic Party for the first time for 58 years, being reduced to 22.8% of the vote and 47 of the 200 *Nationalrat* seats as against 24.4% and 51 seats in 1979. Thereafter opposition within the SPS to continued participation in the federal coalition government came to a head when the party's nomination of female left-winger Lillian Uchtenhagen for a ministerial post failed to secure the support of the other coalition parties. However, a recommendation from the executive in favour of withdrawal from the government was effectively rejected by an emergency party congress in Bern in February 1984 by 773 votes to 511. The SPS contested the 1987 general elections on a platform including ecological objectives; it lost six seats, polling only 18.4% of the total valid vote, the party's representation in the new *Nationalrat* (41 seats) being its lowest since 1919. In the canton of St Gallen the SPS held its two seats in alliance with a Green List for People, Animals and the Environment (*Grüne Liste für Mensch, Tier und Umwelt*).

The 1991 federal elections were also bad for the SPS, which languished on 18.5% of the vote, although the canton-based voting system gave it three additional seats, for a total of 44. Demonstrating its commitment to women's equality by having a rule that at least one third of its election candidates must be women, in 1993 the SPS again became exercised by the resistance of its coalition partners to female ministerial participation when its nomination of Christiane Brunner was rejected, apparently because of her unorthodox life style and outspoken feminism. The SPS promptly nominated another woman, Ruth Dreifuss, and warned that it would leave the coalition if she too were blackballed. The result was that Dreifuss was elected to the government, becoming Interior Minister. Benefitting from a swing to the left in the October 1995 general elections, the SPS recovered its position as the premier party, advancing to 54 seats in the *Nationalrat* on a vote share of 21.8%.

Swiss Democrats
Schweizer Demokraten (SD)
Démocrates Suisses (SD)
Democratici Svizzeri (DS)
   Address. Postfach 8116, 3001 Bern
   Telephone. (#41–31) 311–2774
   Fax. (#41–31) 312–5632
   Leadership. Rudolf Keller (president), Markus Ruf (parliamentary leader), Robert Meyer (secretary)
   The party was founded in 1961 as the National Action Against Foreign Infiltration of People and Homeland (*Nationale Aktion Gegen Überfremdung von Volk und Heimat*), which was later shortened to National Action for People and Homeland (*Nationale Aktion für Volk und Heimat*) and abbreviated to National Action (NA). It called for strict curbs on immigration, an end to the "misuse" of the right to asylum and measures to limit the sale of property to foreigners. It also advocated "the protection of the natural environment, full employment of the Swiss population, political independence, and security, law and order in liberty".
   In 1968 the NA launched a campaign for setting a ceiling on the proportion of foreigners resident in Switzerland and initiated a national referendum to that end, which was defeated by a slight majority in June 1970. Although the government subsequently issued certain restrictive regulations on foreign residents the NA continued its campaign and launched another initiative, which was also rejected by a majority of citizens in 1974. Following an increase in the number of naturalizations the NA undertook a further initiative together with one demanding the submission of all future treaties with foreign countries to a referendum. The Federal Council and Parliament thereupon drafted a counter-proposal which was approved in a referendum in March 1977. In 1981 the NA asked for a referendum on a proposed bill relaxing some of the existing restrictions on foreign workers, and this bill was subsequently, on June 6, 1982, rejected by a large majority of those citizens who took part in the vote.
   In the 1967 elections to the *Nationalrat* the NA gained one seat for its founder, James Schwarzenbach, who left the NA in 1970 and later founded the (now defunct) Swiss Republican Movement. In the 1971 *Nationalrat* elections the NA won four seats (while the Swiss Republican Movement obtained seven). By October 1979 the NA's representation had fallen to two; but in the 1983 elections it rose again to four seats, after the party had contested the elections on a joint list with the Swiss Republican Movement which obtained 3.5% of the vote. In August 1985 Hans Zwicky (who was then president of the NA) asserted that there was no connection between the NA and the newly formed National Socialist Party.
   Despite scoring some local election successes in the mid-1980s, in the general elections of October 1987 the NA lost one of its four seats in the *Nationalrat* and obtained only 2.9% of the vote. The new SD title was adopted prior to the 1991 federal elections, in which the party rose to five seats, having presented a joint list with the Ticino League that took 3.4% of the vote. It dropped back to three seats and 3.1% standing alone in the October 1995 elections.

Swiss Party of Labour
Parti Suisse du Travail (PST)
Partei der Arbeit der Schweiz (PAS)
Partito Svizzero del Lavoro (PSL)
   Address. 25 rue du Vieux-Billard, CP 232, 1211 Geneva 8
   Telephone. (#41–22) 328–1140
   Fax. (#41–22) 329–6412
   Leadership. Jean Spielmann (president)
   The PST was founded in October 1944 by members of the pre-war Communist Party (formed in 1921 but banned in 1939) and left-wing socialists who had been expelled or had resigned from the Social Democratic Party. The party is organized in a dozen cantons, in particular in Geneva,

Vaud, Neuchâtel and Basel (all predominantly French-speaking) and Ticino (Italian-speaking). Formely an orthodox pro-Soviet party, it converted to democratic socialism on the demise of the USSR in 1991. Its reward in the 1991 elections was a tripling of its *Nationalrat* representation from one to three seats, which it retained in 1995 with 1.2% of the vote.

Swiss People's Party
Schweizerische Volkspartei (SVP)
Union Démocratique du Centre (UDC)
Unione Democratica di Centro (UDC)
Uniun Democratica dal Center (UDC)
   Address. 18 Brückfeldstrasse, 3000 Bern 26
   Telephone. (#41–31) 302–5858
   Fax. (#41–31) 301–7585
   Leadership. Ueli Maurer (president), Theo Fischer (parliamentary leader), Myrtha Welti (general secretary)
   The right-wing liberal SVP was founded in its present form in 1971 as successor to (i) the Farmers', Traders' and Citizens' (i.e. Agrarian) Party, which had been formed in Zurich in 1917 and in Bern in 1918, and which was joined by the artisans and former Conservative Liberals of the canton of Bern in 1921, becoming a government party in 1929, and (ii) the former Swiss Democratic Party (founded in 1942), which had its origins in the Democratic Party established in the canton of Zurich in 1867, the Democratic and Workers' Party set up in the canton of Glarus in 1890 and the Democratic Party founded in Grisons in 1942. Since the 1971 union, the SVP has continued to hold the one seat in the federal government which the Agrarian Party had held since 1959 in coalition with the Radical Democratic, Social Democratic and Christian Democratic People's parties.
   In the 1983 general elections the SVP retained its 23 seats in the *Nationalrat* on the basis of 11.1% of the vote. In the 1987 elections the party obtained 25 seats on a slightly reduced vote share, which it increased to 11.9% in 1991 while still winning 25 seats. The October 1995 elections brought something of a breakthrough by Swiss standards, to 14.9% of the vote and 29 seats, only five less than the Christian Democrats (which held two government posts). The SVP's success in 1995 was attributed to its participation, alone among the coalition parties, in the successful campaign against Swiss membership of the European Economic Area and its consistent opposition to accession to the European Union.

Ticino League
Lega dei Ticinesi (LdT)
   Address. 7 via Monte Boglia, CP 2311, 6901 Lugano

   Telephone. (#41–91) 513033
   Fax. (#41–91) 527492
   Leadership. Giuliano Bignasca (president), Mauro Malandra (secretary)
   Based exclusively in the Italian-speaking canton of Ticino, the LdT combines right-wing economic and social policy prescriptions with advocacy of greater autonomy for Ticino within the confederation. It won two *Nationalrat* seats in 1991 on a joint list with the equally right-ring Swiss Democrats. In the October 1995 contest it retained only one, standing on its own.

Women Make Politics!
Frauen Macht Politik! (FraP!)
   Address. Postfach 9353, 8036 Zurich
   Telephone. (#41–1) 242–4418
   Fax. (#41–1) 242–4418
   Leadership. Barbara Huber and Claudia Schätti (joint secretaries)
   The exclamation mark in its title indicating its campaigning orientation, the FraP! seeks to change what it regards as the ingrained resistance to female participation within established Swiss parties by persuading more women to become involved at the political level. It established a bridgehead in the October 1995 elections, winning one *Nationalrat* seat.

Other Parties

Conservative and Liberal Movement (*Mouvement Conservateur et Libéral*, MCL), an extreme right-wing anti-immigration party founded in February 1985 in the canton of Valais with a programme similar to that of the National Front in France.

Green Alliance (*Grünes Bundnis*, GB), left-wing ecologist grouping hostile to the main Green Party of Switzerland, urges the eventual abolition of the Swiss Army; established a presence in the Lucerne cantonal parliament, before contesting the 1987 general elections on a joint list with the Progressive Organizations of Switzerland (POCH), winning four seats and 3.5% of the vote; ceased to be represented in 1991.

Independent Women's Alliance (*Unabhängiges Frauenbundnis*, UF), represented by one member of the Lucerne cantonal parliament from May 1987.

Jura Rally (*Rassemblement Jurassien*, RJ), advocates the creation of "one canton of all six francophone districts" of Jura and for the "liberation" of francophone territory not forming part of the canton.

Jura Unity (*Unité Jurassienne*, UJ), founded in 1975, advocating autonomy for the whole of the Jura as a French-speaking region.

National Socialist Party (*Nationalsozialistische Partei*, NSP), led by Ernst Meister (a former vice-president of what later became the Swiss Democrats), radical right-wing party founded in 1985 "to improve the image of national socialism" and to combat "over-population by foreigners".

Progressive Organizations of Switzerland (*Progressive Organisationen der Schweiz/Organisations Progressistes Suisses*, POCH), led by Georges Degen and Eduard Hafner, left-wing formation based on "scientific socialism" and ecological standpoints, strongest in Italian-speaking canton of Ticino; allied with Autonomous Socialist Party (later a component of the Unitarian Socialist Party) in 1975, 1979 and 1983 national elections, on the last occasion taking three of the four seats obtained by the alliance (with 2.2% of the vote); in 1987 elections the POCH presented a joint list with the Green Alliance which obtained four seats and 3.5% of the vote.

Socialist Workers' Party (*Parti Ouvrier Socialiste/ Sozialistische Arbeiterpartei*, POS/SAP), Trotskyist grouping originally founded in 1969, relaunched in 1980 on a less narrow platform, including environmental issues, allied with Progressive Organizations of Switzerland in 1975 elections, won 0.4% in 1983 general elections.

Swiss Ecological Liberal Party (*Ökologische Freiheitliche Partei der Schweiz/Parti Écologique Libéral Suisse*, PELS), founded in 1986 by Valentin Oehen (a former leader of what later became the Swiss Democrats), claiming to be neither right- nor left-wing but combining ecological concerns with a demand for curbs on immigration.

Swiss Party of the Handicapped and Socially Disadvantaged (*Schweizerische Partei der Behinderten und Sozialbenachteiligten*, SPBS), led by Fritz Butikofer, founded in 1984 with the aim of launching a popular initiative to secure the "right to work" for handicapped people.

Unitarian Socialist Party (*Partito Socialista Unitario*, PSU), led by Dario Robbiani and Werner Carobbio, left-wing socialist grouping based in Italian-speaking Switzerland, founded in January 1988 as a merger of the Autonomous Socialist Party with a section of the smaller Community of Ticinese Socialists (*Communità dei Socialisti Ticinesi*, CST).

Syria

Capital: Damascus

Population: 14,300,000 (1995E)

The Syrian Arab Republic is, under its 1973 constitution, a "socialist popular democracy". It has an executive President, who is secretary-general of the *Baath* Arab Socialist Party and also chairman of the National Progressive Front (NPF), embracing the country's legal parties. These are the *Baath*, the Socialist Unionist Movement (SUM), the Arab Socialist Union (ASU), the Arab Socialist Party (ASP), the Syrian Communist Party (SCP) and (since 1990) the Socialist Unionist Democratic Party (SUDP). Legislative authority rests with the People's Assembly, which is elected for a four-year term by universal adult suffrage of citizens over the age of 18 years and under a simple-majority system in multi-member constituencies. In elections held in August 1994, the *Baath* Party and its allies within the NPF won 167 of the 250 Assembly seats, with the remaining 83 going to independents.

The President is elected every seven years in a nation-wide referendum after nomination as sole candidate by the People's Assembly on the recommendation of the ruling Baath Party. In the presidential referendum held in December 1991, Hafez al-Assad was re-elected for his fourth term of office. The President appoints the Vice-Presidents and the Council of Ministers.

Arab Socialist Party (ASP)
Hizb al-Ishtiraki al-Arabi
 Address. c/o People's Assembly, Damascus
 Leadership. Abd al-Ghani Kannut

The ASP has taken part in government since 1970, normally being allocated one ministerial post. It has been represented in the People's Assembly since 1973, as part of the NPF structure, obtaining six seats in the 1994 August elections. It is anti-Egyptian and seeks a revival of free competition among political parties.

Arab Socialist Union (ASU)
Ittihad al-Ishtiraki al-Arabi

Address. c/o People's Assembly, Damascus

Leadership. Jamal Atassi (leader), Ismail al-Kadhi (secretary-general)

The ASU has long been a "Nasserite" group (subscribing to the socialist ideals of the former Egyptian President, Abdel Gamal Nasser), although its original pro-Egyptian stance has been moderated in the light of tensions between the Syrian and Egyptian governments over the general Middle East situation. The party has been represented in every People's Assembly, as part of the NPF, and took seven seats in the August 1994 elections. It has not been represented in government since 1985.

Baath Arab Socialist Party
Hizb al-Baath al-Arabi al-Ishtiraki

Address. PO Box 849, Damascus

Leadership. Hafez al-Assad (secretary-general, chair of the National Progressive Front), Abdallah al-Ahmar (assistant secretary-general)

The *Baath* (Renaissance) stands for secular pan-Arabism, socialism, anti-imperialism and anti-Zionism. It is historically (but now only theoretically) a regional party of which the Syrian party is one "regional command", others being in Iraq and Lebanon. Founded originally by Michel Aflaq in Syria in the latter part of the 1940s, the Baath absorbed the Syrian Arab Socialist Party in December 1953 and assumed its current name. The party was behind the March 1963 coup (the month after its involvement in a coup in Iraq) and it has held office in Syria ever since, although following a crisis in its ranks in 1966 the party expelled its rightist wing in which Aflaq was prominent. The Iraqi *Baath* returned to power in 1968, having been ousted at the end of 1963, but the theoretical unity of the party was not restored. The Syrian and Iraqi wings became fierce enemies, the former regularly denouncing the latter as a "rightist clique", and both sides have sponsored violent action against the other.

Assad's group within the *Baath* seized power in late 1970 and he has maintained his dominance of the Syrian political scene since that time. The *Baath* has, in turn, consistently dominated the National Progressive Front which it formed as a broad umbrella group in 1972, providing the framework for putting forward approved lists of candidates for legislative elections. In the August 1994 elections, 135 *Baath* candidates were returned.

Socialist Unionist Democratic Party (SUDP)
Address. c/o People's Assembly, Damascus

The SUDP first appeared as one of the constituent parts of the National Progressive Front at the legislative elections held in May 1990. In the 1994 elections it took four seats.

Socialist Unionist Movement (SUM)
Haraka at-Tawhidiyah al-Ishtiraki-yah

Address. c/o People's Assembly, Damascus

Leadership. Sami Soufan (leader), Fayiz Ismail (secretary-general)

Like the Arab Socialist Union (ASU), the SUM proclaims "Nasserite" socialist ideals but has tended to moderate its pro-Egyptian attitude in view of friction between the Syrian and Egyptian governments. The SUM has been represented in government since 1967, and is also represented in the People's Assembly through its membership of the NPF, obtaining seven seats in the August 1994 elections.

Syrian Communist Party (SCP)
Hizb al-Shuyui al-Suri

Address. c/o People's Assembly, Damascus

Leadership. Wisal Farhah Bakdash, Yusuf Faysal

Founded in 1925 (as part of a joint Communist Party of Syria and Lebanon until 1958), the SCP is generally regarded as the largest Communist Party in the Arab world, and was pro-Soviet in orientation until the collapse of the Soviet bloc. It is technically illegal, but is permitted to operate openly and has been represented in the Cabinet since 1966. The SCP is a part of the NPF framework, taking eight seats in the August 1994 elections to the People's Assembly.

Illegal Groups

Communist Action Party (CAP), founded in the 1970s in opposition to the pro-Soviet line of the Syrian Communist Party; was subjected to a government clamp-down in the mid-1980s, when many activists were arrested.

Muslim Brotherhood (*Ikhwan al-Muslimin*), has long maintained an active underground campaign against the Baath Arab Socialist Party and its leadership, most notably in a bloody, yet unsuccessful insurrection in the city of Hama in 1982; more recently there have been indications that the government no longer considers the group a serious threat.

Taiwan

Capital: Taipei

Population: 21,000,000 (1994E)

The government of Taiwan (Formosa) is derived from that which ruled the Chinese mainland prior to the 1949 communist revolution and the establishment of the People's Republic of China. The Taiwan government maintains a claim to legal jurisdiction over the mainland and continues to designate itself as the Republic of China. Martial law, imposed in 1949, was lifted in 1987, this decision opening the way for the legalization of opposition parties. Under the 1947 constitution, representative authority is vested in the National Assembly (*Kuomin Tahui*), which receives legislative proposals from the smaller elective Legislative Yuan (*Lifa Yuan*). Constitutional changes in April 1991 provided for the retirement of all remaining 'senior parliamentarians' who had been elected on mainland China in 1947–48 and granted life terms upon the formation of the Taiwanese government in 1949.

Elections in December 1991 for 325 seats in a new National Assembly resulted in the Nationalist Party (*Koumintang* or KMT) winning 254, the Democratic Progressive Party (DPP) 66, the National Democratic Independent Political Alliance 3 and independents 2. In elections to the 164–member Legislative Yuan on Dec. 2, 1995, however, the KMT achieved only a narrow majority, winning 85 seats, against 54 for the DPP, 21 for the New Party and 4 for independents. Constitutional reforms approved in July 1994 provided for the direct election of the executive President (previously elected by the National Assembly). In March 1996 the incumbent, President Lee Teng-hui of the KMT, was re-elected with 54% of the votes cast.

Democratic Progressive Party (DPP)

Minchu Chinpu Tang

Address. 13th Floor, 399 Nanking East Rd, Sec. 5, Taipei

Telephone. (#886–2) 769-2939

Fax. (#886–2) 765-8189

Leadership. Hsu Hsin-liang (chair), Chiu I-jen (secretary-general)

The DPP is Taiwan's main opposition party. It was formed in 1986 (although the restrictions of martial law still applied at that time) by a dissident movement (*Tangwai*, meaning "outside the party"), which had been set up to promote multi-party democracy. Accorded legal status in 1989, the party supports an independent, sovereign Taiwan which would abandon the claim to mainland China. In the National Assembly elections in December 1991 the DPP won 66 of 325 available seats, but it continued thereafter to increase its representation in the Legislative Yuan, most recently securing 54 seats (out of 164) in the December 1995 polling. In the March 1996 presidential election the party's candidate, Peng Ming-min, came second with 21% of the vote.

The DPP has observer status in the Liberal International.

Nationalist Party

Kuomintang (KMT)

Address. 53 Jen Ai Rd, Sec. 3, Taipei

Telephone. (#886–2) 343-4522

Fax. (#886–2) 343-4524

Leadership. Lee Teng-hui (chair), Wu Poh-hsiung (secretary-general)

Dating from 1894, the *Kuomintang*, or KMT, has been dominant at all levels of government since the proclamation of the Republic of China in 1949. It aims to supplant communism in mainland China, of which it sees itself as the legitimate government, reunifying the country under the "three principles of the people" (nationalism, democracy and social well-being—originally enunciated by Sun Yat-sen, the party's founder).

In 1986 the KMT conceded to demands for a broader political structure, subsequently lifting martial law, legalizing opposition parties and addressing the need to rejuvenate the legislature. Although the KMT secured a landslide victory in the National Assembly elections in December 1991 (gaining 254 of the 325 available seats), its control of the Legislative Yuan declined subsequently. In 1993 members of a younger and more reform-minded New KMT Alliance faction within the party had defected to form the New Party (NP).

In the December 1995 poll the KMT secured a reduced majority (85 of the 164 seats) with only 46% of the vote, its lowest public endorsement since it took power. At the time of the election the majority KMT faction favoured a period of separate international recognition for Taiwan, prior to eventual reunification with mainland China. Ten days after polling two conservative KMT vice-chairs who favoured closer ties with China, Gen. Hau Pei-tsun (a former Prime Minister) and Lin Yang-kang (a former president of the Judicial Yuan), were expelled from the party for violating party rules by aligning themselves with the NP.

The KMT chair and incumbent President, Lee Teng-hui, won Taiwan's first direct presidential election in March 1996, drawing 54% of the total vote.

The KMT is an affiliate of the International Democrat Union.

New Party (NP)
Hsin Tang
Address. 6th Floor, 7 Ching Tao East Rd, Taipei
 Telephone. (#886–2) 393-0930
 Fax. (#886–2) 393-1281
 Leadership. Wang Chien-shien (chair), Jaw Shau-kong (secretary-general)

The New Party was set up in mid-1993 by dissident Nationalist Party (KMT) members in the Legislative Yuan, and merged later that year with the China Social Democratic Party (which had broken away from the Democratic Progressive Party in 1991). The party advocates a "one-China" policy while supporting the concept of direct talks with the mainland communist government. In the December 1995 elections the NP's representation in the Legislative Yuan rose to 21, making it the third largest formation. In the March 1996 presidential election the NP-backed candidate was former KMT vice-chair Lin Yang-kang, who came third with 15% of the popular vote.

Other Parties

China Democratic Socialist Party (CDSP), dating from 1932 and currently led by Wang Shih-hsien; it aims to promote democracy and improve public welfare.

Chinese Freedom Party, founded in 1987, advocating social reform and a policy of détente towards the People's Republic of China.

Chinese Republican Party, founded in 1988, advocating "peaceful struggle for the salvation of China".

Democratic Liberal Party, founded in 1987, aiming to promote political democracy and economic liberty.

Labour Party (*Kungtang*), formed in 1987 to promote the rights of Taiwan's industrial workforce. It is led by Wang Yi-hsiung.

National Democratic Independent Political Alliance, which won three regional National Assembly seats in the 1991 elections.

Workers' Party, formed in 1989 by a radical breakaway faction of the Labour Party.

Young China Party, led by Jaw Chwen-shaw, which aims to recover sovereignty over mainland China, to safeguard democracy and promote links with the non-communist world.

Tajikistan

Capital: Dushanbe

Population: 6,000,000 (1995E)

The Soviet Socialist Republic of Tajikistan declared independence from the USSR in September 1991 as the Republic of Tajikistan, which became a sovereign member of the Commonwealth of Independent States (CIS) in December 1991. The post-Soviet constitution adopted by referendum in November 1994 established an executive presidency, with the President as head of state, chief executive and commander-in-chief, being popularly elected for a five-year term (once renewable consecutively) and having the authority to appoint and dismiss the Prime Minister and other ministers, subject to approval by the legislature. Legislative authority is vested in the unicameral Supreme Assembly of 181 members, also elected for a five-year term by universal adult suffrage.

The Soviet-era Communist establishment remained in power in independent Tajikistan until civil war erupted in mid-1992, when allied pro-democracy and Islamic parties briefly took control, before being driven into opposition and armed insurgency by the resurgent Communists.

In presidential elections on Nov. 6, 1994, interim incumbent Imomali Rakhmonov (who was identified with the Communist Party of Tajikistan, CPT) was returned with 58.3% of the vote. In Assembly elections on Feb. 26 and March 12, 1995, a majority of those elected were stated to have no official party affiliation. In the absence of any official results, reports indicated that the CPT had won about 60 seats, the People's Party of Tajikistan 5, the Party of Popular Unity and Accord 2 and the Tajikistan Party of Economic and Political Renewal 1.

Communist Party of Tajikistan (CPT)

Address. c/o Supreme Assembly, Dushanbe

Leadership. Shodi Shabdollov (first secretary)

Having been the ruling (and only legal) party since 1924 as the republican branch of the Communist Party of the Soviet Union, the CPT entered the era of independence still very much in charge in conservative Tajikistan, with a substantial genuine membership concentrated in areas of high ethnic Uzbek or Russian population such as the northern industrial region of Khodjent (formerly Leninabad). Twelve days after Tajikistan's declaration of independence, a CPT congress voted on Sept. 21, 1991, to convert the party into the Tajik Socialist Party, with a democratic socialist orientation. In response to immediate mass protests, a presidential decreee of Sept. 22 banned the party and nationalized its assets. One day after that, the Communist-dominated Supreme Soviet voted to rescind the prohibition, triggering further popular protests which resulted in the ban being confirmed on Oct. 2. However, the direct election of hard-line Communist Rakhman Nabiyev to the presidency in November 1991 with 58% of the popular vote resulted in the ban being officially lifted in January 1992, whereafter the party resumed activities under the CPT title, while maintaining its new commitment to democratic socialist principles.

The onset of civil conflict in 1992 ranged the Communist-era establishment against the allied forces of the Islamic and pro-democracy opposition, with the establishment emerging victorious, as indicated by the accession of Imomali Rakhmonov to the presidency in November. The Supreme Court's decision in June 1993 to ban the four leading opposition parties served to confirm the CPT in its resumed role as effectively the ruling formation. Several new pro-government parties launched in 1993-94, such as the People's Party of Tajikistan and the People's Democratic Party, were regarded by observers as extensions of the CPT's network of influence, which was strengthened by the presidential election victory of incumbent Rakhmonov in November 1994, although neither he nor his government ministers were identified as having party affiliation. As a result of the February-March 1995 parliamentary elections, at least a third of the elected candidates were acknowledged CPT members.

Democratic Party of Tajikistan (DPT)

Leadership. Shodmon Yusuf, Jumaboy Niyazov, Maksud Ikramov, Davla Koudonazarov

Based in the autonomous region of Gorny-Badakhshan, the pro-Western and strongly anti-Communist DPT was launched in 1990 on a platform advocating Tajik sovereignty within a framework of confederal states. Its candidate in the October 1991 presidential election was Davla Koudonazarov, who came a creditable second on the strength of an alliance with the Islamic Renaissance Party (IRP) against the ruling establishment of the Communist Party of Tajikistan. The DPT was prominent in the "government of national reconciliation" of May-November 1992, but the reassertion of Communist authority in late 1992 forced it into armed resistance. It was one of four opposition parties banned by the Supreme Court in June 1993, amid escalating internal conflict ranging pro-democracy and Islamic forces against the government. Peace talks resulting in a notional ceasefire agreement in September 1994 failed to bring the DPT and other genuine opposition parties into the elections of late 1994 and early 1995.

Divisions between the moderate and hard-line wings of the DPT led to an open split in June 1995, when Shodmon Yusuf was deposed from the leadership but refused to recognize the election of Jumaboy Niyazov as his successor. Claiming to be the authentic DPT leader, Yusuf came to an agreement with the government under which his faction of the party was re-legalized in July, whereas the Niyazov faction entered into a formal opposition alliance with the IRP. Closely associated with the DPT is the Moscow-based Co-ordinating Centre for the Democratic Forces of Tajikistan, led by Otakhon Latifi.

Islamic Renaissance Party (IRP)
Nazdate Islamiye Tajikistan

Leadership. Sayed Abdullo Nuri (chair), Ali Akbar Turadzhonzoda (first deputy chair), Davlat Ousman (deputy chair), Muhammad Sharif Himatzada (military commander)

The IRP was founded in June 1990 as the Tajik branch of a network of Islamic parties which emerged in the last phase of the USSR. Based in the rural population, the IRP has declared its long-term objective to be the conversion of Tajikistan into an Islamic republic, although it rejects the label "Islamic fundamentalist". The party was refused permission to hold its founding congress in Dushanbe in October 1990 and was subsequently proscribed by the presidium of the then Tajikistan Supreme Soviet. It nevertheless took an active part in organizing the mass protests that followed the Dushanbe government's support for the attempted coup by hard-liners in Moscow in August 1991. Legalized in October 1991, the IRP supported the unsuccessful presidential candidacy of Davla Koudonazarov of the Democratic Party of Tajikistan in October 1991.

The IRP was again banned in June 1993, along with three other opposition parties. Two months later a death sentence was passed on an IRP leader, Ajik Aliyev, who had been found guilty of attempting to overthrow the government. The IRP's deputy leader, Ali Akbar Turadzhonzoda, was Tajikistan's chief *kazi* (senior Muslim cleric) until February 1993, whereafter he acted as an opposition spokesman in peace negotiations with the government. Their failure to produce political agreement resulted in an IRP boycott of the presidential and legislative elections of late 1994 and early 1995. The talks were resumed thereafter under the auspices of the CIS and with the OSCE also seeking to act as mediator. However, despite regular ceasefire announcements, armed conflict between Russian-supported government troops and opposition forces intensified in 1995–96, with the IRP's armed wing (called "Defence of the Fatherland") playing a prominent role and drawing support from Tajiks in Afghanistan.

In February 1996 IRP leader Sayed Abdullo Nuri, who was also leader of the United Tajik Opposition (UTO), claimed that forces opposed to the government controlled 70% of Tajikistan's territory. In June 1996, in a statement from his headquarters in exile in Afghanistan, he rejected participation in a a new consultative council set up by President Rakhmanov, asserting that "a fair distribution of power" and a coalition government were needed to achieve national accord.

Party of Popular Unity and Accord (PPUA)
Address. c/o Supreme Assembly, Dushanbe
Leadership. Abdumalik Abdulajanov (chair)

The PPUA was founded in November 1994 on the basis of the unsuccessful presidential election campaign mounted that month by Abdumalik Abdulajanov, a former Prime Minister. Backed by some secular opposition parties, Abdulajanov was defeated by the incumbent but received a creditable 35% of the vote, drawing his main support from the ethnic Russian and Uzbek regions of northern Tajikistan. The PPUA was in part a successor to the Party of Economic Freedom (PEF) founded by Abdulajanov on his resignation from the premiership in December 1993 because of resistance to economic reform in the state bureaucracy. The PPUA was credited with winning two seats in the 1995 Supreme Council elections.

People's Party of Tajikistan (PPT)
Address. c/o Supreme Assembly, Dushanbe
Leadership. Abdulmajid Dostiyev (chair)

Initially launched in August 1993 in the wake of the banning of the main opposition parties two months previously, the PPT was formally constituted in April 1994, apparently as a product of the ruling establishment's wish to demonstrate the multi-party character of the new Tajikistan. Reports that the PPT was intended as a successor to the Communist Party of Tajikistan (CPT) proved to be premature, as the CPT remained in being on its own account. In the 1995 parliamentary elections the PPT was credited with winning five seats in the 181–member Supreme Assembly.

Tajikistan Party of Economic and Political Renewal (TPEPR)
Address. c/o Supreme Assembly, Dushanbe
Leadership. (vacant)

The TPEPR was founded in April 1994 as a pro-market formation aspiring to convert Tajikistan into a capitalist economy, albeit with a social dimension. The new party was credited with winning one seat in the 1995 Assembly elections. On March 8, 1996, the TPEPR leader, Mukhtor Boboyev, was murdered in northern Tajikistan by unknown gunmen.

Other Parties

Badakhshan Ruby Movement (*Lali Badakhshan*), led by Atobek Amirbek, founded in the late 1980s to represent the distinctive Pamiri (Ismaeli Muslim) people of Gorny-Badakhshan, officially demands full autonomy (although a militant faction wants independence), to which end it joined the opposition alliance headed by the Democratic and Islamic Renaissance parties in armed struggle against the Dushanbe government and was banned in June 1993.

Justice (*Adolatho*), founded in 1996 under the leadership of Abdurahmo Karimov.

Justice and Progress Party of Tajikistan (JPPT), led by Safarali Kenjayev and Karim Abdulov, moderate opposition grouping founded in 1996.

People's Democratic Party (*Hizbi-Khalq-i-Demokrati*), formed in 1993 on the initiative of northern business interests, led by Abdujalil Hamidov, who had been Communist Party leader in the Khodjent/Leninabad region in the Soviet era.

Rebirth Movement (*Rastokhez*), led by Takhir Abduzhaborov, founded in 1990 as a nationalist/religious movement advocating the revival of Tajik culture and traditions; participated in the anti-Communist, pro-independence agitation of 1990-91 and in the "government of national reconciliation" of May-November 1992, prior to being banned in June 1993.

Union of Progressive Forces of Tajikistan (UPFJ), led by Karimjon Ahmedov, registered in July 1994, aims to promote ethnic harmony, democracy and economic reform.

Tanzania

Capital: Dar es Salaam

Population: 28,800,000 (1994E)

The United Republic of Tanzania was established in 1964, when the newly independent states of Tanganyika and Zanzibar merged. Under the constitution, executive power is vested in the President of the United Republic, who is elected by direct popular vote for a five-year term, renewable once only. Legislative power is exercised by the (mainly) directly-elected National Assembly, which serves a five-year term. Zanzibar's internal administration provides for a popularly elected President and House of Representatives. In December 1994 a constitutional amendment was introduced ending the convention that the President of Zanzibar would automatically serve as a Vice-President of the United Republic. The ruling Revolutionary Party of Tanzania (*Chama Cha Mapinduzi*, CCM) was the sole legal political party until 1992 when legislation allowing for opposition parties was passed.

Multi-party presidential and legislative elections were held in mainland Tanzania on Oct. 29, 1995, followed by re-runs in seven Dar es Salaam constituencies on Nov. 19. Amid much confusion and opposition claims of malpractice, the official results of the presidential election gave victory to the CCM candidate, Benjamin Mkapa, with almost 61.8% of the vote, while the official legislative results gave the CCM 186 of the 232 directly elective seats plus 28 of 37 nominated women members, for a total of 214 out of 269. Of the opposition parties, the Civic United Front (CUF) was shown as having 24 elective seats and 3 nominated members; the National Convention for Reconstruction and Reform–Mageuzi 16 and 3 respectively; the Party for Democracy and Progress (CHADEMA) 3 and 1 respectively; and the United Democratic Party 3 and 1 respectively.

In separate elections in the islands of Zanzibar and Pemba on 22 October, the CCM's incumbent presidential candidate, Salmin Amour, was narrowly declared the winner with 52% of the votes cast, while in the House of Representatives the party secured 26 of the 50 elected seats, the other 24 going to the CUF. Of ten additional seats filled by presidential nomination, the CCM obtained 6 and the CUF 4.

Civic United Front (CUF)
Address. PO Box 3637, Zanzibar
Leadership. James Mapalala (chair)
The CUF was formed by Mapalala in 1991 from a pressure group, the Civil and Legal Rights Group. In the 1995 elections the CUF presidential candidate, Ibrahim Lipumba, took third place with 6.4% of the votes cast, while in the National Assembly elections the party won 24 of the directly-elected seats and was allocated three of the nominated women's seats. In the Zanzibar presidential poll, the CUF's Seif Shariff Hamad

was narrowly beaten into second place, having secured 48% of the vote.

National Convention for Construction and Reform–Mageuzi (NCCR-Mageuzi)

Address. PO Box 5316, Dar es Salaam
Leadership. Augustine Mrema (chair)

The NCCR-Mageuzi evolved from a broad-based pressure group for constitutional reform. It was launched as a political party in early 1992 and was registered the following year. In the October 1995 presidential election, party chair Mrema (who had resigned from the ruling Revolutionary Party of Tanzania in March 1995) took second place with almost 28% of the vote, while in the elections to the National Assembly the NCCR secured 16 of the directly-elected seats and three nominated members.

Party for Democracy and Progress

Chama Cha Demokrasia na Maendeleo (CHADEMA)

Address. PO Box 5330, Dar es Salaam
Leadership. Edwim Mtei (chair)

CHADEMA was registered in 1993, advocating democracy and social development. In the 1995 elections the party did not put forward a presidential candidate, but won three of the directly-elected seats in the National Assembly and was allocated one nominated seat. It broke ranks with the other main opposition parties by participating in the re-run of the legislative ballot in Dar es Salaam.

Revolutionary Party of Tanzania

Chama Cha Mapinduzi (CCM)

Address. PO Box 50, Dodoma
Telephone. (#255–61) 2282
Leadership. Benjamin Mkapa (leader)

The CCM was formally launched in 1977 upon the merger of the Tanganyika African National Union (TANU) with the Afro-Shirazi Party (ASP) of Zanzibar. Since the adoption of a one-party constitution in 1965, TANU had been the sole party of mainland Tanzania and the ASP the sole party of Zanzibar. Under President Julius Nyerere, the party had pursued a policy of socialism and self-reliance. However, Ali Hassan Mwinyi, who succeeded Nyerere as President of Tanzania in 1985 and as CCM chairman in 1990, implemented free-market reforms and economic liberalization. In February 1992 an extraordinary national conference of the CCM unanimously endorsed the introduction of a multi-party system.

In July 1995 Benjamin Mkapa was selected in succession to Mwinyi as presidential candidate for the CCM. The party reasserted its political dominance in the multi-party elections in October-November 1995, retaining the presidency and achieving an overwhelming majority in the National Assembly, although its victories in the Zanzibar polls were much narrower.

United Democratic Party (UDP)

Address. c/o National Assembly, Dar es Salaam
Leadership. John Cheyo

In the 1995 elections the UDP presidential candidate, John Cheyo, took fourth place with just under 4% of the votes cast. In the National Assembly the party won three of the directly-elected seats and was allocated one nominated seat.

Other Parties

Bismillah Party, its title meaning "In the Name of God", an Islamic fundamentalist grouping formed in Zanzibar by supporters of the island's former Chief Minister, Seif Sharif Hamadi.

Democratic Party, unregistered and led by Rev. Christopher Mtikila.

National League for Democracy (NLD), registered in 1993 under the leadership of Emmanuel Makaidi.

National Reconstruction Alliance (NRA), whose presidential candidate, Kighoma Malima (a former government minister and member of the ruling Revolutionary Party of Tanzania until June 1995), died suddenly in August 1995.

Popular National Party (PONA), chaired by Wilfrem Mwakitwange.

Pragmatic Democratic Alliance, an unregistered party.

Tanzania Democratic Alliance Party (TADEA), registered in 1993 and led by Flora Kamoona.

Tanzania People's Party (TPP), chaired by Alec Che-Mponda.

Union for Multi-Party Democracy (UMD), organized in 1991 by Abdallah Said Fundikira, who had been a prominent figure in the constitutional pressure group that evolved into the National Convention for Construction and Reform–Mageuzi.

United People's Democratic Party (UPDP), chaired by Khalfani Ali Abdullah.

Zanzibar Democratic Alliance–Hamaki, led by Hemed Hilal Mohamed, founded in 1988 by exiled opponents of the govenment, reportedly favouring enhanced autonomy for Zanzibar.

Thailand

Capital: Bangkok

Population: 60,000,000 (1995E)

The Kingdom of Thailand is the only south-east Asian country not to have been colonized by a European power. Modern Thailand came into being in 1932 when a civilian-military group carried out a coup (commonly referred to as a "revolution") which removed the country's absolute monarchical system in favour of a system modelled on the European constitutional monarchies. Since that time military rule has been interspersed with short periods of democratic government.

During the most recent military intervention in politics, between February 1991 and mid-1992, a new constitution came into effect in December 1991. This provided for the creation of a legislative body, the National Assembly (*Ratha Sapha*), consisting of a House of Representatives (*Sapha Poothan Rassadorn*) elected by universal adult suffrage and an appointed Senate (*Woothi Sapha*), and for the appointment of a Cabinet headed by a Prime Minister. A subsequent constitutional amendment in 1992 stipulated that the Prime Minister must be an elected member of the House.

In elections held in March 1992 pro-military parties secured enough seats to form a government, but this quickly fell in the aftermath of the army's violent suppression of pro-democracy demonstrations in May. Fresh elections took place in September 1992 resulting in victory for a coalition led by the Democrat Party (DP). Further general elections to the House of Representatives (enlarged to 391 members) were held on July 2, 1995, and resulted in the following seat distribution: *Chart Thai* Party 92, Democrat Party 86, New Aspiration Party 57, National Development Party 53, *Palang Dharma* Party 23, Social Action Party 22, *Nam Thai* Party 18, Thai Citizens' Party 18, *Seri Tham* Party 11, Solidarity Party 8, Mass Party 3. They ushered in a new centre-right coalition led by the *Chart Thai* and including six other parties.

Chart Thai Party

Address. 325/74–76 Lookluang Road, Mahana-khorn Intersection, Dusit, Bangkok 10300

Telephone. (#66–2) 282-7054

Leadership. Banharn Silpa-Archa (leader)

The right-wing and pro-business *Chart Thai* ("Thai Nation"), which has a substantial military membership, has been one of Thailand's leading parties since its formation in the mid-1970s. In the 1988 elections the party won the most seats, subsequently serving as the core of a governing coalition until the military coup in early 1991. After the March 1992 elections, *Chart Thai* and other pro-military parties formed another coalition (with the now defunct *Sammakkhi Tham*, which had won 79 seats, as the dominant partner). This fell soon afterwards, leading to further elections the following September which resulted in a new government of pro-democracy groups. In the July 1995 elections *Chart Thai* emerged as the largest legislative party, increasing its representation from 77 to 92 seats and forming a new seven-party coalition administration under the premiership of party leader, Banharn Silpa-Archa.

Democrat Party (DP)

Address. 67 Settasiri Road, Samsen Nai, Phay-thai, Bangkok 10400

Telephone. (#66–2) 270-1683

Fax. (#66–2) 279-6086

Leadership. Chuan Leekpai (leader)

The liberal DP, established in 1946, is Thailand's oldest political party. Having won by far the largest number of legislative seats in 1986, the party then experienced factional in-fighting leading to a split in 1988 and a dramatic fall in support in the elections of that year. The DP subsequently served in the *Chart Thai*-led coalition until 1990, when it withdrew into opposition. Emerging as the largest single party in the September 1992 elections, the DP headed a new coalition which ultimately collapsed in May 1995, heralding early elections in July. Although the DP increased its legislative representation to 86 seats, it came second to *Chart Thai*, which formed the core of a new government.

Mass Party
Muan Chon

Address. 630/182 Somdetprapinklao Road, Bangyeekan, Bangplad, Bangkok

Telephone. (#66–2) 424-0851

Leadership. Chalerm Yubamrung (leader)

The right-wing *Muan Chon* was formed in 1985 by dissidents from various government and opposition parties, and was briefly a member of the ruling coalition from 1988 until 1990. Following the July 1995 elections, in which its legislative representation fell from four to three seats, the party joined the new *Chart Thai*-led administration.

Nam Thai

Address. 253/1 Sawankalok Road, Suanchitralada, Dusit, Bangkok 10300

Telephone. (#66–2) 243-6620

Leadership. Amnuai Wirawan (leader)

Nam Thai (variously translated as "Dynamic Thai" or "Leadership for Thailand") was established by its leader in July 1994 upon his resignation as deputy leader of the New Aspiration Party (NAP) and Deputy Prime Minister. In the July 1995 elections the party won 18 seats, subsequently joining the new coalition government headed by *Chart Thai*.

National Development Party (NDP)
Chart Patthana

Address. 10 Soi Phaholyothin 3, Phyathai, Bangkok 10400

Telephone. (#66–2) 270-3104

Leadership. Gen. Chartchai Choonhavan (leader)

Launched in mid-1992, the *Chart Patthana* contested the elections to the House of Representatives in September of that year and won 60 seats. Briefly a member of the Democrat Party-led coalition government between December 1994 and May 1995, the party lost ground slightly in the July 1995 elections, securing 53 seats.

New Aspiration Party (NAP)

Address. 310 Soi Ruamchit, Nakhornchaisri Road, Dusit, Bangkok 10300

Telephone. (#66–2) 243-5000

Leadership. Gen. Chaovalit Yongchaiyut (leader)

The NAP was set up in 1990 as a vehicle for the political ambitions of its leader, a former army commander and self-styled 'soldier for democracy'. Despite his background, Chaovalit was strongly critical of the military's intervention in national

politics in 1991–92. Following the September 1992 elections, in which it won 51 seats, the NAP was a component of the pro-democracy ruling coalition until December 1994 when it withdrew. In July 1995, emerging from the legislative poll as the third ranked party with 57 seats in the House of Representatives, the party joined the new *Chart Thai*-led coalition government.

Palang Dharma Party

Address. 445/15 Soi Ramkhaeng 39, Wangthonlang, Bangkapi, Bangkok 10310

Telephone. (#66–2) 718-5626

Leadership. Thaksin Shinawatra (leader)

Palang Dharma (meaning "Righteous Force") was set up in 1988 by the then governor of Bangkok, Chamlong Sirimaung, who sought to project an image of party integrity. In the July 1995 elections the party's legislative representation fell sharply to 23 seats (down from 47 in September 1992), but it continued in government as a part of the new coalition led by *Chart Thai*.

Seri Tham

Address. 6/69 Kampaengpet-Phayolyothin Road, Samsen Nai, Phyathai, Bangkok 10400

Telephone. (#66–2) 278-4223

Leadership. Arthit Urairat (leader)

Formed in mid-1992, *Seri Tham* is variously rendered as the Liberal Democratic Party, the Justice Freedom Party or simply "Virtuous Freedom"). It joined the Democrat Party-led coalition government in September 1993 upon the departure of the Social Action Party (SAP). In the July 1995 elections the party won 11 seats, three more than in September 1992.

Social Action Party (SAP)

Address. 126 Samsen 28 Road (Soi Ongkarak), Nakhornchaisri, Dusit, Bangkok 10300

Telephone. (#66–2) 243-0100

Fax. (#66–2) 243-3224

Leadership. Montri Pongpanich (leader)

The SAP emerged in 1974 as a conservative outgrowth from the Democrat Party. It obtained a majority in the 1979 elections and was again the leading party in 1983. Internal divisions led to the resignation of the long-time leader Kukrit Pramoj in 1985, and the party's fortunes slipped in the 1986 poll. Runner-up to the *Chart Thai* in the 1988 elections, the SAP subsequently served in the ruling coalition until December 1990 when it withdrew along with the Democrat Party. Kukrit, who had briefly returned to the party leadership in mid-1990, was replaced by Montri Pongpanich the following year. Having secured 22 seats in the September 1992 elections, the party joined the Democrat-led coalition but went into opposition in September 1993. In July 1995 it maintained its legislative representation, becoming a member of the new seven-party coalition government headed by the *Chart Thai*.

Solidarity
Ekkaparb
Address. 90 Ratchadapisek Road, Huay Kwang, Bangkok 10310
Telephone. (#66–2) 246-1881
Leadership. Chaiyot Sasomsap (leader)
Ekkaparb was formed in 1989 from the merger of four opposition parties (*Ruam Thai*, Community Action, Progressive Party and *Prachachon* Party). It briefly acceded to the governing coalition just prior to the 1991 military coup. In both the September 1992 and July 1995 general elections the party won eight seats.

Thai Citizens' Party
Prachakorn Thai
Address. 9/250 Soi Ladprao 55, Lardrap Road, Bangkapi, Bangkok 10310
Telephone. (#66–2) 559-0008
Leadership. Samak Sundaravej (leader)
The right-wing, pro-military *Prachakorn Thai* was launched by its populist leader in 1979. Samak Sundaravej took the party into coalition government between 1983 and 1986, and again in December 1990 until the military takeover in February 1991. Having lent its diminished support to the short-lived pro-military coalition formed after the March 1992 elections, *Prachakorn Thai*'s legislative representation fell to three seats in the September 1992 poll. The party recovered in the July 1995 balloting to take 18 seats, and subsequently joined the new *Chart Thai*-led coalition.

Other Parties

Citizen's Party (*Rassadorn*), electoral support for which dipped sharply in 1992, and which did not contest the 1995 polls.

Democratic Liberation Party, registered after the July 1995 elections.

Siam Principle (*Lak Siam*), launched in 1994 by a breakaway faction from the *Palang Dharma*.

Thai People's Party (*Puangchon Chao Thai*), led by Maj.-Gen. Boonyoong Watthanapong.

Togo

Capital: Lomé

Population: 4,100,000 (1995E)

The Republic of Togo gained full independence in 1960, having previously been administered by France as a United Nations Trust Territory. In 1967 the present head of state, Gen. Gnassingbé Eyadéma, seized power in a bloodless coup and assumed the title of President. Existing political parties were banned, and in 1969 the Rally of the Togolese People (RPT) was established as the ruling and sole legal party. By early 1991 Eyadéma was facing increasing opposition pressure for the introduction of multi-party democracy, and he agreed to the holding of a National Conference, in July and August of that year, to determine the political future. The Conference set up a transitional High Council of the Republic which subsequently engaged in a power struggle with President Eyadéma. Amid the continuing political tension, a multi-party constitution was given approval in a referendum in September 1992. This vested executive power in the President and legislative power in an 81–member National Assembly (*Assemblée Nationale*), both directly elected for five-year terms of office.

Togo's first multi-party presidential elections in August 1993 resulted in victory for the incumbent Eyadéma, although the contest was marked by the absence of any serious challengers and accusations of electoral malpractice. In the legislative elections in February 1994, the opposition Action Committee for Renewal (CAR) and Togolese Union for Democracy (UDT) won 36 and 7 Assembly seats respectively (although the results in three constituencies were subsequently declared invalid by the Supreme Court), while the ruling RPT took 35 seats.

Action Committee for Renewal

Comité d'Action pour la Renouveau (CAR)
Address. c/o Assemblée Nationale, Lomé
Leadership. Yao Agboyibo (leader)

Part of an opposition coalition with the Togolese Union for Democracy (UDT), the CAR boycotted the presidential election in August 1993 but participated in the legislative balloting in February 1994. Initially the party gained the highest number of seats, with 36, although this was subsequently reduced to 34 by a controversial Supreme Court decision which prompted a CAR boycott of the new National Assembly. In the light of the election results, the CAR/UDT coalition declared in March 1994 that CAR leader Agboyibo had been selected for appointment as the new Prime Minister. However, President Eyadéma refused to endorse this, and in April he appointed the UDT leader, Edem Kodjo, as Prime Minister in a move which fractured the unity of the CAR/UDT coalition. The CAR rejected the appointment, continuing to assert that the new Prime Minister should come from within its own ranks, and made clear that the party would not participate in a Kodjo Cabinet. In May 1994 the CAR ended its boycott of the Assembly. However, it again suspended its participation the following November over the continuing controversy surrounding the CAR candidates whose election in February had been invalidated by the Supreme Court. The boycott continued until August 1995, when agreement was reached with the government for the establishment of an independent electoral commission.

Co-ordination of New Forces

Co-ordination des Forces Nouvelles (CFN)
Address. c/o Assemblée Nationale, Lomé
Leadership. The CFN was formed in 1993, comprising six political organizations and led by the (then) Prime Minister, Joseph Kokou Koffigoh. Koffigoh resigned as Prime Minister in March 1994, following the legislative elections the previous month in which the CFN won one seat.

Rally of the Togolese People

Rassemblement du Peuple Togolais (RPT)
Address. Place de l'Indépendance, BP 1208, Lomé
Telephone. (#228) 212018
Leadership. Gen. Gnassingbé Eyadéma (president)

The RPT was established in 1969 under the sponsorship of President Eyadéma, and ruled on a single-party basis until its constitutional mandate was abrogated in 1991 by the National Conference. The Conference, convened in response to increasing opposition to the regime, set up a transitional High Council of the Republic and a serious power struggle subsequently developed between this body and Eyadéma.

In the presidential elections held in August 1993, which were boycotted by the main opposition parties, Eyadéma was confirmed in office with about 96.5% of the votes cast. In the legislative elections the following February, the RPT won 35 National Assembly seats but failed to win an overall majority. President Eyadéma split the opposition ranks in April 1994 by appointing the leader of the Togolese Union for Democracy as the new Prime Minister. RPT members secured the key portfolios in the coalition Cabinet announced the following month.

Togolese Union for Democracy

Union Togolaise pour la Démocratie (UTD)
Address. c/o Assemblée Nationale, Lomé
Leadership. Edem Kodjo (leader)

In alliance with the Action Committee for Renewal (CAR), the UDT boycotted the presidential polls in 1993 but participated in the National Assembly elections in February 1994. The party secured seven seats initially, although the election of one UTD member was subsequently invalidated. Having refused to appoint the CAR leader as the new Prime Minister, President Eyadéma chose UDT leader Kodjo in April 1994 to head a new government. Kodjo's acceptance caused a breach in relations between the UDT and the CAR. The latter refused to serve in the administration which was named in May 1994 and which was drawn mainly from the UDT and the Rally of the Togolese People. A Cabinet reshuffle by Kodjo in November 1995 drew further criticism from the CAR.

Union for Justice and Democracy

Union pour la Justice et la Démocratie (UJD)
Address. c/o Assemblée Nationale, Lomé
Leadership. Lal Taxpandjan (leader)

A small pro-Eyadéma formation, the UJD won two National Assembly seats in the 1994 elections.

Other Parties

Democratic Convention of African People (*Convention Démocratique des Peuples Africains*, CDPA), one of the earliest identifiable opposition movements to emerge under the Eyadéma regime at the end of the 1980s.

Movement of 5th October (*Mouvement de 5 Octobre*, MO5), a militant anti-Eyadéma group led by Bassirou Ayewa.

Nationalist Movement for Unity (*Mouvement Nationaliste de l'Unité*, MNU), led by Koffitse Adzrako.

Pan-African Socialist Party (*Parti Pan-Africain Socialiste*, PPS), a radical party under the leadership of Francis Agbobli.

Party for Democracy and Renewal (*Parti pour la Démocratie et le Renouveau*, PDR), led by Zarifou Ayewa.

Party of Action for Democracy (*Parti d'Action pour la Démocratie*, PAD), headed by Francis Ekoh.

Party of Democrats for Unity (*Parti des Démocrates pour l'Unité*, PDU).

Togolese Alliance for Democracy (*Alliance Togolaise pour la Démocratie*, ATD), led by Adani Ife, whose presidential candidacy in 1993 attracted only about 1.6% of the vote.

Togolese Democratic Party (*Parti Démocratique Togolais*, PDT).

Togolese Union for Reconciliation (*Union Togolaise pour la Réconciliation*, UTR), led by Bawa Mankouby.

Union for Democracy and Solidarity (*Union pour la Démocratie et la Solidarité*, UDS), headed by Antoine Foly.

Union of Forces for Change (*Union des Forces du Changement*), a coalition of organizations, opposed to the Eyadéma regime, under the leadership of Gilchrist Olympio; boycotted the presidential and legislative elections in 1993 and 1994.

Union of Independent Liberals (*Union des Libéraux Indépendants*, ULI), launched by Jacques Amouzou, who contested the 1993 presidential election but came a very distant second to Gen. Eyadéma with 1.87% of the vote.

Tonga

Capital: Nuku'alofa (Tongapatu) **Population:** 98,000 (1995E)

The Kingdom of Tonga, an independent constitutional monarchy within the Commonwealth, was a British Protected State for 70 years prior to achieving full independence in 1970. The Tongan sovereign is head of state and exercises executive power in conjunction with an appointed 11–member Privy Council which functions as a Cabinet. The 30-member unicameral Legislative Assembly consists of the King, Privy Council, nine nobles elected by the country's 33 hereditary peers, and nine popularly elected representatives. In recent years this system has faced an increasingly determined challenge from a pro-democracy movement, members of which founded the country's first formal political party, the People's Party, in August 1994. In the most recent general election, which was held on January 24–25 1996, the pro-democracy movement made a strong showing, retaining a majority of those seats open to popular vote.

Trinidad and Tobago

Capital: Port of Spain **Population:** 1,300,000 (1995E)

Trinidad and Tobago became independent of the United Kingdom in 1962 and was declared a republic in 1976. Under the 1976 constitution the head of state is the President, who is elected by a parliamentary electoral college. Legislative power is vested in a bicameral parliament composed of a 36–member House of Representatives, which is directly elected for five years, and a 31–member Senate appointed by the President (16 of whom are named on the advice of the Prime Minister, six on that of the Leader of the Opposition, and nine at the President's own discretion). Tobago, the smaller of the country's two main constituent islands, achieved full internal self-government in 1987; its House of Assembly has 15 members (12 directly elected and three chosen by the majority party), who serve four-year terms.

In an early general election held on Nov. 6, 1995, the People's National Movement (PNM) and the United National Congress (UNC) each won 17 seats, and the National Alliance for Reconstruction (NAR) won two. In elections to the Tobago House of Assembly on Dec. 7, 1992, the NAR won 11 seats to the PNM's one.

National Alliance for Reconstruction (NAR)

Address. 71 Dundonald Street, Port of Spain
Telephone. (#1–809) 627-6163
Leadership. Joseph Toney (leader)

The NAR originated in the early 1980s as a coalition of moderate, left-wing opposition parties. It was reorganized as a unitary party in February 1986, incorporating the Democratic Action Congress (DAC), the Organization for National Reconstruction (ONR), the Tapia House Movement (THM) and the United Labour Front (ULF). Although the alliance, under the leadership of Arthur N.R. Robinson, won a landslide victory over the PNM in the 1986 general election, it subsequently encountered serious internal divisions and increasing unpopularity. In 1988 a number of former ULF members under Basdeo Panday, who were opposed to Robinson's policies, were expelled from the NAR, forming the United National Congress (UNC) in the following year. The NAR was reduced to two seats in the December 1991 general election, in the wake of which Robinson resigned as leader to be replaced by Carson Charles. The party retained overwhelming control of the Tobago House of Assembly in December 1992, winning 11 of the 12 elective seats. Having been replaced as party leader by Selby Wilson in early 1993, Charles left the NAR to form the National Development Party. In August 1994 Wilson in turn gave way to Joseph Toney.

People's National Movement (PNM)

Address. 1 Tranquillity Street, Port of Spain
Telephone. (#1–809) 625-1533
Leadership. Patrick Manning (leader)

The centre-right and moderate nationalist PNM won every election in Trinidad and Tobago from its formation in 1956 until 1986, when it was heavily defeated by the NAR. George Chambers, who had assumed the leadership on the death in 1981 of the party's founder, Dr Eric Williams, lost his seat in the election and resigned in 1987 to be replaced by Patrick Manning. The PNM recovered

in 1991, winning 21 seats in the December general election, but went into opposition again in 1995 following the November polling in which it failed to win an overall majority. The party held one seat in the Tobago House of Assembly elections in 1992.

United National Congress (UNC)

Address. Rienzi Complex, Southern Main Road, Couva
Telephone. (#1–809) 636 8145
Leadership. Basdeo Panday (leader)

The UNC was formed in 1989 by former ULF members who had been expelled from the National Alliance for Reconstruction (NAR). Having been the runner-up to the PNM in the 1991 general election, winning 13 seats with about 30% of the vote, the party's electoral performance further improved in the November 1995 polling, in which the UNC secured 17 seats and formed a new government in coalition with the NAR.

Other Parties

Movement for Unity and Progress (MUP), launched in 1994 under the leadership of Hulsie Bhaggan.

National Development Party (NDP), established in mid-1993 by Carson Charles, who had been the leader of the National Alliance for Reconstruction (NAR) until his replacement earlier that year.

National Joint Action Committee (NJAC), a left-wing grouping under the leadership of Makandal Daaga, contested its first election in 1981.

National Vision Party (NVP), formed in early 1994 by Yasin Abu Bakr.

Republic Party (RP), launched in January 1994 by Nello Mitchell, who had been expelled from the People's National Movement (PNM) the previous year.

Tunisia

Capital: Tunis   **Population:** 9,000,000 (1995E)

The Republic of Tunisia was declared in 1957, a year after the country achieved independence from France. Under the 1959 constitution executive power is held by the President, elected every five years, who appoints the Prime Minister and the Council of Ministers. The unicameral Chamber of Deputies (*Majlis al-Nuwab*/*Chambre des Députés*) is also elected for a five-year term by universal suffrage (with a minimum voting age of 20). Following the deposition in November 1987 of 'President-for-Life' Habib Bourguiba and his replacement by Gen. Zine El Abidine Ben Ali, the Chamber voted to limit the President to a maximum of three five-year terms.

In presidential elections on March 20, 1994, Ben Ali was the sole candidate (standing for the ruling Democratic Constitutional Rally, RCD) and was officially stated to have been re-elected with over 99% of the votes cast. In simultaneous elections for the Chamber of Deputies, the RCD won all 144 seats contested in the traditional first-past-the-post district list system. Four of the six legal opposition parties shared the remaining 19 seats, reserved under a newly instituted system for parties which did not secure a majority in the constituencies.

Democratic Constitutional Rally
Rassemblement Constitutionnel Démocratique (RCD)
   Address. blvd 9 Avril 1938, Tunis
   Telephone. (#216-1) 560393
   Fax. (#216-1) 569143
   Leadership. Zine El Abidine Ben Ali (chair), Hamed Karoui (deputy chair), Chedli Neffati (secretary-general)

Founded in 1934 as the Neo-Destour Party—a breakaway group from the old Destour (Constitution) Party—the organization led the movement for independence and for a republic, adopting in effect a single party framework between 1963 and the early 1980s. The party used the name Destourian Socialist Party from 1964 to 1988. The change to its present name at the end of that period was intended to reflect a greater political openness under President Ben Ali.

The RCD has a moderate left-wing republican orientation. At a congress held in July 1993 it confirmed its commitment to free-market economic policies and its opposition to Islamic fundamentalist militancy. Despite the controlled and limited multi-partyism implemented since 1981, the RCD has retained its monopoly of power, winning 144 of the 163 seats in the Chamber of Deputies in the 1994 elections against nominal opposition from six parties. In local elections held in May 1995 the RCD won control of all 257 municipalities.

The RCD is a member party of the Socialist International.

Democratic Socialist Movement
Mouvement des Démocrates Socialistes (MDS)
   Address. c/o Chambre des Députés, Tunis
   Leadership. Mohamed Mouada (president)

Legally registered in 1983, the MDS was originally organized in 1977 by a number of former cabinet members from the ruling party who sought greater political liberalization in Tunisia. The MDS boycotted legislative elections in 1986, following the arrest and disqualification of its leader Ahmed Mestiri from running for legislative office, and failed to secure representation in the 1989 poll, after which Mestiri resigned as secretary-general. The party also boycotted municipal elections in June 1990 in protest against the failure of democratization efforts in the country.

In March 1994 the MDS supported Zine El Abidine Ben Ali for re-election as President but challenged the ruling Democratic Constitutional Rally in the national legislative balloting. Although no MDS candidates were successful on their own, 10 subsequently entered the Chamber of Deputies under the new electoral arrangement guaranteeing the opposition a minimal number of seats.

Liberal Social Party
Parti Social Liberal (PSL)
   Address. 3b rue Gandhi, Tunis
   Telephone. (#216–1) 341023

Leadership. Mounir Beji (secretary-general)

Advocating liberal social and political policies and economic reforms, the PSL was officially recognized as a legal party in September 1988 under the name of the Social Party for Progress (*Parti Social pour le Progrès*, PSP). The party assumed its present name in October 1994.

Popular Union Party
Parti de l'Unité Populaire (PUP)
  Address. 7 rue d'Autriche, 1002 Tunis
  Telephone. (#216–1) 289678
  Fax. (#216–1) 796031
  Leadership. Mohamed Belhadj Amor (secretary-general)

The PUP evolved out of a factional conflict within the Popular Unity Movement over the issue of participation in the 1981 legislative elections. It was officially recognized in 1983 as a legal organization. The party failed to win legislative representation in the elections in 1989, but secured two of the 19 seats proportionally allocated in the Chamber of Deputies to opposition parties in March 1994.

Renewal Movement
Mouvement de la Rénovation (MR)
  Address. c/o Chambre des Députés, Tunis
  Leadership. Mohamed Harmel (secretary-general), Mohamed Ali el Halouani (chair)

Formerly the Tunisian Communist Party (PCT), the MR adopted its new name at an April 1993 congress when it was announced that Marxism had been abandoned as official party doctrine. The PCT had been banned in 1963, regaining legality in 1981. In 1986 it boycotted the legislative elections because it was debarred from presenting a "Democratic Alliance" list with the then illegal Progressive Socialist Rally. The party was critical of the government's emphasis on free-market economic policies but initially welcomed President Ben Ali's political liberalization measures in the late 1980s. However, it subsequently became disillusioned over the lack of progress on full democratization, boycotting the June 1990 municipal elections, having earlier failed to win any seats in the 1989 national legislative poll. No MR candidates were successful in the 1994 elections, although four party members were subsequently seated in the Chamber of Deputies under the new electoral arrangement established for opposition parties.

Unionist Democratic Union
Union Démocratique Unioniste (UDU)
  Address. c/o Chambre des Députés, Tunis
  Leadership. Abderrahmane Tlili (secretary-general)

Legalized in November 1988, the UDU is led by a former member of the Democratic Constitutional Rally who resigned from the ruling party to promote the unification of various Arab nationalist tendencies in Tunisia. Under the proportional arrangement for opposition parties, three UDU members were seated in the Chamber of Deputies following the March 1994 elections.

Illegal Groups

Communist Workers' Party (*Parti des Travailleurs Communistes*, PTC), an unrecognized splinter group of the former Tunisian Communist Party; its leader, Hamma Hammani, was imprisoned in 1994.

National Arab Rally (*Rassemblement National Arabe*, RNA), banned following its launch in 1981; the organization advocates unity among Arab countries and is led by Bashir Assad.

Party for Labour and Justice (*Parti du Travail et de la Justice*, PTJ), calling for the "installation of healthy relations between labour and capital", led by Khalifa Abid.

Popular Unity Movement (*Mouvement de l'Unité Populaire*, MUP), formed in 1973 by Ahmed Ben Salah, a former minister who fell out of favour with President Habib Bourguiba and who directed the party from exile. The movement reorganized itself as a political party in 1978 but was unable to gain legal recognition. In 1981 Ben Salah was excluded from a government amnesty and he urged the party not to participate in national elections in that year. This caused a split between his supporters and the faction which broke away to form the Popular Union Party. Although Ben Salah returned to Tunisia in 1988, the government refused to restore his civil rights, thereby preventing his participation in national elections. The MUP is a consultative member of the Socialist International.

Renaissance Party (*Hizb al-Nahda/Parti de la Renaissance*), formed in 1981 as the Islamic Tendency Movement (*Mouvement de la Tendance Islamique*, MTI) by fundamentalists inspired by the 1979 Iranian revolution, and renamed in 1989. MTI adherents were harassed under the Bourguiba regime, and although President Ben Ali initially adopted a more conciliatory approach, the movement was denied legal status on the grounds that it remained religion-based. However, the party's "independent" candidates collected a significant percentage of the total popular vote in the 1989 elections. Despite the party's denials of any complicity in violent or revolutionary activity, the government labelled it a terrorist organization in the early 1990s and took repressive action against it, including sentencing its leader in exile, Rachid Ghanouchi, to life imprisonment.

Turkey

Capital: Ankara **Population:** 61,500,000 (1995E)

Under a new constitution approved by referendum in November 1982, Turkey is a democratic secular state in which legislative authority is vested in a unicameral Grand National Assembly (*Büyük Millet Meclisi*) currently of 550 members, who are elected by universal adult suffrage for a maximum five-year term by a system of proportional representation. Executive power is exercised by a President and a Council of Ministers headed by a Prime Minister appointed by the President subject to parliamentary approval. The new constitutional arrangements were introduced by the National Security Council (NSC), in power since the military coup of September 1980; in accordance with its provisions, the chairman of the NSC, Gen. Kenan Evren, continued as head of state until 1989, when a new President was elected by the Grand National Assembly for a seven-year term. The 1982 constitution bars the formation of political parties on an ethnic, class or trade union basis, as well as those professing communism, fascism or religious fundamentalism. It also specifies, in Article 96, that Assembly deputies are debarred from changing party allegiance once elected (although this provision has been circumvented by the stratagem of founding new parties and then dissolving them prior to mergers with other parties).

Following a partial lifting of the ban on political activity in April 1983, elections to the Grand National Assembly were held in November 1983 under close supervision by the NSC, although the latter body was dissolved the following month in a qualified restoration of civilian rule. By March 1987 martial law had been lifted in all provinces except the four with Kurdish-speaking majorities. Further elections to the Assembly, enlarged from 400 to 450 members, were held in November 1987 under freer conditions, although a stipulation that at least 10% of the valid votes was required for representation restricted the number of parties obtaining seats to three. Prior to those elections, a referendum in September 1987 had produced a narrow majority (50.2%) in favour of lifting the current 10–year ban (until 1992) on over 100 political figures who had been prominent before the 1980 military coup. This decision did not affect the continuing ban on Marxist parties such as the United Communist Party of Turkey (TBLP) or that on militant Kurdish groupings such as the Kurdish Workers' Party (PKK).

The most recent elections, held on Dec. 24, 1995, for an Assembly enlarged to 550 members, resulted as follows: Welfare Party 158 seats (with 21.4% of the vote), True Path Party 135 (19.2%), Motherland Party 132 (19.7%), Democratic Left Party 76 (14.6%), Republican People's Party 49 (10.7%).

Democratic Left Party
Demokratik Sol Partisi (DSP)
  Address. Fevzi Cakmak cad. 17, Ankara
  Telephone. (#90–312) 212–4950
  Fax. (#90–312) 221–3474
  Leadership. Bülent Ecevit (chair), Zeki Sezer (secretary-general)
  The DSP has a social democratic orientation, following the secular and republican principles enunciated by Kemal Atatürk, founder of modern Turkey and of the historic Republican People's Party (CHP). The party was founded in July 1984 mainly by former members of the CHP, which until it was banned following the October 1980 military coup had been led by Bülent Ecevit, who had served two terms as Prime Minister in the 1970s. On the creation in November 1985 of the rival Social Democratic Popular Party (SHP), the

DSP was formally established as a party under the chairmanship of Rahsan Ecevit, wife of the former Prime Minister, who himself remained subject to a 10–year political ban under transitional provisions of the 1982 constitution.

Having accused the SHP of falsely claiming to represent Turkey's social democrats, Rahsan Ecevit in January 1986 concluded an agreement with the conservative True Path Party (DYP) on the need for a "constitution of national reconciliation". In December 1986 the DSP was joined by 20 SHP Assembly deputies (by way of a short-lived People's Party) and thus was able to form an official parliamentary group (then numbering 23 members). Over this period Bülent Ecevit was prosecuted several times for allegedly contravening the political ban to which he was still subject. However, following a September 1987 referendum decision in favour of lifting the ban, he was elected chair of the DSP, with his wife becoming deputy chair. In the November 1987 Assembly elections the DSP failed to achieve the 10% minimum of the valid votes required for representation, although it headed the list of unsuccessful parties with 8.5% of the vote. After the elections Ecevit announced his intention to resign as DSP chair, this being formally accomplished at a party congress in March 1988, when Necdet Karababa was elected as his successor. In January 1989, however, Ecevit made a comeback, being once again elected DSP leader.

The DSP achieved Assembly representation in the October 1991 elections, although it was allocated only seven seats, whereas the SHP and its allies won 88. The lifting in July 1992 of the ban on organization of the CHP gave rise to a fierce struggle between the DSP and the SHP to acquire the mantle of the historic party, this being "won" by the SHP to the extent that the SHP eventually dissolved itself into the revived CHP. The DSP took its revenge in the December 1995 Assembly elections, decisively out-polling the CHP and advancing strongly to 76 seats on a 14.6% vote share. It then participated in talks between the secular parties on forming a coalition government, but these became deadlocked over who should be the Prime Minister, to which post Ecevit laid claim on the strength of his party's gains. The consequence was that the DSP continued in opposition, initially to a government of the secular centre-right parties and from June 1996 to a coalition of the Islamist Welfare Party and the secular DYP.

Motherland Party

Anavatan Partisi (ANAP)
   Address. Karsisi 13 cad. 3, Balgat, Ankara
   Telephone. (#90–312) 286–5000
   Fax. (#90–312) 286–5019

Leadership. Mesut Yilmaz (chair), Ekrem Pakdemirli (deputy chair)

Founded in May 1983 by former senior minister Turgut Özal, the conservative and nationalist ANAP aspires to occupy the political ground held by the pre-1980 Justice Party. It supports a free market economy and closer relations with other Islamic countries, while favouring Turkish accession to the European Union. Launched in the wake of the partial restoration of open political activity in March 1983, the ANAP had some initial skirmishes with the military but was allowed to contest the November 1983 Assembly elections. It won an absolute majority (212 of the 400 seats) against two other parties, whereupon Özal became Prime Minister. By now favoured by the military as a guarantor of political stability, the ANAP subsequently experienced internal dissension between its moderate and Islamic fundamentalist factions; but the party was strengthened by the adherence of 22 independent Assembly deputies in May 1986, following the dissolution of the Nationalist Democracy Party (MDP). In December 1986, moreover, the small Free Democratic Party, founded in May 1986 by other independent deputies who had in many cases previously been members of the MDP, decided to merge with the ANAP (although about a quarter of the FDP Assembly contingent of some 20 deputies decided instead to join the True Path Party (DYP)).

In the November 1987 Assembly elections, the ANAP retained its overall majority, winning 292 of the 450 seats on the strength of 36.3% of the vote. The following month Özal formed a new government notable for the inclusion of two prominent liberals (one of them his own younger brother, Yusuf Özal) and for the exclusion (apparently at the insistence of President Evren) of the then ANAP deputy chair, Mehmet Kececiler, a prominent Islamic fundamentalist. Prime Minister Özal in 1988 proposed a merger between the ANAP and the DYP, with the aim of creating a parliamentary majority large enough to pass constitutional amendments without need to obtain referendum endorsement. However, he was rebuffed by the DYP, whose then leader, Süleyman Demirel, described Özal a "a calamity for the nation".

On Özal's elevation to the presidency in November 1989, he effectively conferred the succession to the ANAP leadership and premiership on the Assembly's Speaker, Yildrim Akbulut. Amid deteriorating economic conditions, Akbulut presided over a catastrophic slump in the ANAP's popular standing, not least because of a furore surrounding the installation of the President's wife Semra as chair of the ANAP's powerful Istanbul section in April 1991. Although supposedly now above party politics, President Özal continued to pull the ANAP strings through his wife and others, as evidenced in June 1991 when Akbulut was defeated in an ANAP leadership contest by Mesut Yilmaz (a former Foreign Minister), who thus became Prime Minister. Persuaded to call early general elections in October 1991, Yilmaz led the ANAP to comprehensive defeat, its Assembly representation slumping from 275 to 115 seats (out of 450), on a vote share of 24%.

In opposition to a centre-left coalition headed by the DYP, the ANAP experienced much factionalism and lost its founder and supreme leader when President Özal died of a heart attack in April 1993. Despite the travails of the resultant Çiller government, the ANAP came under increasing challenge on the conservative/Islamist right from the Welfare Party (RP), to which it lost heavily in local elections in March 1994. When the Çiller government collapsed in September 1995, personal antipathy between Yilmaz and Turkey's first female leader at that stage precluded the obvious solution of an ANAP/DYP coalition. General elections in December 1995 served to chasten both secular centre-right parties; but the ANAP at least gained seats on the strength of the expansion of the Assembly complement from 450 to 550 members, winning 132 seats on a reduced vote of 19.7%.

In protracted post-election negotiations, the ANAP found no basis for co-operation with the RP; instead, Yilmaz and Çiller were sufficiently reconciled to enable the formation of an ANAP/DYP coalition government in March 1996, with the ANAP leader taking first turn as Prime Minister. He had only three months in the top political job, being forced to resign in early June after the DYP had withdrawn from the coalition in late May when Yilmaz declined to back Çiller against allegations of corruption under her recent premiership. The upshot was that the ANAP again found itself in opposition, this time to a coalition of the RP and the DYP. In local elections in June 1996 the ANAP improved marginally on its general election performance, to 21% of the vote, but was again outpolled by the RP.

The ANAP is affiliated to the International Democrat Union.

Republican People's Party
Cumhuriyet Halk Partisi (CHP)
Address. Willy Brandt S. 5, Çankaya, Ankara
Telephone. (#90–312) 468–8922
Fax. (#90–312) 468–8906
Leadership. Deniz Baykal (chair), Fikri Saglar (general secretary)

The original CHP was established in 1923 by Kemal Atatürk, the founder of modern Turkey, and became the country's main force for modernization and secularization. It was the only political party until 1946, thereafter becoming a mainstream moderate left-wing formation which was in power in the 1970s under the premiership of Bülent Ecevit but was proscribed following the 1980 military coup. Successor parties included the Social Democratic Popular Party (*Sosyal Demokrasi Halkci Partisi*, SHP), as well as the Democratic Left Party (DSP) led by Ecevit. Founded in November 1985, the SHP was a merger of the Popular Party (PP) and the Social Democratic Party (SODEP) led by Prof. Erdal Inönü (son of former President Ismet Inönü, a pre-1980 leader of the CHP).

Of the two SHP constituent parties, the PP had been formed in May 1983 under the leadership of Necdet Calp and became the main parliamentary opposition party in the November 1983 elections, winning 117 of the 400 Assembly seats and about 30% of the vote, in part because other left-wing parties had been excluded from participation. In the March 1984 local elections, however, its support slipped to 8%, whereas SODEP (formed in June 1983 but excluded from the November 1983 elections) came in second place with 23.3%. Thereafter the PP became divided as to its future strategy, and Calp was replaced in June 1985 by Prof. Aydin Guven Gurkan, who at first explored the possibility of a merger with the DSP but who in July 1985 signed a unity protocol with SODEP under which the latter would be absorbed into the PP's legal structure. Meanwhile, a proposal that SODEP should itself unite with the DSP had also proved abortive. On the formal accomplishment of the PP-SODEP merger (in November 1985), a number of PP Assembly deputies resigned from the party in protest; nevertheless, the new grouping was the largest opposition group in the Assembly at that point.

Prof. Inönü replaced Prof. Guven Gurken as leader of the new SHP at its first congress in June 1986 and in September 1986 was elected to the Grand National Assembly in one of a series of by-elections in which the SHP polled 22.7% of the vote. In December 1986 the SHP was weakened by the defection of 20 of its Assembly deputies to the DSP (via a short-lived People's Party). Nevertheless, in the November 1987 Assembly elections the SHP emerged as substantially the strongest left-wing party (and still the main parliamentary opposition), winning 99 of the 450 seats and 24.8% of the vote. It was weakened in late 1989 when 10 Kurdish SHP deputies left the party in protest against the earlier expulsion of seven Kurdish deputies who had participated in a Kurdish conference in Paris in defiance of party policy. However, the People's Labour Party (*Halkim Emek Partisi*, HEP) formed by these dissidents in June 1990 contested the October 1991 Assembly elections on a joint list with the SHP, their respective seat tallies being 22 and 66. The outcome was that the SHP became the junior partner in a coalition with the True Path Party (DYP) committed to an ambitious programme of economic and social reform.

The SHP's role as guarantor of a parliamentary majority for the DYP became increasingly difficult in 1992–93. First, most of the HEP contingent opted for independence, forming the Democracy Party (*Demokrasi Partisi*, DP) when the HEP was banned in June 1993 and the People's Democracy Party when the DP was banned in June 1994. Second, the lifting of the official ban on the CHP in July 1992 divided the SHP between those who wished to return to the banner of the historic party and those preferring to maintain the SHP as the authentic successor to the CHP. The formal relaunching of the CHP in September 1992, under the leadership of Demiz Baykal and with 21 SHP deputies declaring support, added to the flux. By June 1993 Inönü was ready to announce his retirement, being succeeded in September by Murat Karayalcins both as party leader and as Deputy Prime Minister. More infighting ensued, until in February 1995 the SHP was formally merged into the CHP under the chairmanship of Hikmet Cetin, a former SHP Foreign Minister and an ethnic Kurd. After some initial uncertainty, the CHP became the DYP's junior coalition partner, with changes in its ministerial team that included the return of Inönü as Foreign Minister.

Participation in an unpopular government became increasingly unpopular in the CHP, which in September 1995 restored Baykal to the leadership on a pledge, carried out immediately, to take the party out of the ruling coalition. In the resultant general elections in December, the CHP was punished by the electorate, winning only 10.7% of the vote and 49 seats, well behind the DSP. Discussions on a broad-based coalition of secular parties (including the CHP and the DSP) came to nothing, so the CHP went into opposition, first to a coalition of the Motherland Party and the DYP and from June 1996 to one of the Islamist Reform Party and the DYP.

The CHP is a member party of the Socialist International.

True Path Party
Dogru Yol Partisi (DYP)
 Address. Selanik cad. 40, Kizilay, Ankara
 Telephone. (#90–312) 417–2241
 Fax. (#90–312) 418–5657
 Leadership. Tansu Çiller (chair), Ali Sevki Erek (secretary-general)

The moderate conservative DYP was founded in May 1983 with the aim of occupying the same political ground as the pre-1980 Justice Party, which had been in government at the time of the October 1980 military coup under the premiership of Süleyman Demirel. The latter was regarded as the principal influence behind the new party (of which Yildirim Avci became the first leader), although at that stage he was barred from political activity by a 10–year ban applied to prominent pre-1980 politicians under transitional provisions of the 1982 constitution. After being excluded from the November 1983 Assembly elections, the DYP took part in local elections in March 1984, coming in third place with some 13.5% of the vote. The following month the state prosecutor applied to the Constitutional Court for a ruling that the DYP should be closed down on the grounds that it was in fact a continuation of a banned party; but this application was rejected by the court in September 1984.

In January 1986 the then DYP leader, Husamettin Cindoruk (who had succeeded Avci in May 1985), signed an agreement with the then leader of the Democratic Left Party (DSP), Rahsan Ecevit, on the need for a "constitution of reconciliation". In May 1986 the DYP was strengthened by the adherence of about 20 independent Assembly deputies, most of whom had previously been members of the Nationalist Democracy Party prior to its dissolution earlier that month. Moreover, in December 1986 not only did a majority faction of the small Citizens' Party formed in March 1986 as a breakaway from the then ruling Motherland Party (ANAP) decide to merge with the DYP but also five Assembly members of the Free Democratic Party disregarded a majority decision to merge with the ANAP and instead joined the DYP.

Süleyman Demirel assumed the leadership of the DYP in September 1987, following a referendum decision that month in favour of lifting the existing ban on him and other pre-1980 political leaders. In the Grand National Assembly elections of November 1987 the DYP came in third place (of only three parties which secured representation), with 59 of the 450 seats and 19.3% of the vote. It therefore remained in opposition to another government of the ANAP, which became increasingly erratic after Prime Minister Özal's elevation to the presidency in November 1989. In the October 1991 Assembly elections the DYP became the leading party, winning 178 of the 450 seats and thereafter forming a coalition with the Social Democratic Popular Party (which later merged into the revived Republican People's Party, CHP), under the premiership of Demirel.

Demirel was elected President in May 1993 following Özal's death in office the previous month, being succeeded as DYP leader and Prime Minister by Tansu Çiller, a youngish American-educated economics professor, who defeated two other candidates to become Turkey's first woman leader. She brought in a new generation of DYP ministers, but economic woes, never-ending Kurdish insurgency in the south-east and an unstable junior coalition partner were only some of the problems with which she had to contend. The CHP's abrupt exit from the government in September 1995 precipitated general elections in December, when the DYP slumped to 135 seats (in an Assembly enlarged by 100 seats) and a vote share of 19.2%, being overtaken as the largest party by the Islamist Welfare Party (RP). Faced with the RP challenge, Çiller sank her personal differences with ANAP leader Mesut Yilmaz and led the DYP into a coalition with the other conservative secular party, with Yilmaz being accorded first occupancy of the premiership under an agreement that it would revert to the DYP later on. This part of the coalition agreement was not tested, however, because Çiller and Yilmaz quickly rediscovered their personal antipathy. When the latter declined to back the DYP leader over corruption allegations against her, the DYP withdrew from the coalition in May on a technical constitutional issue, forcing Yilmaz to resign. Çiller then sank her previous distaste for the policies of the RP, agreeing that the DYP should be the junior coalition partner in the first Islamist-led government of modern Turkey. Within her party, however, there was strong rank-and-file opposition to governmental alliance with the RP.

Welfare Party
Refah Partisi (RP)
Address. Ziyabey cad. 2, Sok. 24, Balgat, Ankara
Telephone. (#90–312) 287–3056
Fax. (#90–312) 287–7465
Leadership. Necmettin Erbakan (chair), Oguzhan Asilturk (secretary-general)

Founded in 1983 as successor to the banned Islamic fundamentalist National Salvation Party, the RP won some 7% of the vote in the March 1984 local elections. It took the same proportion in the November 1987 elections to the Grand National Assembly, thus failing to surmount the 10% barrier to representation. Determined to overcome the 10% hurdle in the October 1991 general elections, the RP headed a joint list which included candidates of what later became the Nationalist Action Party and the Nation Party. The combined list took 62 Assembly seats. Following the elections, however, overall RP representation was quickly reduced to around 40 seats by the preference of deputies of associated parties for their own

political identity. Further local elections in March 1994 yielded a doubling of the RD share of the previous such vote in 1989, to 18.3% (and third place in the party order), with its victories including the mayoralties of both Istanbul and Ankara.

The problems of the post-1991 centre-left coalition government of the True Path Party (DYP) and what became the Republican People's Party (CHP) assisted the RP cause in the December 1995 Assembly elections. The party startled foreign observers by achieving a clear plurality of 158 seats (out of 550) with a vote share of 21.4%, thus establishing its right to take on national government responsibility. The response of the DYP was to conclude a coalition agreement with the Motherland Party (ANAP), as the other major conservative secular party. But this arrangement broke down by May 1996, with the result that the RP was able to reach a coalition agreement with the DYP under which the RP leader, Necmettin Erbakan, became Turkey's first Islamist government leader since the demise of the Ottoman Empire.

On taking office in June 1996, Erbakan sought to allay fears about the RP's intentions by stressing that "the Turkish Republic is a democratic, secular and social state based on law and the principles of Atatürk". At the same time, he indicated that Turkey's longstanding pro-Western orientation would now have the admixture of closer co-operation with Islamic countries, particularly those of central Asia and the Balkans.

Other Parties

Democracy and Peace Party (*Demokrasi ve Baris Partisi*, DBP), led by Refik Karakoc, founded in 1996 to advocate Kurdish autonomy.

Freedom and Solidarity Party (*Özgurluk ve Dayanisme Partisi*, ODP), led by Ufuk Aras, founded in 1996.

Grand Union Party (*Buyuk Birlik Partisi*, BBP), led by Muhsin Yazikioglu, formed in 1993. *Address.* Tuna cad. 28, Yenisehir, Ankara

Labour Party (*Isci Partisi*, IP), led by Dogu Parincek, left-wing formation that won 0.2% of the vote in 1995. *Address.* Mithatpasa cad. 10/8, Sihhiye, Ankara

Nation Party (*Millet Partisi*, MP), led by Aykut Edibali, founded in 1992 as successor to the centre-right Reformist Democracy Party (IDP), itself descended from the original MP; obtained 0.5% of the national vote in 1995. *Address.* Rizgarh Mah. Gayret cad., Sok 2, Ankara

Nationalist Action Party (*Milliyetçi Hareket Partisi*, MHP), led by Alpaslan Türkes, extreme right-wing formation dating from 1948 and known until 1969 as the Republican Peasant Nation Party; dissolved in 1980, it was continued by adherents as the Nationalist Labour Party (*Milliyetçi Çalima Partisi*, MÇP), launched in 1985, prior to resuming its historic name in 1992; narrowly failed to surmount the 10% barrier in 1995, winning 8.2% of the vote. *Address*. Strazburg cad. 36, Sihhiye, Ankara

New Democracy Movement (*Yeni Demokrasi Hareket*, YDH), founded in 1994 by Cem Boyner, an entrepreneur with the conviction that Turkey can become part of the Western world; won 0.5% of the national vote in 1995. *Address*. Kennedy cad. 144, Ankara

New Party (*Yeni Partisi*, YP), led by Yusuf Bozkurt, founded in 1993, won 0.1% of the vote in 1995. *Address*. Rabat Sok 27, Gaziosmanpasa, Ankara

People's Democracy Party (*Halkin Demokrasi Partisi*, HADEP), led by Murat Bozlak, Kurdish formation created as successor to the Democratic Party (banned in June 1994), itself successor to the People's Labour Party (banned in July 1993), which had contested the 1991 elections on a joint list with the Social Democratic Popular Party (later merged into the People's Republican Party); having obtained only 4.2% (and no seats) in the 1995 elections, HADEP came under official pressure in 1996, 18 of its senior members being put on trial in September charged with "leadership of an armed gang". *Address*. Mithatpasa cad. 39/9, Kizilay, Ankara

Renaissance Party (*Yeniden Dogus Partisi*, YDP), led by Hasan Celal Güzel, obtained 0.3% of the national vote in the 1995 elections.

Turkmenistan

Capital: Ashkhabad

Population: 5,000,000 (1995E)

The Turkmen Soviet Socialist Republic declared independence from the USSR in October 1991 as the Republic of Turkmenistan, which became a sovereign member of the Commonwealth of Independent States (CIS) in December 1991. The constitution introduced in May 1992 provides for an executive President as head of state and government, popularly elected for a five-year term. Legislative authority is vested in the 50–member Assembly (*Majlis*), which is also elected for a five-year term. There is also an advisory People's Council (*Khalk Maslakhaty*), which has 50 directly elected members and also includes the 50 *Majlis* deputies, the members of the Council of Ministers, 10 appointed regional representatives and other senior executive and judicial officials.

A presidential election on June 21, 1992, resulted in President Saparmurad Niyazov of the (ex-Communist) Democratic Party of Turkmenistan (DPT) being re-elected unopposed. In a referendum on Jan. 15, 1994, almost unanimous approval was officially stated to have been given to a five-year extension of Niyazov's term, i.e. until January 1999, so that he was not required to seek re-election in 1997. Elections to the *Majlis* on Dec. 11, 1994, resulted in 49 of the 50 deputies being returned unopposed, most of them being DPT members.

Democratic Party of Turkmenistan (DPT)
Address. Gogolya 28, 744014 Ashkhabad 14
Telephone. (#7–3632) 251212
Leadership. Saparmurad Niyazov (first secretary)

The DPT was founded in November 1991 as in effect the successor to the former ruling Communist Party (CP) of the Turkmen SSR, which had been suspended immediately after the attempted coup by

hardliners in Moscow in August 1991 and was officially dissolved by decision of its 25th congress on Dec 16, 1991. At its inauguration, the DPT distanced itself from its predecessor's "mistakes" but declared itself to be the country's "mother party", dominating all political activity but seeking to engender a "loyal" political opposition. In succeeding years very little of the latter made its presence felt, as the DPT maintained a grip on power every bit as firm as that exercised by its predecessor.

In February 1992 President Niyazov gave an outline of his preferred version of a multi-party system in Turkmenistan, suggesting that veteran Communists in cities should form a new communist party, that former CP officials and supporters in rural areas should set up a peasant party, and that everyone else should join the ruling DPT. In a further pronouncement in December 1993, the President said that a recently formed Peasants' Party would eventually be granted official registration, as the first step towards a multi-party system. However, as of mid-1996 there was no indication that such registration had been granted. In January 1994 referendum approval was given to a five-year extension of Niyazov's presidential, to save him the inconvenience of having to seek re-election in 1997. The official figure of a 99.9% "yes" vote was seen by many observers as reminiscent of Soviet-era election results, as was the burgeoning cult of personality surrounding the former general turned President.

Other Groupings

Democratic Development Party, led by Durdymurat Hoja-Mukhammedov, established in December 1990 as a more political version of Unity of Voice, urging the construction of a working democracy. The party gave only qualified support to Turkmenistan's declaration of independence in October 1991, arguing that independence at that time would only serve to strengthen the totalitarian regime in power. Refused permission to hold it in Turkmenistan, the party held its founding congress in Moscow in October 1991, becoming the main component of the *Genesh* (Conference) alliance of Turkmen pro-democracy opposition groups.

Islamic Renaissance Party, branch of the all-Union Muslim party created in the last phase of the USSR, advocates the revival of Islamic values and practices, but appears to have made little headway in tightly-controlled Turkmenistan.

Movement for Political Reforms, Moscow-based movement of Turkmen and other pro-democracy dissidents, contains many former Communist Party members, inclines to the view that the Niyazov regime can be "reformed from within".

Peasants' Party, reportedly formed in 1993 as an unofficial group of agrarian members of the *Majlis*, following President Niyazov's endorsement of creation of such a party; there appeared to be no urgency in granting legal status to the party.

Turkestan Party, pan-Turkic formation advocating the political and economic unification of the Central Asian republics.

Unity of Voice (*Agzybirlik*), led by Shiraly Nurmyradov, founded in September 1989 as an opposition "popular front", banned in January 1990. This small opposition group based in the urban intellectual elite is concerned with the status of the Turkmen language, cultural discrimination against the native population of the country, ecological damage arising from over-production of cotton and poor water supply, and other economic issues. *Agzybirlik* was banned after it had proposed public commemoration (for the first time in Soviet history) of the battle of Geok-Tepe, when the Turkmens had been forcibly incorporated into the Russian Empire. The movement nevertheless held a founding congress in February 1990, adopting a general opposition platform and urging the creation of a multi-party democracy. Thereafter its members were routinely harassed by the authorities, dismissed from jobs, imprisoned, kept under house-arrest and sometimes even shot. Much respected writer Nurmyradov was arrested in the autumn of 1990 and sentenced to seven years' imprisonment on trumped-up charges; international protests secured his release into exile in Moscow in April 1992. Meanwhile, *Agzybirlik* had been granted official registration in October 1991, only to be declared illegal again three months later. Original members of the movement were involved in the creation of the Democratic Development Party.

Tuvalu

Capital: Fongafale, Funafuti atoll

Population: 10,000 (1995E)

Tuvalu, formerly the Ellice Islands, became a fully independent nation in 1978. The head of state is the British sovereign, represented by a Governor-General. Legislative authority is vested in a 12–member unicameral Parliament (*Fale I Fono*) which is popularly elected for up to four years. Executive power is exercised by a Cabinet drawn from, and answerable to, Parliament, and headed by a Prime Minister elected by Parliament. There are no political parties in Tuvalu, but members of Parliament tend to be aligned with the dominant political personalities. Following a general election on September 2, 1993, the resulting Parliament was evenly divided between supporters of the then Prime Minister, Bikenibeu Paeniu, and his predecessor, Tomasi Puapua, and was, therefore, unable to choose a premier. A fresh general election was held on November 25, 1993. The following month the new legislature selected Kamuta Latasi as Prime Minister in preference to Paeniu (Puapua having decided not to stand).

Uganda

Capital: Kampala

Population: 18,500,000 (1995E)

Uganda became an independent state in 1962 after some 70 years of British rule, a republic being instituted in 1967. In 1971 President Milton Obote and his Uganda People's Congress (UPC) regime were deposed by Idi Amin Dada, whose military government was in turn overthrown in 1979 following internal rebellion and military intervention by Tanzania. General elections were held the following year in which Obote and the UPC were returned to power. The current President, Yoweri Museveni, assumed power in January 1986 as leader of the National Resistance Movement (NRM). The NRM had waged a guerrilla war since 1981, firstly against the Obote government and subsequently against the military regime which deposed Obote in July 1985.

The President is assisted by a Cabinet and a legislative National Resistance Council (NRC), consisting of 210 elected and 68 presidentially appointed members. Although political activity is banned, political parties are permitted to exist and the main traditional groupings, the UPC and the Democratic Party, have been represented in the NRM-dominated government. In 1993 the Government published a draft constitution. The following year a Constituent Assembly was elected, on a non-party basis, to debate, amend and enact the new constitution. Having extended the NRM's term of office in November 1994, the Assembly voted in June 1995 to retain the current system of non-party government. The constitution came into effect in October 1995, after which the Constituent Assembly was disbanded.

In non-party presidential and legislative elections on May 9 and June 27, 1996, respectively, President Museveni was victorious in the former with 74.2% of the vote, while the latter resulted in presidential supporters winning a majority in the new 276-seat National Assembly.

Democratic Party (DP)

Address. PO Box 7098, Kampala

Telephone. (#256-41) 233922

Leadership. Paul Ssemogerere (president), Robert Kitariko (secretary-general)

The DP was founded in 1954, attracting strong Roman Catholic support in southern Uganda. Having been banned from the late 1960s, it became the main opposition party to the Uganda People's Congress (UPC) following the parliamentary elections held in December 1980. After the assumption of power by the National Resistance Movement (NRM) in 1986, the DP was represented in the coalition government under President Museveni. Party leader Ssemogerere, who had continued to campaign against NRM dominance and against the regime's refusal to move more quickly to a multi-party system, resigned his post as Second Deputy Prime Minister and Minister of Public Service in June 1995, announcing that he would contest planned presidential elections as the DP candidate. In the event, under the October 1995 constitution party labels were barred in the

May 1996 presidential elections, in which Ssemogerere came a poor second to the incumbent with only 23.7% of the vote. Factors damaging his cause reportedly included his gravitation to an alliance with the unpopular Milton Obote's UPC and his reluctance to make outright condemnation of the militant anti-government Lord's Resistance Army.

The DP is affiliated to the Christian Democrat International.

National Resistance Movement (NRM)

Address. c/o National Assembly, Kampala

Leadership. Yoweri Museveni (leader), Samson Kisekka (chair)

The NRM was founded in early 1981 as the political wing of the guerrilla National Resistance Army in opposition to the Obote government. The armed struggle had been launched when the political party formed by Museveni in mid-1980—the Uganda Patriotic Movement—was deemed to have won only one seat in the December 1980 legislative elections. The NRM assumed power in early 1986, ousting the short-lived military regime which had deposed Obote, and has since been the dominant force within government.

Uganda Patriotic Movement (UPM)

Leadership. Jaberi Ssali (secretary-general)

Co-founded by Yoweri Museveni in 1980, the UPM controversially won only a single seat in the December 1980 legislative elections, prompting a subsequent guerrilla struggle against the Obote government. Having dissolved upon Museveni's formation of the National Resistance Movement, the UPM re-emerged after the NRM took control in 1986 and several of its members were accorded ministerial positions.

Uganda People's Congress (UPC)

Address. PO Box 1951, Kampala

Leadership. Milton Obote (leader in exile), Luwuliza Kirunda (secretary-general)

The UPC is a mainly Protestant formation, with a socialist-based philosophy, dating from 1960. It led the country to independence in 1962 under Milton Obote and was the ruling party until overthrown in 1971. The UPC returned to power, after the ousting of Idi Amin, with a disputed victory in the December 1980 elections. Obote was again overthrown by the military in 1985, but UPC adherents were included within the broad-based government established by Museveni after the National Resistance Movement assumed power in early 1986. Friction has persisted between the government and Obote loyalists, and a number of UPC offshoots have reportedly taken up armed resistance to the Museveni government.

Other Groups

Conservative Party (CP), founded in 1979 by Joshua Mayanja-Nkangi, who had been Prime Minister of the then autonomous Kingdom of Buganda between 1964 and 1966 and who later joined the NRM government.

Lord's Resistance Army, claiming to be fighting a "holy war" against the NRM government, under the leadership of Joseph Kony.

Movement for New Democracy in Uganda, formed in 1994 to campaign for a multi-party political system, and headed by Dan Okello-Ogwang.

Nationalist Liberal Party (NLP), formed in 1984 by a breakaway faction of the Democratic Party; its leader is Tiberio Okeny.

Uganda Democratic Alliance (UDA), a grouping of anti-government elements formed in 1987 and led by Apollo Kironde

Uganda Islamic Revolutionary Party (UIRP), formed in 1993 to promote Ugandan Muslim rights.

Uganda National Unity Movement, an anti-government formation led by Alhaji Suleiman Ssalongo.

Uganda People's Democratic Movement (UPDM), formed in 1986 by disparate anti-Museveni forces active mainly in the north and east of the country; signed a peace accord with the government in 1990.

Uganda People's Freedom Movement, an insurgent group reportedly operating in eastern Uganda under the leadership of Peter Otai, who was previously associated with the pro-Obote Uganda People's Front and its military wing, the Uganda People's Army.

Ukraine

Capital: Kyiv (Kiev)   **Population:** 52,000,000 (1995E)

The Ukrainian Soviet Socialist Republic declared independence from the USSR in August 1991 as Ukraine, which became a sovereign member of the Commonwealth of Independent States (CIS) in December 1991. A new constitution adopted in June 1996 vests substantial powers in the executive President, who is directly elected for a five-year term and who nominates the Prime Minister and other members of the government, for approval by the legislature. Supreme legislative authority is vested in a People's Council (*Narodna Rada*) of 450 members, who are elected from constituencies for a four-year term by universal adult suffrage. In addition to defining Ukraine as a democratic pluralist state, the 1996 constitution also recognizes the right to private ownership of property, including land.

The legislature had previously been called the Supreme Council (*Verkhovna Rada*), the most recent elections to which began on March 27, 1994, continued into a second round on April 2–3 and 9–10 and then into further rounds on July 24 and 31, August 7 and November 20, 1994, by which time 45 constituencies had still not produced the requisite 50% turnouts and/or majorities of 50% of those voting. The distribution of the 405 seats filled by end-1994 was as follows: no party affiliation 227, Communist Party of Ukraine (KPU) 90, Popular Movement (*Rukh*) 20, Peasants' Party of Ukraine 19, Socialist Party of Ukraine 15, Ukrainian Republican Party 11, Congress of Ukrainian Nationalists 5, Labour Party of Ukraine 5, Party for the Democratic Rebirth of Ukraine 4, Democratic Party of Ukraine 2, Social Democratic Party of Ukraine 2, Civic Congress of Ukraine 2, Christian Democratic Party of Ukraine 1, Ukrainian Conservative Republican Party 1, Party for the Economic Rebirth of Crimea 1. The "no party affiliation" deputies included approximately 30 identified with the Inter-Regional Bloc for Reforms and 25 identified with Statehood and Independence for Ukraine. Further balloting for the 45 empty seats at last took place in December 1995, but only 14 were filled. An attempt to fill the remaining 31 seats was made in April 1996 (half way through the parliamentary term), but only six contests were resolved.

In presidential elections on June 26 and July 10, 1994, incumbent Leonid Kravchuk (previously identified with the KPU) was defeated by Leonid Kuchma (Inter-Regional Bloc for Reform, but endorsed by the KPU), who took 52.1% of the second-round vote.

Christian Democratic Party of Ukraine

Khrystiiansko-Demokratychna Partiia Ukrainy (KhDPU)

Address. 11/85 vul. Draizera, 253217 Kyiv

Telephone. (#380–44) 546–7676

Fax. (#388–44) 517–2618

Leadership. Vitaly Zhuravskiy (chair), Irina Komeshko (secretary)

The KhDPU was founded in June 1992 by a moderate splinter group of the more nationalistic Ukrainian Christian Democratic Party (UKhDP). Whereas the conservative UKhDP is based in western Ukraine and supported mainly by Uniate Catholics, the KhDPU represents Orthodox Christians in central and eastern Ukraine, a majority of whom are Russian-speakers, and advocates liberal reforms and the creation of a market economy. The KhDPU won two seats in the 1994 parliamentary elections, one in Transcarpathia and the other in Odessa.

Civic Congress of Ukraine

Grazhdanskii Kongress Ukrainy (GKU)

Address. PO Box 3540, 340000 Donetsk

Telephone. (#380–622) 357464

Leadership. Aleksandr Bazeliuk and Valeriy Meshcheriakov

Based in the ethnic Russian community, the GKU grew out of several movements for regional autonomy that appeared in eastern Ukraine in the wake of Ukrainian independence in 1991, the party being formally constituted at two congresses in June and October 1992. As such it paved the way for the strong revival of left-wing forces in the region in 1993–94, for which it has provided intel-lectual leadership. The GKU stands for a federal Ukraine, the use of Russian as a parallel state language in eastern and southern Ukraine, and close economic and political ties with Russia, although it is not as firmly opposed to market reforms as rival leftist groups in eastern Ukraine. Drawing its main support from Donetsk, Luhansk and Kharkiv, the GKU won two seats in the 1994 legislative elections.

Communist Party of Ukraine

Komunistychna Partiia Ukrainy (KPU)

Address. 1/11 prov. Vynohradnyi, 252024 Kyiv

Telephone. (#380–44) 293–4044

Leadership. Petro Symonenko (first secretary)

The Soviet-era KPU was formally banned in August 1991, but a campaign for its revival began as early as the summer of 1992, culminating in two restoration congresses in Donetsk in March and June 1993. The party claims to be the "legal successor" to the Soviet-era KPU, but avoided declaring the June congress to be the "29th" in the party's history and has been unable to claim former KPU property. The party was officially registered in October 1993, the day after President Yeltsin's troops bombarded the White House in Moscow. Unlike other "successor" parties in Eastern Europe, the KPU remains aggressively anti-capitalist and anti-nationalist. It stands for the restoration of state control over the economy, and for some kind of confederative union between Ukraine and Russia. The KPU's populist nostalgia rapidly gained it support in economically troubled industrial areas of eastern Ukraine, especially in the Donbas (where Petro Symonenko had been second secretary of the Donetsk party under the Soviet regime).

In the mid-1994 presidential elections the KPU gave crucial backing to Leonid Kuchma (of the Inter-Regional Bloc for Reform) in his successful challenge to the incumbent. In the parliamentary elections that began in March 1994 (but were not completed when the present volume went to press over two years later), the KPU emerged as substantially the largest single party, with an initial total of 90 seats (nearly all in eastern and southern Ukraine). The party thus became the fulcrum of potential further conflict between the eastern and western regions of Ukraine. In 1995–96 the KPU put up determined resistance to the new "presidential" constitution favoured by President Kuchma, claiming in February 1996 to have collected 2.5 million signatures in support of a referendum on the issues at stake. However, following the final adoption of the new text in June 1996 (without a referendum), the party leadership announced that it would no longer question the constitution's legitimacy, but would instead mount a campaign for early presidential and parliamentary elections, combined with mass industrial action in protest against government economic policy.

Congress of Ukrainian Nationalists

Kongres Ukrainskykh Natsionalistiv (KUN)
  Address. 21/111 vul. Kreshchatyk, Kyiv
  Telephone. (#388–44) 229–2425
  Leadership. Slava Stetsko (chair)

The extreme right-wing KUN was established in October 1992 by the émigré Organization of Ukrainian Nationalists (OUN) as a means of attracting various small right-wing groups into its ranks. Many in the OUN leadership feared that the organization's name was still controversial, while others preferred to maintain a semi-underground existence. An umbrella organization was seen as the best means for the OUN to return to active politics. KUN has therefore absorbed other rightist groups, while indirectly supporting a variety of independents. KUN's programme commits the organization to supporting "democratic nationalism" and a strong nation state independent in all respects from Russia, including withdrawal from the CIS. Economically, CUN veers between the strongly pro-capitalist orientation of its émigré members, and a recognition of the need for state protection for the enfeebled Ukrainian economy.

The KUN was officially registered in January 1993. Although party leader Slava Stetsko was prevented from standing in a Lviv constituency in the 1994 parliamentary elections, the party had considerable support in western Ukraine, where it elected five deputies to the new parliament in its own name and endorsed several successful non-party candidates.

Democratic Party of Ukraine

Demokratychna Partiia Ukrainy (DPU)
  Address. 93/14 vul. Chervonoarmeiska, 252006 Kyiv
  Telephone. (#388–44) 268–5743
  Leadership. Volodymyr Yavorivskiy (chair)

Founded in December 1990, the DPU is the main party of the nationalist Ukrainian intelligentsia, many of whom were the original founders of *Rukh* (Ukraine's pro-democracy Popular Movement). It advances a civic, territorial conception of nationalism, although it favours a unitary state and opposes autonomy for Ukraine's ethnic minorities. It also advocates strong national defence, exit from the CIS and a social market economy. Under the party's first leader, Yuriy Badzio (1990–92), the party moved to the right, forging a close alliance with the Ukrainian Republican Party (URP). However, at the party's second congress in December 1992 Badzio was replaced by Volodymyr Yavorivskiy, who moved the party back into the political centre and away from a possible merger with the URP. The DPU had 23 deputies in the 1990–94 parliament. Poor organization meant that its representation collapsed in 1994 to an official complement of two deputies (although several successful "non-party" candidates were identified with the party).

Inter-Regional Bloc for Reform

Mizhrehionalnyi Blok Reformiv (MBR)
  Address. c/o Narodna Rada, Kyiv
  Leadership. Leonid Danilovych Kuchma and Vladimir Griniov

Former Prime Minister Leonid Kuchma and former Deputy Speaker Vladimir Griniov (both Russian speakers) announced the formation of the MBR in December 1993. Its political base was the Party for the Democratic Rebirth of Ukraine and the various pro-reform forces grouped in the New Ukraine movement (the latter headed by Griniov), together with the Union of Ukrainian Industrialists and Managers (headed by Kuchma) and a variety of business and party structures in eastern and southern Ukraine (including the Crimea). The MBR adopted the slogan "Strength to the state, prosperity to the people, reason to those in power", its order of priorities for political consideration beginning with the individual citizen and ending with the state. Its three main policy planks are devolution of power to the Ukrainian regions, free market reform and strategic alliance between Ukraine and Russia.

Policy disagreements quickly surfaced between Kuchma and Griniov, the former being less enthusiastic about rapid transition to a market economy than the latter. Nevertheless, in presidential elections in June-July 1994, Kuchma unexpectedly defeated the imcumbent, winning 52.1% in the second round after trailing in the first with 31.3%. Important to his success was endorsement by the Communist Party of Ukraine and the support forthcoming from predominantly ethnic Russian regions in eastern Ukraine. In the 1994 parliamentary elections the MBR returned some 30 supporters in the 1994 elections, mostly from the east-central regions of Kharkiv (Griniov's base) and Dnipropetrovsk (Kuchma's home town).

Labour Party of Ukraine
Partiia Truda Ukrainy (PTU)
  Address. PO Box 3327, 340016 Donetsk
  Telephone. (#388–622) 632630
  Leadership. Yukhym Zvyahilskiy, Valentyn Landyk, Nikolai Azarov
Described as the party of "red directors" in the Donbas, the PTU was founded in December 1992 by Soviet-era industrial managers and trade union officials in ethnic Russian eastern Ukraine. It claims to be a centrist party, but its belief in "the equality of all forms of property" and "the union of state and market forms of regulation of the economy" indicates its less than total enthusiasm for the market economy. The party also supports closer links between Ukraine and the CIS, and a "system of several state languages in Ukraine". In June 1993, after a damaging wave of strikes in the Donbas, President Kravchuk attempted to win the region's support by appointing Zvyahilskiy and Landyk as Deputy Prime Ministers in the Kiev government. The former subsequently served as acting Prime Minister from September 1993 to June 1994. Under their influence, the Ukrainian government moved sharply to the left, placing more emphasis on state regulation and "economic stabilization" and delaying measures to promote privatization and credit control.

The party's three main leaders were all returned as deputies in the 1994 parliamentary elections, along with two other PTU candidates (and a few pro-PTU independents). However,in the Donbas as a whole the party lost out to the more effective populist campaign of the Communist Party of Ukraine. In November 1994 Zvyahilskiy became the target of corruption allegations dating from his earlier tenure as mayor of Donetsk.

Party for the Democratic Rebirth of Ukraine
Partiia Demokratychna Vidrodzhennia Ukrainy (PDVU)
  Address. 11/3 vul. Liuteranska, 252024 Kyiv
  Telephone. (#388–44) 228–3870
  Leadership. Volodymyr Filenko (chair)

The PDVU grew out of the "Democratic Platform" of the Communist Party of Ukraine (KPU), formed in the run-up to the 28th congresses of the Ukrainian and Soviet parties in 1990. After the relative triumph of conservatives at both congresses, 28 Ukrainian deputies left the KPU in July 1990 and formed an initiative group to create the PDVU (which eventually claimed the support of 36 deputies). In the economic sphere, the PDVU combines a pro-market liberal element and a social democratic wing from eastern Ukraine (although a section of the latter later defected to the Social Democratic Party of Ukraine). In the political sphere the party favours decentralization and the maintenance of healthy links with Russia and the CIS (most of its members being Russian-speaking), whilst opposing nationalist policies of Ukrainianization.

The PDVU's drift towards the political centre in 1992–93 cost it support in eastern Ukraine. It was almost wiped out in the 1994 parliamentary elections, winning only four seats, with party leader Filenko being defeated in Kharkiv. Post-election analysis showed that much of its potential support had gone instead to candidates identified with the Inter-Regional Bloc for Reform (which became the "presidential" party in July 1994).

Peasants' Party of Ukraine
Selianska Partiia Ukrainy (SePU)
  Address. 6/29 vul. Maiakovskoho, 35200 Kherson
  Telephone. (#388–5522) 24452
  Leadership. Serhii Dovhan (chair)
The roots of the SePU lie in traditional rural organizations of the former ruling Communist Party of Ukraine, which first established the Peasants' Union of Ukraine in September 1990 and then the SePU in January 1992. While collective farm chairmen and heads of agro-industry usually prefer to remain "non-party" publicly, in practice nearly all of them support the SePU, which has been a powerful force maintaining the flow of huge subsidies to the agricultural sector and obstructing plans for land privatization. In alliance with the Communist Party of Ukraine and the Socialist Party of Ukraine, the SePU polled strongly in the 1994 parliamentary elections, winning 19 seats in conservative rural areas. In the new People's Council, it became the dominant component of the Rural Ukraine faction, which claims 36 members.

Popular Movement
Rukh
  Address. 37/122 vul. Shevchenka, Kyiv
  Telephone. (#388–44) 224–9151.
  Leadership. Vyacheslav Chornovil (chair)

The first attempt to unite all Ukrainian opposition groups in a "popular front" modelled on similar groups in the Baltic republics was crushed by the authorities in the summer of 1988. The second attempt therefore brought in moderate elements from the Communist Party of Ukraine (KPU) and the Writers' Union of Ukraine over the winter of 1988–89, and resulted in the publication of a draft manifesto in February 1989. At this stage, *Rukh* (Ukrainian for "movement") still accepted the leading role of the KPU and refrained from any direct mention of Ukrainian independence. This pattern was largely confirmed by the movement's first congress in September 1989, which elected the writer Ivan Drach as leader. The autumn of 1989 also brought the resignation of the KPU's veteran conservative leader, Volodymyr Shcherbytskiy, and the beginning of the campaign for republican elections, which allowed *Rukh* to expand its influence. *Rukh*'s high-water mark came in March 1990, when the movement's front organization, the Democratic Bloc, won 27% of the seats in the elections to the Ukrainian parliament.

Thereafter, *Rukh* lost its status as the sole opposition group. Other political parties began to appear, and Rukh fell increasingly under the control of its nationalist wing. The various elections and referendums of 1991 showed no advance on *Rukh*'s 1990 position, and the movement effectively split at its third congress in February-March 1992, with the more nationalist wing leaving to found the Congress of National Democratic Forces in August 1992. Vyacheslav Chornovil was left in charge of a rump *Rukh*, which formally turned itself into a political party under his leadership at its fourth congress in December 1992. Under Chornovil's leadership, *Rukh* has taken a centrist-nationalist line on most questions, supporting market reforms and a liberal democratic state united around territorial rather than ethnic patriotism, but also advocating strong national defence and Ukraine's immediate departure from the CIS. On this platform, it won 20 seats in its own right in the 1994 elections and subsequently attracted half a dozen independent deputies into its parliamentary group.

Social Democratic Party of Ukraine

Sotsial-Demokratychna Partiia Ukrainy (SDPU)
   Address. 16/24 vul. Tolstoho, 252032 Kyiv
   Telephone. (#388–44) 293–5919
   Leadership. Vasyl V. Onopenko (chair)
   Ukraine's small social democratic movement first emerged in 1988, when various all-USSR groups became active in the republic. In 1989–90, however, the Ukrainian groups cut their ties with sister organizations in the rest of the USSR, organizing a founding congress in May 1990.

However, the congress resulted in a split, with the SDPU thereafter representing moderates who supported Ukrainian sovereignty and German-style social democracy, while the radicals formed the United Social Democratic Party of Ukraine (OSDPU). At its fifth congress held in Luhansk in September 1993 the SDPU moved back towards the left, announcing its departure from the centrist New Ukraine coalition. It won two seats in the 1994 elections and was strengthened in February 1995 when it absorbed the Ukrainian Party of Justice and the Human Rights Party.

Socialist Party of Ukraine

Sotsialistvchna Partiia Ukrainy (SPU)
   Address. 21/41 vul. Malopidvalna, 242034·Kyiv
   Telephone. (#388–44) 291–6063
   Leadership. Oleksandr Moroz (chair)
   The SPU was the first would-be successor to the banned Communist Party of Ukraine (KPU), formed only two months after the August 1991 coup attempt in Moscow and led by Oleksandr Moroz, the former KPU chair in the Ukrainian parliament. Moroz steered the SPU away from open nostalgia for the old system, but in 1992–94 adopted a populist position, attacking the "introduction of capitalism" and the "growth of national-fascism" in Ukraine. He also called for the reintroduction of state direction of the economy, price controls and "socially just privatization". In the sphere of external policy, the party has condemned "national isolationism", advocating closer economic and political ties with Russia and the other CIS states (its more radical members supporting a restored USSR). Unlike the revived KPU, however, the SPU is generally reconciled to the fact of Ukrainian independence.

In June 1993 the SPU formed an alliance called "Working Ukraine" with the Peasants' Party of Ukraine and smaller left-wing groups, in close co-operation with the KPU, although the latter did not join. The SPU claimed the support of 38 deputies in the Ukrainian parliament in 1992–93 while it enjoyed the advantage of being the only organized leftist successor to the KPU. Its pre-eminence on the left disappeared with the rise of the restored KPU in 1993–94, but it nevertheless won 15 seats in the 1994 elections, after which Moroz was elected chairman of the Ukrainian parliament. By mid-1994 the SPU controlled a parliamentary faction of 25 deputies.

Statehood and Independence for Ukraine

Derzhavna Samostiinist Ukrainy (DSU)
   Address. 20/14 vul. Kurska, Kyiv
   Telephone. (#388–44) 242–2183
   Leadership. Roman Koval (chair)
   The right-wing nationalist DSU was founded in

1990 by a former political prisoner, Ivan Kandyba, who aspired to a reincarnation of the pre-war Organization of Ukrainian Nationalists (OUN). The DSU stands for a powerful Ukrainian nation-state within its ethnographic borders, i.e. including territories in Poland, Belarus and Russia. Membership is not open to non-Ukrainians or to former members of the Communist Party of Ukraine. At the third DSU congress in December 1992, the party's only parliamentary deputy, Volodymyr Shlemko, replaced Kandyba as leader; but Shlemko became increasingly at odds with his deputy, Roman Koval (editor of the main party paper), who began to call for the "ethnic cleansing" of Russians and Jews from Ukraine. The DSU formally split at its fourth congress in December 1993 between supporters of Koval and Shlemko, with the latter subsequently opting to merge with the Organization of Ukrainian Nationalists in Ukraine. In the 1994 elections, 25 of the successful independent candidates were identified with the DSU.

Ukrainian Conservative Republican Party

Ukrainska Konservatyvna Respublikanska Partiia (UKRP)
  Address. 189/6 vul. Volodymyrska, Kyiv
  Telephone. (#388–44) 229–3056
  Leadership. Stepan Khmara (chair)
The UKRP was founded in June 1992 by a right-wing faction of the Ukrainian Republican Party (URP) led by Stepan Khmara. Khmara's UKRP is vigorously anti-Russian; unlike the URP, it is also strongly opposed to compromise with former Communists such as Leonid Kravchuk (President until July 1994), whom Khmara had hounded as a "traitor" to Ukrainian national interests. Khmara has been a leading advocate of a nuclear Ukraine, and of support for ethnic Ukrainians in neighbouring Russian territories. In the 1994 elections Khrnara secured revenge against Mykhailo Horyn, leader of the URP, by defeating him in a Lviv constituency.

Ukrainian Republican Party

Ukrainska respublikanska partiia (URP)
  Address. 252024, Kiev, vul. Prorizna, 27.
  Telephone. (#388–44) 223–0306
  Leadership. Mykhailo Horyn (chair)
The URP was the first non-communist political party to be openly formed in Ukraine in modern times (in April 1990) and the first to be officially registered (in November 1990). The party is the direct successor of the Ukrainian Helsinki Union (1988–90), itself a revival of the Ukrainian Helsinki Group (1976–80). The party bases its ideology on the conservative Ukrainian philosopher Viacheslav Lypynskiy and supports "the Ukrainian character of national statehood", while advocating a tolerant approach to the civic rights of ethnic minorities. However, the party has always had more radical elements within its ranks, including Stepan Khmara, the party's deputy leader until he formed the Ukrainian Conservative Republican Party (UKRP) in 1992. Since independence the URP has been a strong supporter of the Ukrainian authorities, standing for resolute national defence, immediate withdrawal from the CIS and a strong, unitary, presidential republic. Economically, the party supports the creation of "a society of property owners" but opposes "socially unjust privatization".

The URP became the best organized nationalist party in Ukraine in the early 1990s, despite lacking the intelligentsia support enjoyed by the Democratic Party of Ukraine. In August 1992 the party was the main founder of an alliance of conservative parties called the Congress of National Democratic Forces. However, despite strong local organization and fielding a total of 130 candidates, the URP performed poorly in the 1994 elections, when it suffered from its often uncritical support for the Ukrainian authorities. Only 11 URP candidates (and one supporter) were elected, party leader Mykhailo Horyn being defeated by Khmara of the UKRP in Lviv.

The URP is affiliated to the Christian Democrat International.

Other Parties

Christian Democratic Alliance of Romanians in Ukraine, founded in November 1991, represents the estimated 190,000 Romanians and Moldovans who live in the Chernivtsi region of western Ukraine (20% of the local population). The party's official programme calls for greater cultural and linguistic autonomy for the Romanian minority, but some radicals have openly called for Chernivtsi to be rejoined to Romania, which ruled the region from 1918 to 1940.

Green Party of Ukraine (*Partiia Zelenykh Ukrainy*, PZU), founded in September 1990, led by Vitaliy Kononov. Motivated by the 1986 Chernobyl nuclear accident, environmental opposition groups emerged in the late 1980s, leading to the formation of the PZU, with some support from the Communist Party of Ukraine. *Address.* 24 vul. Liuteranska, 242024 Kyiv

Liberal Democratic Party of Ukraine (*Liberalno-Demokratychna Partiia Ukrainy*, LDPU), founded in November 1990, led by Volodymyr Klymchuk. Unlike Vladimir Zhirinovsky's misnamed Liberal Democratic Party of Russia, the LDPU is a genuine centrist party, favouring a managed transition to a market economy, greater stress on individual rights, a federalized Ukraine and friendly relations with Russia. *Address*. 40/110 vul. Bratyslavska, Kyiv

Liberal Party of Ukraine (*Liberalna Partiia Ukrainy*, LPU), founded in Donetsk in June 1993, led by Ihor Markulov (a local businessman and adviser to President Kravchuk until 1993). The party favours market reforms but also supports greater autonomy for the Ukrainian regions and economic union with Russia. It claimed to have returned one candidate (standing as an independent) in the 1994 elections. *Address*. 74a vul. Artema, 340055 Donetsk

National Fascist Party of Ukraine, founded in December 1993, led by Fedor Zaviriukha, based in Lviv, stands for the establishment of a "Greater Ukraine" within the borders of the medieval Kievan Rus, including substantial neighbouring territories in Belarus, Russia and Poland.

Organization of Ukrainian Nationalists in Ukraine (*Orhanizatsiia Ukrainskykh Natsionalistiv v Ukraini*, OUNU), founded in January 1993, led by Ivan Kandyba. The OUNU aimed to re-establish the pre-war OUN Ukrainian nationalist movement, but was disowned by the émigré OUN leadership, which backed the rival Congress of Ukrainian Nationalists (KUN). In the 1994 elections the OUNU was soundly defeated by the KUN in the quest for the nationalist vote. *Address*. 1/6 vul. Aralska, 290017 Lviv

People's Party of Ukraine (*Narodna Partiia Ukrainy*, NPU), founded in September 1990, led by Lepold Taburanskiy, who won 0.6% of the vote in the 1991 presidential elections. *Address*. 1 vul. Naberezhna Lenina, A/S 1235, Dnipropetrovsk

Social National Party of Ukraine (*Sotsial-Natsionalna Partiia Ukrainy*, SNPU), founded in December 1991, led by Yaroslav Andrushkiv, an openly neo-fascist and ethnicist party based in Lviv, which favours the expansion of the Ukrainian state to include all the territory controlled by the early medieval kingdom of Kievan Rus. The party has a paramilitary wing, whose symbols and uniforms are reminiscent of those of the Nazi party. The party's 19 candidates in Lviv in the spring 1994 elections won 2.5% of the local vote.

Subcarpathian Republican Party, founded in March 1992, led by Vasyl Zaiats, contends that the Slav population of the Transcarpathian region in western Ukraine form a distinct ethnic group as Rusyns and are entitled to autonomy (which was endorsed by 73% of local voters in a referendum in December 1991). The party's more radical members have openly called for Transcarpathia to be returned to Hungary, which ruled the region until 1918 and from 1938 to 1945.

Ukrainian Christian Democratic Party (*Ukrainska Khrystiiansko-Demokratychna Partiia*, UKhDP), founded in April 1990, led by Vasyl Sichko, based in the Uniate Catholic population of Galicia, of nationalist orientation. The party's Orthodox wing broke away in 1992 to form the Christian Democratic Party of Ukraine. It is affiliated to the Christian Democrat International. *Address*. 10a/4 vul. Turianskoho, Lviv

Ukrainian National Assembly (*Ukrainska Natsionalna Assembleia*, UNA), founded in September 1991 (in succession to the Ukrainian Inter-Party Assembly of mid-1990), led by Yuriy Shukhevych, umbrella organization of radical nationalists. The UNA has a national-corporatist ideology and supports the building of a "neo-imperial" Ukrainian state, independent of both Russia and the West. Its slogan in the 1994 elections was "Vote for the UNA and you will never be troubled to vote again". Three UNA members were elected, standing without party identification. The UNA also has a notorious paramilitary wing, the Ukrainian Self-Defence Forces (UNSO), which claims to have 5,000 men under arms (despite the passage of legislation in 1993 specifically outlawing paramilitary groups).

Ukrainian National Conservative Party (*Ukrainska Natsionalno-Konservatyvna Partiia*, UNKP), founded in October 1992, led by Viktor Rodionov, small right-of-centre party formed as the result of a merger between the Ukrainian National Party and Ukrainian People's Democratic Party in June 1992.

Ukrainian Peasants' Democratic Party (*Ukrainska Selianska Demokratychna Partiia*, USDP), founded in June 1990, led by Serhiy Plachynda. The USDP has sought to challenge the domination of the Ukrainian countryside by conservative collective farm chairmen and agro-industry bosses. It has failed to have much impact outside Galicia. *Address*. 52/61 vul. Chkalova, 252054 Kyiv

Union for Democratic Reforms (*Obiednannia Demokratychnykh Peretvoren*, ODP), founded in December 1993, led by Serhiy Ustych and Volodymyr Prykhodko. The ODP was founded in the western Ukrainian region of Transcarpathia in December 1993 to represent local *nomenklatura*

and business interests. Two to three independents elected in Transcarpathia in spring 1994 are reportedly close to the ODP.

United Social Democratic Party of Ukraine (*Obiednana Sotsial-Demokratychna Partiia Ukrainy*, OSDPU), founded in May 1990, led by Oleksandr Alin. After a split at the founding congress of the Social Democratic Party of Ukraine in 1990, the OSDPU was formed by the more left-wing faction, who based their social democracy on the pre-1917 tradition of the Ukrainian Social Democratic Workers' Party. The USDPU has remained a small group of left-leaning intellectuals.

Crimean Parties

Communist Party of the Crimea (*Kommunisticheskaia Partiia Kryma*, KPK), founded in June 1993, led by Leonid Grach, successor to the former ruling party banned in August 1991. The KPC is relatively unreconstructed, standing for a revived USSR and state control of the economy. It is a constituent part of the Communist Party of Ukraine and would like to become part of a revived Communist Party of the Soviet Union. Party leader Grach came fourth in the January 1994 presidential elections in the Crimea, with 12.2% of the vote. The party won four seats in the all-Ukrainian elections of March 1994, but only three in the simultaneous elections to the Crimean parliament, where it became an opposition party. *Address*. 24 ul. Budennogo, 333017 Simferopol

Democratic Party of the Crimea (*Demokraticheskaia Partiia Kryma*, DPK), founded in June 1993, led by Anatoliy Filatov. A centrist party, based mainly in rural regions and amongst the Yalta intelligentsia, the DPC favours a policy of national reconciliation in Crimea and has allied itself with moderate Crimean Tatar groups. The DPK favours Crimean autonomy, but believes that the peninsula should remain part of the Ukrainian state.

National Movement of the Crimean Tatars (*Natsionalnyi Dvizheniia Krymskikh Tatar*, NDKT), founded in April 1987, led by Vashtiy Adburaiymov, the oldest Crimean Tatar organization, with roots going back to the protest movements of the 1960s, although its first formal meeting was in April 1987, when the vast majority of Crimean Tatars were still in exile in Soviet central Asia. The NDKT is the most moderate of the three main Crimean Tatar organizations, favouring co-operation and dialogue with the Crimean authorities and rejecting the claim of other Tatar parties to sovereignty over the whole of the

Crimea. On becoming leader in December 1993 (following the murder of Yuriy Osmanov), Adburaiymov formally allied the NDKT with the Russia Bloc (headed by Yuriy Meshkov of the Republican Party of Crimea) for the spring 1994 elections, but the NDKT was soundly defeated in the special elections for the Crimean Tatars, winning only 5.5% of the vote and no seats. *Address*. 15 ul. Sovetskaia, S. Christenkoe, Simeropol

National Party (*Milli Firka*, MF), founded in August 1993, led by Ilmy Umerov, a radical Crimean Tatar group named after the party that attempted to establish an independent Crimean Tatar republic in 1917–18. It rejects all idea of compromise with the authorities in the Crimea or in Kyiv, whom it describes as "occupying powers", and seeks to establish an ethnic Crimean Tatar republic in the Crimea, in which the Crimean Tatar language, culture and religion would predominate. The party supports direct extra-parliamentary methods of struggle, although it has accepted subordination to the much larger Organization of the Crimean Tatar National Movement. Umerov became a Crimean deputy in March 1994.

Organization of the Crimean Tatar National Movement (*Organizatsiia Krymskotatarskogo Natsionalnogo Dvizheniia*, OKND), founded in August 1991, led by Rejep Khairedinov, the largest of the three main Crimean Tatar parties, whose roots go back to a founding meeting in May 1989 in Uzbekistan. Most mainstream Crimean Tatar activists are members of the OKND, including Mustafa Cemiloglu and Refat Chubarov, respectively leader and deputy leader of the Crimean Tatar parliament (*Medzhlis*) elected in 1991. Often referred to as the *Medzhlis*, the OKND stands for "the restoration of national statehood" for the Crimean Tatars in their historic homeland, although the movement is avowedly secular and places heavy emphasis on liberal rights and the rule of law. The OKND's position as the main Crimean Tatar political organization was confirmed in the March 1994 elections to the Crimean parliament, when it won 89.3% of the Crimean Tatar vote and all 14 seats reserved for Tatars. *Address*. 8 ul. Samokisha, 333270 Simferopol

Party for the Economic Rebirth of Crimea (*Partiia Ekonomicheskogo Vozrozhdeniia Kryma*, PEVK), founded in May 1993, led by Vladimir Sheviov, Vladimir Egudin and Vitaliy Fermanchuk, backed by local import/export and tourism business interests. Regarded at its foundation as the local "party of power", the PEVK supported pragmatic market reforms within the framework of an economically independent Crimea, being responsible in 1993 for formulating plans for

Crimean fiscal independence and a Crimean central bank. However, the party's close association with the Crimean leadership of Mykola Bagrov yielded a heavy defeat in the March 1994 Crimean elections, when it was reduced to two seats (plus a further four business "supporters"). It won one seat in the 1994 national elections. *Address.* 2/46 ul. Ushynskoho, Simferopol

People's Party of Crimea (*Narodnaia Partiia Kryma*, NPK), founded in November 1993, led by Viktor Mezhak, one of several offshoots from the Republican Movement of Crimea, originally formed as a moderate alternative to the Republican Party of the Crimea (RPK). The NPK stands for a confederation between Crimea, Russia and Ukraine rather than outright Crimean independence or simple reunion with Russia. Nevertheless, Mezhak withdrew his candidacy for the Crimean presidency in favour of Yuriy Meshkov of the RPK, and in January 1994 the NPK joined with the RPK to form the Russia Bloc, which routed the ruling Party for the Economic Rebirth of Crimea in the Crimean elections of spring 1994, winning 54 out of 94 seats. However, underlying tensions between the NPK and RPK made it difficult for the alliance to operate as a single faction in the new Crimean parliament.

Republican Party of the Crimea (*Republikanskoe Partiia Kryma*, RPK), founded in 1993, led by Yuriy Meshkov, derived from the Republican Movement of the Crimea (RDK), which was formed in August 1991 to campaign first against Ukrainian independence and for the maintenance of the USSR, and then in favour of Crimean independence. The RDK's petition campaign to force the Crimean authorities to hold a referendum on Crimean independence collected 246,000 signatures in mid-1992, forcing the Crimean soviet to agree in May 1992, only to back down in the wake of Kyiv's furious reaction. Thereafter the RDK quarrelled increasingly with the Crimean soviet, led by Mykola Bagrov, and fell victim to a series of internal splits, the rump of the movement becoming a formal political party (the RPK). The RPK organized a second petition campaign in the summer of 1993 to force the resignation of Bagrov and the local soviet, which resulted in the collection of 195,000 signatures, but the campaign was frustrated by the Crimean authorities, who invalidated a sufficient number of signatures for the petition to have no legal force. The campaign to elect a Crimean President in the winter of 1993–94 proved to be the RPK's salvation, in that Meshkov trounced the increasingly unpopular Bagrov by winning 72.9% of the vote in late January 1994. For the March 1994 Crimean elections the RPK was the dominant component of the Russia Bloc, which won 54 out of 94 seats, while simultane-

ously urging local voters to boycott the all-Ukrainian elections held on the same day. The RPC's political platform is dominated by the single theme of securing Crimean independence, while its economic policy is a mixture of populist measures (lowering the price of bread), lower taxes to attract foreign investment and plans for Crimean economic independence. The party's campaign proposal to return Crimea to the rouble zone was quickly forgotten after the elections.

Russian Party of the Crimea (*Russkoi Partiia Kryma*, RusPK), founded in September 1993, led by Sergei Shuvainikov, a splinter group of the Republican Movement of the Crimea, more radically anti-Ukrainian than the Republican Party of the Crimea (RPK), supported by Vladimir Zhirinovsky's Liberal Democratic Party of Russia. Whereas the RPK includes both Russians and Russified Ukrainians amongst its supporters, the RusPK is mainly a party of ethnic Russians. Moreover, unlike the RPK, the RusPK favours outright union between Crimea and Russia, rather than an independent Crimea. Shuvainikov came third in the January 1994 Crimean presidential elections with 13.6% of the vote, but by then his party was beginning to fall apart amongst accusations of bad faith and personal corruption. The party won only one seat in the Crimean parliament in the spring 1994 elections, where it is in opposition to the Russia Bloc alliance headed by the RPK.

Ukrainian Civic Congress of the Crimea (*Ukrainskyi Hromadskyi Kongres Kryma*, UHKK), founded in November 1993, led by Serhiy Lytvyn and Ihor Banakh, based in the ethnic Ukrainian community, opposed to Crimean separatism, failed to elect any candidates in the Ukrainian and Crimean elections of spring 1994.

Union in Support of the Republic of Crimea (*Soiuz v Dodderzhku Respubliki Kryma*, SPRK), founded in October 1993, led by Sergei Kunitsyn, representing traditional industrial interests in the Crimea. It had 20 deputies in the local soviet in 1993 and two deputies in the Kyiv parliament (Yakob Apter and Sergei Kunitsyn). During the Crimean election campaign over the winter of 1993–4 Apter was killed in a road accident and replaced by Kunitsyn as party leader at an emergency congress in December 1993. The SPRK takes a relatively moderate line towards relations with Kyiv and with local Ukrainians and Crimean Tatars. In spring 1994 the SPRK formed the *Yednist*, a coalition between the Crimean Tatar Organization of the Crimean Tatar National Movement and moderate centrist parties, but the coalition made little electoral impact on the 1994 elections, winning less than 3% of the vote.

United Arab Emirates

Capital: Abu Dhabi   **Population:** 2,250,000 (1995E)

The United Arab Emirates (UAE) are a federated state of seven sheikhdoms (Abu Dhabi, Dubai, Sharjah, Ras al-Khaimah, Fujairah, Umm al-Qaiwain and Ajman) without parliament or political parties. The highest federal authority is the Supreme Council of Rulers comprising the seven hereditary rulers of the sheikhdoms. Decisions of the Supreme Council require the approval of at least five members, including the rulers of Abu Dhabi and Dubai. The head of state is the President, who is elected by the Supreme Council from among its members for a five-year renewable term. The Prime Minister and the Council of Ministers are appointed by the President. An appointed consultative Federal National Council with 40 members considers legislative proposals submitted by the Council of Ministers.

United Kingdom

Capital: London   **Population (including N. Ireland):** 58,000,000 (1995E)

The United Kingdom of Great Britain and Northern Ireland is a hereditary constitutional monarchy in which the monarch, as head of state, has numerous specific responsibilities. The supreme legislative authority is Parliament, consisting of (i) a 651–member House of Commons, with a life of not more than five years, directly elected under a simple-majority system in single-member constituencies, with the right to vote being held by British subjects (and citizens of any Commonwealth member country or the Republic of Ireland resident in the United Kingdom) above the age of 18 years, and (ii) a House of Lords, in which some 1,200 peers and peeresses have the right to a seat for life. The latter include hereditary peers and peeresses, life peers and peeresses appointed by the monarch, 16 law peers and 26 bishops of the Church of England. The government is headed by a Prime Minister who is leader of the party which commands a majority in the House of Commons. Each candidate standing for election to the House of Commons has to pay a deposit of £500, which is forfeited if he or she obtains less than 5 per cent of the valid votes in his constituency. Any vacancies arising are filled through by-elections.

Opposition parties in the House of Commons are entitled to receive financial assistance from state funds at an annual rate of £2,250 per seat and £5.10 per 200 votes won in the last general election. To qualify for the subsidy (known as "Short money", after the minister who introduced the arrangement in 1975), a party must have at least two MPs or one and at least 150,000 votes. Under this formula the Labour Party became eligible for approaching £1 million per annum on the basis of its April 1992 election performance.

In general elections to the House of Commons held on April 9, 1992, seats and percentage shares of the vote (for the three national parties) were obtained as follows: Conservative and Unionist Party 336 (41.9%), Labour Party 271 (34.4%), Liberal Democrats 20 (17.9%), Ulster Unionist Party 9, Social Democratic and Labour Party 4, *Plaid Cymru* (Welsh Nationalists) 4, Scottish National Party 3, Democratic Unionist Party 3, Ulster Popular Unionist Party 1. (Northern Ireland parties are covered in a separate section below.)

Conservative and Unionist Party

Address. Conservative Central Office, 32 Smith Square, London, SWIP 3HH

Telephone. (#44–171) 222–9000

Fax. (#44–171) 222–1135

Leadership. John Major (leader), Michael Heseltine (deputy leader), Brian Mawhinney (chairman)

Founded in the 1830s, the Conservative Party regards freedom of the individual under the rule of law as its guiding principle. It believes that political arrangements should be so designed as to give people "the maximum degree of control over their own lives, whilst restricting the role of government so that the state exists for the benefit of the individual and not vice versa". The party stands for wider ownership of property and wealth and for lower taxes on earnings, and is strongly committed to the free enterprise system. Believing in the maintenance of the United Kingdom, it is opposed to devolution of power to Scotland and Wales; it is also opposed to proportional representation and supportive of retention of the hereditary principle in the House of Lords. The party is pledged to the maintenance of strong defences and regards the concept of deterrence as central to the nation's nuclear and conventional defence capability.

The Conservatives trace their history back to the 17th and 18th century, but the modern party was formed by Sir Robert Peel, who established the first Conservative government in 1834, shortly before which the term "Conservative" was first used as opposed to "Tory" (a term of Irish origins applied to members of the political grouping which from 1679 opposed Whig attempts to exclude the future James II from the succession to the throne). The party assumed its present official name in 1912 when it was formally joined by the Liberal Unionists (former Liberals who opposed home rule for Ireland and had supported the Conservative Party since 1886). During World War I the party took part in a coalition government. It was returned to power in 1922 and remained in government for most of the inter-war years (from 1931 as the dominant party in a National government) and in the World War II all-party coalition (under Winston Churchill from May 1940 to July 1945).

In the post-war era the Conservative Party has been led by Churchill (1940–55), Anthony Eden (1955–57), Harold Macmillan (1957–63), Sir Alec Douglas-Home (1963–65), Edward Heath, the first leader elected by the parliamentary Conservative party (1965–75), Margaret Thatcher (1975–90) and John Major (since November 1990). After heavily losing the 1945 elections, the Conservatives were in opposition until 1951 and thereafter in power until 1964. The next Conservative government, under Heath in 1970–74, successfully negotiated Britain's entry into the European Community. After being in opposition from 1974, the party was returned to power in May 1979 under the premiership of Margaret Thatcher (the first woman leader of a major British political party). The party was confirmed in power with large majorities in June 1983 (benefitting from the successful British military action in 1982 to reverse Argentina's occupation of the Falkland Islands) and again in June 1987, although its percentage share of the vote slipped from 43.9% in 1979 to 42.4% in 1983 and to 42.3% in 1987. Thatcher's 1987 victory, with a Commons majority of 102 seats, made her the first British Prime Minister in modern history to win three consecutive terms in office.

Under the Thatcher premiership the Conservatives pursued radical right-wing social and economic policies, with the party's moderate "one nation" wing being increasingly marginalized (and referred to derogatively by the Thatcherites as "wets"). Major reforms included stringent curbs on the powers of trade unions, the promotion of individual choice and market mechanisms within the welfare state structure, the sale of council houses and the privatization of many industries and companies previously under public ownership. Her government also cut income tax rates to pre-war levels (although without appreciably reducing the proportion of GDP spent by the state) and presided over an economic boom in the late 1980s, when for a while there was an actual surplus in government finances. During her third term, however, an attempt to reform the financing of local government so that all residents paid a "community charge", not just house-owners, provoked large-scale opposition to what was dubbed a "poll tax". There were also deepening divisions within Conservative ranks over British membership of the European Community (later Union), which many Conservatives saw as being intent on eroding the national sovereignty of member states.

Thatcher positioned herself on the "Eurosceptic" wing of the party, delivering a celebrated speech in Bruges (Belgium) in September 1988 in which she categorically rejected schemes for a federal European state. However, a series of by-election defeats in 1989–90 weakened her position, which was fatally undermined by the pro-European Sir Geoffrey Howe, who delivered a blistering critique of her stewardship following his exit from the government in November 1990. The speech precipitated an immediate leadership challenge by the pro-European former Defence Minister, Michael Heseltine, who obtained enough first-round votes to force a second round, whereupon Thatcher resigned in the face of almost certain defeat. Two other contenders then entered the lists, including the Chancellor of the Exchequer, John Major, who was regarded as the Thatcherite candidate and for that reason was elected in the second-round ballot by a comfortable margin.

At 47 Britain's youngest 20th-century Prime Minister, Major quickly jettisoned his predecessor's more controversial policies (which he had staunchly supported), including the "poll tax". The Conservatives fought the April 1992 election on a somewhat more centrist platform of further privatization (including British Rail and the coal mines), financial accountability in the National Health Service and freedom of choice in the state education sector. In the sphere of economic policy, they contended that the recession into which Britain had descended in the early 1990s would be much worse under a Labour government. Assisted by public doubts as to the prime ministerial calibre of Labour Party leader Neil Kinnock, the Conservatives won an almost unprecedented fourth term, although by the much narrower margin of 336 seats out of 651 (from an aggregate vote of 14.1 million, representing a 41.9% share). Also almost unprecedented was the massive post-election slump in the Conservative government's public standing, as evidenced by disastrous local election results in 1993 and 1994 and the more threatening loss of several hitherto safe Conservative parliamentary seats to the Liberal Democrats. Contributing factors included Britain's humiliating enforced exit from the European exchange rate mechanism in September 1992, representing a traumatic collapse of government economic policy (but not generating any ministerial resignations) and leading to a ramp of additional taxation in direct breach of the party's election pledge to reduce taxes. Also damaging were related internal Conservative divisions over Europe, evidenced in protracted resistance to ratification of the 1991 Maastricht Treaty creating a European Union (despite the much-trumpeted opt-outs negotiated for Britain by Major), and a never-ending series of "sex and sleaze" scandals featuring prominent Conservatives.

In June 1994 the Conservatives fared badly in elections for the European Parliament, falling from 34 to 18 seats (out of 87) with only 26.8% of the vote and losing several seats in the Conservative heartland of southern England. Further by-election and local election disasters in late 1994 and early 1995, with Labour now the main beneficiary, fuelled increasing Conservative criticism of Major's leadership, which the Prime Minister unexpectedly decided to confront in June 1995, when he announced his resignation as party leader (although not as Prime Minister) to force a leadership election in which he requested his critics to "put up or shut up". Only one Conservative dared to "put up", namely Welsh Secretary John Redwood, representing the Euro-sceptic and anti-centrist wing of the party. Major was duly re-elected in July 1995 with the support of 218 of the 329 Conservative MPs and therefore continued as Prime Minister, immediately elevating Heseltine to "number two" in the government as reward for his crucial support during the leadership contest.

Major's leadership election victory had no impact on the historically low opinion poll ratings being accorded to the Conservative Party, which kept losing by-elections no matter how "safe" the seat. It also, unusually, suffered defections from the parliamentary party, one to Labour in September 1995, another to the Liberal Democrats at the end of the year and a third who became an independent in February 1996, before opting for the Liberal Democrats in October. Yet another by-election defeat in April 1996 reduced the government's overall theoretical majority in the Commons to one and another local election disaster in May all but eliminated the Conservative Party from local government. The following month internal party dissension over Europe intensified when 74 Conservative back-benchers voted in favour of an early referendum on whether Britain should surrender further sovereignty to the EU. An important factor in the latest manoeuvrings was the perceived threat to Conservative re-election prospects posed by the new Referendum Party.

The Conservative Party is a founder member of the International Democrat Union. Its representatives in the European Parliament sit in the European People's Party group (consisting mainly of Christian Democrats).

Green Party

Address. 1A Waterlow Road, Archway, London, N19 5NJ

Telephone. (#44–171) 272–4474

Fax. (#44–171) 272–6653

Leadership. Penny Kemp, Jean Lambert and David Taylor (spokespersons), John Morrissey (executive chair)

The Green Party propagates policies which are based on the principle that people must live in harmony with nature within the limitations of the earth's finite supply of resources. Its aims include unilateral disarmament, a ban on all nuclear as well as chemical and biological weapons, an end to Britain's involvement in NATO, an end to nuclear power generation, material security through a Basic National Income scheme, land reform, decentralization, proportional representation and increased aid for third-world countries in the form of grants not loans.

The party was founded in 1973 as the Ecology Party, which nominated 54 candidates for the 1979 general elections, All of them lost their deposits and gained an average of only 1.2% of the vote in the contested constituencies, the party's best results being 2.8% in two. In the 1983 general elections Ecologists contested 109 seats, the highest vote for any candidate being 2.9%. In September 1985 the party changed its name to Green Party, which in the 1987 general elections fielded 133 candidates, the highest vote obtained by any of them being 3.7%. Meanwhile, the party had elected its first two local councillors in the district elections of May 1986, when its candidates averaged 6% in the wards which it contested.

The Greens seemed to make a breakthrough when they obtained 2.3 million votes (15% of the total) in the June 1989 European Parliament elections in Britain (but no seats). However, internal divisions between the moderates and a radical wing weakened the party in the early 1990s. It was also damaged when well-known television sports commentator David Icke, a party member, announced in 1991 that he was the new messiah sent to save mankind (and also left himself open to charges of antisemitism in a new book). The party obtained only 171,927 votes (0.5%) in the April 1992 general elections, when all 253 Green candidates lost their deposits. Four months later Sara Parkin resigned as leader, stating that because of perpetual infighting "the Green Party has become a liability to green politics". Britain's other best-known environmentalist, Jonathon Porritt, also distanced himself from the party. Nevertheless, the Greens staged a minor recovery in the June 1994 European Parliament elections, winning 3.1% of the vote (but no seats).

Labour Party

Address. 150 Walworth Road, London, SE17 1JT

Telephone. (#44–171) 701–1234

Fax. (#44–171) 277–3300

Leadership. Tony Blair (leader), John Prescott (deputy leader), Tom Sawyer (general secretary)

The party was founded in 1900 as the Labour Representation Committee at a conference held in London attended by representatives of the trade unions, the Independent Labour Party, the Fabian Society and other socialist societies, having been convened as a result of a decision by the Trades Union Congress to seek improved representation of the labour movement in parliament. Later in 1900 two Labour members were elected to parliament. The name of the Committee was changed to the Labour Party in 1906, when there were 29

Labour members in the House of Commons. The first Labour government was in office from January to November 1924 and the second from June 1929 to August 1931, both under the premiership of Ramsay MacDonald, although the latter then headed a National government from which the bulk of the Labour Party dissociated itself.

Labour joined an all-party coalition during World War II and won an overwhelming victory in the 1945 general elections under the leadership of Clement Attlee (party leader from 1933 to 1955). His government carried out many social and economic reforms, among them the National Insurance and National Health Acts, remaining in office until 1951. After 13 years in opposition (for part of which the party was led by Hugh Gaitskell), Labour was narrowly returned to power in 1964 and consolidated its majority in the 1966 elections, on both occasions under the leadership of Harold Wilson, who remained in office until losing the 1970 elections to the Conservatives.

Labour returned to office as a minority administration in March 1974 after becoming the largest single parliamentary party in the elections of the previous month, and subsequently achieved a narrow overall majority in the October 1974 elections. Wilson vacated the leadership in 1976 to be replaced by James Callaghan, who was obliged to enter into a parliamentary pact with the small Liberal Party (later the Liberal Democrats) after Labour's majority had been eroded by by-election losses. In the May 1979 general elections the Labour Party suffered a decisive defeat at the hands of Margaret Thatcher's Conservative Party and was in opposition through the 1980s and into the 1990s.

After the 1979 election defeat Labour's left wing gained the ascendancy within the party, this development contributing to the defection of some right-wing elements and the formation in March 1981 of the breakaway Social Democratic Party (later mostly subsumed into what became the Liberal Democrats). Personifying Labour's "old left", Michael Foot (who succeeded Callaghan in 1980) sought to unify the party on the basis of radical policy commitments, while at the same time moving to expel alleged Trotskyist infiltrators of the "Militant Tendency". Nevertheless, in the June 1983 elections Labour went down to a further heavy defeat, its 27.6% share of the votes being the party's lowest since 1918. In an attempt to repair Labour's public image, the party conference in October 1983 elected Neil Kinnock (then 41) as the party's youngest-ever leader. However, in June 1987 Labour suffered its third general election defeat in a row, albeit with the consolation of having reversed its electoral decline by increasing its share of the vote to 31.6% and its seat total to 229 (out of 650).

Subsequent to its 1987 defeat, Labour revised its policies in key areas, notably by abandoning its commitment to unilateral nuclear disarmament and its opposition to the UK membership of the European Community (later Union, EC/EU), for which the party quickly became a great enthusiast. It also moved towards acceptance of the market economy (subject to "regulation" in the general interest), while remaining opposed to privatization. Nevertheless, Labour was again defeated by the Conservatives in the April 1992 elections, although its seat total of 271 and 11.6 million votes (34.4%) represented a significant improvement. Kinnock resigned immediately after the contest and was succeeded by John Smith, a pro-European Scottish lawyer on Labour's moderate wing. Smith continued with the modernization programme, securing the adoption of "one member one vote" (OMOV) arrangements for the selection of Labour candidates and leadership elections, and led Labour to major advances in the 1993 and 1994 local elections.

Smith died of a heart attack in May 1994 and was succeeded in July, under the new voting arrangements, by another "modernizing" and pro-European lawyer, Tony Blair (41). Meanwhile, under the interim leadership of Margaret Beckett, Labour had won a decisive victory in the June 1994 European Parliament elections, taking 62 of the 87 UK seats with 42.7% of the vote and for the first time in recent memory breaking through in hitherto "safe" Conservative areas in southern and central England. Moreover, the so-called "Blair factor" accelerated Labour's electoral resurgence not only in the 1995 and 1996 local elections but also in parliamentary by-elections. Labour was also boosted in September 1995 by the almost unprecedented defection to its ranks of a sitting Conservative MP.

In a symbolic revision of clause 4 of Labour's constitution, a special party conference in April 1995 approved the abandonment of the party's 77-year-old commitment to "the common ownership of the means of production, distribution and exchange". It was replaced by a general statement of democratic socialist aims and values asserting that the party seeks "a dynamic economy, serving the public interest, in which the enterprise of the market and the rigour of competition are joined with the forces of partnership and co-operation to produce the wealth the nation needs and the opportunity for all to work and prosper". In another significant policy shift, the Labour leadership in June 1996 announced that plans for the creation of directly-elected tax-raising assemblies in Scotland and Wales would be submitted to referendums in each country before the necessary legislation was introduced by a Labour government at Westminster.

The Labour Party is a founder member of the Socialist International. Its representatives in the European Parliament sit in the Party of European Socialists group.

Liberal Democrats

Address. 4 Cowley Street, London, SWIP 3NB
Telephone. (#44–171) 222–7999
Fax. (#44–171) 799–2170
Leadership. Paddy Ashdown (leader), Robert Maclennan (president), Graham Elson (general secretary)

The Liberal Democrats are directly descended from the historic Liberal Party, by way of an alliance and then merger between the latter and the bulk of the new Social Democratic Party, initially under the title Social and Liberal Democrats, which was shortened in late 1989 to Liberal Democrats. The party's federal constitution states that the party "exists to build and defend a fair, free and more equal society, shaped by the values of liberty, justice and community, in which no-one shall be enslaved by poverty, ignorance or conformity". The party is committed to continued British membership of the European Union (EU) and of the North Atlantic Treaty Organization (NATO), while advocating the freezing of Britain's nuclear deterrent capacity at the existing level. It also advocates devolution of power to Scotland, Wales and the English regions, an elected second chamber at Westminister and the introduction of a form of proportional representation.

Of the two components of the Liberal Democrats, the Liberal Party traced its earliest origins to the 17th-century struggle by English Whigs in favour of freedom of conscience and civil rights which led ultimately to parliament rather than the monarch being accepted as the country's supreme authority. (The Scottish term Whig was applied to those who opposed the succession of James II in 1685 on account of his Catholic sympathies.) The term Liberal Party was formally used by Lord John Russell in 1839 in letters to Queen Victoria. Liberal governments then held office for over 50 of the 83 years up to 1914. The National Liberal Federation, set up in 1877, was the national political organization and Liberals were the first to produce party manifestos; they also introduced a national system of education, the secret ballot, the foundations of the welfare state and a reform of the House of Lords. During World War I, when the party led a coalition government under David Lloyd-George, it became divided and began to decline, a process accelerated by the rise of the Labour Party on the strength of universal adult suffrage and its trade union base.

Liberals held office in the World War II coalition government, and Sir William Beveridge, a Liberal MP in 1944–45, was the architect of the post-war National Health Service and other welfare state structures created by the Labour government. By now the Liberals' representation in the Commons was tiny, remaining at six seats in the three elections of the 1950s, rising to nine in 1964 and 12 in 1966, and then falling back to six in 1970. In this period the party was led by Clement Davies (1945–56), Jo Grimond (1956–67) and Jeremy Thorpe (1967–76). Under Thorpe's leadership the party obtained over 6 million votes (19.3% of the total) and 14 seats in the February 1974 elections, although in October 1974 it fell back to 5.3 million votes (18.3%) and 13 seats. Undone by scandal, Thorpe was succeeded in July 1976 by David Steel, who became the first Liberal leader to be elected directly by party members. Steel led the party into the 1977–78 "Lib-Lab pact", under which the Liberals supported the minority Labour government in its pursuit of economic recovery between March 1977 and July 1978. But his hope that the Liberals would thereby acquire a beneficial "governmental" aura was disappointed in the May 1979 elections, in which the party won only 11 seats on a 13.8% vote share.

With the Conservative Party now in power under the radical right-wing leadership of Margaret Thatcher and the Labour Party having moved sharply to the left following its election defeat, the Liberal Party's hopes of presenting a viable centrist alternative appeared to be strengthened in early 1981 when a right-wing Labour faction broke away to form the Social Democratic Party (SDP). In June 1981 the Alliance of the Liberals and the SDP was launched in a joint statement entitled *A Fresh Start for Britain*, in which the two parties agreed not to oppose each other in elections. After winning a number of Commons by-elections on the basis of this agreement, the Alliance contested the June 1983 general elections with an agreed distribution of candidates between the two parties. However, although it garnered 7.8 million votes (25.4% of the total), the yield in seats was only 23, of which the Liberals took 17. The Alliance was nevertheless maintained and contested the June 1987 elections under the uneasy joint leadership of Steel and Dr David Owen (who had become leader of the SDP immediately after the 1983 elections). However, a further decisive Conservative victory and a partial Labour recovery denied the Alliance its minimum target of securing the balance of power between the two major parties: its aggregate support fell to 22.6%, with the Liberals winning 4.2 million votes (12.8%) and 17 seats and the SDP 3.2 million (9.8%) and five seats.

Three days after the June 1987 elections Steel unexpectedly proposed a "democratic fusion" of the two Alliance parties, a proposal which was supported with some reservations within his own party but which divided the SDP into pro-merger and anti-merger factions, the latter including Dr Owen and, at that stage, three of the other four SDP MPs. A subsequent ballot of the SDP membership showed a 57.4% majority of those voting in favour of merger negotiations, whereupon Dr Owen resigned as SDP leader (on Aug. 6, 1987) and launched an anti-merger Campaign for Social Democracy. His successor, elected unopposed by the SDP MPs, was Robert Maclennan, a former Labour MP who had joined the SDP on its formation, had initially opposed merger with the Liberals but was now prepared to negotiate in good faith in accordance with the membership ballot verdict. After both the SDP and Liberal 1987 annual conferences had given overwhelming approval to the concept of a merger, detailed negotiations on the constitution and platform of a unified party took place between the two sides. After one false start, these resulted in a modified policy document (published in January 1988) and agreement that the new party should be called the Social and Liberal Democrats (Liberal Democrats for short). Whereas a first policy document had pledged firm support for British acquisition of the Trident nuclear missile system (notwithstanding the Liberal Party's official commitment to nuclear disarmament), the revised version called for the freezing of Britain's nuclear deterrent at a level no greater than the existing Polaris force, adding that the Alliance's 1987 election commitment to cancel Trident would be considered in the light of realities applying when the new party came to power.

Later in January 1988 special conferences of the two parties each voted heavily in favour of proceeding to a further ballot of their memberships to secure final approval of the merger plan. Both of these ballots showed large majorities in favour of a merger, enabling the new SLD to be formally launched on March 6, 1988, under the joint interim leadership of Steel and Maclennan pending an election for a single leader later in the year. On the declaration of the SDP's final ballot decision in favour of merger, Dr Owen announced the relaunching of the Social Democratic Party as an independent formation. It did not prosper and was dissolved in June 1990.

Meanwhile, in July 1988, the merged party had elected Paddy Ashdown as its leader in succesion to Steel. He led what had become the Liberal Democrats to some improvement in the April 1992 general elections, when the party won 20 seats and almost 6 million votes (17.9% of those cast) on a platform which included a commitment to a general increase in the basic income tax. By June 1994 its Commons representation had risen to 23 seats on the strength of a series of stunning by-election victories in hitherto "safe" Conservative seats. In the same month the party at last achieved European Parliament representation, winning two of the 87 UK seats, although its share of the national vote fell back to 16.1%. Thereafter the Liberal Democrats were somewhat eclipsed by Tony Blair's "new" Labour Party, which gained ascendancy as the main opposition party, although the Liberal Democrats were boosted to 26 Commons seats by two Conservative defectors, one at the end of 1995 and a second in October 1996. The response of Ashdown and other Liberal Democrat leaders to the resurgence of Labour was to make increasingly explicit offers of support for a future Labour government in the event that the Liberal Democrats held the balance of power.

The Liberal Democrats are affiliated to the Liberal International, Their two representatives in the European Parliament sit in the European Liberal, Democratic and Reformist Group.

Plaid Cymru (Party of Wales)

Address. 51 Heol yr Eglwys Gadeiriol/ Cathedral Road, Caerdydd/Cardiff, CF1 9HD, Wales

Telephone. (#44–1222) 231944

Leadership. Dafydd Wigley (president), Karl Davies (general secretary)

Founded in August 1925, *Plaid Cymru* seeks full self-government for Wales based on socialist principles, representation at the United Nations and restoration of the Welsh language and culture. It has contested all elections to the Westminster parliament since 1945 but remained unrepresented until July 1966, when its then president, Dafydd Elis Thomas, won a by-election at Carmarthen. Although the party lost that seat in 1970, it won two others in the February 1974 elections (Carnarvon and Merioneth) and added the Carmarthen seat in October of that year, for a tally of three. The party also built up significant representation in local government. In light of this performance, the then Labour government tabled proposals for an elected Welsh assembly, but the idea was rejected by Welsh voters in a referendum of March 1979.

In the May 1979 general elections *Plaid Cymru* obtained 132,544 votes, holding the Carnarvon and Merioneth seats but losing Carmarthen to Labour. It retained its two seats in the 1983 elections, winning a total of 125,309 votes. In the June 1987 elections the party again moved up to three Commons seats by winning Ynys Môn, although its total vote slipped to 123,595 (7.3% of the Welsh total). A month before that contest *Plaid Cymru* had signed an agreement with the Scottish

National Party under which they were to form a single parliamentary group. The April 1992 general elections yielded the party's best-ever result, four of the 32 seats contested (out of 38 in Wales) being won, including Pembroke North, with an aggregate vote of 148,232 (about 8.5% of the Welsh total). In the June 1994 European Parliament elections, moreover, *Plaid Cymru* advanced to over 17% of the Welsh vote, although without winning any seats.

Scottish National Party (SNP)

Address. 6 North Charlotte Street, Edinburgh, EH2 4JH, Scotland

Telephone. (#44–131) 226–3661

Fax. (#44–131) 226–7373

Leadership. Alex Salmond (leader), Winifred Ewing (president), Alasdair Morgan (general secretary)

The SNP identifies itself as "moderate, left-of-centre" on economic and social questions; its basic aim is Scottish independence within the European Union (EU) and the Commonwealth, with a democratic Scottish parliament elected by proportional representation. The party was founded in 1934 as a merger of the National Party of Scotland and the Scottish Party. It won a by-election at Motherwell in April 1945 but lost this Commons seat in the general elections three months later. Thereafter the SNP held only single seats in the House of Commons: Hamilton from 1967 to 1970, Western Isles from 1970 to 1974 and Govan from 1973 to February 1974. In the February 1974 elections, however, the party won seven seats with 21.9% of the vote in Scotland, boosted by the discovery of oil in the North Sea and the prospect that an independent Scotland would be financially viable on the basis of oil revenues.

In the October 1974 elections the SNP advanced further to 11 seats with 30.4% of the Scottish vote, whereupon the then Labour Party government tabled proposals for the creation of a devolved Scottish assembly. But the tide of pro-independence feeling had ebbed somewhat by the time of the March 1979 referendum on the plans, the outcome being that the 52% vote in favour represented only 32.8% of those entitled to vote (the turnout having been only 63.7%). Basing itself on an earlier decision that a higher real vote in favour would be required, the UK parliament thereupon refused to set up the assembly. In the May 1979 general elections the SNP lost all but two of its seats, although it still polled 17.2% of the Scottish vote. Both of these seats were retained in the 1983 elections, but the SNP's share of the Scottish vote contracted to 11.8% (331,975 votes), which was only slightly more than in 1970. In the June 1987 elections the SNP polled 416,873 votes

(14% of the Scottish total) and won three parliamentary seats. Immediately prior to the 1987 general elections, the SNP signed an agreement with *Plaid Cymru* (Welsh Nationalists) pledging mutual support in parliament.

By-election successes increased the SNP's Commons representation to five seats in the course of the 1987–92 parliament, but the party fell back to three in the April 1992 general elections despite increasing its share of the Scottish vote to 21.5% (629,564 votes), just behind the Conservative Party. The SNP recovered the status of Scotland's second party (after Labour) in the June 1994 European Parliament elections, obtaining nearly a third of the Scottish vote and winning two Euro-seats (compared with one in 1979). In May 1995, moreover, the party increased in Commons representation to four seats as a result of a by-election victory over the Conservatives in which it took 40% of the vote.

The SNP's two members of the European Parliament sit in the European Radical Alliance group, the main component of which is the Left Radical Movement of France.

Other Parties

The proliferation of small right-wing, left-wing and other parties and groups which have been active in Great Britain in recent years includes the following:

British National Party (BNP), led by John Tyndall, an extreme right-wing formation founded in 1960 as an alliance of the League of Empire Loyalists, the White Defence League and the National Labour Party. A split in the BNP was caused by the formation of a paramilitary elite corps (named "Spearhead") under the leadership of Colin Jordan and Tyndall, the rump BNP being one of the founder members of the National Front in 1967. In 1982 the BNP re-emerged as an independent party under Tyndall's leadership, contesting 53 seats in the 1983 general elections (losing 53 deposits) and a smaller number in 1987 (with the same result). Although Tyndall had been sentenced to 12 months' in prison in 1986 for incitement to racial hatred, the party subsequently sought to give a "respectable" face to extreme right-wing politics and to develop contacts with like-minded movements in continental Europe. Standing for "rights for whites" and the repatriation or exclusion of coloured immigrants, the BNP attracted some support in inner city areas of high minority population in the early 1990s. Although its 13 candidates all lost their deposits in the 1992 general elections (achieving an aggregate vote of 7,005), in September 1993 it won its first local council seat in the east London borough of Tower Hamlets, an area of high Bangladeshi settlement. It lost the seat in the May 1994 local elections, although its overall vote in the borough increased. *Address.* PO Box 117, Weling, Kent, DA16 3DW

Communist Party of Britain-Marxist-Leninist (CPB-ML), founded in 1968 by Reg Birch (a trade union official) after his expulsion from the Communist Party of Great Britain (later the Democratic Left); once regarded as the largest British Maoist party, the CPB-ML publishes *The Worker*.

Communist Party of Great Britain (CPGB), led by Mick Hicks, derived from a 1988 breakaway by a hard-line minority faction of the CPGB opposed to the latter's espousal of "Euro-communism", leading to its conversion into the Democratic Left in 1991, whereupon the hard-line group took over the historic party name. The new CPGB is closely aligned with the hard-line co-operative that has retained control of *The Morning Star* (once the official newspaper of the old CPGB). *Address.* 1–3 Ardleigh Road, London, N1 4HS

Co-operative Party, led by P. Nurse (chair) and P. Clarke (secretary), founded in 1917 by the British Co-operative Union (the central body representing British consumer and other co-operatives) in order to secure for the co-operative movement direct representation. The party has been represented in parliament ever since, in alliance with the Labour Party whereby its representatives stand as "Labour and Co-op" candidates. There have been Co-operative members in all Labour governments since 1924. *Address.* Victory House, 10–14 Leicester Square, London, WC2H 7QH

Corrective Party (CP), led by Lindi St Claire, advocating liberalization of the laws on prostitution. A prominent spokeswoman for prostitutes, Ms St Claire has contested general and European elections, without success. An independent Corrective candidate won 140 votes in the 1992 elections.

Democratic Left (DL), led by Nina Temple (secretary) and Mhairí Stewart (chair), founded in 1991 in succession to the Communist Party of Great Britain (CPGB), itself founded in 1920 and for 70 years Britain's main Communist formation with the considerable influence in the labour movement in the post-war decades, although its attempts to establish formal co-ooperation with the Labour Party were consistently rebuffed. For long an orthodox pro-Soviet party, the CPGB had moved to a "Euro-communist" line in 1985 backing the return of a Labour government, despite fierce resistance from a hard-line minority. Having fielded 19 deposit-losing candidates in the 1987 elections, the bulk of the CPGB reacted to the collapse of communism in Eastern Europe in 1989–90 by abandoning Marxist-Leninist theory and launching the DL, whose programme stresses environmentalist concerns and the need for left-wing unity, including co-operation with the Labour Party. The DL did not contest the 1992 elections. *Address.* 6 Cynthia Street, London, N1 9JF

Fellowship Party (FP), led by R.S. Mallone, founded in 1955 on a pacifist, socialist and environmentalist platform, claims to have been instrumental in the establishment of the Campaign for Nuclear Disarmament (CND). It has contested numerous elections without any real success, its single candidate in 1992 winning only 147 votes. *Address.* Woolacombe House, 141 Woolacombe Road, Blackheath, London, SE3 8QP

International Communist Party (ICP), a leftist formation which presented four candidates in the 1992 general elections, who lost their deposits and won only 342 votes in total.

Islamic Party of Britain (IPB), led by David Musa Pidcock, founded in 1989 in part to campaign for the banning of Salman Rushdie's *Satanic Verses* but also for other religions to be brought under the protection of the blasphemy laws currently only giving (notional) protection to the established Protestant Christian faith. Advocating state funding for Muslim schools, the IPB fielded four candidates in the 1992 elections, obtaining a total of 1,085 votes and losing all four deposits. *Address.* 1A Hazelwell Road, Birmingham, B30 2PQ

Liberal Party (LP), led by Michael Meadowcroft (a former Liberal MP), founded as an attempt to keep the historic LP in existence following the formation of what became the Liberal Democrats in 1989. The LP obtained 64,744 votes in the 1992 general elections, although only one of its 73 candidate saved his/her deposit.

Mebyon Kernow (Cornish National Movement), led by R.G. Jenkin (chair) and Len Truran (national secretary), founded in 1951 to campaign for the self-government of Cornwall. By 1960 it claimed to have the active support of three Cornish MPs of other parties, although such became ineligible for membership following the movement's 1974 decision to contest parliamentary elections itself. It has gained representation in Cornish local government, often under the "independent" label, but has failed at national level. *Address.* Trewolsta, Trewirgie, Redruth, Cornwall

Militant Labour Party (MLP), led by Peter Taafe, founded in 1993 by the Trotskyist faction grouped around the *Militant* newspaper which had sought to act as a radical pressure group within the Labour Party in the 1980s, until the Labour leadership had resolved to expel such activists. *Address.* 3–13 Hepscott Road, London, E9 5HB

Monster Raving Loony Party (MRLP), led by (Screaming) Lord David Sutch, Britain's premier "alternative" party, founded in the early 1960s, deserving of a listing in a serious reference work because Sutch (a former rock musician) has contested over 40 by-elections, never saving a deposit but sometimes registering a not insignificant vote, as when he obtained 4.8% in a 1994 contest. Known by many variants of its historic title (and sometimes suffering from the intervention of similarly-named but unrelated parties), the MRLP has significant support in the West Country, where at least one follower has been elected to a local council.

National Front (NF), led by Ian Anderson, far right formation founded in 1967, seeking the restoration of Britain as an ethnically homogeneous state by means of the "repatriation" of coloured immigrants and their descendants. It also seeks to liberate Britain from international ties such as the United Nations, NATO and the European Union, and opposes the international financial system and "big business capitalism", favouring instead small privately-owned enterprises and workers' co-operatives. The NF was founded as a merger of the British National Party (BNP), the League of Empire Loyalists and the Racial Preservation Society. It has nominated candidates in all general elections since its formation, rising to 303 in 1979, but has received only negligible support, although a 1973 by-election in West Bromwich yielded 16.02% of the vote. In the 1970s NF meetings frequently led to serious violence, as opponents mounted counter-demonstrations. The right of NF candidates to hire halls for election meetings was upheld by the High Court in November 1982, but NF marches have been banned under a Public Order Act; moreover, NF leaders have been sentenced for "incitement to racial hatred" under the Race Relations Act. In 1984–85 the NF gained publicity when one of its activists, Patrick Harrington, registered at a North London college, provoking a long confrontation with anti-fascist students. Subsequently, the Front sought to improve its image by electing a new generation of university-educated leaders who developed a new intellectual basis for the movement (described as "new positivism") and publicly distanced themselves from the violent street activism previously associated with Martin Webster (the controversial NF organizer ousted from the party in 1983–84). Nevertheless, internal divisions continued, leading to a split in 1986–87 between a "revolutionary nationalist" group and a "radical nationalist" group in 1986–87, by which time the NF had largely been eclipsed on the far right by the revived BNP. The NF's 14 candidates in the 1992 elections all lost their deposits, obtaining a total of 4,816 votes. *Address*. PO Box 760, London, N17 7SB

Natural Law Party (NLP), led by Geoffrey Clements, launched in Britain and other developed countries in a well-funded attempt to secure electoral support for the mystic Indian religious concepts of the Maharishi once espoused by the Beatles pop group. The supposed bliss of "yogic flying" made little impact on British voters in the 1992 elections, when the NLP's 310 candidates all lost their deposits.

Referendum Party (RP), founded by Sir James Goldsmith in 1994 to campaign on the single issue of its demand for a referendum on British participation in European economic, monetary and political union as envisaged under the 1991 Maastricht Treaty of the European Union (EU). A multi-millionaire businessman with dual French and British nationality, Goldsmith had been elected to the European Parliament in 1994 in France for what became the Movement for France and had announced his willingness to put up £20 million to finance an election campaign by the RP in Britain, targeted at constituencies where the sitting Conservative MP would not declare support for a referendum. His initiative alarmed many Conservative MPs concerned about their majorities in the next elections. A furore erupted in June 1996 over the disclosure that an anti-EU think tank run by "Euro-sceptic" Conservative MP Bill Cash had accepted financial donations from Goldsmith. Cash was obliged to end his indirect connection with the Referendum Party, but received recompense when former Conservative leader Margaret (now Baroness) Thatcher made a "substantial" donation to his think tank. In early October 1996 the former Conservative treasurer, Lord McAlpine, caused a stir by declaring his support for the Referendum Party. *Address*. Dean Bradley House, 52 Horseferry Road, London, SW1P 2AF

Revolutionary Communist Party (RCP), led by Helen Simons, leftist grouping founded in 1981. Its eight candidates all lost their deposits in the 1992 elections, drawing an aggregate vote of 745.

Socialist Labour Party (SLP), launched in 1996 by Arthur Scargill to provide a radical left-wing

alternative to the "new" Labour Party of Tony Blair. As president of the National Union of Mineworkers, Scargill had led abortive trade union opposition to the policies of the Thatcher government in the 1980s, becoming increasingly disenchanted with the line of the Labour leadership. In the new party's first electoral contest, at the Hemsworth by-election in February 1996, the SLP candidate won 5.4% of the vote.

Socialist Party of Great Britain (SPGB), led by Adam Buick, a Marxist formation founded in 1904 in quest of "a world-wide community based on the common ownership and democratic control of the means of wealth distribution and production". In the course of its long history the SPGB opposed both world wars, without success. Its parliamentary and local election forays have also met with regular lack of success. The SPGB has links with similarly named and orientated parties in a number of other developed countries, together constituting the World Socialist Movement. *Address*. 52 Clapham High Street, London SW4 7UN

Socialist Workers' Party (SWP), led by Duncan Hallas, a Trotskyist grouping founded in 1950 as the International Socialists and known under that name until 1977. The SWP has worked towards "the building of a nucleus of a serious revolutionary party", not by infiltrating the labour movement but in influencing it in a leftward direction from outside. It does not rule out the use of force in support of socialist legislation opposed by forces of the right. It has not taken part in recent general elections, but it has led militant campaigns through the Anti-Nazi League and the Right to Work movement. It has also worked to oppose what it regards as the rightward drift in the Labour Party. *Address*. PO Box 82, London E3 3LH

UK Independence Party (UKIP), led by Alan Sked, opposed to what it regards as the unacceptable surrender of British sovereignty to the European Union (EU). Having contested the 1992 general elections as the Anti-Federalist League (its 16 candidates all losing their deposits), the UKIP fought most UK seats in the 1994 European Parliament elections, winning an overall vote share of 1%. *Address*. 16 Manbey Street, Stratford, London, E15 1EU

Workers' Revolutionary Party (WRP), led by Mike Banda, leftist formation which rejects "the parliamentary road to socialism" but has contested general elections. A WRP government would nationalize banks, insurance companies, the media and all major industries, repeal all immigration and anti-union laws, end private education, close down the nuclear power industry, establish workers' militias in place of the army, withdraw British troops from Northern Ireland, leave NATO and seek to replace the European Union by a socialist United States of Europe. Descended from the pre-war Militant Group, by way of the Workers' International League and the Revolutionary Communist Party (among other earlier formations), the WRP succeeded the Socialist Labour League (founded in 1959) and at first worked inside the Labour Party. Since 1974 it has unsuccessfully contested general elections. In 1979 it nominated 60 parliamentary candidates who gained a total of 12,631 votes (and no seats). In the 1983 and 1987 general elections it unsuccessfully contested 22 and 10

seats respectively. In October 1985 the WRP's founder and former leader, Gerry Healy, was expelled from the party after an internal inquiry had found him guilty of gross sexual misconduct against young female party members. This action was opposed by a minority faction that included the party's best-known members, actress Vanessa Redgrave and her brother Corin Redgrave, and led to a split which also reflected internal opposition to moves by the leadership to initiate co-operation with other left-wing groups (including the Labour Party). A more immediate cause of the split was a dispute over the ownership of the party's assets of some £1.5 million. The WRP's two candidates in the 1992 general elections won 330 votes between them.

Northern Ireland

Capital: Belfast   **Population:** 1,650,000 (1995E)

Northern Ireland was created in 1921 as an autonomous component of the United Kingdom of Great Britain and Northern Ireland, its territory comprising six of the nine counties in the historic Irish province of Ulster. In 1972 its Parliament was suspended, and thereafter (apart from a brief period in 1974) it has been ruled directly from Westminster, the responsible member of the UK Cabinet being the Secretary of State for Northern Ireland. Under a bilateral agreement of 1985 the Republic of Ireland, which formally asserts a claim to the region, has a consultative role in its governance, expressed in an Anglo-Irish Intergovernmental Council, a lower-level Intergovernmental Conference, an Inter-Parliamentary Body and administrative structures.

Northern Ireland is represented in the UK House of Commons with 17 seats, due to increase to 18 at the 1997 elections. There is legislative provision for a Northern Ireland Assembly, but the last such body, elected in 1982, was dissolved in 1986 (but may be reactivated). A Northern Ireland Forum, with no legislative or executive functions, was established by elections in 1996 to discuss future constitutional arrangements for the region, which were also at the time of writing the subject of separate talks mainly involving the direct rule administration and representatives of all parties elected to the Forum except *Sinn Féin* (SF).

In the UK general election of April 9, 1992, the 17 Northern Ireland seats (filled by simple majority in single-member constituencies) were distributed as follows: Ulster Unionist Party (UUP) 9 seats (with 34.5% of the vote), Social Democratic and Labour Party (SDLP) 4 (23.5%), Democratic Unionist Party (DUP) 3 (13.1%), Ulster Popular Unionist Party (UPUP) 1 (2.5%). The single UPUP seat was lost in a by-election on June 15, 1995, to the United Kingdom Unionist Party (UKUP).

In the Northern Ireland Forum elections of May 30, 1996, 90 of the 110 seats were filled by direct election in 18 five-member constituencies coinciding with the revised Westminster electoral boundaries. The remaining 20 seats were distributed equally among the 10 parties securing the highest vote-share across the region as a whole, thereby ensuring representation for four parties which failed to win constituency seats. The seats were allocated as follows: UUP 30 (24.7% of the vote), DUP 24 (18.8%), SDLP 21 (21.4%), *Sinn Féin* 17 (15.5%), Alliance Party of Northern Ireland 7 (6.5%), UKUP 3 (3.7%), Progressive Unionist Party 2 (3.5%),

Ulster Democratic Party 2 (2.2%), Women's Coalition 2 (1%), Labour Coalition 2 (0.8 per cent). (All of these parties, except *Sinn Féin*, were invited by the British government to take part in talks. *Sinn Féin* did not participate in the Forum, and the SDLP initially took part but withdrew in July.)

The three Northern Ireland seats in the European Parliament have always been held by the DUP, the SDLP and the UUP. Under a proportional representation system (unlike the rest of the UK), they gained in 1994, respectively, 29.2, 28.9 and 23.8% of first-preference votes.

Alliance Party of Northern Ireland (Alliance, or APNI)

Address. 88 University Street, Belfast, BT7 1HE
Telephone. (#44-1232) 324274
Fax. (#44-1232) 333147
Leadership. Lord (John) Alderdice (leader), Addie Morrow (president), David Ford (general secretary)

Alliance, as the party is usually known, was founded in April 1970 as a centrist, non-sectarian unionist party, drawing support from the moribund Ulster Liberal Party and the moderate (Faulknerite) Unionist Party of Northern Ireland. It advocates the restoration of a devolved government with the sharing of power between the Catholic and Protestant sections of the community. The party, which has tended to have a mainly Protestant following, but Catholic leaders, is generally regarded as a liberal middle-class formation, and is strongly opposed to political violence. It was the only unionist party to support the Anglo-Irish Agreement of November 1985.

It first contested elections in 1973, winning 9.2% of the vote for the Northern Ireland Assembly. In January 1974 it joined a "power-sharing" Executive (provincial government) with Brian Faulkner's faction of the Ulster Unionist Party and with the Social Democratic and Labour Party. (That Executive collapsed in May 1974.) In the May 1975 Constitutional Convention elections Alliance obtained 9.8% of the vote, and its support peaked in the 1977 local government elections, when it came third with 14.3%. In the Assembly elections of October 1982 it won 10 of the 78 seats, with 9.3%. In the June 1983 UK general elections it polled 8% of the vote, and in those of June 1987 9.9%.

John Cushnahan, who had succeeded Oliver Napier as party leader in 1984, resigned in October 1987 and was succeeded by John T. Alderdice (who was ennobled in 1996). In the 1989 local, 1992 general and 1993 local elections the party secured 6.8, 8.7 and 7.7% of the vote respectively, which fell to 4.1% in the 1994 European polls but recovered to 6.5% in the 1996 Forum elections.

Alliance is a full member of the Liberal International, which it joined in 1991. It has had close relations, but no organic link, with the Liberal Party in Great Britain, and subsequently with the Liberal Democrats.

Democratic Unionist Party (DUP)

Address. 91 Dundela Avenue, Belfast, BT4 3BU
Telephone. (#44-1232) 471155
Fax. (#44-1232) 471797
Leadership. Rev. Ian Richard Kyle Paisley (leader), Peter Robinson (deputy leader), Jim McClure (chairman), Nigel Dodds (secretary)

In Northern Ireland the term "unionist" is used of the (mainly Protestant) majority which wishes to preserve the constitutional union of Northern Ireland with Great Britain. This includes a relatively moderate and pragmatic element prepared, to that end, to contemplate concessions to the (mainly Roman Catholic) minority in the region; some in this element favour greater integration with Britain and others restored devolution. The term "loyalist" is used of the other end of the unionist spectrum, that is, those whose nostalgia for the 1922–69 era of Protestant hegemony causes them to favour stern action against republicanism and a return of power to the majority in the region, even if the strengthening of regional institutions may be seen as restricting the authority of the central UK government. Although all unionists are loyalist in the broad sense of loyalty to the British crown, and although all loyalists are unionist in the sense of seeking to maintain the link with Britain, the terms are often used more narrowly to contrast the generally middle-class, conservative unionists with the generally working-class, radical-right loyalists. In this sense the DUP is a right-wing loyalist party, closely identified with its leader's brand of fundamentalist Protestantism and drawing its main support from the urban working class and small farmers.

The DUP is more populist in its approach than the Ulster Unionist Party (UUP, formerly OUP). It is vehemently opposed to any involvement of the Dublin government, which it regards as alien and Catholic-controlled, in the administration of the North. It also opposes the European Union, which it has denounced as a Catholic conspiracy. Paisley, the holder of an honorary doctorate from the Bob Jones University of South Carolina (USA), founded and leads the Free Presbyterian

Church, a fiery sect which provides much of the DUP's support. He was also founder and leader of the DUP's predecessor, the Protestant Unionist Party (PUP), which was formed in 1969 (by the amalgamation of the Ulster Constitution Defence Committee with Ulster Protestant Action) and which in 1970 won two seats in the Northern Ireland Parliament and one in the UK Parliament.

The DUP, founded in 1971 (and formally known as the Ulster Democratic Unionist Party, UDUP), won eight of the 78 seats in the Northern Ireland Assembly in 1973. Paisley was re-elected to the House of Commons in February and October 1974, when the DUP and other groups combined as the United Ulster Unionist Council (UUUC); he was re-elected in 1979, when the DUP gained two other seats, and in the same year Paisley was elected to the European Parliament. (In 1975–76 the party held 12 of the 46 UUUC seats in the inconclusive Northern Ireland Constitutional Convention.)

In the October 1982 elections to the Northern Ireland Assembly the DUP secured 21 of the 78 seats (with 23% of the vote). The DUP's Westminster MPs, re-elected in 1983 (when the party secured 20% of the vote), resigned their seats along with their OUP colleagues in January 1986, forcing by-elections as a form of referendum on the 1985 Anglo-Irish Agreement: all three held their seats, as they did in the June 1987 UK general elections, when the DUP declined to 11.7% (having agreed not to contest any OUP-held seats). Peter Robinson, who had lost prestige in unionist circles by paying a fine imposed for participating in a riot in the Republic of Ireland, resigned after seven years as deputy leader in October 1987, but was reappointed in early 1988.

In the 1992 general elections the DUP increased its vote to 13.1%, retaining its three MPs, and in 1993 it won 17.2% in local elections (down from 17.7% in 1989). Before, during and after the IRA ceasefire of 1994–96 the DUP resolutely opposed any negotiations by political parties or government representatives with *Sinn Féin*. In the 1996 Forum elections it increased its vote to 18.8%.

Sinn Féin (SF)

Address. 51–55 Falls Road, Belfast, BT12 4PD
Telephone. (#44-1232) 230261
Fax. (#44-1232) 231723
Leadership. Gerry Adams (president), Mitchell McLaughlin (chair), Martin McGuinness (vice-president)

Sinn Féin (the name, which means "ourselves" in Irish, is not translated) is one of a small number of parties active in both jurisdictions on the island of Ireland. The Northern membership, which forms a majority within the party, is formally integrated in the all-Ireland structure, although a Northern executive deals with matters specific to what it would term "the occupied area" or "the six counties".

Founded in 1905 as a nationalist pressure group, *Sinn Féin* became associated with militant republicanism. After the partition of Ireland in 1922 it was the political wing of the republican movement, supporting the periodic guerrilla campaigns of the Irish Republican Army (IRA) against British rule. The main party of the Catholic electorate in the North after 1922 was the Nationalist Party, as *Sinn Féin* candidates stood on a policy of refusing to recognize or participate in any of the three parliaments claiming jurisdiction on the island. In the 1955 Northern Ireland parliamentary elections, however, SF won 150,000 votes (some 56% of the Catholic total). The party was banned in Northern Ireland in 1956 (and remained so until 1973).

A period of left-wing activity from 1967 moved *Sinn Féin* to an overtly socialist position, but communal violence in 1969 led to a resurgence of the traditional nationalist tendency. A split in 1970 led to the creation of a "Provisional" Army Council, which rebuilt the IRA to pursue a military campaign against British rule; the political wing of this more militant faction became known as Provisional or (after its Dublin headquarters) Kevin Street *Sinn Féin*, to distinguish it from "Official" (Gardiner Place) *Sinn Féin*. The latter group evolved into the Workers' Party, leaving only one *Sinn Féin* and making redundant the Provisional prefix (which was never formally adopted but is still widely used in the abbreviated "Provos" form).

The Provisional tendency portrayed itself through the 1970s as a classic national liberation movement, adopting Marxist rhetoric for non-American audiences, but in fact having almost no party political activity because of its principle of abstention from the institutions of the "partitionist" states. In the early 1980s, however, the movement was transformed by the emotional reaction and mass demonstrations generated by the hunger strikes of IRA (and other) prisoners, and by the election of abstentionist republican (not, formally, *Sinn Féin*) candidates to the Westminster and Dublin parliaments. *Sinn Féin* capitalized on the hunger strike issue to involve a new generation in its political activities, which broadened to include participation in community issues and contesting local and parliamentary elections. It continued to demand British disengagement from the North and the negotiation of a new all-Ireland framework. In 1981 it won the UK Commons seat which had been held by an IRA volunteer (Bobby Sands) who had died on hunger strike. In the 1982 elections to the Northern Ireland Assembly SF candidates secured 10.1% of the vote. In the 1983 UK general elections SF won 13.1% in Northern Ireland (43% of the Catholic vote), with Gerry Adams (who had become national leader of SF in 1983) being the only SF candidate elected (and holding to the abstentionist policy). By late 1987 SF had some 60 seats on local councils in the North, having won its first in 1983. In the UK general elections of June 1987 SF received 11.2% of the vote; Adams held his seat in West Belfast but lost it to the Social Democratic and Labour Party (SDLP) in 1992, when the SF vote slipped to 10%. In the 1993 local polls the SF vote rose to 12.5%.

From January 1988 *Sinn Féin* had a series of discreet meetings with the SDLP, much to the consternation of the unionist camp, which spoke of a "pan-nationalist pact". The contacts were, however, instrumental in bringing about secret negotiations with the British government in 1991–93, and the announcement of an IRA ceasefire in August 1994. During the ceasefire the party sought to become involved in ministerial-level negotiations with Britain and in all-party talks on a new constitutional framework, but the British government and most unionist parties insisted that substantive talks had to be preceded by the partial or complete disarmament of the IRA. The IRA resumed its bombings in February 1996, since when SF has continued to press for its unconditional inclusion in negotiations, bolstered by its increased share of the vote (15.5%) in the June 1996 elections to the Forum (the proceedings of which SF boycotted because of its continued exclusion from constitutional talks).

The party has no formal international affiliations, although it corresponds with many overseas socialist parties and nationalist movements. It has a particular affinity with the Basque party United People (*Herri Batasuna*).

Social Democratic and Labour Party (SDLP)

Address. Cranmore House, 611c Lisburn Road, Belfast, BT9 7GT

Telephone. (#44-1232) 668100

Fax. (#44-1232) 669009

Leadership. John Hume (leader), Séamus Mallon (deputy leader), Jonathan Stephenson (chair), Gerry Cosgrove (administrator)

The nationalist, centre-left SDLP is the main party of the Catholic minority, and has as its long-term objective the reunification of Ireland by consent; it rejects political violence and seeks co-operation with the Protestant majority. It is the only major party in Northern Ireland committed to the maintenance of the 1985 Anglo-Irish Agreement, and to the institutionalization of the Dublin government's advisory role in respect of

Northern affairs. There are within the SDLP various currents of opinion committed to greater or lesser degrees to traditional nationalism; the social democratic aspect of its ideology has tended to be understated.

The SDLP grew out of the Catholic civil rights agitation of the late 1960s; it was formed in August 1970 by members of the then Northern Ireland Parliament. Two of its founders sat for the Republican Labour Party (including Gerry Fitt, also a Westminster MP, who became leader), one for the Northern Ireland Labour Party, one for the Nationalist Party and three as independents. The new party rapidly overtook the Nationalist Party as the main party of the Catholic community, and it continues to exercise that role.

The SDLP participated with moderate unionist members of the Northern Ireland Assembly in the short-lived power-sharing Executive formed in 1974. John Hume was elected to the European Parliament in 1979, in which year he won the party leadership from Fitt (who left the party, lost his Westminster seat and was later elevated to the British House of Lords). In the 1982 Assembly elections the SDLP won 14 seats, with 18.8% of the vote, but did not take them up because of the opposition of the unionist parties to power-sharing. Hume entered the UK Parliament in 1983; the SDLP advantage over *Sinn Féin* fell to 4.5 percentage points (17.9 to 13.4%), but it recovered ground thereafter. The party won an additional Westminster seat in the 15 by-elections held in Northern Ireland in early 1987, and a third seat in the 1987 UK general elections, with 21.6% of the vote.

In the 1992 general elections it won 23.5% and captured a fourth seat, in West Belfast, from *Sinn Féin*. Hume's central role in bringing about the IRA ceasefire of 1994–96, and in persuading the SF to commit itself publicly to the notion of a negotiated settlement, proved of more electoral benefit to *Sinn Féin* than to the SDLP; in the 1996 Forum elections the decline in the SDLP vote (to 21.4%) contributed significantly to the dramatic increase in the SF vote. The party is a full member of the Socialist International, and at the European Party Hume sits in the Party of European Socialists group.

Ulster Unionist Party (UUP)

Address. 3 Glengall Street, Belfast, BT12 5AE

Telephone. (#44-1232) 324601

Fax. (#44-1232) 246738

Leadership. David Trimble (leader), John Taylor (deputy leader), Josias Cunningham (president), Rev. Martin Smyth (chief whip), Ken Maginnis

As the largest party of the (mainly Protestant) unionist majority in Northern Ireland, the UUP stands for the maintenance of the union with

Great Britain, although since 1990 it has wavered between calling for full integration with Britain and favouring a restored regional government. It is conservative on social and economic issues.

The original Unionist Party, which with the semi-secret Orange Order (still linked organically with the UUP) mobilized the Protestant majority in north-eastern Ireland in defence of the union with Britain, was founded in 1905; it was the monolithic ruling party from the creation of Northern Ireland in 1921 (by the partition treaty which gave the rest of the country autonomy within the British Empire) until the prorogation of the regional Parliament and the introduction of direct rule from London in 1972. During this period of Protestant unionist hegemony, challenged from time to time by upsurges of republican violence, the region was ruled by a Parliament and government based at Stormont, although it continued to be represented in the UK Parliament.

The party fragmented in 1970–73 under pressures arising from the agitation of the Catholic minority for civil rights; the faction informally known as the Official Unionist Party (OUP) was the largest and the most successful in claiming historical continuity with the old Unionist Party, whereas the Democratic Unionist Party (DUP) was the only breakaway party to achieve and retain a significant electoral following. James Molyneaux succeeded Harry West as OUP leader in 1974, and was himself succeeded in September 1995 by Trimble.

The OUP, which during the 1980s gradually reasserted the original title of Ulster Unionist Party (although legally constituted as the Ulster Unionist Council, UUC), has consistently won a large proportion of parliamentary and local council seats, sometimes in coalition with other unionist parties. In 1982 it secured 26 of the 78 seats in the Northern Ireland Assembly, with 29.7% of the vote; in 1983 it won 34% and 11 of the 17 Northern Ireland seats in the Westminster Parliament (losing one in a subsequent by-election). In June 1987 it won nine Westminster seats, with 37.7%, holding them in 1992 with a reduced share of the vote. In 1994 it held its European Parliament seat with 23.8% of first-preference votes. In the June 1996 Forum elections it headed the list of successful parties, winning 30 of the 110 seats on a 24.7% vote share.

The Unionist Party was closely linked for most of its existence with the British Conservative Party, but those ties were considerably weakened during the early 1970s, and were terminated as a result of the Conservative Party's commitment to the Anglo-Irish Agreement.

United Kingdom Unionist Party (UKUP)

Address. 10 Hamilton Road, Bangor, BT20 4LE
Telephone. (01247) 272994
Fax. (01247) 465037
Leadership. Robert McCartney (chair), Anne Moore (secretary)

Not so much a party as the personal vehicle of McCartney, a leading barrister, this body arose to support his successful bid to succeed the similarly independent-minded unionist Sir James Kilfedder (of the Ulster Popular Unionist Party) as MP for the affluent constituency of North Down after Kilfedder's death in 1995. McCartney, formerly a leading member of the Campaign for Equal Citizenship, fought the by-election on June 15 as an independent "United Kingdom Unionist" candidate on a platform of resolute opposition to the involvement of the Republic in what he saw as the internal affairs of Northern Ireland; thus he opposed the Anglo-Irish Agreement of 1985, the Downing Street Declaration issued by the British and Irish governments in 1993, and their joint framework document of February 1995. He was identified with hard-line unionism, although vigorously rejecting the religious sectarianism associated with others of that tendency.

In the June 1996 Forum elections McCartney headed a list which became known as the UKUP, although it was not formally constituted as a party. McCartney was the only UKUP candidate elected to a constituency seat, but two regional-list seats went to the curious pairing of Conor Cruise O'Brien (a former Foreign Minister in the Dublin government representing the Labour Party, latterly a journalist sympathetic to the Northern unionists) and Cedric Wilson (an inveterate protester against "Dublin interference", formerly a member of the Democratic Unionist Party).

Other Parties

Communist Party of Ireland (*Páirtí Cummanach na hÉireann*, CPI), based in Dublin, but its Northern Area, based in Belfast, has a degree of autonomy. The Northern Area organizer is Paul Kernan. The CPI has contested many elections without success, most recently the 1996 Forum elections, in which it won 66 votes. *Address.* PO Box 85, Belfast, BT1 1SR

Conservative Party, at the time of writing the governing party of the United Kingdom; although (unlike the opposition Labour Party) it extended its organisation to Northern Ireland in the late 1980s, following the breakdown of its long relationship with the Ulster Unionist Party, it has failed to achieve a significant following in terms of membership or electoral support. It has constituency associations in several parts of the region, but has local council representation only in the commuter belt of North Down. Despite securing 5.7% in the 1992 general election, and several council seats in 1993, it won less than 0.5% in the 1996 Forum elections. *Address.* c/o North Down Conservative Association, 2 May Avenue, Bangor, Co. Down

Democratic Left, a socialist movement formed in 1992 (when it was known briefly as New Agenda). The product of a split in the Workers' Party (WP), it operates in both parts of Ireland, and has parliamentary representation in the Republic where its more moderate socialist policies quickly won over most of the WP support; in the North, where more members remained with the hard-line WP, Democratic Left failed to achieve a significant following, its local council representation falling in 1993 to one seat. The party stresses non-violent, democratic, progressive and anti-sectarian politics, and supports the peace process. It secured 0.3% of the 1992 parliamentary poll and less than 0.2% in the 1996 Forum elections. The Northern leadership includes Paddy Joe McClean (regional chair) and Seamus Lynch (regional secretary). *Address.* 30 Floral Gardens, Belfast, BT36 7SE

Democratic Partnership, a centrist formation which contested the 1996 Forum elections without success, scoring 0.1%.

The Green Party, chaired by Jude Stephens, this ecologist group has contested elections since 1981, and in the 1996 Forum elections received 0.5%. It has close links with other Green parties, especially in Britain and the Irish Republic. *Address.* 537 Antrim Road, Belfast, BT7 1JR

Independent Raving Looney Ozone Friendly Party (IRLOFP), a joke party whose leader, Dino Martin, contested the 1992 general election, winning 0.1% of the regional vote.

Ingram Society (formerly the British and Irish Communist Organization, B&ICO), a group set up in 1988 to further the "two nations" theory that Northern Ireland is a distinct and legitimate political, cultural and historical entity. The Society, led by Boyd Black, drew support from the Campaign for Equal Citizenship (CEC), a pressure group which sought to persuade British parties to organize in Northern Ireland.

Labour Coalition. Although a single Labour list was put forward in the 1996 Forum elections,

securing 0.8% of the vote and two regional-list seats, its subsequent internal wrangles illustrated the difficulties which have frustrated all efforts to organize a region-wide socialist party across the sectarian divide. The Coalition brought together supporters of a wide range of extinct or obscure, ephemeral and often ideologically incompatible labour formations, including (i) the defunct Northern Ireland Labour Party (NILP), a former affiliate of the Socialist International which had no significant electoral support since 1975, when it secured 1.4% of the vote in constituent elections; (ii) the Labour and Trade Union Groups (L&TU), a network of local democratic socialist formations which contested elections in Belfast, Derry and other centres without success, from 1975 onwards (securing 0.2% in the 1992 general election); (iii) the Newtownabbey Labour Party, which won a single council seat in 1993 for Mark Langhammer (then the only public representative elected on any Labour ticket); (iv) the Labour Party '87, which also contested the 1993 local elections; (v) the Labour Co-ordinating Committee, chaired by Langhammer, which joined and then broke away from the Coalition; (vi) the Labour Movement in Local Government, formed by Paddy Devlin and Robert Clarke in May 1984 as an anti-sectarian socialist group which sought to unite the working class on economic and social issues; (vii) the Labour Representation Committee (LRC), formed in 1984 (succeeding the Campaign for Labour Representation in Northern Ireland) to seek the extension of the British Labour Party to Northern Ireland, to provide an alternative to the nationalist-unionist or Catholic-Protestant divisions; and (viii) Militant Labour, which fought the 1993 council elections without success and is allied with the British and Irish Militant movements. There have also been a number of independent Socialist, Labour or Independent Worker candidates in local, parliamentary and European elections since 1992, but only one (Davey Kettyles), a Workers' Party defector running as a Progressive Socialist, secured a council seat in 1993 (having won 0.1% of the Northern Ireland vote in the 1992 parliamentary polls). *Address.* c/o Northern Ireland Forum, Interpoint Centre, 20–24 York Street, Belfast, BT15 1AQ

Natural Law Party (NLP), contests elections to advertise the beliefs and practices of the Maharishi cult. In the Northern Ireland context it proposes that the ongoing civil conflict, in which 3,100 people have been killed since 1969, can usefully be addressed by a small proportion of the population engaging in meditation and "yogic flying". The party has contested several elections in the region with discouraging results, securing 0.3% in the 1992 general election, 0.4% in the 1994 European polls and 0.05% in the 1996 Forum contest (from which it announced its withdrawal too late to be removed from the ballot papers). *Address.* 103 University Street, Belfast 7

People's Democracy (PD), led by Eamonn McCann and the former Westminster MP Bernadette McAliskey; formed in 1968 as a civil rights group, the PD (also active in the Republic of Ireland) is a Trotskyist group (affiliated to the Fourth International, United Secretariat). It has offered conditional, and often critical, support to the IRA. It has no electoral base.

Progressive Unionist Party (PUP), political wing of one of the two so-called "loyalist terrorist" groupings, in this case the Ulster Volunteer Force (UVF). The PUP was formed in 1980 (succeeding the Volunteer Political Party, VPP) and is led by Belfast city councillor Hugh Smyth, David Ervine and Billy Hutchinson. Although the UVF has been illegal almost since its formation, the existence of the PUP permitted the British government to engage openly in ministerial-level negotiations with it from late 1994, the declared aim of the government being to secure the disarmament of the loyalist paramilitaries. It was widely accepted that the electoral system for the 1996 Forum elections, in which the PUP secured 3.5% of the vote and two seats, was designed to ensure representation for the two parties euphemistically described as "close to the thinking of" the loyalist terrorists. *Address.* 214-216 Shankill Road, Belfast

Protestant Unionist Party (PUP), a Belfast grouping (reviving the name of a precursor of the Democratic Unionist Party); based on an earlier Ulster Protestant League (UPL), the second PUP was founded in 1986 by George Seawright, a Scottish sympathizer of the Ulster loyalist movement, following his release from a prison sentence (imposed *inter alia* for his advocacy of the incineration of Catholics). The leadership, and Seawright's council seat, passed to his widow after his assassination in 1987, but she lost it in 1993 (when she was the party's sole candidate in council elections).

Republican Sinn Féin (RSF), a small splinter group of *Sinn Féin* with negligible support, which does not contest elections to institutions of the "partitionist" states as a matter of principle, and is allegedly linked with an IRA splinter group under a Continuity Army Council.

Socialist Workers' Party (SWP), a Trotskyist formation with perhaps two dozen members in Northern Ireland and no regional office.

Ulster Christian Democrat Party, an obscure right-wing grouping which contested the 1996 Forum elections without success, coming last of the 24 party lists with 31 votes (out of 752,391).

Ulster Democratic Party (UDP), founded in the 1970s (as the Ulster Loyalist Democratic Party, ULDP, dropping the second word in 1992) as a political front for the Ulster Defence Association (UDA). The UDA, a loyalist paramilitary group responsible for many hundreds of murders, mainly of Catholic non-combatants, was eventually declared illegal in 1992; by that time the party had established some distance between itself and the parent organization, presenting itself as quite independent. The UDP, led by Gary McMichael and David Adams, has contested local government elections, securing a handful of council seats by election or defection, but its main role is as a channel of communication with the UDA and the Protestant underclass which supports it. In that capacity it participated in talks with the British government, some at ministerial level, following the loyalist ceasefire declared in October 1994, four months after that of the IRA. It secured only 2.2% of the poll in the 1996 Forum elections, winning no constituency seats, but was accorded two at-large seats under the formula designed to bring the UDP and its associated party, the PUP, into negotiations. McMichael is the son of a UDA commander who founded the ULDP, and who was assassinated in 1987. *Address.* 36 Castle Street, Liburn, Co. Antrim

Ulster Independence Movement (UIM), a pressure group led by Rev. Hugh Ross and Robert McGrath, which draws very limited support, mainly from the rural Protestant community, for its goal of independence for Ulster (meaning some or all of the six counties of Northern Ireland, rather than the nine counties of the historic province of Ulster). The Movement came sixth in the 1994 European Parliament election, with 1.4% of the vote (two other pro-independence candidates securing a total of 0.2%), and it has since lobbied unsuccessfully for admission to the discussions which have taken place between the British government and other parties. In the 1996 Forum elections its vote fell to 0.3%, placing it 14th. *Address.* 316 Shankill Road, Belfast

Ulster National Front (NF), a local section, led by John Field, of one of the competing tendencies of the British fascist National Front. The name may have been superseded by National Democrats (ND), since that London-based NF splinter group announced in 1996 its intention of contesting a Northern Ireland constituency at the next general election. A former NF activist stood in the 1994

European elections an an "Independence for Ulster" candidate, securing 0.1% of the vote. *Address*. PO Box 40, Belfast, BT7 1LY

Ulster Popular Unionist Party (UPUP), the personal vehicle of the late Sir James Kilfedder, founded in January 1980 (as the Ulster Progressive Unionist Party). He continued to sit at Westminster for the affluent North Down consituency which he had represented since 1970 for the Ulster Unionist Party (UUP), and since 1974 as an independent unionist. Kilfedder also served in the Northern Ireland Assembly (as Speaker, 1982–86). He was aligned in most matters with the UUP, although taking a more liberal line on social issues. His unwavering support for the UK government of the Conservative Party was reflected in 1994 in his appointment to chair the new parliamentary Northern Ireland select committee. The UPUP fell into disarray after his death in 1995 and the ensuing by-election was won by a United Kingdom Unionist candidate. The UPUP won a single council seat in 1993, but did not contest the 1996 Forum elections.

Women's Coalition, an *ad hoc* grouping formed to raise the profile of women's issues in the 1996 Forum elections and the subsequent discussions. It obtained just over 1% of the vote and its regional-list nominees, Monica McWilliams and Pearl Sagar, were among only 14 women elected to the 110–seat body, in which they frequently protested that their interventions were not taken seriously. *Address*. c/o Northern Ireland Forum, Interpoint Centre, 20– 24 York Street, Belfast BT15 1AQ

The Workers' Party (WP), a semi-autonomous Northern section of the Dublin-based WP, a Marxist republican party which arose from the "Official" majority faction which remained loyal to the then leadership of *Sinn Féin* in the 1969–70 split, at which time the Northern section of *Sinn Féin* operated under the name Republican Clubs. The associated armed faction known as the Official IRA wound down its activities during the 1970s and was said to have disbanded in the 1980s. The movement's attempts to develop radical anti-sectarian socialist politics in the North, reflected in its change of name to The Workers' Party-Republican Clubs and its subsequent abandonment of the suffix, were hampered not only by the climate of violence in the 1970s and 1980s but by allegations of gangsterism associated with the Official IRA and by factionalism within the political wing, leading to the breakaway of what became the Democratic Left. The WP, which campaigns for peace, full employment and class politics, has been represented on local councils, with one remaining councillor in 1996, but has rarely secured more than 2% of the parliamentary poll, and only 0.6% in 1992; in the 1996 Forum elections its share fell to 0.5%. Organized in both Irish jurisdictions, it is led nationally by a Northerner, Marion Donnelly (president); its Northern chair is Tom French. *Address*. 6 Springfield Road, Belfast, BT12 7AG

World Socialist Party of Ireland (WSPI), a sister party of the Socialist Party of Great Britain, with the same programme and a similarly miniscule following. *Address*. 3 Pym Street, Antrim Road, Belfast, BT15

Independent lists which contested the 1996 Forum elections without success were the **McMullan, Chambers** and **Templeton** lists, **Ulster's Independent Voice**, and **Independent DUP**, each of which scored 0.1% or less.

UK Crown Dependencies

The three crown fiefdoms of Jersey and Guernsey (the Channel Islands) and of the Isle of Man are historically distinct from the United Kingdom, although to all intents and purposes they are British territory and accepted as being such by the vast majority of their inhabitants and under international law. Legally, both entities are under the jurisdiction of the crown rather than the Westminster parliament (in which they are not represented) and neither is part of the European Union *de jure*.

Channel Islands

Capital: St Helier, Jersey   **Population:** 150,000 (1995E)

Located in the English Channel off the French coast, the Channel Islands consisting of Jersey and Guernsey with dependencies, have been attached to the crown of England since 1106. Each of the two islands has a Lieutenant-Governor representing the British monarch and a Bailiff (appointed by the crown) as president of each of the States (legislatures) and of the royal courts. Elections to the States are not held on British party political lines, although in Jersey some elected members have represented the **Jersey Democratic Movement**.

Isle of Man

Capital: Douglas   **Population:** 70,000 (1995E)

Situated in the Irish Sea between Britain and Ireland, the Isle of Man has been a dependency of the crown for four centuries, but retaining its own laws administered by the Court of Tynwald, consisting of a Governor (appointed by the crown), an 11–member Legislative Council and the House of Keys, which is a 24–member representative assembly elected for a five-year term by adult suffrage and which elects eight of the Legislative Council members. In elections to the House of Keys in November 1991 all successful candidates stood without official party attribution, although parties have been active in the past.

Manx Labour Party (MLP), led by E.G. Lowey, moderate left-wing party which commanded a majority in the House of Keys until November 1981, when its strength was reduced to three members. It retained three seats in November 1986.

Manx National Party (MNP), led by Audrey Ainsworth, advocates internal independence from the jurisdiction of the UK Home Office.

Mec Vannin (Sons of Mann), led by Lewis Crellin and J. Bernard Moffatt, founded in 1962 to promote the independence of the Isle of Man as a democratic republic and protection of the Manx way of life. The party has had some success in local elections, even though most Manx politicians are independents. It gained one seat (out of 24) in the House of Keys in 1976, but failed to retain it in 1981.

UK Dependent Territories

At end-1996 the United Kingdom retained sovereignty over 14 overseas territories, of which three (British Antarctic Territory, British Indian Ocean Territory, and South Georgia and the South Sandwich Islands) have no settled population. The other 11 all enjoy substantial autonomy in their internal affairs and the majority have a flourishing party system. Around 97% of the total population of the dependencies is accounted for by Hong Kong, which is due to revert to Chinese sovereignty on July 1, 1997.

Anguilla

Capital: The Valley   **Population:** 9,000 (1995E)

The Caribbean island of Anguilla was a British colony from 1650 to 1967, when it became part of the new Associated State of St Christopher/St Kitts-Nevis-Anguilla. However, the Anguillans repudiated government from St Kitts, and in 1969 a British commissioner was installed following a landing by British security forces. In 1976 Anguilla was given a new status and separate constitution, formally becoming a UK dependent territory in 1980. Constitutional amendments introduced in 1982 (and in 1990) provide for a Governor (as the representative of the British sovereign) with wide-ranging powers, an Executive Council and a House of Assembly. The Executive Council consists of the Chief Minister and three other ministers (appointed by the Governor from among the elected members of the House of Assembly), together with the Deputy Governor and the Attorney-General as *ex-officio* members. The House of Assembly includes seven representatives elected by universal adult suffrage, two *ex-officio* members (the Deputy Governor and Attorney-General) and two nominated members.

A general election on March 16, 1994, following the retirement of Sir Emile Gumbs of the Anguilla National Alliance (ANA) after 10 years in office, failed to produce a majority party. The ANA, Anguilla United Party (AUP) and Anguilla Democratic Party (ADP) each returned two members, while an independent candidate took the seventh elective seat. A coalition administration was formed by the AUP and the ADP.

Anguilla Democratic Party (ADP)
Address. c/o House of Assembly, The Valley
Leadership. Victor Banks (leader)

The ADP was founded in 1981 (as the Anguilla People's Party) by Chief Minister Ronald Webster on his expulsion from the then ruling Anguilla United Party (AUP). The party won five seats in the House of Assembly in subsequent elections that year and Webster was reappointed Chief Minister. In the 1984 polls the party held only two seats, and Webster resigned as leader, to be replaced by Victor Banks. The ADP remained in opposition until the 1994 elections, after which it formed a new coalition government with the AUP.

Anguilla National Alliance (ANA)
Address. c/o House of Assembly, The Valley
Leadership. Eric Reid (leader)

In 1980 the then People's Progressive Party, whose leader Ronald Webster headed Anguilla's government from the separation from St Kitts-Nevis in 1967 until 1977 (when he was replaced by Sir Emile Gumbs), was reconstituted as the

Anguilla National Alliance. Having lost power in the 1980 elections, the ANA again became the ruling party in 1984. Gumbs remained Chief Minister until his retirement in February 1994. In the ensuing elections the ANA won two of the seven elective seats and went into opposition. The ANA is affiliated to the International Democrat Union through its membership of the Caribbean Democrat Union.

Anguilla United Party (AUP)
Address. c/o House of Assembly, The Valley
Leadership. Hubert Hughes (leader)

After losing the leadership of the ruling People's Progressive Party in 1977, Ronald Webster formed the AUP which won the elections in 1980. Webster returned as Chief Minister, but after disagreements within the party he was expelled from the AUP in May 1981. In early elections in June 1981 the AUP lost all its seats. Under the leadership of Hubert Hughes, the revived party won two seats in the March 1994 elections and formed a coalition administration with the Anguilla Democratic Party (ADP), under the chief ministership of the AUP leader.

Bermuda

Capital: Hamilton

Population: 60,000 (1995E)

First settled by the British in 1609 and located in the western Atlantic, the crown colony of Bermuda has enjoyed internal self-government since 1968. The Governor, representing the British sovereign, has responsibility for external affairs, defence, internal security and police. Internal executive authority in most matters is exercised by the Premier and the Cabinet, who are appointed by the Governor but are responsible to the 40–member House of Assembly, which is popularly elected for a five-year term. The Governor also appoints the 11–member Senate, including five on the recommendation of the Premier and three on the advice of the Leader of the Opposition.

In the most recent general election on Oct. 5, 1993, the ruling United Bermuda Party retained power, winning 22 seats in the House of Assembly, against 18 for the Progressive Labour Party. In a referendum on Aug. 16, 1995, voters rejected the principle of independence from the United Kingdom by a 58.8% majority.

National Liberal Party (NLP)
Address. POB HM 1704, Hamilton HM HX
Telephone. (#1–809) 292-8587
Leadership. Gilbert Darrell (leader)
The centrist NLP was formed in 1985 by a breakaway group of Progressive Labour Party members of the House of Assembly led by Gilbert Darrell. The party lost one of its two seats in the 1989 elections and failed to win any representation in October 1993.

Progressive Labour Party (PLP)
Address. Court Street, POB HM 1367, Hamilton HM FX
Telephone. (#1–809) 292-2264
Fax. (#1–809) 295-2933
Leadership. Frederick Wade (leader)
Founded in 1963, the left-wing PLP draws most of its support from the black population and has campaigned for Bermudan independence and an end to British rule. The PLP has been runner-up to the ruling United Bermuda Party in successive elections since 1968, most recently in October 1993, when it won 18 of the 40 seats in the House of Assembly. While favouring independence, the party urged its supporters to abstain in the August 1995 referendum.

United Bermuda Party (UBP)
Address. Central Office, 87 John F. Burrows Building, Chancery Lane, POB HM 715, Hamilton HM CX
Telephone. (#1–809) 295 0729
Leadership. Jim Woolridge (leader)
The conservative and multi-racial UBP has held power continuously since the granting of internal self-government in 1968, gaining its eighth successive general election victory in October 1993 (although with a much reduced share of the vote). In August 1995, following the independence referendum result, Sir John Swan resigned as Premier and UBP leader (positions he had held

since early 1982). Although the UBP as a party did not endorse independence, Sir John and some other UBP leaders advocated a "yes" vote and he had promised to resign in the event of defeat. He was succeeded by the Tourism Minister, Jim Woolridge.

British Virgin Islands

Capital: Road Town, Tortola

Population: 18,000 (1995E)

Located in the Caribbean and under British rule since 1672, the 60 or so islands comprising the British Virgin Islands are a crown colony, with an appointed Governor representing the British sovereign. Under the present constitution, which took effect from 1977, the Governor is responsible for defence, internal security, external affairs and the civil service. The Legislative Council consists of a Speaker, chosen from outside the Council, one *ex-officio* member (the Attorney-General) and 13 directly elected members, representing nine constituency seats and four territory-wide ("at large") seats. The Executive Council, chaired by the Governor, has one *ex-officio* member (the Attorney-General) and four ministers (including a Chief Minister) drawn from the elected members of Legislative Council.

In a general election on Feb. 20, 1995 (when the four "at large" seats were introduced in a reform imposed by Britain despite some local opposition), the Virgin Islands Party retained power, winning six of the 13 elective Legislative Council seats and gaining the support of one of three independent members. The Concerned Citizens' Movement and the United Party won two seats each.

Concerned Citizens' Movement (CCM)

Address. c/o Legislative Council, Road Town, Tortola

Leadership. Omar Hodge (leader)

The CCM was formed in 1994 as successor to the Independent People's Movement, which had itself been formed by party leader Omar Hodge in 1989. In the 1995 general election the CCM won two Legislative Council seats.

United Party (UP)

Address. c/o Legislative Council, Road Town, Tortola

Leadership. Conrad Maduro (leader)

The UP has fought successive general elections since the mid-1970s, and was briefly in government from 1983 to 1986 in a coalition under the premiership of an independent, Cyril Romney. Most recently, in the February 1995 polls, the UP won two seats in the Legislative Council.

Virgin Islands Party (VIP)

Address. c/o Legislative Council, Road Town, Tortola

Leadership. Ralph O'Neal (leader)

Until his sudden death in May 1995, H. Lavity Stoutt had been the long-time leader of the VIP, serving as the islands' Chief Minister from 1967 to 1971, Deputy Chief Minister under an independent Chief Minister from 1975 to 1979, and Chief Minister again between 1979 and 1983 and from 1986 until 1995. Having been returned to power in 1986, the VIP increased its majority in the 1990 election, and then retained power with the support of an independent following the February 1995 poll. Stoutt was succeeded as Chief Minister by his deputy, Ralph O'Neal, and the government majority in the Legislative Council was maintained by the recruitment of another independent member.

Cayman Islands

Capital: George Town, Grand Cayman   **Population:** 27,000 (1995E)

Under British rule from 1670, the Caribbean Cayman Islands were governed from Jamaica until its independence in 1962, when the islands opted to remain under the British crown. The constitution, which was most recently revised in 1994, provides for a Governor, Executive Council and Legislative Assembly. The Governor represents the British sovereign and is responsible for external affairs, defence, internal security and the civil service. The Executive Council, chaired by the Governor, consists of three official members (Chief Secretary, Financial Secretary and Attorney-General) and five other members elected by the Legislative Assembly from their own number. The Assembly includes the three official members of the Executive Council and 15 directly elected members.

For many years there have been no formally constituted political parties in the Caymans. Elections to the Legislative Assembly came to be contested by loose groupings or "teams" of candidates, as well as by independents, but all candidates were committed to the economic development of the islands and the maintenance of colonial status. In the general election on Nov. 18, 1992, 12 of the 15 Assembly seats were won by a grouping called the "National Team", which had been formed earlier that year to express opposition to constitutional amendments then under review.

Falkland Islands

Capital: Stanley   **Population (civilian):** 2,100 (1995E)

Situated in the South Atlantic, the Falklands Islands have been under continuous British rule since 1833, except for a brief period in 1982 when Argentina (which calls them Las Malvinas) asserted its claim to sovereignty by military occupation in early April but surrendered to British forces in June. Under the 1985 constitution, the Falkland Islands and their former dependencies (South Georgia and the South Sandwich Islands) are administered by a Governor representing the British monarch. The Governor presides over an Executive Council with two other (non-voting) *ex-officio* members and three elected by and from the Legislative Council. The latter body has two (non-voting) *ex-officio* members and eight elected by universal adult suffrage. Decisions of the Executive Council are subject to veto by the Governor and the British Foreign Secretary.

All candidates elected to the Legislative Council on Oct. 14, 1993, stood as independents favouring the maintenance of British status and avoidance of unnecessary contact with Argentina until the latter abandoned its claim to sovereignty. The only recognizable political grouping is the **Desire the Right Party**, which has a small following for its platform of greater community self-reliance and reconciliation with Argentina.

Gibraltar

Capital: Gibraltar

Population: 33,000 (1995E)

Located on the southern tip of the Iberian Peninsula, Gibraltar became a British possession under the 1713 Treaty of Utrecht. Under its 1969 constitution, the dependency has a crown-appointed Governor exercising executive authority, a Gibraltar Council under a Chief Minister and a House of Assembly of two *ex-officio* and 15 elected members serving a four-year term. The franchise is held by British subjects and citizens of the Republic of Ireland resident in Gibraltar for at least six months prior to registration as voters. Each voter has the right to vote for up to eight candidates, which is the maximum number that any one party can present in Assembly elections.

In elections to the House of Assembly held on May 16, 1996, the Gibraltar Social Democrats won eight of the elective seats (with 48% of the popular vote) and the Gibraltar Socialist Labour Party the remaining seven (with 39% of the vote). A major issue in these and earlier elections was the Spanish claim to sovereignty over Gibraltar and the local response to ongoing UK-Spanish negotiations seeking to resolve the dispute.

Gibraltar Social Democrats (GSD)

Address. Haven Court, 5 Library Ramp, Gibraltar

Telephone. (#350) 77888

Fax. (#350) 77888

Leadership. Peter Caruana (leader)

The GSD were launched in 1989 as a centre-right party advocating that the government should participate in the ongoing UK-Spanish negotiations on Gibraltar, thus differing sharply from the boycott policy of the then ruling Gibraltar Socialist Labour Party (GSLP). Drawing support that had previously gone to the Gibraltar Labour Party-Association for the Advancement of Civil Rights, the new party won seven of the 15 elective seats in the January 1992 Assembly elections and became the opposition to the further GSLP government. Assisted by subsequent economic problems and a deterioration in relations with Spain, the GSD won the May 1996 elections, taking the maximum possible eight seats with a vote share of 48%.

Gibraltar Socialist Labour Party (GSLP)

Address. Line Wall Road, Gibraltar

Telephone. (#350) 42359

Leadership. Joe Bossano (leader), Ernest Collado (chair), Joe Victory (general secretary)

The party's constitution is modelled on that of the Labour Party of Britain, as it was when the GSLP was founded in 1976. The party's basic aim is "the creation of a socialist decolonized Gibraltar based on the application of self-determination", so that it vigorously opposes Spain's claim to Gibraltar as well as the 1984 UK-Spanish Brussels agreement providing for negotiations on the sovereignty issue. The party was formed as the Gibraltar Democratic Movement (GDM), which contested the 1976 elections with the statutory maximum of eight candidates, of whom four were elected on a platform of "working for the decolonization of the Rock [of Gibraltar] and the creation of a new constitutional arrangement which will guarantee the future of the territory and the people". In 1977 three of these members of the GDM crossed the floor, only one remaining when the GDM changed its name to GSLP.

The party contested the 1980 elections on a socialist programme with six candidates and obtained 20% of the vote and one of the 15 elective seats in the House of Assembly. In January 1984, however, when it fielded eight candidates, it gained all seven opposition seats in the House. The GSLP finally came to power in the March 1988 Assembly elections, when it won eight seats and approaching 60% of the popular vote. As Gibraltar's new Chief Minister, Joe Bossano reiterated his party's election pledge that a GSLP government would not participate in the negotiating process initiated under the 1984 Brussels agreement. The GSLP was confirmed in power in the January 1992 elections, retaining the maximum permissible eight seats but with a vote share of over 70%.

Economic and other difficulties during Bossano's second term, including lack of any progress on the GSLP's self-determination aim, resulted in a seepage of popular support, amid worsening relations with London over the rise of drug-trafficking and money-laundering in Gibraltar. In the May 1996 elections the GSLP was soundly defeated by the Gibraltar Social Democrats, winning seven of the 15 elective seats on a greatly reduced popular vote of 39%.

Other Parties

Gibraltar Labour Party Association for the Advancement of Civil Rights (GLP AACR), led by Isaac Marrache (president) and John Piris (general secretary), founded in 1942 and the dominant Gibraltar party in the post-war decades under Sir Joshua Hassan, who favoured a Gibraltar "with Britain but not under Britain". His retirement as Chief Minister in 1987 was followed by defeat for the party in 1988 by the Gibraltar Socialist Labour Party, whereafter the GLP-AACR was supplanted on the centre-right by the Gibraltar Social Democrats.

Gibraltar National Party (GNP), led by Joseph Garcia, founded in 1991 to promote the idea of self-determination for Gibraltar from a right-wing perspective (as opposed to the left-wing orientation of the then ruling Gibraltar Socialist Labour Party), improved from 5% of the vote (and no seats) in 1992 to 13% in May 1996 (but still with no seats).

Hong Kong

Capital: Victoria

Population: 6,000,000 (1995E)

The British crown colony of Hong Kong is due to revert in its entirety to China on July 1, 1997 (as a special administrative region of the People's Republic), upon the expiry of the 99–year lease on the New Territories, which form some 90% of the total land area of the colony (the other 10% being Hong Kong proper, which had been ceded to Britain in perpetuity under the 1842 Treaty of Nanking). Agreement on arrangements for the reversion was reached between the UK and Chinese governments in September 1984 and was signed in December of that year, with exchange of instruments of ratification taking place in May 1985. In the interim, the colony continued to be administered by a crown-appointed Governor and an Executive Council of three *ex-officio* and up to 12 appointed members, with the representative structure being headed by a 60–member Legislative Council (Legco), which advises the Executive Council and scrutinizes and approves public expenditure proposals. Under a controversial reform package proposed by the Governor and approved in June 1994, Legco's directly representative component was increased from 18 to 20 members (representing geographical constituencies and elected by universal adult suffrage), with 30 members being indirectly elected by "functional constituencies" (such as chambers of commerce and trade unions) and 10 being chosen by an electoral college of the colony's directly-elected district and urban councillors. There are no appointed members in the new Legco, whereas the previous body had included 21 appointed or *ex-officio* members (who had ensured the passage of most government bills).

Elections to the new Legco on Sept. 17, 1995, resulted in the pro-democracy Democratic Party winning 12 of the 20 directly-elected seats (on a turn-out of 36% of the eligible electorate) and seven in the other two categories, for a total of 19 seats, whereas pro-Chinese parties fared badly. In the wake of the poll, official Chinese sources reiterated Beijing's intention to abolish Hong Kong's existing representative structure when it assumed authority in 1997 and to establish new bodies.

Association for Democracy and People's Livelihood (ADPL)

Address. 1104 Sun Beam Building, 469–71 Nathan Road, Kowloon, Hong Kong

Telephone. (#850) 2782–2699
Fax. (#850) 2782–3137
Leadership. Frederick Fung (chair), Lee Yiu-kwan (secretary-general)

The ADPL was founded as a pro-democracy grouping laying stress on the need for economic continuity. It took fourth place in the September 1995 Legco elections, winning two directly-elected seats, one from the "functional constituencies" and one from the electoral college, for a total of four.

Democratic Alliance for the Betterment of Hong Hong (DABHK)

Address. 24/F-2/F China Overseas Building, 139 Hennessy Road, Wanchai, Hong Kong

Telephone. (#850) 2528–0136

Fax. (#850) 2528–4339

Leadership. Tsang Yok-sing (chair), Cheng Kai-nam (secretary-general)

The DABHK was founded in 1992 by various groups and interests favouring accomodation with China and full acceptance of the reversion of sovereignty. It was heavily defeated by the pro-democracy Democratic Party in the September 1995 Legco elections, winning only two directly-elected seats, plus two each in the two indirect sections, for a total of six seats.

Democratic Party (DP)

Address. 401/413 Central Government Offices, West Wing, 11 Ice House Street, Central, Hong Kong

Telephone. (#852) 2537–2471

Fax. (#852) 2397–8998

Leadership. Martin Lee (chair), Law Chi-kwong (secretary-general)

The DP was founded in April 1994 as a merger of the United Democrats of Hong Kong (UDHK) and the Meeting Point group, advocating full autonomy for Hong Kong after the reversion to China in 1997. The UDHK had allied with other pro-democracy groups in the first democratic elections to Legco in 1991 to win 16 of the 18 directly-contested seats. In the September 1995 elections the DP won 12 of the 20 directly-contested seats, plus five in the "functional constituencies" section and two from the electoral college, giving it a total of 19 seats out of 60. It could also expect support from among the 17–strong contingent elected as independents on "China-related" issues and from the Association seven-strong Liberal Party group on economic and social questions. The DP's success was regarded with great opprobrium by the Chinese government, not least because of the party's support for the pro-democracy movement in mainland China.

Liberal Party (LP)

Address. 2/F Shun Ho Tower, 24–30 Ice House Street, Central, Hong Kong

Telephone. (#850) 2869–6833

Fax. (#850) 2845–3671

Leadership. Allen Lee Peng-fei (leader)

The LP was founded in 1993 as a pro-business party favouring accomodation with China in the interests of preserving Hong Kong's economic structure, although rejecting the label "pro-Chinese". It came in second place in the September 1995 Legco elections, winning only one directly-elected seat but taking eight in the "functional constituencies" section, for a total of nine seats. The LP contingent was expected to support the dominant Democratic Party on social and business issues, but to be more cautious on "China-related" matters.

Five groupings won one seat each in the September 1995 Legco elections (none of them in the directly-elected category), namely the pro-Chinese **Progressive Alliance** led by Ambrose Lau, the pro-Chinese **Liberal Democratic Federation,** the pro-Chinese **New Hong Kong Alliance**, the **123 Democratic Alliance** and the **Federation of Trade Unions**. A total of 17 independents were also elected, three of them in the constituency section.

Montserrat

Capital: Plymouth

Population: 12,500 (1995E)

The Caribbean island of Montserrat formed part of the British federal colony of the Leeward Islands from 1871 until 1956, when it became a separate dependent territory. Under the 1960 constitution as amended, Montserrat has a Governor who represents the British sovereign and is responsible for defence, internal security and external affairs (including, from 1989, regulation of the "offshore" financial sector in response to a banking scandal). The Legislative Council consists of the Speaker, seven elected representatives, two official members (the Attorney-General and Financial Secretary) and two nominated members. Executive authority in most internal matters is exercised by a seven-member Executive Council, presided over by the Governor and including the Attorney-General, Financial Secretary and four ministers (including the Chief Minister) drawn from the Legislative Council. In the general election on Oct. 8, 1991, the newly formed National Progressive Party (NPP) secured a majority with four seats in the legislature, the other three seats going to the National Development Party, the People's Liberation Movement and an independent candidate.

National Development Party (NDP)
Address. c/o Legislative Council, Plymouth
Telephone. (#1–809) 491-3600
Leadership. Bertrand B. Osborne (leader)

The NDP was formed in 1984 by business interests advocating economic development, free enterprise and the maintenance of colonial status. In elections in 1987 the party won two legislative seats, but one NDP member subsequently resigned to become an independent. The party retained one seat in the 1991 poll.

National Progressive Party (NPP)
Address. POB 280, Plymouth
Telephone. (#1–809) 491-2444
Leadership. Reuben T. Meade (leader)

The NPP was formed just prior to the general election in October 1991, when it won a majority in the Legislative Council, securing four out of the seven seats. Party leader Meade became Chief Minister.

People's Liberation Movement (PLM)
Address. c/o Legislative Council, Plymouth
Leadership. John A. Osborne (leader)

The centre-right PLM has sought to promote economic development of the island and supports eventual independence. It was the governing party from 1978 until 1991 when, amid allegations of mismanagement and corruption against the Osborne administration, the PLM retained only one Legislative Council seat in the October elections. In February 1993 John Osborne and Noel Tuitt, a former PLM minister, were cleared of corruption and conspiracy charges following a police investigation. Although an opposition member, Tuitt was appointed to the NPP administration in March 1994. The PLM is affiliated to the International Democrat Union through its membership of the Caribbean Democrat Union.

Progressive Democratic Party (PDP)
Leadership. Eustace Dyers (leader)

The PDP, under Austin Bramble, was in power from 1973 to 1977, but its influence has since declined. It failed to win any seats in the 1991 elections.

Pitcairn Islands

Population: 50 (1995E)

Britain's only remaining Pacific dependency, Pitcairn Island was settled in 1790 by the mutineers of *The Bounty* and became an official British possession in 1887, together with three nearby uninhabited islands. Under the 1940 constitution, the Governor (since 1970 the UK high commissioner in New Zealand) represents the British monarch. An Island Magistrate elected every three years presides over the Island Court and the Island Council of 10 members, five of whom are elected annually. There is no party activity among Pitcairn's small and dwindling population.

St Helena and Dependencies

Capital: Jamestown   **Population:** 6,500 (1995E)

Situated in the South Atlantic, St Helena was governed by the British East India Company from 1673 and brought under the control of the crown in 1834. The constitution in force since 1989, applying to St Helena and its dependencies of Ascension Island and the Tristan da Cunha island group, provides for a crown-appointed Governor and Commander-in-Chief, who presides over an Executive Council, which includes five members selected from among their number by a popularly-elected Legislative Council of 12 members. Elections to the latter in the 1970s and early 1980s were contested on a party basis reflecting differing views on the constitutional future of the islands; more recently, however, there has been no party activity, the balloting of June 1993 being conducted on a non-partisan basis.

Turks and Caicos Islands

Capital: Cockburn Town, Grand Turk   **Population:** 14,000 (1995E)

A Jamaican dependency from 1873 until 1959, the Turks and Caicos Islands became a separate British colony in 1962, following Jamaican independence. From 1965 the islands were administratively associated with the Bahamas, until Bahamian independence in 1973. Under the 1976 constitution as amended, executive power is vested in the Governor, who represents the British sovereign and is responsible for external affairs, defence and internal security. The Governor presides over the Executive Council, which includes ministers appointed from among the elected members of the Legislative Council and also *ex-officio* members. The Legislative Council is made up of the Speaker, three nominated members, the *ex-officio* members of the Executive Council and 13 directly-elected representatives.

In a general election on Jan. 31, 1995, the People's Democratic Movement won eight Legislative Council seats, thus defeating the then ruling Progressive National Party (PNP), which took four, with one seat going to an independent candidate (Norman Saunders, who in 1985 had been forced to resign as Chief Minister in a PNP administration after a drugs scandal).

People's Democratic Movement (PDM)
Address. POB 38, Grand Turk
Leadership. Derek H. Taylor (leader)
Founded in the mid-1970s, the centre-left PDM favours internal self-government and eventual independence for the islands. The party won the first elections held under the 1976 constitution, but then went into opposition following defeat in 1980 on an explicitly pro-independence manifesto. Having overwhelmingly won the 1988 elections, and then lost to the Progressive National Party in 1991, the PDM returned to power in the January 1995 poll, in which it gained eight Legislative Council seats.

Progressive National Party (PNP)
Address. c/o Legislative Council, Grand Turk
Leadership. Washington Misick (leader)
The conservative PNP is committed to continued dependent status for the islands. It was the ruling party from 1980 until the suspension of ministerial government and its replacement by a nominated executive headed by the Governor in 1986. This followed a period of domestic political tension in

the islands and investigations by a commission of inquiry into political and administrative malpractices. At the 1988 elections, preceding the islands' return to constitutional rule, the PNP suffered a heavy defeat by the People's Democratic Movement. Having been returned to power in 1991, the party retained only four seats in the January 1995 elections and again went into opposition.

United Democratic Party (UDP)
Leadership. Wendal Swann (leader)

The UDP was formed in 1993 by Wendal Swann following his expulsion from the People's Democratic Movement. The party contested the 1995 elections but failed to win any seats.

United States of America

Capital: Washington, DC

Population: 265,000,000 (1995E)

The United States of America, consisting of 50 member states with a measure of internal self-government, has an executive President elected for a four-year term (by an Electoral College elected directly in each state) and re-eligible once only; he or she is both head of state and head of the executive, whose other members he or she nominates. The executive consists of the President, a Cabinet, executive departments headed by cabinet secretaries and various independent and quasi-independent agencies. The President is elected together with a Vice-President, who succeeds to the office of President if the latter dies in office, resigns or is successfully impeached.

Legislative power is held by Congress consisting of a 100–member Senate and a 435–member House of Representatives. In each state two senators are elected by direct adult suffrage for a six-year term, with one-third of the Senate's membership being renewed every two years. Members of the House of Representatives are elected for a two-year term. There is a traditional two-party system, but the constitutional separation of executive and legislative functions precludes party government in the accepted sense (as the President's party may be faced with a majority of the other party in Congress). Party organization is diffuse, each major party being a coalition of autonomous state parties, which are themselves constituted by county and city parties.

The minimum voting age is 18 years and the registration of voters is controlled by the states. In elections to the House of Representatives, candidates are elected by simple majority in districts of more or less the same population, with the proviso that each state has at least one representative. In each state a governor is elected for a four-year term by popular vote; most state legislatures are bicameral. For presidential elections the number of Electoral College seats per state is determined on the basis of the combined representation of each state in the Senate and the House of Representatives. Under the constitution, Electoral College delegates are at liberty to vote for any candidate, but they normally follow their party affiliation (itself determined by the outcome of the popular vote in each state). Party candidates for the presidency are chosen by a caucus of party leaders or by the voters in primary elections (for which the turn-out tends to be low). In the final elections the delegates vote as a state bloc. The presidential primaries or caucus sessions start 10 months before the national election; a presidential election campaign requires a massive and costly effort. Candidates for nomination as the party's choice for President receive federal grants to cover campaign expenses, provided no private funds are accepted. Candidates for Congress receive no federal funds and are free to accept private contributions.

In the presidential election held on Nov. 3, 1992, the Democratic Party candidate, Bill Clinton, defeated the incumbent, George Bush, thereby breaking the Republican Party's 12-year grip on the presidency. Clinton was inaugurated as President on Jan. 20, 1993. In simultaneous legislative elections the Democrats maintained their hold over both houses of Congress. This was lost at the mid-term elections of November 1994, which left the Republicans controlling 53 Senate seats and the Democrats 47, whilst in the House of Representatives the Republicans won 230 seats compared with 204 for the Democrats and one independent.

Democratic Party

Address. Democratic National Committee, 430 South Capitol Street SE, Washington, DC 20003
Telephone. (#1–202) 863-8000
Fax. (#1–202) 863-8140
Leadership. Donald L. Fowler (national chair), Christopher J. Dodd (general chair), Thomas A. Daschle (Senate minority leader), Richard Gephardt (House minority leader)

While European-style political labels cannot properly be applied to the complex coalitions of interests which make up both major US political parties, the Democratic Party may be broadly defined as occupying the centre-left of the US political spectrum. Supportive of a free-market economy, the party also places emphasis on social equality and civil, labour and consumer rights.

Founded in the early 19th century, the party was originally known as the Republican Party, later as the Democratic Republican Party and then, prior to its first national convention in 1832, as the Democratic Party. It was the dominant party until 1860, when it was split over the issue of slavery, and thereafter held the presidency for only two four-year periods (1885–89 and 1893–97) up to 1913. The Democratic Presidents since that date have been Woodrow Wilson (1913–21), Franklin D. Roosevelt (1933–45), Harry S. Truman (1945–53), John F. Kennedy (1961–63), Lyndon B. Johnson (1963–69), Jimmy Carter (1977–81) and Bill Clinton (since 1993). Democrats have generally controlled both houses of Congress since 1932, although this has not meant that Democratic Presidents could automatically rely on congressional support, particularly in view of the strength of the conservative southern Democrats.

The loss of the presidency in the 1980 election was followed by two further presidential defeats in 1984 (in which Walter Mondale was the Democratic candidate) and 1988 (contested by Michael Dukakis). However, in 1986 the party regained control of the Senate, which it had lost in 1980, and increased its majority in the House of Representatives. In the 1992 elections Bill Clinton won back the presidency for the Democrats (in a contest heavily influenced by the strong performance of an independent candidate, Ross Perot, who was later to found the Reform Party), while the party preserved its congressional majorities. However, the Democrats suffered a devastating setback in the mid-term elections in 1994,

again losing control of the Senate and, more dramatically, losing their majority in the House of Representatives for the first time since 1954.

Having in February 1996 won the Democratic caucuses with 100% of the vote, President Clinton was duly nominated to run for second term in the November 1996 elections at the Democratic national convention meeting in Chicago in August, when Vice-President Al Gore was again nominated as his running-mate.

The Democratic Party is an observer member of the Christian Democrat International and of the Liberal International.

Reform Party

Leadership. Ross Perot (leader)

In the 1992 presidential election Ross Perot, a wealthy Texas businessman, stood as a populist independent candidate, concentrating his campaign on the economic question of reducing the federal budget deficit. Although he came third, he attracted 18.9% of the popular vote, a significant proportion of which, it was believed, would otherwise have gone to the defeated Republican candidate, George Bush. In September 1995 Perot announced that he would form a new party as a challenge to the country's two-party structure, the resultant Reform Party duly nominating Perot as its presidential candidate in August 1996. Shortly afterwards Perot announced his selection of Pat Choate, a prominent market economist, as his vice-presidential running-mate. The Reform Party calls for a balanced budget, term limits for legislators, campaign and lobbying reforms, and a protectionist trade stance.

Republican Party

Address. Republican National Committee, 310 First Street SE, Washington, DC 20003
Telephone. (#1–202) 863-5000
Fax. (#1–202) 863-8820
Leadership. Haley Barbour (national chair), Trent Lott (Senate majority leader), Richard Armey (House majority leader)

The Republican Party, generally more conservative than the Democratic Party, is opposed to over-centralization of government power and in recent years has advocated welfare and tax reforms to reduce public expenditure in those areas, economic growth with due regard to environmental protection, and a strong military defence.

Informally known as the "Grand Old Party (GOP)", the Republican Party was founded in 1854 by opponents of slavery. It unsuccessfully contested the 1856 presidential elections, but in 1860 its candidate, Abraham Lincoln, was elected President with the votes of the country's 18 northern states. Thereafter it held the presidency for all but eight years until the 1912 elections, when it also lost control of the Congress. The party regained the presidency in 1920, but lost it again in 1932 in the shadow of the economic depression. The Republicans did not return to power until the election of Gen. Dwight D. Eisenhower as President in 1952. In 1960 and 1964 Republican presidential candidates were unsuccessful, but the party regained power with the election of Richard M. Nixon in 1968 (although it failed to gain control of Congress). As a result of the Watergate scandal, Nixon became the first US President to resign office (in August 1974), his successor being Vice-President Gerald Ford, who in 1976 narrowly lost the presidential election to his Democratic rival, Jimmy Carter.

In 1980 Ronald Reagan won back the presidency for the Republicans, who also gained a majority in the Senate for the first time since 1952. Although Reagan was convincingly re-elected President in 1984, the party fared badly in the 1986 mid-term elections, losing control of the Senate to the Democrats who also increased their majority in the House of Representatives. George Bush (Reagan's Vice-President) won the presidency for the Republican Party again in 1988, but was ousted after one term by the Democrat, Bill Clinton, in the 1992 elections, which also confirmed the Democratic majority in Congress. In the 1994 mid-term elections, however, the Republicans enjoyed a resurgence, winning control of both congressional houses.

Following the party caucuses and primary elections during February and March 1996, the Republican national convention in San Diego in August confirmed the nomination of Bob Dole as the party's presidential candidate for the forthcoming elections in November 1996, together with Jack Kemp as his running-mate. In May 1996 Dole had announced that he was not only giving up his post of majority leader in the Senate but that he was retiring from the Senate altogether to concentrate on his election campaign against President Clinton.

The Republican Party is a member of the International Democrat Union.

Minor Parties

American Independent Party, originally established to promote the presidential candidacy of the segregationist George Wallace in 1968.

Communist Party of the United States of America (CPUSA), founded in 1919, led by Gus Hall (general secretary).

Democratic Socialists of America (DSA), established under its present name in 1982, led by Alan Charney (national director); a member of the Socialist International.

Greens/Green Party USA, an ecological party which nominated veteran consumer rights campaigner Ralph Nader as its candidate for the November 1996 presidential election.

International Green Party (IGP), led by Randall Toler.

Libertarian Party (LP), formed in 1971 and chaired by Mary T. Gingell, standing for individual freedom, a free-market economy, civil liberties and an anti-interventionist foreign policy; the 1996 LP presidential candidate was Harry Browne.

National Patriot Party (NPP), favouring electoral reform and a flat tax.

National States' Rights Party (NSRP), a right-wing and White supremacist party.

National Unity Party (NUP), subscribing to principles derived from the liberal rather than conservative strand of Republicanism.

Natural Law Party (NLP), US version of the worldwide network of parties promoting the ideas of the Maharishi Mahesh Yogi; its 1996 presidential candidate was John Hagelin.

Populist Party of America (PPA), chaired by Donald Wassall, espousing a nationalist philosophy.

Prohibition Party (PP), chaired by Earl F. Dodge, opposed to alcohol, drug abuse, abortion and euthanasia.

Social Democrats USA (SDUSA), led by Don Slaiman, a member of the Socialist International.

Socialist Labor Party (SLP), led by Robert Bills.

Socialist Workers' Party (SWP), headed by Jack Barnes.

US Taxpayers' Party (USTP), conservative formation advocating the abolition of the Internal Revenue Service and the elimination of federal income tax.

US Dependencies

The achievement of independence by Palau in October 1994 effectively terminated the US government's administration of the United Nations Trust Territory of the Pacific Islands, the other components of which had either achieved full independence or, in the case of the Northern Marianas, opted for US Commonwealth status on the same basis as Puerto Rico. These two territories are covered below, together with the other US dependencies of significance in the Pacific and the Caribbean.

American Samoa

Capital: Pago Pago   **Population:** 52,000 (1995E)

The South Pacific islands known collectively as American Samoa form an unincorporated territory of the United States, administered since 1951 by the US Department of the Interior. Executive authority is vested in a Governor, who is popularly elected for a four-year term. The bicameral legislature (*Fono*) consists of an 18–member Senate chosen by traditional clan leaders, and a popularly elected 20–member House of Representatives. The territory has a non-voting delegate to the US House of Representatives. Local elections are usually contested on a non-party basis but the main US parties contend for higher offices. In November 1992 the Democratic Party gubernatorial candidate, A.P. Lutali, defeated the Republican Party incumbent, Peter Tali Coleman.

Guam

Capital: Agaqa   **Population:** 130,000 (1995E)

The Pacific island of Guam is an unincorporated territory of the United States and is administered by the US Department of the Interior. Executive power is exercised by a Governor elected by universal adult suffrage for a four-year term. The unicameral Guam Legislature has 21 members who are popularly elected for a two-year term. The territory elects one delegate to the US House of Representatives. Political activity mirrors that on the US mainland and is therefore dominated by the Democratic Party and Republican Party. In the gubernatorial election of November 1994, a Democrat, Carl Gutierrez, defeated his Republican opponent, while in simultaneous elections to the Legislature the Democrats retained control with a slightly reduced majority.

Northern Mariana Islands

Capital: Sapian   **Population:** 45,000 (1995E)

Originally part of the UN Trust Territory of the Pacific administered by the United States, the Northern Mariana Islands voted to become a US Commonwealth Territory in 1975, following which a new constitution came into effect in 1978. One of two US Commonwealth Territories (the other being Puerto Rico), its inhabitants have US citizenship. Executive authority is held by the Governor, elected by universal adult suffrage for a four-year term. The Northern Marianas Commonwealth Legislature consists of a directly elected Senate and House of Representatives. Political activity mirrors that on the United States mainland. In the gubernatorial elections of November 1993, the Democratic Party won control of the office of Governor. In legislative elections in November 1995 the Republican Party retained its majorities in both the House of Representatives and the Senate.

Puerto Rico

Capital: San Juan   **Population:** 3,650,000 (1995E)

The Caribbean island of Puerto Rico was ceded by Spain to the United States in 1898 and has, since acquiring Commonwealth status in 1952, been in "free association" with the USA. Although Puerto Rico residents are US citizens they do not vote in US elections and are represented in the US Congress by a Resident Commissioner, elected for a four-year term. Executive power is exercised by an elected Governor assisted by an appointed Cabinet. Legislative power is vested in the bicameral Legislative Assembly, comprising a 27–member Senate and a 53–member House of Representatives; both chambers are directly elected for a four-year term.

In a referendum held in November 1993 on Puerto Rico's constitutional future, 48% of voters opted for continued Commonwealth status, 44% for statehood within the USA and 4% for independence.

New Progressive Party
Partido Nuevo Progresista (PNP)

Address. c/o House of Representatives, San Juan

Leadership. Pedro Rosselló (leader)

Formed in 1967, the PNP advocates a more equitable distribution of wealth and the incorporation of Puerto Rico as a state within the USA. Having broken away from the Popular Democratic Party (PPD), the PNP contested the 1968 elections, winning the governorship and a majority in the House of Representatives. In opposition from 1972, it reorganized to regain the governorship and win a majority in both chambers in 1976. In

1980 it retained the governorship but narrowly lost its legislative majority. After a split in 1983 and a further electoral defeat in 1984, the party's president and unsuccessful gubernatorial candidate, the former Governor Carlos Romero Barceló, resigned. His successor, Baltasar Corrada del Río, failed to regain the governorship from the PPD in 1988. The PNP's fortunes revived in the November 1992 elections, when its leader, Pedro Rosselló, won the gubernatorial poll (with 49.9% of the vote compared to 45.9% for his PPD rival) and the party secured strong majorities in both the Senate and the House of Representatives (with 20 and 36 seats respectively).

Popular Democratic Party

Partido Popular Democrático (PPD)

Address. 403 Ponce de León Ave, POB 5788, Puerta de Tierra, San Juan, PR 00906

Leadership. Héctor Luis Acevedo (leader)

The liberal PPD, which favours the retention and enhancement of Puerto Rico's Commonwealth status, was the dominant political formation from 1940 until a split in the party in 1968 gave a majority in the House of Representatives to the New Progressive Party (PNP). Having regained the governorship and control of the legislature in 1972, the PPD again lost its majority in elections in 1976. In 1980 the party won control in both chambers by a slim margin, although the governorship remained with the PNP until 1984 when the PPD's Rafael Hernandez Colón was returned to office. Hernandez Colón was re-elected in 1988, but his successor as PPD leader, Victoria Muñoz Mendoza, was defeated in the gubernatorial balloting in November 1992 by the PNP candidate. In legislative elections held at the same time the PPD lost the majority it had enjoyed in both the Senate and the House of Representatives, retaining only six and 16 seats respectively.

Puerto Rican Independence Party

Partido Independentista Puertorriqueño (PIP)

Address. 963 F.D. Roosevelt Ave, Hato Rey, San Juan, PR 00918

Telephone. (#1-809) 782-1430

Fax. (#1-809) 782-2000

Leadership. Rubén Berrios Martínez (president)

The moderate left-wing PIP was formed in 1946 and has campaigned for full independence for Puerto Rico as a socialist democratic republic. In the November 1992 elections the party won a single seat in both the Senate and the House of Representatives, and its gubernatorial candidate took third place with 4.1% of the vote.

The PIP is a member party of the Socialist International.

Other Parties

Puerto Rican Communist Party (*Partido Comunista Puertorriqueño*, PCP), founded in 1934, advocates full independence and severance of ties with the United States, but has attracted very little popular support.

Puerto Rican Socialist Party (*Partido Socialista Puertorriqueño*, PSP), formed in 1971 and led by Juan Mari Bras and Carlos Gallisa; seeks the establishment of an independent Puerto Rican socialist republic, but has received only a small percentage of the vote in recent elections.

US Virgin Islands

Capital: Charlotte Amalie, St Thomas

Population: 100,000 (1995E)

Located in the Caribbean east of Puerto Rico, the US Virgin Islands were purchased from Denmark and proclaimed US territory in 1917. The group is an "unincorporated territory" administered under the US Department of the Interior. Executive authority is vested in a Governor, directly elected for a four-year term, and legislative authority in a 15–member Senate, popularly elected every two years. The islands send a non-voting delegate to the US House of Representatives.

Gubernatorial elections held in November 1994 were won by an independent candidate, Roy Schneider, who defeated a Democratic Party contender. Another independent defeated a Democratic Party rival for the islands' seat in the House of Representatives.

Democratic Party of the Virgin Islands

Address. POB 3739, Charlotte Amalie, St Thomas, VI 00801

Telephone. (#1–809) 774 3130

Leadership. Marylyn A. Stapleton (chair)

The party is affiliated to the Democratic Party in the United States. Alexander Farrelly won the gubernatorial elections in 1986 and 1990 for the Democrats.

Independent Citizens' Movement (ICM)

Address. Charlotte Amalie, St Thomas, VI 00801

Leadership. Virdin C. Brown (chair)

The ICM was formed by a breakaway group of the Democratic Party, and one of its members, Cyril E. King, was elected Governor in 1974. He died in 1978 and was succeeded by the ICM's Juan Luis, who was re-elected to an additional term in 1982. At the gubernatorial election in 1986 the ICM candidate was defeated by the Democratic Party contender.

Republican Party of the Virgin Islands

Address. Charlotte Amalie, St Thomas, VI 00801

Telephone. (#1–809) 776 7660

Leadership. Sheron E. Hodge (chair)

The party is affiliated to the Republican Party in the United States.

Uruguay

Capital: Montevideo

Population: 3,200,000 (1995E)

The independence of the Republic of Uruguay was recognized in 1828 after a period in which its territory was the subject of a dispute between Argentina and Brazil. Internal politics has since been dominated by the struggle between the liberal Colorado (red) and the conservative Blanco (white) parties, giving rise to civil wars throughout the 19th century. The Colorados held power continuously from 1865 to 1958 before giving way to the Blancos. The illusion that Uruguay was the Switzerland of Latin America was shattered when in 1971 laws curtailing civil liberties were introduced to give the army a free hand in fighting the Tupamaro guerrillas, and two years later in 1973 the armed forces took power, dissolving Congress and replacing it with an appointed Council of State. Although by 1976 the military promised a return to democracy, their regime of terror continued, with an estimated 6,000 political opponents imprisoned and subjected to torture. With an eye on eventually transferring power to a civilian government, the military regime drafted a new constitution meant to assure the army a say in all national security matters. This was rejected by a plebiscite in November 1980. Amidst mass protests, demonstrations and strikes and an economic crisis, the military finally agreed in August 1984 to elections being held in November, subsequently won by the Colorado candidate, Julio María Sanguinetti. His government was marked by a major controversy over whether a "full stop" (*punto final*) amnesty law should be conferred on all military and police personnel accused of human rights infringements, which was finally approved in a referendum in April 1989. The first fully free elections since the coup were held in November 1989, from which the Blancos emerged as the winning party.

Presidential and congressional elections were held on Nov. 27, 1994. Julio María Sanguinetti of the opposition Colorado Party was elected President. Elections to the Senate ended in a very close result, with the Colorados taking 11 seats, the Blancos 10 seats and the Progressive Encounter nine. In elections to the Chamber of Deputies, the Colorados won 32 seats and the Blancos and the Progressive Encounter 31 each. President Sanguinetti took office on March 1, 1995, when a new broad-based government was sworn in, in which, in addition to the Colorados and the Blancos, the Party for the Government of the People (PGP) and the Civic Union (UC) were represented.

Under the 1966 constitution the republic has an executive President who is assisted by a Vice-President and an appointed Council of Ministers. Legislative power is vested in a National Congress consisting of a 99-member Chamber of Deputies and a 31-member Senate. The Vice-President is a member of the Senate and presides over Senate business but is also permitted to vote. Following the return to civilian rule in 1985 a National Constituent Assembly was installed on July 1, 1985, to draw up a series of constitutional reforms to be submitted to a plebiscite for ratification. An executive presidency was replaced with a nine-member collective leadership but was reintroduced in 1986. The President is elected for a five-year term by direct universal suffrage and cannot be re-elected. The Vice-President, senators and deputies are also elected by proportional representation for fixed five-year terms. Senators are elected from a national constituency and deputies from the 19 regional subdivisions. Under Uruguayan electoral law, the electorate votes for factions within each party itself. The winner of the presidential election has to win the largest number of votes within his party and come from the party which has secured a simple majority among the electorate. Voting is compulsory for all citizens who are 18 or older.

Under Uruguay's referendum law, any citizen can start a petition to hold a referendum, which has to be held if the petition contains signatures of at least 25% of the electorate.

Broad Front

Frente Amplio (FA)

Address. 1367 Colonia 2°, Montevideo

Leadership. Tabaré Vazquez (1994 presidential candidate); Carlos Baraibar (political secretary)

A constituent part of the Progressive Encounter alliance, the FA is itself an alliance of five separate leftist parties formed in 1971. The alliance is a left-wing grouping whose election demands in 1989 included the alleviation of social hardship, the reduction of unemployment and the control of inflation. One of its main policies is its opposition to privatisation.

The coalition originally consisted of 17 parties of such diverse allegiances as the Christian Democratic Party (PDC) and the Communist Party of Uruguay (PCU), and various Colorado and Blanco factions.

Internal divisions caused by former *Tupamaro* guerrillas joining the Front and over the nomination of a presidential candidate led to a serious split in March 1989, with the departure of the PDC, PGP and UC (who together formed New Space—NE). The front nevertheless scored considerable success in the November 1989 elections; Líber Seregni, once more the presidential candidate, came third with 21 per cent of the valid vote. The Front also came third in the congressional elections with 21 seats in the Chamber and seven seats in the Senate.

On a national level, the Front supported a broad campaign against the Blanco government's privatization programme and in Congress voted against proposed austerity measures.

As of April 1992, the Communists were displaced as the dominant grouping in the FA by the Socialists. Although not having a majority in the group's plenum, the influence of the Socialists' Tabaré Vazquez grew. In March 1994 he was declared the alliance's presidential candidate.

The members of the Broad Front alliance are the Communist Party of Uruguay, the National Liberation Movement, the Oriental Revolutionary Movement, the Party for the Victory of the Poor, and the Uruguayan Socialist Party.

Christian Democratic Party

Partido Demócrata Cristiano (PDC)

Address. Yaguaron 1318 bis, Montevideo

Telephone. (#598-2) 908546

Fax. (#598-2) 921044

Leadership. Mario Cayota (president), Adolfo Perez Pierra (secretary-general)

A centre-left party within the Progressive Encounter alliance (alongside the Broad Front), the PDC was founded in 1962 and is an affiliate of the Christian Democrat International. The party was formed as a successor to the Civic Union of Uruguay, a progressive party founded in 1872. The majority decision to join the Broad Front in 1971 caused a more conservative section to split away and form the Civic Union (UC). Like all Broad Front parties, the PDC was banned after the coup in 1973 but was legalized again in July 1984.

In 1988 the Christian Democrats opposed the inclusion of the former *Tupamaros* guerrillas (by now called the National Liberation Movement) in the Broad Front. Soon afterwards, the party had further disagreements with the more left-wing members of the Front when the candidacy of Hugo Batalla, (leader of the Party for the Government of the People, PGP) was not approved for the 1989 presidential elections. The Christian Democrats, together with the PGP and the UC, withdrew from the Broad Front in March 1989 and together formed the New Space alliance, which came fourth in the November 1989 general election. The PDC joined the Progressive Encounter alliance in 1994.

Civic Union

Unión Civica (UC)

Address. Río Branco 1486, Montevideo

Telephone. (#598-2) 905535

Leadership. Luis Pieri (1994 presidential candidate)

The Civic Union was originally a centre-right faction of the Christian Democratic Party (PDC) which split away when the PDC joined the Broad Front in 1971. It was suppressed under the military regime but was allowed to operate again from 1981. It won two seats in the Chamber of Deputies in the November 1984 general elections and its presidential candidate Vicente Chiarino came fourth with 2.3% of the vote. He subsequently joined the Colorado government as Defence Minister. In 1989 the Civic Union joined the Christian Democrat-led New Space alliance.

Colorado Party
Partido Colorado (PC)
Address. Vásquez 1271, Montevideo
Telephone. (#598-2) 490180
Leadership. Julio María Sanguinetti Cairolo (*Foro Batllista* faction); Jorge Pacheco Areco (1994 *Unión Colorado Batllista* presidential candidate); Pablo Miuor (*Cruzada 94* faction); Jorge Battle Ibáñez (1994 *Battlista Unido* presidential candidate and PC secretary-general)

The Colorados emerged from the 1936-48 civil war and were named after the liberals' red flag. The party first came to power in 1865 and governed Uruguay uninterruptedly for 93 years. The party was dominated by the Batlle family— one of whom, José Batlle y Ordóñez, during two terms as President (1903-07 and 1911-15) introduced a wide-ranging social welfare system, and *Batllismo* became synonymous with welfarism and industrial development. Having lost the collective leadership (which replaced the presidential system in 1951-66) the Colorados regained power in the 1966 elections which gave them 50 of the 99 seats in the Chamber and re-introduced the presidency.

The Nov. 25, 1984, elections which marked the end of Uruguay's military rule was narrowly won by the leader of the Colorado "Unity and Reform" faction, Julio María Sanguinetti, with 38.6% of the vote.

Sanguinetti's most controversial policy was the *punto final* ("full stop") law granting amnesty and immunity from prosecution to military and police officers accused of gross human rights violations during the military rule of 1973-85. Although widely opposed, the need to mollify the military was uppermost in the government's mind and the amnesty law was passed by Congress in December 1986 with the assistance of the Blancos.

In the internal selection in May 1989 for the party's main presidential candidate in the November 1989 elections, Sanguinetti's Vice-President and preferred choice, Enrique Tarigo, was beaten by the neo-liberal Jorge Batlle Ibáñez. He came second with 30% of the national vote and the Colorado Party went into opposition with 30 seats in the Chamber and nine seats in the Senate.

As the second largest party in Congress, the Colorados signed an agreement with the new Blanco government pledging support for the government's economic reform programme in return for four ministerial posts (industry and energy, health, tourism, territories and environ-

ment). The agreement with the Blancos was effectively ended in January 1993 following a mid-term cabinet reshuffle. However, the Blancos allowed two Colorado ministers to remain in their posts until May 1994.

Communist Party of Uruguay
Partido Comunista del Uruguay (PCU)
Address. Rio Negro 1525, Montevideo
Telephone. (#598-2) 917171
Fax. (#598-2) 911050
Leadership. Marina Arismendi (secretary-general)

Once the main force in the Broad front, the PCU is a true left-wing party that was founded in 1920. The party originally was the Socialist Party, whose delegates to the 1920 party congress voted by a large majority to join the Communist Third International. Despite initial opposition from its leadership the party nevertheless joined and changed its name, registering as a legal political party the following year. Unusually for a Latin American Communist party, the PCU remained legally recognized for 52 years and regularly had candidates elected to Congress.

The party has also had a strong representation in the trade union movement throughout its history. Together with some small left-wing parties the PCU formed the Left Liberation Front (FIDEL) in 1962, which won several seats in Congress. In 1971 the PCU set up the Broad Front (FA) in conjunction with 16 other left-wing and centre-left parties and groups, and in the general election of the same year the Communists won two of the 18 FA seats in the Chamber.

As a result of the 1973 military coup the PCU was banned and fiercely persecuted. The party's secretary-general, Rodney Arismendi, was permitted to go into exile in the Soviet Union in 1975 but many others continued to be subjected to torture in prison. The PCU continued to be the dominant left-wing force in the Broad Front and took a major part in the campaign for a referendum on the *punto final* amnesty law and contributed to the Front's success in the Nov. 26, 1989, general election in which 21 Broad Front deputies and seven senators were elected. As part of the FA, the third political force in Uruguay, the PCU has remained an active opposition party.

National Liberation Movement
Movimiento de Liberación Nacional (MLN)
Leadership. José Mujica (secretary-general)

The left-wing MLN was founded in 1962 with guerrilla roots. It campaigns for rural reforms and contends that, although the MLN is intent on defending and deepening democracy, people should not renounce the right to defend themselves when known coup-mongers remain in the army.

The MLN was founded by Raúl Sendic Anton-accio as the *Tupamaros* guerrilla group (named in honour of the 18th century Peruvian Indian leader Tupac Amaru). It was originally concentrated in rural areas, motivated by the plight of the sugar cane cutters (whom Sendic had helped organize in the strikes of 1961-62) and seeking to "strike the local oligarchies" without using violence against the person. The group switched its attention to the cities in 1966.

Following the army offensive launched against them in 1972, and the ensuing military dictatorship, the MLN was virtually annihilated. On the return to democracy, most guerrillas were released in an amnesty in 1985, Sendic announcing that the MLN would now be working within the democratic political system. While piloting MLN towards parliamentary involvement, Sendic founded a movement to promote rural reform. Although at first excluded from the Broad Front, the MLN was finally permitted to join in late 1988. In May 1989 it obtained legal recognition as a political party.

Following the departure of the centrist PDC, PGP and UC, the MLN became an influential part of the Broad Front alliance. During 1991, however, relations with other Front members cooled somewhat, amid calls from the MLN to stage new elections for the alliance's leadership.

National Party

Partido Nacional (Blancos) (PN)
   Address. 18 de Julio 2338, Montevideo
   Telephone. (#598-2) 903355
   Leadership. Carlos Alfredo Cat Vidal (president); Luis Alberto Lacalle Herrera (*Herrerista* faction); Gonzalo Aguirre Ramírez (*Renovación y Victoria* faction); Carlos Julio Pereyra (*Movimiento Nacional de Rocha* faction and 1994 presidential candidate); Eduardo Pons Etcheverry (*Divisa Blanca* faction); Alberto Sáenz de Zumaran (secretary-general and leader of *Por la Patria* faction)

The Blancos, who derive their name from the conservatives' white flag in the 1836-38 civil war, were founded by large landowners to defend their interests in the civil wars. The National Party was for a long time the permanent opposition party and only turned to parliamentary politics after the unsuccessful 1904 uprising. It focused mainly on the rural constituencies and did not win national power until 1958 when the Blancos obtained six of the nine seats on the National Executive Council. The party retained a majority in this collective national leadership in the elections of 1962. However, in 1966, when the presidential system was re-installed, the PN lost the elections to the Colorados. The party leader, Wilson Ferreira Aldunate, won the most votes of any single candidate in the 1971 presidential elections, but

lost the election under the aggregate party vote system. He was forced into exile after the 1973 military coup and was imprisoned for six months on his return in 1984. Other reformist PN members who had remained in the country suffered persecution and imprisonment.

For the presidential elections of Nov. 26, 1989, the party selected Luis Alberto Lacalle Herrera, representing the right wing, as its main candidate. He won the presidency with only 37% of the ballot and the party did not perform well in the Congressional elections, taking 13 seats out of the 30 in Senate and 38, only just over a third, in the House of Deputies. In the important elections for the mayorship of Montevideo, held simultaneously, the main Blanco candidate Carlos Alfredo Cat Vidal came second with 27% of the vote.

In early 1990 Lacalle resigned the leadership of the Blanco Party and his presidency of the national executive committee of the party's *Herrerista* faction in order to be able to take up his post as President of Uruguay.

Despite this search for national consensus, the Lacalle government met with sustained opposition from the Inter-Union Workers' Assembly-Worker's National Convention (PIT-CNT), who staged numerous general strikes between 1990 and 1992 against the government's austerity programme, but also from sections of the Colorado Party and even a faction of the Blancos.

By 1992, the business sector was turning against Lacalle in protest at higher corporate income tax and social security contributions along with the removal of tax concessions and protection for the car industry.

At the 1994 polls, four Blancos presented themselves as presidential candidates, none being elected.

New Space

Nuevo Espacio (NE)
   Address. c/o Congreso, Montevideo
   Leadership. Rafael Michelini

This electoral alliance was formed by the Christian Democratic Party (PDC), the Party for the Government of the People (PGP) and the Civic Union (UC) after the PDC and PGP left the Broad Front (FA) in March 1989 following disagreements over the presence in it of the former *Tupamaros* guerrillas, its policies and the choice of presidential candidate for the forthcoming elections.

The New Space alliance backed the moderate campaign of Hugo Batalla, the leader of the PGP, who came fourth in the Nov. 26, 1989, elections with 8.5% of the national vote. The alliance together won nine seats in the Chamber and two seats in the Senate.

In the run-up to the 1994 elections, the PDC left

to join the Progressive Encounter alliance and the Civic Union withdrew to campaign separately. PGP members remained the backbone of the NE and came in fourth in the 1994 election.

Oriental Revolutionary Movement
Movimiento Revolucionario Oriental (MRO)
  Leadership. Walter Artola, Mario Rossi
  A left-wing pro-Cuban former guerrilla group, the MRO has been a part of the Broad Front since its foundation in 1971.

Party for the Government of the People
Partido por el Gobierno del Pueblo (PGP)
  Address. Ejido 1480, Montevideo
  Tel. (#598-2) 987194
  Fax. (#598-2) 982736
  Leadership. Hugo Batalla (secretary-general)
  The leader of this small break-away group from the Broad Front is currently Vice-President of the Republic. The PGP is a consultative party in the Socialist International.

Party for the Victory of the Poor
Partido por la Victoria del Pueblo (PVP)
  Leadership. Hugo Corres (president)
  A relatively recent addition to the Broad Front, the PVP has recently characterised itself as an internal dissenter within the alliance. It has particularly criticised the MRO for its re-advocation of armed revolutionary struggle.

Progressive Encounter
Encuentro Progresista (EP)
  Address. c/o Congreso, Montevideo
  Leadership. Tabaré Vazquez (1994 presidential candidate)
  The EP was formed prior to the 1994 election, in which it came a creditable and surprise third behind the Blancos. The constituent parties in this left-of-centre alliance are the Broad Front (*Frente Amplio*, FA) (see below) and the Christian Democratic Party (*Partido Demócrata Cristiano*, PDC). The EP's third place finish finally broke up the two-party stalemate in Uruguayan politics.

Uruguayan Socialist Party
Partido Socialista del Uruguay (PSU)
  Address. Casa del Pueblo Soriano, 1218 Montevideo
  Telephone. (#598-2) 913344
  Fax. (#598-2) 982548
  Leadership. José Pedro Cardoso (president), Reinaldo Gargano (secretary-general)
  The PSU was founded in 1910 by Emilio Frugoni and reorganized after the majority split away to form the Communist Party (PCU) in 1921. The PSU moved to the left in 1959 and became a founder member of the Broad Front (FA) in 1971 and one of its leaders, Tabaré Vázquez, became the first left-wing mayor of Montevideo in the November 1989 elections.

Other Parties

Blue Party (*Partido Azul*, PA) is led by Dr Roberto Canessa and Armando Val.

Democratic Labour Party (*Partido Demócrata Laboral*, PDL) led by Polpeyo Giansanti.

Federal and Pacific Sun (*Sol Federal y Pacifista*), was formerly the Ecological Green Party led by the 90-year-old Rodolfo Tálice. It is now led by Homero Mieres.

Justice Party (*Partido Justiciero*, PJ) led by Luis Espinola.

Progressive Party (*Partido Progresista*, PP), led by Elías Perdomo.

Workers' Party (*Partido de los Trabajadores*, PT) is a far left-wing party founded in 1984, led by Juan Andrade (who was the party's 1994 presidential candidate).

Uzbekistan

Capital: Tashkent

Population: 22,500,000 (1995E)

The Republic of Uzbekistan declared its independence from the Soviet Union at the end of August 1991. This was confirmed in a referendum on Dec. 29 1991. Simultaneous direct presidential elections were won by the chair of the Supreme Soviet (the then highest legislative body), Islam Karimov, with a reported 86% of the total votes. Also in December 1991, Uzbekistan became a member of the Commonwealth of Independent States (CIS).

A new constitution, adopted in December 1992, provided for a smaller legislature, the 250-member Supreme Assembly (*Oly Majlis*). Elections to this body were held for the first time on December 25, 1994, and on January 8 and 22, 1995. The ruling, former communist, People's Democratic Party (PDP), led by President Karimov, won 69 seats, while the Progress of the Fatherland grouping gained 14. The majority of the remaining 167 deputies, although local council nominees, were also PDP members, ensuring the party's continued domination.

In a referendum held in March 1995 voters almost unanimously backed an extension of Karimov's term of office to the year 2000.

Freedom
Erk

Leadership. Mohammad Salih (chair)

Freedom (Erk), one of the main opposition parties, was established in 1990 as an offshoot of Unity (Birlik), but remains banned by the PDP regime. Its leader was President Karimov's only rival in the December 1991 direct presidential elections.

Independence Path
Istiqlal Yoli

Leadership. Shadi Karimov (leader) Independence Path was formed in 1994, but was not permitted to register to take part in the legislative elections held in December 1994 and January 1995.

Islamic Renaissance Party (IRP)

Leadership. Abdullah Utayev (leader)

The IRP was banned in 1991 under legislation outlawing religious political parties.

Justice (Social Democratic Party of Uzbekistan)
Adolat

Address. c/o Oly Majlis, Tashkent

Leadership. Anwar Jurabayev (First Secretary) Justice was registered as a new political party in February 1995, establishing a parliamentary faction claiming to have the support of nearly 50 deputies in the Supreme Assembly. The party advocates greater social justice and the consolidation of democratic reform.

National Revival Democratic Party
Milli Tiklanish

Leadership. Aziz Qayumov (chair) Including several prominent Uzbek intellectuals, the National Revival Democratic Party was formed in May 1995, favouring democracy and the establishment of a law-based state. The party was officially registered in June 1995.

People's Democratic Party (PDP)

Address. c/o Oly Majlis, Tashkent

Leadership. Islam Karimov (leader)

The PDP, formerly the ruling Communist Party of Uzbekistan, restructured itself as the People's Democratic Party in November 1991. It has since remained the dominant political force under President Karimov's authoritarian leadership. As one of only two parties permitted to register for the legislative elections in December 1994 and January 1995, the PDP secured a landslide majority in the Supreme Assembly. President Karimov reportedly resigned his position as party chair in June 1996.

People's Unity Movement
Khalq Birliki

Reportedly pro-government, the movement emerged as a political formation in May 1995 and was officially registered the following month.

Progress of the Fatherland

Address. c/o Oly Majlis, Tashkent

Leadership. Anwar Yoldashev (chair) Progress

of the Fatherland was formed in 1992. It advocates the development of a market economy, and is supportive of the ruling People's Democratic Party (PDP). It was the only party, other than the PDP, permitted to contest the legislative elections in December 1994 and January 1995, gaining 14 seats in the Supreme Assembly.

Unity
Birlik

Leadership. Abdurakhim Pulatov (chair) Unity, a nationalist and secular organization, was formed in the late 1980s as the first significant non-communist political grouping in Uzbekistan. As one of the main opposition parties—although split in 1990 by the defection of some members to form Freedom (Erk)—Unity has been subjected to repressive measures by the ruling People's Democratic Party under President Karimov, and was outlawed in 1992.

Other Parties

Forum for Democratic Forces, under the leadership of Shukrulla Mirsaidov.

Party of Social Progress of Uzbekistan, led by Fayzulla Ishkanov.

People's Movement of Turkestan, formed in 1991 and led by Bakhrom Hazip. It advocates the unification of those states which were formerly Turkestan.

Samarkand Movement, with a small membership consisting of ethnic Tajiks.

Uzbekistan Society for Human Rights, formed in 1992 and led by Abdumanob Pulatov.

Vanuatu

Capital: Port Vila

Population: 168,000 (1995E)

Vanuatu, the former Anglo-French condominium of the New Hebrides, became an independent republic in July 1980. Legislative authority is vested in a unicameral Parliament, the 50 members of which are elected for four years on the basis of universal adult suffrage. Executive power is exercised by a Prime Minister (who is elected by Parliament from among its members) and by a Council of Ministers, which consists of members of Parliament appointed by the Prime Minister. The President, the republic's head of state, is elected for five years by an electoral college composed of the Parliament and presidents of the regional councils (local government bodies to which a considerable degree of power is constitutionally devolved).

The general election held on Nov. 30, 1995, was contested by three main political groupings: the ruling Union of Moderate Parties (UMP), the Unity Front (UF, consisting of the *Vanua'aku Pati*, the Melanesian Progressive Party and the Tan Union) and the National United Party (NUP). These groupings secured 17, 20 and nine seats respectively. Of the remaining four seats, the *Na-Griamel* and *Fren Melanesia* parties won one each, and two were won by independents. After a confused period of inter-party negotiation, Serge Vohor, the president of the UMP, was elected Prime Minister in December 1995 and formed a coalition government comprising the UMP, NUP and *Na-Griamel*. However, Vohor resigned from office in February 1996 in a political crisis reflecting serious factional divisions within the UMP. He was replaced by his UMP rival, Maxime Carlot Korman, who had been Prime Minister until the November 1995 election and who formed a new coalition with the Unity Front.

Fren Melanesia

Address. c/o Parliament, Port Vila

A small regionalist party, *Fren Melanesia* won a single parliamentary seat in both the December 1991 and November 1995 elections.

Melanesian Progressive Party (MPP)

Address. POB 39, Port Vila

Leadership. Barak Sope (chair)

The MPP was organized in 1988 by a breakaway group from the *Vanua'aku Pati* (VP) led by Barak Sope. In 1989 it absorbed the Vanuatu Independent Alliance Party (VIAP) and the National Democratic Party (NDP). Having returned four representatives to Parliament in the 1991 general election, the MPP contested the November 1995 poll as a constituent of the Unity Front (UF), which won 20 seats. In February 1996 the UF joined the faction of the Union of Moderate Parties (UMP) supporting Maxime Carlot Korman in a new coalition government.

Na-Griamel

Address. c/o Parliament, Port Vila

Leadership. Frankie Stevens (leader)

Na-Griamel was founded by Jimmy Stevens, whose secessionist revolt on the island of Espiritu Santo was put down in 1980. Stevens died in February 1994 (having been released from prison in 1991) and his son assumed the leadership of the movement. *Na-Griamel* participated in the formation of the opposition Unity Front (UF) in late 1994 (despite Frankie Stevens' earlier defection to the government headed by Maxime Carlot Korman of the Union of Moderate Parties), but reportedly switched its allegiance back to the government in February 1995. In the November 1995 general election *Na-Griamel* secured one parliamentary seat, and was subsequently included in the short-lived UMP-National United Party coalition formed by Serge Vohor in December.

National United Party (NUP)

Address. c/o Parliament, Port Vila

Leadership. Fr. Walter Hadye Lini (president)

The NUP was launched by Fr. Lini following his removal as leader of the then ruling *Vanua'aku Pati* (VP) in 1991. In the general election in December of that year the NUP gained 10 parliamentary seats and joined the coalition supporting Maxime Carlot Korman of the Union of

Moderate Parties (UMP). The UMP-NUP coalition was beset by internal problems during 1993 and in August a majority NUP faction led by Lini withdrew its support of Carlot Korman. However, some NUP members defied instructions by continuing to support the government, and were expelled from the party in May 1994 (following which they formed the People's Democratic Party). In the November 1995 general election the NUP won nine seats and, in December, joined the faction of the UMP supporting Serge Vohor in a new coalition government (which survived only until February 1996).

People's Democratic Party (PDP)

Leadership. Sethy Regenvanu (leader)

The PDP was formed in mid-1994 by a former minority faction of the National United Party (NUP) which refused to endorse Fr. Walter Lini's break with the Union of Moderate Parties (UMP) in August 1993. The party formed a coalition with the UMP until the November 1995 general election, in which it failed to retain any seats.

Tan Union

Address. c/o Parliament, Port Vila

Leadership. Vincent Boulekone (leader)

The Tan Union, comprising a breakaway group of deputies from the Union of Moderate Parties (UMP), contested the November 1995 general election as a constituent of the Unity Front (UF). The UF won 20 seats and, in February 1996, joined the faction of the Union of Moderate Parties (UMP) supporting Maxime Carlot Korman in a new coalition government.

Union of Moderate Parties (UMP)

Address. POB 698, Port Vila

Leadership. Serge Vohor, Maxime Carlot Korman (factional leaders)

The francophone UMP was formed in 1980 as a coalition of groups opposed to the *Vanua'aku Pati* (VP) government. Under the leadership of Vincent Boulekone, it came second to the VP in both the 1983 and 1987 elections. Boulekone was replaced by Maxine Carlot Korman after the 1987 balloting and subsequently broke away from the UMP as head of the Tan Union. Following its success in the December 1991 election, in which it won 19 out of 46 seats, the UMP joined with the Fr. Walter Lini's National United Party (NUP) to form a coalition under Carlot Korman's premiership. While a majority NUP group under Lini went into opposition in August 1993, a minority NUP faction (that became the People's Democratic Party) remained in the coalition as the UMP's junior partner. In the November 1995 election the UMP won 17 out of 50 seats. In the subsequent

inter-party negotiations over the formation of a new government, it became clear that the UMP was seriously split between factions led by the outgoing Prime Minister, Carlot Korman, and the party president, Serge Vohor. The party's executive council eventually decided in favour of the NUP as a coalition partner and chose Vohor, rather than Carlot Korman, for the post of Prime Minister. However, in February 1996 Carlot Korman's supporters, together with the opposition Unity Front (UF), succeeded in bringing down Vohor's administration and forming a new coalition.

Unity Front (UF)

Leadership. Donald Kalpokas, Barak Sope, Vincent Boulekone (leaders)

The anglophone UF was formed prior to provincial elections in November 1994 as an opposition formation comprising the *Vanua'aku Pati* (VP), the Melanesian Progressive Party (MPP), the Tan Union, and the *Na-Griamel* movement (which reportedly switched its allegiance to the government in February 1995). In the November 1995 general election the UF won 20 of the 50 seats in the Parliament. In February 1996 it joined the faction of the Union of Moderate Parties (UMP) supporting Maxime Carlot Korman to oust the UMP-National United Party government installed the previous December and form a new coalition administration.

Vanua'aku Pati (VP)

Address. c/o Parliament, Port Vila

Leadership. Donald Kalpokas (president)

The VP was established in the early 1970s as the New Hebrides National Party, adopting its present title in 1977. Under the leadership of Fr. Walter Lini, the party won a majority of seats in the Representative Assembly in November 1979, and Lini formed a VP government which led the country to independence as Vanuatu the following year. Lini then became Prime Minister. Despite the emergence of internal dissent, the VP retained power in the 1983 and 1987 elections. In 1988 the former VP secretary-general, Barak Sope, and four colleagues resigned from the VP and announced the formation of a rival Melanesian Progressive Party (MPP). By 1991 there was diminishing support for Lini's leadership and in the autumn of that year he was ousted and replaced as party leader and Prime Minister by Donald Kalpokas (whereupon Lini and his supporters formed the National United Party). In the wake of the party split, the VP was defeated in the December 1991 general election. The party contested the November 1995 as a constituent of the opposition Unity Front (UF), which won 20 seats. In February 1996 the UF joined the faction of the Union of Moderate Parties (UMP) supporting

Maxime Carlot Korman in a new coalition government.

Other Parties

Efate Laketu Party, a regional party formed in 1982 and based on the island of Efate.

Independent Front, launched in mid-1995 by UMP dissidents under the leadership of Patrick Crowby.

Namake Auti, a northern regional group representing rural interests.

New People's Party, established in 1986 and header by Frazer Sine.

Vanuatu Labour Party, a trade union-based grouping formed in 1986 and led by Kenneth Satungia.

Venezuela

Capital: Caracas

Population: 21,800,000 (1995E)

The Republic of Venezuela achieved full independence from Spain in 1830. It was mostly ruled by *caudillos* ("strong men") and the military until 1945, when Gen. Enisaías Medina Angarita was removed by a coup led by progressive young army officers and supported especially by an ambitious middle class. An interim revolutionary junta was established and a new constitution introduced which for the first time provided for the election of the President and Congress by universal suffrage. The first President elected under the new constitution, Rómulo Gallegos, was deposed by a military coup in 1948, however, and a period of military rule followed. Gen. Marcos Pérez Jiménez, who proclaimed himself President in 1952, alienated all sections of opinion by his corrupt and repressive rule, and was overthrown in 1958 by a popular uprising. The two strongest parties, Democratic Action (AD) and the Social Christian Party (COPEI), have since alternated in office, the former holding power from 1958 to 1968, 1973 to 1978 and since 1983. The AD's Carlos Andrés Pérez, who had been President from 1973 to 1978, again won the presidential elections for the AD in 1988. Harsh economic austerity measures, introduced in 1989, subsequently provoked major social unrest throughout the country which were repressed by use of the army, resulting in the loss of more than 600 lives and the detention of 7,000 people. The continuation of these policies, and the reluctance of sections of the army to be used again as a social pacifier, culminated in a serious coup attempt against Pérez in February 1992 which resulted in 14 deaths and the detention of over 1,000 rebel soldiers.

Under the new 1961 constitution as amended, executive power is vested in the President, who is assisted by and presides over an appointed Council of Ministers and who may not be re-elected. Legislative power is exercised by a bicameral National Congress, the Senate having at least 46 elected members and as life members the ex-Presidents of constitutional governments, and the Chamber of Deputies currently having 199 members. The President and National Congress are directly elected for concurrent five-year terms. Adult suffrage is universal and nominally compulsory. The 22 Venezuelan states and one federal district are autonomous and each has a governor and an elected assembly. Since December 1989 governors are also directly elected.

Presidential elections held on Dec. 5, 1993, resulted in a victory for Rafael Caldera Rodriguez, heading the 17-party National Convergence (CN) coalition. In simultaneous congressional elections, the CN won only a minority of seats. The new government took office on Feb. 2, 1994.

Communist Party of Venezuela

Partido Comunista de Venezuela (PCV)

Address. Edificio Cantaclaro, esq. San Pedro, San Juan Caracas

Telephone. (#58-2) 410061

Fax. (#58-2) 481 9737

Leadership. Ortega Diaz (president), Trino Melean (secretary-general)

Founded in 1931, the party was pro-Soviet and its support seriously dwindled prior to the collapse of the Soviet Union and the eastern bloc. The country's oldest existing party, it operated underground until 1942 and to 1945 as the Venezuelan Popular Union (UPV), a legal front. The party then temporarily split into the PCV, which favoured co-operation with the then Medina government and was legalized by it, and the UPV which opposed this policy.

At the 1960 Moscow conference, the PCV was one of a few Communist parties to support China in the Sino-Soviet split. Under the influence of the Cuban revolution, a number of younger Communist leaders, most notably Douglas Bravo and Teodoro Petkoff, joined activists of the Movement of the Revolutionary Left (MIR) in forming the Armed Forces of National Liberation, which began guerrilla activities in 1962 with Cuban assistance. After two years of internal controversy, the party abandoned its support for the guerrilla struggle in 1967, and Bravo and his followers, who advocated its continuation, were expelled. As a result of its participation in the guerrilla war the party's membership fell heavily and it lost almost all of its influence in the trade union movement.

For the 1988 elections, the PCV formed an alliance with the People's Electoral Movement (MEP), performing so poorly that it needed to re-register its membership in order to qualify for participation in subsequent elections. In 1988 the MAS had also turned down PCV overtures for a common presidential candidate, although there was some co-operation between the two in the concurrent state assembly and national congressional elections. Hector Mujica resigned as PCV leader in August 1991.

Democratic Action

Acción Democrática (AD)

Address. Calle los Cedros, Entre Avenida Los Jabillos y Samanes, La Florida, Caracas

Telephone. (#58-2) 749855

Leadership. Pedro Paris Montesino (president), Luis Alfaro Ucero (general secretary)

Founded in 1936, the AD is nominally social democratic but has promoted deeply unpopular conservative policies when it has been in office. The party was formed by Rómulo Betancourt under the name of National Democratic Party (*Partido Democrático Nacional*, PDN) and was registered as a legal party under its present name in 1941. Its grass-roots support came mainly from organized labour.

Control of the AD in late 1987 went to the faction supporting the charismatic populist and former President, Carlos Andrés Pérez, and opposed to President Lusinchi's austerity policies. Pérez was subsequently selected to fight the December 1988 presidential elections, which he won with 52.91% of the vote. The party, however, won only 97 seats in the Chamber and 23 in the Senate and thus lost control of Congress. After his inauguration in February 1989, Pérez introduced an IMF-approved austerity programme which was followed by days of mass protest, rioting and supermarket looting throughout the country.

Despite regular popular protests and opposition from within the party, Pérez refused to alter his neo-liberal economic policies. He introduced a wide-ranging privatization programme, including that of the state airline Viasa in August 1991, which attracted criticism from the business community for being too sluggish. Furthermore, Pérez was highly criticized from all sides for devoting more of his time to international affairs than to national problems.

As opposition to Pérez mounted within the party, the AD became increasingly dominated by the "orthodox" faction supporting ex-President Lusinchi. This was confirmed in the September 1991 internal party elections when the pro-Pérez "renewalists" won only 44% of the votes. In the party leadership elections at the party convention on Oct. 6, 22 of the 26 posts on the national executive committee went to the "orthodox" wing, as did the presidency of the party.

The November 1991 general strike against cost of living increases and widespread student protest led conservative opposition deputies to warn of a military coup unless emergency measures were taken. These warnings were amply fulfilled when, on Feb. 3 and 4, 1992, rebel army units tried to take over the government palace and presidential residence in an apparent attempt to assassinate Pérez. He narrowly escaped and in a television broadcast rallied loyal troops who put down the uprising. His request to opposition parties to join a "political" Cabinet to help draft policies for the following two years was initially rebuffed, but in March the Social Christian Party (COPEI) accepted two portfolios in a "Cabinet of National Unity". COPEI withdrew from the government in June 1992.

In the national elections of December 1992 the party fared badly at both state and municipal level. To confirm the AD's decline and departure from power, its presidential candidate, Claudio Fermin, was beaten into second place with only 23.6% of the vote, behind Rafael Caldera.

The AD is a member party of the Socialist International.

Democratic Republican Movement

Unión Republicana Democrática (URD)

Address. Quinta Amalia, Avenida Páez, El Paraíso, Caracas

Leadership. Ismenia Villalba

The centrist URD has been a fixture in Venezuelan politics since 1946. Originally opposed to the dominance of the Democratic Action (AD) when it came to power following a progressive military rebellion in 1945, the URD initially supported the AD government's overthrow in the military coup of 1948.

In 1978 the URD had only three congressional deputies, who sat with the Social Christian Party (COPEI) opposition bloc. In the 1983 elections, it supported the New Alternative (NA) and won eight seats in the Chamber and two in the Senate. Since then, it has made little electoral impact, whether standing on its own or in alliances.

Movement of the Revolutionary Left

Movimiento de Izquierda Revolucionaria (MIR)

Leadership. Héctor Perez Marcano (president)

The MIR was founded in 1960 by members of a large left-wing dissident group which split away from the ruling Democratic Action (AD) and included among its ranks 13 deputies and most of the AD's student section. The party's ideology was inspired by the Cuban revolution and in 1962 it began guerrilla operations mainly in rural areas. MIR members were being arrested for "subversion" in 1960 and it was completely banned in 1962. A section of the membership renounced violence in 1965 but the main group, led by Américo Martín and Moisés Moleiro, continued the armed struggle until 1969. In that year MIR accepted the Caldera government's offer of an amnesty and was legalized soon after.

In the 1983 presidential election the MIR supported the candidate of the Movement Towards Socialism (MAS) but stood alone in the congressional elections, in which the party won only two seats in the Chamber. Like the MAS, the MIR became much more pragmatic during the 1980s and in 1988 the two parties joined forces. The resultant electoral alliance won 18 seats in the Chamber and three in the Senate and the MAS-MIR presidential candidate, Teodoro Petkoff, took third place with 2.73% of the vote. The party supported the CN's Rafael Caldera in the 1993 presidential campaign.

Movement Towards Socialism

Movimiento al Socialismo (MAS)

Address. Urb. Las Palmas, Av. Valencia, Qta. Alemar, Caracas

Telephone. (#58-2) 782 7309

Fax. (#58-2) 782 9720

Leadership. Enrique Ocho Antich (secretary-general)

This democratic socialist party was founded in 1971. The MAS was formed by the bulk of the membership of the Communist Party of Venezuela (PCV), a majority of Communist trade union leaders, and almost the entire PCV youth movement, following a split in 1970. The split had occurred after the expulsion of PCV leader and former guerrilla leader Teodoro Petkoff for his open condemnation of the 1968 Soviet invasion of Czechoslovakia and his rejection of both Soviet and Eurocommunist models for the development of Venezuelan socialism.

The party's growing success, however, was hampered in the run-up to the 1983 election when it split into supporters of Petkoff and those who, backing Rangel as the representative of a broad left alliance, broke away from the party. Petkoff, with the support of the Movement of the Revolutionary Left (MIR), won 4.2% (as opposed to Rangel's 3.3%) but the MAS's representation in the Chamber of Deputies fell to 10 seats and to only two in the Senate.

The two parties formed an alliance in 1988 when Petkoff once more stood for the presidency in the December elections, although one sector of the party wanted to support the Democratic Action (AD) candidate, Carlos Andrés Pérez, in order to concentrate the alliance's efforts on the congressional elections. Petkoff came third with 2.73% of the presidential vote, as did the MAS-MIR alliance, which obtained 18 seats in the Chamber and three in the Senate. Because the ruling AD failed to retain its congressional majority the MAS gained considerable influence as part of the congressional opposition block.

After the attempted military coup in early February 1992, the MAS leadership was invited by President Pérez to take part in a "Cabinet of National Unity" to draft policies for last two years of his term. Aware of the compromising position in which this would place the party, the MAS rejected the offer. In March and April, it supported anti-government protests, demanding the restoration of constitutional rights and Pérez's resignation.

MAS joined COPEI in a 1992 coalition that won ten state governorships and supported the National Convergence's Rafael Caldera in his successful 1993 presidential bid.

National Convergence

Convergencia Nacional (CN)

Address. Parque Central, Edificio Tajamar, Mezzanina, Caracas

Telephone. (#58-2) 576 8341

Fax. (#58-2) 576 8214

Leadership. Rafael Caldera Rodríguez (leader), Juan José Caldera (general co-ordinator)

The CN was launched in 1993 as a presidential campaign vehicle for Rafael Caldera, who was successful in December 1993. The CN itself, alongside its electoral ally the Movement to Socialism (MAS), could only manage third place in the lower house poll, winning only 51 of the 199 available seats.

National Opinion

Opinión Nacional (OPINA)

Address. Pájaro a Curamichate 92-2, Caracas 1010

Leadership. Pedro Luis Blanco Peñalver (president)

OPINA is a centre-right party founded in 1961 to promote its own version of "collective integralism". It won a seat in the Chamber of Deputies in 1978, when it endorsed the COPEI presidential campaign. Its own candidate won only 0.5% of the poll in 1983 but the party took three seats in the Chamber. The party has won no seats since.

New Alternative

Nueva Alternativa (NA)

Address. Edif. José María Vargas, esq. Pajaritos, Apdo. 20193, San Martín, Caracas 1010.

Telephone. (#58-2) 563 7675

Leadership. Guillermo García Ponce (secretary-general)

The NA is an alliance of democratic left-wing parties founded in 1982. Its founder members comprised the Martín faction of the Movement of the Revolutionary Left (MIR), the Unitary Communist Vanguard (VUC), the People's Revolutionary Movement (MRP) and the Movement of the Socialist Fatherland (MPS). The member parties have since acted as one in the New Alternative. The NA won two seats in the Chamber of Deputies in the 1983 elections but in 1988 failed to obtain any representation in Congress. Its presidential candidate, Leopoldo Díaz Bruzual, a former Social Christian Party (COPEI) member and ex-president of the Central Bank, was widely criticized on the left and received a negligible numbers of votes. Secretary-general Ponce was among other left-wing leaders to meet with a delegation from the Korean Workers Party (KWP) in the Ecuadorian capital Quito in April 1992.

New Democratic Generation Liberal Party

Partido Liberal Nueva Generación Democrática (PLNDG)

Address. Avenida Andrés Bello, Centro Andrés Bello, Torre Oeste, Piso 12, Officina 122-0, Las Palmas, Caracas 1010.

Telephone. (#58-2) 793 3512

Fax. (#58-2) 793 3512

Leadership. Germán Febres Chaitaing (president)

This centre-right party was founded in 1961 to promote its own version of "collective integralism". Originally called the New Generation (*Nueva Generación*, NG), it forged the PLNDG alliance in 1989 with two smaller groups: Formula One (*Fórmula Uno*, F1) and the Authentic Renovating Organisation (*Organización Renovadora Auténtica*, ORA) to form a legislative alliance called the Venezuelan Emergent Right (*Derecha Emergente de Venezuela*, DEV).

The PLNGD is an observer member of the Liberal International.

Peoples' Electoral Movement

Movimiento Electoral del Pueblo (MEP)

Address. Edificio MEP, Av. Buenos Aires, Urbanización Los Caobos, Caracas

Telephone. (#58-2) 781 7186

Fax. (#58-2) 782 4697

Leadership. Adelso González Urdaneta (general secretary)

The MEP split from Democratic Action (AD) in 1968 and initially was based mainly in the Confederation of Venezuelan Workers (CTV). It achieved some success through alliances, chiefly with the Communist Party of Venezuela (PCV). In 1988 its presidential candidate, Edmundo Chirinos, former rector of the Central University of Venezuela, was supported by the PCV and the Independent Moral Movement but won less than 1% of the vote and its congressional representation fell to two deputies. In 1989 an MEP candidate, Ovidio González, supported by a broad "anti-corruption" front including the Social Christian Party (COPEI), won the governorship of Anzoátegui.

The MEP is a consultative member of the Socialist International.

The Radical Cause

La Causa Radical or *Causa R (LCR)*

Address. Esq. De Pajaritos, Edif. Administrativo, Congreso Nacional, Fracción Causa R, Caracas

Telephone. (#58-2) 541 2412

Leadership. Lucas Matheus (general secretary)

The party controls the 17,000-member union of the steel company Sidor and has its main support base in the Guayana industrial region. The LCR joined the New Alternative (NA) in the 1983 elections but in the 1988 elections stood by itself and won three seats in the Chamber of Deputies, attracting votes away from traditional left-wing parties. The party leader and presidential candidate, Andrés Velásquez, came fifth and in the 1989 gubernatorial elections won the governorship of Bolívar. Opposed to the ruling Democratic Action (AD) and its austerity policies, the LCR openly expressed sympathy for rebel officers who tried to depose President Carlos Andrés Pérez in February 1992. Its then leader, Noé Acosta, was arrested on Feb. 6 in the city of Maracaibo. In March the LCR characterized Pérez's appeal for a "Cabinet of National Unity" as a farce and joined with the Movement Towards Socialism (MAS) in supporting a one-day strike against the government on April 8.

In December 1992 the party won the mayoralty of Caracas. The party came in fourth in December 1993, with 21.9% of the vote.

Social Christian Party

Partido Social-Cristianol Comité de Organizatión Politica Electoral Independiente (COPEI)

Address. San Miguel a Palo Negr, Entre Av. Panteón y Fuerzas, Caracas

Telephone. (#58-2) 519033

Fax. (#58-2) 521876

Leadership. Luis Herrera Campins (president), Donald Ramirez (secretary-general)

Founded in 1946, COPEI is a centrist, Christian democratic party which is the Venezuelan affiliate of the Christian Democrat International. The party was founded by Rafael Caldera as the Organizing Committee for Independent Electoral Policy (*Comité de Organización Política Electoral Independiente*), whose acronym COPEI is still in use despite the party's change of name.

Rafael Caldera was again selected to fight the December 1983 election but, after a particularly vitriolic campaign in which the AD attacked the incumbent Herrera government on economic and personal grounds, lost to the AD candidate winning 34.6% of the vote. The party obtained only 60 seats in the Chamber and 16 in the Senate. In December 1988 the COPEI put forward Eduardo Fernández as its presidential candidate but with 40.42% of the vote once again lost the election to the AD. Its representation in the Chamber, however, increased to 67 seats and in the Senate to 22, making it the dominant party in the majority opposition bloc in Congress.

Following the unsuccessful February 1992 military coup, the COPEI, along with the Movement Towards Socialism (MAS), declined President Pérez's request to the main opposition parties to join a "political Cabinet" of ministers without portfolio to draft policies for the next two years. They characterized the move as a "cosmetic" operation which would not lead to any significant changes in the government's economic policies. However, in early March two COPEI ministers joined a "Cabinet of National Unity", one of whom, Humberto Calderón Beti, was named as the new Foreign Minister. Pérez stated that this provided evidence of COPEI's "sense of responsibility" in agreeing to "demonstrate its solidarity with the Venezuelan democratic government". It also produced a split within the party, with one faction still determined to oppose the government and insisting that Pérez resign. However, COPEI withdrew from the government in June 1992.

In the elections of 1992 the party won a total of ten gubernatorial seats in alliance with the MAS. Then, in June 1993, former President Caldera Rodríguez was expelled from the party for standing as an independent presidential candidate in the December elections. The COPEI nominee, Oswaldo Alvarez Paz, came third behind the victorious Caldera.

Other Parties

National Integration Movement (*Movimiento de Integración Nacional*, MIN) is a nationalist party that was founded in 1977. It is led by Gonzalo Perez Hernández.

National Redemption (*Rescate Nacional*, RN), led by retired general Luis Enrique Rangel Bourgoin, the party's 1983 presidential candidate.

Party of the Venezuelan Revolution (*Partido de la Revolución Venezolana*, PRV) is headed by former guerrilla leader Douglas Bravo.

Socialist League (*Liga Socialista*, LS) was founded in 1974 and is led by Carmelo Laborit. It has had no Chamber seats since 1988.

Vietnam

Capital: Hanoi

Population **Population:** 75,000,000 (1995E)

The Socialist Republic of Vietnam was proclaimed in July 1976, after North Vietnam-backed Communist insurgents had effectively reunified the country in April 1975 by overthrowing the United States-supported government of South Vietnam. (North and South Vietnam had been divided into separate states in 1954, following protracted Communist-led resistance to French colonial authority.) Effective political power has since been exercised by the Communist Party of Vietnam (CPV), the sole legal political party.

In 1992 a new constitution entered into force, which enshrined the market-oriented economic reforms undertaken since the mid-1980s, while ensuring that the CPV maintained its position as "a leading force of the state and society". Under the constitution the National Assembly (*Quoc Hoi*), the highest organ of state power, elects the President (from among its own deputies for a five-year term), the Vice-President and the Prime Minister, and ratifies the Prime Minister's proposals for appointing members of the government.

Elections to the 395–member National Assembly were held in July 1992. Candidates were nominated by the Vietnam Fatherland Front, the CPV-controlled body embracing the country's various mass organizations. In September 1992 the National Assembly elected Gen. Le Duc Anh as President.

Communist Party of Vietnam (CPV)
Dang Cong san Viet Nam
> *Address.* 1C Hoang Van Thu Street, Hanoi
> *Telephone.* (#84–4) 431472
> *Leadership.* Do Muoi (secretary-general)

The CPV is descended from the Communist Party of Indo-China (CPIC), founded in 1930 by Ho Chi Minh and other Communists, which in April 1931 was recognized as an autonomous section of the Third (Communist) International (or Comintern). Born in 1890 as Nguyen Tat Thanh in the Annam province of what was then French Indo-China, Ho Chi Minh (literally "Ho the seeker of enlightenment") had been a founder member of the French Communist Party in 1920 and had subsequently worked as an agent of the Comintern in Asia. Following the formation of the CPIC, a peasant rebellion broke out in Indo-China with Communist backing, after the suppression of which Ho was sentenced to death *in absentia* by the French authorities. After the failure of a further Communist-led uprising in 1940, Ho joined Indo-Chinese exiles on the Chinese border and in 1941 formed the Communist-dominated Viet Minh guerrilla organization, which harried the Japanese during World War II.

Immediately after the Japanese surrender in August 1945 the Viet Minh set up a provisional government in coalition with other nationalist groups and on Sept. 2, 1945, the Democratic Republic of Vietnam was proclaimed in Hanoi with Ho as its President as well as Prime Minister and Foreign Minister. Various attempts to reach a compromise settlement with the re-established French authorities broke down and from late 1946 Ho's Viet Minh guerrillas engaged in bitter hostilities with the French forces which culminated in the decisive defeat of the latter at Dien Bien Phu in May 1954. Meanwhile, at its second congress in February 1951, the CPIC had divided into independent Cambodian, Laotian and Vietnamese formations, the last-named taking the name Vietnam Workers' Party (VWP). Under the 1954 Geneva agreements Vietnam was temporarily divided at the 17th parallel and Ho Chi Minh became both President and Prime Minister of North Vietnam, relinquishing the premiership in 1955 but retaining the presidency and party chairmanship until his death in September 1969.

At its third congress in 1960 the party decided *inter alia* "to promote the national people's democratic revolution in South Vietnam" and "to unify the country on the basis of independence and democracy". The ensuing war against the then government of South Vietnam, which was supported by the United States, ended in the conquest of South Vietnam in April 1975 followed by the reunification of the country as the Socialist Republic of Vietnam. At the fourth party congress held in December 1976, the party's name was changed to Communist Party of Vietnam. Early in 1977 the three mass organizations led by the party–the National Front for the Liberation of South Vietnam (established in 1960), the Vietnamese Alliance of Democratic and Peace Forces (set up in 1968) and the (North Vietnamese) Fatherland Front (dating back to 1955)–were merged in one national Vietnam Fatherland Front with the object of "uniting all political parties, revolutionary mass organizations, progressive classes, nationalities, religions and notables in the country and overseas Vietnamese" and of "ensuring broad unity of all forces loving the country and approving socialism under the leadership of the Communist Party of Vietnam". Other parties included in the Front were the Socialist Party and the Democratic Party.

At the fifth party congress, held in Hanoi in March 1982, Le Duan, then CPV general secretary, declared *inter alia* that the party had established "the dictatorship of the proletariat in the whole country" and had waged two wars—"against the expansionism and hegemonism of the Chinese reactionary leadership" (in 1979) and against aggression in the South by the Cambodian "Pol Pot clique"—and that "a militant alliance between Cambodia, Laos and Vietnam" had also strengthened "militant solidarity with the Soviet Union". He described the task of the party during the 1980s as being to guide the people and the Army "to build socialism successfully and to defend the socialist Vietnamese fatherland". His report also emphasized the need of consolidating party unity, and he criticized members who had "damaged the prestige of the party", warning that they would be expelled.

In the political report presented to the sixth CPV congress in December 1986 by Truong Chinh (general secretary in succession to Le Duan, who had died in July 1986), it was admitted that existing serious shortcomings in the country's economy and social life had "lessened the confidence of the masses in the party leadership and the functioning of state organs". It was expressly acknowledged that the central committee, the political bureau, the secretariat and the Council of Ministers were "primarily responsible for the above-mentioned errors and shortcomings". The report addressed a number of these errors, in particular in economic planning for investment allocation and capital construction in 1976–80, and it found that the target set by the fifth party congress had not been met. Truong Chinh resigned as general secretary during the sixth congress, and Nguyen Van Linh (real name Nguyen Van Cuc) was elected as his successor. In February 1987, amid a series of leadership changes, it was officially revealed that more than 190,000 persons, many of them guilty of serious errors and having sought to acquire wealth and exorbitant privileges, had been expelled from the party.

A further major restructuring of the party leadership took place at the seventh party congress in June 1991, when seven of the 12 CPV politburo members lost their posts, only three secretariat members retained theirs and Do Muoi was elected general secretary in succession to Nguyen Van Linh. Since then the party has been engaged in its own version of economic and political reform known as *doi moi*. Some progress has been made in renovating the Vietnamese economy, especially in the encouragement of private enterprise, but the leadership has been unmoved by the collapse of communism in Eastern Europe and the demise of the Soviet Union, maintaining stern resistance to any moves towards political pluralism.

Western Sahara

Capital: El Aaiún   **Population:** (in dispute)

The former Spanish Western Sahara (consisting of Saguia el Hamra and Rio de Oro) was partitioned between Morocco and Mauritania under a 1975 treaty following Spain's decision to withdraw from a region which it had controlled since the 19th century. However, this decision was not accepted by the territory's principal national liberation movement, the Popular Front for the Liberation of Saguia el Hamra and Rio de Oro (Polisario Front), which proclaimed the Sahrawi Arab Democratic Republic (SADR) in 1976. The SADR has since been recognized by more than 70 countries (and by the Organization of African Unity), despite Morocco's extension of sovereignty over the whole territory when Mauritania officially renounced all claims in 1979.

The protracted and militarily inconclusive conflict between Morocco and the Polisario Front has been the subject of United Nations mediation efforts, envisaging the holding of a UN-sponsored referendum to determine the future status of the territory. However, preparations for such a referendum have repeatedly stalled over the issue of voter eligibility and a date remains to be set. In May 1996 the UN Security Council unanimously recommended the suspension of the UN Mission for the Referendum in Western Sahara (MINURSO) because of lack of the co-operation required for it to complete its assigned task.

Popular Front for the Liberation of Saguia el Hamra and Rio de Oro (Polisario Front)

Frente Popular para la Liberación de Saguia el Hamra y Rio de Oro (Frente Polisario)

Address. BP 10, El-Mouradia, Algiers

Leadership. Mohammed Abdelazziz (secretary-general)

Formed in 1973 to pursue independence for Spanish Sahara, the socialist Polisario Front was initially based in Mauritania, but its political leadership has operated since the mid-1970s from Algeria, although with diminishing backing from the government of that country. A congress in 1982 elected the Front's secretary-general, Mohammed Abdelazziz, as President of the SADR. The Front's main organs are a seven-member executive committee, a 27–member political bureau and a 45–member Sahrawi National Council.

In a post-Cold War climate much less friendly to liberation movements, the military stalemate and reduced financial and material support from Algeria and Libya caused serious problems for Polisario, which suffered from a stream of defections to Morocco, including the SADR foreign minister, Brahim Hakim, in August 1992. On the UN's initiative, Polisario and Moroccan government representatives had their first open meeting in El Aaiún in July 1993, without substantive result. A further such encounter, scheduled for October 1993, was called off by Polisario at short notice in protest against the inclusion of SADR defectors in the Moroccan delegation.

Meanwhile, a new SADR government-in-exile announced in September 1993 featured the appointment as defence minister of the hard-line Brahim Ghali, a known advocate of a resumption of full hostilities if the UN process did not make speedy progress. The suspension of the UN mission in May 1996 raised fears of an imminent resumption of hostilities between Polisario and Morocco, although most observers believed that Polisario did not have sufficient military and manpower resources to mount a major campaign.

Western Samoa

Capital: Apia   **Population:** 162,000 (1995E)

Formerly administered by New Zealand (latterly with self-government), Western Samoa achieved full independence in 1962. The head of state acts as a constitutional monarch with the power to dissolve the unicameral 49-member legislative assembly (the *Fono*) and to appoint a Prime Minister upon its recommendation. The *Fono* is elected by universal adult suffrage for up to five years, although the right to stand for election remains confined to members of the *Matai* (elected clan leaders).

In the general election held on April 26, 1996, the ruling Human Rights Protection Party (HRPP) was returned to power despite a fall in support. The following month the leader of the HRPP and incumbent Premier, Tofilau Eti Alesana, was re-elected Prime Minister by members of the *Fono*.

Human Rights Protection Party (HRPP)

Address. POB 3898, Apia

Leadership. Tofilau Eti Alesana (leader)

The HRPP was founded in 1979 as Western Samoa's first formal political party. Having won 22 parliamentary seats in the 1982 general election, the party won an overall majority in 1985. However, subsequent defections brought down the government headed by Tofilau Eti Alesana at the end of that year. Tofilau Efi formed a new HRPP administration following the 1988 election, and the party's majority was enhanced in polling in 1991. In the 1996 election, the HRPP retained power with the support of independent deputies.

Samoan National Development Party (SNDP)

Address c/o Fono, Apia

Leadership. Tupua Tamasese Efi (leader)

The SNDP was formed in 1988 by an alliance of independents and Christian Democratic Party (CDP) members. The CDP had been formed by Tupua Tamasese Efi prior to the February 1985 general election and, in January 1986, had entered into a coalition government with a dissident faction of the Human Rights Protection Party (HRPP). The SNDP was constituted following the February 1988 election which saw the return to power of the HRPP, and it has since remained the principal opposition party.

Other Parties

Samoa Democratic Party (SDP), formed in 1993 by Le Tagaloa Pita, a previously independent deputy in the legislative assembly.

Samoa Liberal Party (SLP), established in early 1994 and led by Nonumalo Leulumoega Sofara.

Yemen

Capital: Sana'a

Population: 13,000,000 (1995E)

The Republic of Yemen was established in May 1990 through the unification of the Yemen Arab Republic (North Yemen) and the People's Democratic Republic of Yemen (South Yemen). A referendum held in May 1991 approved the country's new constitution. There had previously been no political parties in North Yemen, while South Yemen had been a one-party state. Unification and political liberalization led to the creation of a large number of political groups.

Elections to the country's legislature, the 301–member House of Representatives (*Majlis al-Nuwab*), were held on April 17, 1993, when 80% of the seats were won by the three major parties—the General People's Congress (GPC), the Yemeni *Islah* Party (YIP) and the Yemen Socialist Party (YSP)—which subsequently signed an agreement providing for the creation of a coalition government. Smaller parties won 12 seats, independent candidates 47 and one seat was undeclared. In October 1993 the House elected a five-member Presidential Council, which in turn elected the GPC's leader, Lt.-Gen. Ali Abdullah Salih, as the country's President.

Mounting tensions between the YSP, with its power base in former South Yemen, and the GPC from the North erupted into full-scale civil war between forces from the two former territories in May 1994. The southern leader and former Vice-President of unified Yemen, Ali Salim al-Bid, proclaimed the formation of the independent Democratic Republic of Yemen (DRY) in the South. In the North, which continued to designate itself the Republic of Yemen, YSP members were dismissed from political office and the armed forces. The DRY forces were defeated by the North in early July 1994 and its leadership fled abroad. In October 1994 the Presidential Council was abolished, President Salih was confirmed in office and a new GPC/YIP coalition, excluding the YSP, was formed.

General People's Congress (GPC)
Mutamar al-Shabi al-Am

Address. c/o House of Representatives, Sana'a
Leadership. Lt.-Gen. Ali Abdullah Salih (leader)

The GPC was formed in 1982 in the North as a 1,000–member consultative body rather than a political party. Lt.-Gen. Salih, the long-time President of the Yemen Arab Republic, relinquished his position as secretary-general of the GPC upon assuming the presidency of the Republic of Yemen in May 1990. With the Yemen Socialist Party (YSP), the GPC was responsible for guiding the new republic through a transitional period culminating in the 1993 legislative elections. In the elections the GPC was the most successful party with 123 seats. It subsequently formed a coalition government with the YSP and the Yemeni *Islah* Party (YIP), and took two seats on the Presidential Council. However, the GPC and YSP became increasingly estranged, leading to the 1994 civil war. In October 1994 the GPC formed a new coalition government with the YIP,

further strengthening its position as the dominant partner in a ministerial reshuffle in June 1995.

Yemen Socialist Party (YSP)
Hizb al-Ishtirakiya al-Yamaniya

Leadership. Ali Saleh Obad (secretary-general)

The YSP was formed in 1978 as a Marxist-Leninist "vanguard" party for the People's Democratic Republic of Yemen, and maintained one-party control of South Yemen despite several leadership conflicts until unification with the North in 1990. Upon unification the then YSP secretary-general, Ali Salim al-Bid, was named Vice-President of the new republic, in which the YSP, together with the General People's Congress (GPC) from the North, was charged with the management of the transitional period prior to elections.

Having won 56 seats in the 1993 legislative elections, the YSP was allocated nine cabinet posts in the subsequent coalition government and took two seats on the Presidential Council. However, increasing political tensions between the YSP and the GPC led to the outbreak of civil war in mid-1994 and the short-lived secession of the Democratic Republic of Yemen. Despite the election of a new party leadership after the civil war, the YSP was excluded from the new coalition government which was formed in October 1994.

Yemeni Islah Party (YIP)
Islah
    Address. c/o House of Representatives, Sana'a
    Leadership. Sheikh Abdullah bin Hussein al-Ahmar (leader)
    The YIP, also known as the Yemeni Alliance for Reform, was established in September 1990, attracting support from the conservative pro-Saudi population in northern tribal areas. The party campaigned against the new constitution adopted in May 1991 in alliance with several other groups advocating strict adherence to Islamic law. In the 1993 legislative elections the YIP emerged with 62 seats, subsequently assuming six cabinet posts in the coalition government and taking one seat on the Presidential Council. The party leader was also elected speaker of the House of Representatives.
    In the 1994 civil war the YIP strongly supported President Salih and the northern forces. It formed a new coalition with the dominant General People's Congress in the government announced in October 1994, although it lost ground in a ministerial reshuffle in June 1995.

Minor Parties

Baath Arab Socialist Party, Yemeni version of the historic pan-Arab Baath, returned seven successful candidates in the 1993 elections to the House of Representatives. In early 1995 the party was reportedly a constituent of a Democratic Coalition of Opposition.

Democratic Nasserite Party, pan-Arab socialist grouping which won one seat in the 1993 elections.

League of the Sons of Yemen, founded in 1990 to represent the interests of southern tribes. Although it fielded a substantial number of candidates in the 1993 elections, it failed to win any seats. The leader of the League, Abdul al-Rahman al-Jifri, was a prominent figure in the breakaway Democratic Republic of Yemen in mid-1994 and fled to Saudi Arabia following the North's victory. In early 1995 the party was reportedly a constituent of the Democratic Coalition of Opposition.

Nasserite Reform Party, another pan-Arab socialist grouping which won one seat in the 1993 elections.

People's Nasserite Party, a third pan-Arab socialist grouping which won a single seat in the 1993 legislative elections.

Truth Party (*Al-Haq*), led by Sheikh Ahmad ash-Shami (secretary-general), established by Islamic religious scholars in 1991, secured two seats in the House of Representatives in the 1993 elections.

Yemeni Unionist Alliance, formed in 1990 by intellectuals and politicians from the North and the South to protect human rights, led by Omar al-Jawi.

Yugoslavia

Capital: Belgrade   **Population:** 10,000,000 (1995E)

The one-party regime of the former League of Communists of Yugoslavia collapsed in 1989-90, heralding the breakup of the Yugoslav federation established in 1945. Four of the former constituent republics—Slovenia, Croatia, Bosnia and Hercegovina, and Macedonia—seceded during 1991. The remaining two republics of Serbia and Montenegro declared themselves the Federal Republic of Yugoslavia (FRY) in April 1992.

    Under the 1992 constitution federal legislative power is vested in the bicameral Federal Assembly, comprising a directly-elected 138-seat Chamber of Citizens (108 members from Serbia and 30 from Montenegro) and a 40-member Chamber of Republics (20 each for Serbia and Montenegro, selected on a proportional basis). Serbia and Montenegro each have republican assemblies and each republic has its own directly-elected President. Executive power is vested in a Federal President and government, although the Serbian President and leader of the Socialist Party of Serbia (SPS), Slobodan Milosevic, has been the most powerful political figure in the FRY.

The SPS remains the dominant political party in both the federal and Serbian republican governments, having secured 47 seats in elections to the Chamber of Citizens in December 1992 and 123 of the 250 seats in the Serbian assembly in December 1993. The strongest Montenegrin party at federal and republican level is the Democratic Party of Socialists of Montenegro, which won 17 federal seats and 46 out of 85 republican assembly seats in polling in December 1992.

Democratic Alliance of Kosovo
Demokratski Savez e Kosoves (DSK)
  Leadership. Ibrahim Rugova (president)
  Formed in 1989, the Democratic Alliance (also known as the Democratic League) is the main political expression for the ethnic Albanian majority in the province of Kosovo (now Kosovo and Metohija) in Serbia, the autonomous status of which was ended in 1990 provoking widespread Albanian protest against Serb rule. Advocating independent status for Kosovo, the Alliance won the majority of seats in provincial assembly elections organized by Albanians in May 1992, and Rugova was declared the "President of Kosovo". However, the elections were declared illegal by the Serbian and federal authorities and the assembly was prevented from holding its inaugural session. Elections to the Serbian republican assembly in December 1993 were boycotted by the Alliance.

Democratic Community of Vojvodina Hungarians
Demokratska Zajednica Vojvodjanskih Madjara (DZVM)
  Address. Trg Oslobodjenja 11, Ada
  Leadership. Agoston Andras (president)
  The DZVM, established in 1990, promotes the interests of the ethnic Hungarian minority in the province of Vojvodina in Serbia. In the December 1992 federal elections the party won three seats in the Chamber of Citizens. It retained five seats in the Serbian republican assembly elections in December 1993. The issue of whether or not the party should support an autonomist platform for Hungarians has created internal divisions.

Democratic Party
Demokratska Stranka (DS)
  Address. Terazije 3/IV, Belgrade
  Leadership. Zoran Djindjic (president)
  The DS was formed in 1990 by Dragoljub Micunovic, a respected academic. Having adopted a strongly Serbian nationalistic position, the party split in 1992; Micunovic withdrew from the leadership and a secessionist group formed the Democratic Party of Serbia. In the December 1992 federal elections the DS won five seats in the Chamber of Citizens. In the Serbian republican assembly elections in December 1993 it increased its representation to 29 seats.

Democratic Party of Albanians
Demokratska Partija Albanaca (DPA)
  Address. Selami Halaci bb., Presevo
  Leadership. Ali Ahmeti (president)
  The DPA, formed in 1990, operates among the Albanian community in Presevo, on the Macedonian border. In the Serbian republican assembly elections in 1993 it secured two seats working in coalition with the Party of Democratic Action.

Democratic Party of Serbia
Demokratska Stranka Srbije (DSS)
  Address. Smiljaniceva 33, Belgrade
  Leadership. Vojislav Kostunica (president)
  The DSS, set up in 1992 by a dissident faction of the Democratic Party, won seven seats in the Serbian republican assembly in the December 1993 elections. It has adopted a far-right political and nationalist stance.

Democratic Party of Socialists of Montenegro
Demokratska Partija Socijalista Crne Gore
  Leadership. Momir Bulatovic (president)
  Formerly the League of Communists of Montenegro, the party adopted its present name in 1991. Advocating continued federation, it is the dominant political formation in the republican assembly, having retained a majority of seats in the December 1992 elections. Party leader, Bulatovic, was elected President of Montenegro in a second ballot in January 1993. At federal level the party holds 17 seats in the Chamber of Citizens, and is a constituent of the coalition government led by the Socialist Party of Serbia (SPS).

Liberal Alliance of Montenegro
  Leadership. Slavko Perovic (leader)
  The Liberal Alliance supports independence for Montenegro. In the December 1992 republican assembly elections it took third place with 13 out of the 85 seats.

New Democracy
Nova Demokratija (ND)

Address. Ho Si Minova 27, Belgrade

Leadership. Dusan Mihailovic (president)

The ND was established in 1990 and, in 1992, joined the Democratic Movement of Serbia (Depos) opposition coalition (which was reconstituted in 1995 as the People's Assembly Party). Following the December 1993 republican assembly elections, however, it left the coalition, its six members transferring their support to the government led by the Socialist Party of Serbia (SPS).

Party of Democratic Action
Partija Demokratske Akcije (PDA)

Leadership. Numan Balic, Harun Hadzic, Sulejman Ugljanin, Riza Halili

Muslim-based elements of the PDA (with links to the Bosnian party of the same name) operate in Kosovo and Metohija (led by Balic), in Montenegro (led by Hadzic) and in Sandzak (led by Ugljanin). The PDA in Preveso (in the extreme south of Serbia), under the leadership of Halili, represents ethnic Albanians.

People's Assembly Party
Narodna Saborna Stranka (NSS)

Leadership. Slobodan Rakitic (president)

The NSS was originally formed in 1992 as the Democratic Movement of Serbia (Depos), a coalition of opposition parties including the Serbian Renewal Movement, New Democracy (ND), the Serbian Liberal Party and the Civic Alliance. The coalition secured 20 seats in the 1992 federal polling, and 45 seats in the Serbian assembly elections the following year (although this was subsequently depleted by the ND's secession to support the ruling Socialist Party of Serbia). Depos was reconstituted under its present name and leadership in January 1995.

People's Party of Montenegro
Narodna Stranka Crne Gore

Leadership. Novak Kilibarda (leader)

In December 1992 the People's Party, which advocates maintaining federal ties with Serbia, won 14 seats in the Montenegrin assembly elections and four seats in the federal Chamber of Citizens.

Reform Democratic Party of Vojvodina
Leadership. Dragoslav Petrovic (president)

In the 1992 federal elections the party won three seats in the Chamber of Citizens in coalitions with other parties.

Serbian Radical Party
Srpska Radikalna Stranka (SRS)

Address. Ohridska 1, Belgrade.

Telephone. (#381-11) 457745

Leadership. Vojislav Seselj (president)

The SRP, which was founded in 1991, is an extreme nationalist party advocating the establishment of a "Greater Serbia". It won 34 seats in the Chamber of Citizens in the 1992 federal elections, but its representation in the Serbian republican assembly was almost halved to 39 seats in the December 1993 polling. It also has eight seats in the Montenegrin assembly.

Serbian Renewal Movement
Srpski Pokret Obnove (SPO)

Address. Nusiceva 8/III, Belgrade.

Leadership. Vuk Draskovic (president)

The nationalist SPO was formed in 1990, largely from the personal following of its charismatic leader. The party became the lynchpin of the Democratic Movement of Serbia (Depos—later the People's Assembly Party) opposition coalition in the 1992 and 1993 elections (in which the coalition won 20 federal seats in the Chamber of Citizens and 45 seats in the Serbian republican assembly). The party subscribes to the ideal of a "Greater Serbia".

Socialist Party of Serbia (SPS)
Socijalisticka Partija Srbije (SPS)

Address. Lenjinov Bulevar 6, Belgrade.

Telephone. (#381-11) 457745

Leadership. Slobodan Milosevic (president), Milomar Minic (general secretary)

The SPS was created in 1990 from a merger of the former ruling League of Communists of Serbia and its associated Socialist Alliance. While acknowledging the importance of its links with the Communist movement in the past, the SPS stresses the importance of the democratic electoral process. The party advocates democratic socialism, its manifesto emphasising responsibility and stability. It sees a continuing role for the state in the economy, is opposed to unregulated enrichment and privatization, and advocates solidarity, participation and the defence of the system of social security.

The SPS has, since the declaration of the Federal Republic of Yugoslavia in April 1992, maintained its dominance as the principal partner in governing administrations at federal and republican level. In federal elections in December 1992, the SPS lost its narrow majority (which it had gained in earlier elections the previous May), but remained the largest single party in the Chamber of Citizens with 47 of the 138 seats. In the same month Slobodan Milosevic was re-elected President of Serbia with about 57.5% of the votes. In republican elections in December 1993 the party increased its representation to 123 seats in the 250-member Serbian assembly, thereafter forming a government with the support of the New Democracy party. Milosevic was overwhelmingly re-elected as SPS president by delegates at a party congress in March 1996.

Other Parties

Christian Democratic Party of Kosovo, formed in 1990 and led by Mark Krasniqi.

Democratic Alliance of Croats in Vojvodina (*Demokratski Savez Hrvata u Vojvodini*, DSHV), representing ethnic Croats in the Serbian province of Vojvodina. Its leader is Bela Tonkovic.

Democratic Reform Party of Muslims (*Demokratska Reformska Stranka Muslimana*, DRSM), a left-wing organization led by Azar Zulji.

League of Communists-Movement for Yugoslavia of Montenegro, chaired by Rade Lakusic.

League of Social Democrats of Vojvodina (*Liga Socijaldemokrata Vojvodine*), a moderate leftist formation.

National Peasant Party (*Narodna Seljacka Stranka*, NSS), founded in 1990 and led by Dragan Veselinov.

Nikola Pasic Serbian Radical Party (*Srpska Radikalna Stranka Nikola Pasic*), a nationalist party launched in January 1995 by disaffected members of the Serbian Radical Party.

Parliamentary Party of Kosovo (PPK), a liberal grouping formed in 1990 and led by Veton Surroi.

Party of Yugoslavs (*Stranka Jugoslovena*, SJ), led by Borislav Kosijer.

Peasant Party of Kosovo (*Partia Fshatare e Kosoves*, PFK).

Peasants' Party of Serbia (*Seljacka Stranka Srbije*, SSS), led by Milomir Babic.

Serbian Liberal Party (*Srpska Liberalna Stranka*, SLS), committed to a programme of personal and economic freedom, within a framework of parliamentary democracy. It is led by Nikola Milosevic.

Serbian Unity Party, a nationalist grouping formed in late 1993 with close links to the Socialist Party of Serbia (SPS). It is heavily centred upon the personality of its founder and paramilitary commander, Zeljko Raznjatovic ("Arkan").

Social Democratic Party (*Partia Social-Demokrate*, PSD), a Kosovo-based formation led by Shekelzen Maliqi.

Social Democratic Reformist Party, secured four seats in the Montenegrin republican assembly in the December 1992 elections.

Socialist Party of Montenegro, credited with five seats in the federal Chamber of Citizens in the 1992 elections.

Turkish Peoples Party (TPP), a Kosovo-based party led by Sezair Shaipi.

Yugoslav Green Party (*Zelena Stranka*), under the leadership of Dragan Jovanovic.

Yugoslav United Left, formed in 1995 by Mira Markovic (the wife of the Serbian President, Slobodan Milosevic). It derives from the former ruling League of Communists of Yugoslavia.

Zaïre

Capital: Kinshasa

Population: 40,000,000 (1995E)

The Republic of Zaïre assumed its present name in 1971, having achieved independence from Belgium as the Republic of the Congo in 1960. Mobutu Sese Seko, who took power in a military coup in 1965, has been President since 1970, ruling through the Popular Movement of the Revolution (*Mouvement Populaire de la Révolution*, MPR), which was the sole legal party until 1990, when the introduction of a multi-party system was announced. By February 1991 a large number of new parties had been established. In mid-1991 a National Conference on the political future of the country began, its claims to sovereignty leading to conflict with President Mobutu. The National Conference, which sat until December 1992, dissolved the National Legislative Council (which had been elected in 1987 from a list of MPR-approved candidates) and replaced it with a 453–member transitional legislature, the High Council of the Republic (HCR), but President Mobutu refused to sanction this action.

Political stalemate between the President and the opposition-dominated HCR, which had resulted by early 1993 in the appointment of two rival Cabinets, was broken in January 1994. The HCR and the National Legislative Council (which had been reconvened by Mobutu) were reconstituted as a single body to be known as the High Council of the Republic-Parliament of Transition (*Haut Conseil de la République-Parlement de Transition*, HCR-PT), which the following April endorsed legislation entrusting it with the task of overseeing the activities of a transitional government. The legislation strengthened the position of the Prime Minister and the Cabinet in relation to the President, and set the duration of the transition to democracy at 15 months, during which time a constitutional referendum, as well as presidential and legislative elections, would have to be organized. In June 1994 Léon Kengo Wa Dondo of the Union for the Republic and Democracy was appointed, controversially, to the post of Prime Minister, in which capacity he named a new transitional administration including pro-Mobutu and opposition members. In May 1995 the government confirmed that multi-party elections, scheduled for July 1995, would be postponed, whereupon the HCR-PT voted the following month to extend the transition period for a further two-years.

Democratic and Social Christian Party
Parti Démocrate et Social Chrétien (PDSC)
  Address. BP 4792, Kinshasa-Gombé
  Leadership. André Boboliko Lokanga (chair)
  The PDSC was founded in 1990 and achieved legal status the following year. It is a constituent of the opposition grouping, the Sacred Union of the Radical Opposition. The party is an affiliate of the Christian Democrat International.

Political Forces of the Conclave
Forces Politiques du Conclave (FPC)
  Established in 1993, the FPC is an alliance of pro-Mobutu groups, led by the the Popular Movement of the Revolution. In January 1994 the major constituent parties of the FPC and the opposition Sacred Union of the Radical Opposition (with the exception of the Union for

Democracy and Social Progress) signed an agreement to form a government of national reconciliation. In June 1995 political consensus was reached between the FPC and the opposition resulting in the extension of the period of national transition by two years.

Popular Movement of the Revolution
Mouvement Populaire de la Révolution (MPR)
  Address. Palais du Peuple, angle ave des Huileries et ave Kasa-Vubu, Kinshasa
  Telephone. (#243–12) 22541
  Leadership. Mobutu Sese Seko (chair)
  The MPR was launched in 1967 advocating national unity and African socialism, and opposing tribalism. As the main vehicle of the Mobutu regime, it became the sole legal political party in 1969 and, until political liberalization in 1990,

party membership was deemed to be acquired automatically by all Zaïreans at birth. The MPR is the leading party within the pro-Mobutu coalition, the Political Forces of the Conclave.

Sacred Union of the Radical Opposition
Union Sacrée de l'Opposition Radicale (USOR)

The USOR developed in the course of 1991 as an umbrella group of organizations opposed to the Mobutu regime. Originally drawing on the ranks of the Union for Democracy and Social Progress, the Union of Federalists and Independent Republicans (which was subsequently expelled) and the Democratic and Social Christian Party, the USOR links some 130 anti-Mobutu movements and factions. The existence within the transitional legislature of an expanded radical opposition grouping, known as the Sacred Union of the Radical Opposition and its Allies (USORAL), was announced in late 1994.

Union for Democracy and Social Progress
Union pour la Démocratie et le Progrès Social (UDPS)

Leadership. Etienne Tshisekedi wa Malumba (leader)

The UDPS emerged in the early 1980s as an attempt to establish an opposition party within Zaïre to counter the "arbitrary rule" of the Mobutu regime. Various of its members suffered consequent arrest and imprisonment, and serious splits in its leadership were subsequently reported. The party was legalized in 1991. The UDPS leader, Etienne Tshisekedi, was elected Prime Minister in August 1992 by the national conference, but the legitimacy of his government was resisted by President Mobutu who, in early 1993, appointed a rival administration, so heightening the political impasse. The UDPS did not sign the agreement in January 1994 on the formation of a government of national reconciliation, and supporters of Tshisekedi have continued to insist on the legitimacy of his claim to the office of Prime Minister.

Union for the Republic and Democracy
Union pour la République et la Démocratie (URD)

Leadership. Léon Kengo Wa Dondo (leader)

The URD was expelled from the Sacred Union of the Radical Opposition in May 1994 after a split with supporters within USOR of Etienne Tshisekedi, the leader of the UDPS and designated candidate of the alliance for the post of Prime Minister in a transitional administration to supervise the period leading to general elections. The following month the URD leader, Kengo wa Dondo, was elected Prime Minister by the HCR-PT.

Union of Federalists and Independent Republicans
Union des Fédéralistes et Républicains Indépendants (UFERI)

Leadership. Jean Nguza Karl-I-Bond (leader)

Founded in 1990 and seeking autonomy for Shaba province, the UFERI was initially one of the most prominent groups in the Sacred Union of the Radical Opposition. However, after party leader Nguza Karl-I-Bond had controversially accepted nomination by President Mobutu for the post of Prime Minister in November 1991, the UFERI was expelled from the Sacred Union coalition.

Other Parties

Alliance of African Nationalists (*Alliance des Nationalistes Africains*, ANA), formed in 1994 under the leadership of Théophane Mulula.

Alliance of Republicans for Development and Progress (*Alliance des Républicains pour le Développement et le Progrès*, ARDP), launched in early 1994 with John Milala Mbono-Mbue as party chair.

Congolese National Movement-Lumumba (*Mouvement National du Congo-Lumumba*), formed in September 1994 as a coalition of parties supporting the nationalist aims of former Prime Minister Patrice Lumumba.

Liberal Federation of Zaïre (*Fédération des Libéraux du Zaïre*, FLZ), an association of liberal political groups formed in 1994.

National Democratic and Social Christian Party (*Parti Démocrate et Social Chrétien National*, PDSCN), legalized in February 1994.

National Party for Integral Development (*Parti des Nationalistes pour le Développement Intergal*, PANADI), recognized in 1994.

Renovated Sacred Union (*Union Sacrée Rénovée*, USR), formed in 1993 by recently expelled Sacred Union members, and led by Kiro Kimate.

Union for Democracy and National Social Progress (*Union pour la Démocratie et le Progrès Social National*, UDPSN), recognized in 1994 and led by Charles Deounkin Andel.

Worker and Peasant Party (*Parti Ouvrier et Paysan*, POP), a Marxist-Leninist group founded in 1986.

Zambia

Capital: Lusaka

Population: 9,000,000 (1995E)

After Zambia had gained independence from the United Kingdom in 1964, the next 27 years of its political life were dominated by the republic's first President, Kenneth Kaunda, and the United National Independence Party (UNIP), which was declared the sole legal political organization in 1972. However, in September 1990 the party agreed to the termination of its monopoly on power and to contest elections on a multi-party basis. Accordingly, a new democratic constitution was approved in August 1991, under which executive authority is vested in the President, who is elected by universal adult suffrage for a five-year term (once renewable) at the same time as elections to the 150–member National Assembly. The President appoints a Vice-President and a Cabinet from members of the National Assembly. The constitution also provides for a 27–member consultative House of Chiefs.

Multi-party presidential and legislative elections on Oct. 31, 1991, resulted in a clear victory for Frederick Chiluba and the Movement for Multi-Party Democracy (MMD) over Kaunda and the UNIP.

Movement for Multi-Party Democracy (MMD)

Address. PO Box 365, 10101 Lusaka

Leadership. Frederick Chiluba (president), Godfrey Miyanda

The social democratic MMD was formed in July 1990 as an informal alliance of groups opposed to the then ruling United National Independence Party, and was granted legal recognition the following December. In February 1991 Frederick Chiluba, the head of the Zambian Congress of Trade Unions, was elected party president. In the elections held in October 1991 the MMD, having focused its campaign on the UNIP's poor record of economic management, secured 125 seats in the National Assembly, an overwhelming majority. In the presidential poll Chiluba dislodged Kenneth Kaunda, winning just over 75% of the votes cast.

The MMD government's rigorous IMF-directed economic policies proved unpopular and caused increasing discord within the MMD, as evidenced by the emergence during 1992–93 of the Caucus for National Unity and the National Party (NP) following splits in the party. Further tensions within the MMD culminated in July 1995 in the expulsion of the party treasurer (who announced the formation of the Zambia Democratic Congress) and in the declaration by the MMD vice-president, Levy Mwanawasa, that he would challenge Chiluba for the leadership at the next party conference.

United National Independence Party (UNIP)

Address. PO Box 30302, Lusaka

Telephone. (#260–1) 221197

Fax. (#260–1) 221327

Leadership. Kenneth Kaunda (president)

Dating from 1958, the UNIP under Kenneth Kaunda ruled Zambia from independence until 1991, for most of that period as the country's sole legal political organization. In the multi-party elections held in October 1991, Kaunda suffered a resounding defeat, taking only about 25% of the presidential vote, while UNIP candidates secured only 25 of the 150 National Assembly seats in the legislative elections. Kaunda resigned as party leader in January 1992, although he continued to take an active interest in political developments. In March 1993 the government accused radical elements within UNIP of plotting a coup with foreign backing.

In June 1994 the UNIP joined a number of other parties in launching the Zambia Opposition Front (ZOFRO). Also in mid-1994, Kaunda announced his intention to return to active politics, being elected UNIP president in June the following year, defeating the incumbent Kebby Musokotwane. In October 1995 the government raised questions about Kaunda's nationality, since he had failed to register as a Zambian citizen at independence in 1964 and had retained citizenship of Malawi (his birthplace) until 1970. The issue was reported to throw in doubt his plans to contest the 1996 presidential elections.

Other Parties

Caucus for National Unity (CNU), a dissident group which surfaced within the Movement for Multi-Party Democracy in 1992, calling for democratic reforms and the eradication of corruption, and which subsequently split from the party.

Democratic Party (DP), under the leadership of Emmanuel Mwamba.

Independent Democratic Front, led by Mike Kaira, who also chaired the Zambia Opposition Front (ZOFRO) which was launched in mid-1994.

Labour Party (LP), a part of the Zambia Opposition Front.

Movement for Democratic Process (MDP), led by Chama Chakomboka.

Multi-Racial Party (MRP), founded in 1991 and led by Aaron Mulenga.

National Democratic Alliance (NADA), led by Yonan Phiri and a member organization of the Zambia Opposition Front.

National Party (NP), launched in 1993 by dissidents of the ruling Movement for Multi-Party Democracy (MMD); the first NP chair, Arthur Wina (a minister in previous United National Independence Party and MMD governments), died in September 1995.

National People's Salvation Party (NPSP), headed by Lumbwe Lambanya.

United Democratic Congress Party, formed in 1992 by former Prime Minister Daniel Lisulo.

Zambia Democratic Congress, reportedly formed in July 1995 by Dean Mung'omba, who had been expelled from the ruling Movement for Multi-Party Democracy the previous month.

Zambia Opposition Front (ZOFRO), established in mid-1994 and comprising a number of opposition formations, including the United National Independence Party.

Zimbabwe

Capital: Harare

Population: 10,900,000 (1994E)

The White minority regime in Rhodesia, which had declared unilateral independence from the United Kingdom in 1965, ended in 1979 with the adoption of the Lancaster House Agreement. The following year the country gained full independence as the Republic of Zimbabwe. It has since been ruled by the Zimbabwe African National Union-Patriotic Front (ZANU-PF).

An amendment in 1987 to the 1980 pre-independence constitution vested executive power in the President, who is both head of state and head of government, with a six-year mandate. Previously executive authority had been held by the Prime Minister. When the Lancaster House Agreement on the constitution expired in April 1990, the former bicameral legislature set up at independence was replaced by a single-chamber House of Assembly with a six-year term of office and 150 members (120 elective, 10 traditional chiefs, eight provincial governors appointed by the President and 12 other presidential appointees).

Robert Mugabe (ZANU-PF), who had been Prime Minister since independence, was elected President by the House of Assembly in December 1987. In March 1990 he was directly elected to the presidency for the first time, being re-elected for a second six-year term in March 1996 as the sole candidate. In legislative elections in April 1995 ZANU-PF won an overwhelming victory, taking all but two of the 120 elective seats. In a by-election in November 1995, the party lost a seat to an independent candidate.

Conservative Alliance of Zimbabwe (CAZ)

Address. PO Box 242, Harare

Leadership. Gerald Smith, Mike Moroney (leaders)

The CAZ was formed in 1962 as the Rhodesian Front (RF), a coalition of right-wing white parties opposed to a transition to black majority rule. From Rhodesia's unilateral declaration of independence in 1965 until 1979 the RF held all 50 white seats in the 66–member parliament, and it formed the government until 1978 when a transitional power-sharing administration was set up. In elections in February 1980, which were held as part of the Lancaster House Agreement and which established the black nationalist ZANU-PF government, the RF won all 20 seats reserved for voters on the White roll. However, from 1981, when the party changed its name to the Republican Front, the RF began to lose its monopoly of White representation. In 1984 it adopted its current title and for the first time announced that it would accept non-White members. With the abolition of reserved White seats in 1987 the CAZ ceased to be represented in the legislature. It remains as an extra-parliamentary opposition party whose principal support comes from sections of the White community.

United Party (UP)

Leadership. Bishop Abel Muzorewa (leader)

The UP was established in 1994 by Bishop Muzorewa, the leader of the former United African National Council (UANC) who had briefly been Prime Minister prior to independence. Having boycotted the April 1995 House of Assembly elections, Muzorewa reportedly declared at the end of the year that he would stand in the March 1996 presidential contest. On the eve of polling, however, he announced his withdrawal on the grounds that the contest was unfairly weighted in favour of the ruling Zimbabwe African National Union–Patriotic Front

Zimbabwe African National Union–Ndonga (ZANU-Ndonga)

Address. PO Box UA525, Union Ave, Harare

Leadership. Rev. Ndabaningi Sithole (leader)

Rev. Sithole was the founding president of the Zimbabwe African National Union but broke away from the party in 1977, forming ZANU-Ndonga. Right-wing in outlook and hostile to the ruling ZANU-PF party, ZANU-Ndonga was the only opposition party to gain parliamentary representation in the April 1995 elections, winning two House of Assembly seats with 6.5% of the vote. In October 1995 Sithole was arrested and charged with conspiracy to assassinate President Mugabe and overthrow the government. He was

subsequently released on bail and had yet to face trial at the end of 1995. In December 1995 a Sithole lieutenant, Simon Mhlanga, was found guilty of undergoing illegal guerrilla training in Mozambique, the court finding that he was leader of the Chimwenje armed dissident movement. In January 1996 the Mozambique government ordered the expulsion of all Chimwenje members from its territory.

Zimbabwe African National Union-Patriotic Front (ZANU-PF)

Address. 88 Manica Road, Harare

Leadership. Robert Mugabe (president)

Originally a black nationalist liberation movement, the party was founded in 1963 as the Zimbabwe African National Union, a breakaway group from Joshua Nkomo's Zimbabwe African People's Union, which had itself been formed in 1961. In the mid-1970s ZAPU and ZANU organized military wings to conduct guerrilla operations against the White minority regime. In 1976 Mugabe and Nkomo agreed to set up the Patriotic Front alliance with the objective of achieving genuine black majority rule, although in practice ZANU and ZAPU remained separate organizations. The following year Rev. Ndabaningi Sithole broke away from the Mugabe faction of ZANU to form the Zimbabwe African National Union–Ndonga.

In the pre-independence elections in 1980 (consequent upon the Lancaster House settlement) and in all subsequent elections, Mugabe's ZANU-PF has won substantial parliamentary majorities, most recently in April 1995 when the party secured 118 of the 120 elective House of Assembly seats. In the first direct presidential election in 1990, Mugabe retained office with 78% of the votes cast.

Nkomo's PF-ZAPU was formally incorporated into ZANU-PF in 1989. In 1991 Mugabe announced that he had abandoned plans to introduce a one-party state structure, and the party agreed to delete references to Marxism, Leninism and scientific socialism from its constitution.

Having been nominated as ZANU-PF's candidate in December 1995, Mugabe registered a somewhat hollow triumph in the presidential election of March 1996, the withdrawal of other candidates leaving him effectively unopposed. In a 32% turnout, he was credited with receiving 93% of the votes cast, the residue going to two names that had remained on ballot papers.

Zimbabwe Unity Movement (ZUM)

Leadership. Edgar Tekere (leader)

In 1988 Edgar Tekere, a former secretary-general of the Zimbabwe African National Union-Patriotic Front, was expelled from the party for making corruption allegations against the government and for his criticism of Robert Mugabe's plans, at that stage, to establish a one-party state structure. In April 1989 he launched the ZUM. In the March 1990 general elections the party won two seats in the House of Assembly, while Tekere won 16% of the vote in the presidential poll as Mugabe's only competitor. Having subsequently experienced serious divisions among the party hierarchy, the ZUM reportedly merged with the United African National Congress in early 1994. The party did not gain any representation in the April 1995 legislative elections.

Other Parties

Democratic Party (DP), led by Giles Mutsekwa, founded in 1991 by a breakaway faction of the Zimbabwe Unity Movement (ZUM).

Forum Party of Zimbabwe (FPZ), led by Enoch Dumbutshena, launched in 1993 to advocate free market economics, reductions in government bureaucracy and protection of human rights; drawing its support mainly from among the urban black community, it put up 24 candidates in the April 1995 legislative elections but all were defeated by a wide margin.

National Democratic Union (NDU), led by Henry Chihota, a conservative Mashonaland grouping founded in 1979.

Zimbabwe Active People's Unity People (ZAPUP), led by Matutu Ndela, formed in 1989, putting forward a pro-democracy and free enterprise programme.

Zimbabwe People's Democratic Party (ZPDP), led by Isabel Pasalk, founded in 1989 by Zimbabwe's first female party leader; it advocates an open and free economy and the integration of women into leadership positions.

INDEX

A

Acción Democrática (AD) (El Salvador), 212
Acción Democrática (AD) (Venezuela), 643
Acción Democrática Nacionalista (ADN) (Bolivia)
Accíon Popular (AP) (Peru), 464
ACT New Zealand (New Zealand), 430
Action Committee for Renewal (CAR) (Togo), 576
Action for Unity and Socialism (ACTUS) (Chad), 129
Adolat (Uzbekistan), 638
Afghan Islamic Association (Afghanistan), 2
Afghan National Liberation Front (Afghanistan), 2; 3
African Forum for Reconstruction (Gabon), 264
African Independence Party (Senegal), 510; 512
African Party for Democracy and Progress/And Jëf
   (Senegal), 510; 511
African Party for Independence (Burkina Faso), 103
African Party for the Independence of Cape Verde
   (PAICV) (Cape Verde), 121
African Party for the Independence of Guinea and Cape
   Verde (Guinea-Bissau), 298; 299
African Party for the Independence of the Masses
   (Senegal), 512
African Rally for Progress and Solidarity (RAPS)
   (Benin), 71
African Society for Cultural Relations with Independent
   Africa (ASCRIA) (Guyana), 300
Afrikaner People's Front (South Africa), 529; 531
Agrarian Democratic Party of Moldova (Moldova), 406
Agrarian Labour Party (PLA) (Panama), 454
Agrarian Party of Belarus (Belarus), 57
Agrarian Party of Russia (Russia), 497; 500
Agrarian Party of Slovakia (Slovakia), 519
Agrarian Union (Hungary), 311
Albanian Republican Party (PRS) (Albania), 5
Alerta Nacional (Argentina), 29
Alfaroist Radical Front (Ecuador), 205
"Alfaro Vive, Carajo!" (Colombia), 148
Alianza Democrática—Movimiento 19 de Abril
   (AD-M19) (Colombia), 144
Alianza Liberal (AL) (Nicaragua), 434
Alianza Politica Opositora (APO) (Nicaragua), 435
Alianza Popular Revolucionaria Americana (APRA)
   (Peru), 462
Alianza Republicana Nacionalista (Arena) (El Salvador),
   213
Alliance 90/The Greens (Germany), 278
Alliance for Colombia (AC) (Colombia), 143
Alliance for Democracy and Federation (Burkina Faso),
   102; 103
Alliance for Democracy and Progress (Benin), 73
Alliance for Democracy and Progress (Central African
   Republic), 123; 125
Alliance for Democracy and Social Development
   (Burkina Faso), 101

Alliance for Democracy (APD) (Dominican Republic),
   392
Alliance for Democracy in Mali–Pan-African Party for
   Liberty Solidarity and Justice (ADEMA-PPLSJ)
   (Mali), 392; 393
Alliance for Social Democracy (Benin), 73
Alliance for Social Democracy (Côte d'Ivoire), 162
Alliance (New Zealand), 429; 430
Alliance of Forces for Change (AFC) (Niger), 439; 440
Alliance of Forces for Change (Niger), 439; 440
Alliance of Free Democrats (Hungary), 310
Alliance Party (Fiji), 226
Alliance Party (New Zealand's Associated Territories),
   431
All-India Dravidian Progressive Federation (AIADMK)
   (India), 317
All-India Forward Bloc (India), 319
All-India Indira Congress–Tiwari (India), 319
Al-Mujahidden Party (Guyana), 300
Alternative Socialist Association (Bulgaria), 94; 97
Alternative Social-Liberal Party (ASP) (Bulgaria), 97
Amal (Lebanon), 368; 369
American Popular Revolutionary Alliance—Peruvian
   Aprista Party (Peru), 462
Anguilla Democratic Party (ADP) (UK Dependent
   Territories), 618
Anguilla United Party (AUP) (UK Dependent
   Territories), 618
Angula (Defiance) (Suriname), 552
Arab Socialist Union (ASU) (Syria), 565
Aragonese Party (Spain), 28; 533
Argentine Socialist Confederation (Confederación
   Socialista Argentina, CSA) (Argentina), 28
Armed Forces of Liberia (Liberia), 372
Armenian Christian Democratic Union (Armenia), 31
Armenian Communist Party (ACP) (Armenia), 30; 31
Army of the Poor (EP) (Mexico), 404
Arnulfista Party (Panama), 454
Aruban Democratic Party (Netherlands Dependencies),
   426
Aruban Liberal Organization (Netherlands
   Dependencies), 426
Aruban Patriotic Party (Netherlands Dependencies), 426;
   427
Aruban People's Party/Christian Democracy (Netherlands
   Dependencies), 426; 427
Asociación Nacional Republicana—Partido Colorado
   (ANR-PC) (Paraguay), 460
Assam People's Council (India), 319
Assembly of Islamic Clergy (Pakistan), 449
Association for the Republic–Czech Republican Party
   (Czech Republic), 184
Association of Peasants and Ranchers (ACDEGAM)
   (Colombia), 148
Association of Workers of Slovakia (Slovakia), 519
Association (UK Dependent Territories), 623

663

Australian Labor Party (ALP) (Australia), 35
Australian Labor Party (Australia), 36; 37; 38; 39
Austrian People's Party (ÖVP) (Austria), 41; 42
Authentic Christian Democratic Movement (El Salvador), 211
Authentic Christian Democratic Movement (MADC) (El Salvador), 212
Authentic Institutional Party (PAISA) (El Salvador), 214
Authentic Liberal Party (Panama), 453
Authentic Nationalist Central (CAN) (Guatemala), 292
Authentic Party of the Mexican Revolution (PARM) (Mexico), 402
Authentic Radical Liberal Party (PLRA) (Paraguay), 459
Authentic Revolutionary Party (PRA) (Guatemala), 292
Autonomist Patriotic Party (Overseas Territories and Territorial Collectivities), 259
Autonomous Patriotic Party (Overseas Territories and Territorial Collectivities), 259
Avanzada Nacional (AN) (Chile), 134
Awami League (AL) (Bangladesh), 49-50; 51; 52; 53; 54; 55
Azerbaijan Independent Democratic Party (Azerbaijan), 46
Azerbaijan Popular Front (AKC) (Azerbaijan), 44; 45; 46
Azerbaijan Popular Front (Azerbaijan), 46; 47
Azerbaijan Revolutionary Revival Party (AIDP) (Azerbaijan), 46
Azerbaijan United Communist Party (Azerbaijan), 45

B

Baath Arab Socialist Party (Iraq), 325
Baath Arab Socialist Party of Iraq (Mauritania), 397
Baath Arab Socialist Party (Syria), 566
Bahujan Samaj Party (BSP) (India), 318
Bangladesh Nationalist Party (Bangladesh), 50; 55
Bangladesh Nationalist Party (BNP) (Bangladesh), 50; 53; 54
Barbados Labour Party (Barbados), 55
Basotho Congress Party (Lesotho), 370
Basque Left (EE) (Spain), 539
Basque Left (EE/EuE) (Spain), 540
Basque Left (Spain), 539
Basque Nationalist Party (PNV) (Spain), 538-539
Basque Nationalist Party (Spain), 534
Basque Socialist Party-Basque Left, PSE-EE (Spain), 538; 539; 540
Basque Solidarity (Spain), 148; 538; 539; 541
Battalón América (American Battalion) (Colombia), 148
Bavaria Party (Germany), 273
Belarusan Christian Democratic Union (Belarus), 58
Belarusan Patriotic Movement (Belarus), 59; 60
Belarusan Peasants' Party (Belarus), 58
Belarusan Popular Front (Belarus), 58
Belarusan Popular Front—Revival (NFB-A) (Belarus), 57-58; 59; 60
Belarusan Social Democratic Party (Belarus), 58
Belize Action Movement (BAM) (Belize), 69
Benin Renaissance Party (PRB) (Benin), 70; 74
Bharatiya Janata Party (BJP) (India), 316; 318; 319; 320
Black Action Party (BAP) (Papua New Guinea), 456; 457
Blancos (Uruguay), 633
Bloc for Social Democracy (Benin), 71
Blue and White (Azul y Blanco) (Argentina), 28
Boer State Party (South Africa), 530

Botswana Democratic Party (BDP) (Botswana), 85; 86
Botswana National Front (Botswana), 86
Botswana People's Party (Botswana), 86
Botswana Progressive Union (Botswana), 86
Bougainville Revolutionary Party (BRA) (Papua New Guinea), 458
Brazilian Communist Party (Brazil), 88
Brazilian Democratic Movement (Brazil), 88
Brazilian Democratic Movement (MDB) (Brazil), 89
Brazilian Democratic Movement Party (PMDB) (Brazil), 87
Brazilian Labour Party (PTB) (Brazil), 87; 88; 90
Brazilian Social Democratic Party (Brazil), 87
Brazilian Socialist Party (PSB) (Brazil), 87; 90
British National Party (BNP) (United Kingdom), 607
Broad Front (Argentina), 23
Broad Front (FA) (Uruguay), 635; 637
Broad Front (Uruguay), 634; 635; 637
Broad Left Front (Ecuador), 206
Broad Left Front (FADI) (Ecuador), 203
Broad Party of the Socialist Left (PAIS) (Chile), 136
Buddhist Liberal Democratic Party (BLDP) (Cambodia), 112
Buddhist Liberal Democratic Party (Cambodia), 109; 112
Bulgarian Agrarian National Union (Bulgaria), 97
Bulgarian Agrarian National Union (BZNS) (Bulgaria), 96
Bulgarian Agrarian National Union–Aleksandur Stamboliyski (Bulgaria), 95
Bulgarian Agrarian National Union-Nikola Petkov (BZNS-NP) (Bulgaria), 92; 97
Bulgarian Democratic Forum (BDF) (Bulgaria), 97
Bulgarian Liberal Party (Bulgaria), 98
Bulgarian Social Democratic Party (BSDP) (Bulgaria), 95; 97; 98; 99
Bulgarian Socialist Party (BSP) (Bulgaria), 92; 93; 95; 96; 97; 98; 99
Burundi Front for Democracy (FRODEBU) (Burundi), 106

C

C-47 (Suriname), 552
Calderonist Republican Party (Costa Rica), 159
Cambio 90—Nueva Mayoría (C-90-NM) (Peru), 463
Cambodian National Unity Party (CNUP) (Cambodia), 111; 112
Cambodian People's Party (CPP) (Cambodia), 108; 109; 110; 112
Cameroon People's Democratic Movement (CPDM) (Cameroon), 114
Canarian Coalition (Spain), 534; 539; 541
Canarian Nationalist Party (PNC) (Spain), 541
Cape Verde Independent Democratic Union (Cape Verde), 121
Capital Democratic Party (PDC) (Argentina), 28
Cardenista National Reconstruction Party (Mexico), 403
Carlist Party (Spain), 536
Cartago Agricultural Action (Costa Rica), 159
Catalan Socialist Party (PSC-PSOE) (Spain), 542
Caucus for National Unity (Zambia), 658
Central African Democratic Rally (RDC) (Central African Republic), 125
Central African People's Liberation Movement (MLPC) (Central African Republic), 122; 123; 124; 125

Central African Republican Party (Central African Republic), 125

Central American Workers' Revolutionary Party (Honduras), 307

Central Auténica Nacionalista (CAN) (Guatemala), 292

Central Revolutionary Council-NPFL (Liberia), 372

Centre Alliance (PC) (Poland), 471; 472; 473; 477

Centre Democrats (CD) (Denmark), 185-186; 187; 189; 190; 191

Centre Democrats (Netherlands), 425

Centre (Norway), 443; 444

Centre Party 86 (Netherlands), 421

Centre Party (KESK) (Finland), 231; 233

Centre Party (Norway), 444

Centre Party of Finland (KESK) (Finland), 229; 230; 232

Centre Party (Sweden), 555; 558

Centre (SP) (Norway), 444

Centre (Sweden), 556; 557

Chad National Liberation Front (FROLINAT) (Chad), 126; 127; 129; 130

Change 90—New Majority (Peru), 462; 463; 466

Chart Thai (Thailand), 573-575

Christian Democrat Party (PDC) (El Salvador), 212; 214

Christian Democrat Party (PDC) (Panama), 452

Christian Democratic Appeal (CDA) (Netherlands), 422; 423; 424

Christian Democratic Centre (Italy), 337; 344

Christian Democratic Community Party (KdS) (Sweden), 554

Christian Democratic Community (Sweden), 557

Christian Democratic Labour Party (Poland), 477

Christian Democratic Movement (Slovakia), 520

Christian Democratic National Peasants' Party of Romania (PNTCDR) (Romania), 484

Christian Democratic Party (Argentina), 24

Christian Democratic Party (Brazil), 90

Christian Democratic Party (CDP) (Belize), 69

Christian Democratic Party (CDP) (Western Samoa), 650

Christian Democratic Party (Costa Rica), 159

Christian Democratic Party (DCG) (Guatemala), 295

Christian Democratic Party (El Salvador), 211; 213; 215

Christian Democratic Party of Honduras (Honduras), 305

Christian Democratic Party of Kosovo (Yugoslavia), 655

Christian Democratic Party of Ukraine (Ukraine), 596

Christian Democratic Party (Papua New Guinea), 457

Christian Democratic Party (PDC) (Bolivia), 78

Christian Democratic Party (PDC) (Chile), 131

Christian Democratic Party (PDC) (Ecuador), 205

Christian Democratic Party (PDC) (Peru), 465

Christian Democratic Party (PDC) (Uruguay), 634

Christian Democratic Party (PDCS) (San Marino), 507

Christian Democratic Party (Peru), 464

Christian Democratic Party (Poland), 477

Christian Democratic Party (Uruguay), 636

Christian Democratic People's Party (KDNP) (Hungary), 308

Christian Democratic People's Party (Switzerland), 560; 562; 564

Christian Democratic Solidarity Front (FSDC) (Nicaragua), 435

Christian Democratic Union (CDU) (Germany), 273-275; 277; 278

Christian Democratic Union (HDS) (Bulgaria), 97

Christian Democratic Union-Czechoslovak People's Party (KDU-ČSL) (Czech Republic), 179

Christian National Movement (Poland), 477

Christian National Union (Poland), 472; 477; 478

Christian People's (Belgium), 64

Christian People's (Norway), 443; 444

Christian People's Party (CVP) (Belgium), 62; 64; 67

Christian People's Party (KrFP) (Denmark), 186; 187; 190

Christian People's Party (Norway), 442

Christian People's Party/Progressive and Fishing Industry Party (KF/FFF) (Danish Dependencies), 193; 194

Christian Republican Party (Bulgaria), 99

Christian Social Movement (Movimiento Social Cristiano, MSC) (Chile), 136

Christian Social Party (PSC) (Belgium), 62; 64

Christian Social Union (CSU) (Germany), 274; 277-279

Christian Social Union (CSU) of Bavaria (Germany), 272

Christian Social Union (Poland), 90; 471

Christian Socialist Party (Partido Socialista Cristão, PSC) (Brazil), 88

Christian Socials (Luxembourg), 379

Cinchonero Popular Liberation Movement (MPL (Honduras), 307

Citizen (Kazakhstan), 354

Citizens' Initiative (GI) (Bulgaria), 97

Citizens' Union of Georgia (Georgia), 267; 268

Civic Alliance Party (PAC) (Romania), 484; 486; 487

Civic Alliance (Yugoslavia), 654

Civic Democratic Alliance (ODA) (Czech Republic), 179

Civic Democratic Party (ODS) (Czech Republic), 178; 179-180; 182; 183; 184

Civic Forum (Central African Republic), 124

Civic National Movement (Czech Republic), 183

Civic Opposition Democratic Alliance (ADOC) (Panama), 451-453

Civic Solidarity Union (UCS) (Bolivia), 75; 76

Civic Union (Argentina), 27

Civic Union of Uruguay (Uruguay), 633; 634; 637

Civic Works Movement (Peru), 464

Civilist Renovation Party (Panama), 454

Coalition and Rural People's Union (KMÜ) (Estonia), 220; 221

Coalition for Democracy (CPD) (Chile), 132; 134; 136

Coalition for Open, Honest and Just Government (Palau), 449

Coalition of Ethiopian Democratic Forces (COEDF) (Ethiopia), 225

Coalition of National Liberation (COLINA) (Panama), 454

Coalition of Parties for Democracy (CPD) (Chile), 131; 132

Coexistence (ESWS) (Slovakia), 518

Colorado Party (Uruguay), 633; 635; 636

"Command for the No Vote" (Chile), 132

Committee for Peasant Unity (CUC) (Guatemala), 295

Communal Liberation Party (TKP) (Cyprus), 176; 177

Communist Left Party (Chile), 135

Communist Party (Belarus), 58

Communist Party (Brazil), 89

Communist Party (Greece), 287

Communist Party (Luxembourg), 379

Communist Party (Norway), 444

Communist Party of Argentina (Argentina), 24

Communist Party of Austria (Austria), 42

Communist Party of Bangladesh (Bangladesh), 52; 55

Communist Party of Belarus (Belarus), 60

Communist Party of Bohemia and Moravia (Czech Republic), 180; 183
Communist Party of Bohemia and Moravia (KSČM) (Czech Republic), 184
Communist Party of Brazil (PCdoB) (Brazil), 90
Communist Party of Chile (PCCh) (Chile), 135
Communist Party of China (China), 136
Communist Party of Colombia (PCC) (Colombia), 146; 148
Communist Party of Colombia—Marxist-Leninist (Colombia), 147
Communist Party of Denmark (DKP) (Denmark), 190
Communist Party of Great Britain (CPGB) (United Kingdom), 606
Communist Party of Greece (KKE) (Greece), 286
Communist Party of Honduras (Honduras), 307
Communist Party of India (CPI) (India), 317; 319
Communist Party of India-Marxist (CPI-M) (India), 316; 319; 320
Communist Party of India-Marxist (India), 315
Communist Party of Jordan (Jordan), 350; 351
Communist Party of Kazakhstan (KPK) (Kazakhstan), 353; 354
Communist Party of New Zealand (CPNZ) (New Zealand), 430
Communist Party of Nicaragua (Nicaragua), 436
Communist Party of Norway (Norway), 445
Communist Party of Peru-Red Fatherland (Peru), 466
Communist Party of Slovakia (KSS) (Slovakia), 519
Communist Party of Spain (PCE) (Spain), 534; 536
Communist Party of Tajikistan (CPT) (Tajikistan), 569; 570
Communist Party of the Philippines (PKP) (Philippines), 470
Communist Party of the Philippines–Marxist-Leninist (CPP-ML) (Philippines), 469
Communist Party of the Russian Federation (KPRF) (Russia), 490; 494; 495; 500
Communist Party of Ukraine (KPU) (Ukraine), 593; 594; 595; 597
Communist Party of Uruguay (PCU) (Uruguay), 634; 637
Communist Party of Uzbekistan (Uzbekistan), 638
Communist Party of Venezuela (Venezuela), 643
Communist Party (Tajikistan), 571
Communist Party (Vietnam), 647
Communist Refoundation Party (San Marino), 506
Communist Workers' Party (Sweden), 556
Community (Atassut) (Danish Dependencies), 196
Concentration of Popular Forces (CFP) (Ecuador), 203; 205; 207
Concerned Citizens Movement (St Christopher and Nevis), 503; 504
Concertación de los Partidos por la Democracia (CPD) (Chile), 132
Conciencia de Patria (Condepa) (Bolivia), 76
Confederation for an Independent Poland (Poland), 473
Confederation for Full Democracy in Swaziland (Swaziland), 554
Confederation of Ecuadorian Indigenous Nationalities (Ecuador), 206
Confluencia Socialista (CS) (Peru), 466
Congolese Labour Party (PCT) (Congo), 153; 154; 155; 156; 157
Congolese Movement for Democracy and Integral Development (MCDDI) (Congo), 154; 155; 156

Congress of National Democratic Forces (Ukraine), 594
Congress of Russian Communities (Russia), 498
Congress of Ukrainian Nationalists (KUN) (Ukraine), 596
Conscience of the Fatherland (Bolivia), 76
Conservative Party (Norway), 442; 443
Conservative Party (Colombia), 143
Conservative Party (Northern Ireland), 616
Conservative Party of Labour (PCL) (Nicaragua), 433
Conservative Party of Nicaragua (Nicaragua), 434
Conservative Party of South Africa (South Africa), 529
Conservative Party (Panama), 454
Conservative Party (Poland), 472; 473; 478
Conservative Party (United Kingdom), 602; 604; 606
Conservative People's Party (Danish Dependencies), 194
Conservative People's Party (KFP) (Denmark), 185; 186; 187; 189; 190
Conservative Popular Alliance Party (PAPC) (Nicaragua), 434
Conservative Social Party (PSC) (Nicaragua), 433
Constitución Para Todos (CPT) (Paraguay), 459
Constitution for All (Paraguay), 459
Constitutional Party of the Right (Finland), 233
Convention for the Democratic Alternative (CAD) (Congo), 157
Convention of Democrats and Patriots (Senegal), 510; 511
Convergence and Union (CiU) (Spain), 534; 535; 539; 543
Convergencia Democrática (CD) (El Salvador), 212
Convergencia Nacional (CN) (Venezuela), 645
Cook Islands Labour Party (New Zealand's Associated Territories), 431
Cook Islands Party (CIP) (New Zealand's Associated Territories), 431
Cook Islands People Party (New Zealand's Associated Territories), 431
Co-ordinator of the Nicaraguan Opposition (CON) (Nicaragua), 160; 435
Costa Rican Ecology Party (Partido Ecológia Costarricense, PEC) (Costa Rica)
Costa Rican Peoples' Party (Costa Rica), 160
Country Liberal Party (Australia), 36
Covenant for Poland (Poland), 471; 472; 477; 478
Croatian Christian Democratic Union (Croatia), 168; 169
Croatian Democratic Party (HDS) (Croatia), 165
Croatian Democratic Union (Bosnia and Hercegovina), 82
Croatian Democratic Union (Croatia), 167; 168
Croatian Democratic Union (HDZ) (Bosnia and Hercegovina), 82; 83; 84
Croatian Democratic Union (HDZ) (Croatia), 165; 168
Croatian Democratic Union of Croatia (Bosnia and Hercegovina), 83
Croatian Independent Democrats (Croatia), 165; 167
Croatian National Party (Croatia), 168
Croatian Party of Rights (Croatia), 166; 169
Croatian Party of Slavonia and Baranja (Croatia), 168
Croatian Peasant Party (HSS) (Croatia), 165; 168
Croatian Peasant Party of Croatia (Bosnia and Hercegovina), 83
Croatian Social Liberal Party (Croatia), 168; 169
Croation Democratic Union (HDZ) (Croatia), 166
Czech Social Democratic Party (Czech Republic), 180; 182
Czech-Moravian Centre Union (Czech Republic), 184

D

Dalmatian Action (Croatia), 167; 168
Danish People's Party (Denmark), 188
Death to Kidnappers (MAS) (Colombia), 144; 147
December National Democratic Party (Kazakhstan), 205; 353; 205
Democracia Popular—Unión Demócrata Cristiana (DP) (Ecuador), 205
Democrat Party (Thailand), 574
Democratic Action (AD) (Venezuela), 642; 644; 645; 646
Democratic Action (El Salvador), 212
Democratic Action for Electoral Rescue (ADRE) (Mexico), 404
Democratic Action Party (Malayasia), 387
Democratic Agrarian Party of Romania (Romania), 485; 489
Democratic Alliance (AD) (Chile), 132; 135
Democratic Alliance (AD) (Italy), 340; 341; 344
Democratic Alliance (Brazil), 88
Democratic Alliance (DA'91) (Suriname), 551
Democratic Alliance M-19 (ADM-19) (Colombia), 145
Democratic Alliance of Albania (Albania), 6
Democratic Alliance of Croats in Vojvodina (Demokratski Savez Hrvata u Vojvodini, DSHV) (Yugoslavia), 655
Democratic Alliance of Kosovo (Albania), 5
Democratic Alliance of Kosovo (Yugoslavia), 653
Democratic Alliance Party of Albania (Albania), 5
Democratic Alliance—April 19 Movement (Colombia), 144
Democratic Alternative '91 (Suriname), 461; 551
Democratic and Social Assembly (Concertación Democrática y Social (Paraguay), 461
Democratic and Social Christian Party (Zaïre), 657
Democratic and Social Convention (CDS-Rahama (Niger), 439
Democratic and Social Republican Party (Mauritania), 397
Democratic Coalition of Namibia (Namibia), 418
Democratic Community of Vojvodina Hungarians (Yugoslavia), 653
Democratic Conservative Party of Nicaragua (PCDN) (Nicaragua), 433
Democratic Constitutional Rally (Tunisia), 579; 580
Democratic Convention of Romania (CDR) (Romania), 484; 485; 486; 488
Democratic Convergence (CD) (El Salvador), 215
Democratic Convergence (CODE) (Peru), 464; 465
Democratic Convergence (DC) (Guatemala), 291
Democratic Convergence (El Salvador), 212; 215; 508
Democratic Convergence Party–Convergence Group (São Tomé and Príncipe), 509
Democratic Development Party (Turkmenistan), 587
Democratic Filipino People's Power (LDP) (Philippines), 470
Democratic Force (France), 249
Democratic Forces of National Salvation (Nicaragua), 438
Democratic Front Against Oppression (FDCR) (Guatemala), 295
Democratic Front for the Liberation of Palestine (Jordan), 350
Democratic Front for the Liberation of Palestine (Palestinian Entity), 451

Democratic Front for the Reunification of the Fatherland (North Korea), 358
Democratic Front (FREDEMO) (Peru), 463; 464; 465
Democratic Front (Guinea-Bissau), 298
Democratic Front (Jordan), 350
Democratic Front (North Korea), 358
Democratic Front of French-Speakers (FDF) (Belgium), 66; 67
Democratic Front of French-Speakers (FDF) of Brussels (Belgium), 62; 64; 65
Democratic Institutionalist Party (Guatemala), 289
Democratic Labor Party (Australia), 34
Democratic Labour Movement (DLM) (Guyana), 300
Democratic Labour Movement (Mauritius), 398
Democratic Labour Party (Barbados), 55
Democratic Left Alliance (SLD) (Poland), 475; 478
Democratic Left (Czech Republic), 183
Democratic Left (ID) (Ecuador), 203; 205
Democratic Left (Ireland), 327; 328; 329
Democratic Left (Northern Ireland), 616
Democratic Left Party (Czech Republic), 181
Democratic Left Party (DSP) (Turkey), 583; 584
Democratic Left (United Kingdom), 606
Democratic Liberal Party of Albania (Armenia), 30
Democratic Liberal Party of Armenia (Armenia), 31; 32
Democratic Movement of Kyrgyzstan (Kyrgyzstan), 362
Democratic Movement of Serbia (Depos) (Yugoslavia), 654
Democratic Movement of Serbia (Yugoslavia), 654
Democratic Party (DIKO) (Cyprus), 172; 174
Democratic Party (DP) (Bulgaria), 92; 96; 97; 99
Democratic Party (DP) (Cyprus), 176; 177
Democratic Party (DP) (New Zealand's Associated Territories), 431
Democratic Party (El Salvador), 216
Democratic Party for the Development of Madagascar (Madagascar), 384
Democratic Party (Georgia), 267
Democratic Party (Luxembourg), 378; 379
Democratic Party of Albania (PDS) (Albania), 4; 5; 6; 7; 8
Democratic Party of Albanians (Yugoslavia), 653
Democratic Party of Armenia (Armenia), 30; 163
Democratic Party of Côte d'Ivoire (PDCI) (Côte d'Ivoire), 162; 163
Democratic Party of Free Kyrgyzstan (Kyrgyzstan), 362
Democratic Party of Guinea–African Democratic Party (Guinea), 296
Democratic Party of Guinea–Renewal (PDG-R) (Guinea), 296
Democratic Party of Kurdistan (Iraq), 325
Democratic Party of Latgale (Latvia), 365
Democratic Party of National Confidence (PDCN) (Nicaragua), 437
Democratic Party of National Co-operation (PDCN) (Guatemala), 293
Democratic Party of National Co-operation (PR-PNDC) (Guatemala), 294
Democratic Party of Nauru (Nauru), 419
Democratic Party of Progress (Guinea-Bissau), 298
Democratic Party of Russia (Russia), 494; 500
Democratic Party of Serbia (Yugoslavia), 653
Democratic Party of Slovenia (Slovenia), 521
Democratic Party of Socialists of Montenegro (Yugoslavia), 653

Democratic Party of Tajikistan (Tajikistan), 570
Democratic Party of the Left (PDS) (Italy), 335; 337; 338
Democratic Party of the Right (Albania), 5; 8
Democratic Party of the Virgin Islands (US Dependencies), 632
Democratic Party of Ukraine (Ukraine), 595
Democratic Party (Slovakia), 521
Democratic Party (South Korea), 359
Democratic Party (UK Dependent Territories), 623; 624
Democratic Party (United States of America), 628
Democratic Party (US Dependencies), 630; 632; 633
Democratic Party (Yugoslavia), 653
Democratic Party-National Salvation Front (Romania), 485; 488
Democratic Party-St Maarten (Netherlands Dependencies), 428
Democratic Popular Movement (Ecuador), 203
Democratic Progressive Party (Taiwan), 568
Democratic Rally (DISY) (Cyprus), 172; 173; 174; 175
Democratic Reform Party of Muslims (Demokratska Reformska Stranka Muslimana, DRSM) (Yugoslavia), 655
Democratic Renewal Party (Angola), 21
Democratic Renewal Party (Costa Rica), 159
Democratic Republican Movement (Venezuela), 644
Democratic Revolutionary Front (El Salvador), 213
Democratic Revolutionary Party (PRD) (Panama), 451; 454
Democratic Revolutionary Unity (URD) (Guatemala), 90; 295
Democratic Socialist Party (Partido Socialista Democrático, PSD) (Brazil), 90
Democratic Socialist Reform Movement (ADISOK) (Cyprus), 174
Democratic (Tajikistan), 570
Democratic Tumu Party (New Zealand's Associated Territories), 431
Democratic Union for Social Renewal (Benin), 71
Democratic Union (Guatemala), 294
Democratic Union (Italy), 335; 336; 340
Democratic Union (Mozambique), 413; 414
Democratic Union of Slovakia (Slovakia), 517; 519; 520
Democratic Union of the Greek Minority (Omonia) (Albania), 6
Democratic Unionist Party (DUP) (Northern Ireland), 609; 613; 615
Democratic Unity (UD) (Dominican Republic), 200
Democratische Alternatif '91 (DA '91) (Suriname), 551
Democrats 66 (D66) (Netherlands), 422; 423; 424
Demokratska Partija Albanaca (DPA) (Yugoslavia), 653
Demokratska Partija Socijalista Crne Gore (Yugoslavia), 653
Demokratska Stranka (DS) (Yugoslavia), 653
Demokratska Stranka Srbije (DSS) (Yugoslavia), 653
Demokratski Savez e Kosoves (DSK) (Yugoslavia), 653
Development Party (Estonia), 220
Dignity and Charity (Russia), 497
Directorio Nacional Unificado—Movimiento de Unidad Revolucionario (DNU-MUR) (Honduras), 306
Dominican Liberation Party (PLD) (Dominican Republic), 200; 201
Dominican Revolutionary Party (PRD) (Dominican Republic), 199; 200; 201
Dravidian Progressive Federation (DMK) (India), 315; 319

E

Ecoglasnost Movement (Bulgaria), 96; 97; 99
Ecoglasnost Political Club (Bulgaria), 92; 95
Ecologist Party (Belgium), 65
Ecologists (Romania), 488
Ecology Generation (GE) (France), 238
Ecuadorean Communist Party (PCE) (Ecuador), 203; 204; 206
Ecuadorean Popular Revolutionary Action (APRE) (Ecuador), 204; 207
Ecuadorean Revolutionary Socialist Party (PSRE) (Ecuador), 206
Ecuadorean Roldósist Party (PRE) (Ecuador), 204; 206
Ecuadorean Socialist Party (PSE) (Ecuador), 203; 204; 206
Ecuadorian Conservative Party (Ecuador), 204; 205
Ecuadorian Socialist Party (Ecuador), 204
Efate Laketu Party (Vanuatu), 405; 642
Ejército Zapatista de Liberación Nacional (EZLN) (Mexico), 405
Emergent Movement of Harmony (Guatemala), 294
Encuentro Nacional (EN) (Paraguay), 460
Encuentro Progresista (EP) (Uruguay), 637
Eritrean Liberation Front (Eritrea), 218
Eritrean People's Liberation Front (EPLF) (Ethiopia), 224
Erk (Uzbekistan), 638
Eskimo Brotherhood (IA) (Danish Dependencies), 196
Esperanza, Paz y Libertad (EPL) (Colombia), 147
Estonian Centre Party (EKe) (Estonia), 219; 220
Estonian Coalition Party (EK) (Estonia), 219; 221
Estonian Democratic Labour Party (Estonia), 223
Estonian Greens (Estonia), 223
Estonian Pensioners' and Families' League (Estonia), 219; 221
Estonian Reform Party (Estonia), 219; 220
Estonian Royalist Party (Estonia), 223
Estonian Rural Centre Party (EMK) (Estonia), 221; 222
Estonian Rural People's Party (Estonia), 219; 221
Estonian Rural Union (Estonia), 219
Estonian Social Democratic Party (ESDP) (Estonia), 221; 222
Ethiopian Democratic Union (Ethiopia), 225
Ethiopian People's Democratic Movement (EPDM) (Ethiopia), 224
Ethiopian People's Revolutionary Democratic Front (EPRDF) (Ethiopia), 223; 224; 225
Ethiopian People's Revolutionary Party (Ethiopia), 225
Ethnic Minority Party (New Zealand), 430
Expresión Renovadora del Pueblo (ERP) (El Salvador), 215

F

Farabundo Martí National Liberation Front (El Salvador), 211; 212
Farabundo Martí National Liberation Front (FMLN) (El Salvador), 212; 214; 215
Farmers' Assembly (Estonia), 219
Farmers' Assembly (PK) (Estonia), 221
Farmers' Movement of Slovakia (Slovakia), 516; 518; 519; 520
Fatherland (Kyrgyzstan), 361
Fatherland Party of Labour (Bulgaria), 99
Fatherland Union (Estonia), 222

Fatherland Union (VU) (Liechtenstein), 374
Febrerist Revolutionary Party (Paraguay), 460
Federal and Pacific Sun (Sol Federal y Pacifista) (Uruguay), 637
Federal Party (Partido Federal, PF) (Argentina), 28
Federalist Centre Party (PFC) (Argentina), 28
Federation of Christian Workers (FTC) (Panama), 453
Fianna Fáil (FF) (Ireland), 327; 328; 329
Fiji Christian Party (Fiji), 227
Fiji Indian Congress Party (Fiji), 227
Fiji Indian Liberal Party (Fiji), 227
Fiji Labour Party (FLP) (Fiji), 226; 227
Fiji Muslim League (Fiji), 227
Fijian Association Party (FAP) (Fiji), 227
Fijian Conservative Party (Fiji), 227
Fijian Labour Party (Fiji), 227
Fijian Nationalist Party (Fiji), 227
Fijian Nationalist United Front Party (Fiji), 227
Fijian Political Party (Fiji), 227
Fine Gael (Ireland), 326
Finnish Christian Union (SKL) (Finland), 229; 233; 234
Finnish Rural Party (SMP) (Finland), 229; 231; 233; 234
Finnish Social Democratic Party (SSDP) (Finland), 228; 230; 231; 232; 233
Flemish Bloc (VB) (Belgium), 65
Forum for Democratic Forces (Uzbekistan), 639
Forum for National Recovery (FRN) (Comoros), 151
Forum for the Restoration of Democracy (Kenya), 354
Forward (Danish Dependencies), 195
Forward (Siumut) (Danish Dependencies), 195; 196
Forza Italia (Ireland), 326
Forza Italia (Italy), 337; 342
Forza Italia of Italy (Greece), 286
Forza Italia (Portugal), 479
Free Bolivia Movement (MBL) (Bolivia), 75; 76; 80
Free Democratic Party (FDP) (Germany), 272; 273; 278
Free Democrats–Liberal National Social Party (Czech Republic), 179; 182
Free National Movement (Bahamas), 48
Freedom Alliance (PL) (Italy), 334; 337; 339; 342; 343; 344
Freedom Civil Movement of Kazakhstan (Azat (Kazakhstan), 353
Freedom Civil Movement of Kazakhstan (Kazakhstan), 353
Freedom (Erk) (Uzbekistan), 639
FreeDOM (French Overseas Possessions), 257
Freedom Movement (Austria), 41; 42
Freedom Union (Poland), 471; 472; 477
Freedom (Uzbekistan), 638
FREJUPO (Argentina), 24
Fren Melanesia (Vanuatu), 640
French Communist Party (French Overseas Possessions), 255; 256; 257
French Communist Party (PCF) (France), 238; 241; 242; 246; 247; 252
French Communist Party (Vietnam), 647
Frente Amplio de Izquierda (FADI) (Ecuador), 206
Frente Amplio (FA) (Uruguay), 634
Frente de Unidad Nacional (FUN) (Guatemala), 292
Frente Democrático de Nueva Guatemala (FDNG) (Guatemala), 213; 293
Frente Farabundo Martí para la Liberación Nacional (FMLN) (El Salvador), 213
Frente Grande (FG) (Argentina), 23

Frente Independiente Moralizador (FIM) (Peru), 464
Frente Nacional (FN) (Guatemala), 291
Frente Obrero, Campesino, Estudiantil y Popular (FOCEP) (Peru), 465
Frente Pais Solidario (FREPASO) (Argentina), 24
Frente Radical Alfarista (FRA) (Ecuador), 203
Frente Republicano Guatemalteco (FRG) (Guatemala), 291
Frente Revolucionario de Izquierda (FRI) (Bolivia), 80
Frente Revolucionario de Obreras y Campesinos (FROC) (Nicaragua), 438
Frente Sandinista de Liberación Nacional (FSLN) (Nicaragua), 436
Frente Unido Revolucionario (FUR) (Guatemala), 294
FREPASO Coalition (Argentina), 26
Front for a Country in Solidarity (Argentina), 23
Front for Democracy and Development (FDO) (Suriname), 551; 552
Front for National Unity (FUN) (Guatemala), 290
Front for the Liberation of Mozambique (FRELIMO) (Mozambique), 412
Front for the Liberation of the Enclave of Cabinda (Angola), 22
Front for the Restoration of Unity and Democracy (Djibouti), 198
Front of Allies for Change (Cameroon), 115
Front to Safeguard Democracy (Mali), 393; 438
Fuerza Democrática por la Salvación Nacional (FDSN) (Nicaragua), 438
Fuerza Republicana (FR) (Argentina), 28
Future New Zealand Party (New Zealand), 430
Future of Russia/New Names (Russia), 497

G

Galician Coalition (Spain), 544
Galician Nationalist Bloc (Spain), 544
General People's Congress (GPC) (Yemen), 651; 652
General Union of the Elderly (Netherlands), 425
General Voters' Party (GVP) (Fiji), 227
German People's Union (Germany), 277; 279
German Social Union (DSU) (Germany), 274; 275
Gesher Party (Israel), 331
Gibraltar Labour Party-Association for the Advancement of Civil Rights (UK Dependent Territories), 622
Gibraltar Social Democrats (UK Dependent Territories), 623
Gibraltar Socialist Labour Party (GSLP) (UK Dependent Territories), 622; 623
Good and Green for Guyana (GGG) (Guyana), 300
Greater Romania Party (PRM) (Romania), 486; 488; 489
Green Alliance (Switzerland), 565
Green Alternative (Austria), 43
Green Alternative (GA) (Luxembourg), 379
Green Ecologist Initiative List (Luxembourg), 379
Green Ecologist Party of Mexico (Mexico), 403
Green Left (Netherlands), 425
Green Party (Bulgaria), 93; 95; 97; 99
Green Party in Slovakia (Slovakia), 518; 519; 520
Green Party (Ireland), 327
Green Party of Aotearoa (New Zealand), 429
Green Party of Switzerland (Switzerland), 561; 564
Green Party (SZ) (Czech Republic), 182
Green Union (Finland), 229; 231; 232; 233; 234
Greens (Australia), 35

Greens (France), 236; 252
Greens of Slovenia (Slovenia), 521
Greens (Portugal), 482
Greens Western Australia (Australia), 35
Grenada United Labour Party (Grenada), 288
Group for National Unity and Reconciliation (GNUR) (Solomon Islands), 524
Group for Solidarity (Côte d'Ivoire), 162; 163
Guadeloupe Communist Party (PCG) (French Overseas Possessions), 255
Guadeloupe Objective (French Overseas Possessions), 255
Guadeloupe Progressive Democratic Party (French Overseas Possessions), 255
Guatemalan Christian Democracy Party (DCG) (Guatemala), 290
Guatemalan Christian Democracy Party's (DCG) (Guatemala), 294
Guatemalan Committee of Patriotic Unity (Guatemala), 293
Guatemalan Labour Party (PGT) (Guatemala), 295
Guatemalan Labour Party—National Leadership Nucleus (Guatemala), 295
Guatemalan National Revolutionary Unity (URNG) (Guatemala), 291; 292; 295
Guatemalan Republican Front (Guatemala), 289; 290; 294
Guerrilla Co-ordinating Board (CNG) (Colombia), 148
Guianese Socialist Party (French Overseas Possessions), 254
Guinea-Bissau League for the Protection of the Ecology (Guinea-Bissau), 298
Guyana Labour Party (GLP) (Guyana), 300
Guyana Republican Party (GRP) (Guyana), 300
Guyanese Action for Reform and Democracy (GUARD) (Guyana), 301

H

Hayista Base Movement (MBH) (Peru), 463; 464; 465
Highlanders' Political Union (Georgia), 269
Holy War (Jihad) (Egypt), 210
Homeland Union (Lithuania), 375; 376
Honduran Patriotic Front (FPH) (Honduras), 305
Hope, Peace and Liberty (Colombia), 147
Human Rights Protection Party (HRPP) (Western Samoa), 650
Human Rights Union Party (Albania), 6
Humanist Party (PH) (Spain), 536
Hungarian Christian Democratic Movement (MKdH/MKdM) (Slovakia), 517; 518
Hungarian Civic Party (Slovakia), 517; 518
Hungarian Democratic Forum (MDF) (Hungary), 308; 309 310; 311
Hungarian Democratic People's Party (Hungary), 309
Hungarian Democratic Union of Romania (UDMR) (Romania), 485; 486
Hungarian Justice and Life Party (Hungary), 308
Hungarian Socialist Party (Hungary), 308; 311

I

Independence and Labour Party (Senegal), 511; 512
Independence Party (IP) (Iceland), 313; 314
Independence Party (Morocco), 411

Independence Path (Uzbekistan), 638
Independent Agricultural Movement (Movimiento Independiente Agrario—MIA) (Peru), 467
Independent Citizens' Movement (ICM) (US Dependencies), 509; 632
Independent Democratic Alliance (ADI) (São Tomé and Príncipe), 508
Independent Democratic Union (UDI) (Chile), 134
Independent Ecological Movement (France), 238
Independent Front (Vanuatu), 642
Independent Liberal Party (PLI) (Nicaragua), 433; 435; 436
Independent Smallholders' Party (FKP) (Hungary), 307; 308; 311
Independents' Alliance (Switzerland), 559
Indian National Congress (Nepal), 420
Indian National Congress (Socialist) (India), 317
Indian National Congress–Congress (I) (India), 315; 316; 317; 318; 319; 320
Indonesian Democratic Party (Indonesia), 321
Initiative for Catalonia (Spain), 546
Inkatha Freedom Party (IFP) (South Africa), 528
Innovation and Unity Party (PINU) (Honduras), 305
Institutional Democratic Party (PID) (Guatemala), 293
Institutional Revolutionary Party (PRI) (Mexico), 400; 402
Intellectual Armenian Union (Armenia), 31
Inter-Regional Bloc for Reform (Ukraine), 592; 593
Intransigent Party (PI) (Argentina), 24; 26; 27
Iraqi Communist Party (ICP) (Iraq), 325
Islamic Action Front's (Jordan), 349
Islamic Constitutional Movement (Kuwait), 360
Islamic Democratic Alliance (Pakistan), 448
Islamic Party (Afghanistan), 1; 3
Islamic Renaissance Party (IRP) (Tajikistan), 569
Islamic Renaissance Party (IRP) (Uzbekistan), 638
Islamic Renaissance (Tajikistan), 570
Islamic Revolutionary Movement (Afghanistan), 3
Islamic Salvation Front (FIS) (Algeria), 11; 12
Islamic Unity Party of Afghanistan (Afghanistan), 1; 2
Israel Labour Party (ILP) (Israel), 331; 332; 333
Istiqlal Yoli (Uzbekistan), 638
Istrian Democratic Assembly (Croatia), 167; 168
Italian Democratic Socialist Party (PSDI) (Italy), 340
Italian Federal League (Italy), 337; 342
Italian Liberal Party (Italy), 343; 344
Italian Popular Party (PPI) (Italy), 334; 335; 343; 344
Italian Renewal (Italy), 341
Italian Republican Party (Albania), 4
Italian Republican Party (Italy), 335; 339
Italian Social Movement (Italy), 342
Italian Socialists (Italy), 335
Ivorian Popular Front (FPI) (Côte d'Ivoire), 161; 162; 163
Ivorian Socialist Party (Côte d'Ivoire), 162
Ivorian Workers' Party (PIT) (Côte d'Ivoire), 162
Izquierda Democrática (ID) (Ecuador), 203
Izquierda Socialista (IS) (Peru), 466
Izquierda Unida (IU) (Bolivia), 80
Izquierda Unida (IU) (Peru), 466

J

Jamaica Labour Party (Jamaica), 345
Jamhoori Wattan Party (JWP) (Pakistan), 447
Janata Dal (JD) (India), 317; 318; 319

Janata Party (India), 316
January 31 Popular Front (FP-31) (Guatemala), 295
Javanese Farmers' Party (Kaum-Tani Persuatan Indonesia) (Suriname), 552
Joint List Bloc (Croatia), 165; 166; 167; 168
Joint Opposition Platform (POC) (Equatorial Guinea), 217
June Movement (Denmark), 191
Justice (Social Democratic Party of Uzbekistan) (Uzbekistan), 638
Justicialist Party (Argentina), 23; 25; 26

K

Kanak Socialist National Liberation Front (Overseas Territories and Territorial Collectivities), 260
Karnataka Congress Party (India), 319
Kenya African National Union (Kenya), 354
Khalq Birliki (Uzbekistan), 638
Khmer Nation Party (Cambodia), 112
Korean Workers Party (KWP) (Venezuela), 645
Korean Workers' Party (North Korea), 357; 358

L

La Causa Radical or Causa R (LCR) (Venezuela), 645
Labour Party (Ireland), 326; 328
Labour Party (Mauritius), 398; 399
Labour Party (Mongolia), 409
Labour Party (Mozambique), 413
Labour Party (Netherlands), 422; 424
Labour Party (Northern Ireland), 610; 613; 614
Labour Party of Britain (UK Dependent Territories), 622
Labour Party (Panama), 454
Labour Party (Taiwan), 568
Labour Party (United Kingdom), 599; 603; 605; 606; 607; 608
Lanka Equal Society Party (Sri Lanka), 548
Latvian Christian Democratic Union (Latvia), 364
Latvian Farmers' Union (Latvia), 366
Latvian Green Party (Latvia), 365
Latvian National Conservative Party (LNNK) (Latvia), 365; 366; 367
Latvia's Way Union (Latvia), 365; 366
Lavalas Political Organization (Haiti), 303
League for National Advancement (LNA) (Papua New Guinea), 456; 457
League of Communists of Montenegro (Yugoslavia), 653
League of Communists of Serbia (Yugoslavia), 654
League of Communists of Yugoslavia (Yugoslavia), 655
League of Communists-Movement for Yugoslavia of Montenegro (Yugoslavia), 655
League of Social Democrats of Vojvodina (Liga Socijaldemokrata Vojvodine) (Yugoslavia), 655
Left Bloc Party (Czech Republic), 181
Left Broad Force Party (Partido Fuerza Amplia de Izquierda, PFAI) (Chile), 136
Left Democratic Front (Bangladesh), 52; 55
Left Liberation Front (FIDEL) (Uruguay), 635
Left Party (Sweden), 559
Left Radical Movement (MRG) (France), 237; 242; 248
Left Radical Movement of France (United Kingdom), 606
Left Revolutionary Front (Bolivia), 80
Left Socialist Party (Denmark), 190

Leftist Nationalist Revolutionary Movement (Bolivia), 77
Left-Wing Alliance (Finland), 231; 233; 234
Liberal Alliance (Nicaragua), 434
Liberal Alliance of Montenegro (Yugoslavia), 653
Liberal and Democratic Party of Mozambique (Mozambique), 412; 413; 414
Liberal Democracy of Slovenia (LDS) (Slovenia), 521; 522; 523
Liberal Democratic Convention (CLD) (Equatorial Guinea), 217
Liberal Democratic Party (Belarus), 60
Liberal Democratic Party (Central African Republic), 123
Liberal Democratic Party (Japan), 347
Liberal Democratic Party (LDP) (Japan), 347; 348
Liberal Democratic Party of Russia (Belarus), 57; 59
Liberal Democratic Party of Russia (LDPR) (Russia), 494; 495
Liberal Democratic Party of Russia (Ukraine), 595; 598
Liberal Democratic Party of Slovenia (Bosnia and Hercegovina), 84
Liberal Democrats (Northern Ireland), 610
Liberal Democrats (United Kingdom), 599; 602; 607
Liberal Forum (Austria), 42
Liberal Front Party (PFL) (Brazil), 87
Liberal International (Croatia), 167
Liberal Party (Norway), 442; 443
Liberal Party (Australia), 33
Liberal Party (Bulgaria), 94; 97
Liberal Party (Danish Dependencies), 193
Liberal Party (Denmark), 188
Liberal Party (KTP) (Cyprus), 173
Liberal Party (New Zealand), 429
Liberal Party of Australia (Australia), 35; 36; 37
Liberal Party of Canada (LPC) (Canada), 118; 119; 120
Liberal Party of Honduras (PLH) (Honduras), 304; 306
Liberal Party of Macedonia (LPM) (Macedonia), 381; 382
Liberal Party (Philippines), 469
Liberal Party (PL) (Brazil), 87
Liberal Party (PL) (Colombia), 143; 144; 145
Liberal Party (PL) (Ecuador), 203
Liberal Party (PL) (Panama), 455
Liberal Party (PL) (Paraguay), 459
Liberal Party (Romania), 484; 487
Liberal Party (Spain), 545
Liberal Party (UK Dependent Territories), 624
Liberal Party (Venstre) (Denmark), 186; 188
Liberal People's Party (FP) (Sweden), 554; 557
Liberal People's Party (LKP) (Finland), 229; 230
Liberal Reform Party (PRL) (Belgium), 63; 64; 67
Liberal Republican Party (PLR) (Congo), 157
Liberal Socialist Party (LSP) (Egypt), 209; 210
Liberia Peace Council (Liberia), 372
Liberty Movement (Movimiento Libertad) (Peru), 464; 467
Likud (Israel), 330-333
Lithuanian Christian Democratic Party (Lithuania), 376; 377
Lithuanian Democratic Labour Party (Lithuania), 377
Lithuanian Democratic Party (Lithuania), 375
Lithuanian Independence Party (Lithuania), 376; 377
Lithuanian National Union (Lithuania), 376
Live Differently (AGALEV) (Belgium), 63
Living Forces Rasalama (Madagascar), 384

Lord's Resistance Army (Uganda), 589
Lorenzo Zelaya Popular Revolutionary Forces (Honduras), 307
Luxembourg Socialist Workers' Party (LSAP) (Luxembourg), 378; 379

M

Madhya Pradesh Vikas Congress (India), 319
Mahabini—Dead or Alive (Suriname), 553
Maharastrawadi Gomantak (India), 319
Malawi Congress Party (MCP) (Malawi), 385; 386
Malaysian People's Movement (Gerakan) (Malayasia), 389; 391
Malta Labour Party (MLP) (Malta), 394; 395
Mandela Bush Negro Liberation Movement (BBM) (Suriname), 553
Maneaban Te Mauri (MTM) (Kiribati), 357
Martinique Communist Party (French Overseas Possessions), 256
Martinique Progressive Party (PPM) (French Overseas Possessions), 256
Marxist Party (Australia), 39
Marxist Workers' Party (Peru), 467
Master Democratic Party (Latvia), 365; 366; 367
Mauritian Militant Movement (Mauritius), 398; 399
Mauritian Militant Renaissance (Mauritius), 398; 399
Mauritian Social Democratic Party (Mauritius), 398; 399
Mauritian Socialist Movement (MSM) (Mauritius), 398; 399
Melanesian Alliance (MA) (Papua New Guinea), 456
Melanesian Progressive Party (MPP) (Vanuatu), 640; 641
Melanesian United Front (Papua New Guinea), 456
Meretz (Israel), 332; 333
Metapolitical Unitarian Movement (Colombia), 148
Mexican Democratic Party (PDM) (Mexico), 403
Mexican Socialist Party (PMS) (Mexico), 401; 403
Milli Tiklanish (Uzbekistan), 638
Moderate Alliance (Conservative) (Sweden), 556
Moderate Alliance (MSP) (Sweden), 554
Moderates (Estonia), 221
Moledet (Israel), 332; 333
Mongolian People's Revolutionary Party (MPRP) (Mongolia), 408; 409
Mongolian Social Democratic Party (Mongolia), 409
Montoneros Free Fatherland (Ecuador), 207
Montoneros Patria Libre (MPL) (Ecuador), 207
Morazanista Front for the Liberation of Honduras (Honduras), 307
Moro National Liberation Front (Philippines), 470
Motherland Movement (Panama), 455
Motherland Party (ANAP) (Turkey), 584; 585
Motherland Party (Azerbaijan), 46
Movement for a Democratic Slovakia (HZDS) (Slovakia), 517; 518; 519; 520; 521
Movement for African Independence, Rebirth and Integration (Mali), 392
Movement for Democracy and Development (Central African Republic), 123
Movement for Democracy and Development (Chad), 131
Movement for Democracy (MPD) (Cape Verde), 120; 121
Movement for Democratic Reforms (Belarus), 58
Movement for Dignity and Independence (Argentina), 26
Movement for France (United Kingdom), 608

Movement for Greater Autonomy (Papua New Guinea), 457
Movement for Israel and Immigration (Israel), 331
Movement for Multi-Party Democracy (MMD) (Zambia), 659
Movement for Nationalist Democratization (MDN) (Honduras), 306
Movement for Rights and Freedoms (DPS) (Bulgaria), 95; 97; 99; 100
Movement for Socialism and Unity (Senegal), 510; 511
Movement for Solidarity, Union and Progress (Benin), 72; 74
Movement for the Defence of the Republic (Cameroon), 113
Movement for the Installation of Democracy in Haiti (MIDH) (Haiti), 303
Movement for the Liberation of Angola (MPLA) (Angola), 19; 508
Movement for the Liberation of São Tomé and Príncipe–Social Democratic Party (São Tomé and Príncipe), 508
Movement for the Reconstruction of Poland (Poland), 471
Movement for the Republic (RdR) (Poland), 471; 472; 473
Movement for the Social Evolution of Black Africa (MESAN) (Central African Republic), 124
Movement for Unity and Change (MUC) (Honduras), 306
Movement of Free Democrats (Cyprus), 173; 174
Movement of Integration and Development (Argentina), 27
Movement of Progressive Democrats (MDP) (Burkina Faso), 101
Movement of the Allendist Democratic Left (Chile), 134
Movement of the Revolutionary Left (MIR) (Bolivia), 76; 77; 78; 79
Movement of the Revolutionary Left (MIR) (Venezuela), 643; 644; 645
Movement of the Revolutionary Left-Peru (MIR-Perú) (Peru), 466
Movement of the Socialist Fatherland (MPS) (Venezuela), 645
Movement of Unity (El Salvador), 211
Movement to Socialism (Movimiento al Socialism, MAS) (Argentina), 28
Movement Towards Socialism (MAS) (Venezuela), 644; 646
Movimiento al Socialismo (MAS) (Venezuela), 211; 644
Movimiento Auténtico Demócrata Cristiano (MADC) (El Salvador), 211
Movimiento Bolivia Libre (MBL) (Bolivia), 77
Movimiento de Acción Solidaria (MAS) (Guatemala), 294
Movimiento de Bases Hayistas (MBH) (Peru), 464
Movimiento de Integración y Desarrollo (MID) (Argentina), 26
Movimiento de Izquierda Revolucionaria (MIR) (Venezuela), 644
Movimiento de la Izquierda Revolucionaria (MIR) (Bolivia), 77
Movimiento de Liberación Nacional (Guatemala), 292
Movimiento de Renovación Sandinista (MRS) (Nicaragua), 437

Movimiento de Restauración Nacional (MORENA) (Colombia), 148

Movimiento de Salvación Nacional (MSN) (Colombia), 145; 435

Movimiento Democrático Nicaragüense (MDN) (Nicaragua), 435

Movimiento Electoral del Pueblo (MEP) (Venezuela), 645

Movimiento Emergente de Concordia (MEC) (Guatemala), 290

Movimiento Izquierda Democrática Allendista (MIDA) (Chile), 134

Movimiento Nacional (MN) (Costa Rica), 160

Movimiento Nacional Revolucionario (MNR) (El Salvador), 215

Movimiento Nacionalista Revolucionaria de Izquierda (MNRI) (Bolivia), 77

Movimiento Nacionalista Revolucionario (MNR) (Bolivia), 78

Movimiento Obras Cívicas (MOC) (Peru), 464

Movimiento Popular Democrático (MPD) (Ecuador), 203

Movimiento Renovación Social Cristiano (MRSC) (El Salvador), 215

Movimiento Revolucionario Tupac Amarú (MRTA) (Peru), 468

Movimiento Revolucionario Tupaj Katari—Liberación (MRTK-L) (Bolivia), 80

Movimiento Unitario Metapolítico (MUP) (Colombia), 148

Mozambique National Movement (Mozambique), 414

Mozambique National Resistance (RENAMO) (Mozambique), 412; 413

Mozambique People's Progress Party (Mozambique), 414

Mujaheddin-e-Khalq (Iran), 323

Muslim Brotherhood (MB) (Egypt), 208; 209; 210

Muslim Democratic Party (Bosnia and Hercegovina), 82

Muslims of Russia (Russia), 500

N

Na-Griamel (Vanuatu), 640; 641

Nahdatul Ulama (Indonesia), 322

Namake Auti (Vanuatu), 642

Narodna Saborna Stranka (NSS) (Yugoslavia), 654

Narodna Stranka Crne Gore (Yugoslavia), 654

Nation Party (Turkey), 585

National Accord alliance (Paraguay), 459

National Action Party (Mexico), 401

National Action Party of the Solomon Islands (NAPSI) (Solomon Islands), 524

National Action Party (PAN) (Nicaragua), 435

National Advance Guard (Chile), 134

National Advancement Front (FAN) (Guatemala), 292

National Advancement Party (PAN) (Guatemala), 289; 291; 294

National Alliance (AN) (Italy), 337; 340

National Alliance for Belizean Rights (NABR) (Belize), 69

National Alliance for Democracy and Development (Chad), 128; 129

National Alliance for Democracy and Renewal (Chad), 128

National Alliance for Reconstruction (NAR) (Trinidad and Tobago), 578

National Alliance Party (Seychelles), 513

National Assembly of Community Representatives (Panama), 454

National Awami Party (Muzaffar) (Bangladesh), 49; 52

National Centre of Independents and Peasants (CNIP) (France), 241; 245

National Centre Party (Partido Nacional de Centro, PNC) (Argentina), 28

National Christian Alliance Party (Alianza Nacional Cristiana, ANC) (Costa Rica), 160

National Civic Crusade (Panama), 455

National Coalition (KOK) (Finland), 229; 230; 231; 232; 234

National Coalition Partners (NCP) (Solomon Islands), 524

National Coalition Partners (Solomon Islands), 525

National Conciliation Party (El Salvador), 214

National Confidence Democratic Party (PDCN) (Nicaragua), 435

National Congress for New Politics (South Korea), 359

National Conservative Party (PNC) (Nicaragua), 434

National Convention for Construction and Reform—Mageuzi (Tanzania), 572

National Convention of Progressive Patriots–Social Democratic Party (CNPP-PSD) (Burkina Faso), 103

National Convention Party (Ghana), 281

National Convention Party (Guinea-Bissau), 298

National Convergence (CN) (Venezuela), 642; 644

National Democratic Accord (Chile), 132; 135

National Democratic Action (Netherlands Dependencies), 426; 427

National Democratic Alliance (NDA) (Pakistan), 446; 447

National Democratic and Social Convention (Chad), 127

National Democratic Coalition (Andorra), 15

National Democratic Congress (Grenada), 288

National Democratic Congress (NDC) (Ghana), 280

National Democratic Front (FDN) (Mexico), 403

National Democratic Grouping (Andorra), 14

National Democratic Initiative (Andorra), 14

National Democratic Movement (MDN) (Guatemala), 292

National Democratic Movement (NDM) (Jamaica), 345

National Democratic Party (Belarus), 58

National Democratic Party (Fiji), 227

National Democratic Party (Germany), 275

National Democratic Party (Morocco), 410

National Democratic Party (Mozambique), 412; 413

National Democratic Party (NDP) (Egypt), 209

National Democratic Party (NDP) (Macedonia), 381

National Democratic Party (NDP) (Vanuatu), 640

National Democratic Party (Suriname), 551

National Democratic Rally (Senegal), 510; 511

National Democratic Union of Armenia (Armenia), 31

National Democratic Union (Panama), 451

National Development Party (Trinidad and Tobago), 578

National Encounter (Paraguay), 460

National Federation Party (NFP) (Fiji), 226; 227

National Front (Colombia), 143

National Front (FN) (France), 240; 244

National Front for Change and Democracy (FNCD) (Haiti), 302; 303

National Front for the Liberation of Angola (FNLA) (Angola), 17; 19; 20; 22

National Front for the Salvation of Libya (Libya), 373

National Front (France), 237; 246; 252
National Front (Guatemala), 291
National Front (Iran), 323
National Front (Malaysia), 387
National Front (Northern Ireland), 615
National Front of France (Belgium), 65
National Front (Spain), 537
National Front (Switzerland), 564
National Front (United Kingdom), 606
National Harmony Party (Latvia), 366
National Independence Party (NIP) (Belize), 69
National Innovation and Unity Party (Honduras), 306
National Islamic Front (Afghanistan), 2
National Labour Front (Chile), 134
National League for Democracy (Myanmar (Burma)), 415
National Leftist Revolutionary Party (Bolivia), 80
National Liberal Party (Nicaragua), 434
National Liberal Party (PLN) (Lebanon), 369
National Liberal Party (PLN) (Panama), 453
National Liberal Party (PNL) (Romania), 486
National Liberal Party (Romania), 484
National Liberation Army (Colombia), 146
National Liberation Army (EPL) (Colombia), 145
National Liberation Coalition (COLINA) (Panama), 455
National Liberation Front (FLN) (Algeria), 8; 9; 12
National Liberation Front (FNI) (Peru), 466
National Liberation Front (Georgia), 266
National Liberation Movement (Guatemala), 292
National Liberation Movement (MLN) (Guatemala), 289; 292; 293
National Liberation Movement of Kampuchea (MOULINAKA) (Cambodia), 112
National Liberation Party (PLN) (Costa Rica), 158
National Liberation Party (PLN) (Ecuador), 204
National Movement (Czech Republic), 183
National Movement for a Development Society (MNSD) (Niger), 439
National Movement for Democracy and Development (Benin), 73; 74
National Movement for the Independence of Madagascar (Madagascar), 385
National Opinion (Venezuela), 645
National Opposition Union (Nicaragua), 432
National Opposition Union (UNO) (El Salvador), 211
National Opposition Union (UNO) (Guatemala), 290; 292
National Opposition Union (UNO) (Mexico), 404
National Party (Bangladesh), 50; 53
National Party for Democracy and Development (Benin), 72
National Party (Grenada), 288
National Party (NP) (New Zealand), 428; 429; 430
National Party (NP) (Papua New Guinea), 456
National Party (NP) (South Africa), 527
National Party (NP) (Zambia), 658
National Party of Centrist Democracy (Chile), 134
National Party of Honduras (PNH) (Honduras), 304; 306
National Party of Labour (Benin), 74
National Party of Mozambique (Mozambique), 412
National Party (Papua New Guinea), 458
National Party (PNH) (Honduras), 305
National Party (South Africa), 529
National Party (the former Country Party) (Australia), 36
National Party (Uruguay), 636
National Patriotic Front of Liberia (NPFL) (Liberia), 372

National Patriotic Front of Liberia (NPFL) (Sierra Leone), 515
National Peasant Party (Narodna Seljacka Stranka, NSS) (Yugoslavia), 655
National People's Coalition (NPC) (Philippines), 470
National People's Party (Netherlands Dependencies), 427
National People's Party (NPP) (Pakistan), 447
National Popular Alliance (ANAPO) (Colombia), 144
National Progressive Party (NPP) (Kiribati), 357
National Progressive Patriotic Front (Iraq), 324; 325
National Project (Nicaragua), 437
National Rally for Democracy and Progress (Chad), 129
National Rally for Democracy (Benin), 72
National Rally for Development and Progress (Chad), 129
National Rally of Independents (Morocco), 410
National Reconciliation Commission (CNR) (Guatemala), 295
National Reconstruction Front (Ecuador), 204
National Reconstruction Party (Brazil), 89
National Religious Party (Israel), 331
National Renewal Party (Guatemala), 290
National Renewal (PR) (Chile), 133
National Renovation Movement (MNR) (Panama), 454
National Republic Party (Suriname), 551
National Republican Association—Colorado Party (Paraguay), 460
National Republican Party (NRP) (Guyana), 301
National Resistance (El Salvador), 213
National Resistance Movement (Uganda), 590
National Restoration (France), 252
National Restoration Movement (Colombia), 148
National Revival Democratic Party (Uzbekistan), 638
National Revolutionary Movement (El Salvador), 215
National Revolutionary Movement (MNR) (El Salvador), 212
National Revolutionary Party (Mexico), 400
National Salvation Front (Russia), 493; 500
National Salvation Movement (MSN) (Colombia), 145, 147
National Self-Determination Union (Armenia), 31
National Socialist Party (JSD) (Bangladesh), 50; 52; 55
National Socialist Party (Switzerland), 563
National Unification Party (PUN) (Costa Rica), 160
National Unified Directorate—Movement of Revolutionary Unity (Honduras), 306
National Union (Comoros), 149
National Union for Democracy and Progress (UNDP) (Cameroon), 114
National Union for Democracy and Progress (UNDP) (Congo), 157
National Union for Democracy in the Comoros (UNDC) (Comoros), 149; 151
National Union for Solidarity and Progress (Benin), 73
National Union for the Total Independence of Angola (UNITA) (Angola), 17; 18; 20; 21; 22
National Union of Popular Forces (Morocco), 410; 411
National Union Party (Costa Rica), 159
National United Party (NUP) (Vanuatu), 640; 641
National Unity and Reconciliation Progressive Party (NURPP) (Solomon Islands), 524
National Unity Front (Guatemala), 291
National Unity Pact (PUN) (Honduras), 305
National Unity Party of Georgia (Georgia), 269

National Unity Party (UBP) (Cyprus), 175; 176; 177
National Unity (PUN) (Honduras), 306
Nationale Democratische Partij (NDP) (Suriname), 551
Nationalist Action Party (Turkey), 585
Nationalist Authentic Central (Guatemala), 292
Nationalist Democratic Action (Bolivia), 78
Nationalist Front for Progress (NFP) (Solomon Islands), 524
Nationalist Labour Tendency (TNL) (Honduras), 306
Nationalist Left Party (Peru), 465
Nationalist Party (KMT) (Taiwan), 568
Nationalist Party (Malta), 394
Nationalist Party (Partido Nacionalista, PN) (Brazil), 90
Nationalist Party (Philippines), 469
Nationalist Republican Alliance (El Salvador), 213
Nationalist Republican Liberal Movement (Panama), 455
Nationalist Revolutionary Movement (MNR) (Bolivia), 75; 76; 78
Nationalist Revolutionary Movement of the Left (Bolivia), 79
Nationalist Revolutionary Movement-Historic (MNRH) (Bolivia), 76; 78
Nationalist Workers' Party (Partido Nacionalista de los Trabajadores, PNT) (Argentina), 29
Nepali Congress Party (Nepal), 420
Nevis Reformation Party (St Christopher and Nevis), 503
New Alternative (NA) (Venezuela), 645; 646
New Antilles Movement (Netherlands Dependencies), 427
New Aspiration Party (NAP) (Thailand), 574
New Azerbaijan Party (Azerbaijan), 44; 46; 47
New Dawn Party (Cyprus), 175; 176; 177
New Democracy (Greece), 287
New Democracy (ND) (Andorra), 14; 15
New Democracy (ND) (Greece), 283; 285; 286
New Democracy (ND) (Yugoslavia), 654; 655
New Democratic Generation Liberal Party (Venezuela), 645
New Democratic Party (Canada), 120
New Front (NF) (Suriname), 551; 552
New Frontier Party (NFP) (Japan), 347
New Guatemala Democratic Front (Guatemala), 289
New Hebrides National Party (Vanuatu), 641
New Korea Party (South Korea), 359; 360
New Labour Movement (Fiji), 227
New Labour Party (NLP) (New Zealand), 429
New Land (Overseas Territories and Territorial Collectivities), 259
New Left Party (Australia), 39
New Majority-Change 90 (NM-C90) (Peru), 462
New National Party (NNP) (Grenada), 288
New Party Harbinger (Japan), 346
New Party (NP) (Taiwan), 568
New People's Party (Vanuatu), 642
New Progressive Party (US Dependencies), 631
New Republican Movement (MNR) (Costa Rica), 160
New Royalist Action (France), 252
New Space (Uruguay), 634; 635
New Ukraine (Ukraine), 594
New Union for Democracy (Bulgaria), 97
New Wafd Party (Egypt), 209; 210
New Zealand Democratic Party (NZDP) (New Zealand), 429
New Zealand First Party (New Zealand), 429

New Zealand Labour Party (NZLP) (New Zealand), 429; 430
New Zealand Party (New Zealand), 429
New Zealand Self-Government Party (New Zealand), 429; 430
New Zealand Values Party (New Zealand), 429
Nicaraguan Democratic Co-ordinator (CDN) (Nicaragua), 433; 434; 435
Nicaraguan Democratic Movement (Nicaragua), 437
Nicaraguan Socialist Party (PSN) (Nicaragua), 436
Nieuwe Front (NF) (Suriname), 551
Niger Party for Democracy and Socialism (Niger), 439
Niger Progressive Party–African Democratic Rally (Niger), 439
Nikola Pasic Serbian Radical Party (Srpska Radikalna Stranka Nikola Pasic) (Yugoslavia), 655
Non-Party Bloc for Reform (BBWR) (Poland), 472; 476
Nora Astorga Front (Nicaragua), 438
Northern League (LN) (Italy), 337; 338
Northern League–Federal Italy (Italy), 337
Norwegian Labour Party (Norway), 442; 443; 444; 445
Nova Demokratija (ND) (Yugoslavia), 654
November 13 Revolutionary Movement of Radical Officers (MR13) (Guatemala), 295
Nuclear Disarmament Party (Australia), 35; 38; 40
Nueva Alternativa (NA) (Venezuela), 645
Nuevo Espacio (NE) (Uruguay), 636

O

Olive Tree (Italy), 335; 336; 337; 338; 340; 341; 344
Open Politics for Social Integrity (Argentina), 24
Opposition Civic Democratic Alliance (ADOC) (Panama), 455
Opposition Democratic Alliance (ADO) (Panama), 455; 509
Opposition Democratic Coalition (São Tomé and Príncipe), 509
Opposition National Union (UNO) (Panama), 452
Organization for Popular Democracy–Labour Movement (ODP-MT) (Burkina Faso), 101; 102; 103
Organization of the Crimean Tatar National Movement (Ukraine), 597
Organization of Ukrainian Nationalists in Ukraine (Ukraine), 595; 646
Organizing Committee for Independent Electoral Policy (Comité de Organización Política Electoral Independiente) (Venezuela), 646
Oromo Liberation Front (OLF) (Ethiopia), 224
Oromo People's Democratic Organization (OPDO) (Ethiopia), 224
Our Home is Russia (Russia), 496; 499

P

País Posible (Peru), 467
Pakistan People's Party (PPP) (Pakistan), 446; 447
Palang Dharma (Thailand), 575
Palestine Liberation Organization (Israel), 331
Palestine Liberation Organization (PLO) (Jordan), 350
Palestine People's Party (Palestinian Entity), 450
Pan-African Union for Social Democracy (UPADS) (Congo), 153; 155; 156; 157
Panameñista Party (PP) (Panama), 452

Pan-Armenian National Movement (PANM) (Armenia), 29; 30; 31

Pangu Pati (Papua New Guinea), 456; 457; 458

Pan-Hellenic Socialist Movement (PASOK) (Greece), 283; 284; 286; 287

Pan-Malaysian Islamic Party (PAS) (Malaysia), 390

Papua Party (Papua New Guinea), 457

Papuan National Alliance (Papua New Guinea), 457

Paraguayan Communist Party (Paraguay), 461

Parliamentary Party of Kosovo (PPK) (Yugoslavia), 655

Partido Acción Nacional (PAN) (Mexico), 402

Partido Arnulfista (PA) (Panama), 452

Partido Colorado (PC) (Uruguay), 635

Partido Comunista de Colombia (PCC) (Colombia), 147

Partido Comunista de la Argentina (PCA) (Argentina), 24

Partido Comunista de Nicaragua (PCdeN) (Nicaragua), 433

Partido Comunista de Venezuela (PCV) (Venezuela), 643

Partido Comunista do Brasil (PCdoB) (Brazil), 88

Partido Comunista Paraguayo (PCP) (Paraguay), 461

Partido Comunista Peruano (PCP) (Peru), 465

Partido Comunista Revolucionario (PCR) (Peru), 466

Partido Comunista Salvadoreño (PCS) (El Salvador), 215

Partido Conservador de Nicaragua (PCN) (Nicaragua), 433

Partido Conservador Ecuatoriano (PCE) (Ecuador), 204

Partido da Frente Liberal (PFL) (Brazil), 88; 89

Partido da Reconstrução Nacional (PRN) (Brazil), 89

Partido da Social Democracia Brasileira (PSDB) (Brazil), 87

Partido de Acción Nacional (PAN) (Nicaragua), 434

Partido de Conciliación Nacional (PCN) (El Salvador), 214

Partido de Innovación Nacional y Unidad (PINU) (Honduras), 306

Partido de Izquierda Nacionalista (PIN) (Peru), 402; 465

Partido de la Revolución Democrática (PRD) (Mexico), 402

Partido de Liberación Nacional (PLN) (Costa Rica), 158

Partido del Frente Cardenista de Reconstruction Nacional (PFCRN) (Mexico), 403

Partido del Pueblo Costarricense (PPC) (Costa Rica), 160

Partido del Trabajo (PT) (Mexico), 401

Partido Demócrata Christiano (PDC) (Argentina), 24

Partido Demócrata Cristiano de Honduras (PDCH) (Honduras), 305

Partido Demócrata Cristiano (PDC) (Bolivia), 76

Partido Demócrata Cristiano (PDC) (Colombia), 144

Partido Demócrata Cristiano (PDC) (Costa Rica), 159

Partido Demócrata Cristiano (PDC) (El Salvador), 211

Partido Demócrata Cristiano (PDC) (Panama), 453

Partido Demócrata Cristiano (PDC) (Paraguay), 459

Partido Demócrata Cristiano (PDC) (Peru), 464

Partido Demócrata Cristiano (PDC) (Uruguay), 634

Partido Demócrata Mexicano (PDM) (Mexico), 403

Partido Demócrata Progresista (PDP) (Argentina), 26

Partido Democrática (PD) (El Salvador), 213; 290

Partido Democrático de Cooperación Nacional (PDCN) (Guatemala), 290

Partido Democrático Trabalhista (PDT) (Brazil), 88

Partido do Movimento Democrático Brasiliero (PMDB) (Brazil), 89

Partido dos Trabalhadores (PT) (Brazil), 90; 295

Partido Guatemalteco del Trabajo (PGT)—Nucleo de Dirección Nacional (LN) (Guatemala), 295

Partido Independentista Puertorriqueño (PIP) (US Dependencies), 632

Partido Institucional Democrático (PID) (Guatemala), 289

Partido Intransigente (PI) (Argentina), 24

Partido Justicialista (PJ-Peronist) (Argentina), 25

Partido Liberal Auténtico (PLA) (Panama), 453

Partido Liberal de Honduras (PLH) (Honduras), 305

Partido Liberal Independiente (PLI) (Nicaragua), 434; 645

Partido Liberal Nueva Generación Democrática (PLNDG) (Venezuela), 645

Partido Liberal (PL) (Brazil), 89

Partido Liberal (PL) (Colombia), 144

Partido Liberal (PL) (Peru), 464

Partido Liberal Radical Auténtico (PLRA) (Paraguay), 459

Partido Liberal Radical (PLR) (Ecuador), 205

Partido Mexicana Socialista (PMS) (Mexico), 401

Partido Nacional (Blancos) (Uruguay), 636

Partido Nacional Conservador (PNC) (Nicaragua), 434

Partido Nacional de Honduras (PNH) (Honduras), 306

Partido Nacionalista Renovador (PNR) (Guatemala), 292

Partido Nuevo Progresista (PNP) (US Dependencies), 631

Partido Obrero Revolucionario (POR) (Bolivia), 80

Partido Popular Cristiano (PPC) (Peru), 465

Partido Popular Socialista (PPS) (Brazil), 90

Partido Popular Socialista (PPS) (Mexico), 404

Partido por el Adelantamiento Nacional (PAN) (Guatemala), 291

Partido por el Gobierno del Pueblo (PGP) (Uruguay), 637

Partido Progressista Reformador (PPR) (Brazil), 90

Partido Renovación Civilista (PRC) (Panama), 454

Partido Republicano Calderónista (PRC) (Costa Rica), 159

Partido Revolucionario de Izquierda Nacionalista (PRIN) (Bolivia), 80

Partido Revolucionario de los Trabajadores (PRT) (Mexico), 404

Partido Revolucionario de los Trabajadores (PRT) (Peru), 467

Partido Revolucionario Democrático (PRD) (Panama), 454

Partido Revolucionario Febrerista (PRF) (Paraguay), 460

Partido Revolucionario Institucional (PRI) (Mexico), 400

Partido Revolucionario (PR) (Guatemala), 293

Partido Roldosista Ecuatoriano (PRE) (Ecuador), 204

Partido Social Conservador (PSC) (Colombia), 146

Partido Social Cristiano (Ecuador), 206

Partido Social Cristiano (PSC) (Guatemala), 293

Partido Social Demócrata (PSD) (Guatemala), 293

Partido Social Demócrata (PSD) (Nicaragua), 437; 646

Partido Social-Cristiano/ Comité de Organización Politica Electoral Independiente (COPEI) (Venezuela), 646

Partido Socialista Brasileiro (PSB) (Brazil), 87

Partido Socialista de los Trabajadores (PST) (Colombia), 148

Partido Socialista Ecuatoriano (PSE) (Ecuador), 204

Partido Socialista Revolucionario (PSR) (Peru), 466

Partido Solidaridad (PS) (Panama), 455

Partido Trabalhista Brasileiro (PTB) (Brazil), 87

Partido Unidad Republicano (PUR) (Ecuador), 205

Partido Unidad Social Cristiana (PUSC) (Costa Rica), 159

Partido Unificado Mariáteguista (PUM) (Peru), 466

Partido Unión Nacional (PUN) (Costa Rica), 160

Partido Unión Popular (PUP) (Costa Rica), 160

Partido Vanguardia Popular (PVP) (Costa Rica), 160

Partido Verde Ecologista de México (PVEM) (Mexico), 403

Partij Nationalistische Republiek (PNR) (Suriname), 551

Partija Demokratske Akcije (PDA) (Yugoslavia), 654

Party for Bosnia and Hercegovina (Bosnia and Hercegovina), 82

Party for Democracy and Progress (Burkina Faso), 102

Party for Democratic Prosperity of Albanians in Macedonia (Macedonia), 381

Party for Democratic Prosperity (PDP) (Macedonia), 381; 382

Party for Legal Justice (Estonia), 223

Party for the Democratic Rebirth of Ukraine (Ukraine), 592

Party for the Economic Rebirth of Crimea (Ukraine), 598

Party for the Government of the People (PGP) (Uruguay), 633

Party for the Total Emancipation of Romanies in Macedonia (Macedonia), 382

Party for Unity and Harmony (KTPI) (Suriname), 550

Party for Unity, Work and Progress (Congo), 154

Party for Democracy (PPD) (Chile), 131

Party of Communists of the Moldovan Republic (Moldova), 407

Party of Democratic Action (SDA) (Bosnia and Hercegovina), 82; 84

Party of Democratic Action (Yugoslavia), 653; 654

Party of Democratic Reform (SDR) (Slovenia), 523

Party of Democratic Renewal (Benin), 73

Party of Democratic Socialism (Germany), 279

Party of Economic Freedom (Russia), 497

Party of Entrepreneurs and Tradesmen (Slovakia), 521

Party of National Restoration (Albania), 6

Party of People's Conscience (Russia), 497

Party of Renovation and Development (Guinea-Bissau), 298

Party of Revival and Accord of Moldova (Moldova), 406

Party of Social Progress of Uzbekistan (Uzbekistan), 639

Party of Socialists of Catalonia (PSC) (Spain), 534

Party of the Brazilian Democratic Movement (PMDB) (Brazil), 87; 88

Party of the Democratic Left (SDL') (Slovakia), 517; 518; 519; 520

Party of the Democratic Revolution (PRD) (Mexico), 402

Party of the Masses (Tudeh) (Iran), 323

Party of the Mexican Revolution (Mexico), 400

Party of Yugoslavs (Stranka Jugoslovena, SJ) (Yugoslavia), 655

Patriotic Accord (AP) (Bolivia), 78; 80

Patriotic Action Front (Mozambique), 413; 414

Patriotic Alliance (AP) (Bolivia), 76; 80

Patriotic Front for Progress (FPP) (Central African Republic), 121; 123; 124; 125; 133

Patriotic Front (Frente Patriótica Manuel Rodríguez, FPMR) (Chile), 133

Patriotic Republican Party (Czech Republic), 178

Patriotic Revolutionary Front (FPR) (Nicaragua), 436

Patriotic Salvation Front (MPS) (Chad), 128

Patriotic Salvation Movement (MSP) (Chad), 126; 127; 128; 129; 131

Patriotic Union for National Reconstruction (UPRN) (Congo), 157

Patriotic Union (UP) (Colombia), 145; 147

Peasant Alliance (Poland), 472; 477

Peasant Party of Kosovo (Partia Fshatare e Kosoves, PFK) (Yugoslavia), 655

Peasants' Party of Serbia (Seljacka Stranka Srbije, SSS) (Yugoslavia), 655

Peasants' Party of Ukraine (Ukraine), 594

People, Change and Democracy (PCD) (Ecuador), 205

People's Action Movement (St Christopher and Nevis), 503

People's Action Party (PAP) (Malaysia), 389

People's Action Party (PAP) (Papua New Guinea), 457

People's Action Party (Singapore), 515

People's Alliance (PA) (Iceland), 312; 314

People's Alliance Party (PAP) (Solomon Islands), 524; 525

People's Alliance (Sri Lanka), 547

People's Assembly Party (Yugoslavia), 654

People's Christian Alliance (Papua New Guinea), 457

People's Congress of Kazakhstan (Kazakhstan), 353

People's Convention Party (Ghana), 281

People's (Danish Dependencies), 192

People's Democracy Party (Turkey), 584

People's Democratic Movement (PDM) (Guyana), 301

People's Democratic Movement (PDM) (Papua New Guinea), 456; 457

People's Democratic Movement (UK Dependent Territories), 626

People's Democratic Party (PDP) (Uzbekistan), 638; 639

People's Democratic Party (PDP) (Vanuatu), 641

People's Democratic Party (Tajikistan), 569

People's Electoral Movement (MEP) (Venezuela), 643

People's Electoral Movement (Netherlands Dependencies), 426

Peoples' Electoral Movement (Venezuela), 645

People's Forum (Bangladesh), 50; 52; 55

People's Front for Democracy and Justice (Eritrea), 219

People's Front (Overseas Territories and Territorial Collectivities), 259

People's Labour Movement (PLM) (Guyana), 301

People's Movement (Iceland), 314; 315

People's Movement of Turkestan (Uzbekistan), 639

People's National Congress (PNC) (Guyana), 299; 300

People's National Convention (PNC) (Ghana), 281

People's National Movement (PNM) (Trinidad and Tobago), 578

People's National Party (Jamaica), 346

People's National Party (PNP) (Papua New Guinea), 458

People's Party (Fkfl) (Danish Dependencies), 192; 193; 194

People's Party for Freedom and Democracy (VVD) (Netherlands), 422; 424

People's Party of Montenegro (Yugoslavia), 654

People's Party of Tajikistan (Tajikistan), 569

People's Party (Tonga), 577

People's Progress Party (PPP) (Papua New Guinea), 456; 457

People's Progressive Party (PPP) (Guyana), 299; 300

People's Progressive Party (PPP) (Solomon Islands), 525

People's Progressive Party (The Gambia), 264

Peoples' Renewal Expression (El Salvador), 213

People's Republican Party (Turkey), 586

People's Revolutionary Movement (MRP) (Venezuela), 645

People's Self-Government Party (Russia), 498

People's Solidarity Party (Cameroon), 115

People's Struggle–National Union of Christian Democrats (Lakas-NUCD) (Philippines), 469

People's Union (Belgium), 62

People's Union (Bulgaria), 92; 95; 98; 99

Peoples' Union (Ecuador), 207

People's Union of Kazakhstan Unity (Kazakhstan), 354

People's Union (VU) (Belgium), 63; 66

People's United Democratic Movement and the Swaziland Youth Congress (SYC) (Swaziland), 553

People's United Front (Papua New Guinea), 458

Peoples' United Party (PUP) (Belize), 68

People's Unity Movement (Uzbekistan), 638

Peruvian American Popular Revolutionary Alliance Party (APRA) (Bolivia), 78

Peruvian Communist Party (PCP) (Peru), 466; 467

Phalangist Party (Lebanon), 369

Plaid Cymru (Welsh Nationalists) (United Kingdom), 606

Polish Party of the Friends of Beer (Poland), 478

Polish Peasant Party (PSL) (Poland), 472; 473; 476; 477; 478

Polish Socialist Party (PPS) (Poland), 474; 477

Política Abierto para la Integridad Social (PAIS) (Argentina), 26

Political Forces of the Conclave (Zaïre), 657

Political Spring (PA) (Greece), 284

Political Union of Economists (Latvia), 366

Polynesian Union (Overseas Territories and Territorial Collectivities), 258; 259

Popular Action (AP) (Peru), 464; 465; 466

Popular Christian Party (Partido Popular Cristiano, PPC) (Argentina), 29

Popular Christian Party (PPC) (Peru), 464

Popular Christians (PPC) (Peru), 466

Popular Democracy—Christian Democrat Union (Ecuador), 205

Popular Democratic Front (PDF) (Guatemala), 290

Popular Democratic Movement (MPD) (Ecuador), 206

Popular Democratic Party (PPD) (US Dependencies), 631; 632

Popular Democratic Union (Portugal), 481

Popular Democratic Union (UDP) (Ecuador), 206

Popular Front (Brazil), 90

Popular Front for the Liberation of Palestine (Jordan), 351

Popular Front for the Liberation of Palestine (Palestinian Entity), 450

Popular Front of Workers, Peasants and Students (Peru), 467

Popular Left Front (Frente de Izquierda Popular, FIP) (Argentina), 29

Popular Liberal Alliance (ALIPO) (Honduras), 305

Popular Liberation Army (Colombia), 147

Popular Monarchist Party (PPM) (Portugal), 480

Popular Movement for Belarus (Belarus), 59

Popular Movement for Latvia-Zigerists Party (Latvia), 365; 366

Popular Movement for the Liberation of Angola (MPLA) (Angola), 18

Popular Movement for the Liberation of Angola-Party of Labour (MPLA-PT) (Angola), 17; 20

Popular Movement (Morocco), 411

Popular Movement of Belarus (NDB) (Belarus), 58; 59; 61

Popular Movement of the Revolution (Zaïre), 656

Popular Movement (Ukraine), 592

Popular National Movement (Morocco), 411

Popular Participation Front (FPP) (Guatemala), 292

Popular Party for French Democracy, PPDF (France), 236; 249

Popular Party, PP (Portugal), 480; 481

Popular Party (PP) (Spain), 535; 536; 537; 541; 542; 543; 544; 545; 546

Popular Rally for Progress (Djibouti), 196; 197

Popular Social Christian Movement (MPSC) (El Salvador), 211; 212; 215

Popular Socialist Party (Brazil), 88

Popular Socialist Party (PPS) (Mexico), 403; 404

Popular Socialist Party (PSP) (Chile), 135

Popular Union Party (Costa Rica), 159; 160

Popular Union Party (Tunisia), 580

Popular Unity alliance (UP) (Chile), 135

Popular Unity Movement (Tunisia), 580

Popular Vanguard Party (Costa Rica), 160

Portuguese Communist Party (PCP) (Portugal), 481

Power (Derzhava) (Russia), 498; 499

Pro Patria (Estonia), 221; 222

Pro Patria National Coalition (Estonia), 220; 222

Progress of the Fatherland (Uzbekistan), 638

Progress Party (FP) (Denmark), 187; 188; 191

Progress Party of Equatorial Guinea (PPGE) (Equatorial Guinea), 216; 217

Progressieve Arbeiders en Landbouwers Unie (PALU) (Suriname), 552

Progressive Alliance (Ghana), 281

Progressive Citizens' Party (FBP) (Liechtenstein), 374

Progressive Conservative Party (PCP) (Canada), 118; 120

Progressive Democratic Party (Argentina), 26

Progressive Encounter (Uruguay), 633; 634; 637

Progressive Labour Party (UK Dependent Territories), 619

Progressive Left Coalition (Greece), 283; 284; 285; 286

Progressive Liberal Party (PLP) (Bahamas), 48

Progressive Movement (Cameroon), 117

Progressive National Party (UK Dependent Territories), 626

Progressive Organizations of Switzerland (POCH) (Switzerland), 561; 564; 565

Progressive Party (Iceland), 312; 314

Progressive Party of the Working People (AKEL) (Cyprus), 171; 172; 173

Progressive Party (Partido Progressista, PP) (Brazil), 90

Progressive Party (PP) (Iceland), 312; 313

Progressive Reform Party (VHP) (Suriname), 550

Progressive Renewal Party (Brazil), 90

Proletarian Tendency (PT) (Nicaragua), 436

Protracted People's War (GPP) (Nicaragua), 436

Proyecto Nacional (PN) (Nicaragua), 435

PSP (Brazil), 90

Pueblo Patriótico (UPP) (Ecuador), 207; 632

Puerto Rican Communist Party (Partido Comunista Puertorriqueño, PCP) (US Dependicies), 632

Puerto Rican Independence Party (US Dependencies), 632; 632

Puerto Rican Socialist Party (Partido Socialista Puertorriqueño, PSP) (US Dependicies), 632

Q

Quebec Bloc (Canada), 119
Quebec Party (Canada), 119
Quintín Lame (Colombia), 145; 148

R

Radical Civic Union (UCR) (Argentina), 23; 25; 27
Radical Democratic Party (El Salvador), 215
Radical Democratic Party (RDP) (Bulgaria), 97
Radical Democratic Party (Switzerland), 561; 562; 564
Radical Liberal Party (Paraguay), 459
Radical Liberal Party (PLR) (Ecuador), 203; 204
Radical Liberal Party (RV) (Denmark), 186; 187; 189
Radical Party (France), 238; 247; 249
Radical Party (Italy), 337
Radical Party of France (Denmark), 188
Radical Party of Italy (Croatia), 170
Radical Party (UCR) (Argentina), 26
Rally for Caledonia (Overseas Territories and Territorial
    Collectivities), 260
Rally for Democracy and Development (RDD) (Congo),
    152
Rally for Democracy and Progress (Chad), 129
Rally for Democracy and Progress (Mali), 392
Rally for Democracy and Renewal (RDR) (Comoros),
    149
Rally for Democracy and Social Progress (RDPS)
    (Congo), 152; 156
Rally for the Republic (France), 236; 242; 252
Rally for the Republic (French Overseas Possessions),
    254; 255; 256; 257; 258
Rally for the Republic (Ireland), 326
Rally for the Republic (Italy), 337
Rally for the Republic (Portugal), 479
Rally for the Republic (RPR) (France), 236; 241; 243;
    246; 247; 248; 249
Rally for the Republic (RPR) (French Overseas
    Possessions), 257; 258
Rally for the Republic (RPR) (Overseas Territories and
    Territorial Collectivities), 259; 261; 262
Rally of Republicans (Côte d'Ivoire), 162; 163
Rally of the Chadian People (Chad), 129
Rally of the Togolese People (Togo), 576
Rally of Woodcutters (Gabon), 263
Red and Green Alternative (France), 253
Red Electoral Alliance (Norway), 443
Red-Green Unity List (Denmark), 191
Referendum Party (United Kingdom), 601
Reform Democratic Party of Vojvodina (Yugoslavia), 654
Reform Party (Turkey), 584
Reform Party (United States of America), 628
Reformational Political Federation (RPF) (Netherlands),
    425
Reformed Political Association (GPV) (Netherlands),
    424; 425
Renewal Social Christian Movement (El Salvador), 212
Renovation (Renovación) (Peru), 467
Republic Bloc (Armenia), 30; 31
Republican Force (Argentina), 28
Republican Nationalist Alliance (El Salvador), 212
Republican Party of Armenia (Armenia), 31
Republican Party of Kazakhstan to form the Republican
    Party Azat (Kazakhstan), 353

Republican Party of the Crimea (RPK) (Ukraine), 597;
    598
Republican Party of the Virgin Islands (US
    Dependencies), 633
Republican Party (Partido Republicano, PR) (Chile), 136
Republican Party (PR) (France), 240; 241; 242; 249
Republican Party (PR) (Panama), 455
Republican Party (RP) (Bulgaria), 97
Republican Party (Tjfl) (Danish Dependencies), 193; 194
Republican Party (United States of America), 629
Republican Party (US Dependencies), 630; 633
Republican People's Party (CHP) (Turkey), 581; 584; 585
Republican People's Slavic Movement–Harmony
    (Kazakhstan), 353
Republican People's Union (Benin), 73
Republican Turkish Party (CTP) (Cyprus), 175; 176
Republican Unity Party (Ecuador), 202
Republicans (Germany), 273; 275; 279; 280
Resistencia Nacional (RN) (El Salvador), 215
Restructured Antilles Party (Netherlands Dependencies),
    427; 428
Réunion Communist Party (PCR) (French Overseas
    Possessions), 258
Revolutionary Alliance of Workers and Peasants
    (Nicaragua), 438
Revolutionary Armed Forces of Colombia (FARC)
    (Colombia), 146
Revolutionary Communist League, (LCR) (France), 251
Revolutionary Communist Party (PCR) (Peru), 466
Revolutionary Democratic Liberal Movement (MLDR or
    M-lider (Honduras), 305
Revolutionary Left Movement (MIR-Perú) (Peru), 466
Revolutionary Movement of the Christian Left (MRIC)
    (Ecuador), 206
Revolutionary Party (Guatemala), 294
Revolutionary Party of Tanzania (Tanzania), 571; 572
Revolutionary Party of the National Left (PRIN)
    (Bolivia), 75
Revolutionary Party (PR) (Guatemala), 290; 292
Revolutionary Patriotic Front (Nicaragua), 434
Revolutionary Progressive Nationalist Party (Haiti), 302
Revolutionary Socialist Party (India), 319
Revolutionary Socialist Party (Peru), 468
Revolutionary United Front (RUF) (Sierra Leone), 514
Revolutionary Unity Movement (MUR) (Honduras), 307
Revolutionary Vanguard (VR) (Peru), 466
Revolutionary Workers' Party (Bolivia), 80
Revolutionary Workers' Party (Mexico), 404
Ricardo Franco Commando (Colombia), 148
Right of Centre Party (ROC) (New Zealand), 429; 430
Rijeka Democratic League (Croatia), 167
Roldosista Party (Ecuador), 202
Romanian Communist Party (Romania), 488; 489
Romanian Ecological Party (Romania), 484; 485
Romanian National Unity Party (PUNR) (Romania), 489
Romanian Social Democratic Party (PSDR) (Romania),
    484; 485; 487; 489
Rural Alliance Party (RAP) (Solomon Islands), 525
Russian Movement for Democratic Reform (RDDR)
    (Russia), 496; 497
Russian Movement for Democratic Reform (Russia), 497
Russian Party of Social Democracy (Russia), 496; 499
Russian Social Democratic Union (Russia), 495; 499; 500

Russian United Industrial Party (Russia), 497
Russia's Democratic Choice (Russia), 494; 496; 497; 499
Russia's Regions (Regiony Rossii, RR) (Russia), 497
Rwandan Patriotic Front (FPR) (Rwanda), 500; 501; 502

S

Sabah Democratic Party (Malayasia), 388
Sabah People's Union (Malaysia), 390
Sabah United Party (Malaysia), 387; 388; 389
Sacred Union of the Radical Opposition (Zaïre), 656; 657
Salvadoran Communist Party (El Salvador), 215
Salvadorean Democratic Front (FDS) (El Salvador), 215
Samajwadi Party (India), 316; 318; 319
Samarkand Movement (Uzbekistan), 639
Samata Party (India), 318
Samoa Democratic Party (SDP) (Western Samoa), 650
Samoa Liberal Party (SLP) (Western Samoa), 650
Samoan National Development Party (SNDP) (Western Samoa), 650
San Marino Christian Democratic Party (PDCS) (San Marino), 507
San Marino Socialist Party (PSS) (San Marino), 507
Sandinista National Liberation Front (Nicaragua), 436
Sandinista Renewal Movement (Nicaragua), 437
Sarawak National Action Party (Malaysia), 389
Sarawak United People's Party (Malaysia), 389
Scottish National Party (United Kingdom), 605
Segni Pact (Italy), 335; 339
Self-Government Party (Sjfl) (Danish Dependencies), 192; 193; 194
Sendero Luminoso (Shining Path) (Peru), 463; 467; 468
Senegal Socialist Party (PSS) (Senegal), 510; 511
Senegalese Democratic Party (PDS) (Senegal), 510; 511; 512
Sephardic Torah Guardians (Shas) (Israel), 331
Serbian Democratic Party (Bosnia and Hercegovina), 82; 83; 84
Serbian Democratic Party (Croatia), 168
Serbian Liberal Party (Srpska Liberalna Stranka, SLS) (Yugoslavia), 654; 655
Serbian Radical Party (Yugoslavia), 654; 655
Serbian Renaissance Movement (Bosnia and Hercegovina), 83
Serbian Renewal Movement (Yugoslavia), 654
Serbian Unity Party (Yugoslavia), 655
Seychelles National Movement (Seychelles), 513
Seychelles Party (Seychelles), 513
Seychelles People's Progressive Front (Seychelles), 512
Shining Path (Peru), 466; 467; 468
Shiv Sena (India), 316
Sikkim Democratic Front (India), 149; 319
Simón Bolívar Guerrilla Co-ordinating Board (CNGSB) (Colombia), 147
Simón Bolívar National Guerrilla Co-ordinating Board (CNGSB) (Colombia), 147
Single-Tax Party (Denmark), 188; 189
Sinn Féin (Ireland), 328; 329
Sinn Féin (Northern Ireland), 615; 616
Slavic Assembly of Belarus (Belarus), 60
Slovak National Party (SNS) (Slovakia), 518; 519
Slovenian Christian Democrats (SKD) (Slovenia), 522; 524
Slovenian National Party (Slovenia), 524
Slovenian National Right (Slovenia), 523

Social Action Movement (MAS) (Guatemala), 289
Social Action Party of Honduras (Honduras), 307
Social Action Party (SAP) (Thailand), 574
Social Christian Party (Bolivia), 76
Social Christian Party (COPEI) (Venezuela), 642; 643; 645
Social Christian Party (Guatemala), 293
Social Christian Party (PSC) (Ecuador), 204; 205; 206; 207
Social Christian Party (Venezuela), 644
Social Christian Popular Party (PPSC) (Nicaragua), 437
Social Christian Reformist Party (PRSC) (Dominican Republic), 200; 201
Social Christian Unity Party (PUSC) (Costa Rica), 158
Social Conservative Party (PSC) (Colombia), 143; 145; 146
Social Credit Political League (New Zealand), 429
Social Democracy of the Polish Republic (SRP) (Poland), 472; 473; 474; 477
Social Democracy Party of Romania (PDSR) (Romania), 484; 485; 487; 488; 489
Social Democrat Party (PSD (El Salvador), 215
Social Democratic and Labour Party (SDLP) (Northern Ireland), 609; 612
Social Democratic Front (Guinea-Bissau), 298; 299
Social Democratic Front (SDF) (Cameroon), 113; 114
Social Democratic Hnchakian Party (Armenia), 31
Social Democratic Labour Party (SAP) (Sweden), 554; 555; 556; 557
Social Democratic Party (Benin), 73
Social Democratic Party (France), 249
Social Democratic Party (Guinea-Bissau), 298
Social Democratic Party (Japan), 346
Social Democratic Party (Jvfl) (Danish Dependencies), 192; 193; 194; 196
Social Democratic Party (Nicaragua), 437
Social Democratic Party of Albania (PSDS) (Albania), 5; 6
Social Democratic Party of Austria (SPÖ) (Austria), 41
Social Democratic Party of Cameroon (Cameroon), 116; 117
Social Democratic Party of Croatia–Party of Democratic Reform (Croatia), 169
Social Democratic Party of Germany (SPD) (Germany), 270; 272; 273; 276; 280
Social Democratic Party of Japan (Japan), 347
Social Democratic Party of Slovakia (Slovakia), 518; 519
Social Democratic Party of Slovenia (SDSS) (Slovenia), 522
Social Democratic Party of Ukraine (Ukraine), 593; 597
Social Democratic Party (Partia Social-Demokrate, PSD) (Yugoslavia), 655
Social Democratic Party (PDS) (Brazil), 87
Social Democratic Party (PSD) (Chile), 131
Social Democratic Party (PSD) (Portugal), 478; 479; 481
Social Democratic Party (SD) (Denmark), 185; 186; 187; 188; 189; 190; 192
Social Democratic Party (SDP) (Iceland), 312; 313; 314
Social Democratic Party (Switzerland), 562; 563; 564
Social Democratic Reformist Party (Yugoslavia), 655
Social Democratic Union (Albania), 6
Social Democratic Union of Macedonia (SDSM) (Macedonia), 381; 382
Social Democratic Union (UDS) (Equatorial Guinea), 217

Social Movement for New Democracy (Cameroon), 116; 117

Social Reformist Union (Guatemala), 294

Social Renewal Party (Guinea-Bissau), 298

Socialist Accord (Peru), 466

Socialist Action Party (PASOC) (Spain), 534; 536

Socialist Alliance (Yugoslavia), 654

Socialist Confluence (Peru), 466

Socialist Democracy (Spain), 535

Socialist Federation of Martinique (French Overseas Possessions), 256

Socialist Forces Front (FFS) (Algeria), 11; 12

Socialist Labour Party (SLP) (Egypt), 208; 209; 210

Socialist Left Party (Norway), 443

Socialist Left (IS) (Peru), 463; 465; 466; 467

Socialist Party (French Overseas Possessions), 254; 256; 257

Socialist Party (Moldova), 407

Socialist Party of Albania (PSS, formerly the PLA) (Albania), 5; 7

Socialist Party of Australia (Australia), 35; 38

Socialist Party of Chile (PSCh) (Chile), 131; 135

Socialist Party of Great Britain (Australia), 40

Socialist Party of Great Britain (Austria), 43

Socialist Party of Great Britain (Northern Ireland), 616

Socialist Party of Great Britain (Sweden), 559

Socialist Party of Kazakhstan (SPK) (Kazakhstan), 352; 353

Socialist Party of Labour (PSM) (Romania), 485; 488; 489

Socialist Party of Macedonia (Macedonia), 382

Socialist Party of Montenegro (Yugoslavia), 655

Socialist Party of Peru (Partido Socialista del Perú—PSP) (Peru), 467

Socialist Party of Russia (Russia), 491; 498; 500

Socialist Party of San Marino (San Marino), 506

Socialist Party of Serbia (Bosnia and Hercegovina), 83

Socialist Party of Serbia (SPS) (Yugoslavia), 653; 654; 655

Socialist Party of Serbia (Yugoslavia), 654

Socialist Party of Ukraine (Ukraine), 593

Socialist Party (Overseas Territories and Territorial Collectivities), 261

Socialist Party (Portugal), 479; 482

Socialist Party (PS) (Belgium), 63; 68

Socialist Party (PS) (Ecuador), 203

Socialist Party (PS) (France), 236; 238; 242; 244; 245; 246; 250; 252; 253

Socialist Party (PS) (Portugal), 480; 482

Socialist People's Movement Party (Partido Movimiento Pueblo Socialista, PMPS) (Chile), 136

Socialist People's Party (SFPP) (Denmark), 190; 191

Socialist Recuperation Movement (Movimiento de Recuperación Socialista, MRS) (Chile), 136

Socialist Renovation Current (Colombia), 149

Socialist Union of Popular Forces (Morocco), 411; 412

Socialist Unity Party (SUP) (New Zealand), 430

Socialist Workers' Organization (SWO) (New Zealand), 430

Socialist Workers' Party (Colombia), 148

Socialist Workers' Party (Partido Socialista de los Trabajadores—PST) (Peru), 467

Socijalisticka Partija Srbije (SPS) (Yugoslavia), 654

Solidarity Action Movement (Guatemala), 290; 294

Solidarity Party (Panama), 455

Solidarity (Poland), 471; 474; 475; 477

Solidarity-affiliated Citizens' Movement for Democratic Action (Poland), 473

Solomon Islands Labour Party (Solomon Islands), 525

Solomon Islands Liberal Party (Solomon Islands), 525

Solomon Islands United Party (SIUPA) (Solomon Islands), 525

Somali National Alliance (Somalia), 526

Somali National Movement (Somalia), 526

Somali Revolutionary Socialist Party (Somalia), 525

Somali Salvation Alliance (Somalia), 526

Soqosoqo ni Vakavulewa ni Taukei (SVT) (Fiji), 227

South Tyrol People's Party (Italy), 344

South West Africa People's Organization (SWAPO) (Namibia), 417

South West African National Union (SWANU) (Namibia), 417

Spanish Socialist Workers' Party (PSOE) (Spain), 532; 533; 536; 537; 538; 539; 541; 543; 544; 545; 546

Spirit of '46 party (Malayasia), 389

Sri Lanka Freedom Party (SLFP) (Sri Lanka), 546; 547; 548

Sri Lanka Muslim Congress (Sri Lanka), 547

Srpska Radikalna Stranka (SRS) (Yugoslavia), 654

Srpski Pokret Obnove (SPO) (Yugoslavia), 654

St Lucia Labour Party (SLP) (St Lucia), 504

Standvaste (Suriname), 551

State Reform Party (Netherlands), 424

Sudanese Union–African Democratic Rally (Mali), 392

Surinamese Liberation Army (Jungle Commando—SLA) (Suriname), 552

Swaziland Progressive Party (Swaziland), 553

Swedish People's Party (RKP/SFP) (Finland), 230; 231; 232; 233; 234

Swiss Democrats (Switzerland), 561; 564; 565

Swiss People's (Switzerland), 562

Syrian Communist Party (Syria), 565

T

Ta Belau Party (Palau), 449

Tamil Maanila Congress (India), 317; 319

Tan Union (Vanuatu), 640; 641

Taukei Solidarity Movement (Fiji), 227

Te Tiaraama (Overseas Territories and Territorial Collectivities), 259

Telugu Desam Party–Naidu (India), 319

The Alliance (New Zealand), 429

The Blancos (Uruguay), 636

The Democratic Party (DP) (New Zealand's Associated Territories), 431

The New Front (Suriname), 551

The Radical Cause (Venezuela), 645

Third Nationalist Party (TPN) (Panama), 455

Third Way (Israel), 331

Ticino League (Switzerland), 563

Tigre People's Liberation Front (TPLF) (Ethiopia), 224

Togolese Union for Democracy (UDT) (Togo), 575; 576

True Path Party (DYP) (Turkey), 582; 584; 585

Tupac Amaru Revolutionary Movement (MRTA) (Colombia), 148

Tupac Amarú Revolutionary Movement (Peru), 468

Tupaj Katari Revolutionary Movement (Movimiento Revolucionario Tupaj Katari—MRTK) (Bolivia), 80

Turkish Peoples Party (TPP) (Yugoslavia), 655
Tzomet (Israel), 330; 331; 333

U

Uganda Patriotic Movement (Uganda), 589
Uganda People's Congress (UPC) (Uganda), 589
Ukrainian Christian Democratic Party (UKhDP)
 (Ukraine), 591
Ukrainian Conservative Republican Party (UKRP)
 (Ukraine), 595
Ukrainian Republican Party (URP) (Ukraine), 592; 595
Ulster Popular Unionist Party (Northern Ireland), 613
Ulster Unionist Party (UUP) (Northern Ireland), 609;
 610; 616
Unidad Revolucionaria Nacional Guatemalteca (URNG)
 (Guatemala), 295
Unified Democratic Union of Cyprus (EDEK) (Cyprus),
 172; 174
Unified Mariáteguista Party (Peru), 159; 467
Unión Agrícola Cartaginesa (UAC) (Costa Rica), 159
Unión Camilista-ELN (Colombia), 149
Unión Cívica Radical (UCR) (Argentina), 27
Unión Cívica Solidaridad (UCS) (Bolivia), 28; 76
Unión del Centro Democrático (UCeDé) (Argentina), 28
Unión del Centro Nacional (UCN) (Guatemala), 294
Unión Democrática (UD) (Guatemala), 290
Unión Democrático Popular (UDP) (Peru), 466
Union for Democracy and Development (Mali), 392
Union for Democracy and National Reconstruction
 (Benin), 72; 73
Union for Democracy and Progress (Chad), 129
Union for Democracy and Social Progress (Zaïre), 656;
 657
Union for Democracy and the Republic (UDR) (Chad),
 129
Union for Democratic Renewal (URD) (Congo), 153;
 155; 157
Union for Development and Social Progress (Congo),
 157
Union for French Democracy (UDF) (French Overseas
 Possessions), 240; 253; 255; 256; 257; 258
Union for French Democracy (Overseas Territories and
 Territorial Collectivities), 259; 261
Union for French Democracy (UDF) (France), 235; 242;
 244; 246; 248
Union for Liberation and Democracy (UBD) (Suriname),
 553
Union for Macedonia (Macedonia), 381
Union for National Progress (UPRONA) (Burundi), 105
Union for National Recovery (URN) (Congo), 157
Union for Peru (UPP) (Peru), 462; 465
Union for Renewal and Democracy (Chad), 129
Union for Social Progress and Democracy (Congo), 29;
 156
Union for the New Majority (Unión para la Nueva
 Mayoría, UNM) (Argentina), 29
Union for the Progress of Chile (Chile), 136
Union for the Republic (Congo), 154
Union of Democratic Forces (Bulgaria), 98-100
Union of Democratic Forces (Chad), 129
Union of Democratic Forces (Côte d'Ivoire), 163
Union of Democratic Forces for Progress (Mali), 392
Union of Democratic Forces (Mauritania), 396; 397

Union of Democratic Forces (SDS) (Bulgaria), 92; 93;
 94; 95; 96; 98; 99; 100
Union of Federalists and Independent Republicans
 (Zaïre), 657
Union of Guyanese International (UGI) (Guyana), 301
Union of Macedonia (SM) (Macedonia), 382
Union of Moderate Parties (UMP) (Vanuatu), 640; 641
Union of Muslims of Russia (Russia), 498
Union of Realists (Russia), 497
Union of Social Democrats (Côte d'Ivoire), 162
Union of the Democratic Centre (Argentina), 26
Union of the National Centre (Guatemala), 291
Union of the Navarrese People (UPN) (Spain), 533; 545
Union of the Peoples of Cameroon (Cameroon), 116
Union of the Revolutionary Left (Peru), 466
Union Party (Sbfl) (Danish Dependencies), 192; 193; 194
Unión Patriótica (UP) (Colombia), 146
Unión por el Perú (UPP) (Peru), 465
Unión por el Progreso de Chile (UPP) (Chile), 136
Unión Reformista Social (URS) (Guatemala), 294; 644
Unión Republicana Democrática (URD) (Venezuela)
Unión Sinarquista Nacional (UNS) (Mexico), 403
Unitarian Socialist Party (Switzerland), 565
Unitary Communist Vanguard (VUC) (Venezuela), 645
Unitary Pinochetist Action (Accíon Pinochetista Unitaria,
 APU) (Chile), 136
United Azerbaijan (Azerbaijan), 46
United Bermuda Party (UK Dependent Territories), 619
United Christian Democratic Centre (OHZ) (Bulgaria), 97
United Christian Democrats (Italy), 335; 339
United Civic Party of Belarus (Belarus), 57
United Communist Party of Nepal (UCPN) (Nepal), 420
United Democratic Coalition (DCU) (Portugal), 479; 482
United Democratic Forces (FDU) (Congo), 153; 155;
 156; 157
United Democratic Front (UDF) (Malawi), 386
United Democratic Left (Portugal), 481
United Democratic Movement (Guinea-Bissau), 298
United Democratic Party (Belarus), 58
United Democratic Party (UDP) (Belize), 68; 69
United Development Party (Indonesia), 322
United Force (UF) (Guyana), 300
United Front (India), 315; 316; 317; 318; 319; 320
United Front of the Revolution (FUR) (Guatemala), 293
United Front (UF) (India), 316; 317; 318
United Greens of Austria (Austria), 42
United Kingdom Unionist (Northern Ireland), 616
United Labour Party (St Vincent and the Grenadines),
 506
United Left electoral coalition (IU) (Spain), 536; 537
United Left (IU) (Bolivia), 76; 77; 79
United Left (IU) (Peru), 466
United Left (IU) (Spain), 532; 534; 535; 537; 546
United Liberal Democratic Party (South Korea), 360
United List of Social Democrats (ZLSD) (Slovenia), 522;
 523
United Malays National Organization (UMNO)
 (Malaysia), 390
United National Congress (UNC) (Trinidad and Tobago),
 108; 578
United National Front for an Independent, Neutral,
 Peaceful and Co-operative Cambodia (FUNCINPEC)
 (Cambodia), 110-112
United National Independence Party (Zambia), 658; 659
United National Party (UNP) (Sri Lanka), 547

United National People's Party (UNPP) (Sierra Leone), 514
United New Zealand Party (New Zealand), 428; 429; 430
United Opposition (Seychelles), 512; 513
United Party (UP) (Papua New Guinea), 457; 458
United People (Herri Batasuna) (Northern Ireland), 612
United People's Assembly (Suriname), 551
United People's Movement (St Vincent and the Grenadines), 505
United Republican Party (URP) (Guyana), 301
United Revolutionary Front (Guatemala), 293
United Social Democratic Party (Guinea-Bissau), 298
United Social Democratic Party of Ukraine (OSDPU) (Ukraine), 594
United Socialist Alliance (Greece), 283
United Torah Judaism (Israel), 332
United Traditional Bumiputra Party (Malaysia), 389
United Workers' Party (Israel), 331
United Workers' Party (Mapam) (Israel), 331
United Workers' Party (UWP) (Guyana), 301
Unity (Birlik) (Uzbekistan), 638
Unity Front (UF) (Vanuatu), 640; 641
Unity Movement (Moldova), 407
Unity of the Valencian People (UPV) (Spain), 536
Unity of Voice (Turkmenistan), 587
Unity (Unidad) (Costa Rica), 159
Uzbekistan Society for Human Rights (Uzbekistan), 639

V

Valencian Union (Spain), 533
Vallentine Peace Group (Australia), 39
Vanua'aku Pati (VP) (Vanuatu), 640; 641
Vanuatu Independent Alliance Party (VIAP) (Vanuatu), 640
Vanuatu Labour Party (Vanuatu), 642
Venezuelan Popular Union (UPV) (Venezuela), 643

W

Welfare Party (RP) (Turkey), 582; 583; 585
Western United Front (Fiji), 227

Workers' Front (Vf) (Danish Dependencies), 194
Workers' Liberation Front (Netherlands Dependencies), 428
Workers' Party (Brazil), 90
Workers' Party (Ireland), 326; 328; 329
Workers' Party of Bangladesh (WPB) (Bangladesh), 52
Workers' Party of Jamaica (WPJ) (Jamaica), 345
Workers' Party (Partido de los Trabajadores, PT) (Costa Rica), 160
Workers' Party (Partido Obrero, PO) (Argentina), 29
Workers Party (Partido Obrero Comunista Marxista-Leninista, POCML) (Argentina), 28
Workers' Party (WP) (Northern Ireland), 614
Workers' Revolutionary Party (Australia), 39
Workers' Revolutionary Party (Peru), 467
Workers' Revolutionary Party (PRT) (Colombia), 145
Workers' Socialist Party (Partido Socialista de los Trabajadores, PST) (Argentina), 29
Workers' Socialist Party (PST) (Mexico), 403
Workers' Struggle (LO) (France), 253
Working People's Alliance (WPA) (Guyana), 300
Working People's Vanguard Party (Guyana), 300

Y

Yamin Yisrael (Israel), 332
Yavlinsky-Boldyrev-Lukin Bloc (Yabloko (Russia), 496
Yemen Socialist Party (YSP) (Yemen), 651
Yemeni Islah Party (YIP) (Yemen), 651
Yi'ud (Israel), 333
Yugoslav Green Party (Zelena Stranka) (Yugoslavia), 655
Yugoslav United Left (Yugoslavia), 655
Yukon Party (Canada), 119

Z

Zambia Democratic Congress (Zambia), 658
Zambia Opposition Front (ZOFRO) (Zambia), 658
Zapatista National Liberation Army (Mexico), 405
Zimbabwe African National Union (Zimbabwe), 659; 660
Zimbabwe Unity Movement (ZUM) (Zimbabwe), 660